FROM DAY TO DAY

FROM DAY TO DAY

ONE MAN'S DIARY OF SURVIVAL
IN NAZI CONCENTRATION CAMPS

ODD NANSEN

Edited and Annotated by

TIMOTHY J. BOYCE

PREFACE BY THOMAS BUERGENTHAL

TRANSLATED BY KATHERINE JOHN

VANDERBILT UNIVERSITY PRESS

Nashville

Bioo

Introduction, annotations, and appendixes © 2016, Timothy J. Boyce
Preface © 2016, Vanderbilt University Press
Illustrations by Odd Nansen used courtesy of Marit Greve

Published by Vanderbilt University Press
Nashville, Tennessee 37235
First printing 2016

This book is printed on acid-free paper.
Manufactured in the United States of America

Library of Congress Cataloging-in-Publication Data on file

LC control number   2015042213
LC classification number   D805.G3 N3513 2016
Dewey class number   940.53/18533154—dc23

ISBN 978-0-8265-2100-2 (cloth)
ISBN 978-0-8265-2102-6 (ebook)

CONTENTS

SKETCHES BY ODD NANSEN

INTRODUCTION

by Timothy J. Boyce

I. ODD NANSEN

On a bitterly cold night in mid-January 1942, Odd Nansen listened, with some trepidation, to an ominous knock at the cabin door. He had good reason to be concerned. Nansen and his family, on an extended Christmas holiday in the snowy mountains above Lillehammer, had just tuned in their (illegal) radio to the (highly illegal) BBC Norwegian broadcast. The distinctive musical prelude, the "da-da-da-dum" of Beethoven's Fifth Symphony (Morse code for the letter "V" for victory) had just resounded through the small hut. As it turned out, the timing of the three men who appeared at the door (the district sheriff and two Germans) was entirely coincidental; they suspected nothing. Rather, Nansen was merely asked to come to nearby Lillehammer and then Oslo, where he would be told the reason for the summons. While any such visit in occupied Norway was worrisome, Nansen was probably not overly concerned; he had been called in a year earlier by the Gestapo for questioning and released. It is unlikely he could have imagined at the time that he would not again experience freedom for some three and a half years, until the closing weeks of the war. It is even more doubtful that Nansen could have conceived on that fateful night the circles of hell he would travel before winning that freedom.[1]

Nansen's first night in captivity, after all, began innocently enough. Dinner in the Lillehammer jail, he recorded, was "a lordly meal," consisting of beef olives, cakes, and cloudberries and cream, all topped off by half a bottle of burgundy. By the spring of 1945 and his imminent rescue at the hands of the Swedish Red Cross, however, his surroundings had become an "infernal vale of tears" and a "sink of degradation," filled with "wretchedness and horror." Nansen wondered whether anyone would "believe this when we come to describe it." Indeed he was even unsure he could adequately describe all that he had seen and heard; it "was so horrible, so incomprehensible in ghastliness, that it defies all description." What occurred during those three and a half years, between that first, rather comfortable night and his final, agonized deliverance, is the stuff of his diary, *From Day to Day: One Man's Diary of Survival in Nazi Concentration Camps*, one of the most vivid, horrifying, and humane documents to emerge from World War II.

Nansen was one of approximately forty thousand Norwegians held by the Nazis in prisons and concentration camps in Norway, Germany, and elsewhere during World War

II, this out of a population of just under three million, or approximately that of modern-day Connecticut.[2] Prisoners included members of the Resistance, parents whose children had escaped to England, and those violating the myriad and ever-growing list of infractions promulgated by the regime (which included, besides owning a radio and listening to unauthorized broadcasts, singing patriotic songs, refusing to sit next to a German on the bus, wearing red caps, etc.). Nansen's arrest stemmed not from any particular transgression, but rather from his ostensible designation as a "court hostage," a practice frequently employed by the Nazis in occupied countries against well-connected individuals.[3] For in Norway the Nansen name was better known, and probably more highly regarded, than almost any other.

Odd Nansen's father, Fridtjof Nansen, was a world-class athlete and a pioneering marine biologist. But it was as an intrepid explorer that Fridtjof Nansen secured his place in Norway's pantheon. By the end of the nineteenth century only the polar regions remained unexplored, unmapped, unknown, "as alluring and unknown as the surface of Venus or Mars," in the words of one writer.[4] In an era characterized by rising nationalist sentiment and, for the first time, widespread news dissemination, the exploits of polar explorers, described as a "parade of fanatics,"[5] took on the trappings of the moon race, the Olympics, and the World Cup all rolled into one. Intoxicated by a strange cocktail of scientific curiosity, commerce, and not a little nationalistic vanity, many countries vied for the ultimate prize: the right to stand at the very ends of the earth. The names Amundsen, Scott, Byrd, Shackleton, and Peary all come down to us from this era. Nansen never reached either pole, and so his exploits have been overshadowed by these later explorers. In his time, however, Fridtjof Nansen was the role model all his successors wanted to emulate; his biographer, Roland Huntford, calls him "the father of modern polar exploration."[6]

Fridtjof Nansen burst upon the scene in 1888, when at the tender age of twenty-six, he became the first man to successfully cross Greenland, an island 80 percent covered by an ice cap more than a mile thick in places. The route Nansen chose, from the uninhabited and inhospitable eastern shore to the inhabited western, appealed to Nansen's sense of daring; once launched he either had to reach his goal, and safety, in the west or perish in the attempt. There was no turning back.

Five years later, in 1893, Nansen (still only thirty-one) again ignored prevailing wisdom in his quest to reach the North Pole. He purposely allowed his specially constructed ship to become trapped in the ice; as that ice slowly drifted westward with the current (as Nansen theorized it would) his ship would drift to ever-higher latitudes. Again this plan meant there would be no line of retreat, no fallback plan. Again the lack of a "Plan B" was intentional. As Nansen once explained, "Then one loses no time in looking behind, when one should have quite enough to do in looking ahead—then there is no chance for you or your men but *forward*. You have to do or die!"[7] Appropriately, Nansen christened his ship *Fram* [Forward]. When, midway through his drift, Nansen concluded his approach would fail to bring the ship directly over the North Pole, he decided to double down; he abandoned the safety of his ship and struck out on sledges and skis with only one other companion. They eventually came within 230 miles of the Pole, the farthest north any man had then traveled. Yet in many ways it was the ensuing fourteen months that constituted the most impressive achievement of all. Failing to return to civilization before the onset of the Arctic night, despite traveling seven hundred miles over ice and snow for 146 days, Nansen and his companion hunkered down and lived off the barren land—Robinson Crusoe style—until they could continue on eight months later.[8] Polar bears and walruses provided the food (meat), shelter (fur), light and heat (rendered blubber), and tools (bones and sinews) they needed to survive, cut-off and alone, in the world's most ruthless, remote, and unforgiving environment.[9]

When Nansen finally returned, almost forty months after setting out, "[h]e was like someone returning from the dead,"[10] and was greeted by a delirious nation. His exploits found a particularly receptive audience in Norway, a country nearing the end of a long struggle for independence from Sweden. King Oscar, the Swedish king of both Sweden and Norway, harrumphed that Nansen's deed encouraged "the already more than sufficient very Norwegian megalomania."[11] Not surprisingly, then, when Norway finally achieved its independence less than ten years later, in 1905, adopting a limited monarchial form of government, the fledgling government enlisted Nansen to approach Prince Carl of Denmark to become the country's new king.[12] And it was only natural, when Norway next desired to negotiate a neutrality treaty with the world's then only superpower—Great Britain—that Nansen was named Norway's first ambassador to the Court of St. James's.

Now financially independent from book and speaking royalties describing his feat, Fridtjof Nansen's reputation would have remained forever secure had he then simply retired to his newly constructed estate on the outskirts of Oslo, which he christened Polhøgda, or "Polar Heights." With the end of World War I (in which Norway had remained neutral), however, Nansen was approached by the newly created League of Nations. Determined to prove its relevance, the league engaged Nansen to organize the repatriation of POWs stranded in Germany and Russia. After all, according to one historian, he was "unquestionably the most towering personality of the post-war world."[13] Moreover, Huntford notes, Nansen had by then "developed a visible taste for good works."[14] His assent would prove to be a career pivot that would have dramatic ramifications for the remainder of his life, as well as the worldview of his son Odd.

Fridtjof brought to his new task the same single-mindedness that had characterized his life as an explorer and statesman. Soon he was also leading efforts to alleviate famine in Russia (assisted by a highly regarded young Norwegian named Vidkun Quisling), helping stateless refugees of the Russian Revolution, mediating claims of ethnic cleansing between the Greeks and the Turks, and seeking a homeland for the Armenians. In 1922 Fridtjof received the Nobel Peace Prize in recognition of his various humanitarian accomplishments. The Nansen Refugee Award, named in his honor, was instituted by the first UN high commissioner for refugees in 1954; it is awarded annually in recognition of the recipient's extraordinary service to refugees.[15]

Odd Nansen was born December 6, 1901, the fourth of five children of Fridtjof and Eva (Sars) Nansen. If Fridtjof was a national hero, Eva's family boasted an equally distinguished pedigree. Her father was a highly regarded marine biologist, and her mother, Maren Welhaven, hosted a sophisticated and cultured salon; Maren's brother, Johan Sebastian Welhaven, has been described as "the first poet of consequence in the Norwegian language."[16] Huntford acerbically describes Maren as possessing a "homely, not to say dumpy, figure,"[17] which was unflattering and no doubt true, but entirely understandable; Eva, the baby of the family, was after all her nineteenth child.

According to Odd Nansen's eldest sister, Liv, he more closely resembled Eva: "Odd had her colouring [*sic*], her jaw-line and her dark eyes."[18] And the resemblance wasn't just in looks; Fridtjof once observed, "[Odd] is like me in some things, but in others he is like his gifted mother, and that I like."[19] From both parents Odd inherited an artistic sensibility.

Fridtjof had once thought of becoming a painter, and his striking drawings have left a vivid legacy of his Arctic travels. Eva, according to Liv, was equally attracted to painting and singing before deciding to concentrate on her voice; she was a well-known singer before marrying Fridtjof, performing in all the Scandinavian capitals. Odd also initially considered becoming a painter before deciding on a career in architecture. Certainly his diary sketches attest to a formidable artistic talent.

Although Odd Nansen grew up in a socially prominent and financially secure family, his home life must have been anything but easy. Three days after his sixth birthday, Eva died suddenly of pneumonia. Fridtjof by this time had already embarked on his diplomatic career—he was away in London as Norway's ambassador when Eva died—and between his career and his scientific pursuits, he was often away from Polhøgda for long stretches. If his children suffered from these absences, they may have equally rued his presence, for Fridtjof entertained child-rearing theories that were draconian even for his day and age. Home life resembled nothing so much as a training camp for future polar expeditions. Food was Spartan; Fridtjof insisted on plain old porridge for his children twice a day, morning and evening, every day.[20] Developing self-esteem was never a consideration. Discipline was strict. Fridtjof maintained, "It is naturally a good thing to bring up nice, well-behaved children. But it is not enough, it is just as important to form character and willpower [which] are often developed by harsh treatment."[21] Liv wrote, "Father did not think anything should be easy."[22] Indeed, hardship was woven into his philosophy of life. "[Y]ou have to go through a little hardship now and then in order to enjoy life properly after it. If you don't know what cold is, neither do you know what it is to be warm," he once remarked.[23] In a 1926 address Nansen endorsed the proposition that "Privation and suffering are the only road to wisdom," and he seemed prepared to do his part in imparting wisdom to his sons.[24] Liv recalled one of her father's guiding principles: "he that spareth his rod, hateth his son," and according to Huntford, "[h]e thrashed his sons when he thought it necessary."[25] Emotionally, their father could be just as difficult. He was often moody, aloof, and unpredictable.[26] The children soon learned to read his signals—if they heard him humming a certain melody, they could conclude that "all was well . . . and the barometer was rising."[27] Nansen even forbade Eva from praising or showing affection to their children—he felt it weakened character.[28]

This treatment, now unmediated by the influence of a mother, no doubt toughened Odd Nansen up and unwittingly prepared him for the crucible he would face as an adult. Even so, it scarcely promoted warm familial bonds. As Huntford observes, Odd's "stronger character and robust humour" [*sic*] helped him to survive his childhood "with fewer mental scars [than older brother Kåre]. Still, there remained the barrier between himself and his father." It is thus hardly surprising to learn that by the time Odd was in high school preparing to matriculate to the university, he was living away from Polhøgda with family friends.[29]

Nansen studied architecture at the Norwegian Institute of Technology (NTH) in Trondheim. While there he began an apprenticeship with Arnstein Arneberg, considered the leading architect in Norway during the interwar period. They already knew each other; Arnstein was a neighbor of Polhøgda. Arneberg's commissions included the Oslo City Hall, the Viking Ship Museum, and, after the war, the interior of the UN Security Council chamber, with its distinctive circular seating arrangement.

Nansen played a prominent role in university life. He wrote and illustrated for the NTH student newspaper, and his more theatrical interests were not neglected either. Since 1917 the Student Society of Trondheim has produced a biennial festival that is now one of Norway's largest cultural events.[30] At the heart of each festival is a student revue. Foreshadowing his songwriting and singing abilities while in prison, Nansen acted in or wrote songs for the 1921, 1923, and 1925 productions and directed the 1923 show. A song he wrote for the 1925 show, "*Hjemvě*" [Homesickness], was an immediate success, was subsequently recorded, and is still sung today, almost one hundred years later.[31]

Nansen was soon to taste his own dose of homesickness. Norway's dearth of jobs and his strained relationship with his father (and even more so his stepmother, Sigrun Munthe, whom Fridtjof had married in 1919), prompted Nansen to move to America in 1927, the year of his graduation and his marriage (on August 27) to Karen (Kari) Hirsch.[32] For the next three years he worked for architectural and urban planning firms in New York City. In 1929, with barely two years' work experience under his belt, Nansen and a partner entered the Lehigh Airports Competition, the first contest in America designed to "crystallize public attention upon the need for well-designed and properly planned airports to facilitate the further expansion of commercial and civil aeronautics" by presenting "designs of practical as well as inspirational value to guide the development of airports, present and future."[33] Nansen's was one of 257 designs ultimately submitted (including one by the son of Frank Lloyd Wright). Despite having a plan that a later critic described as "suggest[ing] an eighteenth-century chateau" with its reflecting pools and radiating walkways, Nansen won third place and a $1,000 stipend, no small sum in those days.[34] Nansen's visions for an airport were to be realized less than a decade later when he was commissioned to design the terminals at Oslo's main airport, Fornebu, which opened in 1939 (*sans* reflecting pools).

By early 1930, Fridtjof's failing health (he had had his first heart attack in 1928) drew Odd back to Norway for good.[35] He arrived just in time; his father died May 13, 1930, at Polhøgda. The following year Odd established his own architectural firm in Oslo. If Nansen now hoped he could focus on building a solid, quiet career, events in Europe soon dictated otherwise. Hitler and the Nazis seized power in January 1933, and the persecution of Germany's Jews followed almost immediately thereafter; in that year alone approximately fifty thousand fled the country.[36] In late 1936 several prominent Norwegians, including Professor Fredrik Paasche, Nobel Peace Prize laureate Christian Lous Lange, and foreign minister Halvdan Koht, approached Nansen to organize a formal assistance program for Europe's burgeoning refugee problem.

The decision could not have been an easy one. Nansen faced the pressures of a young and growing family (daughter Marit was born in 1928, followed by son Eigil in 1931 and daughter Siri in 1933) as well as the demands of his nascent architectural practice. Moreover, anti-Semitism was well entrenched in Norway. Indeed, the Norwegian chargé d'affaires in Berne, Switzerland, wrote in 1942 that "there were not many countries in Europe which were more closed to political and Jewish refugees than Norway before the invasion."[37] Nevertheless, Nansen ultimately agreed to form "Nansenhjelpen," or Nansen Relief; in the words of fellow board member Sigrid Helliesen Lund, "he was quite clear about his responsibility as the bearer of the Nansen family name."[38] It is likely his backers hoped the star power of the Nansen name would once again open doors otherwise closed to the persecuted and the powerless.

But Nansen was no mere figurehead, simply lending his marquee name to the enterprise. Myrtle Wright, an English Quaker trapped in Norway following the German invasion who ended up living with Sigrid Lund, once wrote, "The chief initiative in Nansenhjelp came from [Nansen]."[39] Nansen faced three challenges: (1) publicizing the plight of Nazism's victims, primarily the Jews, (2) raising funds, both for operations and for the refugees themselves (discussed below), and (3) setting up offices in central Europe to help with visa applications and the like. For the next three years, assisted by a small group that included Paasche,[40] Lund, Nansen's wife Kari, Kari's sister Signe Hirsch, and family friend Tove Filseth, Nansen threw himself into an arduous cycle of travel, fund-raising, and lobbying. According to Wright, "[Nansen] had an attractive personality and both as an organiser [*sic*] and propagandist was well suited for the work he had taken up."[41]

Nansenhjelpen's work, initially focused on refugees fleeing Germany, took on increased urgency following the German Anschluss of Austria in March 1938 and its seizure of Czechoslovakia's Sudetenland later that year.[42] As Kari observed in a June 1938 letter, "the Jews have a terrible time out in Europe just now."[43] Czechoslovakia's 1,100-mile border with Germany meant that the country, and particularly its capital Prague, served as "haven and host" for both Jewish and non-Jewish refugees fleeing Nazism. Accordingly, Nansen set up a field office there early in 1939 in an attempt to accelerate the visa process, all the while also addressing the plight of refugees in Vienna and in Slovakia's capital, Bratislava.[44]

The problem was daunting, if not overwhelming. After the Sudetenland was detached from Czechoslovakia as a result of the Munich Pact, a cable from the US Legation in Prague revealed that there were more than 90,000 registered (and 10,000 to 15,000 unregistered) refugees in the country, of which approximately 6,700 were Jews. The atmosphere was desperate, as both refugees and Czech Jews frantically applied for visas to any country that would admit them, and there weren't many.[45] US ambassador to Czechoslovakia Wilbur Carr ominously noted at the time, "The suicide toll among the refugees mounts."[46] Meanwhile, Nansen faced popular and governmental resistance, apathy, and downright hostility back home. The Norwegian government, for example, created a formidable burden by insisting on financial support for each refugee (including a sizeable deposit) to ensure they would not become a burden to society, all the while denying those selfsame refugees any opportunity to work out of fear they would steal jobs away from native Norwegians. Adding to Nansen's woes, the head of the Norwegian immigration authority, Leif Konstad, was a pro-Nazi who once had declared that "not a single Jew would be admitted into Norway no matter what the pretext."[47] More locally, Msgr. Josef Tiso, the fascist head of Slovakia, did nothing to halt the attacks on refugees in Bratislava despite Nansen's personal pleas.[48]

On March 15, 1939, Nansen and Kari were in Prague and witnessed firsthand the final disintegration of Czechoslovakia as German troops marched into the city at dawn; Tiso had declared Slovakia's independence (subject to German protection) the day before. The Nansens were unceremoniously evicted from their hotel room/office by the Gestapo in need of good lodgings. All hopes for further assistance faded as the country's trains were suspended and emigration brought to a standstill, but Nansen, in desperation, played his final cards. Another occupant at his new lodgings, the Hotel Alcron, was General Höppner of the Wehrmacht. At Kari's urgings, Nansen confronted Höppner directly, seeking his assistance for the many refugees scheduled to depart that very day. With the general's tacit approval, and behind the backs of the Gestapo, a transport of women and children was allowed to depart, while the men were helped to escape over the border into Poland. Several months later Sigrid Lund returned to Czechoslovakia and oversaw the evacuation of children whose parents were awaiting papers to emigrate from the country.[49]

All told, Nansenhjelpen succeeded in bringing two hundred adults and sixty children to Norway. Despite this herculean accomplishment, Nansen saw little to cheer about. "I felt like an executioner," he somberly admitted in 1940, "because I had to pick only a few hundred to be saved—we had so little money."[50] Three decades later Nansen was still indignant over this treatment: "Neither the Labor Unions nor the [Norwegian] authorities can look back to that time without shame."[51]

With central Europe overrun, and with the outbreak of the so-called Winter War between Finland and Russia in November 1939, Nansenhjelpen shifted its attention to the plight of the Finns. This conflict is barely remembered today, but at the time feelings in America ran high in favor of the Finns, in fact higher in the United States than anywhere outside of Scandinavia. The State Department seriously considered breaking off diplomatic relations with Russia, and the Soviets withdrew their exhibit from New York's 1939 World's Fair for fear of hostile demonstrations.[52] Prominent Americans, headed by Herbert Hoover, Fridtjof Nansen's old friend from their days working together on Russian famine relief, raised money and lobbied for greater involvement. On December 21, 1939, Hoover addressed a crowd of fifteen thousand at Madison Square Garden, and less than a week later Estelle Bernadotte, the American-born heiress and wife of Count Folke Bernadotte of the Swedish Royal Family, organized a benefit concert at Carnegie Hall attended by a roster of dignitaries including senators, the secretaries of war and the navy, Supreme Court justices, and members of the diplomatic corps.

Nansen also sailed for America, arriving in New York on December 23, 1939, "to plead the cause of Finland," which was "putting up a glorious fight for European freedom." Ever the humanist, Nansen focused in particular on a subject "that has not yet been mentioned. That is the refugee problem arising from the war." He crisscrossed the country, often in the company of Folke Bernadotte (who was to play a critical role in his own freedom in 1945), addressing benefit rallies, women's clubs, and student groups. The Midwest, home to many Norwegian Americans, was a key focus. Milwaukee, Madison, and Appleton, Wisconsin, and numerous lesser towns were all stops along the way.[53]

But just as in Norway and Sweden, who were overwhelmingly sympathetic to Finland and yet chose for various reasons to retain their historic neutrality, official US support was frustratingly hard to come by. In typical Nansen style, he recorded in his diary for January 21, 1940: "Sought an audience with Roosevelt today, but have not yet heard anything. Everything is so damn slow and difficult. I wonder if I should just go over to the White House and ring the bell."[54] Nansen never got his audience with Roosevelt, but he continued to lobby in meetings and radio addresses. As late as February 24, 1940, in a speech to the Foreign Policy Association at the Hotel Astor back in New York City, Nansen pleaded for anti-aircraft guns and planes; they were more needed, he claimed, than "sympathy and toasts of goodwill."[55]

Finland's capitulation on March 13, 1940, spelled an end to Nansen's mission in America, and he elected to return to Norway by early April 1940, disappointed at the insignificant results of his efforts. Elsewhere, however, unseen forces were in motion, and the Norway to which Nansen returned was not the one he had so recently left, even if life outwardly appeared the same. It is ironic that the very same edition of the *New York Times* (December 24, 1939) that announced Nansen's arrival on US shores also related, several pages later, that imprisoned Lutheran pastor Martin Niemöller had just been denied permission to attend his parents' golden wedding anniversary notwithstanding the support of several German notables. Niemöller would instead remain in Sachsenhausen. One of the far-reaching consequences of events that winter would include making Nansen a denizen of Sachsenhausen in due time as well.[56]

First, as Nansen was preparing to sail to America, Vidkun Quisling, as head of Norway's fascist Nasjonal Samling (National Unity) or NS Party, traveled in complete secrecy to Berlin and on December 14 and December 18 met with his idol Adolf Hitler for the first time. Quisling made it clear that he was quite prepared to seize the government, by coup if necessary, and to prevent Norway from falling into British hands he was also prepared to welcome a German occupation of the country. Quisling played on German fears that Great Britain would seize Norway first and thus deny Germany strategic access to the Atlantic and cut off vital iron ore imports from Sweden, much of which passed through Norway. Whatever Quisling's exact intentions in initiating these discussions, beyond meeting his hero, establishing his gravitas with Hitler, and obtaining increased financial support for his struggling party, the effect on Germany's end was immediate, indeed electric: Almost before Quisling had exited the Reich Chancellery on December 14, Hitler ordered General Jodl, chief of the Operations Staff of the Armed Forces High Command (OKW), to initiate planning for an occupation of Norway, at Quisling's invitation if possible or by force if without it. By the time of Quisling's follow-up meeting with Hitler a mere four days later, Jodl had a first draft ready.[57]

Second, on February 16, just days before Nansen's Hotel Astor speech, a British destroyer pursued the German tanker *Altmark* up Norway's Jøssingfjord and freed more than three hundred captured merchantmen Britain suspected the *Altmark* was secretly harboring.[58] The event, thereafter known as the Altmark Affair, threw Hitler into a "violent rage." Convinced that Norway could not or would not repel British incursions on her neutrality, Hitler ordered a drastic speeding up of the invasion planning, now code-named *Weserübung*.[59] On March 3, Hitler decided to unleash *Weserübung*, even putting it ahead of *Case Yellow*, the planned "decisive blow" against France and the Low Countries. Thus, as Nansen landed in Oslo in early April, an unsuspecting Norway was fixed firmly in Germany's crosshairs.[60] Indeed, by then the first ships of the German assault force had already put out to sea.[61]

Operation *Weserübung* was launched on the morning of April 9, and German forces quickly overran a woefully unprepared Norway.[62] Overnight Nansen became a marked man. First, his family had been close friends with the soon-to-be-exiled royal family ever since Fridtjof had persuaded Prince Carl to assume the Norwegian throne. Second, Nansen was immediately thrust into the spotlight when the Germans directed him and his team to continue their work on Fornebu Airport, henceforth under the direction of the Luftwaffe. Nansen objected, citing the Hague Convention. After invading a country without even a declaration of war the Germans were scarcely concerned with the niceties of the Hague Convention, and they threatened Nansen with violence. In the end Nansen, who earned the sobriquet *Der schwierige Herr Nansen* [the difficult Mr. Nansen], was able to obtain an acknowledgment in writing from the Luftwaffe general that the Norwegians' work was being carried out under duress. And Nansen's acts of resistance went beyond the passive kind. Following the invasion, he convened at Polhøgda what was to be christened "The Group," a select body of influential people, including Eivind Berggrav, primate of the Norwegian Church; Didrik Seip, rector of the University of Oslo; Jacob Worm-Müller, professor at the University of Oslo; Gunnar Jahn, former minister of finance; Paal Berg, chief justice of the Supreme Court; and Jens Olaf Gjerløw, an influential newspaper editor, to formulate policy for an occupied Norway. Nansen was elected chairman of The Group.[63]

More importantly still, Odd Nansen had clashed with Vidkun Quisling, and Quisling was suddenly now the man on top. To be sure, Quisling's short-lived coup d'état following the invasion (April 9–15, 1940), and the manner of his later 1942 installation as minister-president, made it abundantly clear to all that he and Nasjonal Samling served at the sufferance of their Nazi bosses. Nevertheless, as head of the only legally recognized political party, and later the nominal government, Quisling wielded considerable power in running Norway's affairs. The real overlord of Norway, *Reichskommissar* Josef Terboven, announced in September 1940, "Henceforth there is only one road to a solution calculated to give the Norwegian people freedom and independence. It leads through Nasjonal Samling."[64] Running afoul of Quisling had its risks.

Nansen's well-publicized efforts on behalf of Jewish refugees hardly endeared him to Quisling, whose anti-Semitic official party newspaper, *Fritt Folk* [Free People] had railed against Jewish immigration since its launch in 1936.[65] And Nansen, no shrinking violet, met the challenge head-on. In a 1939 lecture on "The Jewish Problem in Norway," Quisling declared that "all Jews must be expelled immediately from the country." Nansen, in the audience, interrupted Quisling's address with the question: "[Y]ou Quisling, better than most, know the refugees' horrible fate. You do not wish that we should turn them over to certain destruction without lifting a finger to help? To what do you think the Jewish refugees . . . can resort?" Quisling's curt conclusion—"That doesn't concern me!"—laid bare, if any further proof were needed, his lack of empathy for, indeed hatred of, Norway's Jews.[66] As Quisling later solemnly declared: "A Jew is not a Norwegian, not a European. . . . Jews have no place in Europe. . . . For us there can be no compromise."[67]

But the real feud between Quisling and Nansen was even more personal than an argument over the fate of Norway's Jews; it involved Odd's father. Fridtjof Nansen and Quisling had worked closely together in Russia during the 1920s. Out of this grew, according to Quisling's first wife Alexandra, "a contradictory mixture of hero worship and bitter resentment," specifically, resentment over Nansen's failure to give proper public credit to Quisling for his contributions. This bitterness, wrote Alexandra, became acute after Nansen was awarded the Nobel Peace Prize.[68] Never personally close, the two had in any event long since drifted apart, as Quisling's attitude "changed from an avid Russophile to an ardent anti-Communist."[69] Nevertheless, Quisling now fashioned himself as Fridtjof Nansen's spiritual heir and repeatedly invoked the elder Nansen's name in such a way as to imply that, were he alive, Fridtjof would have fully supported Nasjonal Samling's goals and policies. Speeches where Nansen had warned against the dangers of *both* communism *and* fascism were edited to remove any condemnation of the latter.[70] All this was too much for his son, and Odd demanded a personal audience with Quisling. They met July 8, 1940, a month after the last fighting forces in Norway had surrendered and King Haakon VII had fled the country to set up a government-in-exile in England.[71] Nansen, as always, went straight to the point:

> I come to you, Quisling, not because I believe you will pay particular attention to what I have to say, and what I will ask, but because it is a matter of conscience for me to speak. . . . I ask that you first let my father's name rest in peace. You know full well, Quisling, that you cheat when you use Fridtjof Nansen's name in support of your politics.

In response Quisling "stood erect and slammed his fist so hard that the desk shook—thundering his denial and claiming the sacrifices he had made gave him full right to use Fridtjof's revered name." Now backed by the full might of the Nazi occupiers, Quisling wasn't likely to forgive, or forget, what Nansen himself conceded were "my profoundly insulting pronouncements."[72]

Quisling and the Nazis now awaited only the right opportunity to get even. Meanwhile, by the fall of 1941 Nansen's circle was rapidly constricting. Arne Fjellbu, dean of Nidaros Cathedral and a member of The Group, reflected in his diary for October 24 of that year about the gatherings at Polhøgda, "where we this last year have been assembled several times. . . . This evening many were missing. Rector Seip and Professor Otto Mohr [both arrested September 1941] were absent. Director Harald Grieg [arrested June 1941] and Professor Johan Holst [fled to Sweden October 1941] could not be along in the circle. The mood of the gathering was marked by this. . . . Who shall have been taken next time we meet?"[73]

Quisling's chance finally arrived in late December, in the form of British commando raids on the Norwegian coast, dubbed Operations "Anklet" and "Archery," during which the commandos arrested several NS members and carried them back to England. In retaliation for what he termed a "kidnapping . . . in violation of international law," *Reichskommissar* Josef Terboven ordered the arrest of twenty "court hostages," close friends of the royal family, including Nansen.[74] On January 13, 1942, Nansen was picked up at his business partner's cabin. Four days later Terboven informed Quisling that after months of waiting in the wings, he would finally be installed as minister-president of Norway.[75] In assuming this position, Quisling announced that he had merged all royal, governmental, and parliamentary authority in his person, and, as King Haakon had been the head of the Norwegian Church, he would, for good measure, assume that title as well.[76] Although Quisling, with or without titles, was a figure of near-universal derision, Nansen's path to freedom now had but one road, and that road led through Vidkun Quisling. Of all the "court hostages" arrested along with Nansen in January 1942, he was the only one never to be released for the duration of the war.[77]

Following Nansen's arrest, Nansenhjelpen managed to continue operating for a while, providing advice and financial assistance to those refugees who had not yet fled to Sweden, and clothing to prisoners released from captivity.[78] It was finally shut down by the Nazis in the autumn of 1942, just as Norway's version of the "Final Solution" was getting under way.[79]

AFTER THE WAR, NANSEN RETURNED to his professional and humanitarian pursuits. He oversaw the restoration of Polhøgda[80] and resumed work on Fornebu Airport, in which he was eventually assisted by his children Eigil and Siri, both of whom joined his firm as architects. L. Corrin Strong, the US ambassador to Norway (1953–1957) was so taken with a *hytte* [cabin] he saw in Norway designed by Nansen that he commissioned Nansen to design a traditional *hytte* for him as well. Strong went one unusual step further: He had Nansen actually construct the cabin in Norway, let it "season" for a year, then had the structure disassembled, shipped to the United States and reassembled (using Norwegian carpenters, supervised by Eigil) on an island off the coast of Maine, where it stands (complete with grass roof) today.[81]

In addition, Nansen remained deeply committed to humanitarian causes. In 1947 he helped found Én Verden (One World), a "bipartisan and independent organization working for peace and for a world governed by international law." Én Verden is affiliated with the World Federalist Movement, which has consultative status at the UN.[82] In 1950 the director general of UNESCO engaged Nansen as a "temporary consultant" to investigate conditions in Germany, which he duly visited twice that year. Nansen reported that millions of refugees and expellees were in distress, without homes or jobs, and "apt to succumb to extreme nationalistic or other radical ideologies."[83] He recommended UNESCO coordinate the reconstruction efforts of all governmental and nongovernmental agencies to increase their effectiveness, with a particular emphasis on youth activities and education. These recommendations ultimately led in part to the formation of UNESCO's Institute for Education (UIE), the forerunner to the current Institute for Lifelong Learning. According to UNESCO's website, the UIE is "intended as a vehicle to promote human rights and international understanding."[84]

After the war Nansen also published several other books besides *From Day to Day*, including a work on the German postwar refugee problem, a memoir: *Langs Veien: Opplevelser, Møter og Samtaler* [*Along the Way: Events, Meetings and Conversations*], an edited selection of his father's writings in seven volumes (with the assistance of his daughter Marit), and, three years before his death, a more extended treatment of his relationship with Thomas Buergenthal, a young prisoner he befriended in Sachsenhausen: *Tommy: En Sannferdig Fortelling* [*Tommy: A True Story*].

Odd Nansen died in 1973, followed by his beloved Kari in 1985.

ODD NANSEN GREW UP IN THE OVERSIZED SHADOW of his famous father. By the time Odd was born, Fridtjof Nansen was no longer simply a hero or a celebrity, but had passed into the realm of legend. The year Odd turned twenty-one and crossed the threshold of adulthood, his father received the Nobel Peace Prize, an accolade bestowed on few mortals. How much of a burden the Nansen name created for Odd can never be known. One anecdote, however, is revealing. A friend once asked Odd why he had not named his own sons after his famous father. Nansen's reply—"But what if the child grows up and is less gifted than what is anticipated of him? Imagine the horrible burden that this child would have to carry with such an important name."—may well have been as much a projection of his own fears about whether he had measured up to "what was anticipated of him" as an expression of concern for his children.[85]

Odd was certainly the antithesis of his father in many ways. He had none of the blond, Nordic features of his father, whom contemporaries described as "a modern Viking."[86] More importantly, it is nigh impossible to picture him forcing his children to down porridge day after everlasting day, or forbidding Kari to show maternal affection to their children. Nor would any biographer be likely to characterize him as "maintain[ing] his awesome dignity," as Roland Huntford does when describing Fridtjof's polar journeying.[87] Even Fridtjof once admitted to a friend that "[Odd] is very much nicer than I am."[88] Fridtjof was also something of a ladies' man; the index to his biography has a separate heading for his female friends, containing fifteen names in addition to his two wives. Odd Nansen's devotion to his wife and family infuses every page of his diary.

And yet the two did share many traits in common. According to Nansen's wife Kari, who knew them both well, "Odd is terribly like his father in everything."[89] Both were physically imposing people. Fridtjof was an outstanding athlete, tall, strong, and powerful; American reporters in 1939 described Odd as being "built like a football fullback."[90] More importantly, both possessed a strength of character bordering almost on intransigence. Nothing, it seemed, was more important than following one's inner compass, and each appeared willing to sacrifice pretty much everything for its sake. Compare Odd's fateful July 1940 confrontation with Quisling as "a matter of conscience" with the conclusion of another of Fridtjof's biographers that the "spirit of compromise was absolutely foreign to him."[91] Both father and son were incapable of dissimulation. They both seemed ineluctably drawn to the plight of the underdog. In addition to being talented artists, both were extremely fluent writers. Odd's prison diary, composed under the most challenging conditions imaginable, nevertheless reads better than many memoirs and autobiographies carefully crafted with the help of professional editors. Likewise, biographer Huntford concludes, "[Fridtjof] was a master of prose."[92] Odd's sister Liv described their father's writing style: "[Y]ou can see from his manuscripts that he must always have had what he wanted to say clear in his head before he began to write. There are almost no corrections."[93] Odd Nansen's original diary pages similarly evidence almost no corrections. Both father and son had remarkable work habits. Fridtjof "was one of those who work well at night, and often he sat up until five in the morning . . . and by nine . . . he would have had breakfast and dealt with his [mail]."[94] Odd frequently composed his diary late into the night, while all his fellow prisoners slept. And, finally, as we will see, both father and son shared similar ideas and often used eerily similar language to express themselves.

In 1893, Fridtjof Nansen embarked on his polar expedition, a journey that lasted thirty-nine months, testing man's resolve against the natural elements. Almost fifty years later his son also embarked, certainly more reluctantly, on a journey that lasted only slightly longer—forty months—this time testing one's resolve against manmade challenges: selfishness, fear, doubt, and despair. Yet against both, their greatest weapon was the same: their character. In his old age Fridtjof was often visited by his daughter Liv, where they talked "of many things, including literature." In the explorer's youth the Norwegian playwright Henrik Ibsen had made the greatest impression, but more recently Dostoyevsky had become his idol. Fridtjof of course did not live to witness the horrors of World War II, nor could he have foreseen Odd's role in it, but in describing to Liv the newfound significance of Dostoyevsky, he used prescient words that sound uncannily as if he were describing his own son:

> [H]e was taken by Dostoievsky's [*sic*] great humanity, his remarkable insight into suffering, his boundless sympathy, his humility, and his capacity for self-knowledge.[95]

II. THE DIARY

Nansen was already an inveterate diarist at the time of his arrest in 1942, and had been for many years; he even had the presence of mind, when the police arrived, to pack along paper and pen to continue his writing. His secret note taking began with his very first night in jail and continued, more or less daily, throughout his captivity. With an unsparing eye Nansen recorded the casual brutality and random terror that was the fate of a camp prisoner. His entries reveal the quiet strength, and sometimes ugly prejudices, of his fellow Norwegians; his palpable longing for his wife and family; his constantly frustrated hopes for an early end to the war; his horror at the especially barbaric treatment reserved for the Jews. The diary brilliantly illuminates Nansen's daily struggle, not only to survive but to preserve his sanity and maintain his humanity in a world engulfed by fear and hate. Very little escaped his attention. The Norwegian edition, published in 1947, comprised three volumes, and even that represented, according to Nansen, only one-third of the entire manuscript: "most of the private matter has been cut out." The original English version, published in 1949 and upon which the present volume is based, had "again been much reduced," according to translator Katherine John.[96] Even so it is a detailed portrayal of camp life, almost cinematic in its focus and sweep.[97]

Nansen's diary can be divided into four segments, each corresponding to a different stage of his incarceration. For the first seven months of his captivity (January 1942–August 1942) Nansen was held at Grini Prison, Norway's largest concentration camp, located on the outskirts of Oslo.[98] Originally intended as a women's prison and completed in early 1940, Grini was commandeered by the Nazis following their invasion and used first as a POW camp, then as a German Army barracks, and finally after June 1941 as a *Polizeihaftlager*, or police detention camp. Primarily, but not exclusively, designed to hold political prisoners, more than nineteen thousand Norwegians (with a handful of foreigners, such as an occasional captured British commando) spent time at Grini, although the camp's maximum population never exceeded approximately six thousand at any one time. Even this number far outstripped Grini's initial capacity, which required the construction of extra barracks, a process begun in 1942 that engaged Nansen's architectural skills. Camp life in Grini, while unpleasant, was not unbearable for most. In the early months of his captivity Nansen was even allowed outside the camp to pick up building supplies in Oslo. Sometimes a surreptitious meeting with Kari could be arranged. The food was inadequate, but Nansen joked that he could afford to lose a few pounds and still "be none the worse." His status as a hostage and his professional tasks kept him for the most part from unpleasant physical labor. Even so, life was no bed of roses. Others faced the penal gang, beatings, and, occasionally, execution.[99]

From mid-August 1942 until late November of that year, Nansen, along with approximately four hundred other prisoners, was sent more than a thousand miles north, to Veidal Camp, well above the Arctic Circle, to help construct snow shelters designed to keep the mountain roads passable. While creature comforts in the primitive camp were nonexistent, life again was tolerable, even if only barely so. With the onset of winter in earnest (Nansen records the season's first snowfall on August 30), the combination of ever-shorter working days and inhospitable working conditions spelled the return of all prisoners to Grini. Initially, their hard work at Veidal earned Nansen and his coworkers special privileges back at Grini (the right to smoke, read, write, etc.) no longer afforded to others. But prison life in general had by then turned considerably more unpleasant. During the same month as Nansen's return, Germany suffered twin setbacks at El Alamein and Stalingrad, and the outcome of the war suddenly seemed considerably less certain to the SS guards. Concomitant with these setbacks on the world stage, and prompted no doubt in part by these events and in part by Vidkun Quisling's heavy-handed policies, resistance in Norway intensified.[100] By late 1942 the occupation authorities had been stymied in their efforts to Nazify the nation's schools, churches, and organized sports. All this undoubtedly led to a souring of the atmosphere at Grini. Punishment drills were stepped up, as were surprise inspections. As Nansen noted, "It's plain that things are getting more rigorous in every sphere." By August 1943 Nansen had become an irritant to his German overseers—he had never hesitated to speak his mind—and was increasingly deemed to be nothing more than a "contemptible humanist" and "Jew-lover," incapable of adjusting to the New World Order. A good faith attempt by Nansen to increase prisoner cooperation in return for the removal of a notorious camp informer backfired, leaving him demoted to the penal gang, with fewer and fewer privileges.

When a harmless prank subsequently went horribly awry, Nansen found himself slated for deportation to Sachsenhausen; 7,500 other Norwegians also ended up in concentration camps in Europe before the war ended. Rumors of worse treatment at Germany's many camps had already filtered back to Grini. Nansen was warned that he need not entertain any hopes of ever returning to Norway; that his friends might just as well go ahead and erect a monument upon his grave. Despite these warnings and despite plenty of firsthand experience with Nazi methods, the reality of Sachsenhausen proved still worse, far worse, than anyone had imagined.

The diary's final section begins with Nansen's October 1943 arrival in Oranienburg, Germany, site of KL Sachsenhausen. By then the tide of the war had long since turned against Germany: in July Mussolini had been deposed, Hamburg destroyed in a firestorm, Sicily invaded, and the German army mauled on the Russian steppes at Kursk. But the certainty of Germany's defeat and the timing of that defeat were entirely different issues. Hitler's resolve to fight to the last man and Joseph Goebbels' "Total War" initiative meant there would be no repeat of November 1918, no sudden collapse of the home front, no mutinies. Even the opening of the "second front" in Normandy was still almost a year away. And so Nansen would spend another nineteen months in captivity, in Sachsenhausen and, in the war's final weeks, in KL Neuengamme, on the outskirts of Hamburg, where he was moved as part of an evacuation orchestrated by the Swedish Red Cross. Although Nansen spent almost one-half of his entire captivity in Germany, this portion of the diary is considerably shorter than the preceding sections. Undoubtedly the difficulty in concealing a growing manuscript and the dramatically worse conditions prevailing in Sachsenhausen account in large part for this diminished output. And the conditions in Sachsenhausen were considerably worse. As Nansen quickly admitted soon after arriving, "It didn't occur to me that I should ever look back on [Grini] with longing. And now it's happened. [Grini] now looks to me like an idyll compared to this hell."

Sachsenhausen, together with its numerous subcamps, was a sprawling, polyglot community, many times larger than Grini, populated with inmates from practically every country in Europe: Russia, Ukraine, Poland, Germany, Denmark, France, Britain, Belgium, Holland, Denmark, Czechoslovakia, Greece, Romania, Hungary—forty countries in all. Located twenty miles north of Berlin, Sachsenhausen was the first concentration camp built after the SS gained full control of the entire camp system. Constructed in 1936 (around the same time as Nansen was forming Nansenhjelpen), it was expected to serve as a model facility, but in the end no other camp followed its unusual triangular layout.[101] Oranienburg was also home to the Inspectorate of Concentration Camps and served in many ways as the administrative center of the SS; its communications facilities, supply and armament depots, and repair facilities were all sited nearby, and Sachsenhausen's prisoners provided the necessary labor force.[102] Over its nine-year existence, Sachsenhausen and its satellite camps housed an estimated 200,000 prisoners; nearly 70,000 at their peak in February 1945.[103] Nansen's tone perceptibly darkens as soon as he arrives in Germany. Now his goal, his focus, is on staying as healthy as possible and surviving what seems like an interminable

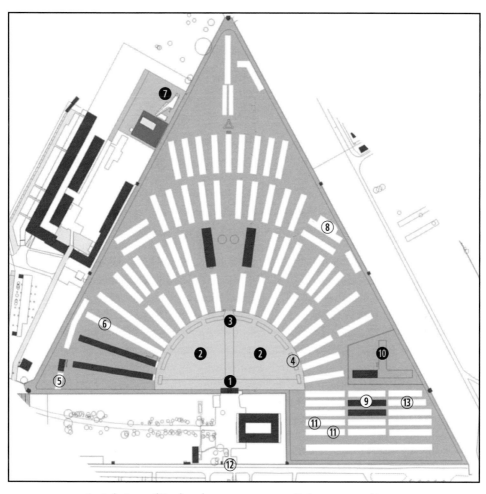

Aerial view of Sachsenhausen. SOURCE: © *hg merz architects*

1   Gatehouse
2   Roll call area
3   Gallows
4   Shoe-testing track
5   Brothel
6   *Revier* III (where Nansen met Buergenthal)
7   *Industriehof* (site of execution trench,
    gas chamber, and crematorium)
8   Delousing unit
9   Block 38
10 Bunker
11 Blocks 18 & 19 (counterfeiting)
12 Outer gate and exit to work stations
    KDW and Herz As
13 Block 58

stay, as the war crawls along with agonizing slowness to its dénouement. Nansen realized all too well that any mishap, any sickness, any infraction with a power-drunk overseer, could render him one of those unfortunates who found themselves "up the chimney," as inmates euphemistically described the crematorium. As one historian observes, "There was no sure way to survive the KL . . . but there were countless ways to die."[104]

Although Sachsenhausen was a concentration camp designed primarily to hold political prisoners, and not a *Vernichtungslager*, or extermination camp, its inmates could be forgiven for failing to detect the difference. By 1943 the camp was equipped with its own gas chamber, crematorium, and even a mobile gallows. Before the war ended between 30,000 and 50,000 of its inmates went up the chimney, dying of neglect, exhaustion, starvation, disease, and outright murder. Death could come for any reason or no reason. In a typical vignette emblematic of life in the camp, Nansen related, "[A] transport of prisoners one day reached the camp. As usual they were counted. . . . There were two men extra. . . . And German figures *must* and *shall* come right. A few revolver shots . . . worked out the sum. The figure was right again, the two were carried away, they had ceased to be superfluous in this world."

Fortunately Nansen did survive even this. His artistic skills landed him in a workshop making toys for the children of the SS; in the corrupt, upside-down world of the concentration camp, his *kommando* [work squad] was even deemed "vital to the war effort" by the authorities. Such desirable work, requiring little exertion and, equally important, providing shelter and heat, ensured survival, but just barely. Rampant disease, filthy conditions, vicious guards; all these and more combined to make for a precarious existence. A critical advantage accorded to all Norwegians (but to virtually no one else in the camp) was the extra food they were allowed via food parcels from the Red Cross. Norwegians, after all, were considered in the Germans' racial hierarchy as akin to wayward Nordic cousins—wayward in their seeming inability to accept the reality of the New World Order—but cousins nonetheless. This advantage enabled most Norwegians to hang on. Despite periodic debilitating attacks of lumbago[105] and a few unpleasant experiences with the punishment squad, Nansen, too, held on.

But it was a close-run thing. By 1945 a tone of desperation, of mental strain, is increasingly apparent in Nansen's entries. As the war reaches its inexorable climax Nansen begins to face the bitter truth that despite his best efforts, the war's end, so ardently desired for so long, might also bring with it the seeds of his own demise. Allied bombing was reaching a saturation level that often counted defenseless inmates among its victims, including some at Sachsenhausen.[106] An interruption in the supply of Red Cross parcels, dependent as their delivery was on Germany's rapidly crumbling infrastructure, could easily reduce the Norwegians to the level of the starved, half-mad, beast-like inmates who formed the bulk of the camp population.[107] Overcrowding—the population of the main camp swelled to more than twice its size between Nansen's arrival and 1945—exponentially increased the dangers of infectious epidemics. Most frightening of all was the very real possibility that the SS might either massacre everyone or else stage their own *Götterdämmerung* and take down the entire camp with themselves in a desperate final convulsion of violence rather than surrender.[108]

Moreover, the dangers were not all physical. One also senses that Nansen's very sanity was at risk. The sheer arbitrariness of life, the stubborn madness with which the Nazis prolonged the war from season to season, the relentless destruction of bodies and minds, was almost more than someone of Nansen's nature could bear. Nansen lamented not just the physical deaths, which were ubiquitous, but the spiritual deaths experienced by even many survivors:

> For it is not only the corpses of human beings which are burned and annihilated here, not only young, strong bodies which have turned into *Muselmenn*, skeletons and crematorium fuel. On this battlefield the young faith and enthusiasm of thousands has gone under as well, the vital spark of thousands has been quenched in darkness and brutishness. Ideals have vanished; human kindness has turned to ice in many a heart; faith in the future, the will and the force of good have withered as the muscles wither up to useless, dry tissue in the skeleton bodies of the *Muselmenn*. Of all mass murders, this is perhaps the worst.

As Wolfgang Sofsky, author of *The Order of Terror*, the groundbreaking study of the concentration camp, warned, "To see too much was life-threatening. . . . Only if you became inured, sheathed yourself in emotional armor, walking past the corpses without taking notice, could you avoid psychological collapse."[109] While on the one hand Nansen could marvel at "how horribly callous we've become," it is painfully evident that he didn't shut his eyes to the suffering; he continued to see "too much." This torment was exacerbated by feelings of helplessness: "It's more than one can stand in the long run, going to bed with these thoughts every night and waking up with them every morning," Nansen confessed less than four months after his arrest, "*and not being able to help, not being able to do anything to stop this madness*" (emphasis added).

Not surprisingly, Nansen's language becomes more desperate as, in the words of one later reviewer, "outrage is piled upon outrage in the same way that corpses . . . were heaped upon one another."[110] Ultimately, even someone as eloquent as Nansen was reduced to near incoherence: "The language is exhausted. I've exhausted it myself. There are no words left to describe the horrors I've seen with my own eyes. How am I to give even a reflection of the hell I was plunged into yesterday?" Only the timely intervention by Count Folke Bernadotte and the Swedish Red Cross in April 1945, in the so-called "white buses" operation, averted what appears to have been Nansen's imminent mental breakdown. Thousands of Norwegians, Danes, and others were ferried, initially to Neuengamme and shortly thereafter to safety in Denmark and ultimately Sweden. When Nansen's odyssey finally ended, the pent-up anticipation, frustration, fear, and relief combined to all but paralyze him:

> One might have thought it would be easy [to write] a message to one's own wife and the children that here I am, safe and well. But no, it seemed to me impossible, insufferable! . . . I felt like crying with despair and rage. . . .
>
> *Dear, darling Kari!* That seemed to be the only thing with any sense in it. I don't know what more I got down. I had to write something, couldn't say I found it impossible. Only a little message—*I'll be home soon!* Surely I could write that much! And so I wrote that and put it in an envelope, and those wonderfully kind people took it away. And here I am, as bankrupt, as confused and as stupefied as ever, out of contact with reality, because it is in fact unbelievable.

MOST FIRSTHAND ACCOUNTS OF WORLD WAR II in general, and of the concentration camp experience in particular, have come to us from memoirs, sometimes composed shortly after the fact and sometimes recalled only after the passage of many years. Diaries are far more rare. Most prisoners were simply too exhausted, mentally and physically, and too focused on survival to bother with recording their experiences. Writing and preserving notes, Primo Levi observed, was "an unthinkable luxury for the Jews and a possibility of no interest to the criminals," two of the largest groups in the camps.[111] Moreover, maintaining any diary was very risky. If William L. Shirer, a US citizen and CBS journalist working in Berlin, could write about his own diary, "[s]ome of my original notes . . . I burned rather than risk them and myself to the tender mercies of the Gestapo; a few things I dared not write down, attempting [instead] to imprint them in my memory," one realizes the infinitely greater risks confronting a concentration camp diarist.[112]

The practical problem of concealment—both the act of writing and the accumulated product—posed a daunting, ongoing obstacle, quite apart from the nearly insuperable task of secreting the manuscript out of the camp itself. The death of the diarist—a fate experienced by 1.7 million concentration camp prisoners—undoubtedly led in many cases to the loss, destruction, or abandonment of his or her work. No one will ever know how many diaries were never started out of sheer fear, how many disappeared with their owners, how many were confiscated by the authorities, how many were destroyed lest they be captured, how many lost in the act of smuggling.[113] Despite Levi's earlier observation, he actually began (once he obtained a less strenuous job as a chemist in the Buna Works) to secretly jot down notes—names, events, etc.—but soon enough decided to destroy it all; "the very act of writing was suspect and highly dangerous," he later recalled.[114]

Whatever the reason, the empirical result remains the same: contemporary accounts from inside the camps are very rare. As Robert Jan van Pelt, the editor of one such diary observes, "While the number of postwar memoirs written by Holocaust survivors is enormous, and the number of diaries and notebooks written during the Holocaust by Jews while they were at home, or in a ghetto, or in hiding is substantial, the number of testimonies that were written in the inner circles of hell, in the German concentration camps, and that survived the war is small."[115]

In this regard Odd Nansen held several advantages. With the exception of a few short intervals, his status as a professional and a court hostage meant that he was usually spared the exhausting physical labor that was the lot of most prisoners, no small matter for a forty-year-old architect with recurring lumbago issues. As van Pelt writes, "Historians of the Holocaust know that the best—that is, the most useful—testimonies of camp life were produced by those who enjoyed a position of privilege and who, as such, were somewhat sheltered from the full horror of the camp."[116] Moreover, as noted, Nansen, like his father, appeared quite capable of functioning on only a few hours of sleep, allowing him time to compose and record his thoughts at length while everyone else snored fitfully away in their bunks. Finally, as we shall see, Nansen was able while at Grini to successfully smuggle out his diary in installments, and he devised an ingenious solution while in Sachsenhausen. As Levi concludes, "the best historians of the Lagers emerged from among the very few who had the ability and luck to attain a privileged observatory without bowing to compromises, and the skill to tell what they saw, suffered, and did with the humility of a good chronicler."[117] It's hard to imagine a more apt description of Odd Nansen.

One of the benefits of wartime diaries, few though their numbers may be, is that they are less subject to the vagaries of memory. "[O]ur memories are not the tape recorders they were once thought to be," writes Ruth Franklin, literary critic and senior editor at *The New Republic*, in her study of Holocaust literature. Diaries, written in real time, are less fallible. Moreover, they don't have the luxury (or burden) of hindsight; events are not filtered through a subsequent lens that deems them significant or irrelevant. Themes are not imposed to make sense of the experience. The benefit of retrospect, the knowledge of what happened next, can easily, even if unconsciously, reshape the narrative of the past. Primo Levi recognized the danger arising from the passage of time. It can create "ever more blurred and stylized memories, often, unbeknownst to [the writer]," he wrote, as they become "influenced by information gained from later readings or the stories of others."[118]

In contrast, in a diary events are transcribed as and when experienced by the writer without concern for their ultimate meaning or significance; they are noted simply because they loom large at the moment or otherwise capture the writer's attention. If "[e]*very* memoir, by definition, is written from the standpoint of the later self," when there is no "later self," as in a diary, the chances of distortion, omission, and commission are minimized.[119] One reviewer of *From Day to Day* noted in 1949, "His book is not the record of a shattering experience recollected in tranquility and turned into a work of art, but the experience itself set down on bits of paper while it was going on."[120] Nansen resisted any impulse to subsequently revisit and reshape events after the fact; other than one section that was lost and had to be reconstructed, "the diary is the original text, with nothing added, corrected, or rewritten."[121]

Diaries lack a historical determinism. This unfiltered approach lends an immediacy, and intimacy, which even a memoir cannot match. We see hopes raised and dashed, fears realized or forgotten, seeming crises fade into insignificance, while insignificant events, such as a practical joke, have far-reaching consequences. When Nansen describes his chance meeting with gentle Olaf Kullmann, "with his odd touch of deep earnestness," he could little guess that he was writing Kullmann's elegy, that in less than two months Kullmann would be sent to Sachsenhausen, and in less than five months he would be dead. And how could Nansen fathom in April 1942 the depths of the Holocaust when he wrote, "I must say that I don't feel confident about what may happen to these Jews [at Grini]." Nansen first hears of the arrival of the new *Lagerkommandant*, Denzer, and wonders "[p]erhaps he may be one long disaster to us all," little realizing that Denzer would be the one who consigns him to Sachsenhausen seventeen months later. Nansen exults on August 20, 1943, that Kari is still able to visit him and that "life is beautiful and wonderful even if Grini should get still fuller of demons than it is now." One month later he was on a transport to Sachsenhausen. And what is one to make of one of the most fascinating entries of all, when Nansen visits a fortune teller on June 19, 1944. The palm reader "[p]redicted that on the 21st or possibly the 20th of July a terrible disaster would befall Germany, which would bring the war to a close." Clearly a lowly prisoner in Sachsenhausen was not privy to the plot to assassinate Hitler. Indeed, the date of the attempt on Hitler's life wasn't even known to the conspirators when Nansen made his visit; it depended entirely on Count von Stauffenberg's ability to attend Hitler's military briefing at his bunker in East Prussia. As we now know, an assassination attempt was indeed made on July 20, but the bomb, hidden in von Stauffenberg's briefcase, was moved at the last minute and the blast, deflected by the heavy briefing table, only slightly injured Hitler while killing four others in the room. It is the province of counterfactual enthusiasts to speculate what effect, if any, a successful assassination would have had on an early termination of the war. At the time of Nansen's June 19 visit, the prediction must have seemed like a fanciful lark; on July 20th it came within a hair's breadth of being realized.[122]

These are but a few of the many examples that make the diary form so unique. And so, in many ways a diary is more like a novel than a history. The protagonist's path is unknown to him; although we can skip ahead and see how it all turns out, the protagonist must experience events as they come, without a roadmap. In reading *From Day to Day* we each time reimmerse ourselves in the world as Nansen experienced it and relive those often terrifying, sometimes uplifting, sometimes humorous, but always unknowable, always uncertain, always worrying, times through his humane and courageous eyes.

The Diary

Nansen's diary served a dual purpose from the very start. It acted primarily as a kind of running blog for his wife Kari, describing events and feelings so that she—whose sporadic visits depended on the whims of the Gestapo, were limited to a mere ten to fifteen minutes, and were under constant supervision—could understand what her husband was really experiencing.[123] But the diary was also a means of processing Nansen's deepest thoughts and emotions. It helped Nansen "arrange my ideas" and thereby relieve his mind of all that weighed on it; it became his "private manner of forgetting."

As noted, maintaining a diary in a concentration camp was not without enormous risk. Less than three weeks into captivity all prisoners were reminded at evening roll call that diaries were strictly forbidden. The resulting tension between Nansen's need to preserve his thoughts and the possible penalties if caught forms a continuous dynamic throughout the ensuing months of his captivity.

Time and again, Nansen admits, "I must write," "I must unburden my memory," "I can't let it alone," and "it's such a blessed help to me, such a comfort." At the same time, the risk of detection weighed on him. "If they should come across these notes . . . it would mean more than five days' solitary confinement, I'm afraid," Nansen remarked soon after his arrest. His family and friends outside Grini felt he was taking "insane" risks keeping such a diary. Even Nansen had to admit that "it would be a fine business if all rocks were happily avoided and then they were to find this document." The stakes got even higher in Sachsenhausen; a Sachsenhausen guard once killed an inmate for leaving an ink stain on a letter, which he suspected might be a secret code.[124] Inevitably, there were some close calls, and inevitably Nansen grew more cautious. In February 1944 a Dutchman was found keeping a diary "and that may lead to disaster [for him]." Even Nansen thought it best to stop at least for a while; the next entry isn't until over a fortnight later. Five months later Nansen again recorded that he had taken a break in writing to be on the safe side. "I somehow felt that they [the camp guards] were wondering very hard what the devil I was doing in secret under the table." Again, that caution didn't last long before Nansen felt the compulsion again—the next entry represented a gap of only nine days.[125]

Added to the strain of engaging in a desperately needed yet potentially lethal undertaking was the task of preserving and then transmitting the diary out of confinement. In Grini concealment proved not to be difficult. "I hide it in such a way that not a devil in hell will find it," Nansen boasted, including one "absolutely safe place": inside the privy. In addition, the camp's boundaries were porous, and well-established channels for smuggling were soon established. It is remarkable that Nansen was able to safely entrust parts of his diary with perfect strangers; he even engaged the services of a Wehrmacht driver, whom he describes as "ungovernable, frankly dangerous," to deliver sections of the diary directly to Kari living at Polhøgda. Insane risks indeed! And yet with the single exception of the seven-week period covering his final days at Grini and his transport to Sachsenhausen, which was lost, all these segments made their way into safe hands.

Nansen's mental burdens increased exponentially when he arrived at Sachsenhausen, since the "exit plan," as it were, for his diary was much more murky. Smuggling opportunities were nonexistent, and the guards let no one in or out of the camp absent a search done with typical Teutonic thoroughness. Nansen had to face the very real possibility that all of his efforts, all of his recorded thoughts and impressions for the final nineteen months of captivity, might come to naught. No matter. The will to record and confide overcame even this new obstacle. Within days of arriving at Sachsenhausen, Nansen admitted, "I'm simply taking the chance that [the time for me to leave here] will coincide with the end of the war, and that all . . . controls will be done away with. So I write hopefully on."

Nansen ultimately hit upon an inspired solution to his dilemma: hiding the diary in the hollowed-out center of his and his friends' breadboards.[126] But even this was not a complete guarantee of safe transit. As late as April 18, 1945, while awaiting evacuation via the Swedish Red Cross, Nansen heard rumors that upon arrival outside of Germany "*everything* [a prisoner had] without exception, is burned." By then, Nansen's friend Frode Rinnan had already been evacuated. All Nansen could do was wistfully speculate, "I wonder if that [Frode's breadboard] escaped?"

All six breadboards did arrive in Norway, intact, and our picture of the inside of the living hell that was a concentration camp is immeasurably richer for it. As Nansen had once speculated, "So many strange moods, so many queer experiences, so much intensely dramatic stuff will emerge again from these pages when I turn to them later on in life." In truth, his diary is far more than a compilation of strange moods, queer experiences, and intense drama. In the words of Christopher Montague Woodhouse, British World War II hero and later Member of Parliament, writing for *The Times Literary Supplement*: "The number of men who have successfully exploited the unique character of the diary as an art-form can still be counted on the fingers of one hand. It might be well worth taking a bet that posterity will place . . . Nansen among them."[127]

Fellow Norwegians

Nansen's diary casts an honest, critical eye on everyone, not least himself and his fellow countrymen. His pride in his fellow Norwegians, his expectation of only the highest standards of decency, patriotism, and solidarity, meant that Nansen was, not surprisingly, often disappointed in their behavior.

In Grini, at least, the conditions of captivity fostered a united front against a single foe: the Nazis and their collaborators. And in this setting Nansen was repeatedly impressed with his compatriots. He frequently remarks on the incomparable bravery of prisoners facing torture and possible death: "These men are fine types of Norwegian patriots." This pride culminated when Nansen was thrown into the camp jail at Grini, on a diet of bread and water, while awaiting transport to Sachsenhausen. Like many such environs, the cell holding Nansen was not really as isolated as it at first seemed. When the jailers were away, an underground communication system immediately established contact, providing moral support and, equally important, cigarettes, letters, and food, all ingeniously delivered to the cell via "string mail" or in a sock tied to a pole slung from window to window. "Here the solidarity and comradeship was better than anywhere else in the camp, better indeed than anywhere else I know of. Unseen, unknown lads . . . some awaiting a death sentence; many with nothing left but hope, and some without even that; all willing to share the little they had with one another, all ready to help a comrade in need with food and clothing, with word and deed. Of all my long time in prison, which lasted forty months, I think those eight days were the most impressive and the best."

At Sachsenhausen, the moral universe became much more complicated. First, there was now an infinitely more layered society, stratified along national (more than three dozen nations represented), political (communist v. noncommunist), religious (Jew v. non-Jew), linguistic (German-speaking v. non-German-speaking), class, educational, and other fault lines, all jockeying for position and privilege. And this contest for the survival of the fittest was engendered in large part by the grim truth that lay behind the cliché: only the fittest were likely to survive in the struggle of all against all. Grini had seen some of its prisoners tortured and even killed, and everyone was usually hungry. But no one had died of malnutrition, exposure, disease, overwork. Within a month of his arrival at Sachsenhausen, Nansen realized the new truth: "Things are different here."

In this new environment, Nansen continued to expect the best from his fellow countrymen, but now they were more often found wanting. "The average Norwegian, even, treats a Ukrainian worse than he would a dog at home." Some Norwegians began to adopt, by virtue of their (relatively) privileged position, the *Herrenvolk* [master race] consciousness of their overlords. This sense of entitlement destroyed one's ability to empathize with the plight of all "others"—Jews, Ukrainians, Poles, and Russian POWs, who had the worst of everything. Nansen rails repeatedly against this smugness, admitting it was a subject on which "I get so easily worked up." Nansen simply could not feel right when he was well off among so many who were not. "The only possible relief is to share the material goods which are divided among us so unequally and unjustly," he decried.

And so it was not without a little bitterness that Nansen realized that despite all this, "no doubt we think ourselves heroes! No doubt we expect to return to Norway as heroes and be feted as such!" Neither selfishness nor self-aggrandizement was in Nansen's DNA, and he had a particularly hard time contemplating it in his own countrymen.

Kari

There was one Norwegian that Nansen never found wanting: his wife Kari. Unfortunately, his chances to interact with Kari declined inexorably as the war continued. Four months into captivity Nansen, sent on an errand into Oslo, was able to meet Kari where "we had a snug little lunch of sandwiches and beer. . . . [W]e could have a proper, quiet talk." Soon thereafter such trips were banned and Nansen was reduced to short, supervised encounters with Kari. At Sachsenhausen, Nansen's lifeline became much more tenuous, consisting of letters (all censored, of course) which were permitted twice per month. In a cruel logic that made sense only to the Nazis, any incoming letter that failed the censor was discarded, but the envelope was delivered, which counted against the twice monthly quota. Well-meaning third parties sending inappropriate letters thus often meant that Kari's letters were returned or discarded, leaving Nansen with nothing more to show for the month than two empty envelopes. And in the Catch-22 world of a concentration camp prisoner, there was no way Nansen could warn anyone of this rule without himself running afoul of the censor. Thus, a letter from Kari, when it made it through at all, was something of a minor miracle and celebrated as such.

Whether it was an all-too-short visit or a letter, this connection was nevertheless crucial to Nansen. Even if they talked of "everything and nothing," seeing Kari was like "drinking vitality and jubilant happiness from an inexhaustible cup." In Sachsenhausen, Nansen observes "absolutely no one, who hasn't been in prison . . . can understand the meaning of a letter from home. I almost think it's the most important thing here—even including food."[128] When a letter arrives, it is "a living breath of home. . . . One is pulled straight back where one belongs." Another letter from Kari is "full of immortality." For his part, Nansen let his diary do the real talking while he was at Grini; at Sachsenhausen Nansen was perversely comforted by the fact that his letters were heavily censored and the diary out of reach for the duration: "I'm glad they know nothing of this at home—or of anything that goes on in German concentration camps."

As Nansen dreamed of the day when he would be reunited with Kari and his family (now grown to four children; his youngest, Odd Erik, was born September 18, 1942, just over nine months after his arrest), he was frightened that his "heart will break with joy." Yet by April 1945, as deliverance was at hand—the Swedish Red Cross was beginning to evacuate Norwegian and Danish prisoners—Nansen began to get cold feet: "[S]uddenly it's as though home and she and the children were so far away—further than ever." Shortly thereafter, now safely in Danish hands, Nansen had a near breakdown. "[A]ll I have been longing for for all these years with all my soul [seemed] more remote than ever." Is it any wonder that upon arrival in Sweden, Nansen could no longer even remember his own telephone number? His love had carried him far, but its very intensity threatened to leave him defenseless once the reality of freedom hit home.

"[E]ven though," as Nansen writes, "most of the private matter [in the diary] has been cut out," in many ways *From Day to Day* can still be viewed as one long love letter to Kari, its originally intended audience of one. Explaining his illicit writing activity to his *Stubenältester* [room leader] in Sachsenhausen, Nansen told him, "I'm writing a love story," a truer description than he perhaps realized or intended. He constantly addresses her with his innermost thoughts. Many of his entries end with a goodnight salutation to Kari. Nansen frets over her pregnancy, is watchful during their visits for any signs of fatigue or despair; he is buoyed by the expectation of the next visit, the next letter. A visit is a "radiant moment." Like a love-struck schoolboy, Nansen confesses that he "could have sat for hours and just looked at her, held her hand . . . and been in heaven." Some of his most poetic writing is to her or about her. On Kari's birthday: "I know your thoughts are going out to me, and they meet mine halfway, and we're together all the same." When Nansen is awaiting another visit: "This place is so quiet that I can hear your heart beating." And perhaps the most poignant line of all, full of pathos, suffering, vulnerability, and love: "I can't do anything without you, not even be in prison." It's not for nothing that Nansen chose to introduce his original work with the final lines from Thornton Wilder's novel *The Bridge of*

San Luis Rey: "But the love will have been enough, . . . There is a land of the living and a land of the dead and the bridge is love, the only survival, the only meaning."[129] It was the bonds of love, more than anything else, that kept Nansen alive, hopeful, and human, during his long days of darkness. Love indeed *was* the only survival, the only meaning.

Resistance

Nansen was a "court hostage"; he was never charged with any offense, although he was in fact involved in the Resistance, what he later called his "wanton playing with fire." He was imprisoned because of his status: who he was, who he and his family were friends with (the royal family), and what he stood for (uncompromising resistance to Quisling and the Nazis). As a hostage he was not treated—at least initially—as badly as most other prisoners in Grini.

The other nineteen court hostages arrested at the same time as Nansen were all subsequently released throughout 1942 and 1943; Nansen alone saw no freedom until the end of the war. It is debatable whether Nansen would have been released early as well even if he had been a model prisoner. After all, as we have seen, Nansen had a unique additional strike against him: he had crossed swords with Vidkun Quisling, the most powerful Norwegian during the war.

In any event Odd Nansen was never a model prisoner. His diary is a record of what often can only be characterized as a low-level guerilla war against his captors. As his father had observed as far back as 1929, "[Odd] is a good boy, and quite intelligent; and he likes to argue—perhaps a little too much."[130] Nansen was the spokesman on behalf of others protesting inhumane conditions; he openly satirized the Germans; he challenged them in debate at every turn, and he never minced his words. In this seeming intransigence Nansen was truly his father's heir. The elder Nansen had never been one to think with the crowd or trim his positions based on what others thought. Fridtjof had attributed this, in a speech once, to "living a great deal alone"—think of all those years on his expeditions—where he had acquired the habit of making up his own mind without asking the opinion of others. Fridtjof also liked to quote Ibsen that "man is strongest who stands most alone."[131]

Nansen's struggles were both subtle and overt. Because of his artistic talents, he was often commissioned by his captors to create cards, paintings, posters, carvings, and the like. As he recognized, such works could serve a dual purpose. Tasked by his jailers with drawing posters encouraging the prevention of lice, Nansen's messages, "Cleanse your land of lice" and "Away with the lice," were, he wrote, "impossible to misunderstand." For a German officer he drew a birthday card with a pig's head showing through a cut-out in the front cover, where it was adorned with a German officer's cap and uniform. Nansen's friends were sure the jibe would be noticed and he would earn a spell in solitary (it wasn't and he didn't).

Nansen's efforts didn't stop at double meanings and sly and not so sly digs at his jailors. He never let an opportunity pass to confront his tormentors and challenge their illusions of ultimate victory. Nansen took comfort that "[n]ot one word has ever crossed my lips that . . . can [be] interpret[ed] as an advance.[132] On the contrary." His philosophy was simple: "[I]t's a kind of treason to hold one's tongue." Having a long political argument with a guard, Nansen admits, "I have never been more rude. The hut was simply gasping for breath." Similar confrontations appear throughout the diary, with guards and with officials, low and high. His jailer-in-chief, Denzer, once invited Nansen during a heated argument (over art) to be as loud as he liked. "[S]uddenly a devil got into me, and I became completely reckless. I threw all precaution overboard. . . . [F]or a long time we stood facing each other . . . shouting each other down and thumping the table. It was delicious to hurl out all I thought—practically without the least restraint. Of course I know it was damned stupid."

Damned stupid, yes, and not exactly designed to win friends in high places. Nansen was reminded often that he was stuck in Grini because his attitude toward National Socialism was "wrong and stiff." But no matter how badly Nansen wanted to be released, no matter how badly he missed his wife and children, there were certain things he simply was not prepared to do to curry favor. Not even suffering accusations in silence. In an early 1943 confrontation, not with some loutish guard but with the very apex of Nazi power in Norway—the feared Gestapo—Nansen describes his performance, its likely consequences, and the principles guiding him:

> For close on two hours we discussed practically everything that has happened in this war . . . and not the least the persecution of the Jews. Of course I couldn't help speaking my mind about it all. No matter for the chances of release. There are certain things one *can't* choke back. Besides, he [the interrogator] was a pretty smart, cunning fellow, who put his questions so infamously that silence would have been tantamount to admissions, which I wouldn't make at any price.

Words that no doubt would have made Fridtjof Nansen proud. Not only had his father's Spartan home life toughened Nansen; Fridtjof's example equipped Odd Nansen to remain true to his own principles even as they were tested in the crucible of the concentration camps. In the final analysis, it is Nansen's diary itself that may constitute his ultimate act of resistance, for as Primo Levi has pointed out, political prisoners made the best historians of the camps because "they realized that testimony was an act of war against fascism."[133]

"It is indeed a curse to be a Jew"

If Nansen and his comrades were regularly subjected at Grini to indignities, humiliations, petty cruelties, and mindless violence, the fate of Norway's Jews was infinitely worse. Almost immediately following Germany's invasion, the mistreatment of Norway's Jewish minority began; the first action targeting Jews—the confiscation of their radios—occurred within the first month. Nansen knew all too well that Nazi ideology held no place for the Jews; he had seen it all firsthand during his earlier work for Nansenhjelpen. If Nansen's experience over the course of his confinement went steadily downhill, the Jews' experience *began* at a much lower level than where his *ended*, and it quickly degenerated into sadism, torture, and, for all too many, death. In the end, of the 772 Jews deported from Norway during the war, only 34 survived to return home, in percentage terms one of the most devastating outcomes for any Nazi-occupied country during the war.[134]

Nansen's first mention of a Jewish prisoner occurs eleven weeks after his arrest. The camp commandant, raging that too little work is being done, comes across an elderly Jew: "He rushed on him like a madman, seized him by the collar, struck him in the face, and raved over a Jew's having indoor work." When informed the man was ill and excused by his doctor from outside work, the commandant explodes: "I don't care in the least what the doctor said! All Jews are to go out!"

This episode was only a mild harbinger of things to come. Fresh on the heels of the Wannsee Conference (January 20, 1942), which coordinated the "Final Solution" to the Jewish Question, life for Jews in all areas controlled by the Nazis was bleak. In a bitter coincidence, on that very same date the police in Norway proclaimed that all Jews would henceforth have a red "J" stamped on their identification papers, the first step toward their ultimate arrest and deportation.[135] Soon thereafter a "trotting gang" was instituted at Grini for the "work-shy" who would have to perform all work on the double. In addition, all Jews "on principle" were assigned to the trotting gang. Thus, while the work-shy could hope through good effort to eventually escape the gang, Jews were consigned to it in perpetuity. Jews were not allowed in the hospital or infirmary, not allowed visitors or letters, and could not purchase tobacco, privileges accorded even to criminals.[136]

The Wannsee Protocols remained highly secret, known only to the most senior Nazi officials. No matter; years of propaganda had already done their work. "All the Germans without exception are Jew-haters, and regard them no more than animals, if as much," Nansen observed. "No [German] will have any scruple about hitting them or satisfying his sadistic tendencies by plaguing and torturing them in other ways." And plague them they did. Nansen is aghast when the trotting gang returns to camp: "Bent, stiff limbed, bespattered from top to toe with camp slush, muck on their faces and hands and striped camp trousers, which one can only just recognize through the grayish brown layer of mud, they stagger in when the command is given." And harassment wasn't confined to work hours: "As we were hastening home in the dark, [Hut] 6 fell in for punishment drill. They had done nothing wrong, but [Hut] 6 is where the Jews live, and the Commandant was drunk and in need of entertainment."

Despite this unconcealed hate on the part of the Nazis, even Nansen was slow to fathom their endgame. When, in April 1942, Nansen concludes that the war will continue through at least another winter, he also concedes, "They [the Jews] won't all survive; that much is certain." But mistreatment, however harsh, is one thing; organized genocide is quite another. Even after the roundup and deportation of Jews in November 1942, with no destination given, Nansen tried to look on the bright side: "Of course they all know they'll all be inside until the war is over; they're not tormented by false hopes of getting out. That helps them unquestionably."[137]

But if Nansen, in his naiveté, was still speculating on their chances for early release, so were many of the Jews themselves. "Auschwitz," the "Final Solution," and "extermination camps" had not yet entered the lexicon of World War II. The departing Jews had assured Nansen, "We can take it all right." In reality most of these men, together with all the women and children, were gassed immediately upon arrival in Auschwitz.[138]

Once in Sachsenhausen Nansen was forced to shed his illusions—fast. Slightly more than a month after his arrival Nansen spoke with a Jew who had been at Auschwitz: "What he told me about that camp was so horrible, so incomprehensible in ghastliness, that it defies all description." His own diary had only recently introduced two new words: "gas chamber" and "crematorium." Even then, the reality was difficult to accept: "They [the Jews from Lublin, Auschwitz, and other camps] told us such things that I shrink from repeating them. I think I must wait and hear still more." Nine days later Nansen was still trying to grasp what he was hearing: "It's impossible—completely impossible to form any picture of the evil revealed here; human comprehension and imagination fall short."

If Nansen's struggle to come to grips with race hatred and genocide had been shared by more of his fellow prisoners, or even his fellow Norwegians, that common moral vision might have ameliorated some of his pain. Unfortunately, all too often Nansen faced a struggle on two fronts, against his captors and his own countrymen. When a fellow Norwegian (and a prominent one at that) offhandedly condemned "these damned Jews," Nansen wasn't surprised; many other Norwegians had done the same. In fact long before that Nansen had realized the futility of his efforts to counteract such prejudice and threw in the proverbial towel: "I've given up defending the Jews."

In addition Nansen had to contend with his own conscience. "[W]hat can one do to help?" Nansen asks on more than one occasion. What indeed *could* anyone do to help stem the tidal wave of hate? Sure, one could supply a scrap of food or provide some words of encouragement, as Nansen did on many an occasion. But what else? Show solidarity by joining the trotting gang? Not likely to alter their fate one bit. Put in a good word with camp authorities? That would be "as hopeless as asking to go home for a little holiday." But the question was not a rhetorical one, not for Odd Nansen, the bearer of the famous Nansen name. His desire to do more, combined with his awareness of how powerless he really was, gnaws at him through the pages of the diary, demanding an answer, until he can contain it no longer: "I felt queer, ill! A sense of impotence grips one by the throat, as though one were suffocating. Nothing can help—not even tears or screaming." In his growing despair, Nansen was reaching a dead end, caught between his need to help and his self-loathing at how little he could actually do. This conflict frames one of the most vivid and wrenching episodes in the entire book.

Nansen visits the isolation area where emaciated Jews are penned in, and what he sees suggests to him a scene straight from Dante's Inferno. Hunger-crazed prisoners fight for scraps of rotten garbage, all the while pursued by truncheon-wielding ex-Wehrmacht soldiers. A Jew who has been beaten collapses at Nansen's feet. Dragged over to the safety of a nearby wall by Nansen, the man regains consciousness. The victim's friend, who had been standing nearby, helps Nansen hold him up. "He explained that he had thought I was going to prop his friend up and kill him, he couldn't believe I only meant to help him. For I wasn't a Jew? What was I? A Norwegian!" Nansen continues to minister to the half-dead Jew, arranging his clothes and wiping away some of the blood. His searing, brutal, self-appraisal of that moment:

> They simply stared at me, both of them, with big, surprised eyes, then [the victim] raised his arm with an effort, as though mustering all his failing strength; his hand reached the level of my head; there he let it sink, and slowly that bony hand of his slid down over my face. It was his last caress, and he gurgled something that his friend translated as, "He says you are a decent man." Then he collapsed along the wall and onto the ground, and I think he died then and there, but I don't know, for I was hurrying off with my face burning.

"A decent man"! I who hadn't even dared to try and stop his tormentor. I who hadn't even cared to risk my own skin by going out into the camp and collecting food for those starving skeletons! *"A decent man"*! If only I could ever raise myself up again from this shadow life . . . and *be "a decent man"*!

Nansen had consistently championed the cause of the Jews, had preached and practiced generosity for all, had worried about postwar forgiveness even while still subject to his captors' whims and caprices, had, through his diary, borne witness to the immense suffering of the Jews and others, had sacrificed his prewar career to help the downtrodden refugees of central Europe. All these actions suggest that, far from having cause to question himself, Nansen may very well have been one of the most decent men to be found in the camp.

Humor

Even life in hell has its share of absurdities, caricature, and irony. Whether it was the absurdities of Nazi leave taking, the strange physiognomy of a guard, or the baleful impact of the Germans—"for them there's no cure"—there *were* things to laugh at. But when life wasn't being comic (which wasn't often), it was nasty, miserable, boring, and dangerous. Yet even here humor could play a useful role in keeping misery at bay, if only for a while. Crammed into the fetid hold of a cargo ship en route to northern Norway, the prisoners begin to lose themselves to the "blackest of despair." Enter Nansen: "Well, this was no time to despair. The thing was to get one's spirits up. I looked at a couple of the other fellows. And we began to laugh. Heavens, how we laughed!" Time and again, when things were bleak, Nansen's response was, "We gave a sigh of relief, and then we burst out laughing again—laughing until we gasped for breath." That ability—to challenge the forces of despair, to deny their intended effect, indeed to turn them on their head and show the world (and perhaps more importantly, oneself) that such forces were not winning, that one could scoff at misery—undoubtedly helps explain Nansen's ability to persevere.

But laughter can also have a darker side when it masks other, equally strong emotions that cannot be or should not be expressed. The concentration camp is at once the most highly regulated society and the most arbitrary, what Primo Levi's biographer calls "its sheer irrational orderliness."[139] When everything is forbidden, rules can be, and usually are, enforced in the most capricious manner possible.[140] And what recourse does the prisoner have? Lacking most outlets, frustration can only be channeled in a few possible directions. When Nansen watched a humiliating punishment drill presided over by gloating guards, he admitted the scene was not without its funny side, and he further conceded that he and a fellow observer had laughed until they cried. "But it was no healthy laughter; we could just as easily have wept with rage and indignation."

Of all the absurdities experienced by Nansen, none approached the events around which his entire prison experience hinged, sending him from Grini to the hellhole of Sachsenhausen. It all started with a harmless practical joke, but one that blew up entirely when the Nazis completely misconstrued its nature and purpose. A search of an infirmary office had unearthed an intentionally fake letter purposely written so that the censor, a fellow Norwegian, could get a good chuckle, as it referred, improbably, to radios, revolvers, and machine guns possessed by the prisoners. The fake letter was indeed so funny that the censor couldn't bear to throw it away, and now the Germans had it. When interrogated about the letter's contents, Nansen writes: "In a flash I saw the comedy, the crazy burlesque—the fundamental Germanism of the whole situation." Unfortunately, his jailors' sense of the absurd was not so finely calibrated. Nansen proceeded to compound his error by admitting, "I could hardly keep from laughing. . . . I'm afraid I didn't manage a sufficiently solemn face, as I remarked that it was only a harmless joke and that the whole thing struck me as comic." Solitary confinement, punishment drills, and transport to Sachsenhausen all soon followed, a heavy price to be paid for Nansen mistaking his captors' capacity for humor. And, indeed, with but two exceptions (one being his birthday), Nansen's last mention of laughter occurs October 6, 1943, the very day of his arrival at KL Sachsenhausen. Thereafter Nansen would have one less resource with which to maintain a sense of equilibrium and cope with the challenges of a lengthy captivity.

The Enemy

Commentators on life in the concentration camp from Sofsky to Levi have remarked on the difficulties of maintaining simple human relationships. According to Sofsky, "[C]ertain fundamental prerequisites for friendships . . . were absent: the freedom of choice, the atmosphere of emotional openness, and opportunities for personal self-presentation." More concretely, Levi observes, "The demand for solidarity, for a human word, advice, even just a listening ear, was permanent and universal but rarely satisfied."[141] Nansen managed to surmount these obstacles. The diary is replete with acts of friendship, whether they be with a discouraged Norwegian, a Hungarian Jew, or a Russian student. This alone would have been sufficient to single him out for special recognition. More surprising is Odd Nansen's attitudes toward his enemy. Despite everything he experienced, Nansen refused to succumb to indiscriminate hate and wholesale group prejudice and rejected the primacy of vengeance in the coming postwar world. It is this expansive humanity that is perhaps the most distinguishing feature of the entire diary.

Nansen recognized that "there are human hearts beating under the uniform jackets [of the Germans]," and he accordingly looked for the tiniest sliver of humanity, the smallest spark of decency, in his oppressors. *Lagerkommandant* Zeidler evinces "undoubted rudiments of humanity." Nansen believes "the human being . . . is gaining" in *Schutzhaftlagerführer* Denzer. He feels *Bauleiter* Gebecke is a human being too, and even admits to a certain liking for Liwa, a stiff-necked guard and confirmed Nazi, "when one gets to know him a little."

All the same, Odd Nansen was a prisoner in a concentration camp and knew full well the pain, frustration, and disappointment that were every prisoner's lot. The Germans are "devil-scum," "a ghastly lot" led by a "maniacal gangster." They converse only by "roars" and "curses" and "bellows," frequently punctuated by kicks and blows. Corruption is endemic, and everyday life consists of orders, counter-orders, and counter-counter-orders. The guards are brutal, mendacious, and childish all at the same time. The authorities take hypocrisy to new heights, whether it's making up fabricated death certificates for those whom they have murdered, or insisting that beds be meticulously made notwithstanding they are crawling with deadly lice.

And even those beating hearts turned out to be anything but pure. Zeidler: "All . . .

must now be taken back. He's a living devil pure and simple." Denzer? Nansen's desires soon "wallow in [his] death and destruction." Gebecke is revealed as nothing more than a "truncated wreck[ ] of humanity," and even Liwa is ultimately unmasked as an informer.

Under these circumstances hatred would have been natural and perfectly understandable; millions of those touched by German brutality exhibited such sentiments for many long years, some for the rest of their lives. And yet despite having his faith so sorely tried, Nansen didn't give up. He remained hopeful, treated each of his captors as an individual, gave them the benefit of the doubt, even as he ruefully admitted, "In a way it would be simpler if none of them were human beings." In the face of others' amazement and no little indignation, Nansen even challenged his hutmates to volunteer for a relief mission to Germany after the war finally ended.

For Nansen the greatest catastrophe was that following Germany's inevitable defeat "evil will dictate the peace and plan the future." He was determined to break the cycle of vengeance, without which yet another European generation might again face renewed conflict. In his postscript Nansen rejected hate, revenge, and retribution: "They lead back to the abyss." Justice, if it meant an eye for an eye and a tooth for a tooth, was also "nothing to aspire to." Legal, political, and diplomatic approaches aroused little confidence in him.[142] Even religion, if it merely ends in "self-communing . . . and . . . thoughts of one's own salvation," was not the solution. Rather, the answer lay in saving the hungry, the homeless, the wretched created by the war. Only through the work of rescue could a common front be created, a front bridging all divisions among peoples: "*the front of human kindness.*" And as we know this was no idle exhortation. In 1947 Nansen spearheaded a relief drive through Europe, dispensing needed medicines and supplies. Later he toured Europe, including Germany, on behalf of UNESCO, advocating for more coordinated aid targeting Germany's youth. In an incredible gesture of magnanimity, Nansen even donated the proceeds of the German edition of *From Day to Day* to German refugees.[143]

Did Nansen's faith bear fruit? Such matters are always difficult to measure. But one small sample may be telling. Young Tommy Buergenthal, whom Nansen rescued while in Sachsenhausen, had plenty reasons of his own to hate the Nazis: they had murdered his grandparents and his father, visited untold suffering upon his mother, and robbed him of his childhood. And Tommy did indeed return to Germany after the war filled with hatred. But looking back over an illustrious career as an advocate for human rights (which career path Nansen "more than anyone else was responsible for my choosing to embark on"[144]), Thomas Buergenthal has perhaps the final word, and the highest accolade: "Odd Nansen . . . not only saved my life but also taught me to forgive."

III. TOMMY

Throughout his captivity, Odd Nansen tried to help those more vulnerable than he, knowing that his meager efforts could hardly provide much amelioration. "[I]t's only so infinitely little one can do to help," he once lamented. The increasingly despairing tone of his entries attests to the hopelessness he often felt when engulfed in an avalanche of misery and despair: "Do you realize, my own Kari, how unspeakably it wrings one's soul to look on—and not to be able to do a thing for [fellow prisoners]?"

And so it was perhaps only natural that when Nansen stumbled upon a ten-year-old Jewish boy in Sachsenhausen's infirmary in mid-February 1945, he wrote, "you went straight to [my] heart." Thomas Buergenthal had somehow survived, since age five, the liquidation of the Kielce Ghetto in Poland, the liquidation of various work camps, and five and a half months in Auschwitz-Birkenau—unlike Sachsenhausen a true *Vernichtungslager* and the symbolic center of the Holocaust—and finally, even the infamous Auschwitz Death March in the dead of winter (fifteen thousand of the more than sixty thousand who started out on the march did not survive, victims of exhaustion, exposure, and Nazi bullets when they could not keep up).[145] Tommy arrived in Sachsenhausen alive, but not unharmed; his feet were so badly frostbitten that several of his toes needed to be amputated immediately to prevent gangrene. Nansen first chanced upon young Tommy, recovering from surgery, when visiting a fellow Norwegian in the same infirmary. Perhaps it was a final piece of luck that brought Tommy to Sachsenhausen instead of the many other camps closer to Auschwitz where the majority of marchers were sent, and that brought Nansen to the infirmary; it's unlikely he would otherwise have ever spotted Tommy at a time when the camp's population had swelled to more than thirty-five thousand inmates.[146]

Nansen was immediately touched by the child, who had seen the very worst of humanity and yet seemed remarkably unaffected by all of the depravity he had witnessed. Tommy delighted to receive the simple gift of a pencil, or some sweets (the first he had seen or tasted in years), while also describing for Nansen with perfect equanimity the operation of Auschwitz's gas chambers. Nansen admitted, "I felt almost like a criminal as I sat there questioning that little angel about such things."

Tommy needed all the help he could get. Nansen describes the infirmary as a "death trap" and "the first step to the crematorium." Fortunately, Nansen had something more than his sympathy to share with Buergenthal; he had food from his Red Cross parcels, the coin of the realm in a camp where thousands were slowly starving. Soon Nansen was not only bringing food to Tommy; he bribed the infirmary orderlies with his extra rations to ensure they kept a special eye on their young ward and kept his name off the list of seriously ill, a sure ticket for going "up the chimney." As Buergenthal writes in his aptly titled memoir, *A Lucky Child*: "Much later I realized that Mr. Nansen['s actions] had probably saved my life."[147] Ultimately reunited with his mother (his father was killed in Buchenwald), Buergenthal emigrated to the United States, attended college, New York University Law School, and Harvard Law School, becoming a world-renowned authority on international law and international human rights. Among his many accomplishments, Buergenthal was a justice of the International Court of Justice at The Hague from 2000 to 2010.

Odd Nansen's intervention was critical to Buergenthal's survival, but Nansen, too, received benefits from their relationship. As he wrote after the war, Tommy's "shining smile and joy over the gifts we had for him almost made us forget where we were and all the threatening darkness that lay before us." More importantly, Tommy "touched something in us which was about to disappear. He called to life again human feelings, which were painful to have, but which nevertheless meant salvation for us all."[148]

The "young Tommy" to whom Nansen in part dedicated *From Day to Day* in 1947, without then even knowing Buergenthal's ultimate fate (and for whom he fruitlessly searched throughout Europe that same year), has now returned the favor and written a preface for this edition, describing, as few can, "The Odd Nansen I Knew."

IV. THE BOOK

The English translation of an abridged version of Nansen's diary was first published in 1949 in America and Great Britain (where its title was *Day After Day*). Critics called it "unforgettable," "profoundly moving," "a classic of its kind," which "will surely rank among the most compelling documents to come out of the [war]." Many reviewers described *From Day to Day* as having an almost documentary feel. Henry Kranz, a former POW, writing for the *Saturday Review of Literature*, lauded Nansen's "rare gift of detached observation."[149] For Bruno Lasker of the *Survey*, it was Nansen's "seemingly unstudied selection of small revealing facts, character sketches [and] even humorous incidents" that produced what Lasker characterized as a "story . . . [of] epic quality."[150] This emphasis on "vivid, concrete details" combined with "sharp character sketches" made for a "continuously engrossing narrative," wrote Orville Prescott, the *New York Times*' long-time daily book critic.[151]

Critics focused both on the book's horrific subject matter and on the uniquely inspiring character of the author. As Emmett Dedmon observed, "the sum of his experiences . . . build up to a climax as terrifying as any Edgar Allan Poe could contrive. . . . Many times you have the feeling that you are reading of Dante's Inferno with a 20th century setting."[152] Nansen's work acts as a "record that will shake the reader with horror again and again," observed the *San Francisco Chronicle*.[153] According to *The Spectator*, the physical conditions of camp life had already been described often and well enough, "but it is doubtful if the psychological atmosphere and the neuroses of internment have ever been so sensitively conveyed."[154] Christopher Woodhouse, writing in the *Times Literary Supplement*, fell back on a literary analogy to describe the book's overall impact: "The first two-thirds of *Day after Day* can only be compared with Dostoevsky's *House of the Dead*; but compared with the last third of Hr. Nansen's book the *House of the Dead* reads like Jane Austen."[155]

Equally impressive to the critics was what Prescott called Nansen's "capacity to rise above the deadly danger of succumbing to the most viciously demoralizing environment ever created by depraved men, to remain cheerful among abominations, to revolt against every cruelty he saw without becoming hysterical or callous, never to lose hope and faith and love."[156] William L. Shirer, writing eight years after his own frightening experience with the Nazification of Germany as a CBS correspondent (recounted in *Berlin Diary*), and eleven years before publishing his magisterial *The Rise and Fall of the Third Reich*, noted how Nansen's book transcended "the unspeakable barbarities" to "remind us in never-to-be-forgotten pages how noble and generous the human spirit can be in the face of terrible adversity." Nansen's diary, Shirer explained, showed "how the Germans behaved when they had a large part of civilized Europe at their feet," and yet, "and this is what makes this record unique—Nansen never gave in nor did he lose his faith in mankind."[157]

Walter Marsden concluded in the *New Statesman and Nation* that it was Nansen's "remarkable humanistic faith which enabled him to look steadily at heroism and martyrdom and evil alike."[158] Several critics noted the complete absence of self-pity at any time during Nansen's captivity. For Orville Prescott, Nansen's "generosity of spirit" aroused "humble admiration"; his diary amounted to a "magnificent and utterly un-self-conscious self-portrait."[159] In the eyes of Anne Goodman of the *New Republic*, Nansen emerged as a "remarkable person," exhibiting a "great, unconscious charm," whose "quick, broad and compassionate personality shines through every page."[160] Alfred Werner (himself a survivor of Dachau), observed in the *New York Times Book Review* that Nansen was "imbued with a spirit of unbelievable humility"; as a result "the reader will, unquestionably, find himself drawn to [him]."[161] In the end one is reminded of Primo Levi's description of his best friend in Auschwitz, Alberto Dalla Volta: "I always saw, and still see in him, the rare figure of the strong yet peace-loving man against whom the weapons of night are blunted."[162]

Notwithstanding such praise, many of the reviewers predicted the possibility of a muted reception. "Don't pass this book by because you've long since been surfeited with horrors," pleaded the *Nation*.[163] Prescott conceded it was "problematical" whether Nansen's "terrible and heartbreaking book" would attract the general attention it deserved. After all, he mused, "Most of us do not care to share even vicariously in print the monstrous suffering of our time."[164] Goodman fretted about those "individuals among us who say they cannot bear to read another harrowing account of the camps."[165] Even Shirer admitted that *From Day to Day* "may get a mixed reception," for "[m]ost citizens, one hears, are fed up with books about the atrocities of the Nazi concentration camps." Shirer could only protest, "But this book is different from all the others."[166] Other reviewers agreed. "What distinguishes this diary from many other books in the same category," wrote Alfred Werner, was Nansen's "keen observation and humanity," his "sympathy for the suffering of all nations," and his "deep understanding of man's frailty."[167] For Goodman, Nansen's humanity gave the diary "a hopeful and even a triumphant note."[168] Christopher Woodhouse summed it up perhaps the best: "[T]here is little in *Day after Day* that cannot be found in a hundred other books. The one difference is that it is a masterpiece."[169]

Masterpiece or not, by 1949 the United States was undeniably suffering from postwar readjustment on the home front while confronting a new and threatening world order. The years between the Norwegian publication and the English translation witnessed an escalating series of confrontations between the Western Allies and their former partner, the Soviet Union. "Our notions about the world were whirling topsy-turvy, enemies turning into friends and vice versa," wrote a GI stationed in Berlin. "It was the start of the Cold War and the Iron Curtain, although the terms had barely been invented."[170] Concentration camp diaries, no matter how eloquent, no matter how humane, no matter how full of insights into the human condition, held little appeal in such an environment.

As the above GI noted, one of the most remarkable developments in the immediate postwar period was the rapid rehabilitation of Germany, or at least West Germany, a beneficiary of the exigencies of the Cold War. Observed one historian, "The Russians were transformed from indispensable allies to implacable foes, the Germans from implacable foes to indispensable allies. In 1945, Americans had cheered as Soviet forces pounded Berlin into rubble; in 1948, Americans organized the [Berlin] Airlift to defend 'gallant Berliners' from Soviet threat."[171] Denazification was officially ended in the American Zone by May 1948 as American policy shifted from one of occupation to one of reintegration. Prosecutions of former Nazis fell off precipitously, and even those previously convicted benefited from generous clemency boards set up by the Allies in 1949 and 1950.[172] In the context of the dawning Cold War, reading about German atrocities became "not just unhelpful but actively obstructive."[173]

For six consecutive weeks Nansen's diary appeared in the *New York Times Book Review*'s "And Bear in Mind" column, a feature initiated by the *Review*'s editors "as a means of calling attention each week to books of literary, scholarly or topical interest, books that might otherwise receive less attention than they deserve." In 1949 only one other nonfiction book had a longer tenure on the editors' list. Nevertheless, *From Day to Day*, the book so many reviewers had called "unforgettable," made it to a second printing and then was quietly all but forgotten.

It would take many years for the world's indifferent attitude toward the Holocaust to change.[174] As historian Peter Novick has observed, even William L. Shirer (an enthusiastic reviewer of Nansen's diary) nevertheless only "devoted 2 or 3 percent of his 1,200-page [bestseller *The Rise and Fall of the Third Reich*] to the murder of European Jewry, a proportion that, to the best of my knowledge, no critic commented upon."[175] Elie Wiesel published *Night*, an account of his experiences in Auschwitz and Buchenwald, in the United States in 1960 (it had previously been published in Yiddish in 1956 and in French in 1958). Finding an American publisher had proven difficult, despite favorable reviews in the French, Belgian, and Swiss press. Wiesel was told, echoing the concerns of Nansen's reviewers, that the topic was too morbid and in any case either too little known or too well known. The first US printing run of three thousand copies took three years to sell.[176]

Primo Levi's experience with his memoir *Survival in Auschwitz* followed much the same trajectory. After completing it in 1946, Levi also had difficulty finding anyone interested in his work. After rejection by six mainstream Italian publishers he finally settled for a little-known amateur operating on a shoestring, which promptly shut down soon after Levi's work was finally issued in 1947.[177] The entire print run of "two thousand five hundred copies . . . was well received by the critics," Levi later wrote, "but sold only in part: the six hundred unsold copies stored . . . in a remainder warehouse were drowned in the autumn flood of 1969. After ten years of 'apparent death,' it came back to life when Einaudi publishing company [a major Italian publishing house] accepted it in 1957."[178] Indeed, initial sales of *Survival* were so discouraging that Levi abandoned his dream of becoming a professional writer and instead returned full time to his chemist's job; he would not even begin his sequel, *The Reawakening*, until thirteen years later.[179] Levi's reception in America was equally chilly. As early as 1946 Levi's cousin in America translated sample chapters of his memoir and submitted them to Little, Brown and Company, which took a pass; as his biographer notes, "In 1946 the subject of Europe's dismal recent past did not engage—indeed it repelled—American readers. . . . [Levi] would have to wait forty years until America took notice of him."[180] Ruth Franklin, in *A Thousand Darknesses: Lies and Truth in Holocaust Fiction*, similarly notes that "[e]ven Anne Frank's *Diary of a Young Girl* did not achieve widespread acclaim until its publication in English in 1952, five years after the original Dutch edition."[181]

Some works never made it into print at all. On the basis of her firsthand conversations with children saved during the war by the Oeuvre de secours aux enfants [Society for Assistance to Children] or OSE, in France, Vivette Samuel, a member of OSE whose father died in Auschwitz, prepared a compilation of accounts she called *Comme des brebis* [*Like Lambs*]. Samuel showed the manuscript to publishers in 1948, and despite its being well received, was told it was "too late . . . or too early." The manuscript remains unpublished, in the possession of the Universal Jewish Alliance in Paris.[182] Even in the world of films, the few dealing with the Holocaust up through the 1960s were not box office hits.[183]

Today *Night*, along with *Survival in Auschwitz* and Anne Frank's diary, are considered among the seminal works dealing with the Holocaust. *The Diary of Anne Frank* is the most widely sold Dutch book of all time; *Night* has since been translated into thirty languages and more than six million copies have been sold in the United States alone.[184] Similarly, NBC's 1978 miniseries *Holocaust* was watched in whole or in part by close to one hundred million viewers in America.[185]

In 1956, less than a decade following the US publication of *From Day to Day*, the editors of *The American Scholar*, the magazine of the Phi Beta Kappa Society, observed its twenty-fifth anniversary by polling a number of distinguished scholars, writers, and thinkers, asking each to nominate one book, published during the preceding quarter-century, that the respondent believed was "the most undeservedly neglected"; that is, "a book which, although of striking merit, did not seem to our correspondent to have received either the critical recognition or the general audience that he or she believed it to deserve."[186]

The responses, from parties as diverse as Aldous Huxley, Lionel Trilling, and John Kenneth Galbraith, naturally covered a wide spectrum of works. But no less a writer than Carl Sandburg, winner of three Pulitzer Prizes, chose *From Day to Day*, describing it as "an epic narrative of life in Nazi concentration camps," which took "its place among the great affirmations of the power of the human spirit to rise above terror, torture, and death."[187]

IN HIS FOREWORD, NANSEN DESCRIBES the almost insuperable problem he faced with his diary at Sachsenhausen, which was neither writing it nor hiding it; these were problems, but manageable ones. Rather, it was the question of how he would take his writings with him when he finally left the camp, given the rigorousness of the Nazis' searches. This conundrum preoccupied him for some time, but it never "stopped me from writing. Even if I were compelled to bury the diary in German soil, I would and must write."[188] Nansen ultimately devised an ingenious solution to his dilemma, and yet his work has been ignored in the intervening years almost as if he had buried it in Sachsenhausen. In the concluding sentence of his postscript, Nansen warned, "What happened was worse than you have any idea of—and it was the indifference of mankind that let it take place!" As Milan Kundera reminds us, "[T]he struggle of man against power is the struggle of memory against forgetting."[189] Lest we forget, this republication of Odd Nansen's diary, in English for the first time in over six and a half decades, illuminates what was almost buried and forgotten, and corrects a long period—far too long—of undeserved neglect.

Timothy J. Boyce
Tryon, NC
February 2015

NOTES

1. All radio sets had been ordered confiscated (except for NS members) in the autumn of 1941; the move was designed to prevent listening to the BBC. Hans Dahl, *Quisling: A Study in Treachery*, trans. Anne-Marie Stanton-Ife (Cambridge: Cambridge University Press, 1999) (hereinafter *Quisling*), pp. 229–30. The order represented "a unique tribute to the ascendancy of the BBC over broadcast services under NS and German control," according to one Resistance member who later wrote of his experiences. Tore Gjelsvik, *Norwegian Resistance 1940–1945*, trans. Thomas Kingston Derry (Montreal: McGill-Queen's University Press, 1979), p. 93 n. The order backfired, inasmuch as determined citizens (like Nansen) continued to listen clandestinely, while the Nazi authorities were deprived of a propaganda outlet. According to historian Bjarte Bruland, four Jews were executed in March 1942 for listening to the BBC. Bjarte Bruland, "Norway's Role in the Holocaust," in *The Routledge History of the Holocaust*, ed. Jonathan C. Friedman (New York: Routledge, 2011), pp. 239, 245 n. 39. See also Richard Petrow, *The Bitter Years* (New York: William Morrow & Company,

Inc., 1974), p. 115. Similarly, diarist Myrtle Wright noted in November 1941 that a teacher was executed for giving news from London radio to two German soldiers. Myrtle Wright, *Norwegian Diary 1940–1945* (London: Friends Peace and International Relations Committee, 1974) (hereinafter *Norwegian Diary*), p. 66. Even in Germany listening to foreign broadcasts and disseminating "lies" was punishable by death. Roger Moorhouse, *Berlin at War* (New York: Basic Books, 2012), p. 208.

The low temperature in Oslo on that night was -13°F. Temperatures in Lillehammer generally run up to ten degrees colder than Oslo. Some of the coldest temperatures ever recorded in Oslo occurred in January 1942. See the website of the Norwegian Meteorological Institute, *www.eklima.no*, accessed January 3, 2013.

For a discussion of Beethoven and the BBC broadcasts, see Matthew Guerrieri, *The First Four Notes* (New York: Alfred A. Knopf, 2012), pp. 211–17. The cabin was owned by Nansen's business partner, Ernst Holmboe. Details regarding Nansen's arrest are from an e-mail from Nansen's daughter, Marit Greve, January 27, 2013.

2. Gjelsvik, *Norwegian Resistance 1940–1945*, p. ix; Samuel Abrahamsen, *Norway's Response to the Holocaust* (New York: Holocaust Library, 1991) (hereinafter *Norway's Response*), p. 2. Norway's population at the time was less than that of Berlin alone. Kevin Sim, *Women at War* (New York: William Morrow and Company, Inc., 1982), p. 106. A similar proportion of internees in the current US population would result in over four million prisoners.

3. "Though the taking of hostages was an ancient custom, much indulged in for instance by the Romans, it had not been generally practiced in modern times. . . . Under Hitler, however, the German Army carried it out on a large scale." William L. Shirer, *The Rise and Fall of the Third Reich* (New York: Simon & Schuster, 1960), p. 957. See also Mark Mazower, *Hitler's Empire* (New York: Penguin Press, 2008), pp. 66, 478; Nikolaus Wachsmann, *KL: A History of the Nazi Concentration Camps* (New York: Farrar, Straus and Giroux, 2015) (hereinafter *KL*), p. 199.

4. Hampton Sides, *In the Kingdom of Ice* (New York: Doubleday, 2014), p. 19. While it was clear by Nansen's time that there was no sea passage through the polar regions, what really existed at the pole was still the subject of the wildest speculations. Among the more fantastical theories, the then president of Boston University published a lengthy work in 1885 theorizing that a hole at the North Pole led to the Garden of Eden. Fergus Fleming, *Ninety Degrees North* (New York: Grove Press, 2001), pp. 233–34.

5. Alec Wilkinson, *The Ice Balloon* (New York: Alfred A. Knopf, 2011), p. 14.

6. Roland Huntford, *Nansen: The Explorer as Hero* (New York: Barnes & Noble Books, 1998) (hereinafter *Nansen*), p. 1. Shortly after his death Nansen was credited with performing "the greatest human exploit of the nineteenth century." Jon Sörensen, *The Saga of Fridtjof Nansen*, trans. J. B. C. Watkins (New York: The American-Scandinavian Foundation/W. W. Norton & Company, Inc., 1932) (hereinafter *Saga*), p. 175.

7. Eric Utne, ed., *Brenda, My Darling* (Minneapolis: Utne Institute, Inc., 2011), pp. 194–95. In Nansen's own account of his expedition he wrote, when contemplating leaving his ship for the dash to the pole: "I cannot imagine any difficulty that will not be overcome when our choice lies between death—and onward and home!" Fridtjof Nansen, *Farthest North* (London: Duckworth, 2000), p. 218. Still later on the voyage he observed, "A wretched invention, forsooth, for people who wish to push on is a 'line of retreat.'" Ibid., p. 230.

8. Nansen, *Farthest North*, p. viii (introduction by Roland Huntford); Sörensen, *Saga*, pp. 155, 160; Fleming, *Ninety Degrees North*, p. 251 (Fleming states the distance was six hundred miles).

9. On New Year's Day 1896, midway through their overwintering, Nansen recorded the outside temperature at 42.2° below zero. Nansen, *Farthest North*, p. 377. Despite their journeying on skis and limited diet, Nansen and Johansen actually *gained* weight (Nansen twenty-two pounds and Johansen thirteen pounds) *after* leaving *Fram*. Nansen, *Farthest North*, p. 411. By contrast, an English journalist in the 1930s estimated that of the more than 1,000 people who had tried to reach the North Pole before 1900, at least 751 had perished in the attempt. Wilkinson, *The Ice Balloon*, p. 4. In some ways Nansen had been preparing all his life for this expedition. He once observed, "While I was in my 'teens, I used to pass weeks at a time alone in the woods. I disliked having any equipment on my expeditions, and managed with a crust of bread and fish which I broiled myself

in the embers. I loved to live like Robinson Crusoe up there in the wilderness." Quoted in Sörensen, *Saga*, pp. 23–24.

10. Nansen, *Farthest North*, p. viii (introduction by Roland Huntford). Even Nansen's first encounter with civilization was unusual: he chanced upon the only other explorer in the area, Englishman Frederick Jackson. That these two should find each other "in the hundreds of thousands of square miles of empty polar cap," was, one historian noted, "an extraordinary stroke of luck." Fleming, *Ninety Degrees North*, pp. 261–62. Nansen always believed himself lucky: "We are born under lucky or unlucky stars. Till now I have lived under a lucky one; is its light to be darkened? I am superstitious, no doubt, but I believe in my star." Nansen, *Farthest North*, p. 146.

11. Quoted in Huntford, *Nansen*, p. 359.

12. Carl agreed to Nansen's request, becoming King Haakon VII, a reign that lasted almost fifty-two years, including all of World War II. See generally, Tim Greve, *Haakon VII of Norway*, trans. and ed. Thomas Kingston Derry (London: C. Hurst & Company, 1983) (Greve was Odd Nansen's son-in-law).

13. Karen Larsen, *A History of Norway* (Princeton, NJ: Princeton University Press, 1950), p. 512.

14. Huntford, *Nansen*, p. 493.

15. Website for the UN high commissioner for refugees, *www.unhcr.org/nansen/503743f86.html*, accessed June 16, 2013.

16. Huntford, *Nansen*, p. 139. Salon guests included "the most distinguished of [Norway's] writers, artists, politicians, and educators," including Nobel laureate Bjørnstjerne Bjørnson. Maynard Cohen, *A Stand Against Tyranny* (Detroit: Wayne State University Press, 1997) (hereinafter *Tyranny*), p. 57. Eva's brother Georg Ossian Sars was also a respected marine biologist, and brother Johan Ernst Sars has been called the "ideological creator of the Norwegian national democracy." Quoted in Larsen, *A History of Norway*, p. 454.

17. Huntford, *Nansen*, p. 140.

18. Liv Nansen Høyer, *Nansen: A Family Portrait*, trans. Maurice Michael (London: Longmans, Green and Co., 1957), p. 186.

19. Utne, *Brenda, My Darling*, p. 83.

20. As one admiring biographer nevertheless concedes, "He . . . was no gourmand." Sörensen, *Saga*, p. 342.

21. Quoted in Huntford, *Nansen*, p. 457.

22. Høyer, *Nansen: A Family Portrait*, p. 186.

23. Quoted in Sörensen, *Saga*, p. 89.

24. Quoted in Utne, *Brenda, My Darling*, p. 202. On his polar expedition Nansen wrote in his diary, "[T]he way to the stars leads through adversity." Nansen, *Farthest North*, p. 204.

25. Quoted in Høyer, *Nansen: A Family Portrait*, p. 204; second quote is in Huntford, *Nansen*, p. 396.

26. Huntford writes, "She [Eva] . . . discovered that when, during their engagement, Nansen had written, 'Now you know what you have in prospect; a gloomy, moody man,' it had been no self-dramatisation [*sic*], but the all too literal truth." *Nansen*, p. 143. See also Alexandra Yourieff, *In Quisling's Shadow*, trans. Kirsten A. Seaver (Stanford, CA: Hoover Institution Press, 2007), pp. 281, 283.

27. Quoted in Huntford, *Nansen*, p. 396.

28. Høyer, *Nansen: A Family Portrait*, p. 163; Huntford, *Nansen*, p. 396. Huntford adds, "[Eva] of course knew how to circumvent this." Ibid.

29. Huntford, *Nansen*, pp. 477, 490, 536.

30. Website of the Student Society of Norway, *www.samfundet.no/informasjon* (in Norwegian), accessed June 28, 2013.

31. Marit Greve jokingly refers to it as "the national anthem of Trondheim." Marit Greve, interview, October 17, 2012.

32. Nansen's older brother Kåre emigrated to Canada in 1929, never to return. With a degree in forestry, he assisted in the development of the ski resort of Mont Tremblant, outside Quebec, where one of the longest ski trails is named Nansen Trail in his honor.

33. *American Airport Designs* (New York: Taylor, Rogers & Bliss, 1930), pp. 7–9.

34. Alastair Gordon, *Naked Airport* (New York: Metropolitan Books/Henry Holt and Company, 2004), pp. 48, 52.

35. Marit Greve, e-mail, May 18, 2012.

36. Anne Ellingsen, "Odd Nansen, Antitotalitær Humanist," in *Humanist* no. 3 (2011) (in Norwegian), p. 67.

37. Quoted in Abrahamsen, *Norway's Response*, p. 4.

38. Sigrid Helliesen Lund, *Always on the Way*, trans. Kathryn Parke (Tempe, AZ: Beverly-Merriam, 2000), p. 38. Also known as Nansenhjelp, Odd Nansen's organization should not be confused with the Nansen Office for International Refugees, set up by the League of Nations following Fridtjof Nansen's death in 1930 as a semi-autonomous body to continue his earlier work on behalf of refugees. Although the organization was awarded the Nobel Peace Prize in 1938 it was dissolved by the league soon thereafter.

39. Wright, *Norwegian Diary*, p. 40.

40. Lund, *Always on the Way*, p. 38; Sigrid Undset, *Back to the Future*, trans. Henriette C. K. Naeseth (New York: Alfred A. Knopf, 1942), p. 26.

41. Wright, *Norwegian Diary*, p. 40.

42. Lund, *Always on the Way*, p. 42.

43. Quoted in Utne, *Brenda, My Darling*, p. 122. The *Kristallnacht* pogrom in Germany on November 10, 1938, further accelerated Jewish emigration. Ian Kershaw, *Hitler, the Germans, and the Final Solution* (Jerusalem/New Haven, CT: International Institute for Holocaust Research/Yale University Press, 2008), pp. 173–83.

44. Livia Rothkirchen, *The Jews of Bohemia and Moravia* (Lincoln/Jerusalem: University of Nebraska Press/Yad Vashem, 2005), pp. 54, 72. Most Austrian refugees fleeing to Czechoslovakia went to Bratislava, Brno, and Prague. Kurt R. Grossmann, "Refugees To and From Czechoslovakia," in *The Jews of Czechoslovakia*, vol. 2 (Philadelphia/New York: Jewish Publication Society of America/Society for the History of Czechoslovak Jews, 1971), pp. 565–77.

45. Rothkirchen, *The Jews of Bohemia and Moravia*, p. 78; Grossmann, "Refugees To and From Czechoslovakia," pp. 565–77.

46. Quoted in Rothkirchen, *The Jews of Bohemia and Moravia*, p. 79. Ilse Weber, a Czech Jew, wrote at the time, "Why did they not think about the Jews there, in Munich? Did Chamberlain not realize the danger in store for the Jews when he sold us out to the Germans?" Ibid., p. 71. Weber was able to save one son through the *Kindertransport*; with her other son and husband she was initially confined to Theresienstadt. When her husband was deported to Auschwitz in 1944, she voluntarily agreed to accompany him. She and her son were gassed upon arrival. Ibid., p. 329 n. 36.

47. Quoted in Abrahamsen, *Norway's Response*, p. 3. Konstad later served in the Quisling-appointed Supreme Court; after the war he was sentenced to five years imprisonment. Ibid. n. 7.

48. Cohen, *Tyranny*, pp. 66–69. Tiso was hanged for treason after the war.

49. Ibid., pp. 63–82; Lund, *Always on the Way*, p. 43. Some, but not all, of the refugees aided by Nansenhjelpen later escaped from Norway into Sweden in late 1942 to avoid the Nazi roundup that sent virtually all of Norway's remaining Jews to their deaths in Auschwitz. Tragically, soon after the German occupation of Norway, several Czechoslovakian parents begged to have their children reunited with them on the belief that Norway was no longer a safe haven. None of these children survived the war. Lund, *Always on the Way*, p. 73. On the other hand, of those who remained all but three were saved. Sim, *Women at War*, pp. 115–22. One Czech refugee who assisted, and was assisted by, Nansenhjelpen was Leo Eitinger. He made it to Norway in November 1939 but was ultimately arrested following the German invasion and sent to Auschwitz. One of the handful of deported Jews from Norway to have survived the concentration camps, Eitinger returned to Norway after the war, testified against Quisling in the latter's treason trial, and pursued a distinguished career in psychiatry, authoring books on the psychological impact of incarceration in concentration camps. The Lisle and Leo Eitinger Prize was established in his and his wife's honor by the University of Oslo to recognize "personal effort and active involvement in human rights." The 1991 recipient was Eigil Nansen, Odd Nansen's eldest son, for his work with refugees. University of Oslo website, *www. uio.no/english/about/facts/human-rights/*, accessed June 16, 2013; Cohen, *Tyranny*, p. 284. Lund was recognized by Yad Vashem in 2006 as being Righteous Among the Nations for her work during

the war in helping Jewish children escape into Sweden. Website of Yad Vashem, *db.yadvashem.org/righteous/righteousName.html?language=en&itemId=5606968*, accessed June 4, 2013.

50. This story was picked up in a variety of local US newspapers. Quote can be found in the *Lima News*, January 11, 1940, p. 10, col. 1. Figures vary considerably on the number of Czechoslovakian Jews murdered before the war ended. Wolfgang Benz, "Death Toll," in *The Holocaust Encyclopedia*, ed. Walter Laqueur (New Haven, CT: Yale University Press, 2001), states 143,000. Ibid., p. 145. Friedman claims as many as 260,000 Czech Jews were murdered. *The Routledge History of the Holocaust*, p. 8. Grossmann's figure is almost 295,000. Grossmann, "Refugees To and From Czechoslovakia," p. 577.

51. Quoted in Cohen, *Tyranny*, p. 64.

52. Max Jakobson, *The Diplomacy of the Winter War* (Cambridge, MA: Harvard University Press, 1961), pp. 191–92.

53. Quoted in the *New York Times*, December 24, 1939, p. 5, col. 4. According to Maynard Cohen, Nansen and Bernadotte were part of a joint Swedish/Norwegian delegation under Bernadotte's direction. Cohen, *Tyranny*, p. 87. The Norwegian economist Trygve Hoff also sailed to America with Nansen.

54. Ellingsen, "Odd Nansen, Antitotalitær Humanist," p. 73. Author Anne Ellingsen confirmed by e-mail that the correct date of the diary entry is January 21, 1940, not January 21, 1939, as originally stated in her article.

55. Quoted in the *New York Times*, February 25, 1940, p. 31, col. 8; Jakobson, *The Diplomacy of the Winter War*, pp. 191–97. Meanwhile, in Britain a volunteer force was assembling (with government blessing) to fight on behalf of the Finns. This force was led by Kermit Roosevelt, Teddy's son and Franklin's cousin, who was already serving as a volunteer in the British army. Jukka Nevakivi, *The Appeal That Was Never Made* (Montreal: McGill-Queen's University Press, 1976), pp. 174–77. The war ended before the volunteers even had a chance to embark. Ibid.

56. *New York Times*, December 24, 1939, p. 8, col. 2. Niemöller, a German theologian, was transferred from Sachsenhausen to Dachau in 1941, well before Nansen arrived. He is best known for the quotation: "First they came for the Socialists, and I did not speak out—Because I was not a Socialist; Then they came for the Trade Unionists, and I did not speak out—Because I was not a Trade Unionist; Then they came for the Jews, and I did not speak out—Because I was not a Jew; then they came for me—and there was no one left to speak for me." He survived the war. Website of the United States Holocaust Memorial Museum, *www.ushmm.org/wlc/en/article.php?ModuleId=10007391* and *www.ushmm.org/wlc/en/article.php?ModuleId=10009392*, both accessed April 28, 2013. There is more than one version of Niemöller's statement; the above is found on the website of the Martin Niemöller Foundation, *www.martin-niemoller-stiftung.de/4/daszitat/a46*, accessed April 24, 2013.

57. Dahl, *Quisling*, pp. 155–58. Other historians emphasize Quisling as the instigator of Hitler's Norwegian designs. For example, Francois Kersaudy writes that "nothing more would have been heard of [an invasion of Norway] but for the appearance at the [Reich Chancellery] in mid-December of a Norwegian named Quisling." Francois Kersaudy, *Norway 1940* (Lincoln: University of Nebraska Press, 1998), p. 38. Christopher Buckley writes in *Norway, The Commandos, Dieppe* (London: His Majesty's Stationery Office, 1951): "That the occupation of Scandinavia formed no part of Hitler's original conception is now certain." Ibid., p. 4.

58. I. C. B. Dear, *The Oxford Companion to World War II* (Oxford: Oxford University Press, 2005), p. 23. A thorough description of the Altmark Affair is found at Henrik O. Lunde, *Hitler's Pre-Emptive War: The Battle for Norway, 1940* (Philadelphia: Casemate, 2009), pp. 26–33.

59. Kersaudy, *Norway 1940*, pp. 43, 45, 48; Nevakivi, *The Appeal That Was Never Made*, p. 107. In a subsequent speech to the Reichstag on July 19, 1940, Hitler described the Altmark Affair as the trigger behind his decision to invade. Dahl, *Quisling*, p. 205. Conversely, the British believed the Altmark Affair signaled the "complete subservience of Norway to German pressure" and began to step up its own naval measures in Norwegian waters. Kersaudy, *Norway 1940*, p. 28 (quoting Lord Halifax).

60. Kersaudy, *Norway 1940*, pp. 37–50; Dahl, *Quisling*, pp. 148–59; Cohen, *Tyranny*, p. 87; Petrow, *The Bitter Years*, pp. 18–44.

61. Johannes Andenaes et al., *Norway and the Second World War* (Oslo: Aschehoug, 1996), pp. 45–46;

Cohen, *Tyranny*, p. 94; Dahl, *Quisling*, pp. 165–67. Simultaneously Quisling was in Copenhagen meeting with a German intelligence officer to provide information about Norway's defenses, and his party newspaper, *Fritt Folk*, was running an editorial on the British threat to Norway. Ibid.

62. Denmark, the other target of *Weserübung*, was even less prepared; it capitulated after only a few hours. Shirer, *The Rise and Fall of the Third Reich*, pp. 694–700. Regarding Norway, see Halvdan Koht, *Norway: Neutral and Invaded* (New York: The Macmillan Company, 1941), pp. 12–13; Hans Christian Adamson and Per Klem, *Blood on the Midnight Sun* (New York: W. W. Norton & Company, 1964), p. 19. As to preparedness, Norway was in some ways worse off in 1939 than it had been in 1914. One historian writes, "Norway found herself less prepared militarily for the Second World War, in which she was forced to take part, than for the First, in which she did not take part." Sim, *Women at War*, p. 85. It had virtually no planes and the Navy's tonnage was less than one-third of its 1914 levels. Lunde, *Hitler's Pre-Emptive War*, p. 9. As to Norway's suspicions, they were more focused on a possible British action than any move by Germany. Kersaudy, *Norway 1940*, pp. 60–62. At a formal affair hosted by the German minister in Oslo only days before the invasion, the guests were shown a "peace film," which turned out to be a gruesome depiction of the bombing of Warsaw; the German minister described it as an example of what happened when a country resisted Nazi attempts to defend itself from England. US minister Florence Harriman recorded, "The audience was shocked, and—this seems strange now—still puzzled, as to why the film had been shown to *them*, to Norwegians." Florence Harriman, *Mission to the North* (Philadelphia: J. B. Lippincott Company, 1941), p. 248. The first American military casualty of the war, Robert Moffat Losey, a military attaché in Sweden, was killed April 21, 1940 in Norway. Although Losey had helped Harriman to escape to Sweden following the invasion, he returned to Norway to rescue other members of the American Legation who were still trapped. He was killed in a German bombing raid on Dombås, a key railway junction two hundred miles north of Oslo. The citizens of Dombås erected a monument in his honor in 1987. J. Michael Cleverley, "The First American Official Killed in This War," *Foreign Service Journal* (December 2003): pp. 66–68; Harriman, *Mission to the North*, pp. 271–75, 281–89.

63. Cohen, *Tyranny*, pp. 109–10. All except Berg were arrested during the course of the war or fled to England. See Kristian Ottosen, *Nordmenn i fangenskap 1940–1945* (Oslo: Universitetsforlaget, 1995) (in Norwegian), pp. 119 (Berggrav), 225 (Gjerløw), 323 (Jahn), and 563 (Seip). Re: Worm-Müller, see website of Norsk Biografisk Leksikon [Norwegian Biographical Encyclopedia], *nbl.snl.no/ Jacob_S_Worm-Müller* (in Norwegian), accessed January 4, 2014.

64. Quoted in Abrahamsen, *Norway's Response*, p. 71; Monica Curtis, ed., *Norway and the War* (London: Oxford University Press, 1941), p. 141. Regarding Quisling's power, Dahl, *Quisling*, p. 207; Ole Kristian Grimnes, "The Beginnings of the Resistance Movement," in *Scandinavia during the Second World War*, ed. Henrik Nissen, trans. Thomas Munch-Petersen (Minneapolis: University of Minnesota Press, 1983), pp. 188–89.

65. Dahl, *Quisling*, p. 121.

66. Quoted in Cohen, *Tyranny*, p. 53.

67. Quoted in Abrahamsen, *Norway's Response*, p. 128.

68. Yourieff, *In Quisling's Shadow*, pp. 208, 280.

69. Abrahamsen, *Norway's Response*, p. 46. Odd Nansen later wrote, "No condition of friendship existed between my father and Quisling. He never participated in any meal or in any form of social gathering in our home." Quoted in Cohen, *Tyranny*, p. 50. Fridtjof once remarked to Odd, "I can never depend on that fellow. He never looks you in the eye." Ibid., p. 51.

70. Ellingsen, "Odd Nansen, Antitotalitær Humanist," pp. 66–67.

71. Koht, *Norway: Neutral and Invaded*, pp. 126–27.

72. The discussion between Nansen and Quisling is quoted in Cohen, *Tyranny*, pp. 182–83. By the end of the meeting Quisling "presented a sorry sight. I no longer considered him a danger. He gave the impression of a man already doomed to death." Ibid. A variant of this meeting is described in David Abrahamsen, *Men, Mind and Power* (New York: Columbia University Press, 1945), p. 106, who places it "in the autumn of 1940," based on a conversation between Nansen and the author's wife.

73. Arne Fjellbu, *Memoirs from the War Years*, trans. L. A. Vigness (Minneapolis: Augsburg Publishing House, 1947), pp. 124–25. Fjellbu ultimately fled to Sweden as well. Ibid., pp. 172–77.

74. Quoted in Joseph H. Devins, Jr., *The Vaagso Raid* (Philadelphia: Chilton Book Company, 1968), p. 196. See also Wright, *Norwegian Diary*, pp. 66–67.

75. Dahl, *Quisling*, p. 236.

76. Wright, *Norwegian Diary*, p. 73; Dahl, *Quisling*, p. 250. Joseph Goebbels, Germany's propaganda minister, confided to his diary that Quisling's claim was "'grotesque' in its shamelessness." Ibid.

77. Nansen wrote in his diary on July 24, 1942, "That confirms what I have believed all the time. Risnæs or Quisling is behind my arrest; court hostage is only a capacious bag for people they are anxious to secure. Personal revenge and other shady motives have dictated the choice." Apart from Nansen, the last remaining hostage, Erik Graff-Wang, was released March 18, 1943. Notwithstanding the enmity between Quisling and Nansen, after the war Nansen helped Quisling's widow Maria when the government attempted to evict her from the apartment she had shared with Quisling before the war. Marit Greve, interview, October 31, 2014; Ralph Hewins, *Quisling: Prophet without Honour* (London: John Day Company, 1966), pp. 360–61.

78. Wright, *Norwegian Diary*, pp. 110, 135.

79. Wright, *Norwegian Diary*, p. 119; Cohen, *Tyranny*, p. 140. Sigrid Lund and Tove Filseth took all of Nansenhjelpen's files to Lund's home immediately after the German invasion and burned them lest they fall into the wrong hands. Wright, *Norwegian Diary*, p. 18; Lund, *Always on the Way*, p. 51. Before the war was over, many of those associated with Nansenhjelpen had fled Norway: Paasche, Lund, and Filseth to Sweden and Koht to England. In addition, Christian Lous Lange's two sons and Lund's only son all ultimately ended up in Sachsenhausen along with Nansen. Another former member of Nansenhjelpen, Ragnar Nordli, fought in the Resistance and was executed in 1944. Wright, *Norwegian Diary*, pp. 137, 157; Lund, *Always on the Way*, p. 76 (Wright mistakenly refers to him as "Ragnar Norli" and Lund calls him "Ragnar Nordlie").

80. Ivar M. Liseter, "Polhøgda, From the Home of Fridtjof Nansen to the Fridtjof Nansen Institute," The Fridtjof Nansen Institute (Revised Edition 2010), p. 16; see website of the Fridtjof Nansen Institute, *www.fni.no/doc&pdf/Hushistorien.pdf*, accessed April 24, 2012.

81. *Portsmouth Herald*, June 18, 1956, p. 5, col. 6; Ingrid Strong (Corrin Strong's granddaughter), telephone conversation, May 14, 2013; *News of Norway*, summer/fall 2013, p. 7.

82. One World website, *www.enverden.no*, accessed March 14, 2012.

83. Memorandum Concerning the German Problem Prepared by Mr. Odd Nansen—Temporary Consultant to the Director-General of UNESCO, Twenty-First Session of the Executive Board of UNESCO (Florence, Italy, May 18, 1950), located at *unesdoc.unesco.org/images/0016/001622/162207eb.pdf*, accessed October 19, 2014.

84. UNESCO website, *uil.unesco.org/home/news-target/the-unesco-institute-for-education-the-forerunner-of-uil-was-founded-60-years-ago/3030bcc674ca496578728d5c4c491b31/*, accessed May 15, 2012.

85. Quoted in Irene Levin Berman, *"We Are Going to Pick Potatoes": Norway and the Holocaust, The Untold Story* (Lanham, MD: Hamilton Books, 2010), p. 157.

86. Huntford, *Nansen*, p. 362; Nansen, *Farthest North*, p. ix (introduction by Roland Huntford).

87. On board the *Fram* Nansen's fellow crew members took to referring to him "with fear and resentment, as Himself." Fleming, *Ninety Degrees North*, p. 243. Only after sailing with Hjalmar Johansen for almost two years and then trekking solo with him to their overwintering site did Nansen finally adopt a familiar form of address; until then they maintained the formalities of "Mr. Johansen," and "Professor Nansen." Ibid., p. 259. Vidkun Quisling, who worked closely with the elder Nansen for several years, was no luckier. Quisling's first wife recalled a dinner party for "our guest of honor, the famous, composed, and frigidly reserved Dr. Nansen (as Vidkun always called him)." Yourieff, *In Quisling's Shadow*, p. 283.

88. Utne, *Brenda, My Darling*, p. 43.

89. Quoted in Utne, *Brenda, My Darling*, p. 122.

90. *Lima News*, January 11, 1940, p. 10, col. 1.

91. Sörensen, *Saga*, pp. 45–46. Similarly, on July 27, 1943, Nansen would confront the powerful *Schutzhaftlagerführer* of Grini Camp, Julius Denzer: "[I]t's become a point of conscience with me to tell you . . ."

92. Nansen, *Farthest North*, p. ix (introduction by Roland Huntford).

93. Høyer, *Nansen: A Family Portrait*, p. 183. Fleming marvels that Fridtjof was able to complete his 300,000 word tome "in an unbelievable two months." *Ninety Degrees North*, p. 265. Both *Farthest North* and *From Day to Day*, based on diaries, were bestsellers. Nansen, *Farthest North*, p. viii (introduction by Roland Huntford).

94. Høyer, *Nansen: A Family Portrait*, p. 183. See also Sörensen, *Saga*, p. 342: "[I]n his later years when the burden became so heavy [he continued his work] often far into the night."

95. Høyer, *Nansen: A Family Portrait*, p. 264.

96. John was the daughter-in-law of painter Augustus John. She translated many works from Scandinavian languages, including those of Icelandic Nobel laureate Halldór Laxness.

97. Since the original publication of the diary only small excerpts from the unpublished portions of the original manuscript have ever been published in Norway, and none in English. Anne Ellingsen published heretofore unviewed portions of the diary in her 2011 article "Odd Nansen, Antitotalitær Humanist." Several diary entries and portions of entries, including that of August 21, 1943, the last of Nansen's to survive before he arrived at Sachsenhausen, appear for the first time in English, and some for the first time ever, translated courtesy of Kari Greve, Odd Nansen's granddaughter.

98. Website of the Lofoten War Museum, *www.lofotenkrigmus.no/e_grini.htm*, accessed November 11, 2013.

99. The exact number of prisoners killed at Grini is unknown, but at least five men and three women were executed and another (Kristian Aubert) beaten to death at the camp during the war. See 1944 Execution Memorial adjacent to Grini Museum.

100. Dahl, *Quisling*, pp. 258, 292.

101. Todd Huebner, "Sachsenhausen Main Camp," in *The United States Holocaust Memorial Museum Encyclopedia of Camps and Ghettos, 1933–1945*, ed. Geoffrey Megargee (Bloomington: Indiana University Press in association with the United States Holocaust Memorial Museum, 2009), vol. 1, part A, pp. 1255–61. The layout of Sachsenhausen, described as "an unwieldy blend of art deco and Jeremy Bentham's Panopticon—proved ill-suited to expansion," and thus failed to serve as a satisfactory model. Ibid., p. 1256.

102. Because of its proximity to the Inspectorate, Sachsenhausen also became the new training center for concentration camp commandants. Daniel Blatman, *The Death Marches*, trans. Chaya Galai (Cambridge, MA: Belknap Press of Harvard University Press, 2011), p. 25.

103. Günter Morsch and Astrid Ley, ed., *Sachsenhausen Concentration Camp: 1936–1945 Events and Developments*, trans. Richard Toovey (Berlin: Metropole Verlag, 2013), p. 133. Because Sachsenhausen was liberated by Soviet forces, was located in the Soviet occupation zone, and later became part of East Germany, it remains one of the lesser-studied camps notwithstanding its being one of the oldest and largest. Jerzy Pindera, *Liebe Mutti: One Man's Struggle to Survive in KZ Sachsenhausen, 1939–1945*, ed. Lynne Taylor (Dallas: University Press of America, 2004), p. ix.

104. Wachsmann, *KL*, p. 226.

105. According to Robert Bjørka, a fellow Norwegian who shared for a time the same *kommando* as Nansen, Nansen suffered from ankylosing spondylitis (also known as Bekhterev's disease), a form of chronic inflammatory disease that primarily affects men and primarily affects the joints in the spine and sacroiliac joint in the pelvis. It can cause eventual fusion of the spine, known as "bamboo spine." Once the inflammation has been reduced, physical therapy is beneficial, but movement during the active inflammatory state only makes the pain worse. The condition can be exacerbated by consumption of starches, which of course constituted a major part of every prisoner's diet. Nansen's daughter Marit Greve confirms that Nansen continued to suffer lower back and hip problems throughout his postwar life. Anne Ellingsen, "Odd Nansen—En Angiver?" in *Humanist* no. 4 (2011) (in Norwegian), p. 71; Marit Greve, interview, October 29, 2014.

106. The first bombing casualties at Sachsenhausen occurred March 16, 1944. By the end of the war Allied bombing had killed thirty-two thousand foreign workers and POWs. Randall Hansen, *Fire and Fury* (New York: NAL Caliber, 2009), p. 286. Richard Overy uses the same figure but suggests these estimates may be overinflated. Richard Overy, *The Bombers and the Bombed* (New York: Viking, 2013), pp. 206–7.

107. Josef Kramer, the commandant of Bergen-Belsen, complained in April 1945, "[I]n the last few weeks it has not been possible to bring in foodstuffs, because the Allies have destroyed all the access roads."

Quoted in Blatman, *The Death Marches*, pp. 134–35. Similarly, the bombardment of industrial concentrations "led to slowdowns and sometimes to total cutoff of food supplies to the camps where [forced laborers] were housed." Ibid., p. 261.

108. On April 18, 1945, Heinrich Himmler issued an order to all concentration camp commanders that "Not a single prisoner must fall alive into enemy hands." Quoted in Blatman, *The Death Marches*, p. 154. "The option of total extermination of the prisoners remaining in the camps was raised repeatedly . . . in the last few months of the war. . . . Anton Kaindl, commandant of Sachsenhausen, testified at his postwar trial . . . that this option was mentioned to him explicitly." Ibid., p. 163. See also pp. 197–217 (discussing the contemplated liquidation of Dachau and Mauthausen by the SS). Another Holocaust historian observes, "The whole process of liquidating the concentration camps . . . turned into a series of atrocities against the prisoners" and proceeds to list a number of massacres. Waclaw Dlugoborski and Franciszek Piper, ed., *Auschwitz 1940–1945*, trans. William Brand (Oświęcim: Auschwitz-Birkenau State Museum, 2000), p. 10. It is estimated that of the roughly 700,000 camp prisoners alive in January 1945, some 300,000, or over 40 percent, were dead by early May. "Never before had so many . . . prisoners died so quickly." Wachsmann, *KL*, p. 544; Blatman, *The Death Marches*, p. 2 (Blatman states that over 35 percent perished on the death marches alone).

109. Wolfgang Sofsky, *The Order of Terror: The Concentration Camp*, trans. William Templer (Princeton, NJ: Princeton University Press, 1997), p. 89. If Sofsky's work provides insights into the theoretical foundations of the concentration camp, Nansen's diary is a concrete, detailed reflection of those insights in action.

110. Emmett Dedmon, *Chicago Sun-Times*, February 6, 1949, p. 8x.

111. Primo Levi, *The Drowned and the Saved*, trans. Raymond Rosenthal (New York: Summit Books, 1988), pp. 18–19.

112. William L. Shirer, *Berlin Diary* (New York: Alfred A. Knopf, 1941), p. vi. Similarly, diarist Myrtle Wright recorded on October 30, 1942, "Now things are really pleasant! Death penalty for having secret papers in the house and not reporting them to the police." Wright, *Norwegian Diary*, p. 111. Wright's diary is a valuable contemporary account of the same events Nansen wrote about while in prison. Like Nansen, Wright worried about detection, so she, too, hid her diary, first in the false bottoms of chicken coops located on Sigrid Lund's property, and later in the war tucked safely away in the University of Oslo's library (where Sigrid Lund's sister-in-law worked) in the section containing Tibetan manuscripts, filed under "'H.7.43'—the King's cypher [*sic*] and the year of deposition!" Still later, Wright again became concerned when the Gestapo raided the library looking for illicit radios ("one never knew when the Gestapo interest might not extend even to Tibetan manuscripts") and it was once again relocated, out into the countryside, where it remained for the duration of the war. The original is now in the Norwegian Resistance Museum in Oslo. Ibid., p. iii.

113. A compelling example of the often precarious existence of a prison diary is afforded by Peter Moen's diary. Moen, a member of the Norwegian Resistance, was arrested February 3, 1944. Held at 19 Møllergata for seven months, he was forbidden so much as a pencil. Nevertheless he kept a diary by painstakingly pricking out letters on toilet paper using a tack. After several pages were composed, they would be dropped through a ventilation grill in the wall. In September 1944 Moen was transported by ship to Germany. While in transit Moen confided to several fellow prisoners the existence and hiding place of his secret diary. En route his ship sank after being struck by either a mine or a torpedo (accounts vary) and all but five passengers aboard (including Moen) drowned. Fortunately one of the five survivors carried with him Moen's secret, and after the war so informed the police. The cell floor at Møllergata was torn up and the diary recovered, intact. It was deciphered and translated into several languages, including English, and published as *Peter Moen's Diary*, trans. Bjorn Koefoed (New York: Creative Age Press, 1951). Similarly, David Koker, a Dutch Jew, kept a diary while imprisoned in the Vught concentration camp in Holland. Portions of the diary were smuggled out of the camp by willing civilian workers until February 8, 1944. It is known that Koker continued to keep a diary after February 8, but on June 2, 1944, he was deported to Auschwitz and later died en route to Dachau; the remaining portions of the diary have never been found. An English translation was published in 2012 under the title *At the Edge of the Abyss*, ed. Robert Jan van Pelt, trans. Michiel Horn and John Irons (Evanston, IL: Northwestern University

Press, 2012). Another Dutch Jew, Rosie Glaser, kept a diary while in a local prison, the Westerbork camp, and Vught. When rumors circulated of an impending transport to Poland, Glaser smuggled the diary out of prison to a former neighbor for safekeeping. Rosie survived Auschwitz but after the war learned that the neighbor's house (and thus the diary) had been destroyed by Allied bombing. She was later able to reconstruct her saga from memory. Even so, her story might have remained unknown had not her nephew found her notes, journals, and letters after her death. See Paul Glaser, *Dancing with the Enemy* (New York: Nan A. Talese/Doubleday, 2013). Even diaries of the famous and powerful can disappear. It is known that Italian dictator Mussolini kept a diary, but it has never been found. Dear, *The Oxford Companion to World War II*, p. 420; John Gooch, "Mussolini's diaries and the 'treasure of Dongo,'" *Times Literary Supplement*, October 17, 2011, found online at *www.the-tls.co.uk/tls/public/article801191.ece*, accessed March 15, 2015.

114.   Quoted in Ian Thomson, *Primo Levi: A Life* (New York: Metropolitan Books/Henry Holt and Company, 2003), p. 183.

115.   The exact number of diaries written in concentration camps will probably never be known. Robert Jan van Pelt cites a study of such diaries that lists fourteen works, seven of which were written by Jews. Nansen's diary is not included in the list, and none of the fourteen diaries identified deals with Sachsenhausen. Moreover, only six of these diaries have ever been translated into English. Koker, *At the Edge of the Abyss*, pp. 11, 65 n. 30 (introduction by Robert Jan van Pelt). Van Pelt also mentions three other journals not mentioned in the previous study. Ibid., n. 31. Wachsmann mentions "dozens" of diaries that have surfaced since the end of the war, including thirty diaries written in Bergen-Belsen alone. *KL*, pp. 20, 639, n. 91. This compares with the millions of men, women, and children sent to the camps during the course of the war.

116.   Koker, *At the Edge of the Abyss*, p. 19 (introduction by Robert Jan van Pelt).

117.   Levi, *The Drowned and the Saved*, p. 18.

118.   Ruth Franklin, *A Thousand Darknesses: Lies and Truth in Holocaust Fiction* (Oxford: Oxford University Press, 2011), p. 11; Levi, *The Drowned and the Saved*, p. 19.

119.   Franklin, *A Thousand Darknesses*, p. 82. Franklin observes that even diaries are not wholly immune from this process: "[A]ll written texts are in some way mediated." Ibid., p. 11.

120.   Anne L. Goodman, *New Republic*, March 28, 1949, p. 24.

121.   Even misspelled names were left as is and were only corrected in the name index that preceded the text in the Norwegian edition. Consistent with Nansen's approach, all name corrections in this edition are shown in the footnotes.

122.   Interestingly, many of the July 20 conspirators ended up spending time in Sachsenhausen. Todd Huebner, "Sachsenhausen Main Camp," p. 1258.

123.   According to Marit Greve, Kari would often read aloud parts of the diary to the wives of other prisoners so that they too could learn of developments within Grini. Marit Greve, interview, October 29, 2014.

124.   Wachsmann, *KL*, p. 223.

125.   Another famous diary to survive World War II was *I Shall Bear Witness: A Diary of the Nazi Years 1942–1945* by Victor Klemperer, trans. Martin Chalmers (New York: Random House, 1999). A Jew but married to a non-Jew, Klemperer avoided deportation and remained a private citizen at large in Germany throughout the war. Nevertheless, he was fully aware of the dangers he ran by keeping his journal: "My diaries and notes! I tell myself again and again: They will not only cost me my life, if they are discovered, but also [my wife] Eva's and that of several others, whom I have mentioned by name." Ibid., p. 364.

126.   The idea to use hollowed-out breadboards may have come from fellow prisoner Robert Bjørka. Bjørka's breadboard (with its own hidden diary) was stolen in Neuengamme (reflecting yet again the fragile existence of such diaries). Ellingsen, "Odd Nansen, Antitotalitær Humanist," p. 78; Robert Bjørka, interview, October 31, 2014.

127.   Christopher Montague Woodhouse, "Of Human Endurance," *Times Literary Supplement*, July 29, 1949, p. 483.

128.   Concentration camp inmate David Koker agreed: "[P]arcels [of food] are technical aids to life. But letters are life itself." Koker, *At the Edge of the Abyss*, p. 130.

129. The excerpt appeared in English in the original Norwegian version.

130. Quoted in Utne, *Brenda, My Darling*, p. 91.

131. Quoted in Huntford, *Nansen*, p. 541.

132. Nansen likely means "advance" as an overture of friendship. In the preceding sentences of the diary Nansen records his disgust at being courted in public by *Lagercommandant* Denzer.

133. Levi, *The Drowned and the Saved*, p. 18.

134. Bruland, "Norway's Role in the Holocaust," p. 232. In the fall of 1942 word of the proposed roundup of Jews leaked out from sympathetic sources within the Norwegian police, and another 1,000 or so Jews (out of a total prewar population of approximately 1,700) were able to escape to Sweden. Sim, *Women at War*, p. 124; Aage Trommer, "Scandinavia and the Turn of the Tide," in *Scandinavia during the Second World War*, p. 246 (Trommer puts the number of escapees at 700).

135. "What Happened in Norway? Shoah and the Norwegian Jews." A publication of the Oslo Jewish Museum from the Exhibition "Remember Us Unto Life," p. 18.

136. Abrahamsen, *Norway's Response*, p. 85.

137. Bjarte Bruland, Norway's foremost expert on the Holocaust, points out that the destruction process went through three phases in Norway. From the invasion until January 1942 [i.e., when Nansen was arrested] was an "indecisive" phase "dominated by single actions . . . and initiatives not necessarily part of a systematic anti-Jewish policy." From January 1942 until October 1942, "signs of a far more destructive intent [were] visible." Only in the final phase [October 1942–February 1943] were there mass arrests, property confiscations and deportations. "Norway's Role in the Holocaust," p. 235.

138. Abrahamsen, *Norway's Response*, p. 125. Sigrid Lund, Nansen's compatriot at Nansenhjelpen, shared the same naiveté. She later wrote, "There has been criticism because the Jews were not sent to safety faster. But people forget that many others were also in danger then, for whom transport to safety seemed even more urgent. It would have been critical for members of the resistance, if they had been captured. Many Jews were seized only because they were Jews, not because they had been involved in the opposition movement. At that time, we didn't realize what was likely to happen to the Jews after they were taken. The pretty word was 'internment.'" Lund, *Always on the Way*, p. 68.

139. Thomson, *Primo Levi: A Life*, p. 160.

140. "The code of rules was terror incorporated. It covered virtually all situations of everyday camp life, prescribing every minute detail for the prisoners. . . . If rules encompass everything, it is impossible not to violate some rule or other. . . . This gave the guards license to act arbitrarily in the name of the rules. . . . Because everything was forbidden to the prisoners, all was permitted for the personnel." Sofsky, *The Order of Terror*, p. 113.

141. Sofsky, *The Order of Terror*, p. 158; Levi, *The Drowned and the Saved*, p. 78.

142. This attitude was shared by his father. In Fridtjof Nansen's Nobel Prize acceptance speech, he observed, "Where is the remedy to be sought? At the hands of politicians? They may mean well enough . . . but politics and new political programs are no longer of service to the world. . . . The diplomats perhaps? Their intentions may also be good enough, but they are once and for all a sterile race which has brought mankind more harm than good over the years." Website of the Nobel Prize, *nobelprize.org/nobel_prizes/peace/laureates/1922/nansen-lecture.html*, accessed January 4, 2011.

143. Thomas Buergenthal, *A Lucky Child* (New York: Little, Brown and Company, 2009), p. 186.

144. Ibid., pp. 163, 189.

145. Nansen records that the temperatures were approximately -12°C, or 10.4°F. "or lower." Odd Nansen, *Tommy* (unpublished English translation by Christopher Smallwood), pp. 86, 90; Blatman, *The Death Marches*, p. 92 (temperatures dropped to -10°C. to -15°C.). Buergenthal's experience is related in Buergenthal, *A Lucky Child*, pp. 86–97.

146. The greatest numbers of marchers were sent on to the Gross-Rosen (fifteen thousand), Buchenwald (fourteen thousand), and Mauthausen (nine thousand), all of which were considerably closer to Auschwitz. Blatman, *The Death Marches*, p. 97.

147. Buergenthal, *A Lucky Child*, p. 104.

148. Nansen, *Tommy*, pp. 109, 84.

149. Henry Kranz, "Norwegian in Nazi Camp," *Saturday Review of Literature*, February 12, 1949, p. 19.

150. Bruno Lasker, *Survey*, March 1949, pp. 177–78.

151. Orville Prescott, *New York Times*, January 21, 1949, p. 3, col. 2.

152. Emmett Dedmon, "Norwegian's Realistic Diary of Nazi Concentration Camp," *Chicago Sun-Times*, February 6, 1949, p. 8x.

153. Joseph Henry Jackson, *San Francisco Chronicle*, February 7, 1949, p. 14, col. 6.

154. *Spectator*, September 29, 1949, p. 40.

155. Christopher Woodhouse, "Of Human Endurance," *Times Literary Supplement*, July 29, 1949, p. 483.

156. Orville Prescott, *New York Times*, January 21, 1949, p. 3, col. 2.

157. William L. Shirer, *New York Herald-Tribune Weekly Book Review*, February 6, 1949, p. 1.

158. Walter Marsden, *New Statesman and Nation*, July 16, 1949, p. 78.

159. Orville Prescott, *New York Times*, January 21, 1949, p. 3, col. 2.

160. Anne L. Goodman, "One of the Survivors," *New Republic*, March 28, 1949, pp. 24–25.

161. Alfred Werner, "Of Man's Inhumanity to Man," *New York Times Book Review*, January 23, 1949, pp. 2–3.

162. Levi, *Survival in Auschwitz* and *The Reawakening*, trans. Stuart Woolf (New York: Summit Books, 1985), p. 57. Dalla Volta did not survive the Auschwitz Death March. Thomson, *Primo Levi: A Life*, p. 192.

163. *The Nation*, February 26, 1949, p. 253.

164. Orville Prescott, *New York Times*, January 21, 1949, p. 3, col. 2.

165. Anne L. Goodman, "One of the Survivors," *New Republic*, March 28, 1949, pp. 24–25.

166. William L. Shirer, *New York Herald-Tribune Weekly Book Review*, February 6, 1949, p. 1.

167. Alfred Werner, "Of Man's Inhumanity to Man," *New York Times Book Review*, January 23, 1949, pp. 2–3.

168. Anne L. Goodman, "One of the Survivors," *New Republic*, March 28, 1949, p. 24.

169. Christopher Woodhouse, "Of Human Endurance," *Times Literary Supplement*, July 29, 1949, p. 483.

170. Peter Wyden, *Stella* (New York: Simon & Schuster, 1992), p. 241.

171. Peter Novick, *The Holocaust in American Life* (Boston: Houghton Mifflin Company, 1999), pp. 85–86.

172. Jonathan Friedman, "Law and Politics in the Subsequent Nuremberg Trials, 1946–1949," in *Atrocities on Trial*, ed. Patricia Heberer and Jürgen Matthäus (Lincoln: University of Nebraska Press in association with the United States Holocaust Memorial Museum, 2008), pp. 91–93.

173. Novick, *The Holocaust in American Life*, p. 85; Richard Bessel, *Nazism and War* (New York: Modern Library, 2004), p. 214 (quote is from Novick).

174. Wachsmann, *KL*, p. 12; Novick, *The Holocaust in American Life*, pp. 85–123; Eugen Kogon, *The Theory and Practice of Hell*, trans. Heinz Norden (New York: Farrar, Straus and Giroux, 2006), p. xvii (introduction by Nikolaus Wachsmann). When first issued in his native Germany in 1947, Kogon's book achieved considerable success (135,000 copies printed), but, like Nansen's diary, was issued "in a much smaller print run" by the time it was translated and published in the United States in 1950. Ibid., p. xvii.

175. Novick, *The Holocaust in American Life*, p. 128. Novick's judgment may be overly harsh, as Shirer repeatedly mentions Hitler's murderous intentions and acts against the Jews and admits that his discussion of the Einsatzgruppen, the "Final Solution," the concentration camps, etc., was nothing more than "a mere summary, which because of limitations of space leave out a thousand shocking details." Shirer, *The Rise and Fall of the Third Reich*, p. 946. Shirer was a journalist, not a historian; his brethren in academia were even slower to the table. Historian Ian Kershaw has pointed out that in the 1960s the Holocaust "had not entered the mainstream of scholarship on the Third Reich. This did not substantially change before the 1980s." Kershaw, *Hitler, the Germans, and the Final Solution*, p. 328. In fact, a conference in 1979 on the Nazi state "did not include a single paper on the Holocaust. Nor, to my recollection, did the 'Final Solution,' or the persecution of the Jews more generally, figure centrally in any of the discussions during the conference." Ibid., pp. 12–13. A 1984 conference in Stuttgart "was the first time an academic conference in Germany had ever been devoted to the persecution of the Jews." Ibid. Focus on concentration camps was equally scant. Wachsmann observes, "In sharp contrast to survivors, the wider academic community was slow to engage with the KL." *KL*, p. 13.

176. Elie Wiesel, *All Rivers Run to the Sea: Memoirs* (New York: Alfred A. Knopf, 1996), p. 325.

177. Thomson, *Primo Levi: A Life*, pp. 228–30. Ironically, much like *From Day to Day*, *Survival in Auschwitz* was out of print by 1949. Ibid., p. 248.

178. Levi, *The Drowned and the Saved*, p. 167. In Italy the title is *If This Is a Man*. Einaudi had rejected the manuscript twice before, in 1947 and 1952. Thomson, *Primo Levi: A Life*, pp. 228–29, 248.

179. Thomson, *Primo Levi: A Life*, pp. 238, 278. In Italy the title is *The Truce*.

180. Ibid., p. 228.

181. Franklin, *A Thousand Darknesses*, p. 90.

182. Perhaps chastened by the experience, Samuel waited another forty-seven years before publishing a memoir of her personal experiences with the OSE, *Sauver les enfants*. It was translated into English (by a child she helped survive through the OSE) and published in 2002 as *Rescuing the Children: A Holocaust Memoir*, trans. Charles B. Paul (Madison: University of Wisconsin Press, 2002). The quoted remarks are found on p. 142.

183. Novick, *The Holocaust in American Life*, pp. 103–4.

184. *New York Review of Books*, October 27, 2011, p. 34; Franklin, *A Thousand Darknesses*, p. 69.

185. Novick, *The Holocaust in American Life*, p. 209. Kershaw attributes awakened popular interest in the Holocaust to this miniseries. Kershaw, *Hitler, the Germans, and the Final Solution*, p. 329. Wachsmann calls the miniseries a media sensation that "played an important part in confronting the public with the Nazi regime and its camps." *KL*, p. 12.

186. *The American Scholar*, Autumn 1956, p. 472.

187. Ibid., p. 496.

188. Nansen was not the only prisoner who thought of burying what he could not keep. Between 1945 and 1970 no less than six manuscripts and note fragments were found buried around Auschwitz-Birkenau. All were written by members of the *Sonderkommando* in charge of the gas chambers and crematoria. As such, they lived slightly more comfortable lives than the average prisoner, but they also knew full well the SS practice of periodically killing off the *Sonderkommando* prisoners; hence their ability and desire to leave behind a written record. The text of several of their accounts can be found at Jadwiga Bezwińska, ed., *Amidst a Nightmare of Crime*, trans. Krystyna Michalik (Oświęcim: Publications of the State Museum at Oświęcim, 1973). See also Nathan Cohen, "Diaries of the *Sonderkommando*," in *Anatomy of the Auschwitz Death Camp*, ed. Yisreal Gutman and Michael Berenbaum (Bloomington: Indiana University Press in association with the United States Holocaust Memorial Museum, 1994), pp. 522–34. According to Cohen the diarists "apparently had an unknown number of partners whose writings have not yet been discovered." Ibid., p. 522. See also pp. 484, 498. More recently, Wachsmann identifies "nine different documents, buried on the grounds of the Birkenau killing complex" that have been recovered since liberation. *KL*, pp. 52–53.

189. Milan Kundera, *The Book of Laughter and Forgetting*, trans. Michael Henry Heim (New York: Alfred A. Knopf, 1980), p. 3.

PREFACE

The Odd Nansen I Knew

by Thomas Buergenthal

When I arrived in Sachsenhausen in February 1945 after surviving the infamous Auschwitz Death March—a three-day march followed by a ten-day train ride in open cattle cars, all in the terrible Polish winter of January 1945—I could barely walk. My frostbitten toes were turning blacker every day; they hurt more and more and the twitching from the nerves in my toes seemed never to stop.

When I could no longer take the pain, I decided to go to the infirmary, even though I had tried for a while to resist doing so. I knew that the SS used the camp infirmaries as showplaces to convince foreign visitors, particularly inspectors from the Swiss International Committee of the Red Cross or the Swedish Red Cross, that the prisoners received good medical treatment. It was common knowledge in the camps, however, that few prisoners who entered the infirmaries ever made it out alive again. "They'll cure you and then they'll kill you," the saying went.

I was operated on shortly after I was admitted to the infirmary. When I opened my eyes again, I was in a bed in a long rectangular room full of patients in beds like mine along both sides of the room. At first, I assumed that both my feet had been amputated. In fact, I only lost two toes; the doctors had been able to save the others. As soon as I was fully awake again, I began to tell myself that I had to escape from the infirmary once I could walk again. But would I be able to do so before they took me away, I wondered?

The rumors that Soviet troops were getting closer and closer to the camp made remaining in the infirmary longer than necessary even more dangerous. "If the SS decides to liquidate the camp," I heard one of my fellow patients say, "they will not take those of us who cannot walk, nor will they leave us behind to be liberated by the advancing Soviet troops. So what do you think they will do with us?" No one answered, but we all knew what the answer would be. I listened and worried, and I missed my father and mother.

Not long after I arrived at the infirmary, a stranger stopped by my bed and introduced himself. "I am Odd Nansen and I am from Norway," he said in German. He was a tall man with a confidence-inspiring smile and eyes that radiated a warmth I had not seen since I had been separated from my father in Auschwitz. We started to talk, and he told me about his children in Norway and that he missed them very much. He asked about my parents, how old I was, whether I had brothers and sisters, and in what camp I had been before coming to Sachsenhausen. After that day he came back a few more times and always brought me cookies and other food I had not eaten in a long time. He was surprised that I could not read or write and promised on his next visit to bring me a pencil, some paper, and a little book. I enjoyed his visits very much and I liked talking with him; he made me feel very happy and grown up. On his last visit he told me that he would have to leave Sachsenhausen in a few days and that he had spoken with the head orderly of my ward to make sure that I would be safe. Then he gave me a piece of paper with his address in Norway and made me promise that I would write to him after the war. I was very sad that he had to leave the camp. He had not only been very kind to me; he was also the only person who came to visit me. In his presence, my toes hurt much less and I could even laugh.

I was liberated from Sachsenhausen in April 1945, became a mascot of a Polish army division fighting under the overall command of the Soviet military, ended up in a Jewish orphanage in Otwock, Poland, and was reunited with my mother in the final days of December 1946, more than two years after we were separated in Auschwitz. It is therefore not surprising that in all the excitement of my new life, I lost Odd Nansen's address and even forgot his name. Almost as soon as I was reunited with my mother in Göttingen, Germany, her hometown to which she returned after her liberation from Ravensbrück, I started to tell her about that wonderful Norwegian who, I was sure, had saved my life in Sachsenhausen. His father was very famous, I told her, so famous that his picture even appeared on a jar of cookies Mr. Nansen had once given me. That prompted my mother half in jest to suggest that the father of my friend must have been a cookie manufacturer. But since that did not get us very far, I continued to remind my mother that we had to find that nice man who had helped me in Sachsenhausen. "After all," I kept telling her, "I promised that I would write to him after my liberation!"

Then, more than a year after I had arrived in Göttingen, my mother came across an article in a newsletter for camp survivors about a Norwegian by the name of Odd Nansen who had published a book about his life in Sachsenhausen. That prompted my mother to suggest that I write to this "Mister Nansen" to ask whether he could help me find my Norwegian friend whose name I had forgotten. I did, of course. After what seemed like a long wait, I received Odd Nansen's reply. His letter arrived together with a big wooden crate filled with food and candy, delivered by two Norwegian soldiers stationed not far from Göttingen. He was the very person I was looking for, Nansen wrote. He had been trying to find me since the end of the war and was overjoyed that I was alive and that I had found my mother. He wanted to know whether we needed anything, particularly food and clothing. He also promised to come to Göttingen and take me to Norway to meet his family and the many "friends" I had in that country who had read all about me in his book, which he had dedicated to me and to some other close friends from Sachsenhausen.

A few months later, my mother accompanied me to meet Odd Nansen at the Hamburg airport, where he was waiting to take me to Norway. I spent the next six weeks—my summer vacation—with the Nansen family in Oslo and in their mountain cabin in the Gudbrandsdalen, about an hour and a half drive from Oslo. The Nansens lived in a large modern house in Lysaker, a suburb of Oslo, very close to the Oslo fjord. Kari Nansen, Odd Nansen's wife, and their four children—Marit, Eigil, Siri, and Odd Eric—treated me almost from the beginning like a member of the family. To Aunt Kari, as she wanted to be called, I became yet another son and felt like one too.

At first, I had to answer many questions, mainly from the Nansen children who had read about me in their father's book. They wanted to know more, particularly how I had found my mother and what it was like to go to school in Göttingen. Although the kids and I usually spoke German with one another, it was different at the dinner table. At least once a week, the language was Norwegian. That meant that I had to learn very fast how to say, "Please pass the food" in Norwegian. We also spoke English and French, which I had started to learn at school in Göttingen. Of course, we laughed a lot because of all the mistakes we kids made trying to speak languages we did not know well. During our meals, "Uncle" Odd would from time to time look around the table with smiling eyes as if to say, "we are finally all together again." The atmosphere in the Nansen home was very happy and relaxed. There were many visitors to the Nansen house, including persons who told me that they had been in Sachsenhausen when I was there and wanted to welcome me to Norway.

I don't remember whether I spent one or two weeks in the Nansen cabin in the mountains. But I have never forgotten how much fun I had hiking with the family in the hills and visiting some nearby farms. On these walks, Uncle Odd and I talked a lot. He told me how the Swedish Red Cross had managed to get the Germans to release the Norwegians and Danes from Sachsenhausen before the end of the war and that he had tried unsuccessfully to take me with him. He had many questions and wanted to know in particular what had happened to me after he left Sachsenhausen and how we learned that my father had died in the camps. In the evenings, we would read and tell stories. Uncle Odd played the guitar and sang Norwegian folk songs accompanied by the rest of the family. There was a lot of laughter all around, frequently about jokes I could not understand. Thinking back to my stay in Norway that summer, I realize that as far as the Nansen family was concerned, the war and Nazi occupation seemed to have been forgotten, despite all the hardships they had experienced. The family was reunited and life was happy and normal again.

I did not see Odd Nansen again until 1951, when he invited my mother and me to come to Cologne for the conferral of a German Peace Prize on Albert Schweitzer, the famous Franco-German humanitarian. Nansen was one of the speakers during these festivities. In his speech—I have kept the text to this day—Nansen pleaded for reconciliation with the German people and an end to hatred. In the meantime, a translation of his *From Day to Day* had been published in Germany, so I was finally able to read it. What made a huge impression on me was that Nansen had donated the proceeds from the German-language edition to programs for the assistance of German refugees. "Why help these people who started the war and murdered so many human beings?" I asked Nansen. He explained that not all Germans had committed these crimes, that it was important to support reconciliation with the German people in general, and to help those in need. Of course, Germans guilty of serious crimes should be punished in the courts. He believed, I still remember him saying, that we had to stop hating all Germans and that hatred only led to more hatred and a never-ending cycle of violence in the world. Over time, Nansen's words led me to rethink my own attitude toward Germany and gradually to rid myself of the hatred I harbored against the German people for killing my father, my grandparents, and other relatives.

A few months later, in December 1951, I left for the United States and did not see Odd Nansen again until 1959 or 1960. We did, however, correspond from time to time. I was already in law school in New York City when Nansen wrote that he would be in town in a few days. We met and talked and talked. I wanted to know what Aunt Kari and the Nansen children were doing. Nansen asked about my plans for the future and I told him that I intended to continue my studies in international law. That pleased him very much.

Unfortunately, I remember little else about our conversation because I was getting ready for my final law school exams and could hardly concentrate on anything else.

In the summer of 1972 I was attending a conference in Uppsala, Sweden, on the "Right to Leave and Return to One's Country," a topic that occupied the human rights community at the time because of the persecution of Soviet refuseniks who were trying to leave the Soviet Union. As the meeting was ending, I decided on the spur of the moment to visit Odd Nansen and immediately changed my ticket to return to the United States via Norway. I had not seen Nansen for quite some time, had heard that he had been sick, and suddenly felt a strong urge to see him again. His book *Tommy* had been published in Norway two years earlier. He had sent me a copy and apologized for taking so long to write it even though he had interviewed my mother and me for it as far back as 1951, when we were together in Cologne. He had been very busy with his architectural firm, he explained, but when he got sick and his doctor "forced" him to retire, he picked up his notes from Cologne and started to write *Tommy*.

We embraced when I entered the Nansen home after arriving from Sweden. He looked thinner and pale, but as we started to talk he seemed to regain his strength and color. He had many questions for me, he said. At first, he wanted to know about my wife and children, whose pictures he had seen some time ago; how were they and when would I bring them to Norway, he asked. He wanted to know what my mother was doing and whether she was well. Then he told me how pleased he was that I was teaching international law and especially human rights law.[1] That was the right subject for a person with my background, he said. He asked whether I thought the United Nations was doing enough to advance the protection of human rights in the world. We discussed that subject and his own work helping refugees. When I noticed that he was getting tired, I started to leave, but before I was able to do so, he made me promise that I would return to Norway with my wife and children; he wanted to meet them, he said. Odd Nansen died a year later.

I would never have forgiven myself had I not decided to stop over in Norway on my return trip from Uppsala. Odd Nansen had not only saved my life, he also enriched it with his philosophy on life. He had a profound influence on me. Whether I knew it or not at the time, my decision to study international law and to work in the human rights field was in large measure inspired by the principles he believed in and lived by.

Timothy Boyce deserves our profound appreciation for producing this magnificent new edition of *From Day to Day*. Odd Nansen needs to be read and to be remembered for what he believed, for the life he lived, and for the wonderful human being and great humanitarian he was.

Thomas Buergenthal
Washington, DC
February 2015

---

1. See W. Augustiny, "Er sprach immer von Tommy," in E. H. Rakette, ed., *Grenzueberschreitungen* 136, at 144 (1973).

"[B]ut worst of all is the thought of the millions of dry eyes staring hopelessly into the future. Eyes that have no more tears. Eyes to which no joy, no sorrow gives warmth or luster any more. Dead, cold, unfeeling eyes, stiffened by gazing on the incomprehensible brutality of fellow men.

"Human heart, do not parch away! May streams of tears come and quench that burning, consuming fire! And in fresh streams from the warm springs of human life nourish the love which is our sole salvation."

Anton, Torgeir, Jacob, Per, Peter, Hans, Henry—and all the many, many more who gave all—and you too, little Tommy! You are those warm springs! From your Elysium the warmth and the faith that will rebuild the world flow toward us. To your living memory I dedicate this book.

—Odd Nansen

A NOTE REGARDING THIS REVISED EDITION

The following edition generally follows the version published in the United States in 1949, with additional text included only in the English version, also published that year under the title *Day After Day*, as well as newly translated text appearing in English for the first time. Certain British uses have been conformed to the American for readability purposes. In the case of any ambiguities or conflict between the American and British usages, the original Norwegian version has been consulted. Also for readability, certain first or last names have been added where only surnames, first names, or initials were used in the diary. Consistent with Nansen's statement, however, that nothing had been added or edited in the text, misspelled Norwegian names are left as is and corrected in the footnotes (Nansen used a name index in the Norwegian version to correct errors). All German names are corrected for historical accuracy, and certain capitalizations have been made consistent. The actual weekday and year, in addition to the date, for each entry is also now shown. The placement of Nansen's sketches has been revised to more closely follow the accompanying text. All footnotes from Odd Nansen are so noted with his initials; all others have been added to this edition for the first time, as have been the introduction, preface, appendices, index, and photographs.

The 1949 edition began with an epigraph from Thornton Wilder's *The Bridge of San Luis Rey* that described love as the "bridge" between the living and the dead. On another page was a quotation (from a source the editor has been unable to identify) and Nansen's dedication. Those elements are reproduced in this edition. The first names in the dedication refer to Anton Bø (executed May 21, 1942), Torgeir Sikveland (executed May 21, 1942), Jacob Friis (executed April 30, 1942), Per Fillinger (executed April 30, 1942), Peter Young (executed April 30, 1942), Hans Michelsen (died July 5, 1944), and Henry Hansen (died April 10, 1944). Tommy is Thomas Buergenthal, author of this edition's preface.

—Timothy J. Boyce

TRANSLATOR'S NOTE

This diary, severely cut by the author for publication in his own country, has again been much reduced in the English version. But there has been no touching up. Minor inconsistencies, the hallmark of a day-to-day record, have not been tampered with. I have tried, in short, to give exactly what was set down, as far as such a thing is possible in another language.

—Katherine John, from the 1949 edition

FOREWORD

by Odd Nansen

THIS BOOK IS A DIARY AND MAKES NO CLAIM to be anything else. I was in the habit of keeping a diary, so it was natural to continue after my arrest on January 13, 1942. Paper and writing materials were the last things I put in my knapsack before going off with the district sheriff and his henchman, up in the mountains at Gausdal. I began to write the very next day in my cell in the Lillehammer county jail and kept it up for nearly three and a half years. For reasons easily understood I wrote the diary in a very small hand on the thinnest of paper. The writing was so small that the typists had to use a magnifying glass.

I never wrote with the idea that what I was writing would be published. I was writing for my wife, to let her know what was happening and how I was getting on—and also to arrange my ideas. Therefore the diary may often seem rather too personal, even though most of the private matter has been cut out. I couldn't cut it all out, I felt, without taking from the diary too much of its character. For it is the case that a prisoner thinks a very great deal about his wife, his children, and home.

Friends, both outside and inside, thought that a diary like this might be of interest beyond my immediate circle. I feel that they may be right, and so here it is. I should explain that it has been cut down to about a third of the original manuscript. I found much that ought to be cut, and could be cut, and it has turned out long enough.

The manuscript of the diary from August [22] to October 4, 1943, was unfortunately lost. As this period was of decisive importance to me, and for what happened later, I have restored it from memory. Otherwise the diary is the original text, with nothing added, corrected, or rewritten.

As time went by inside the barbed wire, writing became a great help to me. It was like confiding in a close friend and relieving my mind of all that weighed on it—it became a private manner of forgetting. I was happy in my invention and grew more and more inventive when it came to hiding it and disposing of what I wrote. At Grini, where I very soon made myself at home, there was no great difficulty. There were hundreds of hiding places that no German ever found out. We had a main storehouse of "illegalities" in the main drain which opened out from the furnace room through a secret tunnel. In pipe shafts in the main building, behind pipes and wires, we had "inflammable" objects, hanging up in bags between the stories. We had hiding places on the farm, in the workshops, under stumps and stones out in the fields, in hollow table tops and legs, in shelves with double bottoms, and in floors, ceilings, and walls in all the buildings in the camp. None of the many searches carried out in my time led to the discovery of anything really vital. Not a single page of the diary ever fell into the wrong hands, not a single important letter or single news bulletin.

We had channels out as well—many and good ones. Many an express message and many a vitally important letter that might mean life or death to those concerned found its way out to freedom in the double bottom of a matchbox, or rolled into a cigarette, or in one of the bits of piping that were always having to go into Oslo for repair. Many hundreds of pages of this diary were gotten out of the camp in the same way. At the Fossum works [a nearby farm and wood mill], at Lysaker station, and in many other places where we called for materials for the *Bauabteilung* [building department] or had other duties, there were good friends who forwarded both mail and parcels and who, with the contact men in Oslo, kept the channels open. And the channels were our vital nerves. It would take too long to mention all who helped, so I mention no one. But honor to them all for their share.

In Germany things were not so good. And I *had* to go on writing. Not that safekeeping was so difficult in that camp. There were fewer searches there. Nor was it difficult to find an opportunity for writing. But the problem was how to take it with me if we were to leave the camp. For that involved a *Filzing*—a search—of body and soul, and nothing illegal might go through. Almost everything was "illegal," and we should probably be going on a transport sooner or later.

This problem occupied me for a long time, but didn't keep me from writing. Even if I were compelled to bury the diary in German soil, I would and must write. Then I made a discovery. Most of the "*Muselmenn*" and others who arrived at or left Sachsenhausen in transports had a breadboard in their luggage. It was like this—the bread ration allotted to each man for the transport was distributed at starting, and it was usual to have a breadboard, or table end, to cut it up on. And that went through the *Filzing*. No greenhorn,* however much on the spot, would regard it as suspicious. Of course! There was the solution. The diary would be inside the breadboard.

I went to work right away. At that time I was in the joinery, and with the aid of my friend Birger Bjerkeng, who was among other things a first-class joiner, I made some breadboards that would serve the purpose. A table end was cut into two leaves with the circular saw. In one a groove was made, the exact size of the manuscript. The two leaves were trimmed and fitted together with the precision of a master-joiner. The manuscript was placed in the groove and pressed down, whereupon the sections were glued together and trimmed off at the edges. No devil could perceive the board to be glued or hollow.

The first board was for me, the second for Frode [Rinnan], the third for Scott [Isaksen], the fourth for Erik [Magelssen], the fifth for Arvid [Johansen], and the sixth for Leif [Jensen]. I carved our names on them and we used them every day until they were covered with knife scratches and spots of grease. In these six breadboards the diary was conveyed to Norway, except for the part I wrote after we left Sachsenhausen, which I sewed into my sleeping bag.

The illustrations in the book I drew partly in the concentration camps, and partly after-

---

* Nansen's used this and similar terms ("the greens," "greenery," "green devils," etc.) as a shorthand for the SS because of their use of gray-green uniforms.

ward, from sketches I made there. Unfortunately many were lost, and therefore the selection is rather unequal. But I felt that such a big book must have a few pictures here and there.

I dare not vouch for the spelling of the German names. If the specimens of the German language are not up to "high German" standards, that is only partly my fault. Nor has it seemed to me of great importance. The Norwegian is more so, and I apologize for any Norwegian names I may have spelled wrong. No harm was meant.

Odd Nansen
Lysaker
November 1946

PART I: GRINI

1942

TUESDAY, JANUARY 13, 1942 ■ At half-past seven the district sheriff of East Gausdal came up to the cottage with two Germans. It was dark. We saw the sheriff's flashlight a long way off. We thought he was hunting radios, as he came just at the suspicious hour.*

It was for me. They said I must come away to Lillehammer, and then to Oslo, where I should be told the reason. I was given time to pack my knapsack. Kari was calm, Marit, Eigil, and Siri cried, poor things, but were smiling bravely through their tears before I left.

So off we went. The car was waiting at the sanatorium garage. The sheriff talked a lot in the car. No doubt he was anxious to gloss over his pitiful role. He wished me a speedy return when he went off at Segalstad Bridge.†

I was put into the Lillehammer county jail. A single cell. When the jailer had gone, a voice in the cell next door asked who I was. It was Odd Wang's voice.‡ He did not know why he had been arrested either, but thought it must be due to a misunderstanding. That I should have been arrested, he said, was natural enough, but that he. . . . No, it was certainly a misunderstanding, which would be cleared up as soon as he got to Oslo and had a chance to explain himself. It had grown late, and we soon lay down. The light was left us until twelve o'clock, and we could read. The plank bed was hard, as plank beds are, but I was not cold, for we were given blankets.

One of the "Germans" turned out to be a purebred Norwegian. At the cottage he pretended to be German. Admiral Tank-Nielsen had spent the night before in my cell.§ I heard about the new actions against special officers and against the friends of the royal family, who were all arrested at this time. I supposed I must come under the latter heading, and if so I should probably be "inside" until the war was over?

WEDNESDAY, JANUARY 14, 1942 ■ Wakened at six o'clock with bread and butter and something by way of coffee. The day passed in reading and a little writing. We were not allowed to smoke, and had had to give up our matches together with our knives. However, I found my lighter in my pocket. It was dry, but I actually got a little flame out of it, enough to light a cigarette. That was before breakfast. When the jailer came in the morning, he dilated his nostrils and said, "You've had a morning smoke, eh?" I had to confess and give up my lighter.

Dinnertime arrived, but I had to wait for mine long after the others. Then came a basket. The jailer looked mysterious and told me not to say anything. "This ain't allowed," he said, and out of the basket came a delicious dinner, with the compliments of Håkon

---

* The ownership of radios by anyone other than NS members was outlawed in September 1941 by the occupation authorities; radios belonging to Jews were confiscated in May 1940. The BBC News Norwegian service would have been broadcasting at 7:30 p.m.; this service was inaugurated shortly after the German invasion.

† Sigrid Undset, Nobel Laureate for Literature (1929), lived in nearby Lillehammer. Her eldest son, Anders Svarstad, reported for duty immediately following the German invasion and was killed in a battle at Segalstad Bridge on April 27, 1940, one of approximately 860 Norwegian soldiers (and 400 civilians) killed during the campaign.

‡ Wang worked in the shipping business in Germany, England, and France before the war. In 1931 he started his own business selling ship supplies, Odd Storm Wang & Co. A/S. He was released January 23, 1943.

§ Carsten Tank-Nielsen (1877–1957) was commander of the Second Naval District, where he played a prominent role in the Altmark Affair. He was incarcerated in Grini for a few days and then released.

Tallaug.* Beef olives, half a bottle of burgundy, cloudberries and cream, cakes, bannocks, and down at the bottom of the basket my friend the jailer had stuck my lighter, and I'm blessed if it didn't light again. In short, a lordly meal. Most of the afternoon I beguiled with trying to swing a lighted cigarette over to Odd Wang's window. I joined my bootlaces to the cord of my knapsack and tied my nailbrush at the end to weight the pendulum. It was a failure but amusing. Later we hit on the idea that he should ring and ask to borrow a cake of soap from me. Thus he got the cigarette—alight in the soapbox. Supper came in to both of us from Odd's father. We lacked for nothing. Before lying down to sleep our second prison sleep, we heard that we were to be taken to Oslo early the next morning.

THURSDAY, JANUARY 15, 1942 ■ The train left about six.

In Oslo we met some of Odd's family, but no Black Maria, so we had to walk to Number 19.† After a last good smoke and a deep draft of fresh air, in we went through an anteroom for biographical records, over the Bridge of Sighs and into Hell.‡

First we were ordered to stand erect with our faces to the wall. A bad habit of sticking my hands into my pockets, which I share with other fairly good Norwegians, produced some frightful bellowing from one of the German guards who stood in the corridor. He had been bellowing a long time before I realized what it was about. Later, when I was unlucky enough to fold my arms across my chest, the bellows burst forth again, this time sealed with a well-directed kick in the pants, and I got my hands down to my sides. But they felt an urge to meet yet again, this time behind my back. Then his screams were loud and ugly and menacing, and he kicked so hard and painfully that the hands shot down of their own accord along the seams of my trousers. I had to stand like that for three quarters of an hour. Then I was called into an office, where I was registered, given a number, and deprived of all my things, except what I might have in the way of food and "harmless" toilet articles. After that I was marched off to a cell with uproar and abuse, first because I went too fast, then because I went too slow, and finally because I went one cell too far, thereby demonstrating that I didn't know how to read.

The cell already had a prisoner—a lawyer named [Jon] Nøkleby, from Drammen.§ He looked ill and had been inside for two months. He was delighted to have a roommate.

Gradually I got wise to the customs and routine of the "house." Up at six o'clock, clean the cell, make the "bed"—I slept on the floor, on a mattress which had only to be rolled up—breakfast, which was served through the peephole in the door by one of the "workers," that is, prisoners who have been in prison for some time and have got the job, then out into the passage to fetch water, and empty refuse, and wash the dishes. Dinner came through the peephole in the door at about twelve o'clock, and supper at about

---

* Håkon Thallaug, a lawyer living in Lillehammer, was himself arrested October 26, 1942, and spent time in Grini and Sachsenhausen before being released January 20, 1945. After the war Thallaug was a council member of Nansen Academy, the Norwegian Humanistic Academy, established in 1939 in Lillehammer and named in honor of Fridtjof Nansen (the school was dissolved for the duration of the Nazi occupation).

† A Black Maria is a police van or paddy wagon. 19 Møllergata was the address of the Gestapo prison. Prior to the war it was Oslo's main police station and jail.

‡ The Bridge of Sighs is an elaborate bridge constructed in 1602 over the Rio di Palazzo in Venice connecting the interrogation rooms of the Doge's Palace to the prison. So named by Lord Byron, it was said to afford the condemned prisoner's last view of Venice before beginning his sentence.

§ Released January 17, 1942. His daughter, Berit Nøkleby, is a historian who has written extensively about Norway's experience in World War II.

five. There was not much else to break the monotony. No doubt strictly speaking I was forbidden to read, but there were a few books in the cell and I embarked on one. Tobacco neither of us had, so that was right out of the question. On the other hand I got a bath. The bathman was County Sheriff Gabrielsen.* We had a pleasant chat. In the cell with me I had a box with a store of food; we shared that and ate it with our supper and breakfast, which was bread and butter and something in the nature of tea or coffee. We were also given a cup of sour milk for breakfast, and a few slices of raw rutabaga for supper. When the dirty slices of rutabaga came in through the little hole, at first I felt exactly like a rabbit.

FRIDAY, JANUARY 16, 1942 ■ In the morning a lout of a jailer came and bellowed something about packing up my things double quick. I was going to Grini, he shrieked. I packed and got out, took an affecting leave of Nøkleby from Drammen, who looked very unhappy at being left alone again with his thoughts, and so, with kicks, cuffs, and yells, was hustled into the "reception," where I got the rest of my luggage back and had to sign that none of it was missing (without a chance to look and see). Odd Wang had now reappeared upon the scene. We were taken down to the prison yard, where a Black Maria awaited us. We were handcuffed to one another. The lout sat down facing us, and laid his right hand on his revolver. He sat like that all the way to Grini. He asked about our professions. I replied in all simplicity that I was an architect. He didn't think much of that, but when Odd announced himself as a professional boxer† he showed marked symptoms of respect. Otherwise our groping attempts to start a conversation miscarried. His only answer was, "That's for Adolf Hitler to decide," whatever we asked.

At Grini we were received in the Vermittlung [Registration Office]‡ by Nils Dybwad and other prisoners who took down what had to be taken down about us.§ Our luggage was gone through. Money and knives were confiscated, but they let us keep our tobacco. Then on we went, up to the "mountain hotel" itself.¶ On the terrace stood Frode Rinnan.** We got a hearty welcome, and he invited us to go in and choose a good room. He was on easy speaking terms with the German who accompanied us, an SS-devil who after all showed some trace of human qualities. His name is Kunz and he is a lathe operator from Worms—mighty smart in his uniform, with the death's-head cap and high, shining boots. And like the rest he delights in bawling one out. On such

---

* Hans Gabrielsen (1891–1965), a lawyer and civil servant, played a key role in organizing the civilian side of the war effort in northern Norway following the invasion. After the war he was a member of the unification cabinet first appointed by King Haakon VII following liberation until elections could be held.–

† Odd is a peaceable businessman. O.N.

‡ The more correct and complete German word is *Vermittlungsamt*. The meaning of any German word or phrase that appears more than once in the text can be found in Appendix IV.

§ A lawyer, Dybwad was released from Grini December 20, 1942.

¶ Another prisoner, writing about Grini in 1943, described it as follows: "It lies in a remote spot, in woodland country surrounded by hills that rise invitingly one above the other. . . . [It] had been converted into a concentration camp by the Germans, who had added twenty-five large barracks huts for living quarters and workshops. Outside the barbed-wire fence, sentry paths connected eight high watch-towers equipped with searchlights and machine guns. Beyond this there was a very high electrified fence then a mine-field."

** An architect and Labor Party politician, after the war Rinnan (1905–1997) was the chief architect for the 1952 Winter Olympics; his work included the design of the famous Holmenkollen ski jump.

occasions a cataract of sound and fury pours from his mouth. One has to have been several months here to understand it.

We were taken up to the third floor and into a big room where the beds stood cheek by jowl in two tiers. Next to it was an annex, a little room with eight beds. We were put in there, and it turned out that for the present we were alone there. When the bawler had gone, we went round saying how d'you do. We were in the middle of the so-called "court gang." There we met Emil Nicolaysen,* Ingar Dobloug,† and very many more, as well as a lot of fathers from Måløy and Bergen imprisoned as hostages for their sons who had gone to England.‡ There were also fathers from other towns and provinces.

Guards' trousers and jacket, a shirt, a pair of drawers, and a pair of boots were issued to us by the lawyer Henning Bødtker, who was in charge of the wardrobe.§ The jacket, shirt, and drawers were too small for me, and the boots unwearable. Everything else was all right.

When I first met Frode, it had been settled that I should have a job with him in the architect's office—according to report an ideal job. The day passed in getting one's bearings; dinner consisted of the famous "storm soup," which was really good. I actually found a bit of meat in it.

SUNDAY, FEBRUARY 1, 1942 ■ I am sitting here alone in my "office." It's Sunday, and I have come here for peace and quiet. This is one's only chance in the week to get some real peace, for today everyone is "free," and all the working places are deserted. I was to get a plan ready by tomorrow for the new block of huts; that was my excuse for coming here. I am reveling in the quiet. Over on the other side of the passage in a cell with a double door, Sejersted Bødtker is on *Dunkelzelle* [dark cell] as a punishment.¶ He has been there a fortnight and has another fortnight to go. He was with Rector [Didrik] Seip of the University.** Seip got out yesterday. I don't think they have been so badly off. At

---

* In August 1942 Nicolaysen was deported to various POW camps in Poland and Germany, including one in Ostrz-eszów, Poland (then named Schildberg by the Nazis), where he remained for the duration of the war.

† Initially arrested as a court hostage, Dobloug was released February 25, 1942, but was rearrested for his involvement with an underground newspaper and confined for a brief time in Bredtveit Prison, northwest of Oslo.

‡ In the first two years of the war, 3,500 men crossed the North Sea in fishing boats and other small craft to England to join British and Norwegian armed forces. German patrolling, and a policy of forcing Norwegians living on the coast to leave their houses during the summer, eventually all but shut down this means of escape.

§ In May 1941 Bødtker (1891–1975), an attorney, signed a circular letter addressed to Reichskommissar Josef Terboven on behalf of the Norwegian Bar Association protesting the attempted Nazification of the legal profession; less than a month later he was arrested along with other signatories. Released July 31, 1941, Bødtker was rearrested during the state of emergency in September 1941 and released again on September 4, 1942. After the war Bødtker served as attorney general of Norway (1945–1962) and auditor of the Norwegian Nobel Prize Committee (1946–1972).

¶ Johannes Sejersted Bødtker (1879–1963), banker and art collector. Among the contemporary art works Bødtker collected were paintings by Axel Revold, Odd Nansen's brother-in-law, and Per Krohg, another prisoner at Grini. As a board member of the National Theater, Bødtker was jailed in 1941 (along with fellow board members Francis Bull and Harald Grieg) for refusing to comply with dictates of the Nazi controlled Ministry of Culture and Enlightenment. He was released July 29, 1944.

** A professor of North Germanic Languages and rector of the University of Oslo, Seip (1884–1963) spent time in Grini and Sachsenhausen; he was later released from Sachsenhausen on Himmler's orders but not allowed to leave Germany until almost the end of the war, when he was personally evacuated by Folke Bernadotte as part of the "white buses" operation. Diarist Myrtle Wright describes him: "His thick-set figure, rough short hair and dry humour [*sic*] were refreshing even in the company of Norwegians who seldom take life tragically and never sentimentally." Seip wrote about his experience after the war in *Hjemme og i fiendeland, 1940–1945* [*At Home and in Enemy Country 1940–1945*].

Frode Rinnan, architect, building superintendent, farming
superintendent, and the Storm Prince's right hand.

other times I feel a positive envy of Sejersted Bødtker, because he is left in peace. The very worst thing about prison life is all these people. There are more than seven hundred of them, and they make a row all day long. Here at the office they are in and out all through working hours, they sit down to pass the time, they talk and smoke. No sooner has one left than another comes in. Not a moment's quiet, not a single little chance to be alone with one's thoughts, to write or draw or whatever else, only something of one's own.

Such is this prison—and to think I have always gone about with the idea that solitude was worse than anything else.

It is three weeks on Tuesday since I was arrested. It seems to me an eternity. I feel as though it had happened in another age, in quite another world. This prison life is so different from what one has been used to. Not that we have a bad time of it, we haven't really—it's true we don't get enough to eat, but to the best of our poor ability and opportunities we have amended that—but the essential strangeness is this living right on top of seven hundred people all round the clock. There is no room to be oneself. In an overcrowded hut one sits up against these people, taking one's meals; at night one lies side by side with them trying to sleep, trying not to hear their deafening snores, while hour after hour creeps by in the darkness.

Neither before, during, nor after working spells can one get away from them; they lie on the beds, sit on stools and tables, stand about in the corridors, talking, smoking, and discussing the selfsame questions over and over. How long will it last? When will Germany have to give in? When shall I get out? So-and-so was let out yesterday, and I'm here for the same thing. Have you heard that So-and-so has been arrested? I wonder why? Do you know anything? Do you *know* anything? Have you heard the latest?—and so on interminably. This atmosphere becomes a heavy and pernicious weight on the mind; insensibly one gives way to it; little by little one slides into the collective. The new arrivals notice it in those who have been here long, until they themselves get like that. Then they leave off noticing. A few more fowls have joined the poultry yard, and the new ones soon learn to cackle just like the rest. Any jarring, distinctive note is quickly muffled and reduced to harmony with the grand chorus.

Mankind's enemy number one, collectivism, is in the process of winning a sly and fatal victory; one must always be on guard if one is not to succumb. Each day is like the next; there are no new problems cropping up. No struggles, no difficulties, everything goes like clockwork—a dreary clockwork. We rise at seven every morning, and make the bed in conformity with German standards—incidentally, an imbecile little farce in itself. Then the different "waiters" bring in the food. It is the same every day; a little pat of butter, three slices of heavy bread, and as many cups of brown water as you please. God knows what it is made of. Oddly enough they call it coffee, but it is weaker than weak tea, and if one hadn't a few saccharine tablets of one's own to slip in, the lukewarm water would hardly have any taste at all. Then comes a break until half-past eight, when we have a roll call, that is, we parade in the yard before the prison. Each section falls in by itself, under the command of its own hut leader. He reports the number on parade, the number sick, and the number "detailed"—prisoners who have been ordered on extra work outside the working places. When the figures have been checked by a so-called *Zugführer* [chief guard],* we parade in working groups and march to the sites.

---

* A *Zugführer* was a police rank equivalent to an SS *Untersturmführer*.

All new prisoners have jobs assigned them by the labor-control office. This office is directed by Erling Steen,* and as far as possible men are given the kind of job that suits their age and health. Beforehand they have been to the doctor, who examines them and gives them a number—that is to say, their life or their physique is appraised. There are four classes of life. Class 1 is the best. The old and chronically ill are put down as 4; they must have indoor jobs or complete exemption. The 3's also have indoor work, while the 2's may have light outdoor work. The 1's get the hardest and heaviest outdoor labor, such as clearing tree stumps, ditching, transport, etc. In the way of indoor jobs there are smithy work, joiner's work, glazier's work, glove making, the architect's office, the stores office, the personnel office, and the surveyor's office, where the work is partly outdoor. The tea gang, or Ceylon gang as they are also called, "roll" tea; that is, they treat the raspberry leaves that have been collected during the summer in the woods and fields round the prison, after a peculiar and original method that consists of rolling the leaves between their palms to a gray-green pulp—the finished product. Light outdoor work includes the shoveling of snow and the lopping of branches along the trout stream; this is done by the so-called trout gang. They clean out the brook where the trout spawn are to be set, and the trees are lopped, it's said, so that the "Storm Prince" can cast a fly in comfort. The "Storm Prince" is *Obersturmführer* [Hermann] Koch,† the superintendent of the prison. It seems to be agreed that he is on the whole a good man for the prisoners. He is on our side in a way, against Victoria Terrace‡ or the highest Gestapo and SS leadership, of which he too is in constant fear. But to return to the daily routine. The first working spell goes on until half-past twelve, which is dinnertime. You either turn up singly in the huts,§ or march there with the whole gang from the place of work. By then the waiters have brought the food up to the passages in large buckets or slop pails. As a rule it is storm soup with one or two bits of meat in it and a powerful lot of groats or it is dried and salted cod, herring and potatoes, or it may be salt coalfish. All this food, whether soup, fish, or potatoes, is eaten from a soup plate, the only kind of plate that has been issued to everyone, along with a spoon, a dinner knife, a fork, and a little cup and saucer. Some have got hold of a container like a chamber pot without a handle. That is better than the plate when it comes to soup, because it holds more. The plate runs over with one helping, and there is quite a long way to carry it from the serving place to the hut. As a rule we get two helpings of soup. To begin with one thinks it an achievement to have swallowed down one, but in the

---

* From 1939 until his death Steen (1891–1961) was chairman of Steen & Strøm, a large retailing and wholesaling concern. He was arrested in June 1941 for his part in protesting the Nazification of Norwegian institutions. After the war Steen became head of the Norwegian Red Cross (1947–1957) and chairman of the Norwegian Refugee Council (1953–1958). Today Steen & Strøm AS is the leading developer and manager of shopping centers in Norway, Sweden, and Denmark. In March 2012 Simon Property Group, Inc., the largest mall owner in the United States, acquired an indirect controlling interest in the concern. Steen was released February 26, 1943.

† *Obersturmführer* literally means "Storm Leader"; Nansen is likely making a play on words when calling Koch the "Storm Prince." All SS ranks, and their US equivalents, can be found in Appendix II.

‡ Gestapo headquarters. Described by a contemporary as "an amazingly ugly building in the wedding-cake style," it was synonymous with torture; prisoners were known to leap to their death from the fourth floor to escape the beatings. One survivor of the experience wrote, "If the walls of Victoria Terrasse [*sic*] could speak they would tell of hundreds of Norwegians who have been tortured and plagued; of tears and blood; of strong young Norwegians who came in well and healthy and who were carried out either as dead men or physical wrecks." The building currently houses the Norwegian Ministry of Foreign Affairs.

§ We called the rooms huts. At that time we were all living in the main building. Later the "barracks" were built. Then everyone moved out of the main building—and lived in huts. Then we called the rooms rooms. O.N.

course of time one feels positively greedy for number two as well. It's the same with fish. To begin with it's hard work to get down one of the unappetizing yellow—brown bits of fish, but in the course of time they slip down more and more easily, not only one but two pieces, besides the regulation three or four potatoes. It sometimes happens that we get barley gruel afterward.

Enough to eat? No, enough is not the word but two big platefuls of soup have a curious deceptive power of filling the belly and creating the illusion that one has had enough. Anyhow a cigarette tastes uncommonly good afterward and so far I have never been short of cigarettes, in spite of the fact that I could only bring in a very few, and though I have distributed them largely in three huts, that is, among over fifty men. Where have they come from? Well, that is a little thriller in itself, which I may find occasion to touch on.

Then comes washing up, and a rest for those who like, and roll call again at half-past one. So at any rate the midday rest is not long. Call-over, parade in working groups and march back to work, until five o'clock, when there is another parade and roll call. Then it is suppertime. For that we have a piece of butter and three bits of bread, as at breakfast. At supper the brown water is called tea, but I can detect no difference between that and the drink we have for breakfast, which is called coffee. Now and then at supper we have a little dab of stewed apple, or even a little cube of cheese, goat's-milk cheese or Gouda. That is the lot. Enough? No, not precisely enough, but I can always get along, my work is not hard. It is worse for the young fellows who have been out stump clearing or on other heavy work. They get too little. Therefore one must make a point of helping them to some more.

After supper there is a free period until nine o'clock, when the light is turned off and everyone must go to bed. You can do anything you like in this "free period." It sounds well, but one must add that the possibilities are rather limited. One can visit other huts and talk. Oddly enough one soon tires of that. I thought it would be so grand to meet all the gallant men assembled here from the worlds of thought and of action. But it wasn't. There is an uncanny sameness about them all. I try to persuade myself that it is the clothes that do it—those queer-looking old guards' uniforms, an equal misfit on every figure, with the striped, filthy dungaree trousers that sit round one's legs like stovepipes, and usually don't even reach the top of one's boots. And then the boots—cashiered, worn-out, mucky boots, usually with twine for laces. The guards' jacket, too, that short, bulgy object, stripped of buttons and epaulettes, sticking out behind over one's rump and usually poking open in front, because it won't go right round, and even the tailor's great exertions in the way of gussets under the arms and in the back and neck, have been in vain and only contribute to an even more bulgy look. On Saturdays and Sundays we put on our "evening trousers"; they are the dark blue ones with the white braid picked off. That is our full dress, and it undoubtedly improves the façade a little, even though the dress trousers also are as a rule ill fitting, both too tight and too short, and leave nothing to be desired in their resemblance to a pair of stovepipes.

But I had reached the evening free period. We can borrow books from the library. There are some good books there too, but most are thrillers and rubbish. But suppose one does get a good book, where can one settle down to get it read? The hut is crowded, and there is always someone talking, who has no wish to read. The passages are crowded with people talking; there is no reading room; the office where I am now is forbidden ground outside working hours, and in bed after nine o'clock it is strictly forbidden to have a light. Nevertheless it is one's salvation to settle there with a cardboard shade and a candle stump. Thank heaven I am in a hut so placed that you have to go through another hut to reach it. So I can hear any inspection in the evening before it reaches my own hut, and can get the shade removed and the candle out in time. In any case it has been all right so far. The flashlight batteries that Kari sent me soon burn out. But now I have been blessed with masses of Christmas candles. They will certainly last out my whole imprisonment.

With reading it is practically impossible to kill the "free period." But writing? The same difficulties make that impossible. Besides there's nowhere to sit. No one has anything but his own little stool, and if there are visitors in the hut—and there always are—then the stools are occupied. Moreover the newly arrived prisoners have no stools in their huts, and the furniture situation will get worse as more come in.

Within the last few days more than thirty prisoners have arrived from 19 Møllergata. They are living in a hut known as the "parachute room." There they sleep one above the other in four tiers, the topmost close up under the roof of the hall, which was designed originally as a gymnasium. The hall is seventy-two square meters [775 sq. ft.] and they have packed seventy-six beds into it. Obviously there's no room for all these men to eat at tables down on the floor, so they live round about on their beds up in the air; a kind of monkey life. It goes without saying that they have not a stool each, not even a shelf each or a peg each to hang up anything. They keep their things in trunks and bags under the lowest bed, and when they have got their food from the slop pails they take it up onto the beds, or they stand outside in the corridor, at the windows, and in other places to eat it. A few of them sit at the table, which is in the "aisle" between the bed feet in the parachute room. If a man fell out of the topmost bunk, in his sleep for instance, he would have a very good chance of being killed, or a very poor chance of coming off without lasting injury. As yet there are not more than thirty-odd men there. But more are always coming, and it seems as if mass incursions were expected hereafter. Today is an anxious day from that point of view. For Quisling is to be proclaimed national leader, and mass arrests and fresh encroachments are awaited, so report has it.*

But about the free period. Sometimes little entertainments are arranged for Sunday evenings, cabaret-like, improvised affairs. They are held in church. The church is a real church. At least it was intended and designed as a church, but now of course it is used as a hut, too. That is where all the strikers live, who were arrested during the state of emergency in September.† They sleep in the main part of the church in four tiers, of which the uppermost is much on a level with the gallery that runs across the back of the hall. Down

---

* Vidkun Quisling (1887–1945) was the leader of the Nasjonal Samling, an anti-Semitic, fascist party that copied the Nazi emphasis on emblems and uniforms and adopted the "*Führer* principle." Quisling was appointed minister-president by the Nazis on February 1, 1942. Arrested May 9, 1945, he was tried and convicted of high treason and executed by firing squad on October 24, 1945. In his youth Quisling worked closely with, and was considered a key assistant to, Fridtjof Nansen during Nansen's 1922 Russian famine relief work. US minister to Norway Florence Harriman wrote in her memoirs that "many people had for a long time regarded him as of unsound mind." The word Quisling is today synonymous with traitor.

† On September 8, 1941, factory workers spontaneously struck over the cessation of the special milk ration they had previously been provided; it was the proverbial straw that broke the camel's back in an environment of steadily worsening food supplies, and became known as the milk strike. Although workers voted to return to the job on September 9, Reichskommissar Josef Terboven declared a state of emergency on September 10, executed two union leaders (who had actually worked to avert the strike), made more than three hundred arrests, and requisitioned all radios owned by anyone other than NS members.

the middle there is a fairly broad aisle leading up to the altar or the stage. The aisle then represents the stalls and pit; the bed feet along the side are side galleries where one can lie and look on. The gallery can be filled in the normal way; it has no beds in it. Only a limited number of the prisoners can get in as audience, but the affairs are highly impromptu and have been badly advertised, so there has been no great concourse of people. And under the circumstances, that is certainly the best way of doing it.

The entertainment varies. The most valuable part of it is perhaps the choral singing, Norwegian patriotic songs, in which all join. It does one good to see political antagonists, rich men, poor men, Communists, labor leaders, men of the Right and of the Left, high and low united in Norwegian music without discord. It is an experience that gives one strength and joy and faith in the future; it is truly valuable, and I believe that the impression goes deep.

Apart from that the programs offer all kinds of "turns" by prisoners with more or less talent. A queer fish named Harris Normann Olsen step dances, sings, conducts the orchestra of mouth organs, and directs the programs in his own style. He is full of gusto and entirely without inhibitions of any kind, can do nothing yet can do anything. He has been five years in the Foreign Legion and has appeared as an "artist" all over the world. Most of his teeth are lacking and a good deal else, but he has genuine high spirits and people enjoy a laugh at him.

We are "free" on Saturdays at half-past twelve, after roll call. That sounds first rate, but when you consider how hard it is to find anything to do, it becomes more dubious. The same applies to Sunday, which is completely free except for roll call in the morning, an hour later than usual, and after dinner at four o'clock. The day gets terribly long unless one can sneak away, as I have done now, and sit here in the office "working." Then Sunday is a marvelous day, which I shall come to long for. I hope this "working plan" can be repeated every Saturday and Sunday.

For work is the very thing one must not lose grip of. And here in prison the watchword is: *Sabotage the work!* Drag it out, do as little as you can, think of things to do that are completely useless! A very dangerous watchword, unless one can find "something else" for oneself, something with real point in it. I almost feel it sinister to watch certain people—how good they've gotten at doing nothing.

MONDAY, FEBRUARY 2, 1942 ■ Eckert, the lunatic German guard, was on the rampage this morning in the passages and inside the huts. When he is in the offing it can be heard a long way. He shouts and curses and roars abuse in an unintelligible language that he maintains to be German. It is the young prisoners who get the brunt of his bullying. He drags them out into the passage, off the seat of the privy when they are sitting there, sets them to knee-bending and all kinds of silly exercises, and has tremendous fun over it. With the older prisoners he is more cautious. After all, he himself is only a puppy of two or three and twenty. But he bellows in the huts too, if the beds are not made right or if there is some sort of untidiness, and there always is. For we have nowhere to put our things; the huts are too crowded for that.

But I personally have a certain hold on Eckert. He went into Oslo with me the other day to keep an eye on me. He is really a good-natured lunatic, and not merely permitted but proposed that I should get someone to buy me things that I could stuff in my pockets.

He had seen nothing and knew nothing.* Of course I made abundant use of the offer, and came back heavily laden with my magic coat. It happened on the way home that at Røa,† where we halted, I met somebody I knew, a young lady who was so overcome by the meeting (I was sitting on the floor of the truck shivering with cold) that she simply had to do something for me. I asked her to get some tobacco. She ran into the shop, where by good luck there was a bulky parcel of cigarettes for me. She came rushing out with the parcel and handed it up to me just as the car began to move—I had only time to wave good-bye and thank you. Eckert was sitting on the floor with me and of course saw everything. The parcel was opened and out poured cigarettes—more than he had ever set eyes on. I think in a way he grew quite tipsy at the spectacle. He offered to take them for me; then later I should have them back, he said. But I didn't give him the lot. I think he pocketed about two hundred; as for me, I stuffed packets down my trousers and into my coat and in all the places that were not crammed already. Another prisoner who was with us also got quite a lot. Between us we must have had close to a thousand cigarettes.

All went well. The only mishap, which might have been fatal, actually befell on the main steps up to the prison, where the truck stopped and we hurried in. Then it was that my left trouser leg came open round the boot, where I had tied it up with a piece of string, and out fell a whole loaf. It rolled right down the front steps and came to rest on the ground, just at the guard's feet. He looked at it and at me, as I came pelting down the steps again (for there was nothing else to be done) and then he smiled. *Gott sei dank!* [Thank God!] I took the loaf and ran up the steps, indoors, and up into the hut. Things kept on tumbling from my trouser leg, but I snatched them up as quick as they fell, and the next minute I was in the hut, saved. Then there was jubilation! It was my sixth successful trip. Every time I had come back loaded to capacity.

So at the moment we want for nothing. Also we distribute to the neighboring huts, and such endless quantities are needed for seventy or eighty men. What can one do with thirty or forty tins of sardines, a few hundred cigarettes, and two or three loaves? Well, they keep one's spirits up, they are bright spots in our existence, and for those engaged they provide some thrilling adventures, intensely thrilling; there is occasion for all one's ingenuity and presence of mind.

In the evening Eckert came and told me a story about how the Lieutenant had seen the loaf I dropped and asked whose it was. Eckert had said that it was his and had got a month's curfew. He didn't mention the cigarettes he brought in for me, but no doubt this story was to make me "forget about them." He was too keen on them himself, and already I should think that most of them are no more. Nor did I find it necessary to mention them. Let him have them; I get a certain hold on him that way.

At Lysaker station, where I have been four times to "superintend" the transport of huts that are sent there by rail and that we fetch away in trucks, I have established a most effective system.‡ The station people ring Kari as soon as I arrive. She comes down with various things on a foot sleigh. I have to "check up" in the inner station office, where I put off the time long and well, mostly in copying out all the freight bills. I have hung up my

---

* Reminiscent of Sergeant Schultz in the 1960s TV sitcom *Hogan's Heroes.*
† A suburb of Oslo.
‡ Lysaker station is approximately four miles west of downtown Oslo; Nansen's home, Polhøgda, was less than a mile away from the station.

magic coat in the outer office, and while I sit checking up inside under guard, my coat is going through such a process that when I come out again it will hardly go on. But it is all right. I have seen Kari three times, and Siri, Marit, and Eigil, who have all been there. As a rule the guard is easygoing, but it sometimes happens, too, that I have a fiend of a man along with me. He keeps an eagle eye open, asks about everything I write, and I expound and hold forth on my completely imbecile job, which has absolutely no connection with common sense. But the guard nods his head, and thinks the work most important and essential. I copied out the selfsame freight bills three times, each time with the same portentous earnestness, the same care and accuracy. The station staff are excellent people, and are in on the secret. They supplement Kari's parcels too, running round the shops, buying things up and stuffing them into my splendid coat with the open inside pockets and the double lining. With a full cargo it does look rather suspicious, and I have to walk very slowly and carefully.

The most exciting trip to Oslo was my first, when I had filled the coat with all the Vienna rolls it would hold, and a little tinned stuff. I had to sit in front of the truck with a guard, squeezed in, that is, between the guard and the driver. It had been tight enough before, even without the addition of the bulging coat. At last I got the worst protuberances over onto my belly and between my legs, so that they didn't stick into my neighbors. I drew a breath of relief when I had got properly settled down in front and we drove away. But the driver began to take an unusual route through the town, and when I questioned him, for I was the guide, he said that he was calling at Victoria Terrace. This was certainly an unpleasant piece of news, but there was nothing to be done but face the adventure in good spirits and with tense nerves.

We halted before the Gestapo palace, and I had to go along up the steps, past the guard, through the corridors in quick time, and into a room full of Gestapo men. There I was to wait. Someone gave me a chair and told me to sit down. Now the thing was that I found a little difficulty in sitting down. Both my trouser legs were stuffed full of Vienna rolls and one thing and another, so that I couldn't bend my knees to any marked extent without a catastrophe. If the string that was holding them together round the bottom had given way, the catastrophe would have taken place on the spot. Thank goodness I found a table edge to sit on, so that I could "sit" with outstretched legs without its being noticeable. For half an hour I sat there conversing with the Germans about this and that, and my heart was in my mouth all the time. It would have been a pretty business if they had conceived a suspicion of my curiously angular and plump trouser legs and my bulging pigeon breast. But it went off splendidly. Finally the driver and the guard came back and we left the room, the guard and driver first, and I in the rear. It was all right going through the corridor, where I had to get by several German guards in a very narrow place with a lot of chairs piled up, then past the guardroom, down the steps, and into the car. I got myself settled in as neatly as the first time, and after that the trip was uneventful right out to Grini.

Outside the *Vermittlung* I had to leave the car. Then a parcel came tumbling out from somewhere on my person. No one saw it happen, but the parcel was left lying on the running board. The guard caught sight of it, picked it up, and ran after me. I made up my mind to deny all knowledge of it. But he said, "I suppose this is something to eat. Put it in your pocket, but at once! Hurry! Hurry up, man!" I did so, scurried off, and got safely by all guards and danger zones and into the hut. That was my first exciting adventure;

since then I have had others, as I said, and I shall doubtless have more in the future. And thus I have set up a branch of the Nansenhjelp here in Grini, which I manage alone. My coadjutors are outside for the present.

TUESDAY, FEBRUARY 3, 1942 ■ Yesterday I began about the crazy Eckert. When he had stormed a while in the outer hut, he came in to us. He always lowers his tone a good many degrees in our little hut. It may be age that calls for a certain deference. He had not much to say this time, but wanted to get hold of me, and beckoned with a half-mysterious air to get me out into the passage. So I went out with him.

In the passage he beckoned me up close and whispered, "What were your stupid countrymen doing last night?" I didn't know what he meant and said so. "Haven't you heard? The big explosion—twenty minutes past three—the whole Eastern Station was blown up!"

This was indeed a juicy bit of news. He said he didn't know much more about it, but assured me that it was true. The news had already spread throughout the whole prison with the speed of lightning, so that his injunction not to tell anyone was superfluous. At any rate I was on no account to say that *he* had said anything. Later I found out from other people that they had heard the selfsame story from the selfsame Eckert. However there were not many who believed it, and when the news gradually expanded to include the Western Station also, there were fewer and fewer who believed it, so it died out in the course of the day.

But in the evening Görtz returned from the town, where he had been all day.* From him we learned that the Eastern Station was still on fire; he had been along that way and seen it. There were five hoses lying outside and the restaurant wing was still burning. He could tell us, further, that the Western Station was on fire too, but that the attempt there had been less successful and on a smaller scale. Moreover he had heard that in the course of the night there were three attempts in all. Those at the railway stations were staged presumably to catch the NS† people and especially the Hirdmen‡ who were on their way home from the festivities in Oslo apropos of Quisling's nomination as minister-president, which took place at Akershus on Sunday.§ As yet these events have not affected us, but God knows what may happen later. Quisling's nomination as minister-president (not national leader, as the first version had it) was the subject of lively comment in Grini— and all over the country, I assume. No one regards these developments as especially tragic; on the contrary, the bigger fool he makes of himself the better.

---

* Gottfred Gjørtz, released August 27, 1942. Nansen also mistakenly refers to him as "Gørtz" later in the text.

† Nasjonal Samling (National Union) Party, the Norwegian fascist party founded by Quisling in 1933. In 1936, the last election prior to the war, NS polled less than 2 percent of the total vote; it never elected a single delegate to Norway's Parliament, the Storting. In 1940 it was still a "minuscule party with only a few hundred members"; after it was declared the only legally permitted party, NS membership rose rapidly, and peaked at forty-three thousand in 1943.

‡ Members of the Hird, a paramilitary organization modeled after the German Stormtroopers (SA), or Brownshirts. "*Hird*" had been the name traditionally given to the retainers in the service of Norway's medieval kings. Approximately 8,500 Norwegians acted as Hirdmen during the war; many were prosecuted and convicted of treason and collaboration following liberation.

§ Quisling was originally slated to be installed as minister-president on January 30, but this was changed at the last minute to February 1; some have speculated that Hitler's jealousy prevented Quisling from celebrating the same day as Hitler's own accession to power in 1933. Akershus is a medieval castle in Oslo. It is currently home to the Norwegian Armed Forces Museum, the Norwegian Resistance Museum, the Ministry of Defense, and, in the Royal Mausoleum, King Haakon VII. Akershus was also the site of Quisling's execution by firing squad in October 1945.

Yesterday evening after supper, and just as we were going to bed, there came an order for a general parade on the square in front of the building. All sorts of guesses and forebodings were flying about. As always at such times we were afraid of a hut inspection, and tried feverishly to clear away all we had "too much" of in the way of foodstuffs and tobacco. But all this clearing up and hiding is quite illusory. A really efficient inspection of any sort or kind would bring all to light. For we have nowhere to put anything away, except in the bed, under the mattress, under the bed, in the privy, in the dustbins, in the trunks and knapsacks, in the washroom, and so on. All equally inadequate. However, this was all carried out in haste by more than seven hundred prisoners, I assume; there can hardly be anyone who has not something in his hut that conflicts with some rule or other.

And so we went down to roll call on the square. A line of guards were drawn up there with their automatics on their shoulders, and the Storm Prince himself, with his spineless old Alsatian bitch, was strutting up and down in front.* For a moment the drastic thought crossed my mind that there was going to be shooting, reprisals for the attempts in Oslo—but only for a moment. It was dark, but the moon was shining down; it was a cold, beautiful winter evening. At last the Storm Prince took up his place. There was a dead silence, everyone waiting in suspense for what he would say.

His speech was magnificent; I should have liked a shorthand report of it. He began by telling us that a letter had now been found proving that the politician Berggrav had known for more than two years that the Norwegian government then in power did not mean to pursue a neutral policy.† But the politician Berggrav had withheld this knowledge from his countrymen. In spite of which he, the Storm Prince, could today inform us that Quisling, leader of Nasjonal Samling, had been appointed minister-president, which meant that Germany had concluded peace with Norway. (Logic?)

He went on to say that despite the fact that Germany had thus concluded peace with Norway, English propaganda was being carried on in this country, and he asked the rector of the university and the chief of police, in particular,‡ to attend to what he was saying now; they knew how this propaganda had been carried on. Even here at Grini, he said, it has been stated today that Quisling is a traitor. That I will not tolerate; at least, he added, not in a German prison. And to show that it will not be tolerated, I hereby forbid the following: *Erstens* [First]: It is forbidden to read. *Zweitens* [Second]: It is forbidden to play games. We waited nervously for *Drittens* [Third] and thought of smoking. But there was no thirdly, only an exhortation to observe these new rules until he himself was made to feel that no one among us retained any such ideas as had been mentioned. With that the session was closed. We could return to our huts and go to bed.

---

* Alsatian is another name for German shepherd, Hitler's favorite dog breed, also favored by those who wanted to emulate the *Führer*.

† Eivind Berggrav (1884–1959) was not a politician but rather the bishop of Oslo and primate of Norway's Lutheran Church. Although Berggrav initially preached noninterference following Germany's invasion, he soon became a vocal critic of the regime, a leader of the Resistance, and as such Quisling's bitter political enemy. When he refused to alter the Church of Norway's liturgical practices in accordance with Nazi policies and helped orchestrate the resignation of Norway's bishops and almost all its pastors, he was arrested in April 1942. Concluding that Berggrav was too powerful to be executed, Quisling had him banished to solitary confinement in his cabin north of Oslo and allowed no visitors, including his wife. With the connivance of his guards, however, Berggrav was able to slip out on several occasions to continue his resistance activities as well as hold furtive meetings in his cabin; he finally escaped from house arrest in April 1945. After the war Berggrav played an active role in ecumenical movements including the formation of the World Council of Churches and as the first president of the United Bible Societies.

‡ Didrik Seip and Kristian Welhaven, respectively.

The occasion of the whole performance was—apart from Sunday's event at Akershus—that two of the prisoners, the Storm Prince's cook and footman, had been asked what they thought of Quisling, and had said they looked on him as a traitor. Both were given the *Dunkelzelle* and are now across the passage here in the "little prison" along with Sejersted Bødtker.

The other day I got my first letter from Kari. She confirms our "forebodings," she has been to the doctor who found it was so.* She writes that she is pleased and happy to have the chance of creating something in this terrible time, when everything is being pulled down and destroyed.

We found a piece of stale bread today, which the dark-cell prisoners had simply thrown out. We shared it, Colbjørn and I; it tasted excellent, better than any cake with our coffee.† Colbjørn is a young architect. He has arrived from Number 19, where he spent two months. He is now my "assistant." Frode is sick, still sick. He has been ill for over a week now. He is stopped up and has been for twelve days, poor chap, otherwise he is O.K.

At roll call after dinner the Storm Prince came to the front again and informed us, through [Kaare] Sydnes,‡ that all books, both borrowed and our own, were to be handed in to the library; in other words that all reading was forbidden until further notice. He also said that all borrowed packs of cards, etc., must be handed in again, but we might keep private ones. And that was that. Therefore playing cards is allowed, but reading is forbidden. It will be tiresome for me, for I don't sleep either in the evenings or in the mornings. My candle or flashlight has been a great comfort to me behind a thick cardboard screen (which I got from [Harald] Grieg in the bookbinding shop)§ when the light is turned out every evening and I lose myself in my book. Heaven knows what I shall do now. But everything tends to adjust itself up here, by degrees, if one has only patience, either until the prohibitions are removed, or until they are forgotten and gradually enforced less and less.

Broch, the lord chamberlain, is equally indignant every day at the treatment we receive here.¶ Not a day passes, indeed hardly a mealtime, without an outburst in his brusque, testy style on how disgraceful it is that one should have to submit to orders and bullying from this *canaille* [riffraff], these ill-bred idiots. He inquires for details whenever anyone has been spoken to or reprimanded; it shall all go into the report he is to send to the King, he says. Everything shall be remembered, nothing shall be forgotten. "They may rest assured of that," he concludes with emphasis, rolling his cigarette of *Karva blå*.** He is truly rich. "Who ever heard of such a thing! The rector of King Frederik's university, the chief constable of Oslo, senior officers of the Norwegian Army, venerable Norwegian citizens, forced to submit to a dressing-down from these vulgarians! No, it's unbelievable!"

---

* I.e., that Kari was pregnant. Their fourth child, a son named Odd Erik, was born September 18, 1942.
† Kjell Colbjørnsen. A fellow architect, Colbjørnsen worked with Frode Rinnan after the war. Nansen referred to him by the nickname "Colbjørn." He remained in Grini and Sachsenhausen until the end of the war.
‡ Released from Grini February 27, 1942.
§ The director of the publishing firm of Gyldendal Norsk Forlag and chair of the Norwegian Publisher's Association, Grieg (1894–1972) was arrested in 1941, along with Francis Bull and Johannes Sejersted Bødtker, for resisting attempts by the Nazi-controlled Ministry of Culture and Enlightenment to control the activities of the National Theater. He was released from Grini September 17, 1942. Following the war Grieg returned to publishing at Gyldendal.
¶ Peter Fredrik Broch, a fellow hostage, was released September 3, 1942.
** A brand of loose tobacco used for rolling cigarettes. *Rød mixture* was also used for the same purpose.

Now and then he turns scarlet all over the face with pure indignation, but the twinkle never leaves his eye.

Today the *Zugführer* had come along to inspect when they were working in the tea gang. One of them had been sitting looking through an autograph book that some collector had left behind. The place is full of these autograph collectors, and their activity has long been forbidden. *Der Zugführer* had asked what sort of book it was, and when it came out had made the devil of a scene, had confiscated the book, and among other things, when questioning members of the tea gang, had said to [Rolf] Pande, on his assurance that he owned no such book, "If you're lying you'll get the *Dunkelzelle*." "Who ever heard of such a thing," hissed Broch, "to talk like that to venerable old Pande, as though he were a schoolboy.* Vulgarians! But it shall not be forgotten! Everything shall be remembered; it shall go into my report to the King." At roll call after dinner today it was impressed on us again that autograph books, diaries, and souvenirs of every kind are strictly forbidden.

Colonel Schiøtz, one of my five roommates, is quite a different type.† He is a military expert, and everything he says is dead serious. His fame as a strategist preceded him to Grini, and he is consulted regularly by young and old on the interpretation of sundry news items, which flow into our prison in great abundance. He sifts them and pours cold water on those rumormongers who stand in need of it, goes round the huts holding little informal chats about the situation on the Russian front, and finds it all very bracing. It keeps him up to the mark, which is a great thing in this place. But now and then one feels tempted—and it does one good, too, I believe—to be a little more enthusiastic and devil may care than he is.

WEDNESDAY, FEBRUARY 4, 1942 ■ Just after supper there came a message that the Storm Prince wanted me on the telephone. I was sitting with Frode; people had been looking for me all over the building and thought there was something wrong. Certain rumors of my accident with the loaf on the front steps had got abroad in the prison and were instantly connected with this order from the Storm Prince. However, he only wanted me to come and see him next morning *früh* [early] with all the drawings for the new block of huts, so that we could thrash it all out with the *Bauinspektor* [building inspector] who was coming next day from Oslo. *Jawohl* [yes], *Herr Obersturmführer, jawohl.*

The new plan was not in very good case; little had been done to it and that little had a shaky and sickly look; indeed I had had no proper drawing materials. So it occurred to me to profit by the occasion and ask the guard to unlock the office; I should have to draw until late in the evening. It went off beautifully. I drew a handsome plan, and by the time I had finished it was half-past ten. I rang through to the guard and asked him to let me out; I had finished my work and must get back to the main prison. (Perhaps I have forgotten to mention that my "office" is in the little prison or "isolation building," at a short distance from the main prison.) Yes, he would come over. I waited and waited, but no guard. I settled down to write, and the time passed. I was well off and had absolutely

---

* Broch (age sixty-two) was actually older than Pande (age sixty); in any event Pande was released less than a month later (February 27, 1942).

† Johannes Henrik Schiøtz (1884–1957) was a Norwegian military officer and historian. For many years Schiøtz edited the *Norwegian Military Journal* and from 1954 to 1956 was director of Norway's Army Museum. Later in 1942 he was incarcerated in Oflag XXI-C in Ostrzeszów, Poland (Schildberg), along with more than one thousand military officers who were rounded up in August 1943. Ostrzeszów is presently home to a Norwegian POW museum.

no longing for my comfortless bed up in the hut. Then the telephone rang and a frantic guard bellowed down it, "You must have patience, man!" I told him I had patience enough and to spare, and he was just to take his time.

And the man took his time; it was not until about half-past twelve that I heard his footsteps and the rattle of his keys in the lock. Then of course he had the wrong key. He had brought the one that fits the other door of the building, where there is now a tuberculosis ward. He asked nervously through the door if he could come in that way. I said he could do that all right, if he had the key of the inner door, between the offices and the tuberculosis ward. He had, and so he went to the other door and let himself in. Came running down the middle corridor and unlocked the lobby door. "Hurry. For heaven's sake! At once! *Sacramento*!* Aren't you ready yet?" and so on.

He was behaving like a madman. I did not realize why until we got outside; then, in a gasping voice, he asked me if I thought it was dangerous to go through the tuberculosis ward. He was brushing himself all over and repeated his question when I asked what he meant. He was exasperated by my stupidity and roared: "Don't you understand anything, man? It's tuberculosis! Tuberculosis, man!" He was in deadly terror of catching it. He had held his breath as well as he could while he was in there, and was now busy brushing off all the germs. On my asking whether he was positive or negative, he disclosed that he had not the faintest idea what that might be. He only knew that tuberculosis was something frightful, something one died slowly of. I gave up trying to explain anything to this bold warrior. He was too German and stupid. At long last I got to bed, and after a highly illegal little read I lay down to sleep, tired for the first time since I came here.

FRIDAY, FEBRUARY 6, 1942 ■ On the morning of the fourth I had a pretty long conference, including an inspection of the whole terrain round the prison, with the Storm Prince and three bigwigs from SS *Bauleitung* [construction management]. Earlier in the morning I went over to the Storm Prince's villa with the plans I had sat over the night before. The Prince was in high good humor and was quite confidential; he hinted that the gentlemen arriving were after all a lot of numskulls, and that he, the Storm Prince, and we architects had a better idea of all that should be done here at Grini. When I advised against setting all the new huts on piles, and urged that in no circumstances whatever should the piles be stuck into the ground without a pile driver, he became really enthusiastic. Indeed that was one of the first things he mentioned to the gentlemen when they arrived: "Herr Nansen is an architect with great experience with hut-building in Norway and especially with substructure and foundation work." However, the gentlemen did not even look my way, and completely ignored the Storm Prince's introduction. Thus the Storm Prince from the very first seemed positively a man of breeding in comparison with those three toughs.

The conference was comic, as conferences between half-educated gangsters usually are. First they rejected the new plan that had been adopted (that was No. 9) and turned up a fresh one. Now one of the toughs had been in Dachau and had seen how the hutments there were laid out; another had been in Buchenwald, and I think that all of them, including the Storm Prince, had been in Oranienburg near Berlin. In such a case it's not easy to

---

* According to one Sachsenhausen survivor, SS guards who had served during the Spanish Civil War picked up numerous Spanish expressions and curse words.

agree. In one place it was flat, whereas another had been rugged and hilly. And obviously that brings up a series of problems which must be well thrashed out, especially when there is to be an electric fence going right round the prison camp, making it impossible for prisoners to escape. Besides, this fence has to be visible all its length from the watchtower, so that the guards can aim their tommy guns or machine guns at any point of it where a prisoner might be escaping. Nor must the terrain be of such a nature or form as to afford the prisoners any sort of cover. In short there were deep problems, and the man who had been in Dachau naturally could not agree with the man who had been only in Buchenwald, where it is flat, to say nothing of the Storm Prince, and then Oranienburg . . .

Now the Storm Prince was a couple of lengths ahead of them in point of age, and the fact that on top of that he *owned* the whole terrain, and could use the first person and address the others with "*Nein, mein lieber Kerl,*" [No, my dear fellow] gave him an advantage which he kept, on the whole, in every round. Moreover, the Storm Prince has lost all his teeth, and that lends his conversation a distinct, not to say an indistinct, character, which had its effect. Of course nobody took any notice of me, and indeed I soon gave up and withdrew from the race. To be sure I have some fatal drawbacks; I am a prisoner and besides I can't shout loud enough. When one's cases are wrong and now and then a word is entirely wrong, somehow one hasn't quite the courage to hurl them out with the true Germanic vigor. And then one may as well give in right away.

They could not agree and decided on an examination of the terrain. Here the Storm Prince got the upper hand in good earnest. For of course he knew his own estate, and could point his cane and expound problems that the others had not seen and considered. For instance, that he had bought up for the property a large and valuable piece of ground, where he meant to have his nursery-garden, on the other side of the brook, which lay low enough to make it difficult to run the electric fence alongside it; in that case the tower would have to be raised or the slope cut out more, and for that he had too little filling material, etc., etc.

The Storm Prince out in the grounds, clad in his short squire's coat with the fur collar, armed with his cane, and followed faithfully by his old Alsatian, a worn-out crock with drooping teats dangling in and out between her legs, is a peculiar sight, and suggests a kind of Junker edition of old Rockefeller on his daily stroll round the farm.* The three other gentlemen, not to mention Prisoner 1380 in the rear,† dropped right out of the picture, each in his way. Their loud Germanic roars, which indicate that they are still present and that they agree or disagree, the gentlemen did not of course leave off, but otherwise they were definitely on the defensive before the Storm Prince.

It was difficult to make quite sure what had been agreed on, and besides my legs were so infernally cold; unfortunately I had only put on shoes, and they are not much good in deep snow. At last, however, the inspection came to an end and I had leave to go.

In the middle of dinner I was sent for to the Storm Prince again. He confided to me that he was very pleased with the result. The new plan, the one temporarily valid now, was simply his own old plan except for one or two points. "Now, my dear Herr Nansen, we

---

*   Junkers were the landed nobility of Prussia, owning great estates. They exerted a dominant influence over German military, political, and diplomatic affairs following the country's unification in 1871 under Emperor Wilhelm (a Prussian).

†   Nansen's prison number while in Grini.

must wait. Just wait quietly, and later carry out my whole old plan. I know these fellows; they talk a lot and have big schemes. They know very little. That is the truth. I know everything better, and just have patience, Herr Nansen, we're going to carry out my old plan; exactly as I planned it at first."

I submitted a list of materials that would have to be bought for the joiner's shop, and asked where I should apply to get the things ordered. Then he clasped me familiarly round the shoulders, and we strutted up and down his room, while he confided to me—to me alone, I was assured—that we must wait now, take it quietly, drag out the work a little, there was no hurry. At the end of next week, perhaps within a fortnight or so, Gebecke, *der Bauleiter* [construction manager], would be coming back from leave, and then I could talk to him about it. Now we mustn't bother any more, but forget it for a while and work at something else, anything else, understand? "I'm sure you understand me, Herr Nansen?" Yes, indeed, I thoroughly understood him; it was, direct and from the highest level, a kind of order to administer loafing and sabotage, in the strictest confidence and in complete understanding.

Yesterday we had a most irregular day. Directly after morning roll call everyone was ordered into the huts again. All work was suspended, and we were to remain in the hut until further orders. Later in the morning there came an order to hand in all our sheets and blankets to [Sejersted] Bødtker. The wildest optimism began to spread. Were we to be set free? Needless to say a number of people had already heard so, and many believed it. However, the fact was that the officers—more than ninety men—were leaving, probably for Jørstadmoen near Lillehammer, to make room for sixty patients who were to be transferred from Ullevål.* The officers had at some time been supplied with Grini blankets and sheets, whereas being prisoners of the Wehrmacht they should have had the Wehrmacht's equipment. We had gotten that instead. Now we were to swap; that was the whole thing.

In addition there was a big change-round in the "sanatorium." The whole south wing of the first floor was to be vacated to make room for a hospital. This removal had its effects on every floor. Beds had to be moved out and in; clothes, equipment, trunks, boxes, chests, bed clothes, and everything conceivable were littered about the passages, and homeless prisoners were running to and fro until they got new huts assigned them.

Evening roll call was dropped in honor of the day, and the lights were not turned off until half-past eight. So it became a saturnalian evening. The real cause of all this turmoil was connected with the transfer of the patients from Ullevål. The fact was, there had been another escape from there. Six men had got away that time. The way it happened with four of them—Wright,† Cappelen,‡ Beck,§ and Simonsen—was particularly styl-

---

* Jørstadmoen was a camp constructed by the Germans north of Lillehammer. Ullevål is Norway's largest hospital, located in central Oslo.

† Carl P. Wright (1893–1961) was a politician; before the war Wright was a member of the Storting, or Parliament, and mayor of Porsgrunn. He and several others had become "ill" after swallowing bacterial cultures. The breakout was originally scheduled to occur on February 1 to coincide with Quisling's installation as minister-president but was delayed until the following night when all conditions were ready.

‡ Didrik ("Dixie") Cappelen (1900–1970). After the war Cappelen served as the prosecutor in treason cases involving Norwegian collaborators and also served as a judge in Skien, Norway, from 1956 until his death. Cappelen was actually freed from Åkebergveien prison, not Ullevål; his escape was moved up from February 1 to January 30 as the Resistance had heard rumors that he might be executed. See also Kristian Aubert below at March 8, 1942.

§ Jens Christian Beck (1920–1943). Unfortunately for Beck, his good luck did not continue to hold. After escaping to England via Sweden following his breakout, Beck joined Company Linge, the Norwegian commando group trained

ish and dramatic. They had been called for by a Norwegian and a *soi-disant* [so-called] Gestapo man, an extremely brutal pair, whose rampaging in the corridors of Ullevål had been something quite extraordinary and had spread fear and horror round about them. They had *Entlassungsschein* [discharge certificates] for four prisoners, signed by Schenk.* (Only a few days before, strict orders had been issued to release no one without a *Schein* [certificate] from Schenk.) All the *Schein* were forged, but the two actors played their part so magnificently that even the men released were in fear of what was going to happen to them now. All of them were men who expected the worst sentences. In the evening, when it was dark, old Dean Skjeseth,† who had witnessed the release, asked his neighbor (a German with a name something like Parsifal) to think of Beck and say the Lord's Prayer (in German, for then I suppose it sounds more forcible). This affecting detail best shows how admirably the job had been carried out by our modern Scarlet Pimpernels.‡

God knows what will happen next time? Here at Grini no one has tried to escape as yet. But then we have been told that if anyone does try, ten or twelve of the other prisoners will be shot. And that's the kind of thing that helps to make one think twice. Certainly there are many here with good reason for clearing out, many who have the worst in prospect, the very worst. But they are all incomparably brave. You couldn't tell that any one of them had the death sentence hanging over him.

Once again I am sitting here alone in the architect's office, and it is evening. Again I have pressing work, and again the humbug has succeeded. The others have already gone to bed; all over Grini it is still and dark.

The silence of a prison is unlike all other silences. It is still more deep and dense and thought-saturated. For many of those over in the main prison it is a terrible thing to contend with. Daylight and being with all the hundreds of others is their salvation. For at night the appalling thoughts come over them. What is going to happen to me? When will my case come up? Suppose it's so far down the list that it never comes up? But *if* it should come up all the same, what are my chances? Has anyone divulged anything? Will it be a death sentence? And what is it like to die? No, no! I *won't* and *mustn't* die now. If only the case could be delayed a few months more, till the summer or perhaps even until the autumn, then I am safe. For the war won't last beyond. Oh, if only there was still some gap in the evidence, so as to need more examinations and more time. Time, time, give me more time, dear God, give me more time. And the prison silence, the deep, dense prison

---

by the British Special Operations Executive (SOE). See March 8, 1942, below. After two scheduled missions were cancelled, Beck made a night parachute drop (his first) into Norway on October 10, 1943, with other saboteurs in connection with Operation Grebe, a plan to sabotage railways in central Norway. All three members of Beck's plane apparently landed in Rambergsjøen, a lake near the Swedish border, and, weighed down with gear and equipment, drowned. Beck's body was never recovered.

* Dr. Schenk was in charge of the prison ward at Ullevål; as he had been friendly to Norwegians, on the night of the breakout he was invited to dinner by another doctor who was a member of the Resistance to guarantee his absence from the hospital and thus avoid unduly compromising him.

† Pastor Kristian Skjeseth was arrested March 7, 1941 (aged sixty), for the sole reason that his son had departed (against his wishes) with the British following their raid on the Lofoten Islands (see February 13, 1942, below); he was released February 19, 1942, less than two weeks following this diary entry.

‡ In the play and novel of the same name by Baroness Orczy, a secret society of English aristocrats helps rescue their French counterparts from daily executions during the French Revolution's Reign of Terror. One historian of Norway claims that "[t]he exploits connected with the many escapes across the Swedish frontier [by the so-called border pilots] were worthy of the Scarlet Pimpernel."

silence returns no answer, but from time to time an echo of the guards' heavy footsteps in the passages or the creaking of their footsteps out in the winter night. And then, as the steps grow distant and the sound of them dies away into the darkness, the thoughts begin again, until in the early morning compassionate sleep dispels them for a few hours.

And here I sit enjoying that silence. Yes, regarding it as a deliverance from all the noise and fuss all day long with all the hundreds of other prisoners. I wonder if I should be afraid of it, too, if I were lying there grappling with the chances I might have in my case, if I had a case.

And by the by, who said I hadn't a case? Who said I needn't worry about the future and what it brings? I am in prison presumably as a hostage, as a court hostage. But the idea of a hostage must surely be that if such and such a thing happens, then the hostage will pay for it? In other words, what happened in France may happen here as well. There a hundred French citizens were shot because a German officer had been killed and the murderer did not give himself up. The hundred, I take it, were also hostages, and a solitary murderer like that can well be imagined in Norway, too.

Impossible, say all the hostages I have discussed it with, but not one of them has the slightest vestige of an argument to put forward why it should be so impossible. Not one of them has even thought the thought out; it is as though it didn't concern them. It can't happen to us. After all we have never done anything. Who would think of touching us?

It was the same when people were coming back from Czechoslovakia and Vienna, and describing the Germans' treatment of the refugees and the Jews. It was just the same. They didn't believe it. One had to resign oneself to the fact that people were not much interested in these everlasting refugees, who probably deserved their fate.* They must have done something or other since they were being persecuted, and in this country we had other things to think of. We had to think first and foremost of ourselves and our own needs, before we began thinking of other nations. Let the Germans go ahead in those countries yonder; they won't come here at any rate. The thought that they might come here was further from these people than the man in the moon. Even after the Finnish war had begun† it never occurred to them that we were in the danger zone, that we Norwegians in old Norway could have anything whatever to be afraid of. We in concentration camps! The idea was ludicrous. Now we sit here gaping at each other . . .

But now I have let the guard know that he can come and let me out of my little private prison. The time is half-past eleven, and it doesn't seem advisable to stay here much beyond that. Good night.

SUNDAY, FEBRUARY 8, 1942 ■ Sunday and Sunday quiet with "overtime work."

Yesterday I was in Oslo. Besides my usual trip for stump-pullers under repair, I was to get hold of a thaw-transformer to thaw out some pipe or other that had frozen during the night. From a place in the town I managed to ring a friend, who got me five hundred cigarettes which vanished into my trouser legs and the lining of my coat. I didn't dare to

---

* Nansen once explained to Johan Scharffenberg, a staunch Norwegian anti-Nazi: "I myself have been in Germany, Austria, and Czechoslovakia. I myself have seen and experienced persecution of the Jews at close quarters. I certainly know, as do you, that no word, no description is powerful enough to tell the truth about that which happened in the midst of us, without a finger being lifted."

† The so-called Winter War began on November 30, 1939, less than six months prior to the German invasion.

take any canned goods this time; I had the devil Stange (the German who has to do with the victualing) in the car with me. We had dropped him at Victoria Terrace and were to pick him up there again.

I rang Kari, but there was no reply—a bitter disappointment. Then I rang [Herman] Reimers and had a cozy chat with him. On the way back we drove round to Godtfred [Bentzen's].* I had to get a resistance coil there for the transformer. Godtfred at once struck the right note with the guard accompanying me. He clapped him on the shoulder and expressed his conviction that the young man was a good fellow. The guard, a lad of twenty, reddened and accepted with a show of reluctance, but none the less very eagerly, the fifty cigarettes that Godtfred in a twinkling had conjured out of a drawer. After that it was of course quite in order that I should pocket another hundred; I had so many friends out there to share with, explained Godtfred, and the guard agreed, happy as a child over his own fifty.

I have just been up in the hut for dinner. It was the usual soup. In honor of Sunday there are no groats in it, and I am inclined to think that several bits of meat can be proved. I've talked to several people who saw them. Recently there has been less soup for each of us, not more than a plateful and a half, and as that is the entire dinner of course we "leave the table" hungry. Storm soup, period. Well, for me it's not so bad, likely enough a slimming cure will be good for me, though I am beginning to feel that I don't have enough to eat. I am getting so slack and apathetic. But it is worse for the youngsters of twenty and thereabouts. They are hungry all day and night. It's almost creepy to see how they collect half-rotten potatoes and scraps of herring or skin and salty, yellow-brown fragments of dried cod left by the others on their plates on fish days.

At two o'clock there is to be a distribution of tobacco. Each man gets half a box of *Karva bla'* or *rød mixture*. That is to last a week. And after that it depends on whether the Prince is in a good mood next Sunday.

Yesterday evening there was to be a cabaret, but it fell through. I stayed on talking with Harris [Olsen] the step dancer, who is an assistant in the doctor's office.

His spirits are imperishable. He is unwearied, and it's remarkable, too, how catching his manner is. It really gets the fellows going. He is Harris to them all, and Harris is enjoying Grini like anything. I think it will be the blackest day of his life when he gets his freedom back. I have written words for his Grini March, which he is mighty proud of, and which he has written down in musical notation. (He can do that, too.) On that account he is always after me to write more. He thinks I am a very great and considerable poet—almost as great a poet as he is a musician, I believe he thinks. He runs round playing the Grini March and tells me about his triumphs. Now he has composed an air, and he wants verses for that. In addition he is working on a fox trot, he has confided to me, and he would like to have all three published afterward. The only thing that troubles him now is that he forgot to write *Words by Odd Nansen* over his march. And now, he showed me, there was no room. He thought me queer when I said I would rather be anonymous.

TUESDAY, FEBRUARY 10, 1942 ■ Today two new patients arrived at the "sanatorium." They were diphtheria patients. They turned up out of the blue and the result was

---

* Reimers, an attorney, had worked with Nansen at Nansenhjelpen. Bentzen was later arrested (in December 1942) and released one month later.

that we in the little prison had to move out of our offices at half an hour's notice to make room for them. That means that the whole of the little prison has become a hospital for epidemic cases. And so that's the end of my cozy time over there, so blessedly peaceful in the evenings, so far away, and so quiet. Heaven knows where we shall be put now with our drawing office. For the moment we have been assigned an empty hut on the third floor of the main prison. But the hut is full of beds and has just been got ready for isolated prisoners, so it seems doubtful if we shall be allowed to keep it. Though for that matter it would be quite like German administration to start using it for offices after it has been especially fitted up for the isolated prisoners, a door bricked up, double doors put in, etc.

However, this removal passed the day, and now everything is at sixes and sevens, so that it will be at least another day before we get straightened out in the place allotted to us—probably to move again in a few days' time. Now I am sitting writing in the hut in the middle of working hours. By my side snores Odd W[ang]. He is ill, really ill; he has such a cold that he is in a sheer state of dissolution. For that matter there are always a lot of sick. I don't observe that they go sick to get off work. Work is after all one's salvation. I daren't even lie down in the daytime; I am so afraid of not being tired enough at night. And then the night is grim. Though by the way I have arranged a book and a little tallow candle in a box inside my little toilet case. One can hardly see that there is a light in my bunk, and it serves its purpose quite well.

WEDNESDAY, FEBRUARY 11, 1942 ■ Strangely enough the days present more variety than one would suppose. Now and then they are almost distinct from one another, indeed something may even happen that somehow sticks in one's memory, and when one thinks about it, may put one in the mood one felt on that particular day. This has been an example. The sun was shining all day in a clear sky, and it was positively warm. The whole camp area lay glittering in the sunshine, breathing idyllic peace. I had a walk down to the "farm," where the tea gang is, to fetch Lange-Nielsen for questioning in the *Vermittlung*.* It is some little distance to walk. On the way there you look out over woods and fields, and today everything was so pretty and bright and cheerful.

About halfway to the farm [Olaf] Kullmann is at work, breaking stones. He has been at work there, road-making, for several months now. That road will get the name of Kullmann's Way. He himself says, with a joyous smile, but with his odd touch of deep earnestness, that no, it has another name; only he's not sure if he may tell. "Yes, out with it now, Kullmann, what's the road called?" "It's called the Way of Atonement," says Kullmann, and becomes quite serious, almost solemn, but the next moment he is smiling all over his face again, laughing and singing away.

A queer fellow. He lives in his own world entirely. It is as if he were engaged on some great task which he has to get done. A task of expiation, perhaps. After a few months he was going to be released, and they wanted him to sign a number of conditions. Nearly all of them he could sign without hesitation. He would not bear arms against the Third Reich. Nor would he agitate for an English victory, nor incite unrest of any kind. No, indeed, he had never even *thought* of doing any of those things. But then came another condition, which he flatly rejected. He was to leave off agitating for his ideas. That he

---

* Fredrik Lange-Nielsen (1891–1980) was an actuary prominent in the Norwegian insurance industry. Arrested in December 1941 for resistance activities, he was released from Grini in May 1943.

wouldn't sign, and accordingly he stayed in prison. Quietly and without a murmur, Kullmann works on at his Way of Atonement.*

Today he was as placid as usual, more so if anything, as he greeted me and smiled in the sunshine, zealously engaged in evening, with a string along the roadside, some big stones he was laying one on top of the other. "Isn't it a wonderful day?" he gushed at me, straightened up, and smiled in the sunshine. He was absolutely radiant with pleasure at the beauty of everything. "Where are you going?" he asked, "or are you just out for a walk?"

I explained that I was to fetch Lange-Nielsen for questioning. "I happened to be in the *Vermittlung*, so I was sent for him."

"Are the Gestapo there?" he asked with interest, and a shadow passed over his face. No doubt he also knew the Gestapo, and that word had the effect of a piercing discord with the sunshine and the landscape and Kullmann's Way, the Way of Atonement. *Gestapo. Questioning.* What an icy sound it has! How raw and cold it is suddenly! No more was said; we only shook our heads, each of us, and I walked on.

A little later I turned and looked back at Kullmann. He was still there, staring in front of him. He was not singing anymore; no doubt he was trying to shake off the gloomy thoughts which had broken in, just because I spoke that one ugly word, Gestapo. Perhaps he's fighting with himself, I thought. Perhaps, even in the gentle Kullmann, that word raises feelings and ideas that one mustn't have upon the Way of Atonement. And now he has to fight himself clear of them.

I fetched Lange-Nielsen. He was questioned by some more than usually gangsterlike Gestapo agents, but he was not beaten up, like so many others. Not this time.

Later in the day I was in the town to fetch drawings, drawing things, tools, and materials. We didn't get off until some time after dinner—the driver, Møller the interpreter, and I. It was a poor trip. I don't want to ask any favors of Møller. I don't want to have any sort of obligation to him. He is sneaking enough and nauseously "understanding" and venal beyond a doubt, but I just can't. Rather let it go. I shall have to wait until another time. A German guard is something quite different. It is somehow cleaner to accept understanding from one of them. But when Møller, the "Norwegian," the NS man and traitor, winks understandingly and thinks himself very fine for "allowing" me to have ten cigarettes, then I feel sick. Therefore I felt sick on this trip to Oslo. Didn't even care about smuggling.

We got back to Grini after supper. A car was just driving out as we arrived. It was a taxicab. In it sat Kari. She saw me and turned back. She had been sitting waiting all afternoon. Had a *Schein* from the Terrace with permission to see me on business. It was lovely to see her again. She looked healthy and fresh and cheerful. It did me an incredible amount of good to sit with her for the allotted ten minutes, talking, hearing her calm

---

* Olaf Kullmann (1892–1942). While a naval officer Kullmann became an outspoken proponent of pacifist ideas (having been influenced by the Kellogg-Briand Pact, which outlawed war). Like Nansen, Kullmann had previously run afoul of Quisling: In 1932 Kullmann's pacifist actions in uniform led Quisling, then Norway's defense minister, to demand he be tried for treason, an event known as the Kullmann Affair. In the end the treason charges were dropped although Kullmann's commission was suspended. He was arrested June 17, 1941, and transferred to Sachsenhausen in April 1942 along with many other Norwegians, including the poet Arnulf Øverland. He died in Sachsenhausen three months later, on July 9, 1942. Øverland subsequently memorialized Kullmann in a poem that reads in part: "It is too small a piece of bread /that he shared. It was his death / (I ate my bread in silent shame / and thus survived him.)" His grand-niece, Kaci Kullmann Five, is presently the chair of the five-person Nobel Peace Prize Committee.

voice and catching the infection of her *joie de vivre*. The ten minutes went like a flash, but it was a lovely flash. If only it's not too long until the next.

FRIDAY, FEBRUARY 13, 1942 ■ The chief topic yesterday in the prison was the rumor of an amnesty. It's said that *Der Herr Reichskommissar,** at the request of the "Minister-President" is deliberating the release of a number of hostages to celebrate the "transfer of power." Of course all the hostages at once begin to cherish the intensest hope that they are to be the ones.

In the first place it's by no means certain that the deliberations will lead to anything at all. And as for the "court hostages" I only hope we shan't get out before all the poor men from Svolvær,† Møre, and other places who have been here many months now. It seems to me that would be bitter; I shouldn't like it at all. Look for instance at a man like Dr. Sven Oftedal,‡ who has been in prison eleven months now as a hostage for the town of Stavanger.§ They have nothing on him. Yet all the same they have kept him shut up nearly a whole year. I haven't heard more than one opinion of Oftedal. All agree that he has done splendidly by the other prisoners. And there are many, many others here who deserve in all conscience to get home to their families and work, far more than the group of well-to-do Oslo people who are in the so-called court gang. It would be marvelous to get out of here; goodness knows there is no attraction in sitting here; one soon gets fed up with it, but let us hope some justice will prevail in these matters.

---

* Josef Terboven (1898–1945). An early Nazi and a protégé of Hermann Göring, Terboven quickly earned a "well-deserved reputation for ruthlessness." In 1934 he married Ilse Stahl, Joseph Goebbels' former secretary and mistress. Appointed *Reichskommissar* (civilian plenipotentiary) on April 24, 1940, he ruled Norway as a dictator. The British Consul General to Zürich described Terboven as "nothing but a gangster [who] should be exposed as such. . . . He is a true fanatic, a man who should not be underestimated." A historian of the period describes him as "at once vain, cunning, brutal and entirely devoid of scruples." His arbitrary and heavy-handed rule quickly alienated the local population. Nor was there any love lost between Quisling and Terboven; Terboven described Quisling as "stupid to the nth degree" and once tried to have him replaced as the head of the NS; on the other hand Quisling's private secretary loved to refer to Terboven as "a small bank functionary from the Ruhr," and "the office clerk from the Ruhr." Upon Germany's surrender in May 1945 Terboven committed suicide by blowing himself up in a bunker on the estate of the Crown Prince, which he had earlier in the war commandeered as his residence.

† The Svolvær raid, also known as Operation Claymore, was an attack by British and Norwegian commandos on the Lofoten Islands in March 1941, the first large-scale commando raid of the war. Its purpose was to destroy several fish oil factories, the source of glycerin used in the manufacture of explosives. Equally significant, the commandos seized a set of rotor wheels for an Enigma cipher machine and its code books, thereby assisting British intelligence in deciphering German naval codes. In addition, Allied forces captured German soldiers and returned with approximately three hundred Norwegians eager to join the Free Norwegian Forces. The raid occasioned severe reprisals by the Germans against the villages of Svolvær and Henningsvær on the island of Lofoten, where houses were burned to the ground and relatives of those Norwegians who had sailed away with the retreating British were arrested and sent to Grini. Svolvær was ultimately converted into the most heavily fortified city in Norway. One contemporary wrote that the decision of three hundred young people to follow the British "after only a few minutes in which to make their decision, tell[s] more about the fighting spirit of the Norwegian youth than any words could do." The very first prisoners at Grini (Nos. 1–64) were hostages from the Lofoten Islands.

‡ Oftedal (1905–1948), a doctor and Labor Party politician, was initially arrested, along with two other prominent citizens of Stavanger, as hostages in reprisal for sabotage in the area. Released in early 1942, he was rearrested in the fall of 1942, imprisoned again in Grini, and in February 1943 sent to Sachsenhausen. See February 16, 1945, below. In the immediate aftermath of the war, Oftedal helped care for ill Soviet, Polish, and Yugoslav POWs left behind in camps in northern Norway by the surrendering Germans. He also served as minister of social affairs in the first postwar unification government. Oftedal died of a heart attack in 1948, age forty-three, a victim of his long incarceration and his responsibilities as a cabinet minister.

§ Stavanger is Norway's third most populous urban area.

For the last fortnight we have had two deafish elderly gentlemen* up here, more than seventy-five years old. One of them was released today, no doubt the other will soon follow. Practically every day they received assurances of getting out. Every evening when they went to bed, they thought, "Well, well, so we'll have to wait till tomorrow." And then they both went snugly off to sleep until the morning. They always kept together, walking up and down on the parade ground every morning and waiting to leave. From a window I overheard a conversation between these two old fellows.

"I say," said one, "did I ever tell you about that time in Edinburgh, when there was a fog?"

Then came a long pause.

"Yes, you did," replied the other.

Long pause again.

"Yes, you see, I was up in Edinburgh, and one day . . ."

And then came—doubtless for the fourteenth time—the story of that time in Edinburgh, when there was a fog.

Obviously the Germans have to keep two such dangerous old foxes shut up.

FRIDAY, FEBRUARY 20, 1942 ■ In the course of the week the fall of Singapore has at last been definitely established. Churchill made his speech a week ago, explaining the why and how.† It was plain that all who had heard him were eminently optimistic, though we haven't got hold of what he actually said. In all probability he didn't gild the situation, but no doubt gave expression as usual to his unshaken faith in the future and the final victory. The certainty he gives our whole world! The victory of which our whole world is as sure as he is! Otherwise the week was not especially eventful.

The great sensation came the day before yesterday. In the midday break we were all ordered to fall in on the square. There they stood in front, the Storm Prince, Kunz, Stange, Schwarz, the *Zugführer* and a number of plain-clothes gentlemen from the Terrace. It was about the amnesty, the long-discussed and yearned-for amnesty, the gift of the new-baked "Minister-President" to the nation. Fifty-two men were called up and fell in separately. They were the Svolvær men, who had been nine months in prison. Everyone was pleased, both those who were getting out and those who still stood in the line. Truly it was high time. In addition there were some men from the [milk] strike gang, those who were arrested during the state of emergency in Oslo last September. It was announced that next week a number of others would be set free, all as a gift from *Der Herr Reichskommissar*, following a request to him by *Der Herr Ministerpräsident*.

Their departure was a moving scene. The Storm Prince took up his post in the *Vermittlung* and shook hands with every man. He too was visibly pleased. Now the Svolvær men were his special favorites, and I quite believe his pleasure was genuine. There is something almost affecting about this queer toothless man who has been put into this devilish job, when one sees him like that, moved and pleased because "his lads" are getting back their liberty. His wish for them all was that they might now behave like good Norwegians. What did he mean by that? There is no doubt he takes an interest in us here and in a way

---

* "Gentlemen" in English in the original Norwegian text; presumably they were both British.

† All British forces in Singapore surrendered to the Japanese on February 15, 1942. With over eighty thousand British, Australian, and Indian soldiers taken prisoner, Winston Churchill called it the worst military disaster in British history.

sympathizes with our fate and rejoices with us whenever there is something to rejoice over. It was a day of joy.

Then came the flip side of the coin. Late in the afternoon it became known that three prisoners had escaped. They had made use of the general disturbance and tumult caused by the departures, and seized their chance to mingle with the liberated men. They were from the Bergen gang. One of them was pretty sure of a death sentence; the others were also on the danger list; at any rate they would have got heavy punishments.

All the same the news was heard with mixed feelings by the other prisoners. For we had been told that if anyone tried to escape ten or twelve others would be shot. It was announced on parade, and besides we all know that everyone has to suffer somehow for all offences. Therefore nervousness began to spread through the prison. Some were sure the severest reprisals would be taken. People were putting on thick clothes after supper, and were sure that there would in any case be a parade with punishment drill or suchlike.

It ended in nothing but the usual parade comedy. Once, and then again, and up to three or four times. Because it's difficult to count. The guards obviously think it next door to impossible; they never get it to tally, and so they have to take it over and over, like a kind of punishment drill, until it comes out right. I strongly suspect them of only *saying* it tallies in the end. Before they finished that night it was long past bedtime, so in the end we were merely ordered to bed.

Not until the next day were certain precautions taken against any repetition of the escape. The whole Bergen gang was locked up. That involved major upheavals. Our little hut was dissolved. The day passed in counting, moving, counting, moving, and counting again. It is now a rule that the architect's office may have the light on until eleven o'clock. So we are in clover.

SUNDAY, FEBRUARY 22, 1942 ■ Today there has been the same hullabaloo, counting, moving, counting, moving. The architect's office, the personnel office, the surveyor's, and *der Rechnungsonkel* [bookkeeper] have moved down to the first floor, where the German guards used to live. The latter have moved down to the north wing of the ground floor, so that all the men living there had to move up, and altogether . . .

We have settled in really comfortably. In here there are six of us. We have our office in another room a few steps away; it is lavishly equipped with furniture, tables, chairs, and cupboards. And I guess we shall do pretty well for food and tobacco, as time goes on. At the moment we're flush. Yesterday when we were expecting reprisals, for we thought there *must* be something after the escape, there was a distribution of chocolate, four whole slabs each. We could scarcely believe our eyes. It looks as though the shutting up of the Bergen gang has been the only consequence of the escape. Let's hope they too will soon come in for relaxation. I am thinking especially of my friend Bryn, the director of the Seaman's School in Bergen.* He is in a tough spot and one could see he was nervous when they shut him up the day before yesterday. He was in the surveyor's gang, along with [Bjørn] Fraser and [Hjalmar] Svae. Those two went off the other day, no doubt to "Bavaria."† That was a melancholy parting. I'm afraid things look bad for them. It was they who stole the

---

* Zakarias Bryn died in the Sonnenburg Concentration Camp in August 1943, age sixty-two.

† A popular name for the Oslo county jail. O.N. Nansen is referring to the Oslo jail at 11 Åkebergveien; it derived its nickname from its prior use as a brewery. Fraser ultimately was sent to various German camps where he survived until the end of the war; Svae escaped from Åkebergveien on March 11, 1942.

German motorboat at Jeløy and sailed for England, but ran aground in Denmark. Their leader [Per] Birkevold, who is now in the hospital, can at any rate have very little chance.* These men are fine types of Norwegian patriots.

MONDAY, FEBRUARY 23, 1942 ■ Today the whole Bergen gang was sent off. We couldn't even say good-bye to them. We stood here at the office window and watched them as they moved off with their trunks and knapsacks, in civilian clothes and under a strong guard of roaring Germans. Bryn waved gallantly as he marched away downhill with the rest.

Otherwise life goes on as before; soon we shall be right back in the old familiar grooves. Yesterday there was even a distribution of tobacco—half a box of pipe tobacco each—as before.

On the very morning the escape took place, the Storm Prince had complained to the Terrace that he had too few men for guard duties. That's what one may call a lucky hit, and it has most likely saved him from unpleasantness. New sentries have been posted, and things have been tightened up a little all round. In the future, it's reported, no one may go into Oslo (except Rinnan, who enjoys the personal favor of the Storm Prince). But no doubt that too will gradually pass off, so that others can have their chance as well. In the meantime we must have patience and enjoy the many and various advantages of prison life as well as we can. For there *are* in fact certain advantages in this life. If we can't exactly call it peace, still it offers much of what is called peace—no telephones, no bother, no nervous hurry to get this and that done in time, no meetings, no importunates coming to see one and to chatter about this and that, no oppressive responsibility for one thing and another.

TUESDAY, FEBRUARY 24, 1942 ■ It is six weeks ago today that I was arrested up in Gausdal. That seems to lie so infinitely far back in time. It's strange how the days fly past. Working hours are positively too short if there is anything one wants to get done. And there is, here in the architect's office. There are songs to write, caricatures to draw, matters to arrange. Recently there have been more and more prisoners wanting free designs for houses and cottages. Some must have them quickly, for they are expecting to get out soon; others have more time, but then as a rule they have also time to enforce their views on architecture, so that the problems gradually become comprehensive and downright wearing.

Our stout, comfortable *Bauleiter* is in the know. He quite realizes that we are working on things we ought not, but he has secured us the personal permission of the Storm Prince to have lights in our rooms until eleven every night, since we have "urgent matters" on hand. In addition he has now procured us a quantity of excellent drawing material. We have even got hold of a copying machine, so that now we can get our caricatures and private jobs copied on the spot. Also he has arranged the purchase of an edging machine, so all our drawings are elegantly bordered. He is in on a certain amount of smuggling, thinks for instance that our bread ration is terribly small. His opinion was that he would starve to death if he had to live on it.

Of architecture he has not the faintest idea. He is a carpenter from Hannover, where

---

* Birkevold was condemned to death; his sentence was later commuted to ten years. He remained incarcerated in German camps until the end of the war.

in civil life he ran a little business. He is homesick for it and has had enough of soldiering, he says. It is badly paid and unattractive altogether. He was on the North Finnish front and was wounded there. He saw and experienced war at close quarters, and it was frightful. Once he saw a Finn cut the throats of four Russians, cut out their Adam's apples and put them away as souvenirs. The Finn explained that he had to have sixteen Adam's apples to get a holiday. Our fat friend *Bauleiter* Gebecke shook his head, which is like an egg the wrong way up, threw out his hand and smiled his broad smile, so that the little mouse teeth stood out between his mighty lips. "That's war," he said. It was something he had once been in, now it was past and gone. His reflections went no further. He was now in Grini, where he had been sent to look after some building work, far, far from the fronts. And here he thought he would have to stay at least two years.

He quite understands that the building work will be so-so. He fully shares our amusement at the way the plans are constantly being changed and that the bigwigs never can agree on how a first-class concentration camp ought to be designed. Today he was grinning all over when he arrived from Oslo with a big copying machine under his arm and announced that the last plan also had been rejected and therefore we were for the moment without a plan. That being so, he said, we had no use for this big machine, and it cost two hundred kroner, but "money is no object," he declared with an even broader grin, which went almost to his ears.

I suggested that we might draw an office hut and build that first, and I turned up a sketch of such a hut. He got interested immediately and by the afternoon had already secured the Storm Prince's consent, so now we can just get on with it and not bother about anyone else. "We won't even show them the drawings," said he. "We'll just build the whole thing, order the materials, and get ahead." Then he sat down and wanted to know how we actually set about building such a hut. I gave him a brisk little lecture on elementary domestic building, accompanied by sketches, and he was very attentive, very docile, and very grateful. After all he has really nothing to do, and if he had, he would be in rather a fix without us to lean on.

SATURDAY, FEBRUARY 28, 1942 ■ Yesterday there was another amnesty, but not what we had expected. None of the Møre men got out, after all this time when they had been counting on their liberty! Probably it's connected with the fact that something has happened down near Ålesund. There is talk of a smack with thirty-one men having made off for England.* One pleasant little rumor says the smack has been taken. That would be a fearful disaster. It looks as though all who make for England are being shot.

Gørtz the plumber, who has been here from time immemorial, no doubt expected to get home to Ålesund with the amnesty. Instead he heard that three sons and a brother had been arrested. The youngest son is sixteen. Gørtz is no longer waiting for an amnesty, but has a good deal else to think of. His business is going to hell, and his wife is delicate and sickly.

However, there was of course great joy among those released. There were about thirty. One of them was Pande the teacher, a strange man, whose behavior has been very fine and who is remarkably well adapted to prison life even at his fairly advanced age. He

---

* On February 23, 1942, the Gestapo arrested twenty-three people on board a boat ready to sail from Ålesund for the Shetland Islands; another twenty who had assisted were arrested soon thereafter. See May 1, 1942, below.

celebrated his sixtieth birthday a month ago. He was by no means overjoyed at leaving—
would really have liked to sit out the rest of the time, he said. Indeed it may be questioned
if we shan't have him back again. The teachers are out in stormy weather, it would seem.
They are all to be forced into an NS organization, but refuse; it looks as though they were
making a stiff resistance and holding out all over the country.* It is the teachers' turn now,
and obviously the clergy's too. Arne Fjellbu was dismissed long ago.† The bishops have
protested jointly and sent in their resignation. Berggrav is dismissed and has to report
himself twice a day.

MONDAY, MARCH 2, 1942 ■ Yesterday we had a cabaret. It was very successful,
I believe. I was one of those who took part, so I cannot judge so easily as when I am a
spectator. Oftedal was lecturer, probably for the last time. He is hoping to be out by next
week, which means this week I should say, and truly he deserves it.

Harris was let loose in the cabaret for ten minutes. He told on the open stage the
crudest story that can ever have been heard from any stage, and that in church, too. It was
strange to see a couple of hundred prisoners lowering their eyes and blushing for him. All
wished themselves away.

Frode and I had a "Trønder section."‡ We finished up with a song we had written
together about the counting. As I said before, we are counted three times a day, morning,
noon, and evening. And the guards can practically never get the figures to tally. They
count and count, add and add, but no, they have to start all over again, not once, but
four, five, six times. No guard has more than thirty or forty men to count. Nonetheless it
is a complete muddle. Not until the *Zugführer* comes rushing up, roaring so that he can
be heard in Drøbak,§ and abusing the guards for *Dummköpfe* [blockheads] and baboons
and bastards, do they get it right, from sheer terror. Needless to say this was a grateful

---

* One of the earliest attempts at the Nazification of Norway began on February 5, 1942, when the newly installed
Quisling government established a Nazi teacher association with compulsory membership. Virtually all teachers
protested the new measure and refused to join the organization. As the standoff continued, the Quisling Ministry of
Church and Education on February 27 declared a month's school holiday due to "the fuel situation." On March 20,
1942, 1,100 teachers were arrested and placed in concentration camps; approximately 200 more were subsequently
arrested. Around 500 of these teachers were sent to Kirkenes, above the Arctic Circle, to labor under atrocious conditions. Ultimately the government was forced to back down, and almost all teachers were freed within several months
of their arrest.

† Born in Decorah, Iowa, Fjellbu (1890–1962) returned to Norway at age ten. On February 1, 1942, the date of Quisling's installation as minister-president, Bishop Fjellbu of the Diocese of Nidaros scheduled an alternative church
service in Nidaros Cathedral in Trondheim. The ceremony with the NS clergyman (at 11 a.m.) celebrating Quisling's
inauguration had a modest congregation; for Fjellbu's ceremony (at 2 p.m.) a large crowd had already gathered when
the police locked an even larger crowd (approximately two thousand) outside in bitterly cold weather, where they
remained and sang until the service inside was concluded. For his actions Fjellbu was dismissed from his post, leading
in turn to a mass resignation in protest by all Norwegian bishops on February 24 and by all but 64 of the Lutheran
Church's 861 pastors on Easter Sunday (April 5, 1942). Fjellbu was progressively banished further and further from
Trondheim and eventually escaped to Sweden. In early 1945 he was appointed by the Norwegian government in exile
as bishop of the northern portion of Norway, which had recently been liberated by the Soviet Army. Following the
war Fjellbu cofounded the World Council of Churches.

‡ Trøndelag is the central region of Norway, of which Trondheim is the unofficial capital. A person from Trøndelag
is known as a *Trønder*. Both Nansen and Frode Rinnan had attended the Norwegian Institute of Technology in
Trondheim and both had written songs for the famous student revue, several of which were well known in Norway.
A Trønder section would have referred to these and similar songs.

§ A town approximately twenty miles south of Oslo on the eastern shore of Oslofjord.

subject for verse. Great was the enthusiasm when in the last verse we both ran mad and started adding, subtracting, multiplying and dividing everything we set eyes on.

SUNDAY, MARCH 8, 1942 ■ Sunday again, in many ways the worst day of all. It is the only day when one may feel that time occasionally stands still. In the first place we have to "sleep" right on until eight, and then there are two long hours for hut-cleaning and breakfast, before parade at ten o'clock. Today the Storm Prince was there in person, dressed the line, which to be sure was rather crooked, and went through his cap drill. He's probably expecting distinguished visitors in the near future, at any rate he absolutely apologized for undertaking the drill. It was not to be regarded as provocative, whatever he meant by that. Besides, he came out with a tremendous favor. Henceforth we were permitted to read from Saturday dinnertime to Sunday night.

Colonel Schiøtz's reaction to the permission to read was the funniest part of all. "Ludicrous! Completely ludicrous!"

"God bless my soul, the things they think of," supplemented Broch.

"Well, I shall *not* avail myself of it," announced Schiøtz after deep deliberation.

"Nor I," said Broch. "Who ever heard of such a thing?"

"No, one must draw a line somewhere," concluded Schiøtz. What he meant is obscure, for it was just the line (from Saturday dinnertime to Sunday night) that was the odd thing, if anything was odd. And as for the fearful threat that Schiøtz and Broch will not read, I should think the Germans can take it.

The inspection of the rooms was carried out after the distribution of tobacco, this time by Kunz alone. Then he is someone other than when he walks silent and bowing behind the Prince. He incessantly makes his noises, which are obviously meant to convey that there is something or other he is not pleased with. One of his standing expressions I have now learned to interpret. It is spelled as follows: "Have you a bird singing in your head, man?" It sounds like a couple of barking dogs knocking down a tool-box.

Now all the others are asleep, and it's almost peaceful for me in the office. Outside the prison gate, across the fields that are covered with our everlasting hut material, a number of people are standing looking. They look at the prison and know that there are hundreds of us inside. And they have their thoughts no doubt. They think that now we're being beaten, now we have to make the beds five and twenty times, over and over until we drop, or we are going through punishment drill until we collapse. I can see their shudders, even all this way off. It reminds me of a day when I stood there myself—also on a Sunday— with the children. Of all I was thinking then, against the background of what I'd heard, and of all I *thought* I saw, though I saw nothing whatever except the large brick building among the spruce firs. Ugh, yes, it sends the shivers right through one, and besides it's getting cold. Let me see, yes, wasn't this the day we were to have rabbit for dinner? Nmm, nmm, rabbit, let's be off home . . .

But there were some who stayed there looking. They forgot dinner, they simply looked and looked, through gratings and walls, which coincided exactly with all they had imagined. And when dusk began to fall their legs turned back toward Røa, but still they kept their faces toward the prison at the forest's edge. And that night at home and next day at the office and all next week they could describe how ghastly it is at Grini. "I was there myself on Sunday, and it was ghastly, it was indeed. I saw Seip; they drilled him for hours right opposite the gate. He was carried in. I'm almost sure it was he, for Seip is a small man, isn't he? And heaven knows if it wasn't the Lord Chamberlain, or perhaps it was Chief Constable [Kristian] Welhaven* or Professor Francis Bull† or Dr. [Hans] Huitfeldt‡ they were beating up while I was there. I heard screams. It's ghastly at Grini. I wanted the real truth about it, so yesterday I took a walk out there myself. I was there for several hours and saw."

Well, an account like that wouldn't be without some semblance of truth. Not long ago a prisoner was killed here. It was Kristian Aubert, the skier from Sørkedalen.§ He was one of the "secret" prisoners. There are nearly always some. They are kept in solitary confinement. No one knows about them officially. They arrive at night; no one must see them. Kristian Aubert was one of them. We came to suspect that he was here before we saw the death sentence in a smuggled newspaper. It was announced that he had died suddenly. But here in the prison, guards had come round the huts on three or four different occasions, asking for Kristian Aubert. They were to take some message or order to someone named Kristian Aubert, and he was supposed to be in the "hotel," they assured us. One night a man was carried out of here on a stretcher, and a few days afterward we read the notice in the paper. Twice two makes four.

We have an old man here named [Lauritz] Sand. He is more than sixty, and they have beaten him to a pulp. They broke his arm twice. They twisted round his fingers and ankles, so that most probably they will never come right again, and they also trod on him and kicked him, so that he is smashed up internally as well. That is what the doctors say who are looking after him. But they failed to twist or torture out of him one word too much. There is a Norwegian we can take off our hats to. He was so moved that the tears ran down his cheeks when Broch greeted him in the King's name, thanking him for what he had done and assuring him that it should never be forgotten.¶

Yes, there are things going on here that can give the man outside the gate cause to shudder. But the prison façade itself always looks the same, as it lies there looming up against the black woods. And the great majority of us behind the façade can stand daylight and sunshine. We look much as when we arrived, if we take off our suits and put on those

---

* Welhaven (1883–1975) served as Oslo's chief of police from 1927 until 1954 except during the war; he was dismissed immediately following Terboven's decree of September 25, 1940, arrested a year later, and spent the remainder of the war in Grini and later in Germany. Reinstated as police chief after the war, Welhaven signed the report on Quisling's execution.

† Bull (1887–1974) was professor of Nordic literature at the University of Oslo and chair of the Board of Directors of the National Theater. When the National Theater would not follow directions from the Nazis, he, along with board members Harald Grieg and Johannes Sejersted Bødtker, was arrested in 1941. When the theater actors were again threatened, it was decided that they should give in, but with the understanding that the public (against whom no reprisals could be taken) would register its opposition by boycotting all performances, and so productions continued, but only for audiences consisting of a handful of NS sympathizers.

‡ Huitfeldt (1876–1969) was a physician to the royal family.

§ Aubert (1909–1942) was the driver of the car that helped smuggle Didrik ("Dixie") Cappelen out of Åkebergveien prison on January 30, 1942. Arrested eight days later, he was the first prisoner tortured to death (February 19, 1942) in Grini. An area in Antarctica was named by Norway in his honor.

¶ Lauritz Sand (1879–1956). Said to be the most tortured man in Norway, Sand (age sixty-two) never divulged any information and so became a legendary figure in the Resistance. Sand owned and operated plantations in the Dutch East Indies prior to the war and only returned to Norway in 1938. Caught in the country when Germany invaded, he was one of the earliest members of the Resistance. King Haakon did not forget Sand's services; he visited him in the hospital after the war while Sand was still recuperating and made him a Knight of the Order of St. Olav. A bust of Sand was unveiled in 1952 near the site of Grini prison, with a single word inscription: "Nei" [No]. Despite Sand's grievous injuries, from which he never fully recovered, he lived until age seventy-seven, dying in 1956.

Lauritz Sand. He was tortured and tormented more than most,
but they never got the better of him.

strange clothes which are called civilian, and which are hanging up in rows in a kind of museum on the third floor, under the curatorship of Henning Bødtker. It's said that he still knows how a tie is tied, and how you make a collar sit round your neck. Altogether he will be a useful man one day when there is a question of . . . well, well, sufficient unto the day . . .

There was a cabaret this evening. Frode was producer. It was his turn. None of us appeared; we had a whole series of new talents, who sang and played with varying success. The choral singing was not very good tonight, everything else was excellent. An evening like that certainly does a lot of good to many who really need a lively song and a good laugh in the darkness of their life. All through the week they are bowed down with anxiety for their families outside, who have nothing to live on and from whom they have perhaps not heard. There were a lot of them in the church this evening, and it really cheered one to see how they warmed up with the bit of gaiety and pleasure that they got from the ballads and the singing and foolery.

One, for instance, a man from Måløy, was sitting there. He is a fisherman. The fishing had been bad this last autumn, he told me, and when he was arrested his wife had nothing but a few kroner, and seven children, all to be provided for. Two had gone to England when the English were there, and through a misunderstanding they hadn't all got away to-gether.* He is a stalwart fellow and used to hard times. "I've been a poor man all my days, but still I never thought it so bad. We've had our food and our bit of livelihood—but now! What's to become of the wife and children now, with me sitting here? Aye, she had a bit of fish in the house, but there were no potatoes, nor anything else either. And when there's no money to buy with, what in the Lord's name are they to do?" I have promised him that his wife and children shall be provided for, he may rest assured of that. I hope they've been provided for long ago, for it's a long time since I sent out word. But until he hears from the wife herself that she is all right, I don't suppose he'll be quite easy. And then there's the point that he has never in his life asked for any help. He has never been in such a position before and therefore can hardly reconcile himself to the idea of other people supporting his wife and children for a time. I have tried to explain that he mustn't look at it like that. It is Norway supporting them, the country and people he is serving by being in here. And indeed it is the very least they can do for him. Tonight he sat in the gallery and smiled and joined in the singing, so that it was a joy to look at him.

There was another man sitting there enjoying the fun—a farmer from up in Øster-dalen. He had five children from zero-seven years old, had also three cows and seven sheep and no fodder for any of them. The wife hadn't a red cent when he left, said he, and he

---

* The coastal islands of Måløy and Vågsøy were attacked December 27, 1941, in a raid (known as Operation Archery) conducted by British commandos and members of Norwegian Independent Company No. 1. Allied forces killed and captured a number of Germans, destroyed fish oil processing plants, and returned with a number of Norwegians who wanted to join the Free Norwegian Forces in Britain. Although the damage inflicted appeared to have little overall strategic value, the raid convinced Hitler to divert additional troops to Norway, where they remained for the duration of the war. The commander of the Norwegians, Martin Linge, was killed during the assault, and the company he led was subsequently named Linge Company in his honor. Over the course of the war Linge Company members were involved in a number of daring and successful exploits. Coincidentally, the British second in command of the Vågsøy raid, John "Mad Jack" Churchill (no relation) was captured on a later mission and ultimately wound up in Sachsenhausen at the same time as Nansen. In retaliation for the raid, the Nazis arrested the nearest male relative of each Norwegian who had escaped to England and sent them to Grini. In addition, Reichskommissar Terboven ordered the arrest of a number of high court officials and Norwegian friends of the royal family as hostages, including Nansen.

broke right down and cried when he came to see me asking for help. The same story here. He had never needed to ask help, had cleared his own land and built his farmhouse and could now feed three cows and seven sheep. But the Germans had taken away his hay this year, and there weren't many potatoes left either when they had taken their cut, and even before, he had scarcely ever had ready cash to buy fodder and provisions. What he had, had gone to pay installments on his loan from the bank, 2,000 kroner. It was a great heavy loan to have on his back, he felt, with a big family and a small farm. All this was weighing the man to earth, so that he was not good for very much when he came to me. But the assurance that his family would certainly be looked after, and the sheep and cows as well, calmed him down. Being together with all the other people here who are in the same boat has also done him good. Tonight he was sitting chuckling high up in the gallery, and joined in the Grini song and was like a new man. Aye, he did see that you might look at it that way, but still it was a poor thing for a man to be so pinched he had to ask help.

That is only one among hundreds of similar cases, and this man is only one among hundreds of sturdy, unassuming, quiet Norwegians who have landed here, and who are alone with their gloomy thoughts and their anxiety for wife and children; long nights and days . . .

Outside they are both willing and prompt in sending help in such cases; it is only a question of getting a message out.

More and more, every day, such messages are finding their way out through the barbed wire; the invisible "illegal" ties between us and the outer world are being knit firmer and surer as the time passes. And the time passes—!

THURSDAY, MARCH 12, 1942 ■ Tonight we've had a farewell party for Oftedal, who is leaving tomorrow. Last night, by the way, there was very nearly a disaster. Suddenly about eleven the Lieutenant walked in, quietly and without knocking. I was busily work- ing on an address to Oftedal, with all kinds of "treasonous" symbols and devices on it. Somehow or other I managed to jerk the drawing away so that it fell on the floor, luckily with the drawing downward. He didn't see it, but could see well enough that we were not drawing huts. There were four or five of us, some reading, others writing; all pretended to be drawing and calculating when he came in. The Lieutenant asked if we were doing things of our own. On my assurance that we were busily engaged on the new workshops, he left the room with an ironic smile. It is queer to feel like a disobedient schoolboy again. And so it must be for [Karl] Oppegaard, who is over fifty.* He looked like nothing but seven cares and seven sorrows and seven times seven guilty consciences, as he sat there with his thriller under his drawing board. (For of course reading is forbidden into the bargain.)

But, as I said, today we've had a pleasant evening. Frode made a good little speech for the guest of honor; we ate a lot of good food, and consumed a number of benzol cocktails. As a matter of fact I was tired. One thing struck me this evening, as on so many other evenings when conversation gets going—here are ten or twelve grown people, many of them outstanding people, business chiefs, politicians, leaders each in his own sphere, men who have achieved social distinction by their ability and intelligence, and what do they talk about? Prison, prison, and again prison. "What did the Storm Prince say today? What

---

* Oppegaard, who was actually only forty-eight at the time, was released October 22, 1942.

did he say when Kunz said that? How did you manage to smuggle this or that in? And do you remember that time and that time?" Such is the substance of all our daily conversations apart from "work." It is almost sinister. Oftedal has a lot to tell about the origins of Grini, both jest and earnest. And yet the whole thing gets to be sinister in a peculiar way, even though we can say with our hands on our hearts that we have had a pleasant evening.

At one moment we got talking of the worst things that have happened here at Grini, at the Terrace and at No. 19. Incredibly frightful things have happened and are still going on. People have been beaten up and tortured and tormented beyond all bounds. Some held, others cracked. No one dare sit in judgment. One man cracked and had the death of others on his conscience: well, he's been shot too. But first he lived through a ghastly time. A little poem on the wall of his cell in No. 19 gave expression to his mental agony. I don't remember how it went, but he does not value or esteem himself as much as a rotten herring.

Sigurd Johansen, [Harald] Thorsvik and [Rolf] Lea used to be roommates here at Grini. None of these three were expecting the worst. All hoped, or were almost sure of a light sentence. Then they were all three shot.* They had only to run away. Sigurd Johansen and Thorsvik had been in Oslo any number of times *without* a guard, and come back here like sheep to the stall. Meekly they let themselves be led to the slaughter. It makes the whole outrage twice as scurvy. First there is a raking in of confidence and upright dealing by every means, and then it is rewarded by a volley of musketry.

What is now lying black and heavy on people's minds is the news that Fraser and Svae have been condemned to death! Now I suppose they are at Akershus, waiting for the time of grace to run out. They can't have much chance to speak of. And poor Birkevold, their leader, who is lying here in the hospital and has been told. He took it splendidly, we heard from one of the male nurses today. He said he was glad to have been told; it was better than lying there knowing nothing. And so he is a hundred percent certain to be shot on his discharge from the hospital, unless something extraordinary happens by then.

SATURDAY, MARCH 14, 1942 ■ Today a lot of new prisoners arrived, some from Bergen and some from Trondheim.† Those from Trondheim were the Ålesund gang. They were on board the boat that was taken and that we heard of a while ago. So it was true, then. There cannot possibly be much hope for them. The Ålesund men (actually there were men from all over the country) had informers on board. They had confided in people whom it's clear they didn't know personally, but who were said to have gotten hundreds of boatloads over in the past. Then they were denounced, and the whole story was already lying on the Gestapo's table. "Explanations" were superfluous.

And so now they're here waiting for the verdict. They expect nothing but the worst. Doubtless their only hope is that enough time may pass before the case comes up. If it takes as long as it has for other passengers to England, they may well have a good chance. Two of these young men were down in our hut this evening, a policeman from Oslo and an Oslo boy named Jakob Friis (a friend of Frode). They discussed the situation calmly and were quite at home with the idea that there was little hope but in time. For the

---

* Sigurd Johannesen (age thirty-seven) and Harald Torsvik (also thirty-seven) were both executed at Akershus on November 20, 1941; Rolf Lea (age fifty) was executed there on November 26, 1941.

† Bergen and Trondheim are the second and third largest cities in Norway (after Oslo), respectively. Trondheim was the Viking capital of Norway, and its kings, including King Haakon VII, were crowned there.

*"Between Battles." Nightmares in the cell
after interrogation at the Terrace.*

moment, as far as that goes, they can take it easy—if they *can* take it easy. And strangely enough there's no doubt they all can. It's almost grisly to hear them talking about it, making jokes about it, laughing and kicking up a row. Why, they even sing a song beginning, "It doesn't matter where we go when we die . . ."

News from the outside is scarce. The reports from Russia continue good. Schiøtz calls them bad. He is always coming down on misplaced optimism. Today's rumor is that the Swedish minister in Berlin has asked for his passports. It is not confirmed, but there is no need to suppose it improbable. Relations between Sweden and Germany are certainly very strained. Now if we should hear in a few days that the rumor was incorrect, that the Swedish minister in Berlin had a conversation with Hitler, none the less I have had my little pleasure from the story that he asked for his passports. It struck a bright little chord which sounded through a whole evening, and there wouldn't be many who broke down when they heard that it wasn't true. I don't care a straw for scientific doubt and reserve, I take the pleasures that present themselves.

SUNDAY, MARCH 15, 1942 ■ Prison Sunday, like all the others. We have to make the bunks so elegantly that there isn't a single crease in blankets or sheets. Our shoes have to stand in a row, in an exact row, and they must be polished both top and bottom. The floor must be washed; the cups and saucers have to stand in a row like Prussian soldiers; toilet things the same. The towels must not hang in view, nor yet any dirty linen, bags, or clothes. From the highest quarter we are recommended to place them under the pillow or the bedclothes, so that they are out of sight. It doesn't matter what the bed may contain and whether it is rumpled or unmade underneath, so long as the topmost cover is smooth and elegant and unwrinkled. And then they must all be made in the same way, or we are in danger of a terrible dressing down from Kunz if he comes alone on the inspection, which takes place in the morning after roll call. Today as it happens the Storm Prince was there, and then Kunz dares not give a single cheep, least of all in our room. Frode is the Storm Prince's favorite, and he always begins talking to him about other things instead of inspecting when he comes into our hut on Sunday morning. Today he shook his head regretfully when he realized that there were actually nine of us in the little room, and that all nine of us worked in the equally modest office. No doubt he realizes that it's not so easy to get output and quality up into the top class.

That Storm Prince is really a strange character. One can't just write him off without ceremony as the usual Gestapo man or German policeman. He is decidedly an individual, with undoubted rudiments of humanity. Also in a peculiar way one almost gets the impression that he is fond of his prisoners, as when he shook hands with all who were released under the amnesty and wished them the best of luck. Or when occasionally he looks into the office or the cell outside inspections and almost apologizes for our being so cramped, and says there shall certainly be an improvement. Or when, with no attempt at concealment, he rejoices in the muddle and dawdling at the *Zentralbauleitung* [central construction authority], and concurs in our doubtful attitude with respect to the final plan. "I dare say it will be altered many times yet," he cackles, but adds that we are sure to come back in the end to his original plan. We must simply have patience. "Patience, my friends."

Other days he may be in quite a different humor, nervous and irritable, and then one must be very careful not to tread on his toes or take any kind of liberty. The other day when we were practicing his eternal comedy of "caps off!" and "caps on!" he suddenly burst into a wild rage. Someone had laughed. And as always he took it personally; Germans are like that. One of the prisoners in my squad hadn't managed to get his cap on properly. It lay flat on top of his head—not so fantastically funny in itself, but when one remembers that the Storm Prince, for the sake of practice, was commanding an imaginary squad of Germans along with us, and that the Lieutenant for this occasion had the role of Terboven inspecting, and finally that the Storm Prince was flying round peering north and south to make sure we were in line, and repeating his "caps off" and "caps on"—with all that it had a quite ungovernably comic effect, the cap lying flat on the head of a portentously solemn prisoner, who dared not budge until we got the order to "schtand at easse."

There were some young lads from Måløy who couldn't help laughing, and simultaneously there was a man who couldn't keep in his wind. That little rifle shot in the silence did its part, too. The Storm Prince was in a frenzy. At first I thought he was going to rush on the nearest Måløy man and tear him to pieces. Instead he invoked the devil a number of times over, and called down death and damnation on all the lot of us if we regarded this as funny. "Here I stand doing my best," he screamed, "and then someone laughs! The devil take you, and the devil and his grandmother fly away with you! You shall get to know another side of me if you take it *that* way." He thundered until the ground shook, and then yelled for [Erling] Steen to translate. Steen did as well as he could, but skipped the bit about the devil, which was really the main content, for the Storm Prince recurred to it incessantly. It passed over and we were allowed to go in when the drill had been gone through once more with admirable precision and in breathless silence. Later Steen explained to the Storm Prince what the laughter was about, and got him to understand that it was not at him or the saluting practice they had laughed. Then he came round again.

The thing was that Terboven himself was to inspect us, and then we were required to be smart fellows. On the day when *Der Herr Reichskommissar* appeared with his court and we "fell in," and he came strolling down the line, the Storm Prince was so nervous that he forgot half his saluting orders as rehearsed. For instance there was the part about looking right and following the visitor with our eyes (and head) until we saw the third man in the rank in front, and then letting our heads go back to "eyes front" with a jerk. The Storm Prince quite forgot that in his flurry! And we were so smart at it! And he also quite forgot the German word of command. He forgot to order "*Presentier Gewehr*," [Present Arms] and we "schtood at easse" as Terboven walked along the front with a gimlet look through his sunglasses. He was certainly not feeling ashamed. Without the least inhibition he stared the prisoners full in the face, and at quite close quarters, too. If anyone had expected that he would lower his eyes, or that a blush of shame would color his hard face when he saw all his victims in a row, that man was disappointed.

The Storm Prince revealed himself at his most servile and cringing. Very likely he was dreaming of a little new star on the shoulder, or wherever they put it. He has talked of that both to Frode and to Oftedal, though at the same time declaring that to him a star more or less was neither here nor there. He was a soldier and did his duty as best he could in the post allotted to him, and that he did whether he had one or more stars, so to him it was a matter of complete indifference whether anyone had thought of promoting or rewarding him for his conscientious efforts. He would fill his post as well as he could, even though one after another of his comrades got more and more stars, and rose and rose. He would . . . well, well.

It may have been something of that kind he was thinking of; it was very likely that which made him so nervous—so nervous that he emphatically threw away his whole stock of chances for more stars, that is, if Terboven has enough military science to have observed these *gaffes* at all. The last I saw of Terboven was his parting with the Storm Prince. I sat and looked on from a window.

A Nazi leave-taking or greeting is altogether something to watch. It is a sheer gymnastic display. Right arms fly up in all directions and at all angles. It looks, if anything, as though the performers were busy slapping at each other, as the arms shoot out right past the other fellow's head. First there is this arm-stretching which both go through on parallel lines, while they smack their heels together so that it can be heard throughout the neighborhood; then they shake each other warmly by the hand, and then off they go again with the arm-stretching, precisely as at first. The hand goes whizzing crosswise right past the other's ear as though the object really were to poke out his eyes. Alas, it was at the handshake that the poor Storm Prince made his final *gaffe*; he was not quick enough in getting his tight gray gloves off, and as Terboven's right hand had already whizzed by his left ear, he had to let the glove alone and return the arm-stretching. Then came the handshake, but the glove would not come off, so he had to clasp Terboven's hand with half a glove off. *Der*

Herr Reichskommissar's fist was bare. Then another mighty lunge with the right arm, and a fresh heel-smacking. And then at last he got his gloves off, but unfortunately there was no one left to shake by the hand, and Terboven had already vanished into his improbably glossy, shining Mercedes, along with adjutant and chauffeur. It was all over.

The inspection inside the prison had been cursory. They had only been to the hospital, which the Storm Prince is very proud of, and where Oftedal had acted as cicerone for the last time.

Apart from the Storm Prince's nervousness and *gaffes*, which one is almost tempted to regret—we are as it were on his side against the Terrace and all its oversnoopers, just as he is really on ours—I should say the whole thing went well.

The philosopher Gebecke's remark to Frode is highly descriptive of the relation between the Storm Prince and the prisoners. "I believe," said Gebecke, "that *der Obersturmführer* Koch would be able to walk about the streets of Oslo free and untouched even after the war." Whether he was here implying a definite outcome of the war I shall not decide, but what he meant is plain enough.

Gebecke is quite alive to the tension between Norwegians and Germans, and would like best of all to take his Solveig* and go posting straight back to his little house in Hannover, with eleven rooms. For he has a little Solveig, whom he is going to marry, a thin little chip of a girl, says Frode who has seen her, and he himself is a great barrel of a man, well over one hundred [kilos, or 220 pounds]. It was therefore scarcely without grounds that the *Rassenamt*,† to which the Germans must apply for sanction if they want to get married, had refused him permission to contract matrimony with the slender girl of his choice. She was not big enough for him; her narrow pelvis would not be able to bear his children, therefore the connection was *abgelehnt* [rejected].

"What did we do then?" said the cunning Gebecke. "Solveig and I, of course, talked this question over thoroughly, and together reached the following solution. I immediately gave my Solveig a child, and later, when the time of the birth approaches, back we shall go to the *Rassenamt* and this time they can't refuse to sanction our union. My child will be there already; that can't be altered, and then I shall at once receive the necessary permission to marry my Solveig, and later I'll apply for leave, so that Solveig and I can go off on our honeymoon. Yes, that's my plan. Pretty good, eh?"‡

There is something almost sympathetic about a man like that, in spite of his incessant first person singular and his undoubted self-absorption. It is *mein Kind* [my child] he talks about the whole time—Herr Gebecke Junior, a new little carpenter of Hannover, who will take over his saw and machines when he is getting old. Then he will simply sit in his house, which has eleven rooms, drinking beer and listening to all the different noises from the saws that his son is working. The big crosscut saw that goes "*krrrrrrrjit,*" and then the little one that goes "*ksksksit,*" and the one that only goes "*kst! kst! kst!*" He is really nice when he sits telling one about those machines of his at home in Hannover. He is like a little boy dreaming boyish dreams of steam engines, cars, trains, and boats!

---

*   A common female name in Scandinavia (Ibsen's heroine in Peer Gynt is named Solveig). Throughout his diary Nansen appears to use it as generic for a typical Norwegian girl.

†   Racial Office. The Rassenamt was the department of the SS Race and Settlement Main Office (RuSHA) charged with safeguarding the racial purity of the SS. SS members were required to apply for a marriage permit prior to the wedding to allow an investigation into the racial purity of their fiancées.

‡   This plan he actually carried out. O.N.

TUESDAY, MARCH 17, 1942 ■ A new man has arrived here, an *Untersturmführer*. I have not experienced him yet, for when he came into our hut along with the Storm Prince I was lying asleep. I was a bit seedy this afternoon. Others however have already had the pleasure of meeting him, and I understand that he is not the type one could precisely wish for. Some even hold that he signifies the opening of a new era at Grini. The reason for his appointment is said to be dissatisfaction in higher quarters with the speed of work here. A high Gestapo officer was here yesterday, and had been growling at the slow tempo and the invisible results. There was to be another kind of dance from now on. And so today was the beginning. It especially concerns the "works," that is, our department, or more precisely the company camp over by the *Vermittlung*, which is to be built. The huts, or sections for the huts, arrived long ago, and are now lying out on the fields and getting ruined, ruined beyond any doubt. I have already had the means of ascertaining how powerfully certain sections have warped. They are lying uncovered, and when the mild weather begins in earnest, it's obvious that the worst will happen.

However, there is to be a change of tempo. The Storm Prince had threatened to order all hands out to work, the tea gang and the hemorrhoids and all who could stand upright. But on a closer scrutiny of the registers in the personnel office, the number of those newly ordered out was reduced to twelve. The leaders of the different gangs were made personally responsible for the work's being done, and for everyone being on the working sites and not leaving without permission. Those whose footwear was bad (this had been complained of, and rightly) would have new boots issued to them. A hundred pairs with wooden soles have in fact arrived today.

Along with the transfer of responsibility to the gang leaders, it has been decided that there shall no longer be guards on the working sites, but that they shall be posted along the boundaries of the terrain. Obviously the Germans are afraid of more attempts to escape. The grounds and the working sites will also be patrolled several times a day, and anyone who leaves the sites without cause will risk being shot at. Incidentally most of the guards are as fed up as we are over this new fuss; of course it means a tighter rein for them too.

From today there is a three-day ban on parcels. Parcels are of great consequence; I am inclined to think we prisoners live better than the people outside. The other evening I counted five different kinds of relish on the table. There was sausage, jam, cheese, herring, and one thing more. It's almost embarrassing the way our tables groan with all the luxuries that our people have scraped together to send us, because they think we're starving. They themselves are assuredly not so well off for food.* At any rate we weren't before I was arrested. Perhaps they dine rather better? Here it is the morning and evening meal that really count for most because of all the odds and ends streaming in. And now I think we're getting method into the consignments, so that there will also be parcels for those whose families are at a distance, or perhaps have nothing to send.

---

* Nansen's daughter Marit remembers that during the war "dandelions could be both soup and salad." Ruth Maier, a young Jewish refugee from Vienna, kept a diary of her experiences including her time in Norway. Her entry for November 19, 1941, reads in part as follows: "The food situation. Butter: . . . Impossible to find dairy butter. Margarine getting rarer. People are using whale oil for frying. Meat: . . . (Almost) unobtainable. . . . Eggs: none. Chocolate: none (queues). Cigarettes: none. Coffee: very little. . . . Cocoa: none. Sugar: little, with ration card." Maier was arrested November 26, 1942, and transported to Auschwitz where she was gassed upon arrival, age twenty-two.

FRIDAY, MARCH 20, 1942 ■ Some busy days have passed. Everything is urgent. No doubt the Terrace has demanded a forcing of the pace, and moreover there is a great influx just now. In all there must be two hundred and seventy teachers to be fitted in here. Shifting and fuss again from morning to night.

Had a visit from Kari and the children the other day, right in the middle of it all. It was a great and joyful surprise. They had announced a ban on parcels and visits, and indeed complete isolation for three days. At first Kari was told the same thing at the Terrace, but she didn't give in. They had promised that she should see me, and in the end she got her *Schein* in the teeth of all prohibitions. Both Kari and the children looked well, and it was grand for all five of us to be able to sit together for a quarter of an hour. Herr Balabanov* who was looking after us let me help myself abundantly to the things they brought. It was a real gala. And now it will be a long, long time before I see them.

The treatment of the new prisoners today was frightful. Kunz punched them in the face and flung them about if they merely didn't understand what he said. And who the deuce can understand what he says? It is far from German. The teachers must have had a fine foretaste of their stay here. I hope they will soon discover that it's not like that every day. The Storm Prince too behaved like a savage. He bellowed in real copybook style, and woe betide those who didn't understand, or put their hands in their pockets, or committed other mortal sins. Altogether it has been such a day as there can only be in a German concentration camp. An atmosphere of gloom settled on the whole camp. We whispered, when discussing who was among the teachers, who got the worst handling from Kunz, and so on. Such a day belongs to calamity, and the rumor that a man has been killed in Number 19 does not fall out of the picture. When one has stood watching Kunz "at work" a while, as I did today, and observed how he can treat people in sight of everyone, it makes one shudder to think what such a fellow would be capable of in a cell alone with a defenseless prisoner. I myself have not been exposed to corporal brutality, but I have seen a little of it and imagination can do the rest.

Creak, creak, creak, outside on the square with every step the guard takes in his enormous boots. It must be cold. The Storm Prince and the lieutenants have just been in here inspecting. I flung this under the drawing board, dipped my writing brush, and bent over the surveyor's map the instant before they stuck their noses in. They did look rather suspicious, but when I had explained that it is urgent to get the map done, and that I had had to give a hand by putting in contours and lettering, and when the Storm Prince himself had sniffed the map up and down a couple of times with an air of connoisseurship, he nodded approval, said good night, and withdrew together with the "Pipe Cleaner," which is our new name for the Lieutenant, because he looks like a pipe cleaner. (The new *Untersturmführer*, who promised to be such a tough the first day but who has turned out a harmless duffer, we call the "Segment," because he looks like that.)

SATURDAY, MARCH 21, 1942 ■ The teachers are streaming in. Yesterday and today two hundred and fifty have arrived, and it looks as though it will continue. One can't deny that there is something melodramatic about this national migration to Grini, but at the same time it is sinister. The treatment they are getting here is still frightful. It was not just a demonstration of welcome. All the Germans yell in copybook style when they come

---

* Eugen Balabanov, a Russian refugee living in Norway who worked as an interpreter at Grini.

across teachers either singly or in a squad, and then they kick and cuff a little for safety's sake, to indicate more precisely what they mean.

This afternoon I had the pleasure of setting a hundred and thirty-five teachers to work shoveling snow and clearing the hut sites on the "upper plateau." It went nicely; everyone got hold of some object or other to indicate work, a pick, a spade, a shovel or something else with which they could either poke at the stumps or "move the snow." Properly they should all have had spades, but we are short of spades, and so we had to eke out with other implements. All went well, and it rapidly developed into a grand-style penal comedy out on the clearing, where the whole gang stood round in the snow and poked. They began to get back their spirits, which perhaps had drooped a little at their reception in the *Vermittlung* and afterward when they were "shown round" inside the hotel. Then the guards came along and began yelling: "Faster, man! Can't you work? Faster, I said; get on, get on! Don't you understand, blockhead? Goddamned Norwegian! And you call yourself a teacher. That's impossible! You'll have to learn something first, blockhead! Get on!" and so on.

But their tour didn't include blows this afternoon, as far as I know. Only bellowing. And one soon gets familiar with the yelling. It is really worse for themselves. In the long run it must be a strain upon the throat and the vocal chords.

All that about its being so ignominious for a cultivated, etc., Norwegian, infinitely far above these ill-bred hooligans, to get all this bawling out—that's nonsense. It isn't in the least ignominious. It is the best demonstration one could wish for of the new system, its methods, and its entire level.

When Kunz comes out on to the front steps during parade, rather nonchalantly dressed, a white jersey pulled up round his fuzzy chin, and shouts for [August] Winkelmann (the barber) to come *sofort* [at once] and shave him, then he has a great moment.*
Winkelmann has then to fall out and run into his barber's shop—where Kunz reclines like an Indian maharajah in the wooden chair—and start lathering.

That is Kunz all over, and that's all of him. He can reach no higher. His imagination doesn't even get as far as a dream of leather upholstery and springs, with which it would otherwise be natural enough for him to fill his matchbox of a brain. No, the demon of power has possessed him, and though he had to sit on a jagged stone under the open sky in the rain, he would not mind in the least, if only Winkelmann came running at his command in the sight of seven hundred people.

As though that man could humiliate us!

Two guards have just been in the lobby with noise and bluster and a rattling of keys. It was [Ole Jacob] Smith-Housken they were after,† and Nils Dybwad and [Rolf] Fremann.‡ They are to dress and go down to the *Vermittlung*. More people are arriving. It is past one. The melodrama continues; the horror spreads. That I should be sitting here in the office zealously engaged in "map-drawing" they obviously found quite in order, even that I should have taken the carbide lamp from the lobby, the one that isn't to be moved or touched. One of them merely muttered something about having to borrow the lamp

---

* Although released July 8, 1942, Winkelmann was rearrested July 7, 1943, and spent the remainder of the war in Sachsenhausen.

† Released June 17, 1942, Smith-Housken was rearrested December 19, 1944, and held at Grini for the duration of the war.

‡ Fremann was released July 8, 1942; rearrested May 5, 1944, and released March 23, 1945.

a moment for Smith-Housken, or something of the kind. I handed it over, waited till Smith-Housken had got dressed and gone away, and then brought it back in here, where I have returned to my "map-drawing."

Very likely still more teachers are arriving tonight, or perhaps it is the barristers' turn. It's reckoned that at least ninety percent of them are O.K. and will refuse to join the new lawyers' union, or whatever its name is. Yes, indeed, the barristers will be coming, and the doctors, and the engineers, and all the lot as time goes on, that is if the NS don't get to realize how hopeless it is, and hit on something to veil their impotence. The attitude outside is firmer, and more splendid than ever. The parents' action against the "new ordering" of children is in full swing, and Minister Skancke is getting protests by the ton, an incessant stream.*

SUNDAY, MARCH 22, 1942 ■ Just back from our evening entertainment in the church. It really was a brilliant evening. All the teachers who were present for the first time were quite enthralled. I talked with a number of them. It had been an experience; why, the place alone is an experience, unique of its kind. I don't know when I've seen a more distinctive theater auditorium, or when I've sung or acted for a more responsive and splendid public. The last two evenings have been on a really high level, and the hall has been packed. The public were standing a long way up the stairs in the background; the gallery could hold no more, and the "bed stalls" were full of prisoners standing, squatting, crouching on all fours, or hanging over the three tiers of beds. On the floor they were standing and sitting right up to the "stage," which is four ordinary tables put together. Today moreover we had found among the teachers a singing teacher, who led the choral singing.

Francis Bull was brilliant; he repeated *Bergljot* and part of Bjørnson's poem to the *Selskabet for Norges Vel*.† He knows everything by heart, and he reaches the farthest corner of the church; you could hear a pin drop when he stops to take a breath.‡

MONDAY, MARCH 23, 1942 ■ Teachers are still streaming in. It looks as though the arrests are going on right and left, and as though the teachers have become the object of the Terrace's utmost fury. No doubt the idea is to convince them, by particularly cordial treatment, that Nazism and its methods are the only right way.

That the rector of a university, a lecturer or headmaster, a shipowner, director, manager, or editor should have to clear stumps, wash floors, roll tea, or shovel snow is damned

---

* Ragnar Skancke (1890–1948), a member of the Norwegian Academy of Science and Letters before the war, became the minister for church and education affairs for the Quisling government and was responsible for the dismissal and/or arrest of priests and teachers who opposed the regime. After the war Skancke was convicted of treason and executed on August 28, 1948, the last person to be so executed in Norway, which thereafter abolished the death penalty.

† *Bergljot,* a poem by Bjørnstjerne Bjørnson (1832–1910), is considered one of his finest examples of lyrical poetry. Bjørnson, winner of the 1903 Nobel Prize in Literature, is viewed, along with Henrik Ibsen, Jonas Lie (the elder), and Alexander Kielland, as one of Norway's greatest writers. He wrote the lyrics for Norway's national anthem, *Ja, vi elsker dette landet—yes, we love this country*. Bjørnson's last major poem, written in 1909 (months before his death), celebrated the one hundredth anniversary of the Royal Society for Development (*Selskabet for Norges Vel*). Many believe it to be his best poem.

‡ A contemporary described Bull as "not at all typically Norwegian. He was pale and elegant, if heavily built, almost affected in his manner of speech, not in any way a sportsman but gentle, giving the impression that his whole interest was in his intellectual studies. His lectures [at the university] were always some of the best attended."

fine and Aryan, to be sure, but it can't possibly give him a better understanding of Nazi theory. Especially when there is a ban on reading as well, and that so strict that not even a "new-ordered" newspaper is allowed through the fence. Kunz's roaring and the kicks of the guards are in point of fact all we really learn here about Nazism. They serve the purpose, goodness they do, but heavens above, how idiotic it all is—.

Between twelve and thirteen hundred teachers have been arrested throughout the country, we heard today. It's natural that the Germans should be in a fuss and fury because the hut-building here doesn't get on. They will need more huts if this is to continue.

SUNDAY, MARCH 29, 1942 ■ We are having strange days at Grini now. The whole of this last week has had a stormy character. The Storm Prince has completely lost his balance. He rages round like a lunatic. Everything is wrong, though he can't exactly point out anything definite. There is too little work being done. The other day he was standing on the terrace in front of the prison just before roll call. The tea gang and some of the other gangs who work on the lower farm were unlucky enough to turn up for the evening roll call a few minutes before the time. Therefore they were shirking. He had an attack of frenzy and bellowed like a wild beast. The tea gang, with Sejersted Bødtker, Francis [Bull], and [Didrik] Seip at their head, had to turn and go back to work again.

Then he caught sight of the stone-breaking gang, marching up outside the gate from the stone quarry. He rushed down to the gate like a gale of wind and started the wild-beast roars again. The stonebreakers with their guards (it is the guards who decide when they shall stop work to go home for meals) had to turn and make their way back. Up he came again to the terrace. On the steps leading into the prison he met an old Jew. He rushed on him like a madman, seized him by the collar, struck him in the face, and raved over a Jew's having indoor work. [Erling] Steen was present at the session; he explained that the man was sick, and that the doctor had pronounced him unfit for outdoor work. "That makes no difference! I don't care in the least what the doctor said! All Jews are to go out! Out I said, out! Do you understand?" And the poor wretch came hurtling out, scared out of his wits, with the maniac at his heels and a stiff, repressed Steen in the rear.

On parade the Storm Prince did some more bellowing and announced that the tea gang was dissolved from now on. The officers, who had been given a single stripe on their arm to show that they were soldiers and not civilian prisoners, now had to rip this stripe off again, for some undetermined reason. Obviously it was just that the Storm Prince needed an outlet for his rage.

One might have thought he would be back in his senses next day at any rate. But no, it went on just the same. Yesterday a thundering order was given for us to work all Saturday and all Sunday. The order was taken cheerfully by all the prisoners, most likely to the great chagrin of the ruling powers.

The poor "baby elephant" Gebecke had interceded for us with the Storm Prince at dinner yesterday. He had got such a fearful dressing down that he was all in a dither when he came and told us. He himself had been ordered to stay here and direct the work both yesterday and today, and, with savage roars, had been accused of siding with the prisoners. He cried when he was telling Frode about it. Real tears were running down his globular cheeks; he shook his big heavy head, gazed at Frode with his big, melancholy blue eyes, and sighed deep and heavily.

As I said, we worked all Saturday and all Sunday, and in good heart. I saw nothing but cheerful faces and a grand *fighting spirit*.* We are definitely underfed; of course it's worst for all those who are now being driven hard out of doors. For ten hours they are doing hard manual work with no extra rations. On the contrary, both yesterday and today less food has been distributed.

The devil behind all this is said to be the Lieutenant. He has been sitting in his room at the villa with a pair of field glasses, and has noted that some of the prisoners out on the works did not swing their pick or spade unintermittently, but stopped for breath now and then. Well, this man obviously believes it possible for a human being to wield a pick or spade, or whatever it may be, ten hours at a stretch. And in his ignorance, combined with genuine devilry, he complains of the discipline and speed of work to higher authorities, that is, the Terrace. No doubt he has an ulterior motive too; he wants to get on. And that's how one acquires merit in the ranks of the Third Reich.

That the Storm Prince should have risen to it, indeed actually run amok on such fallacious grounds, is more peculiar. But he too is a German and an SS man, so what else can one expect.

We have had our entertainment in the church tonight, all the same. It was a splendid show. Francis [Bull] was quite outstanding. The evening was especially arranged for the teachers. That is the central thing at present. For the Storm Prince has given them a chance of joining the new "teachers' union" by nine o'clock tomorrow morning. He reminded them of their families and uttered the most barefaced threats of what would happen to *them* if they didn't join. They were to do it singly. He would have no joint action, thank you. Now they could think it over, each for himself, until nine o'clock on Monday. After that it would be irrevocably too late.

The offer speaks for itself, and indeed there were not many teachers for whom it raised much of a problem. The few who needed it were stiffened up by their colleagues and by the rest of us, especially by other prisoners who have themselves been out in rough weather. This evening in the church, with Francis' unforgettable talk on *Brand* and *Peer Gynt*, finished the job.†

A prisoner who is very unpopular with his mates—a Swede—was in church this evening. Two guards were there as well. Both were drunk as lords. They declared vociferously that three days ago this fellow had volunteered for the SS, that he sneaked to them and told on us. "If we were you," they assured us, "we would take that man and finish him, knock the life out of him, trample him underfoot; he is a dirty swine right through." Their fury was genuine and their contempt for the man unfathomable.

This episode disturbed our evening's program a good deal to begin with. The guards did their best to whisper, which did bring down the tone to that of ordinary loud conversation. But that sort of thing is not very pleasant for the man on the stage, nor is it nice

---

* In English in the original Norwegian version.

† *Brand* (published in 1866 and first performed in full in 1885) and *Peer Gynt* (published in 1867 and first staged in 1876) are both verse plays by Norwegian playwright Henrik Ibsen (1828–1906). Fridtjof Nansen once observed, "If I may use myself as an example, it is no exaggeration to say that my character, such as it is, has been largely of Ibsen's making. The suggestive influence of such poems as '*Brand*' upon the men of my generation has been more than you would easily believe." According to a friend of Fridtjof, "He could recite whole pages of '*Brand*' by heart and in English." Ibsen has been called as a "writer of incomparable 'social' drama which gave him a place of influence in the literature of all western civilization," and some maintain that he is the most frequently performed dramatist in the world after Shakespeare.

for those who are listening. At last it was settled that the man should make himself scarce; running the gauntlet of his fellow-prisoners, he slunk away through the hall with his tail between his legs. It was a pitiable sight. He went to his doom. Up in the passage outside his cell he was received by other guards, who sat in judgment on him. He got a thorough beating in front of everyone, and then he had to stand and repeat after the guards: "I am a dirty character and a bad man and a scurvy comrade. I steal from my comrades and tell tales on them to the guards. I lie and steal. I sneak to the guards and slander my comrades to them. I have volunteered for the SS and yet pretend to side with the prisoners. I am a cheat and a filthy character." He had to say it in German. It was translated by one of the prisoners (Åsebø)* as he went along, and was repeated over and over again. In between he had to do knee-bending till he shammed a faint.

I didn't see anything of this; I was fully occupied with the program in the church. The two drunken guards who had disturbed its opening also disappeared at length. But before they left, we were accorded an unforgettable scene. We sang *Proud Sons of Norway*, about our liberty and laws, our mother wit, our righteous cause, and one of the guards mounted the rostrum in a transport and conducted the singing with heavy, unmanageable arms. His body swung to and fro as well. He was in ecstasies and so were we.

The program continued after the last drunk had staggered out, and it went without a hitch and brilliantly to the very end, which was the national anthem. As I said: Francis was first-rate.

Also we had Robert Andersen on the program for the first time.† He has got his violin in, and he played superbly. It was an experience to hear good music again. The sight of that eminent musician in prison dress and slippers, standing there on the table before the world's most superb audience, and playing Norwegian melodies until there was not a dry eye, made it an experience never to be forgotten. Tired and worn the prisoners sat there, after ten hours' hard labor in woods and fields, in ditches, quarries, and workshops, and they listened. That little time in the church became a tonic rest for mind and soul, and in the roar of applause that went up to the church roof there was genuine gratitude, a deep, unifying sense of the significance of the hour.

MONDAY, MARCH 30, 1942 ■ The frenzy continues. Two hundred and fifty fresh teachers have arrived, and we are expecting still more. They are to be quartered in the garage, a shanty with cement floors and thin wainscot walls. There they are to lie on straw mattresses side by side on the floor, and at night the thermometer is likely to go down well below zero [C or 32° F].

It is frightful to see how the Germans treat them. Kunz stands in the *Vermittlung* and harries them; they all get a vigorous kick in the pants as they go by, and some a blow in the face as well, if they are not brisk enough in handing over their money, knives, or ration cards.

---

* Carsten Åsebøe or Aasebøe (1903–1945), a journalist and a communist, was transferred to Sachsenhausen on April 3, 1942 (see below); in the closing days of the war he was transferred to Bergen-Belsen, where he died April 1, 1945, age forty-one.

† A violinist who toured Scandinavia as a child prodigy, by age sixteen Andersen (1914–1961) was an instructor of violin at the Oslo Conservatory. Immediately after the war he organized and conducted an orchestra made up of musicians who had been interned in camps with him, performing benefit concerts for stricken Norwegian families. In 1948 Andersen moved to Minneapolis, where he taught music at the University of Minnesota, and performed in the first violin section of the Minneapolis Symphony Orchestra. Andersen was released December 15, 1942.

If the Storm Prince happens along, there is more bawling out; some are sure to be so imprudent as to have their hands in their pockets, or perhaps they don't salute in time. If the Storm Prince is near enough, they get a blow in the face; if he is a little way off, he only bellows like a tiger. He has become completely unhinged, he is not accountable any more.

All the teachers are to leave tomorrow morning, both the new and the old. So there will be no more garage nights for the present, at any rate not here. No one knows what it will be like where they're going.

The old lot had a peculiar experience of their own today. They were once more led apart in a body by the Storm Prince; he had something to tell them that none of the other prisoners were to hear. Out on the building site they were drummed together in a great rally round the Storm Prince and his tyke. Since none of the teachers, said the Storm Prince, had accepted his offer, they had proved themselves to lack intelligence. No one must imagine that a pack of dirty teachers could hold up the development of Europe. They had set themselves against the new ordering that was taking place today over our whole continent, and this offense was such that hereafter they must be regarded as ordinary manual workers. They would now be treated accordingly. None of them would ever again be able to engage in any kind of instruction, they were no longer intellectuals; they were manual workers and henceforth would be given nothing but manual work. Then in conclusion some tirades about the new era. And with that the second teachers' meeting was over.

It had a little afterpiece. As some of the teachers were going past the woodshed, suddenly the Storm Prince with his dog and Kunz came popping out. The teacher in front must have been slow in getting his cap off, although the Storm Prince had immediately begun to bellow something unintelligible (everything, without exception *everything* they bellow, is unintelligible, even to those who think they know German). The unlucky teacher got a tremendous blow in the face from the Storm Prince's clenched fist, so that the cap flew off across the field. He was ordered to pick it up and put it on again. He did so. Whereupon he got two blows in the face and a vigorous kick in the behind.

Such are German officers. Such is the new order. It is not surprising that a man of his caliber and with his spiritual equipment should at times get drunk with his power. But now and then the devil and the yahoo in him may disappear again, and one may be absolutely tempted to look on him as a normal human being. If anyone asked me, I should say I think it best for us to keep this man after all. We are beginning to know him, which is always an advantage. We have seen him in every phase. I don't think he has more to reveal. All the same there will be quite a bit for him to atone for afterward, when one adds it up. And there are a lot of people doing that.

FRIDAY, APRIL 3, 1942 ■ Long Friday! [i.e., Good Friday] Indeed it has been. And yesterday deserved to be called Long Thursday. It was a full working day from seven in the morning until seven at night. The guards, the Lieutenant, and the Storm Prince kept after the prisoners all day long. All who don't work, that is, all who don't swing their pick, spade, ax, or whatever the implement may be, without an instant's relaxation, are noted down on a black list. They are to be formed into a trotting column, that is to say a penal column that must carry out all work on the double. They won't be allowed to walk. They must always run, wherever they may be and whatever their errand may be. At first it was a threat; now the Storm Prince has announced that it will be put into practice. He has been forced to do it, he says, to make the prisoners work. They are too lazy and dodge, and he must put a stop to that.

The whole thing is sheer ignorance or devilishness. Dr. [Jørgen] Berner's* representation that the food is quite inadequate was put aside with a shrug of the shoulders and a remark that if Victoria Terrace got to know how much extra food he, the Storm Prince, lets us have in the form of parcels, it would be a fearful business for him. The figures Dr. Berner could produce after accurate computation are as follows: The food we get yields eighteen hundred calories. A manual worker with an eight-hour day should normally have four or five thousand. And here the work goes on for ten hours, at a penal tempo controlled by slave-drivers.

All the same, they shan't get us down that way. All the prisoners are taking it splendidly. The spirit is first class; no one complains out loud. All help each other. Never has there been more solidarity. Never could anyone be prouder of being a prisoner at Grini.

Today something dreadful happened. Fifty men were to fetch their civilian clothes; they were being released. Everyone thought it was an Easter gift, a fresh "amnesty." There were touching farewell scenes, thanks for everything, greetings to everyone outside. Don't be long behind and so long. Then doubt crept in; the choice of men aroused suspicions. There was a long list of Communists among them, and there was [Didrik] Seip, there was Rolf Hofmo,† there was August Lange,‡ and a lot of others, the last who could expect to go free.

They were going to Germany. It passed from mouth to mouth. Do you know anything for sure? Are they going to Germany? Have you heard they are to be sent off? And some had already heard. Others thought they were going to Jørstadmoen, where the teachers have been sent, but soon everyone believed in the German trip. And so it was. The Storm Prince said so himself to Erling Steen, but not until after they had left. They were driven off in German buses, and when we saw that we knew everything. Such equipages are never used for prisoners who have been set free; they have to get themselves to Oslo as best they can.

Frode's name was also on the list, but had been crossed out. That suggests that the Storm Prince needs Frode here in Grini, and has therefore rescued him from this trip. But there it is, fifty of our comrades had to go. It will be no bed of roses. One must almost hope that after all the food situation in Germany is not so bad as we usually rejoice to think it. One thing is certain—the prisoners in the concentration camps don't get more food than others, and as for parcels from Norway, they are likely to be so-so. No, all the

---

* The secretary general of the Norwegian Medical Association from 1925 to 1949, Berner (1883–1964) was one of the leaders of the trade unions' protest against German occupation in 1941. He was released October 24, 1942.

† An athlete and Labor Party politician, Hofmo (1898–1966) helped form the Workers' Sports Federation (AIF) in 1924, of which he was the chairman 1939–1940. He also engineered the merger of the AIF with the NLI (Norway's National Sports Association) to form the Norwegian Confederation of Sport, of which he was the vice chairman from 1946 to 1947. Today it is known as the Norwegian Olympic and Paralympic Committee and Confederation of Sports, the umbrella organization for all of Norway's sports federations. Hofmo spent the remainder of the war in Sachsenhausen.

‡ Writer, educator, and cultural attaché; after the war Lange (1907–1970), whose brother was fellow-prisoner Halvard Lange and whose father was Nobel Laureate Christian Lous Lange, contributed to various works on life at Grini and Sachsenhausen, including the two-volume *Griniboken* [*The Book about Grini*]. Lange remained in Sachsenhausen for the remainder of the war.

ideas one has of this are equally distressing; it is hard to find any bright spot. No wonder it was a dark day, one of the darkest we have had, a genuine Long Friday, not soon to be forgotten. I can still see all the joyful faces of the men who were feverishly pulling on their civilian clothes and sharing out their things among their mates, for now they were to go home. And then the appalling blow it was when the truth dawned on them, when they saw the buses coming, when they were stowed in like sheep, to leave for what is ten times worse than Grini, for the very homestead of evil, for Germany, for a concentration camp in Germany.

It seems clear that the Germans want to have a solid band of more or less prominent Norwegians in Germany, perhaps as a kind of insurance, perhaps to be exchanged later. They want to secure good cards for the final game, the sinister game in which innocent lives and deaths are to be the stake on one side of the table. Let us hope that the development itself will prevent things from going so far.

Out in the world, movement is obviously slow but certainly in the right direction. It's just the damnable time it takes, days, weeks, months, years! and fateful days, weeks, months, years! Many will succumb. Each day costs hundreds of lives. But one must harden oneself and not think like that. There are things that are more important than that the individual should live through it. There are things worse than war.*

Martin Strandli† has arrived here; he had been seven weeks in Møllergata. He came here along with thirty-five others from the same place. He has had a hideous time, has been whipped and tortured and looks deplorable. When he caught sight of me he was quite agitated; he had to come up and put his arms round me, and the tears stood in his eyes. It was easy to see how strongly it affected him to come here and suddenly find himself among comrades. He wouldn't tell a great deal, but by degrees one got enough out of him to form a picture of all he has gone through. They whipped him with steel springs until he could neither stand nor walk. They did it time after time, to make him speak. But he didn't speak. Now they must have given it up. To him Grini seems a mountain sanatorium pure and simple. We are looking after him as well as we can. He has got a job as building foreman here in the office, and yesterday evening he moved into our hut to take the place of Hofmo, who was sent to Germany. In a while we shall get him back in trim all right, and make him forget some of the devilry.

SATURDAY, APRIL 4, 1942 ■ Easter Eve! Thanks to high-mindedness and generosity we had only one hour's extra work today. This was an Easter gift to the prisoners, which was announced on parade at ten o'clock. The prisoners showed a commendable mastery of their rejoicing; a pale smile brushed as it were over the tired faces.

We held a short entertainment in the hospital this afternoon. All the patients were lying or sitting out in the long corridor. The "stage" was just outside Sand's door. Sand's? Or was it the ghost of Sand I saw there, propped up in the bed with pillows? A white-haired, emaciated old man, staring in front of him and sucking mechanically at the pipe he could just hold onto with the hand that was free from bandages and plaster.

He nodded faintly to me when I sat down; I nodded back; it struck me there was

---

* In a speech given February 2, 1940, in Appleton, Wisconsin, while lobbying for aid to Finland during the Winter War, Nansen observed, "There are things in this world worse than war, fates worse than being victims of war."
† Norwegian trade unionist and politician for the Labor Party and, for a time, the Communist Party, Strandli (1890–1973) cofounded the Oslo Building Society and was its chairman (1937–1942).

something familiar about the man. Thus I slowly recognized him, feature by feature. It *was* actually the Sand I knew, the Sand I had lunched with almost daily last spring and summer. Last summer he was going around brisk and springy. Now he was a broken old man; his eyes sat deep in his skull; his cheeks had fallen in; his neck and chin had dried up and contracted. I saw that he could not move. The only living thing about him was the eyes, deep down in their sockets. I don't know what the gangsters have done to him, and I don't want to ask. It must be an atrocious thing that can change a man so. His arm was broken in two places, all the fingers of his right hand were out of joint, his whole body seemed one affliction. He got part of this treatment at the Terrace, part of it here. And it is known who are guilty. I don't know how I managed to perform this evening, only that I got up in my turn and repeated *Norsk sang*, by Collett Vogt,* to Sand, to Sand alone, and tried to put into it all I felt he was a martyr for. I had such a desire to tell him right out that I was burning with pride to be his countryman. But there was a guard standing motionless outside his door, and I could see he understood Norwegian; he was following the program with his face. When I had said that poem, I moved; I couldn't sit any longer facing Sand's door and looking at him. I was to sing some lively songs for the patients, and how was I to get through them with Sand before my eyes? The hell of the German concentration camps is no longer in Germany alone. It makes one shiver to think what may happen before this nightmare is done with. It's said they told Sand that as soon as he recovers they will smash him to bits again until he talks.

SUNDAY, APRIL 5, 1942 ■ Easter Day. We were awakened this morning by Robert Andersen playing the Easter hymn through the corridor until it resounded. *Morn of gladness, ending sadness, ending grief for evermore.* Ah me.

Birkevold was lying out in the hospital corridor last night, listening to our entertainment. I waved to him. He smiled back, but he was a different man from when I last saw him. His mates have been condemned to death. Svae managed to escape, indeed, but Fraser is sitting waiting, yonder in Akershus. And here lies Birkevold, waiting to be condemned in his turn. He is ill; he has a fever, and never surely has a fever that will not yield been more blessed than this one.† May it only last both spring and summer, yes, and far into the autumn for safety's sake. That is his one chance. For it doesn't seem as though they condemn sick people, at all events not yet. One fine day they will probably discover that they can shoot a sick man just as well as a sound one. Birkevold must be lying thinking such thoughts too, poor lad. And the thoughts and griefs that are agonizing him are such as no Easter morning has the power to end or drive away.

I was sitting in the hut while the others were undressing. Every night I have my hour of solitude in the office here, so I was only sitting talking a while. As Martin [Strandli] slipped off his drawers, I saw his thigh and his behind. The whole back part of his body, on both sides of the thighs and down to the knees, was covered with bruises, dark red and blue. Martin was trying to hide it as best he could. He is like that; he doesn't say much about himself and what he must have endured.

I caught a glimpse under his shirttail and asked him to let me see it all, but he declared it was quite all right now. It was a whole month since they had beaten him. "*Then* it really

---

* *Norwegian Song*, by Nils Collett Vogt (1864–1937).
† The fever was no doubt Oftedal's work. O.N.

did hurt," he added. "I had to lie partly on my belly." They whipped him with steel springs with a ball at the tip. It was the ball that was worst, he said. It made open wounds, too. After every blow they had tried to make him talk, had stood over him threatening worse tortures, had laid out all kinds of other instruments of torture round the chair he had to lie across, while the blows hailed down on him. "One of them must have felt sorry for me in the end," he continued, "for they left off beating me, and they didn't use the other tools on me after all. There was a hammer there, which they told me was for crushing finger tips, and there was one of the torturers who looked like a devil. He had an absolutely square face, and his expression and eyes were like a snake's." Here Martin's voice rose and became intense; horror came into it—the horror of that moment. "You know, I couldn't help crying," said Martin finally, "I just couldn't, and I dare say that was what made one of them sorry for me. I'm not a young man either."

He knows the names of the torturers. I wouldn't ask, but someday they will come out. Some day judgment will be passed on these wretches. And so these are Quisling's fellow workers. Traitor becomes a feeble word on this background. *Quisling* is better. Quisling needs no other name. It will live after him in eternal shame and dishonor.

MONDAY, APRIL 6, 1942 ■ In the last few days a number of Jews have arrived. Now there are nineteen in all. Today they were placed together in two huts just across the passage from us. Yells and bellowings from Kunz announced that something was going on this morning. When I stuck my nose out of the office door to see what was up, it got Kunz full in the chest; he was on his way into the architect's office with a delicate commission for me. I was to make two placards *strengsten verboten*," [strictly forbidden] and fix them on the doors of those two huts. For half a second it went through me that no, I wouldn't do that, but I soon realized that a refusal would serve no other purpose than to send him into an ungovernable fury. His calm assumption is that everyone hates the Jews; on that ground, and on that alone, he treats us "Aryan" prisoners as comrades.

I couldn't think up any demonstration but to make the placards like mourning cards, with a wide black border. Now each is fixed on its door, and I have already found that everyone understands my little demonstration—at any rate the Jews, with whom I have been talking this afternoon, poor fellows, in the teeth of the placards.

They are afraid now of being put into a special squad, where they will be bullied and beaten. They have already had more than one sample of such treatment. They come to me and ask if I can't try and do something for them somehow or other. What irony of fate that instead I have to sit making placards forbidding all intercourse between Aryans and Jews, and fix them on their doors myself. That's all the help I can give—unless indeed you count some poor words of comfort that perhaps may reassure them a little. One of them asked anxiously, "Now I suppose we can't go on attending the Sunday evenings in the church?" I told him there was nothing to stop it; no one really knew anything about these entertainments of ours; they were entirely unofficial, and so on. "But to be on the safe side," I added, "you can take care to spread yourselves out, and you'd better dodge out of sight in the unlikely event of any Germans turning up." He was visibly relieved and promised to follow my advice.

I must say that I don't feel confident about what may happen to these Jews. It is not unlikely that they will be put into a special Jewish gang, which may easily degenerate into the most savage beastliness. All the Germans without exception are Jew-haters, and regard them no more than animals, if as much. No one will have any scruple about hitting them or satisfying his sadistic tendencies by plaguing and torturing them in other ways. Even if they are not formed into a special gang, it's easy enough to take them separately on account of the yellow star which is sewn firmly on their jackets, so that everyone may see that here comes a dirty Jew—get out of the way.

WEDNESDAY, APRIL 8, 1942 ■ The guards, the *Zugführer*, and the little Segment (the *Untersturmführer*) openly abuse the Lieutenant, who for that matter is steadily and truly hated by all. The Segment says a lot of queer things about him. He is coming by degrees to realize how matters stand in this country. When he was asked how people in Germany reacted to the occupying forces in the Ruhr after the last war, and what they thought of Germans who played the occupiers' game, he said straight out—fully realizing that the situation in this country now is a complete parallel—that they were traitors pure and simple. Not bad for an *Untersturmführer*. He has said a good deal more besides. He said for one thing that at Grini there were only decent Norwegians, who should all be let out. He had imagined that we were dangerous political offenders, but now he realized that it wasn't so. Slowly but surely a light is dawning on that man. His cerebral activity may not be overwhelming, but what little there is of it is obviously working on the right lines. If there are many like him as the hour approaches, much will adjust itself better than anyone had thought. I believe there will be more and more like him. The guards here listen in to both Motala and England.* They are a long way from Germany now.

THURSDAY, APRIL 9, 1942 ■ It may be a little sign of prison torpor that I consistently put last month in the date. Today I have got it right. For who can forget the ninth of April?† Only April ninth has that sound. And indeed it was a memorable day, at least here at Grini.

A squad or two came back a few minutes early for evening roll call. The Storm Prince was on the square and saw them. He was so furious that he again became completely unhinged. He rushed into the building, followed by the damned Lieutenant, and then began a search through the huts for all who were there without a reason. Roll call was put off until half-past seven, and all the gangs had to go back to the working places. He pounced on those who were standing nearest, no matter who. He was quite wild! Completely wild! Of course he bellowed at the Jews across the lobby with special violence, but I didn't hear of any blows. He only raved and thundered through the corridors like a tempest, with a servile, muttering Lieutenant walking behind, relishing the effect of his reports—he has been making notes every day and pointing out those who didn't work.

The roll call introduced the salvo. To fire it off, the Storm Prince had to get Balabanov up from the *Vermittlung*. He wouldn't trust Steen with the translation of what he was now going to say. A trotting column was to be formed of all the work-shy, whom we had to thank for roll call's being late this evening. All the prisoners whose numbers would be read out were to step forward, and of them a trotting party would be formed, that was to say, a gang that would have to do all its work in *quick* time, and would have to go to and from

---

* Motala, Sweden, equidistant between Sweden's two largest cities (Stockholm and Gothenburg), was the site of Sweden's only long-wave radio transmitting station. The reference to England is of course to the BBC.
† The anniversary of the invasion of Norway.

work in *quick* time, translated Balabanov. The question is whether quick doesn't mean a run. We must wait and see. To this party, which from now on would be permanent again (they have had it before at Grini), belonged "*grundsätzlich alle Juden,*" [all Jews on principle] he proclaimed in a contemptuous snarl. They were always to be in it, along with all who were reported for laziness, disobedience, and so on. They would all get out in a month, if they showed good conduct—only not the Jews. If, on the other hand, they went on showing themselves lazy and ill conducted, further reprisals would be taken against them; they would be forbidden to smoke, to receive parcels, to read, to write, etc. Then the numbers were read out. There was a long list of them, a distressingly long list of good men, picked out wholly at random, because their names had been taken by Kunz or the Lieutenant.

It made one's blood boil. But worst of all was the categorical fate of the Jews. No one asked what they had done or hadn't done. They were Jews and would therefore be punished. The Germans certainly regard it as a final edge on the punishment of the other prisoners that the trotting party *grundsätzlich* consists of Jews, that Aryans are now to be condemned to work with a Jew gang!

All those in the trotting party are to have work of their own and to be driven especially hard. They are to be moved to the parachute room, which is empty since the teachers left; the doors there are to be locked in the free period. They are not allowed to be with others. Among them is a man whose name was taken by Kunz because he was in the dentist's office getting a toothbrush; he wanted it for cleaning the carburetors of the carbide lamps, which it is his job to look after. Only Kunz bellowed so that it was hopeless to explain.

There was one man or perhaps two in the whole trotting gang who may have deserved to be there, and more than twenty were named. Several of those called out were sick into the bargain. Sick men who were in bed in their huts are to be punished for being sick.

Some elderly Jews came to me tonight in despair. They didn't think they would be able to stand this. One of them had tears running down his cheeks. There was not much I could say, but I think that what I did say may have helped all the same, since it established once more that they had us to a man on their side. All of us were prepared to help them with all our power, I said. Keep smiling.*

The youngest ones will get through it all right, but it's a worse prospect for the older ones. They may break up, they may be hounded until they drop. There may be pure Dachau here at Grini. Who can prevent it? What can we do for them when it comes to the point? Slip them a little food. (They are not allowed more than one small parcel a week. With the work before them now, that's the same thing as undernourishment.) Yes indeed, we must give them a bit of food now and then, as long as we ourselves are getting it. But that may well stop. To the "authorities" we may just as well keep our mouths shut about the Jews; putting in a word for them would be as hopeless as asking to go home for a little holiday. They are to be regarded merely as animals, a low type of animal.

If there were a God, He would be bound to stop this now, at least if He is all they make Him out to be: the God of justice, the God of goodness, the God of love. How false and hollow it all sounds today, on this background! Who can speak today of the God of love, the God of justice? Only Germans. Good night!

---

* In English in the original Norwegian version.

FRIDAY, APRIL 10, 1942 ■ Life goes on, but is now becoming a good deal harder to live. The food is getting worse and worse. We have not had potatoes for a long time. We have rutabagas. The rations are altogether too small. The working hours are increasing steadily. Yesterday and today we worked from seven in the morning to half-past seven at night, with two hours for dinner. Of the midday rest half an hour is taken up by roll call, sometimes more. We are to have a full working day tomorrow, Saturday, and the day after, Sunday. The Storm Prince is as frantic as ever. I doubt if he will ever calm down again. All one may unluckily have said in his favor in bygone days must now be taken back. He is a living devil pure and simple. He is chronically yellow green in the face, and truly looks no better than he is. The almost-human characteristics his face no doubt had at one time, at the time when he was a missionary in Madagascar or wherever it was, have completely vanished, leaving nothing but a sinister toothless grimace of an indeterminate greenish yellow color, and a pair of brown, venomous, stinging eyes deep in the shadow of the cap brim with the death's-head and bones on top.

All day long there is at least one guard standing over the trotting gang, driving them on the old Egyptian model. No sooner does one of the unfortunates straighten up than the guard is on him with a roar. His number is taken down on a list, which is to form the basis for continuation in the trotting party. Names are being taken incessantly throughout the day. All who let up for a moment are noted down, Jew or Christian. Sometimes there were three guards standing over them at once. At ten this morning a man was carried indoors; it was old skipper [Ingvald] Walderhaug. The doctor diagnosed a serious heart attack. Walderhaug has a disease of the heart, and said in advance that he was sure he wouldn't get through this, and now he is lying there disabled, perhaps injured for life. He is a man of close on sixty, hardworking, conscientious, and honorable. I know him well; we were in the same hut when I first came.

Outside there is great optimism—"It won't be long now, fellows; it'll soon be the big push now; hold out a bit more and they'll have had it"—and in that style. It does one's heart good to hear such talk, only to hear it, even, I might almost say, if it is based on nothing at all but good healthy optimism. It screws one up quite a few pegs, which one can do with at this black time.

SATURDAY, APRIL 11, 1942 ■ Got sober news from outside today. It is good, but not so blooming as the Grini reporters eventually make it.

For the first time, I notice, I am suddenly beginning to imagine another war winter, another whole long war winter. It's a hell of a thought. But still I shall always get through it. It's worse for a lot of people here. Just think of the Jews. They won't all survive; that much is certain. The mere prison life in itself is more than hard for a lot of people. Indeed God knows what it will be like for me when the months start piling up in earnest. As yet there are only three of them. I know it's bound to be tough as the time approaches when our new baby is expected and Kari has to be alone with everything. Yes, of course there are friends and all sorts of kind people, but it will be tough all the same.

But it is getting late. We have worked a full day and are to have a full day again tomorrow. Saturday and Sunday are abolished. One day something or other will crack here at Grini. One seems to feel it in the air. For it's not only the prisoners who suffer for this insanity. The guards are furious. The drivers give off sparks. The officers are growling, too. The Segment said today to Erling Steen, during a long, candid conversation: "*Der*

Obersturmführer must go, and go he will!" Everyone is burning with hatred of the Storm Prince. At one blow he has become a devil to his whole circle in this melancholy part of the world.

And now he has decided to take in [adjacent] Haga farm. With livestock and buildings, woods and fields, he means to have it expropriated, and that forthwith. The plowing and sowing is to be done by prisoners. He counts on getting three thousand prisoners, and they shall all have something to do. He will go to work wholesale. The Storm Prince has no idea what he's talking about, but there are great sparks crackling through his crazy head; they take the form of model farming, new land, more new land, trout streams, dams, bridges, woods, timber, and teeming fields with trotting parties to weed, dig, sow, plow, harrow, and harvest. The man is a lunatic, that's the ghastly thing about it, a complete lunatic, and it may take his lunatic superiors a long time to discover that his lunacy is too lunatic. He has the power and means to spread much affliction and havoc, much suffering and wretchedness about him still, before his hour strikes.

SUNDAY, APRIL 12, 1942 ■ Glorious April weather. Sunshine from a sparkling light blue sky. Birds chirping, snow loosening, rills chuckling under rotten snow. Spring. Real spring. But seven hundred prisoners are being hounded to work all day long. Who has time to look up and enjoy the spring sunshine?

When the signal went for midday roll call at twelve o'clock, they came streaming up, gang after gang, from all the different working places, tired and fagged, with bent heads, up to the square in front of the prison. There they paraded in long wavering lines to be counted before they were let into their stalls for feeding. Each man's whole body was crying out for food and rest—but no, twenty minutes of the precious midday break went in roll call, today as well, before it came out at length, that everlasting sum, and we could march in. The worst sight is the trotting party with the Jews at its head. Bent, stiff limbed, bespattered from top to toe with camp slush, muck on their faces and their hands and the striped camp trousers, which one can only just recognize through the grayish brown layer of mud, they stagger in when the command is given. They come running on parade; they are not allowed to walk; this is a punishment squad. So that no one shall be in doubt of it, they have all had two white stripes sewn down the back seam of their jackets. No doubt it's meant to be disgraceful to have these stripes on their backs; others are meant to smile and scoff at them in their humiliation. Laugh, gentlemen, please, point at them and laugh! I actually saw some of the new guards doing that (we have had a change of guard again today).

How long are the German people to continue on the road to destruction? How long will it be before generations once more grow up in Germany to whom we can trustfully stretch out our hands? I am afraid that we who have experienced both world-conflagrations never will live to see it. We know the day of reconciliation must come; we will labor to prepare it, but it is a dark, disconsolate outlook. I can't help seeing it so. It's one thing to win the war. To win the war—after all, what sort of illusion is that? No one has ever won a modern war; all have lost, all without exception. The thing is to win the future. I don't deny that the war, the suffering and afflictions may have tempered us for that task, ripened us for it, even roused whole nations and peoples out of torpor. But at the same time the war has thrown us decades back. We have much ground to recover, much to rebuild from the foundations, before we can talk about our winnings. Perhaps we shall have slipped back into the torpor by the time our loss is made up. *Then* who has won the war?

But that leads into dark vistas, and my time is passing. It is after half-past one. There is such a row in the building—as much tramping and bellowing as in broad daylight—that it doesn't seem to me like night. Fresh prisoners are arriving in long columns. No doubt it is our old friends the teachers coming back. They are expected. There has been one long procession since eleven o'clock.

MONDAY, APRIL 13, 1942 ■ It was the teachers who arrived last night, but only a hundred and forty-six of them. The rest have been sent north, first in cattle cars to Trondheim, and from there by boat, probably to Kirkenes.* The choice of those who came here was quite haphazard, young and old mixed, but chiefly old.

At Jørstadmoen near Lillehammer it had been quite appalling. There were close on seven hundred of them. The journey up from here was tough. For twenty-seven hours they were without food, and when they got to Fåberg they had to walk, with trunks, bags, bedclothes, etc., the three or four kilometers [2–2.5 miles] from the station to Jørstadmoen. Cold huts received them. Not a crumb of food. They were allowed two hours' sleep before they had to turn out again. Then at last they got some food, two hundred grams [seven ounces] of bread each, butter and jam. There were no sanitary arrangements except for an ordinary privy. Nor was there any water or washing tubs. They had to melt snow for drinking water, and the washing up was done outside. Then began the day's "work": punishment gymnastics for hours on end, knee-bending, line gymnastics, and "exercises" out on the grounds. They were wading in snow above their knees and at a whistle had to fling themselves down on their backs or bellies. Then came the word "Oslo!" or "Berlin!" and they had to kick out with their legs and make as if they were running. The guards had got some spiteful fun out of it.

In general it was easy to see that the Germans had had strict orders about harrying the teachers—and harry them they did. The same exercises had been gone through in mud. A selection of elderly teachers had to do the goose step; both faintings and heart attacks occurred, but made no special impression on the bold knights of the *Herrenvolk* [master race]. All this was staged to get them to "sign," as it was called, that is, to join the teachers' union. They succeeded in getting twenty-odd members—out of seven hundred men. As for other work, they had had none whatever with any sense in it. They "cleared" snow from the bottom of a hill up to the top. This they did with sticks and bits of board and what else they could find. There were no tools. They also had some frozen sand to poke loose; in short the work was pure idiocy. And then it ended in the camp's being dissolved. Five hundred teachers to the north, the rest here to Grini. The few who gave in and joined were allowed to go home. Poor fellows. They were the most to be pitied!

What will happen to those who have arrived here, nobody knows. Today has passed in medical examination, enrollment, and so on. Doubtless the fun will start tomorrow.

Fresh people are always going into the "trot," as it is now called. All new "guests," except hostages, go straight into the trot.

I have been in Oslo twice today. Both times for bricks and clay. A man whispered to me, "The Finns have attacked the Germans!" "Is that certain?" "Yes, it's quite certain."

---

* Kirkenes lies in the extreme northeastern part of Norway, 240 miles above the Arctic Circle. See August 15, 1942.

That was an epoch-making piece of news, but I can't believe it quite, until I get confirmation of it. So far the report is a bit too meager. For instance, it is possible that the Finns are knocking off an odd German here and there, and that such phenomena (which are not rare even in peacetime Finland) have been magnified into a whole war. I must wait until tomorrow to burst with joy; it would be too exasperating if the whole thing were the fabrication of a man with a gift for drama.

TUESDAY, APRIL 14, 1942 ■ The Segment has got bridge-building on the brain. We are to build two more bridges besides the one we're on now, also a dam and a large gateway in the outer fence. Through the gate and over the bridges it must be possible to drive a tractor, which has been bought. All the Segment understands is that the bridge must be built of "thick" material, really thick, immensely thick. Therefore he has had massive tree trunks carried down, which he intended to lay on other tree trunks, which he intended to lay straight on the ground—on the frozen crust. When I explained that the bridge would very soon go *kaput*, he said he had built a hell of a lot of bridges on an estate in Germany, and that all the lot of them were standing as well as ever to this very day.

I hinted that there might not be frost in the ground in those parts. Oh yes, he said, there was frost, *ach doch* [oh yes], there was frost, but did that worry him? Not likely, all he did was to take his thick tree trunks, that's to say really *thick* tree trunks, thicker than we had in Norway, and much better timber. Those he cut up into pieces or lengths that were exactly equal, "*verstehen Sie?* [understand?] *Pass' mal auf* [Mind this], then I take my tree trunks and lay them side by side, exactly side by side, from one side of the brook to the other, *verstehen Sie? Aber, und das ist wichtig, so pass' mal auf* [understand? But, this is important, so mind this], first I've removed the earth and turf where my logs are to go under the equally long, thick logs; on each side of the brook I lay an even thicker log on each side, *verstehen Sie? Und dann festmachen, und wirklich festmachen mit langen Nägeln, ni?* [understand? And then make fast and really fast with long nails, eh?] *Und drauf, pass' mal auf* [And then, mind this], I take some more thick tree trunks, exactly as long as the breadth of all the others put together, and lay them close, quite close, beside each other across the others, *verstehen Sie, ni?* and to get these tree trunks, which are thick, solid tree trunks, to lie side by side, I take them, *pass' mal auf,* and make them flat along the sides. *Und dann wieder festmachen mit grossen soliden Nägeln* [And then make fast again, with big solid nails]. *Und die Brücke ist da!* [And you have your bridge!]"

The mill goes round like that all the time; it is practically impossible to throw a word of sense now and then into all this twaddle. My objections are simply drowned in fresh tirades. And all the time this strange man has a peculiar gleam in his eye, as though in every microscopic pause a fresh idea of genius were striking him. And out come both ideas and genius in all their glory, so indecently silly that one has to classify the whole man as being in a kind of half-witted infancy that has become permanent.

All the same this half-wit is a human being. There is not much harm in him. An *Untersturmführer* has to bellow; he has three stars on his shoulder and is second in command of the camp; he has to assert himself. But behind the bellowing there is actual kindness shining out of his funny little eyes, which look like two fortuitous holes in an empty box. He is jocose too; when he says "idiot," he says it in a way that may make one laugh, and if we do laugh he doesn't mind, on the contrary; then he's very pleased with himself, then he's made a hit.

It is a bit of a trial to be exposed to him for hours every day. He has developed a certain crush on me; the fact is that in the end I managed to teach him a little about bridge-building and foundations. He kept quiet for whole seconds at a time, blinking his little mouse eyes as though he were hearing a pupil he was pleased with. Then when he had snapped up a little of what I had been saying, and come round briskly and painlessly to the line of action I proposed, he would run off to the working gang who stood there scratching their heads over his last orders and thunder out what I had just said—a direct translation into much better German. So that's the method. First I have to get him alone and tell him how it's to be done. After that he will run round, elated and voluble, repeating it to the working gangs. Now he always comes and asks first; he is quite afraid to say anything without asking. He is downright willing to take orders from me or Frode or Steen, who also have him in their pockets in their own sphere.

Today there were many new arrivals: Trygve Hoff,* Per Krohg,† Lieutenant-Colonel Fredrik Bølling,‡ and many others, who will no doubt slip into the milieu and lend it fresh tones and shades. The motto of "The Whole Nation in Prison" seems to have been adopted. We are expecting more teachers and clergymen.

Tomorrow Kari will be coming; I'm sure of it. I must try to stay at home (!). I must see her now; perhaps she will bring the children as well. That would be splendid. Then we'll all smile again together, anyhow for ten minutes.

WEDNESDAY, APRIL 15, 1942 ■ Kari didn't come. I've stayed at home all day long because I was sure she would be coming. I got the tailor to press my "dinner jacket," I cleaned my boots, shaved and smartened myself up, and then she didn't come. All afternoon I went fussing round the *Vermittlung*, had an awful lot to see to at the office hut, had very little time for inspecting remoter building works. But she didn't come. At last I had to give up; after six no one comes. I was rather low this evening, tired and fagged out.

Today again produced the usual trip with the Segment. Frode and I were at all the bridge works with him, talking them over. When we had finished—it was a long job, first he has to empty out all his nonsense, then we have to say how things should be done, and then he has to repeat it at least four times—well, when that was finished, we took a stroll in the woods with him, and he told us the most pointless stories of the last war, in which he had served four and a half years (so he said). For instance: One day, on patrol at St. Quentin with his rifle, he had come upon an English sentry. "*Ein Engländer!*" [An

---

* Hoff (1895–1982), an economist, had accompanied Nansen to the United States in 1939 to lobby on behalf of Finland in its Winter War with Soviet Russia. He was released July 1, 1942.

† An artist, Krohg (1889–1965) was commissioned after the war to paint the mural that dominates the United Nations Security Council Chamber in New York City. Described as "the most unique feature of the room," Krohg's mural initially met with resistance from the Headquarters Art Panel on the grounds that it might interfere with the delegates' concentration. At the insistence of Arnstein Arneberg, the architect in charge of the interior design of the Security Council Chamber, and Trygve Lie, the first secretary-general of the UN (both Norwegians) the painting stayed put. It was installed in the summer of 1952 in time for the official inauguration of the chamber on August 22, 1952. Krohg was released from Grini on May 19, 1943.

‡ Released September 22, 1942, Bølling was rearrested October 24, 1944, and remained in prison for the remainder of the war.

Englishman!] he ejaculated in tones of horror. He had raised his gun, and the Englishman had disappeared again. *Weg!* [Gone!] Then he had walked on. "*Ja, ja. Ich war damals ein junger Leutnant.*" [Yes, yes. I was then a young lieutenant.]

So he gabbles away, conjuring up a kind of dramatic narrative out of absolutely nothing. In between he tells us how grand everything is at home in Germany, and how rotten everything is in Norway. "Here there's nothing but mud and filth and frost and snow and darkness, but at home where I live the plants are so high already," and then he bends down with his hand above the snow to show us how tall they are.

The news today was great and epoch making, if one could only be sure that it doesn't come from the Grini news agency. *Finland capitulated at nine o'clock this morning!* It is quite certain; someone has been talking to someone who heard it with his own ears. All the same I am putting off my jubilations.*

FRIDAY, APRIL 17, 1942 ■ Kari came about half-past one. When I got word out in the fields somewhere, I forgot everything else, sent the Segment, with whom I had been twaddling, straight to hell, and ran for the *Vermittlung* like a thirsty camel for an oasis. And there she stood in the sunlight, smiling, confident, and sure. Ten minutes, what on earth can one find to say in ten minutes? Why, it takes twenty just to collect oneself. And then that loathsome little twerp Claffy listening to all that's said.† That sweepings of a creature is to decide what we may say to each other!

Five minutes—six—seven—no indeed, we were neither of us counting, only Claffy, but he was counting those little drops of time as though he meant to stick the whole watch into his eye. There was no eleventh minute today, but we got the ten. I feel that I can live on that meeting for a year if necessary.

I can write no more now; something else has happened; there is something going on. Seven shots have just been fired outside; earlier in the evening there were five and then three. No one knows what it is. Practice? Or is there someone making use of the darkness, trying to escape? Some one of the many who have nothing to lose, but everything to gain?

About twelve a guard came up and woke Steen. They wanted to get hold of Rinnan. Frode was wakened and told to dress and go straight down to the *Vermittlung*. To the question what for, the guard replied "*Vernehmung*" [Examination]. Questioning at this time of night? A shiver goes down one's spine at the mere thought. Frode went off taciturn as usual, controlled and tense as a steel spring, and an uncanny feeling settled down on the hut. A little later a car turned out of the *Vermittlung*. So he was going to the Terrace. What can it be? Gracious God, are they going to smash *him* to pieces now? What can those devils mean to do with him? I sat on a long time in the hut with the others. We didn't say much. We didn't know anything; we were only guessing and remembering all the frightful things that happened to others, but to Frode?—No! No! No!

We got a terrible message yesterday; Fraser was shot the day before. It's becoming more than one can stand; I can't go on writing.

Kari, if only you were here now. For it wasn't true what I just wrote; I can't live a year on those ten minutes.

---

* Finland, which fought on the side of Germany against the Soviet Union during the so-called Continuation War, did not in fact surrender until September 1944.

† Claffy acted as an interpreter at Grini. He started as a member of the Hird, but later joined the SS.

Another shot has just gone off. Of course it has nothing to do with Frode; he vanished in the car an hour ago. But it has something to do with one's nerves.

Well, but I must try to sleep; it's no use sitting here waiting. Doubtless Frode won't be coming for a long time. Perhaps he's being tortured now; perhaps at this moment he is face to face with the devils who want to squeeze something out of him. Perhaps they're showing him how they have planned to get it out of him. Perhaps—perhaps! No, this won't do. Perhaps we shall get him back as sound and grand as ever.

SUNDAY, APRIL 19, 1942 ■ Sunday. We have been "free" for the first time since Easter, and we needed it. I've just come from the evening entertainment in the church. The atmosphere was splendid and the program on a high level. And yet I'm sitting here infinitely dreary and despondent. Frode is gone; they took him away in the middle of the other night, and since then we have heard nothing. There were shots, a lot of shots, and shouts and screams and a deafening hullabaloo. It shook one up inside, and my nerves were in the act of going on strike or rather of rearing up on edge and letting fly. I shall never forget the compressed atmosphere of horror that weighed down on everything that night. I didn't get to sleep; I couldn't write; I wasn't capable of reading. I could only lie staring into the darkness. It was an appalling night.

Now it's two days ago, and still we've heard nothing of him. We have had an elucidation of the shots; it was the three building superintendents, Gebecke, Ehling, and the new one in uniform, having a binge in their lodgings on the upper farm. They must have been mighty drunk, for they went completely berserk, smashed up the furniture, tore down the stove, shot at the walls until the splinters flew, pissed on the floor, and bawled and raved like madmen until the small hours, when they pitched headlong into what was left of their bunks. They were all going round with their tails between their legs and drinking water all the next day, and their lodgings looked as though there had been an air raid.

This interlude in prison life makes no great impression on the Germans. I believe it's a feature of good Aryan custom. The Vikings and Germanic bands had such customs too; now they are obviously being revived as a link in the new era. No reprimands, no punishments, except for the hangover they had afterward. Next day Gebecke was sitting in the office, fat and sulky, and describing the excesses of the night. He described the whole thing, all he remembered, and he remembered most of it, especially that he had shot best with the pistol, best of all three. It is worth mentioning that a lot of the shots went in the direction of the prison; I was sitting in the hut, by the open window, and heard the bullets whistle over the roof.

The Storm Prince called me out in front yesterday and asked me in "confidence" if I knew what the trouble was about Rinnan. He said he had believed that Rinnan was a good fellow. I assured him that he was right in thinking so. "He is a quite exceptionally good fellow," I said. "That's what I thought, too," said the Storm Prince, adding with a regretful shrug of the shoulders that he was afraid neither of us could do anything about it.

Today there is a rumor that fru Rinnan has been arrested, and is one of five women who are in solitary confinement in the south wing of this floor.

It would be horrible if it were true. In the first place it's barbarous to take a young mother, all alone, away from two small children when her husband has been in prison nearly a year. Who is to look after the babies, mites of four and two years old? Her family is in Sweden (she is Swedish), and Frode's is in America. In the second place it's alarming, when one thinks of Frode's situation, that his wife should be arrested, too. What on earth can they be after?*

And out of doors it is spring. The sun is pouring down its gold all day long. It only makes the whole thing even more senseless.

After the evening entertainment the Storm Prince came and asked [Erling] Steen what had been going on in the church. Steen said it was no doubt someone playing the violin. The Storm Prince was furious and called it *eine ungeheuere Frechheit* [a monstrous insolence]. [Arne] Scheel had unluckily described it as a cabaret when the Storm Prince asked him.†

Finally he came to me. But he was very restrained then. I confessed that I had arranged the whole thing. He asked how on earth I could have taken it into my head to get up a concert, an entertainment, without asking. *In a prison—but that won't do, it's really monstrous!* I managed to say that it had happened before, that I had supposed it was allowed, that in any case it was quite impromptu. There was no question of supposing anything whatever, said the Storm Prince, I was a grown man after all, I must use my head, I must surely understand that such a thing was impossible?

Thereupon he left me. I got the impression that he wouldn't pursue the matter any further, but I assume we have had our last evening in the church. The Prince was plainly controlling himself all the time and didn't let go; I was expecting a fist in my face, but it didn't come. Unluckily he had heard the singing from the church, the choral singing at the end, a sonorous *God Bless Our Dearest Country*, as he took an evening stroll round the prison with his girlfriend.‡

It's strange, but this doesn't affect me, it seems so damned insignificant. And it would indeed be incredible if we could go on having a spiritual life!

MONDAY, APRIL 20, 1942 ■ It was true about fru Rinnan. She is here. She knew nothing about Frode; she thought he was here. She knew nothing about her children either, for she had been driven straight to Grini without a chance to arrange anything. I haven't talked with her, but saw her through the peephole in the door of her cell when I was indoors inspecting some "building work" that was going on in the women's section.

A letter from Kari. Splendid! Good night.

THURSDAY, APRIL 23, 1942 ■ Today we have had news of Frode. One of the new prisoners had been with him at Number 19 and says he was all right. He hadn't been tortured, but had been imprisoned in a dark cell and questioned for twelve hours. And that's wonderful, if only it's true.

Tomorrow will be an ordinary day again. But it will be easier to work, easier to smile, easier to get on with the others. Good gracious, Kari. The day is coming on with giant strides when there will be no more fence, no more barbed wire, and no more devils to part us.

---

* Like her husband, Hanna-Greta Rinnan remained incarcerated for the duration of the war.
† Scheel was released October 3, 1942.
‡ I.e., his dog.

FRIDAY, APRIL 24, 1942 ■ Had a talk with the Storm Prince in his villa this morn-ing. I wanted information about various things I have to take over instead of Frode. He was comparatively friendly, but in no way "confidential" as he has been from time to time in the past. He made it clear that he has absolutely no grasp of the administration of the work in this prison. What he comes back to all the time is that the prisoners are *lazy*. They must be driven to work; they force him to take drastic measures, and so on. I heard that over and over in reply to all my questions, and left about as wise as I came.

Before leaving I also asked him about the evening performances. I said I was sorry to have arranged one when it wasn't allowed, but explained that we had had these Sunday evenings every week since I arrived here nearly four months ago, and so I thought it was all right. I asked if he couldn't go himself, and convince himself that our program was educational and by no means the reverse. Politics and every form of propaganda would of course be barred. The Prince said he couldn't do that, nor would he have such things got up as a matter of course; it would seem tantamount to a reward for the prisoners, whom on the contrary he meant to punish because they were lazy. And off he went again on that whole sermon. I maintained that the lazy ones *were* being punished now, since they were put in a trotting column, and besides today the trotting column had been moved into a hut of their own (one of the new ones), and so they wouldn't be able to attend the Sunday evenings. That was obviously a good argument. He promised to think about it, and I could bring the matter up again later. He offered me a cigarette.

Otherwise the day has been normal. The trotting gang have had a hard time. Fiendish guards have been standing over them all day; now they are at work on the land down by the *Vermittlung*, full in view of the Storm Prince, who sits at his window with a pair of field-glasses seeing that they work. And then the guards have to bellow, to show that they're "doing their duty," as it's called.

Only one piece of news, which it was grand to get. Fraser is reprieved—ten years' hard labor. Not long ago we heard that he had been shot. That was a bad day. Now this message has arrived and brightened everyone up. They say it's quite certain he is reprieved. This must be wonderful for Birkevold, who is up there in the hospital going through a bad time. Hope for him *must* revive again, even though he was the leader. Ten years—why it's almost mild. If the leader were to get fifteen or something of the kind, it would be joyful news pure and simple; one year or twenty makes no difference at all.

SATURDAY, APRIL 25, 1942 ■ One of the good days. I went off to Oslo with Götling early in the morning. We were at Ullevål for one thing, and did a couple of other errands before returning home. But first we had a snug little lunch of sandwiches and beer at the office. Kari was there, and we could have a proper, quiet talk. The children are all right and Kari too, calm and strong and brave. It was like drinking vitality and jubilant happiness from an inexhaustible cup. Perhaps that may sound queer, but for someone who has been a long time in a concentration camp it's not queer. Nor sentimental either. It *is* so, simply and just like that.

And so these trips into Oslo are of inestimable importance. I almost forget the risk I'm running, and occasionally notice with alarm how cheeky I'm beginning to get. Today I simply took my whole cargo, a bulky parcel that must have weighed twenty kilos [44 pounds] and a smaller parcel of sandwiches, under my arm and marched up to the main entrance, past the guards and other evil powers and into the hut. The big parcel was full of tobacco and tinned stuff and my bag was not empty, either. I walked right up from the garage without so much as trembling at the knees—at least, I think I did tremble for an instant when I caught sight of Schwartz, but it soon passed; I walked impudently on and had it clear in my mind that I would say the parcel contained office requisites, if he asked. Curiously enough he only stared fiercely at me, turned his back, and walked off.

Of course that's how it should be done. Or as we did it the day before yesterday. The surveyor's gang came down to the garage with me, equipped with knapsacks and surveying apparatus, and returned with their goods and chattel as though they were coming back from a surveying trip. But they had great quantities of tinned stuff, tobacco, and other things.

That time I even brought in a bicycle. Frege had said he would like a bicycle. Götling would like one too, but he insists on paying for it. We must let him, to be sure. In my view it's all right to "grease" these fellows, whose assistance is so invaluable.

SUNDAY, APRIL 26, 1942 ■ Sunday again. One week after another slips away into the darkness; they are like gray cats. Now it has become a change to be free on Sunday. If we could only have used this as a day of rest, which most people need. But though morning roll call is put back until ten o'clock, the day gets chopped up by a whole series of regulations. Besides, the only exercise we are allowed is back and forth on the dusty square in front of the prison. Prisoners are prisoners with numbers; they must walk in a row; they must be pale and thin; they are being punished, and they must bear the stamp of it.

The teachers had a sermon from the Storm Prince today. They were called down in front of the *Vermittlung* where the Prince with interpreter (one of the teachers) made his speech. It was in dulcet tones if anything, the usual nonsense about the new era, but this time he started off with a eulogy of the teachers' high intelligence. One can't help remembering his gibes to the exact contrary the last time he spoke to them, when he informed them that a pack of stupid teachers couldn't stop the implacable development of Europe. Today all teachers were enormously intelligent men, who must understand the futility of their resistance. He admitted that some of them might perhaps have grounds for resisting, but if the resistance was the outcome of a vulgar taste for opposition, it would not be tolerated. He had nothing, he said, against a fight with intellectual weapons, where opinions stood opposed to each other, but the teachers must realize that if they had opinions that stood opposed to the only correct development then these opinions belonged to a world now going to its grave.

He invited them to come quietly to him, one by one, when they had thought it over, and join the union. He condemned joint actions of every kind!!! That he was uttering a mass of absurdities and contradictions and muddleheaded phrases he did not grasp, but his hearers noticed it without difficulty. They left the meeting fortified. Now there is no sign of a breakdown.

TUESDAY, APRIL 28, 1942 ■ Both yesterday and today I was in Oslo—yesterday with Götling. That was a very successful and pleasant trip. Today with Bitner. Which was a very unsuccessful and unpleasant trip. Yesterday we ate at the office, delicious sandwiches (imagine me sitting here writing about sandwiches), and Kari was there. Also I had arranged a meeting about the gumboots for the Segment. They were debated from every side, and we are getting fifty more this week and fifty next week. The Segment gave permission to eat in town if necessary.

Today, as I said, I went there with Bitner. He is a surly brute, not a smile, not a pleasant word, not a bite of food, nothing. So that was that. Well, there have to be such trips as well. The Segment was much affronted because the gumboots I fetched today had wooden soles. He said he wanted *real* gumboots, high, good, thick, and all of rubber. Naturally he did. I knew that. I must suggest his making a trip to Oslo with me. It's no good securing opportunities if one is to trail round with a surly vinegar bottle of a driver; in the first place it puts one damned little in the mood for doing anything, and besides one has a feeling that all the time the sour face thinks one up to something wrong or suspicious.

Funnily enough he sent me off alone with a heavy acetylene-gas container that we had collected at Filipstad* and were to deliver somewhere else in Oslo. So I was sent out on my own with the container on my shoulder. For the first and no doubt last time I was plodding along Karl Johan† with a lumping great container on my back—in prison clothes, with blue jersey and blue guard's trousers. I didn't meet anyone I knew, but it was strange to be walking there among "free" civilians without a guard. Of course I could have decamped; of course I could have got away; and of course I thought of it. It didn't exactly seem to me that I owed the driver anything, the surly beggar. I could just have left him to his fate. He only said, "You'll be back, eh?" But it didn't get beyond thinking. I delivered the container on the third floor of Holmgården. (Gracious what a weight it was.)

And then I went back to slavery like a tame, idiotic, cowed prisoner, and sat down to repent in the front seat. I wished it had been someone else who had had that opportunity. Alas, I have had all too many. Constantly when I'm in town I have one or more. But then I feel my place is at Grini; there I can actually do something for others, not much, but a little—more, I believe, than outside—and therefore I find a certain satisfaction in taking on the job. On the other hand there are many, many others who ought to clear off, who need to, and who would have no cause for a second's hesitation if the chance offered, as it is forever offering to me.

With these thoughts I went jogging up the ill-kept road and into our cherished sanatorium. Here there was more turmoil. The teachers were having another course of treatment. All morning they had been driven like beasts. Guards and slavedrivers had been standing over them the whole time, as they toiled in the clay trenches or at the stump-pullers out on the hut sites behind the prison. The trotting gang, on the contrary, had had a peaceful day. It is plain that orders have been given to hound the teachers, hound them to madness or despair.

I should say they were miscalculating when they gave such an order. A few of the teachers have certainly eaten humble pie, but they had already done it when this hell was let loose. Last night or this morning they put their names to the document they were being tempted with. These poor devils were singled out at once, both by the Germans and

---

* A neighborhood in downtown Oslo.
† Karl Johans Gate is the main street in downtown Oslo, connecting the Royal Palace at one end with Oslo Central Station, the main rail station in Oslo, at the other. It was so named in 1852 after King Karl Johan (1763–1844), king of Sweden and Norway. Karl Johan was born Jean Bernadotte in France and served in the French army under Napoleon until 1810, when he was elected heir to the Swedish throne, thereby establishing the royal house of Bernadotte in Sweden, which remains the royal house of Sweden to this day. King Haakon VII of Norway was Karl Johan's great-great-grandson.

by their Norwegian comrades. The Germans made them fall in separately, as though they meant to exhibit them and say, "Look at these poor wretches, look at them, this is how they look, those who betrayed the best in themselves and submitted to save their skins."

And that was how they were looked on by their comrades, boycotted, shut out with their shame. The world can be brutal, and it is today. Some of the twelve are doubtless good people, who could stand no more. They are having a bad time now; they are sure to have even worse.

But after all I don't suppose the Germans see things like that, at least not many of them. Most likely the reasons for the twelve being paraded separately were purely "administrative." The point was that they were not leaving. The others on the contrary got an order to pack their things this afternoon. Once more the corridors were full of the bustle of departure. A hundred and fifty prisoners were swarming round, nervous and distraught. Civilian clothes were given out; trunks, bags, and boxes made their appearance and were packed and roped; friends were saying good-bye; presents were being given and received; the air was buzzing with instructions, greetings, shouts, and explanations. Food was being collected by the sack from all huts throughout the prison, and shared among those going away. This time they shouldn't starve on the journey; we would see to that anyhow. The kitchen people were set to work making unlawful soup; it was poured into unlawful bottles and distributed among the teachers, who were living scattered about in several different huts.

In the midst of all this came evening roll call. When that had been got through, few thought of their supper, everyone of the teachers. There were so many to shake hands with, so many to talk to, so many one had looked forward to knowing, but who were now going away.

Then came the counterorder.

The teachers were not leaving after all, not tonight, perhaps tomorrow, perhaps the day after, perhaps not at all. That supplied a fresh topic of conversation. There were some indeed who calmed down and ate a bit of supper, but minds and huts and corridors were full of this new development. What was the plan now?

An hour later came a fresh order: They *were* to leave. Then the uproar began afresh, packing, distribution of civilian clothes, some of which had now been handed in again, instructions, greetings, handshakes, assurances, presents, wishes, food parcels, and tobacco.

And then they really went off. I stood on the steps and watched them go. One by one they came down with their bags on their backs, with suitcases and boxes under their arms. Bent old men, many of them, but all with a cheerful parting speech: "Au revoir, friends! We won't give in. Thank all the others from us all, for everything here. Everything has been grand. Thanks and au revoir!"

It was thrilling to stand and watch them. None of them knew what they were going to, but they must have thought the worst likeliest, north to Kirkenes where the others went, or perhaps south, to Germany. But whatever might happen to them, one thing was certain—they would hold out.

"Long live our King and country!" The cry was in the air, one could read it on every lip, one just didn't hear it, but that was so blessedly superfluous. Never has it been felt more intensely, never has anyone lived up to it more strongly and splendidly than that silent procession of Norwegian teachers who were now setting out on another journey to the unknown, but with a common goal behind the darkness and fog.

I wished those outside could stand in the blacked-out prison and hear what a transport of prisoners is like. Hearing is enough. Hoarse roars and bursts of fury from half a dozen Germans at a time tear the dark to shreds. When a name is called out, it sounds like a two-inch plank snapping through and being chucked down. Then the person addressed doesn't answer quick enough, perhaps because he didn't recognize his name in that strange disguise, and then there comes a torrent of abuse, echoing far across the moonlit landscape.

Before that avalanche has settled, a fresh one starts. No doubt somebody or other has been too slow, has lost his suitcase or dropped a parcel, and the poor man mustn't die in sin. A hailstorm of German vocables (not likely to be found in any dictionary) comes rushing down on him. And then they strike and kick, too. That's part of it. It is an important link in the new German culture. One stands there dumb with horror and loathing, a mixture of contempt and indignation rises in one almost to the choking point. But then one must laugh instead, for thank God the situation has its comic side. And so we laugh, really laugh a while, until the laughter sticks in our throats.

A violent paroxysm of rage from down in the *Vermittlung* cuts through the night. One can positively see the bloodshot eyes protruding from their deep sockets, and the toothless jaw, for it is the voice of the Storm Prince. Yet another paroxysm; it begins in the depths and ends higher up almost in falsetto; he has no breath left; one can almost hope for a fit of suffocation or perhaps a heart attack. It *must* be wearing; not everyone would have the strength to keep up such outbursts.

And indeed it is the substantial war effort of this man who never has time for anything, and who persuades himself and others that he is useful because he does "his duty."

WEDNESDAY, APRIL 29, 1942 ■ The cold continues. Only in the middle of the day does the sun get a real hold; at night it freezes. A thin layer of ice covers the puddles and ditchwater in the morning, when work begins after the parade at seven o'clock. But it soon thaws, and all the sites round about the works are full of liquid clay gruel and porridge. Things are especially bad for the trotting gang who have to work on the company camp down by the *Vermittlung* (in view of the Storm Prince). They are busy on a large main sewer which cuts obliquely through the whole works. The trench is deep and goes through sheer potter's clay. Then it has to be propped up so as not to collapse, and down in the trench, which is about seven feet deep, there is clay soup up to the knees, in which they have to stand and work all day, with these hogs bellowing and bullyragging if they rest on their spades a moment or stretch their backs.

It's no fun to be works foreman and walk around dry-shod with drawings, pointing and explaining, while these men are fagging themselves crazy down in the trench. The worst thing is to look at the Jews, unaccustomed as they are to such work, bespattered with clay which runs down on their heads from the board they shovel it up on, and from which it is then shoveled further on. A pitiful sight, but what can one do to help? It wouldn't improve matters if one were to throw off one's own jacket and jump down into the clay soup, a thing one could really feel impelled to do, if it were only to show that one was quite prepared to class oneself with the Jews and make common cause with them. Not for *their* sakes, for they know well enough that all the prisoners here are on their side, but for the sake of the guards, the poor German wretches, who actually do stand there hating the Jews. One can see it—let them in general be ever so "decent," ever so "understanding,"

*The "trotting gang" at work in
the trench of the main sewer.*

the Jews they hate, the Jews they've learned to despise. And doubtless they think we do too, we *must*, for doesn't everybody? They don't think further.

This morning I had a long conversation with one of the Ålesund men (who were taken when they were on their way to England in a smack). They are in a tough spot and their future prospects are worse than gloomy. All were caught in the act. The man I was talking with told me that after their arrest the boat was loaded with dynamite and towed out to sea; all the lot were to be blown up out there. He told me they had never been in such wild spirits as on that trip; they had sung and joked and played cards. But then they weren't blown up. It was only a bluff to frighten them and soften them up for questioning. And indeed the examinations came thick and fast, but the Germans got nothing out of them. Nor for that matter were they subjected to torture of any kind; on the contrary they had rather been treated with special kindness, with food and everything of the best. To be sure that's also a method.

It goes without saying that here at Grini they have all been thinking of escape from morning to night. Chances have offered all the time, but no one has taken them. Regard for the others—for there are a lot—must have held them back.

Today it's too late. Today the rest of the gang arrived from Trondheim. They were locked into the church, and at evening roll call all their names were called and they had to fall in in front. They were to pack their things and be ready within five minutes. No one knows what is going to happen to them.

Now, after that, it is night. Outside there is a noise of bellowing and words of command, tramping and uproar. Sixty fresh prisoners are arriving. No one knows who, no one knows where from. Black views wherever one may turn, not a gleam of light. In my mind's eye I see the melancholy face of Jakob Friis, one of those who have had a hundred opportunities of clearing out. Where are they off to now with that young lad? What is he to go through now, what mental agonies, what horrors?

And young [Per] Fillinger, an airman, a brilliantly plucky lad.* He has something special about him, something that gives one a firm belief that he will be there for the last round, and not be cleared away now, so miserably. The Germans offered him a job in the *Luftwaffe*. "Rather shoot me and be done with it," was his reply.

I can't make myself believe these lads will be shot, condemned to death, because they did their duty. I won't believe it. I can't believe it; it would be too senseless, too horrifying.

One of those who arrived from Trondheim had his head in bandages and was led up here by two of his buddies. He had inflammation of the brain, an earache that had worked inward. He had only one chance, said the doctor I discussed it with, to get straight onto the operating table. And what happened? The man, who had of course been taken up to the hospital, where they had begun at once to treat him provisionally, was fetched away and carried down to the church. *That* was his place. It was an order. No hospital for him. The Storm Prince himself had had a look at him and made the decision.

Oh Kari, how terrible it is to be here, and how brutal men can be! It's more than one can stand in the long run, going to bed with these thoughts every night and waking up with them every morning and not being able to help, not being able to do anything to stop this madness. And yet I suppose this is nothing to all the horrors that are going on

---

* See May 1, 1942, below, regarding both Friis and Fillinger.

elsewhere, to all the suffering and terror spreading where the Germans advance and where they settle in.

Outside, the words of command are cracking out; the bellows echo through the night, people are running back and forth, something is going on. I don't know what. Everything is dismal and dark and sinister. But the full moon is shining down from a blue, starry sky, and tomorrow there will be more sunshine and spring. Heavens, what a spring!

THURSDAY, APRIL 30, 1942 ■ This morning, before the rest of us were afoot, they were sent off. The Storm Prince himself was up and made a thundering speech to them, in front of the *Vermittlung*; also he struck them with his riding whip, in a fury. The echo of it all carried as far as our room in the main building, and from the window we could follow the incredible scene that was taking place.

They were sent off in handcuffs, fastened together two and two. Their luggage stayed here, with tags bearing the names and addresses. The home address. [Henning] Bødtker got instructions to take charge of it and send it home to them. Obviously this was to look like a discharge.

The Segment was going around talking of that. He certainly believed it. He knows no better. I had a talk with him. It was all a jumble, first he talked of discharge, then he said they would be back for dinner, by the afternoon at latest, but were to leave again with a transport, with a big transport. He knew nothing, that was plain. I told him about these men, how they were arrested, what they were doing when the Gestapo caught them. He knew nothing about it. He didn't even know that it was a capital offense to leave the country without permission, not to speak of an attempt to get to England. He seemed to be horrified, but brushed it aside; he said he was so tired today.

A gloomy, suffocating silence has lain over the prison today. As the hours stole by, it was as though hope were ebbing, slowly, oh so slowly and painfully, but horribly surely, until evening came, and the last remnant of hope vanished with the sun behind the Bærum Hills.* Now it is night, and only the noise of the guards below disturbs the quiet, the deep uncanny quiet saturated with sleepless hate, with grief, and with gnawing terror of what has happened and what is going to happen.

Are they already shot? Murdered? Perhaps without even a sentence? Or was there some kind of trial? Though what does that matter anyhow?

The man with inflammation of the brain was carried out of the church this morning; he was to go, too. Dead or alive. And why indeed should they bother with his inflammation yesterday, when he was to be shot today? Perhaps it was easiest for him after all. A deliverance! But for all the other twenty-year-olds?

Can it be true that this has happened? Can it actually be true that these lads, with whom only yesterday morning I was talking and joking, are no more? Perhaps they're only being questioned! After all, we've heard of questionings that have taken ten and twenty hours, yes, and more. Perhaps they're only keeping them in Akershus or Number 19, or wherever it is, to squeeze the truth out of them? For none of them has "cracked" as yet; they haven't even had cause. They haven't been pressed hard, at least not those who were here. God grant it may be that. Even if they had to be tortured, yes, even if they had to be exposed to the worst atrocity, it has the effect of a lightening in this black despair. They are

---

* The region northwest of Oslo where Grini Prison was located.

young, strong lads, most of them, just the type who will stand practically anything. And I have never felt it to be truer—while there is life there is hope!

If only I could be sure of meeting them all again!

Here I sit in Frode's place and write, while the clock ticks away, every somber evening, until past midnight. But I can write no more; my thoughts won't sort themselves out. What can one possibly find to hope for? That the Storm Prince will turn into a human being? Or as much of a human being as we used to fancy him? A man who used his riding whip on those poor young men this morning, as a farewell from Grini. Perhaps he knew that they were being sent off to be shot?

The Segment? Poor little ninny. Everyone laughs at him. All shake their heads, his subordinates, his superiors, and the prisoners, right before his comic little caretaker face. His world is jovial; half playfully he sends people into the trotting gang, as though it were a game, a kind of prisoner's base. Yes, the effect is much as though he were employed in a vacation camp or summer boardinghouse to arrange the amusements and the open-air games. The gravity and horror, the game of life and death, passes far over his head.

"Why hadn't you made a good breakfast for the men who were going off this morning?" he scolded Robert Andersen, the cook.

"Because I didn't know they were going off," answered Robert.

"Then make a good dinner for them," returned the Segment, and toddled on with his stick.

A fresh devil has turned up, a young *Oberscharführer*. All day he has been going round the "estate" amusing himself by setting prisoners old and young to knee-bending, frog-jumping thirty yards and so on. Odd [Wang] was walking up from the lower farm this afternoon. As he passed the garage, a strange sight presented itself. Round the corner came a singular figure; it was advancing in curious kangaroo jumps. The figure proved to be Fredrik Gjertsen;* he groaned out in despair, "Is he still after me?" Odd looked round, but could not see a German in any quarter and could make nothing of it. He thought Gjertsen must have gone raving mad. Gjertsen went jumping on down the road, crooked up with long gangling legs and with his bag, which he always carries round his neck, tumbling about him. Odd didn't know whether to laugh or cry; it was undeniably a fantastic spectacle. I saw it too, but from a long way off, right up on the prison terrace. It was the new *Oberscharführer* he was obeying. That was one of his amusements today. Gjertsen had done nothing wrong, nor was he dodging. He had been up in the joinery sharpening a knife.

Well, we must put up with it. We are prisoners in a German concentration camp, and the representatives of the *Herrenvolk* are entitled to have their fun with us.

FRIDAY, MAY 1, 1942 ■ They were shot yesterday morning at ten o'clock, no trial, no red tape. After the Storm Prince's philippic they were driven away, probably straight to Hovedøya† or Akershus. Eighteen brave Norwegian lads are no more. Eighteen atrocious murders that cry for vengeance. Vengeance! I am afraid that one day vengeance will be executed and that no one can prevent its happening. No one can prevent it. God help us all.

---

* Giertsen spent the remainder of the war in Grini and various concentration camps in Europe.
† A small island in the Oslofjord.

It was on the radio at half-past seven this morning. Some prisoners had been listening in the *Vermittlung* guardroom, and it spread at once through the camp. They were shot as a reprisal for two Gestapo men who were killed somewhere in Vestland a few days ago while engaged on their "lawful" work.* The name of every man had been read out; each was like a whiplash, like a stab in the heart, the names of comrades with whom we had been living for weeks, had shared food and tobacco, had joked and laughed, had discussed the situation, theirs and our own, the country's and the world's. Comrades we had grown attached to, a rare band of stout Norwegians, all between twenty and twenty-five years old. They were shot down at ten o'clock yesterday.

If one could only cry one's fill over it; but even that is impossible. There's nobody to go to and cry, not even a little solitary place with a tree, a flower, or a little animal to confide in, a place where one could sit down alone and collect some poor bit of strength.

I thought I should be coming out to you the day before yesterday, Kari, yesterday, today, but something always got in the way. The idiotic Segment or the fool Gebecke or one greenhorn or another spoiled my chance every time. And all I wanted was just to see you a tiny bit, a few minutes, for you would give me back what I can absolutely feel being squeezed out of me to make room for something else, something I'm afraid of, something terrible: *hate*. I know that I could kill now, Kari, I could indeed, yes, and more, I *long* for it.

I was up at the Storm Prince's this afternoon to talk about that garden of his and walked round with him for half an hour. I went round fondling his neck with my eyes; in my imagination I had my hands round it, and I squeezed; I saw his face distorted with pain and turning from yellow-green to dark blue before he expired. I knew then that I wouldn't have let go until it was over. And I would have felt a satisfaction in it. The world would have been a devil the poorer. But I also knew that the reaction would come. And it did come, only because I was thinking such thoughts, so vividly. I have forgotten everything we talked about, every word, and when I got into my cell I just collapsed, exhausted in mind and body.

This morning I told Gebecke about what had happened. He laughed! Openly and un-restrainedly laughed! That round, fat, good-natured, queer, stupid man, whom I had taken for a human being, he laughed when he heard that eighteen of our friends were shot. I wouldn't believe my own eyes and ears. I repeated it; I asked in horror if he understood. "Jakob Friis is dead," I said, "shot down yesterday morning, the man you were in contact with every day, the fair, blue-eyed young man, he is shot, murdered."

I almost screamed it out. But Gebecke didn't bat an eyelash. He only kept the broad,

---

* Eighteen members of the "Ålesund Gang," including Jacob Friis (age twenty-five), Per Fillinger (age twenty-two), and Peter Young (age twenty-one) were executed April 30, 1942, at Trandum Woods, outside of Oslo, in reprisal for the deaths of two Gestapo officers killed April 26, 1942, in a fight with Norwegian agents in Telavåg, near Bergen. Another member of the gang had earlier been beaten to death during questioning, one was shot during reprisals in Trondheim, and four others served prison sentences. German reprisals for the Gestapo deaths were not limited to members of the Ålesund Gang: Terboven ordered all houses in Telavåg (more than three hundred) to be razed, all cattle shot or seized, all fishing boats sunk, all male inhabitants between sixteen and sixty-four (approximately 76) arrested and sent to Sachsenhausen, where many died, and all other inhabitants (approximately 260) interned in Norway. On October 10, 1954, Crown Prince Olav unveiled a memorial to those executed at Trandum that reads (in Norwegian, English, and Russian): "In the combat for freedom during the 1940–1945 war, 173 Norwegians, 15 Soviet subjects and 6 Britons were here in the woods of Trandum executed by the enemy." Nansen dedicated *From Day to Day* in part to the memory of Friis, Fillinger, and Young.

fat smirk on his face and said he had already realized that, but it was no concern of his. The wisest dodge, he said, that dull maggot, was to keep out of everything like that, so that it shouldn't concern one. "I've seen and heard worse things than that," he added with a rounding-off gesture. He withdrew the smile and with a brief "*also*" began to talk about the day's building program. Wrath shot up in me like a great wave; I stammered out something or other, I don't know what; my tongue curled up, I got nothing out, then I simply turned round and walked away from him. And he stood there gaping. He couldn't understand!

Is it really strange that they can make it work in Germany, this barbaric system, when these are the kind of people they have to deal with? These truncated wrecks of humanity! This is what they have become after nine or ten years in uniform, and even so he's one of the very best! God help the German people. God help us all!

SATURDAY, MAY 2, 1942 ■ And life goes on. A Saturday like all other Saturdays. A new camp chief has arrived. Obviously the idea is that the Storm Prince shall go; he was too incompetent. The accounts were in a muddle; he neglected his work all round; he went out shooting crows, magpies, and squirrels instead of seeing to the matters that were piling up on his desk. And no doubt someone complained of him, Balabanov it's being hinted, and probably the Segment too, who did whisper that he must go and that he *would* go. So he was right, even though he can hardly have had much share in it.

It's plain that the Storm Prince realized what was in the wind—indeed he may have had several warnings—but their only effect has been his increasing devilishness to the prisoners, his inordinate fury and its scurvy outcome. The trotting column, the bellowings, the confiscation of days off, the whipping of boys condemned to death—no, we don't lament that he is to go, but I'm afraid that we have also something to expect from the new one. He is named [Julius] Denzer and looks like a Prussian NCO in the full sense of the word. His entrance has been one prolonged bellow. He clearly thought the discipline slack, and has already introduced some "improvements." When he or another officer comes into a cell, the command is no longer to be the Norwegian "Attention!" (That's a poor word with no crack in it.) No, there is to be a roar of "*Achtung!*" [Attention!] until the walls nearly split. He has been giving demonstrations himself, round about in corridors and cells, and Erling Steen had to announce the decree on the line this evening.

And Denzer still has probably a little of everything on his mind; he looks ready to burst with devilment. Perhaps he may be one long disaster to us all. Perhaps after all we shall come to long for the devil we had before, if for nothing else then because at any rate he was lazy and slack about duty. This man has *not* a lazy air; his chest, his riding breeches, and his high boots look as if they would explode with sheer Prussian energy. He roars out all his sentences, has only one degree of power in his voice; it is adjusted roughly to a middle-sized concentration camp. However, as yet we don't know but that after all, under that swaggering deportment, he may have preserved something of the soldier's joviality, blunt and brutal, smelling of beer and honest sweat—the sort the books deal with.

After bedtime came shock number one. Orders went round to all the huts that tomorrow morning we would be wakened at half-past six and parade at eight o'clock, instead of being wakened at half-past eight with parade at ten, as is usual on Sundays. One can do with a night's sleep occasionally. But that's not all. From eight to half-past nine there is to be drill. *Punishment drill!* So it's to start in earnest here, too. We've heard about it from prisoners arriving from other camps, Ulven and Sydspissen,* where this fellow used to be *Lagerkommandant*. So now he's to trim up Grini. At present I am only curious, horribly curious; I can't work up a shudder. There may be others who are shuddering, old people who realize they won't be able to get through an hour and a half of hard drilling, and if it is to be the kind we've heard of, it will not be merely hard but devilish. That may be the idea. That may be how he's planning to write his name in the history of Grini. Well, let us wait.

SUNDAY, MAY 3, 1942 ■ And it was Sunday for God knows which time. Probably there is snow lying even yet in the north slopes of the woods where the wind is coming from. But the birch trees have made ready for springtime, a hint of green enfolds them, rounding their contours against the dark wood behind, and underfoot the grass is taking on fresh color. The yellow torches of the coltsfoot burn in clusters across the fields, and the white anemone is opening to the morning sun. Oddly enough there are no blue anemones here.† It has made a void; it is as though a part of spring were missing.

There are no blues to be seen unless one raises one's head and looks up at the sky. It almost seems as though there were a higher meaning in that. One needs some blue, therefore one looks up at the sky, and then it is so much easier to forget all the other voids, all the rest of this spring that is missing. For the spring heaven is high and boundless. It has nothing that shuts in, no barbed wire, no machine guns, no bayonets, only now and then a gray-black aircraft ventures up toward the blue, like a dirty mark. And high up there it is as though all partitions vanish, yes, even the partition between life and death melts away, and everything is united in a great flood of light. We meet the others again, they nod to us, and we know that the flood of light will reach down to us one day, if we only raise our heads and take it in, let the bright blue enter into our souls and cleanse them.

Roll call at eight o'clock this morning didn't turn out as we were fearing last night. It turned out to be quite ordinary—*caps off and on*—in short a display for the New Broom. Then important visitors arrived. God knows who they were, those fat, disgusting creatures in mufti who stepped out of a shining car and strutted along the front with the Prince, the New Broom, and the Segment. They had some of the worst physiognomies I've ever seen.

The roll call went off accurately and without a hitch. I believe it would have, even if it had been Quisling who stepped out of the car with his court. We can wait; we have time—a confounded lot of it, unfortunately.

The inspection of the huts was awaited with great suspense and anxiety, but came to nothing since it was carried out by the Segment. When he was received with the new "*Achtung!*" he only laughed and waved it off. He had been in to us beforehand, asking us for safety's sake to stick all our *Dreck* (crap) under the beds and make the huts look as neat as possible. "The gentlemen won't bend down," he said, "therefore they won't see what may be under the beds." He shook his head, laughed, and went away.

The Segment is getting more and more pally; more and more it is dawning on him what a gigantic swindle he is mixed up in, what an infamy, and he invariably takes our side. He says quite openly that he is far more at home among the prisoners than with

---

* Concentration camps in Os and Tromsø, Norway, respectively.
† In her portrait of growing up in the Nansen family, Odd Nansen's eldest sister, Liv, wrote, "Our greatest joy in the spring was to find the first wood anemone . . . for Mother. The one who did was always given a reward."

his own people, who all disgust him. "They're all getting crazier and crazier," he said yesterday.

In the midday rest I was summoned to the *Zugwachtmeister** up at the villa. He shut and locked the door, after looking carefully to see that there was no one out in the passage. Then he came up to me and stared me in the face.

He wasn't wearing his uniform—only his training shorts and shirt. The shirt was open at the neck; he had just been shaving; there was still a little shaving soap round his ears.

"You had a friend among those who were shot the other day," he said. "Isn't that right?"

"They were all my friends," I said.

"Yes, but you had a particular friend among them, hadn't you, the fair young man, the one who used to help to unload the trucks?"

"Yes," I said, "that was Jakob Friis; I came to think a lot of him; he was a good friend, a very good comrade."

Tears came into the man's eyes; he managed to stammer out that Jakob Friis had given him a farewell message for me. Jakob had known the last two hours that he was going to be shot, and had entrusted him, the *Zugwachtmeister*, with a message of thanks for everything and a radiant assurance of the certainty they all felt that Norway would be free again. There was no doubt in his mind that it would be so; he only felt it hard and painful to have no share in it. What was going to happen now, they had been long expecting; now he only wanted to say thank you for the company and comradeship. It had been a good time, among their friends at Grini. I was to tell them all and thank them.

Zugwachtmeister Tauber stared disconsolately before him; he had unburdened his heart. He was leaving today, he said, for the Eastern front, and so he had to give me this message, for he didn't know if we should ever meet again.

"I've felt this more than you may realize," he added, "but war is terrible."

He stood with bent head, gazing darkly at the floorboards. His arms hung slack and helpless by his sides—and he was breathing hard. Then suddenly he raised his head and looked at me.

"I hope too with all my heart that one day you'll set Norway free, and that you'll be free men again, free Norwegians in a free Norway, just as he wished," he said strongly, in an unwavering voice.

I made no reply for a long time. We both stood staring at the ground. At last I looked up at him; the tears were running down his cheeks. This big fellow, whom we called "the Ox"—whom all the prisoners had regarded as an especially vicious brute—he was crying, crying over a young Norwegian patriot and his comrades who died without a chance of doing what they had longed to do for their country and their people.

I don't remember now how we parted, *Zugwachtmeister* Tauber and I, but we parted friends. Strange that one should live through that as well—parting from an SS man in friendship. But after that meeting I had to find a place where I could be alone a while. I found it too—in a dark corner of the toolshed on the upper farm, where I sat for some time grappling with my thoughts.

---

* A junior rank in the local, or order, police (Ordnungspolizei, or Orpo) of Nazi Germany, equivalent to a rank between SS *Oberscharführer* and *Hauptscharführer*, or NCO. It was possible to hold dual ranks in both the Orpo and the SS.

I dare say a good while passed before I suddenly became aware that there were a great many things I should have asked the Ox about. Many important things. Had he been there when they were shot? Where were they shot? When? How? Oh heavens—what had I been thinking of, to let slip the opportunity.

I rushed out of the toolshed and went straight back up to the villa. *Zugwachtmeister* Tauber had gone. The prisoner who did his room was there, and told me so. He pointed through the window at the main entrance to Grini—and there, sure enough, I could see one of the big tarpaulin-covered trucks driving through the gateway and disappearing round the bend into the woods. Under the tarpaulin roof there were soldiers; the evening sun glittered on their rifles; they had their full kit and were going away forever. They were leaving for the Eastern front—someone thought he knew—and among them was my friend *Zugwachtmeister* Tauber. He would escape all the questions of which he certainly wasn't free to answer a single one. For it is "*grundsätzlich verboten*" [forbidden on principle] for any German soldier or officer to carry on an "*aussendienstliches Gespräch*" [off-duty conversation] with a prisoner. But even for a German there may be things that rank above prohibitions.

(Later)

No! No! No! This mustn't go on. We must proclaim it through the world, for all to hear. They must come and stop it. Good God, how long are we to wait? Aren't they coming soon? This afternoon twenty-six prisoners were allowed to see their Norwegian lawyers. Their case is coming up on Tuesday. They are men from Jæren, all of them young fellows, accused of planning a trip to England. The lawyers have prepared eighteen of them for the worst.*

One tragedy succeeds the other. No sooner have the Germans committed one outrage than they roll up their shirt sleeves and start in on the next. This time they obviously haven't the external pretext for dropping all proceedings and shooting them down straight off. A germ of hope for their escaping some time tomorrow died a sudden death tonight, when all the twenty-six were assembled and locked into a hut with a guard at the door.

This is German chivalry!

Some say that the *Wehrmacht* will intervene if it gets too bad. It has long been too bad, and have we seen anything of intervention by the *Wehrmacht*? Have any of the lofty generals raised a finger to prevent infamies?†

And yet not all the German people are like that. We know it, but we don't care to know it now. It just can't be helped. The mere sound of the German language will excite loathing for a long time to come. And yet all the same there are human hearts beating under the uniform jackets, as with the *Zugwachtmeister* Tauber just now. Poor man, I

---

* Eighteen men from the west coast village of Jæren had attempted to escape to England twice in September 1941 and twice were thwarted by engine problems. Word of the failed attempts eventually leaked, and all eighteen, together with eight others who had helped with the preparations, were arrested. All but one of the eighteen who had attempted the crossing were sentenced to death in May (the sole exception was instead sentenced to prison on account of his youth).

† Nikolaus von Falkenhorst, the commander-in-chief of German forces in Norway (1940–1944) was sentenced to death for violating the rules of war by implementing Hitler's so-called Commando Order (which required the immediate execution of captured commandos, even those in uniform, in contravention of the Geneva Convention). His sentence was later commuted to twenty years, and he was released in 1953 after serving only seven years due to poor health. Falkenhorst lived another fifteen years, dying in 1968 at age eighty-three.

think I pity him and his comrades more than Jakob Friis. What sort of achievement do *they* have to show?

On a surveying job the other day one of the guards told us that several of his comrades had volunteered for the Russian front. They wanted to get away from here, they couldn't stand it any longer. And they didn't want to go to Germany, for if Germany lost the war it would still mean the end of everything and nothing to live for. Then, he said, far better to die young. And it was plain that he fully realized that Germany would lose, and that he really wished to die and be forgotten. His life was anyhow so ruined. They are grown men, most of the guards, not greenhorns like the last, and they know what they're talking about.

Perhaps it was with such a company of volunteers for the Eastern front that "the Ox" went off the other day?

THURSDAY, MAY 7, 1942 ■ Some days have passed with no opportunity for writing—bad days. The twenty-six men from Jæren are going to and from the court-martial. Early in the morning they go off to Oslo in two cars with an outsize police guard, chained together. Then toward evening they come home, and are kept locked up until the next morning. There is no means of having a real talk with them, only a brief, stolen interchange now and then. From that it appears that they are pleased with the proceedings so far.

Poor lads, they probably see a gleam of light in everything. The mere fact that the proceedings are more or less on the customary civilized model, they see as a dawning hope that perhaps after all . . .

I was in Oslo the other day with Liwa, a driver I already knew. Liwa is a decent man, honest and faithful to his duty. He is a convinced Nazi in his primitive, naive, but stiff-necked way. He has made out something which he thinks good and right in Nazism, and sticks to it like grim death. He knows nothing, but then he doesn't pretend to know anything. He knows only what he has himself experienced and what Hitler has told him. The first has set a brand on his soul; he is a Sudeten German, who didn't have a very good time in Czechoslovakia after the last war. The second he believes like the Bible, or rather instead of the Bible.

We talked a lot on the trip. He likes a chat, but if we get onto questions that demand a more personal view of the meaning and object of existence, he says frankly and honestly that he has never been in the way of thinking about that, and wouldn't be able to discuss it with a man who has "been to college." It's not much use explaining that such things have little to do with academic studies.

The truth he does know is palpable enough. He has a wife and three children. They must be supported. He must earn a living for them and himself. Hitler will look after that. In the old days it was hard enough. The Czechs took the jobs from the Sudetens; they were being pushed out more and more. Hitler was their savior.

Had he got any work from Hitler so far, except war service? No, of course not, but he would afterward, afterward everything would be arranged for the best, there would be joy and gladness! Was he really so sure of that? Didn't he think the war would squander so much of Germany's strength and wealth that there would be too little left to rebuild what the war had pulled down? No. War was merely wholesome. A nation without a war at proper intervals would perish. War made men; soldiering made healthy people with strong bodies! Didn't he think that people could do something for world development even if they hadn't such outstanding muscles in their legs and arms? No, he thought that first the body must be right. Therefore he had an inveterate distrust of everything intellectual. All the learned men he had ever seen looked wretched, he said, held themselves badly and wore glasses. Well, but the new era would be different, and the learned man, too.

And so we talked on, but it was and remained hopeless. He wasn't to be budged out of his little ready-made *Weltanschauung* [world view].

All the same one can't but feel a certain liking for him when one gets to know him a little. I helped him to buy presents for his children. He was touching when I charmed a doll out of unknown hiding places for his five-year-old daughter. He followed the dressing and undressing of the naked little celluloid body, performed, to demonstrate the marvel, by the lady behind the counter, as though it had been his own little daughter she was dressing and undressing. Warmth came into his eyes, which were assuredly straying far away, home to the wife and little ones. He didn't care about the price, and was happy, joyful, and grateful when we strolled out of the shop, he with the doll under his arm.

He had tried in a lot of shops to get a doll like that, but had been told everywhere that they were sold out. And he knew why well enough, but forgot it in his joy at having the doll, which he meant to give his daughter in a month or two, when he got his leave.

We also talked about the eighteen who had been shot, that is, I talked. He listened to me, gravely and in silence, and I could see he was affected. When I had finished, he only said, "Look here, Nansen, I can't speak about things like that. You mustn't talk to me about them."

Kari wasn't in Oslo that day at the appointed time and place. Our friends had said I might be "shadowed" and she didn't want to expose me to any risk. It was a fearful disappointment. I had been looking forward like a child to seeing her again. For more than a week, a fearful week, I had been looking forward to it and longing for it. I was in such heartfelt need of it. Time after time this expedition had been planned, and time after time I was disappointed because something got in the way. It was as though I only kept myself up with the thought of seeing Kari again, only for a little while. Now there I was in the town with a driver who would have allowed it, and she didn't come.

I made myself very useful in the town; a heap of business was dispatched. I delivered Robert's violin to be mended; the Segment had given me permission. I brought back a substantial pile of music, and various materials for the joinery, which it's usually impossible to get hold of. When everything was dispatched, it turned out that Liwa had orders to call at Lysaker station for a cask of train oil.* A wild hope blazed up in me. Perhaps I could get word to Kari. First we went to the stationmaster's office, and I managed to drop a hint. If only we took a little time, the children at any rate would have time to cycle down from Polhøgda.† And we did take just that long, for we had to make up our minds to leave the cask where it was. It was too heavy, we had too much on the truck, and there were too few of us to manage the weight.

But Kari arrived in time, and Siri. It was wonderful, even though it was only a little

---

*   Train oil, or whale oil, is oil obtained from the blubber of various whale species. It was widely used in Norway at the time; immediately prior to the war, whaling employed forty thousand Norwegians.
†   Polhøgda is presently the home of the research foundation Fridtjof Nansen Institute.

glimpse outside the goods office, a fleeting nervous minute, for Liwa didn't like its going on there in the public view. But it was Kari, and she looked well; she smiled that sure, calm smile of hers, but wasn't there anxiety in her eyes? She asked me so sweetly to be careful; she must have been agitated by all this dreadful business going on. Oh, if only I could have set her mind at rest, but it wasn't possible on the square outside the Lysaker goods office, with ten children standing round staring, realizing what was up. Siri was radiantly well and fit. I didn't get a sight of Eigil, unfortunately, and Marit was in bed with a cold.

FRIDAY, MAY 8, 1942 ■ Today there's only one thing to write of, one single thing in all our minds. For eighteen of the twenty-six the death sentence is proposed, as the lawyers said it would be. Six of those eighteen are proposed for death twice over, and for them there is not the faintest hope but in time. It can't be less than a month before the sentences are carried out, but I suppose we daren't hope for an Allied victory within that time. The proposal for the rest was up to fifteen years' hard labor.

That, then, is the prosecuting counsel's report, after what I don't doubt was a brilliant defense by the Norwegian lawyers, especially Leif Rode.* Normally there would be hope that the sentence will not accord with the report, but will be milder. Here that hope is excluded, because the prosecutor also acts as judge. It is like that in a German police court, and this is a police court, not a court-martial. Sentence is to be pronounced tomorrow morning. They are all to go into the town again to hear it read. Will they be coming back? No one knows. Perhaps they are to spend the time of waiting at Grini? It would be a new arrangement, but then it's even a new arrangement that they should come back here every night after the court proceedings. We are hoping they will be here to the last, for if so we can at least take a little care of them on the q.t.

At supper Robert [Andersen] brought word that Anton Bø, one of the Jæren lads condemned to death, had sent for me; he would like a word with me through the door of the cell where they are all locked up together. At the same time Robert asked if we couldn't sing and play a little for them this evening, at any rate in the passage outside their door, if we weren't allowed in. We were not allowed in. The *Zugführer* refused, but dubiously gave us leave to play out in the passage. It would unquestionably have been his duty to refuse that as well.

It was an unforgettable conversation I had with Anton Bø through the keyhole of the death room.

I only got out a word or two. It wasn't as if he needed anything; he was the one with something to give. And it wasn't the hectic speech of a doomed man, with nerves unstrung and judgment disorganized, nor a strained effusion got by heart. No, it was a sedate man's plain, tranquil thoughts, for which he found concise, good expressions. When I asked if there wasn't any message I could take for him or anything at all I could do for him, he only said, "No, all of us have everything worked out and settled, so just let them know the truth. We'll get through it fine! We won't so much as blink! Say that from us, Nansen!"

Later in the evening I asked him to write down what he had said to me. He answered

---

* An Olympic rower, sports official, lawyer, and writer, during the war Rode (1885–1967) often acted as defense counsel in German courts-martial. He was also active in preventing the Nazification of Norwegian sports. After the war Rode served as defense counsel for collaborators and others accused of treason in the legal purge that followed liberation.

that he didn't remember, but he would try. Here it is, on this crumpled scrap of paper, written in a clumsy, childish hand with an illicit stump of pencil.

To him that finds this. Please write a letter home to all my brothers and sisters and dad and mother and say the truth that I took it quite calm, and put what's right besides. The address home is

Ole K. Bø. Nærbø, Jæren

And one to my dear lass, I have gone with her about three years so it's not good to part like this, so write the truth it was for Norway. The address is frk. Berta Halland, Hognestad, Jæren.

Anton Bø

On the other side is written:

For our liberty and laws for Norway's sake it was. That Norway will be free though we fall all of us in here are full sure of that, and a day of reckoning will come and then we all hope them that are left will settle up the right way where it's wanted. [? This word is illegible.] The worst I see these days is the women, they walk about in the court yonder, they walk about and laugh at us as we sit waiting for our death sentence but they are forgiven for my part, for you know the woman fell first in paradise and yet was forgiven. Then we are sure and certain of our God and put all trust in him. Good luck to all them that are coming over, tell them not to go to work like these here.

*Anton Bø, Nærbø, born 29/9/1922.**

After my conversation with Bø, Robert [Andersen] began to play, and it was grand. I'm sure that none who were there will ever be able to forget that concert in the passage outside the condemned men's room. One behind another down both sides of the passage their comrades stood in silence. And there behind the door they were sitting, close together doubtless, to hear better, and still, dead still! I sang a couple of songs, for I had promised Anton. Now I was almost repenting; I felt I couldn't get through it, but the second song didn't go too badly; I recovered my strength and calm, which for a while had left me completely. For that was just after the conversation with Anton, and I could think of nothing else. But I was glad I sang all the same; perhaps it gave the men inside there a little pleasure at any rate, a reminder of their comrades and our evenings down in the church and of the time gone by, which after all had been bright and good.

Robert played again: "Ola, Ola—I Lay Down So Late," then one got a lump high up in one's throat—"Solveig's Song"†—and then at the end "God Bless Thee, Norway, My Fair Land!" We stood bolt upright while Robert played through these verses. We dared not join in, it was forbidden, it could only spoil things for everyone, for the men inside as well, but the words burned into our hearts just the same, and Norway can never have

---

* Executed May 21, 1942, age nineteen.

† Both songs by Norwegian composer Edvard Grieg (1843–1907). The final lines of *Solveig's Song* are: "God give you strength, wherever in the world you go! /God give you joy, when you stand before his judgment seat! /Here I'll wait until you come again /and if you are waiting up above, there we'll meet, my love!"

received a finer, more thrilling tribute than when the men in there struck up the national anthem.

They were not singers, and they began too high, so that it went right up into falsetto, but never have I been more affected by that glorious hymn. It was as if I hadn't known it until then. Every time I hear it again I shall think of the stalwart young Norwegians who sang it in the death cell and who put all their souls into it, all they had to live for.

Here I am again in the doctor's office with my tallow candle behind a screen. But I don't think I can write of anything else but what is taking up all my thoughts. I should have liked really to put down a few words about various changes in the office, new building foremen, a new accountant, and so on. But after all the whole thing is so unimportant. What does it matter if building superintendents fly into a rage and go berserk, or if the new SS *Oberscharführer* and accounts chief demands the impossible with threats of punishment drill and other devilishness? The whole thing is merely ludicrous and petty.

The new accounts chief, Herr Koopmann, has obviously chosen me as a special target. Several times he has been after me, but with no great result. The other day he thought up a refined vengeance, because I was always ready with my alibi when he asked me why I was here or there, or doing this or that. He came to me in the office and gave me a short and simple order to provide him with two brief cases, of the same size and quality as one, belonging to a prisoner, which I borrow when I go into the town. I explained that it was impossible to buy that kind now. He interrupted me and said nothing was *impossible*; that word had been erased from the German language.

"Consequently, what's your answer, when I give you an order?"

I replied that if the order was for that kind of brief case, then it was an impossible order to carry out. They're not to be had; they're sold out—gone long ago! He interrupted again, threateningly, and said it was obvious I needed some drill with him. But then he got an idea. He demanded a German dictionary. We had one—it was Brockhaus—and it was given him. He was right; it hadn't the word impossible. It had only: to become impossible—*sich unmöglich zu machen*. (Then say the Germans are not thorough.)

"For example," said he, "when you have been in prison a year, you've become *impossible* in good society. You're not the man you were. No one will have any more to do with you. Do you see what I mean?"

Of course I saw, and was enchanted that I could tell him so with conviction.

He wriggled his abnormally fat and wobbly backside and waddled out of the room with an air of having given us something very profound and difficult to think over, something that had never occurred to us, something that he, in his sagacity and shrewdness, had put his finger on.

A new building superintendent is coming (number four); he is to be over Gebecke and have his room. Then Gebecke and the others will have the surveyors' room, and that will be that. The hut is too small, I said so from the first, but at that time it was too big, they said.

SUNDAY, MAY 10, 1942 ■ It went as everyone expected. The death sentences have been pronounced, seventeen of them. One was commuted to a milder punishment. I saw them coming back, chained together two and two, under the escort of a dozen soldiers with steel helmets and submachine guns, as usual. At their head was Anton Bø with another man. Anton Bø smiled and nodded to me; so did most of them as they were going by.

No one who saw them would ever have imagined they were coming back from the court where most of them had heard the reading of their death sentence. It was almost more than I could do to smile back.

Midnight, and this must be got away tomorrow, if there's a trip to Oslo. Good night, Kari. Au revoir!

MONDAY, MAY 11, 1942 ■ Of course there was no trip to Oslo. Instead I was informed that henceforth no prisoners will be allowed to go into town under any circumstances. It was a new regulation, and Gebecke, who told me about it, was sorry, but could do nothing. Well, so perhaps that period is over, which for me took so much of its color from those Oslo trips. And this is the beginning of a new one. The worst part is that now most likely I shall see nothing of Kari. The so-called "regulation" monthly visits are so uncertain. They seem to depend entirely on the Gestapo people's whims and the wives' audacity. But Kari is not deficient in that respect, and besides it won't be so long now.

Otherwise there's really no need to mind about the trips to Oslo. They were nerve racking, and perhaps it was lucky that "fate" stepped in and put the brake on, while the going was good. Now and then I could have envied those who were safe in their jobs at Grini and did nothing but absorb food and news, news and food.

My particular friend Koopmann, whom we have named "Venus-bottom" (his backside is massive and feminine, like the man in general), is always giving me fresh commissions. I am to draw this, that, and the other for him, and to procure him, as I said, a number of objects impossible to buy. I am to draw him a chaise longue, and it is to be done by Monday morning. I was told this at midday on Saturday. At the same time he told me that on Monday morning I must have finished the drawings for the enlargement of the upper farm, where he and the other German building men live. A room with an open fireplace, a bedroom, and another living room. The work was to start on Monday morning and be done in two or three weeks. Not a word! It's an order!

It is not nice to think of the men up in 412 [the parachute room]. The waiting time has begun. High up behind the windowpanes we can see their faces, when we are parading on the square. But they smile and wave!

At another window of the main building stands an old man staring out into the darkness every night. It is old [Elling] Sikveland.* He stands there waiting for Torgeir—his son who is condemned to death—to be taken away one night, among the rest.

A lot of old prisoners have gone to No. 19 to be photographed. There is talk of a new big transport to Germany. Many of us have already been photographed, so it's impossible to form any idea of who would be included in a transport if it took place. (I have been photographed myself, for that matter.) All of us regard the German journey as the next worst that can happen to us. The atmosphere of the camp is therefore gloomy, but we try to smile and take it cheerfully. On the whole with grand success—especially for those who are in the danger zone, oddly enough. It is as though the proximity of disaster gave unknown strength and fresh courage!

Now it is nearly two o'clock and I have talked myself out. When shall I see you again,

---

* Released May 19, 1943.

Kari? A lawful visit is drawing on apace now, you must manage it. This place is so quiet that I can hear your heart beating.

TUESDAY, MAY 12, 1942 ■ Churchill has said the war will be over in the autumn! That's the best of today's news. Did Churchill really say so, I wonder, or did he only say something to the effect that it might be over in the autumn, or perhaps merely remark in some connection that *if* the war is over in the autumn. . . ? It's not like Churchill to make that kind of prophecy; he isn't in the habit of embellishing and giving false hopes. His motto has been plain and downright: Blood, sweat, and tears! And he has lived up to it. So if he said so, then, yes, the war will be over in the autumn. He knows what he is talking about, I'm convinced of that. In private I am fancying he said so, and am jubilantly happy about it, but I'm aware that it is a repression of my natural skepticism and emphatic doubt of its being true. One has to do that sometimes, and today I needed it badly.

The day has been so gloomy, for no reason at all. On such days everything goes wrong. Suddenly you catch yourself getting worked up about the silliest things and the big and little shortcomings of your fellow men, for which normally you don't give a hoot, because it's really none of your business. Days like that are no fun. Then one feels the need for a little solitude, but that's impossible in this confounded Grini. All round the clock one is compelled to live in a swarm of fellow creatures, tall and short, thick and thin, stupid and not so stupid, clever and not so clever, congenial and not so congenial. One gets to know all of them by heart, at least nearly all of them. One blesses the quiet ones, one curses the noisy swaggerers, and longs for solitude without a sound.

But I have this time at night in the doctor's office, and I long for it every day, as I used to long to have the architect's office to myself after bedtime.

Now, as ever, tireless music is booming out from the guardroom down below, but it finally becomes a kind of symbol of silence. For it is playing all day as well, but then one can't hear it for all the uproar and to-do. In the evening when the clock is moving toward eleven, it comes out plainer and plainer as one after another of the men falls asleep and conversation dies away. It is the Grini silence approaching, and after eleven it is there. It embraces also the footsteps of the guard out on the square, the tramping of his colleagues up and down the corridor below and their running feet on the stairs. It has always been a mystery to me what they're doing.

So Churchill has said the war will be over in the autumn, and so it hasn't been a bad day.

Erling [Steen] has been in Oslo today; he was called to his old mother's sickbed, it may have been his last sight of her.

THURSDAY, MAY 14, 1942 ■ Up in 412 the seventeen condemned men are sitting staring at the spring through the bars. Two guards are sitting at the door of their cell; no one is allowed to talk with the men inside; no one may see them. Not even old Sikveland, whose son is among them, condemned to death twice over. The old man is toiling away at an appeal to the German authorities; his view is that his son and the others have been condemned on false premises, that they have been condemned for things they haven't done.

I met him out on the square yesterday. He seized hold of me, must have a talk with me; he believed that I could help him. He told me about his son; the boy had fought in the war, had fought hard for his country. He had been accused of plundering the bodies of German soldiers. The old man hissed with indignation and contempt when he spoke of that. His Torgeir do such a thing! No indeed, he was a good lad, Torgeir, and a good Norwegian, and so he believed were all the others, he didn't know them all.

He told me of a plan, well, perhaps he shouldn't talk about it, but he felt that I ought to know. All the parents of these lads would come to Oslo and try and explain to the Germans that it was a mistake. They might be on their way now. Did I think it would help at all? Did I know how long it would be before we heard any more? I told him it was bound to take a good while yet, for the case must first go to Berlin for ratification, then come back here, and then wait for the usual respite for appeal, of ten or twelve days. It was bound to take a month, all in all, before the sentence could be executed.

It was painful to stand there trying to comfort a desperate father, when I didn't myself believe there was any hope.

A male nurse came and called Sikveland away; he is in the hospital now. That brought the conversation to an end. He would look me up again, he shouted as he went off.

The Storm Prince is slipping more and more out of our daily life. It seems certain now that he is to retire and leave the scepter to Denzer. We only see him occasionally walking round with his gun, shooting magpies and crows and perhaps squirrels. Then he goes round "busying" himself a bit with the farm work. No doubt it's a kind of job he has been given to retire on.

SATURDAY, MAY 16, 1942 ■ Everything seems brighter again. I can't actually find any good and sufficient reason, but it's as though there were more smiles around one, more sun and warmth. Perhaps because tomorrow will be the 17th of May.* *May 17th!* It will certainly be a queer place and a queer way to celebrate it. But the tactful vigilance and chivalry of the Germans have not been wanting. They intend us to work tomorrow, first and foremost because it's the 17th of May and second because it's Sunday. But they can't take May 17th away from us, all the same.

We have now four building superintendents, in addition to Venus, as he is called now for the sake of brevity and propriety. They only get in the way and hold up the building work which it's their job to promote. And that is no exaggeration.

Their greatest pleasure is to walk round the sites, pointing and playing the superintendent. Each of them does it in his own way. Gebecke prefers to hang around the circular saw, looking for a chance to demonstrate his accomplishments in that sphere. The business of pointing stakes, especially, he finds as tempting today as two months ago. Unhappily for him we don't point them now; they went too far down into the clay, so now we cut them right off. We can use the saw for that too, as we have it. On such occasions Gebecke is on the spot; he sets the saw going and cuts the first dozen logs himself. Indeed he may stand there for hours dreaming of the saw in Hannover and of Solveig and the son she is carrying, who is one day to be a master sawyer, while Papa Gebecke himself sits on the veranda in the owner's villa with his beer and his cigar. And he cuts log after log, humming the saw's tune: *krrrtj—krrrjt! bssssitj bsss-it!* according as the logs are thicker or thinner.†

---

*   May 17 (Syttende Mai) is Norway's Constitution Day, its most important national holiday, celebrating the adoption of the Norwegian Constitution in 1814.

†   Nansen's description may have been informed by Robert Frost's poem "Out, Out—" (first published in 1916): "And the saw snarled and rattled, snarled and rattled /As it ran light, or had to bear a load."

For Gebecke there isn't any war. He won't hear of it. It doesn't concern him. He is a *Bauführer* [construction foreman], not a soldier. The only thing is the revolver. He has been longing for a revolver in his belt the whole time. He had nothing but a measly bayonet, that's all a *Rottenführer* gets. He who was the best revolver shot in Hannover. He who turned the very general himself pale with admiration when he got his fourth bull's-eye running at the military exercises in nineteen hundred and umpteen, and thereby saved the company's undying honor, and was rewarded by the general in person with a week's *Urlaub* [leave].

But *now* Gebecke has a revolver. A ponderous barker in a black leather case swings from the *Gott-mit-uns* belt out on the slope of his fat stern.* He's got a new cap as well. Doubtless he thought a lot of that too, though he may be unwilling to admit it, so after all there are certain features of the soldier and warrior worth annexing. It's not everyone who has a cap like that, with a wire-framed roof, a straight and shiny peak and those broad eaves round it! No indeed, not even an *Obersturmführer* has a smarter cap. To be sure he has an extra couple of buttons here or there, an invisible little oakleaf on the shoulder or a little stitch of silver thread in his neckband, but on the whole, taking him from a distance and a bit sideways, Gebecke looks just as smart. Solveig will see no difference, for example, and the bigger his revolver the nearer she will think he's got to the rank of general.

And then he's been wounded too. Not *everyone* has the sword badge on his left breast pocket. It tells of his bravery in Finland, where he was in the war, and where he saw a Finn cut the throats of four Russians and cut out their Adam's apples as souvenirs. Yes, indeed, Gebecke knows war and warriors. He smiles a pale, omniscient smile at the thought, but thrusts it far, far away. He has done his military service. For the rest of the time he will be a *Bauführer* at Grini. He thought he was going to be *Bauleiter* and in chief command of all building work, but alas, the plump *Rottenführer* has been superseded. A new *Bauleiter* has arrived, a man with one more button on his shoulder strap. He is named Jantzen and is descended from Norwegian Vikings, he told me. He is quite young, younger than Gebecke, hardly thirty, and knows just as little about building, perhaps still less.

Jantzen has helped himself to the biggest room in the new office hutment, the one that was to be used as a storeroom. The store clerk, Bråthen, now hangs out in a room in the shed behind and under the barn.† It has neither light nor air nor space for human beings, but it will have to do, the *Bauleiter* must have a room, he can't make do with the one that was intended for him. It was too small, far, far too small. *Nein*, he must have space; besides his desk, there must be a little suite with table and armchairs by the south window, and on the floor there is a carpet already down, and in the windows there are curtains already up.

On parade one day they advertised for a decorator. A man reported who had done such work, by his own account. He hung up the curtains and placed the furniture and carpet. Now the room has a genteel appearance, but it's not finished yet. Jantzen called me in yesterday and asked if I could paint some little decorations in the door panels, Norwegian subjects, Vikings or something like that? Yes, I could do that all right, and I got to work.

I sketched a Viking ship with Vikings on board and a gush of foam round the bow.

---

* *Gott-mit-uns* [God with us] was a slogan inscribed on the belt buckles of Wehrmacht soldiers in World War II.
† Gunnar Bråten was released January 16, 1943, rearrested September 21, 1944, and remained in prison in Norway until the end of the war.

It fell on good ground. It was *sehr schön* [very fine]. Then I sketched a brownie* standing crying with an empty beer jug in his fist. That was *sehr schön* too. Then I sketched a troll, also with a brownie cap, grasping his knotted club until the knuckles whiten, and shaking his fist at the man sitting at the high table. It was no good; *that* was *sehr schön*, too.

Heaven knows what I shall think of next time; obviously I can let myself go far without his understanding. For Jantzen is a simple man, very simple, and his mind is a very simple mind.

The building works, incidentally, are of no interest to him at the moment. He must get settled first, and his demands on his environment are not small. At the time when he was a hodman, I suppose he had more than one peep into a boss's office, and ever since the image has haunted him, until now at last he is on the threshold of his own boss's office. Hitler has obtained it for him. *Heil Hitler!* That just shows them, it isn't necessary to be an architect or engineer. *He* made good, with nothing but his bare fists and the common sense that was his dower in the cradle. It's all nonsense, all that studying up hill and down dale. It's a bit of damned snobbery, a little clique that does it just to show off and take all the good jobs in the community from those who really ought to have them. *Heil Hitler!*

"Paint decorations, Nansen; it might be nice too if you painted a house being built, scaffolding and a foundation wall, and then a building superintendent standing pointing, with a drawing in his hand. *Nicht wahr?* [Eh?] *Gutes Motiv, nicht wahr?* [Good subject, eh?] *Sehr schön!* Try that, won't you?

"Or again tools lying crosswise, composed into a decoration, that would be very nice and original. It's a building office, *nicht?* [no?] That kind of thing would just suit a building superintendent's office, as a symbol of his work or of the work he's in charge of, *nicht?*"

Ehling is a good deal older, and a sly fox. He is the eldest of the whole bunch, and the only thing he has in common with them is his taste for beer and his imperfect knowledge of building. He is a civilian, brown all over. In him the predominant feature is the belly. It is enormous, and wholly original in shape. It doesn't start until about the height of his navel, but then it makes up for lost time. It goes straight out. I can imagine the navel hole pointing directly upward, so that for example it would do as the socket for a flagpole. Far out in space the belly makes a sharp turn inward again, and hurries back to rejoin the body at a place where it intrudes distractingly upon physiology, and makes the simplest and most needful things impossible.

"I could tell you a lot about myself," he said the other day, when he had smuggled in to me a bulky parcel of cigarettes, letters, and other things. "A lot about myself I could tell you, politically you understand, in the old days. But never mind, take this and hide it away and burn the letter. It says Ehling somewhere, *nicht?* So it had better be gotten rid of. That kind of letter mustn't have my name in it. You must promise to burn it when you've read it, *nicht?*"

He is not a soldier and doesn't care a straw for the whole regime, but really does take an interest in building questions, even though he doesn't know much about them. He tries to do his job, works hard and runs around until that belly of his jumps up and down

---

* According to Norwegian legend, brownies are good-natured little spirits, akin to fairies. Their name is said to derive from the brown skin they develop from exposure to all elements. Brownies typically appear only at night, to perform good deeds or play harmless pranks. They are rarely seen by humans.

in mighty bounces. He cross-questions me and takes advice, and if I go up to his room, where he sleeps with Gebecke, Venus, and Reinitz, I get half a pint from him, if there's no one else there.

Ehling is one of my hopes now that prisoners are forbidden to go into Oslo. For that matter Gebecke is also usable. Yesterday he came back from the town with a parcel and a letter. I was to have these because I got them a calculating machine and other office equipment. I'm blessed if Venus wasn't in it too; I noticed that from a remark to Gebecke about the parcel Nansen was to have. Well, I can't make any of them out really, but the whole thing is getting to be pure farce.

No sooner have the prisoners themselves been deprived of any chance of getting in anything at all, no sooner have new regulations arrived in sheaves, all designed to tighten the control and restrict the prisoners in all directions, than the Germans themselves take over the smuggling of tobacco and foodstuffs, and moreover act as postmen for highly illegal letters, with the cheeriest accounts of "projects" outside and of the "temperature of the building market" in general.

Indeed I have yet another man in my pay. This one is a *Wehrmacht* driver. He is ungovernable, frankly dangerous. He will do anything whatever. One just has to take care not to ask too much of him. Yesterday he was at Polhøgda. He had two sections of this diary and a letter for Kari. He got a letter and parcel to bring back and was frantic with enthusiasm. He must have had a present for himself too, and was set on going there again with no matter what.

Tonight I have been up in the parachute room with Robert [Andersen], entertaining the new hostages from Telavåg near Bergen.

This is the story: There were two Norwegians living in Telavåg who had come over from England. The cunning fishermen said they knew nothing about them or what they were doing. However, the Gestapo got on their track and sent six or seven men out there. It came to a scuffle and two Gestapo agents were shot, along with one of the Norwegians. The other died later of his wounds.

The Norwegian fisherman who had housed these men was taken into custody, and I should think his fate is sealed. He is in Bergen county jail. Then the rest of the population, men, women and children, were lodged in a school in Fana. Next, the Germans set to on the houses in Telavåg. Three of them were blown up while the arrested men were still there; they saw it with their own eyes. Later, it's reported, the Germans blew up and set fire to all the houses, about a hundred and fifty in all. Four hundred and fifty people made up the whole population. As far as is known they were all arrested. Sixty-six have arrived here. Two of them are weak-minded and one has cancer of the lungs. The women, children under sixteen and men over sixty are interned in the school in Fana.

All the breadwinners are fishermen, poor fishermen, who are now staring into a completely black future. All they possessed has been burned up. It was a tragic audience that gathered round us in the parachute room when we began. But as we played and sang, luster came into their eyes. It was as though they were reviving. When we had finished, the eldest of them came forward and thanked us. He grasped us warmly by the hand and said this had been their salvation. Yes, hearty thanks to all of us, and a couple of big tears rolled down his cheeks. Several came up and shook hands. One could see that it had really meant something to them, and that our entertainment had broken the ice.

SUNDAY, MAY 17, 1942 ■ It's best to forget the 17th of May when you are a Norwegian shut up in a German concentration camp and struggling to make the time vanish, so that it may be the 18th as quickly as possible. So in a way it was no bad thing to have a working day today. But work as I might, and struggle as I might to get the time, the confounded time, to pass, it wasn't possible to forget that it was May 17th. It was in the air, the clear, fresh spring air blowing from the southwest. The sun shone from early morning; the birds were singing, the birches sprouting so that one could absolutely stand and watch how their pale green tops became denser and more copious hour by hour. They flamed against the dark wood behind, which hasn't rightly awakened yet.*

Southward the landscape opens out; there is no dark, grave forest barrier. The sallows too are beginning to dress for the party, as they stand by the spring becks winding down between the fields toward the sea—far, far out yonder. I truly believe we can make out a streak of that too, a silver streak just under the light blue ridge on the horizon. And the mind goes on to seek the glittering fjord, with its islands one behind another, right out to the last skerries† and then still farther out, to the open sea.

And behind rises the blue landscape, up from the ocean and from ridge to ridge with green floes in among them, and with dark and light brown fields like patchwork between the copses and rocky outcrops, and at the back of all, the mountains stand against the spring sky, pale blue with shining flecks of white. It is as though the eye were following the mind upon its free journey. And one sails on along the coast, gazing in rapture at the wonderland within. A rush of warmth goes through one. This is all Norway. And further yet, further north, mountains, fjords, and parishes as far as the land extends, as far as there are Norwegians living, struggling to live, and welcoming each new summer with light and gladness and the spring paean in the heart.

That is the content of the 17th of May; so it has always been, and so it will always be. No one can change it, least of all these Germans, who have no conception of it.

And no one can deprive me of today's tour of Norway; I've been round the whole country and absorbed it with the spring air. I saw it bathed in spring sunshine, beautiful as never before. No, I take it back that one should forget the 17th of May because one's in a German concentration camp. On the contrary, one should remember it and keep it more intensely and fervently than ever.

The men from Jæren up in 412 think the same, I'm sure of that. Twenty-six men shut up in one room, seventeen of them condemned to death, denied every favor; they may not even have a doctor, though several of them need one. Yet all the same they are keeping the 17th of May, these lads from Jæren. The day of liberty! What a day of liberty!

THURSDAY, MAY 21, 1942 ■ Just as I was going in to dinner the day before yesterday Claffy came for me. I was wanted in the *Vermittlung*. *Bauleiter* Jantzen was with him. I thought it must be something about those confounded cigarettes I'd had from Gebecke. The inner office in the *Vermittlung* was packed, as though for a really big meeting. There

---

* In a letter written almost exactly thirteen years earlier, on May 22, 1939, Fridtjof Nansen wrote a friend, "Here from my window in my tower I see the maidenly birches in their bridal veils against the dark pine wood; there is nothing like the birch in the spring."

† Skerries are "islands that stretch by the tens of thousands along Norway's coast. The smaller skerries are mainly bare rock, the larger are fair-sized islands with grass and human habitation."

was Kunz and Schwartz and Claffy and Jantzen and the Segment and a whole lot more. They were waiting for his highness Denzer. My insignificance stood straight as a candle against the wall, cap in hand. Denzer came rushing in like a fresh gale; he swept through the little room as though it had been the throne room in Versailles, and sat down at the desk. He turned straight to me, when he had got hold of the letter opener in one hand like a kind of scepter, and the paperweight in the other, as an orb.

"*Sie sind Herr Nansen, nicht wahr?* [You are Herr Nansen, eh?] You have written a song here in Grini, haven't you? And what a song!"

He was looking at a paper in front of him. Obviously it was my poor little song, and I asked to see it. He shoved it over, and I confessed I had written it.

"Yes, it is already established that you are the author, my dear sir. When did you write it?"

"In January."

"How long have you been in Grini?"

"About four months, since January."

"Yet you are an intellectual, aren't you—an intelligent man?"

"I am an architect."

"You are the son of Fridtjof Nansen?"

"Yes."

"And as such an intellectual and known to all? We have here, gentlemen, a typical example of the spiritual leaders of the opposition, of our enemies. You used to be a Communist, Herr Nansen, isn't that so?"

"No, *Herr Untersturmführer*—I have never been a Communist. I have never concerned myself with politics, only a little with humanism."

"But still you were a Communist, like your father?"

"My father never was a Communist."

"Certainly—why, he was in Russia, and then he took part in everything."

Denzer was visibly annoyed now at having been derailed. His studied oration had missed fire at an essential point, because I had never been a Communist, but only a contemptible humanist. So he skipped that and went for the song again, now with menace in his voice.

I objected that it had nothing wrong in it. Then he raised his voice to a trembling hurricane and assured me that he would make me realize it had something wrong in it, that it was a camouflaged act of sabotage—an enemy war song. He started to read out my poem—of which he had already secured an excellent German translation. It sounded really splendid in German—much better than in Norwegian, to be honest. It never was a good poem, alack, and I've had more than enough of it with the hundred times I've heard it being hummed in Grini. It goes like this:

Proud Sons of Norway, met
From the lathe, the plow, and the net,
Mountain and sea and shore,
Classroom, office, and store,
High and low from shacks or stately homes, and yet
Chips of the same block,

The same old tough Norwegian saga stock,
All of the same strain,
Of the same grain,
The same clear faith in heart and brain!
Here we are Norwegians with prison numbers all;
None of us are grandees and none of us are small;
Lofty and low,
(Pot-bellies too),
Young men and nimble and graybeards and all:
Join all the throng
In a common song!
Grini nursing home will crown
With a halo of its own
Norway's long renown.
Norway let us sing!
Let all voices ring
For our liberty, our laws,
Our mother-wit, still as it was,
For justice and its cause!

When he had read it all through—in a truly rhetorical manner—he looked triumphantly round the audience, as though for applause. All had been listening devoutly, and they now stood in silence, waiting breathlessly for what he would say and do next. Denzer repeated most of what he had said before, that this was a case for swooping down on the intellectual, spiritual leader with an iron hand, and turning to me he said, "The first time I saw you here, I got a wrong impression of you. Your drawing is good. You've done a good job on the building works. You seemed intelligent and polite. I had a very good impression of you. It was wrong. There you see"—he threw out his hand toward the others—"how one can be mistaken."

He faced round on me again.

"You are not worthy of the favors you've enjoyed in this camp. You cannot go on working in the office where you are now. You cannot wear a white stripe."

He made a sign that I was to remove it. I took my jacket off, removed the stripe, and put my jacket on again.

"Therefore," turning to *Bauleiter* Jantzen, "I sent for you, Herr Jantzen, to know whether you require a new man instead of this one, whom you can no longer have in your office. And at the same time I wanted you to hear what sort of fellow you have had in your employ."

Jantzen mumbled something unintelligible—I don't know whether it was yes or no. Probably something in between.

Denzer turned to me afresh—he had still a long tirade left of his oration. He yelled out, banging the table until the inkstand leaped, and something fell on the floor. "We have the power! and we shall use it!! We'll be here a long time yet! Mind that, Herr Nansen."

He looked round in triumph. Then he asked Kunz to take charge of me, until he had decided on my punishment. Kunz shut me up in a single cell on the first floor of the main prison.

He went.

A little later he came back again. I was to go down to the *Vermittlung*. On the way I caught sight of Kari, Eigil, and Siri outside the fence. So Kari did come—I was to see her today, all the same. A wild delight seized me. I might talk to her for five minutes; I mustn't say anything of what had happened. No indeed!

Five minutes' heaven in this hell brought all my nerves back to rest, and balance into all that had been chaos. But the five minutes flew—we talked of everything and nothing. Whether she realized the state of things, I don't know.

When we got back up to the prison, I was allowed to fetch my bedclothes and toilet things. Not the safety razor, for some reason; he said I could come back and shave.

Thus began my first night as a dangerous criminal in solitary confinement. I slept like a log. All the next day passed uneventfully. Indeed what should happen in a single cell that isn't opened more than three times a day, when the meals are shoved in? I get the usual food incidentally, and I've had the contents of my pockets returned, both cigarettes and lighter. This pencil stump I had sent to me on a bit of thread. It's curious how one adapts oneself in time to all kinds of situations.

I've had nothing but a spoon and a bowl for eating with. No knife for the bread; I've had to munch that, buttering it with the spoon as I went along. Kunz promised me a knife. It didn't come until today, the third day, at supper. That made the meal a sheer banquet. Just imagine, slices—cut with a knife—not jabbed with the handle of the spoon.

The cell is thick with dust. The mattresses are stuffed with sawdust and leak abominably. There are six beds, three in a tier. The beds are wire sprung, and with my two blankets I'm extremely well off.

In the bunk over mine there was once a prisoner named Jørsten Johansen.* I can see that from the brown paper lying under the mattress. He got it once upon a time round a parcel from the Red Cross. This is the fourth day.

FRIDAY, MAY 22, 1942 ■ Yesterday afternoon the Segment looked in. He asked if I wouldn't like to paint posters for him. I said I would. If I would rather do that than go to Number 19 Møllergata? I said I certainly would. He said he would see that I got out of here, but I couldn't go back to the office. Then he went. He said something first about this not having been necessary, whatever he meant by that.

Late in the evening, after I had lain down, the *Lagerkommandant* arrived with his whole court. He was striding about and talking fearfully loud and commandant-like along the corridor, inspecting his prisoners. He came in to me as well. I leaped out of bed. With a commanding gesture he signified that I could stay where I was. "Herr Nansen! Hm-hm!! Hmmmm! Alone? Hmmm! *Ja, ja!* Hmmmm! Hmmm! Alone! This shouldn't have been necessary. It would be better to work. Hm! Hmmm! It shouldn't be necessary. You have made a slip. Hmmm! We must do something with you. Pity, but we'll find out what can be done with you. Hm-hm."

---

* Based on the date of Johansen's arrest (October 17, 1941) and transfer to Grini (November 6, 1941) it appears that he was a member of the Jæren Gang, along with Anton Bø, Torgeir Sikveland, and Magnus Mæland. He was executed in Trandum Woods on May 21, 1942, the very day Nansen wrote this entry; Johansen had turned twenty-eight three days earlier.

He cleared and cleared his throat and looked fearfully important. Then he cleared his throat a lot more, then he said "*gute Nacht*," [good night] and then he and the court went off. I said "*gute Nacht*" in return, and the door was shut.

I don't know what he meant—but he wasn't in a temper. Perhaps he really feels it's all a misunderstanding, perhaps he's thinking of some way to make it right again.

I slept like a log all night until seven o'clock, when I was awakened by roll call under the windows. My cell looks out on the square and I can follow the events of the day. So I have been in pretty lively communication with the fellows, too. All necessary messages have gone out; everything seems to be in order. I was to have a change of cell and begin drawing, but when?

I'm doing exercises and taking walks up and down, up and down—three meters [10 ft.] up, three meters down. I've had another shave, and in the shaving gear lay four cigarettes. Kunz knew about them. I was allowed to wash my floor, too. That was a great favor. The Segment was here and said I should soon be getting out. He would see to it.

In the cell next to mine is a man whose name I have forgotten, but it was with him they found *Proud Sons of Norway*. He had forgotten about it, he said one day when we were talking outside the window (we both stick our heads out through the grating) and so it had been lying among his letters or his things, typewritten. Aha! It was at once, then, a case of manifolding, distribution of illegal propaganda. They had vigorously swooped down on him. Whom had he got it from? How many copies did he get? How many had he distributed? How many had he manifolded? Who was the author, and so on.

He had involved himself in contradictions, to spare his mates presumably, and it had ended as a tangle of nonsense. First he was beaten by Kunz and Denzer—plentifully beaten—and then he had been reprieved until three o'clock. Since then he had heard nothing.

He was on bread and water. I told him he was to be there three days; I had heard that when I was before the "tribunal." ("Give the one who lied three days' bread and water!" bellowed Denzer.) Now perhaps his guilt is already expiated; I've heard nothing of him today. The only one left is the poor poet—"*der geistlige Leiter der Opposition*" [the spiritual leader of the opposition]. What the deuce did the Segment mean about my painting posters for him, and about seeing that I got out? Why the blazes does he say that—when he can't do it, really. It's much worse to sit here waiting for uncertainties than to prepare oneself for a fortnight or a month in solitary confinement.

It will be all right; one gradually gets into even this routine. The adaptability of human beings is fantastic.

SATURDAY, MAY 23, 1942 ■ I keep on with my exercises, but I'm all stiff with rheumatism. I can't make it out; I've never been like this before. It's as though I'd been beaten black and blue, which I haven't yet, for some unknown reason. When Denzer was at his height it can't have been far off. A word too much just then—and he'd have set to. I really wasn't so dumb to keep my mouth shut and be the crushed, repentant sinner. That's what they like.

In a cell some way off a woman is sobbing bitterly. There are women too in this "criminal corridor"—most likely specially dangerous women.

I stuck my head out of the window-grating to try and hear where the sound was coming from. No, it wasn't possible to make out, except that it was from a cell nearer the center block. Long, melancholy wails, interrupted by gasps and sobs—now intense, now quieter. It went on unceasingly. Those who were out on the square pulled up and listened. The dreary noise is echoing through the passage too, but doubtless making no impression on Kunz, who is busy out there harrying the washermen. Perhaps they're just in the act of punishing that woman? Perhaps there's something they want out of her? Or is she crying simply because she can't bear it any longer?

Look out the window, my dear! Fill your lungs with the fresh, wonderful spring air. It will give you strength. And word of the future. Don't cry so bitterly; save your tears for the great, incomprehensible moment of rejoicing. Then they will have to flood. No one can stop them till the source is dry; save your tears for that day.

The Segment looked in this morning. First I saw him from the window. He was standing out there with Erling [Steen] after roll call; they were laughing, joking about something or other. Then he called up to me: "*Haben Sie noch Zigaretten?*" [Have you any cigarettes left?]

I shook my head.

"*Ich will Ihnen welche bringen,*" [I will bring you some] he shouted, and went on talking to Erling, probably about me and what he could do for me. For I am certain he would like to do something for me. I'm not mistaken in *him*; he really is a little human being.

Well—he came up with three packets of cigarettes. Had I enough to smoke over Whitsun?* Yes, a thousand thanks, I had. But if I might have clean underclothes? Yes, he would speak to Steen. If I might have a bath? We-ell, that was more doubtful I could see. But after Whitsun he would try to get me out, he said, and went off. Then when Kunz arrived I got the clean clothes.

After I had had breakfast, and gotten the room spring-cleaned I started to take a bath. I was mother-naked when the door again opened. It was the Segment. He had brought a parcel. "*Ein Packet für Sie, Nansen,*" [A parcel for you, Nansen] he thundered furiously, banging the door after him. I blessed him as he jogged off down the passage, his stick thumping on the floor at every step. This was out of the kindness of his heart. I think it's better no one should see this parcel. It contained two packets of cigarettes, four eggs, a sausage, a small packet of crispbread and half a pound of butter. I feel a Croesus,† with supplies for a long, stiff prison stretch to come—indeed a superfluity—but no one to share with. How many in the prison, or for that matter outside it, have eggs for Whitsun?

A moment ago I stuck my head out of the grating to say good-bye to a fellow prisoner who was just being released. "*Kopf einstecken, Mensch!*" [Stick your head in, fellow!] barked out a little jailer puppy who saw a chance of hectoring. And I pulled my head back into the cage and missed saying good-bye. There were several who got free, so Whitsun did bring some joy into the camp. My carpenter has gone off, doubtless committing to the deuce the whole farm extension he was working away on, chivvied incessantly by a whole leash of ignorant *Bauleiters*, who wanted the house done by Whitsun. God knows what happened after I ceased to act as buffer. And God knows what happened about the cabin in the woods, where these blokes were to have rendezvous with girls. Koopmann com-

---

* The Christian feast of the Pentecost, celebrated seven weeks after Easter.
† In Greek and Persian cultures the name Croesus (King of Lydia, 560–547 BC) became synonymous with great wealth.

missioned me to furnish this love nest in a tasteful style with a cabinet for *schnapps*, some comfortable chairs, and a wide bed with room for two. "*Sie verstehen, Herr Nansen, he-he?*" [You understand, Herr Nansen, he-he?]

Really I am living like a prince, that is, a prince in confinement, with nothing to do. With nothing but a little bit of smuggled pencil stump, which I must economize, and some scraps of toilet paper, which must also be used with care. The time goes rather slowly, but I have food enough and clothes enough and water enough and time enough. Oh, this time. If it would only fly away. Times will come—if they would only roll on a bit faster in the meantime.

Torbjørn [Henriksen] was sitting outside in the dusk, talking to the cat.* He told the cat that things were going fine. No special news, puss, but they're going the right way, tip-top.

I heard snatches of the Swedish news last night—from one of the guard's radios. It said something about an American battleship. I was unable to discern what it was. I think it was sunk. Perhaps it was sunk but it will be ok. America has many battleships. And if they lose some, more are ready behind them, and always new ones.†

It's blessedly quiet this evening, a real Whitsun eve. One would almost think that everyone was sitting indoors to receive the blessing. I've never known such a quiet evening at Grini, and here I sit alone into the bargain. I wonder where Kari is today? Sitting alone too? She may be unhappy for my sake; she must have heard I'm "inside." I am writing: Dear Kari, soon all these horrors will be over, and we shall live together again and be happy. I can't do anything without you, not even be in prison.

SUNDAY, MAY 24, 1942 ■ He came again last night, the *Lagerkommandant*, along with the Segment, after I'd gone to bed. It looks as though he had a predilection for that time of day. It gives him an advantage, as it were, when the prisoner is lying down. Once again he was the half-jocose type, who flares up mightily and strikes first, then comes and strokes one afterward—relishing the effect of his power. How he relishes this chance of being human afterward. Well—he said he would send for me tomorrow (that is today), said good night, and went.

The Segment said something about letting me out today. To me he talks in his ordinary voice with a comic, sorrowful countenance, like a sympathetic little bandy-legged bulldog with kind eyes. At the other prisoners he screams and bawls and I think he succeeds in scaring them thoroughly. He is well aware that I see through him, and perhaps is even rather sorry that he should have unmasked to a prisoner who was going to land in the punishment cell; but he is anxious I should realize that *he* is putting things right. It is thanks to him that I'm getting out now. But when?

A little later Kunz arrived, in Whitsun mufti, rather less bad tempered and bellowing than usual. He told me to come along; I was wanted in the *Vermittlung*. In his office on the first floor the Commandant was sitting at his desk with his woman secretary at the typewriter.

"Herr Nansen? Yes indeed, it's Herr Nansen, the champion of freedom. Good day.

---

*   Henriksen was released December 20, 1943.
†   The Battle of the Coral Sea (May 4–8, 1942) resulted in the loss of one American aircraft carrier, the USS *Lexington*. It was the first naval battle ever fought exclusively by aircraft; the opposing United States and Japanese ships never saw each other.

Why, you look well, so big and strong." (He gestured largely with his arms, as though to draw my powerful form in the air.) "Now then, take a seat, please, sit there. Now then . . ."

Then he dictated to his lady all I had said last night; he remembered it to the smallest detail. First he got all my data, then he said that yesterday he had been reading a book by my father—by the Nansen who was with Quisling.

"That was your father, wasn't it?"

"Certainly."

"*Donnerwetter!* [Damn!] There was a man. And you—a pity. You have made a slip. You will reform—make up for it, eh?"

Then came dictation, constantly interrupted by the lady, who didn't know the machine and had to begin over again. Moreover a German lady of consequence came in in the middle, was introduced, and sat down. On it went. He dictated a heap of things, ending with my promise that henceforth I would not infringe the rules of the camp. The document was in the tone a bad boy would use when he was sorry for having disobeyed. With a gesture to the ladies, whom he now had as audience, he explained that this young man was the son of Fridtjof Nansen, the great, famous Fridtjof Nansen, one of whose books he, Denzer, had been reading yesterday.

"No, really," quacked the ladies in chorus. "*Nansen, der grosse Dichter!*" [Nansen, the great poet!] They both looked quite overcome. Denzer was enjoying himself. Well there, to be sure he was no stone; he had a heart, too. Under the uniform it was beating, but duty, duty. However painful it may be, ladies . . .

When I signed the confession, I was dismissed. Kunz was waiting down below. I should be getting out, said Kunz. I was allowed to go round to the hut and fetch my shoes, brush, and comb. I'm getting equipped by degrees. And now here I am again, after a good dinner, waiting for something to happen. Am I to get out? Or is the punishment to last a while longer?

I don't feel very brisk. The rheumatism bothers me. There's an infernal draft in here.

The transport for Germany left yesterday. I was sitting at my window and watched it go. They paraded on the square. First all the fishermen from Telavåg with their bags. All they possessed in the world was in those canvas bags. The rest had been burned or stolen by the Germans. Now they were off to the country of the Germans. It was a melancholy sight; I shall never forget it. The procession was wound up by one of the half-wits, who was being led, and by the two who can't walk, but waddle along like ducks. They are father and son.

Then came the Grini people. Mæland went off, Asbjørnsen and a whole lot of decent men and good comrades. God knows what they are going to.* We must hope it's something better than they expect.

MONDAY, MAY 25, 1942 ■ Afternoon. At last I've got solitude enough—more than enough. But no peace and no work. There is fuss and uproar on all sides and I have nothing to work with. It gets on one's nerves. Also I've acquired a splitting headache—and the

---

* Both Finn Meland and Odd Asbjørnsen were sent to Sachsenhausen, where they remained for the duration of the war.

rheumatism is getting worse. Yes, thank you, I'm a trifle so—so. But when I think of the men in 412 I feel ashamed of myself.

Every morning from my window I see old Sikveland out on the square. He walks about bareheaded, with a long, light-colored stick he has cut. He goes from one to another of the hospital people who are out for an airing. I can see—and hear—that it is his boy he wants to talk about. Poor old man. He has still not given up hope; he still believes that something will save them all and prevent this senseless killing of his boy.

FRIDAY, MAY 29, 1942 ■ On Sunday evening I got out of my cage. It was a few days before I could write again. An affair like that always leaves one a bit jumpy. If they should come across these notes, which I *must* write now to feel comfortable, it would mean more than five days' solitary confinement, I'm afraid.

The condemned Jæren men were shot while I was inside. It was on the morning of Thursday the 21st. Fifteen men were called for in the night. Two were pardoned.

Old Sikveland is more at peace now, since the death sentence has been carried out.* He talks quietly of his son Torgeir, and of what he did in the war and afterward. He describes how they were beaten and tortured at the questionings in Stavanger after their arrest—himself as well. But not a word too much had crossed their lips.

Now they'd shot them every one—all the young fellows—who were the leaders, as they thought—and the others that helped in different ways—they'd got heavy prison sentences. Now, he thought, now he might surely get home to the wife, alone with two daughters on the farm yonder. It was all finished. There was no more to be said now. Not that he had said anything about it—or ever, though they beat him to a jelly, would say anything. But surely now the thing was worked out and finished. The arms have been found, some place in Jæren. It was two machine guns and ammunition that the boy was to take to England. And the whole affair was cleared up now—thanks to the informers, poor chaps. That chap that informed on me—he's said he wasn't sure but that I knew something about those arms. That way I was drawn in. And one of the lads they took—he gave the names of the rest. Aye, you'll have heard that, Nansen—he gave them all. Torgeir found fault with him for that—and thought it was his doing that they were taken and condemned.

I broke in with the remark that it couldn't be pleasant to be that man today. Old Sikveland stared in front of him a long time; it was as though he had to arrange his ideas and to conquer the evil that sprang up in him.

"No," he said slowly and seriously, "it must be terrible!"

Then he began to speak of Torgeir again—about the last glimpse he had of him when he went that night. Torgeir was in front, handcuffed to [Magnus] Mæland.† They followed on two by two, chained together, but erect and upstanding. The whole road down to the *Vermittlung* was full of Germans with rifles at the ready. When they swung off down the road, they all turned at once—as at a given signal—and looked up at old Sikveland, who was standing up there at his window in the hospital, where he had stood night after night, waiting for this moment. They nodded, smiled, and waved to him for the last time.

"They were straight and proud till death," said Sikveland, and his voice trembled

---

* Torgeir Sikveland was executed fifteen days shy of his nineteenth birthday.

† Mæland, a farmhand, was twenty-one.

with pride—not only in his son but in all these young heroes going to their doom with heads erect. Torgeir had the same coat on, said the old man, as he had been wearing in the courtroom at Stavanger, where he had been tortured and beaten. The coat was like a single clot of blood when he came out after the questionings. They had beaten him with something mighty heavy—he believed a strap, with small shot sewn into it. But not a sound had passed Torgeir's lips. Not a word. They would never have got anything out of *him*, if they had beaten him till he was done for.

"That Gestapo agent that took them, and questioned them, he's in Stavanger yet, so they say. [Arnold] Hölscher he was called, and he's the chap that killed Torgeir so to say."

Then he began to tell me about his home in Jæren. He and his had worked that land for ten generations now. The farm was so big that he had meant to divide it into three; then each of his sons would have had his share of it.

"But now I've no son," he said—feebly throwing out both his arms. "One son of mine lost his life in a shooting accident eight years gone. He fell by his own hand so to say. The second died two years before of an influenza or the like. Torgeir was the last I had—and he fell for his country. He knew his part all right, and he did it with a will." Then he was silent again, blinking a little in the sun.

"I can't get to sleep at nights," he said, "I just lie thinking and thinking. I've a bit to think of, too." Then there was another long pause.

"That Sikveland—that young chap that went to England—that was my cousin," he said suddenly, his face brightening. "It wasn't only my Torgeir that went off to the war. Torgeir had thoughts of going along with him, but it didn't happen so. Now if he'd only done that, Torgeir, things would all have been different." He came back again to Torgeir, do what he might.

Now the farm will have to go to one of the daughters—since Torgeir's gone. It was to have been his. He had trained for that. He'd been through agricultural school and several courses, and was well equipped to take over the farm and carry it forward.

They believed in God, these men from Jæren, and put their trust in Him with firm, childlike faith. The night before they were fetched away they had held a prayer meeting. It would be Anton Bø that conducted it, thought Sikveland, who told me. They had sung "A Mighty Fortress Is Our God."* I thought of the night they sang the national anthem.

Old Sikveland is himself, I can see, a religious man, who bows to the will of God. He starts no reflections of his own on God's dealings—never puts forward any "why." He wouldn't presume. He lost his three sons—was himself thrown into prison and subjected to torture while the Germans plundered his goods. That must have been God's will. And yet he thanks God, praises Him, and puts all his trust in Him alone. Strange indeed!

I was standing wondering at this—when the Segment bellowed from the main steps that the two men jabbering down there were to be off at once. And when we looked around, we saw that we were the only ones left on the square, which had been cleared while we were lost in our conversation. We had to decamp in haste, I was by no means entitled to be strolling round. Sikveland vanished in the direction of the hutments behind the prison, bareheaded and wide legged, with his white woolen scarf wound several times round his throat, and that long yellow stick of his clutched in his left fist. He would have

---

* One of the best known of Martin Luther's hymns, based on Psalm 46.

to seek out a new friend with whom he could talk of Torgeir; perhaps the new one might have something to tell about his son that he hadn't heard.

It was the Segment who came on Sunday and let me out. I was to have work, he said, not sit rotting away up here in the cell. "Tomorrow," he said, "you shall build a wall for me in the hospital. Then you shall have an office for yourself, a big room with a drawing board and everything you need for working in your own line as an architect. But," he continued, "you're not going down there again." He pointed down at the office hutment and curled up his nose. "That's no place for you—among those people. It's nothing but a lot of shit and muck. Shits working away at shit. Let them grub on with their rubbish."

I got my jacket and cap on and ran down to parade. Congratulations streamed in from every side. The fellows were in their Sunday best; for it was Whitsun and a day off, and the Sunday best seemed not to be just outside, it went right through. There was good news from the fronts as a treat for me who had been inside and in the dark, and all was sunshine and gladness, until I heard about the Jæren men.

That was a whole week ago, but I haven't got the better of the dark mood that swooped down on me that evening. But one day I suppose I shall be all right again.

With Martin [Strandli's] help I built up the wall on Monday, to the satisfaction of the Segment. The next day I roughcast it, with the help of a man who couldn't roughcast either. I looked like a keg of plaster when I was through. The Segment is still keeping me in cigarettes.

Now here I am, in my own office incidentally, fully occupied with my writing. I have discovered that thin paper and small writing are a fortunate combination. Pages like these can easily be made to disappear in one's baggage, one way or another. And there are quite a lot of ways. I know of quite a few already—and pretty tricky ones. I must write. And the opportunities have never been better.

I have my own office, as I said—actually in the north wing of the first floor, in among the detention cells, where I sat a week ago gaping at the wall. I have it all to myself and have peace all day. But now let me describe how this came about.

When I had finished the bricklaying job I was at a loose end. I waited for the Segment to keep his promise that he would give me an office and some real work. And indeed every time he saw me he said it should be arranged *sofort*. First I must come along to the hospital or some other section to have a look at something that needed doing. There were doorsills to be put in, locks to be changed, signs to be painted. Sign painting he thought should suit me to begin with.

He unfolded to me a sign plan on the grand scale. Over every bed in the hospital there was to be a board. He wanted this painted black, and it was to say in white letters: *Name . . . Beruf* [Occupation] *. . . Geboren* [Born] *. . . Krankheit* [Sickness] *. . . Eingeliefert* [Admitted] *. . .* He had seen that done in other hospitals, and then one could tell at once who was in the bed, what was wrong with him, and how long he had been there. I explained that that was a painter's job. He couldn't see it. I must be able to paint, was his idea. I said I didn't mind trying, if he decided so, but I had never done that kind of thing. Wouldn't it be better to put one of the skilled painters on to that? Right, then I was to put a skilled painter on to it. Afterward he accepted my suggestion that the whole placard should be printed at a printing office in town.

With that I was out of work again. But there were more signs to come. The Segment wanted new inscriptions everywhere. Once he had seen the plaques of compressed sawdust

Old Sikveland tells the story of his son Torgeir.

that the bed signs were made of, his enthusiasm for this material was not to be curbed. Everything was to be painted on compressed sawdust. Wherever there was a vacant space, a sawdust notice was to be hung up, with some valuable legend or other and an arrow pointing right or left. Once again I had to assure him that that was a job for a skilled painter, not for me. Once again the same astonishment that I was not a skilled painter. Once again he accepted a fresh proposal of mine. This time I proposed that the legends, numbers, and arrows should be painted directly on the walls or doors. In the end he was quite enchanted and grateful for this suggestion. Besides, he was out of sawdust plaques. They were used up already for the signs he had ordered at the first go.

The other morning he pulled himself together. Now a room was to be found for Nansen. It must be in the center block, and it must be big and light. The Segment stood in the hut, expounding what it was to be like. It must be at least as big as the hut, and white and handsome. In the window there was to be a big table, where I could have my maps and drawings and everything I needed. I must simply write all that down, then he would go into town himself and get it for me. *Nicht?* And then at the far end of the room I could have my bed and a little table, nicely arranged, and then a washbasin, just like in here.

Now there was nothing lacking but a small bathroom built into one corner. Nobody would have been astonished if he'd proposed that, too. A joke? By no means. It was all seriously meant, and he would certainly have done it for me if I hadn't restrained him. All who were by (there were a number of my hutmates) simply sat there gaping and sniggering. This was indeed a way to treat a discharged convict. In the end it became almost painful. What was the man's idea? Obviously the *Lagerkommandant* had given him a free hand with me; I understood as much later.

Ultimately, then, we sallied out to find me this wonder office. The Segment made straight across the passage to the hut leaders' hut, and asked if I liked that room. If so he would have it cleared. He roared, "*Heraus!*" [Get out!] at the scared and bewildered hut leaders who were sitting there. I assured him that I would on no account have that room.

We wandered on, into the *Vermittlung* people's hut. Same comedy there. With the utmost difficulty I averted the clearing of the room. Then in my despair I cried that I could make do with a table in the window of the center lobby. For a moment he was glad of that, but immediately found out that no, it was impossible. I would get no peace. Why, the door of the water closet was right opposite, and the traffic there would disturb me, not to mention the smell. No! No! It was impossible.

Then we went on to *Einzelhaft* [solitary confinement]. At the west end were the men from Jæren who had been condemned to imprisonment. He was going to throw them out now. He was going to have them out to work. I should have the room if I liked it, and it was big enough. I swore that it was first rate, and so it was decided that I should have it, the very next day. So that was settled—and the Segment vanished into the elevator in the center lobby after asking me to keep an eye on all his signs and sundries for the rest of the day.

The next day came—but not the office. The matter had completely dropped out of the Segment's funny little head. I remained idle all day and the next as well. Each time he saw me, to be sure, he had an attack of guilty conscience, and would then just say in passing that now I must see about getting an office and some work. Once I tackled him and asked what sort of work.

"Fine work! Architectural work! I don't know what. That will be settled outside."

I got no more out of him; he slipped away again, roared at someone further along the corridor and disappeared.

Not until yesterday did he pull himself together once more. He admitted that the plan to clear out the Jæren men wasn't coming off. I couldn't have that room. All the same we went in and looked at it, and once again I managed to empty my pockets of cigarettes for the poor devils. The Segment bellowed a few half-jocose taunts in there, and then strode over to the cell I am in now, which has finally become my office.

I have a commission too, apart from the notices, which, God help me, he still keeps fussing about. I am to draw a gateway! A new main entrance to Grini.

SUNDAY, MAY 31, 1942 ■ Yesterday a fresh lot of guards arrived. There was a tremendous uproar and to-do all the afternoon—parades, saluting and good fellowship. When the Germans start on that it goes on for hours. And people don't go up to each other when they have something to say; they shout it with a Germanic, manly ring in the voice, and they shout it loud, for a hundred and fifty others are shouting at the same moment. Add six large buses with an open exhaust, racing their engines alternately or simultaneously—and the barking of commands—and the moving in and out of more than two hundred men with knapsacks, firearms, steel helmets, trunks, radios, concertinas and high boots—and one can well form a conception of the hullabaloo. It's said they remove the eardrums of the horses they take up to the front—including those they've stolen from Norwegian farmers—so that they shan't take fright at the explosions. One is tempted to believe the soldiers must go through a similar operation. But they're said to have cut the horses' vocal cords too. One can only regret that the parallel at that point breaks down completely.

Denzer, by the way, looked into my *bureau* yesterday with the Segment. As usual he offered me a cigarette. The Segment was eagerly engaged in holding forth about his notices and the other things I was to do for him. Denzer looked the whole time as though he were standing just behind the scenes rehearsing various attitudes that he would strike the next moment in a musical comedy. In very *liebenswürdig* [amicable] style he gave me a light, then he leaned his head back, lit his own cigarette, and cut off the Segment's flow of speech.

He told me that he had seen my drawings on the wall of the architect's office. He expressed his great appreciation of my "art," and asked if I had done all that out of my own head, or if I had used a model. His admiration rose higher yet when I informed him that I had really thought it out on my own. It was especially the brownie with the beer jug that had appealed to him, and he would like to have one "as a souvenir from you!" Whatever I needed for the work I was simply to note down; it would be ordered and sent up here. Denzer would pay for it. *Gel?* [Understand?]

He assured himself that I had paper on which to draw this "*Andenken*," [souvenir] predicted that I should soon get home to my wife, cleared his throat, smiled and *ja*-ed a number of times before getting up again. Then he begged me in an almost confidential, chummy tone not to do any more silly things here in prison, asked if I was all right and liked my new office, if it was light enough, big enough? "*Also—guten Tag!*" [Well then, good day!]

Before he went, he told me that of course he himself used to draw at one time, both with a ruler and freehand. He had thought highly of it ever since, and knew how to appreciate good drawing, good art, and I was an artist. I think the portrait of the man is now pretty clear?

THURSDAY, JUNE 4, 1942 ■ The day before yesterday there was a "purge." After supper everyone was ordered out on parade. First we had high-class drill in German; then began the "purge." In the first place everyone—absolutely everyone who wasn't too ill to walk—was made to turn out. They began by going through the hospital. It was a unique medical examination. All who weren't old and infirm, or hadn't visible defects, so that anyone could see they were disabled, had to dress and fall in. They were reported fit offhand by Denzer in person, and ordered to work from the next day. His examination was short and pithy:

"How old are you? Occupation? Why are you on the sick list? Since when? Nonsense! Out! In Germany all have to work up to twelve hours a day—old or young—rich or poor—all!! They have no time to be ill. Most illnesses can be got over by work! Therefore, young man—out! At once I said! That means quick!"

When the hospital had been combed and decimated, the rest of us had our turn. We were ordered to parade in working groups. Then Denzer started on the gangs. All young men were taken out of gangs that had indoor or fairly light work and transferred to hard outdoor labor. Every group was put through a sieve. A young Jew who is a joiner by trade was dragged out of the joiners' gang, and, with some choice gibes hurled after him, shifted over to the outdoor lot. It was as though he had been trying to keep out of view, so as to avoid working. But Denzer would nab him sure enough, and drag him into the light of day, *verdammter Judenschwein!* [damned Jewish pig!]

The purge lasted nearly three mortal hours.

FRIDAY, JUNE 5, 1942 ■ The purge was a kind of farewell show for Denzer, who is going on leave. He set out today. In the meantime the Segment is to be *Lagerkommandant* and the old one (the Storm Prince) is to be *chief*—whatever that may mean.

SATURDAY, JUNE 6, 1942 ■ Now I'm in the parachute room! I've landed here in the end, after being thrown out of my smart office in *Einzelhaft* the other day, and after a couple of days' homelessness.

The Segment, who has gone quite crazy with his position as Commandant, now flies around screaming and raving, on the best models. There's no point or common sense in anything he says or does. He must think that goes with the position, and indeed he may be right in a way. I have again been set to the idiotic work of drawing posters: *Entry strictly forbidden! Smoking strictly forbidden! Caution! Danger!* And so on. These texts are practical anyhow; they can be stuck up—appropriately—anywhere in the camp.

After being thrown out of my private cell I supported a wretched life in the lobby outside our hut for a couple of days. It was hopeless. People hung over me all day. Pencils, erasers and drawing pins vanished quicker than I got them out of my frail receptacles, and in the end I grew so peevish and sick of it that I told the Segment he must find me a place to work if he wanted me to do anything. He rushed into the hut and was going to throw [Karl] Oppegaard out on the spot. Indeed he was going to throw out everyone who lived there and send them over to one of the new huts. *Nansen is to have a decent office!* Then he rushed round wanting to throw everybody out of their rooms, just like the time before.

At length I suggested the parachute room. Instantly he ordered all my things up there, and here I am with the shoemakers and the painters.

Before Denzer left, he got the picture I painted for him. It was a commission, so I did it in working hours. It represented a farmer with a brownie cap in his empty storehouse. He had an empty beer jug in one hand, and the other was flung out despairingly, while he stood and wept. Empty vats and butter churns, empty bottles and fish pails lay strewn around. Everything was empty. A dying mouse was breathing its last, propped against an empty tub, and by its side lay a gnawed-off ham bone; only the bone was left. An empty churchwarden* lay on the floor, grinning with its black, empty maw. The upper half-door stood open; outside shone the Norwegian spring; there was a blue haze toward the snow peaks in the distance.

He had been wildly enthusiastic. Hilarious! But he had caught the irony. "Everything is empty," he said. "We Germans have eaten it all up!"

SUNDAY, JUNE 7, 1942 ■ Today one of the Tromsø Jews came and poured out his troubles.† If I could only do something? I—dismissed, degraded, and punished—what can I do?

It is indeed a curse to be a Jew.

Grundsätzlich they must be in the trot, with no hope of ever getting out again, let them toil ever so hard. And they do toil. Some time ago, when a number of volunteers were sought to do some work after hours (a water pipe had sprung a leak, it was important to all of us to get it dug up and mended), more than half of the volunteers were Jews. They offered spontaneously, while it took time to make up the rest of the number. They had nothing to gain, and all day (this was in the evening) they had been toiling in the trench under the whip of one of the slave drivers. The overtime went on until midnight.

The Jews worked cheerfully, and didn't spare themselves. I overheard a conversation between two of them, two lads who were passing to fetch some tools. One said, "This is easy work, my word!" The second replied, "Yes, it's like this every day for the rest of them." One couldn't really detect any bitterness in his tone of voice; he was merely stating, quietly and simply, a fact that had just dawned on him, to his astonishment.

To these Jewish lads this work was like a pleasant relaxation! There was no one standing over them and bellowing, no one striking or kicking them. And for a fleeting moment the yellow star they wear on their breasts was doing no harm. It was only showing all who chose to reflect on it that the Jews too can work—spontaneously—even on top of a long day's toil in the clay soup down in the trench. Let the devil have his due—it was they who did most of the heavy work. Their Aryan brothers were a good deal cleverer at getting in a chat and a smoke.

Unfortunately there are also objectionable elements among the Jews who spoil things for their unlucky comrades, and they often spoil them with a vengeance. Every unprepossessing thing they do recoils on all the rest. It's not only the Germans who take that view, it also applies in a high degree to the Norwegian prisoners. The other day a new Jewish

---

* A long-stemmed pipe.
† More than two hundred miles north of the Arctic Circle, Tromsø is Norway's seventh largest city.

prisoner came in. He had tucked away a hundred-kroner note—in his jacket sleeve—in the hope of getting it safely through the search down in the *Vermittlung*. He was found out and came in for a sound thrashing from Kunz's riding whip. Then he was put in *Einzelhaft* on bread and water.

One of our most prominent fellow prisoners said, "Yes, these damned Jews are always trying to save that money of theirs." It slipped out of him quite involuntarily. It didn't occur to him that he was committing a gross injustice in saying so. For how many Norwegians had done the same! Strange that responsible, clever people should be driven with the herd by their lethargic, stupid intolerance, which is "hereditary" in them, and which each imagines to be the result of his own experience.

While I still had my little private office in *Einzelhaft* I had some small experiences, of which I've said nothing. (One grows less jittery as the time passes without any indiscreet investigations to shake one up, so now I have gathered courage and imprudence to mention them.)

One day Øyvind [Hansen]*—Kunz's little "adjutant"—came and told me excitedly that there was a man in one of the cells who was to be shot. He was anxious to send a message to his wife. Could I help? Of course it meant launching out on dangerous adventures once more, but who can refuse to do something for a man about to die? I went to him one morning at a time when all was quiet in the section, and I had assured myself that Kunz had left the main building. I peeped into the cell and caught sight of a gaunt, loose-jointed fellow, with many days' growth of black beard bristling out of his chin and cheeks.

When I breathed a faint *pst!* in through the hole, he started up and approached the door. I asked if there was anything I could do for him.

"Get me a pencil," he said.

I had one on me, and gave it to him.

"I've been wanting so much to write a note to my wife," he continued, "she's just had a child—a son. Our first child. And if it's possible—do you think you could get an answer in, too?"

I promised to do my best and said I should be back in an hour's time; then he must have his little note ready. Yes, he would. He went on to tell me that he had been caught red-handed, smuggling various compromising pieces of information over to Sweden. To the question whether he was alone, he replied that some others had been in it, but he didn't know where they were—or whether they had been arrested at all.

He said he had had a series of examinations. "And they gave me such a beating," he added. The examining judge had said he would be shot. He told me quite coolly—I suppose he had gradually got used to the idea in a way—but in his next request he betrayed his fear of dying. He said he was on a diet for nephritis. The German doctor had diagnosed it. But he thought himself that he had stomach ulcers, and asked if there were no powerful drugs that could make him terribly ill, so that he would go into the hospital. He didn't care what it was, if he only fell ill, terribly ill, and could get out of here.

He gazed at me beseechingly and wildly with the one eye that I could see through the hole. I can see it still. I knew for certain that what he asked was impossible, but I brought myself to say I would try. Ashamed of myself and my cowardice I began to talk of some-

---

* Hansen was sent to Sachsenhausen February 20, 1943, where he remained until the end of the war.

thing else. Wasn't there anything I could get him? Cigarettes? Yes, he smoked, and so I gave him a few cigarettes through the hole, and a number of matches. He was pleased. He told me that for a long time he'd had nothing to read, but now he had got a Bible in.

An hour afterward I called for the letter. It was on a torn-off, crumpled bit of toilet paper, was written indistinctly, almost illegibly, in a clumsy childish hand, and contained surprisingly little.

He was all right now, had a Bible to read, etc.—much that he had already told me. Not one word of danger to his life, not one word even about the gravity of his position. At the end, love to her and their son. The letter went home to her, and an answer has arrived. She is all right, and the boy is splendid. He is so extraordinarily handsome.

Now I can't see him anymore, but I had two scraps of paper from him yesterday. He begged me to find out if his friends had been arrested, and asked if I thought it possible to escape. Finally he asked me for news. That was the content of one piece.

The other said, "Do you think the following is possible: to get me some narcotic or other, so that I'm lying unconscious at feeding time—some day when there's no German doctor about. Then most likely I'd be taken to the hospital. If a doctor there could make out that I had some disease that had to be treated outside Grini, something like cancer for instance. Possibly that I was so damned bad I'd stay here in the hospital for the rest of the war. Perhaps we could get a morphia syringe in and out through the hole. It doesn't matter if I pass out from too much, am done for anyhow."

First the thought for his comrades—and then that almost touchingly childish question about the possibility of escape! How in the wide world could *that* be done?

He has heard nothing of the war since he was placed in solitary confinement a month ago. It's natural that he should long to know if anything big has happened. Is the war any nearer its conclusion? May he hope that it will end before it's too late? "Send me news!" Oh God, if I could only send you some news. But what good can it do you to hear that the Russians are getting on, that Kharkov* has been taken by the Germans, indeed, but after heavy losses, that the Russians in Finland are close to the Norwegian border in the far north, that the position in Cyrenaica† is favorable to the Allies, etc., etc. We have been hearing the same thing now month after month. We're no further on—we're none the wiser—need no less patience to wait—wait—wait until we go mad! Poor boy, what is he to wait for? Which is coming first—death or life?

I heard yesterday that he's supposed to have broken down at the last examination— and "talked." The tactics of the examining judge may have been precisely to fix his mind on the idea that he is to be shot, in order to take away his strength, to make him desperate and confused, so that in the end he'll break down and talk unrestrainedly. And then, when they've got all they want out of him, there will be nothing more to stop them from shooting him. Therefore, friend—hold out! As long as you have more to tell them, it's

---

* Kharkov, the fifth largest city in the Soviet Union, was the object of five battles and changed hands four times. It was originally captured by the Germans on October 24, 1941. The "Second Battle of Kharkov" began on May 12, 1942, when Soviet forces attempted to destabilize German forces before the Germans could launch their expected offensive against Moscow. Despite initial success, the Soviet forces were ultimately routed in what has been called "one of the great German victories and terrible Russian defeats of the war." By the time the battle had ended, the Red Army lost more than 100,000 killed and 200,000 captured.

† The eastern coastal region of modern-day Libya.

your best weapon. Hold on to it! I got this advice smuggled in to him in his bread ration, with Øyvind's help.

This lad's case has had a strong effect on me; it is an actual physical strain to smile and join in the jokes and nonsense among my friends in the hut. For through it all I see the pale, bearded face with the frightened, wandering eyes. And through that again I see the face of Jakob Friis, of Fillinger, Bø, Sikveland—yes, and Viggo Hansteen*—and it becomes impossible to smile and be gay. It's as though it will never, never more be possible, if I can't do something for this one lad.

Then I see other faces in my mind's eye: Kari's, Marit's, Eigil's, Siri's—and another yet—the little round face of the child that is to come.

MONDAY, JUNE 8, 1942 ■ Today the Storm Prince has been storming in a big way. He's using the sunset of his power as chief at Grini to scold and rage for all he's worth in the time that's left him. In a fortnight he will certainly be going for good. Denzer comes back from leave then. The Segment is to take over the farming, and Stange will have the Segment's job with the prisoners, allocation of work, etc. (Now I think of it, God knows what the Segment's job is exactly?) Then I'll probably go over to the farming as well, to design barns and cowsheds and new agricultural works. The Segment said so, but then he says such a lot of things. The *schöne Arbeit* [nice work] that he dangled in front of me has still, apart from the gateway, been confined to poster painting.

THURSDAY, JUNE 11, 1942 ■ Today the Segment really let himself go; he told me that every day he listens in to London in German. I invited Erling [Steen] and myself to his room at half-past seven this evening for a cup of coffee and a cigarette. Then he said, *he* would find himself in prison, too. I invited him, in that case, to come and stay in our hut, where I was sure we should still find means of passing the time. Altogether—we had quite a merry talk. Also I inveigled him down to the cellar of the *Vermittlung*, where I got several packets of cigarettes. Another great and joyful achievement—I got him to make a personal call to Oslo and ask them to send Robert [Andersen's] violin out. In an hour's time Robert had the violin and was transported with joy. He has been rubbing and polishing at it all the rest of the day, until past ten o'clock.

FRIDAY, JUNE 12, 1942 ■ The Segment has no words to express his contempt for the so-called Norwegian summer and his homesickness for more southerly parts, where everything is far different and superior. Otherwise he is still in a good mood. He has been walking around the lower farm disturbing me all morning. I've surveyed the ground for the cowhouse and barn down there with the assistance of two schoolboys, who think they've had a first-rate morning. They're used to toiling a good deal harder at the working places they've been assigned to. That I can contradict the Segment and joke with him, and that what is more, he pays attention to what I say—nay, actually gives in and comes round

---

* A legal adviser to the trade union organization, Viggo Hansteen (1900–1941) was shot by the Nazis on September 10, 1941, in retaliation for the so-called milk strike. His death, along with that of labor leader Rolf Wickstrøm, marked the first two executions by the Nazis during their occupation "and later came to be seen as a watershed in the history of the occupation, dividing it into an earlier period of innocence and a later deadly serious phase in which Quisling's regime came to be regarded as an increasingly brutal oppressive power." Hansteen's wife, Kirsten, became a part of the first postwar coalition government and Norway's first female cabinet minister.

to my ideas and suggestions—that's something new to them. They're used to seeing people cap in hand, dithering and saying *jawohl* when the Segment blusters. If only they don't pick it up now and think this is the method! I'm not sure that it would be a success.

The rheumatism is bothering me. It hurts to sit, it hurts to stand. And there's an infernal draft everywhere except in my bunk, where there's a draft, too.

I had a talk with fru Rinnan through the window today. She asked if anyone had heard anything certain about Frode, and if anyone is sending him parcels. Unfortunately I had nothing to tell, but assured her that he was undoubtedly being looked after. At the first opportunity I'll ask Kari to inquire. I was able to give her news of the children; they are all right.

God knows if Frode is still in Number 19. No one has any definite information. It wouldn't be surprising if he had been sent to Germany. That little family has been hit hard enough in all conscience, dissolved and scattered to the winds. When will they be reunited?

One can't help thinking of the situation after the last world war. What will be the picture that meets our eyes when the curtain goes up on the European scene after this war? If it was dismal and appalling before—what will it be this time?

In the conversations I have had with people here lately, it has been depressing to notice how little these problems are understood. A lot of people are already on the verge of plunging afresh into party politics, which are more to blame perhaps than anything else for the whole wretched business! Party programs—party boundaries, propaganda, lies, class hatred—and the whole wretched business all over again. So that's all it's meant to us—that's all we shall have learned. It's as though party politics had become our religion, and existence without them were unimaginable.

They say the fate of the court hostages is to be discussed by the Germans and NS in the immediate future. Many are inclined to optimism on that account. Of course it's conceivable that they may hit on the idea of letting us out again. There are fourteen left of us out of twenty. The others have gradually been released on account of illness, *Gefäng-nisunfähigkeit* [incapable of serving in prison]. I shouldn't mind getting home to you now, Kari.

SATURDAY, JUNE 13, 1942 ■ Today it's five months since I was arrested. I feel as though it were as many years.

I took a job with the surveyors today to get in a little walk down the Anker road with a small tin box I had to get rid of. It was a lovely walk, too, a glorious morning with really warm, sparkling sunshine and the birds chirping. We were down at the cabin that the building foremen use as a brothel, but which the Segment has discovered and supposedly made a row about. In any case there were no girls living there now. There were three of them at one time. While we were there, Reinitz came for the furniture with a heavy truck. We helped to carry the things out to it. It turned out that they needed the furniture for their new lounge, which is to be inaugurated this evening. There's to be a rare carousal, I imagine. They've been toting boxes and things in there all afternoon. There are not likely to be many of them on the working site in the morning, nor are they likely to be especially *arbeitsfähig* [fit for work] when they arrive toward noon.

The day's best rumors talk of street fighting in Berlin. It's like sheer music in my ears. In that case they're far gone. A German *Sondermeldung* [special bulletin] this afternoon says that Sevastopol has been taken by the Germans.* That's not so good, but in the first place, it's not certain to be true, and second there are no oil wells in Sevastopol. Good night.

SUNDAY, JUNE 14, 1942 ■ Today I've rolled a cigarette for a friend outside. He'll get it on Tuesday, and then on Wednesday no doubt he'll take a bicycle ride on the old Anker road. So Thursday might be a good day for the surveyors to check up the measurements of the old barn. The tinsmith made two neat little drums for me today. They are admirably suited for keeping drawings in—in damp places.

The party in the *Bauleiters'* new quarters assumed dimensions in the course of the night, by what I hear. The *Wehrmacht* drivers were having a party at the same time on the lower farm. Late in the night the two gatherings had made contact and exchanged some civilities. A quantity of furniture had been thrown out of the windows, and Kringlebotn† and two Jæren men (the cowmen) who live down there hadn't got a wink of sleep all night. A particularly joyous item in the night's program had been the mating of rabbits. That absorbed them for a long time. I haven't come across any of the merrymakers today, and I don't suppose many people have. So we had a quiet morning.

After supper there was a little entertainment in the lobby. Robert [Andersen] and a new man, [Leif] Wolfberg,‡ also a violinist, played some duets. At the end I sang a couple of songs. We wound up the performance with the national anthem. It was grand to hear it again; it's been a long time now. We must have more such evenings. I'm sure with caution we can set them going so that there need be no row about it. It's especially for the very youngest lads, I think, that it might be of importance to arrange something, so that they could have something else to think of than just the hardships and dangers of prison life, which very largely engross them now.

MONDAY, JUNE 15, 1942 ■ Have just had another letter from my "forlorn hope," with another morphine or veronal suggestion. It ends like this:

"I've heard no news for five weeks, put down the important things, shall I throw a string out if it's all clear, come back in an hour." On the back is written: "I couldn't take the 'questioning.'" (Underneath the last word is: *Flogging*). "Hope I haven't got anyone into trouble. Myself I'm done for."

Then there is a letter to his wife and one to his professor. This last contains information about a thesis he has nearly finished, and ends thus: "It will be best to get the manuscript off to the press as quick as you can, for if, which is the likely thing, I am shot, you surely won't be allowed to print anything of mine. Put in a dedication to my wife, and thanks to teachers and colleagues. Remember me to all friends, and best wishes to yourself. This is probably the last you'll hear from me. Your friend and pupil," and then the Christian name.

I will let the boy know that they're working hard on his case—that Leif Rode has it—if there is anything he wants to send word of in that connection.

But the lad must have patience yet awhile; he shall have nothing in writing. A few cells

---

* Sevastopol (and approximately ninety thousand POWs) eventually surrendered to the German army on July 4, 1942, after a long and bitter siege.

† Jacob Kringlebotten was released May 17, 1943.

‡ See November 16, 1944, and February 15, 1945, for information on Wolfberg.

down from him are two men who sent news by string to the women's section. The strings and news were promptly discovered and the men locked up indefinitely. Next time the culprits will assuredly not be the only sufferers. To save your life, friend, I'll take risks, and if there is the tiniest bit of hope I'll go far. You must get on without news; perhaps Øyvind [Hansen] will be able to whisper that everything is going fine—first-rate! You must be content with that.

The great and wild news this morning was that the Allies have landed a million men in France. It sounded as though it had taken place during the night. A little simple calculation makes short work of that. Nine thousand tons can carry three thousand men; add tanks, guns, field equipment, food, etc. There must have been a good-sized fleet out in all conscience. Tonight there was another bulletin which confirmed the invasion, and says it's going according to plan. Can one believe that, now?

Claffy has been telling someone or other that one of these fine days there is to be a big release of hostages. He said something about the Terrace carrying out a large-scale weeding of the lists of prisoners, especially hostages. Well, well. Anyhow it will be better to put one's house in order and have everything ready for the march. There are a few things that oughtn't exactly to be lying loose in one's trunk.

TUESDAY, JUNE 16, 1942 ■ I went to Dr. [Håkon] Rasmussen this morning to talk about the young man with nephritis.* I was lying thinking about it last night and came to the decision that I wouldn't take any steps until I heard what [Leif] Rode says about the case. Dr. Rasmussen thought the same. However, he agreed that an acute change for the worse, brought about by some poison or other (he favored morphine, as far as I understood), might give the boy a very slight chance of being transferred to the hospital. There does exist, of course, a danger of the morphine's being traced, in the event of an immediate examination of the stomach contents. Then there will be the devil to pay.

Hans Huitfeldt was released today—one more of the court gang. People have always been saying he would get out; his age was held to be decisive.† Now there are only thirteen of us left, I think. Perhaps that release was the sole result of the "weeding" process?

There are a lot of silly jobs being done here under German direction. One of the worst of all is the putting up of the electric fence round the "inner" prison area (the main prison and the hutments). This fence is to be stretched between concrete posts, which have arrived in great quantities. A good proportion of them are already in place, two and a half meters [just over 8 ft.] apart. They are set deep in the ground. The work is heavy and difficult; the posts have to be carried long distances and are no light weight.

Now it's been decided that after all they're not to be two and a half meters apart, but five meters [16.5 ft.]. So they've started taking up every other one of the posts already placed and moving them further on, together with the posts that have been brought up to their respective holes, dug two and a half meters apart.

It would have been strange if some such counterorder hadn't arrived. It's a feature of the system.

Later on, besides these posts, there are to be barbed-wire barriers. Electric wires are to be stretched between the posts, and moreover a series of inspection towers is to be built—

---

* Rasmussen was released December 21, 1942.
† Huitfeldt was sixty-six.

nine of them apparently. Each of these towers is a small two-story building. The ground floor is to be of solid brickwork with concrete foundations; the upper floor is to be built of wood with windows on every side. In the guardroom on the upper floor there is to be a guard with a machine gun, shooting down those extraordinary prisoners who still insist on trying to crawl over, under, or through the barbed wire, electric wire, netting, and concrete posts to get out, instead of using the main entrance. Well, those will be prisoners who are here about Christmastime, for all this won't be done sooner.

When a couple of the towers are built, I assume they will be pulled down again to be placed a meter farther west. And about Christmastime we shan't be here any longer, I'm convinced of that, though now and then recently a wave of pessimism has crept in on me—genuine pessimism. Suppose Germany should really stand the strain, should have undreamed-of resources with corresponding devilishness to carry this war on to absolute ruin. And suppose we should be dragged down with it! No! Suppose the earth were to burst! This is not me; it's a bad edition of my astral body that says such things—and therefore it isn't thinking. The war will be over by the autumn at the latest, and besides I've made up my mind to get home to Kari in good time for our wedding day on August 27th. So it's true all right about the invasion, and more too. I must hurry up and sleep one more night away. Good night.

WEDNESDAY, JUNE 17, 1942 ■ This afternoon I got a big job from the Storm Prince. (It seems as though he's going to be here some time yet.) I am to design quarters for officers and men, up to thirty of them, with dining room, living room, kitchen, etc., for fifty. I have been working intensively on this commission right on to supper, and after supper too. It is marvelous to have a decent job in hand again, and to find that one hasn't got right out of it. I don't much believe this house will be built, but still it's a clear-cut job that can be worked out freely and unhampered by all that usually gets in the way—economy, for instance. *Geld spielt überhaupt keine Rolle* [Money plays no part at all], and then there is the German weakness for size and pomp, which opens out possibilities of planning quite a stylish establishment. I have positively got my blood up already and could hardly tear myself away from the work. But one must have some sleep as well, and I must write a little first to feel comfortable.

Ole Smith-Housken was released today, so now there are only twelve of us court hostages left.

Denzer came back this afternoon. The Segment is crazier than ever. One can't get anything settled. He says he's going to leave here and never come back again. "What the devil am I doing in Norway? There's not even a summer here—the middle of June and still as cold as midwinter. At home in Germany the potato shaws are so high already, and they'll soon be cutting the hay. No, I'm going home in July and not coming back. To hell with the new cow house and barn and all the rest of it; what's it got to do with me? Draw me a little house instead, for me to build in Germany. A little house with four or five rooms and bath—*gell?*"

"*Jawohl!*"

Such was our conversation today, when I wanted to talk to him about the cow-house plan, on which I'm working, and which was a commission from *him*. The only thing I got out of it all was three packets of cigarettes. I got him to promise them, and then I shepherded him right down to the cellar of the *Vermittlung* and collected them myself. I have to do that or I get nothing. And I can do it with the Segment; that's the good thing about him. Otherwise, as I said, he's hopeless to have to deal with. Today he wanted to paint the stone surround of the main prison entrance black. He took the brush out of the hand of the painter, who was busy with some lettering, and smeared a tremendous blob of black paint right in the middle of the stonework. It'll never come off again. The stone is ruined, even though he afterward gave directions to remove the paint and got a supply of spirit for the purpose. I think he did feel a bit sheepish when he realized the *gaffe* he had made.

No serviceable rumors have arrived today, and no confirmation of the invasion rumors. With a bleeding heart I suppose I must give them up.

FRIDAY, JUNE 19, 1942 ■ Yesterday passed into today—literally. I wasn't in bed last night. I was sitting working in the doctor's office all night, and morning too, right up to two o'clock. It was the Storm Prince's commission—quarters for the permanent staff at Grini. The job would normally take a fortnight before one got some practicable ideas hatched out. I was given two days. But I might work overtime as long as I liked. Fancy that!

The worst of it is that the job got hold of me—like drink. It was fun to be wallowing in architecture again. And the night really went like play.

No sooner had I got the drawings "finished" than I heard that Kari was coming at two o'clock. I had only just time to bathe, shave, and smarten myself up. And Kari came, bringing all the children. It was a radiant moment. Denzer came in as well, to swagger and take a look at fru Nansen, and informed her that he would do all in his power to get me released. Nobody asked him, nor can he do it either, but he'll say it to be on the safe side; then if I am released, he takes the credit. *That's* the idea. Still he went away again; his tactlessness didn't extend over the whole of the allotted time, he only managed to spoil five minutes of it. But then he had gone beyond the rules to let the children in, he told Kari; he imagined it might be nice for them to see their father. Fancy, it *was* nice, Denzer; I made that out with lightning acumen the moment I saw them getting out of the car. Fantastically nice. But Kari looked tired and worn, and now I know my thoughts will begin fingering at that—whether there is anything wrong—and so on, and so on.

Perhaps this visit helps! It was so heavenly.

Kari had heard at the Terrace that I would soon be released, but most likely it was the usual talk. They must be sick of her persistence, I imagine, and say anything to get rid of her.

SATURDAY, JUNE 20, 1942 ■ Now another "forlorn hope" has turned up. He has been driving people over the frontier. He writes on a scrap of paper which a man brought to me, God knows how he got hold of it, that he will certainly to be condemned to death. He wants somebody at home to put something in the food they send him, so as to make him very ill. Poor man; that's always the first thought: If only I could have something that would get me into the hospital; then perhaps I might stay there until the war's over.

SUNDAY, JUNE 21, 1942 ■ Denzer looked into the parachute room today. He was as ridiculous as ever. He looked at my drawings for the permanent staff at Grini and wanted copies of them. He'll see that it's built. Afterward, the Norwegian State will take it over, he said. He's never said such a thing before. On the contrary, it has been plain that he was thinking of Grini as a permanent German concentration camp. He went on to speak of Kari and the children, and ground out some insipid compliments.

His attitude and behavior have changed a bit since he's been in Germany. I was expecting as much; only I didn't know which way he would react. It's gradually becoming clear that the *human being* in him is gaining ground. Dread of the future is also a human trait. A settlement is coming—! One will be called to account—! A certain sum of good deeds to good Norwegians may perhaps be a good thing to have in hand on settling day. And the Norwegian State can take over that building and find a use for it—*gell?* He was anxious for me to say yes. I didn't say anything.

Sleep well, Kari. One Sunday less till we meet again.

MONDAY, JUNE 22, 1942 ■ The morning went like a flash; it was swallowed up in a perspective drawing I made of my new building project. The Segment looked in, wanting to see the villa I have been commissioned to design for the Storm Prince. The other day, after I had been up all night at this housing plan, the Storm Prince commissioned me to design a *Guthaus* [mansion]—for himself, presumably. It was to have a number of spacious halls, living rooms, and drawing rooms, a separate servants' wing, a separate servants' entrance, a garage, a workroom with a separate entrance, three bathrooms, and all kinds of aristocratic arrangements. He had no idea how big he wanted it exactly, but whatever I proposed—and I gradually felt it such a joke that I proposed all sorts—he wanted that, too. "*Natürlich, das muss man haben,*" [Of course, one must have that] was his refrain, as though he were afraid I might believe he wasn't used to living in that style. I thought: Either the man has gone completely megalomaniac, or else he's truly managed to embezzle a good round sum, or perhaps both. His *Guthaus* will run to four or five hundred square meters [4,300–5,400 sq. ft.] at the least, but I've not begun it and don't suppose I shall, either. There seems no doubt that he's going at last after all.

Well, the Segment wanted to see this house. When I had nothing to show him, he told me not to draw it at all. It was all rubbish, he said. "That swindler isn't to have a house. Just leave it alone; he's going away. He only wants to make use of you and get something gratis. Don't you do it."

That's what they're like. Always with their knives in each other; they don't mind vilifying each other to anybody, exposing each other, unmasking their corruption and swindling to the prisoners in all its ugliness. It's not many days since the Segment himself spoke to me about a house, on a modest scale indeed. He hasn't acquired a taste for the polite world and still has small, sober, German-peasant claims on existence. Perhaps he ordered the house because he simply had nothing else to give me when I was dunning him for something to do.

TUESDAY, JUNE 23, 1942 ■ Midsummer eve. It's been a fine day, warm and sunny, but it ended in rain and storm. A strange midsummer eve, but I suppose it's strange enough outside, too. So now we're going toward darker days again.

The fall of Tobruk* holds; I'm afraid there's nothing to be done about it. One must

---

* Tobruk, a Libyan seaport on the eastern Mediterranean near the border with Egypt, fell to the Germans on June 21, 1942, following the Battle of Gazala. One historian has called it "a spectacular German victory" and another "one of

resign oneself. It seems Bardia's* gone the same way, one of the German guards said today, and the Axis is at the Egyptian frontier. What is one to think of that? For the present that it's not true. Next that the war will be decided far from Cyrenaica, and last, just that it may postpone the decision for a while—that's all.

Another German—Herold, Esser's secretary at the Terrace†—said to [Thorvald] Moe‡ today that if it lay with him he would release all the hostages. They made such a lot of work for him. But, he went on, the Russians would soon have had it, and then a lot of amnesties would be granted, in his opinion. They actually believe that! If we had to wait for that amnesty, it would indeed be a fairly distant prospect for the hostages, not to say hopeless. But tomorrow I believe I shall be getting a new "west wind"§ that will chase the bad weather back to Jericho, and if not tomorrow, then we'll get it another day. Time is on our side.

The Storm Prince has commissioned me to have his *Guthaus* done by Monday at the latest. By tomorrow morning he must have the basement plan of the scheme for Grini, and I've done that. I haven't started on his *Guthaus*, but I suppose I'm in for it. He came into the hut while I was lying reading in working hours. He didn't say anything; on the contrary, he was as mild as milk. You see he wanted something out of me. Told me not to get up, and said nothing about the book, which he saw. At one time that would have meant at least a month in the trot or a fortnight in a dark cell.

WEDNESDAY, JUNE 24, 1942 ■ Today I've been absorbed in the Storm Prince's chateau. It's overgrowing all bounds. The man who builds it will have to be a multi-millionaire. I can't be bothered restricting myself. Every time I get a new idea I give it free rein, and the estate is waxing. Now it just looks like open ridicule, but he doesn't see that. Today he was in here nodding approvingly at the design for the ground floor, which is close on four hundred and fifty square meters [4,840 sq. ft.]. He was far from having any reductions in mind. On the contrary, he wanted a *Wintergarten* [winter garden] in the plan, too. He shall have his *Wintergarten*.

He wants a shooting lodge as well now, quite a small shooting lodge, with room for a few guests. That also was to be done by Monday. I said I couldn't manage it. He only wanted a few sketches, he told me then, for a very small shooting lodge. He's going to have something to take away right enough, but God knows what he'll do with it. He must

---

the greatest blows to befall British arms in the Second World War." The German general leading the campaign, Erwin Rommel, was promoted to Field Marshal following the battle; the British commander of the Eighth Army, Neil Ritchie, was sacked. As Churchill explained, "Defeat is one thing; disgrace is another." Rommel pursued the British into Egypt, but losses of armor incurred during the Battle of Gazala led to his eventual halt at the First Battle of El Alamein in July 1942 and defeat at the Second Battle of El Alamein (October–November 1942). Rommel was later implicated in the plot to kill Hitler; due to his prominence he was allowed to commit suicide (October 14, 1944) in order to protect his family.

* Bardia is a Mediterranean seaport in eastern Libya.

† SS *Hauptsturmführer* and criminal commissioner, Wilhelm Esser was Adolf Eichmann's representative in Norway. He compiled lists of Jewish stores and members of Jewish congregations and was responsible for issuing the order in May 1940 for the confiscation of all radios owned by Jews. After the war he was sentenced to prison for eight years.

‡ Moe was transferred to Schokken camp in Europe in October 1942 and spent the remainder of the war in captivity in various European camps.

§ "West wind" refers to news emanating from the BBC and surreptitiously received and disseminated in Grini.

be mad after all, I think, raving, hatter-mad. But for me it's really quite a satisfying job, if there only hadn't been such a rush and if I'd had decent drawing paper.

There's a strange atmosphere around nowadays. Slack. Denzer has completely gone out. It's as though he'd lost all interest in Grini. They say there will be a new *Lagerkommandant* arriving soon. In July? Denzer will be staying too, I suppose, but under him. No doubt the Segment will be staying as well, in some post or other. Altogether it seems there is to be a bit of shifting around, and that probably accounts for a certain casualness all along the line. But it's dangerous for the prisoners; they're getting too slack. When we have another purge one fine day, as it's quite certain that we shall, a lot of people will have to smart for it.

Every day now we can see young lads rummaging in the dustbin for refuse which may be edible. Denzer came across one of them today, and when he grasped the state of affairs he took the lad into the kitchen and gave him a plate of soup. I fervently hope this experience impressed him strongly enough to make him do something about the food situation. If the parcel rationing, for instance, was made a little less strict, so that we might have a parcel every week. One thing is certain: if these boys are not to be injured for life they must have more food. For that matter there isn't one among the prisoners who doesn't go away hungry from every meal. I can't remember having had enough to eat from time immemorial, but it doesn't do me any harm, far from it. I can go on losing weight yet awhile and be none the worse, but it's the young ones, always the young ones who are affected. They can't go on and on being hungry all round the clock.

THURSDAY, JUNE 25, 1942 ■ It was late before I got to the "office" tonight. We've had another labor-allocating comedy on the square. Everyone was ordered out at nine o'clock tonight, and so it began. It lasted only an hour, but there was an icy north wind blowing, so we got stiff and numb as we stood there in the ranks, unable to move. The whole gang had mustered, with Denzer at their head.

The object was to get four hundred and fifty men for the fence-building. It is to be speeded up. There are rumors that the camp is to be got ready for the reception of Russian prisoners of war. Men from the *Zentralbauleitung* have been up here raising Cain two days running among the works people. The German building superintendents were the chief targets. Yelling and screaming, louder and louder—and then at length: "Get more people, in the devil's name! Four hundred and fifty!" But these blokes don't understand that the whole fence job turns on the blasting. Holes have to be blasted for every concrete post (four hundred and thirty of them), sites have to be blasted for every tower (nine of them), and four hundred and fifty men can't blast. There are comparatively few who can, and besides, they're short of tools.

Just let them muddle on. Let them put on so many men that they're treading on each other's feet, making it impossible for [Christian] Henriksen* and his gang to get in with their boring and blasting. Tonight they picked out everything that could crawl, old men, invalids, and schoolboys. A lot of working gangs were dissolved, with the most spirited abuse. Now we should get cracking again!

Denzer is funny enough, but we are getting to know him and his ways and mannerisms. Even funnier are a couple of NCOs who try to copy him—gestures, intonations,

---

* Released May 25, 1943.

and all. It's a talentless effort. Denzer *has* a kind of musical-comedy talent. At any rate he's completely mastered the part he plays, and no one can imitate him, for it simply is his own conception of himself and his calling. But after all, Denzer has changed considerably. There is a kind of good humor about him now, a nauseous, half-sneaking good humor, as though he were trying to approach the prisoners more as their comrade and equal.

That applies especially to the "classy" prisoners, those with names and titles, those whom he includes under the common appellation of *anständige Leute* [decent people]. Those he thinks of himself as meeting afterward for a chummy evening in the beer hall of the house I've designed and which "he will see to the building of." Of course "on a national basis," he added! No doubt he thinks they will be delighted at the chance of an evening's gaiety with their former *Lagerkommandant* some time in the future when we are free, and when the State—*der norwegische Statt*—[the Norwegian State] has taken over the building. Want to see that man! No, my worthy Denzer, our kindest wish for you would be that you might disappear into darkest Germany and stay there, never again to stick so much as that arrogant, stupid face of yours up into the light.

Fifty-four were released today. It has been a red-letter day! All the Møre men got out at last, after about a year in this place as hostages. There was indescribable joy. The old men—and most of them were old—became quite tearful with excitement, their hands shook, and they simply couldn't get their things packed.

There are obstinate rumors that the court hostages are to be released on Saturday. "Thoroughly reliable sources" report a statement by "responsible persons" at the Terrace (who *are* responsible there exactly?) that the court hostages have a good chance of getting out along with seventy-four other hostages one day in the very near future. And Saturday is in the very near future. It is the day after tomorrow! A lot of hostages have a firm belief in this, especially the latest arrivals. It almost hurts to refrain from believing in it, too. For to tell the truth, it would be very nice. When I turn my thoughts loose and give them leave to do a bit of grappling with this rumor, perspectives open out, undeniably, that make me feel strangely giddy.

In spite of the lack of news—and the bad news we have had—the atmosphere tonight is radiant. It's good to see so many being released, and then of course it's good to imagine that next time it will be my turn, especially if the next time is to be Saturday.

Otherwise I've been immersed in work on that damn-fool palace of the Storm Prince's. He was up again today. Smooth as butter. He looked at the design and had no objections to make. He didn't understand any of it. He would rather have had only the shooting lodge, he said, but he had to have the chateau as well, for "entertaining."

FRIDAY, JUNE 26, 1942 ■ I've been absorbed in the Storm Prince's *Guthaus* all day, and have hardly raised my eyes from the drawing board. There has been nothing to raise them for, luckily. A number of internal squabbles and difficulties, with the working gangs and building chiefs and personnel office, which are dished up right and left with the storm soup and slimming fare, I've trained myself not to listen to. For there is something every single day. Some German has been making a row.

I've provided myself with earflaps which I can let down, to shut out Grini and Grini gossip and all that may be described as *griniology*. It's very practical, and I am delighted with the invention.

There was no "west wind" today either. It's been overclouded all day, and wet in the woods and fields. Not surveying weather. There's still a cold wind from the north, and I'm freezing. It isn't summer at all—nor in one's mind either. These damned rumors predict success to the devil, and one can't help being affected by them.

Damnable too that someone should begin talking about the hostages being released tomorrow. One keeps on thinking about it, and I know I'll be disappointed now, if nothing comes of it, even though I've made up my mind not to believe in it. Over in the hostages' hut there is sheer fever—*Entlassungsfeber!* [release fever!] There it's long been dead certain that we go home tomorrow. They're already packing.

Two Grini hostages were released today. Why? If anyone had asked me to point out a man who didn't deserve to be released, and who, frankly, would be the better for a longer spell, I'd have pointed out one of those. He's taking no experience away with him. He'll always believe that it was dashing and plucky to parade in slippers, stand with folded arms in the ranks, talk out loud, and waggle his knees. He'll always believe that one could dodge as much as one liked, if only one "knew the dodge." Every day I've been expecting Kunz or someone else to launch a fast one at his mug and remove a little of his superiority, but now instead he's being released. Well, well—that's the way of things. But even that one contemplates with great joy. A prisoner freed, no matter who, makes joy in Jerusalem.*

SUNDAY, JUNE 28, 1942 ■ I couldn't be bothered writing yesterday. I was tired and not in the mood after a full day's work. Nor was there anything to write about. Unless that we were not released, as everyone had expected. My disappointment failed to materialize. It turned out that I simply hadn't believed a word of it. Now of course tomorrow is to be the day. Many are quite certain of it, as certain as they were before that we should be released yesterday. That's how the days go in a prison.

I had an important message yesterday for my two forlorn hopes. Their cases are both deferred until the autumn. The Germans have too much to do and not enough people. They are now in contact with good lawyers, who both warn them against any drastic step. There's plenty of time to wait now, and every reason to believe the cases will settle themselves, in that the war will play the hangmen the trick of stopping!

Today we've had a real Sunday. A whole day without work, as in the old times. We could sleep until half-past seven and it was lovely. In our hut we actually had eggs and bacon for breakfast, only a small postage stamp of bacon indeed (it was a little bit of Adolf, the cottage pig, that Kari sent me in her last parcel)† and half an egg (hard-boiled), but good heavens what a banquet!

I had a chat with fru Rinnan through a window today, and told her that Frode is getting two parcels a week and that the children are having a splendid time in the country.

MONDAY, JUNE 29, 1942 ■ There was no release today either, but I'm blessed if the optimism doesn't hold. Now it's tomorrow, or at any rate in the course of the week. They're getting ready, betting and waiting. If they only keep it up long enough, the time will pass, and then the optimism will be justified one day.

---

* A phrase out of 2 Chronicles 30:26 describing the celebration of the Passover: "So there was great joy in Jerusalem."
† The Nansens kept two pigs: Adolf [Hitler] and Hermann [Göring].

TUESDAY, JUNE 30, 1942 ◼ No news. Sunshine all day. Work all day. Now I've finished the Storm Prince's rubbish. He goes tomorrow. He looked in this evening. He *is* mad. Also he wants to take the original designs with him. I think of forgetting that. Denzer looked in with a new *Hauptsturmbannoberführer* or something of the kind.* Denzer is a fool. The new man was repellent and loathsome looking. They wanted me to take a commission in the SS. They said they needed men like me. I didn't understand German, also I was busy and went on drawing. The surveyors were out. Nothing new. The box moved three meters west. Cigarettes rolled tonight. Run right out of tobacco. Letters and drawings hidden. *Entlassungsfeber* cooling off. Otherwise nothing of importance, and it's getting close to midnight. It'll soon be quite dark.† Good night, Kari. I'll be coming!

THURSDAY, JULY 2, 1942 ◼ Yesterday I was *detailed*, so I got no writing done. I had to work until two in the morning to get a drawing finished for the *Hauptmann* [Captain]. It was to be delivered at eight o'clock this morning, and was. A singular drawing. The job was to do a caricature of a man I've never seen, and who isn't here. I was provided with a small photograph, in which the man's head was the size of one of the letters in this diary, and the information that he was a whale at carving and eating pig's head. Consequently I depicted the man (who is the captain's adjutant and thirty years old today) standing with uplifted bayonet over a grinning, exceptionally dead, and smoked pig's head on a dish. He was in full uniform. The drawing was placed on another sheet in a folded "birthday card." In the first sheet I cut a hole, following the outlines of the pig's head, so that it grinned through to the front page, which furnished it with a German officer's cap and uniform introduced into a vignette of guns and vine tendrils round the hole. It was audacious, but it got by. It went as I was counting on. They didn't notice the gibe! My friends were sure that it would land me in *Einzelhaft*.

An instance of the level of information among the German officers: Stange and Kunz—*Oberscharführers* both—were round at Erling's today. They had been on a bit of a rampage in the huts; that is, they "inspected" and amused themselves by chucking out and beating up all who were there in working hours, including the sick. Yesterday Kunz threw out a man who was very ill. Today he's gone into the hospital; it turned out that he has scarlet fever. This case was mentioned, and there was talk about the food situation and our not getting enough to eat. It happens almost every day that someone faints or collapses at the working place or on parade. In this connection Erling spoke of the doctors' calorie calculations, which show quite a glaring deficit. Then said Stange, after jeering at this nonsense about calories, which he regards as humbug to cover laziness and ill will: "I, for instance, have never had my calories examined!"

It must be added that Stange has been victualing chief here for many months.

Sevastopol has fallen. It doesn't seem as though we can get away from it, and in Egypt things looked nasty. The Germans have long since crossed the frontier, and announce that

---

* There is no such title; presumably Nansen is showing his contempt for formal SS titles. He was not the only concentration camp inmate to look askance at such titles. In David Koker's diary the Dutch Jew interned at Vught
mentions an "*Oberhauptscharführer*." His editor notes that no such title existed and observes, "David may be using
the designation. . . ironically: the Dutch were amused by the German habit of adding the adjective *ober-* (superior)
even to lowly occupations such as that of waiting on tables."

† Because of Oslo's northern location, the sun does not set until almost 11 p.m. and rises again before 4 a.m. at this time
of the year (i.e., days after the summer solstice).

Rommel is approaching Alexandria. Part of the French Navy is laid up there. What's going to happen? It's a tense situation, and not much fun sitting here with no "west wind." How much is true? How much importance is ascribed to Egypt and Sevastopol? Is this the well-known last offensive before the breakdown? Like the one in August 1918?

SATURDAY, JULY 4, 1942 ■ So one more week has glided into oblivion, and it's Saturday. But no common Saturday. In the morning Kari arrived quite unexpectedly with a visiting permit. Marit was there, too. That was a welcome surprise. On the other hand it may imply that there is to be no release of hostages in the near future. A permit would scarcely be given if that was the idea. Though who knows; logic has never bothered them either at the Terrace or elsewhere. On the contrary; one gets the impression that every-thing is as haphazard as it can possibly be.

I couldn't get any talk with Kari about news, but to judge by her looks and joyous spirits, things are going well. She's hardly ever struck me as so cheerful and optimistic. I'm blessed if Denzer didn't come in today as well, and steal some of our precious minutes with his monkey tricks. I could have sat for hours and just looked at her, held her hand and Marit's, and been in heaven.

SUNDAY, JULY 5, 1942 ■ Tonight we held a big open-air concert out among the huts. A man from Vestland who is a fisherman and actor recited. I ruined three songs plus my voice by trying to make it carry beyond the front rows. The concert ended with the national anthem, which no one sang, but Robert [Andersen] played. Many hundreds of prisoners had found strength through the concert, and now that the Storm Prince is gone forever, perhaps we can resume our Sunday evenings in that form. There will be room for many more than we could get into the church. We must see about arranging the next performance and make a really good evening of it.

Now I'm sitting here after a bright and good Sunday. Will it be the last at Grini? And isn't it the damnedest thing—I can't stop listening to the tempting, seductive, sly voice inside me whispering that perhaps you'll be getting out in this very week that's coming. Perhaps . . . perhaps. . . ! But I've resolved to pay no attention. I won't go mincing round in suspense until disappointment comes and throws me down bang into the darkness. I'll be here until the war is over—you're sure to manage fine, Kari, won't you? I feel tonight as though I had strength and reserves and spirit enough to stay on for years.

MONDAY, JULY 6, 1942 ■ I've nothing to do these days. It looks as though they had clean forgotten me after the Segment went. Never mind; I shall make the time pass all right.

Erling is possessed with *Entlassungsfeber*. Denzer came in to him last night and asked if he'd considered who should take his place if he were to leave. After that he's expecting to be released any day.*

TUESDAY, JULY 7, 1942 ■ An illegal newspaper has taken a powerful grip on itself and forced its way into the lion's den. The truth about Cyrenaica was disheartening. The English have suffered a grave defeat. Churchill makes a clean breast of it and says it has

---

* Steen wasn't in fact released until February 26, 1943.

altered the situation in the Mediterranean. The defeat was highly unexpected, he says, and nothing graver has happened to them since France capitulated. He admits heavy losses, too, and has very little indeed to bring forward by way of comfort and counterbalance. He says they're sending powerful reinforcements. But, he says, the Germans also have reinforcements on the way (God knows where from?), and the whole thing is becoming a race against time for both sides.

WEDNESDAY, JULY 8, 1942 ■ There are twelve *Schein* lying in the *Vermittlung*— twelve *Entlassungsschein*—and there are exactly twelve of us left now in the court gang. An odd coincidence; but certainly a coincidence, a sheer accident. Devil take it; even I can't keep clear of this fever. It's as though I've lost the initiative to start on anything fresh. I have a couple of little house-jobs for fellow prisoners. But I'm not composed enough to set to. I'm afraid this week will have to pass first.

Bjørn Oscar [Andersen]* and I had a funny little scene with Kunz today. Bjørn Oscar was busy washing the floor of the hut, and I was down there in working hours to wash my hands, have a smoke, and take it easy for a bit. It's a joke of ours to converse like aged men, who have been forty years in Grini. We were at it when Kunz turned up in the passage without our noticing. The door was open, and our piping, senile voices carried a long way. Kunz came stalking them to see what this queer thing meant. We went on for some time and didn't see him until the moment when he roared out, "What's up? What's wrong with your voice?"

Bjørn Oscar still kept on with it; I stopped.

Kunz asked again and I tried to explain that it was only nonsense. Bjørn Oscar piped cheerily on, and Kunz had to laugh. He was really *smiling* before he turned and walked out, having clean forgotten to ask what I was doing in the hut in working hours. To be sure he collected himself promptly afterward, returned and rushed into the privy to see if there was anyone dodging there. He found two outdoor workers, took them down to his cellar (under the *Vermittlung*) and gave them a beating with a stick. Later he reported them to the Commandant, and now the poor devils are locked up each in a cell on bread and water.

There was a little breath of "west wind" at noon. The news was scanty but good. The Americans started their own action in Europe on Independence Day, the fourth of July.† Genuine American, with an eye for publicity value in everything. Frode is all right, getting food parcels and well treated; his children are doing excellently. Love to Hannagreta, his wife.

THURSDAY, JULY 9, 1942 ■ Today all at once I began collecting my things, packing, and making everything ready. I hadn't settled it in my mind at all, nor even been thinking of it, but I suddenly got to work as though impelled by an instinct. Now I'm ready to leave. The only unlawful thing I've got now is this scrap of paper I'm writing on. The rest of the diary, the thirteen pages I finished yesterday, are now lying soldered up in a box in the woods near the Anker road. I don't myself know where. If necessary I can easily tear

---

* Released December 20, 1943.
† The United States conducted its first bombing raid of World War II in Europe when six planes joined the British in attacking German air bases in Holland.

this up. It's not worth taking any risks if I *were* to get out tomorrow—or the day after—or later on?

At dinnertime I was called down for questioning in the *Vermittlung*. It was Herold who did the questioning. My entire life was unrolled, from the cradle to the present day. He tried to make out that my mother was a Jewess. They tried the same in an examination at the Terrace when I was first arrested more than a year ago. It didn't work that time, nor yet this. He dwelt a long time on Nansen Relief and its activity, and was avid to pick a quarrel with me about the Jews. He inveigled me into argument and I couldn't stop myself. Besides it's a kind of treason to hold one's tongue.

Then he dwelt a bit on my authorship of the Grini song, but there was really nothing of special interest to him. Clearly the point was just to get a résumé of my whole career and make it look—in its entirety—like a menace to the Third Reich. I was confronted with a good-sized collection of "anti-German" remarks I've made throughout the years in lectures and articles on the refugee question. Herold produced them from a fat briefcase full of documents, on the outside of which, to my great dismay, I saw my name in big letters. All of them were furnished with a source, year, and date. I felt positively flattered by so much attention.

He confronted me with things I was supposed to have said to one of the drivers at Grini. I didn't believe in the Russian atrocities they were using as publicity. Katyn, etc.* The point of interest here is that the drivers tell tales. It must be Liwa. He's the most serious Nazi, and of course for *Parteigenossen* [Party members] informing is a duty. The questioning took up the whole dinner hour and more.

After dinner I was sent for again to sign the report. I couldn't sign; it was quite wrong in many places, tendentiously distorted on vital points. I drew Herold's attention to this, and he was intensely annoyed at being obliged to have it rewritten. I took a huge risk at his request. I signed *in blanco*. He would correct the mistakes, he said, and he had struck out what was wrong, so the manuscript was defaced anyhow. Only the last page was untouched, and it was all right. I signed that. I was sorry afterward.

If he's a swine, as he is of course, he can put anything he likes in the report with my name under it. But then I decided that the whole report is probably neither here nor there. No doubt my fate is settled in advance, and the report is only another document in the great paper mill.

SATURDAY, JULY 11, 1942 ■ Saturday again. This week slipped through one's fingers. There was great suspense this morning. The court gang had high hopes for the day. They

---

* At the Katyn Forest in Russia thousands of Polish military officers were murdered by the Soviet secret police on Stalin's express orders; together with a larger extermination of Polish officers and members of the Polish intelligentsia conducted April–May 1940, it was part of Stalin's plan to deprive the country of its best military and managerial talent. The mass graves were discovered by the German army following its conquest of large areas of western Russia. The Soviet Union only formally acknowledged responsibility for the massacres in 1990, the fiftieth anniversary of the crime. It is estimated that approximately twenty-two thousand Polish nationals were murdered at Katyn and other locations in Russia, Belarus, and Western Ukraine. What is most unusual is Nansen's mention of a possible Soviet atrocity at this early date. Although rumors of the executions had circulated as early as 1942, the Germans later claimed that the graves were not discovered until early 1943, and in any event the official German radio announcement of their discovery, a major propaganda victory, did not occur until April 13, 1943. How this information had already reached Norway nine months earlier is unknown.

titivated as though it were Sunday. Shaved and shining they turned out for morning roll call, and doubtless most of them had been tidying up trunks and knapsacks on the sly, against an emergency, as it were. But the morning passed, exactly like other mornings. And it came dinnertime, and nothing had happened. And it was a dinner like all the other dinners. The fish was perhaps even saltier than usual, the potatoes bluer, the atmosphere more depressed.

One tried to have a nap as usual and look unconcerned, as though it were any other Saturday. It wouldn't do. It was impossible to shut one's eyes, let alone one's ears. And so midday passed. The next spell began. It was long and hard, but nothing happened. Nothing. And evening came.

Now one almost wished oneself unshaved and ordinary, just to have something to hide the disappointment in, for it was not to be concealed. The sarcasms and valiant jokes didn't ring quite true. It couldn't be covered up; one was disappointed, horribly disappointed. So then one had to turn right round, try to recover the peace one had before, the peace accompanying the certainty that one was to be here until the war ended.

It's curious in a hut like this where people live on top of each other month after month. It's no use hiding oneself. One gets so sensitive to fine shades. Without really knowing each other, we know each other through and through, know exactly what's up, even though perhaps we would rather not. One often feels almost tactless, because without wanting to or doing anything about it, one intrudes, as it were, into other people's thoughts, into another man's territory, where one knows and feels oneself unwelcome.

"Why, haven't you gotten out yet?" How many times have I been asked that question today? My examination—which may have been about release—everyone of course has heard of. And then the question comes in passing. And I sit here and *know* I'm not getting out. It's mere madness to think differently. Herold, the questioning—it's all plain enough. They won't let *me* out. And yet?

And I was so snug in my original conviction that I shouldn't get out until the war was over. The idea didn't seem to me at all frightening; I looked out for tasks to occupy me here far ahead; it would have gone first rate, if only this hadn't come—all these rumors— and the questioning. Now the whole thing is overturned. There's no foothold anywhere. It will take time to find one's balance again, to build up one's prison life anew—that is, if it should be necessary?

TUESDAY, JULY 14, 1942 ■ Yesterday it was six months since my arrest. Half a year in prison! And yet I'm lucky, downright damned lucky. I'm only a hostage and have suffered no ill treatment. How easily it might have been different, when I think back over wanton playing with fire. How easily I might have been laid by the heels for something serious. But it *was* a disappointment not to get out now, a genuine disappointment. Really the first I've had here.

There was no sign of an *Entlassung* [release] of hostages today either. On the contrary. At Victoria Terrace it's just been said that hostages must reckon on at least a year's imprisonment. I haven't yet grown so pessimistic as to believe that anyone at all will have to stay on another year, or rather half year, and there's no ground for attaching excessive weight to any remark whatever from the Terrace, but for that matter it agrees with my original view: *We'll be here until the war is over.*

I've moved my office again, this time to a hut that also contains the bookbinding shop with [Harald] Grieg, [Einar] Skavlan,* and Per Krohg. Will it be the last removal? Well, never mind. I haven't much to lose or anything to gain either. But it's midnight. Good night.

WEDNESDAY, JULY 15, 1942 ■ Denzer has apparently ceased to be *Lagerkommandant*. It seems a new one arrived today. Reinhardt† of the Terrace is said to have "installed" him when he was here today. The same Reinhardt carried out an inspection which will no doubt lead to fresh regulations. At any rate the library was closed. "For the present," Denzer had said, to gloss it over a bit. All reading matter is to be removed, the fiat goes, and no one may leave his cell after supper. We were expecting something of the kind. Of course there *had* to be some devilment, something that would hit everyone.

In the hospital section Reinhardt had discovered a bridge diploma on the wall of a cell. It was confiscated and taken off to the Terrace, with some furious remarks about our apparently thinking Grini was a rest home. I drew the diploma. It may turn out awkward enough, though there's nothing in the least offensive about the drawing, unless indeed a border in the Norwegian colors.

There's a report that from now on card-playing is to be forbidden too, and all packs are to be confiscated. That will affect a lot of people, so he's got a bull's-eye there all right.

THURSDAY, JULY 16, 1942 ■ This morning I had a box soldered, and some more chapters disappeared from view. I feel so relieved every time, I almost wish for an inspection and search just to show there's nothing to be found, but before the day is out, off I start again. I can't let it alone. And I should feel a genuine bereavement if these night hours of mine were to get lost. So many strange moods, so many queer experiences, so much intensely dramatic stuff will emerge again from these pages when I turn to them later on in life.

Today the venerable Francis Bull and I put our heads together over a matchbox. Within it lay a small, folded scrap of paper covered with minute writing. It was the news—the "west wind"—direct from London. We look round guiltily, make sure that the door is shut and that there are no "dangerous characters" about. And greedily we suck in the reports from outside, looking like small boys engrossed in a crib sheet at school.

The crib sheet is long and full of matter, and we know this to be the truth, as it comes from London at least. So *that* and *that* was true, but *that* was an exaggerated rumor, and *that* was sheer fabrication. It's a kind of winnowing process. Everything superfluous goes into the waste-paper basket—all the rough sketches, all the false ideas. There remains only

---

* Skavlan (1882–1954) was a journalist, newspaper editor, theater director, and critic. He was editor-in-chief of the newspaper *Dagbladet* from 1915 to 1954, except for a short period when he was theater director for the National Theater (1928–1930) and while imprisoned at Grini for refusing to comply with Nazi editorial demands. At the time of his death *Dagbladet* was the second largest newspaper in Norway. He was released October 19, 1943.

† SS *Sturmbannführer* Hellmuth Reinhard (1911–?). Reinhard was born Hermann Gustav Hellmuth Patzschke. He joined the SS in 1934 and in 1939 adopted the name Reinhard. He was chief of the Gestapo in Norway from January 1942, reporting to Heinrich Fehlis until February 1945 when he returned to Germany. After the war Reinhard reverted to his original name, and thereby escaped notice and prosecution until 1964, when he was discovered to have married his "widow." Tried in 1967 in Baden-Baden, West Germany, Reinhard/Patzschke was convicted of complicity in the murder of Norwegian Jews and resistance fighters and sentenced to five years imprisonment (the prosecution had asked for life). He was released in 1970.

so much as can be used to build on, so much as is fact, whether bad or good. And when the whole sheet has been read through, one can positively feel how much good it did, how it has composed one's mind.

We have a bit of discussion back and forth on what we've heard. We are delighted. We work out the most favorable interpretation possible of what was not clear. We talk in whispers. Then I fold the splendid little scrap again until it's even smaller, put the matches back on top, and pocket the matchbox.

Not a living soul will find the "west wind," not if they open the box and empty all the matches out. For the matchbox has the little peculiarity of a double bottom. And between the two the "west wind" lies folded up, in silence and obscurity. And Francis goes back to his wood carving and I to my architecture with strength renewed and fresh hope in mind and soul.

On days like this the long, tough afternoon spell goes like play. *Whoosh*—it's evening again. Today we've had parcels, several of us, so the larder is rich again. There will be butter and something extra on every slice. As usual the hut is full of smoke from the toasting. We have a griddle, and on that we toast about sixty slices of bread twice a day. It's an incredible improvement to toast this heavy, tough bread. It's more easily digested and much better to eat. Strange that we should be allowed to do this toasting, or rather perhaps that no one should have found out we're doing it. It would be stopped for sure. I can't possibly imagine that anything that does us so much good and gives us so much pleasure can be allowed!

The reading out of the "west wind" in the hut is another of the bright moments of existence. Grunts of satisfaction come from all sides as the bulletins are read. If they say for instance that large numbers of Germans have been killed, the universal glee has an effect of sheer cannibalism. One rubs one's hands and wishes for a much, much higher figure next time. One thinks of Kunz, Stange, and Denzer, or of some Terrace devil, or of course of our native gangsters as well, and one's desires wallow in their death and destruction, without the least restraint.

Overcome evil with good! Who dares to say that today?* And what sense would there be in it? Should Hitler not be overcome? And is it to be done with good? The only question is whether there will be anything left when the struggle is over. *That* is the great catastrophe that threatens, that evil may dictate the peace and plan the future. Then indeed all will have been in vain. But it will never be. I feel convinced that in spite of everything this is not the end; on the contrary, it's rather the beginning.

Today the new prohibitions were specified in detail. All cards, all pictures (including family photographs), and all musical instruments are to be confiscated. We had an extra roll call at nine tonight. The new *Lagerkommandant* was introduced in front. He is called Seitel or Seidler† or something like that, and is the oily little devil who has been going

---

* In 1941 the clergy of the established Church (Lutheran) were increasingly at odds with the occupation authorities, ultimately leading to the resignation of all Norway's bishops and virtually all of its ministers. The opening salvo in this struggle occurred on January 15, 1941, when all seven bishops sent a letter to the Department of Church and Education asking for clarification of the Church's position in a German-occupied Norway. When the answer was unsatisfactory, they issued a circular letter on February 16, 1941, to be read to all congregations. In the concluding paragraph the bishops wrote, "Equally we adjure our people . . . to abstain from violence and wrong. . . . Scripture says: Do not repay evil with evil, but overcome evil with good." Doubtless Nansen had this admonition in mind when writing this entry.

† Alfred Zeidler (1902–?). After the war Zeidler was tried and sentenced to life imprisonment but was released in 1953.

West wind—the news bulletin being studied in the hut at night.

round with Denzer lately. Denzer has been made something called *Schutzhaftlagerführer* [Head of protective custody camp], and the Segment is to be his deputy when he comes back. Working hours have been altered. Now we are to get up at half-past four (!!), work until eleven, and rest until one. Then work until seven as usual, from Monday. But it's late. Good night, Kari.

FRIDAY, JULY 17, 1942 ■ The change of chief created no fuss beyond the extra roll call last night, and then the new vetoes. It's possible for that matter that the vetoes derive from Reinhardt after his tour the other day, and that the new Commandant is "innocent." As yet we don't know this man, but to judge by looks we may have trouble from him.

Tomorrow is Quisling's birthday. Many have high hopes of that scoundrel's fifty-some-thingth anniversary. They believe in an amnesty, and rumors are buzzing. I don't believe in it. I've left off listening to that kind of thing and am getting quite calm again. Today I chopped wood for three hours for a bit of exercise. Now it's dark; I have no candle, so I must stop.

SATURDAY, JULY 18, 1942 ■ Saturday again. This week vanished like a sigh. What on earth became of all the days? What happened? What did I do on Wednesday? On Thursday? Nothing. I was Prisoner 1380, who has really nothing to do, who leads a queer sort of prison life in an office with private jobs for the officers as his chief task, and who is forgotten for weeks on end and left to himself. Perhaps it's not so queer that the days should slip through my fingers, for I have always enough to occupy me. There are a lot of fellows lining up to get drawings for houses, and a good many lining up for help of other kinds. The channels are now oiled and greased; they function excellently and much more quickly than before. Almost every day a couple of hours goes in preparing and arranging the "channel goods." There's a lot to do to it. This week the traffic has been lively. So it was Saturday before I knew it.

Nils Ramm* was out today with a remarkably free-spoken guard. What he said was interesting, and I think perhaps also typical of the ideas of very many Germans today. Nils's first encounter with him was some time ago, when he met him out on the grounds and saluted him according to regulations. The guard had asked him not to salute and said he asked everyone the same; he felt uncomfortable when the prisoners took off their caps to him. His parting words were, "*Guten Tag, Kamerad*" [Good day, comrade].

This previous acquaintance established contact from the first moment, when he went along today on the surveyors' outing. In a corner of the woods they had sat down and talked for more than two hours. The German had told a little about himself. He was married, but to the question whether he had any children he only made the reply, now hackneyed from repetition, that no, in any case they would be nothing but cannon fodder.

They talked about conditions at Grini. The guard said that his countrymen (he was referring to the chiefs from the Commandant downward) behaved in such a way that he often felt ashamed of being a German. But then he added something that shows how even he and others like him are taken in. He said that if *unser Führer* [our Leader] saw or heard how these Germans treated the Norwegian prisoners here, they would all be shot.

What had occurred last night the guard described as an open scandal. In the Com-

---

* Ultimately transferred to prisons in Germany until the end of the war.

mandant's house there had been a positive drunken orgy. Denzer and the Commandant and doubtless a lot of others had been as drunk as lords and had run amok until three or four in the morning—screeched and hooted and thumped and carried on like schoolboys on their first binge—and had awakened the whole camp (only not me, I slept like a top). They kept it up all the rest of the night, and the Commandant turned out on morning roll call dead drunk and stinking. He amused himself by reeling round, seeing that everyone had his jacket buttoned up to the neck. Afterward he took up his stand and stopped all the working groups in turn as they marched past him, because they hadn't saluted properly. It was sickening to see that crapulent fellow staggering about with his loose, malicious, almost sadistic smirk and his half-closed eyes, and to know oneself at the mercy of such a fellow's whims. Now the Commandant and Denzer and the rest of the band are sleeping it off. Balabanov announced that fact loudly and clearly in the *Vermittlung* in the hearing of quite a crowd. He declared that on his next visit to the Terrace he would complain. Here he had to work away all day (sic!)—and then he was kept awake all night by wild shrieks and deafening uproar from those drunken tramps—the men in charge of the camp.

But to return to the German guard. He no longer thought Germany would win, but said that after all it didn't matter who won; in any case we should all be destitute and poverty stricken. That fitted in with a theory he had about the real cause of the war. It was the "big people" in all countries who had engineered it, in his view. The workers and "little people" in the community had got up and on too far; they must be pushed back down into misery. Therefore the "big people" had long been deliberately working for war, and there was an agreement among them, in his view, an international agreement.

He maintains that eighty per cent of the German nation think and believe as he does, but they are gagged and bound, he says. Anyone who tried to speak his mind would inevitably be shot.

He thought the war would—indeed *must*—last a long time. For, said he, the German Army can't be beaten, and if the others should win the war, Germany would be done for—wiped off the map—and the German people would become the slaves of the conquerors. Therefore the Germans must fight to the last man. He realized all right that there would never be negotiations for a compromise peace with the present rulers of Germany, and oddly enough he said, in so many words, which was a trifle inconsistent with his former vague intimations of respect for the leader, that they ought to be wiped out, all the Nazis—vanish from the face of the earth! But he also expressed doubts of the possibility of "reasonable" peace negotiations with the real German people—the eighty percent!

Before they parted, he begged that what he had said might go no further—not even to his comrades—for if it came out, he would be shot. What he told Nils about his wife's parting words is an almost childishly touching proof that we have to deal here with a simple, straightforward character. His wife had asked him to treat the prisoners as his heart prompted—and then the prisoners would treat him in the same way. What a message for a German police soldier to take away with him at this time, when he marches off to stand guard over the infamies of his countrymen!

SUNDAY, JULY 19, 1942 ■ It actually got to three o'clock last night, and yet I didn't manage to write nearly all I had on my mind. And however it came about, I didn't even manage to say good night properly. I simply broke off short and went to bed, without even reading a single page of my unlawful book. Something happened yesterday evening; something happened last night, and something has happened today—Sunday. I just don't know how I'm to get it all in.

Recently I've often noticed with a certain dismay that one's power of indignation is relaxing. What is the use? But today at ten o'clock parade it burst into flame, and it is still burning and quivering within me as I write this. But let me begin at the beginning.

Yesterday evening Felix Tschudi,* as hut leader of Number 8, was called down for questioning along with three or four other men. It turned out that they had been reported by one or more of those in the hut for talking politics and disparaging Hitler and Quisling. Felix had not joined in, but it's his duty as hut leader to see that nothing of the kind takes place and to report every instance of it. He was promptly degraded and dismissed from his post as hut leader. It was Denzer who did the talking; the Commandant was merely there. And Denzer's antics had been quite fabulous. Felix is a shipowner. Aha! *Kapital!* Naturally an opponent of the new era—National Socialism, equality, comradeship between high and low. Naturally, as a shipowner and capitalist he fights against us who are for a new order! Tries to hinder us in our endeavors to create a better, juster world. And in his post of confidence as hut leader he gives the men complete liberty to disparage our leaders, while coming down on those who defend them and understand them.

When he had more or less finished his outpourings, word was sent for all those who lived in Number 8. They had to repair to the *Vermittlung* on the double, driven by Kunz and Claffy, who also had to run. (It was some comfort and satisfaction to see them pounding along, for our chaps were young and nimble and they ran like the devil.) On arrival they came in for a sermon and the news that they were all to have two hours' punishment work right after parade next morning. The Nazi [Kristian] Forsberg was appointed the new hut representative.† Then they were allowed to run back to Number 8 again. It's not yet settled how Felix and the three or four others are to be punished.

At last evening came, and many slept the sleep of the just until well into the "morning hours"—for it was Sunday. (I was sitting writing, and could hear that there was something going on outside late in the night—a lot of people, cars, and din. I'll come to that afterward. First I must describe the end of the other story.) On parade this morning more Germans than usual had turned out, Denzer, Claffy, Kunze,‡ Jantzen, and Reinitz, but the Commandant himself was not there. I suppose he can't have had his sleep out yet.

When the counting was over, it began. Denzer aired his eloquence, and Erling [Steen] had to translate. It was an account of what had happened and a statement that such things would not be tolerated, but would be suppressed with an iron hand. He kept on until he had repeated himself a number of times in every key and with appropriate gestures. Then all foremen and hut leaders were called out, while the others were allowed to march back to the huts. I posted myself at the window of the hut and became witness to an uncommon spectacle on the square.

First these responsible men were put through ordinary drill. All in German, of course.

---

* Released April 12, 1945.
† Released December 20, 1942.
‡ Kunze should not to be confused with Kunz. Kunz was an *Oberscharführer* and had been at the camp a while; *Kunze* an *Unterscharführer* who had just recently arrived. O.N. Kunze was in charge of the trotting gang; after the war he was sentenced to twenty years in prison.

Erling gave the commands as dictated by Denzer who was rushing about giving a performance of his own. He swung his stick, talked in a bass voice, shrilled in a high treble, smacked the stick against his riding boots to emphasize his turns of phrase, spun round on his heels this way and that, squatted down and peered, and demonstrated in word and action all the military drill he could elucidate with his funny, fat body and his stage voice.

It was an effort to keep one's countenance. He was ludicrous, but horrid at the same time. Then they had to set off on the double—round and round—and lastly there was another fall-in. They got a further lecture on the disciplinary rules they were appointed to enforce. They were responsible for their men. An extra little comedy developed from the last order: *Tretet zurück!* [Step back!] That wasn't it! *Weggetreten!* [Dismissed!] that was it, and it was to come out so fast and shrill that it sounded more like hawking. At the same time he demonstrated how this order was to be obeyed. One did a fantastically brisk about turn to the left and then made off, straight backward, for every cent one was worth. One vanished, so to speak, instantaneously. No one who saw his demonstration of this little trick, the vanishing trick, will ever forget it.

Then came the next act. It included everyone from Number 8, *except the informers.* The same drill followed here, the same demonstrations, the same gestures and tirades. They had to march and run and march and run interminably. And at the command *"Hinlegen"* [lie down] they had to throw themselves down on their bellies and lie motionless until they got the command: *"Aufstehen!"* [Get up!] The German swine liked that exercise. They smiled and gloated over the Norwegian prisoners lying in the dust at their feet, while they stood smoking cigarettes, rapping their high boots with their sticks, laughing, chattering, and pointing. It made one's blood boil.

The situation wasn't without its funny side, that is undeniable. Over a hundred men flinging themselves on their bellies and lying just as they came down. There was a collision of bodies and heads, which had a singular effect. I can't deny that both a fellow prisoner and myself laughed until we cried. But it was no healthy laughter; we could just as easily have wept with rage and indignation.

All the Germans took part in giving the commands; it was as though they worked each other up. Reinitz walked about flicking people under the chin if they didn't hold their heads right. Kunze bellowed—and Claffy, yes, indeed, Claffy was in a class by himself. He played the ape to them. It was macabre to see that Norwegian traitor running about ordering his countrymen to fling themselves on their bellies in the dust before their tyrants—his "friends." Ugh, the hangman's assistant!

When that scene was over, it seemed to be the end. Jantzen, Reinitz and the Lieutenant took their leave. All the gangsters shook each other by the hand, gave the *Heil Hitler* salute with raised arms and heel-smacking, thanked each other for being present and behaved like Germans. When they were gone, however, Denzer thought of something he'd forgotten, and sent for the three clergymen—a Catholic priest and two of the established Church—[Arne] Thu* and [Ole] Sæverud.†

Now punishment drill for these three was to begin. An extra little tidbit before lunch. The Catholic was let off, because he had drilled that morning with Number 8. The other

---

* *Time Magazine* reported in its December 25, 1944, issue that Thu, the "vicar of Vestby and veteran Indian missionary, died in . . . Grini last June after being forced to crawl hundreds of yards with his hands behind his back and a latrine bucket in his teeth."

† Released December 2, 1942.

two had to go through it. They had held services, and the same morning, too. Therefore they were now to be punished.

First a speech was made to them by Denzer, and translated by Claffy in the purest idiom of Oslofjord. "You held a service or suchlike, eh? Well, that's forbidden from now on. You can believe and think what you like, but you're not allowed to hold meetings or get at any of the other prisoners. You should have asked leave for your preaching. You knew it was wrong, and that's why you broke the rule. Your Bibles are confiscated, and you're not allowed to do any Bible reading after this."

At this point we heard the bells ringing from Røa church, and then began one of the most infamous and provocatively insulting displays I have ever witnessed. These two clergymen had to run round the square and keep on throwing themselves down in the dust before those thorough-paced hooligans. On one occasion Sæverud hadn't his face right down on the ground. Kunze came along and shoved his head down with one foot so that nose and chin went right into the dust where people are spitting all day long. The bells rang on, proclaiming that it was churchtime. Denzer lit a cigarette and enjoyed his power. Kunze and Claffy gave the orders.

The two priests carried them all out with admirable calm and self-possession, while we others absolutely trembled with rage. This was almost beyond bearing! Two clergymen, broken-winded with running round the square again and again, lying prostrate in the dust before this archgangster, because they had exercised their calling and held a service in prison! And the punishment took place in the middle of churchtime, while the bells were ringing, and the commands were given by a Norwegian traitor!

I can hardly control my indignation even yet, as I sit here. It's been quivering within me all day. Oh, if I could only express my feelings, but I'm at their mercy today.

I am paralyzed, especially after hearing tonight that I'm to be sent to Germany. So *that* was the outcome of the golden dreams. I've told Kari in a letter that will go out with this tomorrow, so I haven't much time to waste; it's past midnight already, and we're to get up at half-past four tomorrow morning. The new order is to begin.

What happened last night was that someone was carried out of here "feet foremost." One of the new arrivals in solitary confinement took his own life in his cell the night before last. He had hanged himself. The doctor was here early next morning, and last night a truck arrived with a crowd of soldiers, who were posted in the square and along the road. The body was removed in the dead of night.

MONDAY, JULY 20, 1942 ■ The actual news that I was to be sent to Germany I took with profound composure. I was almost frightened at myself. But when the thought of Kari and what might happen to her began to get hold of me in earnest, then it was worse. First and foremost I've told her everything today. Of course she must know. Only for an instant I hesitated. How will she take it? She will face it with her head high; she will defy and fight it to the last gasp, for herself, for me, for the child, and for the great cause of life itself.

The factual details known are as follows. Denzer's woman clerk said to Dybwad that "Nansen is being sent away. Yes. Didn't you know? He's to go to Germany." That's all. Well, it's enough. When you add the long questioning, with its obvious attempt to make out a case against me as an enemy of Germany and the New Order (and thus as it were provide a basis for deportation) the whole thing seems more and more probable.

On the other hand there is reason to suppose it all a misunderstanding. The stupid typing wench may have confused Hansen with Nansen, for example. And my friend [Karl Hjalmar] Hansen the tinsmith is obviously going to be sent.* He's just been photographed at Number 19, and that's usually the sign. But after all I have a feeling that it's true, and it's safest to work on that assumption.

TUESDAY, JULY 21, 1942 ■ I got no further yesterday. So much had happened. My thoughts were tired; I had to go to bed. Everything has come at once—Sunday's infamies, this about myself, and also a lot of important news from outside. And to make everything still more somber, heavy, and hard to bear, a comrade has been condemned to death in the police court today. [Paul] Kvamme of Bergen—married with two children. He took it splendidly. There seem to be especially good reasons for thinking he'll be reprieved. I wish to God it may be so.† But it's always the best who are taken. I am thinking of all our comrades who were taken in the past—the elite—while the dregs are seated in the high places, even among the prisoners.

WEDNESDAY, JULY 22, 1942 ■ There's not much to tell today. Denzer and most of the gang have gone on a "boating party" to Larkollen.‡ They come home drunk and nasty in the small hours, I should imagine. It's been a blessedly peaceful day.

Twenty-two fresh prisoners arrived. Ten teachers from Solør. What does that mean? Have they started on the teachers again? No one got out today, I don't think, but the day before yesterday three old hands were released. That was fine. They'd been here well over a year. Now it's so dark that I'm writing blind, so to speak. I don't want to light up, instead I'll go to bed. Good night, Kari, you know the whole story now, and I feel you're taking it calmly. Perhaps it even strikes you as a bit queer that I should fill page after page with this. I've escaped so much. What might not have happened? And indeed nothing has happened yet.

FRIDAY, JULY 24, 1942 ■ Birkevold is to go before the court martial one of these days and will unquestionably be condemned to death. He couldn't stand being ill any longer; he's decided to meet his fate now, whatever it may be. The time got too long and deadly up there in the hospital! Both his buddies escaped dying, no doubt he would, too. Well, let us believe so.

Kari came yesterday—Kari, Marit, and Eigil. I wouldn't believe my own ears when I got word to come down to the *Vermittlung*, my wife had come to see me. She had gone straight to the Terrace and had got a *Schein* at once. It was three sunbeams; it was a great bit of heaven that came in to me in the little room. All my anxiety, all my doubts, all my wretchedness were blown away. Now I don't care what happens. Now I know she'll be all right whatever it is.

---

* Hansen was in fact not transferred to Sachsenhausen in Germany until February 1943; he died in captivity less than two months later, on April 13, 1943, age forty-three.
† Kvamme, who worked on an underground newspaper, was executed at Trandum Woods on August 12, 1942, age thirty-two.
‡ Larkollen, a small village thirty-seven miles south of Oslo, was the landfall on the sea route between Oslo and Copenhagen for several centuries.

She's fighting like a lioness to get me out. Perhaps it may come off? The latest idea is that I may be released for a month or two on parole. She had discussed it with Koch, Terboven's second in command, and is expecting an answer from him one day soon.* Koch, by the way, said something very interesting. I was here because of National Relief and Nansen Relief, he said. Her information that I'm a court hostage was new to him and had astonished him.

That confirms what I have believed all the time. Riisnæs† or Quisling is behind my arrest; court hostage is only a capacious bag for people they are anxious to secure. Personal revenge and other shady motives have dictated the choice. Unfortunately that makes it more likely that they've planned a trip to Germany for me.

When Kari and the children had gone, I went off with the surveyors to pick bilberries.‡ We had the decent guard I wrote of before. We were hardly outside the gate when he asked me if I hadn't just had a visit from my wife and children. When I said yes, he said I should have arranged a meeting with them outside. I objected that it would have been too risky both for him and for us. He didn't seem quite convinced.

It turned out a splendid morning. We found a slope by the woodside beyond the stone quarry where there were a lot of bilberries, and settled down there for the whole afternoon. Kari and the children might have gone there, and we might have been together two or three hours instead of the poor minutes in the *Vermittlung*. A pang went through my heart every time I thought of it.

SATURDAY, JULY 25, 1942 ■ Saturday evenings are long now. Nothing to look forward to any more. Not cards, nor reading, nor singing, nor entertainment. Everything is forbidden. The idea must be for us to sit bolt upright in our rooms and stare into space until eleven o'clock. We're still allowed to stay up until eleven on Saturdays. I tried to visit the hospital this evening. It was old Sikveland I meant to call on; the poor old chap is still there, with a bad heart. The door was locked. *That* wasn't allowed, either. The doctor's office is shut; they've been varnishing the floor. I am homeless and out of work. I'm altogether in a poor way. I've sought refuge in the dentist's office, but here I don't feel so safe. For the door can be opened, I can't get settled here, can't collect my thoughts.

Nothing has happened in the camp today. I've not been to see the Segment yet, but he's sent me two packets of cigarettes. He begins at once. He's his old self. Now the fellows are drying dandelion roots and leaves to smoke. They're digging in the dustbins for cigarette butts or refuse. It had to be forbidden on parade yesterday for reasons of hygiene. So that's forbidden, too.

Prohibitions are hailing down on us. One has to look where one's going now, not to

---

* Hans Reinhard Koch (1902–1997). After spending time after the war as a British POW Koch returned to Germany and practiced law.

† Sverre Parelius Riisnæs (1897–1988), minister of justice in the Quisling government, was arrested following the war and tried for treason, but the trial was eventually suspended when he was declared insane, a decision that remains controversial to this day. Riisnæs was hospitalized from 1948 to 1960, left Norway for Italy in 1974 and thereafter spent many years abroad, returning to Oslo in 1985 for the final years of his life.

‡ Similar to blueberries, bilberries grow wild throughout Scandinavia. America's minister to Norway Florence Harriman observed, "Berries! Not even people who come from Cape Cod, or Berrien County, Michigan, have any idea of what berries there are in this [Norwegian] world, how delicious, and in what varieties. Blue, black, red, orange and yellow—Norwegian berries are as marvelous as the fruits of the tropics, and how Norwegians love them!"

make a false step. There are a fearful number of places where it's forbidden to walk. On the square one may not walk further south than to a vertical line on the facade of the prison, by the north flagpole. It's forbidden not to have a bath. It's forbidden to wear a scarf. It's forbidden to smoke in working hours. It's forbidden to be in places where one doesn't have to be for one's work. It's forbidden to take off too many clothes when the sun shines. It's forbidden to converse with the guards. It's forbidden to go to the dentist if one hasn't toothache. All other treatment is forbidden.

On the whole it's easier to count up what is allowed. Ninety percent of what one does is illegal all the same. Therefore I'm not nervous any more. It's impossible to maintain every veto; no one can keep a check. We're all lawbreakers as a matter of course, from morning until night, from night until morning. That must be the idea, so that there may always be grounds for seizing and if it suits them punishing no matter whom. It would be interesting to see whether it is in fact possible to be law-abiding here, except during sleep or unconsciousness in a permitted place. Outside they're nervous about this diary; they think I take insane risks. I can't stop, and the risks we take to get it out are not so great, I believe, as they may look from outside. Now and then I think it's wrong of me to alarm Kari with it. She has more than enough without. But then I dismiss it again; she'll understand. Now I mean to go to bed early, read unlawfully, and sleep late. Tomorrow's Sunday. No roll call until ten o'clock. Goodness how the time flies.

Good night.

MONDAY, JULY 27, 1942 ■ It's strange to think that in No. 19—indeed, even here at Grini—there are a lot of prisoners locked up in small rooms who would all give anything on earth for a chance to work, outdoors or in. And with those who *have* to work, it seems to be an object to wriggle out of it as much as possible. Of course, these shirkers don't have a good time. Of course they make their existence even more dreary and destructive than it need be. Moreover, they persuade themselves that it's the correct thing to do. *They're sabotaging work for the Germans!* Pretend to be continuing the fight! Stiffen each other up with this imposture, till they believe in it themselves.

It's striking for that matter how the quality of prisoners is going down. The new arrivals are of nothing like the same caliber as those who were streaming in a few months ago. I don't know why it is, but it's undeniable, there's a lot of scum getting in here. Petty saboteurs—men who have walked out of their jobs because they saw some better opportunity, something that was still better paid. Men who have got into fights with Germans or NS people, with whom they have been more or less fraternizing. Black market men. And finally, there are more and more men from the NS, caught out in theft or some other dirty work. It's as though they'd begun to eat each other up now. These elements come to the front here unfortunately, and we have no means of preventing it.

Emil Nicolaysen has been informed that from today he is a prisoner of war. In other words, he is to be sent to Germany. He alone? No indeed, I don't believe it. It concerns us all. Those who are not officers and can't be prisoners of war will be something else—convicts for instance. It's the hostages' turn now. It fits in capitally with what I arrived at long ago. They're planning a big new transport to Germany.

Well, so Emil has now been here six and a half months, has been bullied and savaged like the rest of us. From tomorrow he's an officer and is to be treated with all the deference and honor imaginable. Is to go about in uniform. Is not to work. Has suddenly become the representative of a beaten enemy—an officer—a man of honor—a respectable person. Only Germans can hit on such ideas.

God knows what they'll hit on for the rest of us. But come what will. *This* is it! *This* is when we mustn't fail.

TUESDAY, JULY 28, 1942 ■ It was a queer day, though nothing special happened. I was working on a chimney for the company camp and later on some dedications in books the Germans are to give each other. I had a visit from the Segment and Kunz. They didn't want anything, just came prying and twaddling. I didn't feel like twaddling and had nothing to be pried into. I'd just finished and sent off a small roll when they arrived, and was absorbed in my work with the best conscience in the world. It was lucky I had something to do when the Segment came, or Lord knows what new poster commissions he might have thought of. They were afoot again.

Now a big red moon is balancing on top of a spruce fir on the upper farm. I'm sitting looking at it, and it occurs to me that it offers tiptop bombing weather for tonight. Such thoughts are the romance of our day. Truly a glorious age. We can get absolutely tipsy on gentle dreams of bombs in the moonlight. There are said to have been aircraft over Oslo this morning. They are even said to have been Norwegian aircraft—one perhaps or more, no one knows, for no one here actually saw them. One of these aircraft is said to have drawn an *I* or *J* in the sky. Which is at once construed as *Invasion*, or perhaps *Jøssing*.* It's quite magnificent. Why, there was even an air-raid warning in Oslo. No one actually heard it; they heard that someone else had heard it.

WEDNESDAY, JULY 29, 1942 ■ I didn't get as far as describing yesterday's sensation in camp. Late in the afternoon an order came for all work on the electric fence and building to stop at once. The civilian workers who were engaged on the erection of the fence and the corresponding watchtowers laid down their tools and went home. At the same time orders were given to start erecting a netting fence to enclose a limited area round the main prison. What was the idea? The wildest guessing began, and rumors spread through the whole camp.

Half an hour afterward came the counterorder. The works were to go on as usual. But the civilian workers had already left, and the staking out of the new netting fence had begun, for it was to be ready in a couple of days.

Then came order number three. All work on huts is to be suspended, except in the company camp. The inner netting fence is to be put up. Work on the outer electric fence is to continue *for the present*. Many held of course that the invasion was on the doorstep, if it hadn't begun already, and that the Germans were therefore busy with evacuation plans. They concluded that the camp was to be used for other purposes, and that a big release was at hand. Most people anyhow construed the event in an optimistic sense. I didn't.

A certain nervousness of invasion is asserting itself. The need for more troops is being

---

* The term "Jøssing" derives from Jøssingfjord, the setting for the Altmark Affair. Originally the term was coined by the collaborationist government as a derogatory term to mean anti-Nazi (and thus the opposite of the pro-government Quislings). The attempt miscarried when Jøssing was instead quickly seen as an honorary term associated with Norwegian patriots. Several underground newspapers during World War II used the term in their names, including *Jøssingposten*. The Grini Museum is on Jøssingveien, or Jøssing Way.

felt with increasing urgency. The *Wehrmacht*, the SS, the SD,* and all the incalculable hordes of Germans in the so-called civil administration are needed now at the guns. A purge may be at hand, I think. "The Fatherland calls. Germans! Do your duty!" But then comes another thought, a sudden fancy. The whole thing may simply be explained by two words, two words that embrace interminable romances of unfathomable muddle, whole worlds of incredibility—*German administration.*

Which of these hypotheses is the right one it's hard to say: they both seem equally probable. All the same I think the first has much in its favor. And besides it's much the pleasanter alternative to occupy one's mind with.

Today the work and rumors continue. The bigwigs we had notice of, who were to come and inspect at seven this morning, have not arrived yet and it's nearly twelve. Needless to say a lot of people think this highly mysterious, immediately connect it with this or that and build the most peculiar theories on it. I've had a good deal to do with Germans and have heard of their lauded punctuality. I've never yet known one of them to make his appearance just at the time fixed. I've never yet seen anything happen at precisely the hour appointed.

(Later)

The distinguished visit is canceled. But the camp is seething with rumors and the tension of rumors.

A couple of hours ago (it's now half-past five) the personnel office received a lightning order to draw up lists of the labor needed to finish the building work in progress inside the new inner fence. The rest of the prisoners were going away, some to "other camps," some into freedom. These lists were to be ready in half an hour. Riedel (the over-snooper for the *Baustelle* [building site] in Oslo) was coming here to go through the works and everything.

The office hutment is bubbling with conjecture and argument. No one rightly knows where it's best to be—on one of these lists, and therefore certain of remaining at Grini, or off the lists and faced with the possibility of being sent to Germany, or being sent on road or harvest work somewhere in Norway, of being transferred to another prison in this country, or finally of being released. Almost everyone believes this last to be the likeliest as regards the hostages. They convince themselves and one another of it unceasingly, and laugh loudly and derisively at me, who obstinately stick to my theory about Germany.

Twenty or thirty new cell prisoners have arrived today. That doesn't exactly suggest reduction, but there's so much that doesn't suggest anything. One must never forget that, when one has Germans to deal with.

SUNDAY, AUGUST 2, 1942 ■ The last few days (since I wrote last) have gone in one long hustle. I haven't had a moment's peace to sit down. The evenings have become unsafe. And besides I haven't been in the mood for writing.

On Friday morning we had orders for an extra roll call at twelve o'clock. All had to attend, except the bedridden. All the "Germans" had turned out, with the *Stormdrunk* (the new *Lagerkommandant, Hauptsturmführer* Seidler) at their head. Also some choice

---

* Sicherheitsdienst, the intelligence service for the SS and Nazi Party. Established in 1931, the SD was responsible for identifying political threats to the Nazi Party and its leadership; the actual enforcement work was handled primarily by the Gestapo. Reinhard Heydrich was the head of the SD until his assassination in 1942; Ernst Kaltenbrunner succeeded him. After the war Kaltenbrunner was convicted of war crimes and crimes against humanity and hanged.

specimens of the civilian Gestapo. They were equipped with lots of paper. This had been preceded by feverish activity in the personnel office and the *Vermittlung*, where they were making lists of all the prisoners and the class of criminal they belonged to.

Also the rumors had been raging to quite a phenomenal degree, supported by loose talk from the Segment and Denzer. There was to be a big release; some talked of no less than four hundred. The waves of argument had overflowed all banks, and anyone who stuck to it that all this about release was not very probable got roughly handled. It *was* a big release that was coming; the camp was to be reduced; we'd seen that for ourselves, hadn't we, with the new fence, the cessation of building work, and so on. Besides, the Segment had said so and Denzer, too, so don't you start saying different. Just before parade Denzer had told Erling that something *fröhliches* [joyful] was coming. This latest unction had just had time to flow over the camp when we fell in at twelve o'clock. The tension was colossal; the hostages especially were at bursting point with blissful expectancy. Many must already have been planning their journey home, thinking of the future and happy days.

I had no faith that this meant anything joyful for anyone, and I had said so. In consequence I was in pretty bad odor. I felt convinced that the hostages would *not* be given special treatment, let alone be released. There was also, in my "pessimism," a certain element of design. I've seen so many instances of the havoc *Entlassungsfeber* has made with many of us. From dizzy heights of joyful, tremulous expectation people have been hurled again and again into the abysses of disappointment. It's been like that every Saturday of late, and always there has remained a tiny, thin little thread of hope, on which they've gone on spinning from Sunday onward until by Saturday it's become quite a good stout rope. Then the rope gave with a bang, and there was another heavy fall. The strain involved in these incessantly broken hopes was too much for a lot of people. They grew neurasthenic and their health was shaken. Some of the optimists actually had to go into the hospital.

Well, so we stood on extra parade at twelve o'clock on Friday, waiting for the bomb to go off. Instructions were given for those whose names would be read out to step forward, and fall in on the left wing. Most thought those were the ones who would be set free. Then it began.

The *Stormdrunk* had settled himself comfortably in an armchair on the terrace—like in a ringside seat. He had the usual decadent expression on his blurry face, and was cleaning his nails, polishing them, fiddling with them, holding them up in front of him, and sending them sleepy glances under the heavy eyelids he could scarcely be bothered opening.

One name after another was called out; prisoner after prisoner stepped forward, walked past the nail polisher, and fell in on the left. It began with Bjørn Oscar (Andersen). With that we knew definitely that the performance did not mean release. For Bjørn Oscar was to have been sent to Germany before. Things had an ugly look now. The names came alphabetically, and as the letters were got through, many a sigh of relief could be heard among the ranks, from those who hadn't been called out.

They got to Q, and we waited in suspense. Then they began again at A. The same thing was repeated; sighs of relief went through the ranks like groans. It was impossible to make head or tail of it.

Every theory began cracking; some were already smashed to bits. New ones had to be formed in haste, and flew from man to man. Those who were called out were to remain at Grini. Finally, when all the names had been called, the rest were to be set free, and of course the hostages in particular. That held for a time. Once more they began on A, once more the whole alphabet was gone through, while an abundant harvest of prisoners fell in in ten ranks on the left wing. Then the first hostage was called out, then came another, then several, then many more, and that theory had cracked, too.

The hostages were streaming over to the left wing. When they got to N, my name was read. I had been expecting it. It caused neither shock nor sigh. I walked past the nail polisher. He set his eyelids ajar, pointed at me, and called out something. It was my jacket which wasn't buttoned right up. The sun was broiling hot, and I had opened up a bit at the neck. The breach of regulations led to no further consequences. He sank back into the armchair and continued work on his nails. A flabby, horrid grin and a gleam from the innermost of his yellow teeth was the last I saw of him before the view was blocked by fresh prisoners, streaming incessantly over to the left wing. Soon I was in the midst of a column of three hundred men.

I looked about. There stood Per Krohg, pale but composed, unknown and anonymous, rather crumpled and miserable in that uniform that doesn't fit anyone. Further off Colonel Schiøtz towered up with his guards' cap on. One of the optimists behind me whispered, "So you were right, Odd. Damnation! I'd never have believed it." He had retorted hotly when I was predicting a trip to Germany. By my side was [Ingebrigt] Maurstad* of Måløy, our waiter. He was taking it calmly; no doubt he'd hoped for release, a lot of his colleagues from Måløy were already free, but goodness, who has ever found any system in the Germans' doings? There were several other Måløy men in the lines. [Hildor] Fjære,† the fisherman with the wife and eight children, who have no breadwinner and no money. Erect and taciturn as usual; I knew his mind was at rest. The wife and children were being cared for; then it was all the same to him what became of him. Things would be straightened out in the end.

I missed Nils [Dybwad]. He was not called out. So the surveyors' group was to remain, and presumably all who had to do with the *Bauabteilung*. That was sad, but still I managed to be pleased for his sake. Otherwise there were many well-known faces round about, many a good chap, and if we might keep together, doubtless we'd succeed in welding a pleasant little community, wherever we were to be sent.

We were told nothing of what was going to happen to us, only that the next time the *Sonderkolonnen* [special columns] were ordered out we were to fall in at the same place in the same order as now.

MONDAY, AUGUST 3, 1942 ■ At seven on Friday there was an extra parade of the *Sonderkommando* [special squad]‡ after the ordinary roll call. We were to be medically examined. It was a bit of a world's record in its kind. Over three hundred men were examined in half an hour.

We simply fell in and did a bit of drill under Denzer's circus management. Hauer, the old Austrian staff doctor, stood and watched this imbecile display, as in duty bound. He

---

* Released December 18, 1942.
† Released March 15, 1943.
‡ Not to be confused with the more typical designation of *Sonderkommando*, i.e., special detachments used in extermination camps consisting of Jewish prisoners used to run the gas chambers and crematoria.

looked embarrassed, for Denzer once more surpassed himself, if possible. During one of his most fanciful capers, accompanied by torrents of *Sacramentos* and *Teufels* [devils] in every variety of bellow, he turned to Hauer for a moment half apologetically, and said, "*Die Norweger werden nie Soldaten!*" [The Norwegians will never make soldiers!] Hauer looked at him—I believe with pain—and answered quietly, "*Nein, Gott sei Dank!*"

Eventually, when Denzer had finished, the ranks marched one by one by the doctor, Denzer, and the rest of his court, and fell in again beyond. There was no call-over. No one was exempted. All were pronounced *transportfähig* [fit for transport] and *arbeitsfähig*. Then we were allowed to run.

Saturday came with brilliant sunshine and passed off quietly, but for the hectic rumors that were heaving and bubbling all round. Not until the evening was there a fresh parade of the *Sonderkommando*, after roll call. This time there were to be more men picked out; it was stated that we were to be four hundred in all, we were a hundred short. Members of the Gestapo had turned up, the Commandant, Denzer, and all the rest of the court. There was a call-over, and fresh names were added. Every now and then the call-over stopped, because someone or other was not present. A few had gone into the hospital in the course of the day, among them the unfortunate young Jew Leiba Wolfberg. He had been operated on that morning for a poisoned foot, which I heard later was pretty serious.

Leiba was ordered to turn out, and came hobbling with a stick. His foot bandaged, but without shoe or stocking. Denzer and Kunz at once took him by the scruff of the neck, got him stationed on a pile of planks and ordered the bandage off. Dr. Rasmussen lent a hand, but they were too slow; Denzer tore off the bandage. Kunz struck the young man in the face with his own cap, which he had unluckily kept on. Denzer performed a furious war dance, in which the *Stormdrunk* joined, when he became aware of the facts. "Here's a lazy rascal of a Jew," he screamed, "been trying to dodge by going into the hospital for nothing at all."

Rasmussen had no chance to speak. Poor Leiba was ordered to take his place in the column. He hobbled off, leaning on his stick. Denzer tore the stick from him in a fury, and swung it threateningly over his head; at the last moment he returned to his senses and hurled it with all his might over the new fence, into the wood.

My friend the organ builder, whose name was called before that, had signalized the day by winding a large bandage round his bad leg, and looked uncommonly pitiable as he limped along with a stick. (Yesterday he was running gaily round the square, well again after a long spell in the hospital. He had really been bad.) *His* case was "recognized," but he was not exempted. He also had to limp into place.

Not until nine or ten were we allowed to run, and woe betide those who didn't run. It was no sunshine Sunday. It was raw, cold, and overcast, typical indoor weather, especially adapted to the hatching of rumors. In the middle of all this more than two hundred fresh prisoners have arrived, and today there are to be a hundred more. They're coming from Number 19, from Bredtvedt* and direct from outside. Today for instance ten men came in who've been arrested in a so-called 3rd of August action. It's the King's seventieth birthday, and there may have been some flickers of demonstration in Oslo. I haven't managed to find out yet. I've had other things to think of.

---

* The Bredveit prison was situated in the Bredtvedt (or Bredvet) neighborhood of Oslo. After the war it was initially used to house collaborationist women awaiting trial and was later converted into a women's prison.

Early this morning I got word that Kari and the children were outside the *Vermittlung*. Off I went. Yes, there they all were, brown and cheery and smiling. They had heard everything. Had been sent word and took it with radiant spirit and profound calm. All my apprehension and nervousness was wiped out. That visit drove away the last remnant of my distress at leaving. Now it has ceased to matter. Now I shan't fail again.

TUESDAY, AUGUST 4, 1942 ■ It seems to be settled that we're leaving tonight. We heard yesterday. We parade today at two and are to be issued blankets, boots, etc. At half-past seven tonight, they say, we're to be ready for the start. No one has any idea where we're going. We're to take warm underclothing; therefore some deduce that we're going north, to a colder spot. Others talk about a two-day journey, others again say two hours, and a few are quite sure we're going to Dovre.*

Yesterday was celebrated in a lot of different ways. Four of the court hostages with the lord chamberlain at their head received a visit from their families, and the compliments of the day were exchanged. In our hut we had a big banquet in the evening—stolen vegetables, goose liver, and waffles. It was also a farewell party for us who were to go.

It seemed as though the day were being kept in Oslo, too, for the prisoners streamed in. They began to appear from early in the afternoon. At that time it was mostly women, largely young girls. They had been wearing flowers no doubt, which one might not do on the 3rd of August. Toward evening and through the night there came huge busloads of both women and men. Most of them had had a flower in their buttonhole. I'm blessed if old [Kristian Jens] Delphin the high court barrister wasn't in one of the buses.† Every day for the last thirty or forty years he must have sported a flower in his buttonhole, but not until yesterday had he been pinched for that improper and illegal habit.‡

The chaps in the *Vermittlung* worked at top speed all night, and before they got to bed in the early morning they had entered two hundred and eighty-three "flower-boys" on the rolls. The new prisoners had a good deal to relate about the toughs' fantastic goings-on. Blows and kicks and abuse had resounded through the office without a pause.

Kunz had shaken a girl of eighteen until her teeth rattled, and when she still couldn't make out what he was bellowing, despite this lucid explanation, had struck her in the chest with his fist. An elderly lady had tried to help the girl. "The young lady doesn't speak German!" She got the prompt reply: "Hold your jaw, you old bitch!"

One man had been so damaged in the face that the Germans didn't dare to show him; they kept him inside the guardroom and later placed him in solitary confinement. One of the fellows had had a glimpse of him. Half of his face was bloody and smashed to bits. Another man came in with blood running down his face. He had been struck again while the chaps were watching, but had driven the Germans absolutely frantic with rage by saying calmly as the blows fell on him, "Just wait till the English come!" This admirable comment Claffy had hastened to translate into German.

It was Kunz and Kunze who had seen to most of the "treatment," but the fellows told us that the Segment also had buckled to and followed the example.

---

* A municipality, or district, 140 miles north of Oslo.
† Released eleven days later, on August 14, 1942.
‡ The "parole" (directive) from the Resistance encouraged everyone to wear a flower in their buttonhole. The police pulled the flowers off many people, who then replaced them from flower beds in the parks. Approximately four hundred people in all were arrested.

This superb object lesson in the cultural life of the Third Reich was more than the prisoners can have been hoping for in the morning, when they fixed their fragrant little flowers in their buttonholes. Now they have garnered learning, on which presumably they are to meditate until the war is over. It's to be over in September, according to the latest bulletin.

Everything looks well. Full of optimism and high spirits and in good heart we set off tonight. (If it comes to anything?) May the "west wind" reach us where we're going, too!

Au revoir!

PART II: VEIDAL

1942

WEDNESDAY, AUGUST 5, 1942 ■ We've stopped at Fokstua station for a moment. Since last night about ten we've been in this cattle car. We left Grini just like tourists in grand buses—but at Lysaker station we were loaded into cattle cars like any other cattle.* It's now past nine in the evening. Well, so we're going northward. We still don't know our destination. They talk of Narvik or Namdalen. I'm lying writing on the floor. The morale is grand. There are thirty-four of us in this railcar. There is neither bench nor stool—only floor, roof, and walls, and barely that, so there's a terrible draft, and the smell of a cattle car is not nice. There isn't room for everyone to lie down at once, but we're getting on fine.

THURSDAY, AUGUST 6, 1942 ■ We arrived here at Trondheim about half-past five in the morning after a strange night. Somehow or other we finally got arranged side by side on the floor of the car, all thirty-four of us, and all the lot of us could almost stretch out. It was a frantic squeeze, and the railcars are so narrow that when we stretch out from the long sides (with our heads against the wall) the legs of the man opposite reach to about our hips. It wasn't much of a sleep, but still a kind of rest, which we were in need of. For it was our second night like that.

The worst of it was really the privy question. All the first night and until we arrived at Otta about five in the afternoon we had nothing but an ordinary bucket, which had been issued to us for the purpose. Anyone can imagine what a filthy business it became. The railcars were hermetically sealed. It was strictly forbidden to open the two hatches in ours. By mischance I had been made car leader, because I could speak German, and I was personally responsible for the hatches being kept shut and for everything being in order generally. Otherwise I should be shot, thundered the SS Lieutenant who was in charge of the transport; he repeated it later on, when the train made short halts and the doors were opened so that we could draw a breath of fresh air and get the buckets emptied.

At Hamar we had something to eat for the first time—coarse bread and butter, and after much parleying we were allowed to walk across the railway lines down to Mjøsa† and fetch water in the little field stewpans that had been issued to most of us. The beach was covered with rubbish and filth and the water lukewarm, but still it was flowing. I hope it won't make us ill. The food tasted excellent, as we ate it lying on the floor or sitting on our trunks and knapsacks.

By degrees we learned what to do about the air vents. When we were on a straight stretch of line we raised the hatches, and got a bit of light as well, along with the air. When the line curved, we had to take care only to have the hatch on the outer side of the curve open. Then no one could see it from the carriage in the front part of the train, where the Germans were. In time we almost acquired the art of traveling in this style; we quite got the hang of it, and the morale was high without exception. I sang a bit, but as

---

* Many onlookers and relatives met at Lysaker station to see the prisoners off, including Nansen's older sister Liv, who was "arrested and kept for several days [in Grini] on account of her arguing with one of the guards." Nansen's daughter Marit had hoped to smuggle some tobacco to the prisoners at Lysaker, but after Liv's arrest this proved impossible.

† Mjøsa is Norway's largest and one of its deepest lakes.

long as the train was moving it was as much as we could do to hear our own voices; there was such a rattling and creaking and squeaking in the old broken-down railcar that it was almost a miracle it held together.

Next to me lay Fredrik Bølling; he had not lost his admirable spirits. Beyond him Schiøtz. He was taciturn and repressed, but was getting on all right. [Erik] Graff-Wang came next,* and then a whole lot of Måløy men. A priceless figure in the ensemble was the Pentecoster [Aksel] Sørensen† munching food, with his whole face, cap included, active in the chewing process, or lying half propped up on the pile of luggage in profound slumber, with eyes raised to heaven (under the lids) and open mouth. He looked like a cross between Jeppe på Bierget and a cherub.‡ He is always a great delight to us.

At Otta we had more food, coarse bread and butter, and this time a little slice of smoked sausage, which was supposed to be dinner. Also we were given water, good water, and we sneaked a little of it onto our faces, too, and our hands. That was great. We just managed to exchange a few words with the fellows in the other railcars. The tone was excellent all round, but a lot complained of the stench from the brimming buckets. The time we stopped at Otta was long enough to afford an opportunity for *Abtritt* [privy break] as well. It took place all over the station area and was a spectacle for youth.§ I shall never forget it—colonels and majors and directors and fishermen and workmen—no, I shan't attempt to describe it. But whenever I pass through Otta in days to come, that fantastic scene will spring to memory. Then we got a glimpse of the high mountains through our hatches, but in general I almost think I must have dozed off, for there's nothing more to relate until we reached Trondheim this morning, and here we still are, but in the bottom of a boat.

The whole train was switched onto a siding that took us out on Brattøra, so we realized at once that we were to go on by boat. The first event, after we had packed up and fallen in on the platform, was that our officers had their names called: Bølling, Schiøtz, Abildgaard, Rørholt, Gjertsen, Gjørtz, Aaby¶ and two more. They fell in separately, and presumably were sent home again as prisoners of war.

FRIDAY, AUGUST 7, 1942 ■ Yesterday I was sitting writing down at the bottom of the hold; I sat on the floor with the sketchbook on my knees. Today I've made a step forward; I'm sitting in the engine room with a new friend, the engineer. I copied out the Grini-march for him, with my name beneath. He asked for it. So I'm allowed to be down here in return. The engine drowns every other noise, so that in a way it's "quiet," and no Germans come in here—that's the best of it—nor yet any other prisoners.

But let me take up my narrative where I left off yesterday: When our friends the officers had paraded and marched off, no one knows where, we marched "by cars" down

---

* A court hostage, he was released March 18, 1943.

† Released July 21, 1943. The Pentecosters were a revivalist sect.

‡ The title character in a comedy/farce by playwright Ludvig Holberg (1684–1754). Jeppe's story is similar to that of Christopher Sly in William Shakespeare's *The Taming of the Shrew* (i.e., a drunk who is temporarily hoodwinked).

§ Another prisoner related, "On Otta station the [rail cars] were opened and some 400 men covered the whole station surroundings relieving nature with all speed, just as a south bound train came into the station!"

¶ Olaf Abildgaard, Eystein Gjørtz, and Erling Aaby (or Aabye) remained imprisoned for the duration of the war, spending significant time in various POW camps throughout Europe. Arnold Rørholt was released from Grini on November 9, 1942; thereafter he worked in the Resistance until fleeing to Sweden in January 1945. From 1949 to 1953 Rørholt acted as chief executive of the Royal Norwegian Automobile Club.

to the quay. After a long wait it turned out that we were going aboard a little boat with *Bodø* on it. Since then I've learned that it's the old *Erling Jarl*, which was wrecked on the coast here in 1940 and which has been raised and repaired. We were driven down into the hold and crammed together on every deck, even under the lowest orlop deck, on the very keelson. I was unlucky enough to be one of those who landed right at the bottom. There was nothing to be done but find a place on the floor, get rid of one's things, throw oneself down, and wait for what would happen.

I had a look round. The height under the roof was about a meter and a half [five ft.]. The floor was damp, and foul with all kinds of refuse. Most of the space was taken up with trench barbed wire—a terrible invention. It caught on everything that went near it; one actually had the impression that it was equipped with long tentacles, which reached out with sharp hooks and pulled one in. We could "just" clear that away, said the German guard, who was down there directing things. I objected that it was impossible with one's bare hands. He shrugged and said we would be the sufferers—to him it was *ganz egal* [all the same]. He had only to carry out the orders he had been given, and these were to stow another forty men on the lowest "deck," which had been full long ago.

These were fine prospects, and as there was an appalling stench down there, I asked if they intended to close the hatch at the top, three floors above us, which was the only place from which we got a little fresh air. He nodded and assured me they did. Then I began in earnest to take a gloomy view of life. It couldn't be possible that they meant to shut us up in this rathole! Surely in heaven's name there must be some sane people among them, who realized that this was all but mass murder. We should be slowly poisoned with carbon monoxide, and all of us "quiet down" by degrees, shout and scream for help as we might.

I pictured what it would be like if in addition to all this misery we got a heavy sea and were sick. The idea was so overpowering that everything inside me turned upside down, and I was in the act of starting the tragedy right off. But the prisoners were streaming down the ladder and distributing themselves in among the trusses of barbed wire, herring boxes, and other lumber and cargo, heaped up under the roof right down the stinking, low-pitched hold.

It was curious to see them all crawling in, dragging heavy sacks and trunks after them, while more and still more streamed down the ladder. Their faces were set and serious; undisguised fury shone out of most, dread and indignation from others, while others again were stamped with the blackest of despair. Well, this was no time to despair. The thing was to get one's spirits up.

I looked at a couple of the other fellows. And we began to laugh. Heavens, how we laughed! And there was plenty to laugh at. The Pentecoster Sørensen, for instance, was crawling among his boxes and odds and ends into a bundle of barbed wire. His cap had slipped down on his nose, his eyes were squinting, and his tongue directing the "traffic" among the barbs. He was puffing and panting, and his cherub cheeks were going out and in like a pair of bellows. From time to time he called a halt, sat up and looked about him, assembled all his things, which were now wildly disorganized, and remained there with arms outflung, like a mother hen defending her chickens with her wings. He was still squinting, and his breath came heavily.

I had to leave him there for the time; I caught sight of old skipper [Ingvald] Walderhaug toiling his way through the barbed wire, crook backed and with set teeth, with an indescribable expression of blind rage on his face. That actually seemed comic too, tragic as it was. County Sheriff [Hans] Gabrielsen was sitting peering down from a high "gallery" where he had been stowed in with countless others. His countenance was as steady as usual. He looked as if he had often handled such incidents. One eye gazed round him with its usual sagacity and enterprise, while the other was hidden beneath the eyelid—as usual. Our merriment had gradually attracted attention, and other people began to join in the laughter. It was just as well to laugh, that is, it was much better, and so we yelled with laughter, pointing and enjoying the scene, until we had actually a pain in the midriff.

And our spirits rose again. The first shock began to pass; more and more people realized the colossal funniness of the situation and gave themselves up to it. They began to throw out comments, satirical, encouraging, sarcastic, ironical, and devil may care. Two days at the bottom of a cattle car went off nicely; no doubt we should also manage a few days at the bottom of a herring keg. But we shall never forget it, never! Not if we live to be a hundred. We agreed on that, and that was fortifying, too.

We set about the clearing work. We found a good many old sacks and bits of canvas, which we used partly to shift the barbed wire out of the way; partly we spread it over the wire as a substratum for the "berths," which were rigged up on the piles of stuff close under the roof. We put our backs into the job, and it wasn't long before every man had made himself a kind of nest.

The transport chief, a Lieutenant, came down. I asked him if they really meant to batten down the hatches up there. He said it would have to be done, or we should freeze. I assured him that none of us was afraid of that, and a unanimous chorus from the others obviously convinced him that I was right. He promised that the hatch should be left open. But, if we *should* freeze, we had only to say so, and the hatch would be shut. This positively remarkable display of sympathy gave me the courage to ask if we mightn't also go up on deck, to the privy and so on. We should go up to the privy at once, he promised, but as for going on deck, we should have to wait until we had left Trondheim, then he would see what he could do.

He emphasized afresh that if one man ran away he would be obliged to shoot ten others. He was only doing his duty. If he didn't, he himself would be stood up against a wall, and that, he said, was out of the question. In what form he was picturing an attempt at escape is beyond my understanding. Perhaps he was afraid we should bore a hole in the bottom of the boat and clear off that way? On deck and on the wharf all was green as far as the eye could see, and there was a flash of rifles, automatics, machine guns, and steel helmets.

A stream of privy-goers scrambled up the ladder to the lower deck and formed a line which has been permanent ever since, and doubtless will continue to be so while the voyage lasts. In the daytime it has an unbroken tendency to increase; not until late in the evening is there a balance between the craving and the delivered. Overnight it declines, but never ebbs right away. For there are only a very few who sleep at night; by about four the "day" is in full swing. People get on their legs and begin to move around after sleeping on hard planks or twisting among all kinds of boxes and sacks in a sitting, lying, or upright posture.

As soon as the privy lines had got going the deck was full of prisoners again. I found my way up there too, which gave me the chance for a little extra, parting experience before we left Trondheim.

An empty truck had drawn up before the gangway. They wanted twenty men for a job of loading and unloading. I went along. We drove off to the train we had arrived on. It was still at the same platform. The job was to unload an empty railway car full of barbed wire, mattocks, spades and implements of various kinds. A truck-load was driven off. We waited for the truck to return. Then another load; again we waited. Then the same load came back. Everything was to go back in the railway car. First that load, then the first which we had unloaded down by the boat, and which had to be fetched while we waited.

For our part we couldn't have cared less whether we were hoisting the things from the truck into the railway car or *vice-versa*. We found it a welcome change and were enjoying the fresh air and sunshine.

On an extremely irregular piece of paper from an extremely vulgar place I wrote word to Kari that I was aboard, that we were bound for Kvænangen and probably on to Kirkenes. The message arrived safely at the contact address I gave in Trondheim, but as far as I can learn it's not very probable about Kirkenes. It doesn't seem as if we were going much further than Nordreisa, or perhaps Kvænangen.* There may be a German camp thereabouts, which we are to help with the building of.

We left Trondheim about half-past twelve, and the weather was fine. Through a porthole in the donkeyman's† cabin I saw the town gliding past. The sun was glittering on the cathedral spire. Good lord, how strange it was to be a German convict-prisoner looking at all these dear old familiar objects through a forbidden porthole on the way to an unknown concentration camp.‡

SATURDAY, AUGUST 8, 1942 ■ Bodø. We're lying at anchor out in the harbor. We arrived last night about half-past one, and it doesn't look as though we were in any hurry to move on again. The Lieutenant has been put ashore; they say we're waiting for the Gestapo chief. The weather is marvelous. Nordland is showing itself at its most magnificent. But let me try to bring this narrative up to date.

We had just left Trondheim. Off Agdenes we were allowed to go on deck, and from that moment the voyage actually changed its character. From a gloomy prison transport with some features of horror it became a tourist cruise up the coast. One could at most find fault with the catering, which undeniably was scanty and Spartan, and with the berths, which also left much to be desired. But the weather was bright and fine, and the sea calm. A fairly fresh northwester was blowing, it was a bit cold, but it only stung one's skin refreshingly and brisked up one's spirits.

The old *Erling Jarl* hugged the coast with a former Norwegian whaler—now a German "warship"—as guard ship. Nor were we ourselves unarmed. On the top deck aft an extra little bridge had been put up for an old machine gun. There are always two German guards up there. I'm told that the machine gun is of an old type that has been scrapped in our own army. It's supposed to be completely useless for air defense. It points its barrel

---

* A German concentration camp was situated in Kvænangen, consisting of two subcamps: Veidal and Badderen. In the spring of 1945, as the Germans retreated from the Arctic Front, they adopted a scorched-earth policy and destroyed and burned everything in Norway north of Kvænangen. When Fridtjof Nansen's *Fram*, piloted by Otto Sverdrup, returned from its leg of Nansen's polar expedition, the first inhabited land it reached after its three-and-a-half-year voyage was a small town in the Kvænangen Fjord.

† The donkeyman runs the ship's boiler or engine room.

‡ Nidaros Cathedral (constructed 1070–1330 AD) is an imposing structure in Trondheim; Nansen studied for his degree in architecture in Trondheim.

at the sky, as yet a dazzling, cloudless blue, and to the uninitiated looks pretty fierce with two "Germans" by its side. At any rate it's fierce enough to prevent the ship from counting as unarmed, and that's all that is required. It means we can be bombed or torpedoed in accordance with the Hague Convention, or whatever the convention is that the persevering rake up out of the dust in such cases, to see what decent people agreed on once upon a time.*

Our first distribution of food on board took place late in the afternoon. We had had no breakfast. It must have been the idea that the bread and slice of sausage we got at Otta were to last until the next evening. Now we got a fresh supply of bread, four pieces of half-rotten herring, and a ration of butter. The fellows were ravenous, and the food disappeared as fast as we could give it out. From being a railcar leader I now slipped into another toilsome post. I became group leader, or *ältester*, as the guards call it, of forty men.

Evening came, after our first day on board, and we were all ordered below. "To bed!" To anyone who had seen our berths this expression would have been laughable enough in itself, but still we got the idea, clambered down into the hold, and scrambled and crawled into place. Some had had cabins allotted to them. Even though eight or nine had to sleep in each four-berth cabin, they were like princes in comparison with the rest of us, who had to sleep right down on the keelson and the orlop deck. Besides which we had had an accession in Trondheim of twenty-nine prisoners, mostly Jews, who hadn't got any berths. There were also quite a number of other prisoners who hadn't got a berth below.

When orders were issued for everyone to go below—no one was allowed to stay on deck at night—there were fresh problems to solve. The Germans solved them quite simply. We at the very bottom were ordered further into the hold so that there should be room for another fifty men down there. It was overcrowded as it was; we were sleeping right on top of each other; one could only just step between the bodies if one wanted to pass. And another fifty men were to find room in here. It was sheer madness. I protested, but was ordered to hold my tongue by the "caretaker," who had now come right down and stood there bellowing and directing. The fifty streamed down the ladder.

Soon people were standing with bent backs under the low roof, so densely that it was no longer possible to move. They could only try to sit down where they stood. Even that was attended with the very greatest difficulties. I plucked up courage and protested again; I asked to speak to the Lieutenant, who couldn't possibly permit this. Again the answer was to hold my damned jaw if I didn't want to get into trouble. There was no question of speaking to the Lieutenant, I had only to obey, as he did himself. Room or no room, the order was that another fifty men *should* find room down there. Those instructions were plain enough and German enough. There was nothing to be done but clench one's teeth into a *jawohl* and wait for him to go.

He went at last, but by that time the lowest hold and the orlop deck were so chock full that I believe it would have been impossible to squeeze one more man in. Once again it was the privy line that saved us. No one could refuse to let us go there. So there we went, both that fifty and another fifty. Only one more stair, and we were out on deck with our bedclothes, sleeping bags, and blankets. One of the men found a good place on the fore-deck and lay down, then another, then still another, then a lot more, and soon we were

---

* Recall Nansen's appeal to the Hague Convention when ordered by the Nazis to continue work on Fornebu Airport following the invasion.

lying there close packed. A daring experiment; it had actually been forbidden. But the guards were sympathetic. The little terrier who had been down among us had disappeared, and those who were keeping guard on deck simply let us lie. I haven't a sleeping bag, but I have four blankets, and when I had settled down I felt this was grand. A bit hard certainly, but I wasn't cold.

The Lieutenant came rushing up. I thought, now he's going to chase us down below again. But he didn't. He seemed merely to be nervous of our freezing to death, and he disclaimed all responsibility. I replied that we were used to sleeping out, even in winter in the snow. The Lieutenant looked stupid, shook his head, and vanished as rapidly as he had come. The coast was clear. We had only to lie down to sleep.

At one o'clock I woke up. We had got to Rørvik; the anchor woke me. I didn't get much more sleep that night, I was shivering now; it had turned cold. By four o'clock I was up; we were still at anchor off Rørvik. We must have been waiting for a new guard ship to relieve the other. One arrived about half-past seven, and we continued our voyage.

It was a wonderful morning. The wind had gone round to the east, and the sun was gradually getting hot. After the hardships of the night the prison transport had again become a cruise, with a lot of strange passengers in queer, identical clothes. Only the twenty-nine from Trondheim were in mufti; they might pass for ordinary passengers or Gestapo men or something equally contemptible.

Nordland was just starting in all its glory, with the skerries out to seaward in the glittering sunshine. No, one truly couldn't stand there and think about imprisonment. That mighty landscape, so untamed and sovereign in its power and its almost brutal loveliness, brushed all such petty thoughts aside. It was Mother Norway and we, her sons, who were meeting, and it was a tonic, unforgettable reunion, in spite of all green devils and all green devilry.

When we reached Sandnessjøen we moored alongside the wharf and all of us were ordered below. Thank goodness it wasn't a long stop, for on a hot, sunny day it isn't nice for four hundred men to be crammed together in passages and stairs and cabins aboard a small boat that normally doesn't take even half the number. The whole first class is of course reserved for greens.

We went on late in the afternoon. On we went, northward into wonderland, and once again we were tourists. Unfortunately I had a lot to cope with over the group-leader job. It had occurred to us as reasonable that all the old men, who last night had had to sleep on the floor or sit in a passage or on a stair, should now get a bed to sleep in at the expense of younger fellows who had had the luck to be placed in cabins. It became a prolonged and thankless job. Discontent, squabbling, and tiresomeness. It was depressing to see how difficult it was to get young men and lads to give up their bunks to veterans of sixty and more.

All those over fifty were to have a bunk as far as might be practicable. Then of course there was a crowd of discontented forty-nine-year-olds, so we had to compromise and fuss on for hours, but most of the old men did get a sleep that night, even though we who were arranging it were not very popular.

While we were busy about that, a singular exhibition was taking place on the foredeck. A number of prisoners were milling round each other or standing with their hands stretched upward, grabbing at something that was being thrown down to them. Some of the Germans were throwing slices of damaged sausage to them, and enjoying the spectacle enormously. It appeared that practically the whole store of fat smoked sausage had been spoiled by mold and decay, as it lay piled up under tarpaulins on the foredeck. Somehow or other the Germans had found out that the prisoners wanted it all the same, and so they arranged this degrading exhibition. In their rage for more food—food at any price—food!—otherwise decent Norwegians completely forgot their dignity. They behaved like sea lions at a circus displaying their tricks. They not merely accepted these scurvy alms, but fought like roaring animals to get hold of them, careless of the Germans who stood there laughing until they had to clutch at their bellies, their own well-filled bellies.

One word might have been enough to make the whole flock blush down to the heels of their boots, but there was no chance of saying that word; one could only turn away and try to forget the disgusting spectacle. Only one can't forget it, one carries it about and frets because the Germans have seen one's countrymen like that.

There's another deplorable thing here on board. Not a little is being stolen. Several have had their whole bread ration stolen, or part of it; butter has also vanished, indeed this mean traffic has been carried so far that the thieves have been into their comrades' trunks and stolen food and tobacco. From the German stores on the foredeck they've stolen cheese, sausage, and bread, and from the galley as well. We know who they are, but we are helpless, with no legal machinery of our own, and we shrink from reporting them to the Germans.

One of the donkeymen on board had bought nine loaves in Trondheim with his own money and his own bread [ration] cards, to share out among the prisoners. While he was dividing them up he was called down to the engine room for a moment. When he returned, five loaves had gone. There is no doubt who took them. It was a man who was caught stealing from his mates at Grini some time ago. He got a beating and solitary confinement that time, but obviously it's done no good. There are others, too. Another chap whom we've had our eye on for a long time was caught red-handed today, with a loaf under each arm. He had stolen them from the foredeck. One result of which was that henceforth we are not allowed on the foredeck.

I dare say that can gradually be changed, but now, at any rate, we'll tackle the thieves. We'll set up our own justice, and I don't doubt that we shall manage to clean up.

But I'm confusing the order of events. This time I was sidetracked at Sandnessjøen. The night that followed gave me a good long sleep. I was allowed to sleep in the bunk of one of my friends, the donkeyman, while he was on watch, and when he came back at three in the morning and the other had to turn out, he lay down in his mate's bunk. It was wonderful to get a whole night's unbroken sleep. I hadn't been out of my clothes for three days and nights, and it was a treat just to get them off, slip into a clean pair of pajamas, and also get myself washed and make a decent toilet. I felt like a prince. Rested and full of energy I turned out this morning at about six. We were lying at anchor in Bodø harbor. The town, the mountains, and the channel out to sea lay sparkling in the brilliant sunshine.

Our contacts with the land are becoming more and more numerous, and the Germans are obviously winking at the parcels the crew bring back from their trips ashore. They are not small ones, either. Two hundred kilos [four hundred forty pounds] of whale meat came here "unofficially" today. It is to be shared out unofficially as well and boiled unofficially. Four sacks of carrots arrived in the same way, and a number of little parcels from here and there. The distribution of these things on board among four hundred men, without the Germans noticing, needless to say presents great difficulties. Indeed, it's of course impossible. We must take the risk of the guards being O.K., and I believe they are. We've had many proofs of it already.

This afternoon we shared out the carrots. There were four apiece, valuable vitamins, and tomorrow every man will get half a kilo [1.1 pounds] of whale meat and a whole loaf extra. Four or five hundred loaves have arrived in the same way. A big parcel of bread, fish cakes, herring, and cheese came to me, for distribution, God knows from whom, and also a whole goat cheese.

People are really incomparable. It looks as though they're stripping themselves and giving of their own scanty rations to help an insatiable troop of unknown fellow country-men in captivity.

Without themselves being aware of it, the Germans are organizing a propaganda journey for the new Norway, a triumphal procession up the coast, better than a hundred lecture tours, more effective than all the old worn-out party machines put together. And so this becomes less pointless. One really gets the feeling that one's "war effort" isn't insignificant and vain after all.

SUNDAY, AUGUST 9, 1942 ■ It's been a wonderful day. Except that we couldn't go ashore, we have had no great sense of being prisoners. Both the Lieutenant and the guards, one must say, are reasonable. I slept on deck for a few hours, and it went off excellently. Since then I've had a busy day. The whale meat and bread have been shared out to all the four hundred as extra rations. It was an immense job to arrange this distribution, nor was it managed without the guards detecting it.

I was called down to the *Hauptwachtmeister** with two others to give an explanation. I gave this: We had received the meat and bread as a present from friends on shore, and had been allowed to warm the meat up in the galley. He knew, however, that the things had been brought aboard by the crew. If it happened again, he would report it to the Commandant, and the whole crew would be arrested. This time he would let it pass, and we declared that next time we would ask first. The chap had a bit of a twinkle in his eye throughout, and I realized from the beginning that we needn't be much afraid of him.

We are still lying in Bodø harbor, and have no more idea than yesterday why and for how long. It's said that the *Lofoten* is expected from the south with a lot of tools we are to take with us.

It's been broiling hot today, sunshine from a cloudless sky. I asked the Lieutenant for permission to bathe. It was refused. Alternatively I asked if we might bathe on the foredeck, with the hose. That was allowed, and we had a grand afternoon, after the whale steak and bread. On the foredeck we bathed under a refreshing cataract of glorious sea-salt water, and sunbathed afterward. It was a rare treat; hardly anyone had had his clothes off for five days and nights. There was Sunday peace and a Sunday atmosphere. The idyll became pretty well complete when the Lieutenant himself, in a bathing suit, started paddling about in the ship's dinghy taking the sun.

After the bath we had an entertainment in the sunlight on the upper deck. I sang a number of songs, and others also figured. It really was impressive and strange. No one was

---

* A position (chief watch master) in the Orpo, equivalent to an SS *Hauptscharführer*.

feeling homesick for Grini then at all events. Everyone was full today, really full, and that's no bad thing.

Tonight it's my turn to sleep in a donkeyman's bunk. Odd is sleeping on the sofa. The Odds (as Odd Wang and I are called) have the bunk and sofa turn about every other night. Both the donkeymen are marvelous to us. One day we shall repay them. It's just about midnight, suddenly some air activity has begun; fighters are speeding westward. No doubt a tragedy is imminent out at sea.

MONDAY, AUGUST 10, 1942 ■ In the morning everybody was ordered below. We were going to put in to the quay; also the *Lofoten* was expected at eleven, and we were to take some cargo aboard from it. Our splendid crew with the mates at their head have been bringing in "personal effects" all day on such a scale that I knew all the time something would go wrong in the end. And in fact we heard a report some time ago that a great quantity of parcels had been confiscated. I haven't had it confirmed yet.

While the *Bodø* and the *Lofoten* (which did come about eleven) were close alongside, I made contact with a young and charming girl at a porthole of the *Lofoten*, just opposite the one I was peeping out of. She promised to send word to Kari and also to try and get parcels sent us as soon as our destination was known. She wanted to chuck something over to us, tobacco, books, and a tempting bag of tomatoes, but I managed to stop her. The guards were standing just over our heads and the risk was too great. But at least she would take our messages and see that they were posted from Trondheim, not from the north. She was a technical assistant to a dentist in Harstad and was on the way home from her holidays.

We left Bodø about half-past one. We have had no food since noon yesterday.

Evening. There was a food parade at four o'clock, but at the same time I was called in to the Lieutenant along with Rasmus* and [Jens] Schultz.† We thought, now there's the devil to pay. However, the Lieutenant received us with the utmost amiability and said a whole lot of parcels had come for us from the Red Cross. They were addressed in part to individuals, some to Rasmussen, some to Nansen, he said, but no doubt the idea is to share them all out among the prisoners? He repeated his remark about the Red Cross, and I gradually realized that he *chose* they should be from the Red Cross. Now he would hand them over to us three and would have no more to do with them. Indeed he knew nothing about them! We might dispose of them as we pleased.

We were shown into the saloon. It was littered with tinned goods, butter, and all kinds of groceries. The Lieutenant had opened all the parcels, and the contents were well mixed together in a great heap. It was obviously no use trying to find out what might have been sent to whom. Everything would have to be shared out together. We were allowed to take it away to Rasmussen's office and distribute it as best we could.

The Lieutenant had more to say. A number of boxes had arrived with whale meat (smoked) and split cod, salt cod's roe, and pickled herring. All that we might share out, only below deck. He knew nothing about it, for it had come aboard for the crew, and if we got it from the crew that was our own business. If we cooked the food in the galley, that was a matter between the steward and us. The Lieutenant declined to meddle in it.

---

*   Nansen's nickname for Dr. Håkon Rasmussen.
†   Released November 12, 1942.

There was no doubt that the chap meant kindly by us, and when we thanked him it was in all sincerity.

The distribution took up all the rest of the day. We were sailing up one of the loveliest parts of our whole beautiful coast, but we were down below sharing whale meat into four hundred portions, or sorting out groceries or wrangling with people who came demanding parcels they had ordered from the shore and which they knew had arrived. *Where was the parcel?* We explained the facts, but as a rule they went away furious, with unveiled accusations that we had embezzled the parcels or the greater part of their contents. One of them asserted that he had a claim on goods to the value of three hundred kroner, which he had paid himself, and the goods were supposed to have arrived in a trunk, which he had ordered especially. Another had paid fifty kroner for the same trunk, a third a hundred kroner, and a fourth and a fifth and a twentieth each missed a whole catalogue of things that *must* have come aboard. He had as good as seen them. *Where were his things? Out with them!*

The most unpleasant charges of embezzlement, dishonesty, and pilfering rained down on our heads. It was indeed a grateful task!

We had to go below when we were crossing Ofotfjorden to Lødingen. It was about eight when we put out from the skerries, and we got safely to Lødingen about eleven. Throughout the whole of this crossing we were packed together below, while the Germans put on lifebelts and stayed on deck. A highly illustrative picture of Germans and Norwegians in today's Norway. If anything had happened, we shouldn't have had the faintest chance, sitting like sardines right down on the orlop, and round about in every passage, cabin, and corner, while our protectors walked about with revolvers and lifebelts on.

Our mate and trustee had been drinking wine with the Germans to get them to wink at all the things the crew had brought aboard. It went according to plan. The *Oberwacht-meister* especially was well pickled.* The instructions I had had from the Lieutenant about sharing the foodstuffs he repeated to me at least five times, every time as a profound secret, in a voice resounding with tipsiness. This is a jolly jail.

Now we've just left Lødingen. We bunkered there and lay alongside the wharf for a couple of hours. We're going up through Tjeldsund, one of the loveliest bits perhaps in all Lofoten, but it's midnight and I suppose we may not stay up and watch. I'm sitting peering out through the donkeyman's porthole. As the dark blue and purple mountains glide by in the night like gigantic unreal colossi, my thoughts go southward, down all the lengthy, lovely country and home to her, alone there with the children and perhaps frightened about what's in store for me. That's the only thing that reminds me that I'm a prisoner in a transport on the way to hard labor, and that I'm *not* taking this journey of my own free will, like all my other journeys up north in the past two years.

TUESDAY, AUGUST 11, 1942 ■ It was late at night, but it was so marvelously quiet, I had to sit on enjoying the stillness, talk with it and feel how it dissolves the hard and cold that otherwise so easily tightens up inside oneself. The noise of the waves against the ship's side, and of the bows cutting through the water close by, as the *Bodø* plowed her way northward in the summer night, was like music in my ears, like a subdued prelude to the

---

* Senior watch master in the Orpo, equivalent to an *Oberscharführer* in the SS.

sunrise, which was already flushing up ahead over the mountains. How full of beauty life is, in spite of everything! It was as though *SS Bodø* were steering right into the very dawn.

The darkness began to glow, from blue-black and violet it shaded over into purple, and soon there flamed up in the north a sea of red fire. Then the first sunbeam cut its way through. It struck a high mountain in the west, with a dazzling patch of snow that shivered it and sprinkled its gold like stardust. That was the day breaking.*

It was nearly five in the morning; if I was to get a little sleep before the whole four hundred started their daily trampling, I should have to lie down. I swathed myself in the blankets and I slept like a log the moment my head was down. I didn't wake for three or four hours. We were already in sight of Tromsø, but there was no need to be in too great a hurry. This is the eighth day of the journey, and what a journey!

In such conditions one learns to set store by anything that recalls one's status as a human being. Every drop of water one can get onto one's face or body acquires remarkable value; every chance one has of brushing one's teeth or getting a shave must be seized on without delay, and exploited to the utmost. God knows when there will be another. And while *SS Bodø* was bearing up the channel toward Tromsø, I took time to relish every act of my morning toilet in the donkeyboys' splendid little cabin. Shaved, clean and fresh, like a smiling soap advertisement, I went up into the sunlight about ten o'clock.

Immediately after, there was a food parade, and I had to fall my troops in and distribute food to them—bread, butter, and "dinner," which consisted today of tinned reindeer meat. Eight men to a tin. Yesterday it was a flat tin of herring (for speedy consumption). The bread is like lead, with streaks of damp in it. Before the distribution was over we had arrived in Tromsø harbor, and we had to go below. Then came six or seven hours of misery. It was a broiling hot day, and we were packed together like sardines below deck.

The passages and all the lower decks were impassable with men sitting, lying, or standing, and the temperature, the air, and the morale were not good at all. But contact with the shore had been made five minutes after we put in to the quay. Right down into the donkeymen's cabin came the Tromsø man Conrad Rye-Holmboe† with five hundred cigarettes, and bubbling with optimism and high spirits. How did he get aboard? Pooh, he simply *walked* aboard, scattered a few nods to right and left, and walked on. His rocklike faith that the war would be over in the autumn had a refreshing effect. He had even fixed a date, an ultimatum. The Germans would hold out until November 16th, but not a day more. He would see about contact with us as soon as we found out where we were going. He thought it would be Nordreisa, and there is a bus connection there from Tromsø. We must try and fix things up with the drivers and anyone else we come in contact with.

The distribution of his cigarettes proved a painful business. They had been given to me and two other men, but we shared them out as a matter of course. We gave them to some we knew were in need of them, a packet each, and asked them to share with others in turn. They didn't go very far, and the discontent was great and in part vociferous.

The distribution of the cod's roe later in the day went off better; each man got a big piece weighing nearly half a kilo [1.1 pounds]. But it was as salty as—salt. In the afternoon we left the quay and put out into the harbor, where we cast anchor. We are to lie here

---

*   Sailing north along the coast of Norway in the *Fram* Fridtjof Nansen recorded, "Those never-to-be-forgotten mornings. . . . [T]he day gleaming over the dazzling white snow-peaks!"

†   Rye-Holmboe, one of the first prisoners in Grini (prisoner number 91), had been released May 8, 1941.

until eleven tomorrow, when we are to go on in convoy. We had the chance of a breath of fresh air before night, and deep breaths they were, after six or seven hours gasping below deck.

WEDNESDAY, AUGUST 12, 1942 ■ At eleven o'clock we left Tromsø, in a convoy of four ships altogether. What there is in the other ships one can't tell. Two of them look like guard ships, and no doubt they are.

We're steering into Grøtsund; the goal is certainly Nordreisa. We may expect to be there this evening, about seven or eight. Whether we're to go ashore at once, we don't know. But it's best to be prepared, so today we're sharing out the rest of our private food stocks.

The guards we have now are not to stay up here. They're going back south, on orders from the general, the Lieutenant tells us. It's said that the company of guards on shore will be *Wehrmacht* soldiers with their officers. That sounds promising. As a rule they're much more friendly and understanding than the SS, SD, and all the rest of them. There's no doubt we are to be on road or railway work, which will be directed by the OT (*Organisation Todt*).*

Now I've been out distributing the pickled herring, dried cod, herring tins, and dried milk. It went fairly smoothly, though of course there were some who made a fuss. One of the four boats in the convoy is fully loaded with ammunition. It's going to Kirkenes. Our prison transport is protecting the cargo. German honesty! German warfare! German honor! However, there's nothing to suggest that we shall be going on as far as Kirkenes. We've had orders to pack our things and be ready to go ashore at eight this evening. To Nordreisa, then. We are apparently to fall in by six o'clock.

A little later. We have now anchored up the sound at a place called Oksfjordhamn. We've been ordered below deck, where we're sitting waiting. It's six o'clock now, so there will be no parade at that hour. The shore is covered with hut sections. Perhaps it's here we are to start putting up the huts. There are a number of OT men on the wharf; otherwise everything is remarkably peaceful. We were called on deck a moment ago, but it was only about the distribution of the cheese ration. So it doesn't look as if there were anything urgent on hand. I've sent two men on deck to collect the cheese for my group. And I'm taking the whole thing with profound calm. I think I shall die pencil in hand one day. But not yet awhile.

Eleven o'clock at night; the boat is asleep, and still lying swinging out in the harbor. There was no further talk of roll call, and all those who had packed their things had to start unpacking again. No unaccustomed phenomenon. I escaped, for I simply didn't pack.

Donkeyman number two has just looked in. The Lieutenant had been in the passage talking to some prisoners, and had said we were going on hut work. We should have good food and plenty of tobacco, if we worked well. A whole lot of huts were to be erected. At the beginning of November we should be finished and were to go back south. In a flash I pictured the return journey that's planned for us, in the middle of the autumn gales,

---

* An engineering and construction group involved in vast projects (such as the Autobahn, the Siegfried Line, and the Atlantic Wall) and named after its founder, Fritz Todt. During the war OT relied increasingly on forced laborers from occupied countries, prisoners of war, and concentration camp inmates. Fritz Todt died in a plane crash in February 1942 under mysterious circumstances (he had recently clashed with Hitler); he was succeeded by Albert Speer.

packed together at the bottom of a stinking hold, with the hatches shut, while we roil about in the agonies of sea sickness. Horror of horrors, what an appalling idea. But not for a moment do I suppose it will come to that, if only because the whole thing will be over first. That's what I believe. At least a month shall pass before I change my opinion.

The Lieutenant had said to the skipper that he noticed the crew had been given a lot of letters to send off for the prisoners. He had said it was a very dangerous business, and asked that the crew should get rid of these letters. The donkeyman was a bit scared. I reassured him by saying that it was probably just bluff. If he hid the things in the engine room in a safe place, and didn't take them when he first went ashore at Trondheim, but waited until a bit later, everything was sure to be all right. But of course he must be damned careful. I can hardly imagine they'll bother to search the ship.

THURSDAY, AUGUST 13, 1942 ■ At eight o'clock a roll call was ordered. Just before it there was a meeting of group leaders, in which I didn't take part, unfortunately. I slept too late. That was a bad job, for important questions were being settled, and settled wrong. Word had come that the Germans wanted a return of all the Jews, and of other prisoners whom the sections wanted to get rid of, thieves and scoundrels and worthless elements in general.

Jews and scoundrels were to be picked out and put in a separate camp.

And we were asked to give the Germans a hand. The group leaders were so keen on getting rid of their bad elements that they quite forgot to think what was really implied in pointing them out like this. Consideration for the Jews has never bothered anyone.

That the Germans give the Jews special treatment is a fact we can't change. Nor can we do anything about it if the Germans now pick them out for a special unit, which will no doubt be worse treated and possibly harder worked.

All the same, in complying with the Germans' request or offer to get rid of our scoundrels by pointing them out and getting them stabled with the Jews, we are guilty of a disgraceful action. We are accepting the German view of the Jews; we are endorsing the German division of mankind into two classes—Jews and scoundrels in one, other people in the other.

Unfortunately my (violent) reaction came too late. The disaster had already happened. The Jews were paraded separately on the upper deck and along with them a long list of "undesirables." The two thieves, the Nazis [Kristian] Forsberg and [Tønnes] Førlandsås,* and finally a whole lot of men who with more or less justification were reckoned "inferior" or "difficult."

How this selection had been managed was plain to one and all. The Jews needn't even have asked me. The Germans hadn't done this by themselves.

I'm still fretting because I wasn't at the little meeting to prevent it. For I believe I could have. The group leaders I've discussed it with since either agree with me, or they're ashamed of what they've lent themselves to and try to explain it away.

On the upper deck Jews and dregs were assembled after zealous collaboration between Norwegians and Germans. Damnation! I didn't know what to say to [Leonard] Levin,† when he came to me afterward asking if it was we who had pointed out all these undesir-

---

* Transferred to Sachsenhausen March 20, 1943; released August 16, 1944.
† See February 24, 1943, below.

ables to form a group with the Jews. My answer can't have sounded very convincing, but I had to try and gloss over the want of tact.

Luckily fate came to our aid in some degree. Besides Jews and "undesirables" there will be a good many others in that gang, which is obviously to contain a hundred and sixty men. And there are not that number of Jews and "undesirables" in the transport. Moreover all the Jews are now assembled in a separate group, while a number of the "undesirables" have returned to their own groups for some reason or other. Therefore it doesn't look so ugly now.

In the morning a number of bigwigs came aboard. There was an officer from the *Wehrmacht*, one from the SS, one from the OT, and a civilian. They walked around for a time among our units. Then came an order for all who were or had been officers or NCOs to step forward. There were twenty-three in all. They were fallen in separately and their names taken. Later they heard that they were to stay aboard the ship. The Jews, undesirables, and others, a hundred and sixty in all, were to fall in with their luggage ready packed at eight tomorrow morning. The rest, two hundred and forty, were to fall in with their luggage at half-past seven.

What exactly is to happen nobody knows, but the following seems probable: The first group is to go a little further by boat, to a place called Badderen, where they will be landed. The second—to which I belong—is to be landed here and driven some distance, most likely four or five hundred meters [440–550 yds.] up into the mountains, there to start work along the highway, erecting snow shelters, building snow roofs, etc.

The third group of officers and NCOs, twenty-three men, is no doubt to return with the boat to Trondheim, and probably be sent back to Grini. German administration is flourishing!

While all this was afoot the *SS Bodø* weighed anchor and stood out into the fjord again. We were to search for water, for we hadn't had the tanks filled at Tromsø. After calling at one place where we were turned away, we've now found out another called Hamnes. Here we've been lying at the wharf for an hour.

The day's food distribution has taken place—a third of a loaf, which has now gone dry and crumbly, a dab of butter and a flat sardine tin. This fare is to last us until noon tomorrow. We may possibly get a tiny bit of cheese this afternoon.

Of the court gang only the Odds are left now. One after another has dropped out. Schiøtz and [Magnus] Hagem* went in Trondheim, and now Graff-Wang is going. We lost Nils [Ramm] right back at Grini, and all the others were ill. The Odds are holding out. As Odd said today, "The Odds are always in the final."† I can't help smiling when I think of the night we spent each in his own cell in the Lillehammer jail, when Odd maintained that his arrest was only a misunderstanding; he would be out again in a day or two; it must be a confusion with someone else, a ludicrous error which would of course be cleared up as soon as he got to Oslo. Well, so that obvious mistake has ended up in Finnmark with penal servitude, and as for explaining, he hasn't had a chance yet.

The idea of going up into the mountains is not uncongenial. The Odds are already busy with plans for trout fishing. Both are fishing crazy. The problem is tackle. We have

---

* Hagem was transferred to Schildberg prison on November 19, 1942, and remained incarcerated in Europe until the end of the war.

† Odds (full name Odds Ballklubb) is one of the oldest and best-known soccer teams in Norway; it has won the Norwegian Football Cup more than any other team.

nothing but our hands, but perhaps those can be used too, or perhaps we can do a bit of barter in Hamnes; we are to lie here until nine this evening and it's only five now. We must have a talk with some of the crew.

The only awkward thing about the mountains is that up there we'll probably be living in complete isolation, with no contact with the outer world. And the telegram from Kari about her and the child won't reach me. Suppose, suppose. . . . No, I won't make room for any "suppose." Kari has said I may be easy and dead certain, so I am. *Basta!* [Enough!] Now I'll try to get some fishing tackle.

It's strange how hardened one grows. Here I sat a while ago, romancing about fishing trips in the mountains and one thing and another. As I sat writing, a prisoner died in the next cabin, not three meters [10 ft.] away, and here I am, observing with horror that it has not affected me—to any great extent. The dead man has been carried out, his things have been packed up and removed, another man is already sleeping in his bunk; from the crew's room there is the sound of a concertina; outside I hear the laughter and bellowing of some German sailors, who are splashing about in dinghies.

[Andreas] Dolva was the dead man's name—a driver from Skien.* He was already ill at Grini; he was in bed in the hospital when his name was called. The doctor's statement was ignored, and Dolva ordered to get up and fall in. Then later he was ordered off with the transport in spite of his condition. He was obviously very ill even then. The responsibility lies with Denzer and with him alone. Perhaps he may share it with the German doctor, who must have approved his decision.

Dolva was ill all the way. Lonely and abandoned, far from all who were dear to him, he died a painful death as a prisoner on a German transport with an unknown destination. Dr. Rasmussen tried to get him removed to Bodø hospital. That was refused by the German doctor who came aboard there. Rasmussen has done what he could. The murder was committed by the Germans. It was a murder. The man hadn't even done anything "wrong" when he was arrested. He had been in the neighborhood of a police raid which was carried out in Skein, and had been picked up with the rest as a "demonstrator." For that he had to pay with his life.

We are back at Oksfjordhamn and once more lying at anchor out in the harbor. It's half-past twelve; I'm sitting waiting for the "west wind." It comes every night about this time, I've discovered.†

We didn't get hold of any fishing tackle. The store in Hamnes was shut. Instead I got some little coalfish and haddock. We boiled a huge pot, and had a meal of fresh fish, which I shan't forget in a hurry. We ate our fill of fresh fish! If there is anyone who doesn't know what that means to German convict-prisoners, it's because they've never been German convict-prisoners.

At half-past seven in the morning my unit is to fall in on deck with kit. We're to go ashore. The mountain theory seems to be the right one in our case. They say there's a prison camp up there somewhere. Temporary address, then: No. 1380, Oksfjordhamn, Troms.‡ It was a fine "west wind!" Tip top! Yesterday as well. So long!

---

* Dolva was forty-nine.
† It was the donkeyman who brought us the "west wind." They had a radio somewhere on board, and they listened in to London every night. O.N.
‡ 1380 was Nansen's prison number at Grini.

FRIDAY, AUGUST 14, 1942 ■ It turned out as we heard last night. We paraded at half-past seven, and not long afterward we were ashore. The luggage, thank heaven, was hoisted onto trucks. A lot of people had been afraid we were to carry it. We were paraded in a meadow, counted and divided into fresh groups, divided into fresh groups and recounted, both well and long. Then several bigwigs arrived in a car. They were representatives of the OT and the *Wehrmacht*. The Lieutenant announced that the *Wehrmacht* was to take us over from now on. He hoped we would behave as nicely as we had done so far. (The Lieutenant, who calls me Amundsen* and Nansen alternately, took a special leave of me as I was crossing the gangway, and hoped we should meet again.)

When the sick and old had been placed on a truck, the march began. It was a lovely day with sparkling sunshine. I soon regretted the warm underclothes I had put on. It turned broiling hot. We marched five in a row, a file of young soldiers with rifles on either side. We went further into the dale and up the side of it along the main road. When we had been walking for an hour, we were allowed to rest by a lake. In ten minutes we went on again; now the gradient was steeper; we were going up into the mountains all right. It was delightful to move a bit.

At last we got up to where the snow shelters were being built, and the wide expanse lay before us. There was another short rest before we reached the camp. This lay on a narrow strip at the highest point, where it began to slope down again toward Kvænangfjord. And indeed we had just a glimpse of *SS Bodø* before she vanished round the point far, far below, on her way to Badderen.

The camp is singular. For Spartan equipment it beats all records. We were quartered in three different huts lying inside a barbed-wire barrier. Round the barrier guards are posted at proper intervals. Each hut contains three rooms. In each room a group of thirty men are to sleep. One is to be used as a hospital ward; Rasmus and [Knut] Gard† have settled in there. In the rooms something has been rigged up to stand for beds in two stories. The first story is the floor pure and simple. It is covered with straw—in bins down both the long walls.

The smell of mold hit us in the face as we went in. The woodwork in floor, roof, and walls is green with mold and mildew. On the second story the straw has been put into sacking covers laid close together from outer wall to outer wall down two sides of the room. In the middle of the floor is a rusty stove with a pipe going up through the roof. There's no wood here at present, that we can see. We are far above the tree line, and the mountain is barren. Only a few osiers, a little heather and moss, but mostly stones and moraine gravel. We get a view of it through the cracks in the walls, and through two windows at each end of the room.

In the windows tables have been put up. They won't hold more than twenty men at most altogether, I've calculated. The rest will have to eat in their "bunks," or outside, if the weather permits. The bunks, the tables, and some benches and stools have all been

---

* Roald Amundsen (1872–1928), a Norwegian contemporary of Fridtjof Nansen, was also a prominent polar explorer. He was the first man to reach the South Pole (1911), utilizing Nansen's ship, *Fram*, and the first to successfully navigate Canada's Northwest Passage (1903–1906). Amundsen disappeared in 1928 while part of a rescue mission searching for survivors of a plane that had crashed while returning from the North Pole. His body was never found.

† Gard, a dentist, was ultimately transferred to prisons in Germany, where he spent the remainder of the war. Secretary-general of the Norwegian Dental Association since 1938, he later became the president of the World Dental Federation.

knocked together in a great hurry from unplaned planking material, also with a delicious odor of mold and mildew. The laths composing the table tops are thin and bend, each board separately, according to the weight put on them. The benches also are rickety to a degree; when fully occupied they form an arc, which in the middle comes very near the floor. There is no place for the luggage; every man must have trunks and knapsacks up in bed with him. That will be problematical, for we'll have to sleep pretty close together. Still there's more room than on the orlop of the boat, so we mustn't complain. The sanitary arrangements are confined to a privy accommodating several people, with little screens as stall partitions between the seats. Apart from that we have a brook outside the barbed wire, about a hundred meters [330 ft.] away among the hills. We have to go there to wash ourselves more intensively. This takes place in units, under a strong guard. They're obviously very frightened of our running away.

This evening there arrived a young man in mufti, obviously a kind of works manager for the activity up here. He told us about the working program. We are to work on snow shelters, etc., up to two kilometers [1.2 miles] from the camp. We fall in at seven tomorrow morning and work until twelve. Dinner from twelve to one and work again until six. Roll call at the huts, with counting, at ten in the evening. He seemed a "reasonable" man and we got on well with him. He was "understanding" and as obliging as he could be. But he had ling in his hat and looked horribly German.

There's nothing here of all that we were led to expect. No clothes, no crockery, nothing but what I've already mentioned. How we're to get on is a mystery to me. For instance, we have only one thin pair of trousers each. But more of that tomorrow. Now I've had roll call and must go to bed. I'm stiff enough and tired enough for it too. Good night!

SATURDAY, AUGUST 15, 1942 ■ *German administration!* God save and preserve us from it when this is over. Forevermore.

And *Organisation Todt*, of which people talk so big! Which builds *autobahns*, railways, bridges, and hutments in record time, and sets everyone gaping in amazement at German skill and tempo! How in heaven's name this myth could ever arise, indeed how the Germans have kept things going at all with this caricature of an organization, this world's record in inefficiency, is to me an insoluble puzzle.

Everything done in this peculiar camp is qualitatively inferior to anything I have ever seen. To begin with the actual placing of the camp: If they had searched with lighted lanterns over the whole mountain, they could scarcely have hit on a more exposed place to put it. It lies on the highest point of the "saddle" between two fjords. It falls away abruptly on two sides, and the plateau itself may be perhaps a kilometer [.6 miles] or so broad. The wind up here must be something frightful. Indeed, the rickety huts have had to be fixed to the ground with wire guy lines on each side. So they've had that experience already.

As I said, there's no wood here. We are above the tree line. A kilometer or two [.6–1.2 miles] on either side brings us down into birch forest, where a camp might have lain snug and sheltered, with enough wood around. It's a long way to any water. The brook, as I said, runs at least a hundred meters beyond the camp, in a gorge cut out of the moraine gravel. There again they could have found a building site that would afford shelter and other advantages. Needless to say it's a particularly bright idea that the water-fetching and washing should take place at such a distance that the prisoners have to be escorted to and fro in small groups. It looks as though they had been at pains to plan the whole thing so that the maximum of time may be spent in futilities, and so that the existence of the prisoners may be as complicated as possible.

The inconveniences also fall on those outside the actual prison camp. Outside the fence a number of other huts have been erected of the same type as ours, and some queer Lappish-looking round huts with tent roofs. That's where the *Wehrmacht* soldiers live; and the OT men. All told there is a detachment of about fifty soldiers on guard. They have nothing to do with the building works. They don't give a hoot for them, but interest themselves only in the guard duties and hardly that. They are in the charge of a *Feldwebel*, who in turn has a *Lagerkommandant* over him. The *Lagerkommandant* is a lieutenant, and is also Commandant of the camp at Badderen. He comes over here from time to time in his little car, bringing a hubbub of people, high and low, OT men, civilians and army men, whom I haven't made out yet.

Besides the guards and us prisoners, the camp is teeming with queer creatures, half ci-vilian, half military. They are OT workers. Most of them are apparently from Vienna, but there are also men from other countries, certainly a number of Czechs. We thought at first that they were Russian prisoners of war, but they seem to be detailed men on *Arbeitsdienst* [labor service]. So they are not prisoners, but "volunteers."

These men work on all kinds of jobs in and outside the camp, under the OT's snuff-colored "officials" with the swastika band round their arms. One of these is also in chief command of the work inside the barbed wire. The detailed men have been up here since the early part of May. For three months, then. In that time they have erected our huts and done a certain amount of work in the camp. It doesn't exactly leave one breathless with admiration.

When one sees them at it, one realizes pretty soon that the result can be no great shakes, as to either quantity or quality. After a closer look at their tools, one understands even more. Most things, in the first place, they haven't got. There are no decent hammers. All they have are some things like Lilliputian sledge hammers. None of the axes has an edge, and whetstones are unobtainable. There are no decent joiner's tools. Everything is the cheapest kind of Nuremberg trash, as we called it in the old days. It's ordered and delivered by the bundle. We saw it lying in open railway cars in Trondheim and elsewhere. A large percentage of it was ruined, rusty, or smashed. There is a shortage of decent nails. They have only certain sizes, which they have to make do with.

But above all they're short of decent material. Round, crooked logs and the cheapest kind of boarding material are all that can be had. Those we have to fetch from some old, abortive snow shelters that are being pulled down on other hills not far away. Presumably they are last winter's futile efforts to keep the road open. This year they're to try again. I hardly think it will come off. According to report they're planning to build twenty-two kilometers [13.5 miles] of snow roofs in all. An Oslo firm has it in hand. Perhaps later we'll be put onto it as well.*

They're a melancholy-looking crowd. Spiritless and gloomy, lackluster, gangling and crook-backed they go around, no, they swarm around, to all appearance about as aimlessly as ants in and round an antheap, only a good deal slower in their movements. Perhaps

---

* Veidal lay close to Highway 50 (now the E6), which ran north to the strategically vital town of Kirkenes.

they rather suggest another insect—in a glue pot. The Grini tempo was the speed of an express train compared with this. Grini efficiency might be set up as a pattern for these people.

We're out of most things we need in every sphere. Only a very few have drinking vessels; they have to use the frying pans belonging to the field kit. (Most have brought a field outfit.) A small stewpan and a frying pan have to be used for everything—for shaving water, as a tooth glass, for coffee, for soup, for solid food, and finally to keep bread and butter in, that is if one has any to keep after meals. Most have brought a spoon. Practically no one has a knife and fork. Pocket knives are therefore at a premium, when it comes to cutting bread or spreading butter. Not to mention sheath knives.

When we ask to be given some few of all our needs, the Germans shrug their shoulders, spread their hands out, and are sorry. They say they haven't anything themselves. The only thing of which they give us any hope is a wash basin, one for every four. And indeed we reckon that a great gain, a long step forward. Also we're apparently to have some little enamel bowls for those who have nothing to eat out of. Otherwise crockery is unobtainable. Several have begun to whittle spoons, forks, and knives, and many envy the Chinese their dexterity with chopsticks.

Denzer and the Segment are being cursed without a break. Just think of all we could have brought with us if we'd known what it was like up here, and hadn't believed all their lies about what would be provided on our arrival.

The worst is clothes. The first night was mild, but stiff enough for those who had only brought two thin blankets. What on earth will it be like when autumn sets in and it begins to blow? These half-rotten, leaky huts can't even keep the faintest polar breeze out. Only one suit of underclothes was issued to us, a pair of drawers and a vest. Most have only that. We should be given plenty where we were going, said Denzer and the Segment in chorus.

We must try and wire to Oslo or elsewhere for the most vital things we were swindled out of by those two irresponsible gangsters. As regards laundry the possibilities are confined to the icy brook out yonder. There's no soap, or anything else to wash with. That also would be arranged on the spot, said Denzer and the Segment to silence us, and we believed then that we were going to Borre* or Germany. Instead we've been sent to hell in the very opposite direction, to a Godforsaken mountain glen among a whole gnat swarm of rickety, useless Central Europeans. Useless as cannon fodder, useless at work, but driven to it by the world's greatest figment of an organization—*Organisation Todt*.

Here we sit, then, or rather lie, side by side in the musty straw on the floors, which are laid straight on the damp ground, and look at one another, after having consumed our meals with hands and sticks out of tins and basins and everything so formed that it can hold the food for the little time in question.

Thank heaven a lot of us can laugh. The Odds laugh every time they look at each other, laugh until they get a pain in the belly, at least I do. Talking of the belly: I wish a diet patient could *see* the bread we eat, but I shouldn't wish anyone to eat it. If one has luck, one may get hold of some that isn't moldy. Then one doesn't have to cut away all the green, so there's a bigger ration. That it crumbles away and can't be sliced really makes no difference, since we have nothing but a penknife to manage with.

---

* A village on the west coast of the Oslofjord.

Hut 2 from my corner of the "hutch."

In spite of all this and of the rather gloomy prospects ahead, all of us really feel we're not doing badly. Indeed I almost think we prefer this to Grini, most of us. The mere fact of getting away from Denzer, Kunz, Kunze, Stange and all the gangsters down there feels like a deliverance, for the sake of which one readily puts up with a bit of hardship.

We had a capital dinner today, a new type of storm soup, of a very much better quality than at Grini. It had several bits of meat in it and was thick with beans. Some people really had their fill. Our own cooks had prepared the dinner; in the first place they managed to boil it all in one go, and in the second place to share it out in a jiffy, so that we had even time left for a rest before one o'clock. That impressed the Germans greatly. None of them had thought it possible. Our cooks believe that we shall manage it every dinnertime.

Tonight we've all had coalfish liver; nourishing and good food. Most drank the oil as well. I couldn't, and I took that as a good sign that I'm not undernourished. The Germans were going to throw the liver away!

Henceforth, as I said, we're to do our own cooking, by our own request. I'm already building a kitchen. I have a group of eight men, and in a couple of days it is to be finished. We've taken over a big field kitchen range from the Germans, and the rest we'll manage alone. The "foundation walls" and posts are already up. Tomorrow we'll have sills and roof; and perhaps walls, too. We'll have tarboard on the roof, and we've secured a long pipe to extend the chimney of the field kitchen. Besides which I already have a lot on my program. I'm to see to all kinds of fitting-up jobs with my gang. The others have been working at different things throughout the day.

The foremen are understanding people; one of them, an OT man in charge of the works inside the camp, said to me today, "You must keep moving all the time. We don't ask much, but if any of the senior officers should turn up, everyone must be on the job. Go round picking up stones, or do something."

The *Feldwebel*, who is beyond comparison the Germanest and hardest of these chaps, we call Nob. The civil engineer in charge of the OT work we call Tot, and the chap who spoke to me we call Captain Paunch, because he's round and plump.

Well, it's nearly ten o'clock. I must see to the evening roll call in my hut. There is mist and rain outside. Good night!

SUNDAY, AUGUST 16, 1942 ■ Mist hangs over the mountain, and a biting, ice-cold wind is throwing itself off the mountain sides and going through bone and marrow. I've put on thick winter underclothes and a sweater and a woolen shirt under my jacket. I have a scarf round my neck and mittens on my hands, and still I'm freezing. It's impossible to keep warm on my work. In fact I don't believe any work would keep one warm up here; it's as though an icy undertow were sweeping through the camp and down the dale. It goes right through one.

Today there's been a little more go in the division of labor. Most were sent off, as far as two kilometers [1.2 miles] from the camp, to build snow shelters. They've had the advantage of getting down into the birch slope, where it's warmer. They're not being driven hard. On the contrary, the foremen absolutely curbed their zeal, with shouts of, "*Langsam! Langsam! Leise gehen!*" [Slowly! Slowly! Take it easy!]

Besides the gangs who were sent out to build snow shelters, there is a permanent gang, mostly of oldish men, that stays in camp to work at different jobs here. Among them are joiners and carpenters, who are building our kitchen. Some time tomorrow it should be ready to move into. It's not much to boast of. The framework is made of crooked logs; floor, roof, and walls of unplaned material; all the boards of different widths, wavy and with cracks in them.

All the same we shall make a kitchen of it, and if the menu keeps up to its present standard, everything pertaining to that department will be all right.

Through the window I'm watching a melancholy piece of work in progress. A whole gang has been set to pull up the dwarf birches growing in our "courtyard." Typical of these people. Soon it'll be like a lifeless peat bog inside the barbed wire. They're also going in great force for the osiers, pulling them up by the roots; big patches of moss, earth, and heather come too; everything is being heaped up and burned. A little rain now, and the whole place will have the look of a pigpen. Even the sun-scorched stones with dry lichen and moss on them are being sedulously gathered up and laid in a heap. They too were in a sense alive! The stones had to go. A drilling ground is a monochromatic, plane surface. So is a prison camp. Which is framed, besides, in barbed wire.

It's strange to see the magnificent panorama to the north—through the wire. The fog vanished about six, in time for the evening sun to send us its last warm rays before dropping behind the peak that towers straight up in the west. It shone out far over the mountains to the north, east, and south, and charmed the loveliest colors out of mountain and fjord.

Even Per Krohg was enthusiastic. He was a bit disappointed with the landscape the day he came. It was so much "panorama," and also he was tired, like the rest of us, after a long, exhausting march. But even a panorama half in bird's-eye view like this can give a sense of intimacy when one comes to know it in all its phases. One sits here with a tremendous feeling that this country of ours is the most beautiful in the whole wide world.

MONDAY, AUGUST 17, 1942 ■ Yesterday the "civilian" (with the ling in his hat and buttonhole) was here and expressed his satisfaction with us. In return we expressed ours with the food. He uttered fresh promises, and assurances that he would do everything in his power to meet our wishes in every way. I'm beginning to think it's mostly talk, but at least it's better than abuse and roaring, and one must be thankful for small mercies.

No doubt we'll gradually learn to adjust ourselves. The rooms are beginning to get livelier already. Individuals are fitting themselves up with shelves, ingenious boot racks, and other devices. There's obviously nothing to prevent those who don't work outside the camp from tackling these jobs in working hours, as long as they "keep moving" and don't stand gaping with their hands in their trouser pockets.

Today it's warmer; the sun is shining through a thin veil of cloud, and there's no wind. The night was cold. Many complained this morning of having felt cold, even though they had spread over themselves all the clothes they had. Especially those who sleep in the straw on the ice-cold floor.

One of the first things I shall see to—as soon as we're finished with the kitchen and the washing benches outside each hut—is the raising of the beds off the floor. After that there are a whole lot of useful jobs on my working program. All of them in our own interest exclusively, so those will go without a hitch. The work outside the camp, which of course has been undertaken for purely strategic ends, we must rather sabotage as far as we can.

Now it's raining again. The ceiling thickened as the day went on, and in a single moment fog shut us in. The bitter, ice-cold wind came down off the mountain bringing rain. We're freezing again, and the worst of it is that if we get wet hardly anyone has a decent change, and no one has more than the one thin pair of camp trousers we traveled in. We have only one jacket, too. When you add that the huts are dank and overcrowded, it doesn't need much imagination to picture the state of affairs after six o'clock, when everyone comes back from work. We're obliged to dry the clothes on our bodies. It would be impossible to stay in here if the filthy, wet underclothes of thirty men were hung up to dry, not to mention how unappetizing it would be to eat in the middle of it. Therefore wet days are a disaster to us.

TUESDAY, AUGUST 18, 1942 ■ Last night after supper we had a game of bridge in the sickroom. We stayed there far into the night. I looked into my hut and dealt with the evening roll call at ten o'clock; afterward we went on with the game. When everyone had gone to bed, we wheedled Rasmus into sacrificing a little of his pure spirit in sugared water. It tasted good. I gave up one of my little Christmas candles.

A sentry came in. We put out the candle and threw down the cards, like children caught red-handed in something horribly naughty. He only wanted to ask us to black out, so that the light would not be visible from the road, if anyone should drive past. When I was outside putting up the shutters he called out to me and asked if we had tobacco. I said none to speak of. Then he opened his raincoat, pulled out his tobacco pouch, gave me a good pinch, and said good night. He smiled so nicely that I was on the point of asking him to come in and have a drink. It was raw, cold, and dark outside, and it was raining. But it's better not to let oneself go so far with them. Still the contact was there, he had effected it himself with his friendly handout in the darkness. In a way it would be simpler if none of them were human beings.

It's a bit depressing to see how many people have gone moldy up here these days. Grousing and grizzling are part of the daily routine, and cantankerous clashes take place in every hut several times a day. Perhaps it's not to be wondered at in these circumstances. After all we're living on top of each other and rubbing against each other all the time, when we're not out on the job.

Some are dissatisfied with the food. They deserve a beating. I should like to know if many people in Norway today are better off, not counting the Germans. Of course the stomach may go wrong, and that is certainly happening. Practically all Rasmus's patients have stomach trouble. Rasmus says that all of them have just simply overeaten. Others are dissatisfied with the job they've got; they see others doing lighter work, and then they feel the ravages of envy. It's nothing else. Why should *he*, when *I* don't, etc. They're like small children in a nursery. Even those who are over sixty. Some again are dissatisfied with their bunk, others have a better bed, and so on interminably.

They all complain to the hut leader. I curse that job many times a day. Oddly enough I'm not cut out for a nursemaid. And I used to think I was so patient. I'm not. A few extra blankets were given out. We gave them to the men over fifty. One must have some principle to go on. The sulks, resentment, and outcries began at once, and the hut leaders get the benefit.

Well, we must try and arrange something in the way of evening entertainments, games, and competitions, as one does for children when there are enough of them and one doesn't know what to do to keep them out of mischief.

This afternoon we had distinguished visitors. First there was an inspection by a colonel with his suite. He was in command of this section. Then came no less a person than the general for the whole of North Norway with his train. One must admit that these inspections were as different from those we had been used to at Grini as day from night. There was no Terrace tone here. These were gentlemen. They were thoroughly correct. They listened kindly and courteously to what the prisoners had to say, wanted to hear their requests, took them up in turn, made a note of them, and promised to do what was in their power to comply with them.

Now it's raining again, and nearly midnight. I feel bad knowing nothing of Kari and how things have gone or are going with her. I wonder if the child has come—and when? Good God, what a punishment we've both been given! Good night!

WEDNESDAY, AUGUST 19, 1942 ■ It was a cold night for most of us. The icy wind freshened overnight into a very pretty gale that swept through the gap here, and forced its way through the leaky cabin walls, underneath and up through the floor, making the straw fly, while it howled and whistled round the corners and in the guy lines. The fellows had to get up and put on all the clothes they had, and even that was not nearly enough. There was very little sleep. We're getting to know this place now. In less than half an hour it can change from storm and rain to sunshine and a clear sky.

Last night and today everyone has been busy writing home. We've now had permission for the first time. There is a lot to write of, but very little of it is allowed, so I suspect the censorship will have plenty to do. The safest thing is to say we are all right and getting enough to eat, and then ask to be sent all the things we haven't got, or rather a few of them.

Food being served out in Hut 2, Veidal (all of the "twos" are in the picture).

Rasmus was with the *Lagerkommandant* today in the other camp at Badderen, where the rest of us are, including all the Jews. The camp is above the tree line there as well, but rather lower than ours. It is warmer than this one, a tremendous advantage, and has running water in the huts. Otherwise it sounds as though we're better off on the whole. They have a sickroom, but no doctor. The two Jewish doctors, [Leonard] Levin and [Wulff] Becker, are not allowed to practice.* So because they're Jews a hundred and sixty men are to be without medical aid.

I sit in the sickroom in the evenings and do a little writing. The storm and rain have begun again. The whole house is shaking and rattling and keeping up a terrible din. It's biting cold out. In here there's still some heat in the stove. But it's dark, and now I can't see to write. I daren't light a candle without blacking out, and that's too much trouble. Besides there are a lot of patients sleeping here, and I am a guest. I must get down into the straw by the other Odd and try to sleep until morning.

THURSDAY, AUGUST 20, 1942 ■ The stormy weather lasted all night, and as soon as the fire had gone out in the stoves, the cold started. It was bad last night, even worse than the night before. This morning another couple of men went to Rasmus complaining of pains in the stomach and chest. The cold and the unaccustomed fare are playing havoc

---

* See February 24, 1943, below.

with people's bellies, but we have no serious cases yet, and as yet the sickroom is only an asylum for the seedy. Therefore it can be used as a kind of general office, a camp center, where everything goes on. It is also a dining room for the camp leaders and a meeting place for all who want to hear the latest news or pass on the latest rumor. From early this morning there was constant traffic of trucks, guns, armored cars, and motor bicycles on the main road northward. But none since dinnertime.

It's not easy to decide who has the say here. Germans variously uniformed and equipped run around giving orders and—not least—counterorders. It's often happened that I've received a definite order for my men from Captain Paunch, which has then been countermanded by Nob or Tot. I complain. They shrug their shoulders. . . . German administration! Always the same many-headed monster. To us of course it's all one.

Now the northward traffic has begun again; it's mostly trucks now, presumably with supplies of food and ammunition, how should I know. A few motorcycles with sidecars go sizzling and cracking past, like gray-green streaks. Needless to say this has given free rein to fancy. The rumors are taking shape; already it's reported that the American fleet is lying just off the coast here and the invasion is in full swing. According to what some have thought up, France is already practically taken by the invasion forces. Doubtless by tonight the war will be as good as over. We can begin to pack our trunks. One man says there are two hundred American planes on Spitsbergen* and several airfields have been made there. God knows where they get it from. But notwithstanding: long live optimism. It's a great help.

We have a typical case of beriberi in the sickroom. Rasmus is delighted. He treated a number of them at Grini, and positively chortled with glee if the symptoms made their appearance in the right order, as he had expected. Now he has a guinea pig all to himself up here.

FRIDAY, AUGUST 21, 1942 ■ I was called into the *Lagerkommandant* today; there were a couple of things in my letter he wanted to ask about. I had written between two full stops. *Be careful!* That was suspicious. I explained that I meant Kari was to be careful after the birth, not work too hard, take it easy and look after her health in general. He didn't seem convinced, but he let it stand. I had written that we could receive parcels and letters as at Grini, but that we were under the *Wehrmacht.* That also was very suspicious. I said I had only meant to explain that we were no longer under the SS, and therefore applications should no longer go through the Terrace. He looked rather glum.

Then he questioned me about why I was a prisoner. Hostage? Court hostage? Which of the royal family had I known? The Crown Prince? Good. How often had I met him? How intimate was the acquaintance. Tja! That was all. He folded the letter and put it in the envelope. He didn't strike out anything.

Discipline has been appreciably tightened up. Today a highly German, categorical order was given on the working site. Most people threw off their jackets when the sun began to get warm, but some kept them on because there was rather a cold wind at the same time. Instructions were given that *either* they must all have their jackets on *or* they

---

* Spitsbergen, Norway's largest island, is almost six hundred miles due north of Kvænangen.

Bilberry-picking under guard.

must all take them off. The guards are taking the numbers of those who work badly. Those reported three times will go into a *Sonderkommando* which is evidently to be set up.

This afternoon I was out bilberrying with four other prisoners and two guards. There were many meters between each berry, but it was a lovely outing and a pleasant change. It was strange to be out here on the free, glorious expanse among the mountains and dales, shining and ringing of Norway, and to be in German hands with two soldiers as jailers.

They were *our* berries we had to pick for these robbers, and into the bargain we got a bawling out for picking too few.

If we work hard tomorrow, we're to have Sunday off. But only on that condition.

SATURDAY, AUGUST 22, 1942 ■ A magnificent sunny day. All morning I was out with three other prisoners and two guards, picking mushrooms. We got a whole sackful, I should think close on a hundred kilos [two hundred twenty pounds]. We managed to sneak some for ourselves, and they were so good that they've given us the taste. We must try to get hold of more. The whole place is covered with them. In the afternoon the same gang picked bilberries, but then we had four guards along.

In general the day brought no important news on the local front.

But for me there was one thing that shone out above all others, and transformed existence at a stroke. I had a wire from Kari. The child has not come yet, but everything is fine.

So now she knows where I am, and that I'm all right. The wire hadn't taken so very long, either. It was sent off at noon today, and I got it about six. Which shows me that after all we're not living such an absolutely senseless distance out in the wilds.

SUNDAY, AUGUST 23, 1942 ■ Sunday off. Our work yesterday must have given satisfaction, since we got a day off.

I was at "church" this morning. Pastor [Ole] Sæverud had obtained leave to hold a service. His sermon was written and censored in advance, and one of the German soldiers who is also a clergyman attended the service, which was held out of doors between two of the huts. The prisoners had brought their benches and sat behind each other in rows, as in church. Others lay on the ground or sat on stones along the walls of the huts, or in the windows. In the center of the "chancel" stood Pastor Sæverud in his ordinary prison dress. He had buttoned the blue guards' jacket right up to the neck, and thus obtained a sort of clerical style. His hair, which is generally untidy, stood up like a dark halo and fluttered in the wind, which he had right at his back. The "chancel" itself, the background of this picturesque group, was perhaps what made the whole picture unforgettable: the barbed-wire fence, and the vast upland with the mountains beyond. Outside the fence through the barbed wire we now and then saw a guard patrolling with his rifle; we could also see OT men, Czechs, Poles and German soldiers lounging about, smoking and chatting, like a kind of profane décor in the "chancel." It happened too that a motorcycle was started up, just behind the altar, and chugged coolly through the "sacristy" and out of the picture. Further off we could hear the clattering of planks and boards being unloaded on the road nearby. Only now and then, if the interruptions

Divine service behind the barbed wire at Veidal.

became rather too loud, would Sæverud pause a moment and turn his head toward the presumptuous disturbance, so that the halo-crest rose even stiffer into the air and the whites of his dark brown eyes showed more distinctly as he looked sideways up.

It was thrilling in a way to hear the Creed repeated in these surroundings. Sæverud's thin but clear voice sounded distinctly through or over the responsive muttering of the "congregation," which was like the roar of a distant cataract and blended superbly with the picture. The hymns too had a powerful effect, seeming to vanish over the uplands in the blue air. And then the final benediction. Like the vault of a giant cathedral the great sky arched over us, dazzling blue between the clouds, which like golden sky-galleries piled up from the horizon at the sides of the vault. In luxuriant streams the sun poured its gold down through the heavenly galleries—over the mountains and the wilds—and blessed the solemnity.

MONDAY, AUGUST 24, 1942 ■ Today I've taken in my "big wash." I boiled and washed my clothes yesterday, and this evening they were dry and fine and clean, and I still haven't begun to use one extra change of underclothes. I'm doing first-rate. Tomorrow I must try and get my socks darned. They're having a hard time.

I forgot to say that yesterday we bathed in the brook under guard. Bathed is a strong expression; the brook isn't more than half a meter [20 inches] wide and hasn't much water in it, but still it flows, and one can get wet all over if one turns about. Per Krohg painted a sketch of that scene. He showed me another preliminary sketch: Divine Service. That may be grand. Otherwise he's busy painting for the Tot-*Baurat* [construction superintendent], who nosed him out in the list of prisoners, embezzled him and set him to painting pictures. Now he behaves as if he owned Per Krohg, hide and hair. Everything Per does is the *Baurat's* property, but he has his time to himself, goes about without a guard, and I think really he's thriving on it. He has become enthusiastic over a couple of subjects, and manages to hide away enough sketches for them. Yesterday he became a grandfather, or was it today? He's coping splendidly with this life.

The tobacco shortage is glaring, and beyond all comparison the thing that darkens prison life most. And there are small prospects of getting any for a long time. Several are bartering their watches and valuables for a little tobacco. Some of the civilian workers are turning the situation to good account. The Poles and Czechs are not backward either. One or two decent German guards give me a pinch of tobacco or a cigarette now and then. I'm almost over the worst now. But it *is* a severe privation. Good night!

TUESDAY, AUGUST 25, 1942 ■ The rumors are buzzing. There has been another invasion of France, this time in five places. In one place they've been repulsed, but in four they've kept their ground and got a firm hold. Five hundred German planes are said to have been shot down. How great the Allied losses have been is not reported. The rumors derive from some civilian workers we meet by the roadside.

A group of twenty men have been at work all day seven kilometers [4.3 miles] off, without coming home for dinner. They got back about half-past five and threw themselves on the food like starving wolves: a huge piece of whale meat each (a gift from the local people round about). Even before the worst of their hunger was appeased the news bubbled out, and it was such that one has to hold onto oneself. If only half of it is true, it's epoch making. Just listen: Göring* has landed in England with seventy planes. General Rommel has capitulated in Egypt. Turkey and Brazil have come into the war on the Allies' side. Sweden is trembling on the brink. Two German battalions in Kirkenes refused to march against the Russians; two hundred and thirty officers shot. Finally there has been an attempt on one of the quisling ministers (God knows which). A policeman was shot, and a large reward is offered to anyone who catches the assailant.

This news is no small beer. If one only knew whether these civilian workers were reliable, for they are the source of information.

A really wild optimism is beginning to get hold of me. I pull against it with all my might, but I can feel myself slipping. Heavens, if only some of this were true!

WEDNESDAY, AUGUST 26, 1942 ■ Berry-picking again this morning. As a rule I go along with an old skipper from Florø. A splendid fellow. His son went to England, and now he's inside as a hostage. To this day he's as venomously angry with them as the day he came in, as unbowed, as unchangeably Norwegian.

"If I could just get my hands on one devil of them afterwards, I wouldn't be long in dispatching him."

---

* Hermann Göring (1893–1946). Göring was a prominent member of the Nazi Party, founder of the Gestapo and commander-in-chief of the Luftwaffe, the German air force. In 1941 Hitler designated Göring as his successor, but he fell from favor as the war progressed and the Luftwaffe failed to perform to Hitler's satisfaction. Convicted at Nuremberg of war crimes and crimes against humanity, Göring committed suicide by swallowing poison the night before the sentence of death by hanging could be carried out.

Any attempt to talk him out of this attitude seems hopeless. Surely I didn't think it was possible to avoid a day of reckoning, when every man would have a chance to settle up for all they had done to him. I admitted that it was certainly to be feared, but just for that reason we looked forward with anxiety to the day when we should sink to the Germans' own level. He shook his head and no doubt thought that was soft. Then he caught sight of one of the guards lighting a cigarette, and called out to him: "Hey, you there! Hey, now you can damn well fork out some tobacco." And so he got a bit in his little chewed-up nose-warmer, lit it and thought of anything but blood and revenge.

THURSDAY, AUGUST 27, 1942 ■ Kari's and my wedding day! Perhaps the child will come today? As a wedding present on our fifteenth anniversary. Let me see, if it were born today I couldn't expect a wire until tomorrow at the earliest, that is unless it was born early this morning. Yes, I can surely start awaiting the telegram this afternoon. Just as though I weren't in the thick of waiting already, and long ago. But one must deceive oneself a little to divide the time up, and make it vanish in short stages. That helps.

The guards have torn up their pictures of Göring, it's said today. The man who told us hadn't heard it from any of the guards, but from another prisoner who had no doubt heard it from someone who had seen it. That's always the way.

It's raining today, a steady downpour. It will be bad for those who are out on the job, a long way off. They've no outer clothes to change, but have to go about in their wet rags. For they *have* gone to rags, already. A sorry sight.

Otherwise I have a suspicion that it's the want of tobacco that is lowering morale and resistance. A lot of people moan about things that wouldn't normally bother them.

One of them has thrown in the towel. He *will* look miserable. He beats all records in unshavenness. His hair hangs in tufts round his thin face, or stands wildly up in the air; his dark eyes stare hungrily out of their dark sockets. To be on the safe side he keeps his trousers hanging right down on his thighs, and his braces trail after him along the ground as he moves in agony, hobbling with arms and legs straddled out. For God's sake don't accost him then, for that's what he wants. He's out fishing. He has his jeremiad all ready; it comes wailing out as soon as anyone bites. I said good morning to him today. I was standing washing; he had come from the privy. That was enough. I got the whole rigmarole. He'd been on the run all night, to and fro. Now he could stand no more. The worst of it all was that he'd behaved like an infant in bed last night, and had had to spend the whole morning cleaning up. No, he couldn't stand any more of this. Now they could do what they liked to him, now he gave up. He went to the doctor before breakfast, and this time Rasmus gave in; the fellow was admitted to the hospital, and now he's lying there as the sickest and wretchedest of the whole bunch.

As I said, it's raining today. All work has been suspended. All the gangs have come back in turn, as wet as drowned cats. Now they're lying in their bunks, in underclothes, while their trousers and jackets hang up to dry. Dinner is over, but the rain continues, and looks as if it would go on doing so. The clouds are hanging low, as far as one can see in every direction. I've taken refuge in the sickroom where there is now two hours' silence on strict orders from Rasmus. I'm disturbing nobody with my writing, and it's really quiet here.

We can surely reckon that about a third of our "exile" is over now, and it has gone fast. It's the same here as at Grini; every day may seem miles long to get through, but the weeks nevertheless gallop into eternity, and before one can turn round a whole month has passed, and summer with it. What became of the summer, all told?*

FRIDAY, AUGUST 28, 1942 ■ Today I should really have been out cutting birch twigs for brooms. It was put off to this afternoon. This morning I'm chopping wood.

No, it ended in berrypicking today as well, both morning and afternoon. I haven't picked so many berries in my whole life, nor shall I ever pick so many again. I feel I must be the North European champion at locating bilberries.

The bilberries we had managed to embezzle we stirred up with our sugar ration into an excellent jam, for our abundant supper table. Into the bargain I had gathered a glorious dish of mushrooms, which also adorned the table. We're living like princes. Today moreover large consignments arrived from Tromsø. It was mostly bread, half a loaf extra for each man. Great joy in Jerusalem. But no tobacco. A lot of grumbling in the same Jerusalem. For there came great parcels, and in those parcels there would have been room for lots of tobacco.

There was a parcel for me, from a kindhearted woman named Johanne Marie Andersen.† It contained a double blanket and a whole outfit of good warm underclothes with thick stockings. All woolen. Also two tins of meat patties, three tins of herrings in oil, a slab of cooking chocolate, a big piece of goat cheese, and a packet of cigarettes of my favorite brand. I'm sitting here enjoying number two already. Heavens how I'm enjoying it. I haven't had one like it for a fortnight.

A civilian worker we passed today as we were marching out on our berry trip said to us with a confident, broad smile, "Now you'll soon be free, lads!" It sounded like a fanfare of victory. Far along the road and far down the heather ridges my feet kept time to that marvelous music, and I still have it in my bones, despite all the rheumatism and stiffness in the world. Now we'll soon be free! Now we'll soon be free!

SATURDAY, AUGUST 29, 1942 ■ Things can't possibly go on much longer like this. We're quite stiff with cold, and working doesn't help. The wind goes through bone and marrow. We have no thermometer, but it can't be much above zero [C or 32° F]. There will be a ghastly end to it if we don't get more equipment—oilskins and outer clothes and warm underclothes. I've asked Rasmus to speak to the Commandant. He agrees that this is affecting our health in every way. Cleanliness is also breaking down. Baths are not to be thought of in this cold, and hot water for washing is almost unobtainable. In one room lice were found yesterday.

SUNDAY, AUGUST 30, 1942 ■ Sunday! so they tell me. One of those I'm not likely to forget. After a miserably cold night we woke up—in a snowstorm. The whole mountain was white. It snowed all through the day. In between there were short, clear blinks of

---

*   Another famous concentration camp survivor, Victor Frankl, agreed: "[A] small span of time, like a day, seemed to last an eternity. A larger length of time though, such as a week . . . appeared to fly by incredibly fast. And my fellow prisoners always concurred whenever I said: 'In the camp, a day lasts longer than a week!'"
†   See October 8, 1942, below.

sunlight, but the next moment the blizzard swept through the gap again, whipped us in the face, and soaked our thin trousers. All hands were at work.

It's painful to see the old men out there in the snowstorm, with their teeth chattering. Many have rheumatism, and almost none have anything on their hands. I can't help admiring them—they don't say much. Of course they let out a juicy oath or two, off and on as it occurs to them what they're really going through up here. Then they clench their fists in their pockets and curse, and I'm afraid have something like murder in their minds. The grains of snow hit them right in the face; they smart like needle pricks.

The guards and OTs were nice enough; they were eager in getting a little roof put up that we could stand under when the worst flurries came, and having a fire lit to warm ourselves by. We stood often and long under the roof or round the fire, for now and then the weather grew simply furious. We stood there several hours, shivering and freezing, while our eyes smarted with the smoke. Instead we might have been at home in the huts, doing useful work. But no, that wasn't allowed.

In the afternoon I "decamped." I stayed away a good long time, at least an hour and a half. I took a trip across the mountain to see what it looked like on the other side, and how it felt to be walking alone across an upland once more, or clambering up a scree. It was splendid. In a few long sunbursts I saw the mountains to the east—white mountains and white expanses as far as the eye could reach—and down below, that chink of sea stretching inland—right in to Kvænangsbotn.

It would have been an easy matter just to go on. Who could stop me? This was precisely the kind of day that would be ideal for an escape. To be swallowed up by mist, snow, and wilds, and walk on eastward mile after mile to Sweden—and liberty. This idea intoxicated me for a moment, as I stood on top of the mountain due east of the camp, while the sun was fraying the mist, opening an alluring distant prospect over the white expanses. . . . Then the mist closed in again; hard, pitiless blasts of wind swept over the mountaintop, and just afterward the flurries began afresh. I returned to the working site. No one had noticed that I'd been away.

MONDAY, AUGUST 31, 1942 ■ I was surprised by a guard last night and had to break off. I hadn't blacked out properly. As good luck would have it, it was my tall friend, the one who gave me a handful of tobacco in the dark some time ago. He said nothing about my writing, didn't even ask what it was. He only told me to black out the whole window and then go on with what I was doing. I preferred to crawl into bed.

There was more berrypicking today. Both morning and afternoon. I'm seeing things blue now, and the fingers of my right hand are permanently blue with cold and bilberries. This afternoon we were allowed to pick a few for ourselves, after filling the big twenty-five-liter [6.6 gallon] bucket. First I managed to embezzle a liter [one quart], then I picked two more.

One of the German guards came to me this evening with a whole plateful of caster sugar for the bilberries. They mean really well, a lot of them. It must certainly have been his own idea, and there's no doubt that it came from the heart.

At midday there were guests here. Baalsrud, the road superintendent, visited the camp with his suite. Great was my astonishment when I suddenly caught sight of an old high-school friend, fat and round and serious, in the superintendent's train. I went up to him, squeezed him by the hand and chatted with him for five minutes. We couldn't talk freely; there was a guard there, one who knows Norwegian, but I managed to find out that things were going excellently. Unfortunately he'd heard nothing about Göring or the invasion, but he said he had been traveling without a break and hadn't had any very reliable news for a long time.

It was nice to talk to a friend from outside. He was going straight back to Oslo, and I asked him to look up Kari, give her my love, and say I'm all right. Then he can tell her a little about what it's like here. He left a parcel for me. A wind jacket, some warm clothes, a little tinned stuff, and a little tobacco. God bless him for it! When the need is highest. . . . I've had no tobacco for a long time now. Also I've gladdened quite a lot of old fellows with a few pinches of snuff and a few quids of chewing tobacco, which were also in the parcel. I got a packet of "Teddy." That dreadful, nasty cigarette I am now smoking devoutly, and enjoying. It's wonderful; I've been doing it great injustice for many years. I take back everything I've said about it. It's pretty well the best cigarette I've ever tasted.

From Oksfjordhamn the chaps brought back nothing very epoch making today, no *Dementis* [denials], but no confirmations either. While there's life there's hope!

Kari must have had her child by now, and she's sure to have wired. The telegram may be lying in the post office at Oksfjordhamn. There are a good many letters there as well, which get no further because none of the Germans take charge of them. The prisoners aren't allowed to bring them back. So I'll have to tackle another night and another day in ignorance.

Some hundreds of German prisoners are to be put in the camp which has been built a few kilometers north. They also are to work on building alterations and snow shelters. They are prisoners from Kirkenes—who refused to advance against the Russians. It's said that eighty were shot. So the rumor of a mutiny in Kirkenes holds good. Apparently it's been in the papers too.

TUESDAY, SEPTEMBER 1, 1942 ■ Today, then, is the beginning of a real autumn month. September—the name has autumn and falling leaves in it. Today it's four weeks exactly since we left Grini. No doubt the rest of the time will pass, too. It's not very likely that we'll be kept up here beyond the middle of October; perhaps they may be knocked out even before that.

I've come back from a bilberry trip as stiff as a post. Rheumatism. I thought it would pass off during dinner; usually it does, but today it wouldn't. When the dinner interval was over, I went to Rasmus asking him to give me the afternoon off, and so now I'm lying here. My whole body aches, and my eye sockets are sore. It hurts to look sideways. But then one should only look straight ahead, so it'll be all right.

A man from Tromsø looked into the camp. He brought no good news. He murdered all our glorious rumors, both about the invasion and about Göring. Well, well, we'll just have to resign ourselves. However, he didn't say where his information came from. Whether he'd listened in to London himself, or was well informed in general. I don't feel like giving up all those grand rumors at a blow. I'll stick to them a bit longer, anyhow.

The rheumatism has passed off somewhat during the afternoon. I slept for an hour, and some tablets I got from Rasmus have had a good effect. Probably tomorrow I'll be out bilberrying again.

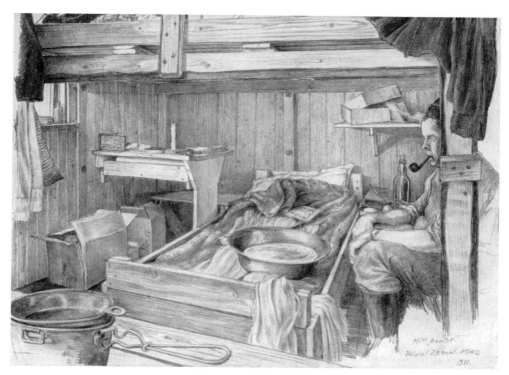

The "Odds'" corner in Hut 2. [Note Nansen's 'office' on the left.]

The old men are gallant chaps. It's extraordinary to see that ninety percent of the sickroom population are young lads. No doubt the old fellows are just as poorly; but things have to be bad with them before they go to the doctor. They're not accustomed to going sick! But anyhow their generation is of a hardier type, which doesn't give up at the first steep place.

Old William Larsen,* a fisherman from Lofoten, was green in the face and almost fainted before he could be persuaded to see the doctor. Then he took a couple of days in bed, but was on the job again long before it was necessary. I've seen him on the job too, I've worked with him. He's always first and takes the heaviest lift. To be able to give one of these men a pipe of tobacco, a bit of plug, or a pinch of snuff is a pleasure that warms one's heart.

One of them, [Kristoffer] Langenes,† has started making me a little "office arrangement," in my bed corner. A bedside table also serves as a chair, and a couple of planed boards out from the wall with legs under them will be the desk. I'll be able to sit writing there in the evenings with my bit of candle in front of me. I'll just put up a screen in the window—a wooden frame with tarboard on it is my idea—and I'll have an intimate little closet all to myself. I'm looking forward to it like a child. As things are now, there's not a moment's peace to be had.

---

* Released December 21, 1942.
† A carpenter from Vågsøy, Langenes was arrested days after the British commando raid there; he was released March 15, 1943.

WEDNESDAY, SEPTEMBER 2, 1942 ■ Truly it's a strange thing that this damnable anti-Semitism is actually a living factor among us. For some reason we've had one of the Jews here from the other camp. Not a day passes but I hear some casual, blackguardly remarks about the Jews, and unfortunately very often indeed they come from just the people who should know better.

I've given up defending the Jews, it's so absolutely useless with men who *won't* understand, who have formed their opinion once and for all from their own "exhaustive experiences." Instead, I try to make them realize how unpatriotic their behavior is today, how German-influenced! But no, they don't see it.

Some of them have also discovered that the theme can be varied interminably, as material for entertainment, wit and brutality. I see nothing humorous in that. I see it only as a distressing example of how little progress we've made in sheer humanity. In all countries— not least our own—the *Herrenvolk* idea is not far off. Certainly we're clear on one point: the Germans are not *Herrenvolk*—but how about ourselves exactly? Is there really anyone superior to us, or as good on the whole? Not that our conceit of ourselves has anything imperialistic about it. We don't aspire to another people's property. We only want to keep what we have, and remain a small nation. But what a nation! What a little pearl among nations! Even where the Jewish question is not involved, our smugness comes out.

I got two parcels today. Both were from Johanne Marie [Andersen]; there was a little note in one. She had just heard from Kari and Siri, and all is well. If only I could get a letter like that! Johanne Marie is touchingly kind. I've written to thank her, and ask her to keep me posted about Kari. For she can make trunk calls. Surely there must be word today? This is getting hard to bear.

Another night is beginning, a long black night, with black thoughts. Uncertainty everywhere. Today I'm slipping for the first time in ages. For the first time in ages I've had that thought again, that the Germans might win the war. That they may possess undreamed-of resources. They may have worked themselves so firmly into the countries they've seized as to succeed in holding them against all attacks. And with that idea come a whole inferno of others of the same kind. One all but gives it all up—one can't be bothered struggling. One "discovers" with horror that it's what one really has believed all along. The other thing—the faith, the certainty, the radiant optimism—was only what one screwed oneself up to. Now it has all collapsed like a house of cards. The worst of it is that one actually feels it restful to let go like this. Of course the last thing one ought to do is sit down and write. Confess one's own miserable weakness and will-lessness to a sheet of paper. It's wretched. An exposure! The unmistakable sign of a weak character. There! Now I've got it out. But one must hide it, hide it as best one can, and keep afloat on the wreckage.

I had a visitor again this evening—[Snarøya] Sælid (the elder, from Polhøgda).* He has a job up here, with Holst-Larsen who is building snow tunnels. He had come straight from Oslo. Last Sunday, the 23rd, nothing had happened yet with Kari and all was well. Everyone at home sent their love. It was good to have the chance of questioning him about all the little things at home—the garden, the house, the wood. I kept at it, wouldn't

---

* Sælid was a longtime caretaker at Polhøgda, tending to the house, gardens, horses, etc. According to Nansen's daughter Marit, Nansen and Sælid had a close personal relationship, and in some ways Sælid functioned as a surrogate father in light of Fridtjof's many absences. Sælid's younger brother had the job after him.

let go of him, I had to have the whole picture. I dare say he thought I'd turned queer. He will be driving back and forth up here all autumn, right on until the snow shelters and tunnels are finished.

Nothing else happened today, except that I got my "office" ready, where I'm sitting writing now while all the rest are asleep. But it's getting on toward midnight; the candle has burned almost right down to my smart, new, planed table top.

THURSDAY, SEPTEMBER 3, 1942 ■ No telegram. No word of any kind. All the same I feel more cheerful today. Yesterday's wretchedness has taken itself off. For some mysterious, inexplicable reason I'm quite calm and convinced that nothing is wrong.

There was a pure-bred Lapp in camp today. He looks after a herd of tame reindeer grazing round about. We see them all the time; there are big, handsome bucks with proud antlers, little shavers of calves and straight, light-footed does. One of them is snow white all over and magnificent. This Lapp apparently owns some of the animals, and the Germans are very keen to get their claws on them. Therefore the Lapp had to come into camp and talk to them. He was as perverse and awkward as he could possibly be.

Could they buy some animals from him? Well, no, it was so difficult to get hold of them at this time of year. Just try it! They run away at once. Rubbish of course, the Lapp had only to go straight up to the herd and pick out any animal he liked. Might the Germans shoot some of them? Well, no, then they might shoot some that weren't his and he would be punished. No, it was quite impossible. Couldn't he try to catch some of his own with a lasso? It ended in his engaging to think that over—for a while. And so we'll see no more of that Lapp, I imagine. To him reindeer are worth more than money. Germans are Germans, and the Lapp is a Norwegian.

FRIDAY, SEPTEMBER 4, 1942 ■ I had some parcels today. Goat cheese, sausages, tinned stuffs, *sunda* [jam], crispbread, tobacco, splendor and joy! Also I had a telegram from Kari, sent off yesterday! *All serene but no news. Your Kari.* She'll be all right.

SATURDAY, SEPTEMBER 5, 1942 ■ The camp's NS member, [Kristian] Forsberg, has got into hot water. He's as work shy here as at Grini. Several times he's tried to go sick, but Rasmus sent him away. He has blabbed to the Germans, and asserts that he's the object of political persecution. The Germans asked Rasmus to write a report on his condition. They got that yesterday, after Forsberg had taken to his bed and refused to go to work or turn out for roll call. He was sent off to work all the same, but returned home with a guard and was allowed to go to bed. He was to have no food, on the other hand; he was too ill. On being told that he pooh-poohed it, saying he had food enough. Why, he had so much that if anyone was short they could come to him.

He was soon to be taken down a peg. The Germans began to harry him in earnest in the afternoon and evening. A special guard kept an eye on him while he was fetching water, carrying boards, planks, and logs, and in general doing all the unpleasant jobs that could be raked up. It's gone on like that all day. It's becoming almost too much of a good thing. Forsberg looks deplorable. Poor chap. He's quite alone. Not a single friend. No one who will even speak to him. And he has all the Germans against him, too. One of them, on hearing that Forsberg was a Nazi and party member, said it was just like that with them, too. All the worst elements, the work-shy, the lazy, and the failures, joined the party to get "employment" and to get on.

If the weather's nice, they're going to let us pick bilberries tomorrow! Those who have been good boys. First we're to pick a liter each for the *Wehrmacht*, and then for ourselves. How generous they are! I think I shall try a water color tomorrow if it's nice weather.

As it was Saturday night we played a game of bridge on the office table, and also treated ourselves to a tinful of coffee with medicinal spirits in it. It tasted delicious. However, in the middle of the game Rasmus was called out on a singular professional visit. One of Holst-Larsen's trucks had run over a cow in a snow tunnel. Now Rasmus had to go and decide whether the cow should be allowed to live. There were jokes about collaboration, etc., but it ended in an agreement that he was to bring back either the cow or a few liters of milk.

SUNDAY, SEPTEMBER 6, 1942 ■ Sunday—a real Sunday. Radiant weather from early morning. We began the day by staying in bed until eight. To wake up at the usual hour of half-past five—we do that from habit—and then just turn over and go to sleep again, when one has collected oneself and really taken in the marvelous fact that it's Sunday off, that's such a treat as I believe no one can understand who hasn't been a convict in *Gefangenlager Veidal* [Prison camp Veidal].

In the old days I never cared to stay in bed in the morning after I'd awakened—even in a good, soft, warm bed. Now it seems to me that I must have been mad. Here I sleep on the bare floor, on a few scanty bits of straw, with two double blankets over me and one under, and I feel it the height of luxury to lie lazing on this couch for an extra hour. So intensely does one relish it, one completely forgets that it's possible to imagine even higher degrees of civilized existence, even more evolved forms of comfort. It no longer strikes me as awkward to clean one's teeth with a flat sardine tin as a tooth glass. It's as though I'd never had anything else to use. The idea of standing washing at a washstand indoors, with hot water in a basin, with a mirror above, is far off and effeminate. No, *we* do these things outside in God's free nature—with ice-cold water—standing in the mud or on stones in the mud along the washing bench on the gable wall. And the towel is gray—practical and handy; it was once white, but that was long ago. I can't conceive how people manage to get them white. I've boiled mine and rubbed and scrubbed it with soap powder and all kinds of "modern" washing stuffs, but the result is an even gray all over—not as before I boiled it, gray in blobs and streaks. I remember Kari saying something about its bleaching white in the sun. I've hung it up in the sun, but the result has still been gray—light gray all over. Now I've decided that it's practical, and have let the matter drop.

Breakfast today beat all records both north and south of the mountains. Eggs and bacon!! Trump that! Rasmus got the eggs as an honorarium for his professional visit to the cowshed last night, and the bacon I got in a parcel. I don't mind betting that there aren't many people today in Norway living in much grander style. That we drink our coffee out of an empty food tin, spread with a penknife, and use a bit of unplaned board as a plate, no one even thinks of minding. No, we're in lordly circumstances.

After breakfast we were allowed to bathe in the brook, in units under guard. I can't remember any bath from a sunny rock by the sea that I've enjoyed more than that romantic bath up here in a brook the size of a medium-sized gutter. It was icy cold and refreshing, and one had to take care not to "dive" just as the soapy water and sediment from some bather higher up was going by. This led to great competition for the highest place. The sun bath afterward was also first rate; fortified in soul and body we returned to the camp, where we immediately went to church.

The service was held in the same way and in the same place as last time. Per [Krohg] got a chance to paint a small study for his picture. A mighty sky, with sunbeams piercing through the clouds, arches or rather towers up over the little flock of people between a few rickety little houses on the ground along the mountains. And then the slight figure of the priest in the middle, with fluttering hair and burning eyes. Houses, priest, and congregation—indeed, even the mountains—look so crushingly small against the mighty, sun-dripping vault of sky. Yes indeed, the subject is grandiose. I tried my hand at it too and made a pencil sketch, but it didn't turn out as I wanted. The sermon was too short today.

I sat on a stool with my back against the urinal. Per was standing by the dustbin, using it as a drawing board. In the middle of the benediction an impious prisoner came and started rippling on the wall behind me, and in the middle of the Lord's Prayer a Viennese waltz, shrill and out of tune, cut in from the German hut beyond the fence. But the congregation listened—no less devoutly—to the clergyman who preached, no less fervently—and Per and I drew and painted no less imperturbably—and the sun poured down its golden rain no less lavishly over all of us—and perhaps the Lord Himself was not so particular about the forms up here in the wilds.

TUESDAY, SEPTEMBER 8, 1942 ■ Fine weather, but cold. I'm surprised I don't catch cold, but it looks as if the air up here saves one from that. Only a very few are troubled with chills. Diarrhea and rheumatism are the worst troubles, and a certain amount of inflammation in wounds. Besides the Germans, of course—and for them there's no cure.

Today my pleasant job continues, of putting shelves up in the main German kitchen. We're still so numerous on that job that there are always one or two standing idle. That's what the Germans are accustomed to. They call it administration, and that's how they set the whole nation to work.

Sælid drove over last night with one of the civilian workers, who needed a doctor. He undermined the invasion rumors, and now I'm compelled to give them up, too. I'm seriously afraid my once firm belief that the war would be decided by the collapse of Germany this very autumn is failing me. To prepare oneself for another year of war is a matter of some difficulty. But if it has to be done, of course we'll make a job of that too. I should hope so indeed!

WEDNESDAY, SEPTEMBER 9, 1942 ■ Last night I gave a little "concert" in the hut after dark. I sang a whole lot of ballads and songs. Our room is in the middle of the hut with a room on each side. One is the sickroom. There are only thin boards in between, so I was entertaining the other two rooms at the same time.

Yesterday I was so imprudent as to help Båstad* by drawing a pattern on a soapbox he's carving for Captain Paunch. Paunch came and saw the box and slobbered with enthusiasm. There was a Tot's name on it then. He asked me to take that out and put his wife's name instead. Also I was to do some more—three for the present.

I've got a peaceful job there, I imagine. Really it suits me very well. I shall have an

---

* Auden Baastad was transferred to Sachsenhausen with Nansen, where he remained for the remainder of the war.

opportunity for both drawing and writing. Indeed I've started carving, too. I've discovered I can do it as well as Båstad, and the worst is that I find it amusing, so amusing that I've been absorbed in it all day, without a glance right or left.

Today I had two parcels, one from the young girl I made contact with through the porthole of the boat in Bodø. A touching parcel. A tin of cod's roe, a tin of field rations, a tin of herring, a packet of Frisco and a quantity of matches. God bless her. Then there was a huge parcel from Leif Andersen, Tromsø.* *He's* quite fantastic. How am I to thank him for all this?

Captain Paunch is going to the Badderen camp and will be there until Saturday. I'm to see that my working group is divided up as usual and does certain jobs, which we've gone through together, while he's away. I'm also to see that two men, [Thorvald] Tønnesen† and Båstad, are reported sick every day and don't turn out. They're to work on *Andenken* the whole time. So am I—while at the same time I'm to be works foreman. He's got quite tame now, Paunch, since I've begun to manufacture *Andenken* for him. One corruption deserves another. Things are looking up. We shall twist both Tots and Nobs round our fingers, and of course there are great advantages in that for us all.

There's one thing I must note down before I stop for the night. A whole mass of goods has reached the camp. I suppose a hundred and fifty new pairs of stockings, straight from the factory, a mass of crispbread and other large quantities of rationed goods. These the Lieutenant has refused to issue. In his view it must be wrong that rationed goods in large quantities can be conjured forth offhand apparently quite outside the rationing quotas. His attitude is comprehensible. It was stupid to send the things in that way. Now the situation is tragi-comic. A great many of the prisoners have no stockings, or they've been wearing their only pair, perhaps a thin pair of cotton ones, for four weeks, and over at the Lieutenant's there are piles of good, new, thick stockings which he won't let us have. No doubt it will end in the sender being hauled up, too. Perhaps we'll get him—or there may be several—out here!

THURSDAY, SEPTEMBER 10, 1942 ■ Another rough, cold, wet day. One of those that lower morale all round and make work a curse in good earnest. I confess I was glad not to have to march out on the snow-shelter job. I am works foreman today, have taken over Captain Paunch's job, and as soon as I had set the men to work I started on my wood carving.

A rumor—the only new one for a long time—says that three boats have been torpedoed in Vestfjord. That's all the news. It's terrible to be without those life-giving reports from outside that made existence livable at Grini. One hardly dares to talk war now; one gets so afraid hearing one's own lurking doubt expressed in words. Pessimism *mustn't* take root here. We can't afford it—not now! The rumors must be good; and so they are, most of them. The others we make away with, pretend we didn't hear them. In our room we listen to [Birger] Eriksrud instead—a fine fellow.‡ He's willing to bet anything whatever that the war will be over before November 15th.

---

* See October 8, 1942, below.
† Tønnesen remained at Grini for the remainder of the war.
‡ Released December 23, 1942, Eriksrud was rearrested November 20, 1944, and released February 19, 1945.

Things are being bought and sold in camp on a large scale. It turns out that Tots and Poles are mad for watches, fountain pens, knives, objects in general! A lot of people are selling their watches for such dizzying sums that the temptation becomes impossible to resist. Others are selling everything they can do without for tobacco. A fountain pen—which must have cost forty or fifty kroner—goes for a couple of fifty-gram [less than two-ounce] packets of bad tobacco. A tiptop sheath knife for the same, or less, according to how insane the owner has been driven by tobacco hunger.

A smart, conscienceless OT devil can exploit this state of distress for the ugliest transactions, and so they do every day. Even people of whom one would expect better are not ashamed to offer their possessions to the Germans with a single abject plea for tobacco written on their faces. Indeed they're not even ashamed to beg cigarette ends, or a pinch of pipe tobacco, or anything, as long as it's tobacco—something to smoke! It's a disgrace. But one must take a very lenient view of it; there's no doubt that the tobacco craving can drive people to absolute desperation that makes them almost irresponsible for their actions.

The maddest of all the tobacco-starved in camp is a man who is now called nothing but Stumperud, because he goes about all day long with one sole idea—to collect stumps [i.e., cigarette butts]. Twice a day he comes into the sickroom to go through the ash trays. It's an agreement; he's not allowed to come oftener. He comes stealing in, quietly, as though to take the butts by surprise, as though they mustn't know of his advent so as not to vanish. He creeps in upon the ash tray, after sighting it from afar. He stares at it hard, with open mouth and madness on his stiffened features. One has the impression that every muscle in his body is tense. Then he takes a little run and throws himself on it.

The whole contents, the ash of burnt matches, scraps of paper, crumbs of refuse, and from time to time—but rarely—real cigarette ends, slide through his grimy fingers. In the hollow of one hand he collects everything he means to smoke. It's by no means only cigarette butts. He takes a good deal of ash as well. Sometimes, he says, it isn't quite smoked out. Not a single grain escapes his painfully exact scrutiny; every mote of what he reckons usable is let down carefully and individually into the hollow of his hand, and thence, as warily as if it were gold dust, poured into an empty tobacco tin. Then, when at length he's finished with one ash tray, his eyes rove wildly and sickly about the room in search of others. He scrutinizes the floor—the ash-tray before the stove—the wood box—the window sills—under and between the beds—the night tables—everywhere! We're looking at him, laughing at him, talking about him. He doesn't give a damn. He answers to the name Stumperud, and thinks it's all as it should be.

The other day Rasmus got him to wash himself, not merely his face and hands, but all over. An enterprise of public utility.

No telegram today either. Good night!

FRIDAY, SEPTEMBER II, 1942 ■ Still no telegram! Still another day and night to wait and trust that everything is fine. Otherwise it's been a good day, quiet and the weather good. I continue as a wood carver, and am positively getting to be quite good at it. My products are exciting the Germans' appetite and unveiled enthusiasm. I should think I'll be on this work for the rest of the time. Per [Krohg] has been "at home" today. He is taking a bit of interest in my trifles, gives me advice, and says they're good. I realize he doesn't mean such an awful lot, but it's encouraging all the same.

Otherwise there's no news in our camp today. However, Rasmus brought back a pretty story from the other camp, where he's been on a professional visit.

A chap called Møte has been ordered by one of the NCOs to wash his shirt.* It was to be washed by twelve o'clock the day after. Of course Møte misunderstood, and thought it was at twelve o'clock the next day that the washing was to take place. He was called in to the *Feldwebel*; he had refused to obey an order; he had been guilty of a heinous offense, an insult to the German *Wehrmacht*.

After the inquiry he was sent outside for a moment, and there he overheard a telephone conversation, allegedly between the *Feldwebel* and the camp Commandant, that is, the Lieutenant here at Veidal. The gist of this conversation was that he had been guilty of a gross breach of discipline, which could not be tolerated. He was to be shot.

When this telephone conversation was over, Møte was called in again and informed that he would be shot for his crime. Three guards with loaded rifles were summoned. Møte was supplied with mattock and spade, and marched out of the camp with the three guards, to a spot where he was ordered to dig his own grave. They asked if he had a family and if he wanted to send a last message. Møte dug and dug, in a cold sweat, answering their questions. In the end they'd given him a thump on the shoulder and said it was all right. The show was over.

Stalingrad is holding out! Today moreover—after an hour's argument with a young puppy of a German NCO—I've made a bet with him that Stalingrad won't fall, as he maintains. The bet is fifty kroner, and a German *Sondermeldung* on the fall of Stalingrad is to be decisive. Of course these bulletins can lie like the very deuce, but one has to take some risks. The mere discussion today was worth the money.

"I am a fanatical Nazi," he said frankly and honestly.

I thanked him for the admission and tried to explain all fanaticism was hampering and dangerous. He shook his confident head, radiating the naïve, blind fanaticism he had just acknowledged, and prophesied that after a time I should undoubtedly be standing where he stood now. He was rather touching, but a tragic figure nonetheless. What will become of a young fellow like that once the truth has dawned on him? The lad is newly married, and sees the future as a bed of roses in the sunshine of a marvelous Hitler paradise, where all Germans will have the job of managing the whole world. Plenty of food, plenty of money, no unemployment—nothing but light and joy for Germans.

This boy was caught at twelve years old. The more he talked, the sorrier I felt for him.

Also we had sad news today. [Paul] Kvamme has been shot! While we were still on the journey.

No one has heard anything of [Per] Birkevold. He was in 412 along with Kvamme, condemned to death and waiting—waiting. Both were sure of a pardon. Both were splendid the day we left Grini; they nodded and waved good-bye and good luck from their window as we went off.

Berlin, Paris and another big town have had an absolutely fearful bombing, so the rumors continue. The Russians are on the Pasvik River,† and also the invasion rumors are beginning to come to life again, with the first million men on the Continent. Unfortu-

---

* Georg Møthe was released December 16, 1942; rearrested January 1, 1944, he was released again February 16, 1944.
† A river that forms part of the border between Russia and Norway.

nately it will need more than a rumor to start me up on that idea again. Finally Judas Lie is said to have blown up.*

My last candle is burned right down.

SATURDAY, SEPTEMBER 12, 1942 ■ Rain and drizzle, drizzle and rain, cold and uninviting all day. I can't deny that I'm glad for my new job on days like this. To be sure my wood carving for Captain Paunch has turned out much too good to land in Germany, but what the hell.

Tonight there came a whole truckload of parcels. A hundred of them. It made a great stir—*Tobacco!?!* It's to be hoped they will be given out tomorrow.

No telegram today either. Tomorrow, then! And so good night.

SUNDAY, SEPTEMBER 13, 1942 ■ The whole mountain was white with snow when we went out this morning. It was real winter and biting cold. Not below zero [C or 32° F] yet, indeed, but not far off. That's all that's wanted for the snow to lie now. We've grown accustomed to this life. If one's bottom and one's knees have come through the trousers, the rest of which are hanging down in tatters over one's legs, well, that's how it is. Not by any means unique. We laugh at it now. At first there was a lot of growling.

Captain Paunch returned fat and smiling from his journey last night. It wasn't until today that he came to inspect his *Andenken*. When he beheld my work of art on his soap-box, at first he was struck quite dumb. Then he liquefied with enthusiasm. He gurgled out some noises which could be interpreted in essence as *ganz fabelhaft—gross—wunderbar* [absolutely marvelous—great—wonderful]. Then he sank down on the bench beside me, where he remained devouring the soapbox with his eyes, which were shiny with melted fat. He turned it this way and that, muttering the same comments all the time, while he puffed and groaned with exertion. Finally he pulled himself together and said he must have one more, one with *Adolf Kulla*† on it. The others I was working on, for the other Tots—including his *Stellvertreter* [deputy]—I could do a bit more offhand, he said; the one for himself I could give a bit of time to, *nicht wahr?* Couldn't I change the name on this one—he liked this pattern so much—and draw something simpler for the man who was to have had it? And up from out of the pork somewhere came a pudgy, fat hand with two (2!) cigarettes in it. A nice man, that Paunch.

At dinnertime there was a distribution of the parcels that came last night. They spread joy and well-being, but there were also of course longing eyes and envy, for by no means everybody got one. I was actually in luck again—had not one but two. One with food and

---

* Nansen is facetiously referring to Jonas Lie (1899–1945), the Quisling minister of police. When the Presidential Board of the Storting was negotiating with the Germans in early 1940 to form a replacement government, Lie was asked about his affiliation with Quisling. He categorically denied belonging to the NS and claimed he would never join it because of ideological differences. Only days later, when Terboven broke off negotiations and imposed an NS-backed government, Lie appeared as a new minister, earning his sobriquet. He died or committed suicide (the evidence is inconclusive) on May 11, 1945. Lie was the grandson of the famous Norwegian writer also named Jonas Lie (1833–1908). Another prisoner in Grini described him as follows: "In wartime Oslo there were few men more feared and hated. Unlike Quisling, whom even his own men knew to be a weak-chinned opportunist, Lie was strong and tough. . . . He looked like a Nazi. He had spotless black jackboots even though it was a mess of mud outside in the streets. He had a barrel chest and an upright bearing that reminded one of a well-trained bear." Lie was high in Terboven's estimation and Terboven even considered at one point replacing Quisling as the head of the NS with Lie.

† His own name. O.N.

good things and a whole little store of tobacco. That was from Ernst [Holmboe].* And one with the most magnificent oilskin coat and another little store of tobacco. That was from Kari. I feel like a Croesus and am sharing out right and left, only wishing it were always so easy to spread happiness and joy.

Now it's evening again, Sunday evening. Outside the rain is pouring down, as it does every night. It's only half-past eight and pitch dark. I'm sitting here in my corner, trying to rest content with the idea that tomorrow or another day, very soon, I'm sure to get the telegram I'm yearning so sorely for. No! I think I must sing a bit; after all it's Sunday evening, and there is still more than an hour until evening roll call. It must be killed somehow, and in the dark.

MONDAY, SEPTEMBER 14, 1942 ■ The singing didn't come off last night. I had the very best intentions, but then [Knut] Gard came and kidnaped me. He had had genuine coffee beans from his wife and had made some real coffee for the doctor's table. It tasted fabulous, and Rasmus felt that the occasion justified an inroad on the medicine cupboard. Out of its multiplicity he conjured forth a bottle of cognac, which he poured out for us in small test tubes. We clinked. It was a sheer festival. First a groaning supper table with all the splendors in the world—several kinds of cheese, honey, grilled coalfish, sardines in oil, sausage, good butter, coffee *avec*. It's quite monstrous that we should be sitting here in profusion while our wives and kind people all over the country strip their larders and hoards to send still more to the poor convicts up north.

When we had gone to bed and the guard had made his round, Odd and I lay chatting. The coffee was doing its work. We talked of different things that had happened to us in these eight months—all the queer situations we've been in. We lay there laughing and laughing, and couldn't stop. The scenes in the railway car especially were not to be borne, so extravagantly funny did they appear to us. Far into the night we lay reminiscing, and so as not to wake up the whole hut, we had to burrow our heads down in the straw when the fits of mirth overcame us. Then a single remark might switch our thoughts and our whole mood into quite a different channel. That was when we remembered all the horrors at Grini, all the comrades who had been maltreated and shot, and now Kvamme. Which strikes me as typical of this life as it has been all along—it has swung from the wildest farce to the blackest and most brutal tragedy, with no transitions.

Today we've had winter weather again. Rain, occasionally mixed with snow, which turned into slush—unfathomable slush. The whole camp looks like a pigsty now, thanks to the meritorious work on it at the beginning, when all the heather and moss inside the barbed-wire fence was removed. It's been biting cold all day, but the chaps have worked hard and not complained. They've got used to it. Indeed, we've been praised for work well done.

I had a wire this morning from Kari. A German brought it. My heart leapt into my throat, and began working like a steam hammer. *Still no news. All serene. Your Kari.* I'll just have to go on waiting. The telegram was sent yesterday. So for that matter the child may have come today.

The day's most important news is that the Lieutenant is going on leave. A new lieuten-

---

* Holmboe was Nansen's business partner in their architectural firm; he owned the cottage where Nansen was staying when he was arrested in 1942.

ant has already arrived, and has inspected the huts with his predecessor. No one will lament that the old one is going away. He was turning out more and more of a bastard. The guards say the new one is a decent chap; they all agreed that the old one was a bastard.

I've got a bunk now—[Kristoffer] Langenes helped me with it. Henceforth I shan't be sleeping on the floor, but like a gentleman—in a tiptop bunk of the finest stolen boarding. Good night!

TUESDAY, SEPTEMBER 15, 1942 ■ A glorious sunny day again. Almost warm. So today I felt almost envious at the sight of all the working groups marching off in the sunshine, while I dived back into the hut to my wood carving. I'm busy carving a German soldier standing on guard in the high north, with Lofoten and the midnight sun in the background. I'm carving deep enough for the soldier to stand out free and plastic. It's an insanely fiddling job, for the whole picture isn't more than half the size of an ordinary business envelope. And indeed this morning, as bad luck would have it, the tool slipped and cut the soldier's head off. Now he stands there like a symbol of the whole German nation.

A German NCO began kicking up a fuss today, when he found out that several men stay indoors making *Andenken* for Paunch. Paunch wriggled around and had a job to prevail on the man to understand and hold his tongue. I suppose there will have to be yet another *Andenken* for him, to stop his mouth. Another NCO—the one I made the bet with—has ordered a carved photograph frame. It is to hold a photograph of his wife, which he has just received, and which has a tendency to make him forget his sacred duty as a national-socialist soldier, and the war, and the Führer, and all the "high and glorious" rest of it.

This evening twelve of our sick people left by bus for Tromsø. First there came instructions—suddenly and without a word of warning—that all who were so ill as to be *arbeitsunfähig* [unfit for work] were to be sent away. They were to parade in ten minutes with all their things ready packed. When they were ready, of course the usual counterorder arrived. They were to wait until tomorrow. But, true to the German system, in another hour's time there came a lightning order that they were to go tonight after all. This time they were to parade in five minutes. And so off they went. God knows where. Most likely they'll be taken to Sydspissen, for instance, into the custody of the German police, and they will hardly profit by the exchange.

No telegram today either.

WEDNESDAY, SEPTEMBER 16, 1942 ■ Now this whole day has gone by too, and no telegram. One will just have to pretend that the event wasn't due until September 15th, and forget this whole desperate month of waiting. And then begin all over again. It can't possibly be much longer now, unless there's something the matter—something they don't want to tell me—and there isn't!

Today I've glued the German's head on and painted the midnight sun behind. I suppose it's too blood red, but what the hell. Anyhow I've never seen it, so how am I to know what it looks like?

The *Lagerführer* [deputy commandant], a Todting, obstinately maintains that we're to leave here on October 15th. We and the Todts. The soldiers are to stay on. I should think November 15th is more likely, but it will be cold and dark in all conscience before we get that length. Now one's thoughts are gradually beginning to occupy themselves with Christmas as a kind of goal to rest on. Norwegian Christmas! Are we to have one? And if not in its proper sense—are we to get home to our dear ones for Christmas? Or shall we be spending it in Denzer's modern hell?

THURSDAY, SEPTEMBER 17, 1942 ■ A quantity of household stuff has been sent us today for distribution—God knows where from. We've had nothing from the Germans. With them it is and will be jabber and empty phrases. All those who were without, got a fork. O splendor! Now we shan't have to eat with our knives or fingers or with wooden spoons. Moreover everyone who was without got a proper spoon, and there was an aluminum dish for all who haven't a saucepan. I got one of these dog's dishes. I don't believe Terboven's dog lives more stylishly, nor any champion silver fox; but there were no cups or glasses. I shall still have to use my empty sardine tin as a tooth glass, I shall still be drinking "coffee" out of a small washbasin or shaving basin. It's all right certainly, but the coffee gets cold so quickly.

The evenings are drawing in fast now. After supper at six the light has gone, and that makes a long evening. It's dusk when we get up in the morning, too. Soon they'll be obliged to cut down the working hours. One can scarcely get through much work up here in the dark. The time we have left will go like a flash no doubt, and then I suppose we'll be off south again? Or are we to be forced to question that, too?

FRIDAY, SEPTEMBER 18, 1942 ■ The mountain lay snow white again this morning. It was biting cold to stand out of doors at one's morning toilet. On the "washstand" lay an inch of snow, and on the "floor" in front was a foot of mud. It may have been only a catlick [i.e., perfunctory] today, but still the program was carried out.

The tall, sympathetic young guard, the one who gave me a pinch of tobacco that night long ago, came in to see me this afternoon. He is the son of a joiner, and he himself wants to be a joiner and interior designer. So he likes talking a bit of shop with me. Or else perhaps it's more of an excuse to chat about things in general.

Today he stayed a long time, and did a lot of questioning and catechizing. About what I thought of conditions here compared with Grini. I told him. Also gave him some naked facts about the treatment inflicted on Norwegians by the SS and SD. I was alive to the risk, for this man is one of the young, convinced Nazis, but I wanted him to know, and I could see it made a powerful impression on him.

He asked me what our attitude would be afterward. What should we feel about Germany and the Germans? I replied bluntly: Hate. Unfortunately hate. And I explained why. He said he understood. Then he asked, "Do you consider Germany to blame for all this?"

"Yes," I replied. "Germany, beyond all doubt, is chiefly to blame. But everyone is to blame."

He made no answer to that. He had no urge to discuss; he only wanted to know my views. At that moment the little guard came in, the one who is a Communist. We dropped the subject. When the tall one had gone, the little one, who stayed behind, told me that the tall one was a convinced Nazi, but a thoroughly decent, honest fellow, who would never misuse what I had said to him.

Then we had a good deal of talk. He talks quite freely, as though we were fellow conspirators. He and his whole family and his wife's family were against Nazism. Quite a number of them had been in prison for long periods on that account. He's a nice little chap, and I have the impression that he's glad to have found someone to talk to at last. With his comrades he doesn't dare exchange a single word about politics. No one dares, he tells me. Neither the course of the war, nor anything connected with it or with the situation in Germany, political and moral, is ever touched on among Germans. Everyone is afraid of all the rest.

These poor young Germans, how appalling things are for them! Take the young NCO, for instance (the one I made the bet with), who informed me today that he had had six years' training to be what he is now. Something like a sergeant.

"Well, but what's your civilian trade? You're married, aren't you? What work will you do in peacetime?"

"I'll continue in *Reichsarbeitsdienst* [Reich labor service]."

What had he learned? He had learned to be a *Führer*, he told me radiantly. It wasn't possible to make the boy understand that in that case he knew nothing—no useful job. Because he doesn't know what it means to know anything. He's going about at twenty years old with the idea that he's been trained as something called a *Führer*. A kind of profession, he doubtless takes it to be. That's what he married on, and what he's building his life on. Poor lad, when some day he wakes up a grown, useless man in a world quite different from the one he dreamed his *Führer*-dreams in.

No telegram has come today, either. I'm sitting looking at the photograph of Kari and our three children on the desk in front of me. The day I'm back home with them, my heart will break with joy; that's what I feel.* The thought almost frightens me. Good night all four.

SATURDAY, SEPTEMBER 19, 1942 ■ Almost at the very moment when I was writing that, the boy was born. For it is a boy. I got a wire about half-past ten this morning. It was signed *Bærum Hospital* and ran: *All well with mother and son.*

I shall be lying in the dark at night wondering what we'll call him! Now I *must* go home soon. It's time this nonsense here came to an end. There's no earthly point in it. It's against nature. It's German!

There was a genuine snowstorm raging when we got up this morning. It had been freezing, too, for the first time. There were icicles hanging from the roof and from the handle of the outer door. Yes, there's no doubt about it—winter has arrived. The snow flurries were thick on every side, and the snowflakes flew about our ears in horizontal stripes when we were out on our usual morning errands.

I for my part wrapped myself well up in the blankets and settled down to sleep again. Not long afterward the morning turmoil was in full swing. But just as it was at its height there came a message not to turn out until further orders. Work was suspended.

The weather held all day, with gleams of sunlight and breaks occasionally, but no sooner had the sun been out long enough to make us think the signal for work would be coming now, than a snow squall rushed up from another quarter which we had overlooked. So passed this memorable Saturday. It became a day off in honor of the little

---

* Fridtjof Nansen also dreamt of his return while on his polar voyage: "[M]y soul is borne . . . to the home-coming! . . . [T]he sufferings of a thousand days and hours melt into a moment's inexpressible joy."

newcomer, and General Winter turned out in person to congratulate me and to give a sample of what he has in mind by way of speeding up the course of events. And truly it looks as if he meant to stay on here. Now the icicles are hanging from the eaves half a meter [20 inches] long; the snow covers the whole mountain and has started blowing into drifts. Winter is positively taking shape. We rejoice malignantly. If this goes on the snow roofs are not likely to be finished, and the German retreat will be snowed in.

In the afternoon there was a distribution of parcels that had arrived from the south. Masses of parcels. There must have been a hundred. Now there are only a very few who haven't had a parcel from home, and they share in the others' plenty. Everyone has something to smoke, and the atmosphere is perceptibly brighter. I had a parcel again, too. Not from home, but from Tromsø. It was a huge sack from Johanne Marie [Andersen]'s mother. In it were two little notes. One to Odd and one to me. Dear Odd (dear Wang) with kind regards from Johanne Marie's mother. Good-bye. And out of the sack came an elegant sleeping bag, cups, dishes, knives, forks, spoons, goat cheese, butter, darning wool, and all the grandeurs in the world. Goodness, how kind these people are!

No sooner had I unpacked this huge sack and put away the things than another parcel came in at the door. With kind regards from Johan Hagerup, Tromsø. Yet another unknown, friendly soul. I shared out to those who had had nothing, and there was gladness and a festal feeling all round.

Would you believe it, there came a third parcel! This was from Trygve Hoff, and contained two tins of tobacco and a bag of sweets. No need to ask if these were welcome. I sent a grateful thought to my friend Trygve for his good deed.

Now we want for nothing. On the contrary, we're living in superfluity. We've received decent table implements, more than enough food, large reserve stocks even, warm bedclothes, and last but not least—something to smoke! Perhaps we're still a bit short of warm clothing, now that winter has set in, but on the whole that problem, too, has adjusted itself. The civilian clothes that have arrived we've now had leave to wear underneath the others. Wind jackets and winter coats we're allowed to use, but so that a restriction may yet remain, it's strictly forbidden to wear civilian trousers on top. We might escape, mightn't we? Across the snowy wilds without skis, heading for London via Sweden. It's best to secure oneself against these contingencies, think the Germans, and keep our trousers.

Newspapers arrived, as well. Old indeed, but with one or two things of interest in them. When the food was consumed and the hut cleaned up for the evening, the chaps sat on, full, lazy, and contented, reading the newspapers round the tables. As we're sitting like that, [Andreas] Onstad* shoves his paper across to [Ole] Iver[sen],† our waiter, and asks him: *Isn't that somebody you know?*

And he points to an item about seamen from Haugesund who have lost their lives while sailing for the Allies. That was how Iver learned that his son was dead. Among the lost was his name, Magnus Iversen, mate, aged twenty-five.‡ Poor Iver. And he took it fearfully hard. He just went and lay down on his bunk, lay and shook with sobs.

---

* Ohnstad remained in Veidal, and later Grini, for the duration of the war.

† Iversen was released November 22, 1942.

‡ Third Mate Magnus Iversen was one of twelve sailors killed when their ship, the tanker *Sydhav*, was sunk March 6, 1942, by the German U-boat U-505. U-505 was subsequently captured by a US naval task force on June 4, 1944, the

SUNDAY, SEPTEMBER 20, 1942 ■ Sunday! It should have been Sunday off, according to the program. Fourteen days we've toiled for a Sunday off, and then late last night there came instructions that, if the weather permitted, we were to work. The Saturday was to count as a Sunday off. It's a swindle, and we all feel cheated today. The working groups were sent out as usual. That in spite of the fact that it was beginning to snow, and it got worse and worse. Indeed it was the roughest day yet for all who were working out of doors. An absolute snowstorm on the naked mountain! Standing nailing boards on snow shelters in such weather, in bad clothes, high up on a ladder, with the squalls blowing round one like smoke, is no treat at all.

One gang was working in the snow squall up on the road. As fast as they cleared, it drifted up again. The job was sheer imbecility—but they were driven to it by a Todt and a guard, who both found it difficult to share that view.

At this moment a service is going on in the hut—in this room. The hymns are buzzing and drawling round my ears. People are getting up and sitting down, as one should in church, while I remain seated on the stool in this corner of mine, well hidden away under the upper bunks. No one can see me here, and my impious little occupation is extremely quiet.

Much more has happened today. I've had the world's most glorious letter from Kari. I'll write about it tomorrow; now it's just on ten. Also Odd [Wang] came back with a couple of first-class rumors, and to conclude, I had a grand business letter from Ernst [Holmboe] and a little letter from Siri.

MONDAY, SEPTEMBER 21, 1942 ■ Far into the night I lay thinking, wide awake and happy. There was so much to think of. All at once a sheer spring of light has washed over me, and hope is budding, and optimism is in the act of outrunning me altogether.

This day dawned rather snowy, and cold. The aspect of the camp has quite changed, it's acquiring more and more the look of a winter camp for whalers up north. The snow has piled up in good-sized drifts, the icicles are hanging lower and lower from the eaves, and rough ice is beginning to form in our "ski tracks"—to outhouses and other traffic centers. There was no talk of suspending work today. We're getting familiar with the winter and the new working conditions it presents. It will be all right, too.

But there was *the* letter from Kari. For it was unique. Either it was sent in some cunning way and meant to be delivered in some cunning way, or else she must have gone completely out of her mind. She writes quite freely and unreservedly about the devils at Victoria Terrace, about ludicrous Gestapo agents, and about the ignorant, silly fellow Claffy at Grini. I couldn't believe my own eyes when I read it. She was especially uninhibited in her mention of Herold (Esser's secretary at the Terrace). Of him she writes that it's incredible that people can become such devils. And then she sums up finally that it's quite incomprehensible how a whole nation can have been made so unfeeling.

This letter has passed the German censorship! It's unbelievable.

---

first capture of an enemy vessel on the high seas since the War of 1812. Following the war U-505 was donated to the Museum of Science and Industry in Chicago, where it remains on display today, the only German submarine in the United States; it was designated a National Historic Landmark in 1989. During the war 706 Norwegian ships were lost at sea, representing almost half of Norway's total maritime tonnage as of December 1939.

But whatever the facts may be, it was a really magnificent letter. Not that I should wish her to write many like that, it might end in disaster, but it was marvelous to read. She's had the whole account. Nico* has been in Oslo, and it was a tonic visit, writes Kari. My stars, what a travel book, she adds with all possible imprudence.

The letter from Ernst was a businesslike and fairly clear account of the situation on the Eastern front. The details he could hardly bring out in the architectonic imagery he employs, but in broad outline he really manages to give quite a clear picture of the situation, without departing for a moment from the most plausible account of our new scheme for an Oslo printing works.

He writes in general that all three schemes (fronts) are sure to be ready for delivery to the respective owners in good time. Well, that must mean he still sticks to it that Germany will break down this very autumn. I sat a long time last night pondering how I was to get back south when it's all over. Of course we shall just be left to our fate and shall have to see about getting home on our own. But we'll manage it all right, even if I should have to walk from here to Polhøgda. Though it would take a desperately long time—that is unless I ran—all the way.

And then I had an enchanting little letter from Siri, too. She tells me about the animals and what she gives them to eat. The rabbits and the pig.† At the end she confesses that she has cut off her braids. Plainly she thinks herself accountable to me for doing it. But she says I'm sure to agree that she looks nicer with her hair short, for it really was ragged, as Mother said when she cut it off. For it was Mother's idea; Siri only got the scissors. Yes, my little Siri, I'm quite sure you look charming whether your hair is long or short. It's not the hair it depends on, when you come down to it. It's all the other things you have so much of, and that come out so enchantingly in your little letter.

Odd [Wang] returned from work yesterday like bad weather, wet and dripping. It had been a beastly day. He had been on his knees in a bog all day, digging holes for the frames of snow shelters, while the snowstorm howled about his ears. The gang hadn't gotten much done, either; the working site is about four miles off, and they had walked there and back.

Odd brought back a couple of first-class rumors. Things are hot now before Stalingrad, but the Germans are on the defensive; they're surrendering in bunches. It sounds promising and far from unlikely. I asked the German NCO today how things were going at Stalingrad. "It looks very gloomy," said he, before he'd rightly considered. "We have all miscalculated," he added.

The all-day workers have just come storming in. Hungry and wet. But they were pleased today. The weather had been mild. In the course of the day it had begun to thaw, and now it's soaking wet outside.

They brought some rumors today as well, including a wholly idiotic one: A million

---

* Nico lives in Trondheim and received from the donkeyman both the section of diary I sent ashore there, and the one I sent with the donkeyman on our arrival at Oksfjordhamn. O.N. Nico, or Nicola Hirsch, was Kari's first cousin; her father and Kari's father were brothers.

† Nansen's daughter Marit relates that one winter the family was reduced to only one rabbit, which they kept with their chickens. Soon the rabbit thought it was a hen: "It climbed the perch . . . in the evenings like the hens, had a siesta in the sitting box . . . every day. Astonishingly, it did not produce an egg."

Germans have surrendered in the Crimea! How this could have happened it's hard to say, but that doesn't matter. It's a fine rumor.

Well, now I must write to Kari and thank her for everything.

TUESDAY, SEPTEMBER 22, 1942 ■ A brilliantly sunny day, with the snow melting and almost warmth in the air. But it's not likely to get rid of all the snow; the cold has fixed it well on the ground, and the drifts are firm already.

Last night there came instructions that we might send an extra letter home and ask for what clothes we need. A general had been round and discovered that we've had none of the clothing he gave us hopes of when he was here before. All bans on the use of civilian clothing were done away with at the same time, even the trouser ban! But to write home now for more clothes is pointless. We'll be leaving here in less than a month, if they keep to the program, and we can scarcely receive clothes from home in less than two or three weeks. It's German method all over. But at least it's a welcome chance to write an extra letter home.

WEDNESDAY, SEPTEMBER 23, 1942 ■ Snow and rain, rain and snow, all day long. All the gangs came in again as the day wore on, soaking wet and tousled. A little later everyone was walking about in drawers and pajamas. For we have only the one pair of trousers, and it has to dry. This attire made the interiors a good deal more lively, and offered many a picturesque if comic subject. There was no more work today; the weather kept on unchanged. A welcome afternoon of rest.

We have started short lectures twice a week in [Hut] number 3. [Hans] Gabrielsen has given a talk on Finmark and the Lapps. Tonight Alf Scott-Hansen was talking about our electricity supply.* On Sunday [Olav] Dalgard† will give a theater causerie. Later on Per [Krohg] is to talk about painting. I may preach architecture perhaps, or I may talk about the refugee problem before, during and after the war!

Unfortunately there are too few who take advantage of these little lectures to get their minds off the everlasting daily problems and the monotonous round in which we move.

Otherwise the days consist chiefly of work, food and rumors.

THURSDAY, SEPTEMBER 24, 1942 ■ Misty, mild. All hands at work. Odd and his gang got up at half-past three last night and went off to Oksfjordhamn, where they're unloading a ship that has arrived with materials. They came back about one in the afternoon, were then relieved by another gang, and had the rest of the day off. Odd says that down in Oksfjordhamn it's still summer, quite green. It's almost queer to think of that—we're entirely reconciled to winter now.

Odd was to try and buy something in the shop down on the quay. He'd never seen any shop so completely sold out. Nothing remained but a few toys. Those he bought and sent

---

* An engineer and film producer, Scott-Hansen (1903–1961) was married to Wenche Foss, a leading Norwegian actress of film, television, and theater from 1939–1950. He was released November 22, 1942.

† Dalgard (1898–1980) was a filmmaker and literary critic. Immediately after the war he published a book of poems about the war: *Gjennom mørkret* [*Through the Darkness*]. Dalgard was chairman of the Norwegian Literature Critics' Association (1953–1955). He was transferred to Sachsenhausen on December 9, 1943, and remained there for the duration of the war.

off south. Of course one must trade, and it isn't often that presents arrive from an uncle in a concentration camp.

Eriksrud brought quite a serviceable rumor back yesterday. He'd got it unsolicited (!) from a civilian worker, who looked devilish reliable, in his view. At Stalingrad the Germans have been driven back eighteen miles, and a million of them are encircled by the Russians. In Finland two hundred thousand Germans have laid down their arms and refused to go on fighting. Just suppose that were more or less true.

Then by Jove I got another parcel today. This one was from my friend in Harstad, the girl in the porthole of the steamer. She had saved up to half a kilo [1.1 pounds] of butter (dairy!), two packets of crispbread, a piece of capital goat cheese, and a tin of sardines. These delicacies the child sends off to a stranger, whom she knows by chance to be in captivity, with best wishes from "the lady in Harstad."

Certain people are still eating too much and have made themselves ill. I realize that this painful fact doesn't look exactly heroic in a diary from a concentration camp, where one expects to read of hunger and misery and nameless hardships. But that's how it is.

FRIDAY, SEPTEMBER 25, 1942 ■ Sleet and slush as usual. Today two of the sick were sent off by bus to Tromsø or further. One was the district sheriff [Agnar] Renolen of Østerdalen.* He has beriberi. In the bus that took them away there were quite a lot from the other camp at Badderen. Twelve of them were released, the rest sick. I went out to see them. They were going south. Home! Really home. Most of them had only been inside a few months.

It seems as though the final date of October 15th were being pushed gently back, for the present, to November 1st. There's not much prospect of our getting away before that. At any rate the snow shelters and tunnels won't be finished earlier—if they get finished at all before it's too late for the winter. One fine day no doubt there will be enough snow to impede transport over here. I dare say we shall have the trucks stuck in the snowdrifts and the food not appearing.

Today there came a useful and in [Hans] Gabrielsen's opinion very reliable rumor: The Germans have given up the attack on Stalingrad. That's short and simple and tells us all we need to know. It means a decisive turning point of the war in the East.

MONDAY, SEPTEMBER 28, 1942 ■ Overcast, cold. I reminded the NCO of our bet. He admitted that he had lost, muttered something about having lost such a fearful lot, and looked wretched that my heart bled for him. He's going away, perhaps to Russia, perhaps somewhere else. He came in to say good-bye. That time he didn't mention the bet. He only said he would come to Oslo after the war. Perhaps he meant to imply that he would settle up then.

Thirteen men were released today. They went happily off in a truck to Oksfjordhamn, and then in a fishing smack to Tromsø, where according to report they will be released. For a moment there was a big lump in my throat and a smarting pain in my chest as I saw those thirteen men, happy and eager, taking the first steps out of the prison gate toward their homes. Then the truck vanished into the tunnel swerving past the camp to north and

---

* Released October 22, 1942.

south like a queer, many-jointed, parti-colored snake, and I dived back into my place of exile—which truly, for a place of exile, is not too bad.

TUESDAY, SEPTEMBER 29, 1942 ■ Good weather, mild, gleams of sun.

Another couple of things happened yesterday, after I'd finished writing. First I got a letter from Kari, written on September 21st, three days after the boy was born. She is radiant, full of spunk, and bursting with *joie de vivre!* The letter hadn't gone through the post. Someone must have brought it north. Rasmus had been on a civilian sick-visit somewhere in the parish, and taken charge of it.

Later in the afternoon, back they came, all the released men who had gone off in the truck. The boat that was to take them to Tromsø had left. Exactly of a piece with everything else. No one is surprised. Now it's the evening of the day after. They're still here. God knows when they'll get away.

I'm not very brisk today. I've got a sore throat, and my head bothers me all the time. They say that more are to be released in a month.

Now the snoring round and over me has begun to make itself heard, and it's nearly ten, when I have to stand up stiff in full uniform and hand over my "*Stube Zwei. Neun und zwanzig Mann—alle hier,*" [Room Two. Twenty-nine men—all here,] as usual. And tonight it's Lazarus on guard; he noses round everywhere to see if he can find anything that's not *peinlich* [scrupulously] and *restlos sauber* [spotlessly clean]! And so good night!

WEDNESDAY, SEPTEMBER 30, 1942 ■ Glorious weather, sunny and mild. The snow is getting less, but is still lying over the whole mountain. At nine this morning the thirteen went off, this time north to Sørstraumen, where apparently there was a chance of getting some boat to Tromsø. It's nearly evening and they've not come back yet, so one may venture to hope that they've really managed to get away.

The brilliant weather and the men leaving have awakened longings. Therefore I've been quite ill today. Oh heavens, if only this confounded time would fly a bit faster, if I could only fall asleep and not wake up again until the day we're going south.*

I feel I'm badly off!

Of course I ought not to sit down and write when I'm like this. I ought to put my things on and take a stroll over the plateau, the glorious, free, open plateau, with the white, white mountains round about, bathed in sunshine. But the barbed-wire fence, envenomed, rusty and hostile, grins at me from all sides, and beyond it a young German is walking up and down with a loaded rifle.

And the stroll on the plateau among the white mountains becomes a few tragic paces in the hopeless slush of this "prison yard," which was once a bit of plateau itself, but which now looks more like a pigsty than anything. And God knows if we're not developing a sinister likeness to pigs as well.

THURSDAY, OCTOBER 1, 1942 ■ Brilliant sunshine, mild.

Thus we start on a new month. October! How autumnal it sounds; it suggests golden foliage, and one's thoughts turn south again, to birch slopes and deciduous woods on

---

* Drifting on the Arctic ice, Fridtjof Nansen observed, "It has always been your great trouble that time flew away so fast, and now it cannot go fast enough to please you."

fire. In my imagination I see all the lovely trees at Fornebu, flaming with all the hues of autumn. I see the Virginia creeper at Polhøgda, fiery red and green, with dark blue berries. I wonder, is anyone decorating the table with it now?

Here it is winter! We were done out of the autumn in a way. It's as if this whole interminable imprisonment has been a continuous winter, and now we're starting off on another one. It is possible that it will be equally long and comfortless? Is it possible that there's to be another war winter?

Hitler made a speech yesterday. The *Winterhilfe* had been reopened.* My little German Communist friend told me about the speech. He'd heard a bit of it, he said, but then he'd fallen asleep, and snored so loud that his comrades had to wake him and tick him off.

My little soldier was pessimistic. He thought the war was sure to last another two years. My suggestion that it would end in November with the total collapse of Germany he didn't believe for a moment. He said he wished it, perhaps even more strongly than myself, but he thought it right out of the question. They were too far gone, too thoroughly subdued and under the whip, to venture on any rising or internal action, in his view. But, he added, no one will convince me but that Hitler and Nazism will go under; that's a hundred percent certain. Don't think I'm a pessimist about that, he added.

The little soldier comes over to me whenever he's off duty. Poor lad, there aren't many bright spots in his existence. The destruction of Germany is no cheerful prospect, but all the same it's what he looks forward to.

I've finished carving and painting another box lid, the third for some idiot of a German, August Hanne. The name is grinning at me with the sea, Lofoten, and the sunset behind. I scraped out that confounded name myself and painted it! A gull is hovering on wide wings over the sea, with one wing piquantly outside the frame. This time I've made a better job of the sky and mountains than on the last one, which turned out syrupy. I must show this one to Per as well, so that he can see I'm not wholly addicted to sweet colors. The frame for the NCO who went away I mean to keep for myself. The little soldier was to take it for him, but I've told him that he shall not have it until I get my bet paid.

Just then a young German soldier who is an interpreter came for a drawing I've done for him. It's a caricature—not wholly unmalicious—of Lazarus. He swore and crossed his heart that he would keep it to himself, and not show it till he and I are out of the danger zone. I think I can rely on him. He's a decent chap; that was my only reason for giving him a drawing. Actually I'm annoyed about it; I should have liked that drawing for myself.

FRIDAY, OCTOBER 2, 1942 ■ Last night I gave more than an hour's entertainment in [Hut] number 6. My public is not fastidious. One might think perhaps that the men's taste would be for ballads and robust humor, but the secret is that they like lullabies, these weather-beaten, filthy, unshaven convicts. And I sing them lullabies! Then they sit as devoutly as in church, and want to hear them *da capo* [from the beginning]. And so I sing *da capo*, and in the flickering glimmer of the candle on the table in front of me I see the faces down along the benches, and up in the bunks—good faces! Faces I shall never forget.

---

* Winter Relief. Winterhilfe was a charitable program run by the Nazi party, similar to one organized during the Weimar Republic, which collected (often under pressure) money and goods, and ostensibly distributed them to needy Germans each autumn and winter. As there was no accounting for collections or disbursements, it has been alleged that the program became increasingly corrupt as the war continued, with donations used to fund Nazi lifestyles rather than the unfortunate.

There were eighteen German convicts up here today, most of them deserters, according to my little soldier-friend, who had spoken to one of them. They had all been transferred here from Yugoslavia. They are living in a camp further north and doing some work for the *Luftwaffe*. Today they stretched a telegraph line across the mountain. They were dressed in German army uniforms, with all badges and piping removed and with a broad yellow stripe down the seams of the trousers. The other soldiers were forbidden to speak to them, let alone give them any food. The little soldier had been had up for talking to them. He told me they were being starved; these eighteen for instance had had nothing to eat since yesterday morning. It was late in the afternoon before they got some food, which they had to stand and eat in the rain.

One of them had been on hard labor for two years; he was as thin as a skeleton. Neither he nor any of the rest would ever get home again, in my friend's opinion. He was deeply stirred by this—and came over to me. He had no one else to talk to, he said. He was quite convinced that they were to be starved, and that it was actually part of the punishment. I suggested slipping them a little food, but the little soldier only shook his head sadly and said: "It's quite impossible Herr Nansen. If I did that I should either be shot or sent to join them, and if you did, it would be a bad job for you. But," he added, "they're working for the *Luftwaffe*, and they help them a bit. The *Luftwaffe* is a decent force. There are a lot of good chaps in it."

That was all the little soldier wanted to talk about today. He was thinking solely of the fate of these boys. And he was deeply depressed. Poor little soldier! Wherever he turns, whatever he thinks of—War! Coercion! Horrors! Hopeless darkness! And at home somewhere in Germany a little girl sits pining for her little soldier in suspense and dread.

All at once it was borne in on me that these poor people are really ten times worse off than us.

SATURDAY, OCTOBER 3, 1942 ■ Rain and rough weather. Misty and gusty.

But now it's evening, and has turned starry clear, with northern lights. I've been drawing all day, only now and then have I started a pretense of wood-carving—whenever Paunch looked in or was in the neighborhood. Though for that matter he says nothing to me these days, whatever I may be doing. He is amiability itself. Under the promise of secrecy he told me today that we were all to leave here on the 12th, and many were to be released, so he said. Of course, he doesn't know much about it, anyhow the last part. And actually it's by no means so certain that we need be enthusiastic, even if it were true. Back to Grini? Or Germany? Both are in the cards, and neither is anything to shout hurrah for.

SUNDAY, OCTOBER 4, 1942 ■ A brilliant sunny day. They say it's Sunday. But I suppose that's just a loose rumor.

I felt like getting out for a bit today, so I went with one of the small gangs, which carries boards just on the other side of the road, on the building site, as we call it. Paunch came up and asked me if I *wanted* to work out of doors. I said I did. Well, if so I was welcome, of course, but otherwise I might do just as I pleased. He wouldn't *order* me out. He was so bland that the fat was running off him. God knows what's up with him, or what he's planning to get out of it.

Later in the day I had quite a long political argument with him. Göring made a speech at twelve, and all the men came home to listen. I asked Paunch, who is now so fat that he rolls rather than walks, whether Göring had any good news. "From now on there will be bigger food rations all round," said Paunch, radiating joy. That was the only thing in the speech that had caught his notice, except that the war would be carried on to victory! Plenty of food—and victory as well. Why the devil should one want more? "We'll take the whole world," he added in his arrogance, "and there will never be war again—and no political discussions. Within a short time you'll have to change completely, Herr Nansen—get a completely new *Weltanschauung!* In two years we can have a talk, and then you must remember what I've said today!"

The whole hut was listening, and it proved a very entertaining half hour. Odd threw in one or two awkward questions, which Paunch couldn't answer at all. He just looked inexpressibly stupid, but prattled faithfully on about the *Führer* and all that he has done, is doing, and is about to do. And these were all facts! He was a sitting bird, I admit. But then I can never have been more rude. The hut was simply gasping for breath. Paunch, however, took it good-humoredly. He slapped me on the back, pinched my arm and thigh, laughed and really thought it very good fun. We agreed to have a talk after the war. That was the result of our argument, and Paunch, content and smiling and hugely confident of victory, rolled out of the door.

MONDAY, OCTOBER 5, 1942 ■ Raw and icy cold, but it improved as the day went on. The sun even came out.

I got a letter off to Kari today by our friend Nilsen, who looked in. His son is getting treatment from Rasmus. Next time he comes he shall take my diary. He'll see that it gets to Tromsø, and then our friends there will take over.

A single new prisoner arrived today from Sydspissen. He told us that all those who left here, happy in their release, are firmly installed in Sydspissen, where it's hellish.* So were all the army men who were sent back from Oksfjordhamn (or from Tromsø). It was the usual rigorous SS concentration camp. So we've been far better off. It's almost amusing to think of one chap who sneaked off with them as an officer. (He was a corporal or something like that.) Truly he had to smart for his smartness. Why this one prisoner came here, why the "released" men are in Sydspissen, why the officers are there after being carted all the way up from Grini to share in the work, and finally why the moon's not made of green cheese, only a German organizer can tell.

TUESDAY, OCTOBER 6, 1942 ■ A thoroughly bad day when one must admit it's an advantage to work indoors. Nothing has happened—no rumors. Odd didn't bring even an amusing story back from the working site. He was rather tired and taken up with what a beastly cold job it was to stand nailing in the snow and blast. It's more and more doubtful, I believe, whether the work here can be finished before the winter sets in. For now winter seems to be at the very door.

Paunch says nothing to me, whatever I'm doing. Today he saw a greeting card I'm doing for Peder Olsen of Sørstraumen, the man who sends us all the food and parcels

---

* Four days prior to the German attack on the Soviet Union in June 1941, all Jewish men in northern Norway were arrested and sent, along with other opponents of the regime, to Sydspissen, which had recently opened. Conditions were described as primitive, and treatment harsh. Jewish prisoners were singled out for extra hard work and brutal punishment drills, and all were ultimately deported to Auschwitz. None of the Norwegian Jews from northern Norway survived the war.

and is so grand to us altogether. The card was tolerably patriotic. A gigantic brownie is popping up behind Veidal Mountain, sweeping away the whole camp with one hand and smirking happily, while the prisoners, nice and fat, come marching out of the tunnel—which is still sprawling unfinished—with the Norwegian flag in the van. Paunch thought the drawing "*prima*" [fine], which is his stock word for everything, as though it were all provisions. He didn't understand any of it, and finally begged me to go on and not let him disturb me.

It looks as though the Todts were making ready for departure. They're in a hurry to get everything done now. They keep talking about the few days that are left. The *Baurat* mentioned a fortnight to Rasmus yesterday, and added that we might be leaving even sooner.

Perhaps it will be safest to "make ready" too.

WEDNESDAY, OCTOBER 7, 1942 ■ Furious snowstorm. The whole mountain is boiling. It's kept on like that most of the night. And—*almost all that can be seen from here of the tunnel is blown down and leveled to the ground.* A sorry spectacle confronted us when it began to grow light enough to distinguish the outlines of what was once the framework. Like a concertina of gigantic length it had folded up, and was now lying in chaos along the road, while the snow piled up in huge drifts in among and over it. Queer that last night I should have been drawing that very theme. The brownie—or the winter troll himself—has been at work and swept the whole thing down, like matchwood. Altogether, two kilometers [1.2 miles] of tunnel framework must have blown down.

Paunch looked in this morning, bundled up in jerseys, coats, wind clothes, and hoods, like a brownie on a trip to the Pole. It was his *Andenken* he was concerned about first and foremost; they must all be finished off without delay. Further, he told us that all the civilian workers in the Holst-Larsen firm together with the whole firm would be locked up. I objected that that wouldn't help an atom, and that it might be cleverer to set them to work putting the tunnel up again. He didn't agree, but held that now the Germans would have to get going on their own account. I also thought that was a brilliant idea, and asked why, in point of fact, they hadn't done it long ago. Well, that civilian firm had insisted that they could manage it, and understood what they were about. For, said Paunch, the Germans had cautioned them all the time against their method of work, erecting the framework first and boarding it afterward! Mere impudence and rubbish. The tunnel was put up under German control, designed and supervised by Germans, against our positive advice and warnings in regard to both the structure and the method of work. The OT was in charge, and it is responsible. But the principle of responsibility consists (as is well known) in everyone's disclaiming all responsibility and finding a *Prügelknabe* [whipping boy] in every situation that calls for one.

How this "disaster" may affect us it's not so easy to say. But the probability seems to be that we shall have to stay up here longer, to repair the damage and complete the work, if that can be done.

Today we could hardly put our heads out of the door. Of work there was no question whatever. It was so impossible that they didn't even let us know it had been suspended.

What a day! Contact with the outer world is completely broken. The road is totally blocked, and it's very doubtful whether it can be cleared again for the next provision transport. If there are difficulties with the food supply, I believe Nobs and Todts and greenhorns will all begin thinking seriously of sending the whole thing to the devil and moving out. Now it's late in the evening, and rather milder, but still blowing like the very deuce. Out of doors it's almost a job to stand upright.

It goes without saying that no news from the fronts has reached us today. On the other hand my friend the little soldier came in and told us that there was a state of emergency in Trondheim for "acts of sabotage against industry," and ten men had been shot.* Among them, he said, was Hirsch Kommisar, the Jew who came here from the Badderen camp. No one could make out why that poor, stocky, little man had been sent, first up here and then south again. He himself apparently thought he was to be used as an interpreter, for he spoke Russian, or to be released. Now he's been shot! Without a doubt wholly innocent. I can't help thinking how little courtesy he got from certain people here, where they had always a hard word on their lips for him. I shudder at our own brutality. Now it's too late to repent.

Another appalling rumor spread in the camp in this connection: [Henry] Gleditsch, the theater director, is said to be one of the ten who were shot.† Henry—shot! The worst of it is that it may be true. He had just the stiff, unbending attitude they would come down on. I've tried to trace the source of this rumor. It went round in a circle and I got back to the starting point without finding anyone who really knew anything. I must try to believe it's a fabrication until further notice. But how could it have arisen? No, there must be something in it. It's terrible, simply, simply, terrible.

I suppose one day we'll get newspapers, and the appalling truth will come out. I dread to think of reading the newspapers. Altogether I dread to think of another day.

I'm not having a bad time. But what's happening is so bad, so bad, that from time to time it's as though one loses faith that one will ever get through it. We're all in the same boat for that matter, and anything may happen to any one of us.

THURSDAY, OCTOBER 8, 1942 ■ Brilliant weather all day. I was out shoveling snow from early morning, staying out all day, and didn't get home until suppertime. It was pretty tiring; I've been niggling indoors so long, but really I enjoyed it. At the same time I got a good view of the storm damage. It was worst up here, not so bad lower down, but all the way the tunnel had drifted full of snow, which we had to shovel out. Per and I shoveled together to begin with. Today he had been included, but later on his *Baurat* came and fetched him away. So then I went on shoveling alone. Well, not alone, but with Gunnersrud of Åsnes‡ and Hansen the Oslo streetcar driver and a lot of other good Norwegians. We shoveled like the very deuce. In the end things went black before my eyes every time I bent down.

Just on the crest of the hill, before we reached the camp, there were two ladies in furs. Before I knew it I had one of them round my neck, and she gave me a resounding kiss.

---

* As a result of several incidents of sabotage and resistance in Trondheim and surrounding areas, culminating in the shooting of two German police officers, Reichskommissar Terboven imposed martial law and selected ten prominent area residents at random for execution as "atonement sacrifices" on October 7, 1942. In subsequent days an additional twenty-four Norwegians already incarcerated in a nearby concentration camp were killed in extrajudicial executions for hostility to the government. All adult Jewish males in Trondheim were also arrested.

† An actor and founder of the Trøndelag Theater in 1937, Gleditsch had resisted Nazi control of the theater and was an outspoken critic of Nazi policies. He was thirty-nine. A stamp bearing his likeness was issued in Norway in 2002.

‡ Johan Gundersrud. Freed May 17, 1943, he was rearrested February 2, 1945, and remained in Norwegian prisons for the duration of the war.

First she had asked if this wasn't Odd Nansen, and I said yes, and then it happened. Afterward I was "introduced." I asked what I already knew—who she was. It was fru [Maja] Andersen, Johanne Marie's mother. She was with fru Matheson Bye.

Fru Andersen was an experience; I would gladly have stayed on talking to her until now, in the guardroom where we were allowed to sit, though it was so hot that we were nearly baked alive. She was salutarily optimistic—dead sure of a "Norwegian Christmas"—brought fresh, cordially cheerful greetings from outside—and was herself like one long breath of fresh air. But now I must have done with superlatives, or I suppose neither Kari nor Leif [Andersen]* will like it.

She had been in the camp for five hours waiting for me. Had come out here, made the whole long toilsome journey, only to see me, and had apparently brought masses of parcels with her—masses to smoke, she whispered. And finally she wanted to know if there was nothing else she could do for us. Fru Andersen made me completely forget my dinner. When she reminded me of it, it had gone right out of my head; I wasn't even hungry any more. Nor did I get hungry afterward. In fact I couldn't eat, though I had had only a couple of bites all day.

At length I had to tear myself away and go in. I got a kiss on the mouth to take with me, and a hug. I'm still a bit dizzy.

But then in the midst of all the joy came the appalling confirmation of the murders in Trondheim. It *was* Henry who was shot. He and a lot of other eminent Norwegians. First the ten, and then, it was announced on the radio today, fifteen more. Terboven himself had been in Trondheim, making a speech in the market place, and had said that what would happen tonight was intended as a warning. And then he had ten men shot. All men in the prime of life.

Good God, what more shall we live through before this is over?

FRIDAY, OCTOBER 9, 1942 ■ Cloudy, raw and cold, with an icy wind all day. Blessed if I hadn't to go through it today as well. Paunch asked nicely if I wouldn't come, too. And after my day's work I'm like a washrag. In the end I literally couldn't bend down and lift a shovelful of snow. I had to bend my knees instead, squat down, and stand up again. That was how I managed the last two hours. It was sheer deliverance to get home and sit down. Heavens, how glad I am we've something to sit on.

My stars, what a reception when I got "home." Two heavy suitcases were lying on my bed. I opened one of them. It was swimming with all the wonders of the world—butter, crispbread, chocolate, woolens, skiing blouse and overalls, oilskins. . . . I had to shut the suitcase and put it under the bed to escape vertigo. The other case was full of illustrated papers and books. Well, God bless them every one. I can find nothing else to say.

We've been hearing gunfire all afternoon. Perhaps there's something going on out at sea?

No news, and no more rumors about the proclamation of a state of emergency throughout the country. That's an appalling possibility, and the thought of it makes one feel quite sick.

---

* Fru Maja Andersen's husband. The Andersens' daughter, Johanne Marie, was married to Kari Nansen's brother Worm Hirsch. They lived in Lysaker, where Johanne Marie's parents eventually relocated (from Tromsø) after the Germans burned most of north Norway in the final year of the war.

But I'm too tired to start thinking of it, let alone writing of it. Now I must lie down and shut my eyes, and presto, I'm back with you, my brave girl! And you conjure with me and my thoughts, and light the light again, if it was blowing out, and so I turn my face to it and sleep sound after all . . .

SATURDAY, OCTOBER 10, 1942 ■ Raw and cold in the morning, but the sun peeped out now and then as the day passed. I've been "working at home." The work consisted of unpacking, sorting, and sharing out the contents of the magic suitcase. It isn't so easy as it sounds to share among hungry wolves. And when it comes to tobacco, they're all hungry all the time!

Today is father's birthday. He would have been 81. He lived, indeed, to see many a 10th of October that was not bright. But he never saw one like this, and for that we must be glad and grateful.

The papers we have had now confirm all the fearful events in Trondheim, but there is not a state of emergency over the whole country. Only in North and South Trøndelag and one district of Nordland. A rumor from Oksfjordhamn today (they're unloading a boat again) says that thirty-five Norwegians have been shot in Trondheim altogether. I hope it's a mistake. Now and then we do get fearfully exaggerated reports from that quarter.

They heard another thing of great interest from the boat's crew—it's a Norwegian boat—that the Germans are requiring Denmark to furnish thirty thousand men for the Eastern Front. There is no Danish reply to hand yet. They can never consent, and if the Germans follow up this insanity it must come to a showdown, which will doubtless put Hitler's "little canarybird"* on a footing with the other occupied countries. Germany will have yet another internal front. Every little helps.

MONDAY, OCTOBER 12, 1942 ■ King Christian has abdicated, they say.† [Johan] Paulsen's wife came to see her husband today,‡ and brought this important piece of news. Well: so that was Denmark's reply, which we've been awaiting since we heard the rumor. King Christian abdicated, and the Germans dismissed the government and installed a *Reichskommissar.*

Hello, old Denmark! The North is beginning to unite, things are working up for the last scene of the last act. Merry Christmas!

---

* The willingness of the Danish government to allow occupation by German forces and cooperate with German demands led Hitler to call Denmark a "model protectorate." This in turn inspired Winston Churchill to call Denmark Hitler's tame "canary."

† King Christian X of Denmark did not abdicate. Unlike King Haakon VII of Norway (his brother), Christian elected not to go into exile and remained in occupied Denmark throughout the war. The precipitating event behind the demand (later rescinded) for thirty thousand troops was known as the "Telegram Crisis." On Christian's seventy-second birthday (September 26, 1942), Adolf Hitler sent him a long congratulatory telegram. Christian replied laconically: "Thank you very much." Hitler was so incensed at this perceived slight that he expelled the Danish ambassador to Germany, recalled the German ambassador to Denmark, issued the demand for troops, appointed a much tougher leader of the occupation army, tasked SS *Obergruppenführer* Werner Best as minister plenipotentiary to rule with an "iron hand," and demanded a more pro-Nazi government. More than six months later (April 19, 1943) at a luncheon attended by Quisling, Hitler was still fuming over Christian's "insolence." During the occupation Christian continued his practice of riding daily through the streets of Copenhagen on his horse, unaccompanied by any guards or servants. Only a week after Nansen wrote this entry (October 19, 1942), Christian fell from his horse; he never fully recovered and remained an invalid for the duration of the war. King Christian died on April 20, 1947 (Hitler's birthday).

‡ Paulsen was released February 15, 1943.

The Trondheim business has developed further. Crowds of people have been arrested. It's said a whole thousand. If the state of emergency is to continue, it's terrible. These people are all in danger of their lives. A massacre may be Terboven's pleasure at any moment. And at a sign from that devil it can be started instantly. And no one—no one! can stop it. A black, fainting feeling comes over one, when one thinks of that appalling fact. A maniacal gangster can do what he likes to us—and no one can stop him.

TUESDAY, OCTOBER 13, 1942 ■ Kari's birthday*—and I have to sit here in the wilds behind the barbed wire and keep it in the society of hundreds of other convicts.

Now you and all of them must be sitting around the table in the dining room at Polhøgda, eating. Rabbit, I should think. It's eight o'clock. And I know your thoughts are going out to me, and they meet mine halfway, and we're together all the same. *Skål* [Cheers] Kari! Many happy returns!

Work on the tunnel is going pretty briskly now. Most of the fellows are out nailing from morning to night. Some are in Oksfjordhamn unloading the boats, which keep arriving, unfortunately. Even a fresh snowstorm would hardly manage to fold the tunnel up now. With this weather and at this speed it's possible that most of the work might be got through in a fortnight or three weeks. But it isn't finished yet—and we're still here—and we may still be here a long time, and still there's no fatal obstacle to a merry Christmas.

WEDNESDAY, OCTOBER 14, 1942 ■ We got the newspapers today. Thirty-five men in all have now been executed under the state of emergency. All the names were in the papers. It's reported that Henry Gleditsch was picked up in the street an hour before they shot him.

THURSDAY, OCTOBER 15, 1942 ■ Filthy weather. It's been a tough day for the outdoor workers, but I've been all right fiddling away indoors. Now they're madly giving fresh orders. One NCO is to have both a box and a photograph frame, and would like a candlestick, too. Paunch is to have more and more all the time. He can't bear to see other people getting anything.

Odd is indoors too, now. He has a new and curious job, whittling can lids for Paunch. He's using empty cans to send pickled herring home to Germany! Odd is a failure at whittling and I suppose makes three or four lids a day. They're to be used on a tin of herring which at most may be worth twenty-five øre or thereabouts [i.e., pennies]. So it's to carry out this highly important work that they transport a man thousands of kilometers.

The tall soldier has just told me that the state of emergency in Trøndelag was canceled three days ago. We may chalk up that at any rate as good news.

The rumors of the Danish King abdicating seem to be sheer invention. The demand for thirty thousand men seems correct, but the rest reduces itself to strained relations. The King and the government have apparently refused to meet the demand.

FRIDAY, OCTOBER 16, 1942 ■ Raw and cold in the morning, but sunny and warm later in the day. Work on the tunnel is advancing quite fast now. Yesterday evening and in the night there was a certain fall of snow, which meant a bit of shoveling today, but

---

* Her thirty-ninth; Kari was born October 13, 1903.

not enough for the "labor reserve" to be called out. It will be exciting to see if they can get the tunnel closed again before the snow comes in earnest. For us I assume it would be desirable.

The *Feldwebel* looked in today for a chat. In the course of the conversation I accused him and his colleagues of having left off thinking. Yes, he said, so we have. At first it seemed a bit comic to us, too, but we gradually got used to it, and now we can see that it's the only right thing. Fancy if everyone had his own opinion; it would never do. It used to be like that in Germany—that was the ruin of us. The squabbling. People never could agree. Our Leader has brought us to agree—united us! There's only one opinion in Germany today.*

Imagine, he said all that with enthusiasm.

In a few minutes the guard will be coming on his evening round, and I must "hand over" my hut as usual. It always goes off painlessly now. It's a long time since Lazarus complained. I think I've broken him of being surly—that evening when I wished him *Gute Nacht*, to show him that was what one said on leaving the hut at that time of day. Then he was so furious that he banged the door until the whole hut shook. Since then he's said *Gute Nacht* every time.

SATURDAY, OCTOBER 17, 1942 ∎ The outdoor and indoor work have gone as usual. Paunch is if possible even more nervous that his confounded boxes won't be finished. He flies around here fussing and interrupting all day. But he's also nervous of the Lieutenant, who might come in and ask what I'm doing. "Then you must tell him," said Paunch today, "that you're sick and doing this to pass the time."

MONDAY, OCTOBER 19, 1942 ∎ [Knut] Gard came back today, after a stay of several days in the other camp. Conditions there were idyllic. For instance, they didn't have lights out until one o'clock on Saturday night. Sunday was a day off, and so on. The *Feldwebel* sat for hours playing chess with one of the Jews in the middle of the working spell, was finally mated, thanked him for the game, and went off. What is one to say?

TUESDAY, OCTOBER 20, 1942 ∎ The *Feldwebel* wants a notice painted, to put up in the road. Can I do it for him? He has powdered colors, and that's all. He thinks I can use gasoline instead of oil. Instead of a brush, which of course there isn't either, I can use an old shaving-brush, he suggested gleefully. As one can see, the camp is splendidly equipped. I suggested train oil, which was accepted. He was delighted with the idea. What can I think of for a brush?

There was a so-called inspection of footwear and underclothes today. We all paraded, in five ranks. Then the Lieutenant walked along the ranks, and we all lifted up one leg and displayed the soles of our boots. We were also supposed to open our jackets and show our underclothes, but that was forgotten. The upshot of the whole is unknown.

We're always having cases of lice. Thank God there have been none in our hut so far. Anyone who has the ill luck to get lice is in a pretty bad way. All the clothes in his

---

* Joachim Fest, who later became the first German biographer of Hitler, was captured in the closing days of the war and ended up in an American-run POW camp. Attending classes on the rudiments of democracy taught by a US Army officer who encouraged debate, Fest was soon told by a fellow German officer: "The [teacher] is very convincing. But the Americans are just guileless people. A man like that doesn't know that freedom always goes wrong in the end."

possession have to be boiled and washed. Bed-clothes too. Meanwhile he has to go about in borrowed drawers and whatever else he can get hold of—which is not much.

WEDNESDAY, OCTOBER 21, 1942 ■ Today it's reported via Per, who had it from his *Baurat*, that we shan't be leaving until November 15th. Most are low spirited at this news. The fellows have just come in, and the rumors are going from mouth to mouth. "Have you heard that the journey's to be put off till the 15th?" "Damn—is that true?" "Who said so?" "Well, that's the very devil!" "Three more weeks! In this cold!" "And so dark as it's getting." "And I've gone and told them not to send anything more."

Then the arguments begin. A skeptic announces that he doesn't believe a word of it, for the reason is supposed to be that they can't get a boat, and as far as he can see, the Germans must be able to requisition a boat whenever and wherever they want one. No one shall persuade him differently.

Someone else has heard that the temperature here can be much more than forty below [also -40°F], and starts conjuring up bogies. Others chime in and declare that's not possible. He sticks to it, and quotes a number of statements by people he has talked to. He thinks we'll pretty well freeze to death. But the darkest of his prophecies are lost in bread and butter and coffee, with which he's now begun to stoke up. The others too are concentrating more and more on food, and by degrees the argument completely dies out.

THURSDAY, OCTOBER 22, 1942 ■ I'm carving and carving nowadays. I've started on a box for Kari. The *Feldwebel* caught sight of it, unluckily. He's to have one the same. Exactly the same. That's the way with all of them. They're like children—can't see anything without wanting it for themselves.

FRIDAY, OCTOBER 23, 1942 ■ The same brilliant weather, but even colder, and the sun is creeping lower and lower. It's not a long way above the mountains now, and hasn't much warmth.

Today there were over seventy men indoors on account of sickness, trouser-patching, and shoe repairs. That was too much for the Lieutenant. All those indoors—except the sick—had to parade especially and give an account of their distress. It was a curious roll call. Many turned out in drawers, others in blankets. The Lieutenant looked rather sheepish and aghast. His tone became polite. Upshot: He would go to Tromsø and "submit the case." We had rather expected a showdown, for there *were* a number of malingerers, too. But at the inspection Bjørn Oscar [Andersen] walked ahead and told each man what to say to the Lieutenant's questions. Everything that goes on turns to farce.

SATURDAY, OCTOBER 24, 1942 ■ There has been a change of weather. It's over-clouded, with the deuce of a north wind and a little snow falling. Now toward evening it looks as though real snow might be coming on. Well, then there will be more shoveling. But thank heaven, at least the tunnel is closed now, except at a couple of meeting places. If they didn't finish what was left today, at any rate they will tomorrow no doubt. When the tunnel is finished there will be two days' rest, says Paunch. Tell that to the marines!*

---

* A phrase originating with British sailors meaning "Go find someone else more gullible to believe it. I don't." Sailors considered themselves well-traveled and worldly-wise, and not as naïve or likely to be fooled as their marine brethren.

There's something quite demoralizing and ghastly about seeing these same people, day in and day out, going in and out of this same hut. Filthy, hungry, cold and bent—joiners, fisherman, workers, lawyers, merchants, tradesmen, technicians, clergymen and teachers. This appalling hovel—stinking of cookery and all kinds of exhalations, jammed full of people—is what has to stand for one's home.

Where we can't move across the floor without elbowing our way and ducking beneath wet, hanging under and outer clothes and boots, where we can't draw breath without inhaling the odors of our neighbors. It's hopeless trying to keep oneself clean, let alone one's things. An indefinable, even layer settles over everything. Even the "clean" clothes one has rubbed and fussed over, boiled and rinsed, look gray, and doubtless *are* gray, and reek unmistakably of train-oil, fat and sundries.

SUNDAY, OCTOBER 25, 1942 ■ The most feverish rumors about Sweden are going around. The Swedes are reported to have sunk a German cruiser which has sunk a Swedish guard-ship, which it refused to obey when given warning to stop. It took place in Swedish waters, then. I don't think I've even mentioned this rumor, I thought it too improbable that the Swedes should have plucked up courage to do anything of the kind. But it seems to be true. Today it was *corroborated* from every quarter, including the best we have, and after that I suppose we must reckon on its really being true. To a rumor that shots have already been fired on the frontier one should certainly add a question mark. For some reason I feel sure that either the Swedes or the Germans will give way.

One doesn't rightly know what to hope and believe. It's terrible to think of yet another small, peaceful nation being drawn into this hell, but I'm afraid I wish it all the same, for many reasons. First and foremost because I believe it will hasten the collapse of Germany, next because it will give Sweden a chance to rehabilitate herself—in our eyes, in the world's—and not least in their own.

TUESDAY, OCTOBER 27, 1942 ■ Brilliant weather—but now the sun is only just above the crest of the mountain. Otherwise a day like all the rest, except for the afternoon, which brought visitors—Jacob Rievertz with his cousin and the cousin's wife.

The news they had was really encouraging. They thought the war would be over before Christmas.

Their visit made a cheerful hour, but now things will be rather hard again, just as I'd resolved to sink that insane hope of a merry Christmas for good. It wears down one's nerves to live in this style, from hope to hope, from rumor to rumor. I'd resolved to have done with it and postpone the end of the war provisionally until the spring, for that matter indefinitely. But now I shall have to give it another chance.

Rievertz & Company were no sooner gone than Paunch arrived. He put his arm round my waist, as his custom is, the greasy swine, and told me with a finger on his lips that we were leaving on November 1st, so I must work like blazes to get all his boxes finished. It was the boxes that interested him, not the going away. Later in the evening an NCO came rushing in, very nervous in case I didn't get finished with *his* box. It had been decided that we were to leave on Sunday.

Now I'm beginning to think it's true. And of course I don't give a damn about the boxes. Now we're going south, nearer home, Kari, and the children. Be things as they may, and come what will—I'm glad to be going back south.

Rievertz had been talking to an NS magnate in Tromsø, who said that within a month fifty of the prisoners here would be released. Among them County Sheriff [Hans] Gabrielsen and Odd Nansen, he said. I don't believe it for a moment, but simply note that it has been talked of.

WEDNESDAY, OCTOBER 28, 1942 ■ Now that we've begun to feel quite sure of leaving on Sunday or thereabouts the work goes easier, even on a day like this. For it's been a nasty one. I'm working full speed on my boxes, while Paunch and other Germans fly around interrupting the whole time, acutely nervous that their things won't be ready.

Per came back at dinnertime with an order for a box for the *Baurat*. He had offered both money and tobacco; Per had said I wouldn't take either, but no doubt I would make a box for him if I had time. When I told Paunch that, he was terrified of the *Baurat's* finding out that we're sitting here making boxes for Todts and Nobs. I was to say I was ill or something. He himself would act quite dumb with the *Baurat* and pretend to know nothing whatever about the box-making. All this the fat swine confided to me in a nervous torrent of words.

I must try and get a box finished for this *Baurat* as well, or he may kick up a row. Ye gods, what a game. Corrupt swindlers the whole lot of them, but with their knives in each other from the top down, in a nervous terror of each other from the bottom up. And then he wants me to help him out in his lie. I'm supposed as it were to have given him *Liebesgaben* [love tokens] in my enthusiasm for his person, *Liebesgaben* which out of love and friendship I've been carving for him in my spare time! For Paunch! Even the *Baurat* will hardly swallow that, I should think.

THURSDAY, OCTOBER 29, 1942 ■ Snowing. Bitter all day and horrible working weather. In the morning it looked like it was turning out to be a regular snowstorm. I'm carving away for dear life.

I've just been out "bathing." We've actually rigged up a kind of bathroom here. We obtained a couple of "Lapp tents"* and set them up in our camp. One we use as a workshop and drying room, the other as a bathroom. Instead of a stove we have an open fireplace in the middle, built of stones. Over it we've placed a trough, in which we heat the water. It was incredibly delicious to get wet all over, rub oneself with soap, and scrub oneself with a brush. I've become a new man, clean from core to surface—but only *to* the surface. For on top I still have filthy trousers. As long as one's underclothes are clean the rest will have to last the time out, and now it can't be much longer.

Our departure on Sunday seems to be coming a bit unstitched. The latest now is that the Lieutenant won't let us go until everyone has proper outer clothes, underclothes, and boots. What we need in that way he'll get from Tromsø. Thinks he. If we're to wait for the clothes the Germans get us, I should think we have a good chance of seeing the spring thaw in Kvænangen.

No news from the fronts today. A Norwegian state policeman has been killed. There are said to have been three men in it, two of them Jews. The Jews have been caught. As a result of this all the Jews in the country above the age of five are said to have been arrested.

---

* Conical tents, similar in style to a tepee.

Rasmus brought this rumor back today from a sick-visit to Kvænangsbotn. It's said to have been in the papers, most of it.*

SUNDAY, NOVEMBER 1, 1942 ■ Sunday off! Fine weather, cold and clear. We had yesterday off too, from about ten or eleven. The Germans were celebrating the completion of the tunnel!

But let me begin at the beginning and make up for lost time; I've been shirking for two days. Well, the day before yesterday Maja Andersen paid us another visit with her friend fru Matheson Bye. We got up a tea party in our hut, where they were both allowed to spend three hours.

After the party we got all the parcels out of the car and took them in to the Germans, who have to look through them. Their car was absolutely loaded with things for us. It was an exceptionally lovely evening. They didn't go until about six, and it had long been dark. The most splendid northern lights I have ever seen were flaming over the whole sky in all the colors of the rainbow—red, green, and yellow against a deep blue sky. Our guests were escorted to the car by a whole troop of attendant swains, who fought to be nearest. If we stay here until Christmas, they assured us, they'll come again. In the evening we went on celebrating until ten o'clock, when we had to go to bed.

It was a real holiday, that Friday, thanks to our two guests, who brisked us up and set our blood flowing. And the festal mood continued next day. We had the time off from about midday. The tunnel was to be celebrated. On that account there was a distribution of five cigars and thirty cigarettes apiece (German rubbish). The Germans held a fête. The Todts under the command of Paunch marched up to the site, where the *Overtodt*† and *Baurat* made speeches. No doubt they bragged about the OT and its fantastic efficiency.

After supper we had a party in the hospital, where Rasmus and [Knut] Gard made a hole in their stock of spirits. Odd [Wang] thawed out in the course of the evening and reached undreamed-of altitudes. All the sick got well in a single night. We kept it up until one o'clock and went to bed in good order.

This day has been one of the quiet ones. A genuine Sunday peace has settled on the whole camp. During the service this morning it was so quiet that it actually made one think of a church Sunday in one of the high dales.

MONDAY, NOVEMBER 2, 1942 ■ The brilliant weather holds, but now the days are so short that our working hours have been cut down. We don't parade until five to eight in the morning, and last night the clock was put back an hour, so we could really have our sleep out. Now everyone is simply waiting for news of our departure, and that makes the time pass, too.

---

* On October 22, 1942, a "border pilot" attempting to smuggle a group of Jews into Sweden was stopped by a suspicious Norwegian policeman; the pilot shot and killed the policeman and attempted to escape. The incident "was used as propaganda to attack Jews in unusually ferocious language" and "was the pretext the German occupation regime and the Quisling regime wanted" to begin the destruction of Norway's Jews. Four days later (October 26) the roundup of all male Jews over age fifteen began; eventually 336 men were arrested. After the German Security Police obtained ship transport to Germany, the Gestapo ordered the arrest of all remaining Jews, which occurred on November 26, 1942.

† There is no such word; this is probably Nansen's slang for someone in a senior position in Organization Todt.

The supply of news is completely at a halt nowadays. Since Maja was here and told us about a big tank battle going on in Cyrenaica, we've heard nothing.* Absolutely nothing!

A German sculptor has written to me, says Kari, asking me to lend him portraits of father. He wants to make a statue of him, to be set up in Fridtjof Nansen Square in Oslo. Who but a German would produce a request like that? He said the Minister-President was certain to approve the idea. Kari replied that I'm in a German concentration camp and have been since January, and that he must return to the subject when I'm released. Perhaps I'll get a day off to attend the unveiling of the monument?

TUESDAY, NOVEMBER 3, 1942 ■ Fine weather, but today we had only just a glimpse of the sun above the mountainside. Tomorrow or the day after it will be completely gone, I should think, and we'll be in the arms of the polar night.

WEDNESDAY, NOVEMBER 4, 1942 ■ We're lucky with the weather. Now it doesn't matter about snowstorms. I'm carving and painting like a maniac, from the first glimmer of morning until I can't see my hand in front of me in the afternoon. It looks as if we might be going any time.

There are wild rumors going round camp today that Von Papen is in Moscow, and that peace negotiations are going on between Germany and Russia.† The Germans are now delighting in the thought that as soon as peace has been made with Russia, which of course is completely done for, they'll take England in earnest! They actually believe that!

SUNDAY, NOVEMBER 8, 1942 ■ Sunday—Sunday off! The same brilliant weather.

Things are brewing up for departure. There's no doubt of it. Today a boat had been seen down on the fjord, heading for Badderen. So now we're all in the clouds. And that's the chief topic of conversation—the journey and how it will go off, what we're to take with us, whether it will be possible to send anything home, what will happen when we get to Grini. No news has made its way in today. Tonight there's a little farewell party in the sickroom.

MONDAY, NOVEMBER 9, 1942 ■ Fine weather. Splendid news from outside. And at last we've had orders to make ready for the start tomorrow. *The start!* Suddenly it comes right home to one. We're leaving. Packing up—I turn dizzy at the thought—to go south. Nearer and nearer to Kari and the children every day. Heavens, how hard to imagine.

The thought of Kunze, Denzer, and all the rest, however, makes me feel sick.

[Birger] Eriksrud brought grand news. He had heard it from a German guard who

---

* This would be the Second Battle of El Alamein (October 23–November 11, 1942).

† Franz von Papen (1879–1969). German diplomat and politician, von Papen served as Germany's chancellor in 1932, and as vice-chancellor under Hitler (1933–1934), after convincing President von Hindenburg that he could control Hitler and the Nazis. Instead, he and the other non-Nazis in the cabinet were soon outmaneuvered, and he resigned following the purge of the SA leadership, known as the "Night of Long Knives," during which many of his close associates were murdered and he narrowly escaped with his own life. Thereafter he acted as German ambassador to Austria (1934–1938) and Turkey (1939–1944). Following the war von Papen was tried and acquitted at Nuremberg; later sentenced by a West German denazification court to eight years in prison, he was released on appeal in 1949. Von Papen had been expelled from the United States in 1916 for his involvement in sabotage activities. The rumors of course were just that.

got it from the German broadcast today. The Americans have landed with a hundred and forty thousand men in Algeria.* Fighting is in progress at Casablanca. Hitler has made a speech and declared that he won't sacrifice another man to take Stalingrad.

The boat we're going with is reported to be a 4,000-tonner. That means we shall have a good deal more room than last time. On the other hand, the boat has probably some beastly German cargo as well which the English might take a fancy to, and such a big boat will have to keep outside the islands a good deal. But it will be all right.

TUESDAY, NOVEMBER 10, 1942 ■ Rainy. No parade—but everyone is to be up at seven and our things are to be packed and the huts "cleaned" by nine. At this moment I'm sitting in my corner, while the waves of packing run high all over the hut. I've had breakfast and did most of my packing yesterday, so I can take it easy and enjoy the sight and sound of this odd spectacle.

It's as though the whole hut—all our domestic comfort—were being pulled up and strewn around with noise and clamor. Everything and everyone is transformed; the door stands wide open, the draft is simply hellish, but we need air! Fresh Norwegian mountain air.

Yes, it looks as though we should really get off, though I'm not entirely convinced yet.

In the midst of this doomsday racket I sit here in my corner looking at the five faces beaming from the desk in front of me. Shall I soon be seeing you again?

WEDNESDAY, NOVEMBER 11, 1942 ■ As I write this, I am in Tromsø, in a big German cargo boat lying at anchor in the harbor.

The actual start from Veidal took place yesterday evening and through the night. I got off on one of the luggage trucks. Late yesterday evening the *Baurat* sent a messenger for the box I was carving for him. Now he's far away, he and his whole army. They pursued me right down to the wharf, the *Baurat's* emissaries, indeed right on board, but I kept them at arm's length and I have the box here. It's mine now.

I had a violent cold even yesterday. Twelve miles on the floor of a truck in the winter weather did it no good. Then we stood freezing on the quay for hours before we could go aboard. Today my whole head is stuffed and I'm not up to much.

The vessel is German—8,000 tons. It's new. We're sleeping in a huge hold on the main deck, which is fitted up with bunks in two tiers. All 350 of us are in here. There's a hubbub, tramping, and to-do all the time. I cleverly selected a place (bunk) for Odd [Wang] and Bjørn Oscar [Andersen] and myself just by the only door of this giant hall. We're up under the roof beneath iron girders, right out in one corner of the hall, and can see far, far up it where people are crawling about like us. And down below they're creeping and crawling in the same way. The narrow fissures between the rows of bunks are chock full of people incessantly going out and in. I've acquired a fresh and deeper understanding of the movements in an anthill.

How long we're to stay here I don't know, but no doubt we'll be taking more prison-

---

* Operation Torch, the Allied landings of approximately 65,000 men in French Morocco and Algeria, began on November 8, 1942. General Dwight Eisenhower commanded the operation. Allied forces achieved complete surprise, and after initial resistance by Vichy French forces, the ports of Algiers, Oran, and Casablanca all quickly fell. It was the first big combined offensive against Axis forces. The North African campaign concluded on May 13, 1943, with the capture of Tunisia, the surrender of over 238,000 POWs, and the elimination of all Axis forces from North Africa.

ers aboard, presumably our own from Sydspissen. Moreover there are 300 teachers from Kirkenes. They are free and not allowed to talk to the rest of us on board. We've found out that they're all right, first-rate morale and full of optimism.

FRIDAY, NOVEMBER 13, 1942 ■ Well, now we're lying at anchor off Bodø. We left Tromsø at seven yesterday morning and got to Lødingen about three. Rasmus was ashore at Tromsø on something that sounded by his account of it like a thorough spree. He met all our friends, and brought back a whole launch full of parcels and things, sacks of potatoes, barrels of herring, and dried cod.

This is a thumping big boat; its name is something like *Moltkefels.** We all sleep in the top hold, and the bunks are in long rows with "streets" between. All the streets debouch into a big open space—the Market Place, as it's already been christened—under the hatch, which is covered and battened down. In the Market Place is the pump, where everyone gets water and most perform their very scanty toilet.

There is a social gathering out in the Market Place tonight, as there was last night. Choral singing can be heard, and individuals recite poems or sing songs of every kind. The whole "town" is on the go; many are lying in their bunks but all join in. The Market Place is bursting with the throng and the streets are jammed full of people. The atmosphere is beastly, as can well be imagined.

We travel only in the daytime. At night we lie at anchor. Tonight we're to lie here off Bodø, tomorrow presumably at Rørvik, and on Sunday we may reach Trondheim, I dare say. And then? But sufficient unto the day . . .

I haven't had my clothes off since we left Veidal, and don't suppose I shall until we reach Grini. Yesterday I pulled myself together by main force and removed my beard.

But the news is grand! The American offensive in Algeria and Morocco is having excellent results. Oran surrendered in five minutes. The offensive in Egypt is advancing with giant strides. Italy is being bombed. Altogether there are big things going on.

Today it's ten months since the district sheriff came and arrested me in East Gausdal. Ten months. It will soon be Christmas!

SATURDAY, NOVEMBER 14, 1942 ■ The day was well advanced before we finally left Bodø. I don't know why. There may have been something going on off the coast. The weather has been bad and windy all day, but not much sea. At reduced speed we've been moving south, steadily and surely, and we're still moving. Now it's midnight.

Odd and I had fire watch from twelve until two. This consists in looking after four stoves in the Market Place and two in different corners of the town. The Market Place is full of card-playing groups now. Fine groups some of them. In one the NS man and legionary [Tønnes] Førlandsås is swanking with his pal. In another the presiding genius is a professional conjurer and cardsharp. Close by sits Pastor Sæverud writing his sermon for tomorrow. Next to him again a couple is absorbed in a game of chess, which a German guard is following with interest.

---

* The *Moltkefels* was used as a troop and passenger transport throughout the Baltic. It later participated in Operation Hannibal, the seaborne evacuation of German troops and civilians from East Prussia in the face of Soviet advances. On April 11, 1945, the ship was sunk by Soviet bombers off the Hel Peninsula (near Gdansk, Poland) with a loss of approximately one thousand lives.

Most of us are counting pretty recklessly and definitely on being set free when we arrive. As I said, I'm not.

SUNDAY, NOVEMBER 15, 1942 ■ In the early hours of this morning we passed Rørvik. Not long after, before we'd got out to Folla, we turned and went back to Rørvik, where we cast anchor. We're still here, and it's nearly midnight. Gale warning? Mines? Submarines? We don't know; we just lie here waiting.

The day passes monotonously. There are only two things one can do—walk about on deck or lie in bed. There's nowhere to sit down. On deck the weather has been nasty, cold, and windy all day, so it's been mostly lying reading trashy novels. It has given me a pain in my back.

MONDAY, NOVEMBER 16, 1942 ■ We're still in Rørvik harbor, waiting. The wind has been something frightful all day. I assume that out at Folla there must be a real storm.

Then came the sensation, well on in the afternoon. It was Rasmus who brought it. There is an alarm of dysentery. Several cases of diarrhea and fever among the teachers may turn out to be dysentery, and if so we shall have to lie in quarantine for an indefinite time. A jolly prospect indeed! To stay aboard here perhaps for weeks and weeks—in this pigsty! Within a short time we shall all be lousy. Lice have already been found.

Now we're anxiously waiting for tomorrow, and what is to happen next. Are we to stay here until the new year? It may take such a devil of a time yet, if the worst should happen. Weeks of quarantine—in Trondheim.

TUESDAY, NOVEMBER 17, 1942 ■ We didn't leave today, for some unknown reason. Food supplies are getting short all round. Neither the Germans, the teachers, nor ourselves have much more than another day's supply. The dinner ration of salt cod—oh, how salty!—was small today, and there was a certain amount of grumbling.

WEDNESDAY, NOVEMBER 18, 1942 ■ This morning about seven we weighed anchor, and at last set off for Trondheim. The wind was pretty slack, but still there was a bit of a sea over Folla—not so much however that there was any seasickness to speak of.

Folla was all alive. There were several boats going southward on the same track. A submarine and a little MTB* passed us. We saw two or three mines exploding on the beach. Our escort vessel shot at mines floating in the channel. It seems quite likely that our delay at Rørvik was due to the mine danger at Folla. The weather was fairly good all day, but showery. It's been raw and cold the whole time, but still we made it, and now we're lying in Trondheim harbor. We got here at about nine. The danger is over.

Trondheim is blacked out, but the new harbor is fully lit; obviously they're working there night and day.† On the other side of the fjord there are also a lot of lights. Some hold that it's a fishing fleet lying there, others think naval vessels. The quarantine flag has been run up on *Moltkefels*.

---

*   A motor torpedo boat, equivalent to a PT boat in the US Navy.

†   During the war the Germans used Trondheim as a major submarine base, known as DORA I. Work on the base began in mid-1941 but was not completed until the summer of 1943; a smaller bunker (DORA II) was started nearby but never finished.

The bread is finished, and the water that comes up in the Market Place is turning brown. But anyhow the sea voyage with its perilous hazards has been got through.

THURSDAY, NOVEMBER 19, 1942 ■ Trondheim—Trondheim—! There it lay in the morning twilight when I went up on deck. Gradually the well-known outlines appeared out of the darkness. Big, black boats were lying around us in the harbor; some were arriving, others leaving, and up in the air some fighter planes were keeping up a deafening racket. Everyone was out on the foredeck, following with interest all that went on. But everyone was prepared to stay on board; we had only to raise our eyes a little, and we could see the yellow quarantine flag floating on the mainmast.

Then came the order to pack and make ready to go ashore in half an hour. The boat was already beginning to heave anchor, and we were gliding in to the quay. Then there was life and bustle and no mistake. Out on deck they came bit by bit—all the clothes, all the boxes, parcels, sacks, trunks, and prisoners. Now we were already alongside, at Brattøra. We were "met" by some German naval men, some OTs, and one or two civilians. A little errand boy with a cycle stood there as well. I asked him to go to Hirsch at Nordre with Odd's regards.* He promised to. So Kari may hear today?

Then came the rain, and not long afterward an order to "clean" our sleeping hall. People volunteered for the job. I was one of them. While we were in the thick of this, heaving all the mattresses onto the floor, sweeping the bottoms of the beds, shaking the mattresses (until the straw and sawdust flew), and then sweeping the floor, there came instructions to stop the work and move in again—all of us. No one was surprised.

Well, well, so then we had to move back all the luggage and take possession of our bunks. Then we were locked in. No one was allowed on deck, of course.

A new tone was making itself heard, a familiar tone—the SD had taken over the guard. "*Los, los, Mensch!* [Hurry, hurry, man!] *Verdammte Arschloch!* [You damned asshole!] *Schweinereien* [Filth], *Schweinehund* [Son of a bitch]," and so on. Yes indeed, we're approaching civilization again. We were counted and checked up in the old way, herded together like cattle, and bullied and shoved and hauled about. There came a multitude of bans, among them a privy ban—that is, one might go if it was extremely urgent, and then one had to stand in a long line before getting there. Two guards stood at the exit door and counted out the men six by six with a steady flow of abuse. One guard went about with a flashlight and saw to it that people were really *sitting* there and that it wasn't just a pretext to get out and smoke.

We've had instructions to be ready to go ashore at nine tomorrow morning.

But the news is fine. Derna and Benghazi have been taken; the Allies have entered Tunis. The papers are writing about Darlan's treachery, and asking: Where is Rommel? Things are looking tiptop.†

Now we've been locked in; no more privy tonight. This will be a snug-looking place tomorrow! But every cloud has a silver lining. The soldiers have shut the doors, and none

---

* Nansen's wife Kari's maiden name was Hirsch; her cousin operated a shop in downtown Trondheim on Nordre Gate (North Street).
† The Libyan cities of Derna and Benghazi were occupied by British forces under General Montgomery following the Second Battle of El Alamein. Francois Darlan was a major military and political figure in Vichy France. In November 1942 he agreed to surrender French troops in North Africa in return for Allied assurances that he would continue to lead French North and West Africa. He was assassinated by a French monarchist on December 24, 1942.

of them is inside. We're smoking and reading until we go to sleep. It's delightful to be doing something forbidden. I say like [Didrik] Seip, "I must live dangerously!" Good night, Kari. It won't be long now.

FRIDAY, NOVEMBER 20, 1942 ■ Bless me, things went pretty much according to plan, except that a brisk snowstorm was raging in the morning. That hadn't been ordered. It took remarkably few hours to get ashore and onto the train, and so here we are, the whole company, distributed in cattle cars with about 28 in each. We've already passed through Støren. There should be hopes of reaching Oslo by tomorrow night. Thank God there are stoves in the cars, or we would have frozen to death; we can see out through the walls and floor.

SATURDAY, NOVEMBER 21, 1942 ■ I got no further yesterday. Before we knew it we were in Opdal, and on we went—Røyse, Drivstua, Kongsvoll—and we actually reached Dombås before ten. I forgot to say that at Støren we were allowed to get out in the snow, and under the windows of a number of citizens' houses we relieved ourselves. The night went by; it's not easy to say or explain how, but it went by. At Hamar we learned that the teachers also had gone south by train. They too had been discharged from quarantine, and more: they were free.

At Hamar we got a couple of slices of bread and a little coffee, and there was the usual watering scene on the railway line at Mjøsa. Goodness, how we looked. Sooty, nasty and unshaven. A number of the cars have no stove. Those who had been unlucky enough to get into them were frozen to the bone. In our car we have colds to a man. I'm leading.

PART III: GRINI

1942

SUNDAY, NOVEMBER 22, 1942 ■ We were in Oslo by about five. First we had a pleasant break at Lillestrøm. Sandwiches and coffee—and something better for some of us. Wives had mustered there. Bjørn Oscar [Andersen's] wife and little daughter got a tolerably bearded, filthy embrace. Fru Eriksrud, fru Gard, and others were there too, brimful of longing and good news. Kari of course couldn't leave the baby, but I had a note from her.*

The idea had actually been to unload us at Lysaker but, perhaps to fool those who had assuredly turned up there for a glimpse of their people, we were shifted on to trucks right back at Loenga and driven direct to Grini, where I am now sitting in Hut 3, *Stube 5*.

It was dark when we arrived, but they lit up the square in front of the main building with the big lamps. Denzer, the *Lagerkommandant*, Kunz, the Rat (pet name for Kunze), and others had turned out, and so we fell in once more, in five ranks—at Grini. Bellows, blows and kicks were in full swing, the first box on the ear had already fallen, and altogether, we were back home.

Yes, it was actually a kind of home-feeling that possessed us, as we stood there. Denzer came up and spoke to me. No, he didn't shake hands, thank God, but wasn't he perhaps on the very point of it? He cross-examined me on what things had been like, and said there had been big changes here as well while we were away. He flung out a hand, as though to display all his glories in one sweeping gesture, pointed proudly at the square, where fresh gravel had been put down (three days ago), and was altogether as complaisant and courteous as a hotel proprietor.

He told me he had reserved two huts for us where we could be isolated, and we should find that a great advantage, he added. For here there's a ban on smoking, reading, writing, parcels and everything imaginable. We know nothing about it, and go on smoking—what we have. No one has told us not to as yet. Our reception was almost cordial. They had been informed that we had worked extremely well, and on that account Denzer had given orders for us to have every kind of easement—we were to have the lightest work too. An extra thick soup had been brewed for us, and we got half a loaf each.

And then we were left completely to ourselves. Not another German disturbed us that night. Unfortunately it was too late to bathe last night, nor did we get our luggage, which had come on separate trucks. And to conclude, no bedclothes were issued to us, so we had to sleep one more night in our clothes, our filthy clothes, unshaven and as filthy as we arrived, for there was no means of washing oneself or making any toilet whatever.

But we met our friends again, and after all that was the event of the day. I went to see Erling Steen—for he's still here, and what's worse, has been degraded to hut leader and spent five days "inside" over a smuggling affair. A young chap named [Even] Evensen—a nineteen-year-old—has been made the new personnel chief.† The Germans can manage him easier than Erling. But Erling was in fine form and the reunion was cordial.

Nils [Ramm] is in the hospital with stomach ulcers.

---

* According to diarist Myrtle Wright, Nansen was greeted by Kari's sister, Signe, who reported that Nansen "looks well."

† Released May 13, 1944.

This has been a working day. But we've had it off. We've only bathed and put ourselves to rights and taken it easy. Heavens, how delicious to have a bath and get some clean clothes on; it's a whole romance in itself.

Otherwise the day has passed in seeing old friends. I had no sooner got into the main building, than I went down to the furnace room and made contact. A matchbox—an admirable matchbox! All in order—radiant greetings! But patience—patience. There's danger here now. Everything is tightened up. One has to tread very softly.

Twenty-five of us were released today. Of course the report is that there's to be a big release soon. Certainly—it goes without saying. But the other day 25 men were sent to Germany. That was something else again.

MONDAY, NOVEMBER 23, 1942 ■ We've not been given any work yet. I spent the morning pottering around and looking at the old places. I had a talk with old [Elling] Sikveland. He's still here, poor chap. Now he's got the idea that Torgeir is alive and in Germany. Poor old Sikveland—he began repeating Torgeir's whole story to me. It took a long time.

I've been talking to Lauritz Sand. He has gradually started to get about a little. It almost seems as though he shall live and be himself again, after all the horrors he has gone through.

In the architect's office there have been changes. First and foremost, Koopmann is gone. He committed embezzlement, was jailed, and later was sent to the Eastern front. The building superintendent, Jantzen, has got kidney disease (i.e. syphilis), and a new one has been appointed. This new man, whom I haven't seen, has been pleased to declare that he won't have me in the architect's office and will have nothing to do with me. God knows why. Presumably I shall be working in an "*Innenarchitektbüreau*" [interior design department] where a man called [Bendt] Winge is designing furniture and decorating.* Well, well, I shan't begin until I have to.

Odd, Bjørn Oscar and I agreed today to move in with our old hut-mates, Martin [Strandli], Nils [Ramm] (when he's better) and [Kjell] Colbjørn[sen]—if we're allowed. I went to Denzer and asked him. He refused, but for an odd reason. We who have been in North Norway are to have special treatment. We're to be allowed to smoke, read, write and everything that's forbidden to the others. Then presumably we shall have parcels and visits too. We're something in the nature of heroes and pets, and now we're to be coddled. I fervently hope it won't be long till Kari and the children pay me a visit, with the new baby.

I also talked with Hannagreta [Rinnan] through the window. Just as smiling and sweet-tempered, but still locked up in a cell, poor thing. She asked how I was getting on, and actually appeared happy that I was back safe and sound. Now she'd been here six or seven months. Frode is still at No. 19. He is a sweeper and I believe comparatively well off. When I've collected myself a bit and got into the way of things, I must try and get her some more little messages from husband and children. There's been a long halt now. The fellows became nervous when capital punishment was introduced for illegal contact

---

* Winge (1907–1983), a furniture designer and interior decorator, was chairman of the Norwegian Interior Architects Association (1951–1954) and president of the National Union of Norwegian Handicrafts (1971–1975). In 1962 he was awarded the Jacob Prize by the Norwegian Design Council, Norway's highest award in design, crafts, and architecture. He was released December 30, 1943.

with prisoners. God knows it's a risk, and one must indeed be careful. Therefore the "west wind" hasn't blown here for the last month.

The news is brilliant. Things are going splendidly in North Africa; one can make out everything between the lines of the newspapers—which we're now allowed to read here. They're even distributed, and when you add the *Whispering Times*, the picture is complete.* But does it mean that the war will be over this year, or by the spring, or by the autumn? After all that means a good deal to all of us, even though we're in no doubt of the final result.

TUESDAY, NOVEMBER 24, 1942 ■ Today most of us were given jobs. I haven't settled yet either with myself or the *Bauleitung* where I'm to work, so I've been loafing today. I've had another bath, shaved and altogether begun to feel like a civilized human being again. *Bauleiter* Niebel sent a message that he wants to talk to me. The same gentleman who announced yesterday that he would have nothing to do with me. Today he's singing another tune. Gebecke, by what Colbjørn says, must have praised me up to the skies, so I'm in danger of landing there after all.

At roll call this evening it was announced that the Germans in their magnanimity mean to let us have a Christmas parcel from home, and that everyone will be allowed to write home once and impart this glorious news. All who lived north of Narvik were to step forward and give their names. (Presumably surprise parcels were to be provided for them by the Germans themselves.) Finally an extremely German and tactful thing: All who were so poor that their families couldn't afford to send a parcel must also step forward and give their names. They wouldn't be forgotten either. Then we were asked if everyone appreciated this, which was really a tremendous favor.

Well, that was cheering. We, who after all had been cherishing some vague idea of getting home for Christmas, we were to have a small parcel. And leave to write a note to our wives and children. Isn't it grand?

Some time ago a search was carried out in all the huts. Everything—absolutely everything eatable—tinned food, butter, sandwich stuff and tobacco, was confiscated—stolen! Martin [Strandli] has found out that yesterday the whole lot was sent to Germany. It's nice that they should be getting some Christmas parcels there, too. After all one can't live entirely on bombs.

WEDNESDAY, NOVEMBER 25, 1942 ■ I must start at once with the all-overshadowing event: Kari has been with me. She came this afternoon, alone. They sent for me while I was out walking somewhere. I realized immediately what for and ran down to the old *Vermittlung*, through a multitude of rooms—and there she was. Oh heavens! What wise man was it who said you never are so near black despair as when you stand on the peak of happiness? I was struggling all the time not to scream or something. I don't know what came over me. It was though I suddenly lost all hope—just when you were with me again at last, when at last I had you in my arms again for one little moment. Why, why?

You said you had hopes of my getting out. I seemed to hear in your voice that you

---

* The name of an underground newspaper. By the fall of 1943, five thousand Norwegians were engaged in editing, printing, and distributing more than sixty underground newspapers; a thousand of these people were imprisoned over the course of the war and more than two hundred died or were executed.

didn't believe it yourself. I felt suddenly with a despairing, overwhelming conviction that I shouldn't get out. I remembered all their fooling of us, and I saw it, all at once, as clear and self-evident that I should be sent to Germany. I got nothing out at all of what I was going to say to you. I only said you looked tired—you smiled—but there were tired lines in your face. Good God, Kari, what can you have thought—I must have struck you as pretty spineless—fainthearted—dismal! But it isn't so; it will pass. It's only now. The reaction at being back here had me in its grip even before you came.

But still I heard that you and the children are all right—that you're not hungry—that you have enough wood—and that all of you are well. The woman interpreter who was there kept on interrupting, forbidding us to speak of this or that. A mad fury with that loathsome creature almost threw me off my balance for a moment. And then the poor ten minutes were up. They have never been shorter, and never more brutally cut off.

It was as though you slipped away from me—and I was left standing, hopelessly lost. I got outside the door—I waved to you—I saw you as in a mist—you waved, and kissed your hand—then you disappeared round the fence. I tore the heart out of my breast and flung it to you, but I didn't even feel that it reached you.

Good God, what's up with me exactly? Have my nerves gone altogether?

I went to see that *Bauleiter* Niebel today. He was a little shaver of a man. He offered me a cigarette to put me in a better temper, he said. Then he explained that I was under Winge, and was to draw from his sketches and directions.

He meant to humiliate me—the shaver! But Winge can't help it, poor chap, and we shall get on all right.

Tonight most of the Jews were sent off—to Tønsberg?* To Germany? Nobody knows. I can't but admire them. All were full of spirit and cheerfulness. We can take it all right, they assured me when I said good-bye. Of course they all know they'll be inside until the war is over; they're not tormented by false hopes of getting out. That helps them unquestionably.†

Many of the North Norway lot in general were sent, too. A man from our room, and among others young Lars Brevig. Poor boy, he looked rather taken aback, but declared pluckily that he'd be all right.‡ His voice shook a little, and I don't think the tears were far off when I said good-bye to him. He can't be more than 18. So *that* was the special treatment we were to get, the reward for our good work in North Norway!

THURSDAY, NOVEMBER 26, 1942 ■ I only just made a start at my new job today. It was an effort to get going. If I'd even had some job that wasn't in my own line, it would have been easier. It's worse to start on something one can do—and find one can't do it. But I shall get over that. Everything works out in the end.

---

* The Berg concentration camp was established in mid-1942. Located near the town of Tønsberg, approximately sixty miles south of Oslo, the camp held political prisoners and Jews awaiting deportation. Although planned for three thousand prisoners, it was never finished and its maximum population at any one time never exceeded between five and six hundred.

† On November 26, 1942, 558 Jews were boarded on two ships in Oslo, the SS *Donau* and the SS *Monte Rosa*. These prisoners were transported to Auschwitz, where most were killed upon arrival. All told approximately 772 Jews (out of a prewar population of approximately 2,000) were deported from Norway during the war; only 34 survived captivity. Most other remaining Jews (more than 1,000) escaped Norway following the German invasion or, forewarned of the impending roundup in late 1942, were able to flee to safety in Sweden.

‡ Brevig, who was not yet nineteen, survived his captivity in Sachsenhausen.

One of the Jews who were at Møllergata yesterday being photographed had had a word with Frode. He looked much the same, was getting on all right, but said they were insanely strict there now. When he was told that things were going *damn well* outside, he answered, "Aren't you just saying that?" So they don't hear anything. Poor fellows, they're living in a sealed tin full of devilry. We at least have the lid off—after a fashion.

FRIDAY, NOVEMBER 27, 1942 ■ It must have been getting on toward two when I put the light out and lay down. No sooner had I dropped off to sleep than I awoke again to find the bottom of my bed giving way. First one cross board fell down, then another, then several—and underneath I could hear Odd [Wang] in full bloom; he was getting the board ends on his head. One, he asserted, fell in his ear, but when I asked sympathetically if it hurt, he assured me it was a pleasure.

As we sat there coming wide awake, a roaring voice was heard through the stillness. It was Denzer's. It was followed by a deafening racket, a tramping of iron-shod boots, shouts, and words of command.

"All out! Paulsen—where's Paulsen? Don't you hear, P-a-u-l-sen! All out at once, *verfluchte mal* [cursed once again]* *sacramento!* In five minutes everyone is to be ready. Out! Out with you!! Get on—get on—get on!!!"

And in a twinkling the hut resounded with tramping feet and feverish activity—the scraping of boots—the racket of tables and chairs upsetting. Prisoners drunk with sleep were tumbling out of their bunks and groping round for their clothes and boots. In less than five minutes we were ready, and out of the hut clattered a noisy train of prisoners. Off to the parade ground! There was no time to discuss what on earth this was all about. The first idea that flashed through my mind was that a prisoner must have escaped. My next was an air-raid warning. My third was that they were going to search the hut (therefore in the darkness and tumult I stuck my diary behind the asbestos plate on the wall by the stove).

Down on the square we fell in. The lights were turned on, so that the square was fully lit. There was the usual eyes right—eyes front—and all the rest of it in German. Then we were counted. We were all present and correct. Now what was it for?

Kunz, the Rat, Stange and all the pirates were equipped with submachine guns. There was a sinister feeling in the air. We stood a long time after the command—*Stillstand!* [Stand still!] Five minutes—ten minutes. Nothing could be heard but the voices of some wrangling Germans a long way off.

Then the fun began. We got the orders *Mützen ab* [caps off] and *Mützen auf* [caps on]. It was the *Lagerkommandant* who gave them, with Evensen the personnel chief translating. When we had spent some time at that, we got the order, knees bend right down. Then there were a whole lot who couldn't—old people, and people with stiff knees—and that gave rise to a lot of roaring and bawling out.

Denzer had now drawn back; it was the *Stormdrunk* (the *Lagerkommandant*) who did the talking. It became more and more obvious that he was tight. Not rather tight—but tight as a drum! Stange was strutting before our hut. People were coughing badly—it was very cold—and especially among us there were a lot of bad colds from the train journey.

---

* The correct German is *verflucht nochmal.*

Suddenly Stange turned to us and said, "Cough! Just cough some more all of you," and with motions of his arm he gave the signal for a general cough. The drunken Commandant was to realize that it was cold and people were feeling it.

There had just been some frightful squabbling between Denzer and the *Stormdrunk*. Denzer must have been expostulating with the other about the cold and the colds. Finally a table was fetched and Stange placed upon it. He was to lead the drill.

On a former occasion the Germans had waxed quite enthusiastic over a new exercise that Stange had picked up from seeing the fellows doing it. It consists purely and simply in bending down and slapping one's knees to keep warm. This was now performed—up and down, up and down—and then it was varied by slapping the back of the man in front, and knee-bendings in four beats. We kept that up a long while.

During these exercises the *Stormdrunk* had been reeling about in front, enjoying his tin soldiers. He had snuffled out some drunken gabble at intervals. I was too far off to see and hear. Then the voice of the personnel chief was raised again. He was to ask if we all sufficiently appreciated the fact that we were to have a parcel weighing two kilos [over four pounds] for Christmas.

"Yes!" from everyone.

Then he asked, "What would you like?"

There was a unanimous cry of, "Tobacco!"

The snuffling voice of the *Stormdrunk* interposed, "*Was wollen Sie haben?—Frauen oder Tabak?*" [What would you like?—women or tobacco?]

He was enjoying himself hugely. That about girls was a terrific stroke of humor—to ask 2,000 prisoners if they would have girls or tobacco—ha ha! Then Evensen went on translating. If we didn't behave nicely, we shouldn't get a parcel. Those who didn't salute the Germans properly wouldn't get a parcel. Those who didn't salute the prisoners with stripes properly wouldn't get a parcel. Those with stripes who didn't salute those without stripes properly when *they* had saluted those *with* stripes properly wouldn't get a parcel, and so on, and so on.

It turned into the wildest farce. But sinister. . . . What might not that man take into his head. And we were all of us at the mercy of his whims and fancies.

It was announced that this was a so-called alarm call-over. There would be one more at night before December 15th, and anyone who wasn't down on the square five minutes after the signal had been given wouldn't get a parcel, *verstanden?* [understood?] At last the performance came to an end. The man had had enough. He wanted to get indoors and go on drinking.

A seething mob streamed out of the square and back to the huts. Some were nearly bursting with laughter, others were furious, and others deeply indignant.

Today Denzer has been talking to Steen. He asked what impression had been made by the events of the night. Erling said that to begin with we all thought it was an ordinary alert—an air-raid warning or what not—but in time we did, Erling added, feel some astonishment. Denzer made no reply for a long time, looked at Erling, and then said, "We will all forget this!"

Well, we can but try.

Later in the night the drinking buddies hit on the idea that it might be fun to close-crop the new prisoners who had just arrived from Stavanger. All the barbers were routed out, and all these poor prisoners—except Sven Oftedal, who was among them, and whom Denzer rescued in a fit of consideration for an old Grini veteran—had their heads cropped, so that they're now going about with heads like billiard balls. I can imagine how the *Stormdrunk* enjoyed himself.

SATURDAY, NOVEMBER 28, 1942 ■ It's just as if the black frost and the mist that lies like a veil over the ground right on until midday were a link in the systematic eeriness enfolding everything and everyone in this Godforsaken spot. I can't get my spirits up again. All I try my hand at is equally intractable. I've written a letter to Kari today—a dreary letter.

SUNDAY, NOVEMBER 29, 1942 ■ The other day a thousand Jews were shipped from Oslo. It's reported that their destination is Poland. Highly probable. Five hundred of the Jews were women and children. All they possessed has been taken. A great deal of it has been sent up here to Grini. Odd is now in the *Verwaltung* [administration building] and is employed in registering the stolen goods.*

TUESDAY, DECEMBER 1, 1942 ■ I fell ill yesterday and was admitted to the hospital for observation. Had insufferable pains in my belly. And here I am in the ulcer ward, in the same room as Nils [Ramm]. There is also a man from Bergen, Christopher Bruun.† A nice chap with stomach ulcers. Both Bruun and Nils keep hard at it reading the papers, reading between the lines, calculating and dividing to make out the position on the fronts.

THURSDAY, DECEMBER 3, 1942 ■ After dinner today, when the men were parading down in the square, I suddenly heard the personnel chief shouting my name. Of course I thought first of release—idiot that I am. I couldn't help it, noticed to my vexation that my heart was beginning to jump up and down, but still had the presence of mind enough to take care of the dangerous pages of my diary, in case anyone should come. Inside the privy I've found an absolutely safe place.

But no one came. I got up and stood in the passage looking out over the hutments; then Odd [Wang] came rushing up. But it was no definite news that made him hurry like that, it was something he was bringing me: cigarettes—tobacco and—a letter from Kari! "*. . . been told by the Security Police that you're not to be released—for security reasons . . .*" It was the *coup de grâce*. And it was hard, I admit; but now I know! Yes, Kari, it may sound odd, but I'm glad of this; I'm at peace now, even though you'll understand that it was a blow.

---

* In late October 1942 Quisling signed a law confiscating all assets owned by Norway's Jews. The accompanying police order gave priority to securities, cash, and jewelry; bank accounts and safe deposit boxes were to be emptied. Moveable property was auctioned off and the proceeds turned over to the state treasury. Not to be left out, Reichskommissar Terboven required that all seized gold, silver, and jewelry be remitted to Germany as a "voluntary contribution to the war effort." A royal commission was set up in 1995 to investigate the issue of confiscations and reparations. The panel produced two reports, a majority report and a minority report, which differed widely over both how much was seized and how much was returned to Jewish survivors after 1945. The Norwegian government ultimately adopted the minority report and allotted $70 million for further compensation.

† Christopher Brun was ultimately transferred to a series of camps in France and Germany, including Natzweiler and Dachau. He died January 7, 1945, age forty-eight, in a Natzweiler subcamp.

FRIDAY, DECEMBER 4, 1942 ■ On his rounds today Leif P[oulsson]* asked if I wouldn't let them discharge me, as they were very short of beds in the hospital. Of course. With that my treatment and my stay in the hospital came to an abrupt end. I'm going to pack this afternoon and am now sitting up in bed writing my swan song.

Just before dinner Denzer looked in. Kindness, loftiness and magnanimity in person. I should have a visit from my wife at least once a month; and with a large, round motion of the arm and a jovial grimace he made it plain that he would work it still oftener. There, now! My state of health? Acidity? Ah yes, acidity. *He* had had that too; disagreeable; oh yes, very disagreeable. He hoped it would pass off. Then he went to have a look at Nils [Ramm], and on hearing that he has stomach ulcers gave him quite a long lecture on the stomach ulcer, its origins and symptoms. So Nils knows now.

Then at last he came out with what he really wanted. I was to make his son a jumping-jack for Christmas. A brownie with a laughing face, a red cap and sprawling legs with glossy boots on. Oh yes, his son—"such a funny little chap." Ha-ha! But of course as I was ill—I was being discharged today? Oh well, then I could still have a try perhaps? First a little sketch that I would show him—*Nicht wahr? Also gut!* [Ok then!] *Gute Verbesserung alle!* [Good improvement in all!] We had some talk about other things as well: about Christmas, about the men who had been up north, who were to have privileges and parcels and tobacco and reading matter. He would see what he could do for us, offered me a cigarette and was altogether as amiable and "gentlemanly" as it was possible for him to be.

In spite of all the sickening features of this scene and of the man in general, it gave me a certain comfort. I haven't him against me; that's always something, of which more can be made.

But now I think I must get packed up and return to hut life—and my "work" of making a jumping-jack for Denzer's son!

SATURDAY, DECEMBER 5, 1942 ■ So yesterday I moved out of the hospital, and Erling [Steen] thought I should seize the opportunity to get myself transferred to Hut 12, back with Colbjørn[sen], Martin [Strandli], [Einar] Skavlan, Francis [Bull], Robert [Andersen], Lorentz [Cappelen Smith],† etc. And here I am.

Just before dinner I was summoned to Denzer, Per Krohg as well, so we went together. A whole performance it turned out. Kari had sent me a big flat parcel, which proved to be a knot-cake.‡ Heavens, what a vision! Denzer must have thought so too. He was indescribable as he opened the parcel and probed its every nook and cranny, as though expecting to find illegal documents or information stuck in somewhere. A slab of choco-late was "examined" in the same way, and at last, the parcel was handed over to me with all manner of gestures and patronizing wishes for "all the best" and a speedy reunion with my family.

Then came Per's turn. His parcel had also been sent through Kari, and thus Denzer

---

* Following the war Poulsson, a doctor, published a study on the mortality and causes of death among Norwegian pris-oners in the Natzweiler-Struthof concentration camp, where he was incarcerated for eighteen months. A landmark in Antarctica is named in honor of Poulsson and his brother Erik, another member of the Resistance.

† Cappelen Smith was released December 8, 1944.

‡ A cake, or pastry, in the shape of a knot, or pretzel.

was led to ascertain that we were old and great friends. Per's parcel was also scrutinized with the greatest acumen, found to be all right and handed over. Per confided to me afterwards that Ragnhild had sent the parcel in answer to his request for some tobacco. There was no tobacco in it. I don't believe Denzer stole it, but there can be no doubt whatever that the tobacco was stolen.

At this juncture the Segment started bellowing; he had meanwhile come into the room. The bellowings were addressed to me, and were to the effect that I had myself to blame for my "misfortune," I needn't have been in prison, I needn't have gone to North Norway, I might have been a free man. For he had just been reading a book about Nansen and Quisling—Ohmygoodnessme! If Nansen had lived, he would have backed the new era, the great Nansen—*mein Gott* [my God]! and Quisling and *Donnerwetter* and altogether! Here Denzer interrupted.

"Just a moment, Seidel!* Quietly! Slowly! Now, then!" And he began a half-hour's lecture. By way of exordium he mentioned for Seidel's information that things were not to be done as fast as he might think, it wasn't so simple, he must remind him that I was a Norwegian, and that I couldn't grasp straight away how just and proper it was for the Germans to have taken Norway, etc. He understood that a hundred percent and had the deepest respect for my attitude. But he would like to point out certain things, certain facts. If the Germans hadn't taken Norway, the English would have. And then where do you think Norway would be today? You see what England's worth today. There was an air attack on Oslo some time ago. They attacked with four planes. What happened? Tja, some lives were lost, some private homes were hit, three of the planes we shot down, only one managed to escape. There you see: That's England today, that's all they're good for. Or see what they're doing now in North Africa! "Imbecile! Completely imbecile!" That was all he had to say of what they were doing there.

Then he passed on to describing the world-dominion of the Germans and of national-socialism. I was national all right, he believed, but I must also become aware of the common people, the masses, socialism, and add that word to "national." "Then we have National Socialism all fixed up—eh?" and he made a stylish gesture with his hands, like a well-bred conjurer after a successful trick. "But it's not so simple. Herr Nansen"—this was to the Segment—"hasn't yet changed his attitude, that takes time; time; slowly! slowly!—"

It looked as if there would be no end to it. But at length, after a short summing-up, he concluded his speech with polite wishes for my birthday, and an assurance and hope that I should soon get home to my family.

I had had the chance to get in one reply, and couldn't resist the temptation. He was talking about Norway's war effort and the volunteers on the Eastern Front. "But," he added, "of course not everyone can be at the front." "No," said I, "there have to be some in prison, too!" He pulled up a moment, failed to catch the irony but flung out his hands and said: "Yes, for the moment that is so—unfortunately—but later it will change," etc. Well, we got away at last, Per and I, each with our parcel, and it was good to draw a breath of fresh air again.

Now here I am in the "new" hut-room. Francis is back from the hospital, where he

---

* The Segment's real name was Seidel.

had been for some time. He gave a splendid little talk on Edvard Storm* this evening after the lights were out and we had the usual survey of the situation at the fronts. In this hut the news editor is usually Colbjørn.

Every evening we have question time. One man puts twelve questions, which the others compete in answering. The attempts are in writing, and the questioner must know the right answers.

SUNDAY, DECEMBER 6, 1942 ■ Even before parade the "west wind" blew according to promise. What it blew was ghastly. Norwegian citizens, children, women and helpless old men are to be wiped out, are being sent to Poland to die. All Jewish men had been arrested earlier. Himmler† has decided that all Jews are to be wiped out before the end of 1942! Something within me cries out: This isn't true! It can't happen, not in this country, not in our Norway! And yet I sit here knowing that man can do it! He has begun, and he will go on. I can see no light anywhere. Only far, far off—and by glimpses—wild hopes shoot out of the thick darkness. Too late! Too late!

This is my birthday—after all. We had a little gathering in the hut. Erling, Odd, Per and Bjørn Oscar, besides those who live here. Kari's knot-cake plus a cup of real coffee made exceptional prison fare. Francis's speech left me quite sheepish and ashamed. I tried to thank him and all my friends. It was a festive board, spread with a white cloth (sheets) with a floral decoration of moss and cowberry-heath in the center, and Kari's cake on a big dish, and Robert's birthday cake on another dish, plus the cups, the massive well-known cups of fragrant, genuine coffee.‡ Besides that it ran to a little square of chocolate each (there were twenty of us) from the slab Kari sent me, and cigarettes which I had received as well. It was a birthday party long to be remembered. Thank you for today, Kari!

MONDAY, DECEMBER 7, 1942 ■ Mild, snowy. It's getting near Christmas, prison Christmas. I am now employed in making a jumping jack for Denzer's son, an exhilarating task, when one has four children of one's own at home who won't have even a greeting from their father. But Denzer is delighted, and carries on as though he were the model for the jumping jack. An idea I thought of using at first, but which I gave up. I shall keep it for next Christmas, and then neither Denzer, Jr., nor Denzer, Sr., will be pulling the string!

TUESDAY, DECEMBER 8, 1942 ■ Today seven officers were sent to Germany as prisoners of war. With them went a good-sized transport of prisoners. Fifty-four from

---

* Norwegian poet, 1749–1794.

† Heinrich Himmler (1900–1945). *Reichsführer* of the SS and head of the Gestapo, Himmler has been called the greatest mass murderer of all time and "the supreme technician of totalitarian police power." In his capacity as overseer of all concentration camps, Himmler was responsible for the deaths of between six and ten million Jews, POWs, political prisoners, gypsies, homosexuals, and others deemed undesirable by the SS. Here is how James McDonald, the League of Nations High Commissioner for Refugees (Jewish and Other) Coming from Germany (1933–1935), described the second most powerful man in Nazi Germany: "Himmler, at first glance, appeared like an experienced title searcher in the office of the Recorder of Deeds of a country county seat. . . . [B]ut those eyes of his; those beady, button eyes, cruel as he was cunning and cunning as he was cruel." Arrested by British forces, Himmler committed suicide on May 23, 1945, rather than stand trial as a war criminal. Allied authorities buried his body in an unmarked grave on the Lüneburg Heath, Germany.

‡ Robert Andersen was a camp cook.

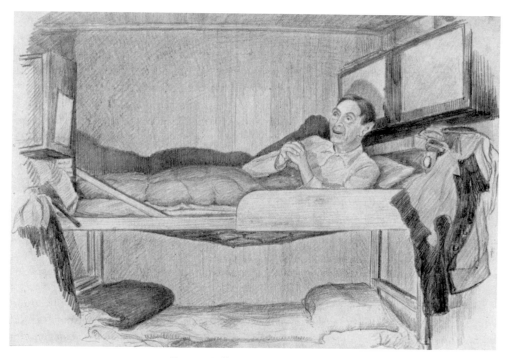

Francis Bull giving a night lecture.

here, forty-three of them from the "film gang," a gang which was arrested some months ago in connection with a performance in the People's House at Grünerløkka,* where a film of the Svolvær raid was shown.

A number of the prisoners had nothing at all to do with the performance. They simply happened to be near the hall and were picked up, too. One of them had been arrested three blocks from the People's House and had no knowledge of the show whatever. He didn't get a chance to explain. Another was taken because he had the ill luck to go to the lavatory—just at the moment when the arrests were taking place. Now they're all on their way to Germany.

Kunz has ordered a jumping-jack as well. So I shall have to do that too. Not that it matters. I suppose I'll be jumping-jack manufacturer for some time to come!

THURSDAY, DECEMBER 10, 1942 ■ Then came a thaw with dripping roofs and mist. The woods are greenish black against the snow, the mist is hanging in the spruce tops and rough mud-colored ice covers all the roads, paths and open spaces in the prison area. The work goes on as usual. But never have I seen the working tempo so low. If one takes a stroll round the different working places, one is quite aghast to see how people are loafing everywhere without disguise. Only when a green man comes along do they seize their tools and begin fiddling with some piece of work. It will end in disaster one fine day.

---

* The People's House is a community center for Norway's labor movement; Grünerløkka is a borough of the city of Oslo.

Inside the workshops work is going on, sometimes quite intensively. But if one looks closer, one will find that it's their own things people are busy with. Christmas presents for their children and wives at home. Knives, boxes, toys and all kinds of objects, which they contrive by some perilous means to send out. For my own part I feel there are much more important things to send, and don't believe I shall take any risks of that kind.

Kunz looked me up in the "office" today with orders to make yet another jumping jack—for the *Lagerkommandant*. Rather different from the one Denzer got, with no further specification.

FRIDAY, DECEMBER 11, 1942 ■ I've finished another jumping jack today, in record time. It's meant for the *Stormdrunk*, and is accordingly a sozzled brownie with an empty brandy bottle in one hand and ditto brandy glass in the other. The rest say I mustn't think of giving that to the Commandant; he'll notice the gibe. I am dead sure he won't. Kunz, who saw the jumping jack this morning, was wildly enthusiastic. *Prima! Prima!*

There was another big binge complete with shooting last night. The whole gang had been on the rampage most of the night, with the *Stormdrunk* at their head. Two of them turned out today with a black eye apiece. Moreover the *Stormdrunk's* secretary had been consoling herself with Claffy all night, and that so thoroughly that she spewed over his uniform, which had to be cleaned today.

SATURDAY, DECEMBER 12, 1942 ■ Thaw, thaw, brown slush and clay soup over the whole prison area, cheerless to behold. Work as usual; my jumping jack number three will soon be finished as well. Christmas is coming on, and people are electing Christmas committees in all the huts, ours too. I've become a member, and so we must set about arranging Christmas in the hut. Good Lord!

The news tonight wasn't specially remarkable. It's getting rather monotonous altogether these days. Tonight Francis reached *Love's Comedy.**

SUNDAY, DECEMBER 13, 1942 ■ Today a live goose has vanished. There are only three left of the four that cackled around the prison area. The probability is that one of the *Herrenvolk* helped himself to it, but of course they want to make out that a prisoner is the thief. In spite of the fact that it would be next to impossible to prepare this delicacy in a hut without being found out, of course it isn't inconceivable that a prisoner may really have taken it. Denzer has asked the personnel office to investigate on the q.t., with the assistance of their sense of smell!

Erling tells us that a whole host of Christmas parcels have come already. More than fourteen hundred, at least three of them for me, he said. I should think the checking and censoring will be very lenient. It isn't only the working tempo which is slack now at Grini. Everything is immensely slack and haphazard. That defective sot of a Commandant leaves his mark on everything to some extent. It's disgusting, but it can be exploited, and is. He and Kunz and Stange, the three worst, are all going home to Germany on Christmas leave,

---

* Another Ibsen play. Although published in 1863, it was savaged by the critics and was not produced until 1873 (successfully) in Oslo; it premiered on Broadway in 1908.

and we may have a pleasanter Christmas with those three well out of the way. I wish to God they were never coming back.

MONDAY, DECEMBER 14, 1942 ■ It was a harder blow than I care to confess when Nils [Ramm] left. He was released today. His whole face beamed, he couldn't straighten it, and everyone rejoiced with him. I was glad too, but when I had said good-bye and given him a message for Kari, I had to hurry out.*

I got the Christmas parcel from home this evening, and there was sadness in that too. "Happy Christmas, father dear!" Not many kilometers off sit Kari and the children, wishing me a happy Christmas—as though I were in America!† Siri had drawn enchanting little cards for every small parcel in the Christmas box, from Mother, from Marit, from Eigil, from Siri, and from Baby, and they sent me the best they have: chocolate, marzipan, sweets, cheese, sardines, goose liver, ham. Good God—why may not these children have their father home for Christmas!

I delivered the last two jumping jacks today. Kunz, the *Stormdrunk*, and Denzer were all present. As I said, the *Stormdrunk* didn't see my joke at all. Nor did Kunz. His brownie had a huge storeroom key in one hand and a gnawed bone in the other. All three in their enthusiasm did an absolute war dance. The result was that they undid the loops in all their jumping jacks. I got them back for repair.

Apparently no one was released today but Nils. So now there are five of us left in the court gang: Schiøtz, Henrik Huitfeldt,‡ Graff-Wang and the Odds. I have a presentiment that soon I shall be the sole survivor of that gang.

WEDNESDAY, DECEMBER 16, 1942 ■ This evening question time, news, Francis—who got to *Brand* and *Peer Gynt*. These evenings in the hut help one over a lot of difficulties and a lot of moping. We have always something to talk about, and blessedly little prison gossip in here, although some is unavoidable.

SUNDAY, DECEMBER 20, 1942 ■ Sunday! Sunday off! But the weather was dreary, and I've seldom worked more intensively from morning to night. But it was work for ourselves and our Christmas plans, so it went like play.

This morning forty-one are set free; it's believed there will be more tomorrow or the day after.

Many are sleeping uneasily tonight. The old immortal *Entlassungsfeber* is raging through the huts. There's only one cure for it: *Entlassung!* And that is in short supply. There's nothing like enough to go round. Moreover, it's too late for many to get home by Christmas, if they're set free. *I* can manage if I get out on the morning of Christmas Eve!

MONDAY, DECEMBER 21, 1942 ■ Rasmus got out today at last. That was a happy event, and he preened himself and shone like a sun when he said good-bye.

I've been toiling all day at my Christmas decorations and hope I shall be able to go on working at them in peace the next few days. Got a huge parcel from Ernst [Holmboe]

---

* Ramm was rearrested during the August 1943 roundup of officers and remained in prison until the war's end.
† Nansen had spent Christmas 1939 in America.
‡ Arrested the same day as Nansen, Huitfeldt was released ten days after this entry (December 24, 1942).

today with all kinds of grandeurs, food and painting things and Christmas ornaments. We rejoice like children over all the trifles we can hang on the Christmas tree, and out of that parcel tumbled stars, bells, little Norwegian flags and lots of other splendid things. Yes indeed, we'll have a fine Christmas tree and an uncommon Christmas.

TUESDAY, DECEMBER 22, 1942 ■ Rainy. Anything but Christmas weather. Slush, mist and heavy showers as the day went on. But what of it? Kari was here today with all our four children. We had a good ten minutes and the whole thing was unique.

Colbjørn and I are working like mad to get the Christmas display finished. We brought our work back to the hut this evening and stayed up until midnight. Francis went on about *Emperor and Galilean** as we worked, and Colbjørn gave us the latest news as he painted an escaping goose (the one that vanished). Now it's horribly late—so I must be pulling up. This was a lovely day!

WEDNESDAY, DECEMBER 23, 1942 ■ "Little Christmas Eve" brought nice weather. Sparkling sunshine, the first for ages, clear sky and frost. This is more like Christmas weather! Have been up to my neck in painting all day and looked neither right nor left.

It's past two; we've been painting and drawing in the hut again tonight. Francis went faithfully on with Ibsen, while Colbjørn and I worked and most of the others snored. Now we must get to bed, or we won't be fit for keeping Christmas tomorrow. About twenty must have got out today.

THURSDAY, DECEMBER 24, 1942 ■ *Christmas Eve!* A strange, but splendid Christmas Eve in its way. And while other Christmas Eves will be merged increasingly in one continuous image of children and candles round the unifying symbol and center of the Christmas fir, this Christmas Eve will always stand out—let us hope alone—in our memory.

And for a Christmas Eve in prison one must say it was magnificent. To be sure we created it ourselves, and thank God for that; not much was done on the other side to procure us any comfort, but that we had a chance to arrange everything, decorations, Christmas trees, Christmas table, songs, etc.—for that we owe the greens a tiny bit of acknowledgment.

There was work until one o'clock, but truth to tell the overwhelmingly greater part of it consisted in finishing off the decoration of the hut rooms and corridors. I think I can safely say that little else of value was done today. At one o'clock there was parade. A Christmas tree had been set up on a table facing the parade ground, with a lot of parcels. Those who hadn't had a parcel from home were being provided for. Ostentatiously of course, and with exhortations to the prisoners to understand and value this to the full. One by one "the poor" and those who lived so far away that nothing had reached them were called up to the tree, where they received their Christmas parcel under the auspices of Denzer himself, to his accompaniment of blessings mixed with hoarse outcries that things weren't going quick enough. It took an inhumanly long time. Spending a whole

---

* A lesser-known play by Henrik Ibsen; although the first edition of the play sold out upon publication in 1873, and Ibsen considered it his masterpiece, the first attempt to stage any part of the work in Norway did not occur until 1903.

hour on parade on such a day is no unmixed pleasure. Still it did come to an end, and the final polish of the huts began.

First of course we had had the Christmas regulations: what's allowed and what's not allowed. We are to have both tomorrow and the next day off. Well, that's grand. There is to be no reading of the Christmas gospel. This was to be a free national festival on a background of good-fellowship, and dogmatic songs, etc., of every kind were forbidden.

Yes, he said a *free* national festival, but the freedom doesn't go so far that one may read aloud from the Bible, as is the custom after all with the great majority of Norwegians.

At five o'clock there was to be a common dinner table for each hut, and Christmas porridge. It was rather behind time, but when it did arrive toward seven it was good, really good, and we got two big platefuls each, with sugar, cinnamon and a lump of butter.*
In our hut we all ate out in the lobby. It was very cozy and successful. The Christmas songs were sung, and there were moments that had a really thrilling effect. Francis made a splendid speech, built on the old fairy tale of Johannes Blessomen† and the giant who drove him home on Christmas Eve, to his native parish, Vågå, the heart of Norway. A cold and bitter journey, but, "You must put up with it, Blessomen!" said the giant. And he got there, home to the goal of his desires, the heart of Norway, where we all long to be, though we shall assuredly have bad times yet before reaching it.

After that the celebrations continued in every room, with another spread—tea and cakes and sweets and anything there was; and truly it was a good deal for a prison! I went and sang in the hospital, first to the whole "staff," then in a couple of wards. When I had finished there it was past ten, and Denzer had decided to call a halt. We went on in the hut until past two. It was a memorable "midnight concert" for a unique audience, which it was a treat to look at and sing to and be among.

Now all are snoring as usual. A thrilling Christmas Eve is at an end. Good night, my darling children, may you have had a snug and happy Christmas Eve out there at Polhøgda! And good night, my splendid Kari! Good night and merry Christmas.

(Henrik H[uitfeldt] was released this afternoon. So he'll just have got home in time for Christmas. Now there are only four of us court hostages left.)

FRIDAY, DECEMBER 25, 1942 ■ Christmas Day has passed in visits to the different huts. A stroll from one art exhibit to another. Everywhere there were amusing things to be seen—here and there something really original, and everywhere spirit, *joie de vivre*, and exuberance. Talents big and small had disported themselves in turn

---

* Nansen wasn't always so fond of porridge. His sister Liv observed that their father Fridtjof was a strong believer in the efficacy of plain food. "We [children] were heartily sick of the everlasting porridge that we had morning and evening. . . . [A]s soon as Father was out of the door with the newspapers and his letters, having had his breakfast," Liv wrote, "we rushed to the window and emptied our plates out of it." While Fridtjof was away in London as ambassador in 1906, his wife Eva wrote him that Odd had refused to eat the Polhøgda porridge. "Yesterday he yelled incessantly and said he would not have it, but then I came in," Eva wrote her husband, "and said that in that case I should have to write to Father, and surely he would not like Father to hear that he had become so fastidious. He at once controlled himself and took his spoon and ate it all up without a grumble. The boy certainly has character."

† A Norwegian folk tale, the story of Johannes Blessomen, who on Christmas Eve, anxious to return from Copenhagen to his home in Vågå, unknowingly accepts a ride with the giant troll, Jutulen, who also is traveling to Vågå, where he lives in a nearby cave. At one point in the journey Blessomen loses his mittens and complains, to which Jutulen replies that he "must put up with it." Jutulporten, the Troll's Gate, is a natural rock formation (and tourist attraction) in Vågå.

on big and little wall spaces, covering them with decorations of every kind, from trolls and brownies to winter landscapes, Grini subjects, and caricatures of fellow prisoners.* Altogether, the hutments were in party dress, and a sense of brightness met one everywhere.

Nor was it only the decking of the houses that produced that impression, but also in a high degree the living people themselves. The whole camp had taken on a new color, a cheerful radiance that must have been there all the time, but simply hasn't always been visible through the mist. And how they sang, those young men! In Hut 9 we found ourselves in a gang of young people who, under their conductor [Dagfinn] Rimestad of Stavanger,† sang better and more zestfully than any I remember hearing. In the afternoon Rimestad went from hut to hut with his singing mates and gave concerts.

I've really been so rejoiced today that I'm quite toned up, have recovered more of my old confidence and faith in Norway's young men, which I must confess had declined a bit after seeing a number of them stream in to fill the huts here. The hunt for food, food, the sport of dodging, and the gray, gray weekday has set its mark on them; but under their shirts, behind the weekday grayness, it would seem that all this exuberance was latent and only waiting to spring out in full bloom! I feel glad at heart, more cheerful than for a long, long time.

SATURDAY, DECEMBER 26, 1942 ■ Truth to tell, holidays in prison soon lose their charm. There's miserably little to do. I can't lie sleeping all day, and this morning I took refuge with [Lauritz] Sand up in the hospital for a couple of hours. He likes to chat, likes to be "received again" among the living. He is now decidedly in a fair way to get better.

It seems as if many people outside were counting on the possibility that the war may be decided this winter. I must confess that for my own part I feel a graver and graver doubt of it. I'm leaning rather to the dark view that after all the Germans will manage to keep going beyond all the dates that have been given them, indeed straight on to ruin, I'm afraid.

Well, perhaps it's this gray weather settling on one's mind. I must stop in time. In spite of Sunday we're to work tomorrow (thank God, say I) from eight till one.

SUNDAY, DECEMBER 27, 1942 ■ So we "worked" from eight till one. But the work which was carried out by these fifteen or sixteen hundred men in these five hours, I should think might have been done by a couple in the same time. Myself I didn't do a stroke.

Tonight Francis resumed his account of Ibsen. We're gradually slipping back into the old grooves, though the Christmas feeling still hangs about us. As long as the Christmas finery is hanging on the walls and the Christmas trees are standing on the tables and there's extra food in the cupboard, we'll hardly settle quite down.

---

* Per Krohg painted a frieze for Christmas; Siegfried Fehmer, a Gestapo officer on an inspection visit to Grini, stopped by Krohg's work and observed, "It is remarkable what a primitive nation can produce under German control." This soon became a byword "and when prisoners were digging ditches in slow tempo or on some other work, they would say to each other, 'It is wonderful what a primitive nation can produce when under German control.'"

† Later sent to Sachsenhausen for the duration of the war.

MONDAY, DECEMBER 28, 1942 ■ This is lamentable Christmas weather, but then it's no bad match for our circumstances. To be sure we have long spells of forgetting, but when we do occasionally pull up and consider how we spend our time here, month after month—well then, it's not just lamentable, it's tragic.

1943

SATURDAY, JANUARY 23, 1943 ■ Odd [Wang] has gone, and I may as well confess that I'm rather low. Not that I grudge Odd his release, God knows I don't, but because there's getting to be such an emptiness round me as time goes on. Odd and I have kept faithful company for more than a year now. We started together in next-door cells in the Lillehammer county jail, and we've stuck together through thick and thin the whole time. And now I'm left alone. Both he and Nils [Ramm], two of the surest and best, have gone away.

MONDAY, JANUARY 25, 1943 ■ It's plain that the Germans have been taken down a good few pegs recently. Thank God this hasn't led to brutality or such-like excesses; on the contrary. The Christmas and New Year idyll has continued, on the whole unbroken, and the devils' return from leave has made no great change. They are tame.

It's said that the other day the *Stormdrunk* reacted to the bulletins from the fronts by taking his radio and throwing it on the floor in a rage. "Take it down to the police mess," he had said. "I've no use for it!" Probably the bottle was at hand, and he resorted to that, instead. But neither have there actually been any exploits in his cups of late. Since he says nothing about all the dodging and so forth that he must see in the camp, one has rather the impression that the fact is he can't be bothered. He's grown more and more apathetic; his malice has lost its energy and initiative; he's gone pale green and is steadily fading.

TUESDAY, JANUARY 26, 1943 ■ The news is splendid. But now the very "best news" is beginning to be in the papers. There is now a balder and balder mention of defeat and ruin. Only they don't call it defeat and ruin. They call it heroism and total war.*

WEDNESDAY, JANUARY 27, 1943 ■ A number of *[Einzel]haft* candidates are before a court-martial every day. Nobody knows how it's going. It's the Kristiansand affair.† It's sinister that this case should have come up for judgment already, over the head of quite a lot of others. Do they want some more death sentences as a warning?

THURSDAY, JANUARY 28, 1943 ■ Ten death sentences have been pronounced in the Kristiansand case. Three men were acquitted, that is, they got sentences of four, eight and ten years. We were sitting reading the "west wind" in the bookbinding shop this morning,

---

* Sigrid Undset once observed, "Ever since Hitler took Czechoslovakia it had become part of youthful jargon to ask, when one doubted something that was said: 'Is it true or is it German?'"
† See February 16, 1943.

Francis, Per, Lindbäck-Larsen,* Nic. Stang† and I, when the message came. There was a faint, almost inaudible groan, and then a dead silence. I don't think any more was said, we just sat like that.

SATURDAY, JANUARY 30, 1943 ■ In the *Bauleitung* today two men were asked by Jantzen if they listened in there. They denied it, but he said he knew they had, adding that if caught they would be shot. Stange burst into the electrical workshop in the smithy unannounced, asking "Where's the radio?" By pure chance they had none there just at the moment (they usually have radios for repairs) and the surprise didn't come off. But it may be repeated and may be a good deal more successful another time. On these grounds there will be a few days' break in the news service.

Tonight we had a discussion in our room on the aims and causes of the war. I didn't join in, I don't know why, I had meant to, but just sat listening. And I was terribly disappointed. There was practically no one but Francis who asserted the idea as a leading force. All the rest wanted to make out that economic forces only lay behind everything. To be sure our young materialists made a sudden change of front where we Norwegians were concerned. *We* were fighting for disinterested reasons as well, for our freedom, against tyranny, while the English, Americans and Russians were fighting on other and inferior grounds!

MONDAY, FEBRUARY 1, 1943 ■ The Commandant and Denzer were at evening roll call. They rampaged a bit over caps off and on, couldn't get it to go quick enough and intimated that we should be left to practice that athletic exercise for two hours, till we had mastered it. This time we got off with a quarter of an hour.

Afterwards Denzer came to the fore and informed us that he had seen several with their jackets unbuttoned and others outside the working places with no jacket. Henceforth everyone apprehended in crimes of that nature would be severely punished. It was no excuse that the jacket was too tight. That was the result of wearing a scarf, and it's forbidden to wear a scarf. Then there was punishment drill for twenty-two men from Kristiansand, and a lecture for all the hut leaders—if anything went on in their respective huts which wasn't allowed, and they didn't report it on the spot, they would be rigorously punished.

It's gradually becoming a vulnerable position to be hut leader. For in every hut, in every room, at every minute of the day unlawful things are going on. People are reading, smoking, dodging, giving lectures, talking about the war, playing cards or chess, indeed, altogether it would be almost quicker to mention the things we do that really are allowed. Denzer also said that he knew as much as they did about everything that went on, for, said

---

* Odd Lindbäck-Larsen (1897–1975), a military officer and war historian. During the German invasion Lindbäck-Larsen was chief of staff to General Carl Gustav Fleisher, commander of the 6th Division. When Fleischer went into exile with the Norwegian government, Lindbäck-Larsen became military chief of staff to Governor Hans Gabrielsen. Lindbäck-Larsen was referred to as Terboven's personal prisoner since he was arrested shortly after a contentious interview with Terboven. He was incarcerated for the duration of the war. After the war Lindbäck-Larsen remained in the military and published a number of military history books, including one on the 1940 northern campaign in Norway.

† Nicolay Stang (1908–1971) was an art historian, cultural writer, and translator whose specialties included antiquity, the Renaissance, and Edvard Munch. He was released April 21, 1943.

he, I have a man in every hut. I almost believe that's true, but then we know these friends of his all right, and we keep an eye on them.

During parade today, Jantzen turned up with a young gentleman in uniform. It proved to be the uniform of the Norwegian legion,* and the young gentleman was Lorang—an architect. He was my assistant at one time, a useless, lazy scamp. The last time I saw him was in Trondheim, where he was working for the Germans. He looked a nasty piece of work even then.

TUESDAY, FEBRUARY 2, 1943 ■ Just for one moment this morning the sun was in the act of breaking through, but then the mist closed in again. The slush is liquid, and it's the same dismal story. Those who had punishment drill yesterday had to wallow in the slush on the square, up again and down again that instant, interminably. Of course, they were wet to the skin all over. This it seems is why they were being punished: One man had been down to the *Vermittlung* on some errand. There he met Denzer's typing-wench. She got a bit "oncoming" in different ways, for one thing picked up a German helmet which was lying there and put it on the chap's head, with the remark that someday *he* would be wearing one like that. "No," said he, "for the English are coming on the 27th."

Just then Denzer arrived, and demanded a repetition of this last remark, and an explanation. The idiot said he'd heard it in [Hut] 7. The scapegoat said he'd heard it from the Kristiansanders, who had just arrived. They stuck together, no one would give anyone away, so they were all punishment-drilled.

It's plain that things are getting more rigorous in every sphere. We've been well off too long now.

WEDNESDAY, FEBRUARY 3, 1943 ■ Stalingrad has fallen, say the Germans, which means it held. The announcement came over the German radio and Chopin's funeral march was played after a three minutes' silence. They're trying to remold their defeat into a kind of impressive memorial ceremony. Let them! Stalingrad held.†

My former assistant Lorang was round "inspecting" today. He's to be Gebecke's deputy in his absence. (Now *he's* got some venereal disease.) Colbjørn was in the architect's office when Lorang came in. Lorang said: "Is there a table of weights for iron bar here?"

Colbjørn: *Nein*
Lorang: Where can I get hold of one?
Colbjørn: *Das weiss ich nicht.* [I don't know.]
Lorang—approaching: Don't you recognize me?
Colbjørn: *Nein.*

---

* The Norwegian Legion was a fighting unit consisting of Norwegian volunteers organized under the Waffen-SS. Although initially assured that they would form a separate unit with Norwegian officers and operate in Finland, the legion was controlled by German officers and saw action principally in the siege of Leningrad. For these and other reasons the number of volunteers, always low, soon declined, and the unit was disbanded in 1943. After the war the survivors were tried as collaborators and received prison sentences, typically of less than three years.
† The Battle of Stalingrad, described as "perhaps the most savage struggle of the war," began on August 23, 1942, and ended with the surrender of German troops on February 2, 1943. Approximately 150,000 Germans were killed in the battle and more than 100,000 taken prisoner, of whom only 6,000 or so survived their captivity as POWs. While Soviet casualties were even higher (some estimate between half a million and one million), the battle represented a catastrophic defeat for the Germans and the turn of the tide on the Eastern Front.

Lorang: Think!

Colbjørn: *Ja-ich kenne Sie nicht.* [Yes, I don't know.]

Lorang: We went to the university together!

Colbjørn: *Meinen Sie die Hochschule in Drontheim?* [You mean the university in Trondheim?]

Lorang: Yes—in 1937.

Colbjørn: *Nein—in meiner Zeit, so weit ich erinnere, war kein Deutscher in der Hochschule.* [No, in my time, as far as I remember, there were no Germans at the University.]

Colbjørn and Lorang were classmates.

He came to me too. But he didn't say *du* to me. He asked what I had done wrong. I said I had done nothing wrong. Why was I in here? He would have to inquire of those who knew. Well, but there must be some reason. "I am a hostage." "For whom?" "Don't ask me!" "Have any of your family gone to England?" "Not to my knowledge!" He gave it up and went. Herr Lorang will have a pleasant stay at Grini, to all appearances.

The *Lagerkommandant* looked in today and ordered three boxes. Good Lord! And I've three others in hand!

THURSDAY, FEBRUARY 4, 1943 ■ Went round to Denzer today; he was in an extra good humor, terribly pleased with himself, and holding forth about it as usual. *En passant* [in passing] he remarked that his brother-in-law had been killed at Stalingrad, and described to me what it had been like there. No prisoners were taken, he assured me, and his brother-in-law had undoubtedly been shot. The struggle was hopeless; battles of encirclement always were, he explained. Hopeless! And then a lot about the heroism of the Germans, of course, and about his young brother-in-law, whose heroism he cashed in on a hundred percent, as though it were himself who had fought to the death at Stalingrad. "It's all madness!" said I. "Yes, it is madness," he admitted. So we agreed about that. When I continued that if things went on much longer in the present style everything would be destroyed, I'm blessed if he didn't agree with *that*. Such was "total" war, he explained. And then seemed terribly pleased about that, too.

Per, Francis and I went to a Lucullian* supper with [Sven] Oftedal, Sejersted [Bødtker] and Leif [Poulsson] this evening, prepared and served by our excellent friend Pinkie [Ragnar] Andersen. Caramel pudding, meat pudding, meatballs and potatoes. To be sure we had to break up in a hurry, on a rumor that the Commandant was on the go in camp, harrying [Hut] number 6. We were in the wrong place, so we had to see about getting "home." As we were hastening homewards in the dark, 6 fell in for punishment drill. They had done nothing wrong, but 6 is where the Jews live, and the Commandant was drunk and in need of entertainment.

Sleep well!

WEDNESDAY, FEBRUARY 10, 1943 ■ It's snowing. Skiing conditions—white forest—white uplands—solitary trails—my God.

Tomorrow Denzer is going off on leave.

---

*   Lucius Lucinius Lucullus (c. 117 BC—57/56 BC). A Roman general and politician who amassed great wealth from his conquests; his banquets were so lavish that his name has come to be associated with luxurious and gourmet feasts.

Kunz has now turned mild as a lamb with me. Perhaps because he's ordered a box from me as well. Why, today he suddenly gave me half a packet of crispbread and some beef-tea cubes. I couldn't believe my eyes.

THURSDAY, FEBRUARY 11, 1943 ■ Denzer went off this morning. Francis [Bull] was examined, for the first time since June 1941. That may well indicate release at last one of these days. He was questioned on all kinds of queer things—from his profession to what he thought of the NS and whether he was related to Hambro.* He answered admirably. It will be sad at Grini without Francis, but if anyone deserves release he does in all conscience.

Eleven condemned men have been pardoned today! The ten from Kristiansand and [Gustav] Neråsen.† They're to be sent to Germany with the forthcoming transport. How that changes the gloomy transport into sheer salvation, the gayest pleasure-trip!

FRIDAY, FEBRUARY 12, 1943 ■ It's moonlit this evening. A sparkling, waxing half-moon—shedding silver across the snowfields.

Last night saw one of the worst outrages in the history of Grini. It was the Jews who were put through it. On parade this morning we could see at once what had happened. The whole square was covered with bloodstains on the snow. Many of the Jews had been crippled. Two broken ribs, a broken shin-bone and a cracked skull are the goodly "result" of the Commandant's and drinking buddy Fiedler's‡ orgy last night.

About three o'clock they reached the stage of wanting amusement. Stange, who most probably was one of the party, was sent to fetch the Jews to the parade ground. He executed this "commission" in a decent way, it's said, and in general took no part in what happened. To begin with they had ordinary drill, and in addition they were ordered to sing and to do all kinds of idiotic things. But by degrees the sadistic appetite awakened, the first blows began to fall. It got worse and worse. Fiedler went for them in complete frenzy. An old Jew of sixty-five was knocked down twelve times in succession. Blood was streaming from his nose, ears and eyes. The "ecstasy" lasted two and a half hours; then at last the poor Jews were allowed to go back to the hut and dress their wounds.

[Knut] Gard, who saw the whole thing from the hospital, said Fiedler's berserk rage was so appalling that at last the Commandant himself reacted and put a stop to it. Today there were more who reacted; even Kunz. Oftedal had been discussing it with him, and Kunz had said that to be sure he got drunk sometimes, but he didn't get like that.

SATURDAY, FEBRUARY 13, 1943 ■ The men for Germany were told that they were leaving at eight o'clock tomorrow morning. They were in mufti tonight and are getting ready. Not a dismal face, all full of optimism.

I'm carving now in the evenings on a great "work." Good night, Kari; it's for you!

---

* C. J. Hambro (1885–1964) was a journalist, editor, author, and Conservative Party politician and is credited with organizing the escape of King Haakon VII, the royal family, key government ministers, and Norway's gold reserves from Oslo following the German invasion in April 1940. President of the Storting (1926–1934; 1935–1945). After the war, Hambro was a delegate to the UN General Assembly (1945–1956) and a member of the Norwegian Nobel Committee (1940–1963). Despite being a practicing Christian, Hambro's family roots were Jewish, and he was particularly vilified by Quisling, who referred to him as "the half-Jew." Hambro and Francis Bull were first cousins.
† See March 1, 1943, below.
‡ Fiedler was married to Commandant Zeidler's secretary.

MONDAY, FEBRUARY 15, 1943 ■ Voroshilovgrad* and Rostov† have fallen!

Today the men for Germany did really get off. They left in five or six big buses, after a tedious parade and going-over on the square this morning. They had the day's news to take away, and could have asked no better provision for the journey. The last we heard of them, they were singing the Grini-march till it resounded.

Otherwise the camp has been quiet. I called on the Segment and got cigarettes. I had to stay with him for an hour, listening to his "amorous" adventure with a Norwegian lady in Berlin. Obviously a common tart who dished up a highly common bedroom-scene in a squalid Berlin hotel. However, in his eyes it was truly a marvelous adventure.

In general it's not till evening that I wake to full consciousness. Then I begin to live. It's just distressing going to bed every night. Francis ended his lecture long ago. Per has gone to bed as well, and the whole organ voluntary is in full swing. It's nearly two o'clock. Also I must write a tiny letter, therefore goodnight.

TUESDAY, FEBRUARY 16, 1943 ■ Brilliant sunshine—west winds and mild. The newspapers bring the most superb admissions of yesterday's news. They lay stress on the enormous advantages involved in the evacuation of Rostov and Voroshilovgrad, which has taken place "according to plan." The mirth when the German communiqués are read aloud is now irrepressible.

New prisoners are streaming in here every day. We must have already made up the number that went to Germany. The prisoners are chiefly from Kristiansand and vicinity. They've got hold of the fringes of a big military organization.‡ But I should think that's as far as they ever will get. What comes in nowadays is good quality.

WEDNESDAY, FEBRUARY 17, 1943 ■ Kharkov has fallen! *Kharkov has fallen! Kharkov has fallen!*§ That's the rhythm of today, its pulse-beat since early morning, when the news spread through the camp. "Hand on your heart—don't tell anyone!"—to begin with; but the news was too big, it couldn't be tucked away, the rejoicing had to find a vent and by degrees the whole camp was dancing to that rhythm: Kharkov has fallen! *Kharkov has fallen! Kharkov has fallen!* The consequences of this event may be enormous. Our "military correspondent" L[indbäck] L[arsen] holds that it is unquestionably the most important event of the war so far. Now practically anything may happen, in his view. The

---

* Now known as Luhansk, a city of approximately 500,000 in southeastern Ukraine, the city was known as Voroshilovgrad from 1935 to 1958 and from 1970 to 1990, when it finally reverted back to its original name.

† Rostov-on-Don, Russia's tenth largest city (population approximately one million) on the Don River near the Sea of Azov. As a railway junction and river port, Rostov was considered strategically important to the Nazis. It was occupied twice by German armies, the second time ending on February 14, 1943.

‡ In early 1943 the Gestapo conducted an extensive roundup of Resistance members in south Norway, arresting four to six hundred men within a few days. One Resistance leader observed, "Milorg [the armed Resistance organization] on the south coast completely shattered. . . . The collapse, and the accompanying arrests, escapes, torture and reprisals, have put fear into people." Many who were rounded up were later executed or died in concentration camps.

§ The third battle of Kharkov began with an attack by Soviet forces, known as Operation Star, in January 1943, with the aim of recapturing lands lost to the Germans during the summer of 1942. Soviet forces captured the city on February 16, 1943. On February 20, however, the Germans launched a counteroffensive, described as "the last offensive operational success the Germans could claim on the Eastern Front," and, despite being heavily outnumbered, reached Kharkov on March 12; the city fell days later following intense fighting. Kharkov, "the most fought-over city in the Soviet Union," was not liberated for good by Soviet forces until August 23, 1943.

golden thoughts of a finish as early as the spring (some even say this winter) are coming back with renewed strength.

THURSDAY, FEBRUARY 18, 1943 ■ A list for a fresh transport to Germany has arrived. Oftedal's name is on it. There are 129 altogether. It's not announced yet, but Bjørn Oscar [Andersen] ran his eye through it before passing it on. His own name wasn't there, nor mine. I wonder however if it won't end in the whole crowd of us going to Germany. I'm beginning to look the possibility in the face for my part, and to that extent am fully prepared.

SATURDAY, FEBRUARY 20, 1943 ■ The sunny weather keeps on, glittering and sparkling, and the roofs dripping and the spring longings wakening. Also it was Saturday today, and even in prison, Saturday is Saturday. Sunday comes next, therefore the evening is praise-God eve.

It's now forbidden to go for walks along the fence. We have really no other tracks to walk in, therefore Sunday's outdoor life ruined as far as that goes, but Sunday is Sunday too—after all. Wherever the Germans see that the prisoners have found something which may be nice for them, at once there comes a ban on that very thing. Regular as amen in church.

Bjørn Oscar had a birthday today, and Colbjørn and I went to the "party." He has unquenchable spirits, Bjørn Oscar, and is now specially on top of the world, since he wasn't on the list for Germany this time either. He thinks he'll be released soon.* Well, God knows! I suppose finally I shall be left alone, of the old lot. But there are still a number of us, anyhow.

SUNDAY, FEBRUARY 21, 1943 ■ There are gloomy prospects unrolling at home now. The labor mobilization is to be launched tomorrow, Monday, with speeches by Terboven and Quisling at Klingenberg.† They say it's to comprise ninety thousand men for Germany.

It turns out that the ten condemned men hadn't been pardoned yet after all. Eight of them were pardoned at a "party" at Terboven's on Thursday. About the last two there are doubts, but there is still hope. They were leaders and received a double death sentence. They're all here still.

TUESDAY, FEBRUARY 23, 1943 ■ Yesterday I shirked and for the first time since God knows how long went to bed with the others. Everyone was surprised: I couldn't be well. Nor was I. But I don't know quite what was wrong. For Kari was here yesterday— and we had a splendid meeting. She had got permission to visit me twice a month. That

---

* Bjørn Oscar was not released until December 20, 1943.

† The disaster at Stalingrad had awakened Germany to the true seriousness of the war, and Hitler demanded that all available resources be mobilized. Accordingly, on February 18, 1943, Goebbels gave his famous "total war" speech. Klingenberg was a cinema in Oslo. Quisling announced a new law: all males between the ages of eighteen and fifty-five and all females between twenty-one and forty were required to register for a National Labor Service. Anyone failing to register was subject to loss of the all-important ration cards. The possibility of forced labor induced many young Norwegians to go into hiding for a time or escape to Sweden.

was grand; only fourteen days, then, till the next time. And fourteen days usually go like smoke. Perhaps they'll begin going slower now for that reason?

But it's two o'clock. Robert [Andersen] gave a lecture tonight, on Beethoven. Per and I were carving as usual. Afterwards Per, Francis and I had our usual midnight snack and chat. We have our little traditions, and our life is pleasant—and uncommon. If only it hadn't been in prison, it would have been downright grand.

WEDNESDAY, FEBRUARY 24, 1943 ■ Mild weather and misery. Last night the Jews were given notice to parade in mufti at eight o'clock this morning. They went off later in the morning. No doubt for Poland. It was a melancholy band. Dr. Becker's face shone out among them. A splendid fellow. "Well, good-bye, Nansen; thanks for everything and au revoir!" No doubt he had his suspicions of what awaited him, but he had evidently made up his mind not to show it. Levin's good-bye was more somber, but he smiled, too.* The others were in a worse state. It hurt to see them going off.

FRIDAY, FEBRUARY 26, 1943 ■ This morning the new transport for Germany was called up. There were a lot of them—about 130—and it took a long time. But there was a beautiful sunrise, and time, of course, we have plenty of.

Erling Steen was released today! That was a great event. His feelings I shall not try to describe. We made the parting brief and painless. So he's gone too, but he deserved it after his faithful and able work here for a year and a half. It's a great loss for Grini that he should be leaving.

Read a letter one of the condemned men has written and sent out to his Solveig. He was a Spanish volunteer in his day.† The letter was magnificent. He is sure she'll take the news of the sentence proudly and calmly. This iron time has its marvelous charm, he writes. Sees a beauty in the fact that he's to die now, and knows that she will also. *Only for love's sake,*‡ he ends the letter, and signs with "Ola-boy," after praising the star that brought her to him on his return from Spain. It was no long-lasting paradise his star prepared for him here on earth, but assuredly rich and bright.

SATURDAY, FEBRUARY 27, 1943 ■ In the morning before we went on parade, our whole hut gathered for a little ceremony out in the lobby. We wanted to take leave

---

* A total of 158 Norwegian Jews (68 men and 90 women and children) were deported aboard the *SS Gotenland*. Of this group 130 were gassed immediately upon arrival in Auschwitz in early March; only six ultimately survived. Both Dr. Leonard Levin and Dr. Wulff Becker perished. The youngest of nine children, Dr. Levin had only recently started his medical practice. One of his older brothers, Marcus Levin, was a friend of Nansen's and worked with him on refugee matters during and after the war. Following the arrest of Leonard Levin and another brother, Sigurd (who also died in Auschwitz), Marcus realized the gravity of the situation and began to make plans for escape; he was able to slip into Sweden (hidden for much of the journey in an armoire) in early November 1942. The Levin family's experience is related in "*We Are Going to Pick Potatoes*" written by Marcus's daughter (and Leonard's niece) Irene Levin Berman. Alerted to the pending roundup of Jews, Berman, who was four years old at the time, her mother, and brother all escaped into Sweden on November 25, 1942, the day prior to the roundup. Berman emigrated to the United States in 1961.

† A small number of Norwegians were among the approximately thirty-five thousand military volunteers from approximately fifty nations who fought in the International Brigades against the Fascists and for the Republicans during the Spanish Civil War (1936–1939).

‡ These words were in English in the original Norwegian text. Probably inspired by Elizabeth Barrett Browning's *Sonnets from the Portuguese*, Sonnet 14: "If thou must love me, let it be for nought / Except for love's sake only. . . . [L]ove me for love's sake, that evermore / Thou may'st love on, through love's eternity."

of the men from our hut who were going south. The hut leader, [Rolf] Bloch Hansen,*
made a short speech, wishing them a good journey, as good a stay as possible and heartily
welcome back to a free Norway. Then we all joined in the national anthem. Old [Sigurd]
Hellik[sen]† replied on behalf of those who were leaving, and concluded with three times
three for a free Norway. Simple enough, almost banal, but in our position and state of
mind anything but banal. The old threadbare forms have acquired a new content. The
hurrahs were not empty, insipid outbursts of rejoicing. There was quite as much pain in
them. Indeed it almost hurt to join in the shouting.

About five o'clock I was told to come at once to the main building. *Regierungsrat*
[government-counselor] Reinhardt of the Terrace wanted to speak with me. Per and a
couple of others were also summoned.

I was taken first. Reinhardt, a young gentleman in mufti with a face as though cut in
marble, from which a snake's eye darted out its sting through thick lenses, offered me a
cigarette and asked if I knew why I was in prison. I said I knew I was a court hostage. Did
I know why these hostages had been taken? I said I understood that it was on account
of the English raid on Måløy a year ago. He nodded and seemed well pleased with these
answers.

Then suddenly he looked straight at me and asked: "What is your attitude toward
communism?" I explained that I had made a statement on it in a former examination, and
repeated what I had said then: that I have always regarded communism as an idealistic
movement, but that I took exception to the methods of violence which were used to
introduce it in Russia; and that I was an opponent of terror and violence and therefore of
dictatorship in every form.

The "examination" was a long one, and developed partly into a heated argument. For
close on two hours we discussed practically everything that has happened in this war and
before it: The encroachments on Czechoslovakia and Poland, the proceedings in the North
and in the other occupied countries, and not the least the persecution of the Jews. Of
course I couldn't help speaking my mind about it all. No matter for the chances of release.
There are certain things one *can't* choke back. Besides he was a pretty smart, cunning
fellow, who put his questions so infamously that silence would have been tantamount to
admissions, which I wouldn't make at any price.

At length I found myself on the redoubt of humanism, which I defended with teeth
and claws. But he despised humanism and its ideas—more I think than anything else.
In his eyes they were diseased and poor-spirited and at times they put him in such a rage
that he seized his hat and announced that he had no further interest in the conversation.
But he kept on just the same. He depicted the atrocities of the Communists and said that
if ten men were shot here in Norway we flared up in horror, but if a hundred thousand
were murdered in Russia we said nothing. And yet, he said, all who were shot in Norway
had been condemned for crimes proved against them. I objected that the ten who were
shot in Trondheim had not been condemned for any crime. He asserted that they were
condemned for military activity. To such an assertion there is no reply.

I said finally that it was difficult to understand the friendly purposes of the Germans
in Norway, for me who had now been kept in prison over a year without trial, especially as

---

* Released June 11, 1943.
† Helliksen, who was sixty-two at the time, survived the remainder of the war in Sachsenhausen.

I had seen and experienced how Norwegians were treated in prison. He would discuss that further with me, he said; and then the interview was over. What exactly was the point of it I can't quite make out. But it may well have been to clear up my attitude to Nazism. If so I'm afraid my profit was meager. At any rate he concluded by saying that I must put up with being regarded as a Communist.

SUNDAY, FEBRUARY 28, 1943 ■ Now Francis has started wood carving too, and a couple more in our room, so we have an absolute wood carver's shop here in the evenings. Francis is priceless when absorbed in this work. Per has done a drawing for him. A nimble Pegasus in a flowery meadow, and a beautiful slender muse with gothic wings. Francis appears enthralled and sunk in his task. All the same he gave a lecture on Bjørnson's work, and now he's lying just in front of me, with a face of pious resignation and his mouth open, sleeping like a log. I am sneezing and coughing and blowing my nose. There's a sheer gale blowing through the room. I must go to bed. Good night!

MONDAY, MARCH 1, 1943 ■ About five this morning the fifteen condemned men were called for and driven away. Everyone realized what it meant when the news spread at morning roll call. Silence fell on the whole square. It was even worse when we heard that the *Lagerkommandant* had gone up to the condemned men the night before and said things so monstrous in their ruffianism that it's almost incredible human beings can sink so low. He had informed them that next morning they were to be shot, and afterwards their dead bodies would be thrown to the winds. He had scoffed at and abused them. Probably he was drunk. It was apparently Ottar Lie who answered:

"Our mission is at an end—we've done our bit—we're ready to die. What happens to our dead bodies is of no interest to us."*

I read the letter one of them wrote to his wife and his two children on toilet paper the night before he was shot. He is sorry, and feels it hard that he may not see her and the children just once more, clasp her in his arms and thank her for all she had been to him, but he submits proudly and calmly to his fate and takes a proud, fond farewell.

He was a Communist. So were all those fifteen. The conflict in which we all stood together may not have been quite the same to them as to many of us. Their aims may not have been the same. But they gave their lives for them. They will stand as shining exemplars among the many other heroes who showed us the way.

[Gustav] Neråsen was one of the fifteen.† Neråsen whose pardon we were happy about.

TUESDAY, MARCH 2, 1943 ■ I forgot to say that we've had all the big skiers out here. The whole Ruud family and the other big jumpers arrived one day last week.‡ They had apparently got up an "all-Norway run," and had a thousand spectators and a hundred

---

* Ottar Lie was executed at Trandum Forest on March 1, 1943, four days shy of his fifty-seventh birthday.

† According to Myrtle Wright, "Neråsen [] had taken home a gun left by the English. After having it on exhibition in his sitting-room he had, unfortunately for him, hidden it in his barn. He was arrested and paid for it with his life." He was forty-seven. Other accounts put the number executed at seventeen, not fifteen.

‡ One of the first efforts in the attempted Nazification of the country was the formation of a Norwegian Sports Association controlled by the Nazis with compulsory membership. Rather than comply, most Norwegians simply boycotted organized sports (as participants and spectators) for the duration of the war. Henceforth sanctioned sporting events included only NS/Nazi types, and few spectators. The Ruud brothers were arrested for engaging in an unsanctioned

taking part. The majority of those taking part were arrested. Most of them seem to be here. It's a fine accession.

FRIDAY, MARCH 5, 1943 ■ At last a few clouds in the sky. It actually has a soothing effect not to be dazzled by the sunrise at morning roll call. But the sun did come out later in the day. And at dinnertime there came word of a visit. And if it wasn't Kari—and Marit. All was well. Marit looked very fit, but I noticed that she's almost grown a bit shy of me, and it went through me like a stab. Have I been away *so* long already? It was only for an instant I had that idea, but long enough to fix the impression—and the idea. May it be wildly idiotic. I can't stand it for my children to drift away.

SATURDAY, MARCH 6, 1943 ■ I've been designing a house for a young fellow from Sandnes. He was well pleased with the sketches I made, but thought the house was rather too big. There's no way of telling whether people here are poor or rich, and it may also be hard to judge what social class they belong to—especially when they talk dialect, and all of course being dressed alike, equally in rags, or equally stained, patched and shabby.

As we sat here putting off the time after dinner—all at once we heard the danger signal "Commandant in the offing!" I for my part vanished through the window, made for the office and began carving at those boxes of his. A moment later there he was. It was the boxes he wanted to have a look at. He said I shouldn't be allowed to leave till I had done the third box as well. I said I hadn't been thinking of it. Then he said I was to be released. I asked if that was true. He said he had been told so. Damnation. Now that trouble's starting again. There's no escape: I can't help occupying my mind with it—can't get rid of it any longer. I dread it—almost more than I rejoice. But when I think it really may be possible that I'm to go home—home!! Just think if that were true! Think! Think!

The news was excellent—but still with no essential points. There has been sabotage in Vemork.* The heavy-water works are destroyed. Four Norwegian-speaking men in English uniform got away. The Knaben molybdenum mines bombed to pieces the other day.† Yes,

---

ski event. According to one Resistance member, the regime's efforts to Nazify the nation's sports organizations "proved to be one of the biggest miscalculations which Quisling and his men made during the whole of the war."

The Ruud brothers, Sigmund (1907–1994), Birger (1911–1998), and Asbjørn (1919–1989), dominated international ski jumping in the 1930s. Birger won the gold medal in the 1932 and 1936 Olympics and a silver medal in 1948, as well as three world championships (1931, 1935, 1937). Sigmund won a silver medal at the 1928 Olympics as well as the 1929 world championship. Asbjørn won the world championship in 1938. All three brothers were awarded the Holmenkollen Medal, Norway's highest skiing award. Sigmund was released from Grini on March 27, 1943, Asbjørn on November 3, 1943, and Birger on February 25, 1944.

* The Vemork hydroelectric plant generated heavy water (deuterium oxide) as a byproduct of fertilizer manufacturing; heavy water can be used in the production of nuclear materials, including weapons. On February 27–28, 1943, ten Special Operations Executive (SOE)–trained Norwegian commandos broke into the heavily guarded complex, destroyed all existing heavy water stocks, and escaped. There were no casualties. A three-thousand-man search by the Germans failed to catch any of the saboteurs even though five of them skied 250 miles in full uniform to Sweden. The SOE later considered Operation Gunnerside, the code name for the attack, the most successful act of sabotage in all of the war, and the German military commander in Norway, General von Falkenhorst, called it "the finest coup I have seen in this war." One of the commandos, Knut Haugland, later accompanied Thor Heyerdahl (whom he met while training in England) on Heyerdahl's famous Kon-Tiki expedition.

† Molybdenum is used to harden steel and is thus used extensively in armaments manufacture, machine tools, and crankshafts. Opened in 1885, the mines in Knaben, forty miles east of Stavanger, were once the largest producers of molybdenum in the world; by 1940 they were the only such mines still operating in Europe. The mines were attacked by Allied bombers twice, on March 3, 1943, and again on November 16, 1943. Molybdenum mining ceased in 1973; the area is now attractive primarily to outdoor enthusiasts.

there are a few things going on—that one must admit. Those who have been made liable for compulsory labor service are to send in their names by the 11th of this month. All are providing themselves with ten forms and filling them up with false, fictitious names. Result: chaos.

SUNDAY, MARCH 7, 1943 ■ Sunday—rest—mud and sunlight. Nothing has happened. Per and I have been carving busily all day. My work of art is advancing, is now really beginning to take shape, but as usual the confounded scale is getting me down. It's utterly too small, and I've squeezed too much into a small surface—so that it becomes a microscopic little fiddling game. Well, well—but then I've never laid claim to more than manual dexterity.

MONDAY, MARCH 8, 1943 ■ Mud, hopeless, sticky, tough, doughy, clay mud, is what chiefly distinguishes the camp at this season. I shudder to think what it will be like when the spring thaw comes in earnest. This place looks frightful even now. The whole area, which once upon a time was beautiful forest floor and open fields with moss, grass, and all kinds of wild plants, has been transformed into a clay puddle of mud, refuse and nastiness, and it's getting worse and worse.

[Fridtjof] Leqvamb was taken and locked up today.* They must have found out that he was communicating with cell prisoners. He's done a grand job.

Francis has given his concluding lecture on B[jørnstjerne] B[jørnson]. Per and I have been talking fresco and mosaic. Sejersted [Bødtker] had a visit from his wife, who declared that we were all to get out soon. All we old hands!! Confound it. One has to listen to such talk. She knew it for certain.

WEDNESDAY, MARCH 10, 1943 ■ Yesterday something fateful happened. It had such an effect on me that when evening came I was quite exhausted and had to pitch into bed.

Sigvart has been jailed, and Nilsen too. Sigvart—or Sigvartsen which is his full name—was the caretaker at Grini, and a free man. Nilsen was his assistant and stoker in the furnace room. Nilsen was also a free man. Both of them carried on extensive and magnificent "relief work" for us prisoners, and were my best connection with the outer world.

Well, so *that* has happened at last. Actually I've been going around in fear of it for a year now. It was too extraordinary that in the midst of all the regulations and rigors and searches and smuggling affairs those two men should be going free and unchecked in and out of the prison. It wasn't credible. One had to ask oneself: How long can this go on? Not that either of them was incautious, that I know of. But still—they *were* on the hunt for "channels." In their almost fairy-tale naïveté and downright silliness there wasn't one of the "acute" German "criminologists" with Denzer at their head to whom it occurred that perhaps Sigvart—and perhaps Nilsen? Month after month went by, one smuggling affair after another was exposed, the victims were punished, and the affairs died down, but

---

* Released April 21, 1944, Leqvamb was rearrested in January 1945 and spent the remainder of the war in Bredtveit prison.

Francis Bull giving one of his many illegal lectures.

Sigvart and Nilsen went out and in, and nothing happened to them. To all appearances not even a suspicion.

It began with Leqvamb. He has kept quiet, I've learned since. But another man—a young lad from Sørland who was caught some time ago writing a letter down in the furnace room (such idiots, then, can people be) was examined, and he must be the one who cracked. God knows what he said, and what will come out. One must hope the whole thing will reduce itself to a "tobacco business." Words have fallen from the Germans pointing that way. Besides, in Sigvart's room up at the villa they've found a number of carved knives, objects he's acquired for tobacco. Uncommonly plausible. Both Sigvart and Nilsen were driven to Møllergata in the evening. They weren't to be left here. They know the Germans too well, perhaps.

Today Denzer has been down preaching in the basement. First in the workshop, then in the furnace room, and then in the little workshop. He described the two arrests, how stupid those two had been—for the sake of such *trifles* they had now lost their jobs and got a prison stretch into the bargain. That about trifles was like music to my ears. For Sigvart, half an hour before he was taken, had borrowed matches from me.* I walked on sharp red-hot needles for the rest of the day, and did nothing but arrange and settle, from end to end, everything that was to be done and said if—!

After evening roll call today another sinister thing happened. Leif [Poulsson] was

---

* Undoubtedly the matchbox contained messages to be smuggled out of Grini.

locked up (this must be the third time). Also Torjussen, Dr. [Arne] Halvorsen, and Seglem.* Nobody knows why yet, but I'm horribly afraid it has some connection with the other matter.

I don't feel safe yet. Safer than yesterday, but the disasters often come in installments. Tomorrow's installment may include me. God knows. And tomorrow is Thursday, normally release day. Heigh-ho! Truly it's no long step from the most azure expectation to the blackest hell-pains, with thoughts of solitary cells and fantasies of flogging and torture. But still this has contributed to put a bit of a damper on my hope of getting out shortly. It will be exciting to see what tomorrow brings.

Surely I ought not to be writing all this down, many will say. And there's no denying it would be a fine business if all rocks were happily avoided and then they were to find this document. But they won't. I hide it in such a way that not a devil in hell will find it, and besides no devil could make out my signs and paraphrases if he did.

THURSDAY, MARCH 11, 1943 ■ Today the Belgians (there are six or seven of them here, a frightful gang who steal like magpies) went through punishment drill. They had to roll in the slush and were permeated with it from the skin out. A pretty senseless form of punishment. Clothing is completely ruined of course. The poor devils, who had stolen five sacks of potatoes and great quantities of swedes, were driven for a whole hour. I looked on for a moment, and saw them when they were through. It was an odd sight: six or seven lighthouses of mud, face, arms, hands, legs and bodies all a monochrome of mud—mud!

The news isn't bad, but the big things are a long time coming. Spring will soon be here, and one will have to put it all off till the autumn. Now I'm pretty sure that's what we must do. Another spring and summer—well, we shall manage it. Tonight Francis began a new course of lectures. This time on Wergeland.† I'm breathing easier now—and observe that I've got over my belief in release.

FRIDAY, MARCH 12, 1943 ■ Today it should be only about a week till Kari's next visit, but perhaps it's best not to expect her so soon. For twice a month doesn't exactly mean every fourteenth day. It's only so nice to think it does.

When the working groups paraded after dinner my name was called. I was to report to Denzer at two o'clock. All my anxiety and nervousness burst into flame again, and a fiery heartburn seized hold of me. But it was only that Denzer had taken a fancy for some small boxes as well. Two of them, one for chessmen and one for cigarettes. Nothing more.

Well, a chat of course—that is, a long lecture on communism, à propos of my conver-

---

* Erik Torjusen was transferred to Sachsenhausen, where he remained for the duration of the war. Halvorsen and Harald Seglem both remained in Grini for the duration of the war.

† Henrik Wergeland (1808–1845). A poet, alternately called "Norway's Byron," "Norway's Pushkin," and "Norway's Victor Hugo," Wergeland advocated for a revision of Clause 2 of Norway's 1814 Constitution, which barred Jews from entering the country. His poetry collections include *The Jews* (1842), the first poem of which, "The Army of Truth," is among his best known, and *The Jewess* (1844). Clause 2 was finally rescinded in 1851, six years after his death. In 1849 Jews from outside Norway (who before the ban was lifted were only allowed into the country on letters-of-safe-conduct) erected a monument at his gravesite in his honor. On it is engraved: "Henrik Wergeland, the indefatigable advocate of freedom and justice for humanity and all citizens." The celebration of Constitution Day (May 17), which Wergeland was one of the first to promote, always includes a ceremony at his graveside. Didrik Seip, rector of the University of Oslo and himself a prisoner at Grini and Sachsenhausen, edited the collected works of Wergeland in twenty-three volumes between 1918 and 1940.

sation with Reinhardt, which I told him about. In his view I wasn't a Communist at all, in fact no decent, thinking person could be a Communist. One had a family *nicht wahr?* and one had to think of it—of the children, of the future, culture; no, it wasn't possible for any intellectual to be a Communist, impossible for a cultivated human being. Thus he twaddled on, in a loud, full-fed, satisfied voice. I've got into the habit of disconnecting entirely when these long outpourings begin. Today I was busy shaping a few questions that I brought out when the shower was over. They were about my work. Might I do a little of my own? My business had gone almost to ruin in the fourteen months I had been inside, and I had no income and a lot of people to support.

He was deeply sympathetic and understanding and wanted me to petition for release. I wouldn't do that, but could consider applying for leave to work. He thought I might draw up an application addressed to Reinhardt, gave me directions on how it should be written, and also promised his help in sending it off.

Leqvamb came out today. His affair had nothing to do with S[igvartsen] and N[ilsen]. Tomorrow no doubt Leif [Poulsson] and the others will be out too, and with that the cellar tragedy will pass into history—I think. That is, except that S[igvartsen] and N[ilsen] are in Number 19 [Møllergata] and will return no more.*

Francis continued on Wergeland. Now everyone is asleep. But I must save my last candle. How am I to get any more now? I can't send word, I see no means to get any of the things that used to make life here a bit more livable. But fresh possibilities may open up. God knows.

MONDAY, MARCH 15, 1943 ■ Well, now I *have* fixed up a splendid little contrivance. An oil lamp! That solves the lighting problem—while also supplying a proper use for the train oil. Why on earth didn't I think of it before? Why, we'd made such lamps upon the mountain. From now on the little flame I need can burn forever, if necessary.

Three great friends of mine got out today. Three trumps from Måløy: [Kristoffer] Langenes, [Hildor] Fjære and [Sigvald] Halnes. I sent them home to Kari. She's sure to look after them, and I sent my love and important messages.

I can't deny that the yearning in one's own heart is rather apt to bolt on such occasions. For long moments at a time one may give rein to the thought—"if it were me." Me packing up my things, putting on my civilian clothes—while congratulating friends stood round me with longing eyes. A wave of paralyzing, drunken happiness surges through one's whole body and breaks on the heart within; at the same instant a telegram about reality reaches it from up in the skull, and there's a painful scene, a dull thud and a stab. Then silence falls again. Prison silence. The whole thing doesn't take long, only a fraction of a minute; but it comes back—over and over.

At evening roll call today Denzer shouted for me. I had to step forward. Again for nothing but a half-whispered conversation, a kind of nauseating intimacy. He said he'd had a letter from Reinhardt, who told him I might have a visit from my wife every fourteen days. Which I already knew. It's sickening to be courted like that in public. But it's no fault of mine. Not one word has ever crossed my lips that he can interpret as an advance. On the contrary. But he delights in having favorites. Erling is free, and Ole Jacob

---

* Theodor Sigvartsen was released from 19 Møllergata on May 25, 1943; a certain Finn Nielsen (also arrested March 9, 1943, and also sent to 19 Møllergata) was released June 30, 1943.

[Smith-Housken]—now he has only me and one or two others left. His "good Norwegian friends."

TUESDAY, MARCH 16, 1943 ■ A fresh transport to Germany is imminent. This time Colbjørn's name is on the list. We must hope he can arrange things with the *Bauleitung*. It would be sad if Colbjørn left. Both for him and for us.

WEDNESDAY, MARCH 17, 1943 ■ At last there came a decent gray day, not a gleam of sunshine, not a moment's lightening, nothing but dreary mist and tough hopeless clay muck everywhere. Capital working weather. And so I've done a lot today. I've been carving like one possessed from morning until night. Carved the foliage on the tree of life in the center of my work—the tree of life from which the future is rising. It's delicious to be absorbed in something, the time goes so quickly, it's noon and evening before one can heave a sigh, and one may catch oneself longing for a new day to come, another gray day. It's like a consumption to waste so much time not being at home. That's the worst of all.

THURSDAY, MARCH 18, 1943 ■ Erik Graff-Wang was released today. So now at last I am alone. The court hostage in person. It's a proud sensation. It will be interesting to see how long he's to be inside.

Denzer appeared at evening roll call with a long sermon, so preposterously translated by [Even] Evensen that we had our work cut out not to shout with laughter. It was a record this time, threats and pats and nursery prattle. Those who were well equipped were to see and help those who were ill equipped, translated Evensen (God knows what Denzer can have said?), and if we did right all would be well. And similar *mots*. And finally the sonorous two-thousand-fold *Yes!* which signifies that we have all understood.

The last time Denzer preached—it can't have been longer than the day before yesterday—there came the following classic Teutonicism, after the saluting order had been stressed: *Whoever fails to salute a German will be shot at!* Simple after all. The German language isn't hard to understand. It goes with a bang as one may say.

Suddenly I've thought of a man who went crazy today. He collapsed this morning over with the tea gang and began raving about a death he had to break to someone or other. He was quite out of his mind; asked Sigmund Ruud, who was sitting next to him, if he had a revolver, and talked a good deal more eerie stuff before he was helped away to the hospital. Poor fellow. It was the call over of the men for Germany this morning he couldn't take.

We had melancholy news today—the kind that helps to make the German transports more sinister. One of the two Hvidsten brothers has died in Germany.* I don't know which it was, but I remember them both so well at Veidal. They used to sing and whistle and were both so cheery. I wonder what they die of yonder. The numbers are mounting up. Are they victims of the bombing? Are they being maltreated or underfed, or is it disease? I always think: It must be typhus surely.

FRIDAY, MARCH 19, 1943 ■ A cloudless sky again, with a blazing sun—which dazzled us even at morning roll call when it came sailing over the tree tops. And then

---

* Harald Hvidsten died in Sachsenhausen on February 27, 1943, age thirty-three; his older brother Håkon survived in Sachsenhausen until the end of the war.

This is a painted wood carving. It represents many a broken dental instrument, many a bloody fingertip, many a curse, and many a loving thought.

nothing happened. I bathed and shaved and made myself smart, for I was expecting Kari today. But she didn't come. Then I suppose she won't come till next week—Monday perhaps! It's rare for anyone to come on Saturday.

The move to get Colbjørn exempted from the German journey didn't come off. [*Bauleiter*] Niebel said he wouldn't apply, because he thought a stay in Germany would do Colbjørn good; he'd noticed that he was anti-German. That was the very deuce. Next moment I went to Denzer. I took a box I had just finished, and planned the campaign minutely. The box part was a hundred percent successful. He was melting with enthusiasm, also Kunz, who threatened to upset my whole plan by being there. Yes, the box was "wonderfully made." "Everything stands out—really marvelous—so natural isn't it?" and he turned and twisted my work of art, held it at arm's length, stuck it right up on his nose, reeled off all the superlatives in the German language.

Then Kunz left, and I began. I told him about Colbjørn. Laid it on thick, said that Niebel must have got quite the wrong impression of him. He wasn't anti-German, but possibly a bit anti-Niebel, I ventured. That went home. One must play on what small strings there are, and the *Bauleitung* is a good old string. I went on to talk about Colbjørn's little daughter and his old father who was ill (so I declared; he's no doubt fit as a fiddle).

Yes, Denzer remembered Colbjørn, that tall young man, but it was a pity I hadn't come sooner, then he would have arranged it. Now he was afraid it was too late. I expressed the view that he could manage it if only he wanted to. I knew he was preening inwardly at this flattery. He promised to do everything in his power to keep Colbjørn here, but was afraid it wouldn't come off. As yet it hasn't come off, and now we've reached midnight, and tomorrow the transport is to leave. They're to parade at half-past seven with all they're taking.

After the hut had been put to rights this evening everyone gathered in the lobby for a short time. Francis said a word or two to those who were going away. We sang the national anthem and Colbjørn replied in a few strong, simple words. Francis didn't lecture this evening. We just sat together talking, and finally we had our night meal together.

Colbjørn has just come up and wrung me by the hand so that I still feel it. *Well, good night then!*—for the last time.

SATURDAY, MARCH 20, 1943 ■ Denzer's whole attempt came to nothing; I strongly suspect him of having forgotten all about it as soon as my back was turned. And so Colbjørn went off—in good heart. The parting was short and hard, as partings should be after all. Now I shall have to try and take over his news service. With my poor memory and with all the frantic Russian and Tunisian and Chinese place names!*

Per [Krohg] has been lecturing this evening, especially on Picasso. Afterward we had a long talk about surrealism, Per, Francis and I. And then we had our night meal. We're grandly off after all.

TUESDAY, MARCH 23, 1943 ■ Today I was summoned to the Commandant and appointed his private architect, with full authority to requisition the labor and materials required to carry out certain tasks he gave me. Terrace, gardens, brickwork, garage, and in conclusion I was also to take over the planning of the dining room in the basement of the Commandant's residence. I was to drop all my other activity and get going at once.

This doesn't really suit me so badly. It gives me an opportunity to get out a bit more into the fresh air, which will be nice when the spring weather comes to stay. And I was delighted at the Commandant's explicit statement that I and my new commissions had no connection with the *Bauleitung*.

WEDNESDAY, MARCH 24, 1943 ■ More sun. But now I've started on my new job and can get a little good out of the sunshine. I keep indulging in strolls about the grounds and am glad to be able to lay aside the whole *Andenken* industry.

MONDAY, MARCH 29, 1943 ■ The whole Mareth line† in English hands, Rommel on the run—6,000 prisoners taken, and the Americans have reached the coast and cut off

---

* Colbjørnsen remained in Sachsenhausen for the remainder of the war.

† The Mareth line was a system of fortifications constructed prior to World War II by the French in southern Tunisia to protect against attack from Italian-held Libya to the east. It fell to Allied forces March 27, 1943.

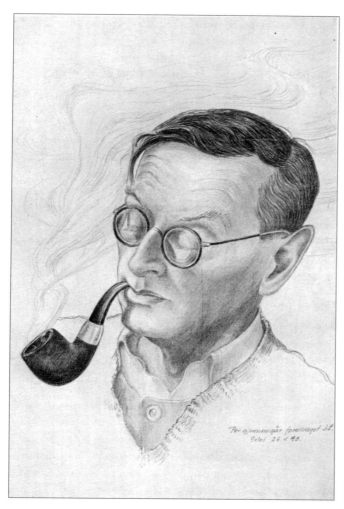

*Artist Per Krohg also gave
illicit night lectures.*

Rommel's retreat!! It's as though a huge load of stones had dropped from our hearts. This must be a really decisive nail in the coffin of the Axis.

I was lecturing in [Hut] 9 this evening; but on the way I fell into one of the worst clay-puddles. I slipped on a greasy plank. I must have given my foot a pretty serious wrench, if indeed I haven't messed up something inside. I thought I heard something give in the ankle. Leif [Poulsson], who was here putting on a bandage, couldn't find anything; but it hurts quite a lot and I can't stand on the leg. I shall have to keep quiet tomorrow anyhow. Hope I can get out of going into the hospital.

Otherwise nothing had happened in the camp. Per [Krohg] has gone to bed, he'd had a black day and wasn't really in spirits till the news came. It took so much out of him that he went to bed. It really can affect one like that.

WEDNESDAY, MARCH 31, 1943 ■ Here I am, resting on my laurels, and here I rested all yesterday without budging—almost. The ankle of my right leg is hopelessly twisted, and to add a final stroke of wretchedness I've got a touch of lumbago. I've had Denzer's exalted leave to stay here and not go to the *Revierstube** [infirmary]. After all it's very pleasant to rest a bit, so on the whole I'm very well off.

The day before yesterday Einar Lund got pneumonia and was admitted to the hospital. Tonight he'd been unconscious since three o'clock—and they were keeping him alive with injections. The worst is feared.

FRIDAY, APRIL 2, 1943 ■ Einar Lund died the night before last.† It was his heart that gave out. I suppose he was too late in going to the doctor. He was an uncommonly good fellow and a good Norwegian. In Kristiansand, after the arrest, he was so beaten up and tortured that he tried to take his own life, because he didn't want to betray his comrades and could stand no more. He escaped death at the time he sought it, but now, when he was just recovering the will to live, death has come and taken him.

On Sunday we're to work. Punishment. There has been more potato stealing and so forth. So, punishment—punishment and prohibitions and the devil and his grandmother.

SUNDAY, APRIL 4, 1943 ■ Sunday again and Denzer & Co. turned magnanimous at the last moment; we got off working this Sunday. I suppose they found out that the punishment would hit them as well.

Yesterday Francis began a course of lectures on Norwegian historians and historical research from Snorre to the present day.‡ He is manifold and inexhaustible and is still going on unmoved, in spite of snores from the different corners of the hut.

MONDAY, APRIL 5, 1943 ■ Denzer left for Berlin today. Apparently his mother is dead. Bombed, perhaps. Kunz is taking over. Per was examined yesterday by Reinhardt, who was here. The examination left him in a mood of sparkling optimism. Now he feels pretty sure of getting out, there was talk of guarantors and everything rosy. I was not sent for. I'm afraid my case has gone down to the bottom of a heap again, and things take time—in Tunis and Russia as well. A confounded lot of it.

Tomorrow Robert [Riefling] goes.§ He heard tonight. Need I say he's happy?

WEDNESDAY, APRIL 7, 1943 ■ Yesterday there seemed no point in writing. I was definitely not much to boast of. I broke my resolutions and gave way again, just went round all day feeling homesick and thinking everything dreary and disconsolate.

Suddenly today Bjørn Eriksen died. He was sitting with [Sejersted] Johannes [Bødtker], joking and laughing—and without the slightest warning, for no reason at all, his head dropped. He was unconscious and a few minutes later he was dead. Apoplexy.

---

*   More commonly referred to as the *Revier*, an abbreviation of *Krankenrevier*.
†   Einar, who was forty-nine, was Sigrid Helliesen Lund's brother-in-law.
‡   Snorre or Snorri, Sturluson or Sturlason (1178–1241) was an Icelandic politician and historian. His history of the Norwegian kings, *Heimskringla*, "a continuous history of Norway to 1177, the like of which few if any other countries possess," holds a special place in Norwegian culture and for a long time was one of the most widely read books in Norway.
§   Riefling (1911–1988), a classical pianist, made his concert debut at age eleven with the Oslo Philharmonic and performed solo at age fourteen. His performing career spanned sixty years, during which he was considered one of Scandinavia's foremost pianists. He recorded nearly eighty albums.

Francis Bull reads Wergeland after the lights are out.

Thirty-three years old, well and brisk, happy at having just escaped the transport to Germany.

My leg has got worse again. It doesn't seem to be an ordinary sprain. I must take it easy again—stay in bed, or sit with my leg up; but I hope I can stay on in the hut.

THURSDAY, APRIL 8, 1943 ■ Things are mighty slack here nowadays. I never see a German, thank God; and they're not around much either. The Commandant appeared today at evening roll call, threatening to send all "dodgers" to Germany or put them in *Einzelhaft*. In that case *Einzelhaft* would be tolerably full up. There would almost have to be *Einzelhaft* all over the camp—in every room of every hut! Why not?

FRIDAY, APRIL 9, 1943 ■ A memorable date! It's now three years since the Ragnarokk broke loose on us, and more than a year of that I've spent "inside."* And as yet there's not much to indicate that I shan't go on. Quite the contrary, I rather think one must say. Today the Nordland tour has suddenly come to life. All the prisoners are to write home and ask for warm clothing etc., "as the prisoner has been assigned outdoor work. For reasons of health you *must* send by return the following clothes:" and then a long list of necessaries to be filled in on the principle of "delete what is inapplicable." Everyone is to write, but it's certain that not everyone will go. So our

---

* The third anniversary of the German invasion of Norway; the term "Ragnarokk" is from Norse mythology to describe the end of the world/judgment day/Armageddon.

people are to send these things all the same, or perhaps the letters won't be sent off to the relatives of those who are not going. God knows. I didn't fill in anything, for two reasons. In the first place I don't believe I shall be going; I went north last year, and moreover I can hardly be sent off with possibly a broken leg. And in the second place I have enough of an outfit for the trip.

We were allowed to "stay up" longer today to finish these letters. But now it's pretty late (nearly two). But I can sleep in the morning, so to hell with that and a lot more.

TUESDAY, APRIL 13, 1943 ■ I'm getting sick and tired of writing when I'm in the dumps. And—confound it!—I am at present. It's all in vain that I struggle to persuade myself and others that I'm O.K. again now. Not until the window shutters have been put up at the regulation blackout hour, that is, right in the middle of a dazzling summer evening, does one sometimes thaw out in the hut air, in the dejected light from the single hanging lamp, and find the good company agreeing with one. For I am in good company. One couldn't wish for much better here—well, if one could forget the friends who have gone away. Nils [Ramm] and Odd [Wang] and . . . one can't forget them. So even at nights despondency and hopelessness may force their way in.

Yesterday Siri-Piri had her tenth birthday! A year ago, when she was nine, I wrote a poem for her, and did a drawing of animals and woods and mountains, and painted it. Everything was so bright and good at that time. Fifteen months' imprisonment have made a change. I remember ending the poem "We'll meet again before you're ten." How dead sure I was that long before that I should be back home with her. How easy and natural it was to write and draw and paint for her—then. And now? I could so easily have done it, I had both time enough and opportunity enough to send it out. But I haven't managed it. It has been utterly impossible.

My leg is in plaster now. I didn't get to Ulleval for an X-ray, so they thought it might as well be in plaster as though it were broken. But they hadn't enough plaster bandages, so the whole thing is just a wretched piece of nonsense. A kind of stiff stocking, roomy and comfortable and no earthly use. It only prevents me from getting on my stocking and shoe or slipper, so I just stay in bed. But it doesn't exactly improve one's spirits. Everything is going well, but not fast enough—in the eyes of a poor convict. The talk of invasion goes on intensively, and belief in it and longing for it increase every day. I must confess that I'm beginning to find it all too easy to adopt a skeptical and doubtful attitude. I'm so sick of English gabble and American bragging.

WEDNESDAY, APRIL 14, 1943 ■ Francis has finished his little wood carving, and his delight in it is touching. He's quite overcome with admiration and pride that he should really have done that himself—well, most of it. For Per and I helped him a bit here and there and gave him advice and so on. But with unequaled care and patience and fervor, he did the main part of it himself. Now he's about to begin a second.

THURSDAY, APRIL 15, 1943 ■ Spring—spring! I can sit in here and feel it, don't need to go out—don't *want* to go out. It's bad enough in here.

Six men were released today. It's said that some of them were prisoners of long stand-

Birthday card for Siri.

ing—ten and eleven months, if one can call that long-standing. One gradually begins to feel like a veteran, among the other veterans.

Stange is packing up today, leaving, never to return. No one will miss him, till we get a new man who's even worse.

Diphtheria is spreading, they've had to take a whole hut as an isolation hut. There's a lot of illness here now, of every kind. Otherwise the days are uniform and colorless.

FRIDAY, APRIL 16, 1943 ■ No more has been heard of the North Norway transport, except that the parcels of "equipment" are beginning to flow in. Per for instance got his today. I thought the letter he wrote to Ragnhild would be kept back, but no, all the letters must have been sent, and two thousand parcels of equipment will be coming for all, whether they're to go or not. A marvelously practical system. Perhaps we'll be going north again after all? I must admit I'm not exactly rejoicing at the prospects of another such journey now, I thought—well, well. One must leave off thinking.

Francis has now begun to talk about Welhaven, Per and I carve.* Now everyone is asleep again, and I'm alone. Ye gods how alone I am.

SATURDAY, APRIL 17, 1943 ■ There is a bright moon tonight, and the stars are flashing in the cold blue night sky; if one stands quite quiet by the open window, one can hear the soughing of the woods and the chuckling of the brook down yonder. If one shuts one's eyes and lets the cold air brush over one's face, it's easy to imagine oneself in the mountains. I wonder when I shall be there again? It's three o'clock—a glorious night. Saturday night again, tomorrow's Sunday, and then Monday—and Kari! Not much more than thirty hours to go.

A good many new prisoners have arrived today and tonight. No one was released.

The Germans are still arresting small boys, right down to the age of thirteen. One fine day I shall probably have Eigil here, he'll soon be old enough to be a dangerous enemy of the State.

TUESDAY, APRIL 20, 1943 ■ But Kari didn't come! Neither yesterday nor today. What's wrong? Yesterday my comfort was that of course she hadn't come because I was to be released today, on Hitler's birthday; amnesty, magnanimity and all that.† But since today it turns out that the birthday child is obviously not in the ascendant (not a flag flying and no demonstrations anywhere) and presumably is gnawing a big birthday carpet, and I'm here as much as ever and without Kari today as well, I can think of no consolation. The clean things I put on on Monday morning will soon be filthy—and to what purpose have I shaved and glamorized myself two days in succession?

Denzer is pretty active these days. Now it's letter writing which enjoys his particular attention. Felix [Tschudi] had written a birthday letter to his little boy, in which he happened to say that Grini was a fine place now, to be sure, with the twenty-three huts that we had built—etc. Denzer had raved like a lunatic; it's forbidden to write about anyone or anything at Grini. He himself made the unsolicited admission that everyone in Oslo knew that much from prisoners who had been released, but it was against the rules to *write* about it! Felix was degraded and condemned to the "trench." Another man who had been guilty of an equally gross offence shared his fate, only in addition his ears were soundly boxed by the lunatic.

WEDNESDAY, APRIL 21, 1943 ■ Nic. Stang was summoned to the Terrace today for questioning. He was a bit nervous. He didn't come back. He was released. His wife

---

* Johan Sebastian Welhaven (1807–1873). Poet and literary critic, Welhaven openly feuded with Henrik Wergeland (although he was romantically involved with Wergeland's sister, Camilla Collett). Welhaven's sister, Maren Sars, was the mother of Eva (Sars) Nansen, Odd Nansen's mother.

† Adolf Hitler was born in Austria April 20, 1889; this was his fifty-fourth birthday.

had brought his civilian clothes there, and he went straight home. *Home!* He's been inside twenty-eight months, and today was his birthday. That's what one may call a birthday! Everyone is rejoicing. Twenty-eight months, most of it at No. 19!

THURSDAY, APRIL 22, 1943 ■ Today Kari came—and she brought the little one and Siri. She was in such a bright mood, so brisk and joyous, and the little one was splendid and Siri enchanting. The baby has two teeth, and he was smiling and laughing and grabbing at my face the whole time. During the visit I managed to smuggle into his knickers an important letter I had written to Kari. One day he shall hear of the time when he was a letter-box.

No news today. The [news] exchange was in the utmost danger for a moment; that was averted, but there will no doubt have to be silence for a few days, unfortunately. However, things are going well out there—I believe. Now it's begun to rain. Good Friday occurred long ago. For this is Easter. But we don't notice it. We're to work tomorrow too.

FRIDAY, APRIL 23, 1943 ■ Today I cut the plaster bandage off my leg. It was doing no good anyhow, and my bunk was full of little bits of plaster. The leg is O.K., only a bit sore in certain positions; but still I'll coddle it a while longer.

SATURDAY, APRIL 24, 1943 ■ Easter Eve after a full working day. Gray and wretched. But we've had a quite outstanding Easter Eve here in [Hut] 6. A festive table with a white cloth (sheets), flowers (palms, white anemones and marsh marigolds)—and the most luxurious dishes, not forgetting a whole bottle of first-rate "benzol liqueur" with the coffee. Francis made a speech, and Per. I made a short little one, and ended with a ballad I wrote this afternoon. It was a memorable evening—everyone said the same.

Now I'm sitting here alone again, while the rain splashes down outside and the others are snoring on every hand. Seldom have they enjoyed a heavier, sounder sleep. It worked out at almost five drams each.* Now we're to have two whole days of rest. It will be a regular Easter even at Grini.

WEDNESDAY, APRIL 28, 1943 ■ Birger Ruud came up to me today and said he had heard Denzer give a long lecture on me this morning. Two NS men had been here trying to persuade Birger to join them in getting sport under way. It may be imagined what luck they had. Denzer had come in during this meeting, which took a long time. He had held forth about the Norwegians' attitude to National Socialism and how stupid they were. Nansen, for example, he said, was kept here because his attitude to National Socialism was wrong and stiff. He had had a lot of conversation with him, he said, and had found him a decent man with many interesting views perhaps, but he wasn't ripe yet! He (Denzer) might of course storm the Terrace and get him released, if he chose, but he wasn't sure it would be fair to the country, for if he were released now, he would join the Jøssings, etc. So that's the state of things. I'm not ripe yet. I wonder if the other court hostages were considered ripe before they got out?

---

* A dram is a liquid measure roughly equivalent to a small shot glass.

FRIDAY, APRIL 30, 1943 ■ Well, at least April didn't wind up without a small event. This afternoon the camp had distinguished visitors. Terboven himself was here with Himmler's deputy and second in command Daluege, the successor of Heydrich. Reinhardt and Fehlis were also of the party.*

The signal for parade came terribly early—half-past five, and there the poor chaps stood for two hours. I got off, for of course I don't parade, I'm still disabled. But my name was called when Terboven reviewed the "troops." Denzer had wanted to "exhibit" me, or possibly his highness in person had expressed a wish to see me. I was reported sick.

Later my name was called again. This time it was Fehlis who wanted me, and a message was sent for me to the hut. The Butcher† rushed in and instructed me to present myself in the personnel room without delay. Their lordships had then concluded the review on the square and Terboven and Daluege had left the camp, while the rest had set off on a tour of inspection round the huts.

Meanwhile I betook myself to the personnel office. There stood Per on the same errand. Fehlis wanted to talk to us. It would be stupid to deny that hope began to blaze up in me. Per obstinately denied that such was the case with him, but, well, I have my own doubts of that. In the half hour we were kept waiting, that crazy hope played havoc with me as it does in such circumstances. My thoughts were already far on the way home. There was only one painful aspect, which I mentioned to Per. It would be terribly hard and cruel for Francis if we were released. Indeed so cruel did I feel it was bound to be that I almost stood there hoping it might not be the case. He was so unhappy and so really touchingly unhappy at the mere idea that Per was going to leave the bookbinding shop and he would be left alone there with people he couldn't really talk to.

While these ideas were still waging war, Blatner came rushing in and said we were to come now. We were called down to the square in front of the main steps, where their lordships' cars were ready to start. The bigwigs were assembled there, obviously in the act of breaking up. Our own augurs, with Reich (acting Commandant) and Denzer at their head, were also standing around. We were shoved forward and pointed at as the two prisoners Herr Fehlis wanted to see.

It was like a kind of cattle show. There we stood, Per and I, stiff, solemn and silent, and on the wall a little distance off I'm blessed if there wasn't another animal. But it was dead, and a dark-red stream of blood was running down the wall onto the gravel. A

---

* Kurt Daluege (1897–1946), an early Nazi and later member of the Reichstag. Daluege rose rapidly in the SS and became its most powerful policeman, second in rank only to Himmler. When Reinhard Heydrich was assassinated by British-trained Czech and Slovak commandos in Prague in May 1942, Daluege succeeded him as acting protector of Bohemia and Moravia, where he was responsible for implementing Himmler's orders to avenge Heydrich's death by destroying the Czechoslovakian towns of Lidiče and Ležáky. In Lidiče men over sixteen were murdered; women were sent to Ravensbrück and the children either murdered or distributed to German families; the village was completely razed. In Ležáky both men and women were killed and the children either "Aryanized" or sent to the camps. Daluege was arrested by US forces in May 1945 and extradited to Czechoslovakia in September 1946. Found guilty of war crimes, he was hanged on October 24, 1946.

Heinrich Fehlis (1906–1945) was head of the Security Police (SiPo), which included the Gestapo, and of the Security Service (SD), or intelligence arm, of the SS in Norway (1940–1945). During the war 151 Norwegians were executed without trial, most on direct orders from Fehlis. At the end of the war he attempted to avoid capture by taking refuge in a German military base in Norway. When discovered and ordered to surrender to Norwegian Resistance (Milorg) units, he chose to swallow poison, then shot himself.

† Wilhelm Heilmann (1911–1992). Nansen interchangeably refers to "Heilmann" or "the Butcher" throughout the diary; Heilmann earned his nickname from his employment as a butcher prior to the war. After the war he was sentenced to jail; released in 1951, Heilmann returned home to Hamburg, Germany.

German had just cut the poor thing's throat with a knife requisitioned from the kitchen. It was a roe deer. No doubt the bigwigs had observed it from the car window as they were driving over—and then I suppose these bold huntsmen, in a noble gusto, had by their united exertions and firearms managed to destroy the nimble little creature—so rare in these parts. There it lay on the stone wall in a dark-red pool of blood, a strange background to the little inquiry which now followed. Fehlis addressed himself first to me.

Did I know why I was imprisoned?

Yes, I knew I was a court hostage.

How long had I been here?

About sixteen months.

My attitude to Germany was hostile?

I had never engaged in politics.

This reply was greeted with an ironic smile.

Never engaged in politics at all? he asked with open and derisive doubt in his voice.

No, never at all.

Reinhardt was standing all the time with a face of stone, staring at me with his infernal snake's eyes behind the glasses. Certainly there would be no help from that quarter, and out on the flank stood Denzer echoing Fehlis's gestures with loud and scornful clearings of his throat at the appropriate points. Never have I despised the fellow more deeply than at that moment. Fehlis went on.

And what about your activity for the German emigrants?

I carried on the Nansen Relief as it has always been carried on—unpolitically and without regard to the race or faith of the individual refugees.

He shrugged his shoulders, so did Reinhardt—and so did Denzer of course, while he repeated the experiment of a sympathetic throat-clearing.

Fehlis had now done with me and addressed himself to Per.

Was he *the* Krohg?

Er-r?

Artist?

Yes.

Was he working here?

Yes, Per was in the bookbinding shop.

Had he no opportunity to work? This was half to Denzer, who instantly burst forth with the utmost complaisance and said yes, of course, there was work done in the bookbinding shop . . .

Yes, but he hadn't meant that kind of work.

Before he could go on, Denzer, with his usual acumen, and with the complaisance of a maître d'hôtel recommending the different glories of his establishment, had caught the idea and said that of course—he could be given any sort of job . . . in the trench? Fehlis smiled: No, that wasn't exactly the kind of work he meant. Then there was a bit of whispering about it, and I gathered that the application for Per to be allowed to carry on his own work was being brought up. And after a question or two about whether Per had been in North Norway, both the "examinations" were over. Denzer made me a sign that we might withdraw. I forgot to say that Fehlis had been so attentive as to ask what was wrong with my foot.

We withdrew, and have now finished both with the episode and with our commentaries. I thought the worst of the lot was Reinhardt; he looked to me like Satan incarnate in German uniform. Per thought Fehlis himself was just as bad. The India-rubber man, the operetta-fool Denzer, isn't even worth talking about. I once made him a jumping jack; it wasn't such a bad likeness. We can hardly be much nearer a release, either of us. Rather the contrary, I'm afraid. Francis can set his mind at rest.

SUNDAY, MAY 2, 1943 ■ Yesterday—which was a day off—I celebrated as usual by shirking the diary. There was another reason as well, namely that from yesterday all blacking out of windows was done away with and therefore all electric bulbs unscrewed. So my little oil lamp would have been visible from outside. My various nocturnal pursuits have thus encountered a new and difficult problem, which I haven't solved yet.

Otherwise yesterday was chiefly remarkable for a cloudless sky and quite heart-rendingly glorious spring weather. Also for a conversation I had with Denzer. Besides which I got a message from Lise [Børsum], who has come here and is in a cell.*

Denzer was in a first-rate mood yesterday right from the beginning of the day. He felt he had managed the distinguished visit quite capitally. He was convinced that the bigwigs had received the very best impression of his outstanding abilities as ringmaster and his rare powers both of criminological insight and of discipline. At an early hour he was up in the hospital, where he settled down on a table in the attendants' room and began a commentary on the solemn occurrence of the day before. He was ecstatic and hilarious in his enthusiasm about himself, the weather and the world at large. The attendants' unlawful books, which were lying open everywhere—since his arrival had been quite unexpected—he missed completely. His never sleeping acumen and vigilance had deserted him for one blank instant, which the attendants did not fail to make the most of, as they lent his outpourings an interested ear and gently slid the books off the table into their laps, and then, still under the table and by divers unseen routes, under the bedclothes in their bunks.

Yes, they agreed that everything had gone off admirably, most admirably. Some of the prisoners of course had made stupid answers, some had lacked the stiff military bearing which was called for at such a moment, and which to every German came naturally and as a matter of course; he demonstrated this involuntary and spontaneous attitude with a colossal jerk, a crashing thud of his heels together, and a movement of the right arm as though he were going to turn a cart wheel. But Germans were Germans, and Norwegians were Norwegians, and there it was. But as he said, on the whole. . . !

Then came parade. He called my name at that parade, also. I made use of the fact to go and see him later in the day. Today—thanks to his rare good humor—I might get in a few words.

It turned out that I was right in this assumption; I got in quite a lot when he had first,

---

* Milly Elise ("Lise") Børsum (1908–1985). A member of the Resistance, Børsum belonged to a network that helped Jews escape into neutral Sweden. After a short stay at Grini she was transported to Ravensbrück concentration camp as a Nacht und Nebel prisoner (discussed in notes following August 21, 1943, entry) until freed as part of the "white buses" operation. After the war Børsum abandoned her prewar life, gave up art and music (she had come from a musical family), divorced her physician husband, and devoted herself to the cause of war veterans and the elimination of concentration camps throughout the world. Børsum cofounded *Nasjonalhjelpen for krigens ofre* (National aid for war victims) in 1947 and was its head from 1966 to 1978. Her daughter Bente, an actress, has performed *Mother*, a monologue in which she plays a range of characters in dramatizing her mother's wartime experience, in both Norway and the United States.

in a gale of noise, reproached me for my foolish conduct the day before, in neglecting so uniquely brilliant an opportunity of bringing out my petition for release. I tried to explain that I didn't see it as a brilliant opportunity for personal conversation—on the square in front of the house, with a crowd of people all round and the cars ready to drive off. I felt, on the contrary, that the situation by no means invited the bringing up of personal requests and difficulties.

But yes, Herr Nansen, that was just what it did invite. Don't you realize that you were face to face with authority, the highest, the supreme authorities, who were actually taking a special interest in you—and in that Krok—Kraa-aag? *Nicht?* You should have said, *Herr Standartenführer* . . .

Here I interrupted with the remark that I didn't know he was a *Standartenführer*. Denzer shook his head despairingly and said that anyhow I must know he was B.D.S.* It was now my turn to shake my own head quite as despairingly and assure him that all these titles and initials were and always would be a riddle to me.

It seemed as if this horrifying revelation and complete exposure brought home to him the insuperable difficulties I had had to contend with down on the square. But then he gave an elegant skip over the floor, as though to intimate that he overleaped these titular prefaces and problems, and went on just the same with what I ought to have said: "I have been in custody a whole sixteen months now, and my wife and three, four (isn't it four), four little children are without means of support. . . . *Herr Standartenführer* [here he forgot that this title was unknown to me]—please let me go home—back to my family and my work!" He didn't *say* that I ought to have fallen on my knees, but there was something in his voice—to which he was trying to give the intonation mine should have had—that made it thoroughly obvious that a kneeling posture would have been the indisputably natural and best-chosen one to adopt immediately before, or perhaps after, proffering the petition.

He went on to say that he had been standing there beside me the whole time thinking that now—now surely Nansen must speak. "Now he'll speak, I thought, now surely he must speak!" He swerved up into falsetto and repeated, "Now surely he must speak! why doesn't he speak? why didn't you look at me? I would have helped you—put in a timely word, my dear Nansen; but what did you do? Nothing, Herr Nansen, nothing! Nothing at all!" He ended right up in falsetto again, dancing round me and gesticulating to show me the despair he had been in on my account.

I chanced to think of the derisive snickering with which he had annotated my replies the day before, and my emotion at his warm interest in my welfare was perceptibly chilled. But now I wanted to speak out a little, and off I went. I should be glad to know if I was still imprisoned as a hostage, or if I was being held on account of my activity for German emigrants. I told him it would be a great satisfaction to me to have that cleared up; then at least, I said, I might perhaps get something to be imprisoned for. And I should like to find out whether it was a necessary condition of release to do *so*—and I raised my right arm 45 degrees. He was amused—his geniality that day was altogether exuberant—and assured me that *that* wouldn't be expected. He invited me to draw up a petition about my wife and children, who were without food or money, etc., etc. Which I declined to do.

---

* BdS was an abbreviation for *Befehlshaber der Sicherheitspolizei und des Sicherheitsdienstes*, commander of the Security Police (SiPo) and Security Service (SD). Heinrich Fehlis was the BdS of Norway.

I talked with Lise today. They've used screws on her, the swine; but she thought of something to tell them which apparently they believed, and then they left off. But she was expecting more examinations, poor girl.

TUESDAY, MAY 4, 1943 ■ Tonight I've hung a couple of blankets across the window and lit my little oil lamp. It would be awkward if a zealous greenhorn were to discover that the pale radiance of the moon or stars is thus prevented from penetrating into our modest room 6, where a wretched little can with a wick in it gives off a nasty reek of train oil from a tiny flickering flame, which only just enables the room's worst malefactor to carry on his shady activities. But there seems nothing else to be done.

Have talked with Lise again and got some important matter, which has been taken care of. I'm afraid Lise is in a tough spot. She has been splendid, done her civic duty and a lot more. Let us hope she'll manage to bamboozle them.

WEDNESDAY, MAY 5, 1943 ■ Before I was up this morning word came that Lise wanted to speak to me. I took up my stand behind the bread truck just outside her window, and the interview went smoothly. Last night they'd used screws on her again. Imagine five men putting a young woman to the vilest torture! They don't believe her after all—and she said she didn't think she could take much more now. "Odd" would have to take cover and disappear. "Jørgen" she thought she could keep out of it, and so on. Later in the day I learned that "Odd" is already under cover, and I managed to let her know. She was visibly—or rather audibly—relieved, and thought she might offer an additional statement of her own accord. I said she must judge that for herself and do as she thought best. Anyhow she needn't be so much afraid of the next questioning. The worst must be over now. Thank God. I managed to throw her a few tablets through the grating (soporific and pain-killing), but she said she didn't hurt so much now.

From today all prisoners under eighteen have been taken out of their respective gangs and are to have extra treatment and their own routine. Are to have gymnastics, football [i.e., soccer] and games for several hours a day, and (this is the plum in the pudding—or the fly in the ointment) are to have three hours daily with Claffy (!) who is to instruct them in the new doctrine. Ideological indoctrination! I don't think there's any grave danger that any of the young gentlemen will be lost, and the other advantages they have received—plus more food than the ordinary rations and half a liter [17 fl. oz. or 2.1 cups] of milk—we can but rejoice at.

Today the newspapers arrived, and with them notice that three more of our companions who went off south are dead. Of the transport that left in I think February, which included [Sven] Oftedal and numbered 131 prisoners from here, 21 are dead. And more death notices are always coming. Oftedal, [Einar] Gerhardsen,* Colbjørn, [Per] Græsli,†

---

* Einar Gerhardsen (1897–1987) was one of the dominant politicians of postwar Norway. As the head of the Labor Party he served as prime minister of Norway in the immediate aftermath of World War II (1945–1951) and again between 1955 and 1965. Gerhardsen is credited with leading postwar reconstruction and with leading Norway into NATO in 1949. At the time of the German invasion Gerhardsen was mayor of Oslo. Arrested in September 1941, he was transferred to Sachsenhausen in April 1943 and returned to Grini in September 1944, where he remained for the duration of the war.

† Per Græsli, a doctor, was arrested in July 1942 for resistance activities and sent to Sachsenhausen May 3, 1943 (two days prior to this diary entry). While in Sachsenhausen he worked in the Infirmary where he contracted a number of

Rolf [Hofmo], Leif [Jensen]* and all the others—where are they? Shall we ever see them again?

THURSDAY, MAY 6, 1943 ■ [Knut] Leinæs† asked Claffy what our friends in Germany were dying of. He answered without hesitation, diphtheria. Asked whether it might not possibly be bombs or clearance work after bombing, he returned a decided negative. There was a diphtheria epidemic all over Germany.

FRIDAY, MAY 7, 1943 ■ A prisoner has escaped! a *hostage* in our hut. A father arrested for his son. He must be mad. Indeed, there are several indications of it. He knew of the threat that ten men would be shot if one escaped. The *Lagerkommandant* appeared on parade and dictated to Evensen all the measures or punishments which were now to be introduced. He was as usual aloof, unsympathetic, exceptionally devilish, but no more so than usual. He said by the way, after recalling the provisions laid down in the event of an escape, that these provisions would be carried out. So it remains in force. It may still happen. But the first thing, anyhow, is to see whether the man won't be caught. No special feeling of uneasiness has arisen, not even in this hut, where the man lived. I must admit I don't quite believe that the appalling provision will be carried out. But I don't feel certain by any means.

SATURDAY, MAY 8, 1943 ■ It proved a quiet night after all. But at morning roll call ten men were picked out. First the five men working in the same gang as the fugitive, then later another five. "In place of that one," Denzer instructed us that the ten were picked. He didn't *say* they were to be shot, and perhaps not very many believed it. But all the same, the threat and horror hung over the camp and over the heads of those unlucky ten.

But it didn't last very long. At nine o'clock there was a signal for general parade. The prisoners came running from all the working places to the parade ground. For the "trot" has been introduced all round, that was one of last night's regulations; I think I forgot to mention it. Everything was to be done on the double. When all were in their places, Denzer stepped forward with his chest out like a strutting cock. He announced that the runaway was caught. This information was greeted with a spontaneous hurrah from the whole body of prisoners.

Denzer preened himself, swelled his chest up almost to bursting point, and resumed his speech. The ten men *who were to have been shot*—said he—will now be sent back to their working places. Now it was touch and go whether his ribs wouldn't pop out of his uniform jacket. For he took the whole thing as a personal ovation. His "sense of justice" (and his marvelous luck) completely intoxicated him. Now indeed—he realized—all the prisoners to a man were his devoted admirers, eating out of his hand.

Those who thought the whole affair was a sham and that the man hadn't been caught at all (and there were many who began to spread this view in the camp) were thoroughly mistaken. Not only had he been caught, but Denzer's offer to deliver up the runaway to

---

ailments; seriously ill when evacuated in the "white buses" operation, Græsli died shortly thereafter, in July 1945, in a Swedish hospital.

* Jensen remained in Sachsenhausen, where he survived the war. His was one of the six breadboards used to smuggle Nansen's diary out of Sachsenhausen.

† Released December 23, 1944.

the prisoners, if he returned to camp, so that they might give him his just deserts, was made good. This afternoon the poor man arrived here. The ten who were to have paid for this man's guilt with their lives were summoned and confronted with him, and were invited to do as they liked with him.

For a moment their leader hesitated, and in that quivering, fateful moment those ten were presented with the chance of teaching the Germans a lesson which they wouldn't have forgotten in a hurry. But alas! the blow that struck the poor, trembling wretch to earth also leveled dignity and pride and shivered the chance to fragments—to the delectation and applause of the Germans, standing there in a body to see how Norwegians settled accounts with their wretches. And then blows came thick and fast; one man spat in the runaway's face, another rushed on him in wild fury, a third gave him a well-aimed punch on the nose, and so on. It was a spectacle so grotesque and sickening that one feels impelled to draw the curtain and hide it.

Now it is right to add that at least two of the ten held their hands. One simply went up to the man, looked at him, and turned away immediately, only saying that he never wished to see him again. The other was the gang leader, who on the German system is responsible for any misconduct on the part of members of his gang during working hours. He showed the man his wedding ring and said he had a wife and five children at home, who had nearly been widowed and orphaned on his account. He was trembling all over and white with rage, but controlled himself. But he didn't speak the timely word.

It's not a question of understanding those ten. Of course we understand them—thoroughly well. Nor is it a question of sympathy for the victim, for he deserved no better (or only because there is a great deal to suggest that the man is hardly in his five wits). The disgraceful thing is that the reaction was German. No one, if he's honest, can help but blush for this episode, and we might so easily have been proud of it.

The day wasn't to decline without more sensations. But the rest were of a very different and, I suppose one must say, more joyful kind. Last night Bizerte fell, and at nine o'clock this morning Tunis!* With that the African campaign is wound up and the Axis chased over into *Festung Europa*.† In the Mediterranean forty-two transports have been sunk, and four destroyers. Good lord! Yes, of course we rejoice. Man is a beast of prey, and we can't help it. They were Germans and Italians, enemies, barbarians, devil-scum!!!

TUESDAY, MAY 11, 1943 ■ I went to work today, and in the evening I turned out for roll call, so now the leg has played its part.

The Lieutenant who was in command of the North Norway transport last year came to see me at the office. He was very amiable and pleasant, and thought it extraordinary that I was still here. Had a lively argument with him about the war. I told him flatly what I thought would be the result of it—to the consternation of the rest. But the Lieutenant's

---

* The Tunisian Campaign, which began shortly after the Allied landings in North Africa in November 1942, culminated in the capture of Bizerte, resulting in the surrender of approximately 250,000 German and Italian soldiers. One historian has observed, "The decision to reinforce North Africa was one of the worst of Hitler's blunders . . . it placed some of Germany's best troops in an indefensible position from which, like Stalingrad, there would be no escape."

† Festung Europa (Fortress Europe) was a term used by the Nazis to describe those parts of occupied Europe they had fortified against invasion by the Allies. But "the destruction of Army Group Centre by the Red Army and the Normandy landings in June 1944 showed just how false the propaganda was."

faith in a German victory was none the less deafening, and strangely immovable. If there are many like him, to be sure they may keep on till they're actually lying in their graves with the coffin screwed down. But then they'll have to give in!

Francis began a new series on Strindberg* tonight. My carving is going badly. I'm worn out. Feel as though I lacked all the vitamins.

WEDNESDAY, MAY 12, 1943 ■ A man in the transport gang was pinched today for trying to smuggle letters from the prisoners out of camp. He stated that he'd had twelve letters. However, he'd had twenty, so things might have gone worse than they did. For what happened was that the twelve were called on to report voluntarily at evening roll call. They stepped forward one by one, till there were eight—nine—ten—eleven, and finally, twelve; but that was counting the smuggler, and so then one more came forward on demand—and that was right. Twenty of course might have come, indeed a lot more for that matter. Nobody could know if his letters had been taken.

But now there followed another awkward and repellant scene. The smuggler, who was "shown to the people," we ourselves were to punish. Not till that was done would there be a lifting of the ban on letters which was now imposed on the whole camp. So the twelve, who were the real sinners, were not to be punished, but the one—who had done his mates a service and taken the big risk involved—he was to be punished—and by his mates. We were to beat him up and make a report to Denzer when it was done. And this was voluntary! God save us! But Denzer wanted to know if we didn't all think it was better for one man to be punished than for the whole camp to suffer. The first time there was no reply. I was standing hoping that it wouldn't be necessary. But Denzer would have a reply, and then came a Yes!—yes! from some hundreds of throats. It was bitter to hear. But *I* might have said no—others certainly would have joined me. Of course we all knew that this punishing would never be done. And indeed later in the evening Denzer was told so.

THURSDAY, MAY 13, 1943 ■ The day had no sooner begun than a new man was pinched for trying to smuggle letters. Truly a splendid proof of the effectiveness of yesterday's judicial proceedings. Though indeed this man must have been an uncommon donkey. He had a placard fixed to his chest with "smuggler" on it in German and Norwegian, and was then posted at attention by the gateway to the parade ground; there he stood till he dropped, about the middle of the day. He had been at attention four or five hours.

This morning I was summoned to Reich. I imagined that now it was the *Bauleitung* for me. But no, it was something quite different. The Germans are having a big party on Saturday, and Reich wanted me to draw caricatures of them all. I had been so long in camp and knew what they looked like, so it would be the work of a moment for me to do caricatures of them, in his view. All the same he had asked me now so that I should have plenty of time—right up to noon on Saturday (this is Thursday), and it would only be about thirty drawings all told! Why, the man was crazy!

---

* August Strindberg (1849–1912). Swedish playwright, novelist, and essayist, Strindberg is considered the father of modern Swedish literature. Interestingly, Strindberg's second wife, Maria Friedrike ("Frida") Uhl, later became the lover of the painter Augustus John (1873–1961), whose daughter-in-law Katherine John translated Nansen's diary into English in 1949.

I tried to explain that it was impossible. He brushed that aside. I wasn't even to get a look at the subjects; I was to draw them from memory! All my refusals, all my assurances that I couldn't do it, were thrown away. I must do it—and I shouldn't do it in vain, he said! Then at last I said I would recruit some of the others and try, but on condition that each of the Germans should "sit" for us. I roped in Per [Krohg], [Alv] Erikstad,* [Joachim] Grøgård,† [Gunnar] Bratlie,‡ and [Bendt] Winge, and it was arranged that we should have every German for five minutes.

At two o'clock we got going in the *Verwaltung*. The "victims" were placed by turns in a chair standing on a chest, and we "artists" took up our places in a circle and began drawing until the sparks flew—the most spiteful caricatures of our tormentors. A certain satisfaction, but repellent all the same. Per was the unhappiest; he grew more and more desperate and finally could stand no more. But we got eleven of them drawn today and are to go on tomorrow. We're to make big drawings (they are to be exhibited from the stage) and each person is to be depicted in a definite situation, specified by Reich himself. The witty dog! For instance, Frau Fiedler§ is to be represented tipsy, carrying a suitcase and a bottle—and she's to be coming out of the German driver Schlägel's room, where she has been spending the night. That must be obvious from the drawing, said Reich.

The Commandant was to be shown tipsy and falling out of "Grandpa's" trap, in which he went for a drive.

Denzer was to be shown as a ringmaster, with the parade ground as the ring, etc., etc. One gets all sorts of commissions, that's certain!

SATURDAY, MAY 15, 1943 ■ Today we were at our caricatures until dinnertime. In the end I couldn't bear the sight of them, let alone feel amused. I was glad when I'd delivered the last and gotten it over. And so I'm sure were others—Per at any rate.

Denzer, as I said, was depicted as a ringmaster in the parade ground with a long whip, while the Butcher stood by with his legs astraddle. As I was on my way to hand over this drawing and some of the others, I met the two Germans in question plus the Commandant in the middle of the square. I had to exhibit my works of art. Denzer grew very stiff in the face when he saw the circus scene, and God knows how it would have gone off if the Commandant hadn't shouted with laughter and slapped his thighs—then of course neither Denzer nor the Butcher could very well be angry. But neither was enthusiastic. At this moment the party is on, and I can imagine more or less how it will develop. Seven tarts were already in the field this afternoon. Yesterday's and today's news pretty strong. Perhaps the best of it all is a sentence in Churchill's broadcast speech from the U.S.A.: "The conference which has just taken place is the last military conference before the

---

* Erikstad (1920–2003), at the time an architecture student, was later city architect for Kristiansand (1950–1987). His most notable work is the concrete church in Grim, a municipality of Kristiansand, built in 1969. He was released March 22, 1945.

† Joachim Grøgaard (1902–1973) remained in Grini until war's end. An artist and illustrator, in 1945 he published a memoir of his incarceration in Grini titled *Tre år under Kunze* [*Three Years under Kunze*]. He also illustrated other books about Grini.

‡ Gunnar Bratlie (1918–1990) was an illustrator and graphic artist. He was imprisoned in February 1943, along with his editor, for his caricature of Quisling and Hitler that depicted Quisling as an unsteady skater being assisted by Hitler. He was released March 22, 1945. A collection of sketches he produced while in Grini was published in 1945 under the title *Skisser I Smug* [*Sketches in the Alley*], the preface to which was written by Francis Bull.

§ *Lagerkommandant* Zeidler's secretary.

armistice."* This statement radiates such optimism and such thrilling power, that it's likely to pass over the whole camp like a burst of sunshine, when it becomes known.

SUNDAY, MAY 16, 1943 ■ Sunday, a cloudless sky—and hardly a German in the field. Last night's party was not a rowdy one. Only a bit of revolver shooting of course, and a certain amount of work today for the glaziers, putting in new windowpanes. But that's just a tame and innocent Germanic parlor game.

I had a long and undisturbed conversation with Lise and with several others in the *Einzelhaft*. The façade was lively today in the sunshine. Heads were sticking out everywhere from all the cells, and there was a positive bubbling and boiling over the whole prison front. The latest news was broadcast, and people arrested for the same affair "exchanged questionings" and reached agreements; altogether there was a delicious atmosphere all round, while the Commandant and his fellows slept off their binge.

MONDAY, MAY 17, 1943 ■ The seventeenth of May. A brilliant sunny day it has been, and in spite of all, the brilliant sunshine found its way into our hearts. A handshake and the compliments of the day wherever we met—out on the working sites, in the passages, on the steps, on the parade ground—was all that was said and done; but it was enough.

At evening roll call came the event of the day: Vidkun Quisling had sought and obtained an amnesty for more than two hundred men. First the names were called, nobody knew why. To begin with people were in dread of being on the list; was it a transport for Germany? Was it some other kind of penal sentence? What was it? Soon there was a rumor of amnesty—and a quivering eagerness to see if one's own name would be called. I can say with my hand on my heart that this time I was not trembling. I was not excited. I felt no disappointment. I knew I shouldn't get out. Now I'm even more certain; me they mean to hold! For that matter no hostages were released, nor any of the really long-standing prisoners. One or two with over a year, but mostly those who have been here the shortest time. A choice amnesty indeed.

Good night, Kari. The next seventeenth of May we shall have together—you and I and our children.

TUESDAY, MAY 18, 1943 ■ Leif [Poulsson] was deposed as *leitender Arzt* [head doctor] today. Denzer has been raving at him lately, calling him a "damned Englishman" and other flattering names. One cause of his fury is that Leif has issued slips of paper, exempting certain prisoners from work some hours of the day, because they were infirm and elderly people.

WEDNESDAY, MAY 19, 1943 ■ In the middle of the afternoon I was up in the hospital. While I was sitting there, word came that Per [Krohg] had been released. I rushed off to the hut. Yes, indeed. There was Per, in mufti, ready to leave. It is needless to say that he was exuberantly happy, and vain to attempt a description of his feelings and ours. He will be a great loss—greater assuredly than I can yet realize. The parting was brief as lightning,

---

* The Washington Conference, code named Trident, took place between President Roosevelt and Prime Minister Churchill and their respective military staffs in Washington, DC, May 11–25, 1943. The final plans for Operation Husky, the invasion of Sicily, scheduled for July 1943, were approved, as was the subsequent invasion of Italy and the cross-channel invasion in 1944. Unfortunately there were to be many more conferences before the war's end.

but painful, and the void is increasing as the hours pass. Our nocturnal trio is crippled; now only Francis and I remain, and we are both, as yet, too strained and anxious to settle down to a duet. It feels worse each time holes are made in the circle.

FRIDAY, MAY 21, 1943 ■ Last night I sent out two "tubes" of the diary and the woodblock to Kari. A German *Wachtmeister** took it. Today Kari has it, I assume.

Lise is under questioning again—has had the screws on her calves again twice, but not screwed up. There's something definite they want to scare out of her—the fiends.

Kari came yesterday. She brought Eigil. It was lovely to see her, but she looked tired, even though she smiled and was plucky. Eigil looked well, he's shooting up and becoming a big boy, while I sit here—and can't be a father to him. That hurts. And it hurts to see the tracings of longing and pain in Kari's face.

The news is what one calls fine. But when will the day break in earnest? When shall we have got so far as to feel impatient for the morning when we lie down at night?

SATURDAY, MAY 22, 1943 ■ When everyone has gone to bed and the camp is quiet, I always stand a while at the window staring out at the night sky; for otherwise there's nothing to look at except the privy opposite. Far away I can hear the Bærum line, or is it the Western line? The thud of wheels against the rails far, far away, and the hooting of the engine. It is like the rhythm of liberty. If one only had a little modest standing place on that train rushing through the spring night away in the southwest yonder.

TUESDAY, MAY 25, 1943 ■ Yesterday I had a bout of lumbago, so I've been lying flat ever since. I can't move much.

THURSDAY, MAY 27, 1943 ■ In the middle of yesterday afternoon I went into the hospital. I felt helpless enough that I might just as well be in a place where others are ill, too.

The news is good, and the whole thing *may* be over before we know it. But it *may* also drag on. Francis has been to see me, but there's no one here who gives lectures. Good night, Kari. Tomorrow I'll see if I can't write something a bit more cheerful.

SUNDAY, MAY 30, 1943 ■ Here I'm lying still and nothing happening. Denzer has gone away. According to report he's going to Prague to sit for the *Untersturmführer* exam (but will probably fail again). Yesterday I had a lot of mail. A letter from Kari, such that it doesn't matter about anything else. She has received the wood block I sent her, and she writes of it and us and the children, of the future, of life, and of our country—in short—!

They bomb and bomb and prate and prate and that's all. Francis comes to see me every day. He is faithful, full of kindness and optimism. I'm all right. Good night, Kari.

TUESDAY, JUNE 1, 1943 ■ So we're starting another month—the midsummer month—under pretty gloomy auspices. Nothing has happened to provide a basis for any special optimism. From London we hear the same old stock phrases that have now been flowing from it so abundantly for more than three years. Hold out! Hold out! And we

---

* Watch master; a non-commissioned rank.

hold out—what in blazes can we do but hold out? Do they suppose we're in the process of giving up? Just wait, they say, a few days or months—or will it be years? First they're going to try to bomb the German and Italian towns to bits. I can't shake off a deep disgust and despair at the kind of warfare on which the Allies now seem to have staked everything.

Today dawned with mist and drizzle and a back more intractable than ever. I'm getting short-wave and massage, but to my shame I don't feel any of it is any use. I've really never been so helpless as I am just now. It's quite out of my power to bend down and pick up anything from the floor, let alone wash my feet—not even sitting. Well, no doubt it will pass off.

FRIDAY, JUNE 4, 1943 ■ Not a speck of news. No releases either. I get up a bit now. Today I couldn't stand bed any longer. It was hot out—real, regular summer.

My old friend Fridtjof Leqvamb and a young student named Ola Bonnevie* and I have formed an "illicit company" (with the support of Dr. [Arne] Halvorsen, who is *leitender Arzt*) whose activity pertains to night and darkness.† Fridtjof and Ola are sure to be a long time in the hospital. Someday their doings will bulk large in the history of Grini.

SATURDAY, JUNE 5, 1943 ■ Evening roll call provided a comedy. The *Lagerkommandant* appeared in a fury and half-seas over.‡ Cucumbers had been stolen, he asserted; it was known who had stolen them, they would have two minutes to come forward, and if no one came forward the whole camp should have a punishment they would never forget.

Two minutes passed, nobody came forward. There were more screaming bouts, then conferences between Reich, Kunze and him, then came a statement that it wasn't cucumbers which had been stolen but chives—now would anyone come forward? The Danish cook up at the Commandant's was called to the front (for some reason which I didn't quite understand), but gradually it must have become apparent that the chives had been cut up there at the Commandant's residence and used in his own kitchen. Both Reich and the Commandant sneaked off with their tails between their legs, and the never-to-be-forgotten punishment was forgotten.

MONDAY, JUNE 7, 1943 ■ My back is not right. I've been moved into a cell for two, which I share with [Kristian] Østberg.§

FRIDAY, JUNE 11, 1943 ■ Germans are the stupidest of God's creatures. At this moment they're rushing about the square and through the passages with tommy guns and all kinds of murderous equipment. God knows on what account, while we, "the illicit

---

* Bonnevie was arrested for producing an illegal underground newspaper, *Half Eight*, named after the time [7:30 p.m.] each evening devoted to the BBC broadcast. He even smuggled a newspaper out of Grini he had produced by eavesdropping on the German's radio reception. In the fall of 1943 Bonnevie was sent to Sachsenhausen, where he remained until the end of the war.

† In the main building the hospital, or *Revier* occupied the second floor of the center block and also the whole third floor of the north wing. *Einzelhaft* occupied all the lower floor of the north wing. Thus from the *Revier* on the third floor we could get in touch by "string mail" with every cell in *Einzelhaft*. It was this vital communication that "the illicit company" maintained every night—when it grew dark enough to hide our primitive tools, moving busily up and down the house front. O.N.

‡ British slang for drunkenness.

§ Remained in Grini until war's end.

company," sit here in the "closet," silently and behind locked doors, writing our dispatches to the south and north wing and out into the world, undisturbed and in complete security. Moreover our "consignments" have been going undisturbed up and down the façade and on all our inscrutable paths, while the Germans bluster and carry on and "see and hear everything."

MONDAY, JUNE 14, 1943 ■ Another day off. But this morning everyone was routed out at quarter past six all the same. About a hundred men were picked for penal labor; they had been reported earlier. Then the rest were allowed to go back to bed.

On an empty stomach these hundred men were kept at work all day till five o'clock. Among them was old [Ingvald] Walderhaug.* Reported for standing idle, which is his job—he's employed as a watchman. He doesn't speak much German, and anyhow what's the use? I managed to give him some food this morning; I left it in a pile of planks, and he took it out and went to the privy. No doubt many of them got something in the same way.

MONDAY, JUNE 17, 1943 ■ Had an awful fright this morning. The Commandant, attended by Kunz, arrived up in the hospital before the devil had his shoes on, and asked for me. [Haakon] Fretheim† came rushing into the cell to warn me; he must have thought that now hell was loose. At the same instant the *Lagerkommandant* appeared in the doorway, shoved Fretheim to one side and went straight to the point: "You are reading a book by Feuchtwanger, *ni*'?"‡ he gave me an angry look under his flaccid eyelids.§ It was a disagreeable awakening, but still I drew a deep breath of relief when I heard what it was about, and told him with an easier mind that such was the case. "Give me the book!" I hunted out the book, which I had, thank God, and gave it to him, with an even deeper sigh of relief. Good Lord, was that all he wanted—was that anything to make such a to-do about?

I looked round—Østberg was lying up there in bed, scared to death—Fretheim stood squeezed into a corner, pale as the whitewashed wall. In the center of the table between the beds lay my sketchbook! I grew hot when I saw it—and I think I turned Fretheim's color. For under the loose, half-open cover of the sketchbook lay *the night's mail from Einzelhaft*. Nor was it quite an ordinary mail! In *Einzelhaft* there were seven Englishmen, taken for "sabotage" in Sørland.¶ We had invited each of them to write a letter to his

---

* Walderhaug, who was fifty-five at the time of this entry, had suffered a heart attack a year earlier (see April 10, 1942, above) while on the trotting gang. He was released one month later, on July 15, 1943.

† Remained at Grini until war's end.

‡ Lion Feuchtwanger (1884–1958) was a prolific German-Jewish novelist and playwright who strongly criticized the Nazis even before their accession to power; after 1933 he was designated by the Nazis as an enemy of the state, and his books were banned. Feuchtwanger ultimately gained asylum in the United States in 1941, and spent the remainder of his life residing and writing in Southern California.

§ On a former occasion Dr. Rietz on one of his rounds had discovered me reading a book by Feuchtwanger, and he must have reported it to the Commandant. O.N.

¶ This refers to John Godwin and six other English commandos who, as members of No. 14 (Arctic) Commando, participated in Operation Checkmate, an attempt to attack German shipping off Norway using two-man canoes to attach magnetic (limpet) mines. After sinking a German minesweeper, all seven were captured May 14/15, 1943. Despite wearing full military uniforms, the prisoners, in furtherance of Hitler's Commando Order, were treated not as POWs but instead were sent to Grini, where they spent their entire stay in *Einzelhaft*. They were ultimately transported to Sachsenhausen at the same time as Nansen. See February 3, 1945, below. In general, British efforts to

people in England—and the Lieutenant, in addition, to send his commanding officer a report of their adventures and of the infamous treatment they were now getting from the Germans.

That very night I had hoisted up these letters and this report by "string mail." They were to be sent out the same morning, and were now lying, a small package wrapped in toilet paper, under the cover of the sketchbook, with a quantity of other string mail. But that package was visible enough, ostentatiously addressed in block capitals:

ENGLISH LEGATION STOCKHOLM

As I got back the use of my mind after the apparition of the sketchbook, and began to think—oh God what thoughts!—I started breathing anything but sighs of relief, and it's incomprehensible to me that the Commandant failed to see the big drops of cold sweat which were absolutely gushing out of my forehead and rolling down into the bed.

"Have you any more books?" asked the Commandant. As though I'd had an electric shock, I started feverishly groping round for more books. At any cost find books! More books! Lots of books! I kept thinking as, in a stream of preternaturally fluent German, I assured him that I had quantities of books—certainly I had books—entertaining books, readers, novels, fine things—oh God! The sweat trickled and my heart was thumping like a steam hammer, as one book after another appeared from hiding places that I scarcely knew of myself. Books by the pile—books, books—only not sketchbooks!!

I was in deadly terror that he would approach and join in the hunt, and catch sight of the fatal sketchbook on the table. I saw him through a mist, the SS cap with the death's-head, that sour-sweet, lazy smirk of his, the impeccable uniform jacket, the jutting balloon-breeches, the riding boots—the riding whip! The riding whip!! I edged cautiously nearer the table—meant to try and snap up the sketchbook and spirit it away by some inexplicable means. But suddenly through the mist I saw Kunz slouching past the Commandant, headed straight for the table! Nonchalantly he flung out one of those long tentacles and seized—the sketchbook! It was as though the world collapsed on my head. What now? I think I shut my eyes—and said the Lord's Prayer forward and backward . . . for ever and ever amen!—while at the same time I lived through Churchill's immortal words: Blood, sweat and tears! But nothing happened. The crash didn't come. I looked up, and there was Kunz waving the sketchbook about in one hand, while he used the other to rummage among the other things on the table. He found nothing of interest there, and turned on me impatiently: "Come now, Nansen! All the books, *ni*'? All! The Jewish books—come on, man, hurry up!" And then—God help us all—he whacked the sketchbook on the table with a resounding thump!

I was expecting to see the "string mail" strewn about the room, dissolved into its little separate slips, and I had already started thinking out my defense before the court-martial. But the age of miracles is not yet over. Nothing happened! Kunz had squeezed the cover so hard with his thumb against the sketchbook that it retained its fateful contents. With the inspiration of despair, I seized my piles of books and held them out to Kunz, heaped them on him, first onto the vacant tentacle and then onto the other, and he had to—God bless our dearest country!—put down the sketchbook! I went on heaping books on him

---

sabotage ships in Norwegian waters were not successful; between 1943 and 1945 fewer than a dozen ships, totaling thirty thousand tons, were sunk or damaged by commandos.

until they reached right up to his chin, meanwhile blessing my own activity as illegal-book center for the hospital.

The Commandant chimed in, announcing to my speechless astonishment that he was aware I had permission both to smoke and to read; he only wanted to find out whether the books I read were *anständige* [suitable]. Then he turned on his heel and left the cell, closely followed by Kunz, round backed and even more crooked than usual with all the blessed books he was laden with.

But the sketchbook lay in peace and innocence on the edge of the table, and whether you believe me or not the little package of English mail had slid out so far that the first two letters of "ENGLISH" were visible beyond the cover.

For the rest of the day I went about in something of a daze after the shock. If it didn't turn me downright "religious," at any rate I promised myself—and others—that henceforth "the things" should be kept a great deal more securely when I was not working.*

SATURDAY, JUNE 19, 1943 ■ Yesterday was a good day because Kari was here, with Eigil and the baby. All three were splendid and we had a fine, happy meeting, even though it was sad when they went away again.

An hour ago a terrific row started in the camp—screams and roars and inarticulate bellowing, in the style we now know too well. I put out the light, rolled up the blind and peered out. The prisoners were streaming from all the huts. Night parade. Denzer was directing the circus act. The electric fence had lit up an hour ago; no doubt there was a suggestion that someone had escaped. I suppose a cat or a squirrel had come in contact with the wire, or it might have been nothing but a short-circuit caused by the rain—for it is rainy and misty. In the end the census came right. To be sure there was a man in [Hut] 5 who hadn't turned out—probably he was asleep in the hut. He arrived, and for a wonder it didn't sound as if he were being struck dead, nor did he get any bawling out that I could hear. There was a census here in the hospital as well, but a pretty casual one.

But then began the circus down in the square. The *Lagerkommandant* came walking up the road—like royalty, together with the Lieutenant. There was "*Mützen ab!*" and "*Augen rechts!*" [Eyes right!] and Denzer trundled off to the gateway, struck an attitude and bawled with standard Aryan vociferation what was going on, and how many prisoners were assembled. The Commandant sauntered over to the personnel chief in the center of the front. Another salute, another "*Mützen ab! und auf!*" and "*Richt euch!*" [Line up!] and "*Augen rechts!*" and "*Augen gerade aus!*" [Eyes straight ahead!] and "*Rührt euch!*" [At ease!] and the rest of it. He can't have been satisfied, for it was repeated over and over and over again, far beyond the verge of parody.

We were kneeling on our beds looking on. Johannes [Bødtker] was in the room with us. Every now and then we had to bury our heads in the pillows, to prevent our roars of laughter from being heard outside. The *Lagerkommandant* left the square, to a further display of the whole ceremony of arm-cranking, bellowing and "*Augen rechts!*" and "*Mützen ab!*" But no, that wasn't the end. He pulled up on the road, and there he remained, calling

---

* I ought to explain that "the things" were usually kept in secret places from the time we received them until they were sent out. One of these hiding places was in the double bottom of a little shelf for toothbrushes, another in the hollow legs of the table, a third in a loose board that could be pulled out of the table top, etc. That morning I had taken the risk of leaving them in the sketchbook, as the "post" was going early the same morning, nor had the Commandant or any of his henchmen ever come inspecting the hospital at such an early hour. It was not yet six. O.N.

for "*Mützen ab und auf!*" again and again, twenty or thirty times. He was never satisfied; it went too slow. Again! Again! Again! Each time, Denzer screamed, bawled, bellowed, seconded by the Commandant on the road, who pointed out where the exercises were being done badly. Again, "*Mützen ab! Ein! Zwei! Sacrament mal! Verflucht mal!*" Curses and commands filled the night air, and the fellows toiled on. I looked at Francis. He was the sheerest master of precision. Nobody was better. But what did that profit him? Again! On the left flank there was someone who couldn't do it. Again!

And we laughed—we couldn't help it. Though it's sinister that grown people should occupy themselves like that in dead earnest. They were sober too. God help us all if that nation is to remain in power much longer. The Negroes in darkest Africa are more evolved. Fish have better brains. Frogs and toads have fine voices in comparison.

MONDAY, JUNE 21, 1943 ■ Rain and mist. A man in *Einzelhaft* has probably broken his back, and can't have much chance of getting over it. The other day he fell on his head from the top bunk onto the stone floor. There can be so many reasons for a thing like that. Today he was sent to Ullevål. I saw him when they were carrying him out. "So I fooled them after all," he said—obviously quite aware that he was done for. He struck one as anything but out of his mind.

From time to time, there are of course many *Einzelhäftlinge* [solitary confinement prisoners] who have become deranged. We have a fellow who is confined here at the sick ward on the same corridor as I. He is totally confused, has tantrums and thinks everybody is after him. In the women's sick ward they have a deranged lady of whom they are very afraid. She is completely out of her mind, screams and carries on, but the worst part of it is that in her condition she has been questioned by Gestapo and in her madness has revealed the most horrendous things—which Gestapo then believes. It might be ominous. There are also others who have become a little soft in the head, and a good many have gotten *Haftpsykose* [prison psychosis]—an unpleasant and dangerous condition.

No news that I care to write of. Bombing and prating. The invasion is coming, they assure us, and we shall wait till we're old and gray—and God knows how far gone we'll all be with *Haftpsykose*.

WEDNESDAY, JUNE 23, 1943 ■ The big news doesn't come at all, the belief in invasion dwindles, and optimism—here in camp at least—is decidedly on the ebb. I've lost four kilos [8.8 pounds]. But I shall work up again. Good night, Kari. A dreary Midsummer Eve—quite the dreariest I've ever known.*

SUNDAY, JUNE 27, 1943 ■ Yesterday at evening roll call it was announced that as the Commandant had noticed many prisoners dodging work of late in spite of repeated warnings, he had decided that the whole camp should be punished by getting nothing to eat on Sunday. This was something new and rather fiendish, as many are undernourished.

But at morning roll call today, Denzer figured in all his incredibility. He made a speech that was unique of its kind. That the day after one of the Commandant's absurdest

---

* Minister Harriman observed, "Next to Christmas the greatest fete of the north is Midsummer Night. . . . It is the great outdoor festivity and the whole population goes out to the fjords, or the mountain tops, drives along the fjord or watches the bonfires and fireworks from boats."

antics he should make undisguised apologies—that we're used to, but today he went even further. He said it wasn't so vital that we should do such a lot of work, provided that man up there (the Commandant) didn't *see* that we were dodging. We must move about the working places, it must look as if we were doing something, at any rate when the Commandant was making his rounds.

This was received with open laughter from the whole body of prisoners—to Denzer's satisfaction. He had, he said, managed to arrange that we should have dinner after all, but not until five o'clock. So the effect of the punishment was that everyone got more food than usual, for as a matter of course there was "scrounging" and "fixing" the whole day through, porridge-boiling and potato-frying and all kinds of cookery, without a single German around to keep a check. The Commandant lay naked on the lawn in front of his house all day, taking the sun. The other Germans were invisible, except Denzer, who followed up his success at morning roll call by "receiving" prisoners who wanted to speak to him.

He invited me, and I went. He asked me to come over to the window. I went to the window, and looked in the direction he pointed out. No, I must come over to his side of the desk and get a proper view. "Look there, up there—there he lies. Do you see him? There—there *he* lies sunbathing. *I* could have done that today when it's Sunday and a day off. But here I am, here at my desk. Why? Because, Nansen, my work is here. Here I have something to do for you, for your comrades, for all in the camp, and I do it, I must do it, I feel impelled to do it. And up there lies he! Do you see him? There—there he lies. I tell you, Nansen, when I was away on leave just now (he was in Prague taking an exam) I was longing to be back the whole time, I knew neither rest nor peace till I got back here to my task, to my prisoners, who I know are in need of me. Look up there! There—there he lies . . ."

If Denzer is not transcendent, no one is.

I seized the opportunity to ask what was the position about those parcels we got when we had visitors—if they weren't extra. "Tja—hm—hm! No, to be sure they weren't extra, those visitors' parcels, to be sure it was only one parcel a month we were allowed, yes, that was so. Hm—hm—*aber!*" [but!] He slapped me on the back, blinked his penetrating criminologist eyes, and did a couple of brisk, elegant dance steps. "*Verstanden?*"

The food came at half past four, for at five o'clock there was parade. A great display. Denzer was once more flaunting in his summer uniform with a white jacket. There was "*Mützen ab!*" and "*Augen rechts!*" first for him and then for Reinhardt, two other Gestapists and the Commandant. There was a fresh call over of the men for Germany. But this time it was almost joyful, for Reinhardt questioned most of them personally and exempted fourteen or fifteen. But the women were not gone through, and Lise is on the list.

MONDAY, JUNE 28, 1943 ■ Sunshine, always sunshine, extravagant sunshine. Wakened this morning by a mighty uproar from the parade ground. It was the transport for Germany which was about to leave. They were already lined up in mufti down on the square. The usual roars and screams from the Germans filled the air, as at other such times. The little cardboard boxes had to be searched, all letters handed over and so on, and such a process can't possibly be noiseless; all are not equally quick at getting their boxes open and strewing their clean clothes and toilet things around on the dusty square. The checking was mostly done with the feet, which were clad in highly polished riding boots. But in the conflict between highly polished riding boots and clean underclothes, a few little toilet things and here and there a sandwich or tin of food, it is decidedly the highly polished riding boots that come off best. Denzer was swaggering around in full summer canonicals, and the whole staff was in activity.

I managed to say good-bye to Lise. She assured me that she was glad of this, and was in good heart. I was to give her love to the children and Ragnar. Bjørn Oscar [Andersen] slipped her a box of cigarettes. Had we been brazen enough, we could easily have given her a hug, too.

THURSDAY, JULY 1, 1943 ■ Thus passed the first half of the year '43, and the second begins with sunshine. Today we've had 33° [C or 91.4°F] in the shade, and naked sun-tanned bodies are the distinguishing feature of the whole camp. Yesterday it was forbidden to appear in drawers, to which most people had confined themselves in this weather; one must be wearing the regulation prison trousers. The result has been that people have simply rolled up the thin dungaree trousers to the middle of the thigh, so that they're just like bathing drawers; otherwise one goes about naked from top to toe. The next ordinance will of course be jackets, too, and a ban on pulling up the trouser legs.

But in general I should think that any outsider who had got a glimpse of the camp today would have described the whole thing as an idyll. The overwhelming majority of the prisoners are standing, sitting, or lying in the sun, now and then having a little go at a wheelbarrow, a spade or some bit of hut section to indicate work; some are strolling inces-santly from one place to another and back again, to make it look as if they had something to do both here and there. But most have thrown over appearances altogether, for there are no Germans about. It's as though this heat had completely paralyzed them as well. They can't be bothered, they are really and patently fed up with the whole business and don't conceal the fact. But it's no doubt safest to count on a reaction one fine day, a fresh "wave of terror" as soon as the worst heat is over and devilry begins to reawaken from its torpor.

SATURDAY, JULY 3, 1943 ■ Saturday and sunshine again, but no news, only bomb-ing—perpetual terror-bombing. All the same the papers are interesting just now. Bigger and bigger admissions.

Here in camp there are incontestable symptoms of dissolution. Denzer himself has sunk to obtaining certain things illicitly through prisoners—or possibly civilians. For which, moreover, he's been confined to camp—for how long I don't know. In general he is busy "rowing."* Still trying, indeed, to hold fast to a single point—hatred of the Bolsheviks. He bellows something about that every day. Yesterday he was talking about it to the hut leaders, and in that connection asked if they didn't read the papers. For after all what's in them can't all be lies, he added. Such a remark in jest or earnest would have been inconceivable only six months ago.

Oddly enough a chap like Kunze doesn't wholly fail to realize what is coming. Ivan [Rosenquist]† in *Einzelhaft* said to him the other day that "in a year from today you'll be

---

* A similar expression in English would be changing one's tack, or changing one's tune, and adopting a different posi-tion or attitude.

† Rosenquist (1916–1994), a geologist, was active in the Resistance intelligence organization (XU) and head of the courier routes to Sweden. He was sentenced to death, but his execution was postponed to allow him to write up

in these cells and we shall be the jailers." Kunze told him that out in camp—that is among the other Germans—they put it at a month. I suppose Kunze doesn't know what to believe, poor hen-brain. He's like a "lamb" these days. Well—a German lamb! Tonight he's drunk. Drunk as an owl. He could hardly keep his feet when he was up here earlier this evening asking for matches. He has the guard tonight.

Talking of guards. Down on the "field" this evening we were entertained by a mirthful sight. In the south watchtower a guard was hanging with his arms and head and half his torso out of the window, sleeping like a log at his post. He slept for more than half an hour at least, for I saw him as long as that.

SUNDAY, JULY 4, 1943 ■ Today I've had a conversation with Denzer. He asked if there was any news, as his custom is, whatever he means by it. It usually signals that he's in a talking mood and would like to start on one of his political numbers. I don't exactly know why it was, but suddenly a devil got into me, and I became completely reckless. I threw all precautions overboard. We came to discuss art. God knows how we got on to it. His arguments were so supremely idiotic that they threw me into despair and I told him straight out that what he was saying was so stupid and unintelligent as to make it difficult to reply. I said it shocked me, it was so totally unaesthetic and so lacking in modesty.

He held up Dürer as the exponent of German art and culture.* He knew of no others, I observed when referring to other medieval masters. But it was mostly about so-called modern art, which, of course, was Jewish—plutocratic art. That I described as Nonsense!—without the least ceremony. Thence we got on to the Jewish question, and in that domain I was not more backward. Several times I asked Denzer not to roar so loud. It became impossible for me to understand him, and, I said, he mustn't think that screaming improved his arguments. He laughed a trifle sheepishly, pleading that he had an extremely powerful voice, that he was a soldier and accustomed to speaking loud; and he invited me to vociferate as well if I liked. I did so and for a long time we stood facing each other in the personnel office, shouting each other down and thumping the table. It was delicious to hurl out all I thought—practically without the least restraint. Of course I know it was damned stupid. He may of course use it against me hereafter if it suits him. But I couldn't stop.

This went on for a couple of hours, during which time—besides [Bernhard] Paus,† who was present from the beginning of the session—the German Hanssen had come in, and finally the NS candidate Meidell-Larsen (the ration-card swindler).‡ Paus was certainly rather aghast at first; especially when I accused Denzer straight out of using stupid, unintelligent arguments, he jumped where he stood—pale against the wall. And he wasn't wholly enthusiastic when from time to time I wound up my vigorous tirades with "*Nicht wahr*, Paus?" But gradually he got more used to it and took some part in the conversation. Hanssen, who is an artist of the Hitler school, looked horrified, but now and then he also

---

his valuable research findings, and he spent the next eighteen months in solitary confinement at Grini completing his doctoral dissertation in geology. Later pardoned, Rosenquist was sent to Sachsenhausen, where he spent the remainder of the war.

* Albrecht Dürer (1471–1528). German artist, engraver, and printmaker, he was considered one of the greatest artists of the Northern Renaissance.

† Less than a month later Paus was transferred to Germany and remained in German prisons until the end of the war.

‡ Gustav Meidell-Larssen was released November 13, 1944.

chimed in with a little laugh in the right places, and with a few remarks and shrugs when he could see they were appropriate. Meidell-Larsen said not a word.

MONDAY, JULY 5, 1943 ■ Today Denzer woke me up. Right down in the square he was thundering at a prisoner who had waved to a poor fellow locked up in the "Parachute" [room]—only a motion of the hand, a little beggarly greeting.* Denzer had seen this from the steps, and was now beside himself with rage. First he gave the man a frightful box on the ear (he's still deaf in that ear this evening), then he fired off a volley of abuse which was worse than most I've heard here, and finally he posted him at attention by the gate, where he has to stand in the rain for several hours. And this was the man who less than 24 hours earlier had been standing roaring at me about culture and refinement!

Later in the day Paus came to see me. He'd just been through another lecture from Denzer, who had thundered for an hour, informing him in that well-known style that I was hopelessly lost, I was too old now, but for him (Paus) there was still a little hope. He might yet be saved. Denzer hadn't slept all night, he said. He had been thinking of his conversation with me. He also said that now he was going to read a book he had of my father's, then he would get hold of me and have some more talk. Very interesting really. Then some of what I managed to say had "gone home."

FRIDAY, JULY 9, 1943 ■ Kari came today—at last. But she looked tired and had nothing like the color she should have had after all that sun. I'm afraid she's working too hard. There was a sadness in her eyes this time, an indescribable sadness, something like dread? No, no such thing!!

SATURDAY, JULY 10, 1943 ■ Sunshine—thunder—rain—rain as though the sluices of heaven were open.

Today there came at last a piece of real news. The invasion of Sicily has begun.† Well. It's not the Continent yet, but a large, important island not much more than a few stone's throws from the toe of Italy. People are hugely optimistic on the occasion. To my distress I can't work up quite so much optimism as the majority. I should think we still have waiting to do.

MONDAY, JULY 12, 1943 ■ Last night I gave my lecture in [Hut] 3. The room was packed full. There was some discussion afterwards, and a lot of people were taken up with the fact that I had appealed to my audience *here at Grini* on behalf of the German people. Well, it wasn't precisely an appeal, but rather a question connected with the situation after the war. Which of us will volunteer for the first relief expedition to the unhappy, misguided people of Germany?‡ Some indeed were indignant at such talk, but that only shows how essential it is to begin thinking of these things straight away, before it's too late.

---

* Perhaps it was nothing more than a little beggarly greeting. In an essay written after the war by Nansen for *Griniboken* titled "Fingerspråket" [finger language], however, Nansen points out that by 1943 a sophisticated sign language had been developed in the camp, primarily to facilitate communications between the men's and women's sections.
† Operation Husky, the invasion of Sicily by 180,000 Allied troops, began on the morning of July 10, 1943. The island was captured by Allied forces on August 17, 1943, opening the way for the invasion of Italy.
‡ Nansen played a leading role for UNESCO in Germany following the war.

We have time and occasionally peace to think out a good deal here at Grini. And I don't believe it's a waste of effort.

Twelve new prisoners came at midday yesterday—the crew of a Danish ship. In jest they had talked of going to England. Into the hole with them.

Today there has been mist and rain from morning to night. After evening roll call we had an agitating sensation. Search of all the huts! During the roll call there came driving into Grini a long train of armed SS soldiers on motorcycles—about seventy of them. They were divided into groups, each under its indigenous SD gangster. Then all of the prisoners were ordered out of the huts, and the soldiers set to work. They stayed in there a long time. Practically everyone had something to be afraid of, and Grini has seldom passed such an anxious hour. Would they discover this or that secret place?—would they find this or that? Oh dear God, let them not find it! Only this once, then I'll have nothing more to be afraid of, everything shall be removed, disposed of, gone; oh my God, this is more than I can stand.

There was feverish activity here in the hospital as well. All at once our secret receptacles were not good enough, we had to find new ones. Johannes [Bødtker] was panic stricken at being in possession of five half-bottles of lager, and wanted to pour them down the sink. The dispenser got them, just for removing them from the hut leader's room. Thousands of kroner which have arrived in these last few days for the next transport to Germany were stuck into air vents, on top of cupboards and under cupboards and behind benches fixed to the wall. God knows which spots weren't suddenly chock full of highly interesting and sensational objects. No one knew whether they might not come here as well.

But they didn't. At long last we saw them emerging from the huts again with their booty. They had parcels and cardboard boxes and whole barrowfuls of different things. Probably books and provisions I suppose, and heaven knows what all. Claffy was up here getting treatment for the sores on his legs. He told us it was tools they were looking for. The *Bauleitung* had lost such a lot of tools. Some they had found. They weren't to take books, only tools, said Claffy, but some had apparently taken books all the same. Claffy, who is rowing with a great splash,* told us reassuringly that the whole thing didn't amount to much.

TUESDAY, JULY 13, 1943 ■ Just a year and a half since my arrest. Brilliant sunshine and good news. About twenty men were released today. All has been quiet and peaceful in camp, no disturbances or consequences of yesterday's raid. The soldiers had behaved very moderately. Indeed, in one hut the Lieutenant had actually taken a quantity of vegetables he found (stolen goods, that is) and dumped them out the window, drawn the hut leader aside and pointed out there with a nod. He could just retrieve the things when they had left.

Today a man from here was condemned to death in a German police court. He is up in the Parachute. His name is [Karsten] Løvstad† and he's been at Grini more than a year,

---

* Presumably Claffy, a Hird and later SS member, was trying to curry favor with the prisoners but doing so clumsily.

† Løvestad (1916–1943), a border pilot described as a "Norwegian Pimpernel," helped smuggle refugees over the border into Sweden. On October 22, 1942, Løvestad was leading a group of nine Jewish escapees when their train was inspected and two of the escapees (one named Hermann Feldmann) were asked to step off the train by a Norwegian policeman. See October 29, 1942, above. Instead, Løvestad drew a gun, shot and killed the policeman and attempted to escape. All parties were ultimately caught; the Jews were sent to their death at Auschwitz and Løvestad was exe-

out in the camp, till this morning he was taken off to court, sentenced to death and shut up in the Parachute.

I've been singing in 350—lullabies for grown men. One can't be sentimental enough for them, and they have no self-consciousness about it. Good night.

THURSDAY, JULY 15, 1943 ■ Sun, sunbathing and slacking. If it weren't for the night work and a number of daily dispatches of various kinds, this would be a life of ruinous idleness. But as long as one has the sense of doing useful work, one may well spend some hours taking the sun—when there is any.

Today the "box"* arrived, quite the most dangerous thing we've received yet. It's already lodged in a spot where no one will find it, yet so handy that it can be got out in a moment. We must think very carefully before getting to work. It will be exciting, but huge fun. Confound the idiots, we'll fool them all right.

Up in the Parachute Karsten Løvstad is struggling with his thoughts. This evening we sent him up a pad of cotton wool dripping with diphtheria germs. He's probably inhaling them now, poor devil. Perhaps we may succeed in making him ill, and that may save his life. It can't be helped if some others up there also get diphtheria. There are thirty-three men. Most likely they're being kept there because it's full up in *Einzelhaft*, where there are 130. We have daily contact with them in our own way. Fridtjof [Leqvamb] is magnificent.

Hannagreta [Rinnan] is now in *Dunkelzelle* as a punishment because she kept on peeping out the window. Poor thing, she's been locked up in a cell fifteen months now. I pass the time of day when we stroll out in the "field." She's back again at the window unlawfully.

FRIDAY, JULY 16, 1943 ■ Today Dr. Rietz was here, and Halvor† seized the opportunity to talk about me and my illness. He had scarcely got a word out when Rietz interrupted him to say, "It's no use talking of release—quite out of the question!"‡ However, what Halvor wanted was to arrange that, as I had chronic sciatica and lumbago, and from time to time was so bad that I couldn't get up, I should be made a fixture in the hospital and given some kind of employment here. Rietz agreed at once, and suggested that I might be employed on propaganda posters for hygiene. Too little was being done

---

cuted at Trandum Forest on September 3, 1943. In one of the more unusual developments arising from this incident, the parents of Hermann Feldmann, Rakel and Jacob Feldmann, frightened by the news reports of the killing and the manhunt for their son, panicked and arrived at the Løvestad farm on October 23, 1942, asking for assistance in escaping as well. Løvestad's brother Haakon and an assistant, Peder Pedersen, agreed to guide the Feldmanns to Sweden, but en route, Løvestad and Pedersen killed the Jewish couple, stole their valuables and money, and sank their bodies in a nearby pond. Both pilots were ultimately implicated after the war, and in 1947 were tried for the murders. In a controversial decision, they were acquitted on the murder charge after arguing that the Feldmanns were old, overweight, and physically incapable of making the arduous twenty-four mile trek to the border, but that to return them to Norway (while the roundup of Jewish men was underway) would have meant likely exposure of the underground railroad on which so many depended. The pilots were instead convicted only of embezzlement for stealing the money and possessions of the Feldmanns. The killing of the Norwegian border policeman was the pretext to justify the roundup of all adult male Jews on October 26, 1942, and all remaining Jews on November 26, 1942, and their deportation to Auschwitz.
* A moving-picture camera. O.N.
† Nansen's shorthand for Dr. Arne Halvorsen.
‡ Rietz was once described as "98% Nazi and 2% doctor."

in camp in that way. Thus my "position" here was assured, and I can breathe easier in the future. Today, besides, I moved in with Fridtjof [Leqvamb], so now we, the two worst, are sharing a cell, which we are arranging and furnishing in tiptop style with an eye to our multifarious business. It's almost too good to be true. But then the Germans are quite uniquely dim witted.

Today something very awkward has happened. One of the "*Einzel*" prisoners was surprised in his cell in the act of reading an illegal letter which had reached him through us. Asked where he had got it, he said he found it on the taboret outside his door and that it had come the back way. The taboret is the stool they get their food off of when the round has been made and the sweepers have left the rations there. The back way is a locked door to the backstairs, and I suppose he mentioned it to spare the sweepers and divert suspicion to someone in the camp, who was to be supposed to have got in with a false key and put the letter on the taboret. Pretty imbecile, but at any rate, as a result of the assertion, all the back doors were instantly equipped with Yale locks. The sweepers were questioned, but flatly denied all knowledge of the affair.

Denzer has been dealing with it right from the start; he doesn't usually give up so quick, but on the other hand he doesn't find out much. However, I suppose it's too optimistic to think this will be the end of it. The letter was sealed, and was most likely from the prisoner's wife. God knows whether the contents were harmless—or the most complete giveaway. It's conceivable that the wife has been arrested and forced to say who carried the letter for her, and that he in turn will be arrested and squeezed till possibly the whole chain is exposed. But for my part I rely on the stupidity of the Germans and on the Norwegians' evasive powers.

SATURDAY, JULY 17, 1943 ■ Sunny, but a day of dark and perilous clouds in our prison sky. This afternoon our worst forebodings were realized. W. caught sight of his wife at one of the barred windows of the women's section. So she must have been arrested today or yesterday. Fru W. had sent the confounded letter to W. who passed it on to the man who was caught.

SUNDAY, JULY 18, 1943 ■ Sunday, and the snowball rolls on. W. was here by half past five this morning. We agreed on what he should say if he were had up today for questioning. At eleven he was summoned to Denzer. A couple of hours later B. was summoned, and it was plain what had happened. What defenses would fall now?

Time passed, and it was late afternoon, then evening. Then both B. and W. were turned loose in camp again. I went to see W. in the hut. It was a pitiful sight. Completely punctured. I thought at first they'd beaten him to a pulp, when I saw him panting on his bunk with a deathlike, distraught countenance. No such thing! He hadn't been struck at all—not yet, said he, only threatened. He had deposed that he threw the famous letter up through the window to the man in *Einzelhaft*. That they refused to believe—Denzer and the *Lagerkommandant*. But when B. came along with the same statement, they believed in it rather more. Still they preferred to think that W. had penetrated into *Einzelhaft* the back way with a false key. That would be so much more criminological! However, W. hadn't been satisfied with naming B.: to embellish his statement he told them the traffic had been going on three or four months. That he had both sent and received letters and parcels. Good Lord, if people would only keep to the agreement. He has gone completely off the rails and is obviously at his wits' end. What may he not come out with if they start beating him?

And after all it's quite ludicrous. Responsible, grown men behave like little brats caught cheating at school, or stealing cakes from the larder at home. For this is all about trumpery. An ordinary love letter—and a little in the way of smokes and ham and provisions, which have been owned up to. I'm sorry for W., but, I must confess, even more exasperated. I tried to stiffen him up. Let's have the courage of our actions, for goodness' sake. *We are at war with the Germans!* One's sense of values mustn't vanish completely because men like that start acting the schoolmaster. Lose your temper! Bang the table! It's for *them* to feel inferior! W. stared at me in alarm, but I think it gave him something to think about.

As a matter of fact I don't believe any more will come of this business. For the thing is that they don't want any fuss and bother with the Terrace. "We must be diplomats!" as Denzer said to the hut leaders today after roll call. "I am a diplomat," he added, preening himself.

MONDAY, JULY 19, 1943 ■ W. was questioned for a couple of hours this morning too. Nothing fresh came up. It was only a "rounding off" of the details and of course a certain amount of roaring from Denzer about Communism, Judaism, etc. Now we can assuredly regard the matter as wound up and buried.

A fresh snowball started last night. It looks just now as if Denzer the criminologist had tasted blood. Four civilian workers were arrested in the new disinfection hut which is being put up, and where these civilians are employed on their night work. We observed the whole drama from our various windows up here in the hospital. There was the usual bellowing and uproar, but we couldn't make out what the civilian workers were being arrested for. They were taken up to the first floor of the main building, where they were examined. We stationed ourselves at the window of 350 just opposite. More bellowing and uproar, but I caught a word here and there. One of the fellows was called Olsen. That was bad. A word that kept on coming was "parcel." Tobacco then, or food! That doesn't specially affect us. We made no more out of the questioning, which didn't last long. Afterwards three of the workers, including Olsen, were put in *Einzelhaft*, while one was released and led off by a guard.

It's really damnable to lose one's outgoing line at the very moment when things are so exciting. But we'll always manage to get a new one fixed up before long.

TUESDAY, JULY 20, 1943 ■ Sunny—while the snowball rolls on. This morning we learned from well-informed circles that all the outgoing mail had been taken and was lying on Denzer's desk, whereas the incoming had been burned by our people, who in the course of the day managed to get down to the furnace room and empty the letterbox. It was a bad job about the outgoing mail, and I spent the greater part of the morning lying in the sun and thinking over what I should say on the subject of my outgoing bulletin to H7.* I got pretty far with my reflections on this theme, but concluded that it must depend entirely on what Olsen had said or might say under questioning.

---

* H7 was a code for Nansen's business partner, Ernst Holmboe; it was also the symbol for the king, Haakon VII, and as such the symbol "H7" was widely used by the Norwegian population as a symbol of defiance to Nazi rule.

Late in the afternoon we suddenly heard that Olsen and the other two were to be let out into the camp. Not long after, we had Olsen's story, short and sweet—none of the letters were taken. Only tobacco! My letter and some others had been prepared for conveyance in the usual style and put into Olsen's shoes before they went to work. Thoresen, the man who was released, had simply put on Olsen's shoes when he went away. He was certainly under guard the whole time, and it wasn't half bad on the spur of the moment, and the scare he must have had. Well, so it passed off that time as well, the whole thing turned into a banal smuggling case. They took some parcels with names on, and the addressees will now get small appropriate punishments. Some outgoing love letters were also taken and no doubt the authors will also get some mild little punishments. Denzer is in a first-rate mood. He feels he's got a couple of sweet little feathers in his cap again.

A really frightful disaster has taken place in the camp. A chief inspector has been appointed, with unlimited authority. He is a prisoner (so they say at least); he is a German, a Nazi, and an informer. A whelp of twenty-two. He's already informed on eight or ten men. Some for want of courtesy, some for the tempo of their work, some for being in the hut without leave, some for potato-stealing. And today he struck a chap in the delousing hut. We'd better poison him perhaps. He was launched and introduced on parade this evening.

Another tragic thing is that [Bernhard] Paus has become a prisoner of war. He was excellent as personnel chief. Who are we to have now?

But the news from outside is still grand, and I'm in better heart and vigor than for a very long time back. I have masses to do, and besides I'm once more coming to believe the autumn will finish it.

THURSDAY, JULY 22, 1943 ■ Have begun on a propaganda poster for the extirpation of lice. A poster against lice can serve two purposes. An inscription like "Cleanse your land of lice," or merely "Away with the lice" will be impossible to misunderstand.

FRIDAY, JULY 23, 1943 ■ Gray weather all day. Actually I had a lot to write about, but Kari didn't come, won't be coming until *next* Thursday, and then I've been sitting up interminably (it's half-past two) writing a poem for Fridtjof [Leqvamb] who is forty-one tomorrow—and then there's been a depressing punishment drill and no news except *Dementis* of the best we heard yesterday, and finally I have a gumboil throbbing away, so I must leave my writing till tomorrow. And even then I forgot to say there has been a fresh call-over for Germany and a devil of a row in the huts, a search, etc., carried out by the Butcher and the new devil-whelp!—the Zebra as they call him, because of all the stripes on his arm. His real name is Fischermann. Ugh, what a day.

SATURDAY, JULY 24, 1943 ■ Yesterday's punishment drills were worse than I thought. They were driven hard for an hour and a half on the football [soccer] field. Hanssen and the Zebra were in charge to begin with. After an hour Denzer arrived and drove them for another half hour. He was wild and went berserk. He struck them with a horsewhip and kicked them. Nilsen, the hut chief, who was among them, and who was put in the punishment drill and demoted when he would not name his comrades and identify who owned the tobacco that was found and seized in the hut, was kicked in the forehead by the Zebra as he lay on the ground. Nilsen has ulcers, and twice has had serious bleeding here at Grini. When he asked Denzer if he could be spared further drill, as he was utterly exhausted, he was told he was malingering, and had to continue. Nilsen was more dead than alive when the drill ended and they marched to the roll call square on the double. When they were ordered to the huts on the double, Nilsen broke ranks and couldn't continue. He had to grab the side of the building so as not to fall down. He said he had to see the doctor; in answer he received a kick and a blow and was ordered to the hut on the double. Today he is in bed. Two or three others were also committed to the hospital. When Denzer learned that Nilsen wanted to see a doctor, he was furious again, called him a malingerer and threatened him with two new hours of punishment drills if the German doctor found that he was healthy. However Dr. Rietz found he was sick, and there were no further punishment drills. Had there been, said Nilsen, Denzer could just as well have shot him.*

This shows the mood in the camp is not light. The way Denzer gets worked up is ghastly. The Zebra may well still be the worst and most disgusting. In the camp there is such a hatred growing for this youngster, who reveals himself more and more as a sadist, and who is given authority to strike and kick, that a disaster might well erupt. But those who should say a word to Denzer about this just stay silent. I am thinking strongly about going to Denzer in the morning and asking for a talk. We'll see. Now I have to go on my nightly expedition. So long!

SUNDAY, JULY 25, 1943 ■ Have just wound up my expeditions. It went off splendidly. For that matter one gets more and more fatalistic. It's the only thing. Damn it, of course I'm nervous and all that, but it's no good, so I've had to cut it out. Certainly I'm careful, heaven help us, I touch the keys as delicately and pianissimo as ever I can. The rest is up to Providence or who or what or whichever. It's an affair of habit like so much else, and it's no more dangerous than a great deal else I have been and am mixed up in at this strange time.

MONDAY, JULY 26, 1943 ■ The news came early this morning and spread like lightning through the camp. Musse has resigned!!† It was on the German news at nine o'clock; some of the prisoners had actually heard it! It was true! Not just a wishful rumor, not a fantasy, but the sober truth. The next few days will be thrilling, and one must allow oneself a few rosy dreams—tonight anyhow. Ever since the morning everyone has been going round in a whirl of glee, passing the compliments of the day wherever they met. Popular wit at once rose to the occasion and framed the new command, "*Musse ab!*"‡

The Germans celebrated the event a good deal more disagreeably. They can't have helped noticing the festive mood of the camp today, and in some of them it has resulted

---

* Sverre Nielsen was sent to Sachsenhausen less than a week later, where he remained until the end of the war.

† Benito Mussolini (1883–1945) seized power in Italy in 1922 and soon became its dictator. In May 1939 he signed the Pact of Steel with Hitler, establishing the Rome-Berlin Axis. With the Allied invasion of Sicily in July 1943, support for Mussolini plummeted, and he was dismissed by King Victor Emmanuel III on July 25, 1943, and arrested. Rescued from prison by the Germans in September 1943, Mussolini agreed to set up a new fascist state in the unoccupied northern portion of Italy, all under German protection. With the war nearing an end in April 1945, Mussolini and his mistress attempted to escape into Switzerland but were captured by Italian partisans and executed on April 28, 1945. "So fell, ignominiously, the modern Roman Caesar, a bellicose-sounding man of the twentieth century who had known how to profit from its confusions and despair, but who underneath the gaudy façade was made largely of sawdust."

‡ A play on the ubiquitous camp command "*Mützen ab*" or "hats off."

in boiling rage. This found a vent in the evening's punishment drill. A punishment column was again selected by the Zebra, who is getting worse and worse. They were put through it over by the German hut. All the SD officers except the *Lagerkommandant* (who was too lazy, no doubt) took part in the punishing, which became an absolute orgy. One young man was hounded until at last he couldn't get up after a "*Hinlegen!*" When he couldn't rise at the command, they kicked him until he fainted. We were looking on from the windows and got word to [Dr. Arne] Halvorsen, who, with a couple of nurses, rushed down to the square to care for the sick man. He was completely done, and is still—more than three hours later—lying on the stretcher only half conscious. They haven't even thought it advisable to move him to a bed.

I wonder how long it will be before that young German prisoner is lynched? Grandpa* and Claffy have openly and directly invited the prisoners to take the Zebra and give him the thrashing of his life. "Just knock him silly so that he won't forget it!" And indeed that's what will probably happen someday. My own fear is that it may happen so decidedly that he'll have no further occasion to remember anything. What the blazes are we to do? I think I must venture it and go to Denzer. If no one else will.

In spite of everything I must say this has been a grand day. It can't last many months now. But what months they may turn out!

TUESDAY, JULY 27, 1943 ■ I went to Denzer at three o'clock and asked to speak to him in private. He sent the lady out and shut the door.

I began by saying that some time ago there were the makings of a system in camp that was based on confidence. Today the scene has completely changed. You have abandoned the line we then thought you were adopting, and have switched over to a new method. You have appointed an informer. A prisoner with authority and full opportunity to spy on his mates, inform against them, indeed actually punish them! I must tell you straight out, Herr Denzer, and it's become a point of conscience with me to tell you, if this goes on we shall have a disaster in the camp one fine day. Hatred of that fellow is increasing daily, and I'm afraid that soon neither you nor I nor anyone else will be able to control it; sooner or later it will bring about a calamity.

Denzer sat listening attentively the whole time. He nodded now and then, to indicate that he was following and fully understood what I said. When I had finished he began his lecture. It was long and diffuse, and purported to explain why he had been compelled to take the step of appointing that man chief inspector. He brought up quite a number of things. The prisoners simply lay and sunbathed during working hours, they smuggled, they neglected in every way to observe the rules of the camp. He thought he had tried all possible means of reaching a good result by gentleness. He had appealed to the men's representatives, asking them again and again to see that rules were kept. He didn't think he had been inhuman in his requirements, but he had found no improvement. And discipline he must demand. It was his duty to see that there was discipline, etc., etc.

Actually there was a great deal of truth in what he said. The discipline in camp has been quite extraordinarily bad and the working tempo of unparalleled slowness. To be quite honest, it has absolutely reached the point of caricature. Which may have been fun, but it has not been well inspired and has done us bad service. Therefore I said to Denzer

---

* The German agricultural chief at Grini. O.N.

that on the whole I agreed with him. Only we believed—indeed, we were convinced—that much more could be achieved by different methods. I began to explain the purely psychological factors governing the attitude of the Norwegian prisoners to the Germans. I asked him to remember that we are at war with Germany. He, Denzer, was my enemy—as I was his. But in spite of the fact that we are opponents in the war now raging, there is nothing to prevent us two from reaching an agreement for the good of both parties. I on my side fully acknowledge that there is much truth in what you say about slackness and want of discipline in the camp, and that it must be corrected. On the other hand I am convinced that you on your side will understand that we can by no means look on you as friends, and find it very difficult to conform to all your rules and principles, which to us are alien and in many cases most uncongenial.

Denzer saw that; he fully understood. Altogether it was amazing how downright friendly he was on this occasion. He repeatedly assured me that my opinions and point of view had his full respect. Then there was a bit of a digression; we got onto the war, to the bombing of open towns. We quite agreed in condemning a bombing war on women and children, I merely pointed out that the Germans had in a high degree been guilty of the same form of warfare. We touched on all sorts of things, but I kept on trying to bring the conversation back to its proper subject.

I described what I had witnessed the day before, when a man had been beaten almost to pulp and carried up to the hospital, and I asked if he knew what crime that man had committed. *Denzer didn't know.* I told him he had been reported because he had to go to the lavatory, which that inspector wouldn't believe. Denzer objected feebly that perhaps he hadn't let his *Vorarbeiter* [foreman] know that he was going to the lavatory? I charged in and asked, "Seriously, Denzer, do you think it reasonable that a fellow should be crippled for life for a possible offense of that kind?" Denzer promptly replied that from now on every case would be scrutinized before punishment drill was meted out. He admitted that this had not been done so far, and that the inspector's statements had been acted on without further ceremony. He admitted further that the drill was very hard—very, very hard.

We got on to comradeship, and I assumed that Denzer was fully conscious of its value. At least he had very often dwelt on it in his speeches. He replied that everything must be built on comradeship. I asked how he got that to tally with the proceedings of the inspector? "Consider, Herr Denzer: that lad, of course, regards it as his business to supply you with a long list of 'criminals' every day, by way of rising in your favor. If he has only a very few names to give you at the end of his day's work, he is sure to be afraid you won't receive him with such goodwill. A lad of his caliber and character is like that." Denzer hastened to say that he didn't at all want a lot of names. "No! Of course not! But don't you realize that the fellow sees it as his business to provide you with them all the same? Can't you see that?" Tja—tja—at any rate if so it was a total misunderstanding. He would speak to Fischermann in private, he said, and let him know that he must show himself a comrade first and foremost and—well, well!—altogether, he would talk to him about things. I urged that it must be possible to find a system, for the good of all, without recourse to informing and brutality. All the representatives could be called together and a foundation laid for mutual trust . . .

Denzer invited me to go ahead and lay it. I refused. "I have no authority, no position—not even a single stripe," I added, pointing to my empty left sleeve. "It's much more than a year since you yourself tore off those stripes, Herr Denzer." "You can have stripes, as many as you please." I declined, would rather not have any. He repeated his request that I would set to work on the lines indicated, and summed up the conversation as follows:

"So you wish me to dismiss the chief inspector?"

I said it was what I had come here to ask.

He said, "Stop a minute, *mein Lieber!* If you can show me results, if, after talking to all the representatives, you can tell me there will be a change—and I see that change, then everything will be well and good."

"Yes, but what can I promise them? May I promise that in that case the inspector will be dismissed?"

"Yes, you have my word for that."

Denzer had now gotten up to go, but I wanted more concessions.

"You must give me a free hand to hold a meeting of all the representatives, in some room with no Germans present, where I can talk to them and set out the case."

"By all means; any time you like!" and he gave me his hand on it.

WEDNESDAY, JULY 28, 1943 ■ At nine this morning all the hut leaders and general foremen were summoned here to the staff room. I gave an account of my interview with Denzer, and proposed that we should take action to improve the conditions, on our own initiative and of our own free will. The proposal was supported by all, and we agreed to call a meeting of all the "striped" in the laundry hut immediately after evening roll call. At that meeting I talked myself warm. It was a large gathering, between two and three hundred men. All seemed to be in agreement on the main question; there was a certain amount of argument, but on fairly trivial points. On the whole I think we are entitled to believe our action has a chance of success.

I have drawn up a memorial to be read out in all the huts this evening by the hut leaders. Tomorrow I mean to go further with Denzer. I shall try to raise the tobacco question—quite the most important of all when it comes to getting the prisoners into a willing frame of mind. Also the question of a short rest in the middle of working spells. But now I must go about my nocturnal business.

I'm looking forward to tomorrow like a child! Kari's coming, with the youngster! Perhaps Eigil and Siri, too.

THURSDAY, JULY 29, 1943 ■ Saint Olav's Day!* It's been a radiant sunny day, and when Kari and the children came we had a radiant sunny meeting! The little one was there, and he was a sight for the gods. Bursting with health and strength, with fine, straight legs, on which he stood up on the barrier. He was all smiles and glee, brown as a nut, and with an expression on his determined little face which was completely disarming. Eigil and Siri also looked radiant, and Kari too; today she'd got the color back in her face,

---

* Olav Haraldsson (995–1030), king of Norway (1015–1028), was instrumental both in uniting Norway and converting it to Christianity. He was killed in the Battle of Stiklestad (July 29, 1030), one of the most famous battles in Norwegian history, and his burial place later became the site for the Nidaros Cathedral in Trondheim. Canonized shortly after his death, he is now considered Norway's patron saint and "eternal King." King Haraldsson's reign is described in Sturluson's *Heimskringla*. In 1847 the Royal Norwegian Order of St. Olav was founded in his memory; it recognizes individuals "for distinguished services rendered to the country and mankind." In 1970, three years prior to his death, Nansen was named a commander in the order.

Visit.

and with the baby on her arm and the other children round her she was more beautiful than anything I know of on earth.

This afternoon the transport left for Germany—126 men it must have been. High spirits all round. No tragic looks. I filmed part of it.

FRIDAY, JULY 30, 1943 ■ I must write now, while the impressions are fresh. About half past seven this morning Johannes [Bødtker] rushed in and said the Commandant was going amok in the camp. On the way up here he had struck eight men with the riding whip he was carrying. He was excessively drunk, his eyes were bloodshot and rolling wildly in their sockets. He was half in mufti—only the riding boots and breeches were regulation, on top he wore a shirt without a collar, open at the neck, and his shirt sleeves were rolled up above the elbows. At the smithy Hegland was standing talking to the goldsmith Holt through the window.* He was interrupted by a cut with the riding whip on his behind. He turned and saw who it was. The *Lagerkommandant* on his side was confused too, when he saw that he had struck an elderly man, a cripple into the bargain (Hegland is lame), with the Red Cross badge and stripes on his arm.† Hegland doesn't speak German and merely pointed to the badge on his arm. The Commandant apologized, and held on to Hegland till someone passed who could speak German and translate his apology. But let no one think he was curbed by that small mistake. He had tasted blood. Now the berserk fit began in earnest. He sent the zealous and obliging Zebra on ahead to fetch up the victims. Here are a couple of examples:

Kjell Olavsen,‡ the diabetic patient, who has Denzer's written permission to stay in the hut till half past seven in the morning on account of his disease, was stopped on his way to work in the hospital by the Zebra, who came running at him and said briefly and peremptorily: "You come along!" The same was said to two others. Olavsen tried to explain why he was out of doors, but couldn't get a word in; he was silenced with a comradely "Shut your mouth, you damned bastard!" Then all three were dragged around for some time, till the Zebra learned that the Commandant had gone into the new kitchen hut.

Off he went there. Inside the Commandant was rushing round like a savage, hitting out right and left; this wasn't swept, that wasn't clean, etc. The three were drawn up in a row in one of the rooms to await his coming. He arrived, and asked what these three had been up to. The Zebra, who had all the time been running after him like a dog, replied that these were the men who were out for a stroll instead of working. "*Jawohl!*" said the Commandant, fondling his riding whip and testing it with his hand.

Olavsen said: "I beg your pardon, that's not correct," and held out his written permit to stay in the hut till half past seven. The Commandant took the slip of paper and read it. "Diabetes!" Saw the signatures: "*Denzer! Fretheim!*" Snorted in contempt and tore the paper to shreds. Then addressed himself to Olavsen: "Well—lout!—so you won't work! You'll go for walks!—ha?" Olavsen repeated that that was not correct, and that he was on his way to work from the hut where he has his insulin injection every morning after parade.

The Commandant asked why he had been arrested and sent to Grini. "Military orga-

---

* Henry Holth was released February 7, 1944.
† Nils Heggland, age fifty-three at the time, was released January 27, 1944.
‡ Kjell Olafsen remained in Grini until the end of the war.

nization!" replied Olavsen; "passive military organization," he added. The Commandant took no notice of the last point, but exclaimed: "*Ach so*—! I knew it by the look of you! Military organization! Diabetes! So!" He was sneering now. "We'll have a look at you!" said he, and ordered Olavsen down into the basement.

Olavsen went first down the stairs; the Commandant, the Zebra and the two others followed. "*Nah*—First the diabetic!" He looked at Olavsen with mad, drunken eyes and shrieked: "Military organization! Diabetic!"—repeated those two words again and again, and then said: "Which military organization?" "Kristiansand!" replied Olavsen, and instantly got such a blow on the ear that he staggered backward. "You know the *Lagerkommandant*, ha? Fast worker, eh?" To all this Olavsen kept replying "*Jawohl!*" standing at attention. "You're going to find that out!"

The Commandant reeked of drink, his eyes were quite yellow and his voice thick, so that it was hard to make out what he said. The Zebra's eyes were wild, and shining with sadism. All the time he kept hanging round, "dressing" Olavsen. Now the Commandant gave the order: "*Verbeugen!*" [Bow!] The Zebra ran up, took Olavsen by the shoulder and "helped" him to bend down, and then came the first blow. It fell across his back. "That was for the military organization! You felt it, ha? Here's for the diabetes!"—and four blows came in succession on his buttocks. As the Commandant struck, he shrieked in ecstasy: "Feels nice—eh?"

Another man was busy straightening nails; he picks old nails out of boards and materials, and sits with a hammer at a small anvil, straightening them out. When the Commandant caught sight of him, he pointed and told the Zebra to fetch him up. The Zebra was off like a rocket, and came back with the unlucky man. Why was he sitting at his work? Why, he had ulcers, and had permission to sit down at work; he had pains in his stomach. The Commandant would see to those stomach pains. Into the washing hut! Everyone in there was ordered out, the Commandant ordered trousers down, the obliging Zebra lent a hand, seized the victim and bent him over, with the poor wretch's head under his arm. Five powerful strokes hailed down on the man, the Commandant shrieking: "That's for the stomach pains! If you have more stomach pains, you shall have five more lashes! *Heraus!*" The man came out with his trousers hanging down over his thighs.

I met a foreman who had seen the Commandant thrash twenty-one men in all. There were a lot more. Both he and the Zebra worked themselves up into a sheer ecstasy. When they had finished down in the camp, they entered the building and came up here to the hospital. He did no beating here. But he dismissed the whole kitchen staff offhand. They were to report to him later, all the lot of them, and go and work in the quarry.

Then he went downstairs and out into the camp again. He still had an appetite. But now Denzer had arrived. He managed to stop him and send him home. But nobody went with him. So he worked in quite a lot more devilry. Down by the company hut he sat down on the grass. There he caught sight of a squad marching. He ordered them up the hill on the double. In that squad they were all infirm, some of them old people. Among them was Ippolo,* a Jew, musician, member of the Budapest Quartet. He has *angina*

---

* István Ipolyi (1886–1955), a Hungarian, was a founding member of the Budapest Quartet, which debuted in 1917. Described as a "sad-eyed, glum-looking musician who sported a mustache," he performed with the quartet until 1936, after which he settled in Norway, where the quartet had spent "many summers rehearsing before each concert season." After the war Ipolyi became a Norwegian citizen, taught music, and published works on musical theory. The Budapest Quartet, which became the quartet-in-residence at the Library of Congress in 1940 and continued

pectoris. He fell headlong, and had a serious heart attack. He was carried on a stretcher up to the hospital, where I saw him. He was given medical treatment and admitted to the *Revierstube*. Jews are not allowed into the hospital, nor strictly speaking into the *Revierstube*, but we didn't care. Ippolo is rather better now. He'll get over this, I dare say; but no thanks to the Commandant.

Tomorrow I'll try to get some more authentic accounts of individual cases. For, by Jove, this shall be heard of. I went to Denzer in the morning, but the Lieutenant was there. I got an appointment for half past five.

He received me quietly and amiably. I was diplomatic and began by talking of something else. I told him about our action and what we had done. He was quite pleased. I suggested a short break in the middle of every working spell. He accepted the idea, and promised to arrange it without delay. I mentioned tobacco. He spoke of the canteen for the 353rd time. But now it's coming. It's settled. By Wednesday of next week at the latest it will have got going. Everyone will be allowed tobacco, he said. Well, not the Jews of course. Jews can't have anything. Not everyone will have the same privileges; some will be allowed to spend five kroners, some ten, and some fifteen. When I asked if those in the lowest class would have any chance of rising, he said they would. If they behaved well and weren't entered in his punishment book.

Then I started on the events of the day. I didn't have to say much. He cursed the Commandant, clenched both his hands, clenched his teeth and hissed. He banged the table with his fist, and called the Commandant "a dammed devil." He confided to me that he hadn't an easy job, with a man like that as his superior. I hinted that our action would suffer, and he went into a fresh paroxysm. I told him about Olavsen, said that the Commandant had also spoken of him (Denzer) with a sneer and thus undermined the respect and discipline we were now trying to build up. I gave him the written permit for Olavsen which the Commandant had torn up. Olavsen had got hold of it afterwards. I mimicked the way the Commandant had read out Denzer's name and Fretheim's. Denzer eagerly seized the bits of paper and assured me he would look into the case.

I gave him a good trump there. "Neither you nor I can prevent this from getting into the Swedish papers, Denzer!" I said. He hissed again and shrieked: "No, it is damnable!!" That stuck all right. Swedish papers have given them something to fuss about before now. Denzer assured me that this shouldn't happen again. He asked me to tell the men—and say that in this affair he was on our side and would do all his power to prevent a repetition of it. More tomorrow; I'm so tired now that I'm seeing double.

SUNDAY, AUGUST 1, 1943 ■ August; there's beginning to be a little taste of autumn. And still nothing definite has happened. Kunz, Heilmann and the Zebra are in pursuit of me. Probably Kunze is in on it, too. They've got hold of the memorial I drew up the other day for the hut leaders. They got Sänger* to translate it into German, in the hope that something I'd written might be suitable for them to use against me.

There was a general parade at twelve o'clock today. The Commandant wanted to

---

to perform until 1967, is considered one of the most successful chamber music ensembles of modern times, one whose name "has become synonymous with chamber music." Interestingly, prior to settling in the United States, the members of the quartet, as stateless individuals with no permanent address, traveled on so-called "Nansen Passports" pioneered by Fridtjof Nansen in the 1920s.

* Max Saenger, a translator, was released April 27, 1945.

announce that the canteen would be opened in the coming week. That was all. It was the first time he had shown himself since the "scandal."

MONDAY, AUGUST 2, 1943 ■ There has been no real change in the camp, except that our action has in fact had distinct results. Both the tempo and the "attitude" have improved considerably all round. Now the vital thing is that Denzer & Company should notice it, and notice it in time, and redeem the promise to me that the Zebra shall be removed.

Tomorrow is the King's birthday. I wonder what that will lead to? On the blackboard where the number of patients in the hospital is shown daily and where every day a fresh date is written, I've helped Johannes [Bødtker], whose job it is, to do a really big and grand figure 3. A very discreet and cautious celebration of the day, one must admit, but still a tiny bit of emphasis—and beggars can't be choosers. Otherwise we're struggling to fix up a tolerably safe line again for outward messages. For the present I've decided to make use of one of the German drivers who is O.K. Pondering whether it wouldn't be a very good trick to have a fountain pen going back and forth—in his pocket. Or several fountain pens, of course. Will write to Ernst [Holmboe] about it.

TUESDAY, AUGUST 3, 1943 ■ *Compliments of the day!* At least the Lord did his part to give it a festal setting. There was brilliant sunshine from this morning early. But it didn't turn out all fête; destiny and a number of Germans willed otherwise. It was the action against me that broke loose today, and now I'm sitting writing in a hut—not even my old hut. This was the way of it:

I made a tour of the camp this morning, and after dinner went off to the Tub [Tuberculosis section]. Johannes [Bødtker] was there. After a glorious sun bath, Johannes was sent for. He was to repair to Denzer instantly with the other hut leaders. Denzer made a furious and utterly crazy speech to them. The speech was larded with outbursts about me and communism, *Sacramento mal* and *Teufel*, and no one understood any of it. Only that the man was beside himself with rage.

Then the Zebra came over to the Tub for me. I was admitted to his lordship Denzer's sight, and then a storm crashed loose—gracious! It's not much use describing Denzer's storms; one has to experience them.

What he said I couldn't possibly repeat, it was one long roar. He read out my memorial and shrieked that it was a piece of impudence and an abuse and showed what I was like. He hallooed that Fischermann (at whom he pointed) had been installed by him and would remain and he assumed responsibility for the consequences. He shouted that he was *Schutzhaftlagerführer* and as such he had the power, it was for him to decide, and he decided *that!!!!!* He shrieked that he was "*Soldat und Kämpfer*," [a soldier and a warrior] and that *Humanität* [humanity] and all the rest of it could go to the devil. In other words he went back on everything, absolutely everything he had promised and said before. All my attempts to speak he brushed off. "I won't hear a single word!" he bellowed. But he didn't say that what I had written was in conflict with our agreement, for he had no doubt ascertained that it wasn't, not in one particular.

I suppose the Zebra, behind his back, had gone to the Commandant, who had then most likely given Denzer a dressing-down for making a pact with me. Now he had to find some means of going back on his word. I was instantly to move out of the hospital, out

Up before Denzer—Kunze is charging these two with filching potatoes.

into a hut, and go to work in the camp. But on account of my "bad leg" I wouldn't be put in the penal column up at the Commandant's house; he also was a human being and paid regard to humanity; but I should be put to some other kind of work somewhere out of doors. And I was to conduct myself like a prisoner, my whole deportment was to be correct, there was to be no more of my going all over the place—and altogether!!

Well, he had done at length. For the last quarter of an hour I had simply stood erect and said nothing. I only looked at him. But I got no nearer making him out.

After supper I moved out to my old room in Hut 12; Francis had just left, so I could take over his bed. Francis is moving over to the Tub, succeeding [Einar] Skavlan, who went off to Ullevål today for a hernia operation. But alas, I hadn't been in my old room five minutes when the Zebra arrived with a form for me. On the form I was assigned to Hut 12, but when he heard I was already there he crossed out the figure 12 in pure devilment and wrote in 3. So then I had to move over here, where I am now writing in the last of the daylight. I don't yet know what job I'm to have.

WEDNESDAY, AUGUST 4, 1943 ■ So then my penal servitude began, after a pretty sleepless night in a bunk with a wooden bottom and a lumpy mattress.

When I'd arranged a few things after morning roll call, I went to the Zebra in the personnel office to get my hard labor meted out. That's his haunt now, and I suppose he's aiming at the job of personnel chief. It ended in my being employed in the wood gang. The working site is in good position facing westward, behind the new canteen hut and among high piles of firewood. Nice people—world champions in dodging, and trained in the admirable warning system for greenery.

I started in at the sawhorse, and all day long I've been cutting up bits of board and paling—with good long sun-breaks to be sure, for the sun was out, and during the afternoon it got really nice and hot. But my back was nearly breaking in two. It was a bit of a transition to be doubled up all day, immediately after "keeping my bed" in the hospital for more than two months. My real, important job I'll get done at the Tub in the dinner interval and here in the evenings. That way there won't be any free time, but it can't be helped. Fridtjof [Leqvamb] can manage the business up there first rate alone, and in our "free time" we'll have the necessary conferences.

All day I've been persecuted by the Zebra. He keeps after me like a gadfly. When I was up being massaged after dinner (for they hadn't said my medical treatment was to stop) the Zebra came peeping into the massage room, and several times he came over to the wood gang, to see if he couldn't catch me out in idleness or absence. But no, Mr. Nansen was on the spot, going full stream!

The news is grand. All initiative is now in the hands of the Allies. People are getting surer and surer that the war will be over in the autumn.

THURSDAY, AUGUST 5, 1943 ■ The second day of my sentence. Things are going splendidly. The time passes rather slowly, that I admit, but still it does pass, and when the sun is out it's grand. I have been sawyer again today, stripped to the waist. My back aches, but when it gets too bad I sit down on the wood-pile for a bit and trust to the warning system. Believe it or not: the canteen has been opened and I've had my first tobacco ration! I'm a tenner, oddly enough; that is, I'm allowed to spend ten kroner instead of five—like most people. But then what does it mean? The fivers are allowed to buy 1.80

worth of tobacco—one box; the tenners 3.20 worth—that is, one box plus the greater part of another, but not the whole. So, as they don't sell halves or quarters, you can't buy more than one box anyhow, unless you choose to spend another 50 øre on a box of cigarettes. And even then it doesn't work out. Even if you add on a bit of plug for 40 øre, it still doesn't work out.

Ernst [Holmboe] was here on a business visit. He brought Marit. She stayed in the car. I asked the interpreter, a decent old booby, if my daughter mightn't come in. He didn't dare. Out of the question. But then one of the German guards came up and asked on his own initiative; he felt it was too bad that Marit shouldn't be allowed to see her father. Then the old chap gave way at once. The guard took the message, and Marit came rushing over, crying bitterly; she had been in such despair because they wouldn't let her see me, poor child. Oh, how it warmed my heart; I do believe she cares a little for her daddy, and now I'm not afraid she may have grown away from me and forgotten me in this time.

I wound up the day by cutting off a fingertip, and have now an interesting bandage on it. A successful day. I feel so light and happy! Now I'll soon be home, Kari!

FRIDAY, AUGUST 6, 1943 ■ Cloudy and cold. A long, bitter day. Truly the spells *are* long in bad, cold weather. The sun is more of a help than I really knew. One learns to value the dinner interval. I've arranged so as to have the Tub as my station and fixed point. There I shave and take a shower every day, as I got into the way of doing in the hospital. And when there's any sun, I take the sun there. All this in the dinner interval. A chat with Leif [Poulsson] and Francis [Bull], a cigarette, and a good rest constitute a great relief after the fatigues of the day.

Francis is now installed in the Tub as a washer and thinks himself in great luck. It's queer to see him functioning as floor washer and dishwasher, but very gratifying to observe how he's thriving over there. He has peace and quiet, a writing table most of the day, and is already in full swing on useful work. When my "time" is out and a job falls vacant in the Tub, it might be ideal to get in there.

They say it's already been in some Swedish papers that the Commandant has been running amok at Grini while drunk and thrashing the prisoners. That's excellent. Delivered on the nail. Yes, this has been a fine day too—after all!

SUNDAY, AUGUST 8, 1943 ■ Sunday! The "day of rest." I've been hard at work all day and so it's gone like smoke. I ventured up to the hospital again, and F[ridtjof Leqvamb] and I did lots of writing, checking and arranging. Finally I was held up there more than an hour just at the busiest time, as Kunze settled down to give a lecture to some prisoners out in the lobby. And Kunze is on my tail, so I didn't dare pass him. Laden with inflammable objects as I was.

Now we've just had evening roll call. The gallant Kunze—the lecturer in the hospital this afternoon—reeling drunk. He may have listened to this evening's news broadcast, and if so I can't blame him for wishing himself out of it. For just listen: this evening it was announced on German radio that a meeting has been called of all German generals! Taken with the day's war bulletins, this news is more significant than anything else. An elated, downright hectic optimism sprang up in our little circle in the Tub kitchen when we heard the news. I almost think that I—*I!*—was the most moderate.

Denzer is now forever laying it down that we're at war with each other—that each and all of us must be regarded and treated as enemies of Germany. I can't help being amused when I recognize my own arguments and sentences, even in reports of his sermons.

MONDAY, AUGUST 9, 1943 ■ A cold, gusty day, with rain and sticky, slippery clay all over the place. One can't go from one hut to another without sliding on clay, without getting one's shoes stuck to the absorbent mass and oneself all wet and muddy. And it is indeed a trial to be working out of doors on a day like this. The sessions are never ending, one gets wetter and wetter, and one can't take shelter even from the worst showers; there's a risk of some confounded greenhorn popping up and taking one's name. The trousers cling to one's thighs, one's shoes gradually get sodden, one's hands grasping the tools grow cold and stiff, and the rheumatism slyly creeps through one's body and settles in. Can one make a complaint? No, not on hard labor, not till one has collapsed and can't move. I'm as stiff as a poker today. I could only just bend down and pick up the bits of wood I was to saw, and when I'd been sawing and sawing for an eternity I'm blessed if my watch had moved, and I myself had stiffened in the bending posture. I feel as though I were still in it, and shudder to think of lying down presently on my wooden bed.

Tonight a few of us had a little birthday party for our youngest colleague in the illicit company—Ola Bonnevie—who was 20 today. I had to make the paternal speech on the occasion, and we had chocolates and cakes in the laundry hut after roll call without being caught.

WEDNESDAY, AUGUST 11, 1943 ■ I'm obliged to mention my rheumatism again, for now I'm almost a cripple. I suppose it's the cold, damp weather making itself felt, and then standing the whole day bent over in one position. I've "attacked" the Zebra for a job where I can work sitting down.

When I was up in the hospital after parade this evening to "arrange" one thing and another, suddenly Bartels and the Zebra turned up. I was in the lobby then, and slipped into the line for the doctor. But those two had caught sight of me and asked what I was doing up there.

"I'm going to the doctor," I explained.

What was the matter with me?

"My feet," I said, for I'm bothered with athlete's foot.

"Yes, and then he has lumbago, haven't you?" the Zebra chimed in.

I said I had.

"And stomach ulcers, eh?"

"Why, yes, Herr Fischermann, I dare say I have."

"And—and—" he stopped to think, "and T.B., eh?" he went on cleverly.

"No, Herr Fischermann, not that. But why all these questions?"

The Zebra turned to Bartels and explained that all my ailments were pure humbug. At that moment I felt like seizing him by the throat and slowly, very slowly, twisting his neck round, but my meditations were interrupted by Bartels, who roared "*Heraus! Heraus!! Sofort!!!*" I asked politely (heavens, how one can!) if I might not see the doctor, but had gotten no further when a fresh "*Heraus!*" resounded through the whole hospital. Well, so then I had to clear out. The Zebra has mobilized these people against me. And it hasn't been difficult. I'd better keep out of view for a good while. However, this will be all right, too.

We nearly had a pretty business today in the hospital. Fridtjof [Leqvamb] didn't censor a letter he'd receive for transmission. He got it from Søren, who'd got it from another man, and so on. It was for fru G.K. Thank goodness, the next link in the postal service had censored it. In clumsy Norwegian-German-Swedish, it said: "*When you get this Brief, report at once to Untersturmführer Denzer.*" That was all. Of course it didn't go!

The facts are obvious. Denzer and Fischermann, the criminologists, were going to bring off a subtle coup. With great acumen they had thought out that if Fischermann were to write a letter (for he knows Norwegian!) to fru G.K., whose husband is in the camp and who is therefore suspected of being in contact with him, and if they got it indirectly to Søren, who is a washerman in the hospital and therefore suspected of being in contact with the women, then they would see if the letter didn't reach her, and then—tableau! But Denzer the criminologist dropped a first-class brick. Not only was the letter not sent, but he was so anxious to know the outcome of his cunning that he couldn't keep quiet till it might possibly have arrived. The day after its dispatch he sent for fru G.K. "You've had an illicit letter!" "No!" "You have! Confess!" I suppose Denzer saw an oak leaf beckoning in the distance,* and he went at it hammer and tongs, but poor fru G.K. defended herself and was completely puzzled. There was a search of her cell, everything was ransacked. Without result. Not a single illegal word, not one illicit chip, nothing. Denzer the criminologist had to enter the affair among those we'll say no more about—I assume.

It remains to trace the course of the letter till it reached Søren. Who is the informer? And will any further steps be taken about it? However, one thing is certain. They have absolutely no clue to Fridtjof. They suspect nothing about anything. They have no more brains than rabbits. But Fridtjof is pretty sure to send on no uncensored letters henceforth.

Not one word or letter which is not of consequence shall go through our department. That has been my invariable principle the whole time, and as long as I was there we kept to it. We had an auto-da-fé every night. One may take a certain risk for comrades who sacrificed a lot for *us* before they landed in here, in fact it would be queer if we didn't; but there's no sense in taking risks to enable lovebirds to tell each other on miles of toilet paper that they love each other. News is first-rate. Wild rumors are circulating about everything imaginable; but let them circulate. The facts will do. Every day is a red-letter day.

THURSDAY, AUGUST 12, 1943 ■ Rain, rain and beastly cold, and I have to go on working in the wood gang. I don't suppose there will be any change, at least not for the better. The foreman of the wood-carving gang, Stamnes,† asked Bartels today if they couldn't have me in the carving shop; he needed a good woodcarver and Nansen was outstanding. "But then you should have heard the din!" said Stamnes. Bartels had flown

---

* In other words, a promotion. The SS used insignia on their collar patch to indicate rank. The use of one or more oak leaves on the collar patch indicated a rank of *Standartenführer*, or colonel, and higher, several ranks above Denzer's rank of *Untersturmführer*, or second lieutenant.

† Harald Stamnæss, a jeweler, was transferred to Sachsenhausen in November 1943, where he remained for the duration of the war.

into a violent rage and called me "damned Jewish lout" and "traitor," etc., for several minutes, and altogether given me a highly flattering character.

It's clear the word has been passed that I am to be persecuted as public enemy number one. Now I've noted in the pack—besides the Zebra—Kunze, the Butcher, and Bartels. I've been told that Kunz is in it too, but I don't know yet. Denzer is behind, and assuredly the Commandant as well, so I haven't many places to appeal if things get too bad. At midday roll call the Zebra came and told me that from today I was forbidden to set foot in the main building, to see the doctor or to have massage or treatment for my lumbago; I must arrange all that some other way. If I dared show myself in the main building, I should be reported and most severely punished, he announced with malicious narrow brown eyes. The whole thing was an order from the *Schutzhaftlagerführer*. Did I understand? Yes, it was impossible to do otherwise.

It took precisely two hours for me to work off my rage. But then the sun came peeping out, and a good deal of blue sky after a cold, rainy morning. Then I could laugh again. If things go too far one day, I'm afraid I may get diphtheria. It would be a blessed deliverance, which might perhaps last until the war is over. But I must wait until Kari has been here on the 17th.

FRIDAY, AUGUST 13, 1943 ■ Friday, the 13th of August. Well, for the first time there has been a Friday the 13th I shan't forget in a hurry. First, in the morning, I learned that the driver had been taken during the night. The green one. They'd found letters in the car. He'd been operating on too big a scale, had been careless, had too many businesses in hand, and so it gave. What has been done to him, poor man, I don't know.

Later on I was sent for, was to report in the personnel office immediately. Learned in a rush that they had found three packets of cigarettes in Fridtjof [Leqvamb]'s cupboard, which he had said came from me. I was at once conducted to Denzer by the Zebra. What followed was a paroxysm of rage from a stark staring lunatic—not a glimmer of sense in it. Those cigarettes. Full stop. Everyone is allowed to smoke now, since the opening of the canteen, but I had no opportunity to say so, no indeed, he didn't want a single word out of me. My package was full! as he said. Thus far and no further! Scoundrel that I was, arch-jøssing, damned humanist, intellectual, etc., etc., over and over again, in a crescendo of rage. Did I understand? *Nein!* said I; it was the only word I got in sometimes, plus of course *ja!* and *jawohl!* where I thought *them* suitable.

I'm not quite sure whether he was only threatening or informing me of a decision, when he said I should be sent packing to Germany, to Buchenwald,* and find out what

---

* Buchenwald was established in 1937 near Weimar, in east-central Germany. The largest camp in Germany, Buchenwald and its subcamps held almost 240,000 inmates during its existence, providing slave labor for nearby armaments factories, quarries, and construction projects. For a time a contingent of approximately three hundred students from the University of Oslo were held at a special "re-education" camp within Buchenwald; see December 2, 1943, below. It is estimated that at least 56,000 prisoners died or were murdered there during its eight-year existence. Notable inmates include Elie Wiesel and Bruno Bettelheim. Karl Otto Koch, the commandant of Buchenwald from 1937 to 1942, previously acted as commandant of Sachsenhausen. The camp was liberated by American forces on April 11, 1945, the first major concentration camp to be liberated by the Western Allies while still occupied. Only days earlier (April 3, 1945) Koch was executed at the camp by the Nazis for corruption. His wife Ilse, known as the "Bitch of Buchenwald," was ultimately sentenced to life imprisonment by postwar German authorities; she hanged herself in jail in 1967.

a German *Kassettenlager* [concentration camp]* was like. I would never come back, he shrieked, adding that the Norwegians might as well put up my "monument" straight away. We are at war, he thundered, and the three million jøssings—*damned jøssing swinehounds!*—would now be made to realize that we are at war!† Millions of Germans are fighting and dying, while the Norwegians do nothing but wallow in food and drink. He was foaming with rage. I couldn't help thinking of the gastronomical excesses of these bold German warriors here at Grini, their luxury *all* along the line, while their countrymen in millions, as he said, are fighting and dying for them.

His audience, Heilmann and the Zebra, *gloated* over the situation. Next they were both instructed to keep the sharpest eye on me, where I was to be put now—in the penal column carrying stones down on the field. And when the bellowing was over, and all directions had been given about my future job, off we went there.

The queer thing is that I'm not the least bit in despair, except for Kari's sake. At the moment I have no line out to which I dare entrust a letter, but I've asked E[rnst Holmboe] to speak to her and tell her everything. She must know, and I have faith that once the situation is in being, she'll be strong and resolute.

In the penal gang things have been going on. The Zebra behaved like a lunatic! He ran after Pastor [Hans] Finstad‡ (who has been banished here on account of prayer meetings held by him and the other clergymen), struck him on the back of the head with a strap or some such thing, and kicked him repeatedly, screaming like mad, "Devil of a pastor! Devil of a pastor! Tonight you can hold a meeting! Understand? Just you hold a meeting! Devil of a pastor! Tonight!" Then he walked off in my direction, but turned back to Finstad, who was walking calmly on with his barrow, and shouted, "But without me!" It's characteristic that everything he says is meaningless.

He came down to the heap of stones, where I was to help in loading the handbarrows, stopped all those who thought they had piled on enough and doubled the load, in fact went on redoubling, until one could only laugh. When two men came to try and lift the first handbarrow he had loaded, they simply stood there, with the shafts in their hands. The shafts cracked, and the barrow didn't move. One could only go on laughing. He didn't mind; he simply ordered them to get a fresh barrow. I begged him to realize that it wouldn't do, but he shrieked that if they could hold prayer meetings and smuggle letters and parcels, they must be able to carry that. He demonstrated with his hands how big and heavy were the letters and parcels they had managed to smuggle. The poor prisoners tottered off with those demented handbarrows, but no, they were to go faster, he kicked and hit them, shrieking that this was hard labor and not a stroll.

I tried to talk to him. No good. A little later I tackled him and asked why he was carrying on like that. Didn't he see how silly it made him look? He calmed down and said he wasn't allowed to talk to me. If Denzer were to come and see him talking to me, he would get "a devil of a row." I of course objected that as personnel chief he could talk to whom he liked where he liked, and again asked him to tell me why he was behaving like that. He

---

*   Nansen most likely meant "*Kazettlager*," that is, KZ-Lager (in German KZ is pronounced "Ka Zett"). The German word for concentration camp was *Konzentrationslager*, typically abbreviated by the SS as "KL," whereas most prisoners preferred the harsher sounding "KZ." "KZ" became the standard abbreviation for the camps in postwar Germany.

†   Presumably the reference to "three million" was intended to incorporate the entire population of Norway at the time.

‡   Finstad remained at Grini for the duration of the war.

The stone-carrying gang, where we went when we fell into disgrace.

dismissed it in the same way again, and said I had only to think, I knew very well, I was just "artful." Then off he went.

SATURDAY, AUGUST 14, 1943 ■ Two new men came into the gang today. Two young fellows. One of them arrived in camp yesterday. He'd brought some cigarettes and a couple of books in his trunk from No. 19 [Møllergata], where he had permission to smoke and read. When the Butcher, who searched his luggage, came on these objects, he told the Zebra to put down his name for the penal gang. The fellow had inflammation of the back and wears an iron corset! He said nothing before going to work. "What's the use? I'd only have got another punch on the nose, and I'd had more than enough already!"

However, stiff, creaking and rheumaticky, we set to, in good heart and contempt for death. It won't be very long now, and we can take this all right. Pastor Finstad, fifty-two and with lumbago like me, led bravely on. He is the Nestor of the gang,* I come next; all the rest are younger. I reeled as I went "home" to dinner, was as stiff as a ramrod and couldn't have bent down to tie my shoelace if I had been paid for it. The small of my back was aching so that each step was agony. I don't think I've ever looked forward to a Sunday as I'm looking forward to the one we shall wake up to tomorrow. Rest, rest; goodness how wonderful it will be.

SUNDAY, AUGUST 15, 1943 ■ Sunday and a day of rest. Did I say that indeed? The day promised well with sunshine and everything; but in the middle of dinner came a lightning order for general parade at quarter past twelve. Every dread foreboding rises up in one's mind on such occasions. Germany? Escape—ten men to be shot? Work for the rest of the day as a punishment for something or other? Fresh discoveries of smuggling affairs? Can the German driver have cracked and told something? Every man has his particular irons in the fire, and is quaking lest it should be his turn now.

But this time it wasn't serious. Simply that Huts 2 and 3 were to be vacated and all the inhabitants distributed among other huts. The moving out was to be done in five minutes, and before we'd got out of our respective huts the *Bauleitung*, with its detailed men, had already started on the erection of a barbed-wire fence round Huts 2 and 3. Of course this gave rise to a lot of guessing and hypotheses. Some held that Sweden had now come into the war and that the local Swedes were to be interned. Others thought Italians, others again were for Norwegian reserve officers or possibly Russians. Johannes [Bødtker] suggested it might be three hundred virgins from Bergen. Same old Johannes! However, as I said, we were distributed among the different huts, all of which are now bursting full; in some of them men even have to sleep on the floor. It really makes no difference, if one has a mattress; the foundation of the beds is only floor too.

MONDAY, AUGUST 16, 1943 ■ The riddle of Huts 2 and 3 was solved this morning. They were for members of the police force. This morning they arrived in trucks and were shut up there.† About half were in uniform, but it's assumed that those in mufti were policemen too.

Erik Magelssen‡ got out into camp today. Is reveling in it—after sixteen months' solitary confinement at Akershus—almost as though he were at liberty. He's become a broommaker. We're well off at Grini after all.

---

* In Greek mythology Nestor was a wise and elderly Argonaut, often dispensing advice to younger warriors.

† When a Norwegian police officer refused to arrest several young girls for evading compulsory labor service, Quisling had the officer arrested and executed and the police put under military law. On August 16, 1943, nearly five hundred policemen were arrested and sent to Grini. Almost half were released in the fall, and the remainder were sent to German concentration camps such as Stutthof near Danzig, Poland, for "retraining." Simultaneously, more than 1,100 army officers were arrested "on the grounds that several Norwegian officers who, following the campaign of 1940 had been pardoned by Hitler after having taken a solemn oath of loyalty, in the meantime had broken their pledge not to take up arms against Germany by participating in underground military activities." As early as the Vågsøy Raid in December 1941 it was discovered that more than a hundred former Norwegian officers had already escaped to England to carry on the fight. The move was motivated in part as a preventive measure against further such defections, and not least by the fear that the presence of such officers would be highly dangerous in the event of an Allied landing in Norway—a fear that haunted the dreams of Hitler until the very end of the war.

‡ Transferred to Sachsenhausen in October 1943, where he remained until the end of the war. Magelssen helped carry home part of Nansen's diary in his breadbox.

TUESDAY, AUGUST 17, 1943 ■ I had a long talk with a German prisoner last night. He was arrested at Stavanger or Saudasjøen for sabotage. He wasn't a member of the party and wouldn't join in party festivals, or do any more than he was ordered and obliged to do; so he was arrested.

He is from Cologne, married, with a little boy of seven. He knew that his house and all he had was smashed and gone in the raids, but nothing about his wife and son—hadn't heard from them in many months. He talked of the situation in his own country and didn't mince words. He was deadly ashamed of his countrymen's behavior over here, and begged me on no account to believe that these were genuine representatives of the German people, the vast majority of whom, he assured me, thought and felt precisely as we did about the new era and its men. He described what he had seen himself in Norwegian prisons, first in Stavanger and then here, and was deeply harrowed, shocked and cast down, but thought with me that most of it was the outcome of desperation and panic. He wasn't quite so optimistic as I about the duration of the war, which he thought might last another six months. Afterwards I sat by the window, gazing out at the dark, dark woody ridges. Just beyond them, only a few kilometers off, all my dear ones were sleeping sound. How fortunate I am compared with this fellow prisoner.

WEDNESDAY, AUGUST 18, 1943 ■ Yesterday morning I noticed that a sore on one finger had inflamed beautifully. The finger was already pretty swollen. To be on the safe side I showed it to the gang foreman; it would be better for him to have seen it, if I had to have it lanced and bandaged during the day. For it was obvious they would suspect me of shamming a sore finger. Before midday it had begun to throb so badly that I asked Leif [Poulsson] to see to it in the dinner interval.

THURSDAY, AUGUST 19, 1943 ■ I didn't sleep well last night. The sore finger was developing, and this morning blood poisoning was in lively evolution. The lymphatic glands under the arm were swollen and painful, and the red streak almost reached my elbow. I couldn't go to work, it would have been madness. If their idea is to wreck one's health, one can't submit tamely.

I went to Leif [Poulsson] after morning roll call. We sent word to [Dr.] Halvor[sen], who was to speak to Denzer. Meanwhile I sat down in the *Revierstube* to wait. I waited on and on, an hour, two hours, three hours. Now the finger was throbbing until I could have screamed. At last Halvor came. Denzer had decided that I might stay in the hut as long as my finger was so bad that I couldn't work. Also I had his gracious permission to go up to the doctor's office and be lanced.

Now I'm sitting in the Tub, it's the dinner interval, and I've swallowed quantities of sulfathiazole pills and am feeling better. It's quite delightful that I'm to stay in the hut. Who would choose to be in the *Revierstube*—that night asylum—when one might be left in peace in the hut, alone and undisturbed, to write, work and read? They're too stupid to be true, and I'm overjoyed.

Yesterday [Bendt] Winge put down my name among others on a list of people who might be considered for new appointments in the architect's office. Bartels, who went through the list to select people, burst into a fresh paroxysm of rage when he reached my name. He started abusing me once more before the whole gang. Idiot, lout, scum, and what has this Herr Nansen ever done? Nothing! Only traded on his father's name, always!

He would have no dealings with that upper-class snob, that low fellow, etc. They'd had enough of Nansen here at Grini.

The persecution has hardly relaxed as yet. The mere sight of me or my name is enough to make them bubble over with fury.

Francis is having a grand time just now. He's busy writing out the talks he's given here at Grini. Thirteen of them, or possibly fifteen. It will be a valuable book.*

Just at that moment I got a fountain pen with a long, detailed report.† Kari is taking it splendidly. Thank heaven! She couldn't get a permit to visit me before tomorrow. It will be exciting to see if it's confirmed.

FRIDAY, AUGUST 20, 1943 ■ They didn't take away my visiting permit! They didn't take away my visiting permit! Tralalalalalala! Hurrah! And Kari has been here, and she was calm and strong and splendid and magnificent, and life is beautiful and wonderful even if Grini should get still fuller of demons than it is now. The devil will soon be fetching them, and we shall hold out all right until then. Goodness how we'll hold out!

SATURDAY, AUGUST 21, 1943 ■ After the sun comes rain, and after joy despair and sorrow.

All my doubts and hopes regarding a new transport to Germany definitively ran aground today.

At this moment the German-transport is lined up in the square dressed in civilian clothes. They will probably be leaving during the afternoon. I do not yet know how many they are, but more and more are being constantly added, and gloom and horror have once again settled as a dark, heavy cloud over the camp. One of those having the hardest time is my friend and roommate Knut E[liassen], a lieutenant in the navy. After twenty-two months in jail, most of the time in Møllergata enduring horrible torture during a total of sixty-three interrogations, he had now somehow managed to get his bearings again and had begun to see life somewhat brighter again. He is married and has a small child. He lives in Holmestrand and during this whole time of horrors has not seen his wife and child. He said that he did not want to see them out there on the road work, where he has been employed recently, despite the fact that it would have been fairly easy to arrange. It would have been so much worse afterwards, he explained to me, biting his pipe shyly and averting his eyes. I did not realize at the time his great pain; how his longing tore him up and how much he worried about his wife and child. He was so introverted and taciturn. He spoke only sparingly of all he had been through; it seemed as if the suffering itself had put its seal on him and closed him up. I managed to get a bit out of him the other day. He had been arrested together with Kristian Aubert and Cappelen and one other. The two others were beaten and tortured to death; Aubert we remember, it was his corpse that was taken out of here one night last spring. "What saved me," said Knut, "was that I slit my wrist. They kicked in Cappelen's rib cage."‡ Knut's attempt at suicide was—as was so many others'—not successful. I hardly think that many have endured more and have had more reason to try to take their life to escape the living hell that anyone who has not

---

* The book was published in 1945 under the title *Tretten Taler på Grini* [*Thirteen Tales at Grini*] and proved very popular.

† That is, the message was smuggled in.

‡ This is likely a reference to Hans "Hasse" Cappelen, who was tortured by the Gestapo. See April 28/29, 1945, below.

experienced can even imagine. I did not pressure him to get more of his story out of him, as he told me he had written it himself, accurately and in every detail, his whole journey since April 9. It is kept safely outside.

Today he was downcast. It came so suddenly, and he had thought that his time of suffering was now over. With one single brutal blow he is right in the middle of it again. Germany! Germany! How fearfully does not this name stand out against the sky—written in blood? How many mothers, wives, fathers and children tremble at the thought that their loved ones may be sent there. And *now*—just before the big showdown! Now, when things are seriously looking brighter—now this veil of misfortune falls over so many unfortunates—and shuts out the sunlight. So close—and yet so distant; maybe more distant than ever? Maybe the veil shall never lift again? I asked Knut if there was anything that I could do for him. He fumbled in his back pocket and pulled out some money. "If you could get this sent to my wife," he said. "She can use it more than I can—now." Tears were now running down his cheek. Tears that no power in world would have been able to stop, and he had a hard time saying just the few words that he uttered. I told him to keep the money, explained that it might come in handy, for bribes and such, when the time was right. I would see to it that his wife and his child would not suffer while he was away, he could rest assured. I shall never forget the look he gave me as I said that. Gratefulness, deep relief and an infinitely tender melancholy could be read in his eyes. Poor boy! He has been severely tested. No wonder he could not control his tears today. They poured uncontrollably down his cheeks. There was nothing to do—he had to get a handkerchief and wipe them away. And he turned away and hid in the innermost corner between two upper bunks, and I could see his shoulders heaving in soundless sobs. If only I could have done something for him, but no thought and no wish is more impossible for me—as the situation now stands. I am probably the one in the camp who can do the least. My star is lowest of all—I realized that latest this morning (but more about that later).

The rest of my tobacco was all I could give him—and some vitamins, etc. It might come in handy after all. And then some encouraging words. Words—words—what do they mean against this ghastly reality. I told him to be fatalistic—and said I was convinced that he would return to Norway—and to his wife and child. He smiled faintly—and then he said that all he had written about what he had experienced since April 9—he thought it might become a book. If he did not return—he added—the book might generate some income for his wife and child. If I could tell his father—in case. I promised to do that, while assuring him that I was convinced he would surely in the near future return to a free Norway and take care of the publishing himself. He held my hand hard and long between both of his, before we parted. I suddenly had a feeling of joy, that I had nevertheless been able to help this boy a little at the last minute. He thanked me so warmly and heartily. I have not seen much of him here, but from the times when we have talked there remains a fresh, strong memory of a personality and rare character. It is as if I have known him for a long time, and I look forward to meeting him again. It is heartwarming to meet people like that. They give one faith in the future.*

Only today I have learned of the following true Zebra story:

Severin Løvenskiold and Per Gjølstad† (forest owner and farmer, respectively) have

---

* Eliassen survived Germany and the war. It does not appear that he ever published his memoir.
† Løvenskiold was released on December 20, 1943, and Gjølstad on December 23, 1943.

been working on the construction of the storage hut. This hut has been finished for a long time, but as the *Bauleitung* doesn't have anything else to put them to work on—they have received orders to continue to "occupy" themselves there. In the last month they have stayed in the attic—and have partly slept the time away. German *Vorarbeiters*, like Kurz, have repeatedly seen them asleep there, without saying anything. It has actually suited them quite well, since they do not have other work for them anyway. This, however, would turn out to be a dangerous habit. Yesterday the Zebra and the Butcher were on the warpath on a raid in the huts. They also came to the storage hut, and the Zebra, who knows the attics well from his own working time there, went straight up the ladder. Up there, Løvenskiold and Gjølstad lay sleeping. Gjølstad woke up, managed to get behind the Zebra, and got away with a punch in the face from the Butcher, who greeted him at the bottom of the ladder. Løvenskiold was in worse shape. He did not wake up until the Zebra kicked him in the back with full force. He sprang up, only to receive a stream of blows to the head. He ducked to avoid the blows. The Zebra then ordered him to stand up straight with his head against the ceiling post so he couldn't avoid the blows, and went at him in full fury, with his fists and with full force.

The two of them were alone in the attic, the Zebra had free range, without any witnesses, and he worked himself up into a mad ecstasy. Yes, because there no longer exists any doubt that the boy is insane. Both Løvenskiold's eyes were "glued shut"—with large bruises on his cheeks and his chin—as well as on the eye itself. But he stood upright and took it all without moving. The Zebra suddenly stopped and said: "If only some of you would hit back! If only some of you would hit back!" And he stared at Løvenskiold up there in the dusky attic with madness and evil in his eyes. "Do you know what would happen then?" he said. Løvenskiold shook his head. "Then I would use this," and he pulled out of his jacket a long, stiletto-like knife and put it to Løvenskiold's chest. I will not attempt to try to describe Severin Løvenskiold's feelings at that moment; he should do that himself sometime.

But anyone who does not understand that there is a sinister reality mixed up in this game must be blind. The point is, briefly and brutally put, that a young, 22 year-old boy, equipped by his superiors with every possible power as well as weapons, walks about among two to three thousand defenseless prisoners looking for an opportunity to commit his first murder. Possibly the first. One cannot think otherwise than that the boy has been "urged" into this by his superiors, on whom the responsibility fully rests. They have understood that the boy might be "used"—that he had "talents" and "abilities" that might be used in a brilliant way. And they have blown on the fire and ignited the madness in him; awakened the demons that dwelt within him. Any obstacle of decency has been thrown overboard. Grini has become a living hell. There surely must, in the name of God, be something possible to do to stop this horrible development!? Are we then to be completely in the power of people like this? Now one can understand a little of the Jews' hopeless destiny—when they are caught.

During the same raid the Zebra and the Butcher came to Hut 15. From there they have a good view of the "punishment field," where "my" gang works, and also of the foundation work for a new hut that is being built opposite Hut 15. They went into the hut, stood by the window and "enjoyed" the view in order to pick out a victim. A moment later one of the Jews was ordered in. Everyone else was ordered to leave the room, but through the window one could see and hear what was going on. The poor Jew was greeted with a blow to the face by Heilmann. He fell—and there was a thump when he hit the floor. Then there were new thumping sounds—it was the Zebra kicking the Jew as he lay on the floor. This drama was short—the Jew fell immediately, and when he later emerged, the blood was streaming down his face. He had done nothing, he was working diligently when he was brought in, but he was Jewish.

Heilmann boasts in his greatest moments that he has helped to hang more than eighty Jews in Poland—and he longs to hang more, he says. He eats himself full every day—got fat and well-nourished during his war service on foreign soil. It is with strange emotions that one reflects on this background—and sometimes thinks of his fellow countrymen who by the thousands sacrifice their lives and blood at the front. How will these hangmen be received—when they return someday to their fatherland—with furs, sardine cans, souvenirs and other stolen goods—instead of iron crosses and medals for bravery and missing arms and legs?

By appointment I went as usual to the doctor at eight o'clock this morning to have my bandage changed. I was alone, and as I passed the first floor, I thought that it might be safest to drop by the personnel office and report that I was going to see the doctor. The prohibition against my entering the main building still is in force. The Zebra was not there, only Meidel-Larsen, and I reported to him and stood for a moment at the door. Then Denzer came rushing in. He saw me, came menacingly up to me and asked what I was doing there. He did not give me a chance to answer, but just repeated his question. I still wasn't able to say more than a few words, which he repeated imitatingly, now in a mounting rage. He hit me; I think he intended to hit me in the face, but he restrained himself and let his hand change direction and hit me in the shoulder instead; then he opened the door and pushed me out with full force.

I finally managed to say that I was at the personnel office to report that I was going to see the doctor. "Then why the hell don't you see the doctor?" he screamed, and a long stream of curses and oaths followed me as I disappeared through the corridor and into the stairwell. A bit further up the stairs I could hear him screaming at the top of his lungs: "Odd Nansen—*der Häftling!*" [the prisoner!] followed by a stream of curses and incomprehensible words. I had to believe that he was calling me, so I ran back. When he saw me again, his rage mounted—if possible—even higher, and he let loose an avalanche of German sounds on a startled crowd of new prisoners and other chance individuals standing round him in the corridor. I concluded from this that my presence was not required, and disappeared again up the stairs.

There was a long line outside of the doctor's office, and I declined—thank God—Johannes [Bødtker's] invitation to wait in his room. A moment later the Zebra stood in the corridor and yelled my name. I had the honor of getting in first, admittedly by being taken by the shoulder and pushed in front of the others standing in line, and got a quick treatment in the presence of the highly interested Zebra. The nurse who changed my bandage was constantly encouraged in his work by the Zebra: "*Schneller! Schneller!* Faster, faster for the devil's sake!" and similar little intimacies. Finally he was done and was about to put the sling round my neck. The Zebra grabbed it and threw it away. "Are you stupid?" he screamed. To me he said on the way to the elevator and in the elevator (I was now going back to Denzer) that I used the sling just to make things seem worse than they really were.

Denzer received me with renewed outbursts of unrestrained cursing in the presence of parts of the clergy: Kunz, Pohl (who has suddenly returned), the Zebra, the female secretary and there might have been even more. This was a good opportunity for a speech—and it came. I grasped that I was the "instigator" at Grini. "No," said I, "it's not true." New rage. I repeated it. He screamed and cursed and declared that I should just dare try coming to the building except to visit the doctor, whom I was allowed to see to get treatment for blood poisoning. I suppose I answered "*Jawohl!*" which ended the session. Denzer had spoken. I had had a new temperature measurement—which reached just below the boiling point, and the barometer still points to storm. But I got to know that I am an instigator! How interesting. How brilliantly sharp he must be. Despite the unpleasantness of it all—and the decided discomfort—the comical aspects are so prominent that I can't help but laugh. He is inimitable in all his helpless comicality. Denzer—showing off at the top of his greatness—acting before a gallery of admiring fellow countrymen. The new age! The Third Reich! The Crusaders! God help us all and free us from them for all time—when we once again—in the not too distant future—get rid of them. Oh yes—I do think that I could "instigate" people to such a prayer—and such a wish—but it would be perfectly superfluous. The other "instigating" I have been doing has been a whole lot more difficult—and has rather taken the opposite direction. He obviously did not like that either. Well, it isn't always easy, is it?

All the new prisoners, who with much to-do were detained yesterday in Huts 2 and 3 with barbed wire and guards, have yesterday and today been released into the camp among the other prisoners. They have been told that they will get light work and have under the prisoner number on their jackets, a pale blue triangle, comparable to our white hostage triangle—none of which has any meaning. The blue one will probably never have any meaning either.

The transport for Germany has left. The buses just departed—it is now six in the afternoon. Rumor has it that Bartels and Heilmann will be leaving. Possibly they are only taking a vacation—and we will have the opportunity to see them again. But it's good to get rid of them for a while anyway. Yesterday, the rumors also said that Denzer was going away too. God grant that it should be true—but now it seems that it was "too good to be true." That the Zebra should leave was also not true. According to the rumors, he should have followed today's transport. But no—it was not so. Nevertheless it is understandable that fantasy should play with these thoughts.

— ◼ —

THAT PROVED TO BE THE LAST of the Grini diary. I went on writing indeed, but the next chapter, which ended with my being sent to Germany, was unfortunately lost. And that was a pity, for it seemed to me one of the most interesting. I shall try, partly from memory and partly with the help of letters that I sent out to my contacts at regular intervals and that have been preserved, to give a short résumé of what took place.

The Zebra, Kunze, Bartels and the Butcher didn't give up, but went ahead. They had succeeded in hurling me from my "pinnacle" into the deepest "degradation" Grini could offer. But they wanted me lower yet. And Denzer and the Commandant assuredly had nothing against it. Denzer because he had a bad conscience and was nursing a hatred that shone out of him whenever I crossed his eye, and the Commandant because he'd just simply taken against me.

They had acquired a zealous colleague in [Kåre] Høvre Johansen, the foreman of the penal gang in which I worked.* From the very beginning he fed Denzer with information that I was the man behind all the sabotage and unrest in the camp. I was the "incendiary," I laughed at Denzer behind his back, slandered him and exposed him to the prisoners in the most blackguardly way. There would be no peace in the camp, declared Høvre Johansen, until Nansen was out of it.

On this background Denzer's sudden, ungovernable rage against me is more intelligible. He was wounded to the depths of his vanity and ran amok.

The Zebra & Company now planned a campaign that was to have far-reaching consequences, and that in its monomaniac stupidity came to surpass anything of the kind we had yet experienced at Grini.

As I said before, I had long been resorting daily to the Tub, where I spent my leisure hours with Francis [Bull], Leif [Poulsson] and several others. For me the Tub had become an inestimable refuge and one bright spot in my otherwise unenviable life.

Leif's name also stood high on the Germans' black list, thanks to his many "escapades" and his fearless attitude. That we two should be "laying our heads together" at the Tub in the dinner interval and in the evenings was a thorn in their flesh. The Zebra resolved to break up the idyll.

One fine day he arrived. There was a search. Cupboards and drawers were emptied—in the kitchen, in the washroom, in the sickrooms, and in the doctor's office, where Leif's desk was turned upside down and the contents tumbled out on the floor. I was at work when this happened, but heard later to my sorrow (and dismay) that the manuscript of Francis's thirteen lectures, which he had just finished, was found in the desk drawer and taken away with a quantity of other things. It had sometimes happened that I wrote up my diary in the evenings or the dinner intervals at Leif's desk, but all my manuscripts were luckily safe elsewhere. That they had found and taken away a number of caricatures and other innocent diversions was a point that no one thought much about. Nor was there any reason to think much of the fact that the Zebra had struck Leif in the face and behaved like a yahoo. It was Francis's manuscript that overshadowed everything else and worried us all. What would be done to Francis?

I looked him up in the evening and tried to cheer him by saying that after all the Ger-

---

* Kåre Johannessen, described by Nansen in the Norwegian version as an "NS traitor and informer," was released December 6, 1944.

mans wouldn't understand a cheep about his talks, even if they had them translated. They were lectures on literature—and no German would grasp the real point of them. "Well, but you see," said Francis, looking like a schoolboy caught in the act and confessing his sins, "I'd written a foreword too, in which I explained the idea of every talk, so unfortunately I'm afraid they *will* understand them!" Oh good heavens! What a disaster! "Well, well," said Francis, "it can't be helped now. We shall have to wait and see. And they can't exactly have my blood for it," he added with a smile, but he looked rather blank.

It didn't occur to anyone that Leif and I would be the worst sufferers. In Leif's drawer they had found a couple of other documents that had seized their whole attention and been of lively interest to them as criminologists. One of these was supposed to be a newspaper called *Grini Tageblatt* [Grini Daily Paper], with the subtitle *Organ der verlorenen Freiheit* [Organ of Lost Liberty]. On the front page under the heading, which incidentally had all the earmarks of a newspaper heading, such as: 2nd year, number 230, date, and so on, there flaunted a caricature of Francis sticking his head out of the prison bars, and there was a long, nonsensical article about him written in Grini German. I had done the caricature and heading, while [Haakon] Fretheim had written the article. Both were harmless and didn't even contain any attack on the greens, though they did smack faintly of derision. Besides this highly important document, they also found in the drawer an article on Leif and one on Sejersted Bødtker, both in the form of so-called *Gutachten* [histories]—those the doctors in the *Revier* drew up on each patient, with personalia, course of the disease, etc. These also were adorned with caricatures. In the one on Sejersted Bødtker there were several, including one of Denzer, to wit, a miniature of the drawing I once did on order from the Germans, for their own *Kameradenschaftabend* [fellowship evening]. Here again the texts had been composed by Fretheim, while the caricatures were from the master hand of Alv Erikstad, a young student of architecture. We only laughed at the thought of this "catch," it never for a moment occurred to anyone that it would have serious consequences. As so often before, we forgot to make allowance for the fact that we were dealing with Germans.

Not long after the search had come to an end and the captured documents been borne in triumph to Denzer's office, the Zebra came rushing back to the Tub, closely followed by the "detectives," Butcher and Hansen. They called on us to hand over the "press." The press that had been used to print *Grini Tageblatt*. Where did we keep it? No one knew anything about a press. But they weren't to be fooled so easily. They would find it all right, if they had to break up the whole floor, and thereupon they started ransacking the house again from garret to cellar. But no rotary press came to light, nor anything else. They left the Tub in a fury, and went racing up to the *Revier*, where they began with a raid on Sejersted Bødtker's room. And there, what did they not find? Not merely a copy of Sejersted Bødtker's *Gutachten*, but also a highly interesting letter from Lauritz Sand to his wife. These were the facts about the letter:

Among the duties of Johannes Sejersted Bødtker, who was hut leader of the *Revier*, was that of reading through all the patients' letters home and seeing that they said nothing wrong. He "snuggled down" to this job in the evenings, and often found a lot of queer things. Many a tender declaration of love did he commit to memory—the old libertine! We were aware of this little idyll, and one day I arranged with Sand that he should write a letter to his wife that would lead censor Johannes to put on at least two pairs of spectacles while he censored it. The letter was to begin quite quietly, "Dear Annie: Now I'm getting on better," and so on. Then it was suddenly to break into Malay (Sand has lived forty years in Java), and in the middle of a sentence there was to be "Sejersted Bødtker." Then he would grow mighty curious.

The letter would go on to say that things had improved at Grini, for now the hut leader went round the rooms every morning with the news—he got it every day on a radio which he kept in his pillow. Indeed a lot of people had their own radios, some kept theirs in the cupboard, others in the mattress, but so ingeniously camouflaged that no devil could find them. Besides which a radio transmitter had been installed in the drawer of the hut leader's bedside table. He would go on to write that now moreover each of the patients had his own machine gun, which they had hidden in their beds, and his own revolver, in addition to a machine gun of large bore built into the kitchen icebox. Much love from Lauritz.

The worthy Lauritz, who was full of mischief, wrote such a letter. It turned out both long and funny, and was written in Malay, French, English, Dutch and Norwegian. So funny did it turn out that Johannes couldn't bring himself to part with it, when it had been "censored" and "confiscated." So there it lay in the drawer, waiting for the Zebra and confiscation. Now they had come! My goodness they had come!

The Zebra, who could read Norwegian, but hardly Malay and the other languages, saw that here—at last—he had shot the parrot!*

Machine guns! Revolvers! Radios! Bubbling with rapture and in complete ecstasy, he performed an absolute war dance with wild yells of "*Sacramento! Hell and damnation!*" Then off he rushed to Denzer with his war booty, followed by his expectant German superiors. Now there would be a clean-up at Grini! There was! And it wasn't long in coming. But long enough for us, who saw that the air was getting thick and the ground a bit hot under foot, to put all our "illegalities" safely away and prepare the façades for the reception of what might come.

That same evening all those implicated were "arrested" and brought before Denzer's throne in turn. When I was ushered into Denzer's office, there was already a strange company standing in the corners and along the walls in the lobby outside, all with their faces to the wall. I caught a glimpse of Johannes in one corner, red as a lobster, and Francis in another, pale and bewildered. Further off stood Fretheim, solemn as a churchwarden. But then I was hustled into the throneroom. Kunz, Kunze, Pohl, Hansen, Bartels, Frau Fiedler, and some more besides, oh, and of course the Zebra, filled the orchestra stalls right up to the throne itself, where Denzer towered with a big, knotty stick in his fist. All gazed expectantly at Denzer, myself not least.

He opened the performance in his own style. "*Du Schweinehund!*" he thundered, rising to his feet. "You rascal! You damned humanist and Jew-lover! You dirty pig! You blasted Communist and incendiary! Your package is full!! Full long ago, do you understand? Do you understand, you damned scoundrel?" He whirled his knotty stick menacingly round his head, and green hate shot lightnings from his eyes. Bartels and Kunze approached me, one on each side, both ready to fly at me on the slightest sign from Denzer. I remember being

---

* The phrase "shoot the parrot" is an expression that derived from target practice, when a wooden (and sometimes a live) target in the form of a bird (the "parrot") was fastened atop a high pole. To "shoot the parrot" meant to "take the prize" by having the best performance hitting the target.

surprised that Denzer should suddenly call me *du*. He'd never done that before. Even in a rage he had always observed the forms. For wasn't he "a cultivated man?"

"*Nein!*" said I, for really what else could I say, "*ich verstehe nicht!*" [I don't understand!] Then I thought for a moment that I was about to have the experience of seeing a man burst. Denzer grew so rabid that he could hardly get sense into his shrieks, his voice broke, the knotty stick whistled aimlessly through the air (but without reaching me, for I was on the other side of the desk) and it looked as if the whole fiery head were definitely exploding and flying to pieces under our very eyes. But his cranium and leather cap band held after all, and in some unintelligible way he managed to collect himself and sign to Kunze and Bartels that they were to bring me round to his side of the desk. They seized an arm each, pinched it tight and rather lifted than led me round the desk to Denzer's place. Now I expected the worst. I was well within reach of the knotty stick. Denzer was frantic, and I was by no means feeling perky. In the center of the desk in front of him lay *Grini Tageblatt. Organ der verlorenen Freiheit*, and Francis's bewildered face, sticking out through prison bars, shone up at me from the page of newspaper. Faithful Francis, friend in need! In a flash I saw the comedy, the crazy burlesque—the fundamental Germanism of the whole situation. And it was a help.

"Where did you print that?" hissed Denzer.

"It isn't printed; it was drawn with a *3B* pencil," I replied.

"Rubbish! Where did you print it? We have means of finding out. We know more than you think, so I advise you to tell the truth." Now he had left off saying *du* and had recovered his criminological dignity and omniscience. I again assured him that the drawing and newspaper heading were not printed, they were pencil drawn, while the article had been typed in the *Revier*. Exultingly he pulled out of his drawer another copy of *Grini Tageblatt*, same issue, same article, caricature and get-up. "Now! where did you print it?" he thundered, in a voice of triumph.

I could hardly keep from laughing. I had drawn three headings for this paper, and three caricatures of Francis. And though almost the same, they were by no means identical. Both the expression on Francis's worried face and the get-up of the drawings in general varied slightly in the two specimens that now lay side by side on the desk. But that had escaped Denzer's eagle eye. He was dead sure that his acumen and skill were this time going to carry off a decisive victory. He'd got me now. It was almost a pity to destroy that touching cocksureness, but it couldn't be helped. I pointed out to him the difference in the two copies, and demonstrated with my forefinger that it would smudge, as it was drawn with a soft pencil. I'm afraid I didn't manage a sufficiently solemn face, as I remarked that it was only a harmless joke and that the whole thing struck me as comic.

His retreat was pitiful. His vanity had received another mortal wound; the hatred of me which had played him this fatal trick surged up anew with untamed force. I shouldn't have let fall that "comic." "*Komisch!*" [Comic!] he bellowed, "*Komisch! Du Lump! Du Schweinehund! Du Spitzbube! Ich bin komisch—he? Du sagst ich bin komisch! Ni'?*" [Comic! You lout! You son of a bitch! You rascal! I'm comic—ha? You call me comic, eh?] Suddenly he thought of pointing at my long hair, which had fallen over my forehead when I stooped to point at the drawings on the desk. "Look at it," he shouted, turning to his audience—which instantly struck up a mutter of appreciation. Fired by this he once more gave his fury the rein, and struck me in the face with his flat, fat hand, so that my hair again fell over my forehead. "Look at the intellectual, the humanist with the lock of hair, the Jew-lover—the incendiary! Isn't he comic?" he shrieked in ecstasy, and with a loud muttering interspersed with yaps and growls the congregation pronounced amen.

Now he was all right again, but there was no further question of *Grini Tageblatt*, and I was no longer allowed to utter a syllable. All my attempts to join in the "conversation" were repelled with a well-directed "*Maul halten*" [Shut up] or "*Halt die Fresse!*" [Shut your trap!] or other such polite names for the organ of speech. He boomed out on a new line—not with imputations of similar offenses, but with sinister prophecies of what would happen to me henceforth. He repeated that "my package was full," and that I would now go to Germany and find out what a real German "*K.Z.Lager*" (*Kazettenlager*) was like. He assured me that I need entertain no hopes of ever getting back to Norway—they could just put up the "monument" upon my grave (once more) straight away, for from the place I was now bound for, people seldom returned alive. Did I understand? I replied that it was impossible to do otherwise. Denzer looked triumphantly round the admiring audience, gave orders for me to be put in *Einzelhaft*, in a dark cell on bread and water, under the strictest guard, and then sank down upon the throne and started on the next item of his program, which must have been a long one that day.

A great, fat, thumping fellow of a German, whom we called Porky, and with whom I was to become better acquainted, was the one who took charge of me. Up we went to the second floor and into *Einzelhaft*, where a well-aimed kick lodged me in a cell with blue glass in the window. I landed on the floor in a corner, and Porky shot a parting curse through the door before he crashed it closed again and locked it. When Porky's big bunch of keys had done rattling and his heavy iron-shod steps had died away along the corridor, silence fell, and I was left sitting on the bare floor alone with my dark-cell thoughts. Only far off in the building somewhere shrieks and uproar could be heard. I suppose Denzer, going on with his program.

How long I sat there brooding over Germans and human beings—whether it was a half hour or a whole—I don't know; but I was roused again by Porky's footsteps in the corridor and the clattering of his bunch of keys at the lock of my door. Next moment Leif [Poulsson] came head first into the cell, under the impulsion of Porky's right boot and a torrent of oaths and curses. Again the door banged to, again Porky's keys rattled, and his steps died away along the corridor—all was quiet. And there sat Leif on the floor beside me.

In the end we laughed, as we had done so often. But this time the laughter may have been slightly forced all the same. Leif had had a rough handling. After his examination by Denzer, which on the whole had behaved like mine, but had been accompanied by more blows, Kunze and Bartels had hauled him off to a ground-floor cell and shut the door. There the two had some private fun out of using Leif's head as a "punching ball." Until they were quite sated they had taken turns punching his face and head, the form and color of which were gradually modified by this Germanic pastime. Then they handed him over to Porky, who promptly dispatched him in to me. And here we were sitting laughing on the floor of the dark cell. But there was nothing to laugh at really. Our trip to Germany was assured, and Denzer's dark threats and prophecies did not exactly hold out a cheerful prospect for the future.

However, before we had sunk very deep in contemplation of it the heavy footsteps were again heard out in the corridor, and immediately afterward the rattling of keys in the lock.

This time it was Erikstad who was shot in as we had been. Poor lad, he was quite bewildered with the doing he had had. His arms flew mechanically up to his face as though to guard it from further depredations when Porky, not omitting the usual oral ceremonies, shut the door with a crash. And indeed his face could not have stood much more if it was to go on reminding one of Alv Erikstad.

It was apparently Denzer himself and Pohl and one or two more who had been in charge of the "fun" with him. Both his jaws and cheeks were violently swollen and took up so much room that it was all his eyes could do to keep the narrow cracks remaining open to them for a look out. His ears looked like hoops of lard, except that they were red, and he couldn't hear much with either of them. He had difficulty in talking. For that matter any explanation of what had happened to him was superfluous.

As we sat gaping at each other, there came a rap on the wall from the next cell. I put my ear to the wall and heard a faint, faraway voice calling something about the air hole. The air hole? What on earth did he mean? Suddenly I remembered that of course the air holes and ventilation channel were *Einzelhaft's* telephone system, and I got down onto the floor and laid my head against the air hole. A voice sounded clearly and distinctly, as though it were in the same room, "Hello?"

"Hello!"

"Is that Fredrik? This is Harald! Who are you?"

I explained who we were and why we were there. The voice explained, "The cell you're in is called Fredrik, mine is Harald. Are you on bread and water?" I was able to say we were, for Denzer had pronounced so.

"Well," came Harald's voice again, "then we'll collect on the house front at eleven to-night." He got no further, for the contact was interrupted by heavy steps and key-rattling far down the corridor.

We looked at each other in astonishment. What on earth did he mean by "collecting on the house front?" What did he mean to collect? We were mystified, and eager for night which was to solve the riddle.

It grew late, as we discussed the events and our prospects; it began to get dark, and as the distant bellowing from Denzer's office came to an end, we judged that there would be no more criminals arriving in our cell that night. Through a hole in the blue paint on our window we saw one after another of the *Herrenvolk* leave the building: Denzer, Pohl, Kunz, Kunze, the Butcher, Hansen, Bartels and at last Porky as well. It was time to get ready for the night. That was soon done. In our cell there was an ordinary two-tier wooden bed but no mattresses or bedclothes. Most of the boards to lie on were missing, but there were enough for one bunk when we placed them rather wide. Indeed there were even a few left over, which could be used as pillows for the two who slept on the floor. Besides the bed our cell contained a great treasure, by no means common to them all—a cold-water sink. Above the door was a wooden shelf, otherwise there was nothing but floor, walls and ceiling.

We agreed that Erikstad must have the bunk the first night; he had most need to sleep in "comfort." He stretched himself out cautiously on the boards and dropped asleep. Leif and I curled ourselves up on the concrete floor, placed a folded handkerchief on the boards as an extra pillow, and lay down to wait for eleven o'clock.

It wasn't long before there came a rap on the wall, and we hastened to the air hole. "Hello, Hello!" It was Harald calling Fredrik, with the following instructions: "When I give two raps on the wall, you go to the window, climb up and stand on the ledge. You raise the top window and stretch out your left arm as far as you can along the wall in our direction, then you'll just be able to reach a pole with a sock hanging from it, which we'll reach out to you. In the sock you'll find bread and potatoes, collected in all the cells along this side of our floor. Be cautious and put everything off if you hear the danger signal. The danger signal is three knocks on the wall. Good night and good appetite."

Such, in all simplicity, was the collection on the house front. The stick with the sock began its wanderings in the far cell nearest the center block and passed from cell to cell. Notice had been given in advance that there were three comrades in Fredrik on bread and water who needed food, and then all were ready to give their share. Fredrik was the last cell but one in the wing, and when we had heard the two raps on the wall and the instructions had been successfully carried out, we had a well-filled sock to help ourselves from. We woke Erikstad, and I can tell you we enjoyed the meal. None of us had had any dinner, and we blessed our new and unknown friends as their hand outs of sandwiches and potatoes vanished quickly into our lean stomachs.

It proved a cold night with little sleep. We were so cold that our teeth chattered, and we were always having to get up and walk up and down the cell to warm ourselves before lying down again on the icy concrete floor and trying to snatch a little nap before the next "cold wave" brought us to our feet again.* Not that we were used to any excess of luxury, but still we had never yet been blessed with a bed like this. Erikstad's bunk was rather better, so he slept pretty well all night.

When Porky arrived about half-past eight the next morning with our breakfast, which consisted of dry bread, we complained of the cold and asked for more clothes or bedclothes. Porky knew what to do. "When one is cold, one does gymnastics!" he lectured, and he was kind enough to start a little private course for us on the spot. First, kneebendings; "*Auf! Herunter!* [Up! Down!] *Auf! Herunter!*"—ten—twenty—thirty times. It made our heads swim, stiff as we were. Then there was lying down on one's belly and raising and lowering oneself with one's arms. I still had my sore finger, and Porky was magnanimous, so I was let off this exercise, but had to keep on with the kneebendings instead. "*Auf! Herunter! Auf! Herunter!*" Porky leaned against the doorpost and jerked his thumb up and down, up and down. The words of command gradually died away; now it was only that fat thumb of his that directed our movements. Up! Down! Up! Down! Leif was groaning like a steam engine, it didn't look as if he could stand much more, but Porky's thumb was unwearied. Up! Down! Up! Down! without a flicker of expression on his large, wicked face with the vacant eyes.

Suddenly Leif got up, scarlet with rage and exertion, and proclaimed in a loud though gasping voice, "I can't go on! I'm ill! My lungs—" "*Maul halten! Schweinehund!*" Porky cut him off. "Ill! Did you say ill? What does that mean? There are only two kinds of men. Healthy men and—dead men! That's all! Understand?"† "*Jawohl!*" thundered Leif in a tone resounding through the corridor. He was burning to say more, but controlled himself.

"What's your occupation?" asked Porky, looking as though he meant to swallow Leif in one mouthful.

"I am a doctor," roared Leif; he's formed the habit of shouting at the Germans, otherwise they always ask again.

---

* On Fridtjof Nansen's sprint to the North Pole he wrote, "We packed ourselves tight into the bag, and lay with our teeth chattering for an hour, or an hour and a half, before we became aware of a little of the warmth in our bodies. . . . [At mealtime] [w]hen this [the cold] was too much for us we walked up and down to keep ourselves warm."

† This was a standard refrain in the camps. The guide to the permanent historical exhibition at Buchenwald states, "'In this camp there are only healthy people or dead people' is a remark ascribed to Camp Commander [Karl] Koch. It is . . . characteristic of the way in which the inmates were treated."

"You are not a doctor," pronounced Porky. "You are a blasted prisoner! A prisoner has no grievances—he has only to obey. I demand discipline! Absolute, blind discipline! Do you understand?"

A fresh "*Jawohl!*" rings through the room and corridor, and with that Porky turns on his heel, forgetting that he hadn't actually finished with the punishment drill, and bangs the door of the cell.

We gave a sigh of relief, and then we burst out laughing again—laughing until we gasped for breath. After all we couldn't sit down and cry! Along with a couple of potatoes we had left from the "house front" the dry bread tasted capital, and we were soon on top again. Erikstad had made a good recovery after his night's sleep, was hearing better already with both ears, and altogether our little trio was in a fair way to getting used to cell life.

Through the holes in the window paint we could follow all that went on out in the square, and in the course of the day we had already made contact with several of our friends in camp. In the dinner interval, when all the Germans had left the main building (they all had dinner up at the Commandant's house) the rapping signal again passed from cell to cell, announcing that "the news" was now on the air hole. First we got the day's war news, fresh from London or Stockholm, and then local bulletins. We learned the fate of our "accomplices." Francis and Johannes had got off lightly, but had each been placed in a penal gang. Fretheim hadn't been so lucky, he had been soundly beaten up and was now in the cell just below us. The Zebra's berserk rage continued; Denzer was at the bursting point; the atmosphere was gloomy and ominous. Something was about to happen! But they had found no more "compromising" papers or other "explosives."* We got out the necessary messages (by string mail at night), and in general procured such directions as we needed for the conduct of life in *[Einzel]haft*. "Hello! Hello! That is the end of the news. We'll be back this evening when Porky has gone!"

Yes, something was about to happen. After evening roll call it came. Darkness had already fallen when there was a signal for general parade. In a single moment the camp was transformed into a swarming anthill. The prisoners streamed onto the parade ground from every side, the air resounded with bellowing and uproar, and in through the gates of Grini thundered two hundred armored soldiers on motorcycles, followed by a long train of cars. Searchlights, roars of command, the racing of engines and the screaming of car sirens rent the night, and horror descended on the camp. What in the name of disaster could be the meaning of this?

From our cell window we had a splendid view of all that went on. Breathless and with our noses flattened against the panes we all followed it, each through his own hole. There came the armored soldiers, marching up the hill from the *Vermittlung* and into the square. Their steel helmets and tommy guns flashed uncannily in the rays of the searchlights and arc lamps, while words of command and heel-smacks went off like volleys of musketry and filled the air. There were "our chaps" marching up with Kunz at their head. More words

---

*   At about this same time Nansen's home at Polhøgda was thoroughly searched for incriminating letters, etc. His diary and letters remained undetected, however, safely hidden in a secret compartment in the rear of the bedroom night table. Nansen's daughter Marit recalls that in their preoccupation with finding hidden contraband, the Germans completely overlooked an illegal underground paper lying in plain sight on top of the same nightstand. Polhøgda had been deemed "off limits" for entry and seizure at the start of the invasion by German authorities when Nansen, learning the house might be requisitioned as a hospital, had informed those same authorities of the historical significance of Fridtjof Nansen's home, library, archives, and burial plot.

of command, more heel-smacking. Denzer was fussing round like a hen going to lay an egg, the prisoners stood at attention like candles in the night, and the Zebra stood on his personnel-chief taboret with dog's eyes, cap in hand, expecting great things. All this he, Fischermann, had staged! He might well be pleased with himself!

The armored soldiers were divided into groups and gradually marched off, each unit led by its "Grini German" to make a search of the huts. One group under Porky turned into the main building. (Better watch out!) But look, a grand, glossy limousine turning the corner of the road. It pulls up on the hill and out steps—yes, upon my soul—none other than Terboven himself in full uniform, with Rediess* at his side and a couple more. A second limousine arrives, with Fehlis and Reinhardt, and then a third, with still more high-ranking devils in leather coats. They move off uphill to the parade ground. The Commandant comes out to meet them in full regalia, halts and faces round with heel-smacking, glove-doffing, and arm-swinging, handshakes, gracious nods, more arm-swinging, glove-donning, and the whole party gets in motion for the square. By this time Denzer doesn't know which leg to stand on—one of the greatest moments of his life has arrived. He dances up to the Zebra in 5-8 time, makes him a feverish sign to set things going, turns right about and like a full-blown hotel proprietor and restaurateur advances to welcome the establishment's exalted guests.

"*Achtung! Stillgestanden!* [Stand at attention!]† *Augen—rechts!*" the Zebra cracks out. He too is enjoying a great moment. And it's going so tiptop! Absolutely without a hitch. Three thousand pairs of eyes follow Terboven and his court; he has now placed himself and suite at a table facing the line. There all the leather coats group themselves about him, and under a dazzling cone of light the whole ballet stands out in spooky brilliance.

In a single flash it was revealed to us what all this meant. Drumhead court-martial! I don't know which of us was the first to speak those uncanny words, but once they were spoken we had not a doubt in our minds that so it was. Drumhead court-martial! Then came a great, oppressive void—like an echo—filling the darkness and silence—and ourselves to the breaking point.

Erikstad must have been the first to say anything. "We're obviously to be shot," said he. Which was not so stupid of him after all, for it broke the silence. It set one's mind in motion and aroused the impulse to contradict. "Nonsense!" said I. "Why in the devil's name should we be shot? Because we drew some harmless caricatures? And Leif because he kept them in an open drawer in the Tub? And Fretheim down below because he wrote a bit facetiously about a couple of fellow prisoners? Don't be silly, man! They can't shoot us for that." Leif reminded me that people had been shot for less, not that he meant to say our fate was sealed. But Germans were quite incalculable. I knew he was right, horribly right, but I refused to admit it. Erikstad stuck to his guns and began pacing up and down the room, repeating at proper intervals that we were obviously to be shot. I stuck to my guns and almost lost my temper. His temper also became rather frayed, nor was Leif particularly chirpy.

---

* Wilhelm Rediess (1900–1945) was the commanding general (*Obergruppenführer*) of SS troops in Norway from 1940 to 1945. According to one historian, "The triumvirate of Hellmuth Reinhard . . . Terboven, and . . . Rediess of the SS, with close cooperation of . . . Quisling . . . set the stage for the identification, registration, roundup, arrest, property confiscation, and deportation of Jews from Norway." On May 8, 1945, Rediess committed suicide in the same bunker as Terboven, who then also committed suicide by blowing up the bunker.

† While both *Achtung* and *Stillgestanden* mean "at attention," *Achtung* is more forceful and used more often in military settings as demanding immediate attention rather than merely standing still.

Thus passed an indefinitely long time. Then we heard heavy footsteps—and once more the keys rattled in the lock. I think we shot a look at each other, one hasty glance, and each had his own thoughts. In the doorway stood Porky and two of the panzer men. We braced up and I reported. "Cell twenty-four with three prisoners. All here!" Porky scanned us fiercely and we felt this was it. Now we were to take our last walk! But the panzers looked uninterested and the order we had been expecting didn't come. We weren't going out at all! They hadn't come for us! Porky had merely come to exhibit three well-trained animals to his two friends. He set us knee-bending and doing push-ups. Up! Down! Up! Down! Up! Down! But our tricks made not the least impression on the panzers. They were bored, and as the show was nearing its climax and Leif was groaning like a steam engine, they turned and walked off, and Porky was left alone in the doorway with his thumb. In the end he got fed up too, slammed the door, and went.

I think I may say we all breathed easier in spite of the gymnastic display, and if I remember rightly Erikstad executed a little private war dance in pure glee, for now the danger was over. For through our peepholes in the window we could see Terboven leaving the square with some of his court—stepping into his limousine and driving off. Praise God, Hallelujah!

The other cells along the corridor were also visited. There were more or less thorough searches of cells and prisoners, but neither automatics nor radios had been discovered. The search and examination in Lauritz Sand's cell in the *Revier* was I suppose the great feature of the day. The cell, including the bed in which he lay, had been fine-combed from floor to ceiling. The yield was nothing but some musical compositions that Fretheim had committed and hidden there.

Then Rediess arrived in person, followed by Reinhardt and a German civilian. They were going to take Sand away for questioning, but Halvor intervened and said that Sand had a broken back and couldn't be moved. So the "court" sat in Sand's room and the questioning began.

By way of preface he was informed that he had only an hour to live, and was urgently advised to tell the whole truth. "Uff da!" said Sand, and prepared for the worst. The letter to his wife was produced. Did he write that? Ye-es, that was right; he had. Didn't he suppose they had men who understood and could translate every language? Yes, Sand had no doubt they had plenty of translators, but he doubted if any of them could translate this letter. Reinhardt, who was now doing the talking, for Rediess had gone, declared they could read every language from Norwegian to Sanskrit. Sand thought that all the same it might be better if he translated for them, there was so little time, and an hour soon passed. They accepted the offer, and Sand got going on his translation.

I would have given a good deal to see Reinhardt's face while the letter was being read to him. For there were a lot of queer things in between the words machine gun, radio transmitter, etc. A lot that was enough to make even a German's lips twitch. "Your grandmother was an old Batavian monkey," for example, or "Kiss my arse you old chimpanzee!" None the less I think most probably Reinhardt's face of stone remained as hard and immovable as ever behind his thick lenses. After all it wasn't so very funny for the big swells of the Terrace suddenly to find themselves with the leading roles in so ludicrous a farce. Suddenly, however, the whole performance was wrecked by Rediess, who came dashing in with shouts of "*Schluss! Fertig! Der Reichskommissar will weg!*" [Finish! Pack up! The *Reichskommissar* is going!] And out they cleared in a hurry, Reinhardt, the civilian, and his papers. Sand's last hour didn't prove to be the very last this time either, and afterward there was a celebration in his cell I should have liked to attend.

It isn't very hard to imagine what had taken place. A report of preparations for mutiny among the Grini prisoners, composed by Denzer, had been sent to Terboven. A panzer *Schnellkommando* [fast squad] had been detailed to unearth the prisoners' radio transmitter, automatics and revolvers. The *Reichskommissar* himself with his court and a special execution squad arrived to hold a drumhead court-martial and dispatch the guilty on the spot. The panzer men returned from their searches with a few stolen carrots and tomatoes and a number of illicit thrillers. That was the whole "catch." Except for *Grini Tageblatt*, a few profound *Gutachten* and Sand's excellent letter. The *Reichskommissar* must have grasped the whole position, and I don't blame him for wanting to get away. Conceivably Denzer's "package" also had begun to be pretty full.

Nor was there any despondency in our dark-cell that night. Even Erikstad was now almost convinced that at any rate the immediate danger was over. But we were still in Denzer's claws—and God only knew what men like that might hit on to constitute revenge for such a disgrace.

We remained eight days in the dark-cell on bread and water, and were given dinner every third day. On the days between we appeased the worst of our hunger "on the house front." We became downright fond of all our unknown comrades along the passage, in "Harald," "Gunnar," "Anton," "Kristian," and whatever all the cells were called. Here the solidarity and comradeship was better than anywhere else in camp, better indeed than anywhere else I know of. Unseen, unknown lads, from every social class and every corner of the country, many of them being tortured under questioning, many filled with the dread of torture; some awaiting a death sentence; many with nothing left but hope, and some without even that; all willing to share the little they had with one another, all ready to help a comrade in need with food and clothing, with word and deed. Of all my long time in prison, which lasted forty months, I think those eight days were the most impressive and the best.

Porky enlivened our existence with frequent punishment drills, and did what he could to make our stay as agreeable as possible. And it was. We got more and more on top. We fixed up contact with the camp and with our friends in it, string mail brought us reports and letters from outside, and we ourselves sent out what was necessary. Pencils, cigarettes and matches we received as well. In the dinner intervals and at night when the greens were gone, we had news, conversation, information on camp affairs, lectures, concerts and entertainments on the air hole. We learned what had happened to our "accomplices," and were reassured on that point. None of them had been very heavily punished, except Fretheim who was in about as tough a spot as we were. We made direct contact with him through the window, exchanged experiences and reached the necessary agreements. Strange that Francis [Bull] got off so cheap, but I suppose his crime was above their heads. We saw both him and Johannes [Bødtker] on parade and going to and from their respective penal jobs.* The camp was gradually subsiding into the old routine, and we felt that after all we were having quite a nice peaceful time.

Therefore it was rather a disappointment when Porky one day announced in his amiable fashion that Leif and I were to pack our things and come along. "Our things" were a crust of bread apiece, so they were quickly packed. It was sad to part from Erikstad, and I think

---

* Francis was assigned to the stone-breaking gang for a fortnight.

he felt it sad to part from us. We had had a fine time together. But the farewell was short and painless, a nod and wink, that was all—a roar from Porky, a crash when the cell door slammed, and Erikstad was left alone.*

We went into the Parachute and we knew what that meant. It was the place for all those condemned to death and all who were sentenced to hard labor and were being sent to Germany.† The latter was no doubt our lot.

We met Lindbäck-Larsen again there, and a lot of other good fellows from the camp who at different times had landed in the Parachute. Many more had come direct from *[Einzel]haft* or No. 19, with no halfway station in the camp itself, so there were also quite a lot of new faces and many new acquaintances to make. There were about forty men in the Parachute when we arrived, at the end of August, but before we left about five weeks later the number had increased to over seventy.

It was a pretty big space, about 70 square meters [750 sq. ft.], and was divided by a thin partition into a smaller and a larger room. Both were practically filled up with bunks and a few tables, benches and stools. The bunks were piled up on one another in four tiers, almost to the roof. Accordingly the floor space in which one could walk about was so insignificant that it was impossible for everyone to squeeze into the two rooms at once. So we lived chiefly "on the heights." A little stump of corridor running crosswise separated the rooms from a couple of closets on the outside, where besides a sink and privy we had two showers with cold and, occasionally, hot water. In this suite we could move about at our pleasure.

Our morning, midday and evening strolls we took in the stump of corridor, round and round, round and round. Conversed and breathed the "fresh air," not all at once of course, but in relays. Our meals we ate partly at the tables, partly in the bunks, and often in corners or in fissures between the bunks. The illumination was rather dim here and there, but as the food appeared a bit the worse for light it didn't matter. It would have been another advantage not to have had a too acute sense of smell. In "leisure moments" we played cards or read novels. Was it allowed? Oh no! But the packs of cards we hid in the wall. They had been smuggled in at different times, or fresh prisoners had simply brought them in without our hosts noticing. And the books? Why, those we got from the library, which was next door to our toilet room. The library was closed and *am strengsten verboten*, with a padlock and all the rest of it. That had been the case from time immemorial, so to speak, and the Germans had forgotten the library. Not so the Parachute crowd. One can do a little fiddling with padlocks—and then the hinges of doors. Well, we were never at a loss for reading matter.

Every Saturday evening we had an entertainment—singing, sketches and recitation. We had lectures too, almost every day. Then we debated—now and then until the fur flew. But that was chiefly when politics were on the carpet. It's a queer thing about politics; they shake communities large and small—yes even the tiny community like ours in the Parachute.

We didn't get enough to eat. That simple fact explains a great deal. The distribution didn't always pass off without growlings from certain hungry throats, though the distributors were elected and did their job as conscientiously and as well as they could. But to divide a box of bad fish and another of bad potatoes into, for example, 62 precisely equal helpings wasn't such a simple task, and precisely equal they had to be. Oh dear, oh dear! More than

---

* Erikstad remained in Grini until his release on March 22, 1945.

† Another prisoner of Grini explained that the Parachute had a double meaning: "[Y]ou needed a parachute to sleep in the upper berths, but the name had even more to do with the 'jump' to the other side" [i.e., death].

a hundred eyes were on every sliver of fish that was dealt out, and the minutest fragment of potato. No, it wasn't easy. Hungry men are not easy. When we had storm soup, it was served in a big bucket or even two buckets. Then there was always something left on the bottom and inside of the bucket. That we called the "scrapings" and there was a tremendous run on it. One could get a whole extra meal out of the scrapings. We all had the scrapings by turns, but some also got them for taking on the washing of the floor and such jobs. Yet even about the scrapings there was always a bit of grumbling.

Almost every day we were in contact with the outer world. This took place usually at one end of the corridor-stump, through the door to which we had a false key. It was quite a young lad, called Daniel, who at great personal risk mounted the four flights in the dinner interval and left things outside the door, while he gave us the needful messages and information through the crack. There was often tobacco; when I had got in touch with those outside, quite a lot came in. For I was an old hand with good connections. The first quarter of plug that reached us I shall never forget. We had had no tobacco for a long time, and there were about 60 of us. A quarter between 60 and exactly the same for each! With a millimeter ruler we had, a Gillette razor blade and a division sum we brought it off. There were a few millimeters each. Leif and I put our millimeters together, shredded them carefully and put them on the radiator to dry. Then we rolled ourselves a cigarette. I took the first puff, deep and fervent. My head swam, and I went flat on the floor. Then we lay down on our bunks, puffed away in turn, and let our heads go round. It was glorious.

We had string mail also, now and then, for the kitchen of the *Revier* was just under our toilet room. But Denzer had placed an informer in the kitchen since the "clean-up," so the string mail was a bit irregular. But we were well supplied both with war news and local information. Also, from the windows facing the square, we could follow all the roll calls, morning, midday and evening, and from certain displays and gestures and grimaces of the fellows down there we formed a pretty good idea of what was going on in camp.

The chief shadow on our life was the calling for condemned men. They were always fetched away at night. The elevator was in the lobby just outside the Parachute, and if we heard it coming up to the third floor at the dead of night we knew what it was for. Then came the heavy footsteps, the rattling of keys in the lock, the darkness suddenly slashed by the cones of light from flashlights, and there were the hangmen standing before us in the room. Pohl, Kunz, Kunze, the Butcher, or Porky, usually with Claffy or Simonsen or some Norwegian traitor. A vigorous Germanism, an oath, or bellow usually opened the performance. Then there was the call-over, and orders to such and such men to pack their things and line up on the floor at once. Three or four names sank heavily into the dark. The dead silence that ensued was soon broken by furious shouts to the condemned men to get a move on with their rag-packing. "No need to be particular! You'll have no more use for them anyhow. The things will go to the Red Cross. Get ready, blast you! Do you think we're going to stay here all night?"

But it was a waste of trouble, their fury had no longer an object, for the condemned men had nothing more to fear—they knew where they were going. Hands were pressed quietly in the dark, good-byes whispered—thanks for everything—love to those at home—and quietly they slipped down to the floor, each with his bundle, into the cones of light from the flashlights. That was the last we saw of them—their faces turned to the light.

I won't try to describe the deathly silence and the darkness that closed behind them. We who were shut in there alone with our leaden thoughts know that one can't write of it. But

I must speak of what happened on one such night—in the deathly silence and the darkness, after they had been taken away.

The condemned men were thrashed in Denzer's office. Muffled blows, hoarse bellowing, furious outbursts and loud laughter from drunken Germans, groans and wailing screams reached our ears. For Denzer's office was directly under the Parachute, two stories under it indeed, but the windows were open. This lasted an interminable half hour. Then silence fell. A moment later cars drove up to the main entrance, and from the window we saw the condemned men, their hands in handcuffs behind their backs, being brought out and stowed away. One had to be carried—the others could walk. There were three of them.

It was on such a night that I first saw something I couldn't have believed possible; but which later—in Sachsenhausen—I was, so to speak, to get used to. One of the condemned men had the bunk over mine. He had been taken away. We were lying there in the dark thinking of him and his comrades. There was dead silence. All at once I heard the man next to me cautiously sitting up in his bunk and creeping out of it. Almost without a sound he clambered into the bunk over mine—where the condemned man had been lying a few minutes before. He rummaged there a little—a cup chinked against a plate—a spoon clattered on the plate-bottom. Then all was quiet again. But in the window I could see his figure, black against the night sky, as he crept into his bunk. He had something hidden in one arm.

The condemned man left behind him a crust of bread and a few decaying potatoes. He wouldn't be wanting them. These objects had changed owners in the dark. That was all.

Suddenly one morning Kunz, Pohl and Claffy came up to the Parachute with a long list of names. Claffy read them out and announced that all whose names were read were to prepare for transport. All would be medically examined by Dr. Rietz except Leif Poulsson and Odd Nansen. No one had any doubt where the transport was to go, and it appeared that Leif and I would be sent to Germany however ill we might be. Denzer had his way and won his little victory, after all. But neither Leif nor I was ill, so we took it calmly.

Now things happened in a rush, and we had some busy hours in the Parachute. There were letters to write home—perhaps the last—things to settle, contacts to arrange, "wills" to draw up and entrust to those who were staying. Our few possessions didn't take long to pack. I got letters off to Kari and two close friends. In case of emergency—after all one didn't know what might happen. Some days before, I had had a smuggled letter from Kari. She realized what was coming and took it splendidly, sure that we should meet again, she and I and all our children. I also got my diary disposed of (unfortunately it was lost afterward).

Then came the good-byes. Our life in the Parachute had not exactly been idyllic; all the same it was a wrench to part from the little community up there on the heights. A fresh gang of condemned men had just come in. We didn't know them very well yet—all the same they helped to make the parting heavier. We knew we shouldn't see them again.

Down in *Haft* on the second floor we got our civilian clothes and our things from the closet. We were allowed to take as much as we could get into a cardboard margarine box, which was issued to each of us. That and one blanket were all we were allowed. So the thing was to get on as many clothes as possible—even if it was warm. Three sets of underclothes, three pairs of socks, two shirts, and two pull-overs I managed to find room for underneath my sports suit. Some friendly souls had smuggled a few cigarettes and

Under cover of darkness, the condemned were fetched away from the "Parachute" to be shot.

tins of sardines in among our things. They came in handy. Our valuables, watches, rings, pocketbooks, fountain pens, etc., were also handed out against a receipt, and then down we went to the square, where big buses were already drawn up and where more than 250 men from the camp had already fallen in. So they were going, too. At the last moment Fretheim was ordered out of our ranks; he escaped the journey and was again consigned to the Parachute, where he remained until peace came.

Among the 250 I caught sight of Erik Magelssen and Frode Rinnan, and already felt more cheerful about the future.

Then, with kicks and roars, came the searching of the margarine boxes, which had to be turned upside down, and clean clothes, toilet things and foodstuffs tumbled out on the ground. Then bodily search, unbuttoning, fingering, kicking and here and there a punch on the nose—and we could pack up again. Then at last we got into the buses and off. I received special parting salutations from Kunze, Bartels and Denzer, all three. The first called me "*Lump*," the second "*Schweinehund*" and the third "*Judenfreund*" [Jew friend]. Too much honor.

I had just a glimpse of Francis, Johannes, and Martin [Strandli] before I left, but couldn't say good-bye to any of them. Perhaps it was better not. Francis was looking blank. I'm sure I was too.

And then the journey began. Grini—dear, detested Grini, with its watchtowers, its electric fence, its filthy huts and all their grief and joy, hope and disappointment, lice and misery vanished behind us in the sunset—and before us lay. . . . Well before us was another bus, raising such a dust that it was impossible to see anything—for the moment.

Erik [Magelssen] and I were in the same bus. Erik is the director of a travel bureau, and felt in his element as soon as all the passengers had taken their seats and the cortège was in motion. There's something strange about movement—even if one is going to hell. At any rate one's getting somewhere—something is happening, the route may be pretty, and isn't the paving celebrated? According to a very congenial interpretation of Einstein's theory of relativity, with which I'm not very familiar, traveling makes one younger. I think there must be something in it. I've traveled a good deal.

Erik lit a cigarette, leaned back in his leather seat, stretched out his long legs, and said something about smoking and traveling. And then we began to laugh. Yes, there's something about travel. As we sped on through woods and fields toward Oslo, our thoughts became more cheerful, our blood began to circulate, and there was new life in our lean and weary bodies. I thought: Erik didn't choose his lifework unadvisedly.

After a longish sight-seeing tour of Oslo we landed at Akershus. In its prison yard we again grew several hours older while nothing happened. Then at last—and now it was pitch dark, 292 prisoners with their guards moved off down to the fortress wharf, where a big black hull loomed up against the night sky. *Isar* we read on it. The deck was crowded with panzer men in full getup with all their kit. Bayonets, submachine guns and steel helmets gleamed in the night. I suppose they were going south on leave—or were they going to the Eastern front, poor devils? A number of prisoners in the cargo would certainly have their *raison d'être* if the Royal Navy should take a fancy to the *Isar*.

The hold was large, we almost all found sleeping room on the floor, and as it was late and the day had been rather tiring, most people slept through our departure. At dead of night the *Isar* glided down the fjord. We were again in motion while the travel agent and

Boarding the Boat. In the dark of night, but under floodlights,
the transport to Germany embarked in Oslo harbor.

his young friends slept a rejuvenating if not entirely noiseless sleep in their big roomy berths.

We were neither torpedoed nor bombed, although we were sailing in convoy with many boats and many guard ships. We saw Sweden in the distance—and may have thought a thing or two, each in his own mind. But nothing much. Now, as so often, the thoughts came and flew away again, noiseless as tired birds. By day we stretched ourselves on deck in the sun, saw Denmark, Hitler's "little canary bird," fading out of view, and had a pleasant time. In the evenings we shivered in the moonlight, watched the phosphorescence in our wake, turned up our coat collars, pulled our hats over our ears, and—traveled on.

Frode told his story, Erik his, and we ours as the *Isar* plowed the Baltic. We sang a little and amused ourselves, as night and day returned four times, before at last the *Isar* glided up the Oder to Stettin.

We were eating well; none of us had eaten so well for many months. Bread with thick layers of dairy butter, and soup with meat in it. It was unbelievable. We reached Stettin all too quickly; we would have liked to travel on like this, on and on, until we were children again. Erik started planning big and awfully cheap pleasure cruises to be run on this model—one day. But then suddenly we were alongside a quay, beside another big pleasure cruiser called the *Donau*.* We had had it in front of us all the way from Oslo—and it held much the same cargo as the *Isar*.

Now the bellowing and kicking began again. Familiar figures with the death's head on their caps came aboard and took charge of the passengers. The idyll was over, and we went ashore, where we were lined up and counted, and counted and lined up again a number of times, as was to be expected. Then we marched a bit and lined up once more. Eighty men were called out and fell in separately, among them Leif [Poulsson] and many other good comrades. No one knew where they were going, no one knew where we were going, and no one knew that many would never meet again. Not until long afterward did we hear that the eighty were NN prisoners† who, after much fatigue and hardship in transport, landed in the notorious *Vernichtungs* [Extermination] camp of Natzweiler in Alsace, from which nearly half were never to return.‡

Erik, Frode and I were left with the rest of our group, now reduced to 212 men. It was

---

* SS *Donau* (Danube) was a freighter used by the Germans as a troop transport in regular service between Oslo, Norway, and Stettin, Germany (now Szczecin, Poland). It was also the ship used to transport Jews to Germany, including the transport of November 1942. On January 16, 1945, the *Donau* sank shortly after leaving Oslo harbor after Resistance fighter Max Manus attached limpet mines below the waterline before it sailed.

† NN stands for "Nacht und Nebel," or Night and Fog, a Nazi program implemented on Hitler's orders in December 1941 whereby political prisoners and resistance fighters were transported to Germany and their whereabouts and fate kept secret; they simply vanished into night and fog. This policy was designed to intimidate residents of Nazi-occupied areas of Europe, on the theory that disappearance without a trace would prove a greater deterrent than public execution. Most NN prisoners were interned at Natzweiler (in Alsace) and Gross-Rosen (in Silesia). It has never been determined how many prisoners were imprisoned or killed under this decree. Field Marshal Wilhelm Keitel, head of the German OKW (Armed Forces Supreme Command) was hanged following the war in part for his role in signing the Nacht und Nebel decree.

‡ Natzweiler-Struthof was a German concentration camp established in the Alsatian village of Struthof, France, the only concentration camp built by the Nazis on French territory. It was specifically designated in 1943 to hold NN prisoners, and the first NN convoy, consisting of 71 Norwegians, arrived June 15, 1943. It was liberated by the Allies on November 23, 1944, the first such camp in Western Europe (the prisoners had already been evacuated to Dachau and other camps). Of the fifty-two thousand prisoners deported to Natzweiler-Struthof from 1941 to 1944, more than twenty thousand died or were murdered; according to Leif Poulsson, of the 504 Norwegians sent to the camp (all

a wrench to part from the others, and we couldn't even say good-bye, for the two groups, with the usual German ceremonial, were marched off different ways. Through a deserted, eerie town we marched. From sooty house fronts windows gaped on us without glass—like eyes put out. Here and there a heap of rubble with twisted girders sticking out of it, bits of brick and fragments of furniture in Babylonian confusion told the gloomy story of the war. Here and there an old woman—or a bent old man—was hobbling along on shaky legs, and one or two scared children peeped out at us from the street doors. No other living thing was to be seen, only ourselves and the green men. Darkness had begun to fall, and our own thoughts were bright no longer.

I was wondering what would happen to Leif, and why we had been separated. We had both been so sure that our fate would be the same—whatever it was. It hadn't even occurred to us that we would go separate ways. And yet here we were, each in his own prison transport, each with his unknown goal! But still it was a comfort to think that we were both among good comrades. Now we must take our chance.

The railway station was on the fringe of the extinct city, and that was where we were bound. Far down a mile-long platform among innumerable railway lines some decayed and solitary cattle cars were awaiting us, with hospitably open doors that yawned for us blackly. Four of the cattle cars were filled up with fifty-three prisoners apiece. But we were allowed to stay out on the platform a bit longer, indeed were actually allowed to go—in relays—over to a distant building for drinks of water and on other needful errands. Some French prisoners of war frequented that building. I suppose they were working in the railway yards. We had no chance to talk to them, but indeed it wasn't necessary, for they had "expressed themselves" on the walls inside the green house. "*En quelques mois la guerre sera finie! Les Boches en retraite sur tous les fronts! A mort les tyrants, les traîtres, les collaborateurs! Vive la France!*" [In a few months the war will be over! The Germans are retreating on all fronts! Death to tyrants, traitors, and collaborators! Long live France!] it said on the walls, in big shaky letters written with bits of charcoal and chalk.

We were among friends and fellow sufferers, that was plain enough. We waved and nodded to them as we left, and they nodded and waved back again.

It proved a toilsome night. It was impossible for all fifty-three to find room on the floor of the cattle car at the same time. We tried every method of sardine-packing, but there were always ten sardines left over. Ten had to stand. Finally we tried a double layer, and that was better, but there wasn't much sleep.

I don't remember when the cars began to jerk and rattle or how long we jerked back and forth in the miles of railway yard outside Stettin before it could be said we were on our way south to Berlin. I think it was about noon of the day after and at the Anhalter Station in Berlin* that we finally got out of our rolling, stinking dark-cells for a breath of fresh air. A fleeting moment, then we were off again.

A journey on the floor of a cattle car has of course its drawbacks. But to the uninitiated it may look worse than it really is. We beguiled the time with singing and entertainment, and the longer it went on, the higher became our spirits. We had food, too—*Isar* dairy

---

classified as NN), 244 died while incarcerated or shortly after liberation. The commandant of Natzweiler from 1941 to 1944, Josef Kramer, was convicted by British authorities and hanged December 13, 1945. See February 5, 1944, below.

* By 1880 Anhalter was the largest rail terminus in continental Europe, accommodating more than forty thousand passengers a day. It was known as Berlin's "Gateway to the World." Heavily damaged in a bombing raid in late November 1943 (shortly after Nansen passed through), it was totally destroyed in a February 1945 raid by the US Army Air Force.

butter and bread and one or two sardine tins emerged from the margarine boxes. What more could we desire?

In the light from a crack in the door where I was lying, I wrote about the strange journey. Unfortunately I didn't manage to preserve that section of diary, but I am certain there was nothing dolorous in those travel notes. We were going on—slowly perhaps, but we were getting somewhere. Something was happening—we were in motion. And as I said, there's something about movement—even if it leads to hell. And that was pretty much where it led.

PART IV: SACHSENHAUSEN

1943

WEDNESDAY, OCTOBER 6, 1943 ■ The diary left off on the train on October 4th, before we reached Sachsenhausen station. Since then developments have been swift and stupefying. As yet we've nothing like settled down—nor even begun to feel our way about. Indeed, we can't even claim to have an idea, as yet, of what this whole place is like. But let me begin at the beginning.

We were in the cattle cars, tired and stiff after a night and a day without sleep or rest. The train stopped at a station with a jerk. A board said Oranienburg. We got "ready" and waited. We were sure to be getting out here. But no. The train jerked us back and forth half a dozen times. There was a squeaking and shrieking of the brakes, the engine puffed and panted and the cars jerked and strained as they were dragged or jostled hither and thither, and every time we tumbled over one another inside the car with our cardboard boxes, sleeping bags, and remaining victuals, which we were trying to eat before we had to get out. Then suddenly the whole train moved on again. It didn't stop until we reached another station, which said Sachsenhausen and was some distance from Oranienburg. There we were ordered out. And soon we heard the old familiar noise: "*Los Mensch! Los! Los! Los!*" Yes, there could be no doubt that we'd reached the terminus and were getting near our destination.

We were lined up on the platform in three ranks and counted by way of a change. It was a country station with an elderly station master, whose entire family was assembled at the door of the station building looking curiously at these prisoners from *Norwegen* [Norway]. Up in the garret rooms on the first floor a married couple sat gazing on us. He in shirt sleeves, with a cutty pipe in his mouth, and she gaping eagerly, no doubt at the queerest of us, wanting to make out what kind of people these were. I don't suppose it was the first prison transport she had gazed on from that window.

The platform and the road outside, which crossed the railway line here, was swarming with children, little boys of four or five. They had all got themselves wooden tommy guns, just like those the SS guards had. With these they took aim at us and blazed away. For we were enemies! They knew that much. The whole column moved off to lively shouting from the guards, ill-looking lads in shabby uniforms, both stained and tattered. "*Los! Los!*"

The little boys ran after us along the road with their tommy guns and had a big afternoon. On one side was a wood of spruce firs, which grew straight out of the sand. Sand, nothing but sand. A cloud of dust flew up at every step. A cloud of fine sand dust—it was like that everywhere, nothing but sand. We passed a number of prisoners who were shoveling sand up into trucks. The prisoners were in striped clothes, blue and white striped like pajamas. They didn't look as if they were overexerting themselves. The working tempo distinctly reminded one of Grini. That was reassuring. After a time we met more squads of prisoners; there were Norwegians among them, who waved and shouted a welcome. Their job was digging out foundations for buildings that were being put up here and there in the fir wood. Then we got to the wall round *Sachsenhausen Schutzhaftlager* [Protective custody camp]. We caught sight of a watchtower, then another, and we recognized the Grini watchtower system. We walked on and on, for the wall was long and the entrance was at the other side, but eventually we did arrive and turned through the *Eingangs-Gebäude* [entrance building] into a huge open space, round which the huts were arranged in a semicircle, radiating out from the center.

The first thing that caught the eye was an inscription of the gable walls of these huts, forming all together a long "maxim" which ran approximately as follows: *There is only one road to freedom. Its milestones are Honesty, Truthfulness, Obedience, Industry, Temperance, Cleanliness and Love of the Fatherland.** It's hard to say whether one was nearer laughing or crying. While it immediately struck one as ludicrous and childish, it was at the same time grotesque and sinister. There was something about the scale that made it monstrous—screamingly German—pure, pure German. It could be no further exaggerated. Couldn't be parodied. It was like seeing the sets of a Chaplin film about a German concentration camp.

The big wrought-iron gateway, *Eingangs-Gebäude*, which we had just marched through proclaimed in shining white letters: *Arbeit macht frei!* [Work makes free!]† How fine! Didn't one seem to feel the fresh breath of the Germanic spirit in person? Tut, there was nothing nasty going on here. Here there was work! Fresh air, honesty, comradeship, fellowship. Just look: Wherever one turned in the big sunny square one encountered huts painted green, flowers, green lawns, and well-kept garden paths between the huts, along the prison wall, and along the electric fence with its well-kept *Todeszone* [deathzone], where nice little placards on the lawns drew one's attention to the fact that one would be shot without warning if one came too near. What a scene of order and cleanliness! What an idyll!

As we stood contemplating all these glories like a crowd of gaping peasants, we got a rather pungent order to face the wall and fall in properly by fives. "*Los! Los!*" It was obviously prisoners who had now taken over the command; German prisoners, who struck one as all "Zebras" together. But perhaps it was only we who had unpleasant memories? They surely couldn't be just lies and fraud, all the fine things written up on those buildings?

I was torn from my meditations by the arrival of a *höherer Offizier* [high-ranking officer]. I suppose the Commandant. He walked along the ranks and looked us over. Then he caught sight of a Negro who was among us, a South African, newly arrested in Oslo. He obviously thought that this was a queer chap. Perhaps he'd never seen a Negro up close. No doubt that was why he called the Negro to the front to have a better look at him. He put some question in German. The Negro shook his head. He mumbled a few words of English, clearly the only ones he knew; then an interpreter took over. There was nothing he wanted to know. Finally he left the Negro and the interpreter at it and walked on. Shifted his cigarette into the other corner of his mouth, said something about not knowing that Norwegians were blacks, and let his gaze wander on down the ranks, with half-closed eyes and slack, fleshy lips. He didn't look unreservedly congenial, that I must admit. It made one shiver to let imagination loose on him. He didn't say anything. After

---

*   The slogan was borrowed from a radio speech given by Himmler on January 29, 1939. "The SS was so taken with Himmler's motto that it was soon displayed in several KL—on signs, roofs, and walls." In Sachsenhausen SS guards would torment prisoners by pointing to the slogan and explaining that there was only one path to freedom: through the crematorium chimney.

†   The phrase first appeared on the gates to Dachau in 1936; it was later added to the gates of Sachsenhausen, Flossenburg, and Auschwitz and apparently to the entrance to the prisoner compound in Gross-Rosen.

sating his curiosity on the Negro he simply walked along the front with his hands stuck loosely in his trouser pockets and was gone.

With a left turn the whole squad moved off across the square and down one of the radiating streets. We passed prisoners of every kind—pale, olive-skinned Czechs, Russians, Slovaks, Ukrainians, Poles, Frenchmen, Dutchmen, Belgians and Norwegians! Most went on with what they were doing and didn't even look up. A new prison transport? As if they hadn't seen hundreds of them come and go, come and go interminably. In sheer defiance many turned the other way. That was by way of a sign that they were old prisoners, I thought as I plodded through the dust cloud in the middle of the column between Frode and Erik.* When we looked at one another, we laughed—not otherwise. There was nothing else to laugh at.

Soon we caught sight of the first friends from Grini—some here, some there. They waved and shouted, "Hi! Hello, Hansen!" "Hi, Jokern!" "Hello, Halvor!" "How goes it, Håkon?" "Is that you, Frode? You don't look too bad!" "Nor you, how long have you been here?" "Are there any more coming?" "Had you a beastly trip?" "Not too bad." "What news from Norway?" "How was it going at Grini?" etc. There was [Carsten] Aasebø. He was the superior and took us under his wing. He had been here almost two years and knew everything, gave advice, told us what and where and how.

The column halted before a hut on the periphery, right out by the outer wall. This was the reception and delousing hut. Aasebø announced that now we had to hand over all our possessions, watches, valuables, money—everything; he urgently enjoined us to hide nothing away. It would be no use, he said, and now especially we must be careful to play no tricks. We would only start a fuss and be sorry.

My thoughts went to the diary, the only cause for nervousness I have now—of that kind. It was in my hip pocket, and here we were to bathe and change our clothes, hand in *everything*. The luggage, sleeping bag, cardboard box and contents, everything except provisions, which we were allowed to take out, was to be handed in and go through the "gasroom" before we got it back—that is, as much of it as they let us keep. The diary problem occupied and disturbed me a good deal. Finally I got hold of an old hand. He advised me just to hand it in. They wouldn't look at it—wouldn't make head nor tail of it. Blockhead! He might simply have offered to pocket it on the spot. I can say that now. Now it's too late. I stuck the diary into my sleeping bag, which went into the gasroom with all the rest, and its fate is still unknown. Some of the men have begun to get their things back today. I haven't had mine yet.

We heard about our old friends here—August [Lange], Halvard [Lange], Sven [Oftedal], Leif [Jensen], Arvid [Johansen], Rolf [Hofmo]. . . .† Yes, they were here—they were all right. Colbjørn was in another camp nearby, but he was doing fine, too. We questioned and catechized, "The ones who died—?" "Ye-es, well, they died—died off like flies—last year and the beginning of this. The chaps fell ill; nearly all of them fell ill, and a lot of them lost their pep and went under—'Went up the chimney,' as we say here." A

---

* One concentration camp survivor later noted, "Newcomers were the lowest form of life in the camp. Newcomers were despised by everyone because they had to prove themselves first."

† Both Jensen and Johansen helped Nansen smuggle his diary out of Sachsenhausen in their breadboards. Halvard Lange (1902–1970) was a politician and statesman, serving as foreign minister (1946–1963; 1963–1965). In his youth Nansen lived for a time with the Lange family and considered Halvard's father, Christian Lous Lange (awarded the Nobel Peace Prize in 1921), as a second father.

little motion of the hand, in a rising spiral with the thumb up, always accompanied this expression, which was in constant use. We learned afterward that the raised thumb was meant to indicate the smoke from the chimney of the crematorium. What did they die of? "*Scheisserei* [dysentery], boils and pneumonia, most of them. They went to the 'ambulance' and if they hadn't over 40 degrees [104°F] of fever they just got a kick in the arse and had to go away. If they had more than 40 degrees they got some pills or so forth—they might be put in the *Revier*—or they might have to go back to the block.* So then they lay and died there. It was too bad about a lot of them. They gave up—couldn't take it."

I asked about a friend from Grini. "Well, now—him—yes, he didn't last long. He was sent to Falkensee, another camp near here.† Then he was suddenly taken bad. So he went into the *Revier* here, pottered round a bit in an easy squad, but took another bad turn, lost his pep, and went up the chimney. Pneumonia, I think it was." Well, yes, it was sad—but otherwise they were all right, got parcels, were allowed to write home twice a month that they were all right, and altogether the Norwegians were well treated.

I asked about another Grini comrade. "Oh—him—he was taken ill too—pretty quick—*Scheisserei* and pneumonia—lost heart and . . ." the lifted thumb told the rest. "But I've come off well, haven't been sick, have eaten and put on weight. Was down to sixty-four kilos [141 pounds], now I weigh seventy-eight [172]—not bad!" He slapped a big, fat belly and laughed. "What was the food like at Grini?"

There was something about that man and the whole business that made me feel uncomfortable. He was of a piece, so to speak, with all we had seen, was as though cut out of the parade ground itself, with its fan-shaped barracks, its inscriptions, and everything. I hadn't as it were the courage to go on asking. Was afraid to hear any more about him, his weight, the comrades who died like flies last year.

We stood round for hours before getting into the first room, where tabs with numbers were issued to us, and where we handed over our money and valuables and all our luggage and signed and filled in a long series of documents and forms—and where we finally had to take off all our clothes, which were put into a sack a man had ready. We were allowed to keep tobacco and foodstuffs, so at the end of the ceremony there we stood, with some tobacco, a bit of bread, and perhaps a little butter in our hands—naked. A slightly odd situation, on which, however, we had no opportunity of brooding for long. With the familiar German cries—in spite of the fact that there were no SS around—we were moved on into the next room. One lined up behind the next pair of naked legs, and thus got quite quickly to a man who was sitting with a big electric bulb in one hand and a hair-cutting machine in the other. He wore a shade over his eyes, and in the eyes themselves I glimpsed the greed of a beast of prey. Before I knew what was happening, he seized me by the arm and pulled me closer. He held out the electric bulb, which also had a shade on it, so that the light fell with unblushing strength and concentration on the lower regions of the belly. He bent forward—very close—and with a couple of brisk professional move-ments of his right hand he had removed all superfluous hair almost before I knew it or

---

* Here the barracks were called blocks. O.N.

† Opened in March 1943 with Norwegian and Soviet prisoners, Falkensee was a subcamp of Sachsenhausen, located on the western border of Berlin. By November 1944 approximately 2,500 prisoners worked as slave laborers for the Demag (Deutsche Maschinenfabrik) factory there, some working on components of the V-2 weapon.

had time to protest. Others didn't get through the process quite so painlessly; streams of blood bore witness to that.

Bereft of this manly ornament, I lined up behind Erik, who had been similarly plundered, in a fresh line. This time it was for the hair on one's head. It went almost as briskly. The hair cutter first took hold of the hair with one hand, fondling it a bit, so to speak; then he set the clipper in it and swept it off with just a few snowplow strokes from the forehead to the base of the skull. One, two, three—and there you stood, naked, bereft of all your hair, with a head that no one had seen before. A curiously squeezed and dented billiard ball with one millimeter of bristle on it. On the floor a great mound of hair was piling up. I suspect them of staging this whole act of the Chaplin film to get hold of the hair to make clothes with.

It was a strangely plucked and reduced assembly that went on into the next room. This turned out to be the bathroom. Our food and smokes we still held faithfully in our hands. Some were lucky enough to have brought soap and toilet things, but as no one had explained either that it was allowed or what the program was to be, most of us had no soap. But bathe we must, it was an order. Well. One lined up in the middle of the room in two rows, under showers fixed in the ceiling and turned on from the same place at the same time. First cold, then boiling hot, then cold again. Everything had to be done in time. I managed to borrow a piece of soap, but so late that the water was turning cold as I soaped myself—and before I got the soap off me, the water had been turned off. A typical mishap. One has to accustom oneself to being a mass man.

Well, I got the soap dried off me with a towel that was handed out on the next "conveyor belt." Then off we went into the next room. We were no sooner through the door than a man came at us with something strange. It turned out to be a stick with antilouse ointment, black and loathsome in appearance. The ointment he had in a big bucket, into which he dipped the stick and splashed a big daub under the belly and under each arm of every naked, shaky prisoner who ventured inside the door. Just on those spots that now lacked their usual ornament, there his stick came down. Then we had to smear that filthy ointment all over with our fingers. It had a pungent smell.

The next item in the program was underclothing, shoes, socks, shirt, pullover, coat and cap. It may sound well. It was nothing but a heap of filthy rags. No one cared a damn whether they fitted or not. You simply had to take the pile that was handed out—whether you were long or short, thick or thin. If you went back and asked to change one of the garments, you got a punch in the face—and asked no more. I couldn't get on anything that was issued to me, but managed to change with one of the others. The prisoners doing the handing out were yahoos, as bad as any German SS men.

I was lucky enough to get hold of a pair of trousers that would go on, even though they only reached halfway down my calves, and a shirt that would go on, even though it wouldn't button round the neck and the sleeves only reached my elbows. The "socks" were something in the way of footbags made of old rags. Of course they didn't fit, so there was nothing for it but to tear them open enough to let one's foot in. There was no warmth in them, but they did afford the foot a kind of protection from the wooden sandals that were issued as shoes. These were a miserable contrivance. They had a kind of toecap nailed on them, usually of thin glove leather. There were also "heelcaps" and "side-pieces" of the same quality. If one managed to get hold of a pair at all the size of one's feet, one might consider oneself lucky—to get the "shoes" to "fit" was impossible. My heels came an inch beyond and thus over the heelcap. I got hold of a bit of twine with which I succeeded in lashing the boards to my feet. In a cap with three hairs on top, a real prisoner's cap of striped cloth; a pair of trousers reaching a little below the knee and threatening to split if I bent down; in a jacket with fringed elbow sleeves, which wouldn't button at the neck, and which was made of blue-and-white-striped pajama stuff; stumbling along on wooden boards, I left that capital establishment with Erik, who looked no better. Now we were genuine convicts and no mistake!

We went out into the open again, under the evening sky. For it had already turned dark and chilly. Straight away we were to find how miserably our new apparel was adapted to keeping out the cold. In a short time everyone's teeth were chattering, and it grew colder and colder, with a starry October sky arching overhead. As yet not all of us had even got into the establishment; there was still a long time to wait, for we were obviously to wait until all had finished.

It was a strange assembly. One could hardly recognize one's friends. Some, who had had beards, looked entirely different. White over their scalps and where the beard had once been, with sunburnt faces, they looked like clowns ready painted and rigged out to charge into the arena.

Oftedal turned up and paid a call on us. He looked well, and it did one good to talk to him. As calm, as balanced, and as sedate as ever. Things *had* been bad here at one time, very bad, indeed absolutely frightful! *Now* they were much better, and the Norwegians especially were well off, better off than the others in many ways. *Unlimited* parcels, for example. It was only a question of getting the dispatch of parcels "under way," and we ourselves would have to wait at least a couple of months. Still we thought that sounded promising. Altogether, Oftedal had a reassuring effect, like oil on some disturbed lake. Moreover he didn't laugh at us for looking so queer. So, involuntarily, we stopped laughing at each other and began to catechize Oftedal about everything between heaven and earth, until I suppose he got sick of it and of us, felt he had done enough for one day and walked off.

Still we had to stand and wait a long time before the last men were ready and we could march off to the hut which is to be our future "home," at least for a more than sufficient time to come. Even then we had a long wait in the open before we could get under cover, but we were now among the huts where the Norwegians lived, and they came out to see us. Work was over, and they had the evening to themselves, until eight or half-past. We were to go into quarantine, like all newcomers. The quarantine is to last a fortnight.

SUNDAY, OCTOBER 10, 1943 ■ Father's birthday. He would have been eighty-two today, if he had lived. If he had lived! The memory of him and his lifework seems completely alien and unintelligible, as though it all belonged to another world. But there are still ties binding us to that world, and we won't allow them to be severed if we can help it. We hold fast to them convulsively, refuse to slide down the precipice that threatens on every side, with its black, hopeless maw. On every hand we see fellow creatures slipping downward. Poles, Russians, Germans, Belgians, Frenchmen, Ukrainians, Dutchmen, Rumanians, Czechs, Hungarians. Their faces grin on one in a sneer of hate, derision and agony. Piles of corpses! Corpses alive and dead! And an appalling stench that threatens to suffocate one. Wherever one turns, always the same nightmare, the same appalling vision. It's as though all these terrible impressions, these ghastly things we have heard and seen, had bewitched us, made us alien to ourselves. We've ceased to know what is happening to us, to be aware of our own reactions.

A deafening row all day long from morning to night—tramping to and fro of wooden soles, moving of benches and stools, tramping on them also. Shrieking, roaring and conversation in one inexorable stream. Not a fraction of a minute's break. Some are eating, some cooking on the stove in the middle of the room, queuing up and wrangling about it, some reading, fighting for newspapers and periodicals, some changing their clothes, some tidying their cupboards, some shaving, some sewing and darning, some playing chess and other games, brawling, or simmering good-naturedly, all the sounds and uproar gathering into one long roar that presses on the eardrums and muffles the working of one's brain.

Suddenly the whole thing is shivered by an "*Achtung!*"—some German *Blockführer* [Block or Hut leader] who comes prying in on us from time to time. Or we are driven out of the block like sheep, to march and drill with our *Blockältester* [Senior Block prisoner] Hans, out in the "streets" or on the parade ground. One loses all power of distinguishing the different experiences. One ceases to know morning from evening, or to care, for what does it matter?

We are to be in quarantine a fortnight, indeed it may be even longer, for last night, when everyone in this block was medically examined, it turned out that one man had scarlet fever. It was [Per] Hareide.* Some may think there are advantages in quarantine. One doesn't have to work; one can lounge about all day with nothing to worry about. It's a hideous mistake to suppose that kind of life is what one has most need of immediately on one's arrival here. More than anything else I should think one needs an occupation. Away at any cost with these appalling thoughts that crowd in! One feels an ungovernable craving to rub out the whole scene that confronts one on every side, as though it were nothing but a fantasy, a bad dream.

Oh, if one could only wake up from this nightmare, wake and find that there exists another reality which is of the light! And this heartfelt wish evolves into an intense yearning, which increasingly takes conscious form in one's mind. The light returns, at first by glimpses like a beacon lamp in the night, then like a fixed light a long way off, steadily approaching, changing to brilliant sunlight. And in the sunlight, suddenly there they are, she and the children, smiling to one in trust and confidence! At last! All one has in life, all one goes on living for, is contained in that vision. All hows and whys are silenced and superfluous. All this horror, even, becomes an episode!

MONDAY, OCTOBER 11, 1943 ■ Every day is bright and clear, sunshine from a clear sky. The nights are starry and biting cold, with a waxing moon in the direction of Berlin. We have had no raids yet, but several alarms. Most of us are cold, day and night. Among the many bans is one on the wearing of a jersey at night, because of the danger of lice! They believe that jerseys attract lice. It's also strictly forbidden to have more than one jersey on, by day as well as night. Breaches of this rule will be severely punished. I am a

---

* Remained in Sachsenhausen until the end of the war.

rule breaker, otherwise I should freeze to the marrow, by day as well as night. I haven't had any of my luggage given out yet, nor yet my sleeping bag. Most people have had theirs.

I'm a bit nervous about my diary which is in the sleeping bag. They'll take it away most likely, but hopefully they will simply put it among my things in the depository. What I'm to do with these pages as time goes on I don't yet know. No one has offered to help me so far. On the contrary. And I should hate to give up writing. It's such a help and comfort.* I'd rather retrench a little. So far I've nothing like arranged my ideas, so what I write for some time to come will no doubt have to be simply a kind of registering of impressions and experiences. I haven't yet made out any daily rhythm. If, now and then, it seems to be taking definite form, it is completely shattered once more by all that others tell me, all that I hear and gradually find out for myself.

Yesterday Anders Daae came along with a young Russian airman, who wanted to see me.† He was taken prisoner with sixteen others at Orel,‡ where he had bailed out after an air fight. They were put in a prisoner-of-war camp at Königsberg.§ They fixed up a radio receiver, were discovered and sent here. This is a hell for Russian prisoners. About fifteen thousand of them have marched through the gate from time to time, and there are only eight or nine hundred left in the camp. The rest have been starved to death, beaten to death or otherwise done away with. Seven of the young Russian airman's comrades were hanged here—I suppose the final punishment for the radio affair in Königsberg. Several of the others have died of starvation and disease.

These hangings take place on the parade ground, and everyone has to look on. Our Norwegian comrades have seen any number of them. Nor are these executions lacking in their "heroic episodes." A German was hanged for attempting to escape. He talked of freedom on the scaffold, freedom for the German people which would soon come. He turned to the Commandant, who attends the executions, and calmly said, Well, it was his turn now, before long it would be the Commandant's.¶ When the rope was put round his neck, he raised his hand and waved and smiled to his comrades for the last time. It must be a good deal worse to look on when the unhappy man or men scream, weep and struggle. Once there were seven hanged at the same time.

Swindling and scrounging go on here in every possible way and on every scale. Practically everything is arranged, and arranged exclusively by bribes. The term "scrounging" is here enlarged to cover everything, from simple theft to bribery, purchase, barter and fraud. If one is trying to get clothes that can be worn, one has to do it by bribing those who have "a foot inside" where the clothes are kept. A cap costs so many cigarettes, or so much food of this or that kind. A pair of trousers, a jacket, a sweater, etc., are priced in the same

---

* In Fridtjof Nansen's diary of his polar expedition he wrote, "My mind is confused. . . . The only thing that helps me is writing, trying to express myself on these pages."

† Daae, a doctor, remained in Sachsenhausen until the end of the war.

‡ Orel, or Oryol, is a city of approximately 300,000; it is 220 miles southwest of Moscow. Captured by the German army on October 3, 1941, it remained occupied until August 4, 1943.

§ The capital of East Prussia, Königsberg surrendered to Soviet troops after a long siege on April 19, 1945. After the war all remaining Germans in the city were expelled by the Soviet Union, which in 1946 renamed the city Kaliningrad.

¶ And indeed Commandant Anton Kaindl (1902–1948) had his turn. Following the war Kaindl was tried by Soviet authorities and sentenced to life imprisonment and forced hard labor in the coal mines at the Vorkuta Gulag, one hundred miles north of the Arctic Circle. He died there in 1948.

way. Of course you can scrounge food too, indeed work as well; everything—absolutely everything!

A Norwegian who is an old inhabitant told me that in "the bad time"—that is, six months, a year, or two years ago, in other words "in the old days" when, as is well known, everything was always worse than it is now—or better if that's the point—in the bad time one could go out into camp and sell a bit of sausage or ham, if one had any to spare, for $20,000, for example. For there was money in unlimited quantities—dollars, pounds, rubles and francs—in notes and gold. There were also precious stones, emeralds, rubies, pearls, diamonds—by the bucket—and all kinds of ornaments and treasures. But none of all these glories could be eaten! Even a multimillionaire might die of hunger, pitiful and helpless, side by side with the poorest and most wretched Ukrainian. The value of his millions became more and more illusory as famine preyed on him, while the value of the bit of sausage or ham rose and rose and burst all habitual standards—all "reasonable" limits—on its way to insanity!

But that calls for an explanation. Money? Jewels? Ornaments? Where did *they* come from?—And to whom did they belong? Multimillionaires? How could this be?

From the great annihilation camps in Poland—Auschwitz,* Lublin† and others— where hundreds of thousands upon hundreds of thousands of Jews were being killed, there came incessantly to Sachsenhausen railway trains full of the clothing, footwear and effects of the murdered Jews. A special squad of many hundreds of prisoners, among them my Norwegian friend, were employed exclusively in ripping open these clothes and shoes, out at one of the factories to which the prisoners were "hired" from the camp. Sewn into the clothing they discovered fortunes in banknotes—and in the footwear, especially in the high heels of the women's's shoes, they found little treasures of jewels. Each day's "catch" was several tubs full of jewels and ornaments and great bundles of banknotes. One has to go back to one's childhood's fairy book, the *Thousand and One Nights*, for a counterpart

---

* Auschwitz, the largest concentration camp and the largest extermination camp established by the Nazis, was situated almost forty miles west of Krakow, Poland. The Auschwitz complex consisted of three main camps, together with a number of subcamps: Auschwitz I (established May 1940), which functioned as a concentration camp and as administrative center for the complex; Auschwitz II (also known as Auschwitz-Birkenau) (established early 1942) was an extermination camp, or *Vernichtungslager*, used primarily for the destruction of Jews; and Auschwitz III (also known as Auschwitz-Monowitz) (established October 1942), was designed as a labor camp to provide workers for nearby chemical works and other factories. Thomas Buergenthal was a prisoner in Birkenau from August 1944 until January 1945; both Elie Wiesel and Primo Levi worked in Auschwitz-Monowitz. At its peak in the summer of 1944, Auschwitz held almost 135,000 prisoners. It is estimated that 1.1 million prisoners died or were killed in Auschwitz. The camp was liberated January 27, 1945, by Soviet forces. The first commandant of Auschwitz, Rudolf Höss, was hanged on April 16, 1947; the second, Arthur Liebehenschel, was hanged January 28, 1948, and the third, Richard Baer, was only discovered and arrested in December 1960. He died while in pretrial custody in 1963. The section of Auschwitz where plundered clothing, shoes, etc., were initially processed was known as "Kanada," an allusion to Canada's supposed riches, particularly its mineral riches.

† The Lublin concentration camp, more commonly known by its nickname "Majdanek," was located in the outskirts of Lublin, Poland, and was the second largest concentration camp after Auschwitz. Its primary purpose was to supply forced labor for the SS, although one historian concludes that at Majdanek, "it [KL labor] was designed only for suffering." Targeted killings and inhuman conditions resulted in a high death toll; Operation Harvest Festival (November 3, 1943) was the largest single-day, single-site massacre of the Holocaust (18,000 Jews). Majdanek was the first major concentration camp captured by the Allies; it was overrun by the Soviet Army on July 23, 1944. When Soviet authorities allowed *New York Times* correspondent H. W. Lawrence into the camp, he wrote, "I have just seen the most terrible place on the face of the earth." The death toll at the main camp alone is estimated at between 80,000 and 110,000.

to all that shining splendor. The robbers too are well represented; for who "owns" all that stolen property? The rightful owners have been put to eternal silence in the gas chambers of Poland, and no one can prevent the SS and the big "factory owners," Himmler, Göring and Goebbels* from taking over the goods. They too must live, and the D.A.W.— *Deutsche Ausrüstungs-Werke* [German equipment-works]†—find they can spare a little time from the production of armaments. Of course they charge a little for their trouble, both the head and the other SS men, one or two buckets of jewels a day and a few piles of banknotes—then Himmler, Göring and Goebbels get the rest—so they think.

But they forget the prisoners, who, in spite of strict control and the most intrusive bodily search at the end of every day's work, have no great difficulty in seeing to it that a considerable proportion finds its way out into the camp. Among the prisoners there are outstanding professionals in the criminal branch. Old jailbirds with experience and skill, they have little trouble in securing a colleague or two among the SS guards on a "commission basis." In brief: It wouldn't surprise me if the world's biggest swindles were taking place in Sachsenhausen. Everything is dead rotten, cold and soulless and horrible behind the prim façade we saw on our arrival, with all its splendid "milestones" to "freedom."

Another typical feature of the whole humbug is that inside the barracks, or "blocks" as they are also called, water is never used at all for cleaning; the beds and bedclothes are never washed. Early and late we have this roaring and display about *peinliche Sauberkeit* [scrupulous cleanliness], and outside and between the barracks are gardens of flowers and little railings along all the paths, of fir branches with the bark on. It looks well-kept and idyllic, and a "visitor" never gets a glimpse of the fact that it only serves as a frame for the most unbounded filth, the worst hatching ground for lice and bacteria. There are no washing materials, I suppose that's one reason. Whited sepulchers. Whited sepulchers they are, indeed. How many have ended their lives in them it's impossible to say. I don't know what or whom to believe. The figures vary. That again is a thing one soon finds out. The looseness with which facts are treated is downright sinister. To achieve a sensation with one's stories, the exaggeration has to be enormous. Otherwise they produce no effect. The everyday reality is so violent, so deadening and brutal. Some say that 40,000 have died here, some 30,000, some less. The prisoners' numbers have now reached about 73,000. Mine is 72,060. There are about 17,000 prisoners in the camp. About 10,000 are on loan to other camps and places of work, so all told the figure of those at present on the records in Sachsenhausen should be over 25,000. Colbjørn is one of those on loan. He is in a smaller camp south of Berlin called Lichtenfelde,‡ and is apparently all right there, except that they are more in contact with the raids. Several barracks in the camp were blown away some time ago, so they have to live in tents to a great extent.

---

* Joseph Goebbels (1897–1945) was Reich minister of information and propaganda. One historian writes, "It is no exaggeration to say that he created Hitler's public image, not merely as a political leader but also as saviour [*sic*] of his people." After Hitler named him "Reich Plenipotentiary for Total War" Goebbels became for a time the third most powerful man in Germany after Hitler and Himmler. On May 1, 1945, the day after Hitler committed suicide, Goebbels had his six children killed and then committed suicide with his wife.

† A company founded by the SS to produce equipment and construction materials for the SS; Sachsenhausen, Buchenwald, Flossenburg, and Mauthausen were all used as sites for this enterprise.

‡ Nansen is most likely referring to Lichterfelde (there is no camp named Lichtenfelde), a satellite camp of Sachsenhausen. Approximately 1,500 prisoners labored in the camp on construction projects and, as the war continued, cleaning up after air raids. Lichterfelde was regarded as a relatively "privileged subcamp" due to its working and living conditions.

The Ukrainians, especially, are the camp's pariah caste and their condition is appalling. Accordingly they die in crowds. We see them round us all day, begging, filching and sneaking about. They look filthy and unkempt, not an intelligible word can they utter, only point at the cigarette butt they want, the potato peelings from dinner they hope to "scrounge," etc. One of them came up to our table the other night. We had had pickled herring. (Only we Norwegians get that, through the Norwegian Red Cross.) Herring guts, skin, bones, scales and filth lay on the table in heaps. This chap came gliding down the table, stole his hand in between our shoulders, seized the herring refuse, and stored it in his cap until the cap was full. Then he emptied it into his trousers and jacket pockets, and continued his "rich harvest." Poor fellow. Someone drove him away. That's what they do here. Harsh words, blows and kicks are the only things that make an impression on them; then they sneak off with their tails between their legs and disappear in the swarm.

What they're doing is of course *am strengsten verboten* and if they're seen will be rewarded with, for instance, twenty-five strokes on the buttocks. Altogether, floggings are the invariable threat. "Twenty-five on the arse" is a standing phrase, and one may get it for anything. Smoking in working hours, for example. One may only smoke three times a day. Before morning roll call, in the dinner interval from twelve to one, and after evening roll call—outside—never in the huts. If one smokes on the sly inside the privy, for instance, one is immediately in danger of "twenty-five on the arse." These floggings also take place in public, and are not, it's said, very pleasant to witness. For work like that they pick out suitable men among the prisoners themselves; these include all sorts of people, even hangmen—willing hangmen. It strikes one that there are remarkably few uniformed SS Germans to be seen in the camp. But all *Blockälteste* (and there are sixty-eight blocks) and *Lagerälteste* [senior camp supervisor], of whom there are three, are Germans. It is they who maintain discipline, and they do it like true Germans and no mistake. They remind me of the man who asked what was the white stuff in poultry dung, and got the completely adequate reply, "That's poultry dung, too!" Yes, indeed, they are Germans, too. God knows why they happen to be on the wrong side—or rather, on the right side of the bars.

Incidentally we seem to be lucky in our *Blockältester*. He's one of the best, and we have had nothing to complain of as yet. He doesn't do much more than his duty, and we can't blame him for doing that. The first time he instructed us in the usual *Blockältester* style on the rules of discipline, work, and mode of life in the camp was an occasion not to be forgotten. He employed and put us wise to all the camp terminology and made frequent use of the upturned thumb to show us what would most likely happen to the majority. He was jovial and pleasant in his way, but hadn't much consolation to give us. He thought that some of us had no doubt a chance of life, but only if we showed him blind obedience and carried out his orders at every point. "*Sonst,*" [Otherwise] he added, pulling a regretful face and shrugging his shoulders, and moving his thumb slowly upward in a spiral. Erik [Magelssen], who hadn't yet found out the exact significance of that peculiar sign with the thumb, ventured to ask, "You, Hans, what does this mean?" And he imitated the sign as best he could. "*Aber Menschenkind doch,*" [But for heavens' sake] roared out Hans in a despairing voice, as though all his teaching had been quite wasted, "Don't you understand? The crematorium! The crematorium, man!" and he brought his thumb up in the most accomplished spiral as high as his arm could reach.

In this camp there is a ghastly multitude of people who "have got like that," and probably will never be any different. There are people here who have been "inside" since 1933. Ten or twelve years in a German prison or concentration camp! Therefore a lot of them of course have gone under, physically and morally. Some have taken to homosexuality. These men are isolated in their own huts. Their unhappy propensity is punishable if detected *in flagranti*. Then the usual punishment is flogging or even hanging. Others have turned into "camp men" and now can hardly be imagined living in a free community. They have turned work-shy, lying, cowardly, and rotten in every way. Others again have as it were gone out; without precisely going under they've simply left off living, so to speak, long before their death. They live on only with a very few essential organs, of which the stomach is the most important. They think of nothing but food, live for food, work mechanically, and react apathetically, except to food—on that they're fanatics. Hoard and grasp it up.

The prisoners are divided into various groups or categories. First and foremost the political prisoners; they have a red triangle before their number. Next come the criminals—thieves, murderers, sexual criminals, swindlers; they have a green triangle before the number. Then we have the antisocial or work-shy, with a black triangle. Then there are the Bible-searchers, a strange little flock, who might be released if they would only abjure their "Bible-searching," one of whose tenets is that Hitler is a false prophet, a danger and disaster to Germany. But none of them will give up this odd conviction.* They have been given a mauve triangle before the number. The homosexuals have also been provided with a triangle of their own, a pink one. Besides which there are a number of other "triangle signs" for SS men, *Wehrmacht* soldiers, and other Germans who for some reason have landed "inside." In addition all prisoners—except the Germans—have a letter before their number, which indicates nationality. Thus we have all an N, the Russians an R, the Poles a P, etc. In many ways the Norwegians are on a special footing, have certain advantages that others haven't, are more respected than other nationalities, perhaps along with the Dutch—and of course the Germans themselves. I suppose the reason is that we are Germanic—and that we receive parcels of ham, sausage, sugar, cigarettes and butter.

TUESDAY, OCTOBER 12, 1943 ■ The same weather, piercingly cold—and clear. Still no raid last night. Expectantly we crawl into bed every night, roll up, in the darkness of the overcrowded sleeping hall, in our disgusting greasy blankets—and disappointed we stagger from our bunks in the morning. Disappointed because we've slept in peace.

Thank goodness it's dark inside, so that at least we can't see those blankets. They *are* fat! The only fat we get. The beds are in three tiers and so close together that they fill up the whole room. Between the rows is a narrow passage in which one has to walk sideways. Two men can't pass in it; one has to clamber up aloft to let the other pass underneath. I'm in the middle of a row, next to Frode [Rinnan]. It's an acrobatic feat to get in and

---

* Jehovah's Witnesses. They were sometimes called "Bible Searchers" or "Bible Students" because their movement originally was called the "International Bible Students Association"; the name Jehovah's Witnesses was only adopted in 1931 by the followers of Joseph Rutherford to distinguish themselves from other Bible student groups. Jehovah's Witnesses (of which Germany had the second largest community after the United States) refused to swear oaths or allegiance to the regime, refused to use the Hitler greeting, and would not render military service. For these reasons they were banned by the Nazis in 1933. Thousands of Jehovah's Witnesses were arrested in the 1930s, and some were sent to concentration camps, where many died as they were for a time mercilessly persecuted for their beliefs.

out of a bunk like that, especially for a man of my build, but I'm beginning to master it. And a good thing, too, for unluckily I've taken to getting up three or four times a night. That's a result of the fare, which is chiefly water, and no doubt of the frost. For I have no underclothing. Only the camp rags. I haven't had my things yet, and there's nothing I can do about them. If I were to go to the *Blockältester*, for instance, or someone else with authority, and tell him I was cold, that I had lumbago (I'm as stiff as an old, old man every morning), and therefore I should like to have my things, I'd only be jeered at. In this place one isn't cold, one isn't ill, one lives as one has to live according to the regulations and "prohibitions"—or else one dies. And both without a sound! *Verstanden?* One can only wait and see. I may get my things before I get pneumonia. And if one gets pneumonia, one hasn't much more use for them.

We live on cabbage soup and potatoes, potatoes and cabbage soup. Both for dinner and for supper we have cabbage soup. It does happen that we have spinach soup and potatoes, that is, it happened once, and no doubt that was cabbage soup too, only the cabbage was green. Erik [Magelssen] holds that it was potato shaws. For breakfast we get another kind of soup with bread crumbs in it—or so-called coffee—with the bread ration, which is small, but of good coarse bread. Butter we get a dab of twice a week. When we have coffee we get something with it, a bit of sausage, some cheesy substance, or jam. All *ersatz* of course; it has a sinister look, but we are hungry.

In general, of course, the food is inadequate. And so people are starving, slowly but surely. Undoubtedly what keeps the Norwegians alive and in relatively good condition is the food parcels from home and from Sweden and Denmark. These parcels are of inestimable importance; we have already made acquaintance with them. Our mates, who have been here a long time and have long been in touch with home, come over to us with tins of sardines, crispbread, cheese, and all the good things on earth, which all disappear like magic, since everyone has still an inner void to fill up before he can get a solid foundation to "work" on. And symptoms that the fare is inadequate are not lacking. Several of the fellows have begun to swell up in the legs. Erik is one of them. But in time no doubt these things will improve. We can't have much to fear. We have been lucky and have already been allowed to send our first letter home. We composed it more or less the same for everyone, so that it should go more quickly through the censorship.

Today at last I got my things. But the diary of course was not there, nor the briefcase of blank paper. Nor yet my shoes. But I got good warm underclothes and socks, and feel comfortable now that I have them on. I brought a set of eating implements; they took those. A bottle of medicine for athlete's foot; they took that. And the meanest thing of all—the picture of Kari and the children, which I had laid under one of the flaps at the bottom of the box—they took that. What a people!

At night, when I lie thinking and thinking, I seem to see the gas chambers where thousands upon thousands of Jews, Poles and others have been killed. The prussic-acid chambers in Lublin camouflaged as bathhouses, which the poor souls enter thinking they're to have a bath. There are men in this camp who come from Lublin, and can describe these things because they have seen them. They're not fantasy. Nor is it a fantasy that in this camp they have cars so constructed that the exhaust flows into the car, which is hermetically sealed. A ten-minute drive in such a car is enough to send anyone to eternity. The cars have been in frequent use. Hundreds of victims have been carried out of them and "gone up the chimney." And there are still several deaths a day, though it's no longer so ghastly as it was—nothing like! There have been times here, when a normal order in the barracks every morning was, "*Tote heraus!*" [dead outside!]—whereupon all who during the night had died in their beds of hunger, cold, exhaustion and disease were carried out and laid in heaps.

WEDNESDAY, OCTOBER 13, 1943 ■ Kari's birthday!* Forlorn—but not alone. Four wonderful children she has with her, and mother, and many, many friends. But all the same I know this will be a hard day for her—even perhaps a little harder than all the other days. Poor, gallant little Kari. God grant that you've heard nothing about this camp—that no one has told you what goes on here.

THURSDAY, OCTOBER 14, 1943 ■ Still we can do nothing but sleep and eat. A little marching after morning roll call, until the floor of the hut is swept and the privy and washroom cleaned, is the only change we have. Everything else is forbidden. Of course it's also forbidden to sit here writing a diary, and God knows what I'm to do with it, let alone how I'm to take it with me when the time comes for me to leave here. I'm simply taking the chance that that will coincide with the end of the war, and that all such controls will therefore be done away with. So I write hopefully on, it's such a blessed help to me, such a comfort—and then the time goes faster.

Now all the others are asleep. For now they've introduced sleeping hours in the middle of the day. From seven until nine in the morning there is to be sleep, and then from one to three. Lights out goes at eight in the evening, and we get up at four. That allows more than enough sleep, for me at least, without these sleeping hours in the daytime. So I prefer to sit up. That of course is forbidden too, but I've squared it with the *Stubenältester* [room leader], a decent old Polish barber who is called Ludwig and who doesn't say anything. I've told him that I'm writing a love story. When he heard that he gave a sly smile, at once delighted and admiring, and told me just to stay where I was. Since then we've had an "understanding."

On account of Hareide's scarlet fever the quarantine is to last another week. So all next week too we'll be going on with this sleeping and eating life, and receiving our impressions through the stories told us by the others. Here is one of the daily "drops," cold, simple, sober and authentic:

Some time ago a transport of prisoners one day reached the camp. As usual they were counted and lined up on the parade ground just inside the main entrance. The figure wasn't right. There were two men extra. The counting was repeated until it was established that there *were* two men extra. The two men were posted at the main entrance under the windows of the gatehouse. They stood there all the rest of the day, and no one gave them another thought. Then came evening roll call, with counting. These two men were still superfluous. Still the figure wouldn't come right. And German figures *must* and *shall* come right. A few revolver shots from a window in the gatehouse worked out the sum. The figure was right again, the two were carried away, they had ceased to be superfluous in this world.

A couple of years ago someone had been careless about illicit smoking in the block. It

---

* Her fortieth.

caught fire and burned to the ground. As a punishment all the prisoners were lined up for two days and nights without food. The temperature was twenty degrees below zero [-4°F]. Thirty men froze to death out of three hundred or so. Our first *Blockältester*, Hans (now we've got a new one called Albert), told us that to scare us off smoking in the block. He himself had taken part in the affair and could guarantee the truth of it. Since then I've had it confirmed from several quarters.

All the same it turns out to be difficult to get the men not to smoke. There are some swine among us who not only smoke illicitly but steal the smokes from their mates. Indeed food is being stolen here as well. It's disheartening, but true. One gradually finds out who the thieves are and gives them a wide berth. That's all. Today we've actually had enough to eat; I think everyone is full and some a bit over. We had potatoes from the canteen, which the others had bought for us. Also dried cod for supper, plenty of dried cod. It's done good all round. The atmosphere is rounder and pleasanter. The stomach is an important organ—even here! Perhaps here especially. I don't want to go to bed, but there's no way out. Good night, Kari.

FRIDAY, OCTOBER 15, 1943 ■ Colbjørn is here on a visit from Lichtenfelde. He looks well, is rounder, apparently in even better form than at Grini. He's very pleased to be at Lichtenfelde and doesn't wish himself back here. They've had a pretty heavy raid there, and take the view that *that's* done with. It went well. Colbjørn is here for medical examination. Everything O.K. He's going back today. It was nice to see him again. A bit of "old times."

Altogether, the fellows here have been kind. We haven't gone hungry, and haven't yet been without tobacco. The cigarettes one can buy in the canteen and which the others have bought for us are as nasty as camel dung and in normal circumstances unsmokable. But here they're as welcome as new bread.

News? We do get some. First of all the daily papers. Naturally they're German papers. But I don't think that the war communiqués are such monstrous lies, and from them we can deduce the main points. Along with those we also get, privately and with all imaginable prudence, fresh news from other quarters. We get it steadily and surely, and on the whole I don't think we're worse informed here than we were at Grini. But in spite of good news and nothing *but* good news from all fronts, I can't get my optimism up again. I still don't choose to admit—not even to myself—that I've given up my belief in a finish this autumn, but I have an idea that something inside me, out of my control and against my will, has already performed that action on my behalf. The radiant optimism at home, Kari's wish for a merry Christmas, and Ernst's assurances that the collapse might come any time, are in my mind, but shrouded more and more in a veil of unreality. Something dreamlike is coming over the entire home scene. What surrounds us here is reality, all the rest was only dream and illusion!

I remember sitting in the "Parachute," dreaming too. It didn't occur to me that I should ever look back on the Parachute with longing. And now it's happened. The Parachute now looks to me like an idyll compared with this hell. Uncle Porky becomes a lovable Christmas brownie, and the daily life up there impresses me as having content and meaning in comparison with this idiot existence, in which one only gets up, eats cabbage soup, does a bit of running round in wooden shoes, a bit of marching, while the block is being "cleaned," goes in and sleeps some more, runs about some more, a bit of "*Mützen ab!*" perhaps, more cabbage soup, more sleep, more idiocy, less optimism—mostly cabbage soup, until at length one gets a feeling of being saturated with that stinking cabbage soup.

FRIDAY, OCTOBER 15, 1943* ■ Well, at last we have some clouds in the sky. That cloudless, empty sky was beginning to get on one's nerves, too. Like everything else. It's milder, but still raw and cold enough. The news is still good; I can't remember when we last had any really bad news. But all the same winter is approaching. We can see we're going to shiver all right unless we get something better to wear than these rags that have been given us. We've started wearing newspapers on our backs, under our waistbands. It's Erik's patent, and a good one.

The worst of our hunger has passed off. The others have sent us up bread and cheese and sardines and sugar and all kinds of things. Now and then we're absolutely gorging. Gracious, how good it is to eat one's fill—or at least nearly. After the cabbage soup one only feels blown out, heavy and uncomfortable. But full? No.

Now the cabbage soup is due again. One can see that by the movement in the room. Those who were sitting down begin to get up. Those who were asleep begin to stream in. Those who were chatting begin to gabble. Over 150 men, without meaning it—without even knowing of it—transform the room into a witches' cauldron of deafening uproar, commotion and bad air. The last is almost the worst, and I needn't explain in detail how it comes about, only mention that the great majority had shed every form of inhibition long before we came here. If two thirds of those who live here and have nowhere else to go were removed, and the rest were "sitting quiet" if possible, the room would be overcrowded by normal standards. It's enough to drive one mad. And I'm on the way. My temples are splitting and I'm on the point of starting to scream!

Two young Russians frequent this block and do odd jobs for cigarettes and a little food or scraps. We call them both Vodka. They're in full swing all day, mending our rags, sewing on numbers, procuring numbers, repairing sleeping bags, etc. Frode and Erik, lazy swine, prefer to sleep while I'm writing. So Vodka gets a handful of our "unsmokable" cigarettes, and everything is tiptop, and the time passes. Heavens, how slowly it passes, and yet how fast too. It's nearly a fortnight since we arrived.

SUNDAY, OCTOBER 17, 1943 ■ Today we've been divided into working groups—chiefly according to trade. They say that quarantine is to end tomorrow after all and that we shall be working from Tuesday. Frode, Erik and I managed to get into the same kommando. Not so bad! But it took a bit of doing. All of us had to fib a little. Erik most, for he had to pretend to be a *Holzgenerator-Expert* [wood-generator expert]. We two gave wood carving and drawing as our trade.

There is now a match being played on the football [soccer] ground between an "Allied" and a German team. On the Allied team are the six or seven Englishmen who were once at Grini, besides a number of Norwegians, and I think a few Dutchmen.† We're not allowed to watch because of our quarantine. Incidentally we've been kept two or three hours

---

*   It is possible that this diary entry was really Saturday, October 16, notwithstanding the original Norwegian text.

†   According the historian of John Godwin's commando raid, when an Allied team at Sachsenhausen defeated a German team at soccer, the Germans "at once put a stop to that sort of contest for ever."

on parade today altogether. They talk of a Frenchman having escaped. Others believe that we're just kept standing out of devilry. We freeze to the bone morning and evening. All have colds, one has pneumonia, two or three diphtheria, and one scarlatina, besides a number with angina. Apart from that all is well—so long as it lasts. If a contagious disease were to break out in earnest in huts like this, of course there are no effective precautions one could possibly take against it. For we're living on top of each other all round the clock. Erik, Frode and I eat out of the same dish, so to speak—but we're thriving admirably on it. Feel like dogs in the same kennel and are happy while we can stick together.

MONDAY, OCTOBER 18, 1943 ■ Tomorrow, apparently, we go to the doctor once again, and also we're to go to the clothing depot and exchange the clothes that don't fit at all. Those who have been given work outside the camp, like Erik, Frode and myself, are to wear striped clothes. The rest will be allowed to swank in mufti.

TUESDAY, OCTOBER 19, 1943 ■ The quarantine is raised. Tomorrow we go out to work. That will be exciting. Possibly we'll have to start on rather moldy jobs; but then after a time we shall be able to "scrounge" ourselves into something else. Everything can be "scrounged." It's repellent, but that's the way here, from top to bottom.

This evening for the first time we paraded on the square. It was an experience in itself to stand there for the first time, with seventeen or eighteen thousand fellow-prisoners. It's an advantage to be tall and get a general view, for that sea of people under the searchlights is worth looking at. People, people—all kinds of people as far as one can see on all sides, a buzz of conversation incessantly interrupted by short German barks of command. "*Stillgestanden! Augen gerade aus! Augen rechts! Augen gerade aus! Richt euch! Rührt euch!*" Some kind of SS man sweeps along the units counting. That lasts a good half hour. Then comes a general command: "*Stillgestanden! Augen rechts! Augen gerade aus! Rührt euch!*"—and then it's over. Gradually they march off the square, each to his own hut. Smoking materials are produced. Cigarettes and pipes shine out everywhere like red eyes in the darkness. A lighter flares up here and there. It tastes damn good, for of course we haven't smoked since dinnertime—one o'clock—and now it's six.

Tonight we paid our first call in another hut. We went round to Arvid Johansen to see how he was getting on. He treated us to biscuits and honey. He was swimming in parcels and good things. One got the impression that the whole hut was doing the same. Ivan [Rosenquist] was at Arvid's table. He's all right, looking well and eating like a bear. A great contrast to the desperate young man who once asked my help to put an end to himself, "at home" in *Einzelhaft* at Grini.

We've managed to exchange some more of our clothes and footwear today. We're all to be zebra-clad. I've got a new jacket and trousers, both rather bigger than the last, but of course not big enough. But later that can certainly be scrounged too. I've also got new sandals which practically sit on my feet, without being lashed with string and with no tender places as yet.

But I must stop—they're bellowing "*Los! Los! Los! Schlafen gehen!*" [Get to sleep!] It's a deafening row. The news good, but scarce! Good night, Kari.

THURSDAY, OCTOBER 21, 1943 ■ Yesterday we started "work." So I had no chance to write. When we got back from work it was already evening and evening roll call. For we have dinner out on the working place, or "kommando" as it's called. You don't ask what kind of work a man has got, but what kind of kommando he's got, and if he likes his kommando.

Well, when we got home it was evening and a fuss and turmoil unparalleled. A battle from the time we get home until we leave again for work the day after. We now have still more men in our room, and the crush is indescribable. The block, which is divided into two wings, A and B, with a washroom and toilet room in the middle, consists, for the rest of four large rooms—two dining and living rooms and two sleeping rooms. The rooms might be more or less the right size for forty or fifty men, and there are a hundred and twenty of us and likely to be more. That it becomes a trial to live in these rooms, and have nowhere else to go is easily understood. Every bite we eat has to fight its way to our mouths and to be piloted round elbows and shoulders, we sit so close—that is if one can *sit* at meals at all. There is barely room for all at once. Erik, Frode and I stick together—more and more and more every day. There's kind of saving in that.

But about that "work" of ours. I'd better start with some account of how yesterday went off. First, morning roll call! It begins in pitch darkness—yesterday there was a mist as well—and lasts on into full daylight. It's a tedious business counting seventeen thousand men. Especially in German—and on the German recipe. When at last they've finished with the counting it's getting light. Then comes the order to fall in by working kommandos, and thus begins the second part of morning roll call, which is the longest. The whole seventeen thousand are let loose on the square, and each has to make his own way to his kommando. To form an idea of how this takes place, one must imagine a giant anthill which has been stirred with a stick or something of the kind, so that all the ants are shaken up and driven out of the hill. That gives a fairish picture of the situation. It's no pleasure to have to smear oneself up against hundreds of people of all sorts, encountering abuse and kicks, indeed even blows. I can't bring myself to curse, hit or kick back—though now and then I must confess I come pretty near. It's so degrading, so horribly symptomatic of what the place can do to one; this method of "getting ahead," this everlasting, disgusting, deafening vituperation!—I believe it's worst of all.

I collided with some German—he gave me a well-aimed kick full on the shin, and let out a stream of German vocables. A prisoner—? Certainly. Most of them are like that.

A little Ukrainian I stumbled over—he muttered something down there in the depths—looked up with a dirty, melancholy face, a beseeching pair of blue eyes—and then he vanished in the throng.

Thus Erik, Frode and I together—for the first time—fought our way through the human swarm, right across the square, to where our kommando was drawn up. "*Kraft-fahrzeug-Depot Wald*" [motor vehicle depot wood] it's called, or KDW. Then we had to fall in once more and be counted over again. They never miss a chance of counting. There was abundant opportunity to meet our friends in the KDW, Arvid among others. Most of the hour we stood there went in chatting and greeting, and counting, of course. A bit of extra counting as well, since it was our first time.

At length it was our turn to march out through the portals of the main entrance, where yet another count takes place as we march through with "*Mützen ab*" and "*Hände angelegt*" [Hands at your sides]. Moving obliquely forward, tense as steel springs, we tramp off down the concrete—the rhythm slamming out like deafening thunder claps as the wooden soles strike on the concrete of the roadway. Right out into the "street" we have to march like that—running a gauntlet of SS NCOs and SS soldiers drawn up with their rifles at the ready, down the whole concrete-paved street outside the electric fence.

SATURDAY, OCTOBER 23, 1943 ■ As I said, the concrete road is outside, but the camp and its adjacent splendors go on interminably, or so it seems, in every direction. The concrete street runs alongside the prison wall, with the electric fence beyond it, on one side of the camp. Across the street lies the SS camp, huts, canteens, *Kameradschaftsgebäude* [recreation building], etc., etc. In other directions there are workshops and all kinds of working places, where prisoners are employed. Our path led into the woods. They are fir woods, German fir woods. That is, the trees stand in rows. Between the rows of firs there are huts and works of every kind. KDW is a separate camp. It is a depot for all sorts of cars, parts and equipment—the main SS depot of the kind—with workshops attached.

On reaching it that morning we were lined up at a hut inside the main entrance, the hut where the SS have their offices. We were to be counted afresh and have jobs assigned us. Erik, who to get into the same kommando as Frode and me was down on the list as a wood-gas generator expert, had been assured that it would work famously. It didn't work at all. The director was unmasked, he's never seen a wood-gas generator close up. As a punishment he was given a hard job in the *Fahrbereitschaft* [motor pool], washing and cleaning cars before they leave the workshops, where they are repaired. Frode and I had better luck; we were at once put on one side: "So these are the two wood carvers. Right, fall in over there and wait." From the very first we realized this was a swindle. We were to be embezzled and do private work for the swine.

When all had been given jobs, the man who had presided at the sorting, Irsch his name was, took us into his office. After some cogitation he decided that for the present, until a room was cleared for us, we were to be in the painting shop under a *Vorarbeiter* who was also in the office and was given instructions to get us paper and pencils, etc., so that we could begin making a few sketches. As for the subjects we were to select for our works of art, Irsch on the spur of the moment could imagine—tja!—he could imagine *"ein Hirsch in der Brunstzeit"* [a deer in the rutting season]. Did we know stags, and what a rutting stag was like? No? Well. Irsch thought again and wrung out of his head another marvelous idea, namely a pair of lovers, or a pastoral subject, as he called it. Then he could imagine yet a third subject—a vase of beautiful roses. All this he had imagined carved in relief (I had told him that relief was my specialty) at the bottom of wooden fruit bowls.

Well, we betook ourselves with Irsch and the *Vorarbeiter* to the latter's painting shop. It was a huge hut, full of cars and people spraying enamel, and so forth. A penetrating enamel smell filled the room, making one's eyes smart. In one corner of the hall the *Vorarbeiter* had a little table and a cupboard; that was his office, and there we were to be for the present.

The *Vorarbeiter* took out of a cupboard some wooden sculptures which had been done by other prisoners before us. He gave them to Irsch, who showed them to us. The first thing that struck me when I saw them was that they were really well carved; so our faces grew pretty long when our friend Irsch said these were specimens of bad workmanship that couldn't be used. He had scrapped this stuff, and those who had done it had lost their jobs. Well, well! This did look promising. Moreover all these things were carved in the round! Sculpture in wood, then, and neither Frode nor I had ever done anything like that. We took up a superior attitude, it wouldn't do to reveal our sinking hearts and our increasing feeling of hopelessness. We echoed the general condemnation of these wood sculptures, showed where they were wrong and put them back with a little shrugging of the shoulders and some long words that were meant to signify, oh well—probably the best they could do, poor chaps—but *we* would show him . . .

Then Irsch went off. We began talking to the foreman. He was a German, named Alfred; at least no one called him anything else. He was from Cologne, an artist and a Communist. Also there was something wrong with his nose; on one side of his face—I think the right—the wing of the nose seemed to merge into the cheek and cheekbone. This gave his whole face and mouth a drawn appearance, while at the same time it fascinated and held one's eye. First we talked of wood carving, drawing and art, then we got onto politics and war and Oranienburg. He had a lot to tell. He's been here eight years. Altogether he'd spent thirteen years of his life in prison. As far back as the last war he was imprisoned as a Communist, then again in the twenties and then after Hitler came. Cold, almost apathetic, scoffing in his attitude to most things, skeptical, destructive and negative, he affected one unpleasantly—especially at first. Now, after a few days, I feel that I'm beginning to place him better. I saw a couple of his paintings the other day. They were thin things—acid, dismal color, and not much life in them. He was pleased with them himself, and proudly called them "quite worthy of exhibit," which they were far from being. But it's admirable that after all these years in prison he has remained in some sense true to his convictions. How much must have been shattered in him with all the years he's been here! Is it at all strange that he's grown bitter and negative?

The day was passed in the painting shop. We weren't working at all. We had paper issued to us. Old printed forms, which we could draw on the backs of! The print showed through, and made it difficult to draw anything. And the pencils they gave us were mere stumps. Alfred had some picture postcards; one of a rutting stag, just the ghastly type of thing Irsch wanted. Well, that was excellent. I did a sketch from the recipe. That was all we achieved that day.

SUNDAY, OCTOBER 24, 1943 ■ I didn't get round to describing the dinner interval. It's something like this: Toward noon people start jogging off to the dining place, which is the highest point of the camp. There, in the open, the soup is doled out to every kommando, which falls in separately. Besides the usual cabbage soup and potatoes we have bread. Two slices with butter and a bit of sausage. A man here and there who has tried to snatch a double ration by parading twice, and so forth, is cursed and thrashed by the foreman. Altogether there are constant episodes to season existence. We have to eat out of doors, unless we want to stand in a dark, overcrowded dining hut, where only the old hands have seats at the table. Arvid, Erik, Frode, Leif and I stick together and form our own little dinner party. We sit or lie on the bare ground, if it's dry—or sit on stones or piles of twigs.

Among the many characteristics of these scenes are the "*Muselmenn*."* They go round

---

* The term "*Muselmann*" was used throughout the concentration camps to denote a prisoner who had reached the stage, through starvation, overwork, abuse, etc., where he was close to death. The term literally means Muslim, although why this name was associated with such prisoners has never been fully determined. Speculation runs from: (1) the headgear worn by many prisoners resembled Muslim headscarves, (2) the fatalistic attitudes of those near death resembled the attitude of religious submission thought to be characteristic of Muslims, (3) the near-death prone state

A "Muselmann."

collecting potato peel in their caps and eating it. Most of them are sallow, skinny Russians or Ukrainians; but there may be one or two of other nationalities dangling around too. "*Muselmenn*" is the name for those who have starved until they're beginning to bear the stamp of the approaching end. They'll soon be going "up the chimney," as it's called. They are much like animals. What they collect and eat is bad pig food, and they look so uninviting, nasty and dirty that watching them can take away one's appetite. They are the

---

of the prisoners resembled the image of a prostrate Muslim during prayers, or (4) the contempt SS guards who had served in the Spanish Civil War felt for those of the Muslim faith translated into a slang term applied to those who had given up any attempt to survive. The majority of *Muselmänner* were Jews, Russians, and Poles—the camp pariahs. As one historian notes, "Although a victim of hunger and misery, the *Muselmann* was despised by the other inmates, kicked and beaten, ultimately left to his or her own devices, or killed. In this way, survivors protected themselves from the menacing visage of their own fate. Before physical expiration, the *Muselmann* died a death that was social." Primo Levi observed, "[I]f I could enclose all the evil of our time in one image, I would choose this image [of a *Muselmann*]: an emaciated man, with head dropped and shoulders curved, on whose face and in whose eyes not a trace of thought is to be seen." The plural of *Muselmann* is *Muselmänner*, not *Muselmenn*, but I have retained Nansen's usage in the text.

most pitiful and dismal gang I have ever seen, walking around in their striped, grimy rags and scrabbling with greedy, shameless fingers between one's feet, down on the ground among pine needles and filth, after refuse which they stuff eagerly into their caps or—if those are filled up—their pockets.

One can't have much of a rest at dinnertime. Of course it's possible to stretch out on the ground, but that's so dusty, and there's so much dirt and rubbish that it isn't very inviting. A few of the older hands have scrounged something to lie on. A bit of canvas or the like. As a rule we just sit on our stones and lean against the trunk of a little fir tree. The whole dinner break lasts an hour, so there isn't very much spare time. When the whistle blows, everyone has to get up and return to the place of work. But that is a long way off in many cases, so a great deal of time is spent in getting to and from dinner. If one adds up all the time we spend every day in roll calls, marching, counting, waiting about, and walking to and from the dinner place, and so on, it comes to at least three hours—often a lot more. And that's German, too.

We didn't stay more than the one day in Alfred's workshop. The very next we settled in here, where we are now, and where we live in quite amazing comfort. It's unbelievable. Frode and I have a whole room to ourselves, with something like a table and any number of splendid chairs, which we contrived to scrounge yesterday after starting off with nothing but a couple of stools. We've got a stove too, and have long since roasted potatoes in the embers; the potatoes we scrounged through our friend Vodka. The other men in the hut are nice chaps; three Norwegians, some Germans, and a Spaniard who are in the fire-service repair shop. A German from the International Brigade, who has been eight years in prison, is especially nice and droll. He is called Peter, is an expert scrounger, good-natured and kindhearted, brought us some coffee and a few mushrooms the very first day, and altogether looks after us and makes us feel at home.

It's a slow business getting hold of drawing materials. We have had two or three pencils issued, a very little plain paper (no print on it but it's wretched paper), and nothing else. But today we've scrounged a little paper through the architect's office. Our "friend" Irsch has looked in a couple of times, without saying much. Tomorrow he wants to see three or four sketches for plates with the prescribed subjects in relief. Yesterday he saw one I had made a drawing of. He condescended to say it was "*ganz nett*" [very nice]; that was an immense "encouragement" of course, and we already feel rather firmer in our chairs.

MONDAY, OCTOBER 25, 1943 ■ Yesterday was Sunday, and it flew by before one knew it. We're beginning to settle down in our new refuge. For a refuge is precisely what it is. A deliverance from the swarm and turmoil everywhere else. Everywhere! "Well, at last we shall have hours and hours of peace again!" is our heart's cry as we sink down, tired and footsore, on our respective chairs and begin slowly planning the day ahead of us.

Footsore, yes! That's a chapter in itself. I have described how I managed to swap my bits of wood for others that were a little better; but in a day or two I had huge blisters on the soles of both feet. It was like walking on red-hot iron with knives in it. We have several kilometers to walk every day, and you can imagine what it's like. Now, after yet another swap, I've rubbed an equally burning, agonizing place on one heel. Simply walking across the floor is unbearable torture, let alone walking to dinner. I'm trying to acquire a technique of keeping my legs stiff, so as to avoid friction inside the shoe. But that demands a slowness of tempo which is not practical when we are marching in column.

Along with the sore feet there is another part of the body that must be mentioned to give an idea of our general condition. That is the stomach! It's full of cabbage. Always full of cabbage—and water. We never feel satisfied, but always full and blown out. A highly disagreeable sensation, which is not improved by all the stories we hear of others who got *Scheisserei* and went up the chimney. Erik's legs are still swelling. A nasty omen. We others have escaped as yet. We're feeding Erik on vitamin B and starches, all we can get hold of, and he's better. Yet still we're all of us in constant, more or less conscious dread of swelling up in the legs and getting diarrhea (dysentery) or some other horror, which will land us in the *Revier*. That's the first step to the crematorium.

I met [Arnulf] Øverland yesterday and had a long chat with him.* He seemed tired, and said he was. He had a tiring job in the gardens. On his feet all day and not allowed to sit down. He hadn't managed to write anything here. He was too tired, and could get no quiet of course. But he is still going strong.

Today we were so industrious and so absorbed in our drawings of plates that we forgot to go to dinner with the others. We failed to hear the bell that rings for the midday break, in pure zeal to do fine pictures for our friend Irsch. But we did get something to eat, though we were late for it. And in the afternoon Irsch arrived, and we had four sketches ready as agreed on. He merely did some grunting, but apparently it meant he was pleased, and he only expressed a little doubt whether our designs would look as well when they were carved in wood as they did in the drawings. This doubt may perhaps be better founded than he realized, but we didn't betray our fears. Anyhow the C.O. of the kommando, a *Hauptsturmführer*, will probably be coming round tomorrow, and as our kommando is only "legalized" as a *Spielzeugkommando* [toy kommando], against his arrival we shall have to have started on sketches and things for various toys. I think of starting in on my famous jumping jacks, that I did so many of at Grini. The "toy kommando" also is of course illegal, but the C.O. is privy to it, that's all.† He may have children for whom he wants Christmas presents. Everything's a swindle—swindle and hanky-panky from end to end. Ugh, what a revolting business, the whole setup—but after all, we've no cause to give a damn. Here the thing is to look after oneself, and we have indeed been lucky in the first round. Old Oranienburgers envy us the job. We can sit indoors when winter comes, have a fire in the stove, cook a little food on it, boil a little "coffee," take it easy, and have peace—really *almost* peace—for several hours every day. These are unique conditions for newcomers. Now if only we could maneuver Erik into an easier job.

TUESDAY, OCTOBER 26, 1943 ■ Today we got a planing bench. That is, not exactly a planing bench, but the remains of two benches that won't join up. But then one can't expect everything. We've also been given tools. Old, blunt, rusty, useless things. A broken keyhole saw that has never been set up, a couple of chisels, a plane, a hammer and other oddments. About the same time, masses of material came tumbling through the door.

---

* Author and poet, Øverland (1889–1968) published a poem as early as 1936 titled "You Must Not Sleep," which warned against the evils of Hitler's Germany. He was arrested in mid-1941 for writing anti-Nazi poetry and continued even while in prison to compose poetry, which was collected and published after the war under the title *Vi Overlever Alt!* [*We Survive Everything!*] William L. Shirer called him Norway's "greatest poet." In 1933 Øverland was tried for blasphemy (and acquitted). He was the last person to be so tried; the law was repealed in 2015.

† As early as the autumn of 1942 the SS Business and Administration Main Office (WVHA) had issued explicit orders to the KLs to abandon all labor details "that were not engaged in work important or essential for the war effort."

Old, used boarding and logs, with paint and nails in them. Now we're to start making toy cars out of this lumber. The *Hauptsturmführer* is coming tomorrow; then we're to be busy on toys, and there are to be lots of shavings on the floor. Joop—that's the foreman—began planing at a log himself, and strewing the shavings about, as a demonstration of how to do it. In the midday break I got more tools from him. A saw file without a handle and a special screwdriver. Later we got a handle, too, but it didn't fit the file. What we're to do with these objects is an open question. They'll hardly do to carve plates with, or be of appreciable use in making toy cars. Well, to some extent they can be used to get the saw going—let us be fair.

WEDNESDAY, OCTOBER 27, 1943 ■ What a *life! What* a life! *What a life!* Desolating! Idiotic! Hopeless! Overwhelming! Paralyzing! How on earth is one to keep one's head above water?

Wherever one turns, swindling and wretchedness, corruption on a scale hitherto unknown. It's worst of all to observe how many of one's Norwegian companions have slipped into this beastliness and acquired the attitude that makes it possible. The Norwegians get much more from home than the other nationalities. Besides the parcels from the Norwegian Red Cross they get similar ones from Sweden and Denmark. Also they have herring, dried cod and train oil. An abundance of goods that are negotiable on the "black market" here. For a herring one can scrounge a great deal. A smart jacket, a good pair of boots, new, warm trousers, and so on. For tobacco one can get anything. One can also scrounge a good job in the same way, and once in the job, one can go on to scrounge oneself tools and better conditions all round. Such is the way of life here that one is forced to regard it as an object, perhaps one's main object, to look after oneself, see that one has enough to eat, enough sleep, and not too much to do. And undoubtedly it is important. In *any* circumstances it is of course essential, only in general it hasn't loomed up as the main point. One's own health and comfort have been matters of course. Things are different here.

THURSDAY, OCTOBER 28, 1943 ■ I think the roll calls are the worst. At least they will be when it gets colder. When we return to camp hungry and worn out, we have to stand and stand and stand interminably on the parade ground—until at last the counting is finished and the figure presented to the *Lagerführer* with a little "ceremony" at the main entrance. And even then we have to stand a while longer before marching—in the dark— to the huts, where the struggle for existence begins in earnest. When I reach the hut in the evening and the office in the morning, after an hour's parade and then an agonizing march on ghastly wooden shoes, my back is breaking in two. I'm afraid I shan't be very fit to walk back to Norway—if *that* should turn out to be the solution in the last act of this nightmare.

But who knows anything of the solution? And what is the good of guessing? Most Norwegians I talk to seem to believe that the very moment Germany collapses and the war is over, there will be a train waiting at Sachsenhausen which will take us straight back to Norway. Or they imagine that a whole squadron of aircraft will arrive instantly to bring us home. It's like talking to very little children who believe in brownies and trolls, and think no farther than the end of their noses.

We've now begun to make toys on a big scale. Cars, dogs, crocodiles and doll's carriages. The wood carving has been temporarily thrust into the background. Still we get no tools, and therefore our activity is tragicomic if anything.

FRIDAY, OCTOBER 29, 1943 ■ Yesterday we heard that after November 1st no more parcels would be forwarded by German railways. That was a hard blow. For we're pretty dependent on what we get from home. We were despairing over it, when Halvard [Lange] gave us the comfort that there was a similar ban last year but then Red Cross parcels were excepted.

Arvid has diphtheria and will probably have to stay in the *Revier* at least three weeks. Erik isn't well and I dare say will land there too. He had a bad cold. We two others are still O.K.

SATURDAY, OCTOBER 30, 1943 ■ The ban on sending parcels in Germany doesn't apply to parcels from abroad, according to today's report, and altogether it won't affect us. That's a great comfort. Almost with shame I must admit that such things play an essential part here. Altogether I'm afraid one is going involuntarily downhill—by fairly imperceptible degrees. We live like sardines in a tin—and however tempting and needful it may be to help one's fellow sardines so that they don't get squeezed to death—it's not possible, since one is being squeezed oneself into silence and immobility.

Everyone is thinking of himself. Everyone is grabbing for himself, few share with others. The average Norwegian, even, treats a Ukrainian worse than he would a dog at home. He *knows* the Ukrainian is starving, *everyone does*, for they get no parcels "from home." He just doesn't think about it, simply drives him away as he would flies or vermin. I suppose the Ukrainians and Russians are the worst beggars, as is natural. Their lives are at stake. The Norwegians did the same thing when *their* lives were at stake. Before they started getting parcels. For a couple of cigarettes, of which the Norwegians get more than other people, they can fool a poor tobacco-starved Russian or other fellow creature out of a whole bread ration—or "bread ball" as it's called here. Indeed some are not ashamed to bargain with herring refuse, which they're going to throw away anyhow and which crowds of *Muselmenn* are waiting to fish out of the dustbin. Not even *that* do they give away! No wonder our friend Alfred, bitterly and with a good deal of jeering contempt, accused the Norwegians of being *"worse than Armenian Jews!"* A harsh judgment, but I'm afraid not entirely unjust. It's as if they had adopted the German *Herrenvolk* consciousness, too. We Teutons! Yes, a Norwegian said that to me the other day, when we were discussing the end of the war and when we might expect to get home to Norway. "Of course we Teutons will be seen to first." I tackled him and he simply saw it as reasonable.

MONDAY, NOVEMBER 1, 1943 ■ Yesterday was Sunday, and for the first time it really made a little change in the succession of days. I actually noticed that half the day was free. After dinner I watched two football matches, and when the matches were over I went sick-visiting.

First I went to see Arvid. He was quite comfortable and not at all bad, but on account of his diphtheria he'll have to stay in the hospital at least a month. Then I went to see Henry Hansen, who has been ill for more than seven months now, hovering between life and death all the time. It was the treatment he got here at the beginning that broke him down. He's been here a year and a half, and they were driven like animals. Worse—like slaves. They got no parcels from home in those days. Talking to Henry Hansen gave me an idea of what things have been like here. We may think ourselves lucky to have arrived so late. For now of course it's quite different. Things are still going on here, certainly! But the camp is so big, there are so many people and phenomena to act as a veil. That ten men were shot one day in camp was something we didn't even notice. It came to us only as a rumor. As I was leaving the hospital yesterday, some men went by with a dead body on a stretcher. It was the body of a German who had just been shot. He had been trying to escape. I must admit that it made no great impression on me. Why should it? I didn't know him.

WEDNESDAY, NOVEMBER 3, 1943 ■ We're manufacturing toys on a grand scale now. Five cars are already finished. Five dogs and five crocodiles lie half-finished on the table before us, and five doll's carriages are piled up in their separate parts on a chair by the wall. We still have nothing but rubbish in the way of tools. We've had no wood-carving tools at all yet, so that work is laid aside for the present.

But the most important thing of all is that we've made contact with home. Both Erik and I have had two parcels of *Kleinigkeiten* [little things] by letter post: cigarettes, butter, cheese, crispbread. Goodness, what a heavenly taste it had, the first cigarette from home! And the dairy butter tasted like an improbable dream!

It's turned colder. We've been permitted to wear a "coat," that is a dressing gown of the same striped cellulose as all the rest of our clothing—and just as tight and tattered and dirty. It's becoming rather cold to eat out of doors, but one can do nothing about *that*. The soup, which is degenerating more and more—it now consists of boiled rutabaga and a little cabbage with potatoes added—gets cold on the way from where it's dished out to our place under a couple of the thousands of little fir trees that stand in rows as far as the eye can see in every direction. It would be a sight for our families to see us at our "picnic dinner"! Filthy and unshaven as highwaymen, in the most peculiar garments, sitting on the ground with our aluminum dishes on our knees, gulping down that appalling cabbage soup that we should hesitate to give the animals at home. Garlanded round about with famished Ukrainians or Russians, all *Muselmenn*, who beg from us our potato peelings and if possible our cigarette butts. They follow our every movement with covetous and hungry eyes, absolutely sharing in every puff of the illicit smoke afterward. They're like flies, you can't wave them off, they come back, encamp, and lie in wait for anything that may fall from our luxurious repast.

A Russian *Muselmann* has discovered that we're good business; so many scraps fall from our table. So he lies down at our feet every day like a faithful dog and watches like a hawk. If we're peeling potatoes, he sticks a bit of paper underneath, so that the peel may fall on it—or in his *Schüssel* [soup bowl] or food satchel. Nothing must go to waste. It's an ugly thing to say, but he's not much more than an animal. One does in fact get into the way of regarding him and his colleagues in that light. They fight for the refuse, too—like animals, and bicker over it—like animals. Snarl, hiss, and show their teeth, and wag their whole bodies at us, asking for more—like animals.

What a life! What an insane, idiotic, wasted life!

THURSDAY, NOVEMBER 4, 1943 ■ Mild and cold by turns. But the nights are always cold—and the roll calls. It's worst for the so-called *Schonungskranken* [convalescent

Daily guests outside the Norwegian blocks.

patients]. The men who are not ill enough to go into the hospital, but who are allowed to stay at "home" in the block and not work. That is, they have to do odd jobs there, unless they've had *Bettschonung* [bed pass], which means that they can stay in bed, because they're running a fever for instance. But they have to turn out for the roll calls, whatever their temperature, and however feeble they may be. Indeed at one time this was carried so far that even corpses, that is, men who had died during the night, had to be carried on parade by their mates to be counted in. The dead and dying often lay on the ground in great heaps of twenty, thirty, or forty men alongside the column.

Today we had a visit from the C.O. of the kommando, a *Hauptsturmführer*. He looked at our various toys, grunted a bit, complained that screws had been used instead of nails, and that the steering wheels of the toy cars had brass wire in them; only steel should be used. He left the premises after giving orders for a specimen of every kind of toy we made. Irsch looked in; he was as sour as vinegar and grunted something about our not working hard enough. Finally he hit on the idea that our place looked like a pigsty, and if we hadn't got it properly cleaned out by Saturday, with shelves for the material, etc., etc., he would chuck us out; now he was tired of these goings-on. Then off he went. As usual we said *Jawohl* in the right places, and when he was gone we had a smoke and went on chatting. No one has been anything like as fortunate as us two. It isn't often we have greenhorns looking in (but often enough!) and then we have to be careful about smoking. But just being able to smoke is quite exceptional. Very few of the others have the chance.

The news is still brilliant. The Moscow Conference is over, and according to report they're "decided" that the war is to be finished this year.* Goodness—if only that could happen!

FRIDAY, NOVEMBER 5, 1943 ■ We've tidied up our office, got it into apple-pie order, put up a shelf, and swept the floor. Over the planing bench we've made a "rack" for tools, so now all the tools are hanging or standing by the wall in a row, and appear to great advantage—from a long way off they look positively serviceable. Irsch was here this afternoon, but found nothing to roar about and went away again with a few quite minor snorts. It's cold today, so dinner out was rather a trial. It's not so easy to peel potatoes and eat cabbage soup with mittens on, in several degrees of frost [i.e., below freezing temperatures]. Frode and I are lucky, with a good warm room to go back to. It's worse for Erik, who works out of doors. We mean to try and get him in here as our assistant. But we'd better wait a little longer.

SATURDAY, NOVEMBER 6, 1943 ■ Another week over. I've had a parcel of clothes from home, all sorts of grandeurs: good warm underclothing, windproof shirt and trousers, leather waistcoat, woolens, etc., etc., plus a quantity of vitamin tablets. All the clothes had to go into the gas chamber to be "deloused," the rest I got straight away. It was marvelous. At least I shan't be *so* cold henceforth.

SUNDAY, NOVEMBER 7, 1943 ■ Yesterday we bathed. That also is a tale in itself. The whole hut, close on three hundred men, bathes at the same time. All are ordered out of the hut simultaneously—and usually when we're in the middle of supper. Then we all have to finish instantly. We roar, halloo, scold, shove, jostle and curse our way through to the cupboards, to our things, and out into the cold. Everything must be cleared away

---

*   The Third Moscow Conference was a meeting of the foreign ministers of the United States, Great Britain, the Soviet Union, and China (October 18–November 11, 1943) to discuss war strategy (they reaffirmed the Allies' commitment to unconditional surrender for Germany) and plans for postwar collaboration. The parties also issued the so-called Moscow Declaration, including a Statement on Atrocities, which provided that anyone participating in war crimes would be tried by the courts of those countries on whose territories the crimes occurred. "Thus, Germans who take part . . . in the execution of . . . Norwegian hostages . . . will know they will be brought back to the scene of their crimes and judged on the spot by the peoples whom they have outraged." The conference served as a prelude to the Tehran Conference (November 28–December 1, 1943), the first meeting of the "Big Three" Allied leaders—Roosevelt, Churchill, and Stalin.

too, for a bit of food or an object of any kind whatever left lying about gets stolen. Just simply stolen—or scrounged. *Stubenälteste* and other "superiors" are not a whit better than anyone else, they too steal like magpies. Not a day passes without something being stolen off the tables—or straight out of the cupboards. Even the boots are stolen off one's feet, as it were, or the outer clothes off one's back, unless one is forever on guard, suspecting one's closest friend of being on the scrounge. It's as though scrounging were all right. That confounded word rubs out one's conscience and honesty. There's no longer a distinction between mine and thine. That's only how it used to be, long ago, in another world! Few really stop to think that that is the world we're fighting for and are to return to some day, and it makes one shudder to realize how unfit most of us will be to live in it. Yes, *most of us*. That is no exaggeration.

I started to write about the bathing. As a rule we line up in the cold for at least half an hour before they let us in. The floor is swimming in water—dirty water. In that we have to stand and undress. Standing on the benches is forbidden, even though we're in stocking feet. The struggle to get one's clothes off, and onto pegs, is hard and intensive. Inside the bathhouse the fight continues; this time it's to get under one of the hundreds of showers in the roof and get a little water on one. All the showers are turned on at once. Often the water that comes out is scalding, so that there are a lot of burns. After a few minutes this hot water is turned off and ice-cold turned on. Then there's more room. But then everyone has to run out and begin the struggle to dry himself with a little pocket handkerchief of a towel and get the clothes onto his damp body. Add that the stone floor is swimming in dirty water, that we're packed like herrings in a barrel, that we have to try and get our feet more or less clean and dry before pulling on our socks, and if possible get them into our boots without stepping in the dirty water. Then add that a lot of Germans are standing roaring and cursing because we're too slow, striking those who have sneaked up on the benches, bawling out those who are clumsy, or stumble, or something, jeering at those who are crippled and therefore can't keep up, and the picture of the madhouse will be pretty accurate. That we don't lose our senses to a man is really a proof of the inconceivable adaptability of the human race.

Yesterday there were letters from Norway. Erik and Frode were in luck, but not I. In Frode's letter his brother said that both Red Cross parcels and those by letter post are forbidden.* All the same there were a lot who did get letter parcels, sent off from Norway after that letter was written. So hope survives. Otherwise we must hope for Swedish and Danish parcels to keep life in us.

MONDAY, NOVEMBER 8, 1943 ■ After snow yesterday it's milder again, so today's dinner in the woods was simply a pleasure. Anyhow we could eat without mittens, if we got up occasionally and had a slapping bout. Sanko (our "regular" Russian; we call him Sanko because he's like a Saint Bernard dog that Frode once had) always turns up before us and is lying in his place when we arrive. He doesn't know a word of German, and as he's always full of suggestions for barter and every kind of scrounging, it's a great struggle to understand what he means. We have to draw and make gestures, and that usually works. Now he's to get us cigarette holders—they make some really nice ones in the

---

* The Quisling government prohibited the Norwegian Red Cross from sending any further parcels to Norwegian prisoners.

camp—and lighters. In return we're to get him herring or tobacco. Yesterday Frode got an excellent pair of boots from him. He had undoubtedly stolen them from the warehouse, that is to say, scrounged them. But everything is done like that. It's what one has to put up with, like it or not.

WEDNESDAY, NOVEMBER 10, 1943 ■ Yesterday I'm blessed if I didn't get three parcels, and the day before my sleeping bag plus a double blanket! Talk of grandeur! The sleeping bag is made to pull over one's head, and with that and a double blanket I'm all right for the winter. Inside the sleeping bag Kari had smuggled I should think two kilos [4.4 pounds] of glorious dairy butter. Also a big bag of Norwegian tobacco, a good many cigarettes and (which brought enthusiastic outcries from Frode) a whole heap of plug! The day before yesterday I received a small package of sardines from Herman [Reimers]. He is faithful.* Yesterday's three parcels were from Kari. Tobacco, butter, crispbread, and other good things, also a whole bottle of train oil and a big jar of real honey. It looks as if we're still allowed *Kleinigkeiten*—and even pretty large *Kleinigkeiten*. Now we feel like Croesuses and can begin to share. The sleeping bag I had has now gone to make another happy. One who was freezing at night in two thin, dirty blankets. There are a lot in that condition, unfortunately.

Unfortunately it seems hopeless to get Erik transferred to us as painter or planer-in-chief. Very likely the foreman Joop has someone else to put in here. Besides he doesn't like Erik, whom he has placed as a "capitalist" on his social register. I suppose Erik's title of director went down the wrong way. And Joop reigns supreme and is hard as flint. It's not much use "talking" to him. If he's taken a thing into his head, so it must be. He's the type that can do everything and knows everything better than anyone else. He also roars louder, kicks harder—and strikes, too; I've seen him in many brutal situations, kicking, striking and bawling out Ukrainians, Russians or Poles who were begging food or trying to line up for it twice.

Joop is a Communist, like all trusted prisoners in this camp. It's extraordinary how the Communists have managed things here; they have all the power in camp next to the SS, and they attract all the other Communists—from other countries—and place them in key positions. The Norwegians, too. Many of the Norwegian prisoners have turned Communist here. Besides all the immediate advantages it offers, most likely they expect Russia to be the big noise after the war, and then I suppose they think it may be handy to have one's color right!

Last night I was talking to our *Blockältester*, a little tub of a man. A Communist—oh, goodness what a Communist. When he and his mates come into power, there would be not merely retaliation, but even more brutality and greater cruelty than the SS uses against us. I could make no headway with my humanism against that ice block of hate and vengefulness, that hard-boiled, hidebound focusing on a new dictatorship!

THURSDAY, NOVEMBER 11, 1943 ■ Yesterday I was talking to a Jew. There actually are a few of them alive in the camp. This one is named Keil, is a watchmaker, and has

---

*   Herman Reimers, an engineer, was the nephew of Herman Reimers the attorney. See March 8, 1942, above. Nansen and the junior Herman Reimers were students together at NTH in Trondheim, and Herman served as Nansen's best man at his wedding.

been in Norway—in Hønefoss, as a German refugee in 1936.* He came here from Auschwitz in Poland. A *Vernichtungslager* [extermination camp] of the worst type. What he told me about that camp was so horrible, so incomprehensible in ghastliness, that it defies all description. He told me that of the Norwegian Jews who were sent there, and I should think all of them were sent, only a very few are still alive; about twenty-five out of twelve hundred was his estimate. I think twelve hundred is too high. (Or is it rather a hope?) Most of them were gassed. Whole transports went straight into the gas chamber and thence into the crematorium. Men, women and children of all ages, from every corner of Europe and every social class. There were five crematoria in the camp, and they were going day and night—and had been for several years.†

Keil's story completely paralyzed me. I asked about Dr. [Wulff] Becker and his brothers.‡ They had all died in the gas chamber. The Kaplan family; only one, the youngest boy, was still alive. He had been spared for some reason, probably because he was in a kommando where they needed him. The whole Shermann family had been killed. And all, all the others! Keil himself had been spared because he was a watchmaker. They needed watchmakers to repair all the hundreds of thousands of watches they were stealing from the dead.§ Now Keil is in the watchmaker's shop here, mending those watches. In other kommandos prisoners are ripping up clothes and footwear. I've already mentioned what sums of money are brought to light, and what fortunes in jewels and so forth come into circulation in the camp, the great "scrounging-mill."

But to return to Auschwitz and Keil. I asked him about Rabbi Samuel.¶ Oh, he died on the steps of a hut. He was returning from work, was done for, just collapsed and was dead. His brother, who was ill, the one we rescued from Dachau (or was it Buchenwald?) at one time, and with much labor got to Norway, he was sent into the gas chamber and died there. Klein, the Klein family; oh, they all died in the gas chamber. Müller, Bernstein, and all, all the rest of them, dead, all dead. Starved to death, beaten to death, worked to death, or sent into the gas chamber. Keil estimated that three or four million Jews had been killed in Auschwitz and in Lublin these last few years. And he thought at least as many Poles had gone the same way—and hundreds of thousands of Russian and Ukrainian prisoners as well.

Today it's twenty-five years since the end of the last world war! A singular jubilee!

We had the dinner of all time, in honor of the day. Raw minced cabbage—pure and

---

* Eugen Keil (1907–1984) was a Hungarian Jew who had learned to be a watchmaker in Hamburg and later escaped Nazi Germany, obtaining asylum in Norway. He survived the war, set up a watchmaking and watch importing business, and became a Norwegian citizen in 1947.

† See November 13, 1944, below.

‡ Wulff Becker (age thirty-five), his brothers Louis (thirty-seven) and David (forty-four), sister Frida (forty-two), mother Mina (seventy-four), and father Mendel (eighty-one) all died in Auschwitz.

§ The repaired watches were then distributed to soldiers of the Waffen SS. Despite gold watches being in particular demand, as well as fountain pens, supply always exceeded demand; by November 1944 SS officials were sitting on more than twenty-seven thousand watches and clocks, as well as five thousand fountain pens.

¶ The chief rabbi of Norway, Julius Samuel (1902–1942) was arrested September 2, 1942. Having been previously arrested, and released in August 1942, Samuel's wife Henriette asked him to consider escaping or going into hiding, but he refused to abandon his congregation. He died December 16, 1942, less than a month after being deported to Auschwitz, age thirty-nine. Henriette and their children were able to escape to Sweden with the assistance of Ingebjørg Sletten-Fosstvedt, a twenty-five-year-old neighbor and member of the Resistance. For her role in saving the Samuel family and others, Sletten-Fosstvedt was bestowed the title of Righteous Among the Nations by Yad Vashem in 1967. Henriette later testified against Adolf Eichmann in his 1961 trial in Jerusalem.

simple. With two half slices of bread and a quarter of a slice of sausage. That was a record. It won't be long until we're eating chaff now! Today it's raining, and for the first time we ate our dinner in the shed. Most likely we shall go on doing so, for there's more room now. The kommando has been split up; the other half eats somewhere else. Unfortunately Erik is in the other half. He's not well these days, but not ill enough to be passed by the doctors in the *Revier*. I suppose he'll have to get pneumonia first, as a man did the other day. He was standing next me on parade, and suddenly collapsed—fainted. We lifted and held on to him, weren't allowed to get him away until the counting was over. Even that was a great favor. I helped to carry him to the *Revier*. Oftedal told us in the evening that he had pneumonia. He had had a temperature of forty degrees [104°F] when he turned out for evening roll call.

Frode is unwell, too. I'm O.K., but God knows there is plenty of opportunity to get ill here—and not much to get well again.

But now it's dark. I can neither write nor work any longer. We're still on our croco-diles; we've made some more animals too, and horses, hares, donkeys and sheep are on the program. It's an imbecile program and an imbecile job, but I shall be all right. Take my word for it!

FRIDAY, NOVEMBER 12, 1943 ■ This is a nasty, cold day and no mistake. Every-thing one touches is raw and clammy. My clothes are grimy, clammy and tattered. Before long they'll all be dropping off me, and it's impossible to scrounge anything new except by means of tobacco or herring or other Norwegian foodstuffs, which one would rather keep for oneself or at least make a better use of.

I've taken some charge of a little Russian student, as frail and wan as a young bird. He came to me some time ago because his father knew mine, had had something to do with him during the Russian relief in 1921–22. That lad shall have the bottle of train oil I got from home. But in small allowances. I'm afraid they would plunder him if he arrived with the whole bottle. He shall have a little butter, bread, sardines, and cheese too. He looks in more need of them than most. I myself am all right in every way, with almost enough at mealtimes, and it's a long time since that was the case.

Opposite me Frode is sitting polishing the crocodiles' feet with a solemnity and convict-routine which are priceless. He's puffing like a walrus, for his nose is completely blocked. The tip is never without a drop hanging from it, for no sooner does one drop off on to the crocodiles' feet than it is relieved by another, which was lurking just behind. Perhaps that's what they mean by crocodile tears?

Darkness is settling on our workshop now, and the lamp has no bulb, so it's a strain on one's eyes. I think of heating a little water in the dinner dish and getting a shave before the evening. One can't possibly manage it "at home" in the block. So long, Kari!

SATURDAY, NOVEMBER 13, 1943 ■ Rain, rain! In such weather one's cheerful, optimistic thoughts are far away. This life seems even more idiotic, more tormenting and interminable. The SS men standing in rows as we march out in the morning after a cold, wet roll call in a biting wind, seem living devils in uniform, in devil uniform with the death's-head on their caps.

Erik had an experience in his dining hut yesterday. A Russian traitor was beaten up by his countrymen. It was an ugly sight. He was beaten to a pulp by ten men frantic with rage, who flew at him like wild beasts. This man had been the Germans' henchman somewhere in Russia. Yesterday they weren't the death of him; he could even stagger back to work without help. But I don't suppose he will last long. August [Lange?], who has just looked in, and who also dines in the other hut, told us that they went for him again today. The foreman Joop arrived and watched the row. It goes without saying that he let it pass. He merely asked them to spare the tables and walls; then he walked off. Russian scores being settled were of no interest to him.

SUNDAY, NOVEMBER 14, 1943 ■ Yesterday I had not only a letter from Kari, but *two*. One was written on the 24th of October and one on the 30th. Splendid letters—in German of a wonderfully personal stamp. She hasn't a grain of self-consciousness about plunging into the sea of language; if there's a word she doesn't know, she puts the Norwegian with a bit of a German *Schwung* [panache]; then it's all right. The censorship thought so too, and of course to me a letter like that, with its queer words and unadulterated Kari stamp, is ten times more precious than one in faultless, alien, and impersonal German. She writes that all of them are thriving, have enough to eat, and are in good health. Both letters are a living breath of home, as it were from another world. One is pulled straight back where one belongs. It's plain that now Kari too has had to quell some of her optimism. Before, she always used to end "Merry Christmas!" now she writes that she doesn't think I'll be home by Christmas, but in the spring! In the spring! Heavens, how glorious it sounded. So distant and alluring, so full of hope! Well then, in the spring, Kari!

Last night there was to be a lice check. No one was to go out after half-past seven. Just then there came an air-raid warning. All to bed as usual and lights out. But when the all clear went we had to get up again, and fall in for a lice and cleanliness inspection. For once it was done properly, so that it really turned out a good thing. A lot of people had to go and wash their feet! One man—a German—was even sent off to the shower, the ice-cold shower, with soap and a scrubbing brush. But then he was a marvel of dirt. They found lice on him as well, and the dirt was in cakes and layers all over him. His head especially looked frightful; that emerged when he was shorn, for he was close-shorn all over. It makes one shudder to think one is rubbing up against men like that all day long.

TUESDAY, NOVEMBER 16, 1943 ■ Today I went over to the Jewish hut, to the fifty Jewish watchmakers. Keil came for me. We were to have gone there together on Sunday, but missed each other.

It was strange to see those Jews. They were men of all ages, all watchmakers employed in this camp on the repair of hundreds of thousands of stolen watches. Practically all these men had lost their families. Their wives and children had been sent into the gas chambers of Auschwitz or Lublin. It was their trade alone that had saved them from the same fate. There's something special about watchmaking; it is a protected trade. All watchmakers are picked out and put in a kommando that works directly under the *Kriegszeugsamt* [war ordnance bureau] (or whatever its name is) in Berlin. In this camp they don't come under the usual camp authorities. They live in an isolated area, have their own roll call, and don't mix with the other prisoners, though oddly enough they are allowed to go about the camp as they please. Queer as it may sound, they're actually favored in a way.

When I arrived at their hut, one of them was playing the cello. His touch was warm and subtle, and it sounded thrilling in the crowded hut, where those shipwrecked men sat round the tables listening devoutly. Harried faces, for the most part. One could read in them directly what these men had gone through, and one realized that the warm notes of the cello bore their thoughts off to vanished days at home with their wives and children. Now all that was gone forever.

I sat there thrilled like all the rest, and there was not much talk. When the concert was over I had only just time to meet a few of them; then I had to leave so as to get "home" to my own hut before closing time. I arranged with Keil that I would come back and have some talk with the different men, so as to hear a little of what they had been through.

Today we have a fresh hand on the job with us. When, even after a fresh intensive effort with Joop yesterday, we failed to get Erik, we made a bid for Rolf Hofmo, and that succeeded. Today he's here in full activity, and thus the toy factory has been enlarged and its production increased.

THURSDAY, NOVEMBER 18, 1943 ■ There was a great sensation today at dinner-time. Rumors of it had been circulating long beforehand—passwords as they're called. We had macaroni in the soup at dinner! Real macaroni, *white* macaroni. We had a lot of potatoes with it too. This has been a big day for most of us. I myself have eaten until blue flames are coming out of my mouth, for we have roast potatoes as well, and a bit of ham Rolf brought.*

We're getting more and more to do. There are regular demands for new types of toys, and if we're to be finished by Christmas we'll have to keep at it all right. I'm busy painting nowadays. Rolf is the joiner; he polishes, files, and puts together. Frode is painting, too. We've gotten pretty handy now.

SATURDAY, NOVEMBER 20, 1943 ■ The night before last there was a big raid on Berlin.† They were American aircraft; the raid began about eight, and we had to go to bed, as usual during raids at that time of day. A process that involves a good deal of uproar, since the lights of course are turned off and a hundred and thirty men have to undress, do the needful, and plunge their way to bed in the black dark. Then it burst forth. Even though it was a long way off, and though the crashes were not so very deafening, they gave a sufficiently convincing impression of the hell it must be where the bombs were dropping. An unintermittent roar of engines told of the myriads of planes involved, and the AA guns hammered away so that the shots merged into one long peal of thunder. The whole sky was incessantly being lit up by explosions, and the blast of them

---

*   A colorful way of describing heartburn.

†   The air raid on November 18 was the opening act in the so-called Battle of Berlin, the longest, most sustained, most costly bombing campaign against a German city in the war. Over a five-month period (November–March), sixteen massed attacks by the British RAF attempted to destroy Berlin and force Germany to capitulate. Despite extensive damage to the city, with thousands killed and hundreds of thousands left homeless, the attempt was a failure. Berlin was the most heavily defended city in Europe, and its size (nineteen times as large as Paris), its wide boulevards, open spaces, and modern buildings all prevented the devastating firestorms that cities such as Hamburg had experienced. The cost to RAF Bomber Command, on the other hand, in lost aircraft and crews was significant. In any event, German morale did not break, war production was not severely diminished, and Germany did not capitulate. Nansen mistakenly identifies the aircraft as American; only British planes (Avro Lancasters, Handley Page Halifaxes, Short Stirlings, and de Havilland Mosquitos) were used by the RAF in their raids, all of which were conducted at night.

made the whole hut tremble like an aspen leaf. A few bombs seem to have fallen nearer Oranienburg; the crash and blast were so powerful that they made one doubt that the hut would stand up. But it did. The attack lasted for an hour, but without a break. The warning lasted for nearly three hours. The whole time I was lying engrossed in the struggle between the forces in me that desired this raid, and those that were reacting against this barbarism—this degrading fashion of making war. But for that matter is there any way of making war that isn't degrading? No, to be sure—! Later we shall return to culture, and all we're fighting for; but now we're fighting!

We were as busy as bees all yesterday, hadn't even time to look up except for food. Our evil genius Irsch was here twice, and complained that the tempo wasn't brisk enough. We thought we should get through the program, three hundred toys, by Christmas. He proclaimed that we wouldn't. No more was said. He counted the toys and went away. The last time he nearly caught me shaving, but I managed to get the shaving things out of sight without his noticing, and to dry the soap off my jaws.

Yesterday I went back to the Jews. Frode came with me. They told us such things that I shrink from repeating them. I think I must wait and hear still more. The man I talked to yesterday, a Slovak, said he would gladly tell me, so that someone might know, even though he didn't get out of here alive. He came from Lublin, and had seen and experienced the worst of the worst imaginable.

MONDAY, NOVEMBER 22, 1943 ■ Sunday turned out a busy day. Unfortunately I had to cancel my visit to the Jews, I had too many other things on hand. There was a cabaret in Block 1, and I had to practice a bit with the guitarist. It didn't go too badly. A crammed house, tumultuous enthusiasm, and tropical heat. At any rate there's nothing wrong with the spirits of the Norwegians, though there may be one or two other things to say against them. Their morale is almost uncomfortably high. Uncomfortably because it exists side by side with the most extreme wretchedness—and because it almost always strikes one as so damned smug. I sang a couple of songs, but noticed that it was an effort, that I was doing it against the grain, because I suddenly—and violently—felt those high spirits and that smugness, which seemed to me to fill the whole room, as an insult to all the hundreds of others who lay dying in their huts in the blackest misery. Food, food, parcels, herring, tobacco, swindling, barter, scrounging, and again food is the main content of our existence—and then no doubt we think ourselves heroes! No doubt we expect to return to Norway as heroes and be feted as such! Even though what we've done, if we've done anything at all, was inevitable. Those who have done something did their duty. Period. It's only in the very few exceptional cases that the duty has been done heroically. My word, there won't be many heroes produced by the body of Norwegians in this place. Such were the thoughts with which I took part in yesterday's performance. I should have kept away. It was I who was on the wrong wave length.

TUESDAY, NOVEMBER 23, 1943 ■ Last night there were three raids on Berlin.* The first alarm went about half-past seven, and the raid started immediately. Frode and I were

---

* According to the RAF, the raid of November 22/23 "was the most effective raid on Berlin of the war." An estimated 175,000 were left homeless. Folke Bernadotte was visiting the Swedish Legation in Berlin that night and called the raid "one of the most terrible [nights] I have ever experienced. . . . The Legation was almost totally destroyed."

at the Jewish block. We had to leave in rather a hurry; everything is blacked out at once, and we had a long way home. It was a strange expedition in the black dark. Hundreds of prisoners were tumbling out of the barracks and beginning a struggle in the darkness to get home to their own. One had to grope one's way, go forward in contempt of death, and take the collisions as they came. It might be people or it might be the whole wall of a hut that suddenly rose right in your path and gave you such a biff in the face or elsewhere that you were all but knocked flat. And it was raining and muddy, so that a closer acquaintance with the ground was not exactly to be wished. Of course we lost each other, but still we got there in the end. And then we had to go to bed and lie in the dark, listening to the bomb crashes and the AA fire and watching the great illuminations of the sky after each explosion.

Today we've had a "stock-taking." We're well ahead with our program, and now know for certain that we shall be able to finish the three hundred toys that have been ordered from us. We have a hundred and eighty done already, and three working weeks left. But no doubt we shall only get more to do when Irsch notices that we can manage the job. But it's good to have a lot to do, the time flies and one hasn't leisure to sit down and let the bad thoughts get hold of one—at least not so much nowadays.

WEDNESDAY, NOVEMBER 24, 1943 ■ Last night there was another heavy raid on Berlin.* It came about seven. We had barely finished supper. It lasted until twenty minutes of ten and seemed to be just as powerful as the last. A few of the explosions shook the whole hut.

This morning Irsch was here and took away 158 toys. He didn't bawl us out today; on the contrary he was almost mild. While we were getting some of the toys ready he employed his time on a little investigation of the room. He peered into a basket we keep on the top shelf. There he found our shaving things, a toothbrush, etc. It's forbidden to have such things at the place of work. He looked at them, put them back, and said nothing. On the table were two empty matchboxes and beside them a heap of unmistakable cigarette ash. He poked the ash with his finger, picked up the empty boxes and threw them into the stove, but still said nothing. We've agreed that this must be regarded as a test, and a proof that he's winking at such things in this *Sonderkommando*. To be sure it's all a swindle, and swindlers are not so particular among themselves. We now smoke with a rather clearer conscience than before, and we boil coffee and beef tea, and roast potatoes and make ourselves as snug as we can.

FRIDAY, NOVEMBER 26, 1943 ■ There was another air-raid warning last night at about eight, but I don't think anything came of it. The state of Berlin must be frightful. The number of dead is now given as more than a hundred thousand, and over a million people are said to be homeless.† There is talk of an ultimatum the Allies have sent to

---

* The RAF later wrote that despite the cloud cover over Berlin, the bombers "aimed their bombs through the cloud at the glow of 11 major fires still burning from the previous night."

† The RAF Campaign Diary noted that the raid heavily damaged the Berlin Zoo and "several large and dangerous animals—leopards, panthers, jaguars, apes—escaped and had to be hunted and shot in the streets." The corollary effect for Berliners, suffering from rationing since even before the war began in 1939, was "a short-lived glut of meat—most of which, thankfully, was unidentifiable."

Germany, giving them until the 27th to capitulate—that is, until tomorrow. I'm afraid it's nothing but a convict fantasy.

We're stuck in our work; the joiner's shop, which saws out our animals and things with a bandsaw, is too slow in delivery, and lately they've refused to let "our man" go on with that rubbish. What's required now is some scrounging. The SS men in the joinery must be greased, and we have to do that in order to go on working for other SS men. Talk of method! And we *must* do it, it's no use complaining and saying we're stuck. That would only mean a bawling out. All yesterday I had to sit designing a doll's house—bedroom and kitchen—with drawings for fittings and all the rest of it, for an SS man in the joinery. Irsch was on no account to see me at it, so whenever someone came to the door I had to whisk the drawings out of sight. Pleasant working conditions! Less might drive one cracked. But one gets into that, too—as though one had never known anything else. Whisking things out of sight has absolutely got into my blood. I suppose I shall be on the *qui vive* [on the alert], ready to hide things I'm working on, long after I get home to the office once the war is over. If it ever is over! And if I ever do get home again.

SATURDAY, NOVEMBER 27, 1943 ■ A frightful raid started after we had gone to bed as usual at half-past eight. It lasted until half-past ten. It was nearer than any of the others and therefore affected us more strongly. And then the night was brilliantly clear, so that the whole tremendous drama unrolled before our eyes on the firmament. Senselessly enough these dramas are beautiful. For long periods at a time the scene is fully illuminated just by the reflection of the big bomb explosions, or light bombs hang in the sky from parachutes, casting a sharp radiance like moonlight over wide areas.* We saw planes caught in the searchlights, but none shot down. They came in waves, with a deafening noise. Somewhere not far from the camp there is a heavy AA battery. The salvos shook the joints of the huts, and each time they came, or each time a bomb explosion shook the ground, a silence fell on the rows of bunks.

What do they talk of, most of them—right in the front line—where the fate of thousands is being decided, where, indeed, our culture's "to be or not to be" is at stake? Why, food! Food again!! The question is whether we shall get any more food parcels! Others are like exultant children, enjoying themselves, pointing and yelling with glee over the fireworks. A huge cluster of phosphorus, sinking with a ghastly majesty into the "inferno," releases cascades of ecstatic yells. The yells that receive it where it falls are of another kind, to be sure.†

SUNDAY, NOVEMBER 28, 1943 ■ The day before yesterday three hundred Berliners arrived in the camp as prisoners. Yesterday thirty-three arrived. All have been shot. That says more than words about the situation and atmosphere on both sides. I suppose these people had broken regulations in some way, or actually demonstrated against the SS.

---

* Nansen is referring to illumination flares dropped to visually mark the appropriate target areas when ground markers could not be employed.

† White phosphorus, a chemical compound, burns fiercely and can produce severe second- and third-degree burns since it can stick to the skin and will burn until completely consumed or deprived of oxygen. In 1944 the chief doctor at Sachsenhausen, Heinrich "Heinz" Baumkötter, initiated tests designed to create a salve to heal phosphorus burns. "During these experiments, prisoners were strapped down onto a table and covered from head to toe with molten phosphorous [*sic*]." See August 12, 1944, below.

Nobody knows. Of course the tale will be that they committed thefts or something like that, unless they're simply reckoned among the casualties.

But it's Sunday. Time to stop already, after loafing all day. We've had no material from the joiner's shop. This afternoon there's a cabaret in [Block] 23. Also I'm going to see the Jews.

MONDAY, NOVEMBER 29, 1943 ■ This time we got a little more peace to listen to the ghastly stories of Lublin, Auschwitz, Warsaw and other towns and camps. Compared to the drama of horror thus unfolded, all the other horrors, atrocities and massacres we know of in the whole history of mankind go, as it were, for nothing. It's impossible— completely impossible to form any picture of the evil revealed here; human comprehension and imagination fall short. One can "follow" up to a point, imagine thousands of Jews, young and old, being sent out in the death transports, see them marching in endless columns, day and night, week after week, month after month, yes, year after year, into annihilation. And yet what one can imagine is still assuredly nothing but a pale reflection of the reality. How those unhappy millions must have longed to die! They must have looked on the gas chambers as a sheer deliverance from the scenes of horror outside. Why that was an easy death! But it wasn't granted to all; hundreds of thousands of the strongest and best—the healthiest and finest young people in their full bloom had first to be "exploited"—their strength had first to be made use of in the death gangs—moving corpses, burning, hanging! And it was their own people they were moving, burning, and hanging—their own! No! I won't make any attempt to repeat what I heard; I can't yet. I must get back from it a little, and also I must hear still more.

Besides the Jews I've spoken of, who are watchmakers, fifty-three in all, there is another special kommando of Jews in the camp, thirty-eight of them, working in a special SS printing shop. This printing shop is in a barrack close by the Jewish hut we were in yesterday, and is surrounded on every side by an impenetrable double fence of barbed wire. I saw it last night. No outsider ever passes through that barbed wire, and none of those inside it ever come out. That printing shop is employed in forging documents and money, turning out all the fraudulent printed matter of which the Third Reich makes use. So much is beyond doubt. But the most horrible thing is that it's taken for granted that the thirty-eight Jews employed in there will never come out to tell what they have done.*

---

*   Operation Bernhard, so named after SS *Sturmbannführer* Bernhard Krueger, who ran it, was a clandestine counterfeiting operation undertaken to destabilize the British economy by flooding the country with fake bank notes. It has been called the most successful counterfeiting operation of all time. At Sachsenhausen this operation, which employed more than 140 prisoners from fifteen countries representing fifty-five trades or professions, was housed in Blocks 18 and 19. Working around the clock, Operation Bernhard ultimately produced notes worth 132 million pound sterling, or almost $6.75 billion in today's dollars. Contrary to Nansen's fears, almost all of the counterfeiters survived the war, including a Norwegian Jew, Moritz Nachtstern (1902–1969), whose family had emigrated to Norway from Poland before the war. Nachtstern was one of only a handful among the 532 Norwegian Jews transported aboard the SS *Donau* on November 26, 1942, to survive. He published his memoirs in 1949, and they were republished in 2006 in conjunction with the opening of the Oslo Centre for Holocaust and Genocide Studies (housed, appropriately, in Vidkun Quisling's wartime residence) and translated into English in 2008 under the title *Counterfeiter: How a Norwegian Jew Survived the Holocaust*. The memoir has been described as "the most reliable and psychologically acute version of the drama as seen from inside Sachsenhausen's Block 19." Many of the counterfeit notes fell into the possession of the Jewish underground after the war and were used to finance the smuggling of refugees into Palestine, as well as the arming of the underground Jewish army there. Bernhard Krueger was never charged with any crime and died in 1989 at age eighty-three.

It was with a sickening sensation of horror that I stood staring at that hut last night in the dusk. I could scarcely take my eyes off it, I felt queer, ill! A sense of impotence grips one by the throat, as though one were suffocating. Nothing can help—not even tears or screaming. Straight from those two hours in hell I went to the cabaret and played the fool! It was strange, but went off all right—though I didn't exactly notice what I was doing. There was a packed house, tropical heat, and ditto atmosphere. "For Norway we're bound," tralalala! Well, there's plenty of variety even here!

TUESDAY, NOVEMBER 30, 1943 ■ The new "routine" we have been given is completely German, with all that that idea implies in the way of "organized chaos" and inefficiency. We get up at half-past four. At a quarter past five there is a general parade. It lasts until about quarter of six. Then all who work in kommandos outside the camp—that is, the majority—have to go back to their huts and wait until half-past six, when there is a parade of working kommandos. That usually lasts half or three quarters of an hour, after which we march out. Thus there are almost three and a half hours between the time we get up and our arrival at the place of work. Add that we get half an hour less at dinnertime, and that evening roll call is postponed to half-past six. This last means that we have between an hour and ninety minutes to wait after we get home before we can turn out for roll call and be counted up again (as we have been three or four times already). To make the whole thing even worse the *Blockältester* has decreed that we are not to have soup or coffee until after evening roll call. So what it means is that we eat the dry bread when we get home about five, and get our coffee or soup toward half-past seven. Bedtime is half-past eight as before. So they've managed to tear our day to shreds, and if *that* was the object, the arrangement is a success at every point.

To us three toy manufacturers perhaps it really matters less than to other people. We are best off at our place of work, so that the half hour off the dinner break (to sit and freeze in) is all the better. Otherwise it makes no great difference to us. But unfortunately that's not the case with the great majority of prisoners. They have to be working out of doors the whole time—soaking, ill clad, chilled and feeble as they are, most of them. If Oranienburg is no longer the decided *Vernichtungslager* it used to be, at any rate it's an "undermining institution" of the first rank.

WEDNESDAY, DECEMBER 1, 1943 ■ Another month begun. The Christmas month! What will it bring, apart from a caricature of Christmas? The Russians are going ahead on a grand scale. It looks as though their plan were still to bring about the decision this year. There's need of it, for our cupboards have long been empty, and we shall soon be sucking on our last cigarette butt. The potatoes are vanishing from our menu more and more (they're going to Berlin); instead we have cabbage and rutabaga soup—no, not instead, but *that* doesn't vanish, unfortunately. If we're to live all winter on that soup and on "bread and tallow," we'll all be *Muselmenn* together, I should think. But sufficient unto the day.

THURSDAY, DECEMBER 2, 1943 ■ There's a great to-do just now in our block about getting the *Betten* [bed] "built" properly. Which means getting the beds made. The *Lager-führer*—or *Rapportführer* [roll call leader] I suppose it is—requires the *Betten* to be built exactly in a certain way. We're forbidden to have anything in our beds except bedclothes.

Muselmenn *waiting for the cabbage soup to be given out. The
two behind the soup kettle could wait no longer.*

Not even sleeping bags are to be tolerated; they're to be put on the top tier of bunks in
the daytime, where they won't show. Otherwise we have no room at all for our clothes
and odds and ends, as there are five of us to a *spinn* [cupboard] in some cases.* The space
assigned to each is more than filled up by one change of underclothes plus eating things.
So the bed is the only place we can resort to. And so we do, in spite of the ban; the only

---

* Nansen shared "spinn 18" with Frode Rinnan, Scott Isaksen, and Erik Magelssen. He and his cohorts liked to make
   a play on words between the Norwegian word for eighteen ("atten," yielding "spinn atten") and the Norwegian word
   for spinach ("spinat").

thing is not to be found out. Not that it's an ideal place to keep anything. The *Schlafsal* [dormitory] is so dirty and disgusting that our families would shed tears if they saw it.

B., who has been made so-called *Stubenältester*, is now running the Germans very close in fuss and screaming. At any rate he's a good mimic. Every word of German he possesses is mixed up with his Norwegian, so his slangings have all the special stamp of Oranienburg. He's forgotten Norwegian words like dormitory, bed, table, hut, cupboard, dish, etc. Here the German words come in—as they do for that matter in the idiom of most people here. In fact it's quite unusual to hear anyone talking about dish and cupboard and bed or bunk. They're called *Schüssel*, *Spinn* and *Bett*.

Another thing they have in common all round is their hatred or contempt for Ukrainians. Just as anti-Semitism is latent in everyone, so also they've adopted this German aversion for Ukrainians, whom they regard, in pure German style, as inferior beings, because they're famished, ill clad (so are all of us who haven't managed to scrounge smart clothes), and come in part from social strata where the level of education, etc., is a good deal lower than that of the average Norwegian. But when it comes to purely human qualities, I often feel that the "Teutons" make the worst showing.

All the students of the university at home are said to have been arrested for refusing to sign a declaration of loyalty.* They're to be sent to Germany, it's said. Perhaps we'll soon have them here. The women students were sent home, while a number of professors were arrested. I suppose the Germans are holding an official "cultural pause." When will it be over? When on earth is it to be over?

FRIDAY, DECEMBER 3, 1943 ■ Last night the Anglo-Americans were back again— with a raid that lasted nearly two hours. The biggest yet, a lot of people think. There are rumors that leaflets have been dropped with an ultimatum to the German people (or the people of Berlin): If they don't provide themselves with a new government before December 20th, they shall have a Christmas they won't forget in a hurry, or (according to some) Germany will be bombed to pieces. Most likely it's an invention.

Yesterday a *Rottenführer* told a gang of prisoners, two of them Norwegians, to dig a pit. They did so, and helped him to pitch into it a quantity of first-class tools, magnetos and car-parts. His reason was that all of it was going to the front. Thus, an act of pure sabotage in front of the prisoners. He's a dead man if they tell tales. Rolf [Hofmo] has spoken with the two Norwegians who were in it, or I should have thought it a fabrication, for it was

---

* In the fall of 1943 the NS Department of Education promulgated new regulations governing admission to the University of Oslo, including one whereby 25 percent of the entering class would be admitted on criteria other than their grades (i.e., students with NS sympathies). This led to immediate protests and in mid-October 1943, ten professors and sixty-four students were arrested. Two days after a fire was set at the university on November 28 (that was blamed on agitators), Nazi officials rounded up more than 1,250 students; 600 were subsequently released but the balance were sent—much like the Norwegian police arrested August 16, 1943—to special camps, 300 to Sennheim concentration camp, a subcamp of Natzweiler-Struthof in the Alsace region, and the balance to Buchenwald, all for "re-education." While the students were treated better than the average prisoner, at least seventeen died in captivity. They were subjected to lectures in racial ideology and Nazi theory, efforts that ended in complete failure as virtually no student volunteered for the SS or adopted Nazi ideology. The University of Oslo never reopened for the duration of the war. According to Quisling's private secretary, Terboven originally had planned to use the arrested students to fight partisans on the Eastern Front. The student action had been taken by Terboven without consulting Berlin, and Hitler was reported to be furious at Terboven for his "tactical ineptitude." Similarly, Himmler felt the arrests served to thwart his goal of recruiting forty to sixty thousand volunteers to fight with the Waffen SS.

a reckless and stupid thing to do. But significant of the atmosphere. It can't possibly last much longer.

SUNDAY, DECEMBER 5, 1943 ■ I didn't write yesterday. Everything was so dreary, so horrible! I was hoping for a letter from Kari which might have put everything right. But there was no letter. Hardly anyone got any mail. It must be the transport difficulties. Erik, Frode and I all had long faces last night. It was a severe disappointment, and what had been dreary and horrible became even worse.

The day before yesterday, when we were just leaving work, there came an order that everyone was to fall in instantly for counting. A man had been missed. It turned out to be a prisoner in the next kommando who had hanged himself somewhere in the woods. As soon as that fact was ascertained, all was forgotten and in order. They had the correct total—including a corpse, which was fetched and driven up on a cart to be counted in!

On the same day the man in charge of the shoe factory, a *Hauptsturmführer*, was arrested for swindling on a large scale. He had had ten thousand pairs of shoes burned to wipe out the traces of his fraud. For the shoes were property stolen from murdered Jews, and he had had them cut up on his own behalf, to secure the ornaments and currency they contained. How much he found is not known, but from previous experience one may safely reckon that immense sums are involved. The man was arrested not for embezzling the valuables but for burning the footwear! Many prisoners, who were employed in the shoe factory and carried out his orders, have been up for questioning, and the case is apparently brewing up to great dimensions. If only it gets big enough, no doubt it will be shelved and stifled. For if that splits open, everything will split. All are implicated in some swindle or other, and that binds them all together in a kind of freemasonry.

Yesterday a prisoner was shot in an attempt to escape. A poor wretch of a Pole, who had first attempted to hang himself. I suppose he could stand no more. Well, so he found peace, and that was doubtless what he longed for.

Every day prisoners are being brought here from Berlin, and they are shot at once. There were eleven yesterday, seven the day before, etc. What they had been guilty of we don't know, but most probably they had been stealing, looting, and exploiting the situation in burning Berlin. Last night we had another raid.

MONDAY, DECEMBER 6, 1943 ■ I didn't get on to the most terrible of all the things that together are making these days heavy and hard to bear. Yesterday a death transport of a thousand men left the camp.

Everyone knows what a death transport is—*ein Todestransport* [death transport]. People who are to be extirpated. Originally a couple of thousand *Schonungskranke* were supposed to be going to Dachau, which passes for a kind of convalescent camp as it were. Then Dachau was changed for Lublin, and the transport temporarily reduced to a thousand men. These were picked out from among the sick. Doctors and hut leaders have had to draw up lists. Oftedal, who at once perceived what was in the wind, has had a big job saving Norwegians from this transport. And he has in fact saved them all—even our friend Henry Hansen, on the pretext that he's on the eve of a new operation that will cure him. Oftedal is doing magnificent work here altogether.

The prisoners who could not be saved were, according to what I learn from various well-informed sources, incurably ill—people on whom the SS could not expect to make

The transport gang was usually made up of Russians and Ukrainians. The huge wagon could contain cabbage leaves, potatoes—or dead comrades.

any "profit" in this camp. For the camp is also run as a business. We are hired out to the surrounding factories, and bring the camp in a large regular income. We three toy manufacturers, for instance, mean a daily revenue of fifteen reichsmarks for the SS.* The shoe factory is a joint stock company (with Himmler as the principal shareholder) that hires labor from the SS and runs moreover on stolen property. A whole series of other factories round about the camp are kept going in the same way, and obviously a large stock of sick "workers" means a big loss, which it is desirable to reduce as much as possible. I believe that is in fact the main reason for the "death transports."

The thousand are said to have been chiefly Russians, Ukrainians, and Poles, with a few of other nationalities as well.

It's strange that they themselves don't realize where they're going; they hope and hope, and cling to life. Even when they had their respective numbers written on their forearm (on the skin) with copying ink, they didn't catch on. This kind of numbering is usual (the Jews in Auschwitz and Lublin had their numbers tattooed on the forearm; Keil has shown me his), and I suppose its object is to facilitate the "sorting" and identifying of the bodies when they're taken out of the gas chambers. For some kind of death certificate must be issued, if only on account of the Germans' hopeless and everlasting passion for protocols, *Schein,* and bureaucracy! Keil also told me that at Lublin some were unceasingly employed

---

*   The SS charged out its inmates to private industry at a rate typically between three and four Reichsmarks per day per prisoner, depending on the level of skilled labor involved. By 1944, as demand rose and the supply of inmates shrank, payments were increased to four to eight Reichsmarks per day. This proved highly profitable for the SS inasmuch as the cost of maintaining the camps equaled about one Reichsmark per prisoner per day.

on the "fabrication" of death certificates giving some "legal" cause of death, appropriately varied, for every one of the extirpated thousands.*

As to whether this death transport will ever get to Lublin at all, or was ever meant to go so far, opinions differ. Some hold that they will merely be sent straight into the gas chambers "round the corner"—in camp. Others maintain that the transport was going to Lublin, but that it had only food for two days, whereas the journey takes at least six. It's said that another transport of six hundred men was to leave today or in the immediate future.

One can't avoid the idea that they may intend to liquidate the whole camp by degrees in this way. Perhaps we're all to go off in transports and have our forearms marked with copying ink. I'm glad they know nothing of this at home—or of anything that goes on in German concentration camps.

Yesterday Frode went to Block 1 to see [Arnulf] Øverland who was in pretty low spirits. His name had been on the transport list, but he was rescued by Sven O[ftedal]. Naturally he feels threatened if there are to be more transports. For he's not strong, and besides he's a hopeless duffer at everything but writing poetry. Now he's in the darning gang, valiantly trying to get a hole or two darned while other people darn ten.

This is my birthday.† I've never known a birthday when the omens were darker, nor ever, I suppose, longed so childishly for the birthday spread at home, with its chocolate and cake. I wonder if you will ever make them for me again, Kari? The Russians are steadily advancing, but we hear nothing of a second front.‡ And Christmas is at hand, and with it 1944. Who dreamed of *that*, when 1943 was drawing near?

WEDNESDAY, DECEMBER 8, 1943 ∎ There has been another day's break. And still the world hasn't gone under. It's enough to surprise one every day.

In spite of the cold, which was a record for this autumn, and the frosty mist, which lay thick over the camp, the day turned out rather more cheerful. I had got the upper hand of my worst thoughts, thanks to the way my friends celebrated my birthday. I received presents. Erik had brought a souvenir of his trade—a kind of puzzle! A slab of wood, the same as those he's busy cutting into three for fuel from morning to night. He had cut it in three, painted the pieces red and packed them up nicely. He accompanied the present with a little speech.

Then Frode arrived with his present and his speech. He wanted to give me something quite personal—as a present should always be—and he had been able to find nothing more personal than a toy I had made myself in our factory—a rocking sheep. And then Frode acted as waiter at the banquet, and he managed to relax our spirits and our laughter muscles until in the end we were quite stiff. It was marvelous to have a laugh again. I laughed until I cried when Frode through the cupboard door—with all the appropriate

---

* Among the most notable, and notorious, such death certificates was the one for three-year-old Gerhard Pohl. His cause of death: "old age."

† His forty-second.

‡ The anticipated location of the so-called "second front" was a matter of much speculation. Hitler was convinced, almost from the start of the war, that it would be Norway and accordingly lavished significant manpower and equipment in an effort to turn Norway into a veritable fortress—*Festung Norwegen*. By the end of the war there were still 350,000 well-equipped German soldiers in the country, or almost one soldier for every ten Norwegians.

Within the image: *Mr. Knott / på hans 52 års dag / Sachsenhausen / 12-4-44*

Director Erik Magelssen in full canonicals—wood-gas-generator expert and "director" of fuel production, member of "spinn atten" and prisoner 72063. Those gloves of his we called the pocket-battleships "Gneisenau" and "Scharnhorst."

gestures—sent "down" an order for four grouse and a bottle of Yquème.* "And get a move on!" And when he gulped down drams and leavings from the dinner in waiter fashion behind the door of the "dumbwaiter," I felt such a burning need to disconnect—and succeeded! Life took on a brighter hue, and it has held since, up to a point anyhow.

We had parcels from the Danish Red Cross yesterday. Cheese and bacon and Ovomaltine, and Ramona-marmalade. We shall be living like princes for some time. Four of those big parcels in the *Spin*.

Yesterday we heard a nasty rumor, which I fervently hope must be untrue. It was that Chr[istoffer] Berg-Hansen, who has arrived here with two others from the camp in Alsace,† is to be sent to Lublin with one of the death transports. B[erg]-H[ansen] left Grini in the same batch as us, and went with the other transport from Stettin—to Alsace. The one that also included Leif [Poulsson] and [Ragnar] Hartvig. Leif has been put in charge of the *Revier* there, so he gets on tolerably, but in general it's an appalling camp, where many go under. They get neither letters nor parcels and have to live exclusively on the prison fare. Of course they die of it in the end. Berg-Hansen and the other two had been ill and unfit for work the whole time, therefore they were on the wrong side of the camp account and had to go. For the present they're in the *Zugangsblock* [new arrival block] in quarantine.

The surly Irsch was here today. He has to bawl one out, and did. We were slow. The thing is that we shall more than finish the program he himself gave us—and he laid it on thick at that time, assuredly thinking: They'll never get through all that. Now he sees we'll do it, so he has to lie his way out of what he said before, by adding that we were supposed to do a whole lot of other stuff. He's a bastard. Well, well, Christmas will soon be here whether we get through or not. Both Frode and I are on the Christmas committee for the block. That means more bother. Decorations, songs, fun and entertainment. If only the joy is forthcoming. And the time. That's important, too.

SATURDAY, DECEMBER 11, 1943 ■ Saturday again! The time flies, but only when one looks back, and one so rarely does. All one's mind and heart are bent on the future. And so it comes about that time moves like a snail, after all.

Every day there is someone executed in the camp, it appears. I just didn't happen to know. They are killed in the gas chambers or hanged or shot in a pit at the crematorium, close by the furnace. Practical. Recently one or more SS men have been arrested every day for embezzlement, theft, and the like. Informing flourishes! There is absolutely nowhere to turn one's thoughts without coming up against rottenness.

It appears that the death transport of a thousand men didn't leave until yesterday. Three of them died here in camp before it went off. They died out on the square, collapsed, could stand no more. They were lucky.

We have already completed our program on the job here, and done far more than three hundred toys. But as I said, the demands have been increased, and we are as busy as ever. Barely a fortnight to Christmas Eve.

---

* A wine produced in southern Bordeaux, France. One wine critic writes that Château d'Yquem is "not only the greatest Sauternes but the greatest wine *per se*."
† I.e., Natzweiler.

SUNDAY, DECEMBER 12, 1943 ■ A letter from Kari yesterday. That was lovely. They're all right, everything seems to be going well with all at home. It was a flaw in my pleasure that Frode heard nothing from anyone. He gets no parcels either, and knows nothing of Hannagreta.

MONDAY, DECEMBER 13, 1943 ■ Yesterday was Frode's birthday;* I completely forgot it until we got home for dinner. Erik and I set to work to brew birthday soup with dried vegetables, bits of ham, and pease meal. But alas, our turn at the stove was too short; we couldn't even get the soup to boil. We had to give it up. One has to arrange that kind of thing at the beginning of the day and get one of the *Schonungskranke* to put the soup on in the morning. Today we've done that, so we'll have to have the "party" today instead.

Otherwise there's not much cause for celebration just now. The particulars of the death transport's leaving camp are horrible. Three men died on the parade ground, as I said before. Sixty-seven died on the way to the railway station. All of them were loaded onto buses in a hall somewhere outside the gates. In that hall civilian women are employed. The way the loading was done drew cries of "Shame!" from these women workers. How many of the poor creatures will die on the train? How many will survive to go into the gas chambers of Lublin—or wherever they get to?

The selection for these transports is one of the most gruesome things imaginable. Whoever has to pick them out must inevitably feel like a hangman. He is, in fact, pronouncing death sentences. One example will be enough to give the idea.

A Russian lad was picked out. He had tuberculosis. He saw it all, fully understood that he was being picked out to die. But he didn't want to die and begged for his life; every day he begged, begged and prayed. The decision rests with a certain August, a ghastly type, an electrician, who is the real "senior M.O." [Medical Officer] of the *Revier*. He, not the doctors, decides who is well and who is ill enough to be thrown out. Lately this August has been better, more like a human being. Anyhow he couldn't bring himself to send the boy, and yielded to his entreaties. There may have been reasons—August has a weakness for boys in more senses than one. However, he had to find someone else, if the boy didn't go. The thousand had to be made up. There was nothing for it but to take the oldest and feeblest of those that were left. He had to do that! No wonder August has now refused to have any more to do with these transports. Next time they can pick out and decide for themselves, he says. Not that it will be any better for another man. But August the electrician is through!

Yesterday a huge transport of Norwegians arrived in camp! Three hundred seventy-four men, mostly from Grini and Falstad.† I don't yet know what acquaintances are in it.

TUESDAY, DECEMBER 14, 1943 ■ There were a thousand men in the transport from Norway; 378 of them came here, the rest were sent from Stettin to other camps. This morning I had a talk with [Carl] Jacobsen the engineer, and Dr. [Paul] Gløersen, who are in this lot.‡ On the whole they were all right, except that all of them are as cold as the very

---

* His thirty-eighth.

† Falstad was a converted former boys' reformatory located north of Trondheim. It is estimated that more than 4,200 prisoners passed through Falstad between 1941 and 1945.

‡ Both Jacobsen and Gløersen survived until the end of the war.

devil. A big collection of underclothing is going on in the Norwegian blocks. Obviously more transports are imminent.

WEDNESDAY, DECEMBER 15, 1943 ■ I went again this morning to see the new-comers in Block 37. I met Hugo Berntsen;* it was a breath of greeting from Room 6 at Grini, from a pleasant bygone time. Hugo was O.K. and had messages from the old gang, all of whom were thriving. But 6 had long been disbanded. One had gone this way and one that. Hadn't I gone into the hospital myself, until I fell further into disgrace. Yes, it's a long time now since 6 had its golden age and we had ours. Last Christmas, for example, which was a pleasant Christmas. What will it be like this year, in Block 24, B-wing, where we've hardly room to sit down all at once?

Berg-Hansen is in the *Revier*; he's had a touch of dysentery, but is better already. The gloomy report that he and the two others from Alsace were to leave with a death transport is dying down, and I fervently hope that it was baseless. Another of the three, Gåserud,† has been put into our block, and I've had some talk with him about the conditions in the camp they come from, Natzweiler it's called, apparently. It's frightful there. Hard work and little food, and all are famished and getting weaker and weaker. His picture of the others and their drudgery was not enlivening. Ragnar Hartvig, for instance, whose legs were swollen and weakened by the torture screws at Victoria Terrace, was thrown out of the *Revier* and put to hard work, carrying stones, and so forth.‡ Leif [Poulsson] doesn't seem to have had much say at first; he was only a nurse; it was an SS doctor who had all the say, and next to him a lot of prisoners with green triangles, BV-ers as they're called, or *Berufsverbrecher* [professional criminals].

We're struggling away at our toys; everything is to be finished by Saturday, and it's Wednesday already. We're scamping more and more, and yet we maintain a quality far above what *they* think *prima-prima*. A ghastly race, in everything they do, wherever they are!

THURSDAY, DECEMBER 16, 1943 ■ There's no doubt that Christmas is approaching. All the kommandos have several men at work, partly overtime work, that is, more than a twelve-hour day, to get their SS masters' toys finished. Our shabby friend Herr Irsch has had a miniature car made for his son in one of the workshops. I haven't seen it, but Joop described it to me. It is all metal, in torpedo form. The inside has padded leather cushions and the outside is enamel sprayed. They say it's a sight. Only millionaires' children in America have ever had the like. And this is made for an SS *Oberscharführer*, by prisoners who are kept here for "important war work"!

There now! Helwig (SS *Scharführer*) has just been in. I thought the door was locked, but it wasn't. He walked straight in and saw me writing. He came up, picked up this sheet and asked if I could really write so small without a microscope. But also, to my intense relief, he said I needn't worry, he hadn't seen anything. Helwig is the only decent one of these chaps here, and I do believe he's O.K. However, he was sufficiently interested in my

---

* Hugo Berentzen remained in Sachsenhausen until the end of the war.
† Berg-Hansen survived in Sachsenhausen until the end of the war, as did Gudbrand Gåserud.
‡ Hartvig was transferred from Natzweiler to Dachau and various other camps before ending up again in Dachau. He survived until the end of the war.

manuscript to study it more closely through a magnifying glass, which he took out of his pocket. He caught sight of Irsch's name, which is at the top of the page, and asked if there was anything about Helwig. I said there wasn't. Then he put down the sheets and started chatting about this and that and nothing at all. I don't think I need worry about him, and Frode had the same impression. So I'm writing calmly on.

SUNDAY, DECEMBER 19, 1943 ■ Yesterday there was a *Kameradenschaftabend*, and we were fully occupied all day getting the things finished, for they were to be distributed among the SS in the evening. Today has been busy too, though of course it was the morning after for the SS, so we haven't had *them* here. We've had Joop instead, and he can be a host in himself. Moreover he now comes on a regular schedule, sneaking tobacco. If I don't offer it he begs, and takes it increasingly as a matter of course that he should have some. Presumably as a reward for "holding his hand over us." The howler! He's got a nasty fit of howling just now. Nor is he backward in hitting and kicking famished, miserable fellow prisoners, especially if there's an SS man about. Most of these old Communists are like that. In reality they're "nazified" through and through, as good slave drivers as anyone. The SS couldn't wish for better henchmen. When the page turns one day, they're all ready to let loose their thunders in the same style the other way round. The prisoners will be a different set of people; that's all.

TUESDAY, DECEMBER 21, 1943 ■ The Christmas committee fell by the ears yesterday. It's B. who is on the warpath against Frode and me; we bite back, and the whole thing is like a nursery. B. staked his position on my not making the Christmas speech, Frode left, and I proposed to the committee to get rid of B. I lost and also left. B. irritates me to the marrow, that I won't deny, but I'm a little dismayed it would go so far. Well, well. Merry Christmas.

MONDAY, DECEMBER 27, 1943 ■ I fell ill on little Christmas Eve [the 23rd], had a temperature of over 39 degrees [103°F], and felt that life was darker, drearier, and more miserable than ever. I had to go and see the doctor at the *Revier* (to be on the safe side; didn't I promise Kari to take care of myself) and so I've been through that ceremony as well. Completely on a par with everything else that goes on here. A long line of rickety individuals lines up after joining in a roll call that lasts an hour—often in ten to twenty degrees of frost [14° to -4°F]. Then I'm blessed if they don't start drilling these people: "*Aufstellung Vordermann!* [Line up!] *Richt euch! Mützen ab! Augen rechts!*" etc. Men on crutches, with their heads, arms and legs in bandages; men in a high fever! A macabre performance, which none but Germans could stage. But here it doesn't really strike anyone as extraordinary. I was given *Bettschonung* after shivering in the line for an hour. I went to bed, in a dark and dismal frame of mind, and the very next day was a lot better.

Then came Christmas, with food, song, entertainments, bother and crush. A strange Christmas. But pleasant too in a way, at least Erik, Scott,* Frode and I had a pleasant little

---

* Scott Isaksen had all along been our "spin comrade" and was the fourth man in our group, which held together through thick and thin while captivity lasted. And further still—O.N. [This last sentence presumably refers to Isaksen's role in smuggling part of the diary.]

*Christmas Eve in Block 24. Arnulf Øverland is reading
his poem "Christmas in Sachsenhausen."*

corner at the table for some time. Joel* also stopped by for a moment and enjoyed some of the feasting, while barrack noise roared around us. The "program" was nothing much, Christmas nonsense and a kind of Christmas atmosphere. But then Øverland arrived. He read his Christmas poem. That was an experience! Anyone who may have thought there

---

* Joel was a German prisoner. A good friend and a rare man, an editor by profession. Twelve years he had spent in German prisons and concentration camps for the sake of his courageous convictions. O.N.

A Christmas tree is lit on "Tyburn."

was anything wrong with *him* was mistaken. He gave the evening content and real life; but heavens, what a risk he took, reading that poem in all the Norwegian blocks. If *that* fell into the hands of the SS, the worst might happen.

All the same, for me there was only one great event of Christmas Eve, 1943; that was the letter from Kari. It arrived as though from heaven—in the middle of Christmas Eve. I managed to get it read the first time squeezed up with others on a bench, then I went off to the dormitory and up into my bunk and read and read—over and over again; and finally I went out into the darkness, among the Norwegian blocks, out on the parade ground. There at last I was alone in black darkness, in the center of the square. Nobody could hear or see me. Facing me was the glimmer of candles from the Christmas tree, which had been lit on "Tyburn," as Øverland relates at the beginning of his poem.* And it's quite true; where the Christmas tree had been set up is where they put up the gallows when someone is to be hanged.

Behind me, on the sentry's balcony of the gatehouse, stood a handful of SS, soldiers with steel helmets, tommy guns and machine guns, ready at the least sign to shatter the darkness and Christmas peace with bellowing and bullets. From the hoarse metal drums of the loudspeakers out on the square there sounded the most pious carols, bringing after all a faint reminder of Christmas. I stood there a long, long time; how long I don't know; but I know I was home in Polhøgda, home with Kari, Marit, Eigil, Siri and the Little

---

* The first line in Øverland's poem "Jul i Sachsenhausen" [Christmas in Sachsenhausen] reads: "A Christmas tree is lit on the gallows!" This poem is included in *Vi Overlever Alt!* Tyburn, a village close to the Marble Arch in present-day London, was the site for public executions, the earliest recorded being in 1196. In 1571, a permanent three-sided gallows, known as the Tyburn Tree, was erected. It remained the principal place of executions until replaced by Newgate Prison in 1783.

One. Certainly I shed a few tears, pitiful and lost in my rags, out there in the dark. But I wouldn't change that moment for anything that life here can offer. And after all it doesn't seem to me such a foolish thing, to shed a few tears. I only felt so scared—and almost happy that I still could.

I took part in a couple of entertainments on Christmas Day, which was a whole day off. Neither my contribution nor the program in general was much to boast of. The first performance began at nine in the morning and was international—a cabaret in which a number of nationalities each had a section. The afternoon and evening were taken up with a concert by the camp symphony orchestra. This is indeed an extraordinary prison. In the midst of all the terror and brutality there exists a big orchestra of prisoners, about forty men. They played a whole section of Grieg. The whole *Peer Gynt* suite. Not as it should be played; but still it was Grieg, and it was music. For a moment one could forget oneself.

My illness is on the mend. I've been given *Schonung** until the new year, but am not using it; we are both more comfortable and more peaceful out on the job. So I've transferred my convalescence here. We loaf as best we can, dissipate in convict style, cook good meals, make coffee and gossip.

1944

SATURDAY, JANUARY 1, 1944 ■ Christmas week and New Year's Eve have gone by almost imperceptibly, and we're in 1944 without more ado! There was no celebration of New Year's Eve in our hut. Most people went to bed, though we were allowed to stay up until ten in honor of the day.

The day before yesterday I was sent for by the chief of this kommando, *Hauptsturm-führer* Steger. What did he want? Why, he'd found out that my name was Nansen and I was the son of—and so on. He'd read a lot about my father, he said, knew of his work for science and humanity, and was sorry I should be exposed to such treatment. Unfortunately he couldn't alter that, nor interfere in any way. I had been consigned to him as a prisoner, and he had to treat me as a prisoner. But he could and would do something to ease the conditions of my work out here. He would place me in a separate room, in a hut where I could be more comfortable, draw, write, read, and so forth. I thanked him, but said I was all right where I was and should appreciate it if he let me go on working there with my friends. He said they meant before long to convert our present quarters into a storeroom. As far as I understood, he was going to let it rest for the present, but Frode would also be transferred to the new quarters when the time came. He also gave me free access to him. I had only to tell the *Unterscharführer* in the anteroom that it was *Häftling* Nansen, and I would be shown right in at any time.

Well, I had no choice but to thank him for all this attention. I felt a bit uncomfortable, but then I remembered Kari's entreaty that I would take care of myself. Here was an opportunity of taking care of myself, and not at other people's expense. This was only a young, awkward, rather tactless, but well-meaning German officer, not a little shamefaced, wanting to prove that he knew a thing or two.

---

* Presumably an abbreviation of *Bettschonung*, or bed pass.

SUNDAY, JANUARY 2, 1944 ■ Joel told me yesterday about the transport of a thousand men that left here some time ago. The death transport! They had had nothing to eat on the way and had never been let out of the trucks in which they were packed. When they got to Lublin, the trucks were driven into a hall, the whole of which was put under gas. All perished. Joel had heard the story from one of the SS guards who accompanied the transport.

I believe I forgot to write about [Ragnar] Juell the chemist, a great friend of mine at Grini. He arrived here with a transport that had been at Kiel. On the very first day at Sachsenhausen he fell ill. It began with influenza, then it turned to pneumonia and finally to inflammation of the brain, and he died at half-past four on Christmas Eve, after nearly twenty-four hours' unconsciousness. Juell was such a radiant optimist. Last summer he was certain the war would end in time for him to go shooting in the autumn—last autumn. He joyfully made a bet with me. We emptied many a glass together in his little dispensary at Grini, and he was an expert at getting rid of the benzol flavor. His cheerfulness and good, steady humor made him an outstanding fellow-prisoner, who only brought light and joy. Now he is dead.*

Thus begins the new year. The year that is to bring the decision. Certainly! Didn't they say that about 1943 just a year ago? And didn't we believe it—from week to week, from month to month—until we came to see that it wasn't true, and that the war would last into still another year, and perhaps take the whole of *that*? For us in this place no year has ever begun more somberly, with more illusions shattered, and with less confidence. None the less we bid it welcome, and once more fix our hopes, our burning wishes, and our ache of longing on the new year. The news is excellent, and all things considered there seems every reason to take a rather more cheerful view of things after all.

MONDAY, JANUARY 3, 1944 ■ I've been *angefordert* [transferred] to another kommando. This is what happened:

An *Unter-* and an *Oberscharführer* were chatting at Scott Isaksen's place of work. They were talking about the League of Nations and Fridtjof Nansen. One of them said Fridtjof Nansen had been to the North Pole, the other said no, that wasn't him, and they had a bit of a squabble over it, until Scott (unluckily) said it was easy enough to find out, since Fridtjof Nansen's son was in the camp as a prisoner. They were interested and curious, and when they heard I was an architect invented a need for one in the kommando. Of course I've no desire to leave here, and the worst of it is that now they think I worked this myself.

We're still idling. I'm afraid there may be a hubbub if we've nothing to show Irsch when he comes. But we don't seem to give a damn.

THURSDAY, JANUARY 6, 1944 ■ The danger of my being transferred to another kommando seems to be averted. Irsch averted it by telling the head of the *Arbeitsdienststelle* [Labor Office], when he rang up to *angefordre* [transfer] me, that I was employed as

---

* Arrested December 19, 1942, Juell arrived in Grini on January 23, 1943; he was transferred to Sachsenhausen December 9, 1943. Juell was forty-eight when he died.

an architect on various plans for the enlargement of the camp out here—work which was just as "vital to the war effort" as the projects of the other kommando!

FRIDAY, JANUARY 7, 1944 ■ The Polish frontier crossed on a four-hundred kilometer [250 mile] front, and in camp the atmosphere is such that we can barely refrain from cheering.* I had such a vivid dream last night about going back home. It was marvelous.

WEDNESDAY, JANUARY 12, 1944 ■ It doesn't affect us so much now if a German officer or NCO stands on the pavement with his riding whip, striking anyone he feels inclined to as we go by, or if our fellow prisoners of the "Communist upper class" start belaboring some Ukrainian, Russian or Pole for something he may have done. An exultant thought is taking root more and more—Soon we'll be out of here; away; home! Through with our trials, sufferings, humiliations, our life of idleness! Home to work and great tasks, home to her and children and home! God grant it!

THURSDAY, JANUARY 13, 1944 ■ Today it's two years since I was arrested. Two everlasting, senseless years. What's become of them? I daren't look back on them. My optimism is paling, too—in spite of good news from the east. When on earth are the *decisive* events coming?

Two men have been taken for listening in to London on the SS radio. They're to have fifty lashes and be sent into the SK [*Strafkolonne* or penal column] for good. It means the end of them.† That's what comes of loose mouths.

MONDAY, JANUARY 17, 1944 ■ I was in the *Revier* yesterday visiting Henry Hansen as usual. A melancholy visit. All round him there are dying men. The man in the next bed was near the end, he lay groaning all the time and already looked like a corpse. Beyond him again a poor wretch lay and wailed; his right arm had been amputated for suppuration. Now he'd made a mess in the bed, and got a fearful dressing-down from bad-tempered, brutal nurses. During the night a neighbor on Henry's other side had died; his whole body from the soles of his feet up to the hips had been full of pus and misery. In these surroundings poor Henry lies in bed, helpless and in pain. No wonder he has gloomy thoughts. And one can do nothing for him, only take him a little plug and a book or two.

FRIDAY, JANUARY 21, 1944 ■ They were back again last night, that is yesterday evening—a big raid.‡ It started after evening roll call. Just another raid. We've gotten so used to it that we've ceased to take much notice.

Saw Henry again on Wednesday. He's going steadily downhill. Now he'd spoken to his Belgian doctor, asking straight out if the doctor thought he would get well. The doctor

---

* On January 6 the Russians captured Rokitno, twelve miles inside the 1939 Polish/Soviet border.
† It was said that the only way out of the SK was "up the chimney." The *Blockführer* of the SK, SS *Hauptscharführer* Richard Bugdalle, was nicknamed "Brutalla" or "Brutalle" and took pride in his ability to kill a man with his hands and his feet. Bugdalle was sentenced by a West German court in 1960 to life imprisonment. He died in 1982.
‡ This was the eleventh massive attack on Berlin since the start of the Battle of Berlin.

had made some evasive answer—"and that was enough for me, you know," said Henry. Then he looked me right in the eyes and said, "It's hopeless!—and so it's just as well to finish down here, for to go home to Norway like this . . ." What was I to say?

There's almost nothing happening, except that the Russians are advancing steadily and surely, while the English and Americans jabber and appoint generals and commanders-in-chief—for what?*

MONDAY, JANUARY 24, 1944 ■ Yesterday I went to see Henry. I go almost every day now; I've found a back way into the *Revier*. He wrote home yesterday. That is, he can't write himself, someone has to do it for him, and he mayn't write anything about himself but the usual phrases—"*Mir geht es gut, ich bin gesund und guten Mutes*" [I am well and in good spirits], etc. That's what his people hear of his condition, and all they'll hear until he is no more. Such is German humanity to prisoners, German thoughtfulness, German—German—German! Oh that I might be delivered once and for all from that concept—German! That I could forget it, rub it out of my consciousness!

Frode is working in the SS office at the entrance for a few days, drawing maps of the camp. It isn't an ideal job; he's surrounded by greenhorns all day long. Meanwhile Rolf [Hofmo] and I are camping alone together. Rolf is making key tags. A ridiculous occupation. Also he cooks food and coffee, but now we've nothing more to cook. Our cupboard is quite bare, and for the first time in ages we have only the camp food to live on. Our tobacco is finished too, and we're getting no more *Kleinigkeiten* or parcels. Yet the worst of all is that I don't hear anything from Kari. The Saturday before last I had an empty envelope from Stockholm, and last Saturday one from Budapest. Someone had written to me from these places and written something that failed to pass the censor. So I get only the empty envelopes. Empty envelopes count as letters, and so Kari's letters go into the wastepaper basket. These kind people don't know the harm they're doing me with their well-meaning letters; and I can't let them know.

WEDNESDAY, JANUARY 26, 1944 ■ It's wet and windy just now; horribly raw, cold weather; typical Sachsenhausen. My sweater and leather jacket are what keep me alive. But it's impossible to shake off my cold. I've had it now since before Christmas, and every day I'm just as blocked up again, after shivering and coughing for hours on the roll calls. Many have bronchitis and many are getting pneumonia; several have pleurisy and several no doubt tuberculosis, unfortunately. We've had a remarkably mild winter so far, hardly any frost, but miserably wet and raw with a biting wind blowing everlastingly through one's marrow every day. God knows if frost wouldn't have been better.

I got a parcel yesterday at last after all four of us had been sucking our paws for a long time. A good deal had been stolen out of it, including nearly all the tobacco, but what I did get is coming in very handy. Otherwise I'm well off just now. Designing a cottage for myself and disposing of my time as I please in this shanty of ours.

---

* On December 24, 1943, General Dwight Eisenhower was appointed supreme commander, Allied Expeditionary Forces, charged with the implementation of Operation Overlord, the Allied invasion of northern Europe. At the time of this diary entry D-Day was less than six months away. Only the day before this entry, on January 20, 1944, General Carl Spaatz was appointed supreme commander of all American air forces in Europe.

SUNDAY, JANUARY 30, 1944 ■ Last night and the night before we had big raids on Berlin.* Heavy stuff it must have been, but only rumors of the destruction find their way here. A four-engined English plane crashed near the camp last night. A lot of people saw it; I must have fallen asleep again. Strange that one actually can sleep with hell loose just outside. Otherwise life is more monotonous than ever. Coughing and hawking—with burning pains in the chest and in arms and legs which are stiff with cold—with dull brains and hopelessly staring eyes, we walk the treadmill—day in, day out. But no, not hopeless! Longing keeps us in life and hope.† Thank heaven!

SATURDAY, FEBRUARY 5, 1944 ■ A couple of men arrived here from Natzweiler the other day. Their account of that camp is appalling. Of a transport (the Christmas transport) of a hundred and twenty men from Norway, twenty-nine have died of pneumonia, and fifty of the rest are in the *Revier* with the same disease. Leif [Poulsson] sent word to [Sven] Oftedal by the two who have just arrived that all the Norwegians in Natzweiler are a hundred percent *Muselmenn*.‡

The news is good, but the invasion remains a myth. There are rumors that now it's coming in a matter of weeks. "Churchill says so!" For example fifty-two weeks? Those fellows always put things so that the words hold good, however it goes. But—it will go all right, Kari!

MONDAY, FEBRUARY 7, 1944 ■ It's biting cold, and we're frozen to the bone. But now as always we have to console ourselves with the reflection that we're better off than so many people. I can't get Leif's message from Natzweiler out of my head. They'll die like flies in the spring, he said. He himself must have been very low; he just "stared in front of him with glassy eyes." They have absolutely no medicines for pneumonia! So to be sure our state is "grand" in comparison.

Wild rumors were circulating yesterday—Sunday rumors. Narvik was taken, for example, and a lot of other sensations that are not even worth mentioning.

SATURDAY, FEBRUARY 12, 1944 ■ Two men escaped some time ago, and on that account a *Portionsperre* [ration cut] has been imposed for some time to come. That means we get no bread with our dinner. It's a sheer disaster for the Russians, Ukrainians and some others. For the bread ration is the essential part of the wretched meal allotted us.

I myself by the way have eaten nothing, neither bread, potatoes, nor cabbage, for many days. I'm really bad. Have got *Scheisserei*. All morning I've been lying dozing on a mattress in the next room; I'm so weak and rickety that I can hardly hold myself up.

---

*   RAF Bomber Command claimed that the raid on the night of January 28/29 was the most concentrated attack of this period, with 677 aircraft participating and 46 lost.

†   On December 31, 1893, Fridtjof Nansen wrote while on his polar expedition, "But longing—oh, there are worse things than that! All that is good and beautiful may flourish in its shelter. Everything would be over if we cease to long."

‡   One Norwegian who arrived in Natzweiler in 1944 recalled the remarks of the camp commandant, Fritz Hartjenstein, upon his arrival: "'*Willkommen. Willkommen in Natzweiler, Vernichtungslager Natzweiler*. . . . Natzweiler is not a *Konzentrationslager*, not a concentration camp. It is a *Vernichtungslager*, a destruction camp. . . . Here you will be dealt with . . . exterminated! . . . That is not a threat. To stamp you out is not a promise, even. It is a fact. You are dead. You have already died. You are . . . you are . . . the *already dead*.'" Hartjenstein was convicted by British and French authorities after the war and sentenced to death, but died of a heart attack while awaiting execution.

I've taken twenty-five M. and B. tablets (which Kari once sent me in a parcel) hoping they may do good;* I've been trying to get to the *Revier* the last day or two, but without much success. The thing is that I can't line up for long at a time; every now and then I have to run off to a certain place. It's "exciting" on parade too, but so far I've managed fine.

There has been a collection of money for the camp *Muselmenn.* Instituted by the Commandant. They call it voluntary, but all have to subscribe something to buy food from the canteen. In the first place, there's little or nothing in the canteen with much food value; secondly, the prices are exorbitant, and thirdly, the whole thing simply means that the SS are in want of money. It's all a swindle to get hold of our money in an apparently "honest," even "high-minded," way.

TUESDAY, FEBRUARY 22, 1944 ■ There's no improvement in my dysentery—for that must be what it is. I went to Gløersen, who offered to get me into the *Revier.* I needed quiet and warmth, he said. But in the *Revier* I should only lie shivering (we're not allowed to take any clothes), so I declined with thanks and mean to try and scramble through as best I can outside of the hospital.

On my way to see Henry yesterday, I passed a stretcher with a corpse on it, which had been left in the middle of the path. A corner of the blanket had been blown aside and uncovered a grinning, purple face, emaciated and staring. A dreadful face. The accompaniment to this idyll was a steady stream of chattering prisoners, who took no notice of the stretcher with the corpse, and an earsplitting dance tune from the loudspeakers all over the camp. When I returned from my visit the corpse was still there and the stream of prisoners was passing the other way, noisy and jabbering as ever. The loudspeakers blared on as before, the infuriated porter—a prisoner like ourselves—was in the act of belaboring and cursing a poor Ukrainian, and the purple face of the corpse was staring up at the rainy sky.

Indoors it was no better. All around lay men sick to death. Some were nearly dead already, were just lying struggling with the last vestiges of life. From outside came the bellowing, grotesque rhythm of the loudspeakers, and suddenly the *Blockältester* rushed in roaring like a maniac that visiting time was over, and there must be absolute quiet in this ward; the visitors must leave! I said good-bye to Henry and went off "home" again—past the corpse on the stretcher, out among the line of fellow prisoners, into the crowded hut. What a life!

August the electrician, who was the real head physician and dictator of the *Revier,* and who has many, many lives on his conscience, was caught *in flagranti* in his room the other day with a little Ukrainian boy. He was promptly sent off in a transport. Many are sighing with relief, but life pursues its uneven tenor. Such things too are part of the daily routine.

THURSDAY, FEBRUARY 24, 1944 ■ Since Saturday the world and life have had a changed and brighter hue, after all. I got a letter! No one, absolutely no one, who hasn't been in prison (and such a prison!) can understand the meaning of a letter from home. I

---

* M & B was the generic name given to an antibacterial compound (sulfapyridine or sulphapyridine), so named after a British chemical company, May & Baker, which developed it in 1939. Its use was later superseded by penicillin and sulphonamides. M & B tablets were credited with successfully treating Winston Churchill's pneumonia in late 1943.

almost think it's the most important thing here—even including food. Kari said she had had two letters returned. Those damned empty envelopes!

Yesterday as we were marching in from work there stood by the gate a curious piece of furniture that produced a disagreeable impression at once, even if one didn't know what it was for. It looked much like an ordinary gymnasium horse, only that it was equipped with a great variety of straps. At evening roll call we learned why the horse had been produced. A prisoner was to be publicly flogged.

After we had stood and shivered longer than usual, interpreters of several nationalities were called for. Then a prisoner was announced to have spread a rumor that he had made for the Commandant, in the tailor's shop where he worked, a pair of lady's riding breeches and a lady's blouse. In return he had been given two loaves and eight marks in *Prämier-schein* [coupons], and some cigarettes, no doubt. Therefore the prisoner in question was to have twenty-five blows with a stick, for the rumor was of course false. Then it began. Unfortunately—or thank goodness—our hut falls in at such a distance from the main building that I couldn't see what was happening. But I heard. Heard the blows falling, one by one, heavily and horribly, and one could imagine, or couldn't help imagining, how the thighs and buttocks of the poor victim were being gradually converted into black pudding. And during the last blows the man's roars of agony carried right to where we stood, about a hundred meters [330 ft.] off. I shan't try to describe what I felt in those ghastly minutes. Nausea and fury were contending in me.

Afterward I got a description of the whole thing from a man who had seen it all close up. First the victim was harnessed firmly to the horse. His legs were lashed to the horse's legs, and then the man was doubled over the horse on his belly, and his arms secured. A sack was fastened down over his head and shoulders and a cloth stuffed into his mouth, to prevent his screams from being heard. None the less those who were nearest heard at every blow a heartrending groan, rising finally to one long roar that pierced through all muffling layers. First he was given thirteen blows with "the big stick," a baton in a leather sheath with lead in it. This is wielded by a stout hangman, a hulking fellow whose job it is. He is a prisoner too—and a political prisoner. Then the man was given twelve blows with a smaller stick, no doubt of the same type; this one is wielded by a second hangman—also a prisoner. When the five and twenty had been reached the Commandant announced that he would now get five more as a special bonus from himself. It was then he bawled so loud that it could be heard all over the camp. When that was over too, the man was "unharnessed," and, in spite of the fact that he could hardly stand, had to go up to the *Lagerführer* and himself report that he had received the punishment. Then the *Lagerführer* spat in his face and cursed him for a *Schweinehund*, with which the ceremony was over.

No one believes that the rumor the man spread was a lie; all are convinced that of course he made the riding breeches and the blouse and got the bribe. His crime is that he spoke of it—and obviously to an informer. Now, after the thirty blows, he's going into the SK, which means a slow form of capital punishment. They're beaten every day there, and the weak soon go under. If they get so ill that they have to go into the *Revier*—that's usually the end. Thousands have gone that way before they "went up the chimney."

Had a talk on Sunday, through an interpreter, with a Russian prisoner of war—a lad of twenty, a Jew and medical student. He arrived in this camp just lately with other Russian prisoners of war. In Block 14 where they are still living, all Jews among them were ordered to step forward. He and three or four others did so immediately. Seven more, who had dark hair, were picked out; they had not reported themselves. Two of them were demonstrably Jews, but the fear of death had kept them from stepping forward. The other five were simply, then and there, pronounced to be Jews, and all seven were led away and shot. Those who had reported as Jews were allowed to live, as a reward for "courage and honesty." The *Herrenvolk* are chivalrous.

It was in the *Revier* I came across this man, with some Jewish children I had gone to see. Eleven little boys who, for some reason, have been spared and sent here from Auschwitz. They are all orphans. Their parents were killed in Auschwitz or elsewhere. The children are all right; they get, comparatively speaking, enough to eat, but nothing at all is being done to educate them or fit them for life. If that goes on for long, of course it will be the ruin of them.*

In general, I go and see Henry H[ansen] whenever I can. I don't rightly know whether he's worse or better.

FRIDAY, FEBRUARY 25, 1944 ■ Nothing is happening just now, I believe I wrote the other day. Well, that is by no means an unqualified truth. The smoke rises from the crematorium chimney without a pause, day and night. Many, many people are being shot or otherwise put to death. The young Russian prisoner of war I met in the *Revier* on Sunday was shot the next day with his three comrades, who had also "confessed" that they were Jews. So the reward for their "honesty" was only a few more days of life. A Dutchman has been found out keeping a diary, and that may lead to disaster. I'm wondering if I shouldn't leave off. Stow this away and stop at least for a while. That kind of thing inevitably makes one a bit nervous.

The scandal of all time has cropped up in camp, but has been hushed up again, since a whole crowd of SS and other prominent men are implicated. The Turkish military attaché was arrested some time ago and spent a week here in "storage." He had bought from a *Hauptscharführer* more than two hundred jewels and $120,000. These he placed in the Bank of Turkey. The Commandant here told him that it was all stolen property, stolen in this camp by prisoners, and called on him to give it all back. The military attaché declared that he was ready to do so, but on condition that he received a clear account of where the valuables had come from, whom they belonged to and how prisoners could lay their hands on such things in a prison camp. The affair was hushed up and the man released.

THURSDAY, MARCH 16, 1944 ■ A few words once more. So much has happened that I must unburden my memory.

---

* The Jewish boys were selected at Auschwitz, many immediately upon arrival at the ramp, by Dr. Arnold Dohmen, to be used as "guinea-pigs" in his medical experiments to determine the cause of hepatitis, which had reached epidemic proportions among German troops by 1941. All eleven survived, in no small part to the interventions of Drs. Sven Oftedal and Per Græsli, and Norwegian Per Roth, a medical assistant in the infirmary. After the war many of these children (whose families had all been killed) emigrated abroad, including to Israel and the United States. As previously noted, both Oftedal and Græsli died prematurely as a result of the mistreatment they experienced in the camps: Græsli in 1945 (age forty-two) and Oftedal in 1948 (age forty-three). Although Per Roth arrived in Sachsenhausen severely injured as a result of brutal interrogations, he recovered and after the war reunited with five survivors in 1995 on the fiftieth anniversary of Sachsenhausen's liberation. A criminal investigation was begun on Dohmen in 1972, who continued to practice internal medicine in Germany, but he was never charged. Dohmen died in 1980, age seventy-three.

I think the first uncommon event after I "laid down my arms" was a vigorous day raid on Berlin. It took place in brilliant sunshine and was, I think, the first raid on Berlin by day.* Two prisoners—one of them Norwegian—and an SS driver were killed. Those were the first air-raid casualties in our camp. I wonder how many there will be before it's all over?

The next important thing, I believe, was the derangement of our idyllic existence up in the "corner." Our "kommando" has been dissolved, and Frode, Rolf and I are scattered to the winds. Rolf went back to his original job, *Holzhacking* [chopping wood]. Frode went into the *Malerei* [drawing], where he's to do placards and of course draw privately for the SS, and I've been placed as a *Schreiber* [clerk] in the *Tischlerei* [carpenters' workshop], that is I have to sit (where I am now) in a glass case of microscopic dimensions along with an *Unterscharführer*, working out the cubic content of all the wood being used in the workshop. A completely imbecile job! Every chip is included; the cubic meter has to be worked out to six decimal points! Also I have to make an occasional drawing of a cottage or a cupboard and so forth. Compared with the habits I had formed in our cozy little room this is a frightful job, but compared with the usual jobs in camp it's one of the very best that could be wished for. The same applies to Frode's, and Rolf also has got nicely settled in to the further manufacture of key tags, in his new place. But it was a frightful transition. Just sitting with that SS man all day is sufficient punishment, and when you add that I have to sit with one buttock practically on the stove, and that the cage, in a corner of the workshop, is a rendezvous for all kinds of greenery all day long, it becomes clear that I'm in some despair at the change. Luckily there are some nice prisoners in this workshop.

However, almost at the moment of this "dissolution" both Frode and I fell really ill. I was the first; I got a very bad throat that took away my voice for several days, and into the bargain it turned out that I had a severe attack of bronchitis. I went to the *Revier* and obtained a *Schonung* the very day after I'd started on my new job. I was at home five or six weeks. The day after that, Frode got scarlet fever. He's in the *Revier* and will probably remain there six weeks. Erik has bronchitis too, so none of us is in very fine fettle.

Last week a ghastly scene was enacted on the parade ground. A man was hanged during evening roll call. When we marched in from work the gallows was already set up on "Tyburn," where the Christmas tree stood. The poor man, who was a professional criminal, had run away and been caught with weapons on him; therefore he was now to be hanged, they announced in various languages. Then it took place. In the searchlight we saw two men up in the space under the gallows, the hangman and his victim. (The gallows was a stout wooden hoop.) We saw the noose put round his neck, saw him fall . . . but he didn't swing, the rope gave way and the man fell right onto the ground, where he sat groaning and clutching at his neck, until an SS man, they say the Commandant himself,

---

* The first daylight raid on Berlin was conducted by the US Army Air Force on March 6, 1944, and was called by Berliners "Bloody Monday." The raid has been called "the turning point in the air war." The damage inflicted on German air forces on this and two follow-up raids in March spelled, in the words of Albert Speer's biographer "very nearly the end of the Luftwaffe." Daylight bombing afforded the Berliners the first opportunity to actually see their attackers and induced a new sense of fear inasmuch as many Berliners were out or at work during the day and away from loved ones and nighttime shelters.

went up and shot him through the head. Even that, they say, didn't finish him. He was shot over again in the *Industriehof* [factory yard], where the "daily" executions take place.*

Yesterday we received Swedish parcels. Not long ago we had a Danish parcel. So we're not short of food.

WEDNESDAY, MARCH 22, 1944 ■ It's two or three o'clock, and we've just experienced a raid at close quarters. Four storage and workshop huts are on fire, also the SS *Wirtschaftsgebäude* [farm building] and an SS dwelling hut. One of the *Fahrbereitschaft* workshops has had its walls and doors blown out. As usual during an alert all the prisoners had to go to the dining hut, where we were packed like herrings in a barrel. It didn't last very long, but those were strange, compressed minutes. When it was over all *Reichsdeutscher* [Reich Germans] and *Norweger* [Norwegians] were ordered on clearance work. The others had to stay behind. Only "Teutons" are asked for in such cases. So we had a chance to inspect it all at the closest range. I don't think there were many who did much work. The matchwood houses were burning merrily, and the whole of the SS dining hut and (as I said) four storage and workshop huts went up, tools and all. The fires are still burning as I write.

THURSDAY, MARCH 23, 1944 ■ Bombs also fell on the prison camp. Half of one hut was burned down, otherwise only minor damage. They say that one man was killed and four taken to the *Revier* with serious injuries. What is certain is that a prisoner was shot for stealing from the ruins. He was caught in the act and shot then and there. No one sees anything strange in that. Served him right, is all they say, with a shrug of the shoulders. The SS and the prisoners appear to be of one mind on this form of justice. I think however that most Norwegians still react against such things. The man shot was a wretched, starving Ukrainian, who saw a loaf that would have burned up in any case.†

SATURDAY, MARCH 25, 1944 ■ I've had a message from Natzweiler, from Leif [Poulsson]. He is ill. He says that if they don't get some medicines, they'll all die like flies during the spring. I've written to Kari, asking her to do all she can to get some drugs for Leif.‡

MONDAY, MARCH 27, 1944 ■ Sunday passed like other Sundays—or weekdays. Most people sleep. I went sick-visiting as usual. Frode is practically well again. He's flaking off now—and has three or four weeks' "vacation" to look forward to. He's heard from

---

* The *Industriehof* was a special area of Sachsenhausen; fenced off from the rest of the camp, it contained the execution trench, shooting facility, gallows, gas chamber, and crematoria. One Sachsenhausen inmate wrote, "Even the victims [of the *Industriehof*] were initially oblivious to where they were going; most were taken there in trucks, or made to walk, along a circuitous route that obscured their destination."

† The night of March 24/25 marked the "swan song" of the Battle of Berlin. Despite immense devastation (almost one-half million Berliners left homeless), the Royal Air Force also suffered unsustainable losses in aircraft and crews. Although bombing of Berlin would continue until the closing days of the war, the Battle of Berlin ended with a defeat for the RAF. "It was just too tough a nut," in the words of one British airman. Beginning in April 1944, Allied air forces were largely diverted to the run-up for Operation Overlord, the cross-channel assault scheduled for June 1944.

‡ The letter arrived. Kari went to Professor Dale who got 400 parcels of drugs sent from Astra to Norwegians in Natzweiler. O.N.

home and found out that Hannagreta has also been sent to Germany. She is in Ravensbrück and probably he'll soon be in contact with her.*

Went to see Henry [Hansen]. *He* has actually improved, and an attempt to get him released and sent home positively seems to be making headway. He's conceived a little hope of it himself, and that helps him on. God grant they can arrange it!

THURSDAY, MARCH 30, 1944 ■ It's hard to do any writing. This confounded glass cage I sit in is full of greenery all day. They come in waves, several at a time, sit down on my drawing table, on the drawing board, sprawl over the stove, fart, belch, and scream, crack jokes, and have their all-Germanic, *grossartig* [marvelous] fun. They're a ghastly lot.

MONDAY, APRIL 3, 1944 ■ Had a splendid letter from Kari yesterday; radiant with joyous optimism. In August—by our *weddingtag* [wedding day], she writes, we'll be together again. It's extraordinary what an effect such letters have. If only they could come a little more often!

WEDNESDAY, APRIL 5, 1944 ■ A prison transport arrived from Auschwitz the other day. It was a ghastly sight. Living skeletons! All except the cook, who was round and fat. He had done the eating for his friends and was immediately "subjected to treatment" here—poor devil! There was a collection of food for them the night they came. They hadn't tasted food for more than three days. They had to be fed cautiously, for they couldn't stand it, starving as they were. So many Lazaruses. Now the camps in Poland are being evacuated . . .

SUNDAY, APRIL 9, 1944 ■ Anniversary†—and Easter Day! What an anniversary and what an Easter! But to hell with it! I had another letter from Kari yesterday. The most glorious letter in the world, full of immortality. It made me so happy. But in the very midst of this rush of joy I got inexpressibly sad news: Henry Hansen is dying. At this moment he may be dead, and I shall never see him again. He was such a splendid fellow, and he fought more gallantly than anyone I've ever seen, but it was no use.

MONDAY, APRIL 10, 1944 ■ I went to see Henry yesterday, but we had had our last talk. He wasn't conscious, was simply fighting his last battle, alone. Henry's bed is just inside the outer door of the ward—in the middle of the traffic, and it was Sunday and visiting time. Prisoners were streaming out and in—it's a big ward, with a lot of visitors. They were elbowing their way as usual; what was it to them that a prisoner lay dying? One of seventeen thousand. They didn't even know him. Besides, they were going to see their own friends, who might be dying too—might be dead already. A window stood open—a little fresh air oozed in like an invisible streak of cold in the oppressive reek that filled the room. And along with this cold air, something else made its way into the sickroom—

---

* Opened in 1939, Ravensbrück concentration camp, approximately fifty miles north of Berlin, was designed primarily to hold women prisoners; it was the second largest women's concentration camp in the German system (only Auschwitz was larger). More than 150,000 prisoners from more than forty countries passed through Ravensbrück by 1945; tens of thousands died from neglect, malnutrition, medical experiments, and gassings—by some estimates as many as 93,000. The last commandant of Ravensbrück, Fritz Suhren, was hanged in 1950.

† Of the German invasion of Norway, 1940.

merry strains from the loudspeaker outside. A shrill, German, female voice with a whole chorus of bellows. And there before me—doubled up under his blanket—Henry lay dying. He stretched his arms out, groping in front of him. I took his hands in mine, stroked his forehead, and pronounced his name. Yes—he quieted down; obviously he had been seeking something and had found it.

Someone gave me a shove, so that I fell forward and had to let go Henry's hands to save myself. And suddenly I realized where I was—in the middle of the crush even here—by a dying friend's bed. Despair seized me in the end, a feeling of impotent revolt against this devilry boiled within me; it was more than I could stand. For the last time I knelt down at his bedside, for the last time I took his cold hands in mine; I stroked his forehead once again, then I turned and fled, out into the turmoil and the crush. I didn't see him again. He died that night at quarter past one.*

Frode is doing well. He'll be in bed another fortnight. Of course we go and see him every Sunday.

WEDNESDAY, APRIL 12, 1944 ■ Everyone in camp is coughing. It's a dangerous climate. The nights and mornings on the parade ground are bitter cold, often below zero [32° F], while the days may work up to a tropical heat. We're now forbidden to wear a coat in fine weather. So at morning roll call and in the early part of the day we're all so cold that our teeth chatter. Naturally, we fall ill. Many are dying. The score is getting worse and worse.

They're bombing and bombing, more and more and oftener and oftener.†

MONDAY, APRIL 17, 1944 ■ There was an "international" yesterday and tremendous feeling. Norway-Germany. For a long time Norway was leading 3-1, and the feeling had reached dangerous heights, but then the Norwegians collapsed and the Germans caught up and more. 5-3 was the result. Which was just as well, or we should doubtless have been paid back somehow or other. It was strange to look on at the match and observe the "international atmosphere" surging through all this wretchedness. Grotesque like everything else. Being a footballer is salvation to a lot of men; they're handled with velvet gloves, given choice jobs and lots to eat, while others are becoming *Muselmenn* and going under.

TUESDAY, APRIL 18, 1944 ■ Erik and Arvid have both got *Schonung*; they're pickled in chills and bronchitis and their voices are gone. I'm beginning to go seedy again myself. It's hopeless to keep well here; and after I promised Kari!

Yesterday a large contingent of BV-ers left here, released to go to the front. Felons and scum are now being enrolled with marks of esteem and comradely gestures. They were presented with gifts and flowers, and were filmed outside the main entrance before leaving. Murderers, men condemned to death, dangerous enemies of society—now they're

---

* Nansen dedicated *From Day to Day* in part to Henry Hansen. He would have turned forty-three the next day (April 11).

† Sixty percent of all bombs dropped over Germany fell after July 1944. A member of the counterfeiter commando in Sachsenhausen described the step up in bombings during April and May 1944: "Day and night, the drone of the B-17s told us that the time of vengeance against the Germans was near. The sound of the engines was music to our ears."

Kameraden; now they're off to fight for *das grosse Vaterland* [the great Fatherland] and *die deutsche Ehre* [German honor]!*

WEDNESDAY, APRIL 19, 1944 ■ We had a terrible raid yesterday just after I'd left off writing; the Heinkel camp was the target.† The workshops there were hit. Four of them, it's reported. But what's worse—a lot of prisoners were killed and a lot more wounded. For so devilish are the arrangements in that camp that the shelters are underneath the halls. A bomb fell in one shelter that holds a thousand men, and they say another was flooded when the water pipe burst. All the doctors were mobilized and seem to have worked all night. So far they're said to have counted about four hundred killed and a hundred injured. Blood transfusions were asked for on a big scale, and a great number of prisoners volunteered. Including many Norwegians.‡

Here in the *Kraftfahrzeugdepot* and other *Waldkommandos* [forest kommandos] the raid was little more than a superb spectacle. Swarm after swarm of planes we saw, high up against the blue; they seemed to be coming from all sides, and the "flak" was thundering. We saw some planes crash to earth; it looked quite unreal. One burst into flames; it flew on, while the crew jumped out with parachutes. Gradually there were a lot of parachutes unfolding, floating high in the air, and gleaming chalk white in the sunshine. The sky was dotted all over with aircraft and exploding shells. It was like a miracle that no more were shot down. We saw only five crash, and there were hundreds of planes. A few immense explosions shook the whole world, but they were a long way off, we saw nothing but the pillars of smoke from the fires in every direction. The *Rottenführer* gave us permission to take cover, that is, we were allowed to go down into a shelter nearby. There they simply threw us out again—for it was packed with SS. Those valiant knights who should have been on duty with steel helmets and extinguishers. We got no cover but what we could obtain by crawling under cars and machines and lying on the ground against the walls of the huts. Cover was highly necessary, and it was almost a miracle that no one was hit by shrapnel, which suddenly began hailing down all round us.

All the time we kept an eye on the scene overhead, and on the parachutes drifting down. One landed on a roof close by the SS camp. It was a young American airman. He got a fairly courteous reception. Another fell by the canal in the *Herzaskommando* [Ace of Hearts kommando];§ he came off worse. I talked to a Norwegian who had seen him falling. When he was thirty or forty meters [100–130 ft.] from the ground, some German

---

* "*Meine Ehre heißt Treue*," "My honor is called loyalty" was the motto of the SS. The use of this phrase is now illegal in Germany.

† The Heinkel *Flugzeugwerke* (Aircraft Works) was the largest satellite subcamp of Sachsenhausen, employing at its peak almost 7,000 prisoners in the manufacture of military aircraft. It is estimated that by early 1945 approximately 230,000 of the 799,000 concentration camp prisoners were involved in Germany's armaments industry; the military aircraft industry was the single largest employer of concentration camp inmates. See February 26, 1945, below.

‡ Dr. Sven Oftedal is credited, along with Dr. Per Græsli, with setting up a blood donation system in which about one hundred inmates participated, most being Norwegians (who were favored because of their better nutritional levels). Donors were given an extra ration of soup and up to two days off from work.

§ The *Herz As* (Heart's Ace or Ace of Hearts) was a large building (a "magnificent but repulsive structure") constructed in the forest near Sachsenhausen, which "accommodated a wireless installation for communication with German [SS] personnel everywhere in the world and its design reflected its strategic importance. . . . The steeply raked roof was five and a half meters [18 ft.] thick; the walls were four meters [13 ft.] thick; the floor plate, four and a half meters [14.75 ft.]; and the inside walls, three meters [10 ft.] thick. The whole building was placed in a young forest, so carefully camouflaged." The origin of this name for the communications center is unknown.

NCOs began shooting at him with revolvers. They missed. When he reached the ground, put up his hands, and advanced toward the Germans, they went to meet him. A blow in the face was the first greeting he received. That was from the civilian German *Bauleiter*. Then came others of the same kind, from other NCOs. They beat him up well, and afterward tore off his uniform. He was left in no doubt of where he'd got to. At length, on the arrival of a *Sturmbannführer*, this treatment came to an end, and he was led away. The *Herrenvolk* had had a chance to air their military honor.

SUNDAY, APRIL 23, 1944 ■ Both the notorious birthday and the days after it passed off quietly.* Indeed things seem to be quieter everywhere. But it may be just as well. For one thing it may mean calm before the storm.

Frode fell ill again yesterday. Fever and influenza through his whole body. Erik is back on the job. Arvid too. They're tolerably well.

MONDAY, APRIL 24, 1944 ■ Frode went back into the *Revier* yesterday. On parade he was already so ill that he had to be helped away. We "called on him" later through the window. He was very bad, poor chap.

THURSDAY, APRIL 27, 1944 ■ Yesterday I was summoned to the political section, and on that account had to stay "at home" in the camp all day. Oh no, it had no connection with *Entlassung*, as of course everyone instantly felt sure. I've broken myself of such ideas. It was something quite different. Kari had sent a letter to the Commandant (she's not backward!) with some photographs of the little one, and asked him in her usual elegant German to let me see the pictures. They were wonderful pictures. The baby looks grand, and I'm going about like a proud cock, showing him to everyone. It wrings one's heart to see these pictures from home, but at the same time it's so infinitely good!

On that occasion I also learned a couple of the reasons why I was sent here. The SS clerk read out a couple of "stanzas" from my *Schutzhaftbefehl* [prison order]: "Pro-Jewish," it said, and "during detention composed an anti-German poem." Good Lord! So they had to fall back on that to get something on me! They must indeed have been keen to get me here. The anti-German part of the Grini march must be the bit about justice,† and it's nice they should admit it themselves.

Yesterday a man was hanged at evening roll call. A Pole who had escaped and been caught again. Once more the "technical apparatus" missed fire. This time the rope was too long, so that when the prisoner fell his feet were touching the ground. Someone dug a hole under them, so that he should hang free. Once more I abstain from trying to describe the impression made on me by this scene.

FRIDAY, APRIL 28, 1944 ■ An action seems to be going on against all Bible-searchers. There are a good many of them in this camp. Apparently they've been issuing a leaflet that says the "leader" will die on a certain day, presumably in the near future. Some of these leaflets are said to have been found within the camp. The object of the action was to get hold of them. As we marched in from work yesterday, all the Bible-searchers

---

* Hitler's fifty-fifth was on April 20.
† Let all voices ring / For our liberty, our laws! / Our mother-wit, still as it was / For justice and its cause!

were picked out, lined up along the square, and *filzet*, that is undressed and searched from top to toe. A number of other prisoners seem to have been taken aside and searched in the same way. There was not a little nervousness among us as we marched in through a gauntlet of SS, *Blockälteste*, and even Gestapists, drawn up in rows between every file of the marching column. For most of us had pipes, cigarette holders, matches and tobacco. All forbidden things.

TUESDAY, MAY 2, 1944 ■ Every Sunday there are football matches. Internationals and other matches. Last Sunday it was Norway-Czechoslovakia and Germany-Poland. Norway won. Poland lost. These matches are hot work now and then. The blood gets up, and sometimes the players go at each other with their fists. In the match between Poland and Germany two players had to leave the field for using their fists, after another two had been carried off disabled. The Poles are red hot against the Germans. Yesterday the teams were composite, Germany-Czechoslovakia against Norway-Poland. The match had to be stopped owing to a pitched battle between the players. They were rolling in the mud of the square and going for each other, while the rain poured down, the referee's whistle squeaked, and the public bellowed. A fine match! Close by people are lying on their deathbeds. Sachsenhausen!

I witnessed a typical little Sachsenhausen idyll yesterday. While the football match was at its height, two prisoners came by with a dead body on a stretcher. Down the whole length of the square, past the roaring onlookers. Suddenly the bearers also became intensely interested in the match. They put down the corpse, each lit his "butt," and they began to follow the game. Then the exciting moment passed, they took up the corpse and pursued their way to the mortuary, to the merry strains of an operetta from the whole chorus of loudspeakers.

SATURDAY, MAY 6, 1944 ■ Yesterday ten of the old *Blockälteste*, formerly condemned for treasonable conspiracy, were sent on a "transport"—that is, a punishment kommando to Klinker.* No doubt a number were yahoos, and they are all Germans. There are only German *Blockälteste*.

A change of system has been going on in camp. The Communist regime has been superseded by a criminal regime. There has always been a struggle for power between the green triangles and the red triangles in camp. Now the green triangles have scored another victory through informing and other devilment, and the red triangles, dominated chiefly by Communists, have been removed from all the leading positions and replaced by green

---

* The *Klinker Grossziegelwerke* (or *Klinkerwerke*), designed to be the world's largest brick factory, was not far from the main camp at Sachsenhausen. Up to 3,500 prisoners worked in the brickworks kommando. Initially intended to supply bricks for massive public works envisioned by Hitler and Speer for after the war, production was instead constantly increased to provide building materials for urban areas steadily destroyed by aerial bombardment; still later the brickworks were used for armaments manufacture, where the large ovens were used to harden shells. Conditions in the *Klinkerwerke* were particularly grim. One Sachsenhausen prisoner observed that "there was not a day that did not bring a death." In fact, Klinker was known as a "death camp," to which authorities in Sachsenhausen consigned prisoners whom they wished to eliminate. The complex was destroyed by Allied bombing on April 4, 1945. The director of the *Klinkerwerke*, Heinrich Freesemann, was particularly brutal, having once killed an American flyer for smoking a cigarette during his interrogation. Freesemann was sentenced to life imprisonment by a Soviet military tribunal after the war; he died in the Vorkuta Gulag in Russia in 1948.

triangles, who are all professional criminals. The Communists were not good, but the criminals are worse, so we have a gloomy prospect.

A Norwegian died the other day after being thrown out of the *Revier* with pneumonia. Twice he went back in and was moved out; the third time he died. An everyday story. Only this time it was a Norwegian, and Norwegians usually get better treatment—for some reason. The other day there was *Filzing* in one kommando. All Norwegians were ordered out of the ranks before it started. We were let off the search. It didn't make us popular.

Frode is out of the *Revier* again, thin, but still going strong. We must get him fattened up.

SUNDAY, MAY 7, 1944 ■ Now the tobacco shortage is glaring. And all round. Erik, Scott and I are all in an equally bad way. We've all sunk to "Mahorka" level. "Mahorka" is canteen tobacco, which means that it has little connection with tobacco, extremely little; it both tastes and smells of death and the devil. But we can "buy" it in the canteen. The "buying" consists in so much being allotted to us, for example seven cigarettes each or a third of a packet of "pipe tobacco," and for that we have to pay pretty much all we have. We earn up to three reichsmarks a month, but all of it is dead sure to vanish on "tobacco" and "beer" before we can take a breath. The "beer" is a sweet liquid, with nothing about it to suggest beer except the color and a lot of stiff froth on top. Good? Far from it, but it's not water, and so far it has been cold, and as I said, we can "buy" that in the canteen, and mustard can be bought too—whole tubs of mustard.

Today by Jove it's Sunday again—horn music and all. For every Sunday the prison orchestra plays on the square when we march out to work and when we come back at dinnertime—but that's all that happens.

MONDAY, MAY 8, 1944 ■ My writing was interrupted yesterday by a raid, but no bombs fell here. It was Berlin that got it again, and the prison camp of Lichtenfelde—that is, prisoners from there, who were working in the Albrechtstrasse in Berlin (the Gestapo headquarters).* Last night a load of corpses was driven into this camp.

There was an entertainment in [Block] 25 yesterday, and I took part. It was fun. But it's terrible to think that while we were doing that, in the mortuary of the *Revier* they were busy shoveling corpses onto a truck. The bodies were so mutilated that they couldn't even count how many there were. Those were the remains of our "comrades," who had gone out to work that very morning at the same time as we did. It's enough to drive one to complete despair when one pulls oneself together occasionally and looks things in the face as they really are. In fact one mustn't do it, not like that; one couldn't go on. Therefore it's right to sing songs while others shovel away corpses.

---

* Hermann Göring, who formed the Secret State Police (**Ge**heime **Sta**ats**po**lizei or Gestapo) in 1933, established its headquarters at Prinz Albrechtstrasse 8, the site of the former School of Industrial Arts and Crafts, soon after the Nazis seized power (its choice was dictated by its proximity to Göring's office and residence). Described as a typical, elegant Wilhelmine mansion, the "house prison" set up in its basement held fifteen thousand political prisoners during its existence; it "very swiftly came to epitomize the Nazi 'terror,'" where "not only the specialized [torture] hardware, but also the specialist torturers were to be found." The building was heavily damaged by Allied bombing during the war and later razed. The site now houses the permanent Topography of Terror Museum. Prinz Albrechtstrasse was renamed Niederkirchnerstrasse in 1951.

WEDNESDAY, MAY 10, 1944 ■ The mortality in camp is getting higher and higher. Lately two or three hundred have died in the *Revier* every month, besides all those who are executed daily or die "in transport," as it's called when they are disposed of by gas or otherwise here in camp. Several Norwegians, too, have died recently. Mostly of pneumonia. This is a perilous climate. Bitter cold at night and sometimes burning hot in the daytime. The fare has been improved somewhat, to stimulate production, but if we hadn't had the parcels from home and from the different Red Cross centers, it would have been a bad job.

Talking of production. Working hours have now been lengthened again. We work from five or six in the morning until six or seven at night. We get up at four and go to bed about nine, and there is no form of rest, except for some few whose jobs permit them to sneak a nap at intervals. To increase production, as I say, the fare is somewhat improved. In spite of which it would be no exaggeration to say that production is from zero to twenty-five percent of normal. The state and temper of the great majority of SS men is slack and indifferent. They don't give a damn, and take the lead in sabotage and laziness. I myself am doing nothing nowadays. Now and then I lie down on a plank in the sun and go to sleep. Today a disabled SS man with one leg came and woke me up. He advised me to lie somewhere else, where nobody could see me, and recommended a big truck in the middle of the square. Frode and I—he woke Frode too—followed his advice. So it goes. While others in other kommandos and other camps are fagging their lives out and dying of hunger and undernourishment. All we can do is to register the cold, sober fact that we've been lucky, very lucky. We lead a life of sheer idleness—and *our* effort isn't going to win any wars.

THURSDAY, MAY 11, 1944 ■ Yesterday I got three big wonder parcels from Sweden. I've no idea who sent them. Goose liver and all kinds of treasures, even real American cigarettes, which were in terrific demand. For a fleeting moment we're all right for smokes again. Invasion gossip fills the atmosphere, and on the whole we're all in the grip of an immense optimism. Or is it only that I've had some tobacco?

TUESDAY, MAY 16, 1944 ■ The rumors went on buzzing and reached their climax on Sunday, when the invasion was announced in the north, south and west. Monday brought its usual cold shower, and yet there's something in the air; I can't get rid of the feeling that things will soon break out in earnest, and now it isn't just the tobacco and letters from Kari.

Erik, Frode, Scott and I, as well as Finn Aanesen,* who has shared our *spin* lately, have been moved from B-wing into A-wing. For now the whole block is Norwegian. A number of prisoners of different nations have been moved out, and now we live in style, with excellent bunks and plenty of room at the table. For the first time in over half a year we've been able to sit down and eat in peace without jogging the next man at every bite, without being spattered with porridge and sprinkled with soup from all the *Schüsseln* passing over our heads, and without being used as "shoe polishers" by all who sat on the inner side of

---

* Arrested for resistance activities in 1941, Aanesen, an engineer, had received his BS in mechanical engineering from the University of Wisconsin in 1921. While at school, he and a group of Norwegian students built the first university ski jump and set many Wisconsin skiing records. After the war Aanesen wrote to a classmate in the United States: "[The rescue by the white buses] was quite a wonderful experience, because none of us really hoped to ever get back."

the bench and walked on it, when getting in or out, in their heavy clog boots—covered with mud and dust. Why, our new conditions are quite grand.

SATURDAY, MAY 27, 1944 ▪ I've been given so-called *Hafterleichterung* [improvement in prison conditions], which consists of two extra pieces of bread a day. I've had no official news of this distinction, notice it only from the extra bread ration, which lies awaiting me every day on my return "home." As I can do without more bread, I give it away. There are plenty in need of it. What further privileges my "new appointment" carries, I don't yet know. They say I shall be allowed to write long, ordinary letters home. What am I to write in them? If at least it meant permission to receive home letters unlimited? But no, I don't suppose it means that. I must look into it today. For this is Saturday—suppose I can write home tomorrow!

I have mentioned that we're being distinctly better fed lately. Yet almost every day we see someone carried off the square at roll call, fainting, dying, or dead from exhaustion, hunger and misery. Those who have been here a long time, and especially those who have no contact with their homes and get no food parcels, are completely, irretrievably undermined, and a slight improvement in the fare is not enough to set them on their feet again. In the *Revier* it isn't often that anybody troubles about them when they're carried in. They get a bed to die in, that's all.

SUNDAY, MAY 28, 1944 ▪ Had a letter yesterday. Kari describes the christening, and how the central figure behaved in church, where he strolled about during the sermon and had a glorious time inside the altar rails. Heavens, what wouldn't I have given to be there, and at the party afterward at Polhøgda!

Kari isn't getting my letters. The last that reached her was of February 16th, she writes. What can be the reason? I get hers now fairly regularly once a fortnight, and it's a great help.

Today is Whitsunday. The only sign is that the SS are crapulent. They had a big Whitsun Eve yesterday. A *Sturmbannführer* in mufti and an *Obersturmführer* had had several over the eight.* They got into a car and drove amok. First they knocked down a gate, then they drove full tilt into a column of prisoners and knocked down a prisoner. The others had to look after him, while the two drunks drove on as before. It was only a prisoner, and he wasn't even Germanic!

TUESDAY, MAY 30, 1944 ▪ Now the air-raid warnings are coming more and more regularly, every day and every night, and more and more I'm getting to believe that *that* is the "second front."

WEDNESDAY, MAY 31, 1944 ▪ So May has gone too, just like that—and midsummer is drawing near. Light summer nights—flowery dresses—warmth and fragrance in the air. The mere thought of violets and lilies of the valley and all the other flowers at home calls up the most wonderful pictures—and memories. But this is Sachsenhausen—nothing, nothing but dusty, filthy, ghastly Sachsenhausen. And nothing happens.

---

* In British military slang "one over the eight" meant one drink too many, that is, intoxicated, the presumption being that the average soldier could safely drink eight pints of beer but no more.

TUESDAY, JUNE 6, 1944 ■ *The invasion started this morning!* In Normandy.* From both sides there were bulletins at noon about heavy fighting. Large forces are said to have been landed from the early hours onward. Also a great number of parachute troops, of course. There is no report of whether they've succeeded in establishing a bridgehead.

It came like thunder from a clear sky. I'd almost given up the idea of that everlasting invasion, that second front that has been haunting our minds for almost three years, and now it's really started! Imagine the inferno! Our own experience of air warfare can be nothing but a pale reflection of the hell now spreading in Normandy, and out over the rest of unhappy France.

WEDNESDAY, JUNE 7, 1944 ■ Yes, one can talk of a festive atmosphere this seventh of June, cynical as it may appear in view of the horrors now being enacted in the West. But there's no denying it, the camp is as though bewitched. People are whistling, singing, smiling, joking; a mood of gaiety has completely gotten the upper hand, and from now on the days will no longer be gray and endless. The decision is approaching, perhaps with giant strides.

THURSDAY, JUNE 8, 1944 ■ Just now the state of affairs in camp is not very pleasant. The action against the German Communists who held most of the key positions is still going on.† Several block leaders have been degraded and sent to other camps—the statement is, to Lieberose,‡ "where they'll be lumped together."§ Instead of these a whole troop of gangsters have been installed. Men who have "sold" themselves to a so-called *Sonderkommission* [special commission], to act as spies and in other shady capacities. In general the "leadership" has again passed to the BV-ers, or criminals. Two or three prize gangsters have been appointed *Lagerälteste*. The head of the police and *Luftschutz* [air raid defense] is a criminal. A ghastly type. A new era of punishments, such as gymnastics for those who put their hands in their pockets, etc., has been introduced. Scott had to take part last Sunday for asking a foreman (also a green triangle) to kiss his arse. These "punishment gymnastics" are conducted by the felon-general and are simply hellish. A bigger insult to political prisoners than being ordered by incendiaries and burglars to crawl about and roll in the filth of Sachsenhausen can scarcely be imagined.

There are rumors of "mass executions" in camp now. Mass executions of Communists.

---

* Operation Overlord, the Allied invasion of Europe, was the largest amphibious invasion in history. More than five thousand ships and twelve thousand aircraft were involved, landing and supporting more than 150,000 troops along five beaches on the Normandy coast of France on June 6, 1944. Allied forces were commanded by General Dwight Eisenhower. Within a month more than a million men, 150,000 vehicles, and 500,000 tons of supplies had been landed on the coast of France.

† In April 1944 a Gestapo special commission was set up to investigate an underground communist resistance organization in the camp. This resulted in the execution in October 1944 of numerous communist functionaries, *Blockälteste*, and others, and the transport in October 1944 of another 103 inmates to Mauthausen, a particularly feared camp.

‡ Lieberose was a subcamp of Sachsenhausen in Brandenburg, Germany, seventy-five miles southeast of Berlin. Note that hereafter in the original text Nansen mistakenly refers to it as Liberose.

§ Because most prisoner functionaries maintained their position through sheer terror, once demoted their days were often numbered. No less an eminence in camp administration than Himmler once explained in a speech: "Okay, so one man is the responsible supervisor . . . with power over thirty, forty, over a hundred other prisoners. Once he becomes a Kapo, he no longer sleeps together with them. It's his responsibility to see to it that they reach the performance target. . . . So, he has to push his men. The moment we're not satisfied with him, he's no longer a Kapo, and he goes back to sleep with his men. But he knows full well that he'll be murdered by them the first night."

One must hope and believe those are only rumors. "But the air is thick." One has to be cautious all round. Mustn't talk invasion or smile.

We've also been forbidden to give food away to anyone from Eastern Europe, that is to Poles, Ukrainians, Russians or Czechs. There is to be a guard between the Norwegian huts every evening, to prevent anyone in these categories from entering the street between the huts. The guards are being equipped with rubber truncheons and are to go for these poor wretches whom starvation and misery have driven to the edge of the abyss. It's appalling. But the worst is that there are Norwegians here who think it right and proper, and trounce them roundly. Still, a good many do help to feed the starved when no one is looking. So I should hope—living as we do in abundance. What lies behind this senseless prohibition is that the Germans themselves want to get hold of the Norwegians' food. All the newly appointed block leaders with their whole rabble of henchmen can be bought for food, cigarettes, soap, etc. Certainly the Communist block leaders were rotten and degraded, too—most of them anyhow—but these are worse.

The *Unterscharführer* in this kommando, who shares my cubicle all day, thinks exclusively and all the time of girls and unfaithfulness. Last night one of his wenches wrote on his cigarette case, in English, "I love you." He had no idea what it meant, and asked me this morning. I told him it meant kiss my arse. His jaw dropped notably and I let it drop.

FRIDAY, JUNE 9, 1944 ■ Things are going the right way in the West; one may now take it as established that they've got a firm and lasting foothold on land. When one hears of this, the biggest and most difficult military operation of all time, one has an overpowering sense of the masterly way in which the whole thing was planned and carried out. All one's forebodings are dispelled, and nothing remains but an overwhelming impression of crushing superiority.

The SS, especially [*Rottenführer*] Follmann, were very greatly cast down both yesterday and the day before; today, however, they've screwed themselves up several pegs. Follmann tells us that all the parachute troops are now being completely exterminated, and the enemy's losses are so great that the landing craft arrive with the white flag up! Now, moreover, the German Air Force is to be thrown in seriously, and so on, and so on. They'll be listening to that today and tomorrow, then no doubt they'll be cast down afresh, and braced afresh with fresh propaganda.

SATURDAY, JUNE 10, 1944 ■ Rolf Nissen, a young student at our table in the block, died the other day.* He was the fourth to die of those who sat at our table in B-wing. The fourth out of twenty-three. But it's no use pausing to think of that. And we don't; we go on living and forget as well as we can. Now and then it strikes me as creepy how well we can.

SUNDAY, JUNE 11, 1944 ■ A biggish transport to Natzweiler, which was to have left at this time and with which a good many Norwegians were being sent, has been postponed for a month. Those who were to go are happy. Now it isn't likely that anything will come of it. Alsace is far west!

---

* Arrested November 29, 1942, Nissen died May 29, 1944, age twenty-five.

MONDAY, JUNE 12, 1944 ■ There was another alert last night. The third night running since the invasion.

It's getting harder and harder to wait "patiently" as one feels more and more certain that the hour of deliverance is at hand.

THURSDAY, JUNE 15, 1944 ■ Unfortunately the transport to Natzweiler left the day before yesterday after all. I sent the concertina with them; it can do more good in that camp.

FRIDAY, JUNE 16, 1944 ■ We are buried alive in an immense common grave, where we creep and crawl about each other like moles. The animal spirits have just enough vitality to see to the bare necessities of survival in this dark-room. There is war here too. All against all. We are conscienceless, without pity for our neighbor, without a thought of anything but scraping our own way and keeping life in our own rickety carcasses. As long as we have enough to live on, and destruction seems to lie outside the immediate circumference, we can even feel a kind of well-being—or so we think. We can actually feel at home together and be jolly. The commonest and funniest and always the most successful jokes are those which play upon the crematorium chimney—that so-and-so will soon be going up that way. Men are dirty beasts after all, and we form no exception, none of us. It's only a delusion to think so.

SATURDAY, JUNE 17, 1944 ■ Yesterday there came a sensation that has jacked up the SS several notches. The new German weapon, Hitler's long-heralded secret that was to decide the war in a twinkling, has been brought into use. London and southern England were the targets of a so-called *Vergeltungsrache*.* We still have no reliable news of the effect; one can't go by the SS, who are dead certain that England will be done for and London leveled to the ground within a short time. The *Rottenführer* [Follmann] was in his glory today; hate and vengeance glittered in his eyes, and behind them, plainly, was a flicker of faith—in victory at the twelfth hour. It will be interesting to see how long the flicker lasts.

Frode went back into the *Revier* yesterday.

MONDAY, JUNE 19, 1944 ■ This community within the walls contains everything, even a fortuneteller—or astrologer, as he calls himself, though he reads hands. He read

---

* The V-1 flying bomb, called a *Vergeltungswaffe*, or vengeance weapon, by the Germans and more derisively "doodle-bug" by the British, was a pilotless, jet-powered bomb. First employed against England on June 13, 1944, thousands of such bombs, together with the V-2, a liquid-fueled rocket (first employed September 8, 1944), were launched through March 1945, when all launching sites were evacuated or overrun by Allied armies. V-1 and V-2 attacks caused tens of thousands of civilian casualties and damaged or destroyed more than a million homes. While the V-1 was cheap and easy to produce, the V-2 was "hideously complex and difficult to make"; both were highly inaccurate and carried a small payload. While some historians emphasize the enormous human and material resources diverted by the Allies to defend against these weapons, the consensus appears to be that they were introduced too late in the conflict, in insufficient quantities, and were employed with almost no strategic oversight and thus had a negligible effect on the outcome of the war. Others point to their enormous cost (perhaps as high as $3 billion, or three-fourths the cost of the Manhattan Project, which produced the atomic bomb) versus the results achieved (the total explosive payload of *all* V-2 rockets was scarcely more than one large Allied bombing raid on Germany) and conclude that the massive misallocation of scarce resources may have actually shortened the war, but contrary to Hitler's predictions, in favor of the Allies.

mine yesterday. Predicted that on the 21st or possibly the 20th of July a terrible disaster would befall Germany, which would bring the war to a close.* The armistice would come immediately afterward, though perhaps not until the beginning of August. I should be home in July or August, he said, whereas most people would have to stay on here until September. He said the secret weapon was bluff.

Nevertheless they've been bombarding London with it nonstop since the 15th of June. For the people of London it may be a rather serious form of bluff. But it will scarcely decide the war.

MONDAY, JUNE 26, 1944 ■ Now a number of the SS in this kommando are going to the front—the youngest here in the joiner's shop, *der Bursch* [the boy], is exulting like a child, won't it be fun. The poor boob.

One hears less and less talk of the new weapon. The SS have quieted down somewhat.

TUESDAY, JUNE 27, 1944 ■ A Ukrainian boy of nineteen was hanged before the gateway at evening roll call last night. Before being hanged he got fifty blows, the first twenty of which were dealt by two of his comrades, two Ukrainian boys from the youth block, chosen haphazard. They were forced on this hangman's job by threats of twenty-five if they didn't do it, or didn't do it properly. Both had their faces punched after they'd begun, for not hitting hard enough. Before the opening of this incredible scene, the "sentence" was announced to all the prisoners in several languages, including Norwegian. The Ukrainian boy had been employed in the shoe factory. There he had taken two leather bags and cut shoe soles out of them. For which he was now to have fifty blows and then be hanged! We couldn't believe our ears. It must be a misunderstanding. We were such a long way off; perhaps we'd heard wrong?

The punishment began. From where I stood I could only see the rubber hose swing through the air, and after the first blow we heard a hoarse, muffled scream; then came a dead silence, one heard nothing but the "thuds" each time the rubber hose sank into his flesh. I didn't count the blows, I looked no more, only tried to turn from this horror, to make a coward's escape; it was unendurable. The two leather handbags the boy had stolen—or scrounged—had been hung up on the gallows by the hangman, one on each post. For the gallows is formed of two posts with a crosspiece on top, in the center of which there is a hook for the rope to pass through. This primitive machine had been tested on the open stage, first by the hangman and then by an SS *Blockführer*, who went up too and pulled on the rope to see if it all held!

Then the flogging was over. The last thirty blows had been dealt by the *Schläger* [beater]. There are several of them, besides the hangman, who has a full-time job with daily hangings and executions in the *Industriehof*. The hangman is the *Vorarbeiter* of a whole kommando which is called the *Krematorien-Kommando* and consists of six or seven men, or possibly double the number; for there is a night shift.

The hangman and the Ukrainian boy appeared on the scaffold. The boy could stand alone; he wasn't pinioned or gagged and seemed to be quite calm, but he was too far off for me to make out his features or any other details. But I saw what we were there to see. The hangman put the rope round his neck and tightened it, took another turn over the

---

* See July 22, 1944, below.

hook and tugged to make sure that all was right, then he stepped down. Another breathless couple of seconds, and the board was kicked away beneath the feet of the Ukrainian boy, who fell. He jerked out desperately with his arms in falling, then we heard a kind of thud as the noose tightened, and he hung swaying. For a long time he went on flapping his arms, trying to scramble up, as it were—as though his neck hadn't broken properly and he was trying to get it done, get it over. Those who were close by and saw it all say that was actually the case; he didn't break his neck in falling and it took five minutes for him to die.*

I don't exactly believe that, but if it had been so it could scarcely have made the crime more horrible and barbarous than it was from beginning to end. The more one thinks of it the more loathsome it becomes, and I thought and thought in the ghastly quarter of an hour we had to stand there after the hanging, before they cut him down. I reflected that the purpose of flogging, if it has any purpose at all but to indulge sadism, must be to prevent a crime from being repeated. In that case hanging would surely be enough. Therefore: The flogging must have been an outcome of the purest sadism, of a craving for the sight of pain, the display of power, the exercise of hate!† And making those two lads from the youth block (boys from thirteen or fourteen up to eighteen years) do the hangman's work on one of themselves, is such unheard-of evil and loathsomeness that it strikes one dumb. Why, the mere fact that there are hundreds of young boys standing in the square to watch these cultural practices—isn't that enough? The men responsible for this, those who fixed the punishment and gave orders for its execution—have such men any right to live? No! They've done enough harm!

Seen in relation to this community of ours, the crime is even more hair-raising. Here where swindling, stealing and lying are part of the daily routine and where our tormentors lead the way with enormous swindles of every kind. Where we're trained to scrounge, and where no one can survive without mastering the system, and making use of it. Here an ignorant Ukrainian boy is flogged and hanged for one of the very smallest bits of scrounging to be met with! No doubt he was going to get himself a little extra soup or a bread ration with the soles, *because he was starving*. Because he too, young as he was, wanted to go on living, overcoming hunger and privations and misery and trying to turn his face toward the light and the future. I did not know you, you poor, brave Ukrainian boy; I do not know what thoughts and feelings filled you as you stood there beneath the gallows, whether defiance or fear. That does not matter. Your manner was dignified and I shall never forget it.

When the Ukrainian boy and the hangman appeared under the gallows, there as a

---

* The boy was Vassily Okselenko, age nineteen. The son of a wealthy farmer, Okselenko was seized at the beginning of the war and sent to Germany as a slave laborer. It is not known for how long or for what reason Okselenko had been sent to Sachsenhausen. It has been suggested that the theft of the leather was a pretext and that camp authorities suspected he was a member of the underground. See October 22, 1944, below.

† Rudolf Diels, the first head of the Gestapo, once observed, "The infliction of physical punishment is not every man's job, and naturally we were only too glad to recruit men who were prepared to show no squeamishness at their task. Unfortunately, we knew nothing about the Freudian side of the business, and it was only after a number of instances of unnecessary flogging and meaningless cruelty that I tumbled [*sic*] to the fact that my organization had been attracting all the sadists in Germany and Austria without my knowledge for some time past. It had also been attracting unconscious sadists, i.e. men who did not know themselves that they had sadist leanings until they took part in a flogging. And finally it had been actually creating sadists. For it seems that corporal chastisement ultimately arouses sadistic leanings in apparently normal men and women. Freud might explain it."

noise and hubbub somewhere on the square. It was a Dutchman, one of the Bible-searchers, screaming a protest against this infamy. One man—of seventeen thousand—dared to react normally! "It's shameful! It's vile!" he screamed. He was seized and led away.

They say there is to be another hanging tonight. Is this the blessing we thought the *Wehrmacht* would bring into the camp? It's said the *Wehrmacht* are to take over; at any rate a lot of *Wehrmacht* officers have arrived, and inspect us every day as we march out and in. They stuck their heads out of all the windows in the main building during yesterday's execution. Were they inquisitive?

THURSDAY, JULY 6, 1944 ■ I had to make a break in my writing. I don't know exactly know why, but I somehow felt that they were wondering very hard what the devil I was doing in secret under the table. And to be on the safe side . . .

I'm beginning to worry about Frode. He's still in the *Revier*. They don't know quite what's the matter with him. The *Revier* is a deathtrap, and the whole establishment an establishment for murder by installments.

THURSDAY, JULY 13, 1944 ■ Last Friday we had another hanging. This was a man who had escaped and during his flight committed "various crimes." A young lad, I think a Pole. We're getting used to it now. That was the fifth hanging since we arrived. Transports are going off, too. All the sick Jews who have been "discharged" from the watchmaking shop because they are sick were sent off yesterday to Auschwitz in Poland, which means quite certainly to the gas chambers.

FRIDAY, JULY 14, 1944 ■ This is France's day of liberty.* They haven't much yet to celebrate. Only a little bit of Normandy, lying in ruins. But it has been delivered from a tyranny whose like the world has never seen, and it can breathe freely. Oh that one could do the same—even among ruins!

SATURDAY, JULY 15, 1944 ■ Yesterday a man escaped from this kommando. A Ukrainian, who had been through rather too much. He had been a long time in the punishment block, had been beaten up and starved, was a *Muselmann*, and now was doubtless trying to get away from it all. We had to "search" until eight o'clock last night, a posse of prisoners, but we didn't find him. Today he was found in one of the halls, under the floor, where he had hidden himself. God knows how long he meant to stay there, and what was his idea altogether. Sheer despair, and lack of courage to kill himself perhaps? What lies before him now won't be nice, but hardly worse than what he's gone through already. He is sure to get at least fifty blows and be put in the SK. It's worse than a death sentence.

Frode is still in the *Revier*; but improving again. He's getting up today for the first time, and soon I hope we shall have him out again.

SATURDAY, JULY 22, 1944 ■ A long time ago I wrote about the fortuneteller who predicted that on July 20th something decisive would happen. *Olsen the Carrier*

---

* July 14 is Bastille Day, the anniversary of the storming of the Bastille prison, Paris, on July 14, 1789, signifying the start of the French Revolution.

(Adam Heinz as the fortuneteller calls him)* would "fall asleep," he said. Dispatched by his own people! And so something of the kind actually took place. An attempt to kill Hitler in his headquarters, in which many were injured, a number gravely and some slightly.† Among these last, according to report, was Hitler himself. Obviously there is a ferment throughout the Reich. Today we have a marvelous rumor that Goebbels was arrested yesterday—by Himmler in person! The feeling among the SS is nervous and insecure. It must be a symptom that all the prisoners had their pocketknives taken away on the night of the attempt. The Commandant has assembled block leaders and foremen, stressed the need for discipline and appealed to them for support, if there should be any disturbance.

Let us devoutly hope that things will move fast now.

TUESDAY, JULY 25, 1944 ■ Olsen the Carrier seems to be in good health. All the forces that were working to put an end to the war have now been bowled over, and the SS is paramount.

On the fronts progress is fantastic, especially in the East.

We went to see Frode on Sunday as usual. This time he was really better.

A little sickroom "interior" is worth including. Frode asked gleefully if I would like to see a *Hauptsturmführer* on the point of death. I almost think I answered enthusiastically that I should indeed. Eagerly he dragged me off. In the next bed lay a yellow, twitching skeleton of a man, already dead to this world. His eyes were nearly glazed already, fixed on the other side; he lay gasping and fumbling a little with his hands. I don't think he was conscious. Next to him, on the further side, lay [Rolf] Randall.‡ Frode and Randall had been lying waiting and betting when he would pack up, the old brute.

As we left the ward again, we ran into [Arnulf] Øverland. When he heard about the half-dead *Hauptsturmführer*, he only asked, "What's the matter with him?"

"Cancer of all the sexual organs, bladder and everything," said Frode.

"Thank goodness, then there's no chance of his recovering," said Øverland.

And then we talked of something else while the loudspeaker thundered out its shrill musical-comedy tunes, and while the *Hauptsturmführer* and many, many others lay taking

---

* "Vognmann Olsen" in the original. A vognmann was traditionally a wagon driver, much like a teamster. Nansen's use of this pseudonym is not clear. The use of **A**dam **H**einz is more obvious.

† On July 20, 1944, a group of disaffected military officers and their civilian allies, under the leadership of Colonel Claus von Stauffenberg, attempted to assassinate Adolf Hitler by detonating a bomb, hidden in a briefcase, during a military briefing held at Hitler's field headquarters in East Prussia. Although the bomb exploded as planned and killed four people in the room, Hitler survived relatively unscathed. The ensuing coup d'état also failed, and the Gestapo immediately initiated a roundup of anyone remotely implicated in the plot. A total of seven thousand people were ultimately arrested. Many others committed suicide prior to their arrest. Almost five thousand were executed and any remaining resistance movement in Germany was crushed. It is worth noting that von Stauffenberg flew to Rastenburg, Prussia, on July 15 to assassinate Hitler and was foiled only when Hitler left the briefing and failed to return. It was not until July 19 that von Stauffenberg was again summoned to Rastenburg to report to Hitler. In other words, the date of Hitler's assassination attempt was not known, even to von Stauffenberg, until the day before his attempt. How the fortune-teller could inform Nansen (on June 18) that July 20 was the crucial date will forever remain a mystery.

‡ Randall (1905–1974) was a film director and writer. For a period of time (1926–1932) he worked in Hollywood and claimed to have a minor role in the 1930 film production of *All Quiet on the Western Front*. In 1946 Randall codirected a film on his wartime experience, *Vi Vil Leve* [*We Will Live*] with Olav Dalgard, another veteran of Grini and Sachsenhausen.

leave, each in his own way, of this infernal vale of tears—and while the Norway-Poland football match was opening before a great concourse of people. Poland won, 3-2.

THURSDAY, JULY 27, 1944 ■ Two biggish transports of rolling stock from the depot here have just left for Poland (or East Prussia) to help with the evacuation. Yesterday a convoy of seventeen trucks left for Königsberg. Erik's chief Lucian went with it. Erik is delighted, sleeping and slacking for all he's worth. He's sure to be away a week, perhaps longer; perhaps he'll never come back! Erik dissolves with ecstasy at the idea.

The day before yesterday we had another *Filzing* as we marched in from work. No doubt they were after weapons that time. *Filzing* always excites great nervousness among the prisoners. It needn't be that they have anything dangerous on them; the mere thought of flogging and torture, face-punching and devilry makes them tremble and in hundreds of cases lose their balance altogether. They throw away everything imaginable—pipes, cigarette holders, trousers, belts, etc., and the road and roadside are strewn with all sorts of oddities, from things like that to loaves and rain capes. Some are so beside themselves with nervousness that the guards think they have something dangerous and make an extra search. A strap which would otherwise have remained snugly round the prisoner's waist he may in sheer terror, because of course he scrounged it, have rolled round the calf of his leg under the trouser. They find it and the case is plain—he stole it. That happened yesterday. The prisoner got several cuts in the face from the strap by way of preface; later it will be the SK no doubt, if not worse. It was one of the *Wehrmacht* officers (whom we believed to be so "humane" and agreeable!) who struck the prisoner in the face.

As I must have mentioned before, we're also forbidden to have unopened tins of food in our cupboards in the block. All one receives is to be eaten up in forty-eight hours, or one may not have more than can be eaten in that time. We're forbidden to give away anything. In that connection I ought to say that the Swedish parcels weigh ten kilos [twenty-two pounds], including between six or seven [thirteen or fifteen pounds], certainly, of tinned stuff. Therefore the regulation becomes impracticable from the moment Swedish parcels are allowed. Only one thing can make it practicable— "giving away," that is, handing over to the *Lagerältester* through the *Blockältester* at least four fifths of the Swedish parcels and whatever else we receive. They say they're given to the *Schonungs-Blocken* [convalescent huts]. We know better. The new tins they bore holes in. That started yesterday. Even the *Kleinigkeiten* are narrowly examined. One reason given is that the tins don't always contain what the label says. Also they're particular about other food, go through the contents of the parcels with care. Whether it's arms, dynamite, or secret documents they're afraid of we don't know. However, that exactly suits the present camp authorities, green and black.* They see it as a means of getting at the Norwegians' parcels. What we're to do I don't know. But presumably the whole thing will slack off in time.

SUNDAY, JULY 30, 1944 ■ Colossal progress in the East. The towns are tumbling like peas out of a sack. Even the German radio is already talking about "southeast of Warsaw."

---

* SS and Wehrmacht, respectively.

Warsaw will be falling this week, one should imagine,* and *then* it isn't far to the German frontier!

TUESDAY, AUGUST I, 1944 ■ Then came August—simply. There is a gleam of autumn in the name. August! Something disconsolate comes with it—like a deep sigh. Is autumn really coming too?

THURSDAY, AUGUST 3, 1944 ■ *The King's birthday!* Sunshine from a clear sky. I, as a royal hostage, ought at least to know how old the King is today. But to my shame I must confess I've lost count. Is he seventy-three or seventy-four?† Or is that a double fault? But still I send my best wishes. What all Norwegians without exception wish for him today is that he may live to return to Norway, to a new day, a new dawn over the land.

And that day is drawing near. They're advancing on all fronts, and the spirits of the SS are getting close to zero. In the glass cage today SS *Rottenführer* Follmann banged the table with his fist and cursed capitalism. I suggested that he was really a Communist. He was startled, but defended himself by referring to darkest Russia—and the Communists in Germany—who would have dragged the country down into wretchedness. Wasn't it now being dragged still deeper into wretchedness? *Ja*—but in battle for the right—and in battle we will go under. It's hopeless—hopeless! To hell with everything! was *Rottenführer* Follmann's sole conclusion.

The two transports that left the depot here for Poland have had a sticky time. The first, under Irsch, has apparently been attacked and the men with it severely wounded. The other, which Lucian (Erik's chief) was with, is said to be either *vernichtet* [exterminated] or *von den Russen geschnappt* [kidnapped by the Russians]. Erik is dancing the can-can. Too good to be true!

FRIDAY, AUGUST 4, 1944 ■ When we got "home" yesterday we were met by the news that there is a ban on parcels. And on smoking. It turned out that the smoking ban applied only to purchases from the canteen—that is of Mahorka—for a fortnight. But the

---

* Although the Soviet army had already reached the eastern suburbs of Warsaw by July 30, 1944, the city was not liberated until January 17, 1945. What transpired between the two dates is one of the most tragic episodes of World War II. On the morning of August 1, 1944, the Polish Home Army, hoping to liberate the city ahead of the Russians (and thus help influence the complexion of the postwar government) commenced an armed uprising against their German occupiers. Inexplicably, the Soviet army did not advance and neither provided help nor allowed Western support for the lightly armed insurgents. The uprising nevertheless lasted sixty-three days. In the end 18,000 Home Army fighters were killed, wounded, or captured; an estimated 150,000 Polish civilians were killed (out of a total population of 720,000 on the west bank), many deliberately massacred by German units. Following capitulation on October 2, 1944, Hitler ordered the remaining population expelled and the city razed. "Despite a critical military situation, in which every last soldier of any age was being impressed into service for the defense of the Reich, thousands of German troops were employed in the ruins of Warsaw, fulfilling the *Führer's* orders. . . . The operation proceeded without a break, day by day, street by street, district by district." By January 1945, when Warsaw was finally occupied by the Soviet Army, more than 80 percent of the city had been destroyed, the victim of either this effort, the uprising itself, the initial 1939 invasion, or the Warsaw Ghetto Uprising of 1942. In the words of one historian, "Warsaw was a modern-day Carthage." In contravention of the capitulation agreement, more than 150,000 inhabitants were sent to slave labor and concentration camps. Among the many consequences of the Poles' defeat was "the final destruction of Polish independence," but also "a sea change in the attitudes at the top in both [Britain and the United States], and their relationship with the Soviet Union would never be the same afterwards." August 1 is now annually commemorated in Poland.

† King Haakon VII was born August 3, 1872; this was actually his seventy-second birthday.

parcel ban is final and permanent. It's not a camp regulation; it came from up above and applies to the whole country and to everyone.

Erik rejoiced too soon. Not an hour after his wild explosion of delight, Lucian with the remains of his truck transport returned from Poland. He had lost seven trucks in a clash with partisans somewhere in Poland, but jumped large as life out of one of the returning trucks, announcing that he was "still among the living," and began cursing and storming on the spot. But he may be sent again. Hope never dies, *it* is total, too!*

TUESDAY, AUGUST 8, 1944 ■ The days pass in sunshine and expectation. Even though they go fast, they go slow! Both in East and West the tempo is now irreproachable from an "objective" point of view. But we are not objective. Those who wrinkle their brows and reflect solemnly and bring out heavy postulates that the war will last a long time—they're bluffing. Only the vexatious thing is that every day proves them right—the know-it-alls!

THURSDAY, AUGUST 10, 1944 ■ No, it doesn't come—all that willy-nilly we're expecting here every day. They're advancing on the fronts certainly, but we want something that goes quicker, something to put the period to it! A violent hubbub, and then finished! But there was only an unsuccessful *attentat* [assassination]. The conspirators were hanged the day before yesterday. One of them, General Höppner, was the general I had to deal with in Prague on the 15th of March, 1939.† The man who helped me with the refugees. Who was a tolerably decent man after all. Now he's been hanged. It's almost symbolic.

SATURDAY, AUGUST 12, 1944 ■ A fresh action has been started, against Communists and other "dangerous" men. Every day people are called for and dragged to the *Industriehof,* from which they either don't come back at all or come back flogged half to death. Prisoners with low numbers, those who have seen and known this camp at its worst, who were here when the murders were committed by thousands, will be dangerous witnesses on the day of reckoning, and it may be from a consciousness that it's close at hand that the Germans are now trying to do away with them. Also there seems to be a tendency to start on those prisoners who were condemned for high treason. According to what I hear, protocols have been drawn up for signature with confessions of the most appalling crimes, committed by the SS, and the prisoners are whipped into signing. Whipped and flogged until they can't stand. An isolation block has been set up for such prisoners. Block 58. The rest of us are enjoined on pain of the worst consequences to keep

---

* Presumably a play on the concept of total war embraced by Joseph Goebbels in his new role—Reich Plenipotentiary for Total War—conferred on him by Hitler in July 1944.

† Erich Höppner (or Hoepner) (1886–1944). Höppner took part in various conspiracies against Hitler in the 1930s, but later commanded troops in Poland and France and for the invasion of the Soviet Union. When Höppner disregarded a Hitler directive in January 1942 not to retreat under any circumstances and executed a tactical withdrawal outside Moscow in the face of a Soviet counterattack, Hitler relieved him of command and dismissed him from the army. Thereafter Höppner reverted to his resistance activities and joined the von Stauffenberg conspiracy (von Stauffenberg was a staff officer in Höppner's 6th Panzer Division in the Polish and French campaigns). He was hanged August 8, 1944, in Berlin. Although an anti-Hitler conspirator, Höppner's reputation has suffered (e.g., a high school in Berlin named in his honor was renamed) after it was learned that Höppner had pursued a brutal, scorched-earth policy in Russia. The war against Russia, he explained to his troops in May 1941, had to be fought "with unheard-of harshness," inspired by "the iron will to achieve merciless, complete annihilation of the enemy."

away. It's also said that a so-called *Stehkommando* [stand kommando] has been set up there. The prisoners have to stand, stand all the time, day after day, till they can stand no longer. Of course they can die of that, too. Only slower than if they were shot, hanged or flogged to death. And perhaps it's *meant* to be slow; possibly some of them will take crimes upon themselves to put an end to it!*

And yet another thing: there is a kind of retaliation in this as well. Against England, or against the enemy, no matter against whom. Vengeance! Hatred and madness find a vent, fanaticism too is becoming total, and darkness, and mankind. Shall we ever, any of us, get home?

A brothel has been established in camp. At first we wouldn't believe it, but now it's a fact. The day before yesterday it was thrown open to the Norwegians. Unfortunately there were some who went, and so that front was broken. There are ten whores. They are from Ravensbrück women's camp, prisoners who have "volunteered" for the sake of being released earlier. The first day was reserved for *Blockälteste* and prominent persons. Then came the turn of the *Reichsdeutsche* and then of all *Germanen* [Germanics]. Only that proud race has access to the establishment, of course on grounds of "medical hygiene," and all is "*peinlich sauber*," there too. *Schein* are issued, you line up five and five and get ten minutes after being passed "*sprungfähig*" [able to jump] on examination of the relevant parts (are they "*peinlich sauber*" and otherwise all right). *Schein* are being bought and sold of course, and thus the cowardly don't have to give in their names in the block, if they feel unchaste desires. The ten poor *Häftlinge*, who were to be released sooner, will certainly have a full-time job.†

MONDAY, AUGUST 14, 1944 ■ Yesterday we had a very stirring Sunday. Altogether there are things going on just now that create a stir. New prisoners by the thousands are expected in camp and have already arrived. Most likely they come from Poland, where one concentration camp after another is being evacuated as the Russians draw nearer.

Yesterday a great influx was expected, two or three thousand. Several blocks were vacated and prepared for their reception. Among these was [Block] 25, where all the Danes, about a hundred and thirty, are quartered with Norwegians. All these Danes and Norwegians were distributed among the other four Norwegian blocks, with the result that we are now living like sardines in tins with multiple layers. Conditions are little short of frightful when you consider, also, that the days are baking hot—and the nights, too. The atmosphere of the dormitory is indescribable from the moment we go to bed, and that although all the windows have been taken out. The dining room is now a nightmare at mealtimes, that is, all the time we're at home in camp, both morning and evening. One has to elbow one's way through naked or half-naked, sweaty, dirty bodies, some covered with boils, others incurably filthy. Yet in the midst of it all we're going around congratulating ourselves that at least they chose our fellow countrymen and Danes to sleep in our beds, sit on top of us at the table, and stand on our feet in the washroom and the *Abort*

---

* The *Blockführer* in charge of the *Stehkommando* (1939–1941), *Oberscharführer* Fitz Ficker, was convicted after the war by a Soviet military tribunal and sentenced to life imprisonment at hard labor. He died in prison in June 1948.

† The brothel, known as the *Sonderbau* or special building, was erected next to the infirmary, directly over the mortuary cellar. When one worker became pregnant, she was executed by order of the head camp doctor, Heinrich Baumkötter. None of the women were released early as promised.

[privy]. It might have been worse. That is, we might have had Poles and Ukrainians. And in spite of all philanthropy and all tolerance—that would have been a number of degrees worse.

This morning, as we marched out to work after the first straitened night, a dismal sight met our eyes on the main road from Sachsenhausen. An endless train of women, children and men. They had been standing there, lined up five and five under guard, for five hours, it's said. They were Poles; some said refugees, others said prisoners, others again that they were Poles who had been saved from the Russians. There were supposed to be three thousand people there, all told; there were babies among them, in their mothers' arms, and young girls and boys. So here we have fresh inmates for the concentration camps which were overcrowded already! And the Germans talk about the Allies making war on women and children!

TUESDAY, AUGUST 15, 1944 ■ The 3,500 people on the road yesterday were refugees from Warsaw. Warsaw is burning. The Germans did it. Completely! One can imagine what is going on there! It's strange that refugees whom the Germans have rescued from the murdering Russians are to go into a concentration camp. From infants to aged people of both sexes.

My last letter to Kari has been returned for the fourth time. This time because the lines were too long, last time because it had been sent once before (I missed my turn) and before that again because there was a sentence too much. *Hafterleichterung* is swell!

WEDNESDAY, AUGUST 23, 1944 ■ All the Germans in camp are now being registered and expect to be mobilized. Gangsters and felons have long been mobilized in great numbers, and now fresh companies of conscripts are always marching off through the gate, while the action against Communists and traitors continues. The other day the former head of the *Arbeitseinsatz* [labor service section] was carried into the *Revier* from [Block] 58—bloody and half killed.

FRIDAY, AUGUST 25, 1944 ■ Romania gave up yesterday.* There again of course it was only a tiny clique of traitors who betrayed their country. It's remarkable how much credit the Germans see in that traitor business. Then there's nothing to be ashamed of. They couldn't help it!

The weather is glorious just now. Sunshine—sunshine—from a clear sky day after day. I sit out of doors a lot, carving. I'm carving a devil at the moment. A devil's head at the bottom of a bowl. I felt like it, and the man the bowl is for was greatly disappointed—very suspicious—and almost angry. So it was quite a success. He doesn't want the bowl. *Prima!* He would prefer a rose, or a marguerite, or some other delicate little flower with leaves. "That would be much prettier—much nicer—eh?"

---

* On August 23, 1944, as Soviet forces entered Romania, King Michael I led a coup d'état that toppled the fascist government of General Ion Antonescu; the timing was dictated by a desire to establish an independent, pro-Western government before the Soviet forces reached Bucharest. Following the coup, King Michael agreed to an armistice, aligned with the Allies, and declared war on Germany. At the Yalta Conference (February 1945), however, Romania was recognized to be within the Soviet sphere of influence and by 1947 King Michael abdicated in favor of a Soviet-dominated Communist government. Romania eventually joined NATO in 2004 and the European Union in 2007.

SUNDAY, AUGUST 27, 1944 ■ Our wedding day! Seventeen years! The third wedding day in prison. So in a way that makes it only fourteen, but fourteen bright, rich years that have made it possible to get through three dark ones. Life has been good to us after all. The wealth it has given us in these seventeen years no one can take from us. It is of eternity and will never die, even though we should never meet again.

MONDAY, AUGUST 28, 1944 ■ Yesterday turned out a great day, as was proper. Wherever one turns one's eye—east, west, north, south—nothing but retreat, and now disastrous retreat, for the Germans. Blow after blow falls on them incessantly, each harder than the last. It seems manifest that they can't take it much longer. Four weeks at most, an elderly and canny Communist has just said to me. Usually he takes a pessimistic view of things. But now there isn't much room for pessimism.

TUESDAY, AUGUST 29, 1944 ■ The terror in [Block] 58 continues. One of its victims has gone into the *Revier*. He's had four hundred blows, and his thighs and buttocks were in such state that they've been removed, amputated. The flesh had been flogged off the bone. He was a Communist, no doubt, and I dare say he had also been helping Russians and Ukrainians with food. Now he meets his fate, his doom from those culture-bearers who are saving Europe from Communism. The master race! God's chosen people!

WEDNESDAY, AUGUST 30, 1944 ■ Once again the specter of winter is becoming visible far off in the haze. Today we had the first real autumn morning. Almost a year has passed since I arrived here. Only another month to go. Is this the month which is to be decisive? Which is to bring the incomprehensible tidings? The tidings which by now one dare hardly mention?

THURSDAY, AUGUST 31, 1944 ■ Yesterday two men were hanged at once on the same gallows at evening roll call. A Pole and a Russian. They had stolen some food in a cellar where they worked. That was all. Again there was something wrong with the "technical apparatus." The ropes were too long. Their feet touched the ground after the drop. One of them was not dead; people ran up and tried to get off his wooden shoes, and when they didn't succeed the hangman lifted his legs off the ground. The victim turned blue in the face, and it looked as though he were suffering the most frightful agonies before he died.

Nor did these two know that they were going to be hanged until they came marching up with their guards and saw the gallows. One exclaimed in Polish, "My God! my God!" The other in Russian, "So long, comrades," looking across and down the ranks, where they stood in silence, thousands of comrades. Both mounted the scaffold bravely, and went calmly to their deaths, without resistance, without a sign of collapse. They were both young lads. Anonymous to most. Two less among many, many hundreds of thousands.

The *Lagerführer* and another man, a *prisoner:*—the dreaded fat *Lagerältester* and informer Kunke of the *Sonderkommission* were seen conversing gaily during the hanging. The *Lagerführer* had actually pointed to the gallows, where the two were hanging, and where people were busy getting their legs off the ground, and had said something that raised a laugh. *We?* Why, we went off to supper, and in the interest of truth we must confess that we enjoyed it as much as usual. Then there was the communiqué from the loudspeaker in the square, then another smoke, if one had it, and then (one's best friend after all) bed and sleep. If only one could sleep into another age!

SATURDAY, SEPTEMBER 2, 1944 ▪ We had splendid news yesterday. They've already reached the German frontier in the West, too. The SS are hanging their heads, but clinging with remarkable unanimity to the rumors of a new weapon that will put an end to the war within a short time.* The specter of gas always comes into one's mind at such moments. Do they mean to try that before going under? For they're going under! We are having an exceptional wave of optimism and have begun to do a little packing.

MONDAY, SEPTEMBER 4, 1944 ▪ Yesterday morning it was announced on the German radio that Finland had capitulated and accepted the Russian terms.† At last! Germany is now completely encircled, and their allies have fallen off one after another. Soon they'll have their backs to the wall and will have to show what they mean by fighting to the last man. I feel by no means convinced that they don't mean it.‡ What may condemned men not do while they have power?

WEDNESDAY, SEPTEMBER 6, 1944 ▪ The development in the West is quite fabulous. Brussels, Antwerp, Flushing, and Breda, yes, and even Rotterdam have fallen. They are on or over the German frontier along the whole Western front, and we are on the heights of optimism and expectancy, while it is more and more obvious that the SS are beginning to understand. They have long since reached what I call the "trunk stage"; all of them are intensely interested in having boxes made to get all "their stuff" away to safety in case "anything" should happen. The joiner's shop has been hard at work on such boxes lately. Of course it is all illegal work. We are now betting on whether the armistice will be this month. There aren't many who venture to bet it *won't be. There is actually reason to believe it will be over this month!* Can it be possible? I daren't think of it. Kari, Kari! Can it be possible?

Something has been going on in camp, something that has changed the "tactics." Suddenly the other day there was a solemn announcement that food once more may be given away, even to people from the East. From whom or from what quarter this order comes I don't know; probably from the Commandant or *Lagerführer*, who, one has the impression, would be quite glad to play a trick on the *Sonderkommission* and its myrmidons.

---

* The first V-2 rocket was launched September 8, 1944. See June 17, 1944, above.

† The so-called Continuation War, of Finland and Germany against the Soviet Union, began on June 25, 1941. After Finland regained territory ceded in the Winter War (1939–1940), the Finnish-Russian Front saw relatively little activity until the Red Army launched a major offensive on June 9, 1944, which resulted in a cease-fire on September 4, 1944, and an armistice on September 19, 1944. The terms of the armistice obligated Finland to expel all German troops from the country, resulting in the Lapland War (1944–1945) against German forces. The scorched-earth policy adopted by the retreating Germans also laid waste to much of northern Norway.

‡ Almost half (49 percent) of all German servicemen who died during World War II were killed in the final ten months of the conflict, or *after* Nansen wrote this diary entry.

THURSDAY, SEPTEMBER 7, 1944 ■ Yesterday another two men were hanged at evening roll call. It seems to be the mode now to have two at a time—on the same gallows. I suppose the sight of two is twice as deterrent. This time the rope was too short. One especially. He didn't fall even a meter, little more than half. It was appalling to watch. He certainly didn't break his neck, but kicked and strained and carried on for many minutes after the drop. The other seemed to die more quickly, but then he dropped half a meter more before the rope tightened. These "accidents" must be deliberate. The conclusion is forced on one. People don't make fateful mistakes at executions so many times.* But it's sinister how little impression it comes to make on one. I noticed with horror that there was joking and talking while the two hung there in convulsions. Yes, during the hanging itself, and among my nearest neighbors!

WEDNESDAY, SEPTEMBER 13, 1944 ■ Well, I made a short break. And indeed that has been the proper characteristic of the days since I last wrote. It looks as though both in the East and in the West they were now rallying for the last decisive blow. After all one can't expect that they'll just continue to roll on and on as fast as wheels can go round, and as though the German frontier were nonexistent. No doubt one must reckon on being faced with a terrific showdown.

Today, however, it looks as though the showdown had begun. They've broken through the German frontier in the West at six different points, and in the last few days the raids have been colossal.† Yesterday we had a fantastic display of aircraft here; wave after wave of hundreds and hundreds of planes appeared from behind the clouds in the West, glittering high up in the sunlight, and pursued their way east or northeast. With a majestic calm, the effect of which was quite overwhelming, they advanced untroubled by the shells exploding round them. Something that looked like an air battle was fought out thousands of meters above our heads in a couple of minutes. Not even that disturbed their course in the least. Utterly unmoved they went on their way, and two or three of the attacking fighters appeared to crash.

The day after I last wrote, another man was hanged at evening roll call. Again something went wrong with the apparatus. He dropped too far and his feet reached the ground.

THURSDAY, SEPTEMBER 14, 1944 ■ One of the dangerous German "gangsters" (i.e. saboteurs) from Berlin who are imprisoned here—most of them in chains—was executed the other day. But he achieved something first. Somehow he had got hold of a pocket-knife, which he smuggled in right to the place of execution in the *Industriehof*, and on the "scaffold" itself he went for the hangman and cut up his face, his chest and several other places, so that they had to take him to the *Revier* in a hurry. Apparently he'll get over it. The death-candidate was handcuffed, so it was a pretty good effort. No one pities the hangman; sooner or later he is sure to be dispatched too, and one can scarcely want a man like that to live.

---

* At the Soviet military tribunal convened in 1947 to adjudicate Sachsenhausen personnel, one of the hangmen, Paul Sakowski, admitted that he and other executioners "purposefully dragged out the hangings to make them more painful." He was sentenced to life imprisonment.

† American patrols from the 1st Army did cross the German border near Aachen on September 11, 1944, creating panic, but the action was not followed up and Aachen was not formally attacked until October 2.

MONDAY, SEPTEMBER 18, 1944 ■ Yesterday a timely word came through the ether: "We are pouring in through the gap in the West Wall."* No more was intercepted, but that will do. It was a glorious Sunday, and morale went up many notches all round.

Executions are taking place every day in the *Industriehof.* Six or eight a day on average, according to someone who can observe every day. The other day four women were taken down into the death-cellar. Two of them were attractive young girls; "beastly pretty," said my informant. They had smiled and nodded, and he was certain they had no idea where they were going or what was going to happen.

Five death-candidates tried to escape the other day. Managed to dodge the hangman and hide. They were found after an exciting chase, all five, and one of them was kicked to death by the hangman. Several people saw that.

The day before yesterday a man was flogged. Twenty-five blows. It was the Dutchman who protested three months ago against German justice. For three months he has been in the SK, and anyone who knows a little about a German penal column in a concentration camp knows what that means. Beating and kicking every day; in those three months he must have had many times the twenty-five blows he was given yesterday before us all. The religious silence that prevailed throughout the whole scene, broken only by the short, soughing thuds of the rubber truncheon on the man's body, and by the poor martyr's groans of pain after every blow, said more than words of what was felt by most of the sixteen or seventeen thousand people who attended this "judicial act."

Some time after the Dutchman had been led away, on that occasion three months ago, I made some inquiries into his fate. One of my Norwegian friends has a job in the secretariat where, in true German style, a card index for every prisoner in the camp is made out and brought precisely up to date from moment to moment. My friend looked up the Dutchman's card. It said, "Subjected to mental examination." The only man in camp who reacted normally must be out of his mind.†

The other day I had punishment gymnastics. I had been "reported" one morning at roll call for turning round and talking to Erik. That of course is highly improper. As I was made to feel. For punishment gymnastics are no joke. That was three days ago, and even now I have the greatest difficulty in moving, let alone bending, sitting down or getting up again.

The gymnastics lasted about an hour and were conducted by one of the greatest brutes in camp, the foreman of the SK, a deserter and ruffian of the worst kind.‡ The job suits him admirably. By doing his work well—making his gymnastics ultrabrutal—he may ingratiate himself and possibly escape being hanged. And ultrabrutal they were. Three

---

* The West Wall, also commonly referred to as the Siegfried Line, was a 250-mile-long series of defensive fortifications constructed by Nazi Germany between 1938 and 1940 along the western boundary of Germany, from Switzerland north to where the Rhine River enters the Netherlands. It has been described as "essentially a position of relatively light defenses with great depth and formidable obstacles," primarily massive mine fields, antitank obstacles, and bunkers. US troops reached the Siegfried Line on September 13, but, rather than frontally attacking this fortified line, the Allies on September 17, 1944, launched Operation Market Garden, the landing of Allied airborne troops in Arnhem, Nijmegen, and Eindhoven, Holland. The goal of Market Garden was to split Holland in two, force a crossing over the lower Rhine River at Arnhem into Germany, penetrate the Ruhr Basin from the north, and accelerate the capture of Germany. The operation ultimately failed completely: of the original 35,000 airborne troops engaged, 1,400 were killed and another 6,000 captured, and the Allies were unable to secure the Arnhem crossing.

† Well-informed prisoners have since told me that the Dutch Bible-searcher finally ended his life on the gallows. I don't doubt it. O.N.

‡ See February 2, 1945, below.

times from Block 14 to the *Revier* and back, that is, three times the diameter* of the parade ground in a frog jump—squatting low with one's arms stretched up in front of one, and jumping along in that posture. A poor devil who began to laugh (for there's no denying that it is ignominiously funny) was kicked and belabored with such absolutely record savagery by the foaming SK bandit that he remained lying in the dust. Later he was carried away. "Dust" is by the way a mild word for the thick, black incrustation covering the whole square. When you consider that fifteen thousand men line up on that square twice a day, and several thousand at other times on the same day, and that all coolly and quite unreservedly spit around them everything they cough and hawk up, you can form a notion of the myriads of bacteria and nastiness contained in this incrustation. When the troops have done a couple of frog jumps the dust is thick a meter above the ground, and one has to breathe after all.

Reeling I got to my feet again when that exercise was over—but alas—only to start another just as hard. Walking in the same doubled-up attitude, that is waddling like a duck. Up and down again the full length of the parade ground. I managed that, too. Then there was running—running on and on. I was reeling and my head swam and I swallowed dust; but I managed. I came through, but many fell and didn't get up. The SK bandit flew at them with boots and stick. Most took no further notice of him. They were carried off.

We had knee-bendings—up and down—ten times, twenty times, thirty times—God knows how many times; and God knows how I got through them, but of course I managed, and of course I could laugh about it afterward, though I'm as stiff as a poker. Next time I don't think I shall laugh. Scott has had punishment gymnastics twice. At any rate I shan't laugh at him next time.

Summer is suddenly and finally over. I suppose it will be necessary to take out the German underclothes, which one expected to have no more use for when one put them away in the cardboard box last spring.

SATURDAY, SEPTEMBER 30, 1944 ■ And thus the hope of getting home for Christmas has broken down. Perhaps it was Churchill's speech yesterday about being prepared for "several months of 1945," perhaps a violent reaction after tense days, perhaps because I've heard nothing from Kari since July 25th, perhaps merely the bad weather. It's an infinitely heavy, painful thought that we're to stay here for another six months—or more.†

THURSDAY, OCTOBER 5, 1944 ■ At last, a letter from Kari yesterday! The last I had was dated July 25; since then I'd had nothing but an empty envelope dated August 12. But now the sun has come out again in my little world, and all is well.

Spotted typhus has broken out in the camp. That may be a bad job. Twenty-three cases yesterday, one in Norwegian Block 2. There is talk of quarantine. Perhaps the kommandos that work outside may be quartered at the place of work. It wouldn't be a bad idea. For the

---

* The diameter was 420 meters [460 yds.]. O.N.

† Churchill, in his address to the House of Commons on September 28, 1944, observed, "I shall certainly not hazard a guess—it could be no more—as to when the end will come. Many persons of the highest technical attainments, knowledge and responsibility have good hopes that all will be over by the end of 1944. On the other hand, no one, and certainly not I, can guarantee that several months of 1945 may not be required."

rest one must keep indoors and watch out for lice.* It may be difficult enough, though to be sure it's been all right so far. But it shall be all right. Die of spotted typhus *now*—that I won't!

TUESDAY, OCTOBER 10, 1944 ■ Father's birthday. He would have been eighty-three.

I have no really big news to produce in honor of the day, and in camp things are as usual. A couple of flogging scenes at evening roll call. No hangings for some time.

FRIDAY, OCTOBER 13, 1944 ■ Kari's birthday! And we'd been so sure that this day at least we should spend together. Once there wasn't a shadow of doubt about it. It was like a light somewhere in the future. That is past now. In front an ominous leaden sky—fresh cloud banks rolling up from all sides—in one's mind the harrowed death's-head faces of the condemned—the hanged men's glassy, staring eyes—the hopeless gaze of the starving from their dark sockets—or the indifferent brutal sneer of those who have long since given up and gone under. Death and the devil! Death and the devil!

And this is your birthday, Kari. I can't help reflecting that it has come on a Friday this year. Friday the thirteenth; what else could one expect? In this landslide of disaster and misery old superstitions have their place.

Still there is little news. Aachen is at last encircled, but if every German town is to take as long, both winter and spring will go.† This is a heavy time. But I had a letter from Kari at the beginning of the month, so I have really no right to be in despair. No indeed, nor am I.

THURSDAY, OCTOBER 19, 1944 ■ Yesterday on our return from work we heard that Himmler was going to broadcast an important statement to the German people. It came at seven o'clock, but we were not allowed to hear it. The loudspeakers in the camp were turned off. Did they feel a bit uncertain of what was coming? We heard about it this morning. It was an announcement that all German men from sixteen to sixty were now to serve at the front. What else he said I don't know, but that is quite enough. Sixteen-year-olds at the front! May we hope this order is so outrageous, so desperate and appalling in its ruthlessness, that it will act as an alarm to the German people?‡

The immediate future will tell. But to speak frankly, I have no great hopes. What I have seen and learned of the Germans and the German attitude is purely disheartening. It does actually seem as if they were all alike—prisoners, SS, or *Wehrmacht*. The same prostrate feebleness and crawling to "authority," that is, to anyone with a higher rank. The

---

* Epidemic typhus, sometimes called "jail fever," is a highly contagious and often fatal fever, transmitted by head and body lice and therefore commonly occurs in crowded, unsanitary environments. It is not related to typhoid fever.

† Aachen, 2009 population 250,000, was the first major German city captured by Allied forces after a prolonged battle in the face of fierce resistance (October 2–21, 1944). The stubborn defense delayed the Allied advance by more than five weeks, cost the Allies eight thousand casualties, and left large portions of the city in ruins.

‡ Himmler read out Hitler's decree establishing the *Volkssturm* [People's Storm], or militia. Although dated September 25, the decree was not publicized until Himmler's speech. "The date [October 18] had been carefully chosen as the anniversary of the highly symbolic 'Battle of the Nations' in Leipzig in 1813, the clash which had brought Napoleon's defeat on Prussian soil. The date was a crucial one in propaganda depictions, resonating in German history and evoking the legendary defense of the homeland by the *Landsturm*, as, faced with slavery at the hands of the French, an entire people rose up to repel the invaders."

same disastrous enthusiasm for everything military. An enthusiasm that one must believe goes deep, in fact so deep that one can't help wondering whether after all it may not possibly be inherited, in the very blood. Normal, grown-up people surely can't regard it as the height of all glory to stand exactly on the dotted line, five and five and one behind another, for a few minutes. And they fag themselves to death every day, several times a day, to get all these thousands of prisoners standing like that for a minute or two. What's the idea? They'd really like to see us all dead. But I suppose they want us even to die in ranks, with "*Vordermann*" and "*Seitenrichtung*"! [Line up with the man in front of you and next to you!] They set to every morning with the same zeal.

And with what zeal they go for their fellow prisoners, when there is a chance of getting them punished for bringing illicit food to the working place! Every morning they go round with a flashlight and seize their victims indiscriminately. If these have any tinned food, woe betide them, they're for Block 38, which means fifteen on the arse at once, and afterward, as long as they remain—a month or perhaps three or more—the most brutal beating up every day. Thirty-eight is a little hell, and we are sent there by our German "comrades," almost exclusively by them. Add that the punishing itself, flogging and face-bashing and all kinds of punishments, is carried out by German prisoners, and the picture of the German "comrades" is complete.* One might add perhaps their unwearied labor "for victory." Not a hint of sabotage, not a moment's rest, and if they have a smoke and are found out, they're ready at once to put the blame on others. If something goes wrong, there are always Ukrainians enough to blame, or others who can't defend themselves in German.

Such, unfortunately, is the picture I have to give of our German "comrades," with a few honorable exceptions. I could paint it in more detail, and support it with hundreds of examples from our daily life here. But let me leave it at that. It's ugly enough in any case. I shudder at the thought of finding afterward that we can never be rid of it. That every German I may come across in the future will call up all these ghastly memories. Yes, that the mere sound of the language will make my blood curdle. For I am certain it will be so. So powerful and ingrained, already, is my aversion to everything German, that I am quite involuntarily getting worse and worse both at speaking and writing it. Sometimes it can be downright physical torture to form a German sentence. There seems to be a yelping, barking and bellowing in the very words and the heavy, clumsy phrases. It's as though I've ceased to believe it possible that anything really fine can be expressed in German.

FRIDAY, OCTOBER 20, 1944 ■ Yesterday a great joy was granted us! When we came back at night, *Lagerältester* Kunke was not longer in the camp. He had been sent on a transport that morning to one of the worst camps, degraded and shorn, and after twenty-five on the arse. It was almost too good to be true, but it had actually happened. It was a friend of his, a "kindred spirit," who had got him into trouble. Kunke had this man admitted to the *Revier* with some fictitious ailment. The fraud was seen through, and Kunke's goose cooked—at last! We sighed with relief. For he was the personal devil behind everything. His might was great. He could order punishments, [Block] 58 and [Block] 38 and SK, and has the lives of many fellow prisoners on his conscience. There is

---

* The *Blockältester* of Block 38, Franz Kernke, was tried after the war and sentenced to only four years after the court "took into consideration . . . that he had been a prisoner and an alcoholic."

only one anxiety to damp our joy now. Who will be *Lagerältester* instead of him? There are scoundrels enough to choose from.

SUNDAY, OCTOBER 22, 1944 ■ The Kunke business was rather different. Even better. Some prominent German prisoner had been consigned to [Block] 58 on Kunke's orders. He asked leave to make a statement. No. He asked to speak to the *Lagerführer*. No. Then one day he escaped from 58 and went to *Lagerführer* Höhne.* What he had to say about Kunke, and could prove, was of such a nature that the *Lagerführer* took action on the spot. He sent for Kunke, who, after some introductory remarks, got "one on the snout." The other *Lagerführer*, Kolb,† turned up, and they dragged Kunke off to the block leaders, where he got twenty-five on the arse after several doses on the snout. He behaved pitiably, crying like a child and screaming. Kolb then took him to 58, where he displayed him to the prisoners. "Here's the man who betrayed you, now it seems to me only fair that you should have a chance to settle up." Then he gave an order for Kunke's best friend in camp, namely the hangman, to come at once, and the hangman was obliged to give his best friend another twenty-five on the arse. After that he was kicked and thumped by the block leaders and the prisoners, until he went off on a transport with his "comrades" from [Block] 58, and that transport is pretty sure to be the end of him.

MONDAY, OCTOBER 23, 1944 ■ It's obvious that there are many sighing with relief since we got rid of the demon Kunke. His people are being distinctly careful. At morning roll call searches and roughhouse episodes have almost ceased. One can gradually begin taking a little food to work again.

I was at a concert yesterday. Again the prison orchestra is allowed to function. It's been a long time now. They played Beethoven, Haydn, Mozart, started a violin concerto by an Italian named Giotta; it was charming, but then there came an alert, and the concert was broken off. It was lovely to hear a little music again, even though their playing is tedious and anemic. There were actually moments when I almost forgot I was in Sachsenhausen, and was going to turn and take Kari's hand.

TUESDAY, OCTOBER 24, 1944 ■ Last night it was announced that all German prisoners condemned for high treason would have an opportunity to volunteer. They were summoned to the *Lagerführer* after roll call, when he informed them that they were being given a chance to recover the esteem of their fellow citizens, etc., etc., and that bygones should be bygones if they volunteered now for war service. They should have twenty-four hours to think it over and an opportunity to discuss the matter among themselves; they were not to make a hubbub in camp, but talk it over with kindred spirits quietly and

---

* SS *Untersturmführer* August Höhn (1904–1982). In 1947 Höhn was sentenced by Soviet authorities to life imprisonment. In 1956 he and others were transferred to West Germany, which released him since West Germany never recognized the legitimacy of the Soviet tribunal. Following a general outcry he was retried in German courts in 1960 and found guilty of "murder in eight instances, accessory to murder in five instances, and accessory to manslaughter in two instances," and sentenced to life imprisonment again. The sentence was reduced to twenty-five years in 1968 as "an act of grace." Released from prison in 1973, Höhn died in 1982.

† SS *Obersturmführer* August Kolb (1893–1962). In 1954 Kolb was sentenced by West German authorities to slightly more than four years for his role in the murder of Vassily Okselenko and for manslaughter in ten other cases; in 1961 he was retried, convicted on an additional charge of assault with fatal consequences, and sentenced to a six-year term with credit for time served. He died in 1962.

privately. *Lagerführer* Höhne imparted this in a restrained and even polite way, and made no threats. What will happen to them if they don't volunteer is left for them to find out, or take a chance on. One or two will volunteer of course, but the majority will doubtless let it alone and, if the worse comes to worst, will die here in camp with such esteem as remains to them rather than die outside with none.

WEDNESDAY, NOVEMBER 1, 1944 ■ A whole week has passed with hardly a sign of life. The main reason is that I have actually been busy. I've begun drawings for our cottage on the scale of 1:50, after thinking and dreaming of it for years. I am dreaming myself so intensely into this cottage with all its details and rooms that I actually long to get to "work" every day. I feel as if I had time for nothing else. The last couple of days I've torn myself away and gone *mushrooming*! Really and truly! A magnificent war effort! I've found a basketful every time, and prepared the contents on the joinery stove to the great enthusiasm of my messmates. We're not living badly now.

In camp a number of things have happened. All the Germans have been enlisted whether they liked it or not. That about volunteering was pretty much a gesture. They were medically examined and passed fit, most of them, and are now waiting to be sent off. Ten years in prison as opponents of this regime, and then out to fight for it, and perhaps die for it.

The day before yesterday eight thousand fresh prisoners arrived in camp. On that account we've had to move still closer together. It's impossible for more than half, at the highest estimate, to sit down to meals, and I daren't even think how much air we have at our disposal per head. I'll work it out some day.

MONDAY, NOVEMBER 6, 1944 ■ SS *Waffenamt* [ordnance department] is one of the kommandos lying near the *Kraftfahrzeugdepot Wald*. Among the jobs in that kommando is the manufacture of one of the famous "new weapons," the *Panzerfaust*.* Work goes on there day and night. When we turn out in the morning, we meet long columns of prisoners coming off the night shift. Day and night, at regular intervals, a little series of three or four shots thunders out from the SS *Waffenamt*; those are the tubes of the *Panzerfaust* being tested. We know the kommando, too, from morning roll call. It falls in next to us, and is distinguished by an exceptionally brutal *Vorarbeiter*, who goes storming up and down the ranks. Also he has a number of willing and apt assistants, who make his job easier. He and his assistants are all of them German "comrades."

At SS *Waffenamt*, some weeks ago, a stamping machine happened to break. This machine is used for stamping small metal plates belonging to the *Panzerfaust* mechanism. The plates are 0.75 millimeters thick, and are placed under the stamp one at a time. If one has the bad luck to put two of them under it, they jam and the machine breaks. This happened while a Pole was serving the machine. He himself took care to repair the damage, went hard at it, and got the thing to rights again in a couple of hours. And he himself reported the incident to the chief, an SS *Sturmbannführer*. The chief said nothing, and the Pole, who had been greatly distressed about the accident, naturally thought the business

---

* Panzerfaust, meaning literally "armor fist" or "tank fist," consisted of a small, high-explosive antitank warhead preloaded on a disposable launch tube, capable of being fired by a lone soldier. During World War II tens of thousands were produced, and since they were capable of penetrating the armor of any Allied tank, spread considerable fear among tank crews.

The gallows cart is coming!

was now in order and finished. Four weeks later, on Thursday of last week, the "hangman's gang" (the crematorium kommando) arrived at SS *Waffenamt* with the "gallows cart." The gallows was set up, and at evening roll call at the place of work, before they marched into camp, the Pole was hanged. A short "sentence" was read by the *Lagerführer*, who came out on a bicycle. The Pole was hanged for "sabotage" on orders from SS *Reichsführer* Himmler. It was the chief, who had said nothing to him when he gave notice of the incident four weeks before, who had reported him and asked for the death penalty. The Pole cried unrestrainedly and heart-rendingly from the moment he was seized until he was swinging.

That was on Thursday. The day after, at the same time, the "gallows cart" with its gloomy kommando again came rolling out to SS *Waffenamt*. The gallows was again raised, and this time two Dutchmen were strung up for the same form of "sabotage." I have talked to a friend of one of them, a Norwegian, who says the Dutchman was a young, exceptionally pleasant and plucky chap. He had just been made a kind of foreman in the workshop where the stamping machine is kept, and was thus "responsible" for everything that took place there. No one in the workshop had intentionally committed sabotage.

That very Friday my informant had been with the Dutchman in the room where they wash and tidy up before going home. The Dutchman was chatting and joking as usual, and proclaimed, among other topics, his firm conviction that the war would soon be over and that he would be home by Christmas. When they went out to roll call they met an SS man rushing round with a bit of paper shouting a name. It was the Dutchman's name. He answered to it. Then he was seized by the shoulder and marched straight up onto the gallows, which, without their knowing it, had been raised on the square. A "sentence" was read out, and two more murders took place. The other Dutchman, who was handcuffed, belonged to the night shift and had come out with the "gallows cart." Both these men had been impressively calm and self-possessed to the very last.

I think I forgot to say that on Wednesday of last week, the day before the first hanging at SS *Waffenamt*, a man was hanged in camp. A BV-er who had been sent out as a partisan, and had escaped and been caught again. That is, he had been "discharged" from here with music and drumroll, and dragged to war for the Fatherland. And now he was brought back here to die on the gallows, as a warning to any who may have been contemplating something of the same kind when their turn comes.

We were called out on parade to attend this ceremony. Otherwise evening roll call has been dropped. Yes, it has! And it's a fantastic easement, a huge advantage, which I should have hastened to put down. It struck me, as we stood lined up for the march to this "gallows roll call," how horribly callous we've become. There we stood, more than four hundred Norwegians (in our block alone), about to go and see a fellow-prisoner being hanged. One would expect such a moment to be marked by gravity, if not by a poignant silence. And there one is, in a chatting, joking, laughing crowd of men and boys, who curse a bit when they collide in the crush or step on each other's feet, throw a quip or an obscenity over their shoulders to the man behind, who is smoking on the sly, and at long last are ready to march off to the scene of the crime, where there is no depression even during the hanging. "*Mützen ab*" while the sentence is being read and repeated in several languages. "*Mützen auf*" when the hangman goes to work. No condemned man is to be honored by his comrades with bared heads! And then at last we can return to the block— to food and foolery. Indifferently the crowd saunters back. Only a very few care who was hanged and why. The thing is to get a place at the table.

WEDNESDAY, NOVEMBER 8, 1944 ■ Marit's birthday. When I was arrested, she was only just thirteen and a little girl. Now she is sixteen and a woman. It's strange. She herself assures me so sweetly and eagerly, in the letter I had from her, that she hasn't grown away from me. But the whole letter shows that she has. Poor little Marit, she can't help it. And besides it's not to oblige their parents that children live their lives. But all the same I miss you badly, my little "fishergirl,"* and if you sometimes miss your daddy too, my wish is only that it may be a blessing for both of us.

THURSDAY, NOVEMBER 9, 1944 ■ When we got back last night, there was another "gallows parade." This time there were two men hanged. Deserters I should think. We hear the announcement of the sentence very badly all this way off, and thank goodness we don't see much either. It's dark at that hour now, and also we're in a spot where the searchlights dazzle us. We only see them drop like two shadows. But that's enough.

The other day a great number of conscientious objectors were hanged in the *Industriehof*. Which for that matter occurs every day. Before they were hanged, the *Lagerführer* asked them if they still refused to serve. They refused. Then one was hanged. The others were asked again if they refused. All said yes. Another was taken up on to the gallows

---

* A pet name for Marit. Nansen enjoyed fishing and before the war would often take Marit along with him. *Fisher Girl* (*Fiskerjente*) is also the title of a novel written by Bjørnstjerne Bjørnson, published in 1868. (Bjørnson frequented the salon hosted by Nansen's maternal grandmother, Maren Welhaven.)

and the rope fastened round his neck. The *Lagerführer* went up and asked him if he still persisted in refusing. He answered yes, and turning to the others, said quietly and firmly that they had only to be steadfast in their faith, the higher powers would protect them. Thus all of them were hanged one by one.*

FRIDAY, NOVEMBER 10, 1944 ■ The first relay of "volunteer" traitors is leaving today at last. In all probability they, like the BV-ers, will be used as partisans. That's the most dangerous thing of all, and few come out of it alive. Peter of the *Feuerwehr* [fire brigade], a great friend of mine, the finest and best German—and Communist—I have ever met, was sent off, alas.

SATURDAY, NOVEMBER 11, 1944 ■ Armistice Day in 1918—and the blood is flowing over the battlefields of Europe, thicker and darker than ever.

Mist and rain, almost snow it's so cold. But I plunged into my cottage scheme "Karistua,"† and dreamed myself away, above the mist, up among white mountains. There the sun shone.

MONDAY, NOVEMBER 13, 1944 ■ The cold gray weather continues. No news from the fronts, except the usual "yardstick reports." How slow we feel it's going, how terribly slow!

Yesterday, Sunday, I passed several hours among Jews. A transport of a thousand Jews has arrived here from Auschwitz, among them two Norwegians. One from Haugesund, an immigrant whom I don't know, and one from Oslo, my friend in North Norway and at Grini, [Leif] Wolfberg, who used to play the violin with Robert Andersen. These two Norwegians and one more, one of the Kaplan boys from Tromsø, must be the sole survivors of the Norwegian Jews who went to Auschwitz—and most of them apparently went there, about 800.

The Wolfberg I met again was quite different from the one I was with at Grini in 1942. That Wolfberg was a sickly, nervous boy, the type of boy one superficially and thoughtlessly calls a "coward." He was afraid of dying at that time, mortally afraid of dying. The Wolfberg I met yesterday had no fear of death; he was no nervous Jewish lad, but a grown man who faced reality unblinkingly, with wide-open eyes. Life was nothing more and nothing less to him than what it gave at the moment—pain or a faint little afterglow of joy. Yesterday it gave him a little joy, the first for a long time. He was glad to meet me, and talked away about "the old days" at Grini, what a pleasant time we had, how different. . . . And then gradually he got talking of the years since. Auschwitz!

I believe it will be hard for posterity, indeed for other people at all, to grasp the depth of suffering and horror of which Auschwitz has been the frame. Still less will it be possible to understand those who have survived it. That they can remain human beings, think and feel and be like human beings. One can't help admiring them, their calm, their cheerfulness, and their resignation. Mixing with these here, one actually gets the impression that they're on a kind of colossal outing. They talk and joke, question and

---

* One concentration camp survivor, writing about his experiences, concluded, "One cannot escape the impression that, psychologically speaking, the SS was never quite equal to the challenge offered them by Jehovah's Witnesses."

† Nansen did build his hytte, or cabin, in the early 1960s, which he christened "Karibu" instead; both names mean "Kari's cabin."

reply, laugh and smile. If one listens and looks more closely, sharpening one's eye and ear, one may indeed, perhaps, hear something hard in the laughter, detect something sad and weary in the smiles, something that must be hopelessness. But no tears or loud despair, no lamentations and scarcely an appeal for a little help. And yet that would be so natural, for they were ravenous; a few were picking up the trodden cabbage leaves and old rutabaga shavings that lay about the field and eating them, while others squatted about the same field at the call of nature. Or if they had asked for a smoke. I was expecting it, but they didn't. I just gave them what I had, and they seized it eagerly and shared with each other; the cigarettes went from mouth to mouth; no one got more than a few little puffs, but they were grateful and glad of that.

All of them were in rags and tatters, like all who come here—all *Zugängere* [new arrivals]. A sad sight in its way, but one we don't notice here; we all look the same. Otherwise most of them looked remarkably well; they were thin indeed and showed distinct signs of undernourishment, but so do most people here (except Norwegians), so one doesn't notice that much either. But none of them looked exactly doomed; they weren't walking skeletons, like so many Russians, Ukrainians, and others that one sees here in camp.* The explanation is a simple one; all who were so far gone either died or were killed in the gas chambers. These were the survivors, the pick of serviceable hands whom they can go on exploiting a while longer, in workshops and other working places, "for victory"! All the rest, sick, old and underage, had been killed. Just like that. They knew what it meant to fall ill or be disabled for any reason; it was the shortest way to the crematorium, and in Auschwitz—or rather in the camp just beside it, Birckenhof—there were five crematoria working without pause day and night—year after year.†

Wolfberg is not a good narrator; one has to drag out of him everything one wants to know, and it's slow work. Perhaps he doesn't feel there's much to tell, just everyday tragedies. And yet he's better than most people, who talk all too easily and fluently. They're apt to overcolor, and besides they're easily tempted by the cheapest sensations. Wolfberg is sober, and if he now and then—rarely—uses a strong word, then one knows it is justified.

THURSDAY, NOVEMBER 16, 1944 ■ I've met Wolfberg several evenings running and talked with him about Auschwitz. There seems to be little doubt that practically all the Norwegian Jews are dead. How many it's impossible to say, but it may be a whole thousand. He knows only of four or possibly five who are still living. Many saw death as a deliverance. One of the Kaplan boys (from Tromsø) and Salomon Schotland (Tromsø)‡

---

* Wolfberg worked as a violinist at Auschwitz-Birkenau and as a musician would have been entitled to slightly better food and clothing.

† Nansen is referring to Birkenau, also known as Auschwitz II. Four, not five, large gas chamber/crematoria facilities (known as crematoria II, III, IV, and V) were constructed in Birkenau between March and June of 1943 (use of crematorium I, in Auschwitz I, had been discontinued around the same time they were put into operation). The last gassings occurred in November 1944, at which time Himmler ordered the destruction of the crematoria to eliminate evidence of Nazi crimes; they were destroyed shortly before the camp's liberation on January 27. In all, approximately 90 percent of all deaths in Auschwitz occurred in Birkenau; approximately 90 percent of these victims were Jews.

‡ Salomon Shotland (1902–1943). Included in the transport to Germany on November 26, 1942, Shotland was killed in Auschwitz less than three months later, on February 11, 1943. A review of Yad Vashem's Central Database of Shoah Victim's Names indicates that Shotland's mother, father, sister, brother, sister-in-law, and eighteen-month-old nephew were all murdered at Auschwitz. The Kaplan (or Caplan) Nansen refers to is likely Herze Kaplan (1913–1943); he was murdered March 3, 1943, less than one month after Shotland. In addition to younger brother Konrad (see immediately below), Herze Kaplan's father and older brother were also killed in Auschwitz.

were at roll call one morning. Schotland said, "Look here, I can't stand any more of this, it's too ghastly, and there's not much sense in our working away here for these swine till we die. I've had enough. Come, let's report at the ambulance!" They agreed without more debate, and asked if Wolfberg wouldn't come too, but he said he would try a little longer, take one more chance. Then they parted, and Wolfberg never saw his friends again.

The youngest of the Kaplan boys, Konrad, was a different type—young (twenty-two) and with more hold on life. Also full of heart and the urge to help others. He had a job on the "ramp," that is, on the platform where the railway cars drew up to the crematorium buildings, with their tragic loads of people mostly condemned to death. Transport after transport from Hungary, from Slovakia, Bohemia, Moravia, Germany, Belgium, Holland, Norway, France, Yugoslavia, the Ukraine, with thousands upon thousands more Jews, came rolling in to that ramp. When the cars had been emptied, the Jews were lined up five and five on the ramp, and a selection was made. All the healthy and able-bodied were picked out; the rest were for the "baths."

All the small children went into the "bath." Every woman with a child in her arms went the same way, and all the old and feeble. This was known to all who worked on the ramp, but the poor creatures who arrived with the transport had no suspicion of it. Therefore it might well seem brutal and incomprehensible to a young, strong woman when Konrad Kaplan came and took the child out of her arms and gave it to an old woman instead. Konrad wanted to save the young woman, and he had to do it like that, with no words or explanations, but peremptorily. For in any case the child and the old woman were going to die.*

Then—when those who were to die had been separated from those who were to live—the death cortege moved off to the crematoria. These contained, besides the gas chambers and the furnaces, which could burn forty-eight corpses at a time, a big dressing room, where they were taken on the pretext that they were to have a bath. They undressed without suspicion and went into the "bath," which was next door. There gas came out of the showers instead of water. How long it was turned on before they died Wolfberg didn't know, nor did he know whether it was a painful death. The road from the bath to the furnace was short. This process has now been going on several years without a break, and in spite of that the five crematoria have been inadequate. They also had to burn corpses out in the open. As fuel they used wood and coal, both in the crematoria and outside. The whole process—stoking, moving corpses and all—was of course attended to by the prisoners themselves. No SS man soiled his hands with such dirty work as Jew-killing.

A little Jewish boy, ten or twelve years old, was to go into the "bath." He didn't want to, and dodged out of the column, but was caught at once. They put him back in the ranks, but he ran away again. Then he was caught and put in a closed truck for the moment, and the door locked. He broke the window and crawled out. The *Lagerführer*

---

* In *Tommy*, a work Nansen published in 1970 that covers the story of Thomas Buergenthal in more detail, Nansen wrote of Konrad Kaplan (who died January 10, 1945, less than three weeks before liberation): "When the Auschwitz camp was later evacuated, the boy still stood on the ramp. Then he had to deal with convoys which were taking the prisoners away. The only thing he could do for his fellow captives was to get them better clothes than the rags they as a rule had. The last I know about him was that he stood half naked and starvation thin and waved to a convoy that rolled away. He had given away his own clothes to those who needed them. It was midwinter, minus fifteen degrees centigrade [5°F]. He never got away from Auschwitz. He stayed at his post, like a captain on a sinking ship. Unknown and as quietly as he did his deed in life, he took his place among the martyrs in the death columns of genocide." Kaplan had just turned twenty-two years old.

felt that that boy had fought bravely for his life and let him live. I suppose a case of Aryan magnanimity. Now the child is an errand boy and on a kind of "easy" footing with the *Lagerführer*, who pats him on the shoulder and plays the uncle.

When Wolfberg said to me that first evening, with a straightforward, unsentimental openness, "I assure you, Odd, I shouldn't care if I were going into the furnace tonight, I'm fully prepared for it," he meant what he said. When he asked me if I thought any of them would come through this alive and get back home after the war, to tell the truth I didn't know what to answer, for there is no denying it would be queer and inconsistent to leave such witnesses alive to tell posterity and the world what has been going on. But then it occurred to me that they might want to have some Jews in the camps just now, to show that even they were treated as human beings and looked after and assisted by the Third Reich—and at the same time, at this eleventh hour of the *Volkssturm* [national militia], they must need labor to the last man, whether he's Jewish, Negro or Germanic—and I said that. "Do you think so?" said he, and it was as though a little gleam of hope shone in his eyes, a grateful little gleam.

Wolfberg and the other Norwegian received a Danish Red Cross parcel each and were delighted.

The day before yesterday seven hundred Jews arrived here from Yugoslavia. They were Hungarian Jews and were all in soldiers' uniforms, or their remains. They had been on the march for ten weeks, all the way from the Yugoslavian frontier, and had scarcely any clothes or shoes left. They were in a miserable condition; many had died on the way; they had dead bodies with them too, and several died on the parade ground, where they had to stand for most of the night after their arrival here. They had wrapped their legs, arms and bodies in paper and sacks picked up by the roadside, to keep warm. No doubt most of them will be going on again, the same way as the others who have been sent off already.*

Yesterday 160 Norwegians arrived from the convict prison in Sonnenburg.† They also were in a miserable state. Six of them went into the *Revier*—T.B.

FRIDAY, NOVEMBER 17, 1944 ■ For the first time in Sachsenhausen, apart from the first month or so, we're short of food. The bread ration, most of which I used to give away, is no longer adequate, and I'm wondering if I shan't begin eating soup again. It's a long time since I did. We've had no butter for a long time, only now and then a kind of grease which goes by that name, and which is doled out to us twice a week, a small dab each. Potatoes too have been getting scarce. We're always having potatoless days, and then there's no "Irish stew" out here on the job—which had become a regular institution and the chief meal of the day. Indeed it's a long time since I ate more than the two meals I have out here. Birger [Bjerkeng]‡ and I breakfast together on a cup of hot "coffee" and sandwiches. We bring the bread with us every day, and we keep a tin here with what we've

---

* The deteriorating war situation in Germany by this time meant that trains were increasingly hard to come by, forcing prospective prisoners to march to their camps instead.

† In 1933 Nazi Germany converted an old prison into a concentration camp for political prisoners in Sonnenburg, a village in eastern Germany. The Norwegians were fortunate to leave when they did; the site is notorious for the massacre of all remaining prisoners (819) by the SS on the night of January 30/31, 1945, prior to their fleeing the camp. The postwar Potsdam Conference detached Sonnenburg from Germany and awarded it to Poland, which renamed it Słońsk.

‡ Bjerkeng was the carpenter who helped Nansen modify the six breadboards that hid his diary. Arrested in April 1941 for espionage (he was carrying a letter from Norwegian authorities in England to the governor of Finnmark province),

smuggled out in the way of sardines, cheese, etc., etc. Everything is forbidden! That's what one does.

At the dinner of Irish stew that I prepare—as I have most freedom I'm the cook—there are four of us—[Arne] Utvik,* [Arne] Holt,† Birger [Bjerkeng] and I. It is an artistic blend of all sorts of things. Potatoes, bouillon, sausage, pâté, ham, carrots, onions, etc., depending on what we have. The dish is already famous, and doubts are expressed as to whether anything approximately as delicious is ever served at home in peacetime. It won't be easy for the wives when these fellows come home with allusions to Irish stew à la Nansen!

TUESDAY, NOVEMBER 21, 1944 ■ Just now a singular patrol is marching round and round the parade ground interminably. All are fully equipped and fitted out and sing and whistle as they walk. That's the "pill patrol." They're being used to test out a new energy pill. How long can they keep going full steam on it? After the first forty-eight hours it's said that most of them had given up and collapsed, although the theory is that after taking this pill one can perform the incredible without the usual reaction afterward. Well, no doubt the Germans could use a pill like that now. The guinea pigs are arrested SA men, so they say.‡ Anyhow they sing and carry on like most Germans—so it hasn't necessarily anything to do with the pills.§

FRIDAY, NOVEMBER 24, 1944 ■ There have been great reductions in working hours, in order to save electric current. We actually get a whole hour's extra sleep in the morning, until quarter past five, and stop at quarter of four in the afternoon. Besides which there will probably be no more work on Sundays. This doesn't fit in very well with the total war effort, about which they make noise enough in general, but it's a most revealing indication of the state of things in the Reich. Of course it's the coal shortage making itself felt. No doubt the Ruhr will soon be going down the drain, and if Upper Silesia goes too, I suppose that will be the end of the coal supplies. And then? Why, God knows if they still won't manage to scrape along.

WEDNESDAY, DECEMBER 13, 1944 ■ One big transport after another is arriving in camp—from Auschwitz, from other camps in Poland, from camps in Germany, and "evacuated" Jews by thousands from Hungary. Two thousand six hundred Jews arrived the other day from Budapest. The transport hadn't taken more than three days. Eighty died on the way, and when they got here they were left standing out in the cold most of the night. Eight died on the parade ground. None had had a drop of water for three days. Food they had brought from home.

---

he was later sent to Germany where he was tried by the Volksgerichtshof, or infamous People's Court. Miraculously acquitted, Bjerkeng was nevertheless sent to Sachsenhausen where he remained for the duration of the war.

* Utvik survived the war.

† Holt remained in Sachsenhausen until war's end.

‡ The SA, or *Sturmabteilung* [literally, stormtroopers] were the original paramilitary wing of the Nazi Party. Known as the Brownshirts, the SA was eclipsed in 1934 by the SS following the so-called Night of the Long Knives, when the SA's leader, Ernst Röhm, and many of its senior officers were murdered.

§ The Nazis experimented with forms of methamphetamine and cocaine as a stimulant for fighting forces during the war. Both Allied and Axis forces pursued the use of stimulants to enhance alertness, especially for flyers, but also for submarine crews needing to be deployed for days on end.

I remember, when the first transport of *évacués* arrived from Warsaw, we were indignant that women, children and the aged should be dragged off in such transports. Now there aren't many who react. Children, some under ten years old, are detained as convicts here and in other camps. The women are sent to camps of their own. The aged are allowed to die here. The process is short, but not painless. It's terrible to see them. Those who come from Poland, for instance, have nothing to put on but the rags issued here, and it's the depth of winter. Only a very few have anything on their feet but wooden boards tied on with straps or string. Of course they get pneumonia, tuberculosis and other illnesses and succumb by the hundreds. They totter round for a while, go into the *Revier* (unless they're Jews, in which case they're not admitted) and there the crown is set on the work, especially in the *Schonungsblocken*, where they're treated more like animals than anything else. If one goes through one of the *Schonungsblocken* (as I have been doing quite often of late), one keeps on seeing living skeletons. Starving Poles, especially those with *Durchfall* [diarrhea] who can't retain any of the miserable fare they get. Diet? One can only laugh. An unknown concept. A Jewish builder from Budapest, whom I've gotten to know, and who was on the terrible march from South Serbia to Germany, told me that one of his arms began to swell up and ache. He went to the doctor, who diagnosed periostitis, put the arm in splints and bandaged it, explaining that it was due to undernourishment and the lack of certain substances in his food. He must eat more, a more nourishing and varied diet—fat for one thing. Merely a gibe, a frigid sneer.

The other evening I was talking to an old Pole in that *Schonungsblock*. He was sixty-seven, but looked ninety-seven; bones, sinews, and skin apart, I'll wager his flesh and stomach didn't weigh five kilos [eleven pounds]. That he could hold himself up was a miracle, but obviously a miracle that would soon cease. He had great difficulty in speaking, and he spoke nothing but Polish. An interpreter translated. He was a Polish peasant from the Warsaw district, and had been "evacuated" here, starving and suffering, starving and suffering; of the rest of his family, children and wife, he knew nothing. They had lost each other during the "evacuation." Now he had *Durchfall* and couldn't eat. He had already gone out, was no longer a man, only a poor, suffering, still living creature waiting for peace. There are hundreds and thousands like him—innocent, harmless, suffering human beings.

THURSDAY, DECEMBER 14, 1944 ■ Yesterday I had a letter from Kari! And one came on my birthday itself. Every one of these letters is a gleam of light in the darkness. I can't help thinking of all the thousands who have no such gleams. How profoundly thankful we should be, we who are well off, who are not in want, and who have good news from our dear ones at home! But these ideas, which arise whenever one looks into the faces of the starving, shattered human beings who surround one everywhere in the camp, make one sad and heavyhearted. It isn't well to be "well off" among so many who are badly off. The only possible relief is to share the material goods which are divided among us so unequally and unjustly. To see a starving, broken-down Ukrainian eat his fill is a far richer and deeper satisfaction than most this life here can offer. But his dog's eyes while he's eating and afterward are unbearable. And it's only so infinitely little one can do to help.

To tell the truth, of the senseless abundance in the Norwegian blocks only a distressingly small amount is given away without a demand for something in return. There is

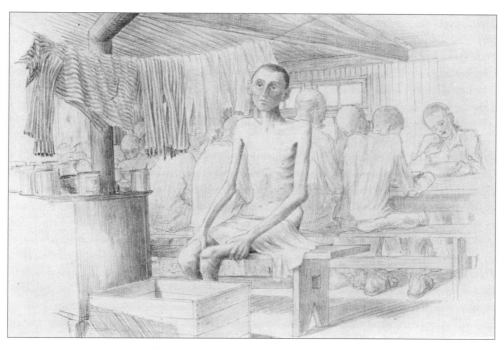

A Ukrainian lad drying his clothes in the hut.

bargaining and scrounging, but not *giving*. Thus it's only the "fittest" and the smart who get anything, those who can steal for others who daren't steal themselves, but find it safer to pay a tin of sardines, a slice of ham, or a bit of cheese for what they want. It's the Ukrainian, the Russian, the Pole who takes the whole risk, and who is hanged or punished if it's found out. The Norwegian owner of sardines, ham, cheese, butter, sausage, tobacco and all the good things that make life here livable and bearable goes scot free. No one suspects *him*. Indeed, so solid is our reputation on this point that if there's a search for stolen potatoes, liquor, or other things, the Norwegians are not searched. Our cupboards are left alone, our possessions are never ransacked, nor our persons touched. Norwegians don't steal—that's what they say. And if a Norwegian happens (and it has happened) to be caught in the act of stealing, or of smoking in working hours, he doesn't get the flogging which the Ukrainian, Pole, Jew, or Russian would have gotten in the same situation. By no means—the Norwegian usually goes scot free; only in a few cases does he get a spell of [Block] 38, and even there the treatment of Norwegians is quite different from that of the other prisoners, who are flogged all the time. Norwegians aren't flogged now. It was different once, in "the bad time," but in those days they had no parcels. And it's those parcels, first and foremost, that have placed the Norwegians on a special footing—not so much the fact that we are "Aryans" and moreover belong to the group of "Aryans" that is purest and that the Germans therefore envy and admire most.

This unfairness has a very bad effect, not only on the relations between the Norwegians and the others, but on the Norwegians themselves, on the individual. We look on it increasingly as a matter of course, look down on others and feel ourselves to be grandees.

I can have a smoke; *I* can take a rest; *I* can do a bit of "moonlighting" work for myself; *ich bin nämlich Norweger!* [I am a Norwegian!] And so we lounge on our way, grocers in spirit and in fact, Jews as that word is understood when we use it as a term of abuse—and we nearly always do, not least in this place. At any rate one would suppose we'd be above *that*. But no! We howl with the Germans and with others: *Verdammte Juden!* [damned Jews!] A Norwegian of my acquaintance, a decent chap on the whole, gave himself away the other day when we got talking of all that these unhappy Jews had to suffer.

"Well, and it serves them right!" said he. "*I* know them; I live in the same block with them. Every day I see what they're like. If one of them gets a parcel, off he goes into a corner and eats it up by himself. Never sharing with anyone, always stealing from each other, always cheating and swindling each other! No, I've had enough of Jews. Thank goodness we had only one at home, in Ålesund. *He* was bad enough."

"Well, you can certainly count on being rid of *him* now," said I. "No doubt he was disposed of in Auschwitz along with a thousand more Norwegian Jews, so you may rejoice, if you can!" And then of course I said a whole lot more, for I get so easily worked up. The thing was that on one of my visits to the Jewish block where this Norwegian lives, I had happened to get a look inside his cupboard. It was as crammed with food and good things as a cupboard can well be. He must certainly have stored up provisions for two or three months ahead. Round him in the block are starving fellow creatures, most of them from Auschwitz. The thought may pass through one's mind—what would the Norwegian have been like if *he* had gone through as much, when even now, without having gone through anything but the ordinary, banal brutalizing process that all go through here, he can keep to himself, in a padlocked cupboard, food and tobacco and all sorts of good things, while people round about him are literally starving? Comradeship, indeed!

As though we didn't steal, too. In our block alone, recently, a whole Swedish parcel and a whole Danish parcel have been stolen, and two Swiss parcels have been opened, looted of cigarettes, and closed up again. Besides which things are stolen daily out of cupboards and pockets. As though we hadn't our egoists and misers! A Norwegian of the highest social class hoarded in his bed, boxes, and cupboard to such a point that action was taken. It was monstrous the amount he had! Then he was said to be ill. For he was a *Norweger*—and not a Jew, not a Ukrainian, Russian or Pole. If a "good" Norwegian steals, he's a "kleptomaniac"—how sad. Poor dear fellow, who would have thought it? There are also "bad" Norwegians who steal, men who have stolen before, who have a bad record, who *are* like that. But it occurs to no one to share the responsibility or to feel that they themselves have a part in the disgrace. No indeed! But the disgrace of a single Jew— whether "good" or "bad"—is divided equally among all Jews. And it's the same today with Poles, Ukrainians, and to some extent Russians in this camp. They are "*grundsätzlich*" scum.

I've talked with a Norwegian who used to live in the wing I've just been writing of. He never had a padlock on *his* cupboard, and in all the time he lived there, nothing was stolen from him. But then he gave away, shared with his comrades, Jew and Gentile. I heard that from the others afterward.

MONDAY, DECEMBER 18, 1944 ■ This year Christmas celebrations are forbidden in any form, nor may prisoners be employed on "Christmas gifts," toys and so forth, nor may material be used for such a purpose. In spite of which this very work is in progress on a big scale in practically every kommando. I am making Christmas cards one after the other, designing Santa Clauses, building blocks, games, and all kinds of illegalities, as though this were the first year of war instead of the sixth, and as though the Germans had great, decisive victories before and behind them, instead of having reached the last lines of the last distressful verse. Finn Aanesen must be about the worst pessimist among us; he bet the other day that the war wouldn't be over by next Christmas. Really there are limits. I immediately bet that it would be over by Easter.

The Jewish builder from Budapest who was in the march from South Serbia to the German frontier has told me some details about that 840 kilometer [520 mile] trek.

"The expedition went off all right to begin with," he said. "We were well treated and well fed, and as most of us were strong and healthy we stood up to its fatigues all right. But then we crossed the frontier into Hungary. One day the guard of Hungarian soldiers and their officers disappeared, and only SS were left.

"We arrived one day at an abandoned brickworks. Never shall I be able to forget what happened there. We had had nothing to eat or drink for two days. When we reached that brickworks, we were completely worn out with hunger, thirst and exertion. Twenty-five names were called out by a *Scharführer*. These twenty-five were taken away, and we heard shots from tommy guns. They shot at them until none was left standing; then they came in and fetched more. (The tears were streaming down his cheeks as he went on talking.) They were our friends . . . my good friends! They were human beings like us . . . they had wives and children! Used for target practice! Nearly two thousand men were killed that night. We were all expecting our turn and felt certain we were all to die. But then they suddenly stopped, and the next day the march continued; we were now only a thousand odd. A number had died of overstrain or had been shot because they couldn't keep going.

"We were now in southern Hungary, and the roads were filled with Swabians (German immigrants with Hungarian citizenship—German "colonists" in Hungary) who were being evacuated. Besides the endless train of trucks full of Swabians, women and children and household goods, the roadway was filled with our own SS soldiers and their transport trucks. We had to run by the roadside. Once we ran twenty kilometers [12 miles] without stopping, in a ditch full of water. The water was above our ankles. The Swabians, women, children and men, struck us with ropes' ends and abused us the whole time as the cause of their calamity. The SS men, who were also Swabians, drove us on with whips and firearms; those who couldn't go on were shot and left in the ditch.

"One day we reached a town. Outside the gate we all had to lie down on our faces in the mud. We lay there a long time, an hour or two, it's impossible for me to say; all of us thought our last hour had come. But we weren't killed, only plundered of all we had in the way of rings, pins, money or watches. Then we were led into the town, to the slaughter-house; in the yard, which was streaming with blood and offal from the slaughtering, a halt was made. Again we were expecting the worst. An NCO demanded to speak to three representatives. Three were chosen; I was one of them. The NCO asked what we would like. We didn't understand him. He asked again what we would like—something to drink or something to eat or something else. We hadn't eaten or drunk for forty-eight hours and said that we would like food and drink. No! We could only ask for one thing, *either* food *or* drink. We agreed to choose water. Our tongues were sticking to our palates. Thirst was really the worst of all. We were given water. We drank like animals and fell sick. I drank three liters. From that moment the natural deaths began.

"We got no food until the next day, then there was an NCO who was well disposed to us. He gave us a live cow. We slaughtered it, and as there were no cooking vessels but an empty gas cask, we got that open and boiled the meat in it. Then I saw for the first time that men are animals. They didn't eat like men, they hurled themselves upon the kill like wild beasts, and scraped and clawed the flesh from the bones with their hands and teeth. It was an appalling sight; I shall never forget it. Nearly a thousand men, dead beat and half mad with hunger, in a slaughterhouse full of blood, slime, and bits of entrails and filth, hurling themselves on and rending in pieces the quarters of a cow boiled in a gas cask. The meat tasted horrible, saturated as it was with gas, and of course we fell even sicker than before. But still it was food, we had something in our stomachs, and that was a relief.

"Then we had to go on. On we went on the double, nearly always on the double. Many ran until they dropped, and if we couldn't drag them along without the guards seeing us, they were simply shot. Oddly enough it was the youngest who suffered most; they had the least stamina. I am forty-three, and I came through, while young men between twenty and thirty had to give in. One man who was done, we had picked up between us and were carrying in a blanket. An SS man saw it, stopped us and said he knew of a much better method. Then he tied a rope around our friend's feet and fastened the other end to the truck. He hadn't been dragged behind the truck long before he died. That was done to many of us. Once when we made a halt, twenty or twenty-five men were picked out and made to kneel down in the road in front of the transport. The photographs of their dear ones they had on them were laid on the ground before each man, and their prayer rugs spread on top. (They were carrying prayer-rugs and prayer-belts and all kinds of religious equipment, for many of them were strictly orthodox.) They were ordered to pray. They might pray to Hitler, they were told, pray to get back home again; it was in his hands. While they prayed, all of them were shot.

"We had *Scheisserei*. One of us had to fall out and relieve himself. He was ordered back, but had already started, and it's impossible to stop in such case. He was ordered to eat up all of his excrement, and forced into it at the point of a revolver. When he had done it, he was shot.

"We got hardly anything to eat. A little bread now and then, and a little water. Otherwise we tried to pick up something eatable by the roadside. We passed fields of potatoes, turnips, rutabaga, beets. If detected, we were shot; but we took the risk, and often managed to get hold of a little something. That was what saved us from collapse.

"A favorite sport with the SS was to order a number of us up into the trees, ten or twelve at a time. They had to climb up high, sit on the branches, and sing Jewish songs. As they sang they were shot down like birds, and the shooting didn't stop until none was left on the branches.

"Thus our days went by for almost three months; then we reached the German frontier. Here the Swabian SS guards were exchanged for German SS, young boys, some of them only fourteen or fifteen. From that moment a complete change took place. There was no more shooting or beating, and we were given food, regular, proper food, for the first time in many weeks. We had now covered a stretch of about 850 kilometers [527 miles] and had taken nearly three months. In that time we had had, altogether, two loaves, on rare occasions a little soup, besides water—also occasionally—and the cow I spoke of. From the German frontier to this camp we traveled by train and were very well treated.

We were in decent second-class carriages, and nothing happened to us before we got here. Here we got a bath—*herrlich!* [wonderful!]—and had these clothes issued to us."

He displayed the rags dangling about him, but not at all by way of complaint; on the contrary, he is pleased with everything in the camp and regards it as a paradise. He says that when they were taken into the bathhouse, there were many who refused to go. They had heard of such baths, and naturally expected this to be one of the same kind, signifying the end of their journey—that fantastic journey which was begun by three thousand men, but of which only eight hundred and fifty saw the end. Some of those who got here, however, were in such a wretched condition that they died a few days later in the *Revier*.

Most of these Jews, incidentally, have already been sent on by transport to another camp. My friend the builder and a few others were detained here by sickness. In addition to the periostitis in his arm, he has caught some infectious disease; we can't go and see him. One touching detail I must relate about this man. I've given him a few clothes and cigarettes and some food. He was very anxious to show his gratitude. One day he came to me with a little thing he wanted to give me as a souvenir, and I had to promise to keep it. It was, he said, the best thing he owned; he had nothing else. It was one of the cigarettes he had had from me, neatly wrapped up in silver paper. I had given him only three that time; I was in low water, too. After the war, he added, he would give me the same present in gold and precious stones.

TUESDAY, DECEMBER 19, 1944 ■ Went to see Rolf [Hofmo] yesterday. He's still in the *Revier*. This must be the fifth month, and we're worried about him. He's been transferred to Oftedal's section, and will at any rate have the best attention and treatment one can get here.

WEDNESDAY, DECEMBER 20, 1944 ■ The day before yesterday the Germans launched an offensive in the West and advanced sixteen kilometers [10 miles] in Luxembourg and Belgium.* Of course the SS are in high feather. In [*Hauptsturmführer*] Steger's office they celebrated with champagne, and Follmann was screwed up several pegs. He started abusing the Americans and English to me, and was half expecting me to agree with his outpourings. I said, "There's really not much point in our discussing this subject. You mustn't expect me to agree with you, and I can see you won't like it if I reply sincerely. I have a country too, *Rottenführer* Follmann, and the fight for mine doesn't coincide with the fight for yours."

He turned white in the face; I wasn't quite sure if he was in a rage, but to be on the safe side I offered him a cigarette and said that all the same we could smoke a pipe of peace together. He wouldn't take one, said in a martyred voice that he preferred to smoke his Mahorka, and began to fill his pipe with that substance.

---

* The Battle of the Bulge began on December 16, 1944, when 200,000 German forces attacked a weakly defended area of the Allied lines in the densely forested Ardennes Mountains of Luxembourg and southern Belgium. It was the largest and bloodiest battle for the Americans in World War II, with nearly 90,000 casualties. By mid-January 1945, superior Allied air power and determined American resistance (such as at Bastogne) spelled the end of the German offensive. German losses of manpower (estimated at 100,000) and armor could not be readily replaced, and Germany was never able to undertake a major offensive again. One historian has remarked, "Hitler's 'last gamble'. . . was extremely short-sighted. It bought a little time at great cost, failed in its object . . . and won back no ground at all."

What children they are! How ignorant, how stupid, how petty minded! But so much the better; the fewer one is forced to respect in any way, the better it is.

FRIDAY, DECEMBER 22, 1944 ■ The world is black as pitch; now the Germans have advanced fifty kilometers [31 miles] in Belgium, and the SS are in uncontrollable spirits; they rage and storm as though they were on the Volga and are fantastic. Truly it's better after all to be a prisoner when things are going badly for them. It looks as though they should be having a hilarious Christmas. To be sure a meter's advance for them today is like six miles a couple of years ago—then what shall we say of fifty thousand meters? Of course they're drunk with it!

TUESDAY, DECEMBER 26, 1944 ■ Christmas 1944 is over and soon we shall be in the New Year. Strange as it may sound, I don't believe that I at least have looked so darkly on the future at any year's end since the war began. But I'm in no condition to see it cheerfully.

1945

WEDNESDAY, JANUARY 4, 1945 ■ Well, I got no further; didn't even manage to say anything of how we kept Christmas. The main reason was that Frode and I, quite on our own, got into a fever of hectic and intense activity. We made up a whole "New Year's revue" in the few days that were left before New Year's Eve.* But first a word or two about Christmas.

A long and detailed program had been drawn up for Christmas Eve. Our hut had been decorated by busy "night workers," and adorned with paintings of Norwegian landscapes, brownies, etc. However, our application to the SS chiefs for leave to celebrate Christmas as planned was, on the 23rd, rejected suddenly and point-blank. Thick red lines through every item, and a red *nein*, of temper and vexation, constituted the reply. Very good! An extra seasoning to the Christmas fare. For we carried out our program unabridged, all but the clergyman with the Christmas gospel; him we dropped. Frode made a speech. There was a joint meal, sandwiches, *Lagerbier* [lager beer], biscuits, crispbread and smokes. There was singing, choral and individual, recitation and a prologue and all kinds of larks. The climax however, this year as last, was Arnulf Øverland with a magnificent poem, which he read himself.

German "magnanimity" in honor of the day extended to half-past ten, when all had to go to bed. But Christmas Day was a day off. No roll call until quarter of nine. Fabulously generous!

When, after a good night's sleep, full fed and contented, I issued forth next morning into the piercing cold winter day, a macabre spectacle confronted me as I was passing the old Norwegian blocks which are now *Revier* blocks. From [Block] Number 2 a couple of skeleton bodies were being carried out and laid on a stretcher, which was on the ground

---

* Both Nansen and Rinnan were students together at NTH and both were members of the Student Society of Trondheim; Rinnan was its chair (1928–1929).

outside the door. The corpses, frozen stiff with arms and legs sticking out in all directions, looked grotesque with their open, staring, glazed eyes. The two bearers bent and broke the arms and legs to make them lie better on the stretcher. They were laid on top of each other; it was too narrow for them side by side. The bearers were smoking cigarettes, and joking and laughing, like all the others who were passing or standing round. For it was Christmas Day, and a day off, and fine weather. I turned and walked on; and then they carried another staring, bristling corpse out of [Block] Number 1.

It's an eloquent proof of what we're like now, that on most of us a "Christmas morning idyll" of this kind has no effect whatever. We go on smoking, go on talking about the war, the Christmas program, the dinner; devote perhaps to the whole matter a brief remark on how "beastly" it is, and then shake it off again.

And we went on parade. It was a long one, in biting cold. Even in good warm clothes, and Swedish boots with soles and snow stockings inside, one felt cold, and it was delicious to get inside the block afterward, to a hot stove, get something hot inside one, and enjoy the "free day." There were hundreds on that parade in thin camp rags, without underclothing, with bare feet on wooden soles, and two of these hundreds froze to death on the parade ground that morning. How many got the *coup de grâce* is unknown. We continued our program on the evening of Christmas Day. Prisoners came in from other blocks; there was a Christmas spirit, food and drink. And a lot of drunkenness. All the prominent *Blockälteste*, *Vorarbeiters*, and their gangs had gotten hold of liquor, God knows how or

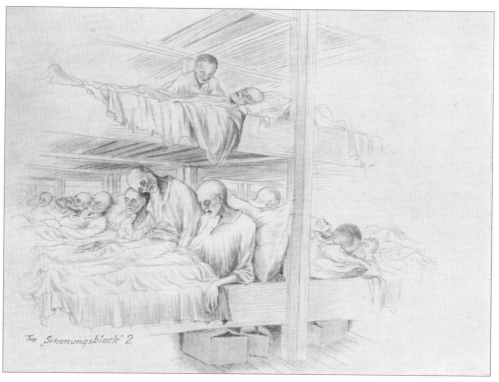

In Schonungsblock 2, *one of the corpse factories.*

where from but drunk they were, and they were staggering round the camp and kicking up a row in the blocks all night through.

FRIDAY, JANUARY 6, 1945 ■ The other day, while I was away from the job, one of them, probably Follmann, had been in my drawer and taken the last page of the diary. There was nothing in it that anyone might not read, but still it's unpleasant. Later I heard that Follmann had gone to a Norwegian in the next workshop to have it translated. He had said threateningly that it was no use translating wrong; the matter would be going further in any case. As I said, the page contained nothing serious, nothing about the SS, nothing about the camp, only about Frode's and my work on a little New Year's revue we got up and something about coffee.

What happened was that the Frenchmen in camp received Christmas parcels. Month after month they had been waiting for the French Red Cross parcels, and here they were—at last! With trembling, bony hands and famished expectation they opened the parcels and found, apart from small crackers, sweetmeats, and little French *raffinements* [refinements], half a kilo [1 pound] of coffee! Almost a jeer at *Muselmenn* who had been expecting food. Food! But the Norwegians had food—sausage, ham, cheese, sardines—and an orgy of exchange began. Coffee! Real coffee! It was marvelous. Frode and I were caffeine-drunk for several days, didn't sleep at night, did nothing but compose and write. It was a kind of fever, a strange kind of reaction from all the dreariness and gloom, from the cold and dark and the German offensive in the West. And the result was a success. We amused both ourselves and others. I wrote, among other things, a song about the bomb nights.

SATURDAY, JANUARY 14, 1945 ■ I've been sacked from Kfz.D.W., simply countermanded, and had to pack my things the same day to return no more. But first something happened. This is Saturday, it must have been on Tuesday evening that my drawers in the glass cage were ransacked by Irsch after working hours. Besides a lot of miscellaneous drawings and papers, and fifteen or sixteen water colors, including many studies of Ukrainians, *Muselmenn*, etc., he took away a rough draft of the bomb song; none of it as dangerous as the page of diary Follmann had secured earlier, for that indicates that there are more pages. It even began in the middle of a sentence. And then those water colors. Irsch had seen them before, a couple anyhow, and said nothing. One can't possibly be hanged for them. No, all in all it's a harmless business, but an incident like that always means a certain amount of trouble.

Well, I returned "home" that day, laden with my drawing things and so on, and went straight off with Scott [Isaksen] to the *Vorarbeiter* at "*Herz As*" to "secure" my transfer there. *Herz As* is the kommando Scott works in, and there are no SS there. That was all right. When we got back to the block we met Erik [Magelssen]. He had news. More trouble! Where were we (Erik and I) on the 5th of January, and where was Nansen on the 3rd? On the 3rd I was at *Herz As* looking about me, and on the 5th we were both at Schützen-Gilde—an outlying kommando—where we were to have gone with a goods truck on a long-planned trip to Berlin, but failed to get off. But we had played truant, and been found out. We could already imagine ourselves in [Block] 38, after twenty-five on the arse—if not worse. Things did look pretty awkward. We started running from pillar to post in search of advice on what to do. At last we found the right man. Before night, the matter was arranged. We could sleep in peace, our man assured us.

And since then I've been hanging about the camp, unemployed, without a kommando. The thing is that one should manage nothing for oneself. One shouldn't go to a kommando without being summoned. One must wait for instructions to come through from the highest authorities in the *Arbeitsdienst*, and no instructions have yet arrived. It really suits me well enough to loaf around here a bit—if only it *is* all right. For that matter another Norwegian hung about like this for two months. The war effort!

My protégés are getting on. The Jew from Budapest totters over to me every day on his swollen legs to fetch his soup—or rather my soup, bread ration, bit of sausage, bag of sugar, etc., etc. And he's improving, slowly but surely. A Belgian architect also comes every day. I've mobilized Arvid [Johansen]. He's grand. He would give the shirt off his back where others would make a hundred objections.

TUESDAY, JANUARY 17, 1945 ■ Yesterday was like a nightmare from morning to night. I don't know how I'm to give a picture of it.

The night before last I received a slip of paper ordering me to go to the *Russen Isolierung* [Russian isolation] next day, to be brought before the *Arbeitseinsatz* and given a *Kommando*. I had a feeling that this boded ill; it's at these *Vorstellungen* [interviews] that transports are made up. But I was assured there would be no question of that in my case.

At eight o'clock precisely I passed through the barrier of the *Russen Isolierung*, an enclosed area between Block 11 and Block 12, housing several hundred Russian prisoners of war who work here, but who for some reason are isolated and not allowed to mix with the other prisoners. Here Jews and *Zugängere* live, until they are assigned a kommando or sent on transports. Here live the "death gangs," under close guard in a separate block. These are gangs of saboteurs or looters from Berlin and other places, often mere boys down to the age of twelve or fourteen.* All these prisoners have black crosses painted on their faces, one on the forehead and one on each cheek. The most dangerous of them are handcuffed day and night, others at night only. Here, too, are deserters who have been caught again and as a rule are waiting to be hanged. The "death gangs" also are waiting to die. Here live the whole SK punishment kommando, *Schuhläufer* [shoe testing kommando] who are being used to test out different types of shoes.†

Well, so I entered this enclosure yesterday morning. As yet there weren't many prison-

---

* In fact, many of these looters were among the 400,000 foreign workers serving as forced laborers in Berlin who were rendered homeless (and starving) by Allied bombing. According to one historian, "The Nazis reacted to the increase in theft and looting by granting wide-ranging powers of execution to the Gestapo at a local level."

† The shoe-testing kommando served a dual purpose. With leather becoming scarce during the war, the regime encouraged firms to develop substitutes, which needed to be tested first. In addition, the SS used the walking detail as a special punishment against targeted individuals. Testers (numbering between 120 and 170 at any one time) had to cover twenty-five to thirty miles daily carrying packs containing up to thirty pounds of bricks or sandbags. According to one Sachsenhausen inmate: "[T]runcheon-wielding SS guards ensured that they kept up a smart pace and sang when required to do so. . . . As an added refinement of torture some were forced to wear boots which were too small for them." Another historian described transfer to the *Schuhläufer* as "practically a death sentence." Dr. Ernst Brennscheidt, the Reich official in charge of shoe testing, was tried by a Soviet military tribunal after the war and sentenced to fifteen years.

ers gathered there, and I thought the whole *Vorstellung* (as it's called) would be over in half
an hour. I was soon to know better and see things differently.

It was icy cold, fourteen degrees of frost [6.8° F], and misty. I was congealed. The
yard began to fill with prisoners, who streamed in through the gate, and out of the blocks
in the enclosure. There were Jews, Hungarians, Belgians, Frenchmen, a German or two,
Slovaks, Poles, Russians, Danes and Norwegians. I began to look closer at them. It was
appalling. The worst were the Jews and other *Zugängere. Most of them were barefoot.* I
went up and spoke to some of them. Were they cold? What a question but what was I
to ask? Those blue, swollen feet of theirs gave the answer. They themselves said that they
didn't feel it much now. It was worst when they first went out. I went to others. One had
a face like an overripe melon, with lips like *Knackwürste* [smoked sausage], cracked, with
matter streaming out of the open, bloody cracks. He could hardly speak. His feet were in
the same pitiful condition, blue with frost and covered with sores. He pulled up the rag
of trouser which hung round his legs, and which he had had to rip up to get his feet and
calves through. He had nothing underneath. A shred of a jacket, and beneath it a tattered
shirt with no buttons at the neck was all he had on above the waist. On his head he wore a
bucket that had once been a felt hat.

I walked on round and met my friend Strauss—my protégé, who has had a *Schonung*
from the doctor for light work. He was to sit, said the doctor, keep warm and eat well.
Now he had to stand here, summoned to the *Vorstellung* for the third time, despite his
Schonung. Strauss was a "veteran" at these *Vorstellungen*, of which I knew nothing. He
knew he would be standing there all day, and had brought some food. I hadn't even had
breakfast, meaning to have it when I got back to the block. Later on he offered me some
of his lunch, but I had lost all my appetite, and I haven't gotten it back yet.

At nine o'clock the call-over began. The prisoners thronged round the announcer, who
stood on a stool calling out the names of those who were to go in and be "presented" to
the august head of the *Arbeitseinsatz* and assigned a *Kommando.* A number of people who
had scrounged their way were called out first so they didn't have to stand about in the
cold. Among them one could observe a lot of Norwegians. Instead, the half-naked Jews
and *Zugängere* had to stand that much longer.

When the announcer had gotten through a bundle of *Schein*, there was usually a long
interval before he started again, and the prisoners dispersed, walked, ran about and did
everything one does in an attempt to keep warmth and life in one. Some dodged away
into the corners between the huts, to smoke or do what else was necessary. Many had
Scheisserei and had to squat down where they happened to be, others couldn't manage
even that, and wet their clothes. It was lamentable! I had some tobacco and rolled a
cigarette. That very instant I had a hundred men round me. A hundred pairs of pleading
eyes. Of course I was used to that. The tobacco vanished, but they stood on. The butt? Or
the chance that there was still a crumb or two in my pocket? I had my pipe. Later on I
smoked it and knocked it out against my heel. Ten men flung themselves down and swept
up the ash, fought for the charred flakes lying in the dirt on the ice crust.

People moved aside. A small "relay" of the death gang, under escort of the "AA
general" (a completely crazy German prisoner who has been promoted head of the air
defense) and his myrmidons were being conducted through the crowd. They were going
to the *Industriehof* to be executed. There were ten death candidates, half naked, thin as

One of the death gangs on the way to the place of execution, conducted by the "AA General." They had black crosses painted on their cheeks and foreheads.

skeletons, starving, battered, worn out. The black crosses on their faces gave the sought-for explanation in all its horror. There was no need to ask. Everyone merely stepped aside, and the detachment passed through to the gate—and was gone. After it came the "general," like a kind of emperor in full dress, with riding boots, bandolier, ax, helmet, parti-colored and inscribed armlet, epaulettes and chin strap. A figure not to be exaggerated in the wildest burlesque. This man, a fellow prisoner, once a Social Democrat, is now living on the pinnacle of his desires.*

Three such relays of the death-marked passed through the yard during the day. One of them consisted of ten small boys. I estimate the age of the youngest at twelve or fourteen at most, but the death crosses on their faces made aged men of them. It made me think of an article I read in the *Völkischer Beobachter*† the other day about some children, down to thirteen years of age, who had been arrested by the English—I think in Belgium. Fancy arresting children! it said. Punishing children! it said. That's what the cruel English do, that's what they'll do in Germany if we surrender, it said. And my thoughts passed on to all the hundreds of thousands of Jewish children who have been sent into the gas chambers in the camps in Poland.

The hours crawled by, we shivered and froze. There came an alert. We were "stacked" into the toilet rooms of the huts. Here as elsewhere, this is done with the stick. I saw one young puppy strike a white-haired, crook-backed old man for not getting out of the way, another "Aryan" using a broomstick on the "crowd," as though the crowd were a danger-ous revolutionary mob, not a starved assembly of wretched, half-dead prisoners. Oh, my dear Aryan with the broomstick, with the handsome scarf, the tailor-made clothes (bought for sardines and lard), I shall take no revenge on you, though my fingers itch. I know you need help as much as the unhappy creatures you're belaboring with your broomstick. Only, may the help not arrive too late. The work of destruction is nearly done. But you don't feel that. Can you feel anything at all when you lift your broomstick and bring it down on the backbone of an elderly, gray-haired, dying Hungarian Jew? If you had even felt a little twinge of guilt for this disaster all round you. But you are guiltless—isn't that so? You always were against Nazism—isn't that so? That's why you're here. And now? You're just helping to keep order—isn't that so? What did you do when human beings were driven like game across the frontiers of Europe, before the catastrophe broke loose? What did you do when the pogroms started in Germany? What did you do when the same attitude began to take root in your own country? Everyone knows what: You shut your door—thought of yourself and your belongings. Now you're awaiting justice, isn't that so?—merely passing away the time, by keeping order. And by justice you mean revenge, isn't that so? Revenge on those who dared to touch your guiltless self—you and yours. Or do you perhaps include the Jews? Try just once and see how it feels. Take that scarf of yours and give it to one of them . . .

---

* Historian Wolfgang Sofsky notes that to some psychologists, the final stage of adjustment among veteran prisoners was often their identification with their oppressors, and observes, "It cannot be denied that prisoners . . . often . . . attempted to conform their appearance to that of the SS by getting hold of old parts of SS uniforms and strutting around in shiny polished riding boots."

† The *Völkischer Beobachter* [*People's Observer*] was the official newspaper of the Nazi Party, known for its virulent anti-Semitism. Alfred Rosenberg (an "utterly muddled man") became its editor in 1923. Its highest circulation, reached in 1944, was 1.7 million. Rosenberg was convicted by the Nuremberg Tribunal and executed October 16, 1946.

Just suppose, in this sick, miserable world, a cry for goodness went up! Might it not be possible? After all!

Strange thoughts in hell perhaps. Here the answers grin at you from all sides. No—no—no—no! But then suddenly you meet a yes. A slip of a lad. A Russian student, twenty-one years old. Was in the fighting at Leningrad, was wounded, captured, racked, tortured, escaped, caught again—more tortures—now here he is, coming toward me. Why are people like this, he asks. Why? Why? He speaks of all he has gone through. Details, heart-rending details. But this young lad is unchanged, he radiates goodness— love of life! Extraordinary. How was it that he didn't go the same way as all the others? He has been through the same.

I asked him what he thought of revenge. *Rache?* [Revenge?] No, he didn't know that word in German, though he speaks it quite well. I explained my meaning. He only looked at me in surprise and again asked why. And I had no answer. I was almost afraid to go on talking to him, the next thing he said might spoil it—turn him into yet another wretched *Muselmann* out for nothing but food—food—something to stuff into his empty, aching belly. But no. He went on talking about himself, his family, his betrothed, his studies. He is a student of architecture from Moscow. Incredible! That boy lay crawling in the dust outside Leningrad with a broken leg, crawling among the dead bodies of hundreds of his comrades, while the shrapnel flew about his ears, until he was at the end of his strength, had to give up and let himself be taken. Since then he has faced one tormentor after another with the same open countenance, the same clear, shining eyes. When we parted, I gave him a tin of sardines that I happened to have on me. He didn't want to take it—no, no. With the "right and dignity" of age I forced him to put it in his pocket.

At two o'clock my name was called. I went into the waiting hut, for we had to wait there an hour before being let in to the throne room.

At last my turn came. The bigwig—an *Oberscharführer* Rose, with glasses on and the general appearance of a human being—asked why I had been turned off my job. I said there were too many architects. Then I added that *Herz As* apparently needed architects, and that I had understood I could have work there. He looked over his spectacles and answered, "*Nein, das kenne ich nicht!*" [No, I know nothing about that!] Then he made a sign that I might go, and dictated to Herr Pflegel, the clerk, "Bad Sarrow!"* That means I'm to go on transport to another camp. All my hopes collapsed at one blow. Transport! Bad Sarrow is a good camp, as far as I know, a small one, where fifty Norwegians are well treated. But to be parted from my friends now, to be pulled up by the roots and be a *Zugänger* once more, begin over again!

I went straight "home." Everyone was at once agog to fix it for me, get my name struck off the list—arrange, fix, scrounge. The rest of the day was spent in talking and fixing, with no visible result. Now I shall just leave it. I'm tired and have lost my appetite.

---

* A subcamp of Sachsenhausen forty-five miles southeast of Berlin, Bad Saarow was set up in 1943 to assist in the construction of (1) offices of the SS, which were relocating from Berlin to avoid the bombings, and (2) a subterranean intelligence center in the nearby Rauener Mountains. The subcamp reached a peak population of 950 prisoners in the fall of 1944. By late 1944 the pressure to staff such work sites meant that fully more than half of all camp prisoners were now held in satellite camps, not the main camps such as Sachsenhausen. Prewar Bad Saarow was a popular resort for Berliners. William Shirer visited the resort on Easter Sunday 1935 and wrote in his diary, "The hotel mainly filled with Jews and we are a little surprised to see so many of them still prospering and apparently unafraid. I think they are unduly optimistic."

Expecting neither one thing nor the other. There is good news, and the war is to be over in March.

THURSDAY, JANUARY 19, 1945 ■ It does indeed look as if the war might shortly be over. The leaf has turned completely. The Russian offensive is fantastic, and in the West the German offensive has long since broken down.*

Now we reckon on being home for Easter. It's so long since we had a wave of optimism. This is a tidal wave! Also I've had a letter from Kari. So what does it matter if I'm sent to Bad Sarrow now?

(Later—two o'clock.)

But I'm not being sent to Bad Sarrow; I'm staying here and going to work in *Herz As*. I've been at the *Arbeitseinsatz* this morning and seen this man and that. First Herr Pflegel, who is the head of the whole *Einsatz* [operation]. He is green (BV), a sardine shark, and a dirty brute. He treads on corpses, but he took my card out of the Bad Sarrow bundle, and crossed out that name on the card.

WEDNESDAY, JANUARY 25, 1945 ■ It's out of laziness that I'm not writing just now. For there's enough to write about. But the life out here at *Herz As* invites laziness, in spite of all that is happening. One can actually do just as much as one chooses, and no more, and without any risk. There are no SS here, only a few civilians who are not dangerous.

But the situation in general has more and more the stamp of panic and dissolution. One transport of prisoners after another is arriving from other camps that have to be evacuated. Yesterday there arrived at Sachsenhausen or Oranienburg station several trainloads of prisoners. Most of them were dead, frozen to death in open railway cars in which they had spent up to three days in frightful cold, as much as seventeen degrees of frost [1.4° F]. An SS man in Kfz.D.[W.], whom I already knew as a human being, told my friends there about his experiences as a railway guard when that transport came in. There were women and children, dead and still alive. The job was to unearth those who still had life in them, and get them into the *Revier*. The dead bodies were taken straight to the crematorium. But the "sorting" at the railway station was no so good as to prevent a call to the *Revier* yesterday, asking them to send a stretcher as it proved that one of the corpses was still alive.

When I hear of this, and that they're dying by the hundreds just now of cold and hunger in this camp alone, without anyone being really affected, indeed without anyone even regarding it as unusual, then it occurs to me that no one will believe this when we come to describe it. You exaggerate, they'll say. It's impossible. After all the Germans are a civilized nation. It's as though a stupefying nightmare were passing over us, and I see it with horror as a mere beginning of what's to come. For it is not only prisoners who are freezing to death. It's not only the lives of prisoners that have ceased to count. The German civil population is going the same way. The eastern towns are being compulsorily evacuated, and by degrees their people will be streaming in on us like a tidal wave. We

---

* The Russian winter offensive began on January 12, 1945. Almost four million men, comprising the 1st Belorussian Front under Marshal Zhukov, 2nd Belorussian Front under Marshal Rokossovsky, 3rd Belorussian Front under General Chernyakhovsky, and 1st Ukrainian Front under Marshal Konev, broke out along a 560-mile front stretching from the Baltics to the Carpathian Mountains, quickly overrunning the depleted German troops, numbering less than one million, facing them.

have been warned that in the course of time there may be seven hundred to a thousand prisoners in each block. Today there are four hundred of us in each, and that's overcrowded; there must be three in two beds just now on average in the Norwegian blocks, and our beds are in four tiers.* In other blocks it's worse. And the Norwegians have every possible advantage. Most have sleeping bags, and all have enough to eat. Imagine all those who have no more than two worn out rags of blankets, no underclothing, no socks, no shoes and no food!

THURSDAY, JANUARY 26, 1945 ■ The accounts of what the evacuated thousands have to suffer are terrible. *Évacués* from the east are constantly streaming toward Berlin.

They arrive on foot or by train. The railway cars are opened, and stiffened corpses roll out. Mothers, children, old people frozen to death as they sit with their heads in their hands or hunched up in the corners. Subways and cellars in Berlin are crowded with refugees, and their condition is appalling. And still the Russians are drawing nearer.

No evacuation plans for this camp seem to be in existence as yet, we hear from SS quarters. God knows what will happen. We can hardly just sit and wait to be liberated by the Russians. A prison transport of twenty-eight thousand, moving west from Auschwitz on foot, was caught up by Russian panzer spearheads. The SS were immediately overpowered and the prisoners released. The Russians just told them that they were free, but must look after themselves, unfortunately they couldn't take charge of them. Perhaps a doubtful freedom; but still! We should always manage, no doubt. But then our qualifications are exceptional, well-nourished as we are, and with good warm clothes. And again one thinks of all the others. Day and night these thoughts torment one. Good God, the things one sees—if one will see, and hears—if one will hear! By the side of one man freezing to death stands another in two pairs of drawers, a ski suit, two pairs of trousers, jerseys, shirts, coats, thick mittens and first-rate boots. He feels chilly and curses at the frost. The man next to him dies without a word. "Well, poor chap; he wouldn't have come through anyhow. Have you anything to smoke? Damn!"

SUNDAY, JANUARY 29, 1945 ■ Yesterday morning a transport of half-dead men left the camp. Thirteen hundred sick people, all of them the wretchedest and feeblest *Muselmenn* that could be exhibited, chosen from the *Revier*, the *Schonungsblocken* and the Tub. Many died at the gate of the *Revier*, where they had to line up in frost and snow, half naked, to be called over. They dropped where they stood, or lay down in the snow and died. "In heaps," said Erik, who was watching. "It was dreadful beyond all description." All of them were nearly dead in advance. Most had been taken straight out of their beds, where at least they might have died in peace and comparative warmth.

Wherever one turns, the destruction of guiltless people is going on like clockwork! With unalterably certain, devilish calculation the camp is gradually being purged of those who in any case are bound to die. Bound to die? Yes, all who look at those poor wretches know at once that they can never be men again. It's a miracle that they can even hold themselves up. They are literally nothing but bones, skin and sinews. All have the same

---

* The population of the main camp of Sachsenhausen, which stood at approximately seventeen thousand when Nansen arrived, swelled to thirty-six thousand (or more than five hundred inmates per block) immediately prior to its evacuation in April 1945.

"expression" on their faces, that is if one can talk of "expressions" and "faces," for they are nothing but skulls, death's-heads, like those that are painted on the death placards along the electric (death) fence round the camp. And death's-heads all look much the same. What an abyss of resignation and suffering stares out on you, without a word, without a sound. How is one ever to be rid of those staring eyes? With horror and repugnance one has to realize that one is gradually getting blunted, and that it's an ineluctable necessity, a kind of self-defense. And in this dance of death criminals are playing their game, swindlers, thugs, bank robbers, pickpockets, cheats. Most of them, raised to positions of authority in the camp, have a free hand within this community. They steal the food out of starving mouths, the clothes off bodies that are freezing to death.

MONDAY, JANUARY 30, 1945 ■ The day before yesterday a transport of two thousand men, mostly Jews, arrived from Auschwitz. Two hundred and sixty were dead. They had spent ten days in open railway cars, coal cars, where they had lain in layers on top of each other. The middle layers came off best, the top and bottom ones had soon frozen to death. They had had no food in all those ten days. Since they arrived, the surgeons in the *Revier* have been at work all the time amputating arms and legs, and other doctors keeping life in those who survived the transport.* But, of course, they're dying in crowds.

THURSDAY, FEBRUARY 1, 1945 ■ Yesterday was the twelfth anniversary of the Nazi regime in Germany, and the *Führer* spoke at night. Of the war situation he said nothing.† I suppose he thought it superfluous. For everyone knows how things are, at least everyone who cares to know. But most of them don't, and to them the leader's words were a welcome, a consolatory, and a much-needed gospel. "Now let the Russians come!" they say. "Just let them come, we shall stop them!" or "They'll be stopped! To be sure!" And many actually think so. But the Russians are rolling on. The *Vorarbeiter* has just come in and announced that they are "*im Kampfraum von Frankfurt an der Oder*" [in the combat area of Frankfurt on the Oder]. It's been broadcast! A hundred kilometers [62 miles] from Berlin! The SS hint that Russian spearheads have got to Eberfelde, forty kilometers [25 miles] from here. Soon one won't know what to believe. In any case I suppose we must expect that there will be no more going out to the kommandos. If evacuation is on the cards, one must suppose they'll set about it in the immediate future; perhaps this very evening? The state of things in camp is as before. But we, that is Norwegians and old prisoners, want for nothing and are unmolested. Only yesterday we received parcels from home. Incredible! One has a feeling that it will go on as long as the war lasts.

FRIDAY, FEBRUARY 2, 1945 ■ Yesterday, after we got back to camp at night, was indescribable. It was almost as though we were already free. All were in smiling spirits, rubbing their hands and breathing deeply. At last! Now it was only a question of hours.

---

* It is probable that Thomas Buergenthal arrived with this group; he, too, underwent an amputation. See February 16, 1945, below.

† This was to be Hitler's last broadcast to the German people. Regarding the war situation, it is worth noting that more than 450,000 German soldiers were killed in the month of January alone, more than either the United States or Great Britain lost for the entire war. Historian Richard Bessel observes, "[O]ver one-quarter of Germany's entire military losses during the Second World War occurred in the last four months, when it was obvious that there was no possibility of a German victory and no military rationale for continuing to fight."

The Russians were just yonder in the trenches. Several wouldn't go to bed, at least not to sleep. The Russians might be there at any moment. One must pack and have everything ready. There weren't many who didn't bring back from the kommando everything they kept there—clothes, food and tobacco. They would never be going out there again! Even the pessimists agreed. That kind of mass psychosis, or hypnosis, always makes me a bit skeptical, but on the whole I believed with the majority that the Russians might arrive any time.

I think the same at this moment, though I'm out here on the kommando as usual, writing again. For we did go out today as well. But it's quite plain that the end is near. Yesterday two *Selbstschutz* [self-defense] companies were set up in camp, one German and one Polish, each, I think, of two hundred men. It's said these companies, which consist of prisoners, have already been given arms. Such a drastic step as that of equipping four hundred prisoners with arms and police authority can surely have but one meaning—that the SS intend to run away when the air gets too thick and leave the camp to itself and/or these four hundred.

And what are they, these four hundred? The two hundred Germans are to be led by a major bandit called Jacob, *Blockältester* in [Block] 13 and the "personality" who leads the punishment gymnastics, or led them, for they seem to be over now.* His men and brothers-in-arms are mostly BV-ers, a gang of brutes who stop at nothing. And then the Poles! The quality of the Poles in camp is sufficiently well known. Among them are to be found the worst *Vorarbeiters* next to the Germans, the biggest bullies, the worst informers, the scurviest "comrades." Who is to be their leader we don't yet know, but one can easily imagine the sort of man it will be. There are enough to choose from. The CO of this whole bandit regime, it's said, is to be the *Luftschutzgeneral*, Manske, the German maniac I've already mentioned, who bullies condemned men. Yes, we may have a merry time. But one must say that it's a conclusion to this nightmare in complete harmony with all that has gone before. The felons in the high places!

This morning, as we paraded in working kommandos, we were met by the unpleasant news that Leo, our "chief" here in the drawing office, had been "called for" at midnight and has not returned. His fate is unknown, but there is reason to fear the worst, as a number of other men were "called for" at the same time, among them a lot of Russian officers and "intellectuals," who are said to have been shot. The BV-er who told us about this and who thinks they've all been "settled" [killed], also thinks this is only the beginning of a purge of everything like prominence and intelligence in the camp. Perhaps not among the Norwegians, Danes and Dutchmen, he adds.

SATURDAY, FEBRUARY 3, 1945 ■ From the brightest and wildest optimism we've been plunged into gloomy pessimism. When we got back from the job last night, we were met by the sinister announcement that the camp is to be evacuated. We're all to start off on a trek. To the great majority the news was thunder from a clear sky, and many still refuse to believe it, such an utterly outrageous impossibility and insanity

---

* Ironically, it was the brutal Jacob who, according to Nansen, first took pity on young Tommy Buergenthal and brought his infected feet to the attention of the Norwegian medical team headed by Sven Oftedal. In *Tommy*, Nansen wrote this about Jacob: "Whatever one can say about him, whatever load of ill deeds yet rests upon his conscience, nevertheless, he was, in [his] own tragic way, a tool in the service of higher powers, who over and over had saved Tommy's life and protected it, in almost miraculous fashion, safe and undamaged through this hell on earth."

does it seem. Forty thousand men on the tramp south, southwest or west, miserably clad, with nothing to eat—for it can be only Norwegians who have any food to take with them—and in a worse than rickety condition. First we heard it as a rumor, and it penetrated slowly into our consciousness, which refused to accept it. Then it came as an official announcement in the block. "The camp will probably be evacuated." *Wahr-scheinlich!* [Probably!] A hope still lingers in the interpretation of that lumpy German word, a little chance that the Russians may be too quick, the possibility of a change of mind with the ensuing counterorder, of which indeed we've known so many that they can almost be taken as the rule. But in that case there is another dark cloud in our sky, a cloud that has grown darker, blacker, and more menacing in the last forty-eight hours. Liquidation! *Vernichtung!*

It is now being said that over two hundred men, including all the lackeys of the *Sonderkommission*, were shot last night. They were a frightful gang indeed, and no one laments them. They were the Gestapo's henchmen among the prisoners. And so that was their reward.

When the truth about the events of the night gradually came out, when we learned that our friends the Englishmen, John and Jack and Tommy and the rest (we knew them right back in Grini), had in all probability been shot,* and the Russian officers and many others, the atmosphere filled with gloom. Rumor also had it that the coming night would be still worse. Last night many were awakened by shots in the camp. This was what happened: When a party of those who had been taken from the blocks under cover of darkness marched out of the gate and turned to the right, they realized where they were going, broke ranks, and ran into the little park there between the walls. The guards opened fire on them, and they were shot down there in the park. The rat-tat of the guards' tommy guns broke the night silence, filling those who lay awake with horror and dread.

Last night I was talking with my protégé Strauss and his friend Lager. Both were quite prepared for it to be the Jews' turn tonight. "We can't die more than once," said Strauss. They were sorry for all the others, who were afraid to die, all who were worse off than themselves.

Last night, as soon as we were told of the evacuation, we began to get ready, though it's not likely that the first evacuation transport can leave until Sunday. People began going through their things, mending clothes and arranging their stock of food. Carrier straps

---

* John Godwin (age twenty-five) and Victor John (Jack) Cox (age twenty-six) were among the seven British commandos imprisoned for their role in Operation Checkmate. Godwin and his crew were housed with the Norwegians in Sachsenhausen until December 8, 1943. In apparent retaliation for the increasingly severe Allied bombings (see November 20, 1943 above, discussing the Battle of Britain), the British were assigned to the SK and forced to participate in the *Schuhläufer* [shoe testing kommando]. Over the next fourteen months it is estimated that Godwin and company marched approximately 12,500 miles. Their murder (along with approximately two hundred others) on the night of February 1/2 was pursuant to an order from Heinrich Müller, chief of the Gestapo, to several camp commandants to liquidate all "dangerous prisoners" to prevent their instigating provocations, etc., when enemy forces arrived. Godwin had previously confided to a fellow Norwegian prisoner that if summoned to his own execution, he would resist, and it appears that Godwin was successful in snatching away a guard's gun and shooting him, leading to a spontaneous uprising that killed several other guards and was quelled only with some difficulty. In 2001, through the efforts of a British survivor, a stone memorial was installed in Sachsenhausen to honor the twenty known and "many still unknown" British and Commonwealth forces who perished at Sachsenhausen or elsewhere during the war. It is unknown who "Tommy" refers to. Not all members of Godwin's team were executed on the night of February 1/2; see February 8, 1945, below.

must be got (scrounged), and if possible a catchall as well. It's obvious that we shall have to leave most of our things behind, for we're to go on foot. Three camps were mentioned, among which we're to be divided: Buchenwald, Schlossenburg,* and Bergen-Belsen.† All who are in good health and under fifty-five are to go on foot, the old and feeble and the sick are to be transported, probably by rail. So the shortest trip will be two hundred and fifty or perhaps more like three hundred kilometers [150–180 miles]. At least a fortnight's march! No doubt it will be much as a German said to me today—one third will die, one third will decamp, and one third will arrive. Thoughts of the second possibility are of course, pretty general. An entertaining idea to play with, but dangerous, and for foreigners rather difficult and chancy to put into effect; though if it is ever to be done, the time is now, when panic is spreading and all the roads are filled with refugees.

Of course we got our last parcels long ago, and the last of our letters from home. From now on we'll just have to wait until it's over. In many ways it will again be worst for those at home. They're sure to hear about the fate of the camp. Poor Kari! This will be a bad time. But this will be all right too!

It's more than strange to go about here knowing that this period will soon be over and something new is to begin, something wholly new and untried! All kinds of possibilities still exist. Anything may happen. Including a *Totalvernichtung*.‡ One must get used to that idea as well; though to die now, when there may be only days left—not to live the life one has dreamed and planned and lived so long on, that would be too senseless.

SUNDAY, FEBRUARY 4, 1945 ■ As early as last night all those without a kommando and all with light work *ohne Anmarsch* [without having to march in formation] were to leave. These include a lot of Norwegians, all the "old hands": [Nic.] Stang, [Christoffer] Berg-Hansen, [Arnulf] Øverland and many others. There was packing and turmoil,

---

* It is likely that Nansen is referring to Flossenburg, as he mentions in the Norwegian edition that the camp was apparently near Nuremberg and approximately 450 kilometers from Sachsenhausen; Flossenburg is in fact 452 kilometers from Oranienburg, and Nuremberg is the closest major city to the camp. Moreover, there is no major German concentration camp named Schlossenburg. Flossenburg was established in 1938 in the Bavaria region of Germany near the border with Czechoslovakia to provide slave labor to the nearby granite quarries owned by the SS; additional subcamps servicing the armaments industry were subsequently established. Nearly ninety-seven thousand prisoners were incarcerated at Flossenburg during its existence; it is estimated that thirty thousand died or were murdered. The camp was liberated by US forces on April 23, 1945, by which time most prisoners had been evacuated to Dachau or had escaped. Days earlier (April 9, 1945) the SS killed several prominent prisoners associated with the July 20 assassination plot against Hitler, including the former head of military intelligence Wilhelm Canaris and theologian Dietrich Bonhoeffer. The last commandant of Flossenburg, Max Koegel, remained at large until June 1946; he committed suicide in his jail cell the day after his arrest.

† Bergen-Belsen was established in 1940 in northwestern Germany. It was initially constructed as a POW camp and in 1943 was converted into a concentration camp for prominent Jews who potentially could be exchanged for Germans interned abroad. Due to overcrowding from transports arriving from camps in the East (the prison population grew from 7,300 in July 1944 to 55,000 in April 1945) deaths from malnutrition and disease (primarily typhus) skyrocketed in the early months of 1945. It is estimated that at least 50,000 concentration camp inmates died or were killed at Bergen-Belsen—35,000 in its final four and a half months alone. It was liberated on April 15, 1945, by British forces. In the fall of 1945 a British military tribunal sentenced eleven Bergen-Belsen SS personnel and prison functionaries to death, including its commandant, Josef Kramer, who was hanged in mid-December 1945.

‡ This was not an idle fear. In January 1945 Himmler ordered the evacuation of the camps in the East, telling their commandants that they were responsible for insuring that "no prisoner should fall alive into enemy hands." Himmler's masseur later reported that in March 1945 Himmler stated if "Germany is going to be destroyed, then her enemies and the criminals in concentration camps shall not have the satisfaction of emerging from our ruin as triumphant conquerors. They shall share in the downfall."

touching farewells and *au revoirs* and all things appertaining. And as it all took place in crowded blocks, in the middle of cooking, eating, bandaging, etc., etc., one can easily imagine the scene of absolute chaos, now and then interrupted by the clerk's whistle (which goes right through one) every time he had to give an order or take back an order given half an hour earlier. People were flying around as though they'd lost their heads and their wits. But here I am again at the kommando, still writing, and the "old hands" are still at home in the blocks. They didn't leave at all. In the dead of night more than three thousand men were called up; the transport could take no more. The Norwegians were not among them, and were left behind.

Poor "old hands." Many of them, after great soul struggles, had conquered themselves and given away what they could find no possible means of taking with them, and then they were left behind after all. Into the bargain we received Danish parcels yesterday, and it's said the Swedish parcels will be coming today or tomorrow. Some, because they don't think, or at least think of no one but themselves, wonder what on earth they are to do with it all.

Yesterday evening I was in Jewish Block 11, where my friend Strauss lived. It was a dismal outlook. Half clad, with no food and no equipment of any kind, they were to set off last night. Undeniably it looked like an extirpation transport. With sinister clearness everything was pointing that way, but we tried to cheer Strauss up, and we gave him the contents of a good Danish parcel to take with him. Good luck to them.

Now the story is that Norwegians and Germans are to stay on in camp, or that the Norwegians are to be sent to a separate camp, God knows where, or a lot of other things more or less reliable.*

MONDAY, FEBRUARY 5, 1945 ■ The "evacuation atmosphere" persists, and the evacuation has begun; several thousand are off already, but on the other hand there are transports coming in all the time, from this and that quarter, and in the most wretched state. On Sunday a transport arrived from Liberose with 160 dead bodies, people who had been crushed and trodden to death on the railway journey.

Strauss went off the night before last or yesterday morning. Shall I ever see him again? If he's to walk he won't last long, for his feet were very swollen and full of water. By train, even in an open railcar, he should have a chance. He was well clad. My young friend the Russian student, whom I'd begun to tutor in architecture, was sent off, too. We gave him a few provisions for the journey and all good wishes. Both he and Strauss promised to write to me after the war, if they lived through it. And the Belgian architect was sent off. Arvid had taken him over and gave him food every day. He wasn't very strong either, he had water in the legs, and was undernourished. But we had dressed him up, so he should have a chance of coming through if it doesn't last too long.

If the *Revier* is to be evacuated there will be great loss of life. Hundreds couldn't possibly survive a transport. Rolf [Hofmo] has now pulled up sufficiently to have a good chance.

---

* What is interesting about this entry is that Nansen is describing exactly what happened; the Norwegians (along with the Danes) were evacuated to a separate camp, Neuengamme, by the Swedish Red Cross. See March 18, 1945, below. At the time of this entry, however, the Swedish government had opened no negotiations with the Germans on this issue, and in fact the Swedish government did not decide that Folke Bernadotte would even conduct the negotiations until February 10.

TUESDAY, FEBRUARY 6, 1945 ■ Yesterday 225 Jews went into the gas chamber. It was a transport from Liberose. All were so wretched and worn out that for most of them death was simply a deliverance. I fear that Strauss has been taken and that the whole "transport" he was to be sent with has gone that way. It's predicted that all the Jews are to be gradually extirpated. The crematorium is busy day and night. The crematorium gang, twenty-five Jews, are on shift work. The previous gang has been "liquidated"; of course they knew too much. These Jews will doubtless go the same way, when they have done their job.

The evacuation continues. Today it's reported that six thousand are going off. It is still the sick and men unfit for work who are being sent. Later, the report is, all Russians, Ukrainians, Frenchmen, Belgians and Poles are to go. An "élite" of twelve thousand Germans, Norwegians, Danes and possibly Dutchmen are to remain in the camp.

In Berlin things are said to be worse than ever. The last raid, I think it was the morning of the day before yesterday, was the biggest and worst yet.* They no longer have a crematorium, and people are dying like flies. Truck after truck of corpses is arriving here for burning. Truck after truck of clothes is leaving the crematorium in a steady stream.

We are living in hell, and it's strange to find that even in such a place people can adapt themselves. If one doesn't leave the Norwegian blocks, and if one shuts one's eyes and ears to all that is going on, and that in the immediate neighborhood (which there is nothing to prevent one's doing, and which many do), why, one may even get a kind of impression that hell is a snug, cozy sort of place, with a lot of fun and comfort, though a bit of a squeeze. The alerts have ceased to be noticed as an interruption. The windows are blacked out, and life inside goes on unaffected by the death and destruction pouring down over fellow creatures a few miles away. Indeed many actually don't know there's an alert, they are so absorbed in their novel, their food, or whatever they may be doing. At night they sleep, sleep and snore and let the world go as it will. Their only thought is: Shall I escape being evacuated? How much longer will it be before I can go home? Will the food run out before then? Will the parcels stop—and the cigarettes and tobacco? We're all like that at bottom, and let no one cast the first stone. Would it be any better if we sat in tears and despair? Besides there are quite a lot who help, I know of more than I used to. It's only certain people who hoard, and whom it takes all one's self-control not to go for. I know one who has *three* Swedish boxes crammed with food, on which he mounts guard like a dragon. Does he know that hundreds of people are dying of hunger in the camp every day? Yes, he's heard of it. I've told him. But his face betrayed no reaction of any kind. What is it to him? Is *he* a Jew or a Ukrainian, a Russian or a Pole? I'm afraid he thinks he's a Norwegian hero!

THURSDAY, FEBRUARY 8, 1945 ■ Yesterday 180 Jews were taken in Block 11, where Strauss also spent the last day. Unfortunately there seems no doubt that they went

---

* On the morning of February 3, 1945, 1,500 American planes dropped more than two thousand tons of bombs on Berlin in the heaviest raid of the war on that city, leaving five thousand dead, wounded, or missing. In total, Berlin, the world's third largest city in 1943, was attacked 363 times during the course of the war. One historian writes, "Berlin attracted more air raids, more aircraft and more bombs than any other German city. . . . It also . . . suffered the largest nonmilitary loss of life of any city in Germany." By May 1945 fewer than one-third of Berlin's buildings remained undamaged.

into the gas chamber. Moreover, there is reason to think that it will be the same with all the Jews.

It seems certain now that our English friends have been shot. Their things have come back. One of them, who for some reason had been forgotten on the list that night, is now in [Block] 58. He woke up when the others were being taken out of the dormitory, and pressed forward to hear what was going on. The *Blockältester* (the dreaded Jacob) was well disposed to him and whispered to him to keep out of sight, but he said that he would stick with his buddies. An SS man caught sight of him and asked in astonishment if there was another Englishman there. His name and number were taken. An hour after the others had been led off, they called for him as well. But an alert came in the way, and he was hurriedly shoved into 58. Careless and haphazard as everything is here, it's possible that he has been forgotten, and that the alert saved his life.*

FRIDAY, FEBRUARY 9, 1945 ■ The evacuation continues. Now almost ten thousand must have gone, but no Norwegians, except for a small transport of those newly discharged from the *Revier*, and a few others who had no working kommando. The transport was going to Bergen-Belsen near Hannover. Activity in the crematorium is undiminished; the burning goes on day and night. In the *Industriehof* too the work is incessant. We are always hearing of Jews and *Muselmenn* going into the gas. Yesterday, we hear, all the sick Russian prisoners of war went. What the truth is, it's hard to say. The camp is in a whirl of rumors and of fear, fear of death.

For the Norwegians, things are falling back more and more into the everyday round. We go out to work every day as usual, and the evacuation excitement is sinking more and more into the background. All the same we're prepared for evacuation orders any day, and indeed for anything at any time.

At *Herz As* I have practically nothing to do. My official task at the moment is to speed the war effort by designing a gardener's lodge for a pretty big estate, which some *Hauptsturmführer* here has scrounged during the war by means of prisoners and swindling. The most remarkable thing about this lodge is that for some obscure reason it's to have no south windows. But I've broken myself of making any comment whatever. Really the surprising thing is that they should want *any* windows in their houses round here, desolate and cheerless as they are to look out of. There are no SS here. That's marvelous. The German civilians trotting around are a pitiful gang of shirkers whose main exertion is to magnify their war effort, magnify it so they won't have to go to war! And so they're building, among other things, a gardener's lodge. A couple of them are actually great, hefty giants in the prime of life, who might be useful at throwing five-ton bombs with their fists, whereas their building qualifications are less than minimal and highly detrimental to the war effort. My first, last and only job out here will be this gardener's lodge, unless indeed the war goes on for another year.

---

* Actually two Englishmen from the John Godwin's Checkmate commando squad avoided execution on February 2: Keith Mayor (age twenty-two), who was apparently simply overlooked, as Nansen mentions, and Alfred Roe (age thirty-nine), who was in the infirmary at the time. Both were subsequently transported to Bergen-Belsen where their true identities were initially concealed. Eventually they were found out; Mayor was executed on April 7, 1945, and Roe died of typhus April 9, 1945, less than a week before the camp was liberated by British troops.

SATURDAY, FEBRUARY 10, 1945 ■ Last night after we got back from work, a transport came through the gateway in a worse than usual state of exhaustion and misery. They were walking skeletons with no proper clothes, and a good many of them barefoot. Some couldn't hold themselves up and were being dragged along by the others. One was being towed along in a blanket. Some fell in the gateway and made desperate efforts to get back on their feet, to avoid the kicks of the SS, who stood on either side of the entrance bellowing *Seitenrichtung!* [Keep in line!] *Aufstehen! Kopf hoch!* [Heads up!] *Finger lang!* [Arms stretched!] and other sprightly exhortations to the half-dead. Those who fell down from exhaustion and yearned, no doubt, to lie forever, were kicked and cursed. "You blasted swine! Get Up! Move on! Quick, you don't need your shoes; just let them lie, idiot! Tomorrow you'll be going into the crematorium anyway! So get on! Don't you hear? Get on! Get on!"

At length all had dragged themselves through the frightful gauntlet in the gateway and on to the square, where they could breathe "freely" and prepare to die. On the march across the square many fell and lay. It was "our" SS men, whom we see every day, and are now and then so ill-advised as to call "good-natured" and "harmless," who kicked those half-dead skeletons, bawled them out and promised them the crematorium. All any of them need is to see the first stone cast, the watchword given, and then they know they're dealing with death candidates; they can just give "nature" free play, they can hit and kick and curse and storm.

We in Block 39 may think ourselves lucky to have such an exceptionally decent old *Blockältester* as Ludwig. He actually wouldn't hurt a fly. And that is unique in the gangster circle he belongs to. Every day we hear of flogging and uproar in other blocks. Begging Ukrainians and others are flung out, kicked and beaten, noted and reported. Before our door, and even inside the hut, there are quite as many beggars. Ludwig roars out, "*Heraus! Heraus! Los! Los!*" But he adds quietly, "If you have your dish, come here! Quickly!" And he takes the dish and fills it with soup, sticks a bit of bread or something else in the "victim's" pocket, and starts roaring again, "*Heraus! Sofort! Heraus, du Schweinehund! Aber schnell!*" and so on. All the time with a twinkle in his eye for us who are watching. But the noise sounds genuine, and any other *Blockälteste* who may be listening take it for granted that Ludwig is of the same caliber as themselves.

But he is not. Ludwig is one of the few who help to preserve something in oneself which must not be lost. For it is not only the corpses of human beings which are burned and annihilated here, not only young, strong bodies which have turned into *Muselmenn*, skeletons and crematorium fuel. On this battlefield the young faith and enthusiasm of thousands has gone under as well, the vital spark of thousands has been quenched in darkness and brutishness. Ideals have vanished; human kindness has turned to ice in many a heart; faith in the future, the will and the force of good have withered as the muscles wither up to useless, dry tissue in the skeleton bodies of the *Muselmenn*. Of all mass murders, this is perhaps the worst.

Saturday again. Nearly the middle of the month, and it's getting to be a long time since we thought it was a question of hours. The pauses have set in again, though hard fighting is reported daily in the news from the fronts.

SUNDAY, FEBRUARY 11, 1945 ■ There were two Norwegians in the transport I mentioned yesterday, which was so manhandled as it passed through the gate. It turned out to be the rearguard of a biggish transport of thirteen hundred men from Liberose. This rearguard consisted of thirty-five or forty men, all of whom were *Muselmenn* or had some injury that made them bad walkers. The Norwegians had sores and blisters on their feet. Yesterday there were only five survivors of this rearguard—the two Norwegians, two Belgians and a German. The rest were killed yesterday. On the way here from Liberose sixty-nine men were shot because they couldn't go on. They were mostly Jews, and the rest Ukrainians, Poles and Russians. All "Easterners," that is. If any of the other prisoners gave out, they got a lift on the "kitchen truck."*

One of the two Norwegians came to our block last night. Both his feet were covered with blisters. "If you have a chance to drive or go by rail, in God's name do it!" said he. "You don't know what you're doing if you choose to walk." (Those who don't think they can manage on foot have now an opportunity to put themselves down for rail transport.) "It's simply hell. All of us threw away everything we had to carry, all but blankets and sleeping bags. A lot threw those away too, and just carried the little food they had."

I think the fellow's blisters had supplanted his judgment. Twelve miles or so a day is not superhuman, even for people out of training. No one in our *spin* is putting himself down for rail transport. We think we can take it, even though we're along in years.

Received two letters from Kari yesterday, but no parcels or *Kleinigkeiten*, though I gather from her letters that she is constantly sending them. It's obvious that fairly widespread mail theft is taking place. The *spin* is empty now. Scraped clean; we have actually nothing but today's dinner, except for dry bread and the "panzer rations" we've put aside for the evacuation march.† Our tobacco is finished, too. But we shall always manage for a few weeks!

MONDAY, FEBRUARY 12, 1945 ■ The language is exhausted. I've exhausted it myself. There are no words left to describe the horrors I've seen with my own eyes. How am I to give even a reflection of the hell I was plunged into yesterday?

It was in the isolation area between Blocks 13 and 14, which was filled with Jews from Liberose. Leif Wolfberg was among them. He had sent for me, so I went. I didn't have much talk with him, I saw that he was all right, he had been getting Norwegian parcels the whole time, and looked "well." But the scene around me took up all my interest, all my thoughts, and nearly all my strength. It was appalling. Dante's inferno couldn't be worse. There were more than a thousand Jews; that is, they had once been Jews and human beings, now they were living skeletons, beastlike in their mad hunger. They flung themselves on the dustbins, or rather plunged into them, head and shoulders, several at a time; they scratched up everything, absolutely everything that was lying in them, potato peel, garbage, rottenness of every kind. They didn't see what they were eating, simply shoved it into their faces, clawed and tore at it, fought over it. They stuck fast in the dustbins, taking them along when they straightened up again, and off they went like that,

---

* As part of the closure of satellite camps around Sachsenhausen, approximately 1,600 inmates were evacuated from Lieberose on February 2, 1945; approximately 1,200 reached Sachsenhausen on February 9/10 after a 120-mile march. Of this group 50 Jewish inmates were shot upon arrival and a further 400 were executed over the next several days. Another 1,350 inmates who were sick or unable to march were left behind at Lieberose, where they were all murdered by the SS (February 2–4, 1945).

† Presumably a reference to an individual daily food ration, much like the K-ration or C-ration used by the US Army in World War II.

De var levende djevler

A transport of Jews has come from Lieberose, and SAW lads in full sadistic ecstasy and armed with rubber truncheons are providing a rich harvest for the crematorium.

two or three skeletons combined into a strange walking caryatid sculpture. But the worst was that the whole time, without a break, the blows from rubber truncheons were hailing down on them. Young lads (SAW lads)* thrashed away at them to their hearts' content. But they took no notice. The instant the tormentors turned away to hit out in another direction, they plunged into the dustbins again. The blood was pouring off them, from their faces and hands and legs. Most were barefoot, and the clothes hung round them in shreds; more great wounds from blows shone through rents and openings in the clothes on their bodies.

The tormentors were indescribable. They were only boys, but the act of striking intoxicated them and drove them wild. I followed them, I saw their faces as they struck, they were no longer human, they were living devils, possessed, transported with ecstasy.

---

* SAW—*Sonder Abteilung Wehrmacht* [Special Department Wehrmacht]. The lads had probably been guilty of *Kameradendiebstahl* [stealing from comrades] and put in a concentration camp for that reason. Here they were supplied with rubber truncheons and the right to strike—the right to kill. They were more than willing. O.N.

They struck whatever they saw, not merely those they saw in the dustbins. They hurled themselves on the crowds like roaring lions, and struck out right and left. The wretched victims went down round them by dozens; that only inspired them, and they went on striking at them as they lay, trod upon them, kicked them, while the blood was streaming from mouths, ears and wounds. Every time they needed a rest, they turned exultantly to their laughing and smiling comrades, laughed back, and gave the truncheon a limber, playful swing round their heads. Then they flew at it again.

A Jew who had been struck ten or twenty times tottered and fell down at my feet. He lay motionless, the blood was running out of his mouth and trickling from one ear. His eyes were bloody and the cheekbones swollen and cracked with blows. One of his lips was cleft and some teeth knocked out. He was barefoot, and his feet covered with frostbite. His trousers had slipped down, so that his matchstick thighs were visible, and through a rent in his shirt one could see his ribs. I bent over him, took him under the arms and raised him; he was light as a child. Wolfberg, who was a little way off, called out don't, it's no use, take care, or something of the kind. Poor Wolfberg, one of them himself, had grown even more hardened, even more callous. *He* didn't mind looking on, this was a commonplace, mere daily fare!

I dragged the Jew to the wall and managed to prop him up against it, and he came to again. He looked at me with such eyes—oh God, such eyes; all the white was red, and the red was running down his cheeks—the brown pupils were dull, as though a film had been drawn over them, and the big eyelids hung over them heavily. Some gurgling noises came from him, I thought he had difficulty in breathing, I tried to straighten him up; still the gurgling noises came, more regularly, it sounded as though he were being choked—but he was crying, crying like a child. A friend of his, who had been standing by for some time, came up and helped me to hold him. He explained that he had thought I was going to prop his friend up and kill him, he couldn't believe I only meant to help him. For I wasn't a Jew? What was I? A Norwegian! He smiled, and something that was meant for a smile appeared on his friend's face too, grotesque grimacings and a thicker stream of gurgling sounds. I felt like a cur; how could I do otherwise? These two Jews, both maimed with blows, for the friend had also been beaten until the blood was running down his face—they had been struck by men of my race, it was men of my race who were doing this to them, to their fellow prisoners! And there they were smiling happily at the sound of the one word "Norwegian," while I stood helpless. I was forbidden even to be where I was, let alone to help any of the abhorred ones. And reason, cold, odious reason, told me baldly that these men were doomed, nobody could save them, not even the best doctors in peacetime. They were too far gone, had already one foot deep in the grave. Only one thought took shape: May death overtake them speedily! May they be sent into the gas chamber this very night! If I had had veronal in unlimited quantities, I would have given it out to hundreds like bread.*

---

* Veronal is the brand name of barbital, a barbiturate or sleeping aid; an overdose can cause death. One German Jew who successfully escaped Berlin in 1937 later wrote that by late 1941 the only way for Germany's remaining Jews to evade a transport was suicide, and the method of choice was an overdose of Veronal: "'The suicides started immediately before the first transport. . . and the number increased very rapidly. People took Veronal. . . .' Barbiturates traded at fantastic prices. . . . [One woman] sold a Persian rug for 1,000 [Reich]marks and invested all the proceeds in Veronal. Her suicide attempt was successful."

I pulled up the trousers of the poor half-dead Jew, fastened them and arranged his clothes as far as was possible, took out my handkerchief and dried a little of the blood from his face. They simply stared at me, both of them, with big, surprised eyes, then he raised his arm with an effort, as though mustering all his failing strength; his hand reached the level of my head; there he let it sink, and slowly that bony hand of his slid down over my face. It was his last caress, and he gurgled something that his friend translated as, "He says you are a decent man." Then he collapsed along the wall and onto the ground, and I think he died there and then, but I don't know, for I was hurrying off with my face burning.

"*A decent man*"! I who hadn't even dared to try and stop his tormentor. I who hadn't even cared to risk my own skin by going out into the camp and collecting food for those starving skeletons! "*A decent man*"! If only I could ever raise myself up again from this shadow life in this sink of degradation, and be "*a decent man*"!

I made my way back to Wolfberg and some other Norwegians who were standing round him. They were watching the scene, which still continued, the tormentors striking more frantically than ever, while the victims drew away, crook backed, their hands protecting their heads and faces, or fell and saved their butchers the trouble of running after them. The dustbin offenses were repeated incessantly. They stuffed the garbage into their pockets, under their shirts, in their caps—what they couldn't stuff in their mouths; they heeded nothing, nothing but food! Food? That beastliness, no pig would have eaten it, no animal, only flies and bacteria would slowly consume it.

A Norwegian said, "Those aren't human beings, they're swine! I've starved myself, but I could never sink to eating sheer filth! It's quite right to keep them off the garbage, and you have to beat them, even that doesn't stop them!" I hurled myself on him and let him have a broadside. It was a solace to see him curl up, for curl he did; he grew quite meek in the end. But a poor, cowardly outlet for all the pent-up forces within me that I felt should have been used for something very different if I had only had the courage. I couldn't stand the place any longer, all I saw increased my impotence, despair, paralysis of dumb disgust at everything, including myself. I got out of it with Arvid [Johansen], who had come with me. We went to the *Revier* to see Rolf [Hofmo]. Thank heaven, he was much, much better. I hadn't seen him for a fortnight, there was a colossal improvement. We stayed a long time; two or three hours, that was forbidden too. At night in the block there was concertina-playing, singing, and high spirits. I sang, too, and made merry! Can it be possible?

TUESDAY, FEBRUARY 13, 1945 ■ From the Tub section of the *Revier* men are constantly being picked out who go direct to the crematorium. Yes, *direct*! Not into the gas chamber first. They get a knock on the head, that's usually enough. One hears screams and single shots when a detachment has gone there. I have long believed that it was only the hopelessly tubercular, those with T.B. in both lungs, who met this fate. Now I hear that in this case too the choice is quite haphazard. A big, strong Pole who has been in the Tub four years and is by no means mortally ill was to be taken the other day. He got word of it, jumped out through the window and hid in the camp. The *Blockältester* took another patient, a Pole or Ukrainian, out of one of the beds and sent him instead. The quota had to be filled to avoid a fuss. It's said that people are sent to the crematorium from this section without even being examined.

Nothing has "happened" yet to the Jews from Liberose. A good many of them died yesterday and the night before. I was talking to Wolfberg again yesterday; he got out to see us. He evidently wasn't expecting to come through this alive, poor fellow, but asked us in a curiously light, easy manner to give his love to common friends if we got through. No crematorium can impress him now, no hangmen, none of these inhuman horrors that still upset me, for a time at least. He is hardened, but at the same time it's remarkable how he has preserved his warmth of heart and his subtle, pliant humanity. He has merely acquired an inexplicable and almost horrid power of shutting it off when necessary. And it is necessary, God knows.

A Norwegian policeman arrived in camp the other day and was put into [Block] 14. He had been interned with the other Norwegian policemen somewhere near Danzig. Some time ago the camp was evacuated on foot. He got sores on his feet and couldn't keep up. They explained where they were going and told him to follow. Then he was left to himself. He went on, following the road, as well as he could alone, begging food at farmhouses and also lodging for the night. But then he forgot the name of the town or camp he was going to. In some little town he reported to the police and explained the matter. They sent three guards with him, and they were to take the train. At the station the guards hung up their coats and rifles and walked off. He was alone once more, for they didn't come back again. So then he met a German officer and reported what had happened. The officer took charge of the coats and rifles and told the man to go on. He went, and at long last he got to Sachsenhausen, where he knocked at the door and asked them to let him in. There was obviously no objection to that, and now he's in Block 14, along with Jews and all future *Muselmenn*.

He must have been a softhead to make no better use of his opportunity. But the story, if it's true, gives an excellent idea of conditions outside the fence. Chaos and dissolution! Valuable information, undeniably, for those who may have been planning to decamp as the three guards did.

The Russians are still advancing. Soon they'll be only a day's march off. All round here they're digging panzer ditches and bunkers, machine-gun nests and trenches. God knows if we're not to see the whole storm at close quarters?

WEDNESDAY, FEBRUARY 14, 1945 ■ Yesterday the total of deaths in the camp (for the previous twenty-four hours) was given as: 150 men in the *Revier*, 46 in the blocks, 14 of the Jews from Liberose, 1,542 men in transports. A day's harvest. Yesterday (the next twenty-four hours) 110 men were "picked out" from the Tub and taken "round the corner," that is, to the crematorium.

The way of it is this: They're called over and lined up for transport (as though most of them didn't know what was coming!). Those in charge of the selection and arrangements even let the delinquents take their blankets and *Schüssel* and any food and oddments they have. They are warmly clad, the SS even help them to button their jackets well up round the neck, look after them, and actually coddle them to quiet their suspicion. This, although the blankets, *Schüssel*, and oddments have returned ownerless to the block from previous "transports." Yet there are a lot who swallow it and believe it's an honest transport they're going on.

One might suppose this fraud, this death farce, to be staged from kindness of heart. No indeed, the motives are strictly practical, the result of years of experience. For it has proved that human beings, even sick people, like animals, are not to be dragged to the slaughter with their own consent. They sometimes use their remaining strength to make a fuss, tear themselves away and run, resist, strike, scream. Then the guards have to start shooting at them, rounding them up again, and there may be all kinds of bother. The attention of strangers might be drawn to this activity, and of course not everyone would understand it straight off, and appreciate it as the hygienic measure it's meant to be. T.B. is infectious, isn't it, one of the worst and deadliest enemies of man. It must be wiped out.

Lately, however, they've left off taking these "transports" round the first corner beyond the gate. They've discovered that the moment they turn to the right round that corner, most people realize where they're going. Many collapse and are troublesome to carry, others make themselves a nuisance for the reasons already mentioned. Therefore the transport now goes right out of the gate, past that fatal corner, and straight through the outer gate, out on to the road into open Germany! And hope springs up! There, you see, all this talk of crematoria is exaggerated! We're only being transferred to a better camp, a convalescent home! They cheer up and on they go, with their fools' blankets and possessions, to the next corner, where they turn to the right round the block and through another entrance to the same establishment with the same yellow chimney, belching heavy smoke day and night. I dare say many think they're only going in here to embark on buses, which will take them to the railway station. When hope has once struck root in a T.B. patient, so I've heard, it's difficult to shake it again. But the "thoughtfulness" and the whole fool's comedy must be at an end from the moment they cross the threshold of the death chamber. When the shots and screams can be heard as far as the *Revier* and other buildings round about, where there are prisoners, what must it be like to be in the "next" room and "be the next?"

A bit of ham from Bjørn H[elland]-H[ansen] "saved" the situation for us yesterday, and a couple of tins of sardines in the same parcel.* Our "panzer rations" were preserved yet another day.

THURSDAY, FEBRUARY 15, 1945 ■ Yesterday there was a "taking out" from *Schonungsblock 2*. They were allowed their blankets and what other things they had. A bus drove right in to the parade ground, where the embarkation took place. With parcels on their backs, parcels on their stomachs and blankets on their shoulders they went off joyously to the parade ground, where they were called over one by one and crossed off a long list. Those crosses were the crosses on their graves. But they didn't know that. Then they were driven out of the camp, right out through both gates. The bus drove round the block and stopped at the other side of the "establishment." A little new hut has been built there. They were marched into it and ordered to take off their shirts, they were to be vaccinated. The inside of the hut looked clean and neat, with white cloths on the tables and two white-clad "doctors." On a table there were several syringes in readiness. One "doctor" gave the injections, while the other "doctor" refilled the syringes and laid them ready on the table. When the prisoner had been injected, a "nurse" led him out of the room by a door opposite the one he came in by, and no sooner was he through this door than he was

---

* A noted Norwegian oceanographer, Helland-Hansen (1877–1957) was a contemporary of Fridtjof Nansen; they even collaborated on a scientific article regarding the effects of sunspots on climate change.

led off to the right, where he fell dead. The rest of his clothes were taken off, and the body went straight on into the crematorium furnace.*

All this was given away by one of the "doctors" while "drunk." For, of course, there's drunkenness as well. Every kind of misery. Several times there have been deaths from methanol poisoning. A Norwegian died not long ago of such "drink," and another went nearly blind.

I'm afraid things look bad for the Jews from Liberose. A number of them, I don't know how many, have already been "taken out," besides all those who die "naturally." Poor Wolfberg. Remember me to everyone, he said. He's prepared all right.†

In the midst of all this wretchedness and horror we have still the *Sonderbau*, the brothel. And as an accompaniment to all these "activities" the loudspeakers thunder, shrill and bellow around the camp, from the time we get back from work at night until we go to bed. Fifth-rate musical comedy, ditto choral singing, military marches, news and propaganda, and sometimes, strangely enough, real music—Bach, Beethoven, Brahms, Schubert, Schumann. But the loudspeakers are so wretched that even that is pretty painful to listen to.

Now there's beginning to be "plenty of room" in the camp. The numbers are fewer than they have been since we arrived.

FRIDAY, FEBRUARY 16, 1945 ■ Figures for the dead, killed and "transported" buzz round us. One has heard this, another that. It's all as certain as amen in church, they've been talking to so-and-so and so-and-so who saw it themselves, or have a friend who saw it. It's practically hopeless to keep any sort of reliable journal of what goes on here. So my notes make no claim to be anything like exhaustive. Nor can I venture to guarantee that everything I write down was precisely as I describe it. I know by experience how things can grow and at times become unrecognizable in their passage from mouth to mouth. But within the limits of my opportunity I have always tried to trace the source and get as near it as possible before writing down the story. And while thus employed I have often found that stories that have gone through many retellings and been a good deal distorted have by no means always grown *worse* than the reality.

The reason is obvious. Figures can easily be exaggerated, hundreds becoming thousands and thousands ten thousands; but the essential thing, the devilry itself, that they were killed, that they were struck and kicked, racked and tortured, that they went about half naked, that they ate out of the dustbins, that they died out on the parade ground or at the gate of the *Revier*, or were clubbed to death by *Blockälteste* and kicked into the privy, where one had to straddle over the corpses to get at the urinals or seats, that the corpses were kept in the bunks as much as several days so that the next man could get the corpse's food rations, that certain SS men or fellow prisoners laughed and diverted

---

* Nansen was omitting one important step: "After [the prisoner was killed], two inmates from the crematorium detail opened the door to the mortuary. . . . There, the gold teeth were pulled out of the corpses of those marked beforehand."

† Leif Wolfberg (aka Leiba, his name in Lithuania where he was born) (1916–?) was one of the handful of deported Norwegian Jews to survive the war. His name was surreptitiously changed on his registration card by fellow Norwegians to "Rolf Berg" and he was evacuated from Sachsenhausen with the "white buses" operation. After the war he taught violin and played with the Norwegian National Orchestra. His rescue at the hands of the Swedish Red Cross is ironic; in 1941 he had escaped into Sweden seeking asylum, only to be deported by Swedish authorities back to Norway and certain arrest.

themselves over the queer antics of a half-dead skeleton when it was hit on the backbone or the skull or the calves of the legs, that some of the "corpses" in the pile of corpses were still living and that they went into the furnace just the same and were burned alive, that Jewish children under ten years old were used as assistants in the crematorium where their parents, brothers and sisters and relations were being killed and burned, and that these children themselves, when they had "seen enough," went the same way (even without going through the gas chamber first)—this and more can simply not be exaggerated. The plain fact is that reality is stronger, more dramatic, and far more gruesome than one can grasp on hearing it recapitulated, normal human imagination falls short, therefore a secondhand account is always paler and more "plausible."

Frode expressed the same thing yesterday. He had come from the *Revier*, had been talking to S[ven Oftedal?]. and heard a little of what is going on. "It's worse than 'the bad time,'" he began. "Only in a slightly different way. It isn't done so openly now, and we Norwegians don't even hear of it all. But what's going on is so immeasurably ghastly. It's far beyond my grasp. My reaction is much the same as when people talk about 'light-years' and astronomic figures."

A little Jewish boy, not ten years old, is in the *Revier*. He comes from Auschwitz. His legs were frostbitten and several toes have been amputated.‡ At Auschwitz he was errand boy in the crematorium. He relates among other things that the most they could take in the gas chamber at a time was two thousand, and then they used two boxes, he said. "But how do you know that?" someone asked him. "Why, because I got the boxes," said the child.

Yesterday Wolfberg was transferred to another block, probably [Block] 58—so I heard from a man who had seen him pass our block with two *Luftschutz* people. Except for them he was alone. That may possibly mean that all the other Jews are to be taken and he was being moved out of harm's way. After all he's a Norwegian, and Norwegians are still "protected." Even the Norwegians in the Tub whose cases are pretty hopeless, and there are a few, are being left in peace. Doubtless they have Sven Oftedal to thank for that. But a Jew? I don't know, and I don't know how I'm to find out what happens to him. 58 is still strictly forbidden ground, and the frightful *Schläger* Ernst is *Blockältester*, with his squire Filip [Olsen] as *Stubenältester*. Filip is a Norwegian lad whom I got to know in North Norway, where he was lazy, difficult, and cross grained, but not ill natured; now he assists the hangmen. Poor Filip, his "golden age" will be short and joyless. When this is over, things look dark for him too, in spite of his long imprisonment and whatever he may once have done that got him inside.

Not counting Filip, whose fate is merely tragic and typical of what may happen to a weak, unsteady lad in this hellish milieu, there are certain Norwegians who should also be equipped with a green triangle. They all have red ones; all are political prisoners, "estimable" patriots. One could indeed collect a pretty bunch of patriots here. It will be another postwar problem what to do with all these scoundrels hiding behind red triangles. Two of them, presumably because their block got too hot to hold them, have volunteered to serve as partisans along with the German greens.

Oh God in heaven, how terrible this is! On all sides robbery and theft, looting,

---

‡ This is Nansen's first mention of Thomas Buergenthal in the diary. The amputation was performed by Norwegian doctors led by Sven Oftedal.

murder, and the guns and bombs booming, and the devils grinning. Isn't this the day of destruction after all? How else had we imagined it?

SATURDAY, FEBRUARY 17, 1945 ■ Yesterday there were Danish parcels, we're rich again. The parcels were brought here in Danish Red Cross cars with their own Danish drivers, who came right into the camp. Some had spoken to them. One of them said, "Next time we'll be coming to fetch you. The cars are waiting!"

Yesterday about thirty Norwegians were taken out on parade at three o'clock and "interned" in the "Russian isolation" for transport. They were all elderly men, apparently selected at random on parade. This transport is expected to leave today, probably for Bergen-Belsen. And so the "principle" of keeping back the Norwegians has broken down.

SUNDAY, FEBRUARY 18, 1945 ■ More Norwegians were picked out for transport in the afternoon and evening. The transport is expected to leave this afternoon. Among those taken yesterday were Arnulf Øverland and Bjarne Aanesen.* The atmosphere in camp in the last few days has become another few degrees more sinister and devil may care. The Norwegians had always felt safe; those who have nerves and "noses" don't feel quite so safe now. *Vernichtung!* now and then appears upon the wall in letters of fire, within the darkroom of the mind.

A gigantic liquor affair in camp is the current sensation. Fifty thousand liters of gin have arrived at Kfz.D.[W.] It wasn't long before the prisoners smelled the stuff and began tapping. The SS soon followed suit, and now they're stealing one against the other, singly or in partnership. Yesterday and today a large proportion of the kommando was pretty plastered. The SS daren't say anything, they're too deep in it themselves. Today Sämmler rang up Irsch and told him that a whole kommando was lying dead drunk in the woods. Nothing was done about it. I have tasted the stuff, it was abominable. Besides, I don't like gin.

MONDAY, FEBRUARY 19, 1945 ■ Yesterday I went to see the little ten-year-old in the *Revier*. Imagine one of Raphael's angels! That's how he looked, one actually had to make sure those weren't wings standing up behind him on either side, but it was the pillow. He was in *R[evier]* III, having a grand time. Everybody knew him, many were taking care of him, and he wanted for nothing. He had enough to eat, and his foot wasn't hurting now.

For two and a half years this child has been in German concentration camps—since he was seven years old! He is a Slovak and used to live in a town near Bratislava. His mother was German—*was*, for it's unlikely that she is still alive; the father was a Slovak, and it seems extremely doubtful whether he's still alive. The first two years he spent with his parents in a camp at Kielce in Poland. They were "all right" and worked in a factory there. After six months the father was sent on a transport. He stayed on a year or so with his mother and was "all right," he said. But then the mother went on a transport, and he was left alone in the world at eight years old. And in what a world!

He was transferred to Auschwitz, where the father was. The father, who was working

---

* Aanesen published a poetry collection in 1945, *Dikt fra Sachsenhausen* [*Poems From Sachsenhausen*], together with Carl Jakhelln, Olav Dalgard, and Lars Magnus Moen.

The Angel Raphael of the Revier, *drawn by Odd Nansen after the war for Thomas Buergenthal.* SOURCE: *Courtesy of Thomas Buergenthal.*

in the camp laundry, happened to see him on the "ramp," lined up with several hundred Jews to be taken to the gas chamber. The father managed to kidnap him and hid him in the laundry under piles of clothes. Later he became an errand boy in the laundry. Before he was ten years old he got to know the horrors in their full extent. He could tell one about the gas chamber, how big it was, how many people it could hold at a time (two thousand), and how many boxes (of gas) they used then (four). He described the dressing room, where they undressed before going into the big hall; it was full of benches, he said, and they had all to hang their clothes up tidily on the pegs and be sure to hang their number tags on the top. No, it wasn't in the big hall there were benches—he laughed at my ignorance—no, they had to stand in there, for they were going to die, and again he smiled his angel smile. Was it possible? No, they couldn't sit down in there, they stood close, close together and died. He sounded surprised that anyone as old as I looked shouldn't know that. It might take about ten minutes; then they were dead, said he almost objectively.

Was the hall like a bath, did the gas come out from cocks in the roof, or how was it? He shook his head at such ignorance. Oh no, it was thrown in to them. The boxes? Now he was quite in despair at my not knowing such simple, ordinary things as that glass containers were thrown in through openings in the wall, and broke as they hit the floor. (About the relation between these glass containers and the boxes I'm not quite clear, but I couldn't go on, I felt almost like a criminal as I sat there questioning that little angel about such things.)

He stayed half a year in Auschwitz; then his father went on another transport. That was last November. The father came to this camp, probably in the same big transport as Wolfberg. But he isn't here now. He was sent on somewhere, and it's very doubtful indeed whether he's still among the living. The child arrived a fortnight ago with another big transport, in which many froze to death or got their arms and legs frostbitten. He knows nothing of his father or mother, and he has no brothers and sisters. He is all alone in the world, alone among strange men in a strange land, at ten years old! Death and destruction, murder, torture and all the devilry of man are familiar to him. Such was his picture of the world—the only picture he had had a chance of forming. He knew nothing, of life—and death—but what he had seen in hell!*

Yet I couldn't make out any stamp, in that little face, of all the horrors he has lived among; the eyes were large and grayish brown, with an open, calm and trustful expression, and smiles were playing round his mouth the whole time. Perhaps there was something nervous about the mouth, yet no, for children smile most when they feel safe and comfortable. There may have been a little shyness too, I don't know, but I realized from the moment Scott (who was with me) pointed it out that his hands had taken over all the symptoms of nervousness. He couldn't keep them still a moment, they were always passing over the blanket, fingering the corners of the sheets, the flaps of his collar; he had a little book, he turned it round and round, turned over the pages, shut it again, took up a pencil Scott had given him, fiddled with it, dropped it, rubbed his forehead, brushed his hand across his face, mouth, ears, hair and back to the corners of the sheets. In perpetual motion. And they were grown-up hands, not like a child's with chubby, stubby fingers and round backs; these were long and sensitive, the fingers finely shaped, transparently pure and delicate with finely modeled palms; beautiful hands, but they didn't seem to belong in Raphael's picture. It was as though this child's whole tragedy had found expression in those little, oversensitive hands, and once one had noticed them, it was impossible to take one's eyes off them.

I took his book and leafed through it. It was a book with pictures of German aircraft, fighters, bombers; I asked if he was interested in that.

"Yes!" with radiant enthusiasm.

"Well, but don't you know what those planes are used for?" I attempted.

"Yes, in the war, to fly high up in the air, high, high up!" and he pointed up as far as he could and laughed gleefully.

---

* Soon after the war began, the Buergenthal family, who were in Poland at the time waiting to emigrate to England, ended up in Kielce, a town in central Poland midway between Warsaw and Krakow. On March 31, 1941 the Kielce Ghetto was established to confine Jews from the town and surrounding areas. In August 1942, the ghetto was liquidated, with most inhabitants executed on the spot or deported to camps such as Treblinka in eastern Poland, where they were killed upon arrival; only one to two thousand inhabitants (of the original twenty-five thousand), survived, including Buergenthal and his parents, who were transferred to a labor camp in late fall 1942. In May 1943, this labor camp too was liquidated (and all the children except Buergenthal murdered); the remaining inhabitants were transferred to nearby work camps. Buergenthal's family was sent to the Henryków Factory, which produced wagon parts. In the summer of 1944 the Henryków labor camp was dissolved. Contrary to Nansen's narrative, Buergenthal, accompanied by his mother and his father [who was actually born in Galicia, a region of Poland], was then sent to Auschwitz-Birkenau (his mother was later sent on to Ravensbrück). Buergenthal's mother survived the war and Tommy was finally reunited with her on December 29, 1946, over nineteen months after the war had ended; Tommy's father (from whom he was separated at some point in the fall of 1944) died in Buchenwald in January 1945.

I showed him a picture of some bombs; did he know what *those* were?

"Of course!" he laughed, "those are bombs!"

"Yes, and what are they used for?"

"To shoot, bomb, blow up!" and he illustrated an explosion with his hands and arms and laughed gleefully.

I said something about bombs and flying machines like that being terrible things that we mustn't care for, but I knew I was going too fast, it would take years to save this little soul. And all at once I felt such a burning desire to take him with me, keep him, protect him and make a human being of him! A thrill of joy, a few good seconds, before I realized the hopeless impossibility of such a plan. I asked him if he had read any of that book. No, he couldn't read. And write? "Can you write me a letter by next Sunday?" No, he said, he couldn't write either. "Well, but your mother must have taught you to read and write at Kielce?" "No, they had the death penalty for that, so she didn't dare," he said with a smile.

Even though I'm pretty thoroughly hardened by this life here and in German concentration camps altogether, and used to hearing and seeing both this and that, these little, smiling replies of his came down on me like bombs.

TUESDAY, FEBRUARY 20, 1945 ■ Today our seventy-two-year-old civilian chief at *Herz As* came in and said we must get hold of some boxes to pack up drawing things and so on, for our transfer to Stettin, but we needn't take everything, he said, for in a couple of months we should be back and would go on working here. Yes, that was his belief! The Russian advance has been stopped now, in their opinion. We're to go to Stettin, twenty kilometers [12.4 miles] from the Russian lines, and rebuild a gasoline factory that has been destroyed by bombs! Can you believe it? The Germans can!

The Norwegians who were taken out for transport (the last "rolling" transport from here, it's said) are still isolated in Block 14. For two days now there have been a thousand men in that one block, while many blocks in the camp are standing empty and there is more room than ever before. And there they are, eating up all the food they took for the journey, after giving away what they couldn't carry!

The liquor scandal at Kfz.D.[W.] is going from bad to worse. Hundreds of liters are now in the prisoners' hands, and bunches of them come back dead drunk in the evening. Yesterday, when Kfz.D.[W.] marched past us, a gust of spirits surrounded them. The kommando leader shrieked in his most vicious German: "The whole Kfz.D.[W.] column stinks of bad gin!" Indeed, marching in through the gate there was a little after-piece. We saw a dead-drunk Pole being conducted, or kicked, across the square to the *Bunker* block.* He was so drunk he couldn't stand, and every time he got on his feet, down he went again for the count at a well-aimed kick from one or more of the SS men, who were enjoying themselves hugely. Poor devil! Afterward I suppose he would be flogged, and the remains

---

* The Bunker Block, also known as the Zellenbau or the Cell Block, was a special prison, located within Sachsenhausen but isolated from the main compound by a high wall, reserved for high-profile political prisoners and for those to be punished for breaking camp rules. One Sachsenhausen prisoner noted that "few incarcerated therein ever lived to tell their friends about it." The SS *Hauptscharführer* in charge of the bunker, Kurt Eccarius, was sentenced to life imprisonment by the Soviets following the war. In 1956 he was repatriated to West Germany and initially received an amnesty. Subsequently convicted twice more for his role in the murder of thousands of inmates, he served only a total of eight and a half years.

of him sent on a transport. Two Norwegians were taken for drunkenness as well, later in
the evening.

Many of the sick are to be sent from the *Revier* with the transport now pending. Rolf
[Hofmo] for one. He looks splendid and will get through it fine. Thank heaven! The
transport is going to Bergen-Belsen near Hannover. It seems to be a good place.

WEDNESDAY, FEBRUARY 21, 1945 ■ The transport still hasn't gone. German
administration is maintaining its traditions to the last. And there are those poor fellows
living on top of each other. Suddenly they're not allowed to come out into camp, and no
one may visit them. It's very strict, what's more!

A Norwegian was driven in to camp from Kfz.D.[W.] in a drunken stupor. They had
failed to revive him, even though he was "detailed" and didn't have to return until nine
o'clock tonight. He landed in the *Bunker*. When we marched out here this morning, we
had to pass through Kfz.D.[W.] by a different "street." A guard with a submachine gun
barred the way past the hut where the spirits were stored. But now so many hundreds
of liters have been scrounged here and there in the kommando, and tucked away by the
prisoners and SS, that there's no further need for anyone to make inroads on the "original
stock." So I suppose the guard will have as peaceful a time as most guards.

THURSDAY, FEBRUARY 22, 1945 ■ Yesterday another couple of cartloads of T.B.
patients were disposed of. They also took the Jewish gang in the crematorium. There were
twenty-six of them. They had been busy wiping out the traces of the murder of twelve
thousand Russians in 1941; that is, they dug up the bones, which had been buried somewhere after defective burning, and crushed them. What was done with them afterward I
don't know; no doubt they were removed or scattered.*

Yesterday a prisoner was sent to the crematorium to put in a broken window in the
mortuary. The window was spattered with blood, and an iron bar was bent, as though
someone had been trying to get out. He learned that it was one of the "corpses," who
hadn't been dead and had awakened down there, where they were working at high
pressure moving corpses from the heap into the furnaces. He had looked into the furnace,
grasped the appalling situation, and made a desperate effort to squeeze out through the
window. Then they shot him. The wall round about the window was peppered with
bullets.

The transport still hasn't gone. One of the dead-drunks from Kfz.D.[W.] has departed
this life. Simply drank himself to death on 82 percent spirits.

SUNDAY, FEBRUARY 25, 1945 ■ The thirty Norwegians who were to be sent on a
transport are still here. Today they're even coming back, after a week's isolation, to their
respective blocks. I've talked with [Hjalmar] Stenstrup,† and his account of that week was

---

* As the SS prepared to evacuate the camp and remove evidence of its crimes, the *Lagerführer* of the *Klinkerwerke*
external camp was ordered by Sachsenhausen's commandant to remove between eight and nine tons of human ash
from the crematorium and dump it into the adjacent Hohenzollern Canal.

† Hjalmar Steenstrup (1890–1945) was heavily involved in the Resistance, couriering funds from the Norwegian legation in Stockholm into Norway and assisting in the escape of refugees from Norway to Sweden. He was arrested in
July 1941 and sent to Sachsenhausen in late 1943. After the war Steenstrup was selected to represent the Norwegian

horrifying. People were dying round them like flies. For they had been stowed away with *Muselmenn* and the disabled. Every day heaps of corpses were piled up in the *Abort* or the washroom. It was part of the daily routine for certain of the "corpses" not to be quite dead. If anyone who hadn't yet got accustomed to this "rough sorting" objected that this or that man was alive and mustn't be put on the heap of corpses, they only said that he would be dying in a few minutes anyhow, so just put him there. And he was put there, and a corpse immediately laid on top of him. There might be life in "dead bodies" at the bottom of the heap.

Another answer to the objection that such and such a "corpse" was still alive was that no, we've got that one's "death-*Schein*," so he's finished, dump him on the pile, he'll soon be dead. They had gone through the "doubtful" cases and made out death-*Schein* for those who in all probability would die during the day. Or what do you think of this act of mercy: There was a call-over. Men were called out one by one and had to fall in by fives, with all their clothes and *Habengut* [worldly goods]. One man's name was called, he didn't come; it was repeated and he tottered up, emaciated, finished. It was plain that he would never stand a transport. Someone came and took his pulse, listened to his heart, said something to the "managers" with a shake of the head—and one of them addressed a group standing by the wall of the hut: "Make room there, will you? Let this man lean against the wall, he's going to die; he'll die in a minute!" They moved aside, the man reached the wall, leaned against it, and immediately collapsed and was dead.

Yesterday when we got back from work there was big news. The Norwegians are being sent to a *Sonderlager* [special camp], it's said. The Swedish Red Cross has been negotiating with Germany, in fact direct with Himmler, and the negotiations have led to a favorable result. We're to leave here! To be evacuated under the protection of the Swedish Red Cross. Orders have come direct from Himmler that the Norwegians are to be taken out of all the kommandos and sent to Neuengamme near Hamburg, which is to be an assembly camp for all Norwegians.* It's also reported that from there we're to be transferred to internment camps in Sweden! Altogether there's no end to all the golden prospects being held out to us. How much of all this is true, it's impossible to judge. However, it's been said officially in certain kommandos that all Norwegians are to be replaced by other men, as they're being sent off "in the very near future." Some say it was Count Folke Bernadotte who conducted these negotiations in Berlin.† Neuengamme, by the way, is known to be

---

concentration camp prisoners at the Nuremberg trials. During trial preparations he took a flight home on December 18, 1945, which crashed outside Oslo, killing him.

* Neuengamme was the largest concentration camp in northwest Germany, less than ten miles southeast of Hamburg. It was initially established in 1938 as a subcamp of Sachsenhausen; by 1940 it had become an independent camp. It is estimated that at least forty-three thousand, and possibly fifty-five thousand, of its one hundred thousand prisoners died by the end of the war due to exhaustion, malnutrition, disease, and violence. The final camp commandant, SS *Obersturmbannführer* Max Pauly, was convicted of war crimes and hanged by the British on October 8, 1946.

† Folke Bernadotte (1895–1948) was the nephew of King Gustaf V of Sweden. In 1928 he married an American, Estelle Manville, heiress to the Johns-Manville fortune. Bernadotte was appointed vice chairman (and de facto head) of the Swedish Red Cross in 1943. He initiated negotiations in Berlin on February 16, 1945, with the goal of transporting interned Norwegian and Danish prisoners to Denmark or Sweden; these efforts ultimately resulted in the "white buses" operation. See March 18, 1945, below. After the war Bernadotte was appointed the first official mediator of the newly formed United Nations, to mediate in Palestine following the UN Partition Plan and the Israeli Declaration of Independence. On September 17, 1948, he was assassinated by elements of the militant Zionist group Lehi (aka the Stern Gang), who were opposed to his proposals.

a bad camp. However, if it's really to be a *Sonderlager* for Norwegians and Danes under the protection of the Swedish Red Cross, there is pretty good reason to believe that the conditions will change a bit.

I need hardly say that the Norwegian blocks are feeling elated—to put it mildly.

MONDAY, FEBRUARY 26, 1945 ■ There is no more news of our fate, but the rumors are spinning on, and the fairest and most joyful prospects are being unrolled. We're to leave here in sunshine buses, to be waited on and tended by Swedish Lottas [military nurses], to have abundance of food and clothing, and all is to be passing well. The days of our distress are over. We're saved!

But otherwise things are just the same. We marched out to work today as usual, and there's no sign of any sudden change.

I hear that all the Norwegians were the object of systematic plundering during their isolation. Partly they *had* to give away provisions to *Blockälteste* and all manner of block personnel and "*angestellte*" [responsible] fellow prisoners to secure decent treatment; partly they were regularly robbed. At night they were robbed all round in their bunks—for they had to take everything they possessed into bed at night and try to brood over it. But they slept too soundly, most of them, and woke with an empty bunk. Empty? Why, they were sleeping two, three, and four in a bunk. The *Muselmann* thieves crept about, insane with hunger and misery, and stole all they could eat and all the clothes they could get on their bony bodies. Can't one understand it? They cling to life, and starvation and terror drive them crazy, desperate! But among these insane creatures there are many accomplished thieves, and the conditions are such that nowhere among them can one be sure of anything one possesses. Things vanish out of one's pockets and out of the cardboard box under one's arm. Indeed, Bjarne Aanesen was standing with all his worldly goods on his back, neatly packed up in a newly-scrounged knapsack; and as he stood among the crush in the lobby, all his worldly goods were cut out of the bag with a knife!

Yesterday, as usual on Sunday, I was in the *Revier*. First I went to see my youngest friend Tommy, the Raphael angel. He was as smiling and sweet tempered as before, and still more communicative. He hadn't done a drawing for me, as he promised. He pleaded that he had tried, but it wouldn't come. I had brought a little parcel of lump sugar, sardines, etc. Scott, who was with me, had some crackers, and Tommy was delighted.

This time he told us a little about the transport from Auschwitz via Heinckel.* The first three days they walked. They had been given some food to take with them, including tinned meat. That was stolen from him right at the start. The blanket he was carrying he threw away; it got too heavy. He walked with several other little boys of his own age. They were alone in the world too—their parents dead, in all probability. Alone in the world, on a prison transport, at ten years old! After three days' march they were stowed into railway cars, two hundred in each car. The cars were open, but had walls. The prisoners stood up, squeezed together, as many as there was room for. So one can imagine what it was like for the little ten-year-olds—right down among the legs of the grown people. The transport took place in the worst period of frost, and took twelve days. The child says people were

---

* After an Allied air strike on April 18, 1944, destroyed the Heinkel factory, it was used as a reception area for camp prisoners evacuated from Eastern Europe.

dying all the time, and that every time someone died the others were glad, for then there was more room. The dead were thrown overboard at once, or another common thing was to sit on the bodies.

"But what did you think of all that, Tommy?"

"I beg your pardon? I don't understand. What do you mean?" (All this in formal German; he never says *du* to "elderly" gentlemen, and is a master of etiquette—polite and prompt spoken.) I explained as best I could what I meant. I didn't really mean anything; what could that child have thought? He supposed I wanted to know what he thought about sitting on the dead bodies, and assured me that he hadn't sat on any, and wouldn't. I asked if they were locked into those railway cars or were allowed to get out at the stations. "Ah! You mean to relieve ourselves!" And he explained that for that purpose there was a hole in the bottom of the railcar for them to use while moving. And a lot of people escaped through that hole, he said. Fifteen from the railcar he was in, and the guards didn't say anything. Indeed why shouldn't they allow those poor wretches a desperate chance like that? Hundreds were dying on the way, freezing to death and being dumped overboard; these others might pass for dead, too—as well first as last. They wouldn't have much chance of avoiding their fate, even in "freedom." Jews! And without food or clothes, in Germany today! Besides there was no doubt a reward for shooting them.

I asked Tommy how many he thought had frozen to death on the way. Oh, lots and lots, *mindestens tausend! Mindestens!* [at least a thousand! At least!] "And you, Tommy, were you very cold?" "Terribly! And I cried terribly. But my hands didn't freeze!" He was proud and glad of that, and held them out, those curiously grown-up nervous hands with the long, sensitive fingers. "But my feet!" and made faces to show how much his feet had hurt.

At Heinckel he was put into the *Revier* with all the other children and many, many more. All had frostbite. He had cried a lot there too, he said rather roguishly—as though he was telling us about some naughty tricks he had played. It was his big toe that hurt most. They had to take off all the skin and flesh, he explained, and it was as thin as that (holding up his thin littlest finger) and quite black. Here they had to cut it off, and the next one too, and that hurt terribly. He must have cried quite a bit here too, but now it was all over and part of a long, interesting story he had to tell. His little playmates he had lost; they had all been sent on somewhere with transports. But there were a lot of "uncles" here who were kind to him, and now he was well off. Only he was in such a hurry, such a great hurry to get up and be well. "But why?" I asked. "You have the time to yourself, and then as long as you stay here you're safe!" He looked at me—almost tolerantly—with those big, sagacious eyes of his and said, "Yes, but if this camp is evacuated—what then? If I'm still lying here and can't run, what will they do to me?"

No, indeed, it wouldn't be much use trying to deceive this ten-year-old or to "cheer him up" on false grounds. Poor little Tommy, what will become of him? Not a single soul can one save. Not if one were to pledge one's own life—and everything belonging to one—not even then.*

---

* In *Tommy* Nansen wrote, "Every possible, or even impossible, plan for getting Tommy with us was thought through hundreds of times, from making him [in]to a Norwegian to packing him in a sack and carrying him with us. But we all knew too well that it was hopeless."

WEDNESDAY, FEBRUARY 28, 1945 ■ So we've even reached the last day of February—just like that. And March is a spring month, and the start of a brighter and brisker period after all. Churchill has spoken again and said things will soon get going for the last time, and the torrent of spirits from Kfz.D.[W.] is flowing with undiminished strength. It's said that 52,000 liters have arrived from an evacuated spirit factory in Breslau, and the camp is drinking; both the green and the striped. A man from B-wing of our block died yesterday in the *Revier*. What he drank I don't know, but anyhow he died of it. And he had a wife and children at home. My God!

FRIDAY, MARCH 2, 1945 ■ The days and nights are filled with raids, and the AA guns are heard no more. "No wonder," says a civilian here, "for all the soldiers have been sent to the front and the 'flak' has to be worked by women and *Hitlerjugend* [Hitler youth]. In the first place they don't know how to fire, second they're afraid of the bang, and as they're short of ammunition anyway they just let it alone. Practically no German fighters are going up. There's no more gas. The fires in Berlin and other places can't be put out. They haven't the water or the men. Along the roads from here to Küstrin* and other parts of the front the trucks are standing one behind another. No gas! Why in heaven's name do they go on with this madness?" The man who said that is a hundred percent Nazi!

SUNDAY, MARCH 4, 1945 ■ Sunday—perhaps our last in Sachsenhausen. Tonight we're all to turn out on parade. It almost looks as if we were going! Obviously to Neuengamme, the assembly camp (?) for further transport (?) to Norway (?) or Sweden (?).

Prisoners from Ravensbrück arrived here yesterday. A few Norwegians too. And eighty children, from four to eight years old; dangerous to the Third Reich! A good many born in concentration camps. The women in Ravensbrück have had a dreadful time. Mostly muselwomen. The parcels that were sent from here to the Norwegian women were stolen for the most part. They were all addressed to a *Vertrauensmann* [reliable woman]. The Commandant played the unbelievably shabby trick of saying that *one* prisoner couldn't possibly be allowed eighty parcels; she might have twenty, and she got those. He took the rest.†

MONDAY, MARCH 5, 1945 ■ Our journey really seems to be coming off. Yesterday all the outlying kommandos arrived in camp. From Falkensee, Klinker, Lichtenrade, Lichtenfelde‡ and all the rest of them. Colbjørn was among them, and many others. But there was no roll call at six as we expected. And we went off to work today as well, as though nothing were going to happen.

The children from Ravensbrück were little gypsies, fantastically pretty and charming, and starved and musical. Some of them were given a meal in Norwegian Block 16, and

---

* Presently Kostrzyn, Poland, it is approximately seventy-two miles due east of Sachsenhausen.
† The commandant of KZ Ravensbrück from August 1942 until the end of World War II, SS *Sturmbannführer* Fritz Suhren, was tried for his crimes by French authorities and executed June 12, 1950. Prior to arriving at Ravensbrück, Suhren had served as *Lagerführer* of Sachsenhausen.
‡ All subcamps of Sachsenhausen.

sang and played in return. Fabulous—strange, like so much else in this camp, where darkness and light, death and life, heaven and hell walk side by side.

I was in the *Revier* on Sunday as usual. Little Tommy (Bürgenthal) was much better. He had been up walking about on that foot of his. He's being coddled like a prince there, and terribly spoiled no doubt. Scott and I brought sugar and things for him, and Arvid arrived with crispbread and sardines, so at least he won't go hungry just yet awhile. But what will happen to him when we leave? When the camp is evacuated? When the war is over? I said good-bye to him yesterday, and don't expect to see him again. He readily promised to write to me when the war is over, and learned my address by heart. I'm sure he'll remember it.* I asked if he would like to come to Norway. After the war, he said, he would come, but he would bring Father and Mother. Poor child! He has seen thousands die, has handled corpses with his nervous little grown-up hands and knows this world, as it has been revealed to him; but it never occurs to him for a moment that Father and Mother may be dead. Father and Mother are alive; he doesn't know where, but after the war they'll look for him, and he'll look for them, and then they'll find each other and go home to the little town in Slovakia, where the father kept a little hotel.

Tommy said good-bye with a smile, and was delighted with a silver pencil I had given him, a pencil with red, blue, green and black lead in it and a gadget to change the colors. He thanked me prettily, in old-fashioned phrases, and promised again to write me in Oslo, Norway, when the war was over; and yes, he knew he had promised to call me uncle, it was a little difficult at first, but he wouldn't forget. "That is my duty!" said he. I suppose he's heard quite a lot about duty, and he must have thought it fitted in here, that grand word.

Little Tommy! If only your fellow-creatures thought a fraction as much about their duty to you as you do about yours to them, all your prospects would be brighter than they are today. Thank God you don't realize that, and may you never come to realize the abyss of vile injustice which has been done you! May there be such a future in store for you that all this frightful, this unintelligible cruelty will be expunged from your mind. May you discover that life is not like that, the world is not as it looked to you from the floor of the cattle car, when you cried because you were so terribly cold. May you one day grasp and experience its richness, and all the warmth and joy, all the beaming light which are reflected in those big eyes of yours, too shrewd for a child's, and which are a reminder and evidence of what you were meant to be.

Of course all imaginable rumors are circulating about our fate. Some think we'll be leaving tonight or tomorrow, some of course think the day after, some are more cautious and think it will be during the week. But all are quite certain we're to leave, unless the Russians suddenly. . . . Machine-gun nests are being dug round about, and barbed-wire barriers put up. It looks as though they mean to defend themselves from hut to hut through the whole "Prussian forest" round here. All the thousands of cars that have been standing in the woods are being towed away and gradually driven off by rail. There's no gasoline whatever, so not a car moves a yard under its own steam. Most of them are ruined from standing out in the rain and snow. All the SS I know have now arrived at a full

---

* Although Tommy did forget Nansen's address (and name) he ultimately reunited with Nansen in 1948 and visited him many times thereafter throughout Nansen's lifetime.

understanding that all is lost. A number of them talk about the last shot in their revolver being for themselves. For they will die rather than be put in chains. Capture by the Russians, to them, suggests the rattling of fetters loaded with heavy ball—and Siberia. But there's a great run on the spirits in Kfz.D.[W.] just now.

WEDNESDAY, MARCH 7, 1945 ■ Now it actually looks as though our days in this camp were numbered. Today may be our last out here on the kommando. For as we marched out this morning all the *Vorarbeiters* of the different kommandos outside the innermost ring of guards were kept back by the *Oberscharführer* who is the *Führer* of all the kommandos. He told them that from tomorrow all the *Norweger* were to stay in camp. In other words we must put our house in order, pack our *Klamotten* [clothing] and make the arrangements necessary for departure after such a long time.

And then we must say farewell. No farewell can ever have been as easy and full of joy as this will be—nor any I have to take henceforth, as long as I live. Nothing shall I sink into oblivion, if possible, with more delight than all I am saying good-bye to here. The leaky, dirty, lopsided huts among the fir trees, and those everlasting, anemic desert trees in ranks, and all the cars, tanks, tractors, buses and trucks scattered about among the trees—as though dropped down from the thunder-clouds overhead. The way out here every morning and every evening. How well I know every boring tree, every branch, every little bypath, every puddle! And how I shall forget them! What orgies of oblivion it all gives food for!

I've got hold of a little pair of mittens for Tommy. I'll send them, if I haven't an opportunity of going there once more.

THURSDAY, MARCH 8, 1945 ■ But we went out to our kommandos today as well. All of us! And there's really nothing in the camp to suggest that we shan't go on. So one must give up believing anything, just wait and see. And let nothing disappoint one. But there's no denying that the days seem longer, now that the waiting has grown so intense.

FRIDAY, MARCH 9, 1945 ■ Here I still am, doing nothing. My time is my own and I could easily make some use of it, but no, it comes to nothing. We'll be going soon. That must be the cause. Now they've gotten so far with the journey as to draw up a list (about fourteen hundred men) of those who are to leave in the first batch. There are to be two batches.

Yesterday it was announced that the Anglo-Americans have crossed the Rhine—at last. Cologne has fallen.* In the East, Stettin is about to fall; there are Russian attacks at Küstrin, where they've driven in a wedge that comes pretty near us and Berlin. We're always thinking we hear the thunder of the guns from the front now, and we have alerts all the time. They come regularly every night before bedtime, so we have to go to bed, and often eat, too, in pitch darkness. Otherwise my mind and thoughts are elsewhere—far, far away.

---

* Cologne, Germany's fourth largest city and the capital of the Rhineland, was captured March 6, 1945; the Rhine River was crossed at Remagen, approximately thirty miles south of Cologne, on March 7, 1945, when the Ludendorff Railroad Bridge, the last remaining bridge over the Rhine, was captured by elements of the US 9th Armored Division. Within a week, seven US Army divisions had crossed over to the east bank of the Rhine, the last barrier to Germany's interior.

TUESDAY, MARCH 13, 1945 ■ On Saturday we were out on the kommando for the last time. When we got back in the evening there was a disruption mood and travel fever in all the Norwegian blocks, as though we were leaving straight away. Fourteen or fifteen hundred men are to go in the first batch. Packing went on until far into the night; the luggage was always getting too heavy or too bulgy and one had to begin again. It was one o'clock before we groped our way to bed in pitch darkness to the sound of an alert. But we didn't get much sleep. It was as though the journey, the unbelievable journey away from Sachsenhausen, had already begun. The journey we have dreamed of day and night and pictured in a hundred different ways. We lay there, I did anyhow, staring up into the dark, while our thoughts were on a circular tour and would take no rest. And thus we got to four o'clock, and half-past, and it was morning again.

The usual roll call and morning bustle. The Commandant's roll call took place from ten o'clock onward. Call-over, falling in, alphabetically—*zu fünfen!* [by fives!] *Seitenrichtung!*—again! The Commandant made a speech, after walking down the lines with lowered eyes. I suppose it was our footwear that especially interested him—or doesn't he like looking people in the face? He said we must be well clad. No one was to leave in zebra clothes, and all whose shoes were bad should have new ones, he promised. All must be newly shaved and in clean clothes before leaving. When that would be he couldn't say yet, but in the very near future. We must behave nicely as long as we remained in camp, and respect its discipline. Buses would be sent for us, and there would be room for thirty in each bus. That was all; with that we might return to the huts, where we still are, and it's already Tuesday afternoon, and not the faintest sign of departure.

Life in the huts these days is one long trial. The hut is crammed with people day and night. Saturday evening was "utilized" for delousing. In the delousing establishment we were stripped and our sleeping bags and clothes put through the "gas," while we ourselves were sent into the bath and afterward examined under the stomach through a magnifying glass. Of course there was an alert as we stood naked waiting for our clothes, while others were standing under the showers and others naked in the anteroom. At last it was over, we got our deloused clothes and sleeping bags, returned to the block and got into beds which must have lice in them, if there was any point in this delousing at all! A good example of German thoroughness.

On Sunday afternoon we went to the *Revier* as usual, and saw Tommy for the very last time. He was doing splendidly and was delighted with two games we'd gotten for him, as well as a big bag of lump sugar. I played with him and lost. He was delighted, but felt it was rather sad that I should lose. Poor, lovable, splendid little Tommy! It was such a wrench to say good-bye—worse than anything in all your "old uncle's" prison life. For the very first time he saw you, you went straight to his heart. But that was something you didn't realize, and I'm glad.

Rolf [Hofmo] is quite himself again, going out for walks and looking better than ever. He leaves with the first batch.

FRIDAY, MARCH 16, 1945 ■ Yesterday so much happened that I put off writing until today. In the morning the first three hundred men on the list (up to and including F) had orders to parade with their luggage. At last! Exodus and uproar, a fresh wave of travel fever, fresh optimism. The three hundred and fifty, after parading on the square, were placed in the bathhouse. They were left there through the day, and one began to get used to the idea that they would now have several days there; that's what usually happens. Then came the alert, and one of the heaviest raids we have ever witnessed. It was on Oranienburg, and camps and buildings in the immediate neighborhood of Sachsenhausen were leveled to the ground.

From the moment the first bombs dropped, we realized that this was more our concern than usual. For in general we've gotten used to taking very little notice. But the bomb thuds this time were not to be stifled. At every deafening crash, and one had the impression that whole showers of bombs were coming down, the huts shook so that everything hanging on the walls or standing loose on shelves fell to the floor, and every moment we were expecting that the roof would lift in the blast and the walls collapse on us. But they stood up, for a wonder. The raid lasted two hours—that is, it didn't stop, only quieted down a bit, and the planes stopped coming; otherwise it's still on, twenty-four hours later, and has been all the time, with an unbroken series of exploding time bombs. During the raid the whole of Oranienburg and the district up to this camp were larded with bombs, a large proportion of them time bombs. All night long colossal explosions have been shaking the huts in all their joints.

A women's camp at Auerverken (armament factory) not far from here was entirely wiped out during this raid. The dwelling huts and workshops were systematically leveled to the ground. All the women were in the huts, and those in the first rows were all killed* (they were German apparently), while the others got out by degrees and escaped from the camp, under and over the electric fence, which had no current then, as the power station had had a direct hit. The survivors have arrived here. They began streaming in only a few hours after the raid. A couple of blocks were cleared for them, and now they're quartered opposite us, in Blocks 36 and 37. A large contingent of women in a camp of men who haven't seen any women for months or years is of course a huge sensation, and that is no doubt the main reason why the blocks they're living in are barred off and have guards posted both front and back. But through the windows communication is in full swing all day. Our block has grown very popular and has visits all day long from the curious of all ages. They line up for the privy and the washroom so as to gaze on the beauties on the other side, who for their part are no more backward and crowd up to the windows, waving, smiling, preening and cooing like doves. Yes, here we have the ancient and eternal game in full swing—despite the fact that less than twenty-four hours ago these daughters of Eve were running for their lives from falling and burning huts, among dying, dead and mutilated sisters.

SUNDAY, MARCH 18, 1945 ■ There weren't many who could still bewitch one with their feminine charms. Most of them were thin and ravaged. But the youngest, most thoughtless and forgetful put themselves forward, smoothed their hair, moistened their lips (they know what it takes all right), and leaned against the window so that their profile could be seen—the whole profile—not just the face! Others, perhaps chiefly those who had no such profile, seated themselves at the windows in picturesque attitudes. And in

---

*   More than three hundred female prisoners at the Auer-Werke factory died during the raid, "most of them because they did not have permission to leave their places of work during the attack." It is estimated that Allied bombing ultimately killed thirty-two thousand foreign civilians (i.e., forced laborers), POWs, and concentration camp inmates over the course of the war.

spite of guards and barbed wire and barriers of planks and blankets, a Norwegian got in there yesterday. He was caught and clapped in the lockup, where he remained four hours, until midnight, when he went off with transport batch number two.

For now the transport is in full swing. The first batch, whom I left in the bathhouse when the raid started, stayed there until midnight of the same day. Then they were led out onto the *Strasse* [street] between the gates. The Commandant made another impressive little speech, to the effect that they must behave properly and not run away. The Swedish government was responsible for no one's doing so, and if anyone escaped notwithstanding, further transports would be suspended.

Then the outer gate was opened, and in came a Swedish officer nearly seven feet high, the head of the Red Cross expedition. Outside stood thirteen white-enameled buses with Swedish flags and Red Cross emblems painted on them.* Salutes were exchanged, and the first bus was filled up with the first thirty men. Never have Norwegians in a German concentration camp been stiffer and smarter on parade, and never has anything gone off more punctually and smoothly—despite the fact that there was not a "*Los! Los!*" to be heard, not a single "*Seitenrichtung*" or "*Zu fünfen!*" or "*Aufstehen!*" or any of their bellows of command. I hope it made some impression on the SS who were there—just as a little parting hint. All the luggage was taken by Swedes in white Red Cross uniforms, and stowed away under tarpaulins on the roofs of the buses. Each man received a parcel of food and *cigarettes*—with the warning that it must last a couple of days, and so off they went.

Well, that was Thursday night. Last night, or rather this morning, for they were in the bathhouse from midnight to five o'clock, the next batch left. That was up to and including Jensen, the big family in the letter J. The destination is Neuengamme, where we'll be in a separate camp, still under German guard; but they say the Swedes are still negotiating about us and about access to the new camp for their own people. So for the Norwegians, as usual, everything is going capitally. Otherwise there is still great wretchedness in the camp. It's better than it was, but first and foremost because those who were worst off are dead.

Even this morning, nearly three days after the raid, time bombs were still exploding. The condition of Oranienburg is said to be indescribable. Thousands of people were killed. Dead men are lying in the ruins, and bits of people lying around everywhere. They have no water or electricity. We are without them in camp as well, and the lavatories can no longer be used. Holes have been dug in the ground between the huts, and what a sight! Thank God it isn't warm yet! Water has reached a premium. They've already begun to deal in it—or *schieben* [traffic in], as it's called.

---

* The rescue effort initiated by Count Folke Bernadotte under the auspices of the Swedish Red Cross is now commonly referred to as the "white buses" operation for the white-painted buses used. Initially Bernadotte was only permitted to assemble Scandinavian (Norwegian and Danish) prisoners at Neuengamme, near the Danish border. More than 5,000 prisoners were transported to Neuengamme from various German camps, with the largest contingent (2,200) coming from Sachsenhausen. Subsequent negotiations between Bernadotte and Himmler allowed the release of Scandinavian prisoners for transport to Sweden via Denmark. The first such evacuations occurred on April 9, 1945. By the time the white buses operation had ended, between 17,500 and 21,000 prisoners had been rescued, including 8,000 Scandinavians and the remainder from more than twenty other countries (including nine Americans).

MONDAY, MARCH 19, 1945 ■ We're waiting and waiting to get off. I still don't know if I'll be in this lot. For the rest of the *Revier* are going, and they'll take two buses. Yesterday we had another heavy raid. Three bombs fell close to the camp; one was a direct hit on a shelter. Everyone was killed.

NEUENGAMME

WEDNESDAY, MARCH 21, 1945 ■ I am now sitting in a rathole of a hut in a pigsty of a camp known as Neuengamme. The long-desired, alluring Neuengamme. But let me give some account of how it happened.

On Monday evening (the day before yesterday) a list was called over that got part of the way through N. Then came packing and good-byes, and at eleven o'clock, in pitch darkness, but under a starry sky, we were stumbling across the square to the bathhouse. A lovely night, "worthy" to be the last in Sachsenhausen. We got cold standing still, and began walking about between the huts for the last time. Deserted "streets," lit only by a pale and slightly veiled young half-moon. The outlines of the camp loomed dark and sinister against the night sky; from the square the hut gables looked like the teeth of a gigantic semi-circular saw; one felt it could only be the dark that prevented one from seeing the blood running down them. I stood a long time on the square, and let my gaze pass from tooth to tooth. Cleanliness—Honesty—Obedience—Truthfulness—and Love of the Fatherland!* And the blood ran down and dripped onto the sand of Sachsenhausen, as it has done for many years without stopping.

About one o'clock we got into the bathhouse, and there we stayed, packed like herrings in a barrel, until four. Then we had to fall in outside. Obviously the cars had come. Just as we were marching off, there was an alert. Back into the bathhouse! Another hour in the crush, then the all clear sounded, and out we went again. This time out through the gate, on through the furthest gate; it was as though we sprouted wings and flew out, to where the row of white buses stood and the voice of the brother nation could be heard. Before I knew it, I was in a soft comfortable seat in the first bus, with a Swedish Red Cross parcel (including a hundred cigarettes!) in my lap. Oh heavens—to be sitting in a Swedish bus with Swedes, or let us say—with human beings! The fairy tale had begun!

We weren't long in starting. For the last time we saw the wall, the watchtowers, the SS camp, the guards at the crossroad, the barrier where the road turns off to Kfz.D.[W.], and all the *Waldkommandoen*, which we marched along every day, morning and evening. Soon the last of the camp vanished from our sight, and we were heading west, for something new, unknown, but so enticing!

I must go on tomorrow. Now it's nearly midnight, and three hundred men are lying snoring round me.

---

* Another prisoner of Sachsenhausen later observed, "I realized later that there was a bitter irony in the fact that the word 'Love' was painted on the gable of the barrack . . . where the Penal Kommando was housed, because a prisoner typically did not survive more than two weeks in that Kommando."

THURSDAY, MARCH 22, 1945 ■ If you remove the avenues from the North German landscape, nothing remains but a flat desert, strewn with *Dörfer* [villages]. The buses took us from *Dorf* to *Dorf* through interminable avenues, straight lines cutting up the desert, mile after mile, into polygons, rectangles and triangles. A landscape of tedium, and, with all the endless numbers of refugees and prison transports we met or passed, a sinister landscape. At the entrance and exit of every village and town they had built tank barriers; everything bore the stamp of preparations to defend each yard of German soil, and might therefore indicate that the war isn't nearly over yet, if it depends on the German leaders. We passed one or two prison camps as well, and in the fields we saw prisoners working, women and men.

The trains—or caravans—of refugees covered all the roads. It looked as though the whole country were full of gypsy gangs. Everything gave the impression of disintegration and confusion, hopelessness, misery and disaster. But we sat smugly in Swedish Red Cross buses on our way to safety. The days of our distress were over! So we thought.

At last we turned down a side road, and immediately afterward all eleven buses drew up before the entrance to Neuengamme concentration camp.

The first thing we encountered as we got out of the buses and stretched our stiff legs was a stink of garbage and unadulterated sewer. A stink that has pursued us ever since, only we've gotten more used to it. The next thing was couple of SS men who began with *Seitenrichtung* and *Zu fünfen!* And all the rest of it straight away. "Liberty" was at an end; our happiest hours for many years past were over, we had to take up our cross again and march into a fresh prison. The "cross" was heavy, though not so heavy as it was to be. As well as the "luggage" we each had our Danish parcel to carry, and the camp itself turned out to be a kilometer from the outside entrance, where the buses had to stop, though there was a good, wide road going right up. But the Swedes were to come no further, and for a more than sufficient reason, as we understand now after seeing the inside, which, one must say, defies description.

We came out on a middle-sized concrete square surrounded by huts, which again were surrounded with barbed-wire fences, behind which we caught a glimpse of friends from the previous transports. We were called over, lined up five and five, and at length marched through the barb-wire enclosure and thence into a hut. But what a hut! The filth was positively sticking out of it, and it smelled of everything that smells bad. The hut was a single open room, eight meters wide and fifty or sixty meters long [26 ft. × 154–196 ft.]; the floor was divided up into hutches filled with straw, and on the straw were blankets. One got the feeling that the straw and blankets were alive with lice, though we couldn't see them yet. We were to be better acquainted!

However, the first thing to do was to secure a place in the sty, and Arvid, Erik and I had the luck to plump down in a corner by the entrance. Handy for getting out—one never knew. There we got rid of our things, and then we went out to inspect the conditions. The "courtyard"—the space between our hut and the next—was narrow as a drain and long as a disaster, for flush with our hut and built onto it was a long, lower *Abort* hut. It was the same opposite. All the huts belonged to the courtyard, but outside the one just opposite there was barbed wire. For in that hut there were condemned men, deserters and others. We saw them; they were standing up against the barbed wire, begging cigarette butts and so on. They looked worn out and miserable. The whole yard was pretty much an open sewer, which stank even worse than the inside of the huts. Although the weather was dry and had been for a long time, puddles filled the holes in the concrete, and the grooves and cracks. What they were puddles of, the smell betrayed, and the condition of the gully holes and the drain they were supposed to lead to was also beyond all doubt. The filth was everywhere, in thick layers; it was worse than a pigsty. The hut was the stall where the beasts were kept at night, the courtyard the outer sty.

But we were tired. We had been done out of a night's sleep, and the journey had been strenuous and agitating, so we were soon sleeping soundly and heavily in those hutches of ours.

SATURDAY, MARCH 24, 1945 ■ I've been hard at work arranging a hut they've let us have as a hospital, and haven't managed to bring these notes up to date. There's no doubt that we have come to a *Vernichtungslager*—a real extermination camp—and the Swedish Red Cross has obviously been taken in.

There is already typhus in the camp. The dungheaps lie open, sewage and filth are afloat everywhere. Lousy, sick, and dying *Muselmenn* drag themselves around and hang begging on the barbed-wire fences round our yards. One has a sense of wading in and swallowing bacteria and bacilli. Every day a hundred or a hundred and fifty men are dying in the camp, which contains eight thousand prisoners altogether, or possibly twelve thousand. The figure varies, for fresh transports keep arriving and also transports are going out all the time.

Several of the chaps have been in the crematorium cellar looking at enormous piles of *Muselmenn* corpses, more than the furnace can burn. Also there's a fuel shortage. Shooting and hanging, too, go on here continually.* A gallows grins at the sky in the far corner of our courtyard. Yesterday I saw a number of our crowd sitting comfortably at their meal on the trapdoor under the gallows. Most of those executed seem to be SS men, including Norwegians and Danes who have been caught in desertion or sabotage. They have a purple band on their sleeves with *Torsperre* [gate closure] on it, and all of them are waiting to die. One gets into the way of seeing them there without pausing to reflect on their fate. After all they deserve it more than thousands of innocent *Muselmenn* who are starving and freezing to death.

Those Norwegians who were sent to Bergen-Belsen from Sachsenhausen a few weeks before the Swedish action got going have had a terrible time. There are two camps at Bergen-Belsen. *Lager 2* is a genuine *Vernichtungslager*. There were no roll calls there; they only counted how many went in and how many corpses went out again. It was undoubtedly intended that all who went there should die and be seen no more. By mistake the Norwegians were put in *Lager 2*. They were there only three days before getting out again and into the other camp, but that was enough. They slept on the concrete floor, which was partly under water. The old prisoners were dying in crowds. It was a common thing there to get hold of a corpse to sleep on, so as to keep dry. Nor was cannibalism a rare phenomenon. One Norwegian saw a prisoner cut the liver out of a dead body and eat it. All

---

* One historian estimated that of the approximately fifty-two thousand who lost their lives at Neuengamme, twenty-eight thousand died in the last six months of the war. As Nansen observed in *Tommy*, "If death paced through the streets of Sachsenhausen, it galloped here [in Neuengamme]."

this and much, much more can be told of it, and will assuredly be told some day by those who have been through it themselves. But I suppose no one will believe them, for want of imagination to conceive such things.

A number of the Norwegians who went to Bergen-Belsen have arrived here as *Muselmenn*. They turned into *Muselmenn* in a few weeks. Most, however, are still there; they were too ill to be removed, and the Swedes weren't allowed into that camp; no doubt it was too ghastly. Most of those who were left behind, more than twenty men I think, have spotted typhus.

Yesterday 108 Danes arrived from Porta camp in Westphalia.* *Muselmenn* every one, sheer skeletons. Eleven of them were admitted to our *Revier*, which is still nothing but an empty hut; we've got as far as shoveling the dirt out and washing it.

In Porta the prisoners were driven until they dropped. The Danes turned into *Muselmenn* in a few months. They had been there six months, and out of two hundred odd, sixty-five were dead. Of the Danish Red Cross parcels they got only the crispbread; ham, tobacco, butter, jam, sugar and the like were stolen by the SS. And the crispbread also was torn from them by organized gangs of Russian prisoners, who fell on them and plundered them to the skin—taking their clothes as well. No wonder they were *Muselmenn* and near death. Now they smiled palely, feeling that their days of toil and distress were over. This was paradise, this was salvation! This pigsty!†

Today the first transport came in from the south, from Dachau.‡ A number of the Alsace men were in it. The loss of life among them had been great, oddly enough even after they left Natzweiler and were distributed through many different camps in South Germany. Many died of pneumonia, many of tuberculosis and other ailments, but most of hunger and exhaustion pure and simple.

Today, moreover, a fresh transport arrived from Sachsenhausen. Now there are only six hundred men left there, and they may all come at once, in a couple of days. In general the transports are beginning to come in from several quarters. It's strange to see old friends again and hear who is alive and who is dead. It's as though enormous expeditions to Central Africa or other perilous quarters of the globe were coming back after being cut off from the world for several years. People stream out to meet them with all sorts of questions, but first and foremost: Who is dead? How many are still alive?

---

* A subcamp of Neuengamme. A number of subcamps were located in Porta Westfalica, Germany, the gateway to Westphalia.

† One Norwegian who had spent almost a year at Natzweiler had this to say of Neuengamme: "At Neuengamme . . . we were bombed harder than ever before in the war, but otherwise the camp was like heaven: food, more than we'd seen in a year was laid out for us that week. . . . Even the bunks were a treat."

‡ Located in southern Germany, northwest of Munich, Dachau was the first concentration camp established by Nazi Germany, on March 20, 1933, less than sixty days after Hitler took power. It is estimated that more than two hundred thousand prisoners from more than thirty-seven countries were incarcerated in Dachau, and more than forty thousand died there and in surrounding subcamps, primarily from disease, malnutrition, and suicide. Famous prisoners included Martin Niemöller (transferred from Sachsenhausen to Dachau in 1941), Leon Blum (three-time French prime minister), Franz Halder (head of the German army General Staff until 1942), the psychologist Bruno Bettelheim, psychiatrist Victor Frankl, and, for a time, Vladek Spiegelman, whose story is recounted in the book *Maus*, by his son Art Spiegelman. It was the second camp to be liberated by the Western Allies, on April 29, 1945. The last four commandants of Dachau either committed suicide or were executed by the US military tribunal.

SUNDAY, MARCH 25, 1945 ■ Of the 504 men who "passed through" Natzweiler camp, nearly half are dead. Mauthausen camp was the worst,* according to those who have been in both. All who arrived yesterday from Dachau and Mauthausen, about three hundred there may be, are now with the students who arrived before us, in quarantine. Therefore it's difficult to talk with them, but we manage. The "courtyard" of the quarantine block runs parallel to the "courtyard" of Block 11, and is divided from it by a strip of "garden," a ribbon of plowed-up earth with dung spread over it and a huge dungheap in the middle, which stinks abominably. This strip of earth has a barbed-wire fence on each side, and along these fences stand hundreds of Sachsenhauseners, all shouting across at once to hundreds of Dachau men and students.

It's a deafening uproar and almost impossible to hear the answer to one's question—that is, if the man on the other side has been lucky enough to catch it. But there one learned of brothers who were dead, and how they died, and heard their last greetings. There one met friends whom one believed to be dead, but here they were again, large as life; many of them skin and bone, many in a wretched state, with teeth knocked out, with shattered arms or legs and ruined health—but alive! The deaths were bellowed out, reached anxious, straining ears through a tremendous din, pierced the heart like arrows—while hoarse shouts telling of life and hope went to other hearts like sunbeams, bringing joy, ineffable and inconceivable joy! The impression one receives is that of one giant catastrophe that has swept over us all—and cut us down in swathes. We may still be far from port—this is only some of the wreckage, washed ashore here at Neuengamme. At home are widows—hundreds—who know nothing.

I heard certain news of Leif [Poulsson]. He is all right, and coming later.

One sight I saw yesterday afternoon is in my mind the whole time; it is like a permanent background, a kind of horizon to all that passes on the stage in front of me. The sight of hundreds of corpses, piled on top of one another in the mortuary, as high as houses. Arvid and I went there. I wanted to see. It was appalling. There might have been three or four hundred corpses. Not ordinary corpses; these were three or four hundred skeletons; they reminded one of lean, plucked chickens; these weren't human beings—so small and miserable. The numbers, the overwhelming numbers, I suppose completely threw out one's sense of scale. But the faces and those ghastly hundreds of pairs of staring eyes, those gaping mouths and pain-distorted features—they were human. Those of human beings who had lived, suffered and died. And all those hundreds were only three days' harvest! They were piled on top of each other with all their heads, or rather skulls, the same way. The bodies took up no more space than the heads, so they lay flat. For there were only bones left, covered with skin. Some were bloody, with running sores and colorful bruises where they had been struck, others pale as wax. A Norwegian was lying just at our feet; the "attendant" showed him to us; he had died of typhus. The attendant was going to turn him over for us, for he lay face down on the concrete floor, but just then an SS man came

---

* Mauthausen, also known as Mauthausen-Gusen, was a large labor camp complex established in 1938 near Linz, Austria, following Austria's annexation by Germany. Many of its prisoners died as a result of the Nazis' *Vernichtung durch Arbeit* (extermination through labor) policy, especially at the adjacent granite quarries. Due to the destruction of its records, the number of prisoners killed at Mauthausen is unknown; estimates range between fifty-five and ninety-five thousand. The camp was liberated May 5, 1945, by the US 11th Armored Division, the last concentration camp to be freed. The commandant of Mauthausen, Franze Ziereis, was killed trying to escape in May 1945. Among Mauthausen's survivors was Simon Wiesenthal, who became a noted Nazi hunter following the war.

in. It turned out to be an *Obersturmführer*, and he started roaring about what the hell we were doing here! I'm afraid we looked silly. I couldn't get out a word. Before me thundered this infuriated *Obersturmführer*, staring at us with a countenance revealing all the qualities of the race, while behind us was the stare of three or four hundred pairs of eyes. I don't know which was more horrible. At last Arvid got out that we had missed our way. The *Sturmführer* invited us to spend three days in the mortuary, if we were so disposed. I think he meant it; he looked like that. But the storm blew over, we were allowed to go in peace, and tumbled out with a few threats hurled after us.

This afternoon I've had a somewhat original "building conference." My plans for a *Revier* are ready and "passed," and therefore I called the "building committee" together—after some previous negotiation with two green-triangle bandits who are to deliver the materials. For the situation is that through legal channels we can get nothing done. Practically all material is in the hands of black-market traders and BV-ers. Everything is paid for in cigarettes. I brought the two green-triangles along to the meeting, and after some bargaining it was agreed that for 5,500 cigarettes they should give us all the materials we need for our hospital. These include 500 square meters [5,400 sq. ft.] of plywood, 800 meters [2,600 ft.] of nailing strips, ceiling moldings, floor moldings, doors and windows, nails and tools, materials for an electrical system with 35 light fixtures and finally, a sanitary facility, with two washbasins, two sinks, a washing tub, a hot water heater, a bath tub, and all necessary pipes, plumbing and tools for hot and cold water in all taps.

After all one must admit that it's a good bargain; it won't be more than about two cigarettes per head, with the camp's present number of Norwegians and Danes. I should like to know how many people have erected a hospital with two hundred beds as cheap as that. Tomorrow the materials are arriving—then we must get the trucks unloaded in a jiffy, so that no one sees, and the day after they'll start building; and we're doing it all ourselves. Of course, this form of purchase is repellant, but for us it means life-saving on a big scale.

Now I'm really tired after a busy day. Good night, Kari!

WEDNESDAY, MARCH 28, 1945 ■ We've had a harrowing night, and I must write while the impressions are still fresh. It began about half-past ten last night, when orders came for a number of us, about twelve hundred Norwegians and Danes, to move into the *Schonungsblock*, a two-story brick building that looks quite grand from outside, but the inside of which no one could forget in a hurry, after one look at it. The misery passed all bounds and baffled all conception. In every bed there were three or four, indeed sometimes five or six men. It sounds incredible, but I saw them. Certainly they were lying on top of each other, but most of them were nothing but skeletons and didn't take up much room. And they lay quiet; they hadn't the strength to move. *They were there to die!* and many were already dead! The whole interior of the building was one inferno, a waiting room of death worse than could be conjured up in the wildest fantasies. Unattended, those poor creatures lay in their beds; some had tuberculosis, others dysentery and typhus, others open wounds and running venereal diseases and all conceivable and inconceivable sufferings of every kind. Those with *Durchfall* and *Scheisserei* who lacked the strength to hoist themselves out of their bunks, which were in three tiers, and they were the majority, relieved themselves where they lay. One can imagine what the bunks looked like, and the bunks below. The straw was antique, and the blankets hadn't been shaken, let alone washed, for years; they lay on the bunks like stiff cakes of filth. On the floors and up the walls the dirt lay in thick, hard layers, and when one entered the building, the stench that met one is unimaginable. In the passages, in the washroom, in the well of the staircase, inside the wards, and in the beds corpses lay around.

And now these people were to clear out, to make room for more Norwegians in the camp. And we were to move in after them. The SS intended us to move into the house and get into the *Muselmenn's* beds just as they were. Into the cakes of ordure and the filth, into the same straw that has lain in the bunks for years, collecting every known species of bacterium and bacillus and every variety of human excrement! Here we have German *Sauberkeit* in a nutshell; that's what it is. The covers must be smooth and the edges flush like rulers in a row, there must be nothing on the blankets, nothing under the beds; what the blankets are concealing, though it were a dungheap, is of no interest, provided it's as smooth as a dance floor. Yes, even if there are corpses under the blankets, rotting away, that's quite in order so long as they are invisible. I mention this last because in the cleaning that followed, dead bodies actually were found, hidden in the straw of the bunks. Their bedmates "kept" the bodies there so as to get an extra helping of soup or an extra bread ration. I suppose they pulled the corpse's arm out when the waiter came round with the food, and helped the dead hand to take hold of the *Schüssel* and the loaf. This trick is well known in practically all German concentration camps, including Sachsenhausen.

However, the SS had miscalculated if they thought they could get Norwegians and Danes in their right senses to move in and go to bed in this hell of filth. Our block doctor unhesitatingly took the responsibility of going against orders, and gave directions for a general spring cleaning of the whole house from floor to roof. And then began a cleanup the like of which this camp and its rulers, at any rate, had never seen. Hundreds of Norwegians and Danes went at it—literally—in contempt of death all night through, and are still at it, far on in the afternoon. Every bunk and every board in every bunk was carried out to the washrooms, scraped, and washed with Lysol and chlorine. Floors and walls were scraped and washed in the same way. In some places one had to hack the dirt off. One gang relieved another. About four in the morning all the *Muselmenn* were out and all the corpses removed. It wasn't merely that there were corpses all over the place, but they dropped and turned to corpses on their way out, poor creatures. They were taken to the baths and washed. Many died when the cold water was turned on them. Of thirty who were admitted to the *Revier* for some reason, sixteen were dead this morning.

There is not a shadow of doubt that they would have died in any case, only a little slower perhaps, which means that their sufferings would have lasted a little longer still. But to other prisoners, witnessing this gruesome spectacle in "their" camp, we, who were to blame, must appear in the most unfavorable light. Here come thousand after thousand of "well-fed" Norwegians and Danes (though in fact we have our *Muselmenn* too)—and to make room for us, many times that number of other prisoners—Russians, Poles, Ukrainians, Dutchmen, Frenchmen, and others—have to clear out of their blocks and squeeze together in rooms that were overcrowded already. There are three, four or five of them in every bunk, and the bunks are eighty centimeters [thirty-one and a half inches] wide. Now every Norwegian and every Dane is to have his own bunk; one man in each bunk! Of course it causes bad feeling and the other prisoners can't see—or understand—why it is, let alone why it should be so. They take this as they have taken all the other cruel dispensations of fate that have filled up their lives day in, day out, for many, many years;

but the bitter thing is that in the gallery of their mortal enemies we now have a place. It was we who took their bunks and huts from them, we who drove them out of "house and home," out on a transport. And what a transport means to them, they all know too well.

SATURDAY, MARCH 31, 1945 ■ Yesterday the long-expected Swedish commission arrived, a festive scene in itself.

Representatives were summoned, for Count Folke Bernadotte, who was at the head of the commission, demanded to speak to them. They had a long conference before the Swedes were shown round the camp. Sverre Løberg was brilliant.* He gave a clear account of conditions, and neither the Commandant, the *Lagerführer*, nor any other of the SS dared to butt in and stop him. The conversation was in "Scandinavian." So the Swedes were well informed when they began their inspection. First they all went into the brick block, which was now in a highly presentable state. But then they went on to Block 6, one of the worst, where our fellows were sitting eating on top of each other in their hutches on the floor. For the Germans the tour must have been an exceptional Canossa-pilgrimage, and in fact they didn't seem to be enjoying themselves.† They said nothing, nor could they prevent the Swedes from keeping up a lively conversation with us, and with others whom we met in the different blocks. The Swedes saw everything and heard everything, and I think we may well say that for us it was a big and successful day. Accordingly our spirits were very high. The mere sight of the Swedes among us was a colossal encouragement, and when you add their radiant optimism about the end of the war and our future fate, no wonder it was as though a fresh spring breeze swept through the Norwegian and Danish camp.‡

I stood and watched a transport of *Muselmenn* leaving the camp today in Swedish buses. The Swedes have had to undertake their transport to obtain more space in the camp. It was a pitiful sight. Most of the *Muselmenn* had too little strength left to succeed in hoisting themselves on to the running board by their arms. They had to be lifted in. Some fell down before they got that length, and remained lying on the ground, where SS men—*Lagerführer* Thuman himself—and foremen were kept busy shoving them in

---

* Løberg (1905–1976) was an early member of the Resistance in Skien, Norway, along with Dixie Cappelen. Arrested August 30, 1940, he was the first Norwegian sentenced to jail for his activities. During the war he was incarcerated in thirty different jails, prisons, and concentration camps. Immediately following his rescue by the white buses, Løberg returned to Germany to search for any remaining Norwegian prisoners. After the war he was elected to the Storting (1945–1969) as a member of the Labor Party.

† The pilgrimage to Canossa refers to a penitential journey taken by Henry IV, emperor of the Holy Roman Empire, in early 1077 to the fortress of Canossa (in Parma, northern Italy) seeking the forgiveness of Pope Gregory VII, who had provisionally excommunicated him. More generally, to "go to Canossa" has come to mean any unwilling act of penance or submission. Hitler's biographer, Ian Kershaw, describes Hitler's January 1925 meeting with the minister president of Bavaria following his release from Landsberg Prison: "The meeting with Minister President Held on 4 January . . . went well. No one else was present. Hitler was prepared to act humbly. It was his 'journey to Canossa.'"

‡ In the unpublished draft copy of his account of the final days of the war, *The Curtain Falls*, Bernadotte wrote, "[I]n the company of the camp commandant I inspected the various barracks and spoke to the Norwegians and Danes only fleetingly. I'd heard, however, that some people I knew before had been transferred to Neuengamme, and I asked the commandant if I could see them personally—particularly one of them I was anxious to meet: Fridtjof Nansen's son, the architect Odd Nansen, who I'd worked together with in 1940 in America. It was quite strange to see him now as just a number among this infinitely large band of prisoners." What appears in the published version is: "While in America I had met Odd Nansen, the brilliant young architect son of the famous explorer Fridtjof Nansen; we had . . . become great friends. When he was brought before me and I saw him snatch off his cap and stand to attention as all prisoners were required to do when in the presence of a German of rank—the commandant was with me—I boiled with anger."

among the ranks and standing in front of them, so that they shouldn't be "visible" to all the Swedish drivers. Then they were carried into the buses. Simply shoved in pell-mell—whereupon the doors were shut and locked. It was as though the situation were "saved" if only they got off, away from this camp! If they arrived as corpses, it didn't matter to *Lagerführer* Thuman; on the contrary, he would be glad—then *he* wouldn't be the one called to account. So Thuman thinks! But it may be that he thinks wrong!

All these *Muselmenn*—most of them already doomed—lit up with ineffable joy and hope when they saw the white Red Cross buses turn into the concrete square and grasped that they were to leave in them. For many it was too much altogether, they hadn't the strength to grapple with so fantastic, so marvelous a prospect—they collapsed and died—literally—of joy! Then off they went. They went to Braunschweig, and there they were marched into a new hell.* The fairy tale endured thus far and no farther. There the hope gave way, and the dream of rescue vanished. Again the barbed wire closed round them, again the days were to be an unbroken series of nameless sufferings, until death takes pity on them and gives them peace. "Charity begins at home," said one of the Swedes to me, shaking his head sorrowfully.

The days of our distress, there is reason to think, are over; we have more than cause enough to rejoice, and to be grateful to the Swedes for what they have done for us. But one thing is certain: If we had known that something was being done for the others, to relieve their sufferings, the joy would have been greater and more wholehearted for all of us. We haven't been in want, at least not most of us from Sachsenhausen. There are, indeed, Norwegians and Danes who have suffered and have been on exactly the same footing as the rest. Even among us the death rate has been pretty high. But none of that can drive away the gnawing sense of undeserving and unfairness in our being preferred to other people who are worse off, and who are going under and dying while we live in plenty.

The commission with Bernadotte at their head went through every block. They had words of encouragement for all—words which were brought out when they were gone, canvassed and interpreted, magnified and deepened in every conceivable way.

I spoke to Runberg† about a number of things we needed to get the *Revier* fixed up, asked for instance if the Swedes could send us cement, sanitary equipment, chlorine, etc. "We-ell, we could of course—but we shan't have time!" replied the professor. Afterwards that became our motto—for he made the same promising reply whenever it fitted in. The Count threw out similar hints past the very noses of the Commandant and the *Lagerführer*. Judge if we were gleeful! To see SS men—and those the very highest hangmen in our world—being treated like air! "Is that the fiend you were telling me about?" the Count said afterwards to Sverre Løberg out on the square—and pointed to the *Lagerführer*. The fiend from Lublin, Thuman.‡

Yes, it was a big day and a marvelous experience for us all. Now the only danger is of

---

* There were a number of subcamps of Neuengamme in Braunschweig.

† Gerhard Arvid Rundberg was the supervising doctor for the Swedish Red Cross medical team. He later wrote a book on his experiences, *Rapport från Neuengamme* [*Report from Neuengamme*].

‡ SS *Obersturmführer* Anton Thumann (1912–1946). Known as a particularly vicious guard, Thumann later admitted to participating in a liquidation of several dozen prisoners who were massacred on April 21 and 23, 1945 (three weeks after the above diary entry) in connection with the evacuation of Neuengamme. Thumann was tried after the war by British authorities and hanged on April 8, 1946.

our becoming altogether too arrogant, too overweening. There are signs of it even now. Some people won't work anymore, simply refuse and stand on their "rights"; it's not in accordance with the "contract." As though we knew of any "contract!" As though anyone had told us we were anything but ordinary *Schutzhäftlinge* [protective custody prisoners], as we have been all along! But it will be all right when people have calmed down again, and it dawns on us that the war will not be over for a few days yet.

SUNDAY, APRIL 1, 1945 ■ Today is Easter Sunday and the first of April, and the camp has a day off. To be sure for us that's no advantage. For we were locked into our barbed-wire streets and aren't even allowed into the other Norwegian blocks. But morale is tiptop, for the Swedes were here again yesterday. Not Bernadotte, but three of the others with Professor Runberg at their head, and they brought eight Lottas, who from today are to start regular work in the *Revier*. They're coming every day in the future! It's unbelievable!

The little *Standortarzt* [senior camp physician]* tagged along yesterday as well, fiddling about with my drawings under his arm, but I don't think even that time he managed to produce "his" plans for our new *Revier*. No one took any interest in him, poor chap, he was superfluous wherever he tried to put himself forward. The Swedes drew up new long lists of our requests, which are now beginning to include such things as musical instruments! Bernadotte is negotiating in Berlin. Apparently he's trying to get us moved on again even before the end of the war, let us hope to Sweden. "It's incredible what Bernadotte has achieved so far, why shouldn't he achieve that, too?" said one of the Swedes.

TUESDAY, APRIL 3, 1945 ■ The day was prefaced by an announcement that from today we're no longer *Schutzhäftlinge*, but civilian internees. All who were to parade for work this morning could go back to bed. That solves the problem of whether we're obliged to work or not. Evidently not. We can idle all day long.

Today a number of transports arrived in camp. They were the outlying kommandos, all of which have been recalled. Most of them were on the Lüneburg Heath, southward in the Hannover direction; in Hannover, it's said, they're already fighting. What are they going to do with all these fresh hundreds? They'll have to be put on top of the others, who were on top of one another before. But that doesn't affect us. We think it's cramped for *us*, with two in a bunk, but what is that to the state of things for the rest of them? Oh, the pitiful, the wretched sight if one merely looks out through the barbed wire, and now it's to be still worse. For most of the new arrivals were *Muselmenn*. How many of them, I wonder, will end up on the heap in the mortuary? After dragging through a time of starvation here, after standing by the barbed-wire enclosure round the Norwegian blocks and staring at all the plenty that is positively oozing out the doors and windows. One could get them to do anything whatever for a bit of smoked sausage. Smoked sausage which many of us have had enough of for the rest of our lives. They try

---

* The *Standortarzt* was Alfred Trzebinski, who according to Professor Rundberg "made an unpleasant impression on most of us. . . . I had to ask myself now and again if he was really a doctor." Convicted for his role in the Bullenhuser Damm murders by a British military tribunal, Trzebinski was hanged on October 8, 1946, along with Anton Thumann and Max Pauly, the commandant of Neuengamme. See April 10, 1945, below.

to sell things to us for food or cigarettes. They steal cups, knives, and spoons, hide them in their rags and hurry off to the barbed-wire fence, where they make desperate efforts to find a buyer. They fall out among themselves because one has snatched a purchaser from under another's nose.

Yesterday all the bread from the Norwegian and Danish blocks was distributed in the camp. The handbarrows with the bread were all but plundered; desperate *Muselmenn* had actually to be kept off by force. One *Muselmann* had got a big bag of crumbs and was tottering over the concrete square on his matchstick legs. His wooden shoes dragged along the concrete with a little bang at each step. Both arms were squeezed against his chest, round the bag of breadcrumbs, and he looked fearfully around as though every moment expecting a rap from the well-known rubber truncheon, or to be plundered by his "comrades." But all went well, no tormentor appeared, and he was nearly across the square, the most dangerous part of the way to the corner he had selected to sit down in and eat and eat.

But the poor fellow had taken no account of dangers from below. Suddenly one of his wooden shoes stuck in a crack in the concrete. For one quivering instant he struggled desperately to free himself, but too late. When the shoe loosened he was already lying flat on space, but still he squeezed the bag in his arms, as though clinging to the last straw. Then—just before reaching the ground, he had to give up and let go. He failed to ward off the crash, so his head came down heavily on the hard concrete, his arms were stretched out and his legs asprawl, the bag was torn and all the breadcrumbs flew out over the concrete like a cloud. He lay motionless, but within a fraction of a second he and the bag and all the breadcrumbs were covered by a shouting, struggling, desperate swarm of *Muselmenn*! Before many seconds had passed, there wasn't a breadcrumb as big as a grain of sand left on the square. The flock of sparrows moved off, scattering in pursuit of fresh spoil, but on the concrete their "comrade" still lay on his face, with his thin arms spread, and his bony hands bent in a last desperate effort to clutch at the vanished treasure. After a time some *Muselmenn* who had been sent by a Kapo* arrived and carried him away. On the concrete where his head had lain there was a red spot. Soon that will be gone, too.

THURSDAY, APRIL 5, 1945 ■ Yesterday Bernadotte was here again with his suite. They brought good news. All our women are to be sent to Sweden at once, also all those with chronic and prolonged illnesses, a number of the students, and Rector Seip and his wife (who are leaving this very day).

SATURDAY, APRIL 7, 1945 ■ Yesterday a transport came in from the south. I got word that Leif [Poulsson] was in it, and ran off to the *Revier*.

All I had heard about his being all right, in fine form, and comfortably well off since he was made *leitender Arzt* at Natzweiler came crashing down at one blow. An emaciated,

---

*   Kapos were prisoner functionaries assigned by the SS to supervise work kommandos or carry out other administrative tasks in a concentration camp. As such they held virtually unlimited power and were often selected for their ruthlessness and brutality. In almost all camps the position was held by German prisoners. The origin of the word remains unclear. Note that this is Nansen's first use of the term; apparently it was not used in Sachsenhausen.

white-haired old man, who could scarcely hold himself up, came stumbling toward me at the ambulance. It was Leif. I gasped for breath, I hardly knew him.

"Heavens—is that you, Leif?" was what escaped me.

"Yes—is that you, Odd," said Leif, trying to make it sound cheerful. We stood looking at each other.

"How are you, Leif?" I asked, for I felt I had to say something.

"Fine, thanks," said Leif, of course he had to answer in the same style, but with that he collapsed—onto a chair that was standing there. Then we gripped each other by the hand, and then we could say nothing for a long time.

Afterward we got Leif to bed and gave him the best we had to eat—eggs, milk and white crackers, but he couldn't get much of it down. We had to dilute the milk with water, and a couple of spoonfuls of egg and a little bit of cracker was all he could manage. I tried to get a little out of him about what he had gone through, but on that subject he was taciturn. At the end of the time at Natzweiler before they had to evacuate he had been a little better off. They had received medicines and a bit more to eat. Since then he had been in several camps and suffered with the others, until at last he landed in a camp south of Stuttgart as a doctor. That was the worst of all the camps he had been in. There everyone was starving. The camp was so tucked away that the Swedes would scarcely have found it if the Norwegian seamen's pastor in Hamburg hadn't been so indefatigable in tracing the Norwegians who were hidden away there. At last he found it out, and the Swedish relief commission came at the eleventh hour.*

By then thirteen of the twenty-nine Norwegians who had reached the camp in January of this year were dead and the rest nearly dead. The dead had gone under from exhaustion, typhus or pneumonia, but chiefly from exhaustion, as everywhere else. Leif hadn't been so easy to get down; he is tough. But his sunken cheeks, the lines of weariness in his face, and his whole emaciated figure are more expressive than words of what he has gone through and of all the distress, suffering and ruin he has seen and experienced. He wouldn't tell us much about himself; we got that from Asbjørn Halvorsen, his friend and loyal assistant through thick and thin in the *Revier* of many camps.†

He was in the bunk next to Leif. He seems to have come through it better, was still as

---

* Nansen is referring to the assistant pastor of the Norwegian Seamen's Church in Hamburg, Conrad Vogt-Svendsen. The remarkable story—of how Vogt-Svendsen compiled the names and locations of Norwegian prisoners with the help of a sympathetic German interpreter, Hiltgunt Zassenhaus—is wonderfully told in Zassenhaus's memoir *Walls: Resisting the Third Reich—One Woman's Story*. Zassenhaus had been hired to supervise the pastor's visits but instead helped him smuggle food and vitamins into the prisoners and, further, kept a card index system tracking where Norwegian prisoners were located. Zassenhaus emigrated to the United States in 1952 and practiced medicine in Baltimore. The only German to be awarded the Royal Norwegian Order of St. Olav for her actions, Zassenhaus was nominated by members of the Norwegian Parliament for the Nobel Peace Prize in 1974. She died in 2004, age eighty-eight.

† Asbjørn "Assi" Halvorsen (1898–1955) was a world famous soccer player and coach, playing on and subsequently coaching the Norwegian national team, which won a bronze medal at the 1936 Olympics (defeating Germany). In his role as secretary general of the Norwegian Football Association (NFF) he was active in the Norwegian sports boycott during the German occupation, which resulted in his arrest and incarceration in Grini and Natzweiler. Halvorsen's stature in the world of soccer and his reputation allowed him to obtain extra benefits (food, etc.) which he passed along to his comrades. After the war Halvorsen resumed his role as secretary general of the NFF; in 1955, while on a business trip for the NFF, he was found dead in his hotel room, age fifty-six, presumably a victim of his long incarceration.

strong as a bear, but enfeebled by spotted typhus, from which he had just recovered—if only the fever would pass off.

"If the Swedes had arrived a week later, Leif would never have got back," said Asbjørn. To begin with, in the last camp, Leif had been able to get through his medical rounds every day. Then that was too much for him; one day in every week he had to stay in bed himself to collect his strength—then two days—then three—then four. And when the Swedes arrived, he could only drag himself round, among dying comrades, one day in the week. The other days he was in bed himself, waiting for the end. It was the last straw, I gathered, when Asbjørn went down with spotted typhus.

"The lice were crawling and swarming about in millions," said Asbjørn. "It was useless to try and protect oneself from them." They were without delousing agents, drugs, food, clothes and everything a human being, not to mention a sick man, needs. They were harried by spotted typhus and all kinds of diseases, and there as everywhere else they were surrounded by thieves, scoundrels, swindling, devilry, bottomless misery, beastliness and filth on all sides. On this background the white buses shine whiter than anyone can grasp who hasn't himself experienced them.

Here also death is riding through the camp. The main *Revier* is being evacuated; all T.B. patients and all who can't get well in two or three weeks are to go (to Bergen-Belsen rumor has it), and we know what that means. All the Jews in camp, and oddly enough there are still a few here, are to go as well, besides a number of other prisoners. At this moment *Hundertschaft* [groups of one hundred] after *Hundertschaft* is passing out through the gate. I've just been out looking at them. A walking cortege of live corpses. Some being dragged along by their comrades; some already lying on the concrete, apparently lifeless.

SUNDAY, APRIL 8, 1945 ■ Today the Norwegians who were left in Bergen-Belsen arrived, but eleven of those left behind there died, and two Danes. Only ten Norwegians and one Dane got here, all with spotted typhus. Those who died, died of spotted typhus. The condition of Bergen-Belsen is appalling; about a thousand are dying there every day.*

And that same Bergen-Belsen was described to us in Sachsenhausen as a good camp. A recreation camp, we heard, and all who were to go there were pleased about it. Indeed they fought over who was ill enough to go with those transports. Actually it was intended that all our sick and old people should be taken there, while the rest of us were to go on foot. That would have been a catastrophe of sinister dimensions. Doubtless it was the Swedes who saved us from it.

But a thousand live corpses left here for Bergen-Belsen today. I wrote a little about it yesterday, but that I wrote in the morning. I saw more. I saw the *Muselmenn* being called over and lined up outside the blocks where they live. They came staggering out of the darkness, couldn't drag their feet along, and a Kapo stood there helping them with a rubber truncheon. He struck them, so that they fell headlong down the steps of the brick building, at the same time cursing them in the usual way. If they couldn't get up again, they were lifted and stood up "*Zu fünfen*," supported by their neighbors. Five and five clinging together and forming one continuous line, which by some obscure means

---

* Anne Frank was among the many thousands dying of typhus at Bergen-Belsen. The exact date of death for her and her sister Margot is unknown; recent research indicates that it was likely during the month of February 1945. The camp was liberated by British forces on April 12, 1945.

In Neuengamme concentration camp. One of the Muselmann
transports starting out on its last journey.

didn't overturn, they "marched" through the gate. Some fell, but were picked up again and dragged on. There a whole row fell on their faces; a Kapo was on them with his whip, and up they got in some inexplicable manner and oozed on, their wooden shoes clattering and scraping on the concrete. To think they didn't just lie down and die where they were! Surely they might have been permitted to do *that* at least! But no! They're to be tortured to the last breath. And they've been so cowed that they drag themselves to the spot where they're meant to drop. Do you realize, my own Kari, how unspeakably it wrings one's soul to look on—and not be able to do a thing for them? Can you realize how they sear one's heart, the looks of hatred and contempt that some of them threw on me in the gateway?

MONDAY, APRIL 9, 1945 ■ Five years ago! Five hard, cruel years, long as a disaster.* But the next five will be different, and be lived differently! In camp the day was marked by little celebrations, speeches, poems and songs. Rather on the old recipe, rather threadbare in style, rather too many big words in advance perhaps. But if only we can live up to them, all is well.

The first transport of the sick to Sweden went off today. Leif was in it. It wasn't so painful saying good-bye to him as it was to see him again. He promised to write to Kari. They're driving to Flensburg, where Danish Red Cross cars are waiting. But things are beginning to look urgent now. Bremen has fallen, and the Allies are probably less than a hundred kilometers [62 miles] from here. If the advance goes on like this, they may be here any day. It's said the SS are busy preparing to evacuate the camp. Here as in Sachsenhausen, they've destroyed the card indexes of the dead. The documents, as they call them, have been burned; there is to be no trace of how the victims were murdered. This process has already been going on some days. Shelves and drawers are already empty in the clerical office of the *Revier*, and the staff of prisoners are awaiting orders to evacuate. They've reached the knapsack stage, and one can get a good price for a serviceable knapsack now. Those prisoners who are left in the camp, outside our barbed wire, are expecting to have to go on foot. Where, nobody can guess. Nor does anyone at present know what will happen to us next.

TUESDAY, APRIL 10, 1945 ■ There are alerts all the time, and many raids not far off. The other day they got a powder factory quite near here, also Altona in a heavy raid. The Swedes are inclining more and more to the view that we shan't be staying here long, and that we're unlikely to be able to carry out much of all we're planning.

Today I went to see a band of Jewish children who are kept here, as they were in Sachsenhausen—as guinea-pigs. At one end of the *Revier* hutments, with a concealed entrance, they live in a little room. There are ten boys and ten girls, from four to twelve years old. First one enters a small backyard, where there's a big cage of actual guinea-pigs—for the same purpose as the Jewish children. The yard also contains a heap of coal and a rubbish heap.

There were hardly ten square meters [108 sq. ft.] to move about in. That was the only place where the children could get outside into the fresh air. Otherwise they lived in the

---

* The fifth anniversary of the German invasion of Norway.

small room inside; it was almost filled up by their beds, which were in two stories, and where they slept two in a bed. They were attractive little things, French, Dutch, Belgian and Polish. All of them came from Auschwitz. One boy of eight had spent four and a half years in concentration camps.

When I asked what kind of experiments were made on these human children, the *Häftlingsarzt* [prisoner doctor] who was "showing me around" put a warning finger to his lips: it mustn't be talked about, but the children had had injections. What kind of injections? Again the finger on his lips, and out it came in a whisper: *Tuberculose!* Were the men who had conducted the experiments really competent scientists? *Ach—ja*—a German professor with some name like Wiesmeyer or Biesmeyer! But the children didn't look as if they had taken any harm, and none of them seemed to have tuberculosis. None of the children who had been there were dead, nor had there been very much sickness. At the moment one of them, the son of the head of the Rothschild Institute in Paris, had pneumonia. But he was well cared for and apparently improving already. And they were obviously getting enough to eat and led a carefree life in a way, with no understanding of what was happening to them and around them.

My friend the *Häftlingsarzt*, who had obviously grown fond of the little ones, answered with a worried shake of the head when I asked what would become of them if the camp were evacuated. He wanted me to ask the Swedish commission if they couldn't do something for them! I will—but am prepared in advance for that also being in vain, like most of what one tries to do for other fellow-prisoners.

As a matter of fact it isn't only these children who are experimented on. The whole block at the end of which they lived turned out to be full of wretched creatures of the usual *Muselmenn* type, and they too are the objects of different kinds of experiments. Whether they die of these experiments or of something else, really in a sense doesn't matter. For die they must! Indeed, if any good came of the experiments they wouldn't have died in vain.* And that's more than one can say of million after million.

---

* Nansen's forebodings proved all too true. Less than two weeks after his visit, on April 20, all the children, together with their Jewish caretakers—two Dutch aides and two French doctors (which presumably included the *Häftlingsarzt* Nansen was speaking with)—were dead, murdered to hide the evidence of this Nazi crime. The children were taken to a satellite camp, a converted school on Bullenhuser Damm Street in Hamburg, injected with morphine, and then hanged in the school's basement. The young boy with pneumonia was Georges-André Kohn, the son of Armand Kohn, director of the Rothschild Institute, the largest Jewish hospital in France. Kohn and his entire family had been arrested August 17, 1944, one week before Paris was liberated, and placed on the last deportation train to leave Paris. The fate of Georges-André, who would have turned thirteen on April 23, was doubly tragic. As the deportation train headed east, his twenty-one-year-old brother Philippe and eighteen-year-old sister Rose-Marie escaped along with others. Georges apparently wanted to join them, but was prevented by his father, who feared reprisals against those who remained behind; both Philippe and Rose-Marie survived the war. The doctor Nansen was speaking with was likely Professor Gabriel Florence, since Florence's German was good enough to allow him initially to be used in the camp as an interpreter. Florence, a renowned scientist, had previously been nominated for a Nobel Prize.

Nansen's hopes regarding the research were misplaced. The experiments—conducted by a Dr. Kurt Heissmeyer—were later characterized by a medical panel as "useless for scientific research and . . . in no way enriched it." Heissmeyer had attempted to prove, among other things, that "racially inferior" people were more susceptible to the disease. After the war Heissmeyer opened a medical practice in East Germany, unrecognized until 1963. Convicted in 1966 and sentenced to life imprisonment, he died of a heart attack the following year. At a court hearing Heissmeyer was asked why he did not confine his experiments to guinea pigs. He responded: "'For me there was no basic difference between human beings and guinea pigs.' Then he corrected himself: 'Between Jews and guinea pigs.'"

WEDNESDAY, APRIL 11, 1945 ■ Between the *Revier* and the next block outside the Norwegian camp they've just been putting up a double barbed-wire fence. Russians, Poles, and others have been doing the work, and have had many a whack from the rubber truncheons of the Kapos because they didn't work fast enough, or for trying to barter with the Norwegians through the barbed wire. Today, with roars and lashes, they were set to pull it all down again. Yesterday they started a foundation for some building between the fences. For this old bricks and rubble were used. Today the whole thing was shoveled up again and driven away.

A transport of Danes came in today. Two hundred from one of the outlying kommandos. Most of them were skeletons. A number couldn't stand; they were carried or supported into the *Revier*.

Frode has gone sick again. Now he's being sent home, and that's good. He can't rightly grasp it himself yet. Home! Free! No indeed, it must be incomprehensible.

FRIDAY, APRIL 13, 1945 ■ Frode left yesterday. It's queer to be without him. But I'm glad, he needed it and deserved it more than a lot of people. When the next transport will be leaving is uncertain, but probably tomorrow.

I feel as though I were living in a half-reality. Now that these long and terrible years may soon be over, now that the hour of deliverance seems immediately at hand—suddenly it's as though home and she and the children were so far away—further than ever. It's as though I were being whirled along in a current so rapid that I can't get out of it; am only a part of it, with no personal existence.

SUNDAY, APRIL 15, 1945 ■ Sunday and a "day off." But here as elsewhere in the years gone by, all days are alike—more or less. These days are merely longer than usual, because we have more to wait for. Over six hundred of the sick have already left. Finally sores on the feet became a qualification; those who put themselves forward got the chance. But negotiations are going on now in Berlin to have us all evacuated.

MONDAY, APRIL 16, 1945 ■ Today the word is that we must be prepared for evacuation at an hour's notice. It's also said that half the camp is to be transported to the Danish frontier straight off, while the other half is supposed to be starting out on foot, and being picked up on the way by the returning buses. Nothing definite is known about anything.

Nor do we know how far they've now advanced against Hamburg. There is talk of fighting going on already in the southeast corner of the town. Lüneburg is said to have been taken, it's about twenty miles from here. Fresh transports of Norwegians and Danes are coming in all the time; almost all convicts now.

WEDNESDAY, APRIL 18, 1945 ■ The front is drawing nearer. This morning we had some planes over, and we're always hearing guns and machine-gun bursts. The planes set fire to a cargo boat at a wharf a couple of kilometers from here. Really it isn't war now, in the usual sense; it's more an occupation we're witnessing.

Huge transports of prisoners are leaving here every day. Whither no one knows. We merely suspect the very worst. The smoke from the crematorium chimney, which on certain days rolls out black and thick and settles with a loathsome stench over the camp,* is a reminder that the "harvest" here is still in full swing, while at the same time columns of *Muselmenn* are being lined up on the square and marched through the gateway, to railway cars south of the camp, where they are stowed away and left—often for days and nights before they roll off. Where?

We are hoping to evade the occupation, or things may well be protracted. The next transport leaves tomorrow morning. If one only knew that now one was off to Sweden!

I've heard an unpleasant rumor that everything we take with us and all the clothes we have on, *everything* without exception, is burned when we arrive. Whether in Denmark or Sweden I don't know, but that's the vital point. If it's in Sweden, I shall always manage to save my little odds and ends from the flames. If in Denmark, it may be worse. For it may be the Gestapo's last form of *Filzing*. It would be provoking to lose this diary after I've kept it going so assiduously. I'll have to seduce a Swedish Lotta into taking it. But then Frode took a breadboard with him. I wonder if that escaped? *But now Frode is in Sweden!*

THURSDAY, APRIL 19, 1945 ■ A transport from our *Revier* was to leave this morning. Everyone was ready. Then came word that all transports were suspended until further notice. The reason is unknown. It seems most likely to be something military. The professor [Rundberg] tells us that Count Bernadotte flew to Denmark today, and is now on his way here by car. He's going to try and continue the negotiations, and if possible obtain permission for us to be evacuated.† However, not even an evacuation is free from peril. Six or seven Danish buses have been shot up, and one of the drivers got a bullet through his thigh. That was on the way back from Denmark. Road transports may be a problematic business henceforth.

The Swedish view of affairs in case of occupation is rather dark. The professor actually said that in the event we must expect to stay here a good long time, and even mentioned six months. Half a year! That's a painful thing to swallow. Most people laugh and regard it as a good—or bad—joke; but it was by no means meant for one. But so deep rooted is this Norwegian attitude that of course we come first! Aren't we Norwegians? And the Swedes are here to save *us*, aren't they? First Norwegians—oh yes, and Danes!—and then the others. One has a hard struggle to preserve one's faith in mankind, and it's the individuals, not the masses, who save it.‡

But when darkness comes, and night sinks down over all the suffering and wretchedness, then the masses split up and become individuals, each whispering in the dark a beloved name.

---

* One survivor of Sachsenhausen observed, "[T]he colour [*sic*] of the smoke . . . carried information disclosing one of the many secrets of the camp. When the regular prisoners were burned, the smoke was light-grey because there was no fat in the corpses. However, the smoke was dense and black when well-nourished people were burned, people who were brought directly to the crematorium from outside the camp."

† Bernadotte received permission to evacuate all Scandinavian prisoners from Neuengamme over the Danish border on April 19; by April 21 Himmler agreed that all such prisoners could go to Sweden.

‡ In 1921 Fridtjof Nansen wrote to a friend, "It is the individual and not the masses who can save the world from the misery of our times."

FRIDAY, APRIL 20, 1945* ■ I am writing in the bus. The bus to freedom. We're going northward through Germany, over the North German plain. We're not far from Lübeck, but our destination is farther north, we hope in Sweden. Word came last night after we had gone to bed. We were to be roused at four and to be ready by six. We're to take as little as possible; no more clothes than we could put on, and the minimum of food.

There wasn't much sleep last night. At least not for me. Most of the night I was walking about outside. I couldn't bring myself to go to bed on this last night. Besides, there was brisk activity out of doors. Incessant alerts. Bombs crashing, cannon booming, and machine guns crackling on all sides. One had a sense of being in the midst of it—though it wasn't so, for no bombs fell in the camp, no shrapnel and no shells. Even that had become unreal. All the same there was uproar in the camp. Some prisoners had been stealing parcels somewhere. They were rounded up and flogged. Their shrieks and roars sounded horrible in the moonlit night, among the bomb crashes and the long-drawn-out sinister wail of the alerts. Hundreds of prisoners were busy carrying their mattresses out onto the square, and emptying the straw there in a great heap. Why? Was it to be burned, with its millions of lice and bacilli? I don't know. The heap was still there when we left this morning. Like all activity under German orders, this was accompanied by roars and shrieks and infuriated commands and curses. Which gave that last night, too, a "home-like," familiar melody.

At this moment we've made a halt in Lübeck. We've just driven through the center of the town and seen the destruction. Precisely the finest part of Lübeck had been laid in ruins, and yet Lübeck must be one of the towns that got off cheapest.

FRIDAY-SATURDAY, APRIL 27–28, 1945 ■ What on earth am I to write? It's as impossible today as on all the other days that have passed in one long whirl of unreality and fairy tale. I am no longer in Germany! I am in Denmark, at a country house; Møgelkær is its name, outside Horsens,† and I've already been here more than a week! It's unbelievable. And what have I not experienced in that week? Only it seems so hopelessly impossible to describe. Where am I to begin, where am I to stop, what am I to write?

The day before yesterday I was to scribble a message to Kari, only a hurried greeting, a few words on a scrap of paper, with the mudguard of a truck to write on. One might have thought it would be easy—a message to one's own wife and the children that here I am, safe and well. But no, it seemed to me impossible, insuperable! Every word became a great intrusive toad, and Kari and the children, all that is dear to me, all I have been longing for for years with all my soul, more remote than ever. I felt like crying with despair and rage.

---

*   April 20 was also the date Sachsenhausen was evacuated; thirty-three thousand prisoners were forced to march north until they were finally liberated by Soviet forces (May 3–6, 1945). Approximately three thousand sick inmates were left behind, including Tommy Buergenthal. One historian writes, "The reason the sick inmates were left, when strenuous efforts had been made in earlier months to liquidate large numbers of them, is unknown." The camp was liberated on April 22 by Russian and Polish forces.

†   Most prisoners evacuated to Denmark in the white buses operation were initially interned at Frøslev, a concentration camp outside of Flensburg, Denmark. When Frøslev was unable to accommodate all the evacuees, a provisional camp was established at Møgelkær, six miles south of Horsens. Gerhard Rundberg persuaded Walter Schellenberg, Himmler's deputy, to allow all prisoners at Møgelkær to be transferred to Sweden, and a convoy of those prisoners began on April 27.

And kind, helpful Danish people were standing waiting for me, to take the message and smuggle it off. Aid to Norway!

Dear, darling Kari! That seemed to be the only thing with any sense in it. I don't know what more I got down. I had to write something, couldn't say I found it impossible. Only a little message—*I'll soon be home!* Surely I could write that much! And so I wrote that and put it in an envelope, and those wonderfully kind people took it away. And here I am, as bankrupt, as confused, and as stupefied as ever, out of contact with reality, because it is in fact unbelievable.*

Just listen to this: I lay on a mattress on the lawn, resting in the sunshine with some friends. A German guard came by—for there are German guards here too, with rifles and everything. He bent down to us and sneaked out of his pocket a little tin of shoe polish, screening it carefully in the hollow of his hand, looking nervously around and whispering, "*Für Tabak!*" [For tobacco!] He wanted to barter with us. Hasse Cappelen,† who was lying beside me, was the first to grasp the situation; he turned furiously on the German: "Don't you know that's forbidden? Be off with you!" And the German hastily thrust the shoe polish back into his pocket, glanced around in terror lest any of his superiors might have seen or heard anything, and scuttled shamefacedly off with his tail between his legs. We went on with our conversation as though nothing unusual had happened—and nothing had. Things are like that here. So completely has our world been turned upside down. Is it strange that one should be confused and still unable to fit oneself into this reality.‡

---

* Such reactions were not atypical. Filip Müller, a member of the *Sonderkommando* at Auschwitz, described his liberation: "Although it may seem incredible, I had a complete letdown or depression. That moment, on which for three years all my thoughts and secret desires were concentrated, did not awaken any happiness or any other feeling in me."

† Hans ("Hasse") Cappelen (1903–1979), a lawyer and brother of Didrik ("Dixie") Cappelen, was a member of the Resistance. After being severely tortured by the Gestapo he spent time in a number of concentration camps, including Natzweiler, Dachau, Neuengamme, Gross-Rosen, and Buchenwald, before being evacuated to Neuengamme again. He was the only Norwegian prisoner to testify at the Nuremberg trials and for a time was chairman of the Norwegian Association of War Prisoners. In 1966 he published a book about his captivity, *Vi Ga Oss Ikke* [*We Did Not Give Up*].

‡ On April 28, 1945, the last entry date in Nansen's diary, Italian dictator Benito Mussolini was executed by Italian partisans. Dachau was liberated the following day. Adolf Hitler committed suicide in his Berlin bunker two days later, on April 30. Nazi Germany surrendered on May 8, and the following day Vidkun Quisling was arrested in Oslo. King Haakon VII returned to Norwegian soil on June 7, 1945, five years to the day after he had been forced to flee to England. Odd Nansen was ultimately reunited with his family in Oslo on June 9, 1945.

POSTSCRIPT

by Odd Nansen

ONE DAY AT THE BEGINNING OF MAY (1945) I was going to telephone my wife, from Ramlösa in Sweden, to let her know that I was out of Germany safe and sound—and I had forgotten our telephone number. The number that has been ours all along! The lady at the exchange had to help me.

I can still absolutely feel that sharp pang that accompanied this tiny tragedy amidst the flood of inconceivable joy. It was like a fleeting shadow of something painful that had to retreat before all the light and life beginning to wake and grow.

Dear reader! Have you too, by any chance, a bad memory? Have you too been in despair at times over the tricks it has played you? Let us try to find consolation in all the things we forget more easily than other people. Things that ought to be forgotten. Things it only hurts to remember with pitiless distinctness. There are many such things. And forgetfulness can be the gentle medicine of a pitying fate.

This diary has taught me that. For I, too, have read it—for the first time.

Much was worse than I seemed to remember. And yet I know that words are too pale to describe most of it. And another thing: What my companions and I saw and experienced is little and pale in comparison with what many, many others saw and lived through in the worst camps. The figures, scale and efficiency of the Third Reich's *Vernichtung* rose to heights that no one had dreamed of, and that few have grasped to this very day. Human brutality and self-obliterating degradation sank to depths that no one thought possible. Normal human imagination can encompass only a narrow interval on that sinister scale. No wonder memory falls short. No wonder that many who experienced nothing of it are unable to realize it. Many of those who lived through it themselves can grasp it no longer. The experiences were often so violent, the impressions so overwhelming, and they themselves so stunned by them that that they were unable to record them for the mind's eye. Had simply to let them go again and make room for fresh ones. Such oblivion is merciful. Only one must never, never let it become indifference.

With inconceivable sacrifices the war was won. Won? Well, that is a debatable point. Can a modern war ever be won? If we look at Europe, indeed at the whole world after this war, I think we shall agree that we have all lost. Or was it for the conditions and the "peace" that have settled down on the world today that we offered up such great sacrifices?

Some time ago, almost three years after the end of the war, I made a journey through the ravaged countries of Europe—on both sides of the so-called iron curtain. I did not take the main roads. No one showed me what I was to see. I looked for it myself and found it. A joyless darkness and a gray misery from the Russian frontier in the East to the Atlantic in the West. Ruins! Ruins of houses, ruins of human beings, ruins of the labor and toil of centuries.

Dear reader! Can you picture children in thousands—yes, in millions—with pleading eyes within dark sockets never kindled by joy, with white, sunken cheeks, with sharp, narrow, crooked shoulders, with ribs like washboards, with pot bellies and matchstick legs that can scarcely carry them—and naked! Can you hear them crying bitterly over the gnawing pains of hunger inside them?

Can you picture the army of the mothers, skinny and wasted, with bony arms that squeeze the dying child despairingly to their empty breasts—and can you realize what an incessant and unbearable suffering their lives have become?

Can you picture the endless, silent train of men, with dull and vacant looks, tottering to work that does not bring in enough to feed them and their families like human beings for even three out of the seven days in the week?

And on top of that, can you picture the droves of refugees—millions of them? Outcast, starving people drifting about in the darkness of Europe. I met them on the roads, half naked and miserable, dragging themselves on to an unknown goal. I met them in the camps, where they congregated in their last struggle for life. In cellars under the ruins, in the bomb-shattered towns, wherever there was shelter from the pitiless cold of the elements and their fellow men.

War victims—those who were not lucky enough to die. The frontiers are being closed as before. The Jews are persecuted as before. The terror whips are plied as before. The human hearts are freezing as before. And the number of unhappy, persecuted, dying fellow creatures is increasing at a sinister rate from day to day, as before. Three years after the war. Hitler may leer out of his darkness, well pleased. Can you see all that and grasp it? Can you sustain the burden of knowing that that is a faithful picture of a great part of the population of Europe today?

Another picture rises up. The only one I can compare it with. The picture of a concentration camp. A *Vernichtungslager!* It was the same there. Dulled and blinded to the misery, want and ruin of others, people staggered round on the hunt for food, food. Immune to horrors and brutality, they walked over corpses to secure a bit of bread, a rotten potato, or a few withered cabbage leaves.

There too there were some who lived at ease—as there are today even in the worst-off countries of Europe. A kind of upper class of the privileged—people who came out on top, either by virtue of their origin and race, their advantageous political color, or their well-developed mastery of the corrupt and degrading methods which alone open the way to a more human existence.

The whole world seems to have become a *Vernichtungslager* of that type, and we have already reached the stage where the sole problem for the individual seems to be to feather his nest and try to keep his head above water as long as possible.

That is the result of the war. Are we not entitled to record as much today—three years after?

No, it is not pessimism. It is never pessimism to look facts in the face. It is a duty.

Can you not imagine the disease, crime, vileness, brutality and dull animalism that shoot up and propagate under such conditions like mushrooms after rain? And do you not realize the deadly peril it involves not only for those people themselves but for us all? For our whole culture? Don't you feel an irresistible impulse to do everything in your power to change those ignoble and disastrous conditions? And yet, mingling with the cries from the ruins of Europe is the cry for another war—as a solution of the difficulties.

Politicians, statesmen, businessmen, economists—all are talking of the possibility of a new world war, and are focused on it in their mode of thought, their work, and their plans. Few are actively focused on averting it. Focused on an attempt to remove the conditions that make it possible. And while the talk of war, atom bombs and every kind of technical devilry fills the atmosphere around us, the fate of the world is hanging by a thread. But the fate of the world—the future of our civilization—does not depend on atom bombs, any more than it depends on lethal gases and bacteria, on oil, or on any of the products of far-advanced human science and technical perfection. It depends on the coming generation. It will be for them to steer the world into a safe harbor—or to shipwreck. It will be for them to decide how we shall apply our technical knowledge—to construction or to ruin.

Suppose there should be no coming generation? Or that it should be weakly, poisoned, stunted in body and soul, unable to cope with its tasks, let alone to change the course that is now being followed and that seems to be leading straight to destruction? And remember, it was we who set that course, and we are responsible for it.

The future must be built and secured by living men. It can't be done by the sick and starving, or by dead bodies.

Here, in my judgment, we are at the very core of the postwar problem that outweighs all the others. How is the coming generation equipped for this work of rebuilding the world and carrying it forward? And what can and must we do to strengthen it and lighten its labor on this, the hardest and most difficult task that any generation has ever faced?

The problems impose themselves. It is no use denying it. They absolutely force themselves on one—a multiple host of problems that we cannot evade or make away with. But what tasks worth coping with have ever been easy? We must bear in mind that our so-called civilized communities are prodigiously involved mechanisms in which the great, simple human truths, principles and ideals are frighteningly easy to submerge in the daily network of random trifles, disagreements and detail conflicts of every kind—among individuals, classes and nations.

One thing is certain: hate, revenge and retribution are not the way. They lead back to the abyss. We should have experience enough by now to know that. If we nourish the rising generation on them it is tantamount to spiritual murder and to signing the death sentence of our culture. I am thinking of the rising generation in all countries, for no country has escaped the disaster. And not least, I am thinking of the rising generation in countries that lost the war.

Whatever one might feel about the Germans and others who were fighting against one's country during the war, surely in the course of time, even though it may require some effort, one can think and feel differently about the growing generation, wherever it is growing up. It does not square with any justice that they should suffer for the sins of their fathers.* Let

---

* In a 1951 keynote speech at a conference in Germany, Nansen addressed the debate under way about Germany's participation in the 1952 Olympics: "It is unjust and senseless to punish the children for the sins of their fathers. But

them have a fair chance. Don't forget that it is they who must rebuild Europe, along with you and me. We are in the same boat. If they sink, we sink as well. Don't let us be like the wise man of Gotham, who sawed off the bough on which he was sitting.

In Europe today, there are several hundred thousand occupation troops. A large proportion of these have been forbidden to fraternize with the people of the occupied country, and they have commonly been forbidden to share their superfluity of food with the starving civil population.

The spirit that dictates that is mad. Think what the occupying armies could achieve if in addition to—and in complete accord with—their military task, they were employed on positive relief work! Suppose they came not merely as occupiers, but also as helpers and friends. Not merely with rifles, but with bread. That indeed would be a new type of soldier. The Germans certainly have never come across one like that. And indeed who has? But suppose they were to come across him one day—and not only one, but tens of thousands of them. Think what enormous significance it would have for those young soldiers themselves, and they are part of the rising generation, to find the way to good works.

I don't believe that the lawyers with all their justice and all their probity will create peace and understanding, at least not on the principles that now seem to prevail. Nor, truly, have all the exertions of the politicians had much success—that is, if they really have been directed by a sincere will to peace.

I don't believe that the diplomats with all their diplomatic shrewdness will find the way through iron curtains and barriers now dividing peoples and nations. Their plans and message, if they have one, seem to go under in the heaps of paper by which the world is being suffocated.

The message for which bleeding humanity craves is neither legal, political nor diplomatic. A starving man does not need revenge to feed him up, he needs food. A sick man does not need a political program to get well, he needs drugs and doctors. A shivering man does not need diplomatic agreements to get warm, he needs clothes and shoes and a roof over his head.*

If some of them should strike you as being your enemies, because they were on the other side of the war front, do you really think that is the vital thing? They are human, too. They too have a country, a home, a family they love. They too are longing for peace. Perhaps also they are longing to meet you!

Love your enemies was the command of Him who wished peace on earth. Surely the hardest, the most rigorous, and perhaps the harshest of all commandments.

If He, the Prince of Peace, had been among us today and talked like that, how do you suppose we should have received His message? Don't you think, dear reader, to be honest, that we should have shrugged and smiled condescendingly at that good-natured softy of a carpenter who was going round preaching anything so sky blue, naïve and childish as *faith in goodness* in the world? Who thought He could build on anything so ridiculous as *human*

---

that is what is sought to be done when Germany's young people are kept out of associations [designed to promote] international cooperation."

* In Fridtjof Nansen's 1922 Nobel acceptance lecture "The Suffering People of Europe," he concluded, "Where is the remedy to be sought? At the hands of politicians? They may mean well enough . . . but politics and new political programs are no longer of service to the world. . . . The diplomats perhaps? Their intentions may be good enough, but they . . . [have] brought mankind more harm than good over the years. . . . In my opinion, the only avenue to salvation lies in cooperation between all nations on a basis of honest endeavor."

worth? And—if He had become too persistent in His zeal, too great a nuisance to our conscience, with His eternal truths and fussing—don't you think we should have overthrown Him, stoned Him and crucified Him?

Yet His commandment still remains, and has remained through the ages—unshaken, written in the sky with letters of gold, high above the din and the fumes of blood from our sink of degradation. Unassailable. Simple. Strong and everlasting. *Love your enemies.*

Who would dare presume to raise that demand today, in a world where even to recall it passes for an unforgivable weakness, a betrayal of justice? *Justice!* What is justice exactly, since it counts for more than anything else? An eye for eye and a tooth for a tooth. That is justice, if I remember right—in all its harshness and heartlessness. Truly nothing to aspire to, no ground or principle to build a new world on. We know the world that was built on that principle. It is the one trembling today on the verge of the abyss.

Just suppose that, from tormented, starving, fear-ridden humanity, instead of the cry for justice, there arose a cry for kindness—for love! The wellhead and deepest ground of all life, and goal of its eternal longings.

In the echo of that cry from human hearts a new justice would be created, the outlines of a new, more human world would appear, and the way to it would open.

Don't you think the Carpenter from Nazareth was pointing toward a world like that? And do you suppose there is any other way there?

Dear reader, now perhaps you are looking back to the title page of this book to see if I happen to be a parson. But I am not. Nor is this postscript going to end by calling on you to turn to God and beg Him to find a way for you. For I believe that you must find it yourself. The way through Him may be the right one—perhaps for many. But often it appears to stop in self-communing, and lose itself in zealous thoughts of one's own salvation. As if that were an object when millions of fellow creatures, indeed whole communities around you, are going to ruin!

The first object, which must and shall be attained if our culture is to survive, is a practicable, unsentimental object: to save those millions from destruction. And there is no time to lose. Every day costs many valuable human lives that *might have been* saved!

It is not a question of yourself. Neither of your soul's salvation, nor your body's weal or woe, nor the righteousness of your heart or brain. It is a question of the life and death of millions of fellow creatures. The "to be or not to be" of our culture.

The dying do not ask if you have the true faith before accepting your helping hand if you stretch it out. You stretch it out; it is clasped; there is no question or reply—and yet you have learned the richest and profoundest secret of life. With rocklike certainty you know all at once that your own salvation too, your own happiness, lies in doing *good works.* And therefore it is the sum of these that must save the world.

Through the work of rescue our faith in human value will be revived. And along with it will come, besides the good will, a recognition of the duties and the responsibility that democracy has need of to endure. On that "ground of faith," and that alone, it will be possible, through and across all the other fronts that now split up the peoples and nations, to create *one* strong front, the most important of all, the only one that can open the way to a new world: *the front of human kindness.*

Dear reader, I shall stop now. This book has turned out long enough, and it may have been heavy going. But when you go to your bookseller for a new one, don't say to him as so many do, "Now I've had enough of these wretched prison books. Give me some better kind of thing. I can't stand any more of that misery." For those who say that show they haven't understood what they read or why it was written. I don't think they have had anything like enough!

Accounts of what happened in the shadow of the Nazi dictatorship have ceased to be sensational reading, or entertainment. They are a call to arms! And they are burningly topical as long as there is still a danger that it may happen again.

The worst crime you can commit today, against yourself and society, is to forget what happened and sink back into indifference. What happened was worse than you have any idea of—and it was the indifference of mankind that let it take place!

Lysaker
October 1948

One of the breadboards used at meals, here shown with pages of Nansen's diary hidden inside. The paper for this section of the diary was the finest quality of thin drawing paper, "war booty" from Russia, used by the Germans as wrapping and toilet paper. "Scrounged" from a storeroom by Nansen. Nansen's breadboard is on display at the Norwegian Resistance Museum in Oslo. The one pictured belonged to Erik Magelssen, one of Nansen's friends. SOURCE: *Photo by Timothy J. Boyce*

19 Møllergata: The Gestapo prison in Oslo. SOURCE: *"Møllergata 19 Oslo 18jun2005" by J. P. Fagerback. Licensed under BSD via Wikimedia Commons*

Two views of Grini Prison, taken shortly after the war. The aerial view shows the main building and the various newly constructed huts; the second photo is of a guard tower. SOURCE: *Courtesy Bærum Library, Norway*

Roll call at Grini. SOURCE: *US Library of Congress*

Victoria Terrace—Gestapo headquarters. SOURCE: *"Victoria Terrasse in Oslo Norway" by Leifern/Leif Knutsen—Own work. Licensed under CC BY-SA 3.0 via Wikimedia Commons*

Quisling installed as minister-president at Akershus. From left to right: Josef Terboven (with right arm raised in a Nazi salute), Quisling, and Wilhelm Rediess. SOURCE: *Norwegian Resistance Museum, Norway*

Lagerkommandant *Alfred Zeidler and* Schutzhaftlagerführer *Julius Denzer.* SOURCE: *Photo taken at Grini Museum by Timothy J. Boyce*

The SS Donau, *the ship used to transport Norway's Jews to Germany.*
SOURCE: *Norwegian Resistance Museum*

Leonard Levin, wearing his university cap. Born May 31, 1905; arrested April 1, 1942; transported February 25, 1943; murdered in Auschwitz. SOURCE: *Courtesy of Irene Levin Berman*

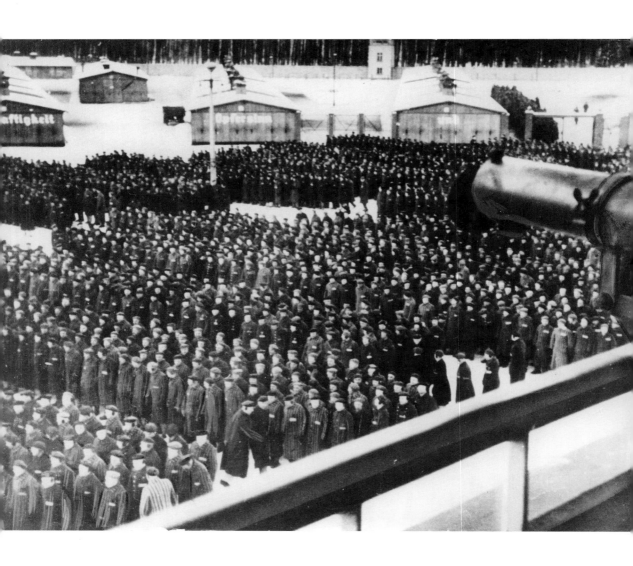

Roll call at Sachsenhausen. Note the inscriptions on the sides of the huts.
SOURCE: *Bundesarchiv, Bild 183-78612-0003/unknown photographer*

Entry gate at Sachsenhausen.
SOURCE: *Photo by Timothy J. Boyce*

Marching home from work—Sachsenhausen.
SOURCE: *Bundesarchiv, Bild 183-78612-0002/unknown photographer*

Remains of Sachsenhausen's execution trench and crematorium. SOURCE: *Photos by Timothy J. Boyce*

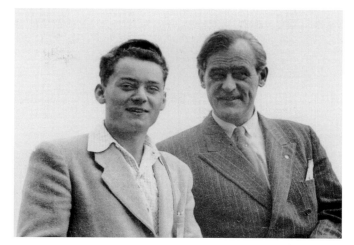

Thomas Buergenthal and Odd Nansen together, 1951.
SOURCE: *Courtesy of Thomas Buergenthal*

*Odd Nansen first arriving in Oslo after three and a half years
of captivity. From left to right, Eigil, Siri, Kari, Odd, Odd
Erik and Marit.* SOURCE: *Courtesy of Marit Greve*

APPENDIX I

Regarding Concentration Camps

ALL OF GERMANY'S CONCENTRATION CAMPS were administered and guarded by a separate unit of the SS (i.e., *Schutzstaffel*, meaning protection squadron or defense corps). Originally formed to provide security for Nazi Party meetings and as a personal bodyguard for Hitler, the SS ultimately grew into one of the most powerful organizations of the Third Reich. SS members had to prove their racial purity back to the year 1700, although this requirement was relaxed as the war progressed. For its emblem the SS used two Teutonic runes—a parallel jagged double SS. All SS units were also distinguished by the death's head (*totenkopf*), or skull and crossbones, insignia on their hats; in addition, the SS-*Totenkopfverbände*, responsible for administering the concentration camps, wore a death's head on their collar insignia. Camp administration was divided into five departments:

1.   Commandant's Office (or *Lagerkommandant*). While considered the highest camp authority, the *Lagerkommandant's* actual powers were quite limited. The *Lagerkommandant* was sometimes assisted by one or more deputies, or *Lagerführers*.

2.   Political Department/Gestapo. This department dealt with prisoner files, carried out interrogations, ordered executions, and issued death certificates.

3.   Internal Service Operations/Labor Deployment (*Schutzhaftlagerführer*). The *Schutzhaftlagerführer* was the standing representative of the commandant, responsible for the day-to-day operation of the *Schutzhaftlager* [protective custody camp], the inmate compound, and as such the second most powerful SS man in camp. Three important functions reported directly to the *Schutzhaftlagerführer*:

    A.   Roll Call Leader (*Rapportführer*). The *Rapportführer* presided over daily roll calls, maintained prison population numbers, and prepared reports on punishment.

    B.   Labor Service Leader (*Arbeitseinsatzführer*). The *Arbeitseinsatzführer* organized prison labor, assembled work squads (*Kommandos*) by prisoner qualifications (real or feigned).

    C.   Block (or Barrack) Leader (*Blockführer*). The *Blockführer* ensured discipline and cleanliness of his assigned block(s).

4.   Administration (*Verwaltung*) was responsible for food, clothing, building maintenance, etc.

5.   Medical services (*Lagerarzt*) was responsible for the infirmary (*Revier*).

There were relatively few SS assigned to each camp, which nevertheless continued to swell in size and population throughout the war. For example, in 1942 the SS manpower quota for Sachsenhausen, which then held well over ten thousand prisoners, was only 256 people. The solution adopted by the SS to the problem of governing such large bodies was to create a second, parallel organizational structure made up of the camp prisoners themselves to administer their own affairs. In fact, as the camps grew, the SS contented itself with sporadic spot checks. All other aspects of everyday camp life were dominated by the so-called prisoner functionaries.

At the top of the prisoner structure was one or more senior camp leaders (*Lagerälteste*). Appointed by the SS, the *Lagerälteste* were representatives of the prisoners' vis-à-vis the Nazis and in turn received orders from the SS. Each *Lagerältester* enjoyed considerable leeway in the selection of his subordinates, the senior block prisoners (*Blockälteste*). The *Blockältester* for each block, or barrack, in turn took orders from his SS equivalent, the *Blockführer*. Each *Blockältester* literally exercised the power of life or death over his charges. The *Blockältester* was assisted by one or more room leaders (*Stubenälteste*), which he selected. Although *Blockälteste* could be arbitrarily selected from among the camp prisoners, certain characteristics defined their ranks. First, they were almost invariably German; non-Germans were typically not allowed into any position of authority, certainly not over German prisoners. Jews were never allowed to hold any position in the camp. Second, *Blockälteste* were drawn from either the political or criminal prisoners. In fact, most camps experienced a fierce struggle between the political prisoners (wearing red triangles) and the green-triangle criminal prisoners (sometimes referred to as BV-ers, or *Berufsverbrecher* [professional criminals]) for the perks their position provided. One of the fiercest struggles between the reds and the greens occurred in Sachsenhausen, as is recounted by Nansen. Third, the prisoner leaders, together with the *Vorarbeiters*, or leaders of the various *Kommandos*, or work squads, demonstrated their loyalty to their SS masters by treating fellow prisoners as brutally as, if not more so, than the SS did. According to historian Wolfgang Sofsky, they "shouted louder than the guards, and were quicker to swing their clubs and strut around like petty potentates." They imitated, and exceeded, their masters in cruelty in order to remain in their privileged positions. Not surprisingly, the more brutal they were, the faster and more violent their downfall was should they ever lose their privileged position. As Sofsky notes: "[A]s soon as the SS removed the truncheons from their hands, their hours were numbered."

This summary is based upon Wolfgang Sofsky, *The Order of Terror: The Concentration Camp*, trans. William Templer (Princeton, NJ: Princeton University Press, 1997), pp. 98; 106–13; 122–44 (the quotes are found on pp. 136 and 140, respectively); Harry Stein, *Buchenwald Concentration Camp 1937–1945: A Guide to the Permanent Historical Exhibition*, trans. Judith Rosenthal (Göttingen: Wallstein Verlag, 2004), pp. 49, 99–101, 136; and Robert Jan van Pelt, *The Case for Auschwitz* (Bloomington: Indiana University Press, 2002), p. 230.

APPENDIX II

SS Ranks and US Army Equivalents

The following are SS ranks referred to throughout the diary,
together with their US Army equivalent.

Oberführer. No equivalent rank (can be described as Senior Colonel)
Standartenführer. Colonel
Obersturmbannführer. Lieutenant Colonel
Sturmbannführer. Major
Hauptsturmführer. Captain
Obersturmführer. First Lieutenant
Untersturmführer. Second Lieutenant
Hauptscharführer. Master Sergeant (highest enlisted rank)
Oberscharführer (Wehrmacht: Feldwebel). Sergeant First Class
Scharführer. Staff Sergeant
Unterscharführer. Sergeant
Rottenführer. Corporal

APPENDIX III

Timeline

December 17, 1858	Eva Sars born
October 10, 1861	Fridtjof Nansen born
1888–1889	Fridtjof Nansen crosses Greenland
September 6, 1889	Fridtjof Nansen marries Eva Sars
1893–1896	Nansen expedition to North Pole
December 6, 1901	Odd Nansen born
October 13, 1903	Karen (Kari) Hirsch born
October 26, 1905	Norway achieves independence from Sweden
December 9, 1907	Eva Nansen dies (age forty-nine)
December 10, 1922	Fridtjof Nansen receives Nobel Peace Prize
August 27, 1927	Odd Nansen marries Kari Hirsch/moves to America
November 8, 1928	Marit Nansen born
Spring 1930	Odd Nansen returns to Norway/Fridtjof Nansen dies at Polhøgda (age sixty-eight)
June 18, 1931	Eigil Nansen born
1931	Odd Nansen starts own architectural firm
January 30, 1933	Adolf Hitler appointed chancellor of Germany
May 17, 1933	Vidkun Quisling founds Nasjonal Samling (NS) Party
April 12, 1933	Siri Nansen born
May 11, 1934	Thomas Buergenthal born in Ľubochňa, Czechoslovakia
Summer 1936	Construction of Sachsenhausen/Summer Olympics in Berlin
Fall/Winter 1936	Odd Nansen forms Nansenhjelpen (Nansen Relief)
November 9–10, 1938	Kristallnacht: 267 synagogues destroyed, thirty thousand Jews arrested
September 1, 1939	Germany invades Poland; start of WWII in Europe
December 1939	Nansen visits United States for aid to Finland
February 16, 1940	Altmark Affair in Jøssingfjord
April 9, 1940	German invasion of Norway
April 24, 1940	Josef Terboven appointed *Reichskommissar* of Norway

June 7, 1940	King Haakon VII flees Norway to establish the government-in-exile in London; Norway surrenders (June 9)
June 12, 1941	Grini opened as a *Polizeihäftlingslager*
June 22, 1941	Operation Barbarossa: Hitler invades Russia
December 7, 1941	Japanese attack on Pearl Harbor
January 10, 1942	Norwegian minister of police Jonas Lie orders all identification cards of Jews to be stamped with "J"
January 13, 1942	Odd Nansen arrested, sent to Grini Prison
January 20, 1942	Wannsee Conference to coordinate the "Final Solution" to the Jewish problem
February 1, 1942	Vidkun Quisling installed as minister-president
March 7, 1942	First execution of Norwegian Jews takes place (four shot in Trondheim)
August 5– November 22, 1942	Nansen sent to Veidal Camp (Kvænangen) to work on snow tunnels
September 18, 1942	Odd Erik Nansen born
October 22, 1942	Border pilot attempting to help nine Jews escape to Sweden kills border policeman; Jews are blamed
October 26, 1942	With the October 22 shooting as a pretext, all Jewish men over age fifteen arrested
November 8, 1942	Operation Torch: Allied invasion of North Africa
November 26, 1942	Norwegian Jews deported to Auschwitz; most sent immediately to gas chambers
February 2, 1943	German 6th Army surrenders at Stalingrad
July 25, 1943	Mussolini deposed
October 6, 1943	Odd Nansen arrives at Sachsenhausen Camp, Germany
June 4, 1944	Allied forces occupy Rome
June 6, 1944	D-Day, the Allied invasion of northern Europe begins
July 20, 1944	Assassination attempt on Adolf Hitler
December 16, 1944	Battle of the Bulge: Hitler launches Ardennes offensive
January 17, 1945	Thomas Buergenthal starts Auschwitz Death March
February 16, 1945	Odd Nansen meets Tommy Buergenthal
February 19, 1945	Count Folke Bernadotte's first meeting with Himmler to negotiate the release of Scandinavian prisoners
March 7, 1945	Allied forces cross the Rhine River
March 20, 1945	Odd Nansen to Neuengamme via "white buses"
April 22, 1945	Sachsenhausen (including Buergenthal) liberated
April 28, 1945	Odd Nansen evacuated from Neuengamme on "white buses" to Denmark, then Sweden
April 30, 1945	Hitler commits suicide
May 7, 1945	Germany surrenders to Allies
May 8, 1945	V-E Day. Allied military mission arrives in Norway to coordinate German capitulation
May 9, 1945	Quisling arrested

June 7, 1945	King Haakon VII returns to Norway
June 9, 1945	Odd Nansen returns to Oslo and is reunited with family
October—November 1945	Soviet military tribunal tries sixteen Sachsenhausen camp functionaries; all are convicted
October 24, 1945	Quisling executed at Akershus Castle
Fall 1947	Nansen journeys through Europe as far as the Black Sea to assess conditions and the need for humanitarian help; also searches for Tommy Buergenthal
1950	Odd Nansen visits Germany on behalf of UNESCO
December 4, 1951	Thomas Buergenthal arrives in United States
1970	Odd Nansen awarded the Order of St. Olav
June 27, 1973	Odd Nansen dies (age seventy-one)
May 28, 1985	Kari Nansen dies (age eighty-one)

APPENDIX IV

Glossary of Repeated German Words and Phrases

ab. off
aber. but
Abort. privy
Achtung. attention
Andenken. souvenir
Arbeitsdienst. labor service
Arbeitseinsatz. labor service section
arbeitsfähig. fit for work
auf. on
aufstehen. get up
Augen rechts. eyes right
Augen gerade aus. eyes straight ahead
Bauabteilung. building department
Bauführer. construction foreman
Bauleiter. construction manager
Bauleitung. construction management
Baurat. construction superintendent
Bettschonung. bed pass
Blockältester. senior block prisoner
Blockführer. block leader
Dementis. denials
donnerwetter. damn
Dunkelzelle. dark cell
Durchfall. diarrhea
Einzelhaft. solitary confinement
Entlassung. release
Entlassungsfeber. release fever
Entlassungsschein. discharge certificate
Fahrbereitschaft. motor pool
Filzing. search

gel. understand
Gott sei dank. thank god
grundsätzlich. on principle
Gutachten. histories
gute Nacht. good night
Guthaus. mansion
Hafterleichterung. improvement
        in prison conditions
Häftling. prisoner
heraus. get out
Herrenvolk. master race
Herz As. ace of hearts
hinlegen. lie down
Industriehof. factory yard
jawohl. yes
Kamerad. comrade
Kameradenschaftabend. fellowship evening
Kleinigkeiten. little things
Kraftfahrzeugdepot. motor vehicle depot
Lager. camp
Lagerältester. senior camp prisoner
Lagerführer. deputy commandant
Lagerkommandant. camp commandant
Leitender Arzt. head doctor
los. hurry
Luftschutz. air raid defense
Lump. lout
Maul halten. shut up
mein Lieber. my dear
Mensch. man; fellow

Mützen. caps
nein. no
nicht. no
nicht wahr. eh
Norweger. Norwegian
peinlich. scrupulous
prima. fine
rechts. right
Reichsdeutscher. Reich Germans
Revier(stube). infirmary
richt euch. line up
rührt euch. at ease
sauber. clean
Sauberkeit. cleanliness
Schein. certificate
Scheisserei. dysentery
Schläger. beater
schnell. fast
Schonungsblock. convalescence hut
Schonungskranke. convalescent patient
Schüssel. soup bowl
Schutzhaftlagerführer. head of
    protective custody camp

Schutzhäftling. protective custody prisoner
Schweinehund. son of a bitch
Seitenrichtung. keep in line
Sonderkommando. special squad
Sonderkommission. special commission
Sondermeldung. special bulletin
stillgestanden. stand at attention
strengsten verboten. strictly forbidden
Stubenältester. room leader
Teufel. devil
verflucht mal. cursed once again
Vermittlung. registration office
Vernichtung. extermination
Vernichtungslager. extermination camp
verstanden. understood
Verwaltung. administration building
Vorarbeiter. foreman
Weltanschauung. world view
Zentralbauleitung. central
    construction authority
zu fünfen. by fives
Zugängere. new arrivals
Zugführer. chief guard

SOURCES FOR FOOTNOTES

Foreword: Re: Uniforms: Arthur Hayes, *SS Uniforms, Insignia & Accoutrements* (Atglen, PA: Schiffer Military History, 1996), pp. 34, 48. See David Koker, *At the Edge of the Abyss*, ed. Robert Jan van Pelt, trans. Michiel Horn and John Irons (Evanston, IL: Northwestern University Press, 2012) (hereinafter *Abyss*), p. 252: "Where they [the SS guards] walk in their green uniforms, the lines separate."

January 13, 1942: Re: BBC broadcasts: Olav Riste and Berit Nøkleby, *Norway 1940–45* (n.p.: Aschehoug, 1994), pp. 22, 35; Tore Gjelsvik, *Norwegian Resistance 1940–1945*, trans. Thomas Kingston Derry (Montreal: McGill-Queen's University Press, 1979) (hereinafter *Resistance*), p. 93. Re: Undset: Sigrid Undset, *Return to the Future*, trans. Henriette C. K. Naeseth (New York: Alfred A. Knopf, 1942), pp. 22, 57; Arne Ording, Gudrun Johnson, and Johan Garder, *Våre falne* [Our fallen] *1939–1945* (Norwegian government, 1951), pp. 272–73, found at *da2ornament uib. no/cgi-win/WebBok.exe?slag=lesside&bokid=vaarefalne4&sideid=273&storleik=* (in Norwegian), accessed July 23, 2015. A strong critic of Hitler whose works were banned in Nazi Germany, Undset fled to Sweden in the summer of 1940, thence across Russia, across the Pacific to San Francisco, and to New York, where she remained until the war's end, pleading the cause of Norway and of Europe's Jews. She died June 10, 1949. German losses amounted to almost 5,300 killed, wounded, or missing; British, French, and Polish losses were just under 5,000. Henrik O. Lunde, *Hitler's Pre-Emptive War: The Battle for Norway, 1940* (Philadelphia: Casemate, 2009) (hereinafter *The Battle for Norway*), pp. 541–44 (citing none other than fellow Grini prisoner Odd Lindbåck-Larsen). Re: Odd Wang: Kristian Ottosen, *Nordmenn i fangenskap 1940–1945* (Oslo: Universitetsforlaget, 1995) (in Norwegian) (hereinafter *Nordmenn*), p. 656 [Ottosen was a prisoner at numerous concentration camps including Sachsenhausen, Natzweiler, and Dachau]; *freepages.genealogy.rootsweb.ancestry.com/~kielland/slekt/per00624.htm*, accessed May 7, 2012. Re: Tank-Nielsen: Ottosen, *Nordmenn*, p. 619; website of the Norsk Biografisk Leksikon [Norwegian Biographical Encyclopedia] (hereinafter NBL website), *nbl.snl.no/Carsten_Tank-Nielsen* (in Norwegian; all such web entries are in Norwegian) (by Harald Rinde), accessed July 15, 2015; see Florence Harriman, *Mission to the North* (Philadelphia: J. B. Lippincott Company, 1941), where the US minister to Norway (1936–1940) wrote, "I had already heard many stories about the Admiral [Tank-Nielsen] and his busman's holidays. When off duty, he used to disguise himself as a fisherman and spend his nights on fishing craft and trawlers up and down and in and out the fjords, ferreting out belligerent craft who had no business in neutral waters." p. 240.

January 14, 1942: Re: Thallaug: Ottosen, *Nordmenn*, p. 623; *runeburg.org/hvemerhvem/1973/0556.html* (in Norwegian), accessed June 5, 2012; website of Store Norske Leksikon [Great Norwegian

Encyclopedia] (hereinafter SNL website), *snl.no/Nansenskolen* (in Norwegian; all such web entries are in Norwegian), accessed October 7, 2013; website of Nansen Academy, *nansenskolen. no*, accessed October 7, 2013.

January 15, 1942: Re: Nøkleby: Ottosen, *Nordmenn*, p. 488; Berit Nøkleby, e-mail, February 12, 2014. Re: Gabrielsen: NBL website, *nbl.snl.no/Hans_Gabrielsen* (by Ivan Kristoffersen), accessed July 15, 2015.

January 16, 1942: Re: Dybwad: Ottosen, *Nordmenn*, p. 171. Re: Grini: Leif Hovelsen, *Out of the Evil Night*, trans. John Morrison (London: Blandford Press, 1959), p. 27. Re: Rinnan: Ottosen, *Nordmenn*, p. 535; NBL website, *nbl.snl.no/Frode_Rinnan* (by Wenche Findal), accessed July 15, 2015. Re: Nicolaysen: Ottosen, *Nordmenn*, p. 467. Re: Dobloug: Ottosen, *Nordmenn*, p. 169. Re: Escapees to England: Gjelsvik, *Resistance*, p. 72; Jacob Worm-Müller, *Norway Revolts Against the Nazis* (London: Lindsay Drummond, 1941) (hereinafter *Norway Revolts*), p. 120; Ole Kristian Grimnes, "The Beginnings of the Resistance Movement," in *Scandinavia during the Second World War*, ed. Henrik S. Nissen, trans. Thomas Munch-Petersen (Minneapolis: University of Minnesota Press, 1983) (hereinafter "The Beginnings of the Resistance Movement"), p. 205. Re: Bødtker: Ottosen, *Nordmenn*, p. 152; *runeberg.org/hvemerhvem/1973/0099.html* (in Norwegian), accessed October 8, 2013; Myrtle Wright, *Norwegian Diary 1940–1945* (London: Friends Peace and International Relations Committee, 1974) (hereinafter *Norwegian Diary*), pp. 56, 64.

February 1, 1942: Re: Bødtker: Ottosen, *Nordmenn*, p. 152; NBL website, *nbl.snl.no/Johannes_ Sejersted_B%C3%B8dtker* (by Jon Gunnar Arntzen), accessed July 15, 2015; Worm-Müller, *Norway Revolts*, p. 76. Re: Seip: Ottosen, *Nordmenn*, p. 563; Sune Persson, *Escape from the Third Reich: Folke Bernadotte and the White Buses*, trans. Graham Long (London: Frontline Books, 2009) (hereinafter *Escape*), pp. 35, 39, 153; Folke Bernadotte, *The Curtain Falls*, trans. Count Eric Lewenhaupt (New York: Alfred A. Knopf, 1945), pp. 44, 94–95; quote is found at Wright, *Norwegian Diary*, p. 40; NBL website, *nbl.snl.no/Didrik_Arup_Seip* (by Finn-Erik Vinje), accessed July 15, 2015. Himmler released Seip to allow him to continue his research on ancient Nordic history (a subject close to Himmler); instead Seip provided intelligence on German activities and tracked the whereabouts of interned Norwegian prisoners. Re: Steen: Ottosen, *Nordmenn*, p. 589; Wright, *Norwegian Diary*, pp. 56, 64; SNL website, *snl.no/Erling_Steen*, accessed March 26, 2013; Steen & Strøm website: *www.steenstrom.com/company*, accessed April 1, 2013; *Wall Street Journal* website, *online.wsj.com/article/SB1000142412788732478440457814505 51764443658.html*, accessed April 1, 2013. During the war Quisling furnished his newly commandeered home, Gimle, "including furniture in the dining hall seating over a hundred, which had been bought from Oslo's largest store, Steen and Strøm." Hans Dahl, *Quisling: A Study in Treachery*, trans. Anne-Marie Stanton-Ife (Cambridge: Cambridge University Press, 1999) (hereinafter *Quisling*), p. 267. Re: Victoria Terrace: Wright, *Norwegian Diary*, pp. 32, 42; "The Gestapo at Work in Norway" (The Royal Norwegian Government Information Office, 1942), p. 31. Re: Quisling: Dahl, *Quisling*, pp. 3, 236–38; David Abrahamsen, *Men, Mind and Power* (New York: Columbia University Press, 1945), p. 108. The *Times* of London wrote, "Quisling has added a new word to the English language. To writers, the word Quisling is a gift from the gods. If they had been ordered to invent a new word for traitor they could hardly have hit upon a more brilliant combination of letters. Actually it contrives to suggest something at once slippery and tortuous." Quoted in Richard Petrow, *The Bitter Years* (New York: William Morrow & Company, 1974), p. 5; Harriman quote is in Harriman, *Mission to the North*, p. 255. The house in Oslo that Quisling occupied during the war is today home to the Center for Studies of Holocaust and Religious Minorities. Re: The milk strike: Riste and Nøkleby, *Norway 1940–45*, pp. 33–34; Gjelsvik, *Resistance*, pp. 45–47.

February 3, 1942: Re: Gjørtz: Ottosen, *Nordmenn*, p. 227 [Nansen mistakenly spells his name Gjørts in the name register he includes in the Norwegian edition, *Fra Dag til Dag* (Oslo: Dreyers

Forlag, 1946) (in Norwegian) (hereinafter Name Index)]. Re: NS party: the quote is from Bjarte Bruland, "Norway's Role in the Holocaust," in *The Routledge History of the Holocaust*, ed. Jonathan C. Friedman (New York: Routledge, 2011) (hereinafter "Norway's Role in the Holocaust"), p. 234; *Resistance*, p. 14 n.; Samuel Abrahamsen, *Norway's Response to the Holocaust* (New York: Holocaust Library, 1991) (hereinafter *Norway's Response*), pp. 2, 47. Re: Hirdmen: Gjelsvik, *Resistance*, p. 33 n.; Abrahamsen, *Norway's Response*, p. 53. According to Sigrid Undset, "The word [Hird] is really borrowed from Anglo-Saxon, a fact our local Nazis resented very much when they learned it from one of our most famous professors of philology." Undset, *Return to the Future*, p. 18 n. 3. Re: Quisling's installation as minister-president: Dahl, *Quisling*, pp. 236, 238 n. 70. Re: Alsatians: Joachim Fest, *Not I: Memoirs of a German Childhood*, ed. Herbert A. Arnold, trans. Martin Chalmers (New York: Other Press, 2013), p. 141 n. 23. Re: Berggrav, see generally Edwin Robertson, *Bishop of the Resistance* (St. Louis: Concordia Publishing House, 2000); Dahl, *Quisling*, pp. 245–60, 357. Koch's remarks were apparently based on Reichskommissar Terboven's speech at Quisling's installation that "present[ed] a great deal of revealing information he had gathered concerning Bishop Berggrav's role as a private peace broker in Berlin and London in 1939–1940." Ibid., p. 248; *Time*, April 19, 1943, pp. 78–79; *Time*, December 25, 1944, pp. 53–56; Gjelsvik, *Resistance*, pp. 34–35; NBL website, *nbl.snl.no/Eivind_Berggrav* (by Gunnar Heiene), accessed July 15, 2015. Re: Colbjørnsen: Ottosen, *Nordmenn*, p. 160. Re: Sydnes: Ottosen, *Nordmenn*, p. 608. Re: Grieg: Ottosen, *Nordmenn*, p. 233; NBL website, *nbl.snl.no/Harald_Grieg* (by Egil Tveterås), accessed July 15, 2015; Wright, *Norwegian Diary*, p. 96; Worm-Müller, *Norway Revolts*, p. 76. Re: Broch: Ottosen, *Nordmenn*, p. 143. Re: Pande: Ottosen, *Nordmenn*, p. 509. Re: Schiøtz: Ottosen, *Nordmenn*, p. 560; SNL website, *snl.no/Johannes_Henrik_Schi%C3%B8tz*, accessed October 10, 2013; Gjelsvik, *Resistance*, p. 110.

February 4, 1942: See *young-israeli-poland.blogspot.com/2010/07/ambiguous-symbolism-of-wannsee-for.html*, accessed May 2, 2011, for an account by a Sachsenhausen survivor of the use of Spanish curse words by SS guards.

February 6, 1942: The escapes from Ullevål and Åkebergveien are recounted in Maynard Cohen, *A Stand against Tyranny* (Detroit: Wayne State University Press, 1997) (hereinafter *Tyranny*), pp. 202–4. Re: Wright: Ottosen, *Nordmenn*, p. 666; *stortinget.no/no/Representanter-og-komiteer/Representantene/Representantfordeling/Representant/?perid=CAWR*, accessed May 20, 2014. Re: Cappelen: Ottosen, *Nordmenn*, p. 155. Re: Beck: Ottosen, *Nordmenn*, p. 110 [Ottosen erroneously places his escape at February 7, 1942]; *spycom.org/WW2/5_HJEMMEFRONT/5D/index.htm* (in Norwegian), accessed July 10, 2015; SOE personnel files at British National Archives, file HS 9/111/8. Re: Skjeseth: Ottosen, *Nordmenn*, p. 573; Arne Fjellbu, *Memoirs from the War Years*, trans. L. A. Vigness (Minneapolis: Augsburg Publishing House, 1947) (hereinafter *Memoirs*), p. 99. Re: Scarlet Pimpernels: Karen Larsen, *A History of Norway* (Princeton, NJ: Princeton University Press, 1950), p. 555. Nansen's quote to Scharffenberg is found in Cohen, *Tyranny*, p. 78.

February 8, 1942: Re: Reimers: Marit Greve, e-mail, May 22, 2015. Re: Bentzen: Ottosen, *Nordmenn*, p. 113 [Ottosen spells his name Gottfred Bentzen; there are some discrepancies between Nansen's and Ottosen's spellings of first names].

February 11, 1942: Re: Lang-Nielsen: Ottosen, *Nordmenn*, p. 395; NBL website, *nbl.snl.no/Fredrik_Lange-Nielsen* (by Inger Døving), accessed July 15, 2015; Wright, *Norwegian Diary*, p. 181. Re: Kullmann: Ottosen, *Nordmenn*, p. 389; NBL website, *nbl.snl.no/Olaf_Kullmann* (by Stein Ørnhøi), accessed July 15, 2015; Dahl, *Quisling*, pp. 90–94; Wright, *Norwegian Diary*, p. 41. Kullmann died of double pneumonia. His family was not allowed to receive his ashes, and his death could be announced in the papers, but not the place of his death. "Such notices however speak for themselves; they appear long after the date of death and the lack of information indicates that the circumstances were unusual." Wright, *Norwegian Diary*, p. 85. Re: Kaci

Kullmann Five: *nobelpeaceprize.org/en_GB/nomination_intro/members/*, accessed May 21, 2015. Øverland's poem can be found in *Sverdet Bak Døren: Dikt* [*The Sword Behind the Door: Poems*] (Oslo: Aschehoug, 1956).

February 13, 1942: Re: Terboven: first quote is from Mark Mazower, *Hitler's Empire* (New York: Penguin Press, 2008), pp. 104–5; the Consul General quote is in Abrahamsen, *Norway's Response*, p. 69; Dahl, *Quisling*, p. 188; H. Franklin Knudsen, *I Was Quisling's Secretary* (London: Britons Publishing Company, 1967), pp. 113, 114, 120; Berit Nøkleby "Adjusting to Allied Victory," in *Scandinavia during the Second World War* (hereinafter "Adjusting to Allied Victory"), p. 313; the final quote can be found in Francois Kersaudy, *Norway 1940* (Lincoln: University of Nebraska Press, 1998), p. 150; Robert Wistrich, *Who's Who in Nazi Germany* (New York: Macmillan Publishing Co., 1982) (hereinafter *Who's Who*), p. 313. As will be seen, a number of Nazi and NS figures resorted to suicide at the end of the war. One historian observes, "Indeed, one of the most remarkable features of the collapse of Nazi Germany was the large number of suicides that accompanied it . . . and it is revealing that so many people who identified with Nazism chose to kill themselves rather than face life in a postwar world." Richard Bessel, *Nazism and War* (New York: Modern Library, 2004), p. 186. Apparently Terboven's dim view of Quisling was shared by General Nicholas von Falkenhorst, the commanding general of all German troops in Norway. Aage Trommer "Scandinavia and the Turn of the Tide," in *Scandinavia during the Second World War* (hereinafter "Scandinavia and the Turn of the Tide"), p. 246. Re: Svolvær: Joseph H. Devins, Jr., *The Vaagso Raid* (Philadelphia: Chilton Book Company, 1968), p. 38 (who points out that fish oil was also desperately needed by the Germans as a source of vitamins for its submarine crews); Dahl, *Quisling*, p. 221; Ohto Manninen, "Operation Barbarossa and the Nordic Countries," in *Scandinavia during the Second World War* (hereinafter "Operation Barbarossa"), p. 141; Worm-Müller, *Norway Revolts*, pp. 116–20 (the quote is found on p. 116); website of the Lofoten War Museum, *www.lofotenkrigsmus.no/e_lofotraid.htm*, accessed July 1, 2013. Re: Oftedal: Ottosen, *Nordmenn*, p. 489; Cohen, *Tyranny*, p. 252; Worm-Müller, *Norway Revolts*, p. 42; NBL website, *nbl.snl.no/Sven_Oftedal_-_2* (by Bodil Wold Johnson), accessed July 15, 2015.

February 22, 1942: Re: Bryn: Ottosen, *Nordmenn*, p. 146. Re: Fraser and Svae: Ottosen, *Nordmenn*, pp. 212 (Fraser), 604 (Svae); Cohen, *Tyranny*, pp. 192–93. Re: Bavaria: see Wikipedia website, *en.wikipedia.org/wiki/%C3%85kebergveien*, accessed October 6, 2013. Re: Birkevold: Ottosen, *Nordmenn*, p. 125; Cohen, *Tyranny*, pp. 192–93.

February 28, 1942: Re: Ålesund incident: Riste and Nøkleby, *Norway 1940–45*, pp. 51–52; Cohen, *Tyranny*, pp. 189–90. The "export group" based in Ålesund had been infiltrated by Henry Rinnan, a notorious Norwegian traitor who was executed after the war. Hans Adamson and Per Klem, *Blood on the Midnight Sun* (New York: W. W. Norton & Company, 1964), pp. 230–31. In addition to escapes to England, some fifty thousand Norwegians escaped into Sweden during the war. Persson, *Escape*, p. 226. Re: teacher arrests: Riste and Nøkleby, *Norway 1940–45*, pp. 40–43; Grimnes, "The Beginnings of the Resistance Movement," p. 197; Gjelsvik, *Resistance*, pp. 61–63; Wright, *Norwegian Diary*, pp. 75–76. Re: Fjellbu: Fjellbu, *Memoirs*, pp. 138–42; Wright, *Norwegian Diary*, pp. 70–71, 75–76; *Time*, December 25, 1944, pp. 53–56; *Time*, January 22, 1945, p. 64; NBL website, *nbl.snl.no/Arne_Fjellbu* (by Øyvind Norderval), accessed July 15, 2015. Fearing he might be ordered to cancel the service, Fjellbu had used a secret stairway to enter the church. *Memoirs*, p. 138. His diary states the temperature outside the church was -13˚F. Ibid., p. 141.

March 2, 1942: Marit Greve, e-mail, June 2, 2012. According to Marit Greve, both Nansen and Frode Rinnan were among the most talented songwriters during their student days.

March 8, 1942: Re: Welhaven: Cohen, *Tyranny*, p. 138; Wright, *Norwegian Diary*, p. 64; NBL website, *nbl.snl.no/Kristian_Welhaven* (by Jørn-Kr. Jørgensen), accessed July 15, 2015; Dahl,

Quisling, p. 415 n. 85; Ottosen, *Nordmenn*, p. 658. Re: Bull: Riste and Nøkleby, *Norway Revolts*, p. 76; Wright, *Norwegian Diary*, p. 57; NBL website, *nbl.snl.no/Francis_Bull*, accessed July 15, 2015. Re: Huitfeldt: SNL website, *snl.no/Hans_Ludvig_Carl_Huitfeldt*, accessed October 17, 2013; *dagtho.blogspot.com/2012/02/hm-king-harald-v-of-norways-75th.html*, accessed October 17, 2013. Re: Aubert: Ottosen, *Nordmenn*, p. 103; *www.specialforcesroh.com/showthread.php?15152-Aubert-Kristian-Gunnar*, accessed February 22, 2011. Re: Sand: Ottosen, *Nordmenn*, p. 553; NBL website, *nbl.snl.no/Lauritz_Sand* (by Arnfinn Moland), accessed July 15, 2015. Re: Måløy: Gjelsvik, *Resistance*, p. 75; I. C. B. Dear, ed., *The Oxford Companion to World War II* (Oxford: Oxford University Press, 2005) (hereinafter *Oxford Companion*), p. 973. A number of other consequences followed from Operation Archery. The Norwegian government in exile, which knew little of the attack until it was already over and announced to the general public, objected to its lack of involvement in planning, leading to greater coordination between the British and Norwegian military staffs. Devins, *The Vaagso Raid*, p. 188. Also, Hitler ordered German naval forces to be concentrated in Norwegian waters to better repel a possible Allied invasion that Hitler was convinced would occur. Accordingly, a number of capital ships, including the battleship *Tirpitz*, were transferred; none of them thereafter played a significant role in the war. Ibid., pp. 204–5. Re: Mad Jack Churchill, Ibid., pp. 64, 75; B. A. James, *Moonless Night* (London: William Kimber, 1983), pp. 129–30. Churchill was described as "one of those splendid military eccentrics upon whose presence in its ranks the British Army so rightfully prides itself." Devins, *The Vaagso Raid*, p. 52. He would allegedly go into battle carrying a two-handed claymore sword and bagpipes. Ibid.

March 12, 1942: Re: Oppegaard: Ottosen, *Nordmenn*, p. 505. Re: Johannesen: Ottosen, *Nordmenn*, p. 334. Re: Torsvik: Ottosen, *Nordmenn*, p. 634. Re: Lea: Ottosen, *Nordmenn*, p. 407.

March 14, 1942: Re: Trondheim: Harriman, *Mission to the North*, pp. 122–23.

March 15, 1942: Re: Rassenamt: Robert Michael, *Nazi-Deutsch/Nazi German* (Westport, CT: Greenwood Press, 2002), p. 323.

March 16, 1942: According to an article in *Viking*, the magazine of the Sons of Norway, Solveig was the most popular girl's name in 1920 and 1925. *Viking*, August 2015, p. 21 (the top girl's name in 2014 was Nora).

March 17, 1942: Re: Food: Marit Greve, e-mail, May 27, 2015; Ruth Maier, *Ruth Maier's Diary*, ed. Jan Vold, trans. Jamie Bulloch (London: Vintage Books, 2010), pp. 372–73. See also Arne Lie, *Night and Fog* (New York: W. W. Norton & Company, 1990), p. 81: "[After two occupation winters and the invasion of Russia], [b]eef had long ago disappeared, and so had fresh fruit. We got occasional fish, and potatoes and onions were still available, but things were very tight. Sugar was like gold. So was coffee."

March 20, 1942: Re: Balabanov: Nansen, Name Index.

March 21, 1942: Re: Winkelmann: Ottosen, *Nordmenn*, p. 664. Re: Smith-Housken: Ottosen, *Nordmenn*, p. 580. Re: Fremann: Ottosen, *Nordmenn*, p. 214. Re: Skancke: Hans Dahl, Guri Hjeltnes, Berit Nøkleby, Johan Ringdal, and Øystein Sørensen, ed., *Norsk Krigsleksikon 1940–45* [Norwegian War Encyclopedia 1940–45] (n.p.: J. W. Cappelens Forlag, 1995) (in Norwegian) (hereinafter *Krigsleksikon*), pp. 381–82 (by Øystein Sørensen).

March 22, 1942: Re: Bjørnson: SNL website, *snl.no/Bj%C3%B8rnstjerne_Bj%C3%B8rnson* (by Giuliano D'Amico), accessed June 1, 2015. Re: Bull: Wright, *Norwegian Diary*, p. 40.

March 29, 1942: Re: *Brand*: Roland Huntford, *Nansen: The Explorer as Hero* (New York: Barnes & Noble Books, 1998) (hereinafter *Nansen*), p. 428; Brenda Ueland, *Me: A Memoir* (Duluth, MN: Holy Cow! Press, 1994), p. 247; Michael Meyer, *Ibsen: A Biography* (Garden City, NY: Doubleday & Company, Inc., 1971), pp. 247–48, 267–71, 406, 410, 546, 741; Larsen, *A History of Norway*, p. 469; website of the National Library of Norway, *ibsen.nb.no/id/1430.0*, accessed June 1, 2015. It appears that Nansen's feelings about Ibsen may not have been fully reciprocated.

When nearly the whole population of Oslo [then known as Christiania] turned out to the quayside to greet Nansen upon his return from the North Pole in 1896, a friend of Ibsen's found him on a deserted downtown street and asked why he was not at the reception. "Ibsen's face stiffened. 'No,' he replied, almost angrily. 'This is an Indian deed to be celebrated with an Indian dance, at which I don't belong.' And he walked on." Meyer, *Ibsen: A Biography*, p. 741. Meyer mistakenly refers to Nansen's return from his Greenland voyage, but the date of the episode (September 1896) indicates that it was the polar voyage instead. Re: Aasebøe: Ottosen, *Nordmenn*, p. 684. Re: Andersen: Ottosen, *Nordmenn*, p. 90; Cohen, *Tyranny*, p. 282; *The Wisconsin State Journal*, April 4, 1949, opinion page, col. 4; *The Winona Daily News*, October 24, 1955, p. 8.

April 3, 1942: Re: Berner: Wright, *Norwegian Diary*, pp. 64, 91; Ottosen, *Nordmenn*, p. 121; SNL website, *snl.no/Jørgen_Haslef_Berner%2Fnorsk_lege*, accessed December 19, 2011. Re: Hofmo: Ottosen, *Nordmenn*, p. 295; NBL website, *nbl.snl.no/Rolf_Hofmo* (by Matti Goksøyr), accessed July 15, 2015. Re: Lange: Ottosen, *Nordmenn*, p. 395; NBL website, *nbl.snl.no/August_Lange* (by Andreas Schanke), accessed July 11, 2015. Re: Nansen quote: *Appleton Post-Crescent*, February 3, 1940, p. 10, col. 2. Nansen had used almost the same words in a speech in Milwaukee the preceding night. See *The Milwaukee Journal*, February 2, 1940, local news, p. 1, col. 4. Re: Strandli: SNL website, *snl.no/Martin_Strandli*, accessed March 2, 2011; Ottosen, *Nordmenn*, p. 597.

April 14, 1942: Re: Hoff: NBL website, *nbl.snl.no/Trygve_J_B_Hoff* (by Arne Bonde), accessed June 2, 2015; *New York Times*, December 24, 1939, p. 5 col. 4; Ottosen, *Nordmenn*, p. 295. Re: Krohg: Ottosen, *Nordmenn*, p. 387; Ingeborg Glambek, "The Council Chambers in the UN Building in New York," *Scandinavian Journal of Design History*, vol. 15, 2005, pp. 8–39. The painting can be viewed at *www.gardkarlsen.com/new_york/Per_Krohg_painting_security_council.jpg*, accessed October 21, 2013. In the small world of World War II Norway, Krohg had been a pupil of Axel Revold in the area of decorative fresco painting; Revold in turn had married Odd Nansen's older sister Irmelin ("Immi") in 1929. Larsen, *A History of Norway*, p. 531; Huntford, *Nansen*, p. 536. Re: Bølling: Ottosen, *Nordmenn*, p. 153.

April 17, 1942: Nansen, Name Index.

April 19, 1942: Re: fru Rinnan: Ottosen, *Nordmenn*, p. 535 [Ottosen states that Rinnan remained at Grini and 19 Møllergata for the duration of the war, but Nansen's diary entry of March 27, 1944, indicates that she was transferred to Ravensbrück]. Re: Scheel: Ottosen, *Nordmenn*, p. 558.

April 28, 1942: *oslo-norway.ca/attractions/karljohansgate.html*, accessed October 22, 2013; SNL website, *snl.no/Karl_Johans_gate*, accessed October 22, 2013. Note that Nansen misspelled Telavåg as Televåg in the original text, which I have corrected.

April 30, 1942: Ottosen, *Nordmenn*, p. 223.

May 1, 1942: Riste and Nøkleby, *Norway 1940–45*, pp. 51–52. Gjelsvik, *Resistance*, pp. 78–79; Cohen, *Tyranny*, pp. 148–49, 189–90; Grimnes, "The Beginnings of the Resistance Movement," p. 201; *www.specialforcesroh.com/showthread.php?16403-Fillinger-Per-Andreas*, accessed July 23, 2015; *www.memorialmuseums.org/eng/staettens/view/712/Monument-in-Trandum-Forest#*, accessed October 17, 2013. Note that Nansen misspelled Telavåg as Televåg in the original text, which I have corrected.

May 2, 1942: *en.wikipedia.org/wiki/ulven_concentration_camp*, accessed March 3, 2011; *lofoten-krigsmus.no/e_grini2.htm*, accessed March 3, 2011.

May 3, 1942: Re: Anemones: Liv Nansen Høyer, *Nansen: A Family Portrait*, trans. Maurice Michael (London: Longmans, Green and Co., 1957), p. 10. Re: Jæren Gang: Cohen, *Tyranny*, pp. 190–92. Re: Falkenhorst: Wistrich, *Who's Who*, p. 72; Lunde, *The Battle for Norway*, pp. 83–84 n.

38. Re: Hitler's Commando Order: William L. Shirer, *The Rise and Fall of the Third Reich* (New York: Simon & Schuster, 1960) (hereinafter *Rise and Fall*), pp. 955–56. Other Nazi generals, including Anton Dostler and Alfred Jodl, were executed after the war for their involvement in implementing the Commando Order.

May 7, 1942: Re: Whaling: Harriman, *Mission to the North*, p. 41. Re: Polhøgda: *www.fni.no/polhogda.html*, accessed January 18, 2011.

May 8, 1942: Re: Bø: Ottosen, *Nordmenn*, p. 151 [Ottosen incorrectly lists May 9, 1942, as the date members of the Jæren Gang, including Bø, were executed. May 9 was the date of their sentencing.] Re: Rode: NBL website, *nbl.snl.no/Leif_S_Rode* (by Magne Bolme), accessed July 15, 2015.

May 11, 1942: Ottosen, *Nordmenn*, p. 566.

May 16, 1942: Ottosen, *Nordmenn*, p. 147.

May 17, 1942: Fridtjof Nansen quoted in Ueland, *Me: A Memoir*, p. 253. Re: Skerries: Adamson and Klem, *Blood on the Midnight Sun*, p. 83.

May 21, 1942: Ottosen, *Nordmenn*, p. 342.

May 23, 1942: Re: Henriksen: Ottosen, *Nordmenn*, p. 287. Re: Coral Sea: Cesare Salmaggi and Alfredo Pallavisini, *2194 Days of War* (New York: Gallery Books, 1979), pp. 238–43.

May 24, 1942: Ottosen, *Nordmenn*, pp. 441 (Meland), 101 (Asbjørnsen).

May 29, 1942: Re: Sikveland, Ottosen, *Nordmenn*, p. 566. Re: Mæland: Ottosen, *Nordmenn*, p. 461; Nansen, Name Index.

June 7, 1942: Re: Hansen: Ottosen, *Nordmenn*, p. 268. Re: Kharkov: Andrew Roberts, *The Storm of War* (New York: HarperCollins, 2011), p. 175; John Keegan, *The Second World War* (New York: Viking, 1989), p. 223; Williamson Murray and Allan Millett, *A War to Be Won* (Cambridge, MA: Belknap Press of Harvard University Press, 2000), p. 277; Gerhard Weinberg, *A World at Arms* (Cambridge: Cambridge University Press, 1994), pp. 296, 412 (the quote is Weinberg's); Dear, *Oxford Companion*, p. 511. Re: Hansteen: NBL website, *nbl.snl.no/Viggo_Hansteen* (by Harald Berntsen), accessed July 15, 2015; Gjelsvik, *Resistance*, pp. 46–47, 124; Wright, *Norwegian Diary*, p. 64; Dahl, *Quisling*, p. 232 (the quote is from Dahl). Myrtle Wright notes that the police were actually looking for "another man, Buland, but he happened by chance to be out of the house on an autumn berry-picking tour, and Wickstrøm was arrested in his place." *Norwegian Diary*, p. 63.

June 13, 1942: Re: Sevastopol: Murray and Millett, *A War to Be Won*, pp. 277–78; Weinberg, *A World at Arms*, pp. 411–13.

June 14, 1942: Ottosen, *Nordmenn*, p. 379.

June 16, 1942: Re: Rasmussen: Based on Nansen's diary entry December 21, 1942. Ottosen puts the release date at December 22, 1942; Ottosen, *Nordmenn*, p. 528. Re: Huitfeldt: Ottosen, *Nordmenn*, p. 304.

June 23, 1942: Re: Tobruk: Churchill is quoted in Keegan, *The Second World War*, pp. 331–32; Murray and Millett, *A War to Be Won*, pp. 269–70; the German victory quote is from Weinberg, *A World at Arms*, p. 350; the British defeat quote is from Roberts, *The Storm of War*, pp. 133–34. Re: El Alamein: Keegan, *The Second World War*, pp. 336–37; Roberts, *The Storm of War*, pp. 284–301; Weinberg, *A World at Arms*, p. 431; Murray and Millett, *A War to Be Won*, p. 271. Re: Rommel's promotion: Roberts, *The Storm of War*, p. 299; Murray and Millett, *A War to Be Won*, p. 270. Re: Rommel's suicide: Roberts, *The Storm of War*, p. 299. Re: Esser: Abrahamsen, *Norway's Response*, pp. 6, 75; Dahl et al., *Krigsleksikon*, p. 84 (by Berit Nøkleby); Per Ole Johansen, "Norway," in *The Holocaust Encyclopedia*, ed. Walter Laqueur, p. 449 (New Haven, CT: Yale University Press, 2001); Bruland, "Norway's Role in the Holocaust," p. 235. Re: Moe: Ottosen, *Nordmenn*, p. 451.

June 25, 1942: Ottosen, *Nordmenn*, p. 286.

June 26, 1942. Interview, Marit Greve, October 2, 2015.

June 30, 1942: Koker, *Abyss*, p. 114.

July 8, 1942: Re: Andersen: Ottosen, *Nordmenn*, p. 84. Re: bombing raid: Salmaggi and Pallavisini, *2194 Days of War*, p. 270.

July 9, 1942: Re: Katyń: Allen Paul, *Katyń: Stalin's Massacre and the Triumph of the Truth* (De Kalb: Northern Illinois University Press, 2010); Dear, *Oxford Companion*, pp. 506–8.

July 14, 1942: Ottosen, *Nordmenn*, p. 571; NBL website, *nbl.snl.no/Einar_Skavlan* (by Kjersti Hustvedt), accessed July 15, 2015.

July 15, 1942: NBL website, *nbl.snl.no/Hellmuth_Reinhard* (by Berit Nøkleby), accessed July 15, 2015; Abrahamsen, *Norway's Response*, pp. 5, 75–76.

July 16, 1942: Re: Pastoral letter: Grimnes, "The Beginnings of the Resistance Movement," p. 194; Worm-Müller, *Norway Revolts*, p. 99–101. The text of the pastoral letter can be found at Monica Curtis, ed., *Norway and the War* (London: Oxford University Press, 1941), pp. 147–54. Re: Zeidler: Dahl et al., *Krigsleksikon*, p. 454 (by Berit Nøkleby).

July 18, 1942: Ottosen, *Nordmenn*, p. 527.

July 19, 1942: Re: Tschudi: Ottosen, *Nordmenn*, p. 637. Re: Forsberg: Ottosen, *Nordmenn*, p. 209. Re: Kunze: Dahl et al., *Krigsleksikon*, p. 238 (by Berit Nøkleby). Re: Thu: *Time*, December 25, 1944, p. 56; Ottosen, *Nordmenn*, p. 629. Thu died June 27, 1944. Re: Sæverud: Ottosen, *Nordmenn*, p. 612.

July 20, 1942: Ottosen, *Nordmenn*, p. 263.

July 21, 1942: Ottosen, *Nordmenn*, p. 390.

July 24, 1942: Re: Koch: Dahl et al., *Krigsleksikon*, p. 217 (by Robert Bohn). Re: Riisnæs: Paul Vigness, *The German Occupation of Norway* (New York: Vantage Press, 1970), pp. 227–28; Dahl et al., *Krigsleksikon*, pp. 352–53 (by Nils Johan Ringdal). Re: Bilberries: Harriman, *Mission to the North*, p. 135.

July 29, 1942: Re: SD: Michael, *Nazi-Deutsch/Nazi German*, p. 372; Koker, *Abyss*, p. 188 n. 315; Wistrich, *Who's Who*, pp. 166–67.

August 2, 1942: Re: Maurstad: Ottosen, *Nordmenn*, p. 440. Re: Fjære: Ottosen, *Nordmenn*, p. 205.

August 3, 1942: Dahl et al., *Krigsleksikon*, p. 97 (by Berit Nøkleby).

August 4, 1942: Re: Delphin: Ottosen, *Nordmenn*, p. 167. Re: King's birthday: Wright, *Norwegian Diary*, p. 89. Re: Paroles: Dahl, *Quisling*, p. 324.

August 5, 1942: Wright, *Norwegian Diary*, pp. 96–97; Marit Greve, e-mail, June 18, 2013.

August 6, 1942: Re: Graff-Wang: Ottosen, *Nordmenn*, p. 229. Re: Sørensen: Ottosen, *Nordmenn*, p. 613. Re: Abildgaard: Ottosen, *Nordmenn*, p. 77. Re: Aaby: Ottosen, *Nordmenn*, p. 678. Re: Rørholt: Ottosen, *Nordmenn*, p. 548; Dahl et al., *Krigsleksikon*, p. 363 (by Berit Nøkleby).

August 7, 1942: Huntford, *Nansen*, p. 483; Fjellbu, *Memoirs*, p. 94.

August 10, 1942: Ottosen, *Nordmenn*, p. 562.

August 11, 1942: Re: Nansen quote: Fridtjof Nansen, *Farthest North* (London: Duckworth, 2000), pp. 43–45. Re: Rye-Holmboe: Ottosen, *Nordmenn*, p. 298 [Ottosen lists him under "Holmboe"].

August 12, 1942: Randall Hansen, *Fire and Fury* (New York: NAL Caliber, 2009), pp. 81–82; Michael, *Nazi-Deutsch/Nazi German*, p. 305; Dear, *Oxford Companion*, pp. 870–71.

August 13, 1942: Re: Førlandsås: Ottosen, *Nordmenn*, p. 219. Re: Hagem: Ottosen, *Nordmenn*, p. 248. Re: Odd soccer team: See team's official website at *www.odd.no* (in Norwegian). Re: Dolva: Ottosen, *Nordmenn*, p. 169.

August 14, 1942: Ottosen, Nordmenn, p. 221; Australian Dental Journal, June 1966, p. 211; Science 113, no. 2945, June 8, 1951, pp. 665–68.

August 15, 1942: Vincent Hunt, *Fire and Ice: The Nazi's Scorched Earth Campaign in Norway* (Gloucestershire, UK: The History Press, 2014), pp. 14–15, 166–67.

August 25, 1942: Re: Göring: Wistrich, *Who's Who*, pp. 101–5; Dear, *Oxford Companion*, pp. 388–89.

August 27, 1942: Quoted in Wolfgang Sofsky, *The Order of Terror: The Concentration Camp*, trans. William Templer (Princeton, NJ: Princeton University Press, 1997) (hereinafter *The Order of Terror*), p. 73.

September 1, 1942: Re: Larsen: Ottosen, *Nordmenn*, p. 404. Re: Langenes: Ottosen, *Nordmenn*, p. 396.

September 2, 1942: Marit Greve, e-mail, April 18, 2014.

September 9, 1942: Re: Baastad: Ottosen, *Nordmenn*, p. 154. Re: Tønnesen: Ottosen, *Nordmenn*, p. 640.

September 10, 1942: Re: Eriksrud: Ottosen, *Nordmenn*, p. 193.

September 11, 1942: Re: Møte: Ottosen, *Nordmenn*, p. 462. Re: Lie: The quote is from Lie, *Night and Fog*, p. 20; Gjelsvik, *Resistance*, p. 212; Knudsen, *I Was Quisling's Secretary*, p. 114; Worm-Müller, *Norway Revolts*, pp. 59–60.

September 13, 1942: Marit Greve, interview, August 22, 2011.

September 18, 1942: Nansen, *Farthest North*, p. 124.

September 19, 1942: Re: Ohnstad: Ottosen, *Nordmenn*, p. 489. Re: Iversen: Ottosen, *Nordmenn*, p. 319. Re: U-505: *minnehallen.no/skip_2/sydhav-mt* (in Norwegian), accessed January 25, 2014; *www.uboat.net/allies/merchants/crews/person/52776.html*, accessed January 25, 2014; *www.uboat.net/allies/merchants/ships/1405.html*, accessed January 25, 2014; *www.warsailors.com/singleships/sydhav.html*, accessed January 25, 2014; *www.uboat.net/boats/u505.htm*, accessed January 25, 2014; *www.msichicago.org/whats-here/exhibits/u-505/*, accessed January 25, 2014; Nøkleby, "Adjusting to Allied Victory," p. 318.

September 21, 1942: Re: Nico Hirsch: Marit Greve, e-mails, September 5, 2011; May 18, 2012; June 2, 2012. Re: Rabbit: Marit Greve, e-mail, May 27, 2015.

September 23, 1942: Re: Scott-Hansen: Website of the Internet Movie Database, *www.imdb.com/name/nm0779940/*, accessed January 26, 2014; NBL website, *nbl.snl.no/Wench_Foss* (by Lise Lyche), accessed July 15, 2015; Ottosen, *Nordmenn*, p. 562. Re: Dalgard: NBL website, *nbl.snl.no/Olav_Dalgard* (by Kari Gaarder Losnedahl), accessed July 15, 2015; Ottosen, *Nordmenn*, p. 164.

September 25, 1942: Ottosen, *Nordmenn*, p. 533.

September 30, 1942: Nansen, *Farthest North*, p. 199.

October 1, 1942: Shirer, *Rise and Fall*, p. 264. According to Shirer, "Many a workman lost his job because he failed to contribute to Winterhilfe or because his contribution was deemed too small." Ibid.

October 5, 1942: "What Happened in Norway? Shoah and the Norwegian Jews." A publication of the Oslo Jewish Museum from the Exhibition "Remember Us Unto Life," pp. 14, 17; Abrahamsen, *Norway's Response*, pp. 83–84.

October 7, 1942: Re: State of Emergency: Grimnes, "The Beginnings of the Resistance Movement," p. 201; Dahl, *Quisling*, p. 280; Gjelsvik, *Resistance*, p. 77; Abrahamsen, *Norway's Response*, pp. 97–99. According to Willy Brandt, who fled to Norway to escape Nazi persecution and later served as chancellor of West Germany (1969–1974), the hostages were shot on the morning of October 7, 1942, after they had learned the previous evening on the radio about their execution; see Abrahamsen, *Norway's Response*, p. 98 n. 14. Re: Gleditsch: Ottosen, *Nordmenn*, p. 227; Wright, *Norwegian Diary*, p. 105; NBL website, *nbl.snl.no/Henry_Gleditsch* (by Thoralf Berg), accessed July 15, 2015; website of the Internet Movie Database, *imdb.com/name/nm0322398/*, accessed February 4, 2014.

October 8, 1942: Re: Gundersrud: Ottosen, *Nordmenn*, p. 243. Re: Andersen family: Marit Greve, e-mail, November 18, 2014.

October 10, 1942: Re: Denmark: Shirer, *Rise and Fall*, p. 700; David Lampe, *Hitler's Savage Canary* (New York: Skyhorse Publishing, 2010).

October 12, 1942: Re: Telegram Crisis: Dahl, *Quisling*, p. 303. "[E]ven while the German 6th army was being bogged down at Stalingrad and Rommel's Africa Corps was pushed onto the defensive at El Alamein, Hitler spared time to replace his Plenipotentiary in Denmark . . . [because of the insult]." Manninen, "Operation Barbarossa," pp. 125–26; Jeremy Bennett, *British Broadcasting and the Danish Resistance Movement, 1940–1945* (Cambridge: Cambridge University Press, 1966), p. 84; website of the Danish Monarchy, *kongehuset.dk/publish.php?dogtag=k_en_fam*, accessed August 14, 2011.

October 16, 1942: Fest, *Not I*, p. 308.

October 24, 1942: Christine Ammer, *The American Heritage Dictionary of Idioms* (Boston: Houghton Mifflin Company, 1997), pp. 646–47.

October 29, 1942: Re: Tents: *www.chebucto.ns.ca/Culture/Shifting_Boundaries/tents1.html* (cached), accessed March 16, 2011. Re: Shooting: The quote is from Bruland, "Norway's Role in the Holocaust," pp. 239–43; Petrow, *The Bitter Years*, p. 116; Wright, *Norwegian Diary*, p. 109.

November 4, 1942: Wistrich, *Who's Who*, pp. 230–32; Lawrence Malkin, *Krueger's Men* (New York: Little, Brown and Company, 2006), p. 141; Abrahamsen, *Norway's Response*, p. 92; Fest, *Not I*, pp. 17, 23, 41, 83.

November 9, 1942: Dear, *Oxford Companion*, pp. 634–38; Roberts, *The Storm of War*, pp. 301–8 (Roberts claims that 230,000 Axis forces were captured); Weinberg, *A World at Arms*, pp. 431–47; Max Hastings, *Inferno* (New York: Alfred A. Knopf, 2011), pp. 364–67; Murray and Millett, *A War to Be Won*, pp. 271–73.

November 13, 1942: Charles Koburger, *Steel Ships, Iron Crosses, and Refugees* (New York: Praeger, 1989), p. 93, table 6.3.

November 18, 1942: Re: MTB: Dear, *Oxford Companion*, p. 596. Re: U-Boat bases: Jak Showell, *Hitler's U-Boat Bases* (Annapolis, MD: Naval Institute Press, 2002), pp. 53–58, 190.

November 19, 1942: Marit Greve, e-mail, September 5, 2011.

November 22, 1942: Re: Nansen: Wright, *Norwegian Diary*, p. 115. Re: Evensen: Ottosen, *Nordmenn*, p. 196.

November 23, 1942: Re: Winge: Ottosen, *Nordmenn*, p. 664; NBL website, *nbl.snl.no/Bendt_Winge* (by Sigrid Rømcke Thue), accessed July 15, 2015. Winge's furniture is discussed in *The New Yorker*, May 28, 1960, p. 109. Re: Whispering Times: Riste and Nøkleby, *Norway 1940–45*, p. 36; *www.desertwar.net/war-cross-norway.html*, accessed February 6, 2014; Norwegian Resistance Museum.

November 25, 1942: Re: Berg: Abrahamsen, *Norway's Response*, p. 119. Re: Deportations: The number of deportees (and the overall Jewish population in Norway) is inexact and several sources cite slightly different numbers. Bjarte Bruland, one of the foremost Norwegian authorities on the Holocaust, uses 771 in his introductory essay in Moritz Nachtstern and Ragnar Arntzen, *Counterfeiter: How a Norwegian Jew Survived the Holocaust*, trans. Margrit Rosenberg Stenge (Oxford: Osprey Publishing, 2008) (hereinafter *Counterfeiter*), p. 10, and he uses 772 in "Collaboration in the Deportation of Norway's Jews: Changing Views and Representations," in *Collaboration With the Nazis: Public Discourse after the Holocaust*, ed. Roni Stauber (London: Routledge, 2011), p. 129. Samuel Abrahamsen cites a tabulation of deportation lists at the Yad Vashem Archives listing 761 Jews. *Norway's Response*, p. 148. As to the prewar Jewish population, Stauber uses 1,700 in *Collaboration With the Nazis: Public Discourse after the Holocaust*, p. 6, as does Per Ole Johansen in "Norway," p. 446, and, by implication, 770 deportees. Abrahamsen uses 1,600, *Norway's Response*, pp. 2–3. Dahl mentions a royal commission that estimated the number of Jews in Norway at 2,173, "of whom around 770 were deported." *Quisling*, p. 287 n. 27. For firsthand accounts of the effort to warn the Jews and their flight to Sweden, see Sigrid Helliesen Lund, *Always on the Way*, trans. Kathryn Parke (Tempe, AZ: Beverly-Merriam, 2000), pp. 65–71, and Irene Levin Berman, *"We Are Going to Pick Potatoes"* (Lanham, MD: Hamilton Books, 2010). Re: Brevig: Ottosen, *Nordmenn*, p. 142; Foundation White Buses to Auschwitz website *www.hvitebusser.no/* (in Norwegian), accessed March 17, 2011.

November 29, 1942: Re: Confiscations: Abrahamsen, *Norway's Response*, pp. 90–91; Bruland, "Norway's Role in the Holocaust," p. 240; Per Ole Johansen, "Norway," p. 450. Re: Reparations: Dahl, *Quisling*, p. 286 n. 24. The minority report was prepared by Berit Reisel, the daughter of Holocaust survivors, and historian Bjarte Bruland. For a description of the so-called "Skarpnes Committee," named after its chairman, Olaf Skarpnes, and the minority report, see the website of the Jerusalem Center for Public Affairs, *www.jcpa.org/phas/phas-10.htm*, accessed January 6, 2015.

December 1, 1942: Ottosen, *Nordmenn*, p. 144.

December 4, 1942: Ottosen, *Nordmenn*, p. 523; website of the Australian Antarctic Data Centre, *data.aad.gov.au/aadc/gaz/display_name.cfm?gaz_id=115781*, accessed February 24, 2014.

December 5, 1942: Re: Smith: Ottosen, *Nordmenn*, p. 580. Smith's granddaughter Lulli is married to Todd Akin, a former six-term Republican congressman for Missouri's 2nd Congressional District. Re: knot-cake: Marit Greve, e-mail, January 16, 2012.

December 6, 1942: Re: Himmler: Wistrich, *Who's Who*, pp. 138–42; Dear, *Oxford Companion*, p. 416; Winston Churchill, *The Second World War: Triumph and Tragedy* (London: Folio Society, 2000), p. 423; McDonald's quote is found in James McDonald, *Refugees and Rescue: The Diaries and Papers of James G. McDonald 1935–1945*, ed. Richard Breitman, Barbara McDonald Stewart, and Severin Hochberg (Bloomington: Indiana University Press in association with the United States Holocaust Memorial Museum, 2009), p. 118. As early as 1935 McDonald publicly resigned in protest from his position as High Commissioner for Refugees (Jewish and Other) Coming from Germany to call attention to the plight of refugees, accusing the Nazi government in his resignation statement of "the demoralization and exile of thousands of human beings." The full text is available at *dl.wdl.org/11604/service/11604.pdf*, accessed June 25, 2015. McDonald later became America's first ambassador to the State of Israel. US State Department website, *history.state.gov/countries/israel*, accessed February 27, 2014.

December 12, 1942: Meyer, *Ibsen: A Biography*, pp. 200–1, 365–66, 386; Internet Broadway Database, *www.ibdb.com/production.php?id=395562*, accessed July 22, 2015.

December 14, 1942: Re: Ramm: Ottosen, *Nordmenn*, p. 527; Børre R. Giertsen, ed., *Norsk Fangeleksikon: Grinifangene* (Oslo: J. W. Cappelens Forlag, 1946) (hereinafter *Fangeleksikon*), p. 49 (in Norwegian). Re: Huitfeldt: Ottosen, *Nordmenn*, p. 304.

December 22, 1942: Meyer, *Ibsen: A Biography*, pp. 377–78, 384.

December 24, 1942: Re: Porridge: Høyer, *Nansen: A Family Portrait*, pp. 122, 141. Re: Blessomen: *gonorway.com/norway/counties/oppland/vaagaa/763ab4a1aac7bd7/index.html*, accessed July 20, 2015.

December 25, 1942: Re: Krohg: Wright, *Norwegian Diary*, pp. 177–78. When the war ended, Fehmer donned a private's uniform and tried to blend in with captured Wehrmacht soldiers. He was known to be fond of his pet German shepherd, however, and when he was caught inquiring about his dog on a tapped phone line, he was captured, convicted of war crimes, and executed at Akershus Castle on March 16, 1948. Cohen, *Tyranny*, pp. 272–73; Dahl et al., *Krigsleksikon*, p. 93 (by Berit Nøkleby). Re: Rimestad: Ottosen, *Nordmenn*, 534.

January 26, 1943: Undset, *Return to the Future*, p. 21.

January 28, 1943: Re: Lindbäck-Larsen: Ottosen, *Nordmenn*, p. 414; NBL website, *nbl.snl.no/Odd_Lindb%C3%A4ck-Larsen* (by Reginald Norby), accessed July 15, 2015. Re: Stang: Ottosen, *Nordmenn*, p. 587; NBL website, *nbl.snl.no/Nic_Stang* (by Hans Fredrik Dahl), accessed July 15, 2015.

February 1, 1943: Dahl, *Quisling*, pp. 227–28; Marc Rikmenspoel and Jason Pipes, "Norwegian Volunteers in the German Wehrmacht in WWII," in *www.feldgrau.com/norway.html*, accessed March 22, 2011; Dahl et al., *Krigsleksikon*, pp. 67–68 (by Jan Egil Fjørtoft).

February 3, 1943: The quote is in Donald Miller, *The Story of World War II* (New York: Simon & Schuster, 2001), pp. 70–76; Bessel, *Nazism and War*, pp. 136–37; Murray and Millett, *A War to Be Won*, pp. 283–91; Weinberg, *A World at Arms*, pp. 447–55; Dear, *Oxford Companion*, pp. 823–25.

February 11, 1943: Dahl, *Quisling*, pp. 143, 222; Cohen, *Tyranny*, p. 53 (quoting Nansen); NBL website, *nbl.snl.no/C_J_Hambro* (by Paul Thyness), accessed July 15, 2015. See C. J. Hambro, *I Saw It Happen in Norway* (New York: D. Appleton-Century Company, 1940).

February 15, 1943: Re: Voroshilovgrad: Weinberg, *A World at Arms*, p. 458; Martin Gilbert, *The Second World War* (London: Folio Society, 2011), p. 469. Re: Rostov: Hastings, *Inferno*, p. 313; Gilbert, *The Second World War*, p. 469.

February 16, 1943: Gjelsvik, *Resistance*, pp. 81–82.

February 17, 1943: Hastings, *Inferno*, pp. 313, 380; the first quote is from Murray and Millett, *A War to Be Won*, pp. 293–94, 298, 391 (quote is on p. 294); the second quote is from Roberts, *The Storm of War*, pp. 409, 425, 522 (quote is on p. 425); Weinberg, *A World at Arms*, pp. 458–59, 467, 605. Some historians use slightly different dates.

February 20, 1943: Ottosen, *Nordmenn*, p. 84.

February 21, 1943: Dahl, *Quisling*, p. 298; Cohen, *Tyranny*, p. 166; Wright, *Norwegian Diary*, p. 146; see Roger Moorhouse, *Berlin at War* (New York: Basic Books, 2012), pp. 336–41, for a description of Goebbels' speech. Unlike Dutchmen, Belgians, or Frenchmen conscripted into the labor service during the same period, the Norwegians who participated all remained in Norway. Trommer, "Scandinavia and the Turn of the Tide," p. 248.

February 24, 1943: Abrahamsen, *Norway's Response*, pp. 133–34; Berman, *"We Are Going to Pick Potatoes,"* pp. 75–79. Ottosen incorrectly dates Levin's death in Auschwitz at January 19, 1943, *Nordmenn*, p. 409, and Becker's at February 17, 1943, *Nordmenn*, p. 111.

February 26, 1943: Robert Rosenstone, "International Brigades," in *Historical Dictionary of the Spanish Civil War, 1936–1939*, ed. James Cortada (Westport, CT: Greenwood Press, 1982), pp. 267–69.

February 27, 1943: Re: Hansen: Ottosen, *Nordmenn*, p. 267. Re: Helliksen: Ottosen, *Nordmenn*, p. 284.

March 1, 1943: Re: Lie: Ottosen, *Nordmenn*, p. 412; Wright, *Norwegian Diary*, pp. 152–53. Re: Neråsen: Ottosen, *Nordmenn*, p. 465; Wright, *Norwegian Diary*, p. 156.

March 2, 1943: Quote is from Gjelsvik, *Resistance*, p. 23; Grimnes, "The Beginnings of the Resistance Movement," p. 192; Riste and Nøkleby, *Norway 1940–45*, pp. 26–27. Diarist Myrtle Wright observed, "This [boycott] decision . . . is the more remarkable when it is realised [*sic*] that a sportsman is at his prime for a very limited number of years." *Norwegian Diary*, p. 36. Ottosen, *Nordmenn*, p. 542 (Asbjørn and Birger) and p. 543 (Sigmund). The skiing results of the three brothers can be found on the website of the International Ski Federation, *data.fis-ski.com/global-links/search-a-athlete.html?listid=%lastname=ruud*, accessed June 18, 2015. Information on the Holmenkollen medal can be found at *self.gutenberg.org/articles/holmenkollen_medal*, accessed July 21, 2015. Birger Ruud's silver medal at the 1948 Olympic Games at St. Moritz (at age thirty-six) was quite unexpected; he attended as the assistant coach to the ski-jumping team and only replaced a younger skier the night before the competition.

March 6, 1943: Re: Vemork: Riste and Nøkleby, *Norway 1940–45*, pp. 59–60; M. R. D. Foot, *SOE: An Outline History of the Special Operations Executive 1940–46* (London: British Broadcasting Corporation, 1984), pp. 210–11. Foot, the official historian of the SOE and an officer with the British Special Air Service during World War II, concluded, "If SOE had never done anything else, 'Gunnerside' would have given it claim enough on the gratitude of humanity." Ibid. Seven tons of water and thousands of kilowatt hours of energy go into the making of a single ounce of heavy water. At the time of the German invasion annual output amounted to a few hundred pounds; by the fall of 1941 that had increased to three thousand pounds, with German demands for even more. Adamson and Klem, *Blood on the Midnight Sun*, pp. 113–74. Haugland, the last surviving member of the Kon-Tiki expedition, died December 25, 2009, age ninety-two. Obituary at *New York Times*, January 4, 2010, *www.nytimes.com/2010/01/04/world/04haugland. html?_r=0*, accessed May 20, 2013. He was the first director of the Norwegian Resistance Museum and for a time the director of the Kon-Tiki Museum. Ibid. An earlier British attempt to sabotage the heavy water plant was an abject failure when both gliders carrying the assault team crashed; those who survived the crash were all captured and executed. After the Gunnerside raid the Germans were nevertheless able to restore heavy water production. When the plant was subsequently subjected to air raids, however, the Germans decided to move all heavy water stocks and equipment to Germany; the SOE was again able to sabotage the ferry used as the transport, sending everything to the bottom of Norway's Lake Tinnsjøen, one of the deepest lakes in Europe. In any event Germany was by that time no longer actively attempting to develop an atomic bomb. Dear, *Oxford Companion*, pp. 973–74. Re: Knaben: *Norwegian Diary*, p. 154; *www.mindat.org/loc-48314.html*, accessed April 1, 2013; *New York Times*, March 4, 1943, p. 2 col. 3, 5; November 17, 1943, p. 1 col. 4, 5; p. 12 col. 3. Officials considered the Knaben mines and refining plant "of greater economic and industrial importance . . . than any other target in Norway." Ibid. (At the time this article was written the Vemork raid was still highly classified and confidential.)

March 8, 1943: Ottosen, *Nordmenn*, p. 408.

March 10, 1943: Ottosen, *Nordmenn*, pp. 633, 252, 563.

March 11, 1943: Re: Henrik Wergeland: *The Army of Truth: Selected Poems by Henrik Wergeland*, trans. Anne Born, G. M. Gathorne-Hardy, and I. Grøndahl (Madison: University of Wisconsin Press 2003), pp. xiii–xx; Abrahamsen, *Norway's Response*, p. 33; Larsen, *A History of Norway*, pp. 416–21. Re: Constitution Day celebrations: Marit Greve, e-mail, January 16, 2012.

March 12, 1943: Re: Sigvartsen: Ottosen, *Nordmenn*, p. 566. Re: Nielsen: Ottosen, *Nordmenn*, p. 468.

March 18, 1943: Ottosen, *Nordmenn*, p. 307.

March 20, 1943: Ottosen, *Nordmenn*, p. 160.

March 29, 1943: Dear, *Oxford Companion*, pp. 561–62.

March 31, 1943: Michael, *Nazi-Deutsch/Nazi German*, p. 246.

April 2, 1943: Ottosen, *Nordmenn*, p. 420; Myrtle Wright (who was living with Sigrid Lund at the time) wrote in her diary: "[Lund's death] was a great shock for, though we had been prepared that he might never come out alive, it was not in this way." Wright, *Norwegian Diary*, p. 158.

April 4, 1943: Larsen, *A History of Norway*, pp. 69, 80, 87; Sverre Bagge, *Society and Politics in Snorri Sturluson's Heimskringla* (Berkeley: University of California Press, 1991), pp. 1, 8. Heimskringla is available online in English: *www.gutenberg.org/author/Snorri_Sturluson*. Quote is from Larsen, *A History of Norway*, p. 87.

April 5, 1943: Ottosen, *Nordmenn*, p. 533; Cohen, *Tyranny*, p. 187; NBL website, *nbl.snl.no/Robert_Riefling* (by Idar Karevold), accessed July 15, 2015; *www.bach-cantatas.com/Bio/Riefling-Robert. htm*, accessed September 18, 2011.

April 9, 1943: Andy Orchard, *Cassell Dictionary of Norse Myth and Legend* (London: Cassell, 1997), pp. 128–29.

April 16, 1943: Larsen, *A History of Norway*, pp. 420–21; NBL website, *nbl.snl.no/Johan_Sebastian_Welhaven* (by Sigurd Aa. Aarnes), accessed July 15, 2015.

April 30, 1943: Re: Daluege: Dear, *Oxford Companion*, pp. 218–19, 540; Wistrich, *Who's Who*, pp. 43–44; Daniel Blatman, *The Death Marches*, trans. Chaya Galai (Cambridge, MA: Belknap Press of Harvard University Press, 2011), p. 413. All told, approximately five thousand people were killed in retaliation for Heydrich's death. Foot, *SOE: An Outline History of the Special Operations Executive 1940–46*, p. 201. The ferocity of the Nazi response contributed to the later forced expulsion of three million Germans from the Sudetenland when Czechoslovakia's borders were restored after the war. Ibid. Re: Fehlis: Cohen, *Tyranny*, p. 273; NBL website, *nbl.snl.no/Heinrich_Fehlis* (by Berit Nøkleby), accessed July 15, 2015. Re: Heilmann: Giertsen, *Fangeleksikon*, p. xxiii. A fascinating story of how a fellow Grini prisoner, Leif Hovelsen, abused Heilmann while guarding him after the war, and then more than fifty years later sought to find him and ask his forgiveness, can be found at *www.forachange.net/browse/1585.html*, accessed July 23, 2015. Leif Hovelsen's father, Carl, is considered the father of Colorado skiing, which he introduced and promoted while he lived in the United States (1904–1921). Leif Hovelsen, who was the 2009 Grand Marshal of the Steamboat Springs, Colorado, Winter Carnival (which his father also started), died in 2011. Leif Hovelsen, *The Flying Norseman* (Ishpeming, MI: National Ski Hall of Fame Press, 1983).

May 2, 1943: Re: Børsum: NBL website, *nbl.snl.no/Lise_B%C3%B8rsum* (by Guri Hjeltnes), accessed June 23, 2015; Bente Børsum, telephone interview, April 24, 2012. Re: BdS: Michael, *Nazi-Deutsch/Nazi German*, p. 91.

May 5, 1943: Re: Gerhardsen: Ottosen, *Nordmenn*, p. 223; Obituary in *New York Times*, accessed at: *www.nytimes.com/1987/09/20/obituaries/einar-gerhardsen-dies-at-90-led-norway-as-welfare-state*, accessed November 25, 2014. Re: Græsli: Ottosen, *Nordmenn*, p. 235; Ording, Johnson, and Garder, *Våre falne*, pp. 721–22, found at *da2.uib.no/cgi-win/WebBok.exe?slag=lesside&bokid=v aarefalne1&sideid=721&storleik=* (in Norwegian), accessed July 23, 2015. Re: Jensen: Ottosen, *Nordmenn*, p. 329.

May 6, 1943: Ottosen, *Nordmenn*, p. 407.

May 8, 1943: Re: Tunis: Rick Atkinson, *An Army at Dawn* (New York: Henry Holt and Company, 2002), p. 537; the quote is from Williamson Murray, "The World at War 1941–45," in *The Cambridge Illustrated History of Warfare*, ed. Geoffrey Parker (Cambridge: Cambridge University Press, 1995), p. 322. Re: Festung Europa: Dear, *Oxford Companion*, p. 275.

May 11, 1943: Michael Meyer, *Strindberg: A Biography* (Oxford: Oxford University Press, 1987). Frida's relationship with Augustus John was a stormy one, which John later characterized as "a long and by no means idyllic tale of misdirected energy, mad incomprehension, absurdity and even squalor." Ibid., p. 570.

May 13, 1943: Re: Erikstad: Ottosen, *Nordmenn*, p. 193; website of the State Archive of Kristiansand, *www.arkivportalen.no/side/aktor/detaljer?aktorId=no-a1450-05000000079144*, accessed September 23, 2011. Re: Grøgaard: Ottosen, *Nordmenn*, p. 235; website of Norsk Kunstnerleksikon [The Norwegian Artist Encyclopedia] (hereinafter NKL website) (in Norwegian, all such entries in Norwegian), *nkl.snl.no/Joachim_Gr%C3%B8gaard* (by Sonia Hagemann), accessed September 23, 2011. Re: Bratlie: NKL website, *nkl.snl.no/Gunnar_Bratlie* (by Bodil Sørensen), accessed March 19, 2014; Ottosen, *Nordmenn*, p. 138.

May 15, 1943: Dear, *Oxford Companion*, p. 877; Salmaggi and Pallavisini, *2194 Days of War*, p. 377.

June 4, 1943: Ottosen, *Nordmenn*, p. 135; Wright, *Norwegian Diary*, pp. 78, 151, 198. Bonnevie was a close personal friend of Sigrid Lund's son, Bernti, who was also in Grini at the time.

June 5, 1943: *dictionary.reference.com/browse/half-seas-over*, accessed March 12, 2014.

June 7, 1943: Ottosen, *Nordmenn*, p. 673.

June 14, 1943: Ottosen, *Nordmenn*, p. 655.

June 17, 1943: Re: Fretheim: Ottosen, *Nordmenn*, p. 214. Re: Feuchtwanger: website of the US Holocaust Memorial Museum (hereinafter USHMM), *www.ushmm.org/wlc/en/article.*

php?ModuleId=10006081, accessed April 16, 2014. Re: Godwin: Kenneth Macksey, *Godwin's Saga* (London: Brassey's Defence Publishers, 1987), pp. 108–15. A précis of Godwin's report was successfully delivered to the British naval attaché in Stockholm. Ibid. Re: British sabotage efforts: Trommer, "Scandinavia and the Turn of the Tide," p. 254.

June 23, 1943: Harriman, *Mission to the North*, p. 153.

July 3, 1943: Ottosen, *Nordmenn*, p. 539; NBL website, *nbl.snl.no/Ivan_Th_Rosenqvist* (by Lars Walløe), accessed July 15, 2015; Dahl et al., *Krigsleksikon*, p. 359 (by Berit Nøkleby).

July 4, 1943: Re: Dürer: Jane Hutchinson, *Albrecht Dürer: A Biography* (Princeton, NJ: Princeton University Press, 1990). "[N]o Western artist has been more consistently admired than Dürer." Ibid., p. 190. Re: Paus: Ottosen, *Nordmenn*, p. 511. Re: Meidell-Larssen: Ottosen, *Nordmenn*, p. 441.

July 5, 1943: August Lange and Johan Schreiner, ed., *Griniboken* (Oslo: Gyldendal, 1946), pp. 280–82.

July 10, 1943: Dear, *Oxford Companion*, p. 779.

July 13, 1943: Ottosen, *Nordmenn*, pp. 428–29. The Feldmann's story is particularly well told in Ted Olson, "Death at Skrikerud Pond," *Harper's Magazine*, May 1953, pp. 65–71.

July 16, 1943: The website of the Lofoten War Museum, *www.lofotenkrigmus.no/e_grini2.htm*, accessed May 12, 2014.

July 20, 1943: Re: Holmboe: Marit Greve, e-mail, September 29, 2011. Re: Haakon VII: Gjelsvik, *Resistance*, pp. 14–15.

July 24, 1943: Ottosen, *Nordmenn*, p. 469.

July 26, 1943: Dear, *Oxford Companion*, pp. 598–601, 674. The quote is from Shirer, *Rise and Fall*, p. 997.

July 29, 1943: Larsen, *A History of Norway*, pp. 98–105; website of the Order of St. Olav, *www.kongehuset.no/artikkel.html?tid=28662&sek=28559*, accessed May 14, 2014.

July 30, 1943: Re: Holth: Ottosen, *Nordmenn*, p. 300. Re: Heggland: Ottosen, *Nordmenn*, p. 280. Re: Olavsen: Ottosen, *Nordmenn*, p. 490. Re: Ipolyi: website of All Music, *www.allmusic.com/artist/budapest-quartet-q8269/biography*, accessed September 28, 2011; SNL website, *snl.no/Istv%C3%A1n_Ipolyi*, accessed September 28, 2011; Nat Brandt, *Con Brio* (New York: Oxford University Press, 1993), pp. x, 4, 16, 36, 62, 63. All quotes are from Brandt. Brandt further states that Ipolyi was freed during the war through the personal intervention of Count Folke Bernadotte, whereupon he fled to Sweden. Ibid., p. 63. Ottosen on the other hand maintains that Ipolyi was released January 21, 1943, but rearrested April 20, 1943, and imprisoned in Bredtveit, Grini, and Berg until the end of the war. *Nordmenn*, p. 316. Described as having suffered a nervous breakdown as early as 1936, Ipolyi later recalled of his incarceration: "Every night, going to bed, I am remembering the horrible feelings I had on the evenings in the concentration camp, never knowing what the next day will bring." Brandt, *Con Brio*, pp. 62–63.

August 1, 1943: Ottosen, *Nordmenn*, p. 551.

August 12, 1943: Ottosen, *Nordmenn*, p. 587.

August 13, 1943: Re: Buchenwald: Dear, *Oxford Companion*, p. 132; Harry Stein, *Buchenwald Concentration Camp 1937–1945: A Guide to the Permanent Historical Exhibition*, trans. Judith Rosenthal (Göttingen: Wallstein Verlag, 2004) (hereinafter *Buchenwald Concentration Camp*), p. 253; Evelyn Zegenhagen, "Buchenwald Main Camp," trans. Stephen Pallavicini, in *The United States Holocaust Memorial Museum of Camps and Ghettos, 1933–1945*, ed. Geoffrey Megargee (Bloomington: Indiana University Press in association with the United States Holocaust Memorial Museum, 2009) (hereinafter *USHMM Encyclopedia*), vol. 1, part A, pp. 290–95; Flint Whitlock, *The Beasts of Buchenwald* (Brule, WI: Cable Publishing, 2011); David Hackett, ed., *The Buchenwald Report* (Boulder, CO: Westview Press, 1995), pp. 1, 43, 337, 341; USHMM website, *www.ushmm.org/wlc/en/article.php?ModuleId=10005198*, accessed November 21, 2011. Re: KZ: Nikolaus Wachsmann, *KL: A History of the Nazi Concentration Camps* (New York: Farrar, Straus and Giroux, 2015) (hereinafter *KL*), p. 635 n. 9. Re: Finstad: Ottosen, *Nordmenn*, p. 202.

August 16, 1943: Re: Police and Army arrests: Riste and Nøkleby, *Norway 1940–45*, pp. 70–72; Gjelsvik, *Resistance*, pp. 108–10; Trommer, "Scandinavia and the Turn of the Tide," p. 246; the quote is from Dahl, *Quisling*, pp. 311–14; Devins, *The Vaagso Raid*, p. 196; Frode Færøy of the Norwegian Resistance Museum, e-mail, May 27, 2012. Re: Magelssen: Ottosen, *Nordmenn*, p. 432.

August 21, 1943: Re: Eliassen: Ottosen, *Nordmenn*, p. 182. Re: Løvenskiold: Ottosen, *Nordmenn*, p. 428. Re: Gjølstad: Ottosen, *Nordmenn*, pp. 226–27.

Post August 21, 1943: Re: Johannessen: Nansen, Name Index; Giertsen, *Fangeleksikon*, p. 207 (Ottosen apparently does not have an entry for Johannessen in *Nordmenn*). Re: Parrot: website of the Skiven (Bergen) Guesthouse, *www.skiven.no/index2.php?pid=23&lang=en*, accessed June 29, 2015. Re: Fridtjof Nansen: Nansen, *Farthest North*, p. 280–82. Re: Karl Koch's remark: Stein, *Buchenwald Concentration Camp*, p. 57. Re: Polhøgda search/status: Marit Greve, interview, October 29, 2014; Cohen, *Tyranny*, p. 104. Re: Rediess: Abrahamsen, *Norway's Response*, p. 6; NBL Website, *nbl.snl.no/Wilhelm_Rediess* (by Berit Nøkleby), accessed July 7, 2015. Re: Bull: Wright, *Norwegian Diary*, p. 196. Re: Erikstad: Ottosen, *Nordmenn*, p. 193. Re: Parachute room: Lie, *Night and Fog*, pp. 130–31. Re: *Donau*: Riste and Nøkleby, *Norway 1940–45*, p. 63. Re: Nacht und Nebel: Dear, *Oxford Companion*, p. 625; Lie, *Night and Fog*, pp. 150–51; Shirer, *Rise and Fall*, pp. 957–58; Sofsky, *The Order of Terror*, p. 285; Wistrich, *Who's Who*, pp. 168–69. Re: Natzweiler: Leif Poulsson, "Rates and Causes of Death Among Male Prisoners NN in Germany," *The Journal of Norwegian Medical Association*, no. 19 (1946). Poulsson states, "It is obvious that even the prisoners with the best constitutions and with the best intention could not fail to succumb sooner or later." Ibid. See also *www.natzweiler-struthof.com/Natzweiler-Struthoftimeline. htm*, accessed March 9, 2012; *www.struthof.fr/en/media-library/comparative-timeline/*, accessed October 4, 2011; Jean-Marc Dreyfus, "Natzweiler-Struthof," trans. Gina Cooke, in Megargee, *USHMM Encyclopedia*, pp. 1003–11. Re: Anhalter: Moorhouse, *Berlin at War*, pp. 184, 201–2.

October 6, 1943: Re: Slogan: Wachsmann, *KL*, p. 100 (the original formulation was "There is a path to Freedom. Its milestones are: obedience, diligence, honesty, orderliness, cleanliness, sobriety, truthfulness, readiness to make sacrifices, and love of the fatherland."). According to Wachsmann, prisoners composed their own slogan: "There is a path to the SS. Its milestones are: stupidity, impudence, mendacity, boasting, shirking, cruelty, injustice, hypocrisy, and love of booze." Ibid., p. 101. Re: "Arbeit macht frei": Wachsmann, *KL*, pp. 100, 657 n. 136. Re: Newcomers: Kevin Sim, *Women at War* (New York: William Morrow and Company, Inc., 1982), p. 225. Re: Lange: Ottosen, *Nordmenn*, p. 395; Gjelsvik, *Resistance*, p. 67; NBL website, *nbl.snl.no/Halvard_Lange* (by Knut Einar Eriksen), accessed July 1, 2015; interview, Marit Greve, October 15, 2015. Re: Falkensee: Klaus Woiner, "Falkensee [with Staaken]," trans. Stephen Pallavicini, in Megargee, *USHMM Encyclopedia*, pp. 1299–1302.

October 10, 1943: Ottosen, *Nordmenn*, p. 270.

October 11, 1943: Re: Fridtjof Nansen: Nansen, *Furthest North*, p. 151. Re: Daae: Ottosen, *Nordmenn*, p. 172. Re: Orel: Gilbert, *The Second World War*, pp. 282, 524; *infoorel.ru/* (in Russian), accessed March 28, 2014. Re: Königsberg: Gilbert, *The Second World War*, p. 766; *www.konigsberg.ru/eng/kaliningrad/history-of-konigsberg*, accessed August 18, 2014. Re: Kaindl: Jonathan Friedman, "The Sachsenhausen Trials," in *Atrocities on Trial*, ed. Patricia Heberer and Jürgen Matthäus (Lincoln: University of Nebraska Press in association with the United States Holocaust Memorial Museum, 2008) (hereinafter "The Sachsenhausen Trials"), pp. 162, 167, 168. The exact date of Kaindl's death "is known only by Russian authorities." Ibid., p. 181

n. 47; Günter Morsch, ed., *Murder and Mass Murder in Sachsenhausen Concentration Camp 1936–1945*, trans. Richard Toovey, Catherine Hales, and Gabriel Fawcett (Berlin: Metropol Verlag, 2008) (hereinafter *Murder and Mass Murder*), p. 116. Re: Auschwitz: Sofsky, *The Order of Terror*, pp. 251, 262–63; Robert Jan van Pelt, *The Case for Auschwitz* (Bloomington: Indiana University Press, 2002), pp. 158, 216; USHMM website, *www.ushmm.org/wlc/en/article.php?ModuleId=10005189*, accessed August 28, 2012; website of the Auschwitz-Birkenau Memorial and Museum, *en.auschwitz.org/h/index.php?option=com_content&task=view&id=6&Itemid=6*, accessed August 28, 2012; Charles Sydnor, "Auschwitz I Main Camp," trans. Franciszek Piper; Gerard Majka, "Auschwitz II-Birkenau Main Camp"; Florian Schmaltz "Auschwitz III-Monowitz Main Camp [aka Buna]," in Megargee, *USHMM Encyclopedia*, pp. 204–20; Raul Hilberg, "Auschwitz," in Laqueur, *The Holocaust Encyclopedia*, pp. 32–44. Re: Kanada: Wachsmann, *KL*, pp. 377–78. At one point thirty-six barracks were devoted to storing the plunder of Auschwitz, but even that capacity "could not keep up with the pace of genocide, and luggage piled up between the . . . barracks or had to be moved to other sites." Ibid.; Malkin, *Krueger's Men*, p. 108; Andrzej Strzelecki "The Plunder of Victims and Their Corpses," in *Anatomy of the Auschwitz Death Camp*, ed. Yisreal Gutman and Michael Berenbaum (Bloomington: Indiana University Press in association with the United States Holocaust Memorial Museum, 1994), pp. 250–66. Re: Majdanek: Elizabeth White, "Lublin Main Camp [aka Majdanek]," in Megargee, *USHMM Encyclopedia*, pp. 876–79; Dear, *Oxford Companion*, p. 555; official website for the State Museum at Majdanek, *www.majdanek.eu/articles.php?acid=45*, accessed April 1, 2014; USHMM website, *www.ushmm.org/wlc/en/article.php?ModuleId=10005190*, accessed March 31, 2014. All told, the SS and police murdered approximately forty-two thousand Jews during Operation Harvest Festival. Wachsmann, *KL*, pp. 330–31; suffering quote is on p. 344. Lawrence's quote can be found in Jon Bridgman, *The End of the Holocaust: The Liberation of the Camps* (Portland, OR: Areopagitica Press, 1990), p. 20. Re: Goebbels: Wistrich, *Who's Who*, pp. 96–100; Dear, *Oxford Companion*, p. 387. Re: D.A.W.: Sofsky, *The Order of Terror*, p. 284; USHMM website, *www.ushmm.org/wlc/en/article.php?ModuleId=10007399*, accessed April 7, 2014. Re: Lichterfelde: Thomas Irmer and Klaus Leutner, "Berlin-Lichterfelde," trans. Stephen Pallavicini, in Megargee, *USHMM Encyclopedia*, pp. 1274–77; *www.berlin.de/mauer/mauerweg/lichterfelde_griebnitzsee/index.en.php*, accessed October 5, 2011. Re: Jehovah Witnesses: Eugen Kogon, *The Theory and Practice of Hell*, trans. Heinz Norden (New York: Farrar, Straus and Giroux, 2006), pp. 33–35; Morsch, *Murder and Mass Murder*, pp. 78–84; Cohen, *The Order of Terror*, pp. 121–22; James Irvin Lichti, "Model Denomination or Totalitarian Sect? Jehovah's Witnesses in Nazi Germany," in Friedman, *The Routledge History of the Holocaust*, pp. 358–74; USHMM website, *www.ushmm.org/wlc/en/article.php?ModuleId=10005394*, accessed July 1, 2015.

October 17, 1943: Macksey, *Godwin's Saga*, p. 123.

October 24, 1943: Sofsky, *The Order of Terror*, pp. 25, 199–205, 329 n. 5 (the first quote is on p. 25). Primo Levi further observed, "Their life is short, but their number is endless; they, the *Muselmänner*, the drowned, form the backbone of the camp, an anonymous mass, continually renewed and always identical, of non-men who march and labor in silence, the divine spark dead within them, already too empty to really suffer. One hesitates to call them living: one hesitates to call their death death, in the face of which they have no fear, as they are too tired to understand." Primo Levi, *Survival in Auschwitz* and *The Reawakening*, trans. Stuart Woolf (New York: Summit Books, 1986), p. 90.

October 25, 1943: Re: Øverland: NBL website, *nbl.snl.no/Arnulf_%C3%98verland*, accessed July 15, 2015; William L. Shirer, *The Challenge of Scandinavia* (Boston: Little, Brown and Company, 1955), pp. 99–100. Karen Larsen describes Øverland as one "who with passionate anger attacked evils and injustice, entering into the social conflicts of the day as one who himself was sharing the sufferings of the oppressed." *A History of Norway*, p. 528; *www.washingtonpost.com/news/volokh-conspiracy/wp/2015/05/08/norway-repeals-blasphemy-law-in-response-to-charlie-hebdo-murders*, accessed July 2, 2015. Re: War work: Wachsmann, *KL*, pp. 405–6.

November 4, 1943: Gilbert, *The Second World War*, pp. 546–47. The Moscow Declaration excluded those major war criminals whose crimes were not limited to one geographical area; they would be tried and punished in accordance with a subsequent joint declaration. This declaration, adopted by twenty-three countries on August 8, 1945, as the "London Agreement on the Punishment of the Major War Criminals of the European Axis," called for the establishment of an International Military Tribunal (IMT). It was the IMT that prosecuted twenty-four of the most senior Nazi officials at Nuremburg. Website of the Avalon Project, *avalon.law.yale.edu/wwii/moscow.asp*, accessed June 2, 2014; Jonathan Friedman, "Law and Politics in the Subsequent Nuremberg Trials, 1946–1949," in *Atrocities on Trial*, ed. Patricia Heberer and Jürgen Matthäus (Lincoln: University of Nebraska Press in association with the United States Holocaust Memorial Museum, 2008), pp. 75–76.

November 7, 1943: Persson, *Escape*, p. 37.

November 10, 1943: Marit Greve, e-mail, May 22, 2015.

November 11, 1943: Re: Keil: website of Terra Buskerund, *www.historieboka.no/Modules/historiebok_tidsepoke_tema_artikkel.aspx?ObjectType=Article&Article.ID=2150&Category.ID=1305* (in Norwegian), accessed June 23, 2012. Re: Becker family: website of Yad Vashem, *db.yadvashem.org/names/nameResults.html?lastName=becker&lastNametype=THESAURUS&place=Norway&placeType=THESAURUS&language=en*, accessed July 2, 2015; Ottosen, *Nordmenn*, p. 111. Re: Watches: Wachsmann, *KL*, p. 379. Re: Samuel: Abrahamsen, *Norway's Response*, p. 86; *www1.yadvashem.org/righteous_new/norway/sletten.html*, accessed April 4, 2011; Ottosen, *Nordmenn*, p. 553; Wright, *Norwegian Diary*, p. 93.

November 18, 1943: Marit Greve, interview, October 28, 2014.

November 20, 1943: Dear, *Oxford Companion*, p. 98; Moorhouse, *Berlin at War*, pp. 320–25; Max Hastings, *Bomber Command* (New York: The Dial Press/James Wade, 1979), pp. 295–309; Hansen, *Fire and Fury*, pp. 141–57 (Hansen places the start of the Battle of Berlin at August 23, 1943); A. C. Grayling, *Among the Dead Cities* (New York: Walker & Company, 2006), pp. 61–64. Grayling points out that "weather conditions were consistently against [Bomber Command's] Berlin forays." Ibid.

November 23, 1943: Web archive of RAF Bomber Command, *webarchive.nationalarchives.gov.uk/20070706011932/www.raf.mod.uk/bombercommand/nov43.html*, accessed April 2, 2014; quote is from Folke Bernadotte, *Instead of Arms*, trans. from Swedish (Stockholm: Bonniers, 1948), pp. 49–54. Bernadotte further relates "an incident . . . which was rather typical of the German mentality, at least . . . during the Hitler regime." Upon exiting the burning Legation, Bernadotte happened upon a fire brigade unable to proceed any further down the bombed-out street, whereupon he asked for their assistance. "[The chief] refused categorically. He had been ordered to extinguish a fire some blocks further on. This and nothing else was his task. . . . Orders were orders. The Legation could go on burning." Ibid., pp. 51–52.

November 24, 1943: Web archive of RAF Bomber Command, *webarchive.nationalarchives.gov.uk/20070706011932/www.raf.mod.uk/bombercommand/nov43.html*, accessed April 2, 2014.

November 26, 1943: Ibid. The food quote is from Moorhouse, *Berlin at War*, p. 94. According to a Berlin resident, "particularly tasty were the crocodiles' tails. . . . Later on, bear ham and bear sausage were a particular delicacy." Ibid.

November 27, 1943: Maurice Smith, "Pathfinder Story," *Flight Magazine*, May 2, 1946, pp. 441–47; May 9, 1946. Re: Phosphorus: Friedman, "The Sachsenhausen Trials," p. 166.

November 29, 1943: Nachtstern and Arntzen, *Counterfeiter*. The quote about Nachtstern's memoir is from the introduction written by Lawrence Malkin, Ibid., p. 24; Malkin, *Krueger's Men*, pp. 10, 69, 95, 116, 190, 195; Jon Kalish, "The Counterfeit Saga(s): What Really Happened at Sachsenhausen?" *The Forward*, June 25, 2008, available online: *forward.com/articles/13635/*, accessed August 27, 2012. The movie "The Counterfeiters," winner of the 2007 Oscar for Best Foreign Language Film, is a fictionalized treatment of Operation Bernhard based loosely on the lives of two real prisoners, Adolf Burger and Salomon Smolianoff. *www.imdb.com/title/tt0813547/awards?ref_=tt_awd*, accessed July 22, 2015.

December 2, 1943: Re: Spinn 18: Marit Greve, interview, October 17, 2012. Re: Student arrests: Gjelsvik, *Resistance*, pp. 112–18; Dahl, *Quisling*, pp. 317–19 (Dahl puts the number of arrests at 1,100); Knudsen, *I Was Quisling's Secretary*, p. 146; Trommer, "Scandinavia and the Turn of the Tide," p. 246 ("about 1,200 arrests"); Frode Færøy, e-mail, May 27, 2012; website of University of Oslo, *www.uio.no/english/about/facts/how-uio-changed-norway/nazis/closed.html*, accessed April 29, 2014; Stein, *Buchenwald Concentration Camp*, p. 175.

December 6, 1943: Morsch, *Murder and Mass Murder*, p. 124; Blatman, *The Death Marches*, p. 43; Jerzy Pindera, *Liebe Mutti: One Man's Struggle to Survive in KZ Sachsenhausen, 1939–1945*, ed. Lynne Taylor (Dallas: University Press of America, 2004) (hereinafter *Liebe Mutti*), pp. 75, 83. Ian Kershaw suggests the cost of maintaining a prisoner may have been as little as eighty *pfennige* a day. Ian Kershaw, *Hitler, the Germans, and the Final Solution* (Jerusalem/New Haven, CT: International Institute for Holocaust Research/Yale University Press, 2008), p. 66. Re: Death certificates: Wachsmann, *KL*, p. 340. Re: Second front: Nøkleby, "Adjusting to Allied Victory," pp. 309–10.

December 8, 1943: Tom Stevenson, *The New Sotheby's Wine Encyclopedia* (New York: DK Publishing, Inc., 1997), p. 93.

December 13, 1943: Website of the Falstad Centre Museum, *falstadsenteret.no/en*, accessed July 4, 2015.

December 14, 1943: Ottosen, *Nordmenn*, pp. 320 (Jacobsen), 228 (Gløersen).

December 15, 1943: Re: Berentzen: Ottosen, *Nordmenn*, p. 114. Re: Berg-Hansen: Ottosen, *Nordmenn*, p. 117. Re: Gåserud: Ottosen, *Nordmenn*, p. 246. Re: Hartvig: Ottosen, *Nordmenn*, p. 271.

December 27, 1943: Re: Poem: Arnulf Overland, *Vi Overlever Alt!* (Oslo: H. Aschehoug & Co., 1945) (in Norwegian), pp. 119–22. Re: Tyburn: Website of Spartacus Educational, *www.spartacus.schoolnet.co.uk/LONtyburn.htm*, accessed June 1, 2011.

January 2, 1944: Ottosen, *Nordmenn*, p. 351.

January 7, 1944: Gilbert, *The Second World War*, p. 567.

January 13, 1944: Pindera, *Liebe Mutti*, p. 58; Friedman, "The Sachsenhausen Trials," pp. 166, 182 n. 67; Open-air exhibition "Stones for 'Germania'—Shells for 'Final Victory'" at Sachsenhausen Memorial.

January 21, 1944: Re: Bombing: Salmaggi and Pallavisini, *2194 Days of War*, p. 476. Re: Appointments: Ibid.; Michael Korda, *Ike: An American Hero* (New York: Harper, 2007), pp. 430–32; Carlo D'Este, *Eisenhower: A Soldier's Life* (New York: Henry Holt and Company, 2002), pp. 469–70.

January 30, 1944: Re: Bombing: Web archive of RAF Bomber Command, *webarchive.nationalarchive.gov.uk/20070706011932/www.raf.mod.uk/bombercommand/jan44.html*, accessed May 6, 2014. Re: Fridtjof Nansen: Nansen, *Farthest North*, p. 144.

February 5, 1944: Lie, *Night and Fog*, pp. 140–41; Ottosen, *Nordmenn*, p. 411.

February 12, 1944: Re: M&B tablets: Marit Greve, e-mail, June 14, 2012. Re: Churchill: Milton Wainwright, "How Two Antimicrobials Altered the History of the Modern World," *Microbiology Today*, February 2007, pp. 16–18; Max Hastings, *Winston's War* (New York: Alfred A. Knopf, 2010), p. 353.

February 24, 1944: Astrid Ley and Günter Morsch, *Medical Care: The Infirmary at Sachsenhausen*

Concentration Camp 1936–1945, trans. Richard Toovey (Berlin: Metropol Verlag, 2013) (hereinafter *Medical Care*), pp. 338–61.

March 16, 1944: Re: Daylight raids: Donald Miller, *Masters of the Air* (New York: Simon & Schuster, 2007), pp. 271–74; Roberts, *The Storm of War*, p. 450; Speer's biographer (Joachim Fest) is quoted in Hansen, *Fire and Fury*, p. 177; Moorhouse, *Berlin at War*, p. 348. Moorhouse quotes a Berlin diarist concerning the differences between the British and American raids: "In contrast to the British night raids, which usually last for about forty-five minutes, the American daylight raids go on for two or three hours. Whereas the British prefer to attack on dark nights and in bad weather, the Americans like daylight and clear skies . . . [.] The British drop their bombs quickly and at random—'carpet bombing' is their specialty—while the Americans prefer to take their time and make two or three trial runs over the target before releasing their bombs." Ibid. Re: *Industriehof*: Pindera, *Liebe Mutti*, p. 83; quote is from Morsch, *Murder and Mass Murder*, pp. 16, 28.

March 23, 1944: Moorhouse, *Berlin at War*, pp. 324–25; quote is from Hastings, *Bomber Command*, p. 309.

March 27, 1944: Dear, *Oxford Companion*, pp. 726–27; Website of Ravensbrück Memorial, *www. ravensbrueck.de/mgr/neu/english/index.htm*, accessed October 28, 2011; USHMM website, *www. ushmm.org/wlc/en/article.php?ModuleId=10005199*, accessed April 11, 2011; Suhren escaped from British custody in November 1946 just as the first (of seven) Hamburg Ravensbrück trial was to commence. Captured by the Americans after three years on the run, he was turned over to French authorities who were conducting their own trials of Ravensbrück personnel (the British trials having all concluded). The French condemned him to death and executed him in June 1950. Michael J. Bazyler and Frank M. Tuerkheimer, *Forgotten Trials of the Holocaust* (New York: New York University Press, 2014), pp. 129–37.

April 10, 1944: Ottosen, *Nordmenn*, p. 262.

April 12, 1944: Ian Kershaw, *The End: The Defiance and Destruction of Hitler's Germany, 1944–1945* (New York: Penguin Press, 2011) (hereinafter *The End*), p. 79; the quote is from Avraham Krakowski and Avraham Yaakov Finkel, *Counterfeit Lives* (New York: C.I.S. Publishers, 1994), p. 199.

April 19, 1944: Re: Heinkel: Alexander Jossifidis, "Oranienburg [*Heinkel-Werke*]," in Megargee, *USHMM Encyclopedia*, pp. 1333–34; Morsch, *Murder and Mass Murder*, p. 124; Blatman, *The Death Marches*, pp. 43–44; Pindera, *Liebe Mutti*, pp. 107–10; the website of the Sachsenhausen Memorial, *www.stiftung-bg.de/gums/en/*, accessed August 17, 2014. Re: Blood donation: Ley and Morsch, *Medical Care*, pp. 108–12. Re: Herz As: Pindera, *Liebe Mutti*, p. 96.

May 6, 1944: Günter Morsch and Astrid Ley, ed., *Sachsenhausen Concentration Camp 1936–1945 Events and Developments*, trans. Richard Toovey (Berlin: Metropol Verlag, 2013), pp. 38, 42; Morsch, *Murder and Mass Murder*, pp. 24, 98; Sofsky, *The Order of Terror*, pp. 177, 187, 327 n. 21; Friedman, "The Sachsenhausen Trials," pp. 162, 167, 181 n. 47. The quote is from Moorhouse, *Berlin at War*, p. 242. See also website of Sachsenhausen International Committee, *www. internationales-sachsenhausen-komitee.eu/content/ueberuns_uk.htm*, accessed May 14, 2013.

May 8, 1944: *Site Tour "Topography of Terror": History of the Site*, trans. Pamela E. Selwyn and Toby Axelrod (Berlin: Stiftung Topographie des Terrors, 2010), pp. 65, 73; the quote is from Moorhouse, *Berlin at War*, pp. 230, 235. Himmler took over control of the Gestapo in 1934.

May 16, 1944: Ottosen, *Nordmenn*, p. 681; *The Wisconsin Engineer* 50, no. 5 (January 1946): p. 11; in 1936 Aanesen was granted a US patent for an "apparatus for sticking strips on to continuously moving webs of paper and the like." US Patent No. 2,062,280.

May 28, 1944: *www.phrases.org.uk/meanings/271100.html*, accessed April 19, 2011.

June 6, 1944: Keegan, *The Second World War*, pp. 369–89; Weinberg, *A World at Arms*, pp. 686–95; Roberts, *The Storm of War*, pp. 461–78; Hastings, *Inferno*, pp. 513–21.

June 8, 1944: Re: Gestapo commission: Morsch, *Murder and Mass Murder*, pp. 114–16. Re: Demoted Kapos: Sofsky, *The Order of Terror*, p. 314 n. 19.

June 10, 1944: Ottosen, *Nordmenn*, p. 477.

June 17, 1944: Benjamin King and Timothy Kutta, *Impact: The History of Germany's V-Weapons in World War II* (Rockville Centre, NY: Sarpedon, 1998), pp. 1–3, 222–23, 242, 309–29; Roy Irons, *Hitler's Terror Weapons: The Price of Vengeance* (London: HarperCollins, 2003), pp. 114–26, 167–95. Michael Neufeld makes a compelling case that the Nazis' "rocket program built an institution and a weapon that made little sense, given the Reich's limited research resources and industrial capacity—a perfect symbol of the Nazis' pursuit of irrational goals with rational, technocratic means." Michael Neufeld, *The Rocket and the Reich* (New York: The Free Press, 1995), p. 278. In a compelling coda to Neufeld's analysis, he points out that more people [i.e., concentration camp prisoners] died producing the V-2 than died being hit by it. Quoted in Wachsmann, *KL*, p. 454.

June 27, 1944: Re: Okselenko: Morsch, *Murder and Mass Murder*, pp. 108–12. Re: Diels: Quoted in Philip Metcalfe, *1933* (Sag Harbor, NY: Permanent Press, 1988), p. 240. Sofsky has observed, "Public corporal punishment was a stage presentation of absolute power. Thousands were compelled to watch as their fellow prisoners, initially reduced to total defenselessness, were then forced to lie in a humiliating position and flogged. The helplessness of the victims symbolized the powerlessness of the entire prisoner society. The shameful ordeal was aimed against not only the delinquent prisoners, but the onlooking public as well. It was meant to deter, intimidate, humiliate, and degrade." *The Order of Terror*, p. 219.

July 22, 1944: Shirer, *Rise and Fall*, pp. 1028–82.

July 25, 1944: Website of the Internet Movie Database, *www.imdb.com/name/nm0709680/*, accessed May 8, 2014.

July 30, 1944: The quote regarding Warsaw's destruction is from Norman Davies, *Rising '44: The Battle for Warsaw* (New York: Viking, 2004), p. 437; the quotes regarding the outcome of the battle are from Weinberg, *A World at Arms*, pp. 709–11. The quote re: Carthage is from Alexandra Richie, *Warsaw 1944* (New York: Farrar, Straus and Giroux, 2013), pp. 648–49.

August 10, 1944: Shirer, *Rise and Fall*, pp. 1028, 1035, 1070–71; Wistrich, *Who's Who*, pp. 152–53; Höppner quoted in Bessel, *Nazism and War*, p. 114.

August 12, 1944: Re: *Stehkommando*: Friedman, "The Sachsenhausen Trials," pp. 163–67, 181 n. 47; USHMM website, *digitalassets.ushmm.org/photoarchives/detail.aspx?id=1099381*, accessed May 4, 2012. Re: Brothel: USHMM website, *www.ushmm.org/wlc/en/article.php?ModuleId=10005199*, accessed April 11, 2011; Ley and Morsch, *Medical Care*, pp. 180–81. The first camp brothel was opened in June 1942 in Mauthausen. Wachsmann, *KL*, p. 412. Baumkötter was sentenced to life imprisonment in 1947 by a Soviet tribunal but released in 1956 as a "non-amnestied war criminal"; returned to Germany, he was retried in 1962 and convicted of accessory to murder and sentenced to eight years, with credit given for time served. Friedman, "The Sachsenhausen Trials," pp. 162–72, 182 n. 66; Ley and Morsch, *Medical Care*, pp. 188–90. Baumkötter died in 2001, age eighty-nine.

August 25, 1944: Mark Axworthy, *Third Axis Fourth Ally* (London: Arms and Armour, 1995), pp. 22–27, 175–83, 198–209.

September 4, 1944: Re: Finland: D. G. Kirby, *Finland in the Twentieth Century* (London: C. Hurst & Company, 1979), pp. 129–47. Re: German casualties: Kershaw, *The End*, p. 379.

September 7, 1944: Friedman, "The Sachsenhausen Trials," pp. 163–68. According to author Jonathan Friedman, Sakowski presents a "truly disturbing case." Far from being a fanatical Nazi, Sakowski had fought in Spain against Franco. Offered the job of hangman in return for better living conditions, however, Sakowski "readily accepted." Ibid., p. 166. Another Sachsenhausen prisoner, Jerzy Pindera, recalled a different kind of botched hanging: A Russian prisoner was once led to the gallows, only to protest that the execution order from Himmler referred to someone else with the same name, but with a different birthdate. "After a few, very long minutes, the *Rapportführer* made his decision. He ordered that the execution of the prisoner at the gallows proceed. Then he ordered that the correct prisoner be brought to the gallows, had Himmler's order read for the second time and ordered the second prisoner hanged. The corpses of both prisoners were put in the same coffin." Pindera, *Liebe Mutti*, p. 72.

September 13, 1944: Salmaggi and Pallavisini, *2194 Days of War*, p. 583.

September 18, 1944: Re: West Wall: J. E. Kauffmann and Robert Jurga, *Fortress Europe: European Fortifications of World War II*, trans. H. W. Kaufmann (Cambridge, MA: Da Capo Press, 2002), pp. 62–63, 74–76. Re: Market Garden: Salmaggi and Pallavisini, *2194 Days of War*, pp. 588–89; Cornelius Ryan, *A Bridge Too Far* (New York: Simon & Schuster, 1974); Gilbert, *The Second World War*, p. 689.

September 30, 1944: Robert James, ed., *Churchill Speaks: 1897–1963* (New York: Barnes & Noble Books, 1998), pp. 834–35. In the same speech Churchill also observed, "[T]o get the nations out of their terrible frenzy of hate, to build up something like a human world and a humane world—it is that [which] makes it so indispensable for us to struggle to shorten, be it even by a day, the course of this terrible war." Ibid.

October 5, 1944: Sofsky, *The Order of Terror*, p. 209; website of the Centers for Disease Control and Prevention, *www.nc.cdc.gov/travel/yellowbook/2014/chapter-3-infectious-diseases-related-to-travel/rickettsial-spotted-and-typhus-fevers-and-related-infections-anaplasmosis-and-ehrlichiosis*, accessed May 22, 2014; website of World Health Organization, *www.who.int/ith/diseases/typhusfever/en/*, accessed May 22, 2014.

October 13, 1944: Re: Aachen: Dear, *Oxford Companion*, p. 1. Kershaw, *The End*, p. 91; see also the photo of Aachen following p. 230.

October 19, 1944: Re: *Volkssturm*: Kershaw, *The End*, pp. 86, 106. Re: Kernke: Friedman, "The Sachsenhausen Trials," p. 170.

October 22, 1944: Re: Höhn: Morsch, *Murder and Mass Murder*, p. 134; Friedman, "The Sachsenhausen Trials," pp. 162–73. Morsch states that Höhn's initial sentence was twenty-five years hard labor, not life. Re: Kolb: Morsch, *Murder and Mass Murder*, p. 112; Friedman, "The Sachsenhausen Trials," pp. 171, 182. Friedman refers to the Ukrainian prisoner as "Wassilenko" and Morsch as "Vassily Okselenko," although from the descriptions of the prisoner's infraction and subsequent punishment it is clear that they are referring to the same person.

November 6, 1944: Chris Bishop, ed., *The Encyclopedia of Weapons of World War II* (New York: Barnes & Noble Books, 1998), p. 208.

November 8, 1944: Marit Greve, e-mail, June 30, 2014.

November 9, 1944: Kogon, *The Theory and Practice of Hell*, p. 34.

November 11, 1944: Marit Greve, e-mail, May 30, 2013.

November 13, 1944: Re: Auschwitz: Sofsky, *The Order of Terror*, pp. 251, 262; USHMM website, *www.ushmm.org/wlc/en/article.php?ModuleId=10005189*, accessed August 28, 2012; website of the Auschwitz-Birkenau Memorial and Museum, *en.auschwitz.org/h/index.php?option=com_content&task=view&id=6&Itemid=6*, accessed August 28, 2012; Charles Sydnor, "Auschwitz I Main Camp," trans. Franciszek Piper; Gerard Majka, "Auschwitz II-Birkenau Main Camp"; Florian Schmaltz, "Auschwitz III-Monowitz Main Camp [aka Buna]," in Megargee, *USHMM Encyclopedia*, pp. 204–20; Raul Hilberg, "Auschwitz," in Laqueur, *The Holocaust Encyclopedia*, pp. 32–44. Re: Wolfberg: Abrahamsen, *Norway's Response*, p. 131.

November 16, 1944: Re: Shotland Family: Ottosen, *Nordmenn*, p. 565; website of the Yad Vashem Central Database of Shoah Victim's Names, *db.yadvashem.org/names/nameResults.html?lastName=shotland&lastNameType=THESAURUS&place=tromso++Norway&placeType=THESAURUS&language=en*, accessed July 3, 2015. Re: Kaplan (also known as Caplan) Family: Ottosen,

Nordmenn, p. 155; website of the Yad Vashem Central Database of Shoah Victim's Names, *db.yadvashem.org/names/nameResults.html?lastName=caplan&lastNameType=THESAURUS&pl ace=tromso&placeType=THESAURUS&language=en,* accessed July 3, 2015. Re: Konrad Kaplan: Ottosen, *Nordmenn,* p. 155; Odd Nansen, *Tommy* (unpublished English translation by Christopher Smallwood), pp. 37–38, 119. Re: Trains: Wachsmann, *KL,* p. 457. Re: Sonnenburg: Kaspar Nürnberg, "Sonnenburg," trans. Stephen Pallavicini, in Megargee, *USHMM Encyclopedia,* pp. 163–66; website of the Museum of Martyrdom Victims Sonnenburg Camp, *www.slonsk.pl/ asp/pl_start.asp?type=14&menu=69* (in Polish), accessed June 10, 2014.

November 17, 1944: Re: Bjerkeng: Ottosen, *Nordmenn,* p. 126; Marit Bjerkeng (Bjerkeng's daughter), e-mails, June 3, 2014, and July 4, 2014. According to Shirer "the People's Court . . . soon became the most dreaded tribunal in the land. . . . One got the impression . . . that most of the unfortunate defendants . . . received a death sentence." *Rise and Fall,* p. 269. Re: Utvik: Ottosen, *Nordmenn,* p. 644; website of North Karmoy Historical Society, *www.n-kh.no/index. php?s=artikkel&artid=100* (in Norwegian), accessed May 9, 2011. Re: Holt: Ottosen, *Nordmenn,* p. 300.

November 21, 1944: Re: SA: Shirer, *Rise and Fall,* pp. 38, 42, 219–22. Re: Experiments: Ley and Morsch, *Medical Care,* pp. 365–70; Wachsmann, *KL,* p. 435.

December 20, 1944: Kershaw, *The End,* pp. 155–60; Murray and Millett, *A War to Be Won,* pp. 463–71; Roberts, *The Storm of War,* pp. 503–10; quote is from Keegan, *The Second World War,* p. 447.

January 17, 1945: Re: Looters: Morsch, *Murder and Mass Murder,* p. 209; the quote is from Moorhouse, *Berlin at War,* pp. 118, 130–34. Re: Shoe testers: Ley and Morsch, *Medical Care,* pp. 362–65; the first quote is from James, *Moonless Night,* p. 123; Friedman, "The Sachsenhausen Trials," pp. 163, 168; the second quote is from Moorhouse, *Berlin at War,* p. 243. Re: Prisoners imitating the SS: Sofsky, *The Order of Terror,* p. 313 n. 15. Re: *Völkischer Beobachter:* Shirer, *Rise and Fall,* pp. 42, 49, 1141–43. Re: Bad Saarow: Andreas Weigelt, "Bad Saarow," trans. Stephen Pallavicini, in Megargee, *USHMM Encyclopedia,* pp. 1265–66; Wachsmann, *KL,* p. 466; William L. Shirer, *Twentieth Century Journey: The Nightmare Years 1930–1940* (Boston: Little, Brown and Company, 1984), p. 161.

January 19, 1945: Kershaw, *The End,* pp. 167–76; Blatman, *The Death Marches,* pp. 73–74.

January 25, 1945: Dr. Horst Seferens, Brandenburg Memorial Foundation, e-mail, December 16, 2014; Mazower observes, "By early 1945, there were more than 700,000 inmates, and some 40,000 guards, in twenty badly overcrowded major camps and another 165 SS-run labour [*sic*] camps." *Hitler's Empire,* pp. 307–8.

February 1, 1945: Bessel, *Nazism and War,* p. 166.

February 2, 1945: Nansen, *Tommy,* pp. 99–106.

February 3, 1945: Re: British soldiers at Sachsenhausen: Gilbert, *The Second World War,* pp. 493, 739; Macksey, *Godwin's Saga,* pp. 101–41. Macksey states that Godwin's crew was only able to survive its ordeal in the SK with the "food which continued to be provided by [the] Norwegians, who went on caring about the British as if they were of their own people." Ibid., p. 129; Blatman, *The Death Marches,* pp. 126–27; Morsch, *Murder and Mass Murder,* pp. 136–38; James, *Moonless Night,* p. 162; *Sunday Mirror,* November 11, 2001, found online at *www.thefreelibrary/com/_/print/PrintArticle.aspx?id=79940224,* accessed March 9, 2012; the website of the Commando Veterans Association, w*ww.commandoveterans.org/cdoGallery/v/ WW2/Operation+Checkmate/,* accessed March 9, 2012, and *www.commandoveterans.org/ cdoForum/posts/list/832.page,* accessed April 1, 2013; *British Navy News,* February 2011, p. 25; a photo of the memorial can be found at: *en.wikipedia.org/wiki/File:Sachsenhausen_memorial.jpg,* accessed March 9, 2012. For his "great gallantry and inspiring example" John Godwin received a posthumous Mention in Despatches. Re: Flossenburg: Todd Huebner, "Flossenbürg," in Megargee, *USHMM Encyclopedia,* pp. 559–65; USHMM website, *www.*

ushmm.org/wlc/en/article.php?ModuleId=10005537, accessed April 2, 2012. Re: Bergen-Belsen: Wachsmann, *KL*, pp. 335, 337; Thomas Rahe, "Bergen-Belsen," trans. Stephen Pallavicini, in Megargee, *USHMM Encyclopedia*, pp. 277–81; Blatman, *The Death Marches*, pp. 132–35; Wistrich, *Who's Who*, p. 178; USHMM website, *www.ushmm.org/wlc/en/article.php?ModuleId=10005224*, accessed February 10, 2012. Re: Himmler's order: Kershaw, *The End*, pp. 228–30, 330.

February 4, 1945: Persson, *Escape*, pp. 67–70.

February 6, 1945: Kershaw, *The End*, pp. 190–91, 236; Moorhouse, *Berlin at War*, pp. xv, 333, 356 (quote is on p. xv). For information on Berlin, see Hansen, *Fire and Fury*, pp. 103, 150; James, *Moonless Night*, p. 167 n.1. The total tonnage dropped on Berlin was 42 percent greater than the next highest city (Cologne). Richard Overy, *The Bombers and the Bombed* (New York: Viking, 2013), p. 301.

February 8, 1945: Macksey, *Godwin's Saga*, pp. 138–44. Macksey puts Mayor's death at April 11, 1945, but the Commonwealth War Graves Commission lists it as April 7, 1945, which I have used. See the website of the War Graves Commission, *www.cwgc.org/find-war-dead/casualty/2463774/*, accessed April 1, 2013. Apparently at least one other Englishman survived the executions of February 2, 1945: John Starr, an SOE agent who had been captured in France. Starr was not housed in the SK with Godwin's crew, and so was overlooked. When he was later summoned to the SK, Jacob, the *Blockältester* who had helped Tommy Buergenthal and Keith Mayor, also convinced Starr to slip into a column then leaving Sachsenhausen for Mauthausen. Starr survived this camp as well and returned to England after the war. His story is told in Jean Overton Fuller's *The Starr Affair* (London: Victor Gollancz Ltd., 1954). Starr, like Macksey, attributes the ability of the British prisoners to survive in Sachsenhausen to the food shared with them by the Norwegians. Ibid., p. 112.

February 11, 1945: Morsch, *Murder and Mass Murder*, p. 146; Blatman, *The Death Marches*, pp. 164–65; Andreas Weigelt, "Lieberose [aka 'Liro']," trans. Stephen Pallavicini, in Megargee, *USHMM Encyclopedia*, pp. 1325–27; Morsch and Ley, *Sachsenhausen Concentration Camp 1936–1945*, p. 127; Wachsmann, *KL*, p. 557.

February 12, 1945: Moorhouse, *Berlin at War*, pp. 115, 178–79. Peter Wyden, *Stella* (New York: Simon & Schuster, 1992), p. 102 (quoting in part testimony of Hildegard Henschel, wife of Moritz Henschel, the last head of the Berlin Jewish community, at the trial of Adolf Eichmann). Between October 1941 and the summer of 1943 between three and four thousand German Jews slated for deportation committed suicide; toward the latter part of the deportation process upwards of 10 percent of Berlin's Jews awaiting deportation resorted to suicide. Dan McMillan, *How Could This Happen: Explaining the Holocaust* (New York: Basic Books, 2014), pp. 188–89. Even those who had escaped the Nazis turned to Veronal in their despair, among them one of the most popular writers of the 1920s and 1930s, Stefan Zweig, who along with his wife ended his life with Veronal on February 23, 1942, in Petropolis, Brazil. George Prochnik, *The Impossible Exile* (New York: Other Press, 2014), pp. 345–48. Of course there were other methods for taking one's own life. On the evening of March 19, 1938, William L. Shirer and Edward R. Murrow found themselves in a quiet bar in Berlin. Murrow suggested a change of scene—the previous evening in the same bar he had witnessed a "Jewish-looking fellow" pull an old-fashioned razor from his pocket and slash his throat. William L. Shirer, *Berlin Diary* (New York: Alfred A. Knopf, 1941), p. 109.

February 14, 1945: Re: Helland-Hansen: Huntford, *Nansen*, p. 493.

February 15, 1945: Re: Teeth: Morsch, *Murder and Mass Murder*, pp. 36, 42, 67. Re: Wolfberg: Persson, *Escape*, p. 35; website of Document.no, *www.document.no/2011/03/m%C3%B8te-med-norsk-j%C3%B8de/* (in Swedish), accessed December 20, 2011; book review of *Escape*, *www.*

olalarsmo.com/bernadotte.htm (in Norwegian), accessed December 20, 2011; website of Edition HH, *www.editionhh.co.uk/ab_pjh.htm*, accessed March 8, 2011.

February 16, 1945: Nansen, *Tommy*, p. 106.

February 18, 1945: Ottosen, *Nordmenn*, p. 681.

February 19, 1945: Thomas Buergenthal, *A Lucky Child* (New York: Little, Brown and Company, 2009), pp. 38–66. Buergenthal's father, as noted, was born in Poland, not Slovakia; he had relocated to Ľubochňa, Slovakia (from Germany where he was then living) shortly after the Nazi's seizure of power in 1933. See also Nansen, *Tommy*, pp. 5–25. In an e-mail on January 15, 2015, Thomas Buergenthal noted that the date and location of his father's death is based on new information which has come to light since *A Lucky Child* was first published. Information on the Kielce Ghetto and the fate of its inhabitants can be found in Marek Maciagowski, *People to People* (Kielce, Poland: Jan Karski Society, 2009), which can be found online at the website of the Jan Karski Society, *en.jankarski.org.pl/images/2014/people.pdf*, accessed July 9, 2015.

February 20, 1945: Re: Bunker Block: Friedman, "The Sachsenhausen Trials," pp. 163–74, 182; the quote is from James, *Moonless Night*, pp. 147–58. Eugen Kogon writes, "I am not exaggerating when I say that a separate book would have to be written on the concentration camp prisons, called 'Bunker.' It would be a bloodcurdling collection of documents." *The Theory and Practice of Hell*, p. 225. B. A. James writes, "The full extent of the atrocities committed during the years . . . Eccarius was in charge will never be known, because few prisoners incarcerated therein ever lived to tell the tale." *Moonless Night*, p. 212.

February 22, 1945: Open-air exhibition "Stones for 'Germania'—Shells for 'Final Victory'" at Sachsenhausen Memorial.

February 25, 1945: Re: Steenstrup: NBL website, *nbl.snl.no/Hjalmar_Steenstrup* (by Inger Døving), accessed July 15, 2015. Re: Neuengamme: website of the Neuengamme Concentration Camp Memorial, *www.kz-gedenkstaette-neuengamme.de/index.php?id=20*, accessed May 16, 2011; Hermann Kaienburg, "Neuengamme Main Camp," trans. Stephen Pallavicini, in Megargee, *USHMM Encyclopedia*, pp. 1073–81. Re: Bernadotte: Persson, *Escape*, pp. 7, 72; Ralph Hewins, *Count Folke Bernadotte: His Life and Work* (Minneapolis: T. S. Denison & Company, 1950), p. 90; Folke Bernadotte, *Last Days of the Reich* (London: Frontline Books, 2009), pp. 9–22 (introduction by Sune Persson); see generally, Bernadotte, *Instead of Arms*. The chairman of the Swedish Red Cross was Bernadotte's uncle, Prince Carl, who was more than eighty years old at the time. Bernadotte's wedding to Estelle Manville was attended by 1,500 guests; when Estelle's father, Hiram Manville, died in 1944, age seventy-one, he was described as one of the wealthiest men in America. The *Milwaukee Journal*, June 27, 1944, p. 1 col. 2. Johns-Manville, the company he founded, filed bankruptcy in 1982 in the face of overwhelming asbestos-related lawsuits; it is now a wholly owned subsidiary of Warren Buffet's Berkshire Hathaway Inc. The impetus behind Bernadotte's initiation of negotiations were rumors that all camp inmates would be liquidated before they could be liberated by Allied forces, as well as the urgings of Norwegian diplomat Niels Christian Ditleff, who was stationed in Sweden during the war. At the time of Bernadotte's assassination the Stern Gang was led by Yitzhak Shamir, who later became the prime minister of Israel (1983–1984; 1986–1992). Regarding Bernadotte's murder, Kati Marton writes, "[N]ot one of the hit team would ever spend a night in jail or face a court of justice." Kati Marton, *A Death in Jerusalem* (New York: Pantheon Books, 1994), p. 240. Bernadotte's aide Ralph Bunche succeeded in negotiating an armistice between Israel and its Arab neighbors in 1949, for which he received the Nobel Peace Prize in 1950. In 1995 foreign minister Shimon Peres apologized to Sweden on behalf of Israel for the murder.

February 26, 1945: Buergenthal, *A Lucky Child*, p. 96; Alexander Jossifidis, "Oranienburg [*Heinkel-Werke*]," in Megargee, *USHMM Encyclopedia*, pp. 1333–34.

February 27, 1945: Nansen, *Tommy*, pp. 114–15.

March 4, 1945: USHMM website, *www.ushmm.org/wlc/en/article.php?ModuleId=10007773*, accessed July 1, 2014.

March 5, 1945: The story of how Buergenthal and Nansen found each other after the war is wonderfully told in Buergenthal, *A Lucky Child*, pp. 176–84.

March 9, 1945: Kershaw, *The End*, pp. 254, 258; USHMM website, *www.ushmm.org/learn/timeline-of-events/1942-1945/remagen*, accessed July 9, 2015.

March 16, 1945: Alexander Jossifidis, "Oranienburg [*Auer-Werke*]," in Megargee, *USHMM Encyclopedia*, pp. 1332–33; Hansen, *Fire and Fury*, p. 286. Richard Overy uses the same figure but suggests these estimates may be overinflated. Overy, *The Bombers and the Bombed*, pp. 206–7.

March 18, 1945: Website of the Swedish Red Cross, *www.redcross.se/om-oss/historik/vita-bussarna/* (in Swedish), accessed December 15, 2011; Persson, *Escape*, pp. 247–49; Sune Persson, "Folke Bernadotte and the White Buses," in *'Bystanders' to the Holocaust: A Re-evaluation*, ed. David Cesarani and Paul Levine (New York: Frank Cass, 2002) (hereinafter *Re-evaluation*), p. 243. See in general Bernadotte, *The Curtain Falls*, for a summary of all events related to the white buses operation. The book was a bestseller upon publication, although Bernadotte was subsequently criticized by some for exaggerating his role in the mission, especially a blistering attack by historian H. R. Trevor-Roper, who accused Bernadotte of being a "transport officer, nothing more." H. R. Trevor-Roper, "Kersten, Himmler, and Count Bernadotte," *The Atlantic Monthly*, February 1953, pp. 43–45. Much of the factual bases for Trevor-Roper's conclusions have since been discredited, and a more reasoned consensus credits Bernadotte with playing a major role in the success of the mission, but concludes he also perhaps claimed more credit for himself than was justified by the facts. Persson, *Escape*, p. 72; Amitzur Ilan, *Bernadotte in Palestine, 1948* (New York: St. Martin's Press, 1989), pp. 25, 38, 43.

March 21, 1945: Pindera, *Liebe Mutti*, p. 45.

March 24, 1945: Re Neuengamme deaths: Persson, *Escape*, p. 123; Nansen, *Tommy*, p. 120. Re: Natzweiler prisoner: Lie, *Night and Fog*, p. 207. Re: Porta: Joseph Robert White, "Porta Westfalica/A II Barkhausen [aka Porta I, Kaiserhof], Lerbeck-Neesen, Hausberge 'Hammerwerke,'" in Megargee, *USHMM Encyclopedia*, pp. 1166–68. Re: Dachau: Barbara Distel, "Dachau Main Camp," trans. Stephen Pallavicini, in Megargee, *USHMM Encyclopedia*, pp. 442–50.

March 25, 1945: Re: Mauthausen: Robert G. Waite, "Mauthausen," in Megargee, *USHMM Encyclopedia*, pp. 900–903; Robert Abzug, *Inside the Vicious Heart* (New York: Oxford University Press, 1985), pp. 106–7.

March 31, 1945: Re: Løberg: Ottosen, *Nordmenn*, p. 426; NBL website, *nbl.snl.no/Sverre_L%C3%B8berg* (by Lars Hellberg), accessed July 15, 2015. Re: Canossa: Ian Kershaw, *Hitler, 1889–1936: Hubris* (New York: W. W. Norton & Company, Inc., 1999), p. 262. Re: Bernadotte: The first quote is in Persson, *Escape*, p. 148, and the second quote is in Bernadotte, *The Curtain Falls*, pp. 81–82. Re: Rundberg: Persson, *Escape*, pp. 86, 148; "The White Buses" report by the Swedish Red Cross, found at *harbourofhope.com/wp-content/uploads/2012/06/HoHTheWhiteBuses.pdf*, accessed July 3, 2014. Re: Thumann: Blatman, *The Death Marches*, p. 162; website of the Holocaust Research Project, *www.holocaustresearchproject.org/othercamps/majdanek.html*, accessed December 27, 2011.

April 1, 1945: Re: Trzebinski and Pauly: Günther Schwarberg, *The Murders at Bullenhuser Damm*, trans. Erna Baber Rosenfeld with Alvin H. Rosenfeld (Bloomington: Indiana University Press, 1984) (hereinafter *Bullenhuser*), pp. 37–45, 92–106, 150–53; the Rundberg quote is found on p. 32.

April 3, 1945: Günter Morsch, "Formation and Construction of the Sachsenhausen Concentration Camp," in *From Sachsenburg to Sachsenhausen*, ed. Günter Morsch (Berlin: Metropol Verlag,

2007), p. 183. Some believe "kapo" derived from the Italian "*capo*" meaning "boss," while others believe it derived from the German "*Kameradschaftpolizei*" or "police comrade."

April 7, 1945: Re: Vogt-Svendsen: Persson, *Escape*, pp. 39–40, 81, 169; Hiltgunt Zassenhaus, *Walls: Resisting the Third Reich—One Woman's Story* (Boston: Beacon Press, 1974). Zassenhaus writes, "[W]henever a prisoner could not be located, my file gave the answer." Ibid., p. 246; see also Sim, *Women at War*, pp. 175–221. Re: Halvorsen: Ottosen, *Nordmenn*, p. 252; NBL website, *nbl.snl.no/Asbj%C3%B8rn_Halvorsen* (by Per Jorsett), accessed July 8, 2014.

April 8, 1945: Website of the Anne Frank House Museum, *www.annefrank.org/ImageVaultFiles/id_17535/cf_21/one-day-simply-weren.pdf*, accessed July 9, 2015.

April 10, 1945: Website of The Children of Bullenhuser Damm Association, *www.kinder-vom-bullenhuser-damm.de/_english/the_story.html*, accessed April 19, 2015; website of the Neuengamme Concentration Camp, *www.kz-gedenkstaette-neuengamme.de/en/exhibitions/bullenhuser-damm/*, accessed April 19, 2015; Schwarberg, *Bullenhuser*, pp. 107–19; the quote regarding Heissmeyer's experiments is on p. 116 and his testimony is on p. 114. Georges-André's story is related in Susan Zuccotti, *The Holocaust, the French, and the Jews* (New York: Basic Books, 1993), pp. 202–3, and in more detail in Jeremy Josephs, *Swastika Over Paris* (New York: Arcade Publishing, 1989), which is dedicated to Georges-André Kohn. Of the Kohn family members who remained on the train, only the father Armand survived; his wife and twenty-two-year-old daughter died in Bergen-Belsen and his mother died in Auschwitz. Armand died in 1962 without ever learning Georges' fate. During the war Nazi doctors conducted experiments on more than twenty thousand prisoners; several thousand died in the process or shortly thereafter, others were murdered to hide the crime, and still others suffered lifelong disabilities as a result of their experience. Wachsmann, *KL*, p. 429.

April 18, 1945: Pindera, *Liebe Mutti*, p. 55.

April 19, 1945: Re: Bernadotte: Dahl, *Quisling*, p. 359. Re: White Buses: Bernadotte, *The Curtain Falls*, pp. 96–98; Cesarani and Levine, *Re-evaluation*, p. 247; the quote is from Blatman, *The Death Marches*, p. 162. According to Bernadotte, the impetus behind Himmler's decision to allow the total evacuation (after just having ordered no further transports of any kind) was the negative publicity surrounding the liberation of Buchenwald and Bergen-Belsen, which occurred only days earlier. Re: Fridtjof Nansen: quote is in Huntford, *Nansen*, p. 501.

April 20, 1945: Website of the Places of Remembrance 1933–1945, *orte-de-erinnerung.de/de/en/institutions/institutions_liste/death_march_memorial_site_in_the_below_forest/*, accessed July 8, 2014; Blatman, *The Death Marches*, pp. 165–66; Buergenthal, *A Lucky Child*, pp. 104–14.

April 27–28, 1945: Re: Møgelkær: Persson, *Escape*, p. 193. Re: Liberation: Müller's quote is found in Primo Levi, *The Drowned and the Saved*, trans. Raymond Rosenthal (New York: Summit Books, 1988), p. 72 [Müller wrote a memoir titled *Eyewitness Auschwitz: Three Years in the Gas Chambers* (New York: Stein and Day, 1979)]. Re: Cappelen: Cesarani and Levine, *Re-evaluation*, p. 264; Cappelen's testimony (January 29, 1946) can be found in the Proceedings of the International Military Tribunal, vol. 6, pp. 278–87, and can be accessed online as part of the Avalon Project of the Yale Law School at: *Avalon.law.yale.edu/imt/01-29-46.asp#cappelen*, accessed November 29, 2011. Re: Odd Nansen's return: Marit Greve, e-mail, March 30, 2015.

Countless books have attempted to explain the phenomena of Hitler, the Nazis, and Germany in World War II. One of the most succinct is offered by historian Francois Kersaudy: "Few destinies can be as amazing as that of the homeless, unemployed painter from Vienna who, in less than two decades, had made himself the absolute master of Germany. He had certainly been powerfully helped by the rancours [*sic*] of defeat, the fear of communism, a devastating economic crisis, the near-sightedness of the big German industrialists and the ineptitude of his political rivals. Yet none of the above would suffice to explain this solitary, uncultured and unbalanced Austrian's meteoric rise to power, unless one were to take into account his fanatical singleness of purpose, high degree of opportunism, and complete lack of scruples, added to an astonishing personal magnetism, undeniable talents both as an actor and as a stage manager, and of course an unrivalled ability to browbeat and paralyse [*sic*] through an expertly balanced combination of secrecy, surprise, verbal abuse and concentrated violence." *Norway 1940*, p. 37.

Postscript: Re: Sins of children: Quoted in Buergenthal, *A Lucky Child*, p. 187. Re: Politicians, etc.: website of the Nobel Prize, *www.nobelprize.org/nobel_prizes/peace/laureates/1922/nansen-lecture. html*, accessed December 1, 2014.

ACKNOWLEDGMENTS

REPUBLISHING ODD NANSEN'S DIARY has been a labor of love from start to finish, but it could never have succeeded without the help and support of countless individuals along the way. For fear of leaving someone out, I, like Nansen, will not try to name them all; as Nansen says, "honor to them all for their share." There are, however, a few individuals I would like to thank for their special contributions.

Marit Greve, Nansen's eldest child, was thirteen years old when he was arrested, old enough to understand the seriousness of her father's plight and to remember well the dangers and difficulties of occupied Norway. Her memory remains undimmed more than seventy years later, and she has patiently answered the many, many questions I have posed since we first met on the back lawn of Polhøgda in the summer of 2011. Many of the insights into Nansen's diary entries would have remained impossible without her knowledge of the events of 1942–1945. Marit is a wonderful friend, self-effacing to a fault, and the inheritor of her father's wit and humor. To come to know Marit as I have is truly one of the unexpected, but deeply cherished, joys of this undertaking.

As Odd Nansen was an indefatigable diarist, I confess to being something of an indefatigable reader; I always need a book in my hand. Many of these books have been enjoyable, indeed memorable. But only Thomas Buergenthal's memoir *A Lucky Child*, a story of struggle and survival, altered my life. Tom's memoir led me to the remarkable Odd Nansen and Norway's experience in World War II. For that introduction I will remain forever grateful to Tom. In January 2011, soon after his return from The Hague, I sought Tom out to discuss my interest in Nansen and my desire to see his diary back in print. Since that first meeting Tom has been a terrific resource, mentor, and source of encouragement. My debt is great, and I only hope I've done justice to the man who played such an important and inspirational role in his own life.

As I became more and more interested in Odd Nansen and his diary, I began to share my passion with groups that might also be interested in the story. After speaking with the Nashville, Tennessee, chapter of the Sons of Norway, an audience member named Dr. Sten Vermund introduced himself and offered to help me with my search for a publisher. Sten (whose grandfather, Torvald Bergfjord, spent time in Grini as prisoner no. 3477), introduced me to Vanderbilt University Press, and this book is the result of that wonderful association. Along the way Sten has never failed to respond promptly to any of my inquiries, notwithstanding his own high-powered career as a world expert in childhood infectious diseases. One such e-mail apologized for its brevity, explaining that Sten was in a pickup truck on his way to give a talk to a medical school in Karachi, Pakistan.

I thank my wife Tara for putting up with the demands this project has imposed over the years and for her encouragement during the inevitable setbacks along the way. I dedicate my efforts here to the memory of my parents, Thomas and Rose Boyce, and especially to my grandchildren Timothy Michael Boyce and John Finnegan Boyce; hopefully they will someday benefit from reading this book as much as I have from working on it.

INDEX

As noted in the Introduction, the original spelling of Norwegian names in the diary has been left unchanged, and the corrected spelling added in the appropriate footnotes. For purposes of the Index, that order has been reversed: the correct spelling is listed first, with the spelling variations of the name used in the text added in parentheses. Where only first names are known, they are listed alphabetically. Bold numbers refer to photos or illustrations.